Language for Life

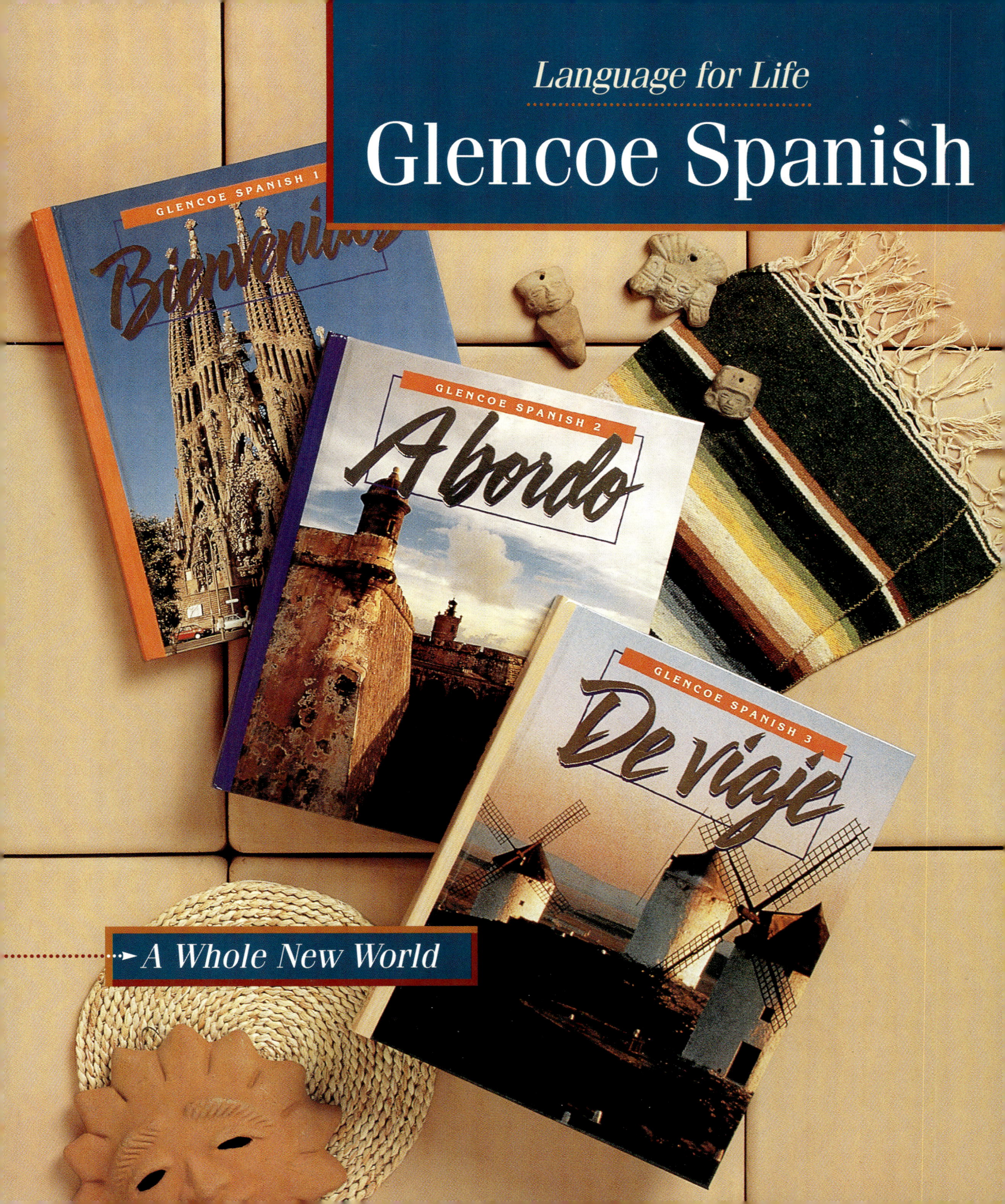

Glencoe Spanish

GLENCOE SPANISH 1
Bienvenidos

GLENCOE SPANISH 2
A bordo

GLENCOE SPANISH 3
De viaje

▶ *A Whole New World*

Student Edition

Step-by-Step: Logical Language Sequencing

There is an amazing amount of experience behind *GLENCOE SPANISH*—classroom experience with teachers just like you, and students just like your own.

Real-life contexts, the heart of this program, help students build practical skills. Logical language sequencing provides a solid foundation for language learning and retention.

Objectives for Success

Set the scene... and the pace

As soon as they begin each chapter, students know what skills they are expected to master. Introduced by colorful photographs, chapter openers:

- *clearly list objectives*
- *set the chapter theme*
- *give students a glimpse of the Spanish-speaking world*
- *promote curiosity and interest in building skills*

CAPÍTULO
7
LOS DEPORTES DE EQUIPO

OBJETIVOS
In this chapter you will learn to do the following:
1. talk about team sports and other physical activities
2. tell what you want to do or prefer to do
3. tell what you can do
4. identify people's nationalities
5. discuss differences between football as it is played in the U.S. and in Hispanic countries
6. discuss the role of sports in Hispanic society

178

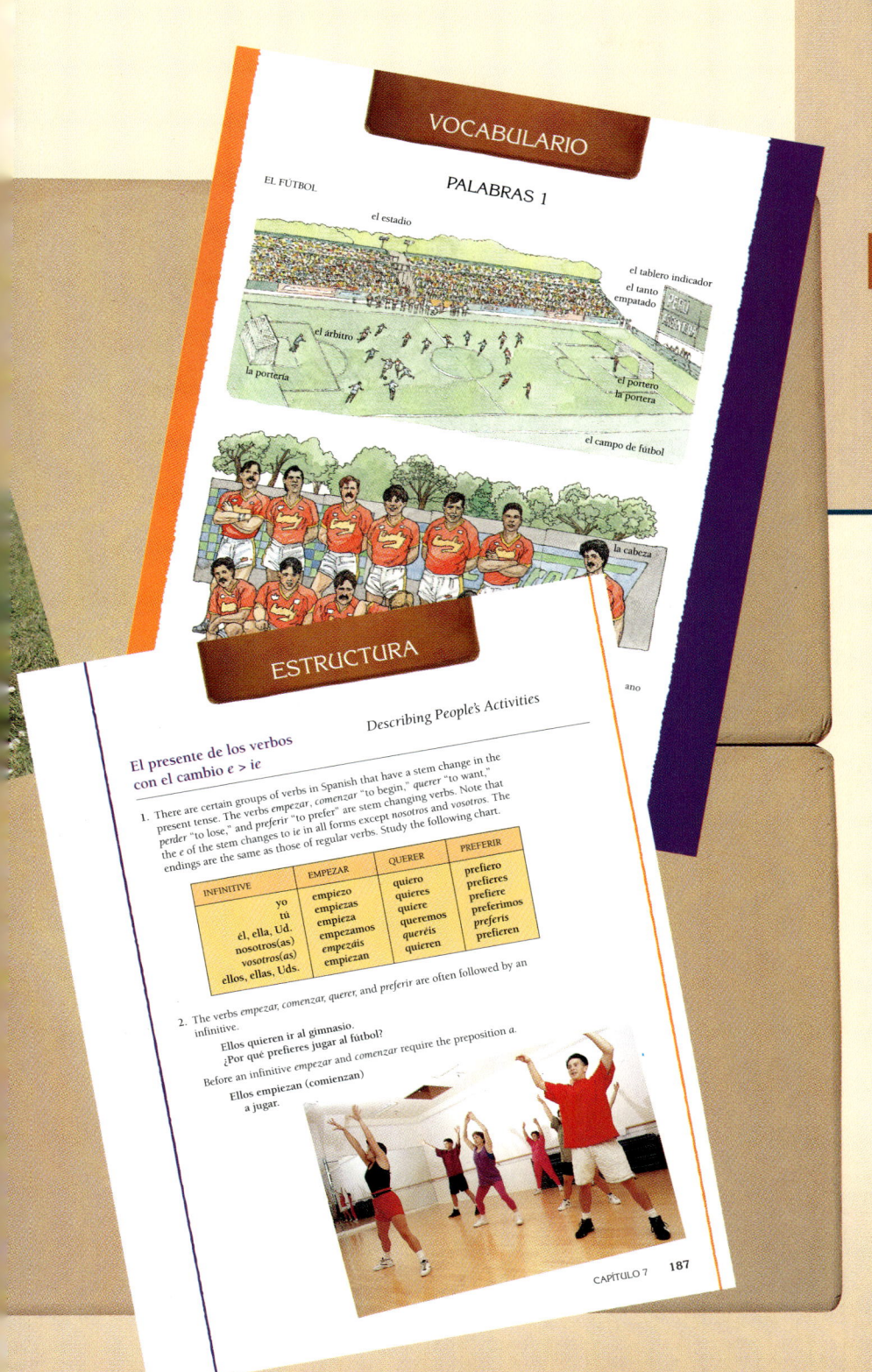

NEW! The Interactive Textbook
Glencoe Spanish CD-ROM Program
The **entire textbook** and **much more** are on the CD-ROM program. It includes video, audio, animation, and record and playback opportunities.

NEW! Spanish for Spanish Speakers Book
This book contains readings that challenge the native speakers and increase their vocabulary and grammar skills.

Vocabulario
multilevel presentation means they'll master meanings more effectively
With **GLENCOE SPANISH,** the difference is in the presentation. Vocabulary is always introduced under the umbrella of an overall theme. New words are presented both individually and in context and are followed by Ejercicios and interactive Comunicación activities. With this culturally integrated, multilevel presentation, students can transfer new words to real-life situations with ease.

Estructura
clear explanations with concrete results
Students start with clear, concise structure explanations, then practice new grammar in carefully controlled exercises. Students build confidence by practicing these contextualized exercises before trying the open-ended Comunicación activities that follow. Your students will be challenged, yet comfortable, learning their new language.

Student Edition

Comunicación
Students have numerous opportunities to use what they have learned in real-life communicative situations.

Conversación
A conversation is presented *after* the students have practiced the vocabulary and structure, enabling them to use these elements in a real-life situation.

Actividades de Comunicación
These occur *3 times* in every chapter. Students practice the language they have learned in a variety of formats. Student-centered, lively activities encourage creative interactive participation. Some written communicative activities are presented.

Lectura
skill building—with every reading
Through these engaging reading selections (all in Spanish), students can apply new grammar skills, study the proper usage of new vocabulary words and develop their critical-thinking skills—*all at the same time.*

Realidades
cultural insights complete the connection
Spectacular photographs and realia give students visual insight into the Spanish-speaking world—providing opportunities for discussions on the similarities and differences that exist between these cultures and Hispanic cultures in the United States.

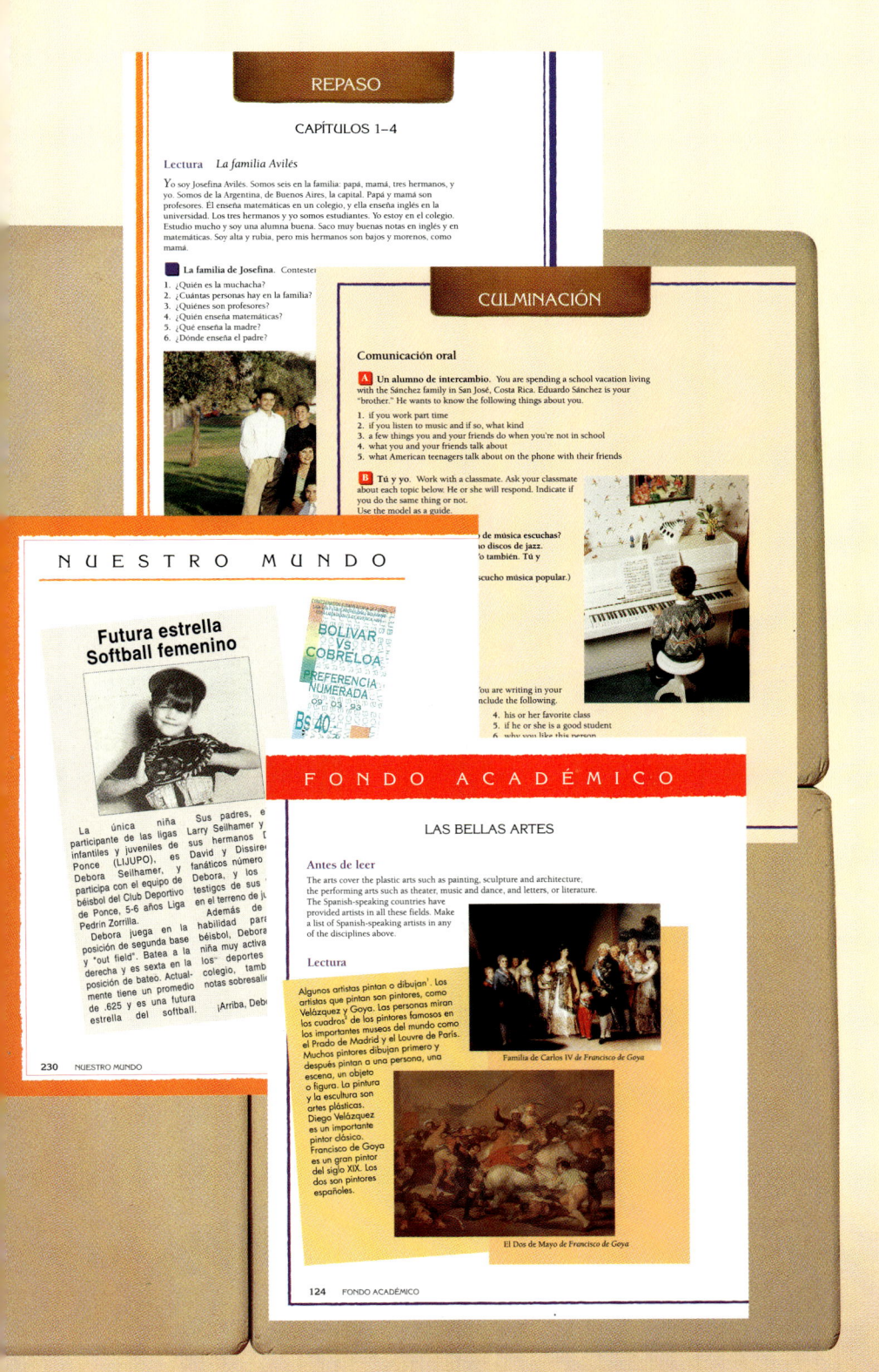

Culminación
integrates and evaluates one chapter at a time
Oral and written activities at the end of each chapter require students to integrate and evaluate the language and cultural concepts they've just learned. The *Reintegración* exercises help students build skills incrementally by recalling important words, expressions and structures from current—and previous—chapters.

Fondo Académico
explores other disciplines without leaving the language
Through interdisciplinary readings in the natural sciences, social sciences, and the arts and humanities, your students are encouraged to stretch their Spanish reading skills and gain meaningful insight into Hispanic cultures.

Nuestro Mundo
"hands-on" realia
Even more reading, culture and realia are provided in *Nuestro Mundo*...no other program gives you more.

Repaso
recycling and review
Every fourth chapter is followed by *Repaso* sections that recycle main vocabulary and structure points. New, stimulating exercises, activities and dialogues help students expand language skills.

Teacher's Wraparound Edition

Your One-Source, One-Stop Teaching Tool

NEW! Interleaf Sections for Teachers

Preceding every chapter, they contain additional teacher material such as Print and Multimedia Resources, Scope and Sequence and information about various program components.

Teacher's Wraparound Edition

Our comprehensive **Teacher's Wraparound Edition** gives you everything you need to introduce, explain and expand lessons—all in one place and all at a glance—so you're always flexible and always prepared.

The **Teacher's Wraparound Edition,** with pages identical to the student edition, plus teaching suggestions and techniques, enriches and expands every page. Activities encourage students to participate and communicate in pairs or cooperative learning groups.

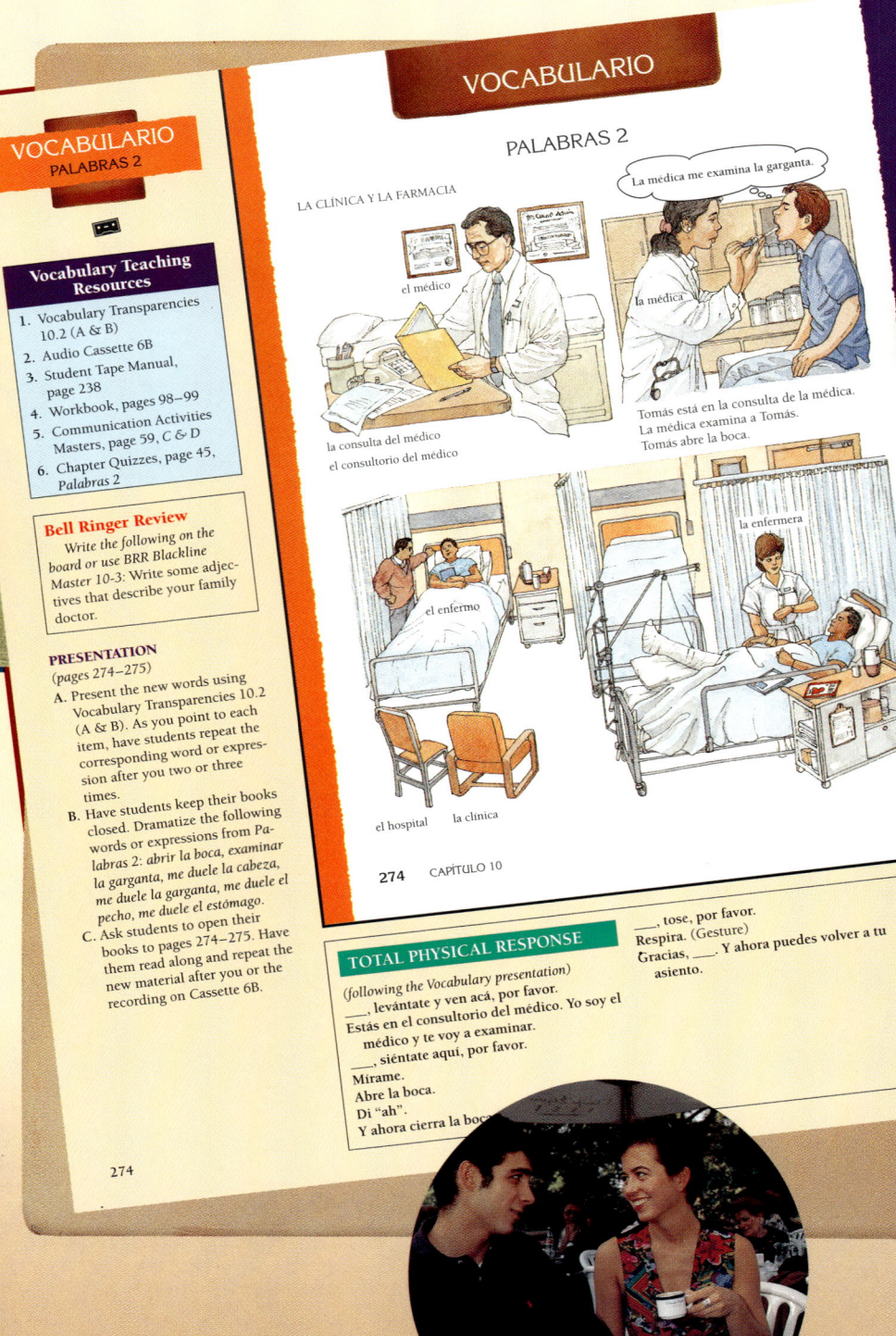

Key topics include:

- Chapter Resources
- Bell Ringer Reviews
- For the Younger Student
- Geography Connection
- Vocabulary Expansion
- Cognate Recognition
- Informal Assessment
- Learning from Photos and Realia
- Reteaching
- Additional Practice
- Independent Practice
- Art/History Connection
- Total Physical Response
- Cooperative Learning
- Did You Know?
- Critical-Thinking Activities
- For the Native Speaker
- Chapter Projects

RECYCLING
Bring back previously learned vocabulary by asking ¿Dónde te duele? and point to your stomach, head, arm, foot, finger, and hand.

Vocabulary Expansion
You may wish to give students the following expressions related to a routine visit to the doctor's office.
explicar los síntomas
hacer una diagnosis
tomar la presión (tensión) arterial
tomar el pulso
tomar una radiografía

COGNATES
Have students repeat carefully the cognates at the bottom of page 275. Meaning should cause no problem.

ABOUT THE LANGUAGE
1. Explain to students that many nouns that end in -ama, -oma come from Greek, and they take the article el. For example: el síntoma, el programa, el problema, el drama.
2. Many of the nouns that end in -osis take the article la. For example: la diagnosis, la prognosis.

CROSS-CULTURAL CONNECTION
En los EE.UU. es relativamente reciente que hay muchas señoras médicas. En España y en Latinoamérica no es nada reciente. Siempre ha habido muchas señoras que practican la medicina.

FOR THE NATIVE SPEAKER
1. Ask students about childhood diseases they may have had. If they don't know their names in Spanish, tell them: sarampión, paperas, tos ferina, varicela (measles, mumps, whooping cough, chicken pox). Ask them to describe the symptoms of each.
2. Remind students that there are a number of professions in the medical field: doctores(as), farmacéuticos(as), técnicos(as), enfermeros(as). Ask them: ¿Cuál es la función de cada profesión? ¿Qué preparación se necesita para ejercer una profesión? ¿Cuál es la importancia de cada profesión en cuanto a la salud del público? ¿Te gustaría ingresar en una de esas profesiones? ¿Por qué sí o por qué no?

Me duele la cabeza.
Me duele la garganta.
Me duele el pecho.
Me duele el estómago.

el farmacéutico
la farmacéutica
la receta
las pastillas
las píldoras
los comprimidos
la farmacia

Tomás va a la farmacia. La farmacéutica lee la receta. Ella vende (despacha) los medicamentos.

Nota: Here is a list of cognates related to health and nutrition. You can easily guess the meaning of these words.

la dieta
las vitaminas
la proteína
los ejercicios físicos
los ejercicios aeróbicos
el síntoma
la alergia
la dosis
la diagnosis
los carbohidratos
la fibra
las calorías
la droga

CAPÍTULO 10   275

Teacher's Classroom Resources

More Things to Do . . .
and More Ways to Do Them

Teacher's Classroom Resources

Evaluation, reinforcement and extra practice are all easy to access...and integrate...with the comprehensive resources found in *GLENCOE SPANISH Teacher's Classroom Resources*.

The *Writing Activities Workbook and Student Tape Manual* is a two-part workbook that offers:

- *Additional writing practice* to reinforce the vocabulary and structure topics in each chapter.

- *Activity sheets* students use when listening to the audio cassette recordings.

Additional resources include:

- *Bell Ringer Reviews* serve as short warm-ups that recycle vocabulary and grammar from previous chapters.

- *Communication Activities Masters* provide further opportunities for students to practice their communication skills in Spanish.

- *Situation Cards* are sets of guided conversational situations correlated to each chapter.

- *Overhead Transparencies Binder* includes five categories of colorful transparencies: *Vocabulary, Grammar/Pronunciation, Communication, Maps and Fine Art.*

NEW! Lesson Plan Booklet
Detailed plans for every chapter help teachers choose effective lesson formats.

NEW! Performance Assessment Tests
Task-based tests provide an alternative approach to measure student learning.

- *Chapter Quizzes* are designed to help both students and teachers evaluate students' mastery of a specific vocabulary section or structure topic.

- The *Testing Program* consists of three different types of tests: *discrete point tests, chapter proficiency tests* on blackline masters and the *Computer Software Practice and Test Generator Program.* The software component allows teachers to print out ready-made tests or to customize tests.

- The *Video Cassette* and *Videodisc Programs* capture the flavor of Hispanic culture in the student text while reinforcing vocabulary and structure chapter-by-chapter. The video is accompanied by a *Video Activities Booklet.*

- The *Audio Cassette Program* includes recorded material for each chapter of **GLENCOE SPANISH.** Also available in *CD format.*

- *CD-ROM Programs* enhance and expand upon what is in the textbook. They can be used for makeup, practice, reward or as a full-class presentation. Students receive immediate confirmation of their responses, written and oral.

Components

Glencoe Spanish...

The Difference Between Ordinary and Extraordinary!

Unlock Student Potential with the Power of Glencoe Spanish.

Level 1

0-02-641001-X	Student Edition
0-02-641002-8	Teacher's Wraparound Edition
0-02-641003-6	Writing Activities Workbook & Student Tape Manual, SE
0-02-641004-4	Writing Activities Workbook, TAE
0-02-641017-6	Student Tape Manual, TE
0-02-641008-7	Audio Cassette Program with Student Tape Manual, TE
0-02-641009-5	Audio Compact Disc Program with Student Tape Manual, TE
0-02-641031-1	Bell Ringer Reviews
0-02-641022-2	Communication Activities Masters
0-02-641023-0	Situation Cards
0-02-641026-5	Transparency Binder
0-02-641005-2	Chapter Quizzes with Answer Key
0-02-641007-9	Testing Program with Test Cassettes Binder
0-02-641006-0	Testing Program Booklet with Answer Key
0-02-641018-4	Video Cassette Program with Video Activities Booklet
0-02-641019-2	Videodisc Program with Video Activities Booklet
0-02-641021-4	Video Activities Booklet with Video Script
	Practice & Test Generator
0-02-641027-3	IBM
0-02-641028-1	Apple
0-02-641029-X	MacIntosh
0-02-641032-X	Spanish for Spanish Speakers
0-02-641033-8	Spanish for Spanish Speakers, TAE
0-02-641053-2	Performance Assessment Tests
0-02-641054-0	Lesson Plans
0-02-646102-1	CD-ROM (Class Disk Package)
0-02-641025-7	Teacher's Classroom Resources

Level 2

0-02-646118-8	Student Edition
0-02-646119-6	Teacher's Wraparound Edition
0-02-646120-X	Writing Activities Workbook & Student Tape Manual, SE
0-02-646121-8	Writing Activities Workbook, TAE
0-02-646127-7	Student Tape Manual, TE
0-02-646125-0	Audio Cassette Program with Student Tape Manual, TE
0-02-646126-9	Audio Compact Disc Program with Student Tape Manual, TE
0-02-646138-2	Bell Ringer Reviews
0-02-646131-5	Communication Activities Masters
0-02-646132-3	Situation Cards
0-02-646134-X	Transparency Binder
0-02-646122-6	Chapter Quizzes with Answer Key
0-02-646124-2	Testing Program with Test Cassettes Binder
0-02-646123-4	Testing Program Booklet with Answer Key
0-02-646149-8	Video Cassette Program with Video Activities Booklet
0-02-646128-5	Videodisc Program with Video Activities Booklet
0-02-646129-3	Video Activities Booklet with Video Script
	Practice & Test Generator
0-02-646135-8	IBM
0-02-646136-6	Apple
0-02-646137-4	MacIntosh
0-02-646139-0	Spanish for Spanish Speakers
0-02-646141-2	Spanish for Spanish Speakers, TAE
0-02-646147-1	Performance Assessment Tests
0-02-646148-X	Lesson Plans
0-02-646103-X	CD-ROM (Class Disk Package)
0-02-646133-1	Teacher's Classroom Resources

Level 3

0-02-646362-8	Student Edition
0-02-646363-6	Teacher's Wraparound Edition
0-02-646384-9	Writing Activities Workbook & Student Tape Manual, SE
0-02-646364-4	Writing Activities Workbook, TAE
0-02-646385-7	Student Tape Manual, TE
0-02-646368-7	Audio Cassette Program with Student Tape Manual TE
0-02-646369-5	Audio Compact Disc Program with Student Tape Manual, TE
0-02-646379-2	Bell Ringer Reviews
0-02-646382-2	Communication Activities Masters
0-02-646373-3	Situation Cards
0-02-646375-X	Transparency Binder
0-02-646365-2	Chapter Quizzes with Answer Key
0-02-646367-9	Testing Program with Test Cassettes Binder
0-02-646366-0	Testing Program Booklet with Answer Key
0-02-646380-6	Video Cassette Program with Video Activities Booklet
0-02-646381-4	Videodisc Program with Video Activities Booklet
0-02-646383-0	Video Activities Booklet with Video Script
	Practice & Test Generator
0-02-646376-8	IBM
0-02-646377-6	Apple
0-02-646378-4	MacIntosh
0-02-646374-1	Teacher's Classroom Resources

GLENCOE
McGraw-Hill

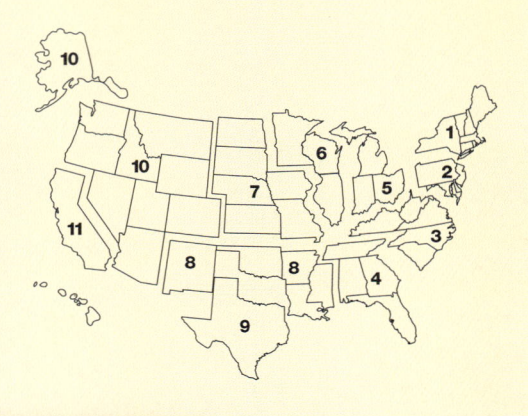

For more information, contact your nearest regional office or call 1-800-334-7344

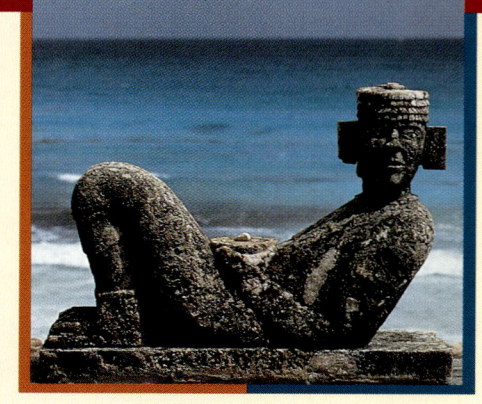

FL 91269-5

1. Northeast Region
Glencoe/McGraw-Hill
15 Trafalgar Square #201
Nashua, NH 03063-1968
Phone: 603-880-4701
Phone: 800-424-3451
Fax: 603-595-0204

2. Mid-Atlantic Region
Glencoe/McGraw-Hill
P.O. Box 458
Hightstown, NJ 08520-0458
Phone: 609-426-5560
Phone: 800-553-7515
Fax: 609-426-7063

3. Atlantic-Southeast Region
Glencoe/McGraw-Hill
Brookside Park
One Harbison Way, Suite 101
Columbia, SC 29212
Phone: 803-732-2365
Phone: 800-731-2365
Fax: 803-732-4582

4. Southeast Region
Glencoe/McGraw-Hill
6510 Jimmy Carter Boulevard
Norcross, GA 30071
Phone: 770-446-7493
Phone: 800-982-3992
Fax: 770-446-2356

5. Mid-America Region
Glencoe/McGraw-Hill
936 Eastwind Drive
Westerville, OH 43081
Phone: 614-890-1111
Phone: 800-848-1567
Fax: 614-899-4905

6. Great Lakes Region
Glencoe/McGraw-Hill
846 East Algonquin Road
Schaumburg, IL 60173
Phone: 708-397-8448
Phone: 800-762-4876
Fax: 708-397-9472

7. Mid-Continent Region
Glencoe/McGraw-Hill
846 East Algonquin Road
Schaumburg, IL 60173
Phone: 708-397-8448
Phone: 800-762-4876
Fax: 708-397-9472

8. Southwest Region
Glencoe/McGraw-Hill
320 Westway Place, Suite 550
Arlington, TX 76018
Phone: 817-784-2113
Phone: 800-828-5096
Fax: 817-784-2116

9. Texas Region
Glencoe/McGraw-Hill
320 Westway Place, Suite 550
Arlington, TX 76018
Phone: 817-784-2100
Phone: 800-828-5096
Fax: 817-784-2116

10. Western Region
Glencoe/McGraw-Hill
709 E. Riverpark Lane, Suite 150
Boise, ID 83706
Phone: 208-368-0300
Phone: 800-452-6126
Fax: 208-368-0303
Includes Alaska

11. California Region
Glencoe/McGraw-Hill
15319 Chatsworth Street
P. O. Box 9609
Mission Hills, CA 91346
Phone: 818-898-1391
Phone: 800-423-9534
Fax: 818-898-3864
Includes Hawaii

Glencoe Catholic School Region
Glencoe/McGraw-Hill
25 Crescent Street, 1st Floor
Stamford, CT 06906
Phone: 203-964-9109
Phone: 800-551-8766
Fax: 203-967-3108

Canada
McGraw-Hill Ryerson Ltd.
300 Water Street
Whitby, Ontario
L1N 9B6, Canada
Phone: 905-430-5088
Fax: 905-430-5194

International
The McGraw-Hill Companies
International Marketing
1221 Avenue of the Americas
28th Floor
New York, NY 10020
Phone: 212-512-3641
Fax: 212-512-2186

DoDDS and Pacific Territories
McGraw-Hill School
Publishing Company
600 Delran Parkway
Delran, NJ 08075
Phone: 609-764-4586
Fax: 609-764-4587

GLENCOE SPANISH 2
A bordo

Protase E. Woodford

Conrad J. Schmitt

GLENCOE
McGraw-Hill

New York, New York   Columbus, Ohio   Mission Hills, California   Peoria, Illinois

Copyright © 1997 by the Glencoe/McGraw-Hill School
Publishing Company. All rights reserved. Except as permitted
under the United States Copyright Act, no part of this
publication may be reproduced or distributed in any form or by
any means, or stored in a database or retrieval system, without
prior permission of the publisher.

Printed in the United States of America.

Send all inquiries to:

Glencoe/McGraw-Hill
15319 Chatsworth Street
P.O. Box 9609
Mission Hills, CA 91346-9609

ISBN 0-02-646119-6 (Teacher's Wraparound National Edition)

1 2 3 4 5 6 7 8 9   RRW   02 01 00 99 98 97 96

CONTENTS

Introduction   T 5

Features and Benefits   T 6

Interdisciplinary Readings: *Fondo Académico*   T 13

Series Components   T 14

A bordo, Organization of the Student Textbook   T 15

Suggestions for Teaching the Student Textbook   T 18

Organization of the Teacher's Wraparound Edition   T 24

Additional Ancillary Components   T 29

Cooperative Learning   T 34

Suggestions for Correcting Homework   T 37

Student Portfolios   T 38

Pacing   T 39

Glencoe Spanish 2 *CD-ROM Interactive Textbook*   T 42

Spanish for Spanish Speakers: *Nosotros y nuestro mundo*   T 44

Additional Spanish Resources   T 46

ABOUT THE AUTHORS

Conrad J. Schmitt

Conrad J. Schmitt received his B.A. degree magna cum laude from Montclair State College, Upper Montclair, NJ. He received his M.A. from Middlebury College, Middlebury, VT. He did additional graduate work at Seton Hall University and New York University.

Mr. Schmitt has taught Spanish and French at the elementary, junior, and senior high school levels. He was Coordinator of Foreign Languages for Hackensack, New Jersey, Public Schools. He also taught Spanish at Upsala College, East Orange, NJ; Spanish at Montclair State College; and Methods of Teaching a Foreign Language at the Graduate School of Education, Rutgers University, New Brunswick, NJ. He was editor-in-chief of Foreign Languages and Bilingual Education for McGraw-Hill Book Company and Director of English language Materials for McGraw-Hill International Book Company.

Mr. Schmitt has authored or co-authored more than eighty books, all published by Glencoe, a division of Macmillan/McGraw-Hill, or by McGraw-Hill. He has addressed teacher groups and given workshops in all states of the U.S. and has lectured and presented seminars throughout the Far East, Europe, Latin America, and Canada. In addition, Mr. Schmitt has travelled extensively throughout Spain, Central and South America, and the Caribbean.

Protase E. Woodford

Protase "Woody" Woodford has taught Spanish at all levels from elementary school through graduate school. At the Educational Testing Service in Princeton, NJ, he was Director of Test Development, Director of Language Programs, Director of International Testing Programs and Director of the Puerto Rico Office. He was appointed "Distinguished Linguist" at the U.S. Naval Academy in 1988. He is the author of over two dozen Spanish and English language textbooks for schools and colleges. He has served as a consultant to the American Council on the Teaching of Foreign Languages (ACTFL), The National Assessment of Educational Progress, The College Board, the United Nations Secretariat, UNESCO, the Organization of American States, the U.S. Office of Education, the United States Agency for International Development (AID), the World Bank, the Japanese Ministry of International Trade and Industry, and many ministries of education in Asia, Latin America, and the Middle East. In 1994 he was invited to chair the National Advisory Council on Standards in Foreign Language Education.

INTRODUCTION

Welcome to **Glencoe Spanish**, the junior high and high school Spanish series from the Glencoe Division of McGraw-Hill School Publishing Company. Every element in this series has been designed to help you create an atmosphere of challenge, variety, cooperation and enjoyment for your students. From the moment you begin to use **Glencoe Spanish**, you will notice that not only is it packed with exciting, practical materials and features designed to stimulate young people to work together towards language proficiency, but that it goes beyond by urging students to use their new skills in other areas of the curriculum.

Glencoe Spanish uses an integrated approach to language learning. From the introduction of new material, through reinforcement, evaluation and review, the series' presentations, exercises and activities are designed to span all four language skills. Another characteristic of this series is that students use and reinforce these new skills while developing a realistic, up-to-date awareness of Hispanic culture. **Glencoe Spanish** incorporates a new feature in which Spanish is used as the medium of instruction for a series of interdisciplinary presentations in the areas of natural sciences, social sciences, and the arts and humanities. The Teacher's Wraparound Edition you are reading has been developed based on the advice of experienced foreign language educators throughout the United States in order to meet your needs as a teacher both in and out of the foreign language classroom. Here are some of the features and benefits which make **Glencoe Spanish** a powerful set of teaching tools:

- flexible format
- student-centered instruction
- balance among all four language skills
- contextualized vocabulary
- thorough, contextual presentation of grammar
- an integrated approach to culture

FEATURES AND BENEFITS

Flexible Format While we have taken every opportunity to use the latest in pedagogical developments in order to create a learning atmosphere of variety, vitality, communication and challenge, we have also made every effort to make the **Glencoe Spanish** series "teacher-friendly." And this is where flexibility comes in.

Although the Student Textbook and the Teacher's Wraparound Edition provide an instructional method, every minute of every class period is not laid out. Plenty of room has been built in for you the teacher to be flexible: to draw on your own education, experience and personality in order to tailor a language program that is suitable and rewarding for the individual "chemistry" of each class.

A closer look at the most basic component, the Student Textbook, serves as an example of this flexibility. Each chapter opens with two sections of vocabulary (*Vocabulario: Palabras 1* and *Palabras 2*) each with its own set of exercises. *Vocabulario* is followed by *Estructura,* consisting of a series of grammar points, each with accompanying exercises. But there is nothing which says that the material must be presented in this order. The items of vocabulary and grammar are so well integrated that you will find it easy, and perhaps preferable, to move back and forth between them. You may also wish to select from the third and fourth sections of each chapter (the *Conversación* and *Lectura y Cultura* sections) at an earlier point than that in which they are presented, as a means of challenging students to identify or use the chapter vocabulary and grammar to which they have already been introduced.

These options are left to you. The only requirement for moving successfully through the Student Textbook is that the vocabulary and grammar of each chapter eventually be presented in their entirety, since each succeeding chapter builds on what has come before.

In the Student Textbook, there is a marked difference between learning exercises (*Ejercicios*) and communication-based activities (*Comunicación*), both of which are provided in each chapter. The former serve as their name implies, as exercises for the acquisition and practice of new vocabulary and structures, while the latter are designed to get students communicating in open-ended contexts using the Spanish they have learned. You can be selective among these, depending on the needs of your students.

The abundance of suggestions for techniques, strategies, additional practice, chapter projects, independent (homework) assignments, informal assessment, and more, which are provided in this Teacher's Wraparound Edition—as well as the veritable banquet of resources available in the wide array of ancillary materials provided in the series—are what make **Glencoe Spanish** truly flexible and "teacher-friendly." They provide ideas and teaching tools from which to pick and choose in order to create an outstanding course.

Student-Centered Instruction Glencoe Spanish Today's classroom is comprised of students who have different learning styles, special needs, and represent different cultural backgrounds. The emphasis on student-centered instruction provided by **Glencoe Spanish** allows the teacher to capitalize and deal positively with such diversity and encourage students to become involved in their own learning.

Glencoe Spanish anticipates the requirements of today's classroom by offering ideas for setting up a cooperative learning environment for students. Useful suggestions to this end accompany each chapter, under the heading Cooperative Learning, in the bottom margin of the Teacher's Wraparound Edition. Additional paired and group activities occur in the Student Textbook (*Comunicación*), and in other headings such as Additional Practice in the Teacher's Wraparound Edition.

Besides cooperative learning strategies, **Glencoe Spanish** contains many other student-centered elements that allow students to expand their learning experiences. Here are some examples: suggestions are offered in the Teacher's Wraparound Edition for out-of-class chapter projects on topics related to the chapter theme. In Level 1, there is a topic called "For the Younger Student," activities aimed primarily at stimulating the middle school/junior-high student.

In the Student Textbook, new grammatical material is divided into "bite-sized" lessons, so as not to be intimidating. The Writing Activities Workbook provides a self-test after every fourth chapter, so that students can prepare alone or in study groups for teacher-administered quizzes and tests. The Audio Cassette Program allows students to work at their own pace, stopping the tape whenever necessary to make directed changes in the language or to refer to their activity sheets in the Student Tape Manual. The Computer Software element consists of not only a Test Generator for the teacher, but a Practice Generator for students, with which they can practice vocabulary and grammar items at their own pace.

These and other features discussed elsewhere in this Teacher's Manual have been designed with the student in mind. They assure that each individual, regardless of learning style, special need, background, or age, will have the necessary resources for becoming proficient in Spanish.

Balance Among All Four Language Skills
Glencoe Spanish provides a balanced focus on the listening, speaking, reading, and writing skills throughout all phases of instruction. It gives you leeway if you wish to adjust the integration of these skills to the needs of a particular individual, group or class. Several features of the series lend themselves to this: the overall flexibility of format, the abundance of suggested optional and additional activities and the design of the individual activities themselves. Let's look at some sections of a typical chapter as examples of the other two characteristics mentioned.

If the suggested presentation is followed, students are introduced to new words and phrases in *Vocabulario* by the teacher, and/or by the audio cassette presentation. The focus is on listening and speaking through modeling and repetition. The *Ejercicios* which accompany the *Vocabulario* section can be done with books either closed (accentuating listening and speaking) or open (accentuating reading, listening and speaking). However, these *Ejercicios* can just as well be assigned or reassigned as written work if the teacher wishes to have the whole class or individuals begin to concentrate on reading and writing. Throughout the *Vocabulario* section, optional and additional reinforcement activities are suggested in the Teacher's Wraparound Edition. These suggestions address all four language skills. Later in each chapter, students are asked to combine the material learned in *Vocabulario* with material from the grammar section (*Estructura*) using a combination of listening, reading, writing, and speaking skills in the process.

Reading and writing activities are brought into play early in the **Glencoe Spanish** series. The authors realize that communication in Spanish includes the use of reading and writing skills and that these skills are indispensable for the assimilation and retention of new language and the organization of thought. Students are launched into writing, for example, as early as Level 1, Chapter 1, through the use of brief assignments such as lists, labeled diagrams, note taking or short answers. Longer writing activities are added in later chapters. These textbook activities are further reinforced in the Writing Activities Workbook.

Let's take a closer look at how each of the four skills is woven into the Student Textbook, the Teacher's Wraparound Edition and the ancillary materials.

Listening You the teacher are the primary source for listening, as you model new vocabulary, dialogues, structure and pronunciation, share your knowledge of Spanish culture, history and geography, talk to students about their lives and your own, or engage in culturally oriented activities and projects. It is your ability to use Spanish as much as possible with your students, both in and outside of the classroom, which determines how relevant and dynamic their learning experience will be.

Glencoe Spanish offers numerous ways in which to develop the listening skill. There are teacher-focused activities, which provide the consistent modeling that students need. Teachers who use the Audio Cassette Program will find that these recordings help students become accustomed to a variety of voices, as well as rates of speech. And activities in which students interact with each other develop listening spontaneity and acuity.

In the Student Textbook, new vocabulary will be modeled by the teacher. Students' attention on the sounds of the new words can be maximized by presenting this material with books closed and using the Vocabulary Transparencies to convey meaning. Following each *Palabras* segment are several *Ejercicios* for practicing the new vocabulary. These can also be done with books closed. After the two *Palabras* segments comes *Comunicación,* in which students may work in pairs or groups and must listen to each other in order to find information, take notes or report to others on what was said in their group. In *Estructura,* students listen as the teacher models new grammatical material and then are given a chance to practice each structure in several *Ejercicios*. Once again, closing the book will provide increased focus on the listening skill. The next section of each chapter is *Conversación,* in which a real-life dialogue is modeled either by the teacher or by playing the recorded version from the Audio Cassette Program. The dialogue is followed by several communication-based activities, where students must listen to and interact with their peers. In **Bienvenidos** (Level 1), *Conversación* also contains a *Pronunciación* segment, covering an aspect of pronunciation related to the chapter material. Here again, students will be listening either to teacher or recorded models. The last section of each chapter, *Culminación,* offers more listening-intensive activities (*Comunicación oral*) where students must be able to understand what their partners say in order to play out their role.

In addition to the Student Textbook, the Teacher's Wraparound Edition offers several other listening-based activities correlated to the chapters. Some of these listening activities are "Total Physical Response" (Level 1) and "Pantomime" (Level 2). Here students must perform an action after listening to a spoken command. There are further listening-based activities suggested under the heading "Cooperative Learning" and often under "Additional Practice," both of which occur in the bottom margins in each Teacher's Wraparound Edition chapter.

The Audio Cassette Program has two main listening components. The first is practice-oriented, wherein students further reinforce vocabulary and grammar, following directions and making changes in utterances. They can self-check their work by listening to the correctly modeled speech, which is supplied after a pause.

The second part of the program places more attention on the receptive listening skills. Students listen to language in the form of dialogues, announcements, or advertisements—language delivered at a faster pace and in greater volume—and then are asked to demonstrate their understanding of the main ideas and important details in what they have heard. The Student Tape Manual contains activity sheets for doing this work. The Teacher's Edition contains the complete transcript of all audio materials to assist you in laying out listening tasks for your class.

More listening practice is offered through the Video Cassette Program. This material corresponds to and enriches that in the Student Textbook, and gives students a chance to hear variations of the language elements they have been practicing, as spoken by a variety of native speakers from different parts of Latin America and Spain. Students' listening comprehension can be checked and augmented by using the corresponding print activities in the Video Activities Booklet.

Speaking Most of the areas of the Student Textbook and the Teacher's Wraparound Edition mentioned above simultaneously develop the speaking skill. After hearing a model in the

Vocabulario or *Estructura* sections, students will repeat it, either as a whole class, in small groups, or as individuals. From these modeled cues, they will progress to visual ones, supplied by the Vocabulary Transparencies or the photos and graphics in the textbook. The real thrust in the *Ejercicios* accompanying these two sections is to get students to produce this new material actively. Then, in *Comunicación,* students have the opportunity to adapt what they have learned by asking for and giving information to their classmates on a given topic. Here, and in the *Conversación* sections, students are engaged in meaningful, interesting sessions of sharing information, all designed to make them want to speak and experiment with the language. The suggestions in the "About the Language" feature in the Teacher's Wraparound Edition enrich speaking skills by offering variants of expressions and speech mannerisms currently popular in Hispanic culture, especially among teenagers, so that from the start your students will be accustomed to speaking in a way that is accurate and reflective of contemporary Spanish. In Level 1, Chapter 1, for example, this feature discusses the variations of *muchacho(a)* /*chico(a)*, the difference between *bolígrafo* and *pluma,* and provides information on the use and formation of nicknames, among other things. Previously presented material is constantly recycled in the communication-based activities, so that students' speaking vocabularies and knowledge of structure are always increasing. For this purpose, beginning with Level 1, Chapter 3, each *Culminación* section contains a *Reintegración* segment. The length of speech is increased over time, so that when students complete Level 1 (***Bienvenidos***) they will have acquired an appreciation of the intonation and inflection of longer streams of language. To assist you in fine-tuning your students' speech patterns, the *Pronunciación* section occurs in each chapter of Level 1.

The speaking skill is stressed in the first part of each recorded chapter of the Audio Cassette Program, where pauses are provided for the student to produce directed, spoken changes in the language. This is an excellent opportunity for those students who are self-conscious about speaking out in class to practice speaking. The Audio Cassette Program gives these students a chance to work in isolation. The format of making a change in the language, uttering the change and then listening for the correct model improves the speaking skill. The Audio Cassette Program can serve as a confidence-builder for self-conscious students, allowing them to work their way gradually into more spontaneous speech with their classmates.

The packet of Situation Cards provides students with yet another opportunity to produce spoken Spanish. They place the student into a contextualized, real-world situation. Students must ask and/or answer questions in order to perform successfully.

Reading Each chapter of the Student Textbook has readings based on the chapter theme. The first reading, *Lectura y Cultura,* is accompanied by a comprehension check and an exercise called *Estudio de palabras,* which focuses on useful strategies for vocabulary-building and recognizing word relationships, which students can carry over into other readings. The second reading, *Descubrimiento Cultural,* is optional and is to be read for more specific and detailed information about the theme of the chapter and as a stimulus for discussion on this theme. In the next section of each chapter, *Realidades,* students again use their reading skills albeit to a lesser degree. While the *Realidades* section is primarily visual in nature, students nevertheless are referred to numbered captions to learn more about the photographs shown in this two-page spread.

After every four chapters of the Student Textbook, **Glencoe Spanish** provides a unique section called *Fondo Académico*. This presentation is designed to use reading as a means of bridging the gap between Spanish and other areas of the curriculum. Three separate readings are offered, one in each of the three areas of natural sciences, social sciences, and arts and humanities. Here students have a chance to stretch their reading abilities in Spanish by reading basic information they may have already learned in other academic subjects. Although the material has been carefully written to include themes (as well as words and structures) which students have learned in previous chapters, it contains the most challenging readings. The *Fondo Académico* sections are optional.

The Writing Activities Workbook offers additional readings under the heading

Un Poco Más. These selections and the accompanying exercises focus on reading strategies such as cognate recognition, related word forms and the use of context clues.

In addition to the reading development above, students are constantly presented with authentic Spanish texts such as announcements from periodicals, telephone listings, transportation schedules, labeled diagrams, floor plans, travel brochures, school progress reports and many others, as sources of information. Sometimes these documents serve as the bases for language activities, and other times they appear in order to round out a cultural presentation, but, in varying degrees, they all require students to apply their reading skills.

Writing Written work is interwoven throughout the language learning process in **Glencoe Spanish**. The exercises, which occur throughout the *Vocabulario* and *Estructura* sections of each chapter in the Student Textbook are designed in such a way that they can be completed in written form as well as orally. Frequently, you may wish to reassign exercises which you have gone through orally in class as written homework. The Teacher's Wraparound Edition makes special note of this under the topic "Independent Practice." At the end of each chapter of the Student Textbook, direct focus is placed on writing in the *Culminación* section, under the heading *Comunicación escrita*. Here there are one or more activities that encourage students to use the new vocabulary and structure they have learned in the chapter to create their own writing samples. These are short, and may be descriptive, narrative, argumentative, analytical or in the form of dialogues or interviews. Often a context is set up and then students are asked to develop an appropriate written response.

The Writing Activities Workbook is the component in which writing skills receive the most overt attention. All of the exercises in there require writing. They vary in length from one-word answers to short compositions. They are designed to focus on the same vocabulary and grammar presented in the corresponding chapter of the Student Textbook, but they are all new and all contextualized around fresh visual material or situational vignettes. Since they often have students making lists, adding to charts and labeling, they provide an excellent means for them to organize the chapter material in their minds and make associations which will help them retain it. As students' knowledge of Spanish increases, longer written pieces are required of them. One workbook section entitled *Mi Autobiografía* has students write installments of their own autobiographies. This is an effective way of stretching student writing skills. It also challenges students to personalize the Spanish they have been studying.

Students are also asked to make implicit use of writing almost everywhere in the series. They are constantly taking notes, listing, categorizing, labeling, summarizing, comparing or contrasting on paper. Even the Audio Cassette Program and the Video Cassette Program involve students in writing through the use of activity sheets. By choosing among these options, you can be sure that your students will receive the practice they need to develop their writing skills successfully.

Contextualized Vocabulary

From the moment students see new words at the beginning of each chapter in **Glencoe Spanish**, they see them within an identifiable context. From the start, students learn to group words by association, thereby enhancing their ability to assimilate and store vocabulary for long-term retention. This contextualization remains consistent throughout the practice, testing and recycling phases of learning.

In the *Vocabulario* section, each of the *Palabras* segments contains a short exchange or a few lead-in sentences or phrases which, together with interesting, colorful visuals, establish the context of the topic. Other vocabulary items which occur naturally within this topic are laid out among additional visuals, often as labels. The result is that students see at a glance the new language set into a real-life situation which provides "something to talk about"—a reason for using it. The accompanying exercises enrich this context. Each *ejercicio* practice item is related to the others within the set, so that when taken together they form a meaningful vignette or story. In other sections of the chapter, these words and phrases are reintroduced frequently.

Moreover, future chapters build on vocabulary and grammar from previous ones. Chapter themes introduced in Level 1 are reintroduced in Level 2 along with additional related vocabulary. Special attention has been given vocabulary in the reading sections of the series as well. For example, in *Lectura y Cultura,* students are encouraged to stretch their vocabularies in order to get as much meaning as possible from the selections. In addition to glossed words and frequent use of cognate recognition, the corresponding *Estudio de palabras* is there to help them with this. Another example is the *Fondo Académico* section after every four chapters. The selections here include glossaries of the most important new vocabulary items, and the accompanying activities put implicit understanding of vocabulary to the test.

Thorough, Contextual Presentation of Grammar

A quick look through the chapters of *Bienvenidos* (Level 1) and *A bordo* (Level 2) will show the role grammar plays in the overall approach of the **Glencoe Spanish** series. Although grammar is by no means the driving force behind the series, it is indeed an important aspect. In **Glencoe Spanish**, grammar is presented as one of seven sections in each chapter. What makes this series particularly effective is that, as well as being thorough, the presentation of grammar runs concurrent with, and is embedded in, the chapter-long situational themes. Students are presented with Spanish structure both directly, as grammar, and as a set of useful functions that will aid them in communication, in expanding and improving their Spanish across the four skills, and in learning about Hispanic culture as well as other areas of the school curriculum. Another important series characteristic is that the presentation of grammar has been divided into short, coherent "doses," which prevent grammar from becoming overwhelming to the student.

As you use this series you will see as you teach the various grammar topics that student interest remains high because each exercise relates to a communicative topic and the format always varies. As is the case with the vocabulary exercises, the individual practice items in the grammar section are related to each other contextually, in order to heighten student interest.

You will find that it is easy to move in and out of the teaching of grammar, dipping into the other sections of a chapter or other components as you see fit. The grammar segments are short and intelligently divided. Each one provides a good sense of closure: if they are taught in one section they are included as much as possible in the others; and they have a coherent contextual theme.

Aside from the Student Textbook and Teacher's Wraparound Edition, with their focus on grammar in the *Estructura* section of each chapter and in the *Repaso* after every four chapters, **Glencoe Spanish** offers students opportunities to practice grammar in other components as well. Chapter by chapter, the Writing Activities Workbook provides ample tasks in which students must put to writing the new structures on which they have been working in class. The Audio Cassette Program includes recorded sections in every chapter of the Student Tape Manual which correspond directly to *Estructura* in the Student Textbook. The Computer Software Program's Practice Generator contains additional grammar-based exercises. Students' knowledge of grammar is evaluated in the Chapter Quizzes and in the Testing Program. And each grammatical structure is practiced in other components, such as the Communication Activities Masters, Situation Cards and Video Cassette Program.

An Integrated Approach to Culture

True competence in a foreign language cannot be attained without simultaneous development of the awareness of the culture in which the language is spoken. That is why **Glencoe Spanish** places such great importance on culture. Accurate, up-to-date information on Hispanic culture is present either implicitly or explicitly throughout every phase of language learning and in every component of the series.

The presentation of Spanish in each chapter of the Student Textbook is embedded in running contextual themes, and these themes richly reflect the varied cultures of Hispanic America, Spain and Hispanic communities in the U.S. Even in chapter sections which focus primarily on vocabulary or grammar, the presence of culture comes through in the language used as examples or items in exercises, as well as in the content of the accompanying illustrations, photographs, charts, diagrams, maps or other reproductions of authentic documents in Spanish. This constant, implicit inclusion of cultural information creates a format which not only aids in the learning of new words and structures, but piques student interest, invites questions and stimulates discussion of the people behind the language.

Many culturally oriented questions raised by students may be answered in the two sections devoted to culture: *Lectura y Cultura* and *Realidades*. Through readings, captioned visuals and guided activities, these sections provide fundamental knowledge about such topics as family life, school, restaurants, markets, sports, transportation, food, hotels, offices and hospitals, among many others. This information is presented with the idea that culture is a product of people—their attitudes, desires, preferences, differences, similarities, strengths and weaknesses—and that it is ever changing. Students are always encouraged to compare or contrast what they learn about Hispanic culture with their own, thereby learning to think critically and progress towards a more mature vision of the world. For more information on this unique feature, see the Teacher's Manual section immediately following, and also the section entitled ORGANIZATION OF THE STUDENT TEXTBOOK.

All of the cultural material described in the Student Textbook can be augmented by following a variety of suggestions in the Teacher's Wraparound Edition. There are guidelines for culturally rich instruction and activities, as well as useful, interesting facts for the teacher, under headings such as Chapter Projects, Geography Connection, History Connection, Critical Thinking Activity, Did You Know? and others. Throughout the TWE there are sections entitled About the Language. In each of these sections, teachers are given regional differences for lexical items such as *el carril, la pista, la vía, la banda,* and *el canal* for lane of a highway, or *el autobús, la guagua, el camión,* and *el micro* for a bus. In addition to lexical regionalisms, explanations are given for structural variations: *contestar* vs. *contestar a*; *jugar* vs. *jugar a*.

INTERDISCIPLINARY READINGS:
FONDO ACADÉMICO

This distinctive feature of **Glencoe Spanish** allows students to use their Spanish skills to expand their knowledge in other areas of the school curriculum. The interdisciplinary readings, called *Fondo Académico,* occur in the Student Textbook after chapters 4, 8, 12, and 16. They consist of three different readings on topics chosen from the natural sciences, the social sciences and the arts and humanities. Each reading topic is accompanied by pre- and post-reading activities. In the *Fondo Académico* sections, students may read about the metric system, for example (Level 1, pages 352 and 353): the history of its development, the values of its respective units and how it compares to the English system. They may read and talk about great Spanish painters, such as Velázquez and Goya (Level 1, pages 124, 240 and 241), and learn details which help to put the work of these artists in perspective *vis à vis* other major events in world history. Or they may learn about what effects the arrival of the Europeans to the New World had on what the world eats (Level 2, pages 110 and 111). Aside from providing basic information about the above topics—*Diego Velázquez es un importante pintor clásico* (Level 1, page 124), for example— the readings have a Hispanic perspective. They include insights that students might not receive if they were reading about the same topic in an American textbook. In the selection about Velázquez, for example, we read: *En el siglo XVII Flandes es parte del imperio español* (Level 1, page 241). By using these interdisciplinary *Fondo Académico* readings, you can open up two-way avenues of exchange between the Spanish classroom and other subject areas in the school curriculum. These readings will also allow your students to exercise critical thinking skills, draw conclusions, and begin to interrelate the knowledge coming to them from fields which they formerly considered unrelated to Spanish. Perhaps the social studies, art, or science teachers in your school will have the pleasure of hearing from your students, "I learned in Spanish class that..." or conversely, students will have outside knowledge about a topic to bring to discussions in your class.

It is hoped that these readings with interdisciplinary content will make this kind of cognitive connection more common in the overall learning process. Of course, students are building their Spanish language skills while learning about the other subject areas. The selections in *Fondo Académico* recycle as much as possible the structures and vocabulary from previous chapters. Glossed words contribute to vocabulary-building, while the accompanying activities encourage discussion in Spanish around the topic.

SERIES COMPONENTS

In order to take full advantage of the student-centered, "teacher-friendly" curriculum offered by **Glencoe Spanish**, you may want to refer to this section to familiarize yourself with the various resources the series has to offer. Both Levels 1 and 2 of **Glencoe Spanish** contain the following components:

- Student Edition
- Teacher's Wraparound Edition
- Writing Activities Workbook & Student Tape Manual, Student Edition
- Writing Activities Workbook, Teacher's Annotated Edition
- Student Tape Manual, Teacher's Edition (tapescript)
- Audio Program (Cassette or Compact Disc)
- Overhead Transparencies
- Video Program (Videocassette or Videodisc)
- Video Activities Booklet
- Computer Software: Practice and Test Generator
- Communication Activities Masters
- Bell Ringer Review Blackline Masters
- Situation Cards
- Lesson Plans
- Chapter Quizzes with Answer Key
- Testing Program with Answer Key
- Performance Assessment
- *CD-ROM Interactive Textbook*
- *Nosotros y Nuestro Mundo*

A BORDO: ORGANIZATION OF THE LEVEL 2 STUDENT TEXTBOOK

Initial Review The Level 2 textbook begins with six review sections, A through F, which together make up the initial Repaso. These sections review all of the salient grammatical points and vocabulary topics presented in Level 1 (***Bienvenidos***). Review sections A, B, and C reintroduce content that was presented in Level 1, Chapters 1-8. Review sections D, E, and F review material that was presented in Level 1, Chapters 9-18. The Overview topic in the corresponding Teacher's Wraparound Edition points out more specifically which grammar topics and vocabulary are being reviewed in each of these sections. For example, *Repaso* section A reviews vocabulary needed to describe people, school and home (Level 1, Chapters 1 through 4). From a grammatical perspective, this section reviews agreement of adjectives, the present of the verbs *ser, ir, dar* and *estar* and the contractions *al* and *del*. (Level 1, Chapters 1 through 4). Each initial *Repaso* section includes practice exercises and activities to help students further internalize these review topics.

Following the initial *Repaso*, each chapter of *A bordo* is divided into the following sections:

- *Vocabulario (Palabras 1 & Palabras 2)*
- *Estructura*
- *Conversación*
- *Lectura y Cultura*
- *Realidades*
- *Culminación*

After every fourth chapter, the following special sections appear:

- *Nuestro Mundo*
- *Repaso*
- *Fondo Académico* (interdisciplinary readings)

Vocabulario The new vocabulary is laid out in two segments, *Palabras 1* and *Palabras 2*. Each of these presents new words in a cultural context in keeping with the theme of the chapter. Ample use is made of labeled illustrations to convey meaning and to provide an interesting introduction to the new vocabulary. The contextual vignettes into which the vocabulary items are embedded make use of the same grammatical structures which will be formally addressed in the chapter, and recycle words and structures from previous chapters. Accompanying each *Palabras* segment is a series of *Ejercicios* requiring students to use the new words in context. These *Ejercicios* employ techniques such as short answer, matching, multiple choice and labeling. They are always contextual, forming coherent vignettes, and they lend themselves well to any variations you might wish to apply to their delivery (books open, books closed, done as a class, in groups or pairs, or written for homework). Wrapping up the *Vocabulario* section is *Comunicación*, a segment consisting of communication-based activities which combine the new words from both *Palabras* sections. These are more open-ended activities, requiring students to personalize the new language by performing such tasks as gathering information from classmates, interviewing, taking notes, making charts or reporting to the class.

T15

Estructura This is the grammar section of each chapter. It is conveniently and logically divided into two to four segments to aid in student assimilation of the material. Each segment provides a step-by-step description in English of how the new grammatical structure is used in Spanish, accompanied by examples, tables and other visuals. Each segment's presentation is followed by a series of flexible *Ejercicios,* designed along the same lines as those which accompany the *Vocabulario* section, and focusing on the grammar point. As in *Vocabulario,* the presentation of the new structures and the subsequent exercises is contextualized: examples as well as items in the exercises are never separate and unrelated, but always fit together in vignettes to enhance meaning. These vignettes are directly related to the overall chapter theme or a theme from a previous chapter. The *Estructura* section makes regular use of the new vocabulary from *Palabras 1* and *Palabras 2,* allowing for free interplay between these two sections of the chapter. This thorough yet manageable layout allows you to adapt the teaching of grammar to your students' needs and to your own teaching style.

Conversación Now that students have had a chance to see and practice the new items of vocabulary and grammar for the chapter, this section provides a recombined version of the new language in the form of an authentic, culturally rich dialogue under the heading *Escenas de la vida*. This can be handled in a variety of ways, depending on the teacher and the class and as suggested by accompanying notes in the Teacher's Wraparound Edition. Teacher modeling, modeling from the recorded version, class or individual repetitions, reading aloud by students, role-playing or adaptation through substitution are some of the strategies suggested. The dialogue is accompanied by one or more exercises which check comprehension and allow for some personalization of the material. Then students are invited once again to recombine and use all the new language in a variety of group and paired activities in the *Comunicación* section. New vocabulary and expressions are sometimes offered here, but only for the sake of richness and variation, and not for testing purposes. Every chapter in Level 1 also contains a *Pronunciación* segment which appears after the *Conversación* section. It provides a guide to the pronunciation of one or more Spanish phonemes, a series of words and phrases containing the key sound(s), and an illustration which cues a key word containing the sound(s). These pronunciation illustrations are part of the Overhead Transparency package accompanying the series. *Pronunciación* can serve both as a tool for practice as students perform the chapter tasks, and as a handy speaking-skills reference to be used at any time.

Lectura y Cultura This is a reading about people and places from Hispanic America and Spain, offering further cultural input to the theme of the chapter and providing yet another recombination of the chapter vocabulary and grammar. As is always the case with **Glencoe Spanish**, material from previous chapters is recycled. Following the reading and based on it is *Estudio de palabras*—an exercise that gives students a chance to experiment with and expand their Spanish vocabularies by using strategies such as searching for synonyms, identifying cognates, completing cloze exercises, matching and others. Next comes a series of comprehension exercises based on the reading (*Comprensión*), and finally the *Descubrimiento Cultural,* where more cultural information is offered. The *Descubrimiento Cultural* is optional in each chapter.

Realidades These pages are intended as brief but enjoyable visual insights into the Spanish-speaking world. The two pages of this section are filled with photographs of scenes that are pertinent to the chapter theme. Each photograph is identified with a caption, thereby providing some additional reading practice. Students are encouraged to formulate questions about what they see, and to compare and contrast elements of Hispanic culture with their own. The *Realidades* section is optional in each chapter.

Culminación This wrap-up section requires students to consolidate material from the present as well as previous chapters in order to complete the tasks successfully. *Culminación* provides an opportunity for students to assess themselves on their own and to spend time on areas in which they are weak. You the teacher can pick and choose from these activities as you see fit. The first segment of *Culminación* consists of *Comunicación oral,* where students must use the Spanish they have learned to talk about various aspects of themselves: likes, dislikes, favorite activities, hobbies or areas of expertise, among others. This is followed by *Comunicación escrita,* which encourages students to apply their knowledge of Spanish in written form. The *Reintegración* segment recalls selected items of vocabulary and grammar from previous chapters. It is short and not meant as a comprehensive review, but rather as a quick reminder of important words, expressions and structures. Finally, the vocabulary words and expressions taught in the current chapter are listed categorically under the heading *Vocabulario,* serving as a handy reference resource for both the student and the teacher.

Nuestro Mundo This feature occurs after chapters 4, 8, 12 and 16 in the Student Textbook. *Nuestro Mundo* presents students with bits of "hands on" realia taken from Hispanic newspapers, magazines and documents. Each piece of realia is accompanied by a variety of activities designed so that students must use their Spanish skills in order to understand what they see. In the *Nuestro Mundo* feature after Level 1, Chapter 4 for example, students are presented with an actual report card from a school in Chile. The accompanying activities have students answer direct questions about it, use critical thinking skills to talk about how the school might be organized and use context clues to guess at the meaning of some of the Spanish the report card contains.

Repaso This review section, designed to coincide with the more comprehensive Unit Tests in the Testing Program, occurs after chapters 4, 8, 12, and 16 in the Student Textbook. In each Repaso, the main vocabulary and grammar points from the previous four chapters are recycled through a variety of new exercises, activities and dialogues. While in the individual chapters new grammar was divided into smaller, "bite-sized" portions to aid in the planning of daily lessons and help students assimilate it, now it is reviewed in a more consolidated format. This allows students to see different grammatical points side by side for the first time, to make new connections between the different points, and to progress toward a generative, "whole grammar." For example, in the first Repaso following Level 2, Chapter 4, formation of the *imperfecto* for several verbs, as well as a review of the uses of the *imperfecto* versus the *pretérito,* are reviewed together on three pages, accompanied by explanations and various exercises. Previously these concepts were distributed over Chapters 1 through 4 of Level 2. Of course every possible combination of vocabulary and grammar does not reappear in the *Repaso*. However, by carefully going through these exercises and activities and referring to the preceding chapters, students will be encouraged to make necessary connections and extrapolations themselves and therefore develop a true, working knowledge of the Spanish they have studied. The *Repaso* is designed to be used by students studying alone, in unguided study groups or as a whole class with teacher guidance.

Fondo Académico This is a unique, interdisciplinary feature of **Glencoe Spanish** which allows students to use and expand upon the Spanish language skills they have been studying, while at the same time applying them to useful topics in the areas of the natural sciences, social studies and the arts and humanities. This material is presented in the form of three readings, one from each of the above areas, accompanied by photos and illustrations. To stimulate discussion and aid in comprehension, there are pre-reading and post-reading activities. The reading selections are more vocabulary intensive than those in the regular chapters. A Spanish-English glossary is provided for each one. The focus here is on the interdisciplinary content rather than the language itself. By engaging your students in some or all of these readings, you will encourage them to stretch their Spanish reading skills in order to obtain useful, interesting information which will be of great service to them in their other academic courses. And you will be giving students the opportunity to judge for themselves the added insight that the study of Spanish offers to their overall education.

SUGGESTIONS FOR TEACHING THE LEVEL 2 STUDENT TEXTBOOK

Teaching the Initial Review Chapter in Level 2

The first day of class, teachers may wish to reiterate the importance of the Spanish language, and reasons for continuing the learning process in the second year. Some suggestions are:

- Show students a map (the maps located in the back of the Student Textbook can be used) to remind them of the extent of the Spanish-speaking world.
- Have students discuss the areas within North America in which there is a high percentage of Spanish speakers. Ask them to name local Spanish-speaking sources including any individuals or groups they may know in their community.
- Make a list of place names such as San Francisco, Los Angeles, El Paso, Las Vegas, or names in your locality that are of Spanish origin.
- Explain to students the possibility of using Spanish in numerous careers such as: government, teaching, business, (banking, import/export), tourism, translating.
- The first day teachers will also want to find out whether their students used a Hispanic name in last year's Spanish class. If not, this is a good time to give students a Hispanic first name, or to let them take a new one, if they wish.

The *Repaso* sections A through F in *A bordo* are designed to give students a concise review of all the essential material taught in *Bienvenidos* (Level 1) in a systematic fashion. Each section is designed to take two or three days of instruction. *Repaso* Sections A, B and C review material from Level 1, Chapters 1 through 8; sections D, E and F review the content of Chapters 9 through 18. Depending upon the amount of material covered in first year Spanish, student aptitude, and your own teaching preference, you may decide to review some or all of the *Repaso* sections at the beginning of the school year. Many teachers will use the *Repaso* sparingly, delving into these sections as required in order to ensure a smooth transition into new material beginning with Chapter 1 of *A bordo*. Above all, we would urge you not to spend more than a few weeks on the *Repaso* before moving along to Chapter 1. It is always possible to return to these review sections later if necessary.

Teaching Various Sections of the Chapter

One of the major objectives of the **Glencoe Spanish** series is to enable teachers to adapt the material to their own philosophy, teaching style, and students' needs. As a result, a variety of suggestions is offered here for teaching each section of the chapter.

Vocabulario

The *Vocabulario* section always contains some words in isolation, accompanied by an illustration that depicts the meaning of the new word. In addition, new words are used in contextualized sentences. These contextualized sentences appear in the following formats: 1) one to three sentences accompanying an illustration, 2) a short conversation, 3) a short narrative or paragraph. In addition to teaching the new vocabulary, these contextualized sentences introduce, but do not teach, the new structure point of the chapter.

A vocabulary list appears at the end of each chapter in the Student Textbook.

General Techniques

- The Vocabulary Transparencies contain all illustrations necessary to teach the new words and phrases. With an overhead projector, they can easily be projected as large visuals in the classroom for those teachers who prefer to introduce the vocabulary with books closed. The Vocabulary Transparencies contain no printed words.
- All the vocabulary in each chapter (*Palabras 1* and *Palabras 2*) is recorded on the Audio Cassette Program. Students are asked to repeat the isolated words after the model.

Specific Techniques

Option 1 Option 1 for the presentation of vocabulary best meets the needs of those teachers who consider the development of oral skills a prime objective.

- While students have their books closed, project the Vocabulary Transparencies. Point to the item being taught and have students repeat the word after you or the audio cassette several times. After you have presented several words in this manner, project the transparencies again and ask questions such as:

  ¿Es un teléfono celular?
  ¿Qué es?
  ¿Es el interlocutor?
  ¿Quién es? (Level 2, Chapter 1)

- To teach the contextualized segments in the *Palabras*, project the Vocabulary Transparency in the same way. Point to the part of the illustration that depicts the meaning of any new word in the sentence, be it an isolated sentence or a sentence from a conversation or narrative. Immediately ask questions about the sentence. For example, the following sentence appears in Level 2, Chapter 2, page 33: [Pablo] **hizo sus compras en el supermercado.**

Questions to ask are:
¿Pablo hizo sus compras en la carnicería o en el supermercado?
¿Quién hizo sus compras en el supermercado?
¿Dónde hizo Pablo sus compras?
¿Qué hizo Pablo en el supermercado?

- Dramatizations by the teacher, in addition to the illustrations, can also help convey the meaning of many words such as *cantar, bailar,* etc.
- After this basic presentation of the *Palabras* vocabulary, have students open their books and read the *Palabras* section for additional reinforcement.
- Go over the exercises in the *Palabras* section orally.
- Assign the exercises in the *Palabras* section for homework. Also assign the corresponding vocabulary exercises in the Writing Activities Workbook. If the *Palabras* section should take more than one day, assign only those exercises that correspond to the material you have presented.
- The following day, go over the exercises that were assigned for homework.

Option 2 Option 2 will meet the needs of those teachers who wish to teach the oral skills but consider reading and writing equally important.

- Project the Vocabulary Transparencies and have students repeat each word once or twice after you or the audio cassette.
- Have students repeat the contextualized sentences after you or the audio cassette as they look at the illustration.
- Ask students to open their books. Have them read the *Palabras* section. Correct pronunciation errors as they are made.
- Go over the exercises in each *Palabras* section.
- Assign the exercises of the *Palabras* section for homework. Also assign the vocabulary exercises in the Writing Activities Workbook.
- The following day, go over the exercises that were assigned for homework.

Option 3 Option 3 will meet the needs of those teachers who consider the reading and writing skills of utmost importance.

- Have students open their books and read the *Palabras* items as they look at the illustrations.
- Give students several minutes to look at the *Palabras* words and vocabulary exercises. Then go over the exercises.
- Go over the exercises the following day.

Expansion activities

Teachers may use any one of the following activities from time to time. These can be done in conjunction with any of the options previously outlined.

- After the vocabulary has been presented, project the Vocabulary Transparencies or have students open their books and make up as many original sentences as they can, using the new words. This can be done orally or in writing.
- Have students work in pairs or small groups. As they look at the illustrations in the textbook, have them make up as many questions as they can. They can direct their questions to their peers. It is often fun to make this a competitive activity. Individuals or teams can compete to make up the most questions in three minutes. This activity provides the students with an excellent opportunity to use interrogative words.
- Call on one student to read to the class one of the vocabulary exercises that tells a story. Then call on a more able student to retell the story in his/her own words.
- With slower groups you can have one student go to the front of the room. Have him or her think of one of the new words. Let classmates give the student the new words from the *Palabras* until they guess the word the student in the front of the room has in mind. This is a very easy way to have the students recall the words they have just learned.

Estructura

The *Estructura* section of the chapter opens with a grammatical explanation in English. Each grammatical explanation is accompanied by many examples. Verbs are given with complete paradigms. In the case of other grammar concepts such as the *imperfecto* versus the *pretérito*, many examples are given in order to contrast these two past tenses. Irregular patterns are grouped together to make them appear more regular. For example, the subjunctive of verbs like *pedir* and *poder* are taught together in Chapter 12. Whenever the contrast between English and Spanish poses problems for students in the learning process, a contrastive analysis between the two languages is made. Two examples of this are the reflexive construction in Level 1 and the subjunctive in Level 2. Certain structure points are taught more effectively in their entirety and others are more easily acquired if they are taught in segments. An example of the latter is the presentation of the direct and indirect object pronouns. In Level 1, Chapter 10, the object pronouns *me, te, nos* are presented immediately followed by *lo, la, los, las* in Chapter 11, and *le, les* in Chapter 12. Both direct and indirect objects are then consolidated in Level 2 in the *Repasos* section, and are later recycled in chapter 5, and 6.

Learning exercises

The exercises that follow the grammatical explanation are presented from simple to more complex. In the case of verbs with an irregular form, for example, emphasis is placed on the irregular form, since it is the one students will most often confuse or forget. In all cases, students are given one or more exercises that force them to use all forms at random. The first few exercises that follow the grammatical explanation are considered **learning exercises** because they assist the students in grasping and internalizing the new grammar concept. These learning exercises are immediately followed by test exercises—exercises that make students use all aspects of the grammatical point they have just learned. This format greatly assists teachers in meeting the needs of the various ability levels of students in their classes. Every effort has been made to make the grammatical explanations as succinct and as complete as possible. We have purposely avoided extremely technical grammatical or linguistic terminology that most students would not understand. Nevertheless, it is necessary to use certain basic grammatical terms.

Certain grammar exercises from the Student Textbook are recorded on the Audio Cassette Program. Whenever an exercise is recorded, it is noted with an appropriate icon in the Teacher's Wraparound Edition.

The exercises in the Writing Activities Workbook also parallel the order of presentation in the Student Textbook. The Resource boxes and the Independent Practice topics in the Teacher's Wraparound Edition indicate when certain exercises from the Writing Activities Workbook can be assigned.

Specific Techniques for Presenting Grammar

Option 1 Some teachers prefer the deductive approach to the teaching of grammar. When this is the preferred method, teachers can begin the *Estructura* section of the chapter by presenting the grammatical rule to students or by having them read the rule in their textbooks. After they have gone over the rule, have them read the examples in their textbooks or write the examples on the chalkboard. Then proceed with the exercises that follow the grammatical explanation.

Option 2 Other teachers prefer the inductive approach to the teaching of grammar. If this is the case, begin the *Estructura* section by writing the examples that accompany the rule on the chalkboard or by having students read them in their textbooks. Let us take, for example, the positioning of direct object and indirect object pronouns when they are used together in a sentence. The examples the students have in their textbooks (Level 2, page 126) are:

Elena me dio el regalo.	**Elena me lo dio.**
Carlos nos preparó la comida.	**Carlos nos la preparó.**
Papá me compró los tenis.	**Papá me los compró.**
El profesor nos explicó las reglas.	**El profesor nos las explicó.**

In order to teach this concept inductively, teachers can ask students to do or answer the following:

- Have students identify the subjects of all the sentences.
- Have students find a pronoun which refers to a person in all the sentences.
- Ask: What do we call these pronouns which refer to people, but which are not the subjects of the sentences?
- Have students identify the direct objects in the sentences in the left column.
- Have students identify the direct objects in the sentences in the right column.
- Ask: What do we call these pronouns which have replaced the direct objects?
- Ask: How many object pronouns are there in each of the sentences in the right column?
- Ask: When a sentence has two object pronouns, which comes first, the direct object pronoun or the indirect object pronoun?
- Ask: Where do both of these pronouns occur in relation to the verb?

By answering these questions, students have induced, on their own, the rule from the examples. To further reinforce the rule, have students read the grammatical explanation and then continue with the grammar exercises that follow. Further suggestions for the inductive presentation of the grammatical points are given in the Teacher's Wraparound Edition.

Specific techniques for Teaching Grammar Exercises

In the development of the **Glencoe Spanish** series, we have purposely provided a wide variety of exercises in the *Estructura* section so that students can proceed from one exercise to another without becoming bored. The types of exercises they will encounter are: short conversations, answering questions, conducting or taking part in an interview, making up questions, describing an illustration, filling in the blanks, multiple choice, completing a conversation, completing a narrative, etc. In going over the exercises with students, teachers may want to conduct the exercises themselves or they may want students to work in pairs. The *Estructura* exercises can be done in class before they are assigned for homework or they may be assigned before they are done over. Many teachers may want to vary their approach.

All the *Ejercicios* and *Comunicación* activities in the Student Textbook can be done with books open. Many of the exercises such as question-answer, interview, and transformation can also be done with books closed.

Types of exercises

Question exercises The answers to many question exercises build to tell a complete story. Once you have gone over the exercise by calling on several students (Student 1 answers items numbered 1,2,3; Student 2 answers items numbered 4,5,6 etc.), you can call on one student to give the answers to the entire exercise. Now the entire class has heard an uninterrupted story. Students can ask one another questions about the story, give an oral synopsis of the story in their own words, or write a short paragraph about the story.

Personal questions or interview exercises
Students can easily work in pairs or teachers can call a student moderator to the front of the room to ask questions of various class members. Two students can come to the front of the room and the exercise can be performed as follows—one student takes the role of the interviewer and the other takes the role of the interviewee.

Repetition of a conversation See Level 2, Chapter 4, page 89 as an example. After students complete the exercise, they can be given time either in class or as an outside assignment to prepare a skit for the class based on the conversation.

Conversación

Specific Techniques Teachers may wish to vary the presentation of the *Conversación* from one chapter to another. In some chapters, the dialogue can be presented thoroughly and in others it may be presented quickly as a reading exercise. Some possible options are:

- Have the class repeat the dialogue after you twice. Then have students work in pairs and present the dialogue to the class. The dialogue does not have to be memorized. If students change it a bit, all the better.
- Have students read the dialogue several times on their own. Then have them work in pairs and read the dialogue as a skit. Try to encourage them to be animated and to use proper intonation. This is a very important aspect of the *Conversación* section of the chapter.
- Rather than read the dialogue, students can work in pairs, having one make up as many questions as possible related to the topic of the dialogue. The other student can answer his/her questions.
- Once students can complete the exercise(s) that accompany the dialogue with relative ease, they know the dialogue sufficiently well without having to memorize it.
- Students can tell or write a synopsis of the dialogue.

Comunicación

Specific Techniques The *Comunicación* section presents activities that assist students in working with the language on their own. All *Comunicación* sections are optional. In some cases, teachers may want the whole class to do all the activities. In other cases, teachers can decide which activities the whole class will do. Another possibility is to break the class into groups and have each one work on a different activity.

Lectura y Cultura

Specific Techniques: Option 1 Just as the presentation of the dialogue can vary from one chapter to the next, the same is true of *Lectura y Cultura*. In some chapters teachers may want students to go over the reading selection very thoroughly. In this case all or any combination of the following techniques can be used.

- Give students a brief synopsis of the reading selection in Spanish.
- Ask questions about the brief synopsis.
- Have students open their books and repeat several sentences after you or call on individuals to read.
- Ask questions about what was just read.
- Have students read the story at home and write the answers to the exercises that accompany *Lectura y Cultura*.
- Go over the *Estudio de palabras* and *Comprensión* in class the next day.
- Call on a student to give a review of the story in his/her own words. Guide them to make up an oral review. Ask five or six questions to review the salient points of the reading selection.
- After the oral review, the more able students can write a synopsis of *Lectura y Cultura* in their own words.

It should take less than one class period to present *Lectura y Cultura* in the early chapters. In later chapters, teachers may wish to spend two days on those reading selections they want students to know thoroughly.

Option 2 When teachers wish to present *Lectura y Cultura* less thoroughly, the following techniques may be used:

- Call on an individual to read a paragraph.
- Ask questions about the paragraph read.
- Assign *Lectura y Cultura* to be read at home. Have students write the exercises that accompany the *Lectura*.
- Go over the *Estudio de palabras* and the *Comprensión* the following day.

Option 3 With some reading selections, teachers may wish merely to assign them to be read at home and then go over the exercises the following day. This is possible since the only new material in *Lectura y Cultura* consists of a few new vocabulary items that are always footnoted.

Descubrimiento Cultural

The optional *Descubrimiento Cultural* is a reading selection designed to give students an in-depth knowledge of many areas of the Spanish-speaking world. You can omit any or all of this reading or you may choose certain selections that they would like the whole class to read.

The same suggestions given for the *Lectura y Cultura* section of each chapter can be followed. Teachers may also assign the reading selections to different groups. Students can read the selection outside of class and prepare a report for those students who did not read that particular selection. This activity is very beneficial for slower students. Although they may not read the selection, they learn the material by listening to what their peers say about it. The *Descubrimiento Cultural* can also be done by students on a voluntary basis for extra credit.

Realidades

Specific Techniques The purpose of the *Realidades* section is to permit students to look at highly appealing photographs from the Spanish-speaking world and to acquaint them with the many areas where Spanish is spoken. The *Realidades* section contains no exercises. The purpose is for students to enjoy the material as if they were browsing through pages of a magazine. Items the students can think about are embedded in the commentary that accompanies the photographs. Teachers can either have students read the captions in class or students can read the captions on their own.

ORGANIZATION OF THE TEACHER'S WRAPAROUND EDITION

One important component, which is definitive of **Glencoe Spanish** and adds to the series' flexible, "teacher-friendly" nature, is the Teacher's Wraparound Edition (TWE), of which this Teacher's Manual is a part. Each two-page spread of the TWE "wraps around" a slightly reduced reproduction of the corresponding pages of the Student Textbook and offers in the expanded margins a variety of specific, helpful suggestions for every phase in the learning process. A complete method for the presentation of all the material in the Student Textbook is provided—basically, a complete set of lesson plans—as well as techniques for background-building, additional reinforcement of new language skills, creative and communicative recycling of material from previous chapters and a host of other alternatives from which to choose. This banquet of ideas has been developed and conveniently laid out in order to save valuable teacher preparation time and to aid you in designing the richest, most varied language experience possible for you and your students. A closer look at the kinds of support in the TWE, and their locations, will help you decide which ones are right for your pace and style of teaching and the differing "chemistries" of your classes.

The notes in the Teacher's Wraparound Edition can be divided into two basic categories:

1. Core notes, appearing in the left- and right-hand margins, are those which most directly correspond to the material in the accompanying two-page spread of the Student Textbook.

2. Enrichment notes, in the bottom margin, are meant to be complimentary to the material in the Student Textbook. They offer a wide range of options aimed at getting students to practice and use the Spanish they are learning in diverse ways, individually and with their classmates, in the classroom and for homework. The enrichment notes also include tips to the teacher on clarifying and interconnecting elements in Spanish language, Hispanic culture, geography and history—ideas that have proved useful to other teachers and which are offered for your consideration.

Description of Core Notes in the Teacher's Wraparound Edition

Chapter Overview At the beginning of each chapter a brief description is given of the language functions which students will be able to perform by chapter's end. Mention is made of any closely associated functions presented in other chapters. This allows for effective articulation between chapters and serves as a guide for more successful teaching.

Chapter Objectives This guide immediately follows the Chapter Overview and is closely related to it. Here the emphasis is on the lexical and structural objectives of the chapter.

Chapter Resources The beginning of each chapter includes a reference list of all the ancillary components of the series that are applicable to what is being taught in the chapter, including the Writing Activities Workbook and

Student Tape Manual, Audio Cassette Program, Overhead Transparencies, Communication Activities Masters, Video Cassette Program, Computer Software: Practice and Test Generator, Situation Cards, Chapter Quizzes, and Test Booklets. A more precise version of this resource list will be repeated at the beginning of each section within the chapter, so that you always have a handy guide to the specific resources available to you for each and every point in the teaching process. Using these chapter and section resource references will make it easier for you to plan varied, stimulating lessons throughout the year.

Bell Ringer Reviews These short activities recycle vocabulary and grammar from previous chapters and sections. They serve as effective warm-ups, urging students to begin thinking in Spanish, and helping them make the transition from their previous class to Spanish. Minimal direction is required to get the Bell Ringer Review activity started, so students can begin meaningful, independent work in Spanish as soon as the class hour begins, rather than wait for the teacher to finish administrative tasks, such as attendance, etc. Bell Ringer Reviews occur consistently throughout each chapter of Levels 1, 2, and 3.

Presentation Step-by-step suggestions for the presentation of the material in all segments of the six main section headings in each chapter —*Vocabulario, Estructura, Conversación, Lectura y Cultura, Realidades,* and *Culminación* are presented in the left- and right-hand margins. They offer the teacher suggestions on what to say, whether to have books open or closed, whether to perform tasks individually, in pairs or in small groups, expand the material, reteach, and assign homework. These are indeed suggestions. You may wish to follow them as written or choose a more eclectic approach to suit time constraints, personal teaching style and class "chemistry." Please note however, that the central vocabulary and grammar included in each chapter's *Vocabulario* and *Estructura* sections are intended to be taught in their entirety, since this material is built into that which occurs in succeeding chapters. In addition, answers for all the *Ejercicios* in each segment are conveniently located near that exercise in the Student Textbook.

Because the answers will vary in *Comunicación* activities, they are usually not provided. However, the Presentation notes do suggest tips for modeling correctness in student responses to these activities. Besides this running presentation, the teacher notes offer other topics for enrichment, expansion and assessment. A brief discussion of these may help you incorporate them into your lesson plans.

About the Language Since Spanish is such a growing, living language, spoken in so many different places of the world by people of different cultures and classes, the usage and connotation of words can vary greatly. In this section, information is offered on their differences. The most important feature of this section is the presentation of regionalism. In the student text itself, we present those words that are most universally understood. The many regional variants are given in this About the Language section.

Vocabulary Expansion These notes provide the teacher handy access to vocabulary items which are thematically related to those presented within the Student Textbook. They are offered to enrich classroom conversations, allowing students more varied and meaningful responses when talking about themselves, their classmates or the topic in question. Note that none of these items, or for that matter any information in the Teacher's Wraparound Edition, is included in the Chapter Quizzes, or in the Testing Program accompanying **Glencoe Spanish**.

Cognate Recognition Since the lexical relationship between Spanish and English is so rich, these notes have been provided to help you take full advantage of the vocabulary-building strategy of isolating them. The suggestions occur in the *Vocabulario* section of each chapter and are particularly frequent in Level 1 in order to train students from the very beginning in the valuable strategy of recognizing cognates. Various methods of pointing out cognates are used, involving all four language skills, and the activities frequently encourage students to personalize the new words by using them to talk about things and people they know. Pronunciation differences are stressed between the two languages. The teacher notes also call attention to false cognates when they occur in other chapter sections.

Informal Assessment Ideas are offered for making quick checks on how well students are assimilating new material. These checks are done in a variety of ways and provide a means whereby both teacher and students can monitor daily progress. By using the Informal Assessment topic, you will be able to ascertain as you go along the areas in which students are having trouble, and adjust your pace accordingly or provide extra help for individuals, either by making use of other activities offered in the Teacher's Wraparound Edition or devising your own. The assessment strategies are simple and designed to help you elicit from students the vocabulary word, grammatical structure, or other information you wish to check. Because they occur on the same page as the material to which they correspond you may want to come back to them again when it is time to prepare students for tests or quizzes.

Reteaching These suggestions provide yet another approach to teaching a specific topic in the chapter. In the event some students were not successful in the initial presentation of the material a reteaching activity offers an alternate strategy. At the same time, it provides successful students another chance to further consolidate their learning.

History Connection Following these suggestions can be seen as a very effective springboard from the Spanish classroom into the history and social studies areas of the curriculum. Students are asked to focus their attention on the current world map, or historical ones, then they are invited to discuss the cultural, economic and political forces which shape the world with an eye on Hispanic influence. The notes will assist you in providing this type of information yourself or in creating projects in which students do their own research, perhaps with the aid of a history teacher. By making the history connection, students are encouraged to either import or export learning between the Spanish classroom and the history or social studies realms.

Geography Connection These suggestions encourage students to use the maps provided in the Student Textbook as well as refer them to outside sources in order to familiarize them with the geography of Hispanic America and Spain. These optional activities are another way in which **Glencoe Spanish** crosses boundaries into other areas of the curriculum. Their use will instill in students the awareness that Spanish class is not just a study of language but an investigation into a powerful culture that has directly or indirectly affected the lives of millions of people all over the globe. By studying geography, students will be urged to trace the presence of Hispanic culture throughout Europe and the Americas. The notes also supply you the teacher with diverse bits of geographical and historical information which you may decide to pass on to your students.

Description of Enrichment Notes in the Teacher's Wraparound Edition
The notes in the bottom margin of the Teacher's Wraparound Edition enrich students' learning experiences by providing additional activities to those in the Student Textbook. These activities will be helpful in meeting each chapter's objectives, as well as in providing students with an atmosphere of variety, cooperation and enjoyment.

Chapter Projects Specific suggestions are given at the start of each chapter for launching individual students or groups into a research project related to the chapter theme. Students are encouraged to gather information by using resources in school and public libraries, visiting local Hispanic institutions or interviewing Spanish-speaking people or other persons knowledgeable in the area of Hispanic culture whom they may know. In Level 2, Chapter 2, for example, they are asked to keep track of new vocabulary for foods which they like. At chapter's end they make up a shopping list or a menu of things they would like to order in a restaurant. These projects may serve as another excellent means for students to make connections between their learning in the Spanish classroom and other areas of the curriculum.

Learning from Photos and Realia Each chapter of **Glencoe Spanish** contains many colorful photographs and reproductions of authentic Spanish documents, filled with valuable cultural information. In order to help you take advantage of this rich source of learning, notes have been provided in the way of additional, interesting information to assist you in highlighting the special features of these up-to-date realia. The questions that appear under this topic have been designed to enhance learners' reading and critical thinking skills.

Total Physical Response (Level 1) At least one Total Physical Response (TPR) activity is provided with each *Palabras* segment that makes up the *Vocabulario* section of the chapter. Students must focus their attention on commands spoken by the teacher (or classmates) and demonstrate their comprehension by performing the task requested. This strategy has proven highly successful for concentrating on the listening skill and assimilating new vocabulary. Students are relieved momentarily of the need to speak—by which some may be intimidated—and yet challenged to show that they understand spoken Spanish. The physical nature of these activities is another of their benefits, providing a favorable change of pace for students, who must move about the room and perhaps handle some props in order to perform the tasks. In addition, Total Physical Response is in keeping with cooperative learning principles, since many of the commands require students to interact and assist each other in accomplishing them. In Level 2, Total Physical Response is replaced by a Role-play or Pantomime activity.

Cooperative Learning Several cooperative learning activities has been included in each chapter. These activities include guidelines both on the size of groups to be organized and on the tasks the groups will perform. They reflect two basic principles of cooperative learning: (a) that students work together, being responsible for their own learning, and (b) that they do so in an atmosphere of mutual respect and support, where the contributions of each peer are valued. For more information on this topic, please see the section in this Teacher's Manual entitled Cooperative Learning.

Additional Practice There are a variety of Additional Practice activities to complement and follow up the presentation of material in the Student Textbook. Frequently the additional practice focuses on personalization of the new material and employs more than one language skill. Examples of Additional Practice activities include having students give oral or written descriptions of themselves or their classmates; asking students to conduct interviews around a topic and then report their findings to the class. The additional practice will equip you with an ample, organized repertoire from which to pick and choose should you need extra practice beyond that in the Student Textbook.

Independent Practice Many of the exercises in each chapter lend themselves well to assignment or reassignment as homework. In addition to providing extra practice, reassigning on paper exercises that were performed orally in class makes use of additional language skills and aids in informal assessment. The suggestions under the Independent Practice heading in the bottom margin of the Teacher's Wraparound Edition will call your attention to exercises that are particularly suited to this. In addition to reassigning exercises in the Student Textbook as independent practice, additional sources are suggested from the various ancillary components, specifically the Writing Activities Workbook and the Communication Activities Masters.

Critical Thinking Activities To broaden the scope of the foreign language classroom, suggestions are given that will encourage students to make inferences and organize their learning into a coherent "big picture" of today's world. These and other topics offered in the enrichment notes provide dynamic content areas to which students can apply their Spanish language skills and their growing knowledge of Hispanic culture. The guided discussions suggested derived from the chapter themes invite students to make connections between what they learn in the Spanish program and other areas of the curriculum.

Did You Know? This is a teacher resource topic where you will find additional details relevant to the chapter theme. You might wish to add the information given under this topic to your own knowledge and share it with your students to spur their interest in research projects, enliven class discussions and round out their awareness of Hispanic culture, history or geography.

For the Younger Student (Level 1 only) Because *Bienvenidos* is designed for use at the junior high and intermediate level as well as the high school level, this topic pays special attention to the needs of younger students. Each chapter contains suggestions for meaningful language activities and tips to the teacher that cater to the physical and emotional needs of these youngsters. There are ideas for hands-on student projects, such as creating booklets or bringing and using their own props, as well as suggestions for devising games based on speed, using pantomime, show and tell, performing skits and more.

For the Native Speaker This feature has been provided with the realization that the modern Spanish-as-a-second-language class in the U.S. often includes students whose first language is Spanish. These students can provide the class, including the teacher, with valuable information about Hispanic culture as well as the language they use in their everyday lives. For the Native Speaker invites them to share this information in an atmosphere of respect and trust. There are often lexical and structural variations in the parlance of native speakers from different areas of the Spanish-speaking world. For the Native Speaker points out, or asks the native speakers to point out, many of these variations. When such variations are caused by the interference of English—for example, the inclusion of the indefinite article with professions and nationalities (*Juan es un médico*)—the interference is pointed out, and native speakers are guided in practicing the corrected structure. Such correction is handled with sensitivity. The idea is more to inform native speakers that borrowed words and structures are not used in all situations, rather than to make value judgments as to which language is right and which is wrong.

ADDITIONAL ANCILLARY COMPONENTS

All ancillary components are supplementary to the Student Textbook. Any or all parts of the following ancillaries can be used at the discretion of the teacher.

The Writing Activities Workbook and Student Tape Manual

The Writing Activities Workbook and Student Tape Manual is divided into two parts: all chapters of the Writing Activities Workbook appear in the first half of this ancillary component, followed by all chapters of the Student Tape Manual.

Writing Activities Workbook The consumable workbook offers additional writing practice to reinforce the vocabulary and grammatical structures in each chapter of the Student Textbook. The workbook exercises are presented in the same order as the material in the Student Textbook. The exercises are contextualized, often centering around line art illustrations. Workbook activities employ a variety of elicitation techniques, ranging from short answers, matching columns and answering personalized questions, to writing paragraphs and brief compositions. To encourage personalized writing, there is a special section in each chapter entitled *Mi Autobiografía*. The workbook provides further reading skills development with the *Un Poco Más* section, where students are introduced to a number of reading strategies such as scanning for information, distinguishing fact from opinion, drawing inferences and reaching conclusions, for the purpose of improving their reading comprehension and expanding their vocabulary. The *Un Poco Más* section also extends the cultural themes presented in the corresponding Student Textbook chapter. The Writing Activities Workbook includes a Self Test after Chapters 4, 8, 12 and 16. The Writing Activities Workbook, Teacher Annotated Edition provides the teacher with all the material in the student edition of the Writing Activities Workbook plus the answers—wherever possible—to the activities.

Student Tape Manual The Student Tape Manual contains the activity sheets which students will use when listening to the audio recordings. The Teacher's Edition of the Student Tape Manual contains, in addition, the answers to the recorded activities, plus the complete tapescript of all recorded material.

The Audio Program (Cassette or CD)

The recorded material for each chapter of **Glencoe Spanish**, Levels 1 and 2 is divided into two parts — *Primera parte* and *Segunda parte*. The *Primera parte* consists of additional listening and speaking practice for the *Vocabulario* (*Palabras 1 & 2*) and the *Estructura* sections of each chapter. There is also a dramatization of the *Conversación* dialogue from the Student Textbook, and a pronunciation section. The *Primera parte* concludes with a *dictado*.

The *Segunda parte* contains a series of activities designed to further stretch students' receptive listening skills in more open-ended, real-life situations. Students indicate their understanding of brief conversations, advertisements, announcements, et cetera, by making the appropriate response on their activity sheets located in the Student Tape Manual.

Overhead Transparencies

There are five categories in the package of Overhead Transparencies accompanying **Glencoe Spanish**, Level 1, and four for Level 2. Each category of transparencies has its special purpose. Following is a description:

Vocabulary Transparencies These are full-color transparencies reproduced from each of the *Palabras* presentations in the Student Textbook. In converting the *Palabras* vocabulary pages to transparency format, all accompanying words and phrases on the Palabras pages have been deleted to allow for greater flexibility in their use. The Vocabulary Transparencies can be used for the initial presentation of new words and phrases in each chapter. They can also be reprojected to review or reteach vocabulary during the course of teaching the chapter, or as a tool for giving quick vocabulary quizzes.

With more able groups, teachers can show the Vocabulary Transparencies from previous chapters and have students make up original sentences using a particular word. These sentences can be given orally or in writing.

Pronunciation Transparencies (Level 1 only) In the *Pronunciación* section of each chapter of *Bienvenidos*, an illustration has been included to visually cue the key word or phrase containing the sound(s) being taught, e.g., Chapter 3, page 79. Each of these illustrations has been converted to transparency format. These Pronunciation Transparencies may be used to present the key sound(s) for a given chapter, or for periodic pronunciation reviews where several transparencies can be shown to the class in rapid order. Some teachers may wish to convert these Pronunciation Transparencies to black and white paper visuals by making a photocopy of each one. There are no pronunciation transparencies for Level 2. However, the Level 2 teacher may wish to use the Level 1 transparencies from time to time to remind students of the importance of developing good pronunciation habits.

Communication Transparencies For each chapter in Levels 1 and 2 of the series there is one original composite illustration which visually summarizes and reviews the vocabulary and grammar presented in that chapter. These transparencies may be used as cues for additional communicative practice in both oral and written formats. There are 16 Communication Transparencies for Level 1, and 16 for Level 2.

Map Transparencies The full-color maps located at the back of the Student Textbook have been converted to transparency format for the teacher's convenience. These transparencies can be used when there is a reference to them in the Student Textbook, or when there is a history or geography map reference in the Teacher's Wraparound Edition. The Map Transparencies can also be used for quiz purposes, or they may be photocopied in order to provide individual students with a black and white version for use with special projects.

Fine Art Transparencies These are full-color reproductions of works by well known Spanish-speaking artists including Velázquez, Goya, and others. Teachers may use these transparencies to reinforce specific culture topics in both the *Realidades* sections, as well as the optional *Fondo Académico* sections of the Student Textbook.

The Video Program (Cassette or Videodisc)

The video component for each level of **Glencoe Spanish** consists of one hour-long video and an accompanying Video Activities Booklet. Together, they are designed to reinforce the vocabulary, structures, and cultural themes presented in the corresponding Student Textbook. The **Glencoe Spanish** Video Program encourages students to be active listeners and viewers by asking them to respond to each video *Escena* through a variety of previewing, viewing and post-viewing activities. Students are asked to view the same video segment multiple times as they are led, via the activities in their Video Activities Booklet, to look and listen for more detailed information in the video segment they are viewing. The Video for each level of **Glencoe Spanish** begins with an Introduction explaining why listening to natural, spoken Spanish can be a difficult task and therefore why multiple viewings of each video *Escena* are required. The Introduction also points out the importance of using the print activities located in the Video Activities Booklet in order to use the Video Cassette Program successfully.

Video Activities Booklet

The Video Activities Booklet is the vital companion piece to the hour-long video. It consists of a series of pre-viewing, viewing, and post-viewing activities on Blackline Masters. These activities include specific instructions to students on what to watch and listen for as they view a given *Escena* in the video. The Video Activities Booklet also contains a Teacher's Manual, Culture Notes, and a complete Transcript of the video soundtrack.

Computer Software: Practice and Test Generator

Available for Apple II, Macintosh and IBM-compatible machines, this software program provides materials for both students and teacher. The Practice Generator provides students with new, additional practice items for the vocabulary, grammar and culture topics in each chapter of the Student Textbook. All practice items are offered in a multiple choice format. The computer program includes a randomizer, so that each time a student calls up a set of exercises, the items are presented in a different order, thereby discouraging rote memorization of answers. Immediate feedback is given, along with the percent of correct answers, so that with repeated practice, students can track their performance. For vocabulary practice, illustrations from the *Vocabulario* section of the Student Textbook have been scanned into the software to make practice more interesting and versatile.

The Test Generator allows the teacher to print out ready-made chapter tests, or customize a ready-made test by adding or deleting test items. The computer software comes with a Teacher's Manual as well as a printed transcript of all practice and test items.

Communication Activities Masters with Answer Key

This is a series of Blackline Masters which provide further opportunities for students to practice their communication skills using the Spanish they have learned. The contextualized, open-ended situations are designed to encourage students to communicate on a given topic, using specific vocabulary and grammatical structures from the corresponding chapter of the Student Textbook. The use of visual cues and interesting contexts will encourage students to ask questions and experiment with personalized responses. In the case of the paired communication activities, students actively work together as they share information provided on each partner's activity sheet. Answers to all activities are given in an Answer Key at the back of the Communication Activities Masters booklet.

Situation Cards

This is another component of **Glencoe Spanish** aimed at developing listening and speaking skills through guided conversation. For each chapter of the Student Textbook, there is a corresponding set of guided conversational situations printed on hand-held cards. Working in pairs, students use appropriate vocabulary and grammar from the chapter to converse on the suggested topics. Although they are designed primarily for use in paired activities, the Situation Cards may also be used in preparation for the speaking portion of the Testing Program or for informal assessment. Additional uses for the Situation Cards are described in the Situation Cards package, along with specific instructions and tips for their duplication and incorporation into your teaching plans. The cards are in Blackline Master form for easy duplication.

Bell Ringer Reviews on Blackline Masters

These are identical to the Bell Ringer Reviews found in each chapter of the Teacher's Wraparound Edition. For the teacher's convenience, they have been converted to this (optional) Blackline Master format. They may be either photocopied for distribution to students, or the teacher may convert them to overhead transparencies. The latter is accomplished by placing a blank acetate in the paper tray of your photocopy machine, then proceeding to make a copy of your Blackline Master (as though you were making a paper copy).

Lesson Plans and Block Scheduling

Flexible lesson plans have been developed to meet a variety of class schedules, including block scheduling. The various support materials are incorporated into these lesson plans at their most logical point of use, depending on the nature of the presentation material on a given day. For example the Vocabulary Transparencies and the Audio (Cassette or Compact Disc) Program can be used most effectively when presenting the chapter vocabulary. On the other hand, the Chapter Quizzes are recommended for use one or two days after the initial presentation of vocabulary, or following a specific chapter grammar topic. Because student needs and teacher preferences vary, space has been provided on each lesson plan page for the teacher to write additional notes and comments adjusting the day's activities as required.

Block Scheduling This type of scheduling differs from traditional scheduling in that fewer class sessions are scheduled for larger blocks of time over fewer days. For example, a course might meet for 90 minutes a day for 90 days, or half a school year. While there are a number of different block scheduling configurations in use, the one provided in these lesson plans consists of a 90 minute Spanish class.

For schools themselves, the greatest advantage of block scheduling is that there is a better use of resources. No additional teachers or classrooms may be needed, and more efficient use is made of those presently available in the school system. The need for summer school is greatly reduced because the students that do not pass a course one term can take it the next term. These advantages are accompanied by an increase in the quality of teacher instruction and student's time on-task.

There are many advantages for teachers who are in schools that use block scheduling. For example, teacher-student relationships are improved. With block scheduling, teachers have responsibility for a smaller number of students at a time, so students and teachers get to know each other better. With more time, teachers are better able to meet the individual needs of their students. Teachers can also be more focused on what they are teaching. Block scheduling may also result in changes in teaching approaches, classrooms that are more student centered, improved teacher morale, increased teacher effectiveness, and decreased burn-out. Teachers feel free to venture away from discussion and lecture to use more productive models of teaching.

Block scheduling cuts the time needed for introducing and closing classes in half. It also eliminates half of the time needed for class changes, which results in fewer discipline problems.

Flexibility is increased because less complex teaching schedules create more opportunities for cooperative teaching strategies such as team teaching and interdisciplinary studies.

Chapter Quizzes with Answer Key

This component consists of short (5 to 10 minute) quizzes, designed to help both students and teachers evaluate quickly how well a specific vocabulary section or grammar topic has been mastered. For both Levels 1 and 2, there is a quiz for each *Palabras* section (vocabulary) and one quiz for each grammar topic in the *Estructura* section. The quizzes are on Blackline Masters. All answers are provided in an Answer Key at the end of the Chapter Quizzes booklet.

Testing Program with Answer Key

The Testing Program consists of three different types of Chapter Tests, two of which are bound into a testing booklet on Blackline Masters. The third type of test is available as part of the computer software component for **Glencoe Spanish**.

1. The first type of test is discrete-point in nature, and uses evaluation techniques such as fill-in-the-blank, completion, short answers, true/false, matching, and multiple choice. Illustrations are frequently used as visual cues. The discrete-point tests measure vocabulary and grammar concepts via listening, speaking, reading, and writing formats. (As an option to the teacher, the listening section of each test has been

recorded on cassette by native Spanish speakers.) For the teacher's convenience, the speaking portion of the tests has been physically separated from the listening, reading, and writing portions, and placed at the back of the testing booklet. These chapter tests can be administered upon the completion of each chapter. The Unit Tests can be administered upon the completion of each *Repaso* (after every four chapters).

2. The Blackline Master testing booklet also contains a second type of test, namely the Chapter proficiency tests. These measure students' mastery of each chapter's vocabulary and grammar on a more global, whole-language level. For both types of tests above, there is an Answer Key at the back of the testing booklet.

3. In addition to the two types of tests described above, there is a third type which is part of the Computer Software: Practice and Test Generator Program (Macintosh; IBM; Apple versions). With this software, teachers have the option of simply printing out ready-made chapter tests, or customizing a ready-made test by selecting certain items, and/or adding original test items.

Performance Assessment

In addition to the tests described earlier, the Performance Assessment Tests provide an alternate approach to measuring student learning, compared to the more traditional paper and pencil tests. The performance assessment tasks include teacher-student interviews, individual and small-group research tasks with follow-up presentations, and skits that students perform for the class. The Performance Assessment Tests can be administered after every fourth chapter in the textbook. They appear in conjunction with the *Repaso* following Chapters 4, 8, 12, and 16.

COOPERATIVE LEARNING

Cooperative learning provides a structured, natural environment for student communication that is both motivating and meaningful. The affective filter that prevents many students from daring to risk a wrong answer when called upon to speak in front of a whole class can be minimized when students develop friendly relationships in their cooperative groups and when they become accustomed to multiple opportunities to hear and rehearse new communicative tasks. The goal of cooperative learning is not to abandon traditional methods of foreign language teaching, but rather to provide opportunities for learning in an environment where students contribute freely and responsibly to the success of the group. The key is to strike a balance between group goals and individual accountability. Group (team) members plan how to divide the activity among themselves, then each member of the group carries out his or her part of the assignment. Cooperative learning provides each student with a "safe," low-risk environment rather than a whole-class atmosphere. As you implement cooperative learning in your classroom, we urge you to take time to explain to students what will be expected of every group member—listening, participating, and respecting other opinions.

In the Teacher's Wraparound Edition, cooperative learning activities have been written to accompany each chapter of the Student Textbook. These activities have been created to assist both the teacher who wants to include cooperative learning for the first time, and for the experienced practitioner of cooperative learning as well.

Classroom Management: implementing cooperative learning activities

Many of the suggested cooperative learning activities are based on a four-member team structure in the classroom. Teams of four are recommended because there is a wide variety of possible interactions. At the same time the group is small enough that students can take turns quickly within the group. Pairs of students as teams may be too limited in terms of possible interactions, and trios frequently work out to be a pair with the third student left out. Teams of five may be unwieldy in that students begin to feel that no one will notice if they don't really participate.

If students sit in rows on a daily basis, desks can be pushed together to form teams of four. Teams of students who work together need to be balanced according to as many variables as possible: academic achievement in the course, personality, ethnicity, gender, attitude, etc. Teams that are as heterogeneous as possible will ensure that the class progresses quickly through the curriculum.

Following are descriptions of some of the most important cooperative learning structures, adapted from Spencer Kagan's Structural Approach to Cooperative Learning, as they apply to the content of *Bienvenidos* (Level 1).

Roundrobin Each member of the team answers in turn a question, or shares an idea with teammates. Responses should be brief so that students do not have to wait long for their turn.

Example from *Bienvenidos*, Preliminary

Lesson H, Days of the week:

Teams recite the days of the week in a roundrobin fashion. Different students begin additional rounds so that everyone ends up needing to know the names of all the days. Variations include starting the list with a different day or using a race format, i.e., teams recite the list three times in a row and raise their hands when they have finished.

Roundtable Each student in turn writes his or her contribution to the group activity on a piece of paper that is passed around the team. If the individual student responses are longer than one or two words, there can be four pieces of paper with each student contributing to each paper as it is passed around the team.

A to Z Roundtable

Using vocabulary from *Bienvenidos*, Chapters 8 and 14, students take turns adding one word at a time to a list of words associated with plane or train travel in A to Z order. Students may help each other with what to write, and correct spelling. Encourage creativity when it comes to the few letters of the alphabet that don't begin a specific travel word from their chapter lists. Teams can compete in several ways: first to finish all 28 letters; longest word; shortest word; most creative response.

Numbered Heads Together

Numbered Heads Together is a structure for review and practice of high consensus information. There are four steps:

Step 1: Students number off in their teams from 1 to 4.
Step 2: The teacher asks a question and gives the teams some time to make sure that everyone on the team knows the answer.
Step 3: The teacher calls a number.
Step 4: The appropriate student from each team is responsible to report the group response.

Answers can be reported simultaneously, i.e., all students with the appropriate number either stand by their seats and recite the answer together, or they go to the chalkboard and write the answer at the same time. Answers can also be reported sequentially. Call on the first student to raise his or her hand or have all the students with the appropriate number stand. Select one student to give the answer. If the other students agree, they sit down, if not they remain standing and offer a different response.

Example from *Bienvenidos*, Chapter 2, Telling time

Step 1: Using a blank clock face on the overhead transparency, or the chalkboard, the teacher adjusts the hand on the clock.
Step 2: Students put their heads together and answer the question: *¿Qué hora es?*
Step 3: The teacher calls a number
Step 4: The appropriate student from each team is responsible to report the group response.

Pantomimes

Give each team one card. Have each team decide together how to pantomime for the class the action identified on the card. Each team presents the pantomime for ten seconds while the rest of the teams watch without talking. Then each of the other teams tries to guess the phrase and writes down their choice on a piece of paper. (This is a good way to accommodate kinesthetic learning styles as well as vary classroom activities.)

Example from *Bienvenidos*, Chapter 4 vocabulary

The teacher writes the following sentences on slips of paper and places them in an envelope:

1. *Hablan.*
2. *Hablan por teléfono.*
3. *Estudian en la biblioteca.*
4. *Escuchan discos.*
5. *Miran la televisión.*
6. *Preparan una merienda.*
7. *Toman un refresco.*
8. *Bailan.*
9. *Cantan.*
10. *Llegan a una fiesta.*

Each team will draw one slip of paper from the envelope and decide together how to pantomime the action for the class. As one team pantomimes their action for 30 seconds, the other teams are silent. Then the students within each team discuss among themselves what sentence was acted out for them. When they have decided on the sentence, each team sends one person to write it on the chalkboard.

Inside/Outside Circle Students form two concentric circles of equal number by counting off 1-2, 1-2 in their teams. The "ones" form a circle shoulder to shoulder and facing out. The "twos" form a circle outside the "ones" to make pairs. With an odd number of students, there can be one threesome. Students take turns sharing information, quizzing each other, or taking parts of a dialogue. After students finish with their first partners, rotate the inside circle to the left so that the students repeat the process with new partners. For following rounds alternate rotating the inside and outside circles so that students get to repeat the identified tasks, but with new partners. This is an excellent way to structure 100% student participation combined with extensive practice of communication tasks.

Other suggested activities are similarly easy to follow and to implement in the classroom. Student enthusiasm for cooperative learning activities will reward the enterprising teacher. Teachers who are new to these concepts may want to refer to Dr. Spencer Kagan's book, *Cooperative Learning*, published by Resources for Teachers, Inc., Paseo Espada, Suite 622, San Juan Capistrano, CA 92675.

SUGGESTIONS FOR CORRECTING HOMEWORK

Correcting homework, or any tasks students have done on an independent basis, should be a positive learning experience rather than mechanical "busywork." Following are some suggestions for correcting homework. These ideas may be adapted as the teacher sees fit.

1. Put the answers on an overhead transparency. Have students correct their own answers.
2. Ask one or more of your better students to write their homework answers on the chalkboard at the beginning of the class hour. While the answers are being put on the chalkboard, the teacher involves the rest of the class in a non-related activity. At some point in the class hour, take a few minutes to go over the homework answers that have been written on the board, asking students to check their own work. You may then wish to have students hand in their homework so that they know this independent work is important to you the teacher.
3. Go over the homework assignment quickly in class. Write the key word(s) for each answer on the chalkboard so students can see the correct answer.
4. When there is no correct answer, i.e., "Answers Will Vary," give one or two of the most likely answers. Don't allow students to inquire about all other possibilities, however.
5. Have all students hand in their homework. After class, correct every other (every third, fourth, fifth, etc.) homework paper. Over several days, you will have checked every student's homework at least once.
6. Compile a list of the most common student errors. Then create a worksheet that explains the underlying problem areas, providing additional practice in those areas.

STUDENT PORTFOLIOS

The use of student portfolios to represent long-term individual accomplishments in learning Spanish offers several benefits. With portfolios, students can keep a written record of their best work and thereby document their own progress as learners. For teachers, portfolios enable us to include our students in our evaluation and measurement process. For example, the content of any student's portfolio may offer an alternative to the standardized test as a way of measuring student writing achievement. Assessing the contents of a student's portfolio can be an option to testing the writing skill via the traditional writing section on the chapter or unit test.

There are as many kinds of portfolios as there are teachers working with them. Perhaps the most convenient as well as permanent portfolio consists of a three-ring binder which each student will add to over the school year and in which the student will place his or her best written work. In the **Glencoe Spanish** series, selections for the portfolio may come from the Writing Activities Workbook; Communication Activities Masters; the more open-ended activities in the Student Tape Manual and the Video Activities Booklet, as well as from written assignments in the Student Textbook, including the *Comunicación escrita* sections. The teacher is encouraged to refer actively to students' portfolios so that they are regarded as more than just a storage device. For example, over the course of the school year, the student may be asked to go back to earlier entries in his or her portfolio in order to revise certain assignments, or to develop an assignment further by writing in a new tense, e.g., the *pretérito*. In this way the student can appreciate the amount of learning that has occurred over several months time.

Portfolios offer students a multidimensional look at themselves. A "best" paper might be the one with the least errors or one in which the student reached and synthesized a new idea, or went beyond the teacher's assignment. The Student Portfolio topic is included in each chapter of the Teacher's Wraparound Edition as a reminder that this is yet another approach the teacher may wish to use in the Spanish classroom.

PACING

Sample Lesson Plans

Level 2 (*A bordo*) has been developed so that it may be completed in one school year. However, it is up to the individual teacher to decide how many chapters will be covered. Although completion of the textbook by the end of the year is recommended, it is not necessary. Most of the important structures of Level 2 are reviewed in a different context in Level 3 (*De viaje*). The establishment of lesson plans helps the teacher visualize how a chapter can be presented. However, by emphasizing certain aspects of the program and de-emphasizing others, the teacher can change the focus and the approach of a chapter to meet students' needs and to suit his or her own teaching style and techniques. Sample lesson plans are provided below. They include some of the suggestions and techniques that have been described earlier in this Teacher's Manual.

STANDARD PACING

	Days	Total Days
(*Repaso A-F*)	2 days per section	12
Capítulos 1-16	8 days per chapter	128
Testing	1 day per test	14
Repaso (4)	2 days each	8
Nuestro Mundo, Fondo Académico (3 [optional])	2 days each	8

	Class	Homework
Day 1	*Palabras 1* (with transparencies) exercises (Student Textbook)	*Palabras* Exercises (written) Writing Activities Workbook: *Palabras 1*
Day 2	*Palabras 2* (with transparencies) exercises (Student Textbook)	*Palabras* Exercises (written) exercises from Student Textbook (written) prepare *Comunicación* Writing Activities Workbook: *Palabras 2*

Day 3	present *Comunicación* one *Estructura* topic exercises (Student Textbook)	exercises from Student Textbook (written) Writing Activities Workbook (written)
Day 4	two *Estructura* topics exercises (Student Textbook)	exercises from Student Textbook (written) Student Tape Manual exercises
Day 5	one *Estructura* topic exercises (Student Textbook)	exercises from Student Textbook (written) Writing Activities Workbook (written)
Day 6	*Conversación* (pronunciation) *Comunicación* Audio Cassette Program	read *Lectura y Cultura* *Estudio de palabras*
Day 7	review *Lectura y Cultura* *Comprensión* questions Video Program	read *Descubrimiento Cultural* and *Realidades*
Day 8	review homework *Comunicación oral* Situation Cards	*Comunicación escrita*
Day 9	Communication Activities Masters Communication transparency	review for test
Day 10	Test	after Chapters 4, 8, 12: *Repaso* conversation

Repaso (review) and *Fondo Académico* (optional) sections

Day 1	grammar review	exercises in Student Textbook and Workbook
Day 2	correct homework *Comunicación*	review for Test
Day 3	Unit Test	pre-read *Fondo Académico*, first selection (optional)
Day 4	*Fondo Académico*, first selection (optional)	*Fondo Académico*, second selection (optional)
Day 5	*Fondo Académico*, third selection (optional)	*Fondo Académico*, second selection in-depth (optional)

ACCELERATED PACING

	Days	Total Days
(Repaso A-F)	1 day per section	6
Chapters 1-8	8 days per chapter	64*
Chapters 9-16	7 days per chapter	56
Test	1 day per test	16
Repaso (4)	2 days each	8
Nuestro Mundo, Fondo Académico (4 [optional])	2 days each	8

	Class	Homework
Day 1	*Palabras 1* (with transparencies) exercises (Student Textbook)	*Palabras* exercises (written) Writing Activities Workbook: *Palabras 1*
Day 2	*Palabras 2* (with transparencies) exercises (Student Textbook)	*Palabras* exercises (written) Exercises from Student Textbook (written) prepare *Comunicación* Writing Activities Workbook: *Palabras 2*
Day 3	present *Comunicación* two *Estructura* topics	exercises from Student Textbook (written) Writing Activities Workbook (written)
Day 4	two *Estructura* topics	exercises from Student Textbook (written) Writing Activities Workbook (written)
Day 5	*Conversación* present *Comunicación* Audio Cassette Program	read *Lectura y Cultura* *Estudio de palabras* and *Comprensión*
Day 6	*Descubrimiento cultural* (optional) *Realidades* (optional) Video Cassette Program Communication Activities Masters	*Culminación*
Day 7	review *Culminación* Situation Cards Communication transparency	review for test
Day 8	Test	After Chapters 4, 8, 12, 16: *Repaso*

*Note: After Chapter 8, the teacher may choose among the *Culminación* activities on days 6 and 7, thereby eliminating one day.

Repaso (review) and *Fondo Académico* (optional) sections

Day 1	*Repaso* exercises	review for Test
Day 2	Unit Test	
Day 3	*Fondo Académico*, first selection (optional)	*Fondo Académico*, second selection (optional)
Day 4	*Fondo Académico*, third selection (optional)	

GLENCOE SPANISH 2 CD-ROM INTERACTIVE TEXTBOOK

The *Glencoe Spanish 2 CD-ROM Interactive Textbook* is a complete curriculum and instructional system for high school Spanish students. The four-disc CD-ROM program contains all elements of the textbook plus photographs, videos, animations, and games to enhance and deepen students' understanding of the Spanish language and culture. Although especially suited for individual or small-group use, it can be connected to a large monitor or LCD panel for whole-class instruction. With this flexible, interactive system, you can introduce, reinforce, or remediate any part of the Spanish 2 curriculum at any time.

The CD-ROM program has three major components - Contents, Games, and References. The Contents contain all the components of the Spanish 2 *A bordo* textbook. These components have been enhanced with photographs, live video, animations, and audio. In addition, there are readings and activities specifically for native speakers, as well as self-tests. These latter elements are unique to the CD-ROM program.

The Contents Menu

The following selections can be found in the Contents menu.

Vocabulario Vocabulary is introduced in thematic contexts. New words are introduced, and communication activities based on real-life situations are presented.

Estructura Students are given explanations of Spanish structures. They then practice through contextualized exercises. One of the grammar points in each chapter is enhanced with an electronic comic strip with which students can interact.

Conversación Interactive video enhances this feature comprised of real-life dialogues. Students may listen to and watch a conversation and then choose to participate as a character as they record their part of the dialogue.

Lectura y cultura Readings give students the opportunity to gain insight into Hispanic culture. They are also able to hear the readings in Spanish. The similarities and differences between Hispanic and U.S. culture are emphasized.

Hispanoparlantes This activity is intended to help native speakers formally learn more about the structual and grammatical aspects of their primary language. It has been added exclusively to the CD-ROM program to challenge and inspire native speakers.

Realidades In *Realidades*, students discover the similarities and differences that exist among various cultural groups in the Spanish-speaking world, including Hispanic cultures in the United States. The narration for each photograph and live-video segment is done by a native speaker from the part of the Hispanic world featured. This gives students insight into the variations in the Spanish language.

Culminación Chapter-end activities require students to integrate the concepts they have learned. There are oral and written activities as well as activities aimed at building skills, and a vocabulary review linked to the glossary.

Prueba The self-test provides a means for students to evaluate their own progress.

At the end of each four chapters are three features: *Nuestro Mundo, Repaso,* and *Fondo Académico.* These selections may also be found in the Contents menu.

Nuestro Mundo This activity provides students with additional readings centered around Hispanic cultures and real-life situations.

Repaso In the *Repaso* section, students participate in a variety of review activities.

Fondo Académico These activities enable students to practice their Spanish reading skills through interdisciplinary readings that provide insights into Hispanic cultures.

The Game Menu

The Game menu gives users access to *El Gran Concurso* (Discs 1 and 3) and *La Vuelta a España* (Discs 2 and 4). Each game reviews the vocabulary, grammar and culture topics that have been presented in the four chapters contained on that particular CD-ROM disc.

The Reference Menu

Maps, verb charts, and the Spanish-English/English-Spanish glossaries can be selected from this menu. The maps include Spain and North Africa, South America, and Central America.

For more information, see the User's Guide accompanying the *Glencoe Spanish 2 CD-ROM Interactive Textbook.*

SPANISH FOR SPANISH SPEAKERS:
NOSOTROS Y NUESTRO MUNDO

This two-level series has been designed for the teaching of Spanish at the secondary school level to native speakers of Spanish residing in the United States. Each of the sixteen chapters takes into account the diversified background of these students—many of whom have a very strong command of the Spanish language and others who have a somewhat limited knowledge of the Spanish language. The textbook also attempts to take into account the specific problems facing the teacher of classes with native Spanish speakers. In some cases, the native-speaking students are placed in separate courses and in other cases, they are in classes with English-speaking students learning Spanish as a foreign language. For these reasons, *Nosotros y nuestro mundo* can be used as a basal textbook in courses for native speakers, or it can be used as an adjunct to the **Glencoe Spanish** series in classes that have both native speakers of Spanish and English. In the latter case, it is presumed that teachers will have less time with their students and a fair amount of the material will need to be acquired by students through independent study or cooperative group work.

Organization

Each of the sixteen chapters is divided into six parts:

- *Nuestro conocimiento académico*
- *Nuestro idioma*
- *Nuestra cultura*
- *Nuestra literatura*
- *Nuestra creatividad*
- *Nuestras diversiones*

Nuestro conocimiento académico This section of each lesson serves several purposes. It exposes students to important information that is presented in other disciplines of the school curriculum. In some cases, it may contain material that students have learned in another course, or it may present information that for one reason or another, they have not previously studied. In addition to the reading topic itself, this section also introduces students to higher level vocabulary that they seldom encounter in Spanish when taking other courses in English.

Many native Spanish-speaking students have an extensive vocabulary on topics related to home, school, family, and everyday activities. Many of these same students, however, possess a limited vocabulary on topics such as geography, economics, finance, medicine, literature, art, music, etc. This is particularly true for students who have lived in the United States for many years and who have been educated in English. It is also true for students who are recent arrivals to the United States and who, for one reason or another, have received little formal education in their native country.

Nuestro idioma It is a known fact that native speakers of Spanish do not need the same type of grammatical/structural or syntactical information about their language as do individuals who are acquiring Spanish as a foreign language. The native speaker has no difficulty responding with *Hablo...* in reply to a question with *¿Hablas...?* The English speaker, on the other hand, needs a great deal of practice before he/she will be able to respond using a proper verb form.

The material in the *Nuestro idioma* section deals with linguistic principles and problems specific to the native speaker. *Nuestro idioma* deals with all of the following areas: grammar/structure, spelling, pronunciation, morphology, etc.

In this section we have taken into account the regional differences in the Spanish spoken by the many native-speaking groups in the U.S. Particular attention has been paid to the Spanish spoken by Mexicans, Mexican-Americans, and of those groups from the Caribbean basin. The Spanish of other areas is also dealt with.

Much attention is given to linguistic problems that arise from living in a bilingual environment—the superimposition of English, for example. In the units that deal with these specific problems, we have been extremely careful to differentiate between *regionalismos* and *vulgarismos* while taking into account that one of the most fascinating aspects of language is that it is forever changing and while many changes are completely acceptable, others are less so.

Nuestra cultura The *Nuestra cultura* section is an extremely important part of each chapter. It serves to introduce students to the tremendous cultural wealth of the Spanish-speaking world both within and outside of the United States.

In this section the word *hispano(a)* is used frequently. Although the word *hispano(a)* can have political overtones and some prefer the use of the word *latino(a)*, we use *hispano(a)* to refer to anyone whose mother tongue is Spanish. In addition, each native speaker of Spanish has his or her own cultural identity: Mexican-American, Mexican, Puerto Rican, Cuban, Nicaraguan, Spaniard, etc.

Nuestra literatura The *Nuestra literatura* section of each lesson introduces students to the literature of the entire Spanish-speaking world. Most selections are of famous authors throughout history as well as contemporary writers. (The works of some lesser-known writers are also represented if we felt the topic would be of particular interest to your students.) In this section, there are examples of the various literary genres: poetry, fable, prose, short story, novel, legend, etc.

Nuestra creatividad The *Nuestra creatividad* section provides students with much opportunity to brainstorm. Many of the activities start with very simple tasks and progress to having students add more information until they finally produce a story, essay or speech on their own. The activities themselves are quite self-explanatory. Some have the students working in groups, others have them working independently. The creative activities deal with both oral and written expression. Students are given the opportunity to write paragraphs, to develop short stories, and to write poetry on their own. They will also give different types of speeches: expository, persuasive, etc.

Nuestra diversiones The *Nuestras diversiones* section of each chapter is something to be enjoyed by both students and teachers alike. Here we include magazine and newspaper articles from periodicals that are available in Spanish in the United States. Students are given the opportunity to sit back, read, and enjoy the material. Hopefully this type of reading activity will develop the desire for students to read on their own--now and in the future.

You can decide how thoroughly you wish to cover a particular article. You may just have the students read it once on their own, or you may wish to ask comprehension questions about it. You may also have students retell what they read in their own words. They may do this either orally or in writing.

ADDITIONAL SPANISH RESOURCES

For detailed information about a particular Spanish-speaking country, you should contact individual embassies.

Embassies

Argentine Republic
1600 New Hampshire Ave. NW
Washington, D.C. 20009
(202) 939-6400

Bolivia
3014 Massachussetts Ave. NW
Washington, D.C. 20008
(202) 483-4410

Chile
1732 Massachusetts Ave. NW
Washington, D.C. 20036
(202) 785-1746

Colombia
2118 Leroy Pl. NW
Washington, D.C. 20008
(202) 387-8338

Costa Rica
1825 Connecticut Ave. Suite 211 NW
Washington, D.C. 20009
(202) 234-2945

Cuban Interest Section
2630 and 2639 16th St. NW
Washington, D.C. 20009
(202) 797-8518

Dominican Republic
1715 22nd St. NW
Washington, D.C. 20008
(202) 332-6280

Ecuador
2535 15th St. NW
Washington, D.C. 20009
(202) 234-7200

El Salvador
2308 California St. NW
Washington, D.C. 20008
(202) 265-3480

Guatemala
2220 R St. NW
Washington, D.C. 20008
(202) 745-4952

Honduras
3007 Tilden St. NW
Washington, D.C. 20008
(202) 966-7702

Mexico
1911 Pennsylvania Ave. NW
Washington, D.C. 20006
(202) 728-1600

Nicaragua
1627 New Hampshire Ave. NW
Washington, D.C. 20006
(202) 939-6570

Panama
2862 McGill Terrace NW
Washington, D.C. 20008
(202) 483-1407

Paraguay
2400 Massachusetts Ave. NW
Washington, D.C. 20008
(202) 483-6960

Peru
1700 Massachusetts Ave. NW
Washington, D.C. 20036
(202) 833-9860

Spain
2700 15th St. NW
Washington, D.C. NW 20009
(202) 265-0190

Uruguay
1918 F St. NW
Washington, D.C. 20006
(202) 331-1313

Venezuela
1099 30th St. NW
Washington, D.C. 20007
(202) 342-2214

Tourist Offices

Mexican Government Tourism Office
405 Park Ave.
New York, New York 10022

Tourist Office of Spain
8363 Wilshire Blvd.
Beverly Hills, CA 90211

Mexican Government Tourism Office
10100 Santa Monica Blvd. Suite 224
Los Angeles, CA 90067

Spanish Embassy Education Offices

The Spanish embassy's education offices offer materials and information free of charge to teachers of Spanish.

Consejería de Educación
Embajada de España
1350 Connecticut Ave., NW #1050
Washington, D.C. 20036-1701

Oficina de Educación
Consulado General de España
150 Fifth Ave. # 918
New York, N.Y. 10011

Agregaduría de Educación
Consulado General de España
6300 Wilshire Blvd. # 1740
Los Angeles, CA 90048

Oficina de Educación
Consulado General de España
2655 Lejeune Road # 1008
Coral Gables, FL 33134

Oficina de Educación
Consulado General de España
1405 Sutter St.
San Francisco, CA 94109

Centro de Recursos de Español
University of Southern California
3424 S. Hoover Blvd. #B-29
Los Angeles, CA 90089-0031

Centro de Recursos de Español
University of New Mexico
4125 Carlisle Blvd., N.E.
Albuquerque, NM 87107-4806

Centro de Recursos de Español
Florida International University
University Park
Miami, FL 33199

Centro de Recursos de Español
University of Houston
416 Agnes Arnold Hall
Houston, TX 77204-3784

Books, Periodicals

Librería Hispánica
115 Fifth Ave.
New York, New York 10003

Ediciones Universal
Librería y Distribuidora
Universal
P.O. Box 450353 (Shenandoah Station)
Miami, Florida 33245-0353

Midwest European Publications
915 Foster St.
Evanston, Illinois 60201

The Spanish Bookstore
10977 Santa Monica Blvd.
West Los Angeles, CA 90025

Spanish-Language Newspapers Published in the U.S.

El Diario La Prensa
143 Varick St.
New York, New York 10013

Diario Las Américas
2900 NW 39th St.
Miami, Florida 33142

La Opinión
1436 South Main St.
Los Angeles, CA 90015

U.S. Distributor of Spanish Magazines and Newspapers

Roig
29 West 19th St.
New York, NY 10011

Spanish Language Radio and Television Broadcasts in the U.S.

Local Spanish Radio Stations

City	Radio Station Call Letters
Boston	WUNR
Chicago	WCRW, WEDC
Denver	KBNO
Houston	KEYH, KLAT, KXYS
Los Angeles	KLVE, KALI, KSKQ, KTNG, KWKW
Miami	WCMG, WOCN, WQBA
New York	WADO, WBNX, WJIT
Philadelphia	WTEL
San Antonio	KCOR, KEDA, KFHM
San Francisco	KBRG

Local Spanish Television Stations

City	TV Station Call Letters
Chicago	WCIU/TV, WSNS/TV
Houston	KRIV/TV
Los Angeles	KMEX/TV, KVEA/TV
Miami	WLRN/TV, WLTV/TV
New York	WNJU/TV, WXTV/TV
Phoenix	KTVW/TV
Sacramento	KCSO/TV
San Antonio	KWEX/TV
San Francisco	KDTV/TV, KTZO/TV

Classroom Magazines

To obtain Spanish-language magazines designed for use in the classroom, write to:

¡OYE!
2931 East McCarty St.
Jefferson City, MO 65102-3710

LISTO
2931 East McCarty St.
Jefferson City, MO 65102-3710

Hispanic American Posters

To buy Hispanic American posters, contact:

Joanne Beardsley
Quarten Manufacturing
444 N. Michigan Ave.
Suite 1600
Chicago, Illinois 60611
(312) 644-8600

Teacher Resources

Network of Educators on Central America
1118 22nd St., NW
Washington, D.C. 20037

GLENCOE SPANISH 2
A bordo

Protase E. Woodford
Conrad J. Schmitt

GLENCOE
McGraw-Hill

New York, New York   Columbus, Ohio   Mission Hills, California   Peoria, Illinois

About the Cover

The fortress of El Morro was built by the Spaniards in the 16th Century. Located on a point of land overlooking the entrance to San Juan, Puerto Rico, its purpose was to protect the city from attacks by English and Dutch pirate ships. Today, El Morro is a symbol of Puerto Rico's rich Spanish heritage.

Copyright © 1997 by Glencoe/McGraw-Hill. All rights reserved. Except as permitted under the United States Copyright Act, no part of this publication may be reproduced or distributed in any form or by any means, or stored in a database or retrieval system, without prior written permission of the publisher.

Printed in the United States of America.

Send all inquiries to:
Glencoe/McGraw-Hill
15319 Chatsworth Street
P.O. Box 9609
Mission Hills, CA 91346-9609

ISBN 0-02-646118-8 (Student Edition)
ISBN 0-02-646119-6 (Teacher's Wraparound Edition)

1 2 3 4 5 6 7 8 9   RRW   99 98 97 96

Acknowledgments

We wish to express our deep appreciation to the numerous individuals throughout the United States who have advised us in the development of these teaching materials. Special thanks are extended to the people whose names appear here.

Kristine Aarhus
Northshore School District
Bothell, Washington

Kathy Babula
Charlotte Country Day School
Charlotte, North Carolina

Veronica Dewey
Brother Rice High School
Birmingham, Michigan

Anneliese H. Foerster
Oak Hill Academy
Mouth of Wilson, Virginia

Sharon Gordon-Link
Antelope Valley Unified High School
Lancaster, California

Leslie Lumpkin
Prince George's County Public Schools
Prince George's County, Maryland

Loretta Mizeski
Columbia School
Berkeley Heights, New Jersey

Robert Robison
Columbus Public Schools
Columbus, Ohio

Rhona Zaid
Los Angeles, California

CONTENIDO

REPASO

A	LOS AMIGOS Y LOS CURSOS	Los verbos en -ar R-4
		Los verbos ir, dar y estar R-7
B	LAS ACTIVIDADES	Los verbos en -er, -ir R-14
		El verbo ser R-16
		Los artículos y los sustantivos R-18
		La concordancia de los adjetivos R-20
		El presente progresivo R-21
C	LOS VIAJES Y LOS DEPORTES	El presente de los verbos de cambio radical R-28
		Los verbos con g en la primera persona R-30
D	EL INVIERNO Y EL VERANO	El pretérito de los verbos regulares R-38
		Los complementos directos e indirectos R-40
E	LAS VACACIONES Y LAS ACTIVIDADES CULTURALES	El pretérito de los verbos irregulares R-46
		El verbo gustar R-49
F	DE CAMPING	Los verbos reflexivos R-54
		El presente de algunos verbos de cambio radical R-56

CAPÍTULO 1

UNA LLAMADA TELEFÓNICA

VOCABULARIO	PALABRAS 1 El teléfono 2
	PALABRAS 2 Cuando llamaba a mi abuelita 6
ESTRUCTURA	El imperfecto de los verbos en -ar 10
	El imperfecto de los verbos en -er e -ir 11
	El imperfecto de los verbos ir y ser 13
	Los usos del imperfecto 14
CONVERSACIÓN	Una llamada telefónica 16
LECTURA Y CULTURA	El teléfono de ayer y de hoy 18
REALIDADES	Telecomunicaciones 22
CULMINACIÓN	Comunicación oral y escrita 24
	Reintegración 25

CAPÍTULO 2
DE COMPRAS

VOCABULARIO	PALABRAS 1 De compras 28
	PALABRAS 2 En el supermercado 32
ESTRUCTURA	El imperfecto y el pretérito 36
	Dos acciones en la misma oración 39
	Los verbos como *querer* y *creer* en el pasado 41
CONVERSACIÓN	Fui de compras 42
LECTURA Y CULTURA	De compras 44
REALIDADES	Tiendas, mercados y supermercados 48
CULMINACIÓN	Comunicación oral y escrita 50
	Reintegración 51

CAPÍTULO 3
EL CORREO

VOCABULARIO	PALABRAS 1 La correspondencia 54
	PALABRAS 2 El correo 58
ESTRUCTURA	El futuro de los verbos regulares 62
	El comparativo y el superlativo. Formas regulares 64
CONVERSACIÓN	En el correo 66
LECTURA Y CULTURA	Escribiremos una carta 68
REALIDADES	El correo y la correspondencia 72
CULMINACIÓN	Comunicación oral y escrita 74
	Reintegración 75

CAPÍTULO 4
UN ACCIDENTE Y EL HOSPITAL

VOCABULARIO	PALABRAS 1	Los accidentes 78
	PALABRAS 2	En el hospital 82
ESTRUCTURA		El futuro de los verbos irregulares 86
		El futuro de otros verbos irregulares 87
		El comparativo y el superlativo. Formas irregulares 89
CONVERSACIÓN		Una visita al hospital 90
LECTURA Y CULTURA		Hospital del Sagrado Corazón —¡Ya voy! 92
REALIDADES		La salud y la medicina 96
CULMINACIÓN		Comunicación oral y escrita 98
		Reintegración 99
NUESTRO MUNDO		Noticias de Telecom y un anuncio de AT&T 100
REPASO		Capítulos 1-4 102
FONDO ACADÉMICO		Las ciencias naturales: El sonido 106
		La sociología: Medicina y sociedad 108
		La historia: Los alimentos en la historia 110

CAPÍTULO 5
EL COCHE Y LA GASOLINERA

VOCABULARIO	PALABRAS 1	El coche 114
	PALABRAS 2	La estación de servicio 118
ESTRUCTURA		El potencial o condicional Formas regulares 122
		El potencial o condicional Formas irregulares 124
		Dos complementos en una oración *me lo, te lo, nos lo* 126
CONVERSACIÓN		En la gasolinera 128
LECTURA Y CULTURA		Los carros en Latinoamérica 130
REALIDADES		La ciudad y el tráfico 134
CULMINACIÓN		Comunicación oral y escrita 136
		Reintegración 137

CAPÍTULO 6
EL HOTEL

VOCABULARIO	PALABRAS 1 En la recepción	140
	PALABRAS 2 En la habitación	144
ESTRUCTURA	El presente perfecto 148	
	Los participios irregulares 151	
	Dos complementos con *se* 152	
CONVERSACIÓN	En la recepción del hotel	154
LECTURA Y CULTURA	Los hoteles en España y en Latinoamérica	156
REALIDADES	¿Cómo es tu hotel favorito?	160
CULMINACIÓN	Comunicación oral y escrita	162
	Reintegración 163	

CAPÍTULO 7
A BORDO DEL AVIÓN

VOCABULARIO	PALABRAS 1 Dentro del avión	166
	PALABRAS 2 En el aeropuerto	170
ESTRUCTURA	Los tiempos progresivos 174	
	La comparación de igualdad con adjetivos y adverbios 176	
	La comparación de igualdad con sustantivos 177	
CONVERSACIÓN	A bordo del avión	178
LECTURA Y CULTURA	Un vuelo interesante	180
REALIDADES	El mundo de los transportes aéreos	184
CULMINACIÓN	Comunicación oral y escrita	186
	Reintegración 187	

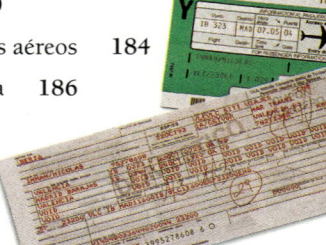

CAPÍTULO 8
LA PELUQUERÍA

VOCABULARIO	PALABRAS 1	¿Cómo te peinas? 190
	PALABRAS 2	Necesito un corte de pelo 194
ESTRUCTURA		La colocación de los pronombres de complemento 198
		Acabar de con el infinitivo 201
CONVERSACIÓN		En la peluquería 202
LECTURA Y CULTURA		Nuevos peinados en Latinoamérica 204
REALIDADES		El cabello y el cuidado personal 208
CULMINACIÓN		Comunicación oral y escrita 210
		Reintegración 211
NUESTRO MUNDO		Los hoteles y sus servicios 212
REPASO		Capítulos 5-8 214
FONDO ACADÉMICO		Las ciencias: La meteorología 218
		Las ciencias sociales: La historia 220
		Humanidades: La mitología 222

CAPÍTULO 9
LA COCINA

VOCABULARIO	PALABRAS 1	¡A cocinar! 226
	PALABRAS 2	En la cocina 230
ESTRUCTURA		El imperativo formal. Formas regulares 234
		El imperativo formal. Formas irregulares 236
		La voz pasiva con *se* 238
CONVERSACIÓN		¿Yo? ¿En la cocina? 240
LECTURA Y CULTURA		Una receta 242
REALIDADES		La producción de los alimentos 246
CULMINACIÓN		Comunicación oral y escrita 248
		Reintegración 249

CAPÍTULO 10

LA CARRETERA Y LAS DIRECCIONES

VOCABULARIO	PALABRAS 1 Las direcciones 252	
	PALABRAS 2 ¡Maneja con cuidado! 256	
ESTRUCTURA	El imperativo familiar. Formas regulares 260	
	El imperativo familiar. Formas irregulares 261	
	El imperativo negativo 263	
	Los pronombres con el imperativo 264	
CONVERSACIÓN	¿Dónde está? 266	
LECTURA Y CULTURA	Las direcciones a Maldonado 268	
REALIDADES	¿Me puedes decir cómo llegar? 272	
CULMINACIÓN	Comunicación oral y escrita 274	
	Reintegración 275	

CAPÍTULO 11

LOS BUENOS MODALES

VOCABULARIO	PALABRAS 1 ¿Cómo te comportas? 278	
	PALABRAS 2 Modales y costumbres 281	
ESTRUCTURA	El subjuntivo 285	
	Formación del subjuntivo 286	
	El subjuntivo en cláusulas nominales 288	
	El subjuntivo con expresiones impersonales 290	
CONVERSACIÓN	¿Por qué no nos tuteamos? 292	
LECTURA Y CULTURA	Buenos modales y fórmulas de cortesía 294	
REALIDADES	La etiqueta y el buen comportamiento 298	
CULMINACIÓN	Comunicación oral y escrita 300	
	Reintegración 301	

CAPÍTULO 12
FIESTAS FAMILIARES

VOCABULARIO	PALABRAS 1	¡Feliz cumpleaños! 304
	PALABRAS 2	¡Feliz Navidad y próspero Año Nuevo! 308
ESTRUCTURA		El subjuntivo de los verbos de cambio radical 312
		El subjuntivo con verbos como *pedir* y *aconsejar* 313
		El subjuntivo con expresiones de duda 315
		El subjuntivo con expresiones de emoción 316
CONVERSACIÓN		El cumpleaños de Lupe 318
LECTURA Y CULTURA		Desde el nacimiento hasta la muerte 320
REALIDADES		Las celebraciones 324
CULMINACIÓN		Comunicación oral y escrita 326
		Reintegración 327
NUESTRO MUNDO		Noticias y notas sociales 328
REPASO		Capítulos 9-12 330
FONDO ACADÉMICO		Las ciencias naturales: La nutrición 334
		Las ciencias sociales: España y las gentes del libro 336
		Las humanidades: La quiebra 338

CAPÍTULO 13
LA NATURALEZA Y LA LIMPIEZA

VOCABULARIO	PALABRAS 1	Por el sendero 342
	PALABRAS 2	Tengo que lavar mi ropa 346
ESTRUCTURA		El infinitivo o el subjuntivo 350
		Repaso del pretérito de los verbos irregulares 352
CONVERSACIÓN		En la lavandería 354
LECTURA Y CULTURA		Isabel la naturalista 356
REALIDADES		Algunos lugares interesantes para visitar 360
CULMINACIÓN		Comunicación oral y escrita 362
		Reintegración 363

CAPÍTULO 14

EL DINERO Y EL BANCO

VOCABULARIO	PALABRAS 1	¿Necesitas dinero? 366
	PALABRAS 2	¿Tiene Ud. una cuenta en este banco? 369
ESTRUCTURA		El imperfecto del subjuntivo 373
		Usos del imperfecto del subjuntivo 374
		Cláusulas con *si* 377
CONVERSACIÓN		En el banco 378
LECTURA Y CULTURA		El dinero es oro 380
REALIDADES		La industria bancaria en el mundo hispano 384
CULMINACIÓN		Comunicación oral y escrita 386
		Reintegración 387

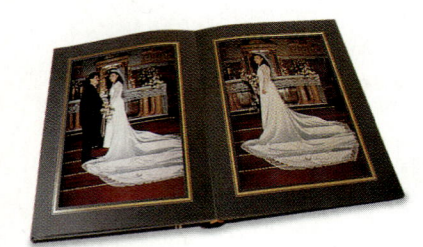

CAPÍTULO 15

AMIGOS, NOVIOS Y EL MATRIMONIO

VOCABULARIO	PALABRAS 1	El compromiso 390
	PALABRAS 2	La ceremonia 394
ESTRUCTURA		El subjuntivo en cláusulas adverbiales 398
		El subjuntivo con *aunque* 400
		El subjuntivo con cláusulas adverbiales de tiempo 401
CONVERSACIÓN		¿Te estás enamorando? 404
LECTURA Y CULTURA		El amor es una cosa divina 406
REALIDADES		La pareja y su día de bodas 410
CULMINACIÓN		Comunicación oral y escrita 412
		Reintegración 413

CAPÍTULO 16

LAS CARRERAS Y EL TRABAJO

VOCABULARIO	PALABRAS 1 El trabajo o el oficio	416
	PALABRAS 2 En busca de empleo	420
ESTRUCTURA	El subjuntivo en cláusulas relativas	424
	El subjuntivo con *ojalá*, *tal vez*, *quizá(s)*	425
CONVERSACIÓN	Me interesa el mercadeo	426
LECTURA Y CULTURA	El español y su carrera	428
REALIDADES	Profesiones y oficios	432
CULMINACIÓN	Comunicación oral y escrita	434
	Reintegración	435
NUESTRO MUNDO	Los medicamentos	436
REPASO	Capítulos 13-16	438
FONDO ACADÉMICO	Las ciencias: El hombre, ¿enemigo de la naturaleza?	442
	Las ciencias sociales: La economía	444
	Las humanidades: Las bellas artes	446

APÉNDICES

Mapas   451

Verbos   455

Vocabulario Español-Inglés   481

Vocabulario Inglés-Español   511

Índice gramatical   529

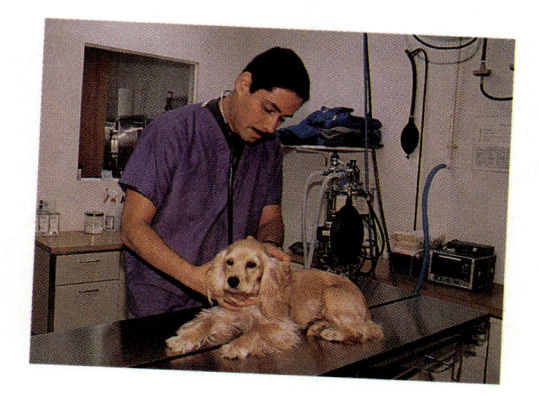

xiii

LEVEL 2 A BORDO
Scope and Sequence

Topics	Functions	Structure	Culture
REPASO A pages R1-R9 School After-school activities	How to talk about going to school and classes you are taking How to express location and how you feel How to discuss what activities you do after school	Los verbos en *-ar* Los verbos *ir,* y *estar*	School and classmates
REPASO B pages R10-R23 Greetings and farewells Leisure-time activities	How to greet someone How to ask where someone is from How to talk about where you live How to describe people and things How to discuss leisure activities	Los verbos en *-er* e *-ir* El verbo *ser* Los artículos y los sustantivos La concordancia de los adjetivos El presente progresivo	Home life Friends
REPASO C pages R24-R33 Plane travel Team sports	How to talk about taking a trip by plane How to discuss a soccer match How to talk about what you want to do	El presente de los verbos de cambio radical Los verbos con *g* en la primera persona	Travel Sports
REPASO D pages R34-R41 Winter and summer seasons	How to talk about summer and winter activities How to talk about vacations	El pretérito de los verbos regulares Los complementos directos e indirectos	Vacations
REPASO E pages R42-R49 Vacations Cultural activities	How to talk about traveling by train How to discuss visiting a museum, theater, or a movie How to talk about eating at a restaurant	El pretérito de los verbos irregulares El verbo *gustar*	Cultural activities
REPASO F pages R50-R57 Camping	How to talk about camping How to talk about daily routines	Los verbos reflexivos El presente de algunos verbos de cambio radical	Camping with friends

Repaso Print Resources

Blackline Masters Teacher's Classroom Resources

Lesson Plans

Workbook   Pages
- Repaso A   R1–R5
- Repaso B   R6–R13
- Repaso C   R14–R20
- Repaso D   R21–R26
- Repaso E   R27–R32
- Repaso F   R33–R38

- 15 Bell Ringer Reviews   1–6

Testing Program
- Listening Comprehension: R1; R4; R7; R10; R13; R16
- Reading and Writing: R2-3; R5-6; R8-9; R11-12; R14-15; R17-18

Repaso Multimedia Resources

CD-ROM Interactive Textbook Disc 1

Repaso Student Edition
- Repaso A: Los Amigos y los cursos
- Repaso B: Las actividades
- Repaso C: Los viajes y los deportes
- Repaso D: El invierno y el verano
- Repaso E: Las vacaciones y las actividades culturales
- Repaso F: De camping

Introduction to the *Repaso*

The *Repaso* sections A through F in *A bordo* are designed to give students a concise review of all the essential material taught in *Bienvenidos* (Level 1) in a systematic fashion. Each section is designed to take two or three days of instruction. *Repaso* Sections A, B and C review material from Level 1, Chapters 1 through 8; sections D, E and F review the content of Chapters 9 through 16.

Depending upon the amount of material covered in first year Spanish, student aptitude, and your own teaching preference, you may decide to review some or all of the *Repaso* sections at the beginning of the school year. Many teachers will use the *Repaso* sparingly, delving into these sections as required in order to ensure a smooth transition into new material beginning with Chapter 1 of *A bordo*. Above all, we would urge you not to spend more than a few weeks on the *Repaso* before moving along to Chapter 1. It is always possible to return to these review sections later if necessary.

REPASO A

OVERVIEW

There are six *Repasos* (A-F) at the beginning of *A bordo*. *Repasos* A-C cover the material in Chapters 1-8 in *Bienvenidos*, and *Repasos* D-F review the material in Chapters 9-16.

Repaso A reviews vocabulary needed to describe a school, as well as school and after-school activities. The regular *-ar* verbs and the verbs *ir, dar,* and *estar* are reviewed.

REVIEW RESOURCES

1. Workbook, *Repaso A*
2. Bell Ringer Review Blackline Masters
3. Testing Program

Pacing

Repaso A should take three to four days depending on the length of the class, the age of the students, and student aptitude.

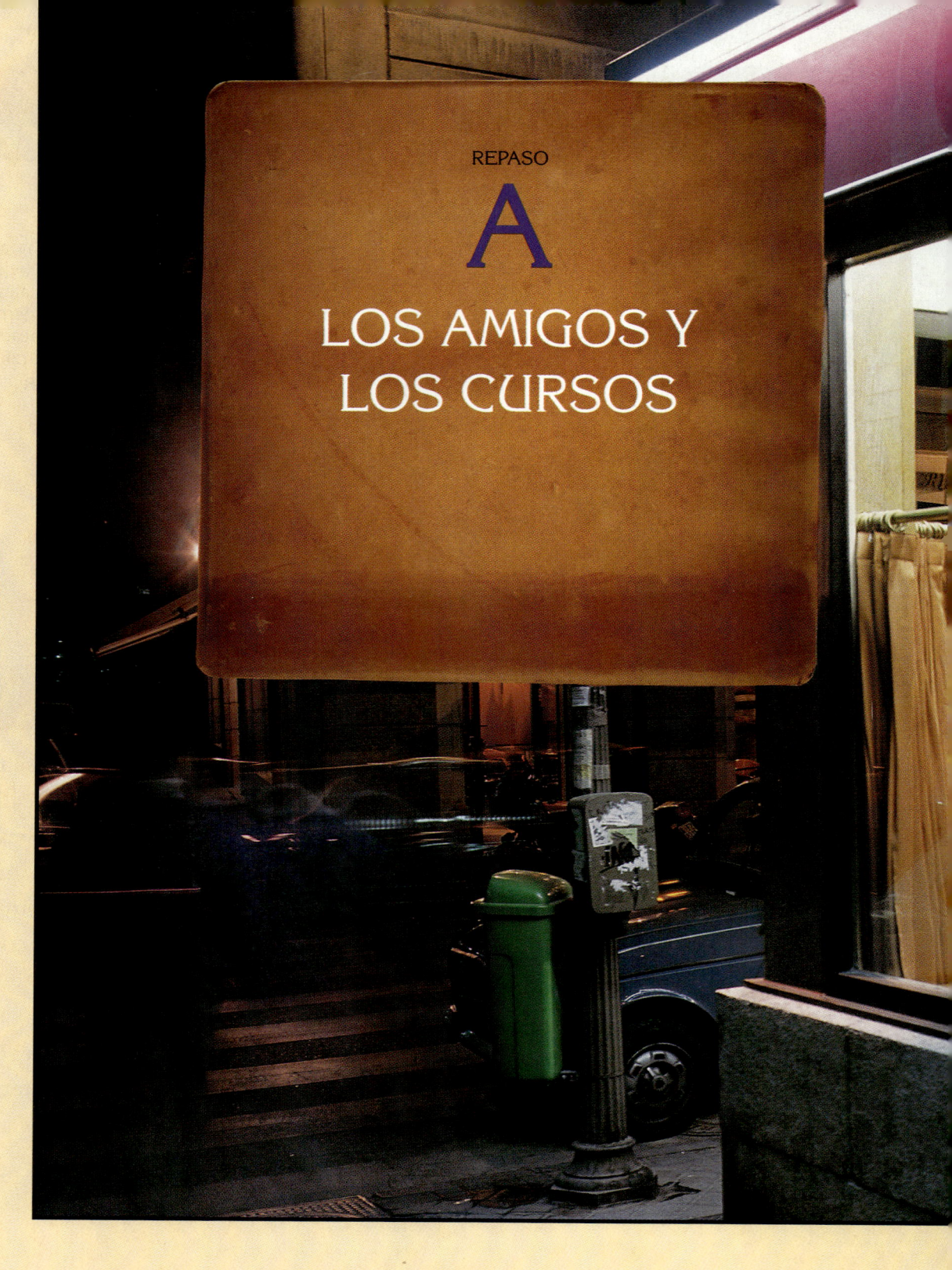

REPASO A

LOS AMIGOS Y LOS CURSOS

LEARNING FROM PHOTOS

1. Have students say as much as they can about the photo on page R-1. You may wish to ask students the following questions: ¿Están en la escuela los amigos? ¿Dónde están? ¿Cuántos muchachos hay? ¿Cuántas muchachas hay? ¿Es moderno el café?
2. Have students tell what they think each student ordered at the café.

VOCABULARIO

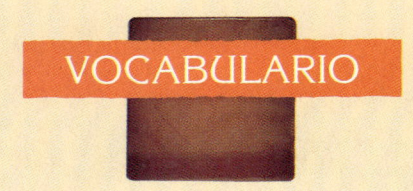

Vocabulary Teaching Resources

1. Workbook, *Repaso A*
2. Bell Ringer Review Blackline Masters

Bell Ringer Review

Write the following on the board or use BRR Blackline Master R-1: Make a list of expressions that you remember from last year that can be used to describe some school activities.

Los alumnos

PRESENTATION *(page R-2)*

Have students repeat each line after you with books open.

Ejercicios

PRESENTATION *(page R-2)*

Ejercicio A

Before going over Exercise A, you may wish to ask more detailed questions about each sentence. For example: *¿Quiénes van a la escuela? ¿Adónde van? ¿Cómo van?*

ANSWERS

Ejercicio A
1. Los alumnos van en el bus escolar.
2. Ellos llegan a las ocho menos cinco de la mañana.
3. Hablan con su profesor.
4. El profesor enseña.
5. Están en la sala de clase en la escuela.
6. Los alumnos van al café.
7. Toman una merienda. (Toman un refresco.)

Vocabulary Expansion

Churros are a type of deep-fried Spanish doughnut. They are narrow and twirled. A *porra* is also a fried doughnut, but it is larger and thicker than a *churro*.

R 2

VOCABULARIO

Los alumnos

Los alumnos van a la escuela en el bus escolar.
Ellos llegan a la escuela.
Un alumno habla con el profesor.
El profesor enseña.
Los alumnos estudian.
Están en la sala de clase.
Después de las clases, los alumnos van a un café.
Toman una merienda en el café.
Toman un refresco.

A En la escuela. Contesten.

1. ¿Cómo van los alumnos a la escuela? ¿Van a pie, en carro o en el bus escolar?
2. ¿A qué hora llegan a la escuela, a las ocho menos cinco de la mañana o a las ocho menos cinco de la tarde?
3. ¿Con quién hablan los alumnos en la escuela, con su profesor o con sus parientes?
4. ¿Quién enseña, el alumno o el profesor?
5. ¿Dónde están los alumnos ahora? ¿Están en la sala de clase en la escuela o están en casa?
6. ¿Adónde van los alumnos después de las clases? ¿Van a la escuela, a la tienda de discos o al café?
7. ¿Qué toman en el café? ¿Toman una merienda o un refresco?

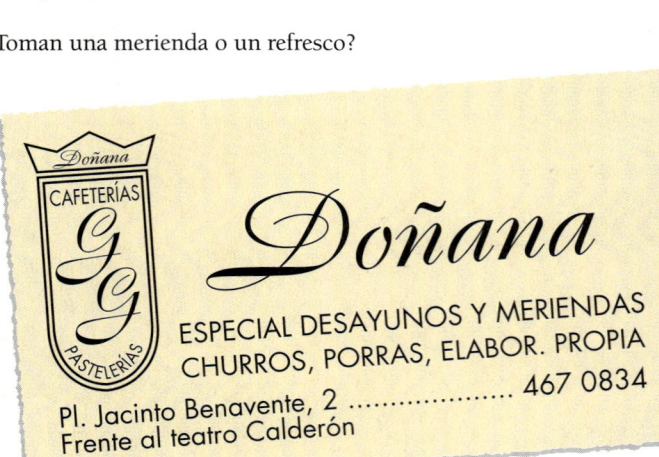

Doñana
CAFETERÍAS GG PASTELERÍAS
ESPECIAL DESAYUNOS Y MERIENDAS
CHURROS, PORRAS, ELABOR. PROPIA
Pl. Jacinto Benavente, 2 .... 467 0834
Frente al teatro Calderón

R–2

LEARNING FROM PHOTOS/REALIA

1. You may wish to ask the following questions about the photograph on page R-2: *¿Quién enseña? ¿Cuántos alumnos hay en el grupo? ¿Son alumnos serios? ¿Es interesante o aburrida la clase? ¿Qué opinas?*
2. With regard to the realia on page R-2, ask students: *¿Cuál es el nombre de la cafetería? ¿En qué calle está? ¿Cuál es el número de teléfono? ¿Cuáles son las especialidades de esta cafetería?*
3. Note the abbreviation *Elabor.* for *Elaboración*. *Elaboración propia* means all products are produced, in this case fried on the premises.

B ¿Qué hacen? Escojan.

1. ¿Cómo van los alumnos?
   a. a la escuela   b. a las ocho   c. a pie
2. ¿Quién enseña?
   a. el profesor   b. en la escuela   c. español
3. ¿Quiénes hablan?
   a. por teléfono   b. los alumnos   c. el profesor
4. ¿Cuándo llegan?
   a. en el bus   b. con sus amigos   c. a las ocho
5. ¿Qué estudian?
   a. en la escuela   b. mucho   c. álgebra
6. ¿Adónde van?
   a. en casa   b. al café   c. hoy

Café Chapultepec

Lago Mayor 2ª Sección
Bosque de Chapultepec
Cd. de México

teléfonos

273 9935
6043
9494

(No se requiere reservación.)

Un colegio en Puerto Rico

Ejercicios

PRESENTATION (page R-3)

Expansion of *Ejercicio B*
You may wish to have students make up questions about the answer choices. For example: ¿Adónde van los alumnos? ¿Cuándo van? ¿A qué hora van?

ANSWERS

Ejercicio B
1. c
2. a
3. b
4. c
5. c
6. b

GEOGRAPHY CONNECTION

El Bosque de Chapultepec es un parque famoso en la Ciudad de México. Los domingos por la tarde los capitalinos van al parque donde dan un paseo o toman una merienda. En el parque hay un castillo famoso, el Castillo de Chapultepec. En el siglo XIX sirve de residencia para el emperador Maximiliano.

HISTORY CONNECTION

The grounds of Chapultepec Park were once (in the early 1500s) the favorite gardens of the Aztec emperor Montezuma.

LEARNING FROM PHOTOS/REALIA

1. You may wish to ask the following questions about the photograph on page R-3: ¿Es grande la escuela? ¿Es bonita? ¿Llevan uniforme los alumnos? ¿Llevan sus libros en una mochila? ¿Es una escuela mixta? ¿Están llegando los alumnos a la escuela o están saliendo de la escuela?
2. Regarding the ad on page R-3, ask students: ¿Cuál es el nombre del café? ¿En qué ciudad está? ¿Cuántas líneas telefónicas tiene? ¿Es necesario tener una reservación para ir al Café Chapultepec?
3. Central High School in San Juan, Puerto Rico, has quite an excellent reputation. For many years it was the most prestigious academic high school in the city. Many famous people graduated from there. Today it is a school for students specializing in music.

ESTRUCTURA

Bell Ringer Review

Write the following on the board or use BRR Blackline Master R-2: Make a list of after-school activities.

Structure Teaching Resources

1. Workbook, *Repaso A*
2. Bell Ringer Review Blackline Masters

Los verbos en -ar

PRESENTATION *(page R-4)*

A. Write the three infinitives from page R-4 on the board and underline the endings. Write the forms for just one verb *(hablar)* and have students provide the endings for the other verbs. Have the class repeat each form in unison.

B. Read each of the explanations in steps 2-5 and call on an individual to read the sentences that illustrate the point.

ESTRUCTURA

Los verbos en -ar

1. Review the forms of regular -ar verbs in Spanish.

INFINITIVE	HABLAR	TOMAR	CANTAR
ROOT	habl-	tom-	cant-
yo	hablo	tomo	canto
tú	hablas	tomas	cantas
él, ella, Ud.	habla	toma	canta
nosotros(as)	hablamos	tomamos	cantamos
vosotros(as)	*habláis*	*tomáis*	*cantáis*
ellos, ellas, Uds.	hablan	toman	cantan

2. Remember that the subject pronouns can be omitted in Spanish.

   (Yo) Hablo español.
   (Tú) Hablas inglés.
   (Nosotros) Estudiamos mucho.

3. To make a sentence negative, put *no* before the verb.

   El profesor enseña. Los alumnos no enseñan.
   Los alumnos toman exámenes. Los profesores no toman exámenes.

4. You use *tú* when speaking to a friend, a family member, or any person who is the same age as yourself.

   Antonio, (tú) hablas español, ¿no?

5. You use *Ud.* when speaking to an older person, someone you do not know well or anyone to whom you wish to show respect.

   ¿Habla Ud. inglés, señor López?

LEARNING FROM REALIA

Have students tell what the advertisement on page R-4 is for.

C **En la escuela.** Contesten.
1. ¿A qué hora llegan los alumnos a la escuela?
2. ¿Cuántas asignaturas toman?
3. ¿Sacan notas buenas o malas?
4. ¿Estudian mucho o poco?
5. Y tú, ¿a qué hora llegas a la escuela?
6. ¿En qué llevas tus libros?
7. ¿Qué asignaturas estudias?
8. ¿Qué notas sacas?

Ejercicios

PRESENTATION (*page R-5*)

Ejercicio C
Do Exercise C first with books open. You may then wish to have students read it for additional reinforcement.

ANSWERS

Ejercicio C
Answers will vary.
1. Los alumnos llegan a la escuela a las…
2. Los alumnos toman… asignaturas.
3. Ellos sacan notas…
4. Estudian mucho (poco).
5. Yo llego a la escuela a las…
6. Yo llevo mis libros en una mochila.
7. Estudio…
8. Saco… notas.

COOPERATIVE LEARNING

1. Have students work in pairs. One makes up a question about the illustration on page R-5 and the other one answers. They can then reverse roles.
2. Have students work in pairs to write a paragraph about the illustration. They can each volunteer some words and expressions. They will then put the words and expressions into sentences and then into a paragraph. As a final step, they will edit the paragraph to find any errors. You may wish to give students the word *casco* (helmet).

PRESENTATION (page R-6)
Ejercicio D
A. Do Exercise D with books open.
B. Call on individuals to supply the correct verb form.
C. Then have two students read the conversation aloud with as much expression as possible.

Ejercicio E
Note If students ask about *fotos instantáneas*, explain to them that *las fotos* is a shortened form of *las fotografías*.

Ejercicio F
After having individuals provide the correct verb forms, you may call on one or two students to read the entire exercise aloud.

Expansion of *Ejercicio F*
Call on one student to retell the information in Exercise F in his/her own words.

ANSWERS
Ejercicio D
1. hablas
2. hablo
3. hablas
4. estudio
5. hablamos
6. escuchamos

Ejercicio E
1. bailamos
2. toca
3. toca, cantan
4. Preparan
5. Tomas
6. miramos

Ejercicio F
1. estudia
2. trabaja
3. estudia
4. hablan
5. cantan
6. estudio
7. trabajo
8. saco
9. hablamos
10. cantamos
11. tocamos
12. toman
13. miramos
14. miramos
15. escuchamos
16. hablamos

R 6

D **¿Qué lenguas hablas?** Completen.
—Oye, Paco. Tú ___ (hablar) español, ¿no?
　　　　　　　　　1
—Sí, (yo) ___ (hablar) español. Y tú también ___ (hablar) español, ¿no?
　　　　　2　　　　　　　　　　　　　　　　　　3
—Sí, pero no muy bien. Yo ___ (estudiar) español en la escuela. En la clase de
　　　　　　　　　　　　　　4
　español nosotros ___ (hablar) y ___ (escuchar) cintas.
　　　　　　　　　　　5　　　　　　　6

E **En la fiesta.** Completen.
1. Durante la fiesta nosotros ___. (bailar)
2. José ___ el piano. (tocar)
3. Mientras él ___ el piano, Sandra y Manolo ___. (tocar, cantar)
4. ¿ ___ Uds. refrescos para la fiesta? (preparar)
5. ¿ ___ tú fotos instantáneas durante la fiesta? (tomar)
6. Sí, y todos nosotros ___ las fotografías. (mirar)

F **Un muchacho en un colegio de Santiago.** Completen.
Ricardo es un muchacho chileno. Él ___ (estudiar) en un colegio de Santiago,
　　　　　　　　　　　　　　　　　　　1
la capital de Chile. Ricardo es un muchacho listo. Él ___ (trabajar) mucho en la
　　　　　　　　　　　　　　　　　　　　　　　　　　　　2
escuela. Él ___ (estudiar) inglés. En la clase de inglés los alumnos ___ (hablar)
　　　　　　3　　　　　　　　　　　　　　　　　　　　　　　　　　　　4
mucho. A veces ellos ___ (cantar) también.
　　　　　　　　　　5
　Yo ___ (estudiar) español en una escuela secundaria en los Estados Unidos.
　　　6
Yo también ___ (trabajar) mucho y ___ (sacar) muy buenas notas en la clase
　　　　　　7　　　　　　　　　　　8
de español. En la clase nosotros ___ (hablar)
　　　　　　　　　　　　　　　　9
mucho con el profesor. A veces, nosotros ___
　　　　　　　　　　　　　　　　　　　　10
(cantar) y ___ (tocar) la guitarra.
　　　　　11
　Después de las clases, los amigos ___ (tomar)
　　　　　　　　　　　　　　　　　12
una merienda. A veces nosotros ___ (mirar) la
　　　　　　　　　　　　　　　　13
televisión. Cuando no ___ (mirar) la televisión,
　　　　　　　　　　14
nosotros ___ (escuchar) discos o ___ (hablar)
　　　　　15　　　　　　　　　　　　16
por teléfono.

R–6

LEARNING FROM PHOTOS
Ask students to describe the people in the photo on page R-6. You may wish to ask questions such as: *¿Es alumno el señor? ¿Qué es el señor? ¿Es alumna la muchacha? ¿Lleva uniforme la muchacha?*

INDEPENDENT PRACTICE
Assign any of the following:
1. Exercises and activities on student pages R-2–R-6
2. Workbook, *Repaso A*

Los verbos *ir,* *dar* y *estar*

1. Review the forms of the irregular verbs *ir, dar,* and *estar*. Note that they are irregular in the *yo* form. All other forms conform to the pattern of a regular *-ar* verb.

INFINITIVE	IR	DAR	ESTAR
yo	voy	doy	estoy
tú	vas	das	estás
él, ella, Ud.	va	da	está
nosotros(as)	vamos	damos	estamos
vosotros(as)	*vais*	*dais*	*estáis*
ellos, ellas, Uds.	van	dan	están

2. Remember that *estar* is used to express location and how you feel.
   ¿Dónde está Roberto? Está en casa.
   ¿Cómo estás? Estoy bien, gracias.

3. The preposition *a* often follows the verb *ir*. Remember that *a* contracts with *el* to form one word *al*.

   Voy al café. No voy a la tienda.

Los verbos ir, dar y estar

PRESENTATION *(page R-7)*

When going over the explanation, emphasize the fact that the *yo* forms of these three verbs follow the same pattern. Have students repeat *voy, doy,* and *estoy*. Then point out that all other forms are the same as those of a regular *-ar* verb.

LEARNING FROM REALIA

Ask students what the ad on page R-7 is for (crossword puzzle book). You may wish to give the word *crucigrama* for crossword puzzle. Ask them the price of the magazine and where it comes from (Spain, the price is 150 *pesetas*).

Ejercicios

PRESENTATION (page R-8)

Ejercicio G

It is recommended that you first do Exercise G as an oral activity with books closed. Call on individuals to respond.

PAIRED ACTIVITY

You may also do Exercise G as a paired activity. One student asks the questions and the other responds. After item 4, they can reverse roles.

ANSWERS

Ejercicio G

Answers will vary.
1. Voy a la escuela…
2. Sí, (No, no) estoy en la escuela ahora.
3. Estoy en la clase de …
4. Sí, (No, no) voy a la escuela con mis amigos.
5. Vamos a la escuela a pie (en coche, en el bus escolar).
6. Sí, (No, no) estoy con mis amigos ahora.
7. Sí, (No,) ellos no están en la clase de español también.
8. Sí, (No,) el/la profesor(a) de español (no) da muchos exámenes.
9. Después de las clases vamos a…

R 8

G **Entrevista.** Contesten.
1. ¿A qué escuela vas?
2. ¿Estás en la escuela ahora?
3. ¿En qué clase estás?
4. ¿Vas a la escuela con tus amigos?
5. ¿Cómo van Uds. a la escuela?
6. ¿Estás con tus amigos ahora?
7. ¿Están ellos en la clase de español también?
8. ¿Da el/la profesor(a) de español muchos exámenes?
9. ¿Adónde van tú y tus amigos después de las clases?

LEARNING FROM REALIA

The ad on page R-8 contains many cognates. Ask students: *¿De qué clase de exámenes hablan? ¿Qué universidad es? ¿Dónde está la universidad? ¿Cuándo es el examen para el tercer período? ¿Cuál es el número de FAX de la universidad? ¿Cuál es la dirección de la universidad?*

Ask students to figure out as many of the subjects as they can.

Comunicación

A **Las actividades.** With a classmate prepare a list of activities you do. Separate the activities you have listed into two categories:

    EN LA ESCUELA   DESPUÉS DE LAS CLASES

Then write a paragraph telling what you do in school and what you do after school.

B **¿Adónde vas?** With a classmate make up a short conversation using each of the following verbs. Use the model as a guide.

    Estudiante 1: ¿Adónde vas?
    Estudiante 2: ¿Quién, yo? Yo voy a la biblioteca.
    Estudiante 1: ¿Sí? Tomás va a la biblioteca también.

1. ir
2. hablar
3. tocar
4. mirar
5. estar

C **¿Cómo soy…?** Describe yourself to your partner in terms of what you are not. Reverse roles.

    No soy alta; no soy rubia…

Un colegio en la Argentina

R–9

Comunicación

PRESENTATION (page R-9)

These activities encourage students to use the language on their own. You may let them choose the activities they would like to participate in.

ANSWERS

Actividad A
  Answers will vary.

Actividad B
  Answers will vary according to the model and cues provided.

Actividad C
  Answers will vary.

HISTORY CONNECTION

The school *"Colegio Nacional Nicolás Avellaneda"* is named for the Argentine journalist and politician (1837-1885) who was president of Argentina from 1874-1880. During his presidency Argentina first exported grain and frozen beef to Europe.

LEARNING FROM PHOTOS

Ask students the following questions about the photo on page R-9: *¿Qué estudian las muchachas? ¿Dónde están ellas?* All the equipment is known as *aparatos de laboratorio*.

INDEPENDENT PRACTICE

Assign any of the following:
1. Exercises and activities on student pages R-7–R-9
2. Workbook, *Repaso A*

R 9

REPASO B

OVERVIEW

Repaso B reviews greetings, salutations, and farewells. In addition, it recycles vocabulary related to activities that can take place at home, school, or during leisure time. The structures reviewed are the present tense of regular *-er* and *-ir* verbs, the irregular verb *ser,* the agreement of articles and adjectives and the present progressive.

REVIEW RESOURCES

1. Workbook, *Repaso B*
2. Bell Ringer Review Blackline Masters
3. Testing Program

Pacing

Repaso B should take four to five days depending on the length of the class, the age of the students, and student aptitude.

REPASO

B

LAS ACTIVIDADES

R-11

LEARNING FROM PHOTOS

The cathedral and the fairground depict the festivities during the *fiestas patronales*. The *fiestas patronales* are traditional in towns and cities in Spain and Latin America. Virtually all towns and cities have a *santo patrón* (patron saint) whose day is celebrated with religious ceremonies and entertainment. In larger cities the *fiestas* may last a week or more with bullfights, dances, contests, sporting events, and concerts.

If you have native speakers in your class, ask them the patron saint of their family town or city, when the *fiestas* take place, and how they are celebrated.

The word for "ferris wheel" is *la noria gigante* or *la rueda mágica*; a "merry go round" is *el tíovivo* or el *carrusel*.

R 11

VOCABULARIO

VOCABULARIO

Los amigos

¡Hola!
¡Hola! ¿Qué tal, Jesús?
Bien, ¿y tú?
Muy bien, gracias.
¡Chao! ¡Hasta luego!
¡Adiós! ¡Hasta luego!

A **Hola.** Say "hi" to a friend in class.

B **¿Cómo te va?** Ask a friend in class how things are going.

C **Adiós.** Say "so long" to a friend in class.

Dos mexicanos

Es Rafael Salas.
Él es de México.
Rafael es mexicano.

Es Carmen Grávalos.
Carmen es mexicana también.
Carmen y Rafael son de Guadalajara.
Viven en Guadalajara.
Ellos son alumnos en el colegio Hidalgo, en Guadalajara.

En el colegio Rafael y Carmen…
 leen libros y periódicos.
 escriben con lápiz y con bolígrafo.
 comen en la cafetería.
 ven un partido de fútbol.

R–12

Vocabulary Teaching Resources

1. Workbook, *Repaso B*
2. Bell Ringer Review Blackline Masters

Bell Ringer Review

Write the following on the board or use BRR Blackline Master R-3: Make a list of expressions used for greeting people and saying good-bye to them.

Los amigos

PRESENTATION *(page R-12)*

A. Review the expressions used for greeting people and saying good-bye that students listed in the Bell Ringer Review above. Then have the class repeat the conversation on page R-12 after you.

B. Call on two students to read the conversation to the class.

Expansion Call on pairs to improvise, changing the conversation in any way that makes sense.

Dos mexicanos

PRESENTATION *(page R-12)*

A. Have students repeat each line after you with books open.

B. You may wish to point to the map of Mexico on page 454 as you review the pronunciation of *México, mexicano,* and *Guadalajara.*

C. Some simple gestures will help review the meaning of *leer, escribir, comer,* and *ver.*

ANSWERS

Ejercicio A
 Hola.

Ejercicio B
 ¿Qué tal?

Ejercicio C
 Chao. (Hasta luego. Adiós.)

R 12

ADDITIONAL PRACTICE

1. You may wish to ask the following questions concerning the statements after *Dos mexicanos:* ¿Quién es de México? ¿De qué nacionalidad es Rafael? Y Carmen Grávalos, ¿de qué nacionalidad es ella? ¿De dónde son ellos? ¿Dónde viven? ¿Dónde estudian? ¿Qué leen? ¿Con qué escriben? ¿Dónde comen?

2. Have students say as much about Rafael and Carmen as they can.

3. Have students change the names of Rafael and Carmen to names of students in the class and then change all the information as necessary.

D Rafael y Carmen. Contesten.
1. ¿De dónde es Rafael?
2. ¿De qué nacionalidad es?
3. Y Carmen, ¿de qué nacionalidad es ella?
4. ¿De dónde son Rafael y Carmen?
5. ¿Dónde viven ellos?
6. ¿Dónde son alumnos?

E Expresiones. Pareen.
1. leer
2. escribir
3. vivir
4. aprender
5. vender
6. comer
7. ver
8. ser
9. subir
10. beber

a. mucho en la escuela
b. al quinto piso
c. una novela
d. un alumno bueno y serio
e. una carta con bolígrafo
f. una limonada
g. en una casa particular
h. una emisión deportiva
i. discos en una tienda en el centro comercial
j. carne, ensalada y papas

F La familia. Completen.
1. La familia ___ en la cocina o en el comedor.
2. La familia ___ la televisión en la sala.
3. Después de la comida mamá ___ una carta a una amiga.
4. Papá ___ el periódico.
5. La familia ___ en una casa privada. La familia no ___ en un apartamento.

G Sustantivos y verbos. Pareen.
1. escribir
2. comer
3. vender
4. beber
5. aprender
6. vivir
7. leer

a. la venta
b. el aprendizaje
c. la escritura
d. la lectura
e. la vivienda
f. la comida
g. la bebida

R–13

INDEPENDENT PRACTICE

Assign any of the following:
1. Exercises on student page R-13
2. Workbook, *Repaso B*

Ejercicios
PRESENTATION (*page R-13*)
It is suggested that you go over all the exercises once in class before assigning them as homework.

Ejercicio D
It is recommended that you do Exercise D as an oral activity with books closed.

Ejercicio E
You may wish to give students a few minutes to go over the exercise before calling on individuals to respond aloud. Exercise E determines if students understand the meaning of the verb.

Expansion of *Ejercicio F*
Upon completion of Exercise F, call on one individual to retell the story about the family in his/her own words.

Ejercicio G
The object of this exercise is to help students recognize new words based on the knowledge of another related word.

ANSWERS
Ejercicio D
1. Él es de México.
2. Él es mexicano.
3. Carmen es mexicana.
4. Rafael y Carmen son de México.
5. Ellos viven en Guadalajara.
6. Son alumnos en el colegio Hidalgo.

Ejercicio E
1. c
2. e
3. g
4. a
5. i
6. j
7. h
8. d
9. b
10. f

Ejercicio F
1. está
2. mira
3. escribe
4. lee
5. vive, vive

Ejercicio G
1. c
2. f
3. a
4. g
5. b
6. e
7. d

R 13

ESTRUCTURA

Structure Teaching Resources

1. Workbook, *Repaso B*
2. Bell Ringer Review Blackline Masters

Los verbos en -er, -ir

Bell Ringer Review

Write the following on the board or use BRR Blackline Master R-4: Answer the following questions in as many ways as you can.
¿Qué comes?
¿Qué aprendes?
¿Qué escribes?
¿Qué ves?

PRESENTATION *(page R-14)*

1. Have students repeat the forms of *comer* and *vivir* after you.
2. Write the verbs *leer* and *subir* on the board and have students give you the endings.

ESTRUCTURA

Los verbos en -er, -ir

1. Review the forms of regular -er verbs and -ir verbs.

INFINITIVE	COMER	VIVIR
STEM	com-	viv-
yo	como	vivo
tú	comes	vives
él, ella, Ud.	come	vive
nosotros(as)	comemos	vivimos
vosotros(as)	coméis	vivís
ellos, ellas, Uds.	comen	viven

2. Note that all forms of -er and -ir verbs are the same except *nosotros* and *vosotros*.

Nosotros comemos.   Nosotros subimos.
Bebemos.   Escribimos.

SE SIENTE...	CON GANAS DE COMER...	¡LO QUE DEBE COMER!
Triste	Alimentos reconfortantes	Sopa, avena, macarrones con queso
Enojada	Alimentos duros crujientes	Palomitas de maíz, apio, manzana
Segura	Comidas picantes	Jugo de tomate con especias, *crudités* con salsas
Avergonzada	Alimentos cremosos	Bananas, yogur descremado
Excitada	Algo dulce	Galletitas "María", caramelos, mazapanes
Tensa	Alimentos salados	Sopa de vegetales, galletitas saltinas
Nerviosa	Alimentos ricos en carbohidratos	Pastas, papas y pan integral
Cansada	Alimentos ricos en proteína	Queso, carne magra y maní

R–14

LEARNING FROM REALIA

1. Have students look at the realia on page R-14 and tell what its message is. The article describes what people want to eat and what they should eat when they are feeling sad, angry, tired, etc.
2. You may wish to ask students how many "states" or feelings they recognize from the list. You may also ask them to identify as many foods as they can.

H **Personalmente.** Completen.
1. Yo ___ en ___. (vivir)
2. Yo no ___ en ___. ___ en ___. (vivir)
3. Yo ___ en la calle ___. (vivir)
4. En casa, yo ___ con mi familia. (comer)
5. Nosotros ___ en la cocina. (comer)
6. Después de la comida yo ___ el periódico. (leer)
7. A veces yo ___ una composición para la clase de inglés. (escribir)

I **Pregunta.** Make up a question for each sentence in Exercise H.

J **Vivimos en los Estados Unidos.** Contesten.
1. ¿Dónde viven Uds.?
2. ¿Viven Uds. en una casa particular?
3. ¿Viven Uds. en un apartamento?
4. ¿Escriben Uds. mucho en la clase de español?
5. Y en la clase de inglés, ¿escriben Uds. mucho?
6. ¿Comprenden Uds. cuando la profesora habla en español?
7. ¿Reciben Uds. buenas notas en español?
8. ¿Aprenden Uds. mucho en la escuela?
9. ¿Leen Uds. muchos libros?
10. ¿Comen Uds. en la cafetería de la escuela?

R–15

Ejercicios

PRESENTATION (page R-15)

Ejercicio H
A. Call on each individual to complete two sentences.
B. After going over Exercise H once, call on one individual to read the entire exercise.

Ejercicio I
Students can make up more than one question about each statement.

ANSWERS

Ejercicio H
Answers will vary for items 1-3.
1. vivo
2. vivo, vivo
3. vivo
4. como
5. comemos
6. leo
7. escribo

Ejercicio I
1. ¿Dónde vives?
2. ¿No vives en…? ¿Vives en…?
3. ¿Vives en la calle…?
4. En casa, ¿comes con tu familia?
5. ¿Comen Uds. en la cocina?
6. Después de la comida, ¿lees el periódico?
7. ¿Escribes una composición para la clase de inglés?

Ejercicio J
Answers will vary.
1. Vivimos en…
2. Sí, (No, no) vivimos en una casa particular.
3. Sí, (No, no) vivimos en un apartamento.
4. Sí, (No, no) escribimos mucho en la clase de español.
5. Sí, (No, no) escribimos mucho en la clase de inglés.
6. Sí, (No, no) comprendemos cuando la profesora habla en español.
7. Sí, (No, no) recibimos buenas notas en español.
8. Sí, (No, no) aprendemos mucho en la escuela.
9. Sí, (No, no) leemos muchos libros.
10. Sí, (No, no) comemos en la cafetería de la escuela.

LEARNING FROM REALIA

Ask students to say all they can about the ad on page R-15. You may wish to ask questions such as: ¿Qué venden? ¿Cuáles son los precios? ¿Dónde están las casas? ¿Para quiénes es el anuncio?

ADDITIONAL PRACTICE

Have students look at Exercise E on page R-13 and ask them to make up original sentences using the expressions they made by combining the verb with an appropriate completion.

El verbo *ser*

PRESENTATION (*page R-16*)

Have students open their books to page R-16 and repeat the verb forms after you.

Ejercicios

PRESENTATION (*page R-16*)

Ejercicio K

Call on two students with good pronunciation to read the conversation to the class.

Expansion of *Ejercicio* K

Call on a student to retell the story of the conversation in his/her own words.

El verbo *ser*

Review the forms of the irregular verb *ser*.

SER	
yo	soy
tú	eres
él, ella, Ud.	es
nosotros(as)	somos
vosotros(as)	sois
ellos, ellas, Uds.	son

K La nacionalidad. Practiquen.

—Roberto, tú eres americano, ¿no?
—Sí, hombre. Soy americano.
—Y tu amiga, ¿es ella americana también?
—¿Quién, Alejandra?
—Sí, ella.
—No, ella es de España.
—Pero Uds. son alumnos en la misma escuela, ¿no?
—Sí, somos alumnos en la escuela Monroe.

R–16

LEARNING FROM PHOTOS

1. You may wish to ask the following questions based on the photograph at the top of page R-16: *¿Dónde está la muchacha? ¿Es ella alumna? ¿En qué escribe? ¿Con qué escribe? ¿Es una clase pequeña o grande?*
2. Have students look at the photo at the bottom of page R-16 and make up sentences using the following words: *alumnos, amigos, hermanos, serios, divertidos.*

L **Roberto y Alejandra.** Contesten según la conversación.
1. ¿Quién es americano?
2. ¿Quién es de España?
3. ¿Son ellos alumnos en la misma escuela?
4. ¿En qué escuela son ellos alumnos?

M **Personalmente.** Contesten.
1. ¿Quién eres?
2. ¿De dónde eres?
3. ¿De qué nacionalidad eres?
4. ¿Cómo eres?
5. ¿Qué eres?
6. ¿Dónde eres alumno(a)?

N **Dos ecuatorianos.** Completen con *ser*.

Marisa Contreras ___(1)___ de Guayaquil. Y Felipe Gutiérrez ___(2)___ de Guayaquil. Los dos ___(3)___ ecuatorianos y los dos no ___(4)___ de la capital.

¿De dónde ___(5)___ Uds.? ¿___(6)___ Uds. de la capital de su país?

Nosotros ___(7)___ de ___ .

Ecuador

Catedral de Guayaquil

Guayaquil

R–17

PRESENTATION (page R-17)
Ejercicios L and M
It is recommended that both these exercises be done orally with books closed.

Expansion of Ejercicio M
After completing Exercise M, call on an individual to tell all about himself/herself.

ANSWERS
Ejercicio L
1. Roberto es americano.
2. Alejandra es de España.
3. Sí, son alumnos en la misma escuela.
4. Ellos son alumnos en la escuela Monroe.

Ejercicio M
Answers will vary.
1. Yo soy…
2. Yo soy de…
3. Yo soy…
4. Yo soy…
5. Yo soy…
6. Soy alumno(a) en la escuela…

Ejercicio N
1. es
2. es
3. son
4. son
5. son
6. Son
7. somos

GEOGRAPHY CONNECTION
Have students locate Guayaquil, Ecuador on the map of South America, page 453. Guayaquil was founded in 1536. Simón Bolívar and José de San Martín met there in 1822 to complete plans for the liberation of South America from Spain. Guayaquil is Ecuador's major port. It has a population of over 1.5 million.

COOPERATIVE LEARNING
Upon completion of Exercise N, have students work in groups of three or four. Each group makes up a story about Marisa and Felipe. Have them come up with as many statements as possible.

INDEPENDENT PRACTICE
Assign any of the following:
1. Exercises and activities on student pages R-15–R-17
2. Workbook, *Repaso B*

R 17

Bell Ringer Review

Write the following on the board or use BRR Blackline Master R-5: List as many classroom objects as you can.

Los artículos y los sustantivos

PRESENTATION *(page R-18)*

As you go over the explanation, have students repeat the words and example sentences after you. Point to a specific person or object as you use the definite article.

Los artículos y los sustantivos

1. Many Spanish nouns end in *-o* or *-a*. Most nouns that end in *-o* are masculine and most nouns that end in *-a* are feminine. The definite article *el* accompanies a masculine noun and the definite article *la* accompanies a feminine noun.

MASCULINO	FEMENINO
el muchacho	la muchacha
el colegio	la escuela

2. Many Spanish nouns end in *-e*. It is impossible to tell the gender, masculine or feminine, of nouns ending in *-e*.

MASCULINO	FEMENINO
el arte	la calle
el café	la clase
el deporte	la tarde
el padre	la madre

3. To form the plural of nouns ending in the vowels *o*, *a*, or *e*, you add an *-s*. To nouns ending in a consonant, you add *-es*. Note that *el* changes to *los* and *la* changes to *las*.

MASCULINO	FEMENINO
los muchachos	las muchachas
los deportes	las calles
los profesores	las ciudades

4. In Spanish, you use the indefinite articles *un* or *una* to express "a" or "an." Note that these articles change to *unos* and *unas* in the plural.

SINGULAR	PLURAL
un muchacho	unos muchachos
una muchacha	unas muchachas

LEARNING FROM PHOTOS

You may wish to ask the following questions about the photograph on page R-18: *¿Cuántas personas hay en la fotografía? ¿Están corriendo ellos? ¿Están corriendo por la calle?*

O **El muchacho y la muchacha.** Completen con *el, la, los o las.*

___ muchacho es cubano y ___ muchacha es puertorriqueña. Sus padres son
  1   2
de Ponce en el sur de ___ isla. Ahora ___ dos muchachos viven en ___ ciudad
                       3   4   5
de Miami. Ellos viven en ___ misma calle y van a ___ misma escuela.
                          6   7

P **El plural.** Cambien cada oración a la forma plural.

1. El muchacho es moreno.
2. La muchacha es rubia.
3. El alumno es serio.
4. La escuela es buena.
5. La ciudad es grande.

El parque de bombas, Ponce, Puerto Rico

R–19

Ejercicios
PRESENTATION *(page R-19)*

Ejercicio O
After completing Exercise O, have one student read the entire exercise as a story.

Ejercicio P
Have students write the plural sentences. Then have them close their books, read the plural sentences, and put them back into the singular.

ANSWERS
Ejercicio O
1. El
2. la
3. la
4. los
5. la
6. la
7. la

Ejercicio P
1. Los muchachos son morenos.
2. Las muchachas son rubias.
3. Los alumnos son serios.
4. Las escuelas son buenas.
5. Las ciudades son grandes

GEOGRAPHY CONNECTION
Have students locate Ponce on the map of Puerto Rico (page 454). The brightly painted firehouse on page R-19 is a very popular tourist attraction.

LEARNING FROM PHOTOS
The *Parque de bombas* in the photo at the bottom of page R-19 is in the central plaza of Ponce, Puerto Rico. It was built as an exhibit hall for an exposition in 1882.

R 19

Bell Ringer Review

Write the following on the board or use BRR Blackline Master R-6: Make a list of words you know that can be used to describe people.

La concordancia de los adjetivos

PRESENTATION *(page R-20)*

A. Draw a stick figure of a boy and a girl on the board. Each time you give a masculine form, point to the boy. Each time you give a feminine form, point to the girl.

B. Have students repeat all the example sentences aloud.

La concordancia de los adjetivos

1. Adjectives agree with the nouns they describe. If the noun is feminine, the adjective must be in the feminine form. If the noun is plural, the adjective must be in the plural form. Review the following.

	FEMENINO	MASCULINO
SINGULAR	la amiga rubia una muchacha seria	el amigo rubio un muchacho serio
PLURAL	las amigas rubias unas muchachas serias	los amigos rubios unos muchachos serios

2. Adjectives that end in *-e* have two forms. To form the plural you add an *-s*.

   el edificio grande
   los edificios grandes

3. Adjectives that end in a consonant also have two forms. You add *-es* to form the plural.

   el curso fácil   los cursos fáciles
   la lección fácil   las lecciones fáciles

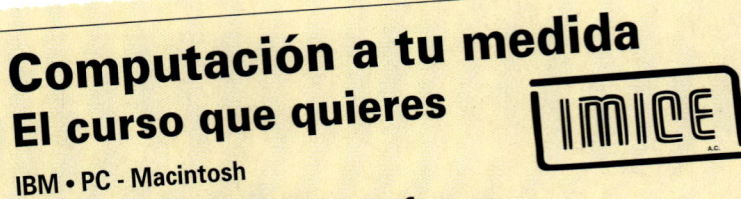

Computación a tu medida
El curso que quieres   IMICE

IBM • PC - Macintosh

El único instituto que ofrece:
• Una computadora por alumno
• Un solo plantel para que nuestros directivos te atiendan personalmente
• Cursos adecuados a tus posibilidades económicas y disponibilidad de tiempo

INFÓRMATE

Pitágoras 931   Eugenia   536-8926, 543-4575, 682-7118, 682-6993 y 687-8293
FAX: 536-89-26

LEARNING FROM REALIA

Ask students what they think the ad on page R-20 is for. The word for "computer" in Latin America is usually *computadora*. In Spain the word is *ordenador,* from the French *ordinateur.*

Q **Las dos muchachas.** Describan a las muchachas.

R **El amigo.** Describan a un(a) amigo(a).

El presente progresivo — *Describing an Action in Progress*

1. The present progressive is used in Spanish to express an action that is presently going on. It is formed by using the present tense of the verb *estar* and the present participle. To form the present participle of most verbs you drop the ending of the infinitive and add *-ando* to the stem of *-ar* verbs and *-iendo* to the stem of *-er* and *-ir* verbs. Study the following forms of the present participle.

INFINITIVE	HABLAR	LLEGAR	COMER	HACER	SALIR
STEM	habl-	lleg-	com-	hac-	sal-
PARTICIPLE	hablando	llegando	comiendo	haciendo	saliendo

2. Note that the verbs *leer* and *traer* have a *y* in the present participle.

   leyendo   trayendo

3. Study the following examples of the present progressive.

   ¿Qué está haciendo Elena?
   En este momento está esperando el avión.

R–21

Ejercicios
PRESENTATION *(page R-21)*

Ejercicios Q and R
After going over these exercises, you may have students describe the boy and the girl in the photos on page R-19. They can also describe the group on page R-16.

ANSWERS
Ejercicios Q and R
Answers will vary.

El presente progresivo
PRESENTATION *(page R-21)*
A. You may have students call out any verb they can think of. Write the present participle of that verb on the board and have students repeat it.
B. Call on students to read the example sentences on page R-21 aloud.

Ejercicios

PRESENTATION (page R-22)

Ejercicio S

RECYCLE

Exercise S reinforces vocabulary related to plane travel presented in *Bienvenidos*.

It is recommended that you do the exercise first orally with books closed. You may wish to do the exercise a second time without providing the cued response.

Ejercicios T and U

Encourage students to be as original as possible in making up their sentences.

ANSWERS

Ejercicio S
1. Los pasajeros están llegando al aeropuerto.
2. Están llegando en taxi.
3. Están viajando a Europa.
4. Están haciendo el viaje en avión.
5. Están facturando el equipaje en el mostrador de la línea aérea.
6. La agente está revisando los boletos y los pasaportes.
7. Los pasajeros están saliendo de la puerta número siete.
8. Están abordando el avión.

Ejercicio T
Answers will vary.
1. (No) Estoy comiendo…
2. (No) Estoy hablando…
3. (No) Estoy estudiando…
4. (No) Estoy bailando…
5. (No) Estoy escribiendo…
6. (No) Estoy aprendiendo…
7. (No) Estoy trabajando…
8. (No) Estoy haciendo un viaje…
9. (No) Estoy leyendo…
10. (No) Estoy saliendo para España…

Ejercicio U
Answers will vary.

S ¿Qué están haciendo en el aeropuerto? *Contesten según se indica.*

1. ¿Adónde están llegando los pasajeros? (al aeropuerto)
2. ¿Cómo están llegando? (en taxi)
3. ¿Adónde están viajando? (a Europa)
4. ¿Cómo están haciendo el viaje? (en avión)
5. ¿Dónde están facturando el equipaje? (en el mostrador de la línea aérea)
6. ¿Qué está revisando la agente? (los boletos y los pasaportes)
7. ¿De qué puerta están saliendo los pasajeros para Madrid? (número siete)
8. ¿Qué están abordando? (el avión)

T Yo (no) estoy… *Formen oraciones.*

1. comer
2. hablar
3. estudiar
4. bailar
5. escribir
6. aprender
7. trabajar
8. hacer un viaje
9. leer
10. salir para España

U ¿Qué están haciendo ahora? *Digan lo que están haciendo.*

1. Mi madre
2. Mi padre
3. Mis primos
4. Mis hermanos
5. Yo
6. Mis amigos
7. Mi novio(a) y yo

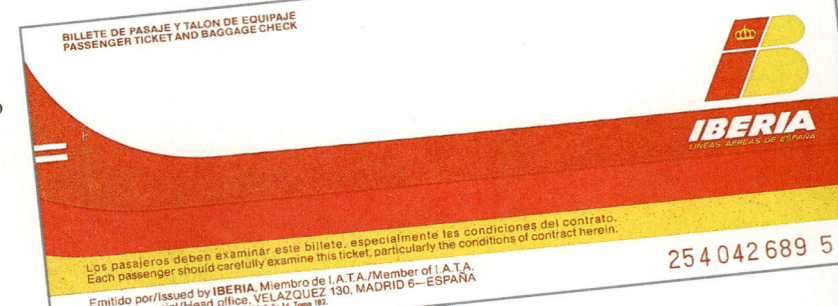

LEARNING FROM PHOTOS

The taxi in the photograph on page R-22 is at the airport in San Juan, Puerto Rico. The airport is named for Luis Muñoz Marín, the first elected governor of Puerto Rico. If you have any students from Puerto Rico, you may wish to ask them to give a brief report on Muñoz Marín to the class.

Comunicación

A **En la cafetería.** You have just met a new student in the school cafeteria. Tell him or her what your nationality is, what languages you speak, what classes you are taking, how many brothers and sisters you have and what their ages are. Reverse roles.

B **Las categorías.** With a classmate make up a list of words you know that describe a person. Then divide the words into the following categories.

descripción física
personalidad
características positivas
características negativas

Continue to work together. Then decide upon a person that fits into all categories and give a complete description of the person.

C **Soy…** Write a postcard to a pen pal in Puerto Rico. Tell him or her what you look like; where you are from; and where you go to school. Describe your school and after-school activities.

El observatorio de Arecibo, Puerto Rico

Un edificio de apartamentos en el viejo San Juan, Puerto Rico

La catedral de Ponce, Puerto Rico

REPASO C

OVERVIEW

Repaso C reviews vocabulary dealing with plane travel and organized team sports. It also reviews the following structure points: the present tense of stem-changing verbs, the verbs *hacer, poner, traer, salir, tener,* and *venir.*

REVIEW RESOURCES

1. Workbook, *Repaso C*
2. Bell Ringer Review Blackline Masters
3. Testing Program

Pacing

Repaso C should take three to four days depending on the length of the class, the age of the students, and student aptitude.

REPASO C

LOS VIAJES Y LOS DEPORTES

R 24

DID YOU KNOW?

Tennis has become very popular in Spanish-speaking countries. The number of international champions from Latin America and Spain increases yearly. You may wish to ask students to identify as many world-class Hispanic tennis players as they can.

VOCABULARIO

Vocabulary Teaching Resources

1. Workbook, *Repaso C*
2. Bell Ringer Review Blackline Masters

Bell Ringer Review

Write the following on the board or use BRR Blackline Master R-7: Write down as many words and expressions as you can think of that have to do with airports or air travel.

Un viaje a Lima

PRESENTATION *(page R-26)*

A. Have students share the words they wrote down for the Bell Ringer Review above.
B. Now have students repeat each sentence of the conversation after you.
C. Call on pairs of students to read the conversation aloud with as much expression as possible.

ANSWERS
Ejercicio A
1. Jorge va a Lima.
2. Sale mañana.
3. No, no tiene que ir a Lima.
4. Sí, quiere ir.
5. Va a ver un partido de fútbol.

VOCABULARIO

Un viaje a Lima

—Hola, Jorge. ¿Qué haces, hombre?
—Pues, voy a hacer un viaje a Lima.
—¿A Lima? ¿Cuándo sales?
—Salgo mañana.
—¿Por qué tienes que ir a Lima?
—No tengo que ir. Es que quiero ir.
—¿Qué vas a hacer en Lima?
—Pues, la Argentina juega contra el Perú.
—¡Verdad!

A **Un viaje a Lima.** Contesten según la conversación.

1. ¿Adónde va Jorge?
2. ¿Cuándo sale?
3. ¿Tiene que ir a Lima?
4. ¿Quiere ir?
5. ¿Qué va a hacer en Lima?

COOPERATIVE LEARNING

Have students work in pairs and prepare a conversation that takes place at an airport when checking in for a flight. One student is the airline agent and the other is the passenger.

LEARNING FROM REALIA

Have students locate Argentina and Peru on the map of South America on page 453. Ask them to tell, in Spanish, where they are located on the continent. Ask what is shown on the brochure for Argentina on page R-26. It is a glacier–*un glaciar.* It is the *Glaciar Perito Moreno,* in *lago Argentino,* in the province of Santa Cruz.

B En el aeropuerto. Contesten según el dibujo.

1. Los pasajeros hacen un viaje a ___.
2. Los pasajeros están en ___.
3. Ellos llevan (tienen) ___.
4. El agente revisa sus ___ y sus ___.
5. Es el ___ número 110.
6. El vuelo sale para ___.
7. ___ a las 9:20.
8. Los ___ van a abordar el avión.

C Los deportes. ¿Qué deporte es?

1. hay cinco jugadores en el equipo
2. hay once jugadores en el equipo
3. el portero guarda la portería
4. los jugadores encestan el balón
5. los jugadores juegan en el campo de fútbol

Ejercicios

PRESENTATION (page R-27)

Ejercicio B
1. Have students look at the illustration as they complete the sentences in Exercise B.
2. Go over the exercise once calling on individuals to do the items. Then have one student reread the entire exercise.

Expansion of Ejercicio C
You may wish to have students say as much as they can about each sport they identify.

ANSWERS

Ejercicio B
1. Managua, Nicaragua
2. el aeropuerto
3. su equipaje (sus maletas)
4. boletos, pasaportes
5. vuelo
6. Managua
7. Sale
8. pasajeros

Ejercicio C
1. El baloncesto
2. El fútbol americano
3. El fútbol
4. El baloncesto
5. El fútbol

COOPERATIVE LEARNING

Have students work in groups of three or four. Have each group make up and answer as many questions as they can about the illustration on page R-27.

ESTRUCTURA

Structure Teaching Resources

1. Workbook, *Repaso C*
2. Bell Ringer Review Blackline Masters

Bell Ringer Review

Write the following on the board or use BRR Blackline Master R-8: Write down as many words or expressions as you can think of related to each of the following sports: *el fútbol, el básquetbol, el béisbol.*

El presente de los verbos de cambio radical

PRESENTATION *(page R-28)*

A. Have students repeat all the verb forms after you.
B. Then have students repeat all the *nosotros* forms.
C. Now have them repeat all the *yo* forms to contrast the stem change.

ESTRUCTURA

El presente de los verbos de cambio radical

1. Review the forms of *e > ie* stem-changing verbs. Note that the stem changes in all forms except the *nosotros* and *vosotros*.

INFINITIVE	EMPEZAR	QUERER	PREFERIR
yo	empiezo	quiero	prefiero
tú	empiezas	quieres	prefieres
él, ella, Ud.	empieza	quiere	prefiere
nosotros(as)	empezamos	queremos	preferimos
vosotros(as)	*empezáis*	*queréis*	*preferís*
ellos, ellas, Uds.	empiezan	quieren	prefieren

2. Review the forms of *o > ue* stem-changing verbs. Note that the stem changes in all forms except the *nosotros* and *vosotros*.

INFINITIVE	VOLVER	PODER	DORMIR
yo	vuelvo	puedo	duermo
tú	vuelves	puedes	duermes
él, ella, Ud.	vuelve	puede	duerme
nosotros(as)	volvemos	podemos	dormimos
vosotros(as)	*volvéis*	*podéis*	*dormís*
ellos, ellas, Uds.	vuelven	pueden	duermen

3. Remember that the stem of the verb *jugar* also changes to *ue*.

JUGAR	
yo	juego
tú	juegas
él, ella, Ud.	juega
nosotros(as)	jugamos
vosotros(as)	*jugáis*
ellos, ellas, Uds.	juegan

D **Un juego de fútbol.** Lean.

El juego de fútbol empieza a las dos de la tarde. Hoy juegan los Osos contra los Tigres. Cuando empieza el segundo tiempo, el tanto queda empatado en cero. Los jugadores vuelven al campo. Todos quieren ganar, pero si el tanto no queda empatado, un equipo tiene que perder. ¿Quiénes pierden? Durante el último minuto del partido los Osos meten un gol. El portero de los Tigres no puede parar el balón y los Osos ganan.

R-29

Ejercicios

PRESENTATION (page R-29)

Ejercicio D

Have students open their books to page R-29. Call on individuals to read two or three sentences each.

LEARNING FROM REALIA

1. Have students say all they can about the sports page. You may wish to ask: ¿De dónde es el periódico? ¿De qué dos equipos habla? ¿Cuántos goles marca Perú? ¿Y cuántos marca México?
2. Have students find the expression "pole vault" (*salto de garrocha*).

R 29

Ejercicios

PRESENTATION (*page R-30*)

Ejercicios E–H
All of these exercises can be done orally with books closed.

Ejercicio E
You may wish to intersperse the questions while students read Exercise D on page R-29.

Expansion of *Ejercicio E*
Call on one student to retell the entire story in his/her own words.

ANSWERS

Ejercicio E
1. Empieza a las dos de la tarde.
2. Los Osos juegan contra los Tigres.
3. El tanto queda empatado en cero.
4. Los jugadores vuelven al campo.
5. Todos quieren ganar.
6. Si el tanto no queda empatado, tiene que perder un equipo.
7. Los Tigres pierden.
8. El portero de los Tigres no puede parar el balón.
9. No, los espectadores no duermen durante un partido.

Ejercicios F–H
Answers will vary.

Ejercicio I
1. empezamos
2. queremos
3. perdemos, podemos

Ejercicio J
1. empiezo
2. quiero
3. pierdo, puedo

Bell Ringer Review
Write the following on the board or use BRR Blackline Master R-9: **1.** Write a list of words for all the members that can make up a family. **2.** Write a list of words you could use to describe a house or apartment.

R 30

E **Los Osos contra los Tigres.** Contesten según la lectura.
1. ¿A qué hora empieza el juego de fútbol?
2. ¿Quiénes juegan?
3. ¿Cómo queda el tanto cuando empieza el segundo tiempo?
4. ¿Quiénes vuelven al campo?
5. ¿Qué quieren todos?
6. ¿Tiene que perder un equipo?
7. ¿Quiénes pierden?
8. ¿Qué no puede parar el portero de los Tigres?
9. ¿Duermen los espectadores durante el partido?

F **Lo que quiero hacer.** Tell five things you want to do.

G **Lo que Pablo prefiere hacer.** Tell five things Pablo does not want to do. Tell what he prefers to do.

H **Lo que podemos hacer.** Tell five things you and your friends can do.

I **El partido de hoy.** Completen.
1. Hoy nosotros ___ a jugar a las dos. (empezar)
2. Nosotros no ___ perder. (querer)
3. Si nosotros ___ el juego de hoy, no ___ jugar mañana. (perder, poder)

J **El partido de hoy.** Cambien *nosotros* a *yo* en las oraciones del Ejercicio I.

Los verbos con *g* en la primera persona

1. Review the forms of the irregular verbs *hacer, poner, traer,* and *salir*. Note that they all have a *g* in the *yo* form.

INFINITIVE	HACER	PONER	TRAER	SALIR
yo	hago	pongo	traigo	salgo
tú	haces	pones	traes	sales
él, ella, Ud.	hace	pone	trae	sale
nosotros(as)	hacemos	ponemos	traemos	salimos
vosotros(as)	*hacéis*	*ponéis*	*traéis*	*salís*
ellos, ellas, Uds.	hacen	ponen	traen	salen

R–30

COOPERATIVE LEARNING ACTIVITY

Have pairs of students prepare short conversations for the following situations:
1. in the taxi (the passenger and the driver): The passenger should tell the driver where he/she wants to go; ask how long it will take; and ask how much it costs. The driver should answer the questions.
2. at the airline counter (the traveller and the airline agent): The agent should ask for the tickets; and whether the traveller has suitcases. The traveller should answer and ask what time the plane leaves and from what gate it leaves.

2. The verbs *tener* and *venir* also have a *g* in the *yo* form. In addition, the *e* of the infinitive stem changes to *ie* in all forms except the *nosotros* and *vosotros*.

INFINITIVE	TENER	VENIR
yo	tengo	vengo
tú	tienes	vienes
él, ella, Ud.	tiene	viene
nosotros(as)	tenemos	venimos
vosotros(as)	tenéis	venís
ellos, ellas, Uds.	tienen	vienen

3. The expression *tener que* followed by an infinitive means "to have to."

   Tenemos que estudiar.
   Tenemos que tomar un examen final.

K Un viaje imaginario. *Contesten con sí.*
1. ¿Haces un viaje a España?
2. ¿Haces el viaje en avión?
3. Antes, ¿haces la maleta?
4. ¿Qué pones en la maleta?
5. ¿Cuándo sales?
6. ¿Sales para el aeropuerto en taxi?
7. ¿A qué hora viene el taxi?
8. ¿A qué hora tienes que estar en el aeropuerto?
9. ¿Tienes mucho equipaje?
10. ¿A qué hora sale el vuelo para Madrid?

INDEPENDENT PRACTICE

Assign any of the following:
1. Exercises and activities on student pages R-26–R-31
2. Workbook, *Repaso C*

Los verbos con g en la primera persona

PRESENTATION *(pages R-30–R-31)*

A. Have students repeat all the *yo* forms in the chart on page R-30.
B. Then point out to students that all the other forms are the same as those of regular *-er* or *-ir* verbs.
C. Have students repeat all the forms of *tener* and *venir* from the chart on page R-31.
D. Have students repeat all the *yo* forms one more time: *hago, pongo, traigo, salgo, tengo,* and *vengo*.

Ejercicios

PRESENTATION *(page R-31)*

Ejercicio K
1. It is suggested that you do Exercise K orally with books closed. Note that this exercise emphasizes the irregular *yo* form.
2. After going over the exercise once, calling on individuals, do the exercise again. Have one student do items 1-5 and another do items 6-10.

ANSWERS

Ejercicio K
1. Sí, hago un viaje a España.
2. Sí, hago el viaje en avión.
3. Sí, antes hago la maleta.
4. Pongo (mi ropa) en la maleta.
5. Salgo a las…
6. Sí, salgo para el aeropuerto en taxi.
7. El taxi viene a las…
8. Tengo que estar en el aeropuerto a las…
9. Sí, tengo mucho equipaje.
10. El vuelo para Madrid sale a…

PAIRED ACTIVITY

Exercise K can be done as a paired activity. One student asks a question and the other one answers. They then reverse roles.

Ejercicios

PRESENTATION (page R-32)

Ejercicio L
Have individual students complete each item.

Ejercicio M
After going over Exercise M, call on individuals to give as much information about their family or their home as they can.

ANSWERS

Ejercicio L
1. hace, pone, sale
2. hacemos, ponemos, salimos
3. haces, pones, haces, sales
4. hacen, ponen, hacen, salen
5. hago, pongo, hago, salgo

Ejercicio M
1. Tengo una familia grande (pequeña).
2. Tengo… hermanos y… hermanas.
3. Tenemos una casa particular (un apartamento).
4. La casa (el apartamento) tiene… cuartos.
5. Sí, tenemos un carro.
6. Sí, tenemos una mascota. Tenemos un perro (un gato).

Note For information concerning the terminology for step relatives, see *Bienvenidos*, Teacher's Wraparound Edition, Chapter 6, page 155.

L **La maleta.** Completen con *hacer, poner* o *salir*.

1. Juan ___ su maleta. Él ___ una camisa en la maleta. Él ___ para Málaga.
2. Nosotros ___ nuestra maleta. Nosotros ___ blue jeans en la maleta porque ___ para Cancún, en México.
3. ¿Tú ___ tu maleta? ¿Qué ___ en la maleta? ¿Por qué ___ la maleta? ¿Para dónde ___?
4. Mis padres ___ su maleta. Ellos ___ muchas cosas en la maleta. Ellos ___ su maleta porque ___ para Miami.
5. Yo ___ mi maleta. Yo ___ blue jeans y T shirts en mi maleta. Yo ___ mi maleta porque ___ para la Sierra de Guadarrama donde voy de camping.

M **Mi familia y mi casa.** Preguntas personales.

1. ¿Tienes una familia grande o pequeña?
2. ¿Cuántos hermanos y cuántas hermanas tienes?
3. ¿Tienen Uds. una casa particular o un apartamento?
4. ¿Cuántos cuartos tiene la casa o el apartamento?
5. ¿Tienen Uds. un carro?
6. ¿Tienen Uds. una mascota? ¿Tienen un perro o un gato?

LEARNING FROM ILLUSTRATIONS

Have students say all they can about the illustration on page R-32. Have them describe everything the young man is packing. You may wish to ask: ¿Cómo es el señor? ¿Dónde está? ¿Qué hace? ¿Por qué? ¿Qué deporte juega él? ¿De quién es la foto?

Comunicación

A **¿Adónde vamos?** With a partner decide on a place each of you wants to go to. Tell how you're going to get there and what you're going to do there. Then ask each other questions about your trip. Write a paragraph about your partner's trip. Then compare what each of you has written.

B **Los deportes.** With your partner decide what sport you want to talk about. Make a list of words that describe this sport. Then put the words into sentences and write a paragraph about the sport. Read your paragraph to the class.

Partidos de clasificación - marzo

FECHA	EQUIPO DE CASA	EQUIPO VISITANTE	SEDE	GRUPO
		Turquía		Europa 2
miércoles 10	San Marino			Europa 4
miércoles 24	Chipre	Checoslovaquia	Limasol	1
	Italia	Malta	Palermo	2
	Países Bajos	San Marino		
sábado 27	Austria	Francia	Viena	Europa 6
				Europa 4
miércoles 31	Gales	Bélgica		3
	Dinamarca	España		3
	Irlanda	Irlanda del Norte	Dublín	5
	Hungría	Grecia		1
	Suiza	Portugal	Berna	2
	Turquía	Inglaterra		

C **Mi familia y mi casa.** You and your partner will take turns saying something about your family and your house or apartment. Write down what the other person says. Then compare your families and your house or apartment.

D **Quiero…** Work with a classmate. Each of you will make a list of things you want to do but can't do because you have to do something else. Then compare your lists and see how many things you have in common.

R-33

Comunicación (page R-33)
These activities encourage students to use the language on their own. You may let them choose the activities in which they would like to participate.

ANSWERS

Actividades A-D
Answers will vary.

GEOGRAPHY CONNECTION
Some countries on the schedule, whose names the students may not recognize, are: *Chipre* (Cyprus); *Países Bajos* (Netherlands); *Gales* (Wales); *Suiza* (Switzerland); *Bélgica* (Belgium); *Irlanda del Norte* (Northern Ireland).

LEARNING FROM REALIA
Ask students the meaning of *Fecha, Equipo de casa* (home team), *Equipo visitante, sede* (site), *grupo*. Have students identify as many countries on the list as they can.

You may wish to ask questions such as: *¿Quiénes juegan el sábado, 27? ¿Dónde juegan ellos?*

INDEPENDENT PRACTICE
Assign any of the following:
1. Exercises and activities on student pages R-32–R-33
2. Workbook, *Repaso C*

R 33

REPASO D

OVERVIEW

Repaso D reviews vocabulary related to the winter and summer seasons. The structure points reviewed are the regular preterite and direct and indirect object pronouns.

REPASO

D

EL INVIERNO Y EL VERANO

LEARNING FROM PHOTOS

You may wish to ask the following questions about the photo on pages R-34–R-35: *¿Es un barco de motor o un barco de vela? ¿Cuántas velas tiene? ¿Es grande o pequeño el barco? ¿Cuántas personas hay en el barco? ¿Qué llevan? ¿Qué tiene el joven a la izquierda? ¿Qué opinas, es un lago o el mar? ¿Cómo está el mar, revuelto, (turbulento, bravo) o calmo (manso)?*

REVIEW RESOURCES

1. Workbook, *Repaso D*
2. Bell Ringer Review Blackline Masters
3. Testing Program

Pacing

Repaso D should take three to four days depending on the length of the class, the age of the students, and student aptitude.

R– 35

R 35

VOCABULARIO

VOCABULARIO

¿Qué hicieron en el verano?

Los amigos pasaron el fin de semana en la playa.
Nadaron en el mar.
Tomaron el sol.
Alquilaron un barquito.
Esquiaron en el agua.

En la estación de esquí

El invierno pasado María del Carmen esquió.
Ella subió la montaña en el telesquí.
Bajó una pista para principiantes.
Desgraciadamente perdió un bastón.

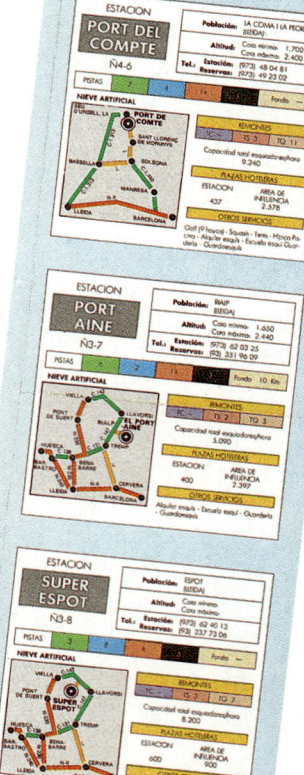

Vocabulary Teaching Resources

1. Workbook, *Repaso D*
2. Bell Ringer Review Blackline Masters

Bell Ringer Review

Write the following on the board or use BRR Blackline Master R-10: You are preparing the weather report for your Spanish class. Sketch the following conditions:
1. Hace calor.
2. Hace viento.
3. Hace mucho sol.
4. Llueve.
5. Está nublado.

¿Qué hicieron en el verano? En la estación de esquí

PRESENTATION *(page R-36)*

Note The sentences in the first group recycle material from *Bienvenidos*, Chapter 11. The sentences in the second group recycle material from *Bienvenidos*, Chapter 9.

A. Use gestures and a few simple dramatizations to reinforce the meaning of the expressions *pasar el fin de semana, nadar en el mar, tomar el sol, alquilar un barquito, esquiar en el agua, subir la montaña, bajar una pista,* and *perder un bastón.*
B. Have students repeat the sample sentences after you.

R 36

R–36

A El verano. Contesten.

1. ¿Qué tiempo hace casi siempre en el verano?
2. ¿Tienes vacaciones en el verano?
3. ¿Adónde vas?
4. ¿Te gusta nadar?
5. ¿Nadas mucho? ¿Dónde?
6. ¿Esquías en el agua?
7. ¿Qué usas como protección contra el sol?
8. ¿Qué llevas para protegerte los ojos?

El Grao Gandía

B El invierno. Contesten.

1. ¿Hace frío donde tú vives en el invierno?
2. ¿Vives cerca de las montañas?
3. ¿Esquías de vez en cuando?
4. ¿En qué suben los esquiadores la montaña?
5. ¿Qué tipo de pista bajan los buenos esquiadores?
6. ¿Qué necesitas para esquiar?

C Las vacaciones de Julia. Contesten.

1. ¿Julia pasó sus vacaciones en un balneario o en una estación de esquí?
2. ¿Ella nadó mucho?
3. ¿Nadó en el mar o en la piscina?
4. ¿Aprendió ella a hacer el esquí acuático?
5. ¿Ella tomó mucho sol?
6. ¿Volvió a casa muy bronceada?

D ¿En qué estación? Escojan y escriban en otro papel.

EN VERANO   EN INVIERNO   EN LAS DOS

1. Hace buen tiempo.
2. Hace frío.
3. Hace calor.
4. Nieva.
5. Llueve.
6. Hay mucho sol.
7. Hay mucho viento.
8. Está a dos grados bajo cero.

Ejercicios

PRESENTATION (page R-37)

Ejercicios A, B, and C
Exercises A, B, and C can be done with books open or closed.

Ejercicio D
Exercise D is to be done with books open.

ANSWERS

Ejercicio A
Answers will vary.
1. En el verano casi siempre hace calor.
2. Sí, tengo vacaciones en el verano.
3. Voy a…
4. Sí, (No, no) me gusta nadar.
5. Sí, (No, no) nado mucho. Nado (en la piscina, en el mar).
6. Sí, (No, no) esquío en el agua.
7. Uso crema protectora.
8. Llevo anteojos de sol.

Ejercicio B
1. Sí, (No, no) hace frío donde vivo en el invierno.
2. Sí, (No, no) vivo cerca de las montañas.
3. Sí, (No, no) esquío de vez en cuando (nunca).
4. Los esquiadores suben en el telesquí.
5. Los buenos esquiadores bajan una pista difícil.
6. Necesito esquís y bastones.

Ejercicio C
Answers will vary.
1. Julia pasó sus vacaciones en un balneario (en una estación de esquí).
2. Sí (No), ella (no) nadó mucho.
3. Nadó en el mar (en la piscina).
4. Sí (No), ella (no) aprendió a hacer el esquí acuático.
5. Sí, ella tomó mucho sol.
6. Sí, volvió a casa muy bronceada.

Ejercicio D
1. en verano
2. en invierno
3. en verano
4. en invierno
5. en las dos
6. en verano
7. en las dos
8. en invierno

COOPERATIVE LEARNING

Have teams create dialogues based on the contexts presented in Exercises A, B and C on page R-37. Teams may elect to work in pairs. Have each team present one of its dialogues to the class.

INDEPENDENT PRACTICE

Assign the following:
1. Exercises on student page R-37

ESTRUCTURA

Bell Ringer Review

Write the following on the board or use BRR Blackline Master R-11: Make a list of as many items of clothing as you can think of.

Structure Teaching Resources

1. Workbook, *Repaso D*
2. Bell Ringer Review Blackline Masters

El pretérito de los verbos regulares

PRESENTATION *(page R-38)*

A. Have students repeat the verbs in steps 1 and 2 after you.
B. Write one form of a verb on the board and challenge volunteers to fill in the rest of the paradigm.

GEOGRAPHY CONNECTION

Ixtapa is on the Pacific coast of Mexico, north of Acapulco. Because of the beautiful bay at Ixtapa, the Mexican government decided to develop the area for tourism. The area is referred to as Zihuatanejo-Ixtapa. Zihuatanejo is an old, picturesque town, Ixtapa is new and modern.

ESTRUCTURA

El pretérito de los verbos regulares

1. In Spanish you use the preterite to express an action that took place in the past. Note that the preterite endings are different from those used for the present tense. Review the forms of the preterite of regular verbs.

INFINITIVE	HABLAR	COMER	ESCRIBIR
yo	hablé	comí	escribí
tú	hablaste	comiste	escribiste
él, ella, Ud.	habló	comió	escribió
nosotros(as)	hablamos	comimos	escribimos
vosotros(as)	*hablasteis*	*comisteis*	*escribisteis*
ellos, ellas, Uds.	hablaron	comieron	escribieron

2. In the preterite the verb *dar* is conjugated the same way as an *-er* or *-ir* verb.

DAR
di
diste
dio
dimos
disteis
dieron

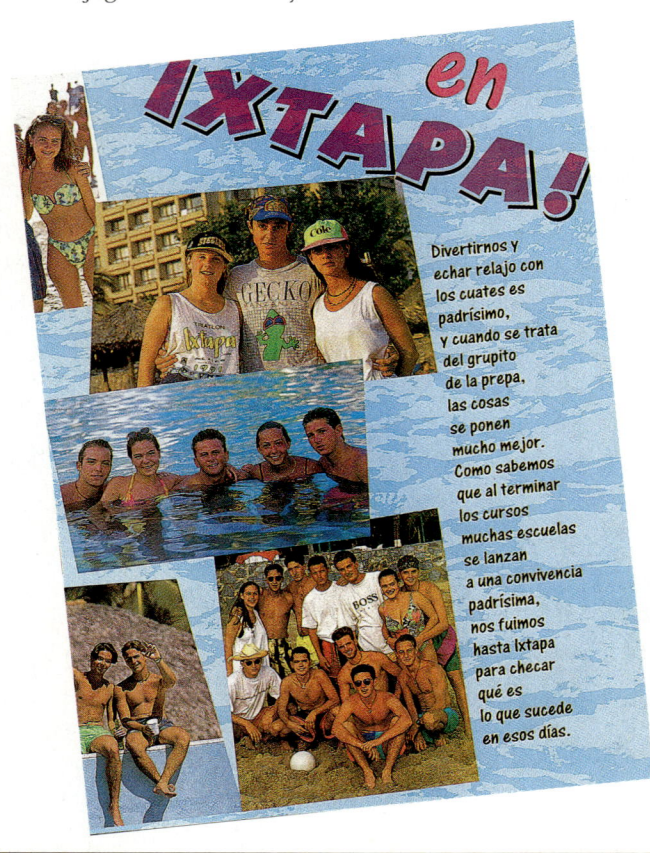

R-38

LEARNING FROM REALIA

Have students scan the realia on page R-38. Point out that there are some colloquialisms in it: *los cuates (los amigos), padrísimo (muy bueno, simpático), checar (averiguar, chequear).*

Cuate literally means "twin." In Mexico the expression is used to mean a close friend, a "buddy."

R 38

E **No contestó nadie.** Practiquen la conversación.

ENRIQUE: Felipe, te llamé anoche pero no contestaste.
FELIPE: Sí, es verdad que no contestó nadie. Anoche mis padres salieron y yo también salí.
ENRIQUE: ¿Salieron juntos?
FELIPE: No, no salimos juntos. Mis padres comieron en un restaurante con algunos amigos y yo vi una película fantástica en el cine Metropol.

Completen según la conversación.

Anoche Enrique ___(1)___ a Felipe pero nadie ___(2)___ el teléfono. No ___(3)___ nadie porque los padres de Enrique ___(4)___ y Enrique ___(5)___ también. Pero ellos no ___(6)___ juntos. Sus padres ___(7)___ en un restaurante con algunos amigos y Enrique ___(8)___ una película estupenda en el cine Metropol.

F **¿Qué hiciste anoche?** Preguntas personales.

1. ¿Saliste anoche?
2. ¿Comiste en casa o en un restaurante?
3. ¿Viste una película?
4. ¿Miraste una emisión deportiva en la televisión?
5. ¿Llamaste a un(a) amigo(a) por teléfono?
6. ¿Hablaron Uds. en inglés o en español?
7. Después de la conversación telefónica, ¿salieron juntos?
8. ¿Vieron una película en el cine?
9. ¿Estudiaron?
10. ¿Escribieron una composición para la clase de inglés?

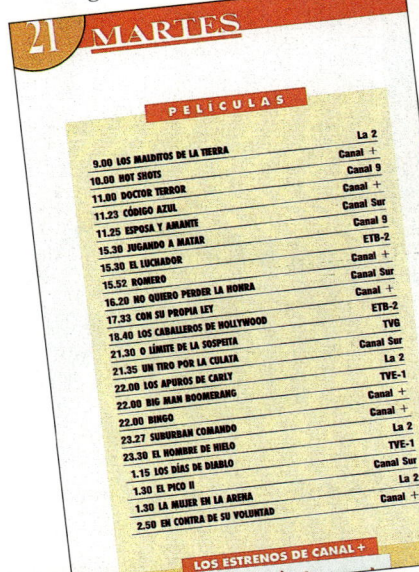

R–39

INDEPENDENT PRACTICE

Assign the following:
1. Exercises on student page R-39

Ejercicios

PRESENTATION (page R-39)

Ejercicio E
A. Call on two students to read the conversation aloud using as much expression as possible.
B. Then have students complete the paragraph that follows.

Expansion of *Ejercicio E*
A. Have students make up questions about each sentence of the conversation.
B. Have one student retell all the information in his/her own words.

Ejercicio F
Exercise F should be done first as an oral exercise with books closed. Students can then read and write the exercise as additional reinforcement.

ANSWERS

Ejercicio E
1. llamó
2. contestó
3. contestó
4. salieron
5. salió
6. salieron
7. comieron
8. vio

Ejercicio F
Answers will vary.
1. Sí, (No, no) salí anoche.
2. Comí en casa (en un restaurante).
3. Sí, (No, no) vi una película.
4. Sí, (No, no) miré una emisión deportiva en la televisión.
5. Sí, (No, no) llamé a un(a) amigo(a) por teléfono.
6. Hablamos en inglés (en español).
7. Sí, (No, no) salimos juntos después de la conversación telefónica.
8. Sí, (No, no) vimos una película en el cine.
9. Sí, (No, no) estudiamos.
10. Sí, (No, no) escribimos una composición para la clase de inglés.

Los complementos directos e indirectos

PRESENTATION (*page R-40*)

A. When presenting step 2, draw a box around the direct object in the sentences on the left.
B. Circle the direct object pronouns in the sentences on the right.
C. Draw a line from the noun to the pronoun to demonstrate that they represent the same person or thing.
D. Have volunteers read the sample sentences aloud.

Ejercicios

PRESENTATION (*page R-40*)

Ejercicio G
Exercise G can be done with books open or closed.

ANSWERS

Ejercicio G
1. … lo tienes.
2. … lo tienes.
3. … lo tienes.
4. … la tienes.
5. … la tienes.
6. … los tienes.
7. … los tienes.
8. … los tienes.
9. … las tienes.
10. … las tienes.

Los complementos directos e indirectos

1. The object pronouns *me, te, nos* function as both direct and indirect objects.

DIRECT OBJECT	INDIRECT OBJECT
Roberto me vio.	Y él me habló.
Él nos invitó.	Nos escribió una invitación.

2. The object pronouns *lo, la, los,* and *las* are always direct objects.

Compré el traje de baño.	Lo compré.
Compré la crema bronceadora.	La compré.
Compré los esquís acuáticos.	Los compré.
Compré las toallas playeras.	Las compré.

3. The object pronouns *le* and *les* are always indirect objects. Note that they are often clarified by a prepositional phrase.

   María le dio un regalo { a él. / a ella. / a Ud.

   María les dio un regalo { a ellos. / a ellas. / a Uds.

G *Aquí lo tienes.* Sigan el modelo.

   el bañador
   Aquí lo tienes.

1. el bañador
2. el traje de baño
3. el tubo de crema
4. la toalla playera
5. la crema bronceadora
6. los anteojos de sol
7. los boletos para el telesquí
8. los esquís
9. las raquetas
10. las pelotas

R–40

LEARNING FROM PHOTOS

You may wish to ask questions about the photos on page R-40. For example: *¿Para qué es la nivea? ¿Para qué son los anteojos de sol? ¿En qué estación del año usamos un traje de baño?*

H **¿Qué quiere Carlos?** Completen con el pronombre.

JESÚS: Teresa, aquí tienes el teléfono. Carlos ___ llama.
TERESA: ¿Carlos ___ llama? ¿Qué quiere él?
JESÚS: No sé. Pero creo que ___ quiere decir algo.
TERESA: Carlos, ¿por qué ___ llamas?
CARLOS: ___ quiero hablar porque ___ voy a decir algo muy importante.
TERESA: ¡Qué va! No ___ tienes que decir nada importante. ¿Por qué ___ estás tomando el pelo?

I **En el aeropuerto.** Completen con *le* o *les*.

La señora López llegó al mostrador de la línea aérea en el aeropuerto. Ella ___(1) habló al agente. ___(2) habló en español. No ___(3) habló en inglés. Ella ___(4) dio su boleto al agente y él lo miró. Ella ___(5) dio su pasaporte también. El agente ___(6) dio a la señora su tarjeta de embarque. A bordo del avión los asistentes de vuelo ___(7) hablaron a los pasajeros. ___(8) dieron la bienvenida a bordo y ___(9) explicaron el uso del equipo de emergencia.

Comunicación

A **Las vacaciones.** Tell your partner about a winter vacation you would like to take. Reverse roles and then report to the class.

B **En el verano.** With a classmate make a list of words and phrases you know pertaining to summer weather and summer activities. Take turns making up questions using these words and answering each others' questions.

Ejercicios

Ejercicios H and I

PRESENTATION (page R-41)

Exercises H and I are to be done with books open.

ANSWERS

Ejercicio H
1. te
2. me
3. te
4. me
5. Te, te
6. me, me

Ejercicio I
1. le
2. Le
3. le
4. le
5. le
6. le
7. les
8. Les
9. les

Comunicación

PRESENTATION (page R-41)

These activities encourage students to use the language on their own. You may let them choose the activities in which they would like to participate.

ANSWERS

Actividades A and B
Answers will vary.

COOPERATIVE LEARNING

After completing Exercises H and I, have teams use them as models for their own conversations. You may wish to have half the class use Exercise H as a model, while the other half uses Exercise I.

INDEPENDENT PRACTICE

Assign the following:
1. Exercises and activities on student pages R-40–R-41

REPASO E

OVERVIEW

Repaso E reviews vocabulary related to vacations and cultural activities, presented in *Bienvenidos* Chapters 11 and 12, as well as vocabulary associated with rail travel. The structure reviewed is the preterite of irregular verbs and the verb *gustar*.

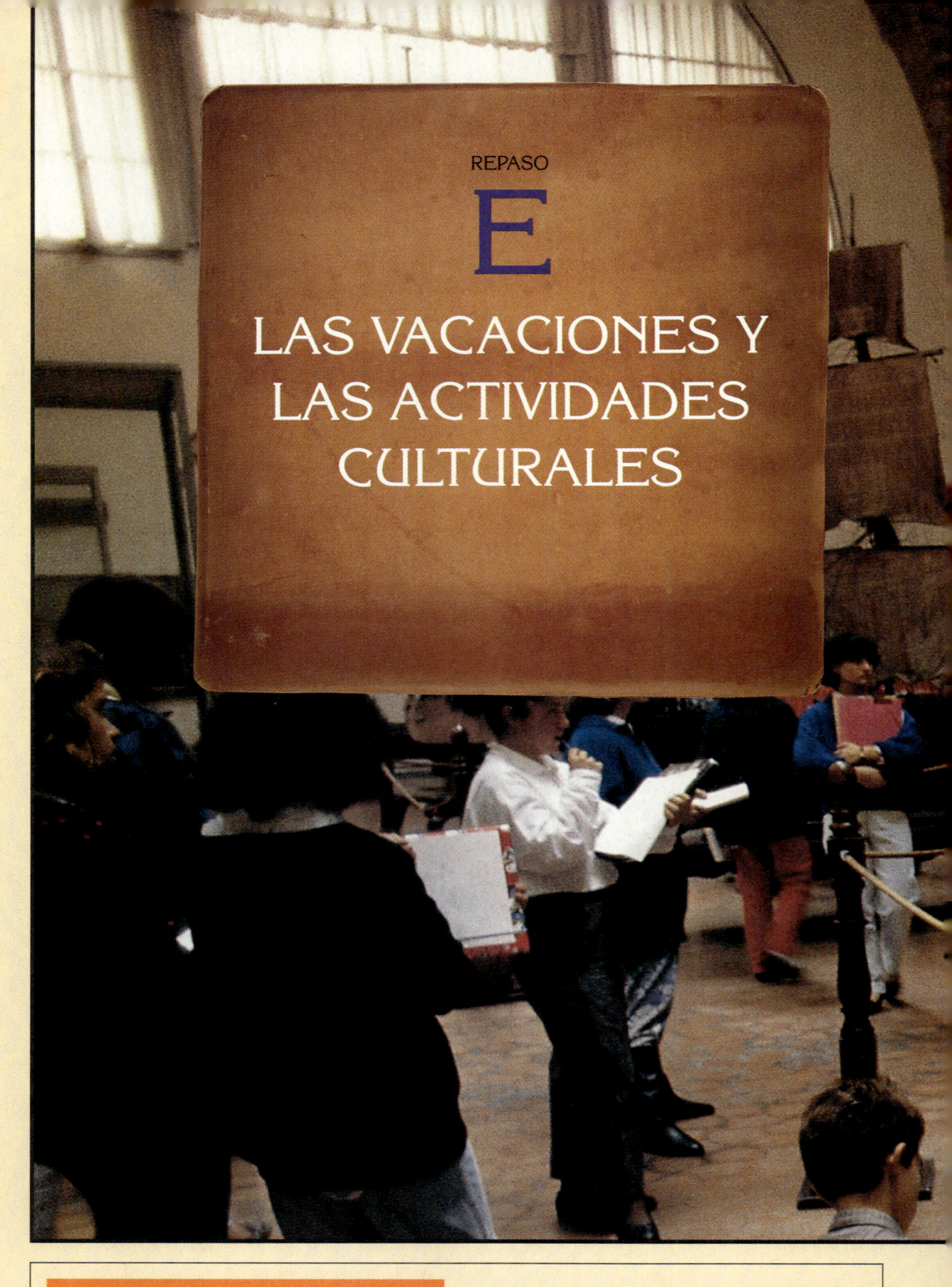

REPASO E
LAS VACACIONES Y LAS ACTIVIDADES CULTURALES

LEARNING FROM PHOTOS

You may wish to tell students that the photo on pages R-42–R-43 is in the Museo Marítimo in Barcelona, Spain. You may also wish to ask the following questions: ¿Están visitando un museo los alumnos? ¿Están mirando un barco moderno o antiguo? ¿Qué están escribiendo? ¿En qué están tomando sus notas?

REVIEW RESOURCES

1. Workbook, *Repaso E*
2. Bell Ringer Review Blackline Masters
3. Testing Program

Pacing

Repaso E should take two or three days depending on the length of the class, the age of the students, and student aptitude.

VOCABULARIO

Vocabulary Teaching Resources
1. Workbook, *Repaso E*
2. Bell Ringer Review Blackline Masters

Bell Ringer Review
Write the following on the board or use BRR Blackline Master R-12: Divide the following list of words into three categories: **frutas/legumbres/carne**.
la banana
la naranja
el pollo
la cebolla
la patata, la papa
el tomate
la carne de res
las habichuelas
la manzana

PRESENTATION *(page R-44)*
A. Call on two volunteers with good pronunciation to role-play the conversation for the class.
B. Have the class repeat in unison the conversation after you.

Ejercicios
PRESENTATION *(page R-44)*
Ejercicio A
Exercise A can be done with books closed.

Extension of *Ejercicio A:* Speaking
After completing Exercise A, have an individual retell the story in his/her own words.

ANSWERS
Ejercicio A
1. Felipe fue a Sevilla.
2. Sus primos, Sandra y Rafael, lo acompañaron.
3. Fueron en tren.
4. Les fue bien.

R 44

VOCABULARIO

ALFREDO: ¿Cómo fuiste a Sevilla?
FELIPE: Fuimos en tren.
ALFREDO: ¿Fuimos? ¿Quiénes te acompañaron?
FELIPE: Mis primos, Sandra y Rafael. ¡Qué viaje más bueno! En el coche-comedor nos sirvieron una comida excelente.
ALFREDO: ¿Una comida excelente a bordo de un tren?
FELIPE: Sí, pedí lomo (biftec) a término medio y el mesero lo trajo (sirvió) en seguida. ¡Exquisito!
ALFREDO: ¿Y qué hicieron en Sevilla?
FELIPE: Pues, fuimos al Alcázar, a la Torre del Oro y vimos una exposición de Murillo en el museo.

A En Sevilla. Contesten según la conversación.

1. ¿Quién fue a Sevilla?
2. ¿Quiénes lo acompañaron?
3. ¿Cómo fueron a Sevilla?
4. ¿Qué tal fue el viaje?
5. ¿Dónde le sirvieron un lomo exquisito?
6. ¿Cómo lo pidió Felipe?
7. ¿Qué hicieron Felipe y sus primos en Sevilla?

"El regreso del hijo pródigo" de Bartolomé Esteban Murillo

R–44

PANTOMIME
Call on students to act out the following:
**Espera el tren en la sala de espera.
Compra un periódico y una revista.
Compra un billete.
Consulta el tablero para verificar la hora de salida del tren.
Ve al andén.**

LEARNING FROM PHOTOS
You may wish to tell students that the author of the painting on page R-44, Bartolomé Esteban Murillo (1617-1682), is known for the biblical and religious themes in many of his works. Murillo was born in Sevilla and was a contemporary of another famous Spanish painter from Sevilla, Diego de Velázquez.

B **Mi restaurante favorito.** Preguntas personales.

1. ¿Cuál es un restaurante que te gusta?
2. ¿Cuándo fuiste la última vez?
3. ¿Qué pediste?
4. ¿Te gustó?
5. ¿Te sirvió bien el mesero?
6. ¿Te trajo la cuenta?
7. ¿Le dejaste una propina?
8. ¿Cómo pagaste?

C **En la estación de ferrocarril.** Completen.

1. Los pasajeros esperan el tren en ___ .
2. Despachan los billetes en ___ .
3. Venden periódicos y revistas en ___ en la sala de espera.
4. Los pasajeros consultan ___ para verificar la hora de salida o llegada de su tren.
5. ___ ayudan a los pasajeros con su equipaje.
6. El tren sale del ___ número cinco.
7. El tren no salió ___ ; salió con retraso.

D **¿Qué es?** Identifiquen.

1. lugar donde presentan obras teatrales
2. lugar donde ponen películas
3. lo que se levanta al empezar una representación teatral
4. donde se proyecta una película
5. donde hace la gente cola para comprar entradas
6. el que pinta cuadros
7. lugar donde hay exposiciones de arte

INDEPENDENT PRACTICE

Assign the following:
Exercises on student pages R-44–R-45

5. Le sirvieron un lomo exquisito en el cochecomedor del tren.
6. Felipe lo pidió a término medio.
7. Fueron al Alcázar, a la Torre del Oro y vieron una exposición de Murillo en el museo.

Ejercicios

PRESENTATION (*page R-45*)

Ejercicios B and D
Exercises B and D can be done with books closed

Extension of *Ejercicio B*:
Speaking/Listening
After completing Exercise B, invite students to talk about their favorite restaurants.

Ejercicio C
Exercise C is to be done with books open.

ANSWERS
Ejercicio B
Answers will vary.
1. Un restaurante que me gusta es...
2. Fui...
3. Pedí...
4. Sí, me gustó.
5. Sí, el mesero me sirvió bien.
6. Sí, me trajo la cuenta.
7. Sí, le dejé una propina.
8. Pagué con dinero en efectivo (con tarjeta de crédito).

Ejercicio C
1. la sala de espera
2. la ventanilla
3. el quiosco
4. el tablero (de llegadas, de salidas)
5. Los mozos
6. andén
7. a tiempo

Ejercicio D
1. el teatro
2. el cine
3. el telón
4. la pantalla
5. la taquilla
6. el pintor
7. el museo

ESTRUCTURA

Bell Ringer Review

Write the following on the board or use BRR Blackline Master R-13: Make a list of routine activities that you did yesterday.

Structure Teaching Resources

1. Workbook, *Repaso E*
2. Bell Ringer Review Blackline Masters

El pretérito de los verbos irregulares

PRESENTATION *(pages R-46–R-47)*

Note Although it is necessary to expose students to these verb forms, it is recommended that you do not emphasize them, since so many of them are not used frequently in the preterite.

A. Ask students to open their books to pages R-46 and R-47. Lead them through steps 1-3.
B. Have students repeat the verb forms after you.
C. In step 2, call on volunteers to read the sample sentences.

R 46

ESTRUCTURA

El pretérito de los verbos irregulares

1. Review the following forms of verbs that are irregular in the preterite.

INFINITIVE	ESTAR	TENER	ANDAR
yo	estuve	tuve	anduve
tú	estuviste	tuviste	anduviste
él, ella, Ud.	estuvo	tuvo	anduvo
nosotros(as)	estuvimos	tuvimos	anduvimos
vosotros(as)	*estuvisteis*	*tuvisteis*	*anduvisteis*
ellos, ellas, Uds.	estuvieron	tuvieron	anduvieron

INFINITIVE	PONER	PODER	SABER
yo	puse	pude	supe
tú	pusiste	pudiste	supiste
él, ella, Ud.	puso	pudo	supo
nosotros(as)	pusimos	pudimos	supimos
vosotros(as)	*pusisteis*	*pudisteis*	*supisteis*
ellos, ellas, Uds.	pusieron	pudieron	supieron

INFINITIVE	QUERER	HACER	VENIR
yo	quise	hice	vine
tú	quisiste	hiciste	viniste
él, ella, Ud.	quiso	hizo	vino
nosotros(as)	quisimos	hicimos	vinimos
vosotros(as)	*quisisteis*	*hicisteis*	*vinisteis*
ellos, ellas, Uds.	quisieron	hicieron	vinieron

INFINITIVE	DECIR
yo	dije
tú	dijiste
él, ella, Ud.	dijo
nosotros(as)	dijimos
vosotros(as)	dijisteis
ellos, ellas, Uds.	dijeron

2. *Saber, poder,* and *querer* have a meaning in the preterite that is different from the normal meaning of the infinitive.

   Carlos lo supo ayer.   *Carlos found it out (learned about it) yesterday.*
   Elena lo pudo hacer.   *(After much effort) Elena managed to do it.*
   José no lo pudo hacer.   *(He tried but) José couldn't do it.*
   Teresa no quiso ir.   *Teresa refused to go.*

3. The following verbs have a stem change in the preterite.

INFINITIVE	PEDIR	SERVIR	DORMIR
yo	pedí	serví	dormí
tú	pediste	serviste	dormiste
él, ella, Ud.	pidió	sirvió	durmió
nosotros(as)	pedimos	servimos	dormimos
vosotros(as)	pedisteis	servisteis	dormisteis
ellos, ellas, Uds.	pidieron	sirvieron	durmieron

E **No sé.** Sigan el modelo.

   ¿Quién lo hizo?
   No sé quién lo hizo.

1. ¿Quién lo supo?
2. ¿Quién lo dijo?
3. ¿Quién lo trajo?
4. ¿Quién lo puso allí?
5. ¿Quién lo hizo?
6. ¿Quién vino?
7. ¿Quién lo pidió?
8. ¿Quién lo sirvió?
9. ¿Quién durmió?

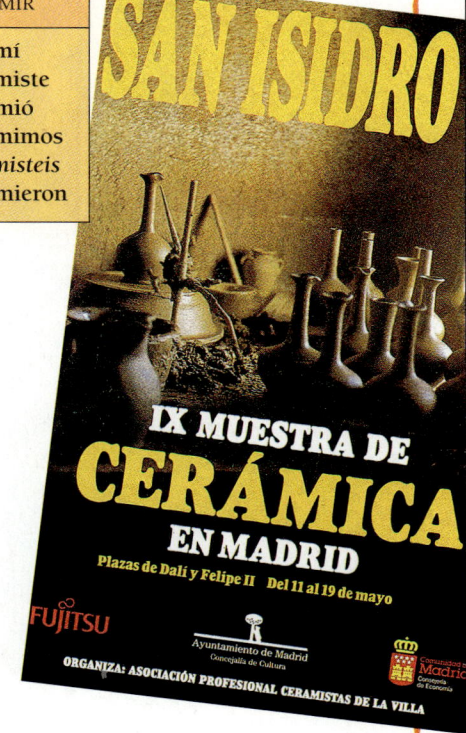

R–47

PRESENTATION (page R-48)

Ejercicios F and G
Exercises F and G can be done with books open or closed.

Extension of Ejercicio G
After completing Exercise G, call on a volunteer to recount the information in story form. Have him/her add as much information as possible to embellish the story.

ANSWERS

Ejercicio F
1. Roberto no vino porque no quiso venir.
2. No vine porque no quise venir.
3. Elena no vino porque no quiso venir.
4. Elena y sus amigos no vinieron porque no quisieron venir.
5. No vinimos porque no quisimos venir.

Ejercicio G
1. Fuimos al restaurante.
2. Yo pedí langosta.
3. Mi amigo pidió biftec.
4. El mesero nos trajo la comida.
5. Nos sirvió muy bien.
6. Yo le pedí la cuenta.
7. Él nos trajo la cuenta.
8. Él la puso en la mesa.

F **Nadie vino.** Contesten según el modelo.

¿Por qué no viniste?
Yo no vine porque no quise venir.

1. ¿Por qué no vino Roberto?
2. ¿Por qué no viniste tú?
3. ¿Por qué no vino Elena?
4. ¿Por qué no vinieron Elena y sus amigos?
5. ¿Por qué no vinieron Uds.?

G **En el restaurante.** Cambien las oraciones al pretérito.

1. Vamos al restaurante.
2. Yo pido langosta.
3. Mi amigo pide biftec.
4. El mesero nos trae la comida.
5. Nos sirve muy bien.
6. Yo le pido la cuenta.
7. Él nos trae la cuenta.
8. Él la pone en la mesa.

R–48

INDEPENDENT PRACTICE
Assign the following:
Exercises on student pages R-47–R-48

LEARNING FROM PHOTOS
Have students name the foods and ingredients on page R-48 in Spanish. Some of them are, *tortillas, tamales, chiles rellenos, salsa, guacamole, langosta, biftec con papas fritas, arroz con frijoles negros, chiles, aguacates, cebollas, tomates.*

El verbo *gustar*

The verb *gustar* is used to express "to like." It takes an indirect object the same as verbs such as *interesar* or *sorprender*.

> Me gusta mucho el arte.
> Me interesa el arte.
> ¿A Ud. le gustan los cuadros de Goya?
> Sí, me gustan mucho.
> A mis amigos les gusta la obra de Orozco.
> Les gustan los murales mexicanos.

"El Quitasol" de Francisco de Goya

H **Los gustos.** Contesten.

1. ¿Te gusta la literatura?
2. ¿Qué autores o escritores te gustan?
3. A tu mamá, ¿le gusta leer revistas?
4. ¿Qué revistas le gustan?
5. A tus amigos, ¿les gustan los deportes?
6. ¿Qué deportes les gustan?
7. ¿Te gustan los deportes también?
8. ¿Cuál es el deporte que te gusta más?

Comunicación

A **Un almuerzo.** You and two classmates are planning a lunch for your teacher. Decide the day and time to have lunch, what to serve, what you need to buy, and who will prepare the food. Then explain your plans to the class.

B **Somos cultos.** This semester you and two classmates are members of a committee that plans cultural activities for your school. Make a list of possible activities taking into consideration what students in your school like or don't like. Then explain your choices to the class.

LEARNING FROM PHOTOS

In regard to the photo on page R-49, you may wish to ask students what they know about Francisco de Goya. Refer to Chapter 2, page 30 of this Teacher's Wrap-around Edition for more information on Goya.

INDEPENDENT PRACTICE

Assign the following:
Exercises and activities on student page R-49

El verbo *gustar*

PRESENTATION (*page R-49*)

Lead students through the explanation on page R-49 and have them repeat the sentences after you.

Ejercicio H

PRESENTATION (*page R-49*)

First go through Exercise H, calling on a different individual for each item. Then have one volunteer read the entire exercise to the class.

ANSWERS

Ejercicio H

Answers will vary.
1. Sí, me gusta la literatura.
2. Los autores (escritores) que me gustan son:...
3. Sí (No), a mi mamá (no) le gusta leer revistas.
4. Las revistas que le gustan son:...
5. Sí (No), a mis amigos (no) les gustan los deportes.
6. Les gustan el...
7. Sí (No), a mí (no) me gustan los deportes también (tampoco).
8. El deporte que me gusta más es el...

Comunicación

PRESENTATION (*page R-49*)

These activities encourage students to use the language on their own. You may let them choose the activities in which they would like to participate.

ANSWERS

Actividades A and B

Answers will vary.

REPASO F

OVERVIEW

Repaso F reviews vocabulary related to camping. The structures reviewed include reflexive verbs and the present tense forms of radical-changing verbs.

REPASO F

DE CAMPING

LEARNING FROM PHOTOS

In regard to the photo on pages R-50–R-51, tell students this is a section of the Sonora desert in Northern Mexico. You may wish to ask the following: *¿Es árido o húmedo el clima? ¿Es una selva tropical o un desierto? ¿Son muy verdes las plantas?*

REVIEW RESOURCES

1. Workbook, *Repaso F*
2. Bell Ringer Review Blackline Masters
3. Testing Program

Pacing

Repaso F should take two to three days depending on the length of the class, the age of the students, and student aptitude.

VOCABULARIO

VOCABULARIO

Vocabulary Teaching Resources

1. Workbook, *Repaso F*
2. Bell Ringer Review Blackline Masters

Bell Ringer Review

Write the following on the board or use BRR Blackline Master R-14: Write at least five things you do when you are on vacation.

De vacaciones

PRESENTATION (page R-52)

Note The sentences in both groups recycle material from Chapter 16 of *Bienvenidos*.
A. Call on a different volunteer to read each sentence.
B. Ask questions about each sentence. For example: *¿Quiénes van de camping? ¿En qué duerme cada uno? ¿Dónde ponen los sacos de dormir? ¿Dónde preparan la comida? ¿Quién se levanta? ¿Qué hace José? ¿Dónde tiene la ropa José? ¿Qué saca? Luego, ¿qué hace?*

Ejercicios

PRESENTATION (page R-52)

Ejercicio A
Exercise A deals with camping. It is to be done with books open.

ANSWERS
Ejercicio A
1. Sí
2. No
3. Sí
4. Sí
5. No
6. No
7. No

De vacaciones

Los Santana van de camping.
Cada uno duerme en un saco de dormir.
Ponen los sacos de dormir en la carpa.
Preparan la comida en el hornillo.

José se levanta.
Se lava y se cepilla los dientes.
José tiene la ropa en una mochila.
Saca un blue jean, un par de tenis y una camiseta.
Luego se viste y se desayuna.

A De camping. ¿Sí o no?
1. Los Santana van de camping.
2. Duermen en una hamaca.
3. Preparan la comida en el hornillo.
4. José se levanta por la mañana.
5. Tiene la ropa en una maleta.
6. Se viste de una manera elegante.
7. No se desayuna.

LEARNING FROM ILLUSTRATIONS

Have students say as much as they can about the illustration on page R-52.

B ¿Qué hace el muchacho? Describan.

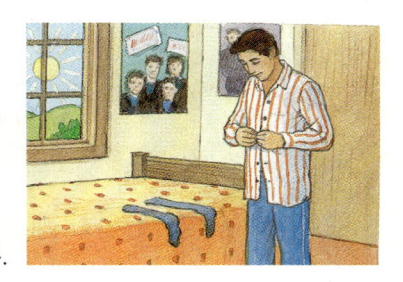

1.
2.
3.
4.
5.
6.

C La muchacha. Escojan.

1. La muchacha se mira en ___ .
   a. el espejo   b. la pensión   c. el hornillo

2. Los jóvenes dan una caminata por ___ .
   a. el camping   b. las sendas del bosque   c. el camión

3. Ella se baña y ___ .
   a. se cepilla   b. se lava el pelo   c. toma una ducha

4. En ___ hay muchos árboles.
   a. la orilla   b. el bosque   c. el saco

R–53

Ejercicios

PRESENTATION (*page R-53*)

Ejercicio B
Exercise B deals with daily routines and reflexive verbs. It is to be done with books open.

Expansion of *Ejercicio B*: Speaking
After completing Exercise B, call on individuals to tell about their morning routines before coming to school.

Ejercicio C
Exercise C deals with camping. It is to be done with books open.

ANSWERS
Ejercicio B
1. El muchacho se acuesta.
2. El muchacho se levanta.
3. El muchacho se peina.
4. El muchacho se viste.
5. El muchacho se desayuna.
6. El muchacho se pone el abrigo.

Ejercicio C
1. a
2. b
3. b
4. b

INDEPENDENT PRACTICE

Assign the following:
Exercises on student pages R-52–R-53

R 53

ESTRUCTURA

Bell Ringer Review

Write the following on the board or use BRR Blackline Master R-15:

Match the following words:
1. cepillar   a. la cena
2. lavar   b. el almuerzo
3. peinar   c. el desayuno
4. vestir   d. el lavado
5. desayunar   e. el vestido
6. almorzar   f. el cepillo
7. cenar   g. el peine

Structure Teaching Resources

1. Workbook, *Repaso F*
2. Bell Ringer Review Blackline Masters

Los verbos reflexivos

PRESENTATION (page R-54)

A. Copy some of the samples from the table on the board or on an overhead transparency.
B. Circle the reflexive pronoun in each sentence, underline the subject pronoun and draw a line from the reflexive pronoun to the subject pronoun to stress that they refer to the same person.
C. Explain to students that *no* comes right before the reflexive pronoun.

ESTRUCTURA

Los verbos reflexivos

A reflexive verb is one in which the action reflects back to the subject. The subject does the action of the verb to itself. The verb is always accompanied by a reflexive pronoun. Review the following.

INFINITIVE	LAVARSE	LEVANTARSE
yo	me lavo	me levanto
tú	te lavas	te levantas
él, ella, Ud.	se lava	se levanta
nosotros(as)	nos lavamos	nos levantamos
vosotros(as)	*os laváis*	*os levantáis*
ellos, ellas, Uds.	se lavan	se levantan

INFINITIVE	ACOSTARSE
yo	me acuesto
tú	te acuestas
él, ella, Ud.	se acuesta
nosotros(as)	nos acostamos
vosotros(as)	*os acostáis*
ellos, ellas, Uds.	se acuestan

D **Yo.** Preguntas personales.

1. ¿A qué hora te despiertas?
2. ¿A qué hora te levantas?
3. ¿Te desayunas en casa?
4. ¿Te cepillas los dientes antes o después del desayuno?
5. ¿Te peinas o te cepillas el pelo?
6. ¿Te afeitas?
7. ¿Te miras en el espejo cuando te afeitas o cuando te peinas?
8. ¿A qué hora te acuestas?

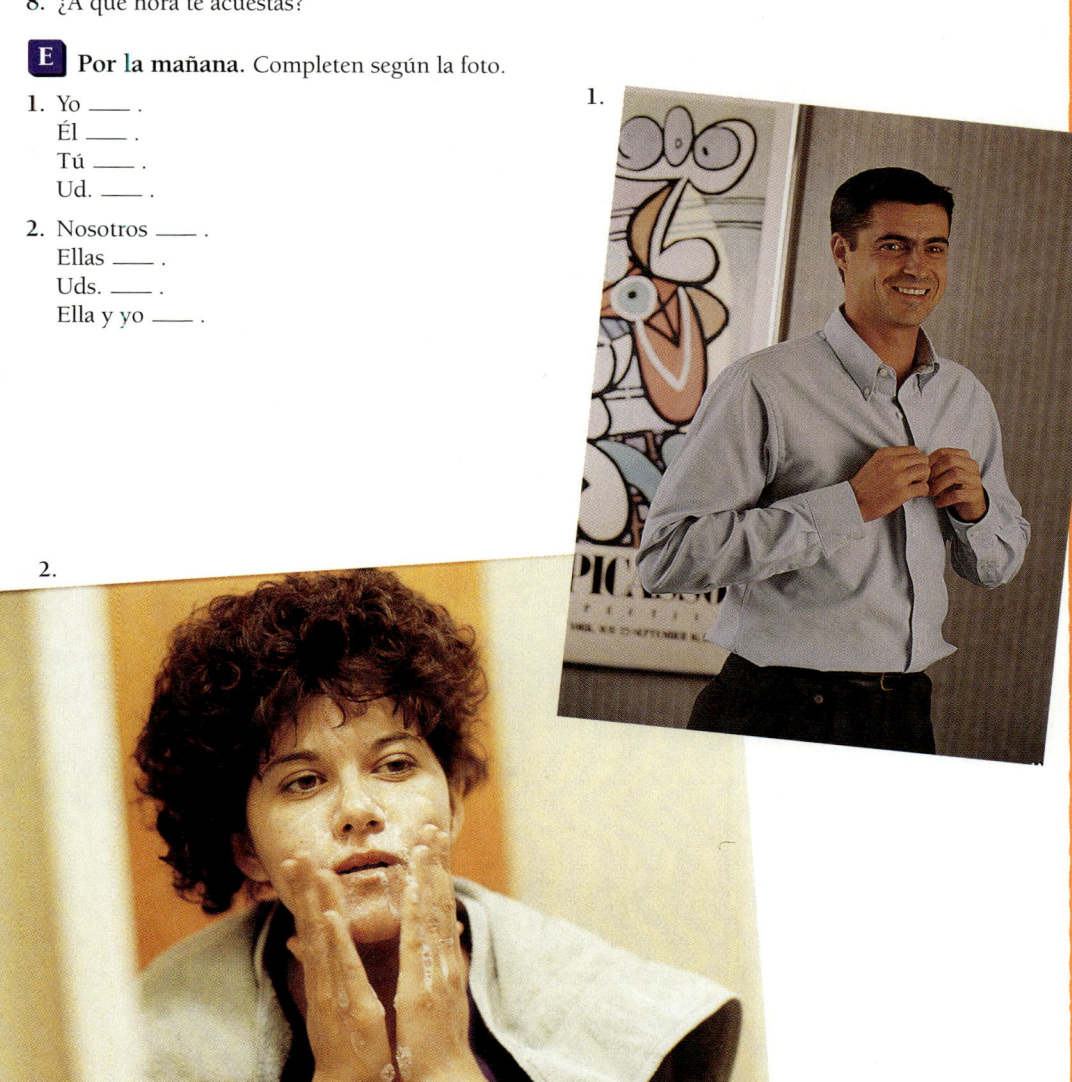

E **Por la mañana.** Completen según la foto.

1. Yo ___ .
   Él ___ .
   Tú ___ .
   Ud. ___ .

2. Nosotros ___ .
   Ellas ___ .
   Uds. ___ .
   Ella y yo ___ .

R–55

Ejercicios

PRESENTATION (*page R-55*)

Ejercicio D
Exercise D can be done in pairs, with partners changing roles so that each partner gets a chance to ask and answer the questions.

Ejercicio E
Exercise E is to be done with books open.

ANSWERS

Ejercicio D
Answers will vary.
1. Me despierto a las…
2. Me levanto a las…
3. Sí, (No, no) me desayuno en casa.
4. Me cepillo los dientes antes (después) del desayuno.
5. Me peino (me cepillo) el pelo.
6. Sí, (No, no) me afeito.
7. Sí, me miro en el espejo cuando me afeito (me peino).
8. Me acuesto a las…

Ejercicio E
1. me visto
   se viste
   te vistes
   se viste
2. nos lavamos
   se lavan
   se lavan
   nos lavamos

INDEPENDENT PRACTICE

Assign the following:
Exercises on student page R-55

R 55

El presente de algunos verbos de cambio radical

PRESENTATION (page R-56)

A. Have students open their books to page R-56. Lead students through steps 1 and 2.
B. Have them repeat the verb forms aloud.
C. Insist that students pronounce the verb forms correctly. If they do, they will be able to spell them correctly.

Ejercicios

PRESENTATION

Ejercicio F

Exercise F emphasizes that the spelling changes occur in all forms except *nosotros* and *vosotros*.

ANSWERS

Ejercicio F
1. Me visto y salgo para el restaurante.
2. Prefiero ir a un restaurante económico.
3. Pido un biftec.
4. Lo pido casi crudo.
5. El camarero me sirve.
6. ¿Repite Ud. el postre?

El presente de algunos verbos de cambio radical

1. Verbs such as *pedir, servir,* and *repetir* change the *-e* of the infinitive stem to *-i* in all forms of the present tense, except *nosotros(as)* and *(vosotros[as])*.

INFINITIVE	PEDIR	SERVIR	REPETIR
yo	pido	sirvo	repito
tú	pides	sirves	repites
él, ella, Ud.	pide	sirve	repite
nosotros(as)	pedimos	servimos	repetimos
vosotros(as)	*pedís*	*servís*	*repetís*
ellos, ellas, Uds.	piden	sirven	repiten

2. *Preferir* changes *-e* to *-ie* and *dormir* changes *-o* to *-ue* in all forms except *nosotros(as)* and *(vosotros[as])*.

INFINITIVE	PREFERIR	DORMIR
yo	prefiero	duermo
tú	prefieres	duermes
él, ella, Ud.	prefiere	duerme
nosotros(as)	preferimos	dormimos
vosotros(as)	*preferís*	*dormís*
ellos, ellas, Uds.	prefieren	duermen

F ¡Todos no! ¡Solamente uno(a)! Den la forma singular.

1. Nos vestimos y salimos para el restaurante.
2. Preferimos ir a un restaurante económico.
3. Pedimos un biftec.
4. Lo pedimos casi crudo.
5. Los camareros nos sirven.
6. ¿Repiten Uds. el postre?

LEARNING FROM REALIA

Refer students to the restaurant ads on page R-56. You may wish to ask them the following questions: ¿Cómo se llaman los restaurantes? ¿Qué tipo de cocina sirven en Domine Cabra (Bar del Teatro, Hacienda el Tapatío)? ¿Dónde están?

Comunicación

A **Lleva una blusa roja y…** Describe to your partner what outfit someone in class is wearing but don't tell him or her the name of the person. Your partner has to guess the name of the person. Take turns describing several people.

B **¿A qué hora te…?** In groups of three take turns telling each other at what time you do the following activities on weekends.

1. levantarse
2. desayunarse
3. cepillarse los dientes
4. lavarse
5. vestirse

20.- Bolso bandolera (9.975). Jersey viscosa (5.975). Blusa seda (5.475). Collar piedras alambre (1.375). Collar terracota (975). Cartera (4.375). Monedero (975). Americana lino-seda (13.975). Blusa seda natural (8.975). Falda viscosa delavada (4.975). Capazo paja (1.875). Gorro paja (1.275). Jersey algodón (6.475). Botines ante (3.975). Cinturón piel (2.975). Cinturón piel (3.575). Cinturón piel (2.875). Cinturón piel (2.975).

R–57

Comunicación

PRESENTATION *(page R-57)*

These activities encourage students to use the language on their own. You may let them choose the activities in which they would like to participate.

ANSWERS

Actividades A and B
Answers will vary.

INDEPENDENT PRACTICE

Assign the following:
Exercises and activities on student pages R-56–R-57

LEARNING FROM REALIA

Have students scan the description of each item. This is a beneficial activity as students can pick up a few new words very easily.

R 57

CAPÍTULO 1
Scope and Sequence pages 1-25

Topics	Functions	Structure	Culture
Telephone

Telephone etiquette | How to make a telephone call in a Spanish-speaking country

How to use proper phone etiquette

How to describe people, things, and events in the past

How to relate habitual routine actions in the past | El imperfecto de los verbos en -ar

El imperfecto de los verbos en -er e -ir

El imperfecto de los verbos ir y ser

Los usos del imperfecto | Spanish telephone etiquette

Telephone service of the past vs. today in Spanish-speaking countries

Palacio de Comunicaciones in Madrid

A telephone token for a public phone in Chile |

CAPÍTULO 1

Situation Cards
The Situation Cards simulate real-life situations that require students to communicate in Spanish, exactly as though they were in a Spanish-speaking country. The Situation Cards operate on the assumption that the person to whom the message is to be conveyed understands no English. Therefore, students must focus on producing the Spanish vocabulary and structures necessary to negotiate the situations successfully. For additional information, see the Introduction to the Situation Cards in the Situation Cards Envelope.

Communication Transparency
The illustration seen in this Communication Transparency consists of a synthesis of the two vocabulary (Palabras 1&2) presentations found in this chapter. It has been created in order to present this chapter's vocabulary in a new context, and also to recycle vocabulary learned in previous chapters. The Communication Transparency consists of original art. Following are some specific uses:

1. as a cue to stimulate conversation and writing activities
2. for listening comprehension activities
3. to review and reteach vocabulary
4. as a review for chapter and unit tests

CAPÍTULO 1
Print Resources

Lesson Plans

Workbook
	Pages
◆ Palabras 1	1-2
◆ Palabras 2	3
◆ Estructura	3-6
◆ Un poco más	7-9
◆ Mi autobiografía	10

Communication Activities Masters
◆ Palabras 1	1-2
◆ Palabras 2	3-4
◆ Estructura	5-7

8 Bell Ringer Reviews   7-8

Chapter Situation Cards A B C D

Chapter Quizzes
◆ Palabras 1	1
◆ Palabras 2	2
◆ Estructura	3-6

Testing Program
◆ Listening Comprehension	1
◆ Reading and Writing	1-4
◆ Proficiency	123
◆ Speaking	141

Nosotros y Nuestro Mundo
- ◆ Nuestro Conocimiento Académico *Las ciencias: ¿Cómo funciona el teléfono?*
- ◆ Nuestro Idioma *El tiempo imperfecto*
- ◆ Nuestra Cultura *Los medios de comunicación*
- ◆ Nuestra Literatura *"La lengua castellana"* de José Mercado
- ◆ Nuestra Creatividad
- ◆ Nuestras Diversiones

CAPÍTULO 1
Multimedia Resources

CD-ROM Interactive Textbook Disc 1
Chapter 1 Student Edition
- ◆ Palabras 1
- ◆ Palabras 2
- ◆ Estructura
- ◆ Conversación
- ◆ Lectura y cultura
- ◆ Hispanoparlantes
- ◆ Realidades
- ◆ Culminación
- ◆ Prueba

Audio Cassette Program with Student Tape Manual
Cassette	Pages
◆ 2A Palabras 1	203-204
◆ 2A Palabras 2	204
◆ 2A Estructura	205
◆ 2A Conversación	206
◆ 2A Segunda parte	206-208

Compact Disc Program with Student Tape Manual
◆ CD 2 Palabras 1	203-204
◆ CD 2 Palabras 2	204
◆ CD 2 Estructura	205
◆ CD 2 Conversación	206
◆ CD 2 Segunda parte	206-208

Overhead Transparencies Binder
- ◆ Vocabulary   1.1 (A&B); 1.2 (A&B)
- ◆ Communication C-1
- ◆ Maps
- ◆ Fine Art (with Blackline Master Activities)

Video Program
◆ Videocassette	
◆ Video Activities Booklet	1-3
◆ Videodisc	
◆ Video Activities Booklet	1-3

Computer Software (Macintosh, IBM, Apple)
- ◆ Practice Disk
  - Palabras 1 y 2
  - Estructura
- ◆ Test Generator Disk
  - Chapter Test
  - Customized Test

1B

CAPÍTULO 1

CHAPTER OVERVIEW

In this chapter students will learn how to make a telephone call in a Spanish-speaking country and to communicate with an operator when necessary. They will also learn the proper expressions for beginning and ending a telephone conversation. The formation and basic uses of the imperfect tense are presented in this chapter. The cultural focus of Chapter 1 is on Spanish telephone etiquette and a comparison of telephone service of yesterday and today in Spanish-speaking countries.

CHAPTER OBJECTIVES

By the end of this chapter, students will know:
1. vocabulary associated with making and receiving telephone calls
2. vocabulary associated with various types of phones, both older and more modern
3. the formation of the imperfect
4. the uses of the imperfect

CHAPTER 1 RESOURCES

1. Workbook
2. Student Tape Manual
3. Audio Cassette 2A
4. Vocabulary Transparencies
5. Bell Ringer Review Blackline Masters
6. Communication Activities Masters
7. Computer Software: Practice and Test Generator
8. Video Cassette, Chapter 1
9. Video Activities Booklet, Chapter 1
10. Situation Cards
11. Chapter Quizzes
12. Testing Program

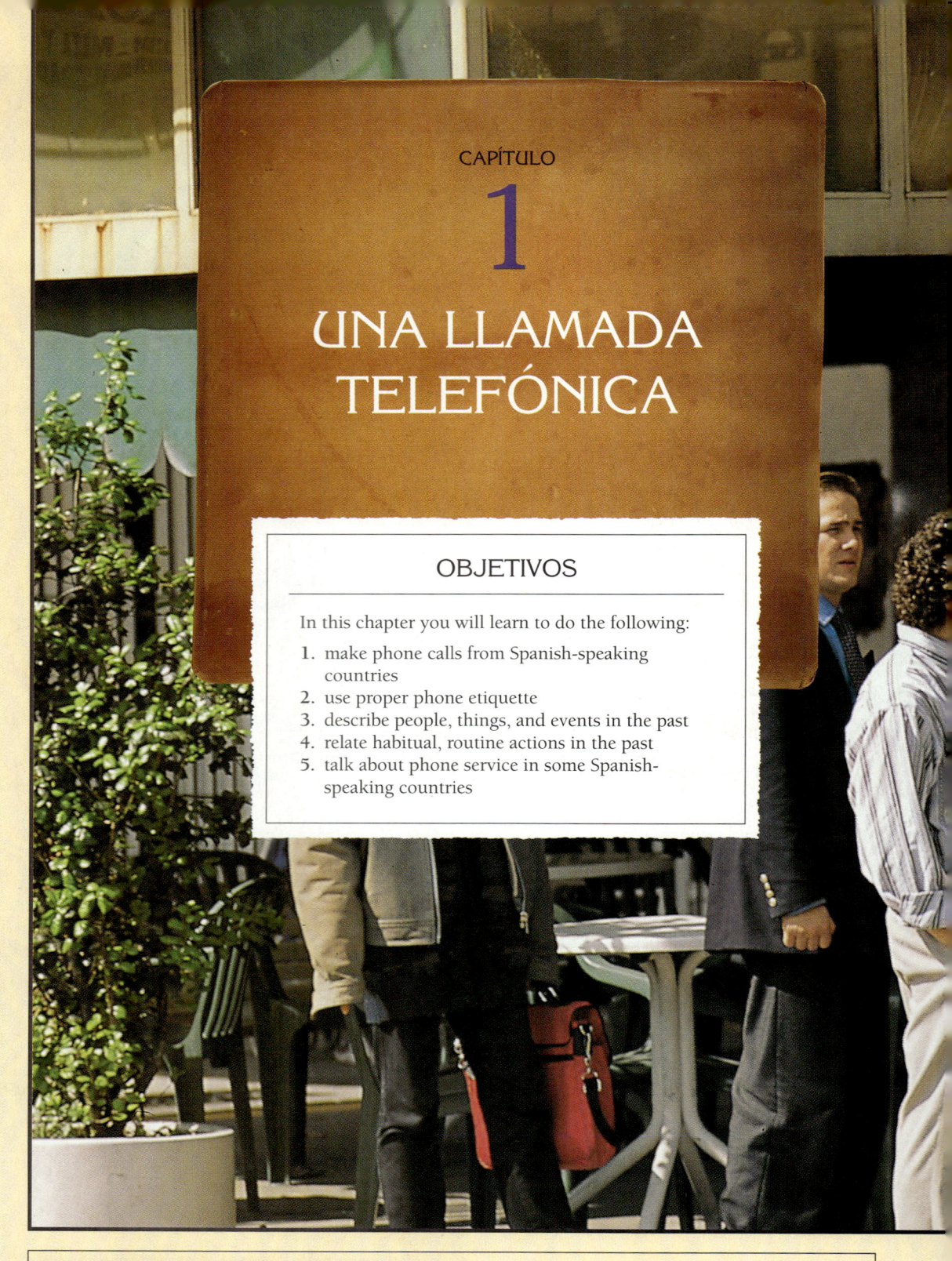

CAPÍTULO 1

UNA LLAMADA TELEFÓNICA

OBJETIVOS

In this chapter you will learn to do the following:
1. make phone calls from Spanish-speaking countries
2. use proper phone etiquette
3. describe people, things, and events in the past
4. relate habitual, routine actions in the past
5. talk about phone service in some Spanish-speaking countries

CHAPTER PROJECTS

(optional)
1. Have students prepare advertisements for *las páginas amarillas* of a Spanish phone book using the ads on page 5, 8, and 21 as a model.
2. Have students prepare a pamphlet for Spanish-speaking visitors to the U.S. which explains how to make calls from a public telephone.

Telefónica de Argentina

Pacing

Chapter 1 will take eight to ten class sessions. Pacing will depend on the length of the class period, the age of the students and student aptitude. (See the Teacher's Manual for additional suggestions on pacing.)

Note on Interrogatives

The most common interrogative wording throughout *A bordo* is inverted word order: *¿Es Juan americano? ¿De dónde es el muchacho?* However, students will sometimes encounter the upward intonation pattern, *¿Juan es americano? ¿Él es de qué nacionalidad?*, since it is so frequently used in many areas of the Spanish-speaking world, particularly in the spoken language.

LEARNING FROM PHOTOS

1. After presenting the new vocabulary for Chapter 1, you may wish to ask the following questions about the photo: *¿En qué país está la gente? ¿Quieren hacer una llamada telefónica? ¿Hacen cola (fila) delante del teléfono? ¿Están llamando de un teléfono privado o público? ¿Está en una cabina el teléfono?*

CRITICAL THINKING ACTIVITY

(Thinking skills: drawing conclusions)
 Vamos a mirar la fotografía en la página 1. *¿Qué opinas? ¿Qué tipo de clima tiene la Argentina? ¿Qué tiempo hace?* Students learned about the reverse seasons in *Bienvenidos*. See if they remember.

VOCABULARIO
PALABRAS 1

Vocabulary Teaching Resources

1. Vocabulary Transparencies, 1.1 (A & B)
2. Audio Cassette 2A
3. Student Tape Manual, *Palabras 1*
4. Workbook, *Palabras 1*
5. Communication Activities Masters, *Palabras 1, A & B*
6. Chapter Quizzes, *Palabras 1*

Devise procedures for BRRs

Bell Ringer Review

Write the following on the board or use BRR Blackline Master 1-1: Answer the following:
1. ¿Hablas inglés y español?
2. ¿Hablas otro idioma?
3. ¿Cuántos idiomas hablas en total?
4. ¿Te gusta hablar por teléfono?
5. Cuando hablas por teléfono, ¿en qué lengua hablas generalmente?

Note All the TPR activities in *Bienvenidos* were presented in the *tú* form. The role-playing activities in *A bordo* will vary. Some will use *tú*, others will use *usted*. This gives students the opportunity to hear the *usted* command form which they will be learning in this textbook.

PRESENTATION (pages 2-3)

A. Have students close their books. Introduce the *Palabras 1* vocabulary using Vocabulary Transparencies 1.1 (A & B). Have students repeat the words after you or Cassette 2A as you point to the appropriate illustration on the transparency.
B. If possible, use props such as a telephone, telephone book, coins, a telephone card, etc., to help teach the new vocabulary.

VOCABULARIO

PALABRAS 1

EL TELÉFONO

la clave de área (el prefijo telefónico)
el prefijo del país (031) 701 228 6534
el número de teléfono

la guía telefónica

(714) 925 2345
el número equivocado

el teléfono público

la ranura
el disco
el auricular,
la bocina

la cabina telefónica

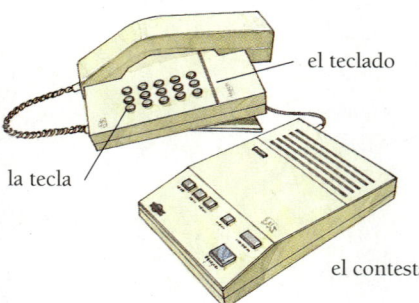

el teléfono de (a) botones
el teclado
la tecla
el contestador automático

el teléfono celular
el teléfono inalámbrico

2 CAPÍTULO 1

PANTOMIME

(following the Vocabulary presentation)

___, levántese Ud.
Venga acá, por favor.
Tome la guía telefónica.
Abra la guía telefónica.
Mire adentro.
Busque un número.
Vaya al teléfono.
Abra la puerta de una cabina telefónica.
Entre.
Introduzca la moneda.
Descuelgue.
Espere el tono.
Hable.
Cuelgue.
Gracias, ___. Vuelva a su asiento y siéntese.

hacer una llamada telefónica

llamar por teléfono

telefonear

descolgar el auricular

esperar el tono (la señal)

introducir la moneda

marcar el número

El teléfono suena.

El teléfono suena ocupado.
La línea está ocupada.

Están hablando.

el interlocutor

¡Hola! ¿Está el señor Salas, por favor?

¿De parte de quién?

Un momento, por favor.

De parte de la señorita Romero.

CAPÍTULO 1   3

C. Ask yes/no or either/or questions to elicit the new vocabulary. For example: ¿*Cuelgo o descuelgo?* ¿*Es una guía telefónica o una operadora?* ¿*Es un teléfono de botones o un teléfono con teclado?*

ABOUT THE LANGUAGE

1. The greeting used when answering a telephone varies from region to region. You will hear *Buenos días, hola, aló, diga, dígame, bueno.*
2. Another term for area code is *el código de área.*

Vocabulary Expansion

You may wish to give students additional vocabulary for different types of telephone calls.

una llamada local (urbana) local call
una llamada interurbana toll call
una llamada de larga distancia long distance call
una llamada internacional international call
una llamada de cargo revertido collect call

CROSS-CULTURAL COMPARISON

In certain areas of countries like Spain, Mexico, and Argentina, public coin phones are being replaced with phones that take a *telecarta*. *Telecartas* contain various amounts of time units and are priced accordingly. The more time units on a card, the more it costs. The *telecarta* can be used for local, long distance, and international calls. An international call takes many more time units per second than a local call. The number of units used for each call is automatically calculated and deducted from the *telecarta*.

ADDITIONAL PRACTICE

Have students look at Vocabulary Transparencies *A & B* again. As they look at them, have them make up questions about the illustrations. They can call on classmates to answer their questions.

Use a mixture of yes/no + info questions

Ejercicios

PRESENTATION (pages 4-5)

Ejercicio A
Exercise A can be done with books open.

Ejercicio B
Exercise B can be done with books open or closed.

Extension of *Ejercicio B*
After completing Exercise B, call on a student to summarize the information in the exercise.

Ejercicios C and D
Exercises C and D can be done with books open.

ANSWERS

Ejercicio A
1. Es un teléfono público.
2. Es un teléfono con disco.
3. Es la guía telefónica.
4. Es el número de teléfono.
5. Es el auricular.
6. Es el teclado.

Ejercicio B
Answers will vary.
1. Sí, (No, no) hago muchas llamadas telefónicas.
2. Llamo ...
3. Mi número de teléfono es...
4. Mi prefijo telefónico es...
5. Sí, (No, no) tengo un teléfono inalámbrico.
6. Mi teléfono tiene...
7. Sí, (No, no) tengo un contestador automático.
8. Sí, (No,) mis amigos (no) dejan mensajes cuando no puedo contestar el (al) teléfono.

Ejercicios ¿Qué es?

1.
2.
3.
4. 741-5928
5.
6.

A ¿Qué es? Identifiquen.
1. ¿Es un teléfono público o privado?
2. ¿Es un teléfono con disco o un teléfono de (a) botones?
3. ¿Es la guía telefónica o la cabina telefónica?
4. ¿Es el número de teléfono o la clave de área?
5. ¿Es el auricular o la ranura?
6. ¿Es el disco o el teclado?

B Una llamada telefónica. Preguntas personales.
1. ¿Haces muchas llamadas telefónicas?
2. ¿A quién llamas?
3. ¿Cuál es tu número de teléfono?
4. ¿Cuál es tu prefijo telefónico?
5. ¿Tienes un teléfono inalámbrico?
6. Tu teléfono, ¿tiene disco o botones?
7. ¿Tienes un contestador automático?
8. ¿Dejan tus amigos mensajes cuando no puedes contestar el teléfono?

4   CAPÍTULO 1

COOPERATIVE LEARNING

Have students work in groups and discuss what they think the conversation is about in Photo 1 of Exercise A.

[Handwritten note at top: "Can be done as a partnered activity. Print these onto cardstock & have students place these in order. Then review with a magnetic set."]

C **Haciendo una llamada telefónica.** Pongan las oraciones en orden.

Hago una llamada telefónica.
Mi interlocutor contesta.
Espero el tono (la señal).
Descuelgo.
Espero la contestación.
Tenemos una conversación.
Marco el número.
Cuelgo.

[Handwritten note: "This could also be a quiz section"]

D **Va a llamar por teléfono.** Escojan la respuesta apropiada.

1. Está sonando ocupado.
   a. ¿No hay tono?
   b. Están hablando (comunicando) entonces.
   c. ¿No contesta nadie?
2. ¡Hola!
   a. ¿De parte de quién?
   b. ¡Hola!
   c. Lo siento. No está.
3. El señor Salas, por favor.
   a. Sí, está sonando.
   b. ¿De parte de quién, por favor?
   c. Favor de colgar.
4. ¿Está el señor Salas, por favor?
   a. Lo siento, no está.
   b. No, favor de colgar.
   c. Sí, lo siento.

CAPÍTULO 1   5

ANSWERS
Ejercicio C
1. Hago una llamada telefónica.
2. Descuelgo.
3. Espero el tono (la señal).
4. Marco el número.
5. Espero la contestación.
6. Mi interlocutor contesta.
7. Tenemos una conversación.
8. Cuelgo.

Ejercicio D
1. b
2. b
3. b
4. a

ABOUT THE LANGUAGE
Until recently, *discar un número* was used as well as *marcar un número*. With the disappearance of rotary phones, the term *discar* is becoming less commonly used.

INFORMAL ASSESSMENT
(Palabras 1)
Have individuals give simple instructions in their own words for making a telephone call.

INDEPENDENT PRACTICE

Assign any of the following:
1. Workbook, *Palabras 1*
2. Communication Activities Masters, *Palabras 1, A & B*
3. Exercises on student pages 4-5
   (See suggestions for homework correction in the Teacher's Manual.)

VOCABULARIO
PALABRAS 2

Vocabulary Teaching Resources

1. Vocabulary Transparencies 1.2 (A & B)
2. Audio Cassette 2A
3. Student Tape Manual, *Palabras 2*
4. Workbook, *Palabras 2*
5. Communication Activities Masters, *Palabras 2, C & D*
6. Chapter Quizzes, *Palabras 2*
7. Computer Software, *Vocabulario*

Bell Ringer Review

Write the following on the board or use BRR Blackline Master 1-2: Answer personally:
1. ¿Tienes abuelos?
2. ¿Dónde viven tus abuelos?
3. ¿Los visitas con frecuencia?
4. ¿Les hablan por teléfono de vez en cuando?
5. ¿Cuándo telefoneas a tus abuelos?

PRESENTATION (pages 6-7)

A. Read the sentences aloud about *abuelita* as students follow along with their books open. Explain to them that the little boy is talking to her.
B. Show the Vocabulary Transparencies A & B. Give a sentence and have students identify the illustration the sentence is about.
C. Call on several individuals to read the sentences aloud.
D. Call on several students to summarize the story about *abuelita* in their own words.

VOCABULARIO

PALABRAS 2

CUANDO LLAMABA A MI ABUELITA

Cuando yo era niño, telefoneaba a abuelita.

Yo adoraba a mi abuelita.
Y abuelita me adoraba.
Nos queríamos mucho.

Cuando yo llamaba, abuelita contestaba en seguida.
Ella contestaba en cuanto sonaba el teléfono.
Yo tenía conversaciones alegres con abuelita.

CAPÍTULO 1

Cuando era niño, yo vivía en Madrid.

Y abuelita vivía en Mérida, en Extremadura.

CAPÍTULO 1

GEOGRAPHY CONNECTION

Mérida está en la provincia de Badajoz, en Extremadura. Es en esta región de España donde se ven las mejores ruinas romanas de todo el país. El teatro romano de Mérida es famoso. Aún hoy se presentan obras clásicas en este teatro.

ADDITIONAL PRACTICE

You may wish to ask the following questions as you present the vocabulary.
¿A quién telefoneaba el niño?
¿A quién adoraba? ¿Se querían mucho el niño y su abuela?
¿Estaba contenta la abuelita cuando el niño la llamaba? ¿Dónde vivía ella? Y el niño, ¿dónde vivía?

Ejercicios

PRESENTATION (page 8)

Ejercicio A
Exercise A can be done with books open or closed.

Ejercicio B
You may wish to have students close their books first. Read each cue to them followed by the three choices. Call on volunteers to give the correct answer.

Ejercicio B: Paired Activity
You may also do Exercise B as a paired activity. One student reads the cue and the other supplies the correct answer.

Ejercicio C
Exercise C can be done with books open.

ANSWERS

Ejercicio A
1. Sí, José adoraba a su abuelita.
2. Sí, llamaba a su abuelita por teléfono.
3. Sí, quería mucho a su abuelita.
4. Sí, su abuelita contestaba el teléfono.
5. Sí, ella contestaba en seguida.
6. Sí, contestaba en cuanto sonaba el teléfono.
7. Sí, José tenía muchas conversaciones con su abuelita.
8. Sí, ella estaba contenta cuando su nieto la llamaba.

Ejercicio B
1. a
2. c
3. b
4. c

Ejercicio C
1. c
2. e
3. f
4. g
5. b
6. a
7. d

8

Ejercicios

A Cuando José era niño. Contesten.
1. Cuando José era niño, ¿adoraba a su abuelita?
2. ¿Llamaba a su abuelita por teléfono?
3. ¿Quería mucho a su abuelita?
4. ¿Contestaba abuelita el teléfono?
5. ¿Ella contestaba en seguida?
6. ¿Contestaba en cuanto sonaba el teléfono?
7. ¿Tenía José muchas conversaciones con su abuelita?
8. ¿Ella estaba contenta cuando su nieto la llamaba?

B José y su abuelita. Escojan.
1. Cuando José era niño, él ___ mucho a su abuelita.
   a. telefoneaba   b. visitaba   c. escribía
2. Él quería mucho a su abuelita. Él la ___ .
   a. detestaba   b. contestaba   c. adoraba
3. Cuando José llamaba a su abuelita, ella ___ en seguida.
   a. llamaba   b. contestaba   c. hablaba
4. Él tenía muchas conversaciones ___ con su abuelita.
   a. tristes   b. aburridas   c. alegres

C Un pequeño diccionario. Pareen.
1. llamar por teléfono   a. la clave de área
2. querer mucho   b. discar
3. en seguida   c. telefonear
4. una conversación   d. la señal
5. marcar   e. adorar
6. el prefijo telefónico   f. inmediatamente
7. el tono   g. una charla, una plática

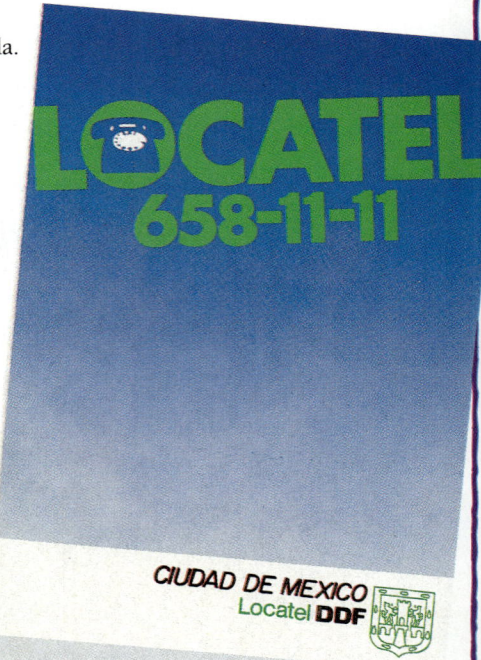

8   CAPÍTULO 1

COOPERATIVE LEARNING

Have teams of four make up as many short telephone conversations as they can based on various situations. Following are some suggestions:
1. ordering a pizza
2. calling several wrong numbers in a row
3. getting a homework assignment from a friend.
4. ordering something from a catalog

INDEPENDENT PRACTICE

Assign any of the following:
1. Workbook, *Palabras 1*
2. Communication Activities Masters, *Palabras 2, C & D*
3. Exercises on student page 8

Comunicación
Palabras 1 y 2

A **Una llamada.** You are in Mexico City making a phone call.

1. Someone responds. Say "hello."
2. You are calling Guadalupe Ortiz. Ask if she is there.
3. The person asks who is calling. Respond.

En la Ciudad de México

B **Un número equivocado.** You call a friend, but a stranger (your partner) answers and tells you that there is no one there by that name. You tell the stranger what number you dialed, and he or she tells you that the phone number isn't wrong but the area code is, and gives you the area code you dialed. Apologize. Then reverse roles.

1. (615) 988-6454 María / (715)
2. (917) 356-3303 Tomás / (817)
3. (402) 248-5417 Eduardo / (202)
4. (513) 751-2083 Camila / (313)

C **Para llamar por teléfono...** Ud. está en una calle de una ciudad de los Estados Unidos y ve a un turista latinoamericano que está tratando de hacer una llamada desde un teléfono público. Explíquele al turista cómo utilizar el teléfono público.

D **Una llamada internacional.** Ud. quiere hacer una llamada internacional. Llame a la operadora (un[a] compañero[a]) para averiguar cómo marcar directamente. La operadora le pregunta a qué ciudad va a llamar y le da las instrucciones. Luego cambie de papel con su compañero(a).

PAÍS	PREFIJO DEL PAÍS	CIUDAD	CLAVE DE ÁREA
Argentina	54	Córdoba	51
Bolivia	591	La Paz	2
España	34	Barcelona	3
Nicaragua	505	Managua	2
Perú	51	Lima	14
Venezuela	58	Maracaibo	61

CAPÍTULO 1

Comunicación
(Palabras 1 and 2)

PRESENTATION *(page 9)*

These activities allow students to use the chapter vocabulary in open-ended situations. Select those you consider most appropriate.

ANSWERS

Actividades A-D
Answers will vary.

INFORMAL ASSESSMENT

Give students a minute to tell what they would say in the following situations:
1. answering a phone
2. forgetting a number
3. getting a wrong number
4. leaving a message

LEARNING FROM PHOTOS

Have students describe the photo at the top of page 9 in their own words. What do they think the girls are doing?

ESTRUCTURA

Structure Teaching Resources

1. Workbook, *Estructura*
2. Student Tape Manual, *Estructura*
3. Audio Cassette 2A
4. Communication Activities Masters, *Estructura*, A-D
5. Chapter Quizzes, *Estructura*
6. Computer Software, *Estructura*

El imperfecto de los verbos en -ar

PRESENTATION *(page 10)*

A. Have students open their books to page 10. Read step 1 to them.
B. Write one of the *-ar* infinitives given in step 1 on the board. Then cross out the infinitive ending leaving just the stem.
C. Write the verb forms on the board in paradigm order.
D. Alongside the paradigms, write the endings. (See chart page 10.)
E. Have students repeat the verb forms aloud.
F. Now read step 2 to the class.

Teaching Tip It is strongly recommended that you do not give students the English equivalents for the imperfect tense. Students must grasp the concept that the imperfect is used to express an ongoing, continuing action. Its beginning and end points are unimportant. When students hear that "used to" is an English equivalent of the imperfect, it confuses them and interferes with the concept because "used to" implies "but no longer," suggesting an end at a given point in time.

Ejercicios
ANSWERS
Ejercicio A
   Answers use the same verb form as the question.

10

ESTRUCTURA

El imperfecto de los verbos en *-ar*

Talking About Habitual Past Actions

1. Spanish has two simple past tenses. One tense is the preterite which you have already learned. The preterite is used to express actions that started and ended at a definite time in the past. The other tense is the imperfect. Study the forms of regular *-ar* verbs in the imperfect.

INFINITIVE	HABLAR	LLAMAR	ENDINGS
STEM	habl-	llam-	
yo	hablaba	llamaba	-aba
tú	hablabas	llamabas	-abas
él, ella, Ud.	hablaba	llamaba	-aba
nosotros(as)	hablábamos	llamábamos	-ábamos
vosotros(as)	*hablabais*	*llamabais*	*-abais*
ellos, ellas, Uds.	hablaban	llamaban	-aban

2. The imperfect tense is used in Spanish to express a habitual or repeated action in the past. When the action or event began or ended is not important.

   La familia Duarte siempre tomaba sus vacaciones en julio.
   A veces pasaban una semana en la playa.
   De vez en cuando alquilaban una casa en las montañas.
   A ellos les gustaban mucho sus vacaciones.

Ejercicios

A **Cuando yo estaba en la escuela primaria.** Preguntas personales.

1. ¿Cómo se llamaba tu escuela primaria?
2. ¿Dónde estaba?
3. ¿Caminabas a la escuela o tomabas el bus escolar?
4. ¿A qué hora llegabas a la escuela?
5. ¿Qué materias estudiabas?
6. ¿Sacabas buenas notas?
7. ¿A qué hora empezaban las clases?
8. ¿Y a qué hora terminaban?

10   CAPÍTULO 1

FOR THE NATIVE SPEAKER

   The imperfect tense form of *-er* verbs is not a problem. Sometimes, however, you may hear native speakers use the archaic form of certain *-er* verbs. They will say *traiba* for *traía*, for example. Have students practice the imperfect tense of these verbs by doing the following exercise.

1. ¿Qué (atraer) ___ a los jóvenes a este lugar?
2. Pues, ellos (creer) ___ que había mucho que hacer.
3. Y tú, ¿lo (creer) ___ también?
4. Sí, porque (leer) ___ mucho acerca de este lugar.
5. ¿Quién te (traer) ___ los periódicos?
6. Nadie. Yo los (leer) ___ en la biblioteca.

B **Mi abuelita.** Preguntas personales.
1. ¿Adorabas a tu abuelita?
2. ¿La llamabas a veces por teléfono?
3. ¿Tú marcabas el número o mamá lo marcaba?
4. ¿Hablabas mucho con tu abuelita?
5. ¿La visitabas de vez en cuando?
6. ¿Estaba contenta tu abuelita cuando Uds. la visitaban?
7. ¿Uds. compraban regalitos para su abuelita?
8. ¿Tú le dabas los regalitos?

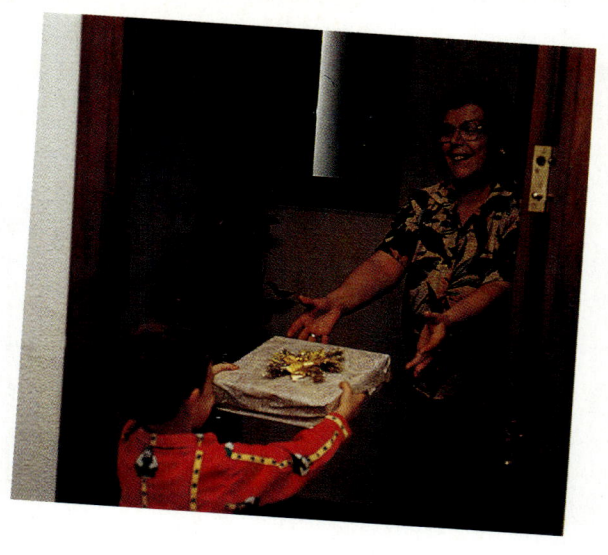

El imperfecto de los verbos en *-er* e *-ir*

Talking About Habitual Past Actions

1. Regular *-er* and *-ir* verbs have identical forms in the imperfect tense.

INFINITIVE	COMER	LEER	VIVIR	ASISTIR	ENDINGS
STEM	com-	le-	viv-	asist-	
yo	comía	leía	vivía	asistía	-ía
tú	comías	leías	vivías	asistías	-ías
él, ella, Ud.	comía	leía	vivía	asistía	-ía
nosotros(as)	comíamos	leíamos	vivíamos	asistíamos	-íamos
vosotros(as)	*comíais*	*leíais*	*vivíais*	*asistíais*	*-íais*
ellos, ellas, Uds.	comían	leían	vivían	asistían	-ían

2. The *-er* and *-ir* verbs that have a stem change in the present tense do not have a stem change in the imperfect.

querer	quería, querías, quería, queríamos, *queríais*, querían
poder	podía, podías, podía, podíamos, *podíais*, podían
decir	decía, decías, decía, decíamos, *decíais*, decían

3. The imperfect of *hay* is *había*.

   Había tres teléfonos en la casa.

CAPÍTULO 1   11

FOR THE NATIVE SPEAKER

When changing *hay* to the imperfect, many students want to use *habían* when followed by a plural noun. Emphasize to them that this is incorrect. It is always *había*. *Hay* has only one form in every tense, i.e. preterite—*hubo*, future—*habrá*, etc.

LEARNING FROM PHOTOS

You may wish to ask the following questions about the photograph on page 11: ¿A quién visitaba el niño? ¿Qué le traía? ¿Cómo estaba su abuelita? ¿Quién le daba el regalo?

Bell Ringer Review
Write the following on the board or use BRR Blackline Master 1-3: Answer personally.
1. ¿A qué escuela vas ahora?
2. ¿Cómo se llama la escuela?
3. ¿Cuántos cursos estás tomando este semestre?
4. ¿Quién es tu profesor(a) de español?
5. ¿Te gusta la clase de español?

ANSWERS
Ejercicio B
1. Sí, (No, no) adoraba a mi abuelita.
2. Sí, (No, no) la llamaba por teléfono.
3. Yo (mamá) marcaba el número.
4. Sí, (No, no) hablaba mucho con mi abuelita.
5. Sí, (No, no) la visitaba de vez en cuando (nunca).
6. Sí, (No,) abuelita (no) estaba contenta cuando la visitábamos.
7. Sí, (No, no) comprábamos regalitos para nuestra abuelita.
8. Sí, (No,) yo (no) le daba los regalitos.

El imperfecto de los verbos en -er e -ir

PRESENTATION *(page 11)*
A. Have students open their books to page 11. Read steps 1-3 to them.
B. In step 1, write the infinitives of the verbs *comer* and *vivir* on the board. Then cross out the infinitive endings, leaving just the stems.
C. Then write the forms of *comer* and *vivir* on the board. Underline the endings.
D. Have students read all the verb forms aloud.
E. Follow the same procedure with step 2 on page 11. Then lead students through step 3.

RECYCLING
Have students redo Exercise B on page 11 in the present.

Ejercicios

PRESENTATION (page 12)

Ejercicio A
Exercise A can be done with books closed or open.

Extension of *Ejercicio B*
After completing Exercise B, call on one student to do the entire exercise and retell the story in his/her own words.

Ejercicio C
Exercise C gives students practice using questions with the *Ud.* form.

ANSWERS

Ejercicio A
Answers will vary but should include the imperfect form of the verb.

Ejercicio B
1. vivía
2. vivía
3. prefería
4. tenía
5. quería
6. hacía
7. visitábamos
8. visitaba
9. venía
10. traía
11. abría

Ejercicio C
1. …, ¿dónde asistía Ud. a la escuela superior?
2. ¿Qué clases prefería Ud. cuando era joven?
3. ¿Escribía Ud. mucho en la escuela?
4. ¿Leía Ud. mucho tambien?
5. ¿Qué tipo de libros prefería Ud. (leer)?
6. ¿Recibía Ud. buenas notas?
7. ¿Tenía Ud. novio(a)?
8. ¿Sabía Ud. que quería ser profesor(a)?

GEOGRAPHY CONNECTION

Adjuntas está en el centro mismo de Puerto Rico. Está en las montañas y casi siempre hace fresco. Adjuntas es un pueblo muy pintoresco. Alrededor del pueblo hay cafetales. Esta región es conocida por la producción de café.

Ejercicios

A **Cuando yo era niño(a).** Preguntas personales.

1. Cuando tú eras niño(a), ¿dónde vivías?
2. ¿Cuántos cuartos tenía la casa de tu familia?
3. ¿Uds. tenían un coche (un carro)?
4. ¿A qué escuela asistías?
5. ¿A qué hora salías para la escuela?
6. ¿Y a qué hora salías de la escuela?
7. ¿A qué hora volvías a casa?

B **Sandra quería mucho a su abuelito.** Completen.

Cuando Sandra era niña, ella ___ (vivir) en San Juan, Puerto Rico. Su abuelo ___ (vivir) en Adjuntas. Él ___ (preferir) vivir en el campo, en las montañas. Él ___ (tener) una casa bonita en Adjuntas. Sandra nos habla.

—Yo ___ (querer) mucho a abuelito. Yo le ___ (hacer) muchas llamadas telefónicas. Nosotros ___ (visitar) a abuelito con frecuencia. Y él nos ___ (visitar) en San Juan. Cada vez que él ___ (venir), me ___ (traer) un regalito. Yo ___ (abrir) sus regalitos en seguida.

Adjuntas, Puerto Rico

C **Nuestro(a) profesor(a) de español.** Pregúntenle a su profesor(a).

1. dónde asistía a la escuela superior
2. qué clase o clases prefería cuando era joven
3. si escribía mucho en la escuela
4. si leía mucho también
5. qué tipo de libros prefería
6. si recibía buenas notas
7. si tenía novio(a)
8. si sabía que quería ser profesor(a)

12 CAPÍTULO 1

DID YOU KNOW?

Adjuntas is one of the world's major producers of citron which is used in making fruit cakes.

INDEPENDENT PRACTICE

Assign any of the following:
1. Workbook, *Estructura*
2. Communication Activities Masters, *Estructura, A & B*
3. Exercises on student pages 10-12

El imperfecto de los verbos *ir* y *ser*

Talking About Habitual Past Actions

The verbs *ir* and *ser* are irregular in the imperfect.

INFINITIVE	IR	SER
yo	iba	era
tú	ibas	eras
él, ella, Ud.	iba	era
nosotros(as)	íbamos	éramos
vosotros(as)	ibais	erais
ellos, ellas, Uds.	iban	eran

Ejercicios

A **En el quinto grado.** Preguntas personales.

1. Cuando tú estabas en el quinto grado, ¿a qué escuela ibas?
2. ¿Quién era tu maestro(a)?
3. ¿Era simpático(a)?
4. ¿Y cómo eras tú en el quinto grado?
5. ¿Ibas a la escuela con tus amigos?
6. ¿Cómo iban Uds. a la escuela?
7. ¿Quiénes eran tus amigos en el quinto grado?

B **Mis vacaciones.** Preguntas personales.

1. Cuando tú eras muy joven, ¿ibas a la playa o a las montañas?
2. ¿Ibas con la familia?
3. ¿Esquiaban Uds. o nadaban?
4. ¿Iban Uds. en carro o en tren?
5. ¿Era largo el viaje?

Una clase de quinto grado en Venezuela

CAPÍTULO 1   13

LEARNING FROM PHOTOS

You may wish to ask the following questions regarding the photo on page 13: ¿Es una escuela primaria, intermedia o secundaria? ¿Es una escuela mixta o es solamente para niños o niñas? ¿Levantan la mano los niños? ¿Por qué levantan la mano? ¿Llevan uniforme los alumnos? ¿Qué tiempo hace en Venezuela? ¿Tiene ventanas la sala de clase (el aula)?

COOPERATIVE LEARNING

Have students work in groups. Have the members of each group compare some things they did with their grandparents when they were very young. Have them describe their grandparents.

El imperfecto de los verbos *ir* y *ser*

PRESENTATION (page 13)

A. Write the infinitives of the verbs *ir* and *ser* on the board.
B. Write all the forms on the board in paradigm order. Have students repeat all the forms after you.
C. When going over the verbs *ser* and *ir*, stress the importance of learning these verbs since they are used very often.

Ejercicios

PRESENTATION (page 13)

Ejercicios A and B
Exercises A and B can be done with books closed or open.

Extension of *Ejercicios* A and B: Speaking
After completing Exercises A and B, call on individual students to do each exercise in its entirety, retelling the story in their own words.

ANSWERS

Ejercicio A
Answers will vary.
1. Iba a la escuela… cuando estaba en el quinto grado.
2. Mi maestro(a) era…
3. Sí,(No) él (ella) (no) era muy simpático(a).
4. Yo era muy…
5. Sí, iba a la escuela con mis amigos.
6. Íbamos en…
7. En el quinto grado mis amigos eran…

Ejercicio B
1. Cuando yo era joven, iba a…
2. Sí, (No, no) iba con mi familia.
3. Esquiábamos (Nadábamos) (No esquiábamos y no nadábamos).
4. Íbamos en carro (en tren).
5. Sí,(No,) el viaje (no) era largo.

Note Since students never try to say or write *vía*, etc., we have not presented *ver* as an irregular verb.

13

Bell Ringer Review

Write the following on the board or use BRR Blackline Master 1-4: Write a description about any person you know. Write as much as you can about him/her in a couple of minutes.

Los usos del imperfecto

PRESENTATION *(page 14)*

A. Emphasize the fact that the imperfect is used for description in the past.
B. Ask students to open their books to page 14. Read the sentences in step 2 as if they were part of an ongoing story in the past.

Ejercicios

PRESENTATION *(page 15)*

Ejercicios A, B, and C
Exercises A, B and C can be done with books closed or open.

Extension of *Ejercicios A and C*: Speaking
After completing Exercises A and C, call on individual students to do the entire exercise, retelling the story in their own words.

Extension of *Ejercicio B*
After completing Exercise B, call on individual students to describe *Don Quixote* and *Sancho Panza*.

Los usos del imperfecto — *Uses of the Imperfect*

1. The imperfect tense is used to express continuous, repeated, or habitual actions in the past.

   Cuando yo era niño, me acostaba temprano.
   Tomaba mucha leche.
   Todos los días yo aprendía algo nuevo.
   Yo iba a la escuela con mis amigos.
   Nosotros nos divertíamos.

2. The imperfect is also used to describe persons, places, events, things, weather, and time in the past.

Location	El joven Felipe estaba en la capital.
Age	Tenía sólo dieciocho años.
Appearance	Era grande y tenía los ojos azules.
Physical condition	El pobre muchacho estaba cansado.
Emotional state	Estaba triste.
Attitudes and desires	Quería volver a casa. Tenía ganas de ver a su familia.
Date	Era el veinte de diciembre.
Time	Eran las diez de la noche.
Weather	Hacía frío y nevaba.

   ¿Y por qué no podía volver a casa si quería?
   Porque era soldado. Estaba en el ejército.

14 CAPÍTULO 1

ADDITIONAL PRACTICE

Have students describe the young man in the photo on page 14.

FOR THE NATIVE SPEAKER

History and grammar can be combined. Ask students to write a physical description of the following historical figures using the imperfect tense. Porfirio Díaz, el Emperador Maximiliano de Austria, Benito Juárez, Emiliano Zapata, Francisco Villa, el padre Hidalgo.

Ejercicios

A El joven soldado Felipe. Contesten.

1. ¿Cómo se llamaba el joven?
2. ¿Cuántos años tenía?
3. ¿Cómo era?
4. ¿Tenía los ojos castaños?
5. ¿Dónde estaba?
6. ¿Y cómo estaba?
7. ¿Adónde quería ir?
8. ¿A quiénes tenía ganas de ver?
9. ¿Cuál era la fecha?
10. ¿Qué hora era?
11. ¿Qué tiempo hacía?
12. ¿Por qué no podía volver a casa?

B Don Quijote y Sancho Panza. Contesten.

1. ¿Quién era alto? (Don Quijote)
2. ¿Quién era bajo? (Sancho Panza)
3. ¿Quién tenía un asno? (Sancho Panza)
4. ¿Quién tenía un caballo? (Don Quijote)
5. ¿Quién era idealista? (Don Quijote)
6. ¿Quién era realista? (Sancho Panza)
7. ¿Quién quería viajar? (Don Quijote)
8. ¿Quién quería volver a casa? (Sancho Panza)
9. ¿Quién quería conquistar los males del mundo? (Don Quijote)
10. ¿Quién estaba loco? (Don Quijote)

C ¿Cómo estabas? Preguntas personales.

1. Nadie contestó al teléfono. ¿Cómo estabas? ¿Estabas contento(a) o triste?
2. La señora no estaba. ¿Cómo estabas, contento(a) o triste?
3. No saliste bien en el examen. ¿Cómo estabas, contento(a) o triste?
4. Tenías cuatro años. ¿Cómo eras, viejo(a) o joven?
5. Querías dormir. ¿Cómo estabas, cansado(a) o contento(a)?
6. Querías beber algo. ¿Tenías sed o hambre?
7. Querías comer algo. ¿Tenías sed o hambre?
8. Tenías fiebre. ¿Estabas bien o enfermo(a)?

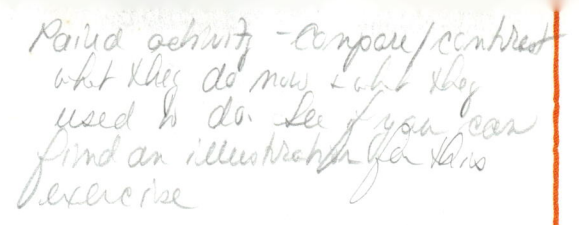

"Don Quijote" de Pablo Picasso

CAPÍTULO 1   15

INTERDISCIPLINARY CONNECTION

If students have read any part of *Don Quixote* in a literature class, have them tell anything they can about this famous Spanish novel.

ANSWERS

Ejercicio A
1. Él se llamaba Felipe.
2. Tenía sólo dieciocho años.
3. Él era grande (alto).
4. No. Tenía los ojos azules.
5. Estaba en la capital.
6. Él estaba triste.
7. Él quería ir a casa.
8. Tenía ganas de ver a su familia.
9. Era el veinte de diciembre.
10. Eran las diez de la noche.
11. Hacía frío y nevaba.
12. No podía volver a casa porque era soldado. Estaba en el ejército.

Ejercicio B
1. Don Quijote era alto.
2. Sancho Panza era bajo.
3. Sancho Panza tenía un asno.
4. Don Quijote tenía un caballo.
5. Don Quijote era idealista.
6. Sancho Panza era realista.
7. Don Quijote quería viajar.
8. Sancho Panza quería volver a casa.
9. Don Quijote quería conquistar los males del mundo.
10. Don Quijote estaba loco.

Ejercicio C
1. Estaba triste.
2. Estaba triste.
3. Estaba triste.
4. Era joven.
5. Estaba cansado(a).
6. Tenía sed.
7. Tenía hambre.
8. Estaba enfermo(a).

INDEPENDENT PRACTICE

Assign any of the following:
1. Workbook, *Estructura*
2. Communication Activities Masters, *Estructura, C & D*
3. Exercises on student pages 13-15
4. Computer Software, *Estructura*

CONVERSACIÓN

Bell Ringer Review

Write the following on the board or use BRR Blackline Master 1-5: You want to tell a friend something but he/she isn't home. Write a message for your friend.

PRESENTATION *(page 16)*

A. Have students close their books. Present the conversation by reading it aloud or playing Cassette 2A.
B. Now have students open their books and read along as you model the conversation a second time.
C. Allow time for pairs to practice the conversation. Then call on volunteers to present it to the class in as realistic a manner as possible. You may wish to use toy telephones as props.
D. After several pairs have presented the conversation, ask the comprehension questions on page 16.
E. Call on a volunteer to retell the story in his/her own words.

Ejercicio

ANSWERS

1. La señorita Solís hace la llamada.
2. No, la línea no está ocupada.
3. Sí, alguien contesta.
4. No, la Srta. Irizarry no contesta.
5. No, no está.
6. Sí, la señorita Solís deja un mensaje.
7. La puede llamar mañana por la mañana.
8. Sí, ella lo tiene.

16

CONVERSACIÓN

Escenas de la vida *Una llamada telefónica*

SRTA. SOLÍS: ¡Hola!
EMPLEADA: ¡Hola!
SRTA. SOLÍS: ¿Está la señorita Irizarry, por favor?
EMPLEADA: ¿De parte de quién?
SRTA. SOLÍS: De parte de Elena Solís.
EMPLEADA: Un momentito, por favor.
(Vuelve)
EMPLEADA: Lo siento, pero la señorita Irizarry no está. ¿Quiere Ud. dejar un mensaje?
SRTA. SOLÍS: Sí, me puede llamar mañana por la mañana. Ella tiene mi número.
EMPLEADA: De acuerdo, señorita.

Una llamada para la señorita. Contesten según la conversación.

1. ¿Quién hace la llamada, la señorita Irizarry o la señorita Solís?
2. ¿Está ocupada la línea?
3. ¿Contesta alguien?
4. ¿Es la señorita Irizarry quien contesta?
5. ¿Está la señorita Irizarry?
6. ¿Deja un mensaje la señorita Solís?
7. ¿Cuándo la puede llamar la señorita Irizarry?
8. ¿Tiene ella su número de teléfono?

> Srta Irizarry,
> La llamó la Srta. Solís. Dice que la puede llamar mañana.
> Teresa

16   CAPÍTULO 1

CRITICAL THINKING ACTIVITY

(Thinking skills: problem solving)
   Read the following to the class or write it on the board or on a transparency:
   La Srta. Solís cree que la Srta. Irizarry tiene su número de teléfono. Si la Srta. Irizarry no tiene el número de la Srta. Solís, ¿qué puede hacer la Srta. Irizarry para poder llamar a la Srta. Solís?

Comunicación

A **En México.** Ud. está haciendo una llamada telefónica en la ciudad de México. Quiere hablar con la Sra. Carmen Casals.

1. Someone else (a classmate) answers the phone. Find out if Mrs. Casals is there.
2. The person asks, *¿De parte de quién?*
3. The situation is reversed. You are answering the phone. Say something.
4. The call is not for you. Find out who is calling.
5. Tell the person to hold a moment.

B **En Buenos Aires.** Ud. está hablando con Carlos Benedetti. Él es de Buenos Aires, Argentina. Carlos quiere saber lo que Ud. hacía en la escuela primaria. Hable con Carlos.

> Estudiante 1: Yo jugaba con mi perro en el patio de mi casa.
> Estudiante 2: Yo también jugaba con mi perro.
> (Yo no. Yo no tenía perro.)

C **No estoy.** Trabaje con un(a) compañero(a) de clase. Ud. quiere invitar a un(a) amigo(a) a su casa. Ud. llama, pero su amigo(a) no contesta. El contestador automático interviene. Deje un mensaje a su amigo(a). Su compañero(a) escribe el mensaje y luego lo lee a la clase.

D **Cuando era muy joven.** Prepare una lista de las actividades que a Ud. le gustaba hacer cuando era muy joven. Luego indique si lo hacía por lo general en el verano, en el invierno, en casa o fuera de casa. Luego compare su lista de actividades con la lista de otro compañero de clase. ¿Qué cosas hacían los dos?

CAPÍTULO 1   17

LECTURA Y CULTURA

Bell Ringer Review
Write the following on the board or use BRR Blackline Master 1-6: Match the words that are related to one another.

1. llamar   a. el teléfono
2. telefonear   b. el disco
3. contestar   c. la llamada
4. responder   d. la introducción
5. discar   e. la contestación
6. introducir   f. la respuesta

READING STRATEGIES
(page 18)

Pre-Reading
Give students a brief oral summary (in Spanish) of the reading.

Reading
A. Call on an individual to read two or three sentences.
B. Ask questions about the sentences just read and call on volunteers to answer them.
C. Continue in this way until the entire selection has been read and discussed.

Post-reading
Assign the reading selection and the exercises for homework. Go over the exercises the following day.

Teaching Tip Call on students other than the reader to answer your comprehension questions. Most students have difficulty comprehending what they are reading when reading aloud, since they tend to concentrate on pronunciation.

Expansion: Speaking After going through the reading selection, have pairs role-play the situation. One student plays the part of the small child. The other the grandparent.

LECTURA Y CULTURA

EL TELÉFONO DE AYER Y DE HOY

José Luis Carrera nos habla.

Cuando yo era niño, me encantaba usar el teléfono. Este aparato me fascinaba. Mamá me dejaba (permitía) telefonear de vez en cuando a abuelita. Yo mismo marcaba el número. Mamá me ayudaba un poco porque a veces yo marcaba un número equivocado. Nuestro teléfono tenía disco y a veces mi dedo pequeño resbalaba[1] y no marcaba el número correcto.

Algunas veces yo llamaba a abuelita desde un teléfono público; cuando nosotros íbamos de compras, por ejemplo. Recuerdo bien que mamá iba a un café o a un estanco de tabaco donde compraba una ficha[2]. Papá me tomaba en sus brazos y me levantaba porque yo no podía alcanzar[3] la ranura del teléfono y yo quería introducir la ficha. Luego papá descolgaba y me daba el auricular (la bocina). Papá marcaba el número y yo esperaba la contestación. Cuando abuelita contestaba, yo oprimía[4] el botón. Si no oprimía el botón, yo podía oír a abuelita pero ella no podía oír lo que yo decía. La ficha caía cuando yo oprimía el botón y si no oprimía el botón, no había conexión.

Pero hoy, todo es diferente. Y yo, no soy viejo. Soy estudiante en un colegio mayor. Cuando hablo de las llamadas que yo hacía a abuelita, es cuestión de hace unos diez años. Y hoy, ¿comprar una ficha para hacer una llamada? ¿Oprimir un botón para hacer conexión? ¡De ninguna manera! Se puede hacer una llamada desde un teléfono público con una moneda o tarjeta de crédito. Ya no hay más fichas. Y nuestro teléfono privado en casa, no tiene disco. Es un teléfono de (a) botones. Tiene un teclado, no un disco. Y tiene una carta de memoria para los números que usamos con frecuencia. ¿Me quiere mandar un fax? No hay problema. Y yo tengo también un teléfono inalámbrico que tiene una distancia de emisión y recepción de 40 kilómetros. Aquí estoy en el jardín de nuestra casa. Creo que voy a hacer una llamada. ¿A quién? A abuelita. Adoraba a mi abuelita y la sigo adorando.

—Aló, abuelita. Te habla tu José Luis.

—José Luis, mi vida. ¿Cómo estás?

[1] resbalaba *slipped*
[2] ficha *token*
[3] alcanzar *reach*
[4] oprimía *pushed*

18 CAPÍTULO 1

ADDITIONAL PRACTICE
After reading and discussing the *Lectura* and completing the exercises, have students summarize in their own words the steps José Luis took to place a phone call.

Estudio de palabras

Una llamada. ¿Cuál es la definición?

1. dejar
2. telefonear
3. equivocado
4. el auricular
5. adorar

a. no correcto
b. la bocina
c. permitir
d. querer mucho
e. hacer una llamada telefónica

Comprensión

A Una llamada a abuelita. Contesten.

1. ¿Quién nos habla?
2. ¿Qué le fascinaba cuando era joven?
3. ¿A quién llamaba frecuentemente?
4. ¿Quién le ayudaba a marcar el número?
5. ¿De dónde llamaba José Luis con más frecuencia, de su teléfono privado o de un teléfono público?
6. Cuando hacía la llamada de un teléfono público, ¿qué compraba su mamá?
7. ¿Quién lo tomaba en sus brazos?
8. ¿Por qué?
9. ¿Qué quería hacer José Luis?
10. ¿Cuándo oprimía el botón José Luis?
11. Si no oprimía el botón, ¿quién no podía oír la conversación?

B Por teléfono. ¿Sí o no?

1. Aún hoy es necesario comprar una ficha para hacer una llamada telefónica en muchos países hispanos.
2. Es posible usar una tarjeta de crédito para pagar una llamada.
3. Los nuevos teléfonos, los aparatos más modernos, tienen disco.
4. Un teléfono de (a) botones tiene un teclado.
5. José Luis tiene un teléfono inalámbrico que es móvil (o portátil).

CAPÍTULO 1   19

Estudio de palabras
ANSWERS
1. c
2. e
3. a
4. b
5. d

Comprensión
ANSWERS
Comprensión A
1. José Luis Carrera.
2. Le fascinaba usar el teléfono.
3. Llamaba a su abuelita.
4. Su mamá le ayudaba a marcar el número.
5. Llamaba de su teléfono privado.
6. Su mamá compraba una ficha.
7. Su papá lo tomaba en los brazos.
8. Porque él no alcanzaba la ranura del teléfono.
9. Quería introducir la ficha.
10. Cuando contestaba la abuelita.
11. Su abuela no podía oír.

Comprensión B
1. no
2. sí
3. no
4. sí
5. sí

LEARNING FROM PHOTOS
You may wish to ask the following questions about the photo on page 19: ¿Quién está haciendo una llamada telefónica? ¿Quién la está ayudando? ¿Dónde la tiene su papá? ¿Qué está haciendo en este momento la niña?

INDEPENDENT PRACTICE
Assign any of the following:
1. Workbook, *Un poco más*
2. Exercises on student page 19 (See suggestions for homework correction in the Teacher's Manual.)

Descubrimiento Cultural
(The Descubrimiento section is optional.)

Bell Ringer Review
Write the following on the board or use BRR Blackline Master 1-7: ¿Sí o no?
1. Los teléfonos celulares son relativamente recientes.
2. Hoy día es posible discar muchos números directamente (en automático).
3. Los teléfonos nuevos tienen disco.
4. Los teléfonos nuevos tienen teclado.

PRESENTATION (page 20)
You may present the *Descubrimiento Cultural* as you would any other reading selection, or you may wish to use it as a silent reading exercise.

DESCUBRIMIENTO CULTURAL

Hace poco en España y muchos países de Latinoamérica, uno tenía que comprar una ficha para hacer una llamada de un teléfono público. Como hacía la mamá de José Luis, la persona que quería hacer la llamada tenía que ir a un café o a un estanco (donde vendían tabaco) para comprar la ficha. Y para hacer una llamada interurbana (de una ciudad a otra) o una llamada de larga distancia, era necesario comunicarse con el operador o la operadora. Hoy día es posible marcar o discar directamente, aun para hacer una llamada internacional. Sólo hay que marcar el prefijo del país, la clave de área (el prefijo telefónico) de la ciudad y el número deseado.

Hablando de operadores o telefonistas, es interesante notar que hasta recientemente en los Estados Unidos casi siempre eran mujeres que trabajaban de operadoras. En los países hispanos siempre había operadores varones[1]. Ahora hay mujeres y hombres que son operadores en los Estados Unidos y en los países hispanos.

Muchos aparatos telefónicos permiten discar o marcar sin tener que levantar el auricular. Y no es necesario marcar de nuevo el último número marcado porque el teléfono tiene memoria para llamar automáticamente el último número marcado.

20 CAPÍTULO 1

Hoy en día muchos comercios[2] españoles y latinoamericanos, y también muchas familias, tienen teléfonos celulares con cartas de memoria para los números llamados con frecuencia. Muchos de esos aparatos son conectables a telecopiadoras y computadoras (ordenadores).

En muchos países, incluso algunos países hispanos, los teléfonos son un monopolio del Estado. Generalmente el servicio telefónico es parte del "Ministerio de Comunicaciones" que también controla los telégrafos, el correo y, a veces, la radio y la televisión.

En algunos países hispanos es muy difícil ser "abonado" de la compañía de teléfonos, es decir, obtener un teléfono privado. Por eso los teléfonos públicos son muy importantes y muy usados. Con frecuencia se puede ver a unas cuantas personas haciendo cola[3] para usar un teléfono público.

[1] varones *males*
[2] comercios *businesses*
[3] haciendo cola *lining up*

ANTENAS
tecno

LA REVOLUCION AUDIOVISUAL

Ver la cara del otro lado del hilo telefónico: televisión y teléfono, unidos en un invento que sólo podía ser japonés... dado su tamaño.

CAPÍTULO 1 **21**

LEARNING FROM REALIA

1. ¿Qué significa "ver la cara del otro lado del hilo telefónico"?
    a. *ver el otro lado del teléfono*
    b. *ver a la persona con quien Ud. está hablando por teléfono*
    c. *ver una pantalla*

2. Ask students: ¿Quiénes inventaron el aparato? ¿De qué tamaño es? ¿Es pequeño o grande?

REALIDADES

(The Realidades section is optional.)

Bell Ringer Review

Write the following on the board or use BRR Blackline Master 1-8: Use the following words in a short sentence.
hacer una llamada telefónica
descolgar
discar
hablar
colgar

Note The purpose of this section is to have students look at and enjoy the beautiful photographs that bring to life the content of the chapter. You may wish to have students read the information that accompanies each photo aloud or silently.

REALIDADES

El Palacio de comunicaciones, en Madrid, es un edificio maravilloso **1**.

Es un teléfono público en Argentina **2**.

Una central telefónica antigua **3**.

Una guía de teléfonos de la Ciudad de México **4**.

Aquí ven Uds. una ficha que uno tenía que introducir en la ranura de un teléfono público en Chile **5**.

PRESENTATION (pages 22-23)

A. Allow students to enjoy the photos and talk about them.
B. Call on volunteers to read the captions aloud. Then have the class discuss the information.
C. You may want to share the following information regarding **Photo 1**: *El Palacio de Telecomunicaciones es un edificio bellísimo en el centro de Madrid. Está en la Plaza de Cibeles, llamada sólo "Cibeles" por los madrileños. La plaza toma su nombre de la diosa griega, Cibeles, a quien vemos aquí en su carroza en el centro de una fuente fabulosa.*

23

CULMINACIÓN

RECYCLING

The *Comunicación oral* and *Comunicación escrita* activities allow students to use the vocabulary and grammar from this chapter in open-ended settings. They also provide an opportunity to recycle vocabulary and structures from *Bienvenidos*. Have students do as many of the actividades as you wish.

Comunicación oral
ANSWERS

Actividades A, B, and C
Answers will vary.

INFORMAL ASSESSMENT

These activities lend themselves to assessing speaking and listening abilities. Following are some grading suggestions:
5: Complete message conveyed, precise control of structure and vocabulary.
4-3: Complete message conveyed, some structural or vocabulary control errors.
2-1: Message partially conveyed, frequent errors.
0: No message conveyed.

GEOGRAPHY CONNECTION

Have students look at the map of Spain on page 452 and locate the cities mentioned on this page: Salamanca, Málaga, Alicante. Ask students the following: *¿Cuáles de estas tres ciudades están en la costa? ¿Están en la costa de qué mar? ¿Qué ciudad está en el sur? ¿Qué ciudad está en el este?*

Comunicación escrita
ANSWERS

Actividades A, B, and C
Answers will vary.

24

CULMINACIÓN

Comunicación oral

A **Llamo a mi amiga.** You are spending the summer studying Spanish in Salamanca, Spain. You call a friend whom you met in school.

1. You know it is not your friend who answered. Find out if he or she is there.
2. The person who answered wants to know who is calling.
3. He or she tells you that your friend is not in. Find out if you can leave a message.
4. Give him or her your message.

B **La clave de área.** Ud. está haciendo una llamada telefónica de Málaga a Alicante, en España, pero no tiene la clave de área para Alicante y tampoco tiene una guía telefónica. Llame a un(a) operador(a), (un[a] compañero[a] de clase). Explíquele su problema y su compañero(a) le va a ayudar.

C **Los veranos de mi juventud.** Pregúntele a un(a) compañero(a) de clase lo que él o ella hacía con frecuencia durante sus vacaciones de verano. Pregúntele adónde iba, con quiénes, lo que hacía, etc. Luego cambien de papel (de rol) y comparen sus vacaciones.

Comunicación escrita

A **Me llamo...** Escriba los siguientes datos personales para un amigo o una amiga venezolano(a) que Ud. conoció recientemente.

1. su nombre (de Ud.)
2. su dirección
3. su número de teléfono
4. su clave de área

B **Un trabajo colectivo.** Divide into groups to create a story sentence by sentence in the past. The first person will write a sentence for Category 1 on a piece of paper and pass it to the next person. The second person will read the sentence and continue the story by writing a sentence for Category 2, and so on. When the story is completed, choose a student to read it to the class.

1. fecha
2. las condiciones del tiempo
3. los personajes y el lugar
4. descripción física o emocional de los personajes
5. sus actitudes
6. sus deseos
7. sus acciones habituales

    Esudiante 1: Era el tres de enero.
    Esudiante 2: Hacía mucho frío.
    Esudiante 3: Yo estaba en San Francisco con mis amigos.

24   CAPÍTULO 1

DID YOU KNOW?

La historia de Salamanca comienza en la época del general cartaginés, Aníbal (247-183 a. de C.). Todavía hoy cruza el río Tormes un puente construido por los romanos. La Universidad de Salamanca fue fundada en 1223 por Alfonso XI de León. Es la universidad más antigua de España.

INDEPENDENT PRACTICE

Assign any of the following:
1. Exercise on student page 25
2. Workbook, *Mi autobiografía*
3. Chapter 1, Situation Cards

C **Me gustaba...** Escriba dos párrafos sobre todo lo que a Ud. le gustaba hacer cuando era muy joven. Si es posible, escriba un párrafo sobre lo que Ud. hacía aún antes de asistir a la escuela primaria. Luego, describa lo que hacía en la escuela primaria.

Reintegración

A **A la playa.** Contesten.
1. ¿Fuiste a la playa durante el verano?
2. ¿Cuánto tiempo pasaste allí?
3. ¿Nadaste mucho?
4. ¿Con quién fuiste a la playa?
5. ¿Tomaron Uds. el sol?
6. ¿Te pusiste crema protectora?
7. Y tu amigo, ¿se puso crema protectora también?
8. ¿Se divirtieron Uds. en la playa?

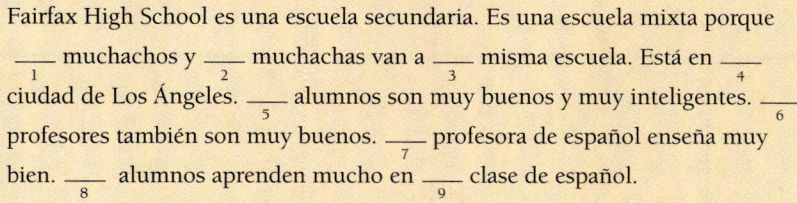

B **La escuela.** Completen con *el*, *la*, *los* o *las*.

Fairfax High School es una escuela secundaria. Es una escuela mixta porque ___₁ muchachos y ___₂ muchachas van a ___₃ misma escuela. Está en ___₄ ciudad de Los Ángeles. ___₅ alumnos son muy buenos y muy inteligentes. ___₆ profesores también son muy buenos. ___₇ profesora de español enseña muy bien. ___₈ alumnos aprenden mucho en ___₉ clase de español.

Vocabulario

SUSTANTIVOS		VERBOS	OTRAS PALABRAS Y EXPRESIONES
el teléfono	la tecla	hacer una llamada	¿Está (el nombre de una persona)?
la llamada	el teclado	llamar por teléfono	¿De parte de quién?
el/la interlocutor(a)	la señal	telefonear	Un momento, por favor.
la guía telefónica	el tono	descolgar (ue)	Están hablando.
el número (de teléfono)	el tono de ocupado	esperar	Suena ocupado.
el prefijo	la línea	introducir	La línea está ocupada.
la clave de área	el contestador	marcar	en seguida
el código de área	ADJETIVOS	discar	en cuanto
el prefijo del país	público(a)	sonar (ue)	de (a) botones
la cabina telefónica	privado(a)	colgar (ue)	siempre
la ranura	celular	adorar	de vez en cuando
la moneda	inalámbrico(a)		con frecuencia
el auricular	automático(a)		a menudo
la bocina	equivocado(a)		
el disco	ocupado(a)		

CAPÍTULO 1   25

Reintegración
RECYCLING
These exercises review and recombine material learned in *Bienvenidos* with vocabulary and structures from this chapter. Exercise A reviews the preterite of regular and irregular verbs. Exercise B reviews definite articles.

ANSWERS
Ejercicio A
  Answers will vary.

Ejercicio B
1. los   6. Los
2. las   7. La
3. la   8. Los
4. la   9. la
5. Los

Vocabulario
The words and phrases in the *Vocabulario* have been taught for productive use in this chapter. They are summarized here as a resource for both students and teacher. The *Vocabulario* also serves as a convenient resource for *Culminación* activities. There are approximately 20 cognates in this list.

VIDEO
The video is intended to reinforce the vocabulary, structures, and cultural content in each chapter. It may be used here as a chapter wrap-up activity. See the *Video Activities Booklet* for additional suggestions on its use.

INTRODUCCIÓN AL VIDEO (0:00:00)

INTRODUCCIÓN (0:02:26)

EL TELÉFONO PÚBLICO (0:03:47)

STUDENT PORTFOLIO

Have students keep a Spanish notebook with their best written work from *A bordo* in it. These writings can be based on assignments from the Student Textbook, the Workbook, and Communication Activities Masters. In the Workbook, students will develop an organized autobiography (*Mi autobiografía*) which may also become a part of their portfolios. Written assignments in this chapter that may be included in students' portfolios are the *Actividades escritas* from pages 24-25 of the student text, and the *Mi autobiografía* section from the Workbook.

CAPÍTULO 2
Scope and Sequence pages 26-51

Topics	Functions	Structure	Culture
Food Grocery Quantity	How to shop for food in a Spanish-speaking country How to ask for the quantity you want How to find out prices How to differentiate between continuous habitual actions in the past and those completed at a definite time How to express two past actions in the same sentence	El imperfecto y el pretérito Dos acciones en la misma oración Los verbos como *querer* y *creer* en el pasado	Hispanic vs. American food shopping customs A *hipermercado* Traditional market in Mexico

CAPÍTULO 2

Situation Cards
The Situation Cards simulate real-life situations that require students to communicate in Spanish, exactly as though they were in a Spanish-speaking country. The Situation Cards operate on the assumption that the person to whom the message is to be conveyed understands no English. Therefore, students must focus on producing the Spanish vocabulary and structures necessary to negotiate the situations successfully. For additional information, see the Introduction to the Situation Cards in the Situation Cards Envelope.

Communication Transparency
The illustration seen in this Communication Transparency consists of a synthesis of the two vocabulary (Palabras 1&2) presentations found in this chapter. It has been created in order to present this chapter's vocabulary in a new context, and also to recycle vocabulary learned in previous chapters. The Communication Transparency consists of original art. Following are some specific uses:

1. as a cue to stimulate conversation and writing activities
2. for listening comprehension activities
3. to review and reteach vocabulary
4. as a review for chapter and unit tests

CAPÍTULO 2
Print Resources

Lesson Plans

Workbook
	Pages
◆ Palabras 1	11-12
◆ Palabras 2	13
◆ Estructura	14-16
◆ Un poco más	17-20
◆ Mi autobiografía	21

Communication Activities Masters
◆ Palabras 1	8-9
◆ Palabras 2	9-10
◆ Estructura	11-12

7 Bell Ringer Reviews
9-10

Chapter Situation Cards A B C D

Chapter Quizzes
◆ Palabras 1	7
◆ Palabras 2	8
◆ Estructura	9-11

Testing Program
◆ Listening Comprehension	5
◆ Reading and Writing	6-8
◆ Proficiency	124
◆ Speaking	142

Nosotros y Nuestro Mundo
- ◆ Nuestro Conocimiento Académico *Las ciencias: La agronomía*
- ◆ Nuestro Idioma *Pretérito y pretérito imperfecto*
- ◆ Nuestra Cultura *La agricultura y la cocina*
- ◆ Nuestra Literatura *"Tierra"* de Gregorio López y Fuentes
- ◆ Nuestra Creatividad
- ◆ Nuestras Diversiones

CAPÍTULO 2
Multimedia Resources

CD-ROM Interactive Textbook Disc 1
Chapter 2 Student Edition
- ◆ Palabras 1
- ◆ Palabras 2
- ◆ Estructura
- ◆ Conversación
- ◆ Lectura y cultura
- ◆ Hispanoparlantes
- ◆ Realidades
- ◆ Culminación
- ◆ Prueba

Audio Cassette Program with Student Tape Manual
Cassette	Pages
◆ 2B Palabras 1	209-210
◆ 2B Palabras 2	210
◆ 2B Estructura	211
◆ 2B Conversación	211
◆ 2B Segunda parte	211-213

Compact Disc Program with Student Tape Manual
◆ CD 2 Palabras 1	209-210
◆ CD 2 Palabras 2	210
◆ CD 2 Estructura	211
◆ CD 2 Conversación	211
◆ CD 2 Segunda parte	211-213

Overhead Transparencies Binder
- ◆ Vocabulary 2.1 (A&B); 2.2 (A&B)
- ◆ Communication C-2
- ◆ Maps
- ◆ Fine Art (with Blackline Master Activities)

Video Program
◆ Videocassette	
◆ Video Activities Booklet	4-6
◆ Videodisc	
◆ Video Activities Booklet	4-6

Computer Software (Macintosh, IBM, Apple)
- ◆ Practice Disk
  - Palabras 1 y 2
  - Estructura
- ◆ Test Generator Disk
  - Chapter Test
  - Customized Test

26B

CAPÍTULO 2

CHAPTER OVERVIEW

In this chapter students will learn vocabulary and structures associated with food and grocery shopping, including expressions useful in searching for items, specifying quantities, and talking about prices. They will learn the difference between the imperfect and the preterite. The cultural focus of Chapter 2 is a comparison of Hispanic and American food-shopping customs.

CHAPTER OBJECTIVES

By the end of this chapter, students will know:
1. basic food vocabulary and the names of some important food items
2. vocabulary associated with various types of shops common in the Spanish-speaking world
3. vocabulary needed to order specific quantities
4. the contrasting uses of the preterite and the imperfect
5. how to use the preterite and the imperfect in the same sentence

CAPÍTULO 2

DE COMPRAS

OBJETIVOS

In this chapter you will learn to do the following:

1. shop for food in a Spanish-speaking country
2. ask for the quantity you want
3. find out prices
4. differentiate between continuous, habitual actions in the past and those completed at a definite time
5. express two past actions in the same sentence
6. talk about the food-shopping practices in Spanish-speaking countries and contrast them with those in the United States

CHAPTER PROJECTS

(optional)

Tell students that as they progress through the chapter, they are to keep track of the names of their favorite foods as they learn them. This vocabulary is important, since these are the words students will probably use most when ordering in restaurants or shopping. At the end of the chapter, have students make up personal shopping lists and "dream" restaurant menus.

CHAPTER 2 RESOURCES

1. Workbook
2. Student Tape Manual
3. Audio Cassette 2B
4. Vocabulary Transparencies
5. Bell Ringer Review Blackline Masters
6. Communication Activities Masters
7. Computer Software: Practice and Test Generator
8. Video Cassette, Chapter 2
9. Video Activities Booklet, Chapter 2
10. Situation Cards
11. Chapter Quizzes
12. Testing Program

Pacing

Chapter 2 will take eight to ten class sessions. Pacing, however, will vary according to the length of the class period, the age of the students, and student aptitude.

LEARNING FROM PHOTOS

You may wish to give students the following additional vocabulary to identify the beautiful produce at this market: *las setas*, *los champiñones* (mushrooms), *los kiwis* (kiwi), *el melón* (melon), *las peras* (pears), *las naranjas* (oranges), *las manzanas* (apples), *las cerezas* (cherries), *la col roja* (red cabbage), *los pimientos* (peppers), *la berenjena* (eggplant), *las zanahorias* (carrots), *las judías verdes* (string beans), *las habas limas* (lima beans), *las alcachofas* (artichokes), *la lechuga* (lettuce), *el perejil* (parsley), *el berro* (watercress), *los espárragos* (asparagus), *las remolachas* (beets).

VOCABULARIO
PALABRAS 1

Vocabulary Teaching Resources

1. Vocabulary Transparencies, 2.1 (A & B)
2. Audio Cassette 2B
3. Student Tape Manual, *Palabras 1*
4. Workbook, *Palabras 1*
5. Communication Activities Masters, *Palabras 1, A & B*
6. Chapter Quizzes, *Palabras 1*

Bell Ringer Review

Write the following on the board or use BRR Blackline Master 2-1:
Write a list of all the foods you already know in Spanish. Keep your list because you will use it again soon.

PRESENTATION (*pages 28-29*)

A. Tell students they are about to learn some new food items. Review the food vocabulary from Chapter 15 of *Bienvenidos*, using the Vocabulary Transparencies from that chapter. You may wish to have students use the words in a sentence.
B. Now model the new words on pages 28 and 29 using Vocabulary Transparencies 2.1 (A & B), plastic replicas of food, or large pictures. Have students repeat the words and phrases in unison. Review by pointing to the items as you ask *¿Qué es?*
C. Once the new words have been presented orally, have students open their books to pages 28-29 and read them.

28

VOCABULARIO
PALABRAS 1

DE COMPRAS

- el pan
- la panadería 
- el pastel
- la pastelería
- la carne 
- la carnicería 
- el pescado
- la langosta
- los mariscos
- los camarones
- la pescadería 
- las legumbres
- las frutas
- la verdulería
- el pasillo 
- el supermercado

28 CAPÍTULO 2

ROLE-PLAY

Getting Ready
Using posters or pictures of stores, set up areas of the classroom as *la panadería, la pastelería, la pescadería, la carnicería,* and *la verdulería*. Dramatize the meaning of *muéstreme*.

(student), **levántese.**
Vaya a la panadería.
Tome pan.
Dé el pan a ___.
Vaya a la carnicería.
Compre un pollo.
Vaya a la verdulería.
Compre legumbres.
Vaya a la pastelería.
Indíqueme una tarta.
Vaya a la pescadería.
Compre mariscos.
Vaya a la caja.
Pague.

el hipermercado

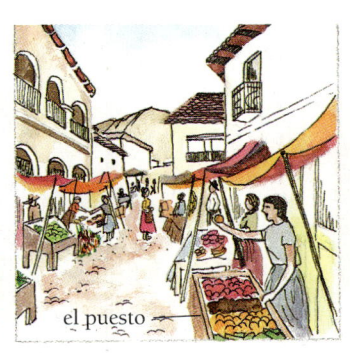

el puesto

el mercado

el carrito

La señora empujó el carrito.
Empujó el carrito por los pasillos.

ALGUNOS COMESTIBLES

las papas,
las patatas

la lechuga

las habichuelas,
los frijoles

las judías verdes

el arroz

las manzanas

las naranjas

las uvas

las fresas

la piña

la carne de res

la ternera

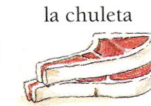

la chuleta

el cerdo

el jamón

el lechón

los huevos

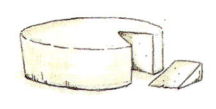

el queso

la leche

la mantequilla

CAPÍTULO 2   29

COOPERATIVE LEARNING

Teams of four sit in a circle. One member names a food item, simultaneously tossing a sponge ball to a teammate. The teammate must name the place where that item can be purchased, quickly name a new food item and toss the ball to another.

DID YOU KNOW?

El hipermercado is a large store that sells food as in the supermarket. However, unlike the supermarket, other types of merchandise are also sold in a *hipermercado*.

D. Ask either/or questions during your presentation. For example: ¿*Es una pescadería o una carnicería? ¿Es un carrito o un puesto?*
E. Now ask other questions. For example: ¿*Va la señora de compras? ¿Va ella al supermercado? ¿Qué empuja por los pasillos?*

RETEACHING (Palabras 1)
Have students tell whether they like or don't like each of the following items: *el pan, la leche, los huevos, la carne de res, el queso.*

COGNATE RECOGNITION
Point out the cognates that appear in *Palabras 1: el pastel, las frutas, el supermercado, el mercado, las patatas.*

ABOUT THE LANGUAGE
Names for food items vary from region to region.
1. *Las papas* is used in all of Latin America, *las patatas* in Spain.
2. Beans vary quite a bit: *frijoles, habas, habichuelas.*
3. *Las naranjas* are *las chinas* in Puerto Rico.
4. *Las fresas silvestres* (wild strawberries) are very popular in some areas when in season.
5. *La carne de res* is *el bife* in Argentina.
6. *El cerdo* can also be *el puerco* or *el chancho.*
7. Fresh ham in some areas is *el pernil.*
8. *El lechón* is used in most of Latin America for suckling pig, *el cochinillo* in Spain.
9. Other words for *el pastel* are *la torta, la tarta,* and *el queque.*
10. In Spain, small *camarones* are called *gambas.*
11. Vegetables are either *las legumbres, las verduras,* or *los vegetales.*

29

Ejercicios

PRESENTATION (*page 30*)

Ejercicio A
Exercise A can be done with books open.

Ejercicio B
Listening
Focus on the listening skill by doing Exercise B with books closed. Then do the exercise again with books open.

Ejercicio C
Exercise C can be done with books either open or closed.

Extension of *Ejercicio C*
After completing Exercise C, call on volunteers to talk about their likes and dislikes. Elicit as much of the new food vocabulary as possible.

ANSWERS

Ejercicio A
1. Es el pastel.
2. Es el pescado.
3. Son frutas.
4. Son mariscos.

Ejercicio B
1. Fue a la panadería.
2. Fue a la frutería y a la verdulería.
3. Fue a la pescadería.
4. Fue a la carnicería.

Ejercicio C
Answers will vary, but will contain *me gustan* or *me gusta*.

Ejercicios

A ¿Qué es? Identifiquen.

1. ¿Es el pan o el pastel?
2. ¿Es la carne o el pescado? 
3. ¿Son legumbres o frutas? 
4. ¿Son mariscos o frutas? 

B ¿Qué compró y dónde lo compró? Contesten.
1. María quería comprar pan, ¿adónde fue?
2. Carlos quería comprar frutas y legumbres frescas, ¿adónde fue?
3. Teresa quería comprar mariscos, ¿adónde fue?
4. Francisco quería comprar carne, ¿adónde fue?

C Mis preferencias. Preguntas personales.
1. ¿Te gustan las papas?
2. ¿Te gusta una ensalada de tomates y lechuga?
3. ¿Te gusta más la carne de res o la ternera?
4. ¿Te gusta el cerdo?
5. ¿Te gustan las fresas?
6. ¿Te gusta el queso?

LEARNING FROM PHOTOS

You may wish to ask the following questions about the photos on page 31.
1. (top) ¿Dónde está la gente? ¿Qué están comprando? ¿Están frescas las legumbres? ¿Cuáles son algunas legumbres que ves en el mercado?
2. (bottom) The painting is *La vendimia* (the grape harvest). Goya (1746-1828) is considered to be one of Spain's greatest artists. He painted *La vendimia* between 1786-1787. It now hangs in the Prado museum. Ask students to describe the painting in as much detail as possible. You may wish to ask questions such as: ¿Quiénes son las personas en el cuadro? ¿Quiénes están vestidos elegantemente? ¿Qué lleva la joven en la canasta?

D **¿A qué grupo pertenecen?** Clasifiquen los comestibles.

　　legumbres
　　frutas
　　carne
　　mariscos

1. los camarones
2. las manzanas
3. la ternera
4. el lechón
5. las uvas
6. las habichuelas
7. el jamón
8. las naranjas
9. la piña
10. las judías verdes

E **Un supermercado o un mercado.** ¿Sí o no?

1. Un supermercado tiene puestos.
2. Hay muchos pasillos en un supermercado grande.
3. Los clientes empujan carritos por los puestos del mercado.
4. Los clientes empujan carritos por los pasillos del supermercado.
5. En el hipermercado venden comestibles, ropa y otras mercancías.

"La vendimia" de Francisco de Goya

CAPÍTULO 2　　31

Ejercicios

PRESENTATION (page 31)

Ejercicio D
　Exercise D can be done with books open.

Ejercicio E
　Exercise E can be done with books either open or closed.

ANSWERS

Ejercicio D
1. mariscos
2. frutas
3. carne
4. carne
5. frutas
6. legumbres
7. carne
8. frutas
9. frutas
10. legumbres

Ejercicio E
1. no
2. sí
3. no
4. sí
5. sí

INFORMAL ASSESSMENT
(Palabras 1)
　Check for understanding by naming a store and having students name as many items as possible that might be purchased there.

RETEACHING (Palabras 1)
　Have students open their books to pages 28-29. Ask them to name any stores on these pages that are found in their own local shopping area. Ask them to use *hay* and any location information they can give in Spanish. For example: *Hay una pastelería en la avenida Wyckoff.*

INDEPENDENT PRACTICE

　Assign any of the following:
1. Workbook, *Palabras 1*
2. Communication Activities Masters, *Palabras 1, A & B*
3. Exercises on student pages 30-31
　(See suggestions for correcting homework in the Teacher's Manual.)

VOCABULARIO
PALABRAS 2

VOCABULARIO

PALABRAS 2

EN EL SUPERMERCADO

un paquete de zanahorias congeladas

una lata (un bote) de atún

un envase de crema

una botella de agua mineral

un frasco de mayonesa

una tajada (lonja) de jamón

un envase de detergente líquido

una caja de jabón en polvo

un rollo de papel higiénico

la canasta

la bolsa de plástico

Nota: To ask the cost of a food item whose price fluctuates frequently, Spanish speakers will ask, ¿A cuánto está(n) _____ ?. ¿Cuánto es? and ¿Cuánto cuesta? are used more often for merchandise. To find out the total cost of several food items you would ask, ¿Cuánto es? or ¿Cuánto le debo? When you are shopping, a clerk will often ask if you want something else, ¿Algo más? If you want something else, you will tell the clerk what you want. If you don't want anything else, you will respond, No, nada más, gracias, ¿Cuánto es? or ¿Cuánto le debo, por favor?

32 CAPÍTULO 2

Vocabulary Teaching Resources
1. Vocabulary Transparencies 2.2 (A & B)
2. Audio Cassette 2B
3. Student Tape Manual, Palabras 2
4. Workbook, Palabras 2
5. Communication Activities Masters, Palabras 2, C & D
6. Chapter Quizzes, Palabras 2
7. Computer Software, Vocabulario

Bell Ringer Review
Write the following on the board or use BRR Blackline Master 2-2:
Take the list of foods you wrote for Bell Ringer Review 2-1 and divide them into the following categories: **carnes, pescados y mariscos, legumbres, frutas, pasteles, otro.**

PRESENTATION (pages 32-33)
A. Model the new words using Vocabulary Transparencies 2.2 (A & B), plastic replicas, food containers, or pictures of food. Follow the procedures outlined in *Palabras 1*, pages 28-29.
B. Have students repeat the words and phrases after you or Cassette 2B.

Vocabulary Expansion
When teaching *agua mineral*, you may wish to add the expressions *con gas* and *sin gas*, since they are so frequently needed when ordering water.

ADDITIONAL PRACTICE
Give students the name of an item. Then have them ask the price:
  los zapatos
  el periódico
  los huevos
  los huevos, la mayonesa y el agua

María estaba en la carnicería.
Compró un kilo de carne de res.

Pablo fue al supermercado.
Él hizo sus compras en el supermercado.
Él pagó en la caja.
Mientras él pagaba, el joven ponía sus compras en bolsas de plástico.

CAPÍTULO 2   33

COGNATE RECOGNITION
Point out the following cognates which appear in this section: *plástico, detergente, líquido, rollo, papel higiénico, mayonesa, botella, mineral, crema, paquete.*

ABOUT THE LANGUAGE
1. When ordering *medio kilo* or *quinientos gramos* of something, people will often say *una libra,* even though it is not exactly a pound.
2. The word for "slice" varies from region to region. Very common are *una tajada* and *una rebanada.* Other terms are *la lonja, una rueda,* and *una rodaja.*

PAIRED ACTIVITY
One partner gives a quantity. The other gives an item one can buy in that quantity. For example: Student 1: *Una botella.* Student 2: *Una botella de agua.*

ADDITIONAL PRACTICE
You may wish to ask the following questions as you present the sentences on page 33. *¿Dónde estaba María? ¿Qué compró en la carnicería? ¿Cuánto compró? ¿Adónde fue Pablo? ¿Qué hizo en el supermercado? ¿Dónde pagó? ¿Qué hacía el joven mientras Pablo pagaba? ¿De qué eran las bolsas?*

33

Ejercicios

PRESENTATION (page 34)

Ejercicios A, C, and D
Exercises A, C, and D can be done with books open.

Ejercicio B: Listening
Focus on the listening skill by doing Exercise B with books closed. Then repeat the exercise with books open.

ANSWERS

Ejercicio A
1. una lata
2. un paquete
3. un rollo
4. un envase
5. una botella
6. un rollo
7. un paquete (una bolsa)
8. una tajada
9. un paquete
10. un paquete, una lata (un bote)
11. una bolsa, una caja
12. una caja, una botella

Ejercicio B
Some answers will vary.
1. Sí, Pablo fue de compras ayer.
2. Fue al supermercado.
3. Hizo sus compras en el supermercado.
4. Siempre hacía sus compras en el mismo supermercado.
5. Sí, pagó en la caja.
6. Él puso las compras en bolsas de plástico.
7. Sí, ponía las compras en las bolsas mientras Pablo pagaba.

Ejercicio C
1. Los huevos están a 90 pesos la docena.
2. Las chuletas de cerdo están a 700 pesetas el kilo.
3. La lechuga está a 130 pesetas cada una.
4. Las fresas están a 2.000 pesos la caja de medio kilo.

Ejercicio D
Answers will vary.

RETEACHING
(Palabras 2)
Have students turn to page 29. Ask them to tell whether they like each item shown or not.

34

Ejercicios

A ¿Qué es? Identifiquen.
1. _____ de sardinas
2. _____ de servilletas de papel
3. _____ de toallas de papel
4. _____ de yogur
5. _____ de leche
6. _____ de papel higiénico
7. _____ de fresas congeladas
8. _____ de jamón
9. _____ de tacos
10. _____ de habichuelas negras
11. _____ de arroz
12. _____ de detergente

B De compras. Contesten.
1. ¿Pablo fue de compras ayer?
2. ¿Adónde fue?
3. ¿Dónde hizo sus compras?
4. ¿Siempre hacía sus compras en el mismo supermercado?
5. Ayer, ¿pagó Pablo en la caja?
6. ¿En qué puso el joven las compras?
7. ¿Ponía las compras en las bolsas mientras Pablo pagaba?

C En el mercado. Contesten según se indica.
1. ¿A cuánto están los huevos? (90 pesos la docena)
2. ¿A cuánto están las chuletas de cerdo? (700 pesetas el kilo)
3. ¿A cuánto está la lechuga? (130 pesetas cada una)
4. ¿A cuánto están las fresas? (2.000 pesos la caja de medio kilo)

D En el mercado. Completen la conversación.
—Sí, señor, ¿qué desea Ud. hoy?
— _____ , por favor.
—¿Y?
—Quisiera _____ .
—¿Algo más?
—No, _____ , gracias. ¿Cuánto _____ ?
—1.200 pesos.

34   CAPÍTULO 2

LEARNING FROM REALIA
Have students peruse the ad on page 34. Have them check how many words they already know. Tell them to try to learn some new words that they don't know.

INDEPENDENT PRACTICE
Assign any of the following:
1. Workbook, *Palabras 2*
2. Communication Activities Masters, *Palabras 2, C & D*
3. Exercises on student page 34
4. Computer Software, *Vocabulario*

Comunicación
Palabras 1 y 2

A **En una pastelería.** You are in a pastry shop. You are admiring some chocolate cookies *(galletas de chocolate)*. A classmate will be the sales clerk.

1. Point to the cookies and tell the clerk you would like some.
2. He or she wants to know how many.
3. He or she asks if you would like something else. Tell him/her no.
4. Ask him/her how much the cookies are.
5. You're not sure if you have to pay at the cashier's. Ask.

B **En la carnicería.** You are in a butcher shop in Monterrey, Mexico. You want some pork chops. A classmate will be the butcher.

1. Ask the butcher the price.
2. Try to find out how many chops there are in a kilo.
3. Tell the butcher you want four chops.
4. The butcher asks if you want something else.
5. Ask him how much you owe.

C **Mis favoritos.** Con un(a) compañero(a) de clase, preparen cada uno una lista de los comestibles que le gustan y que no le gustan. Luego compartan los resultados. ¿Cuántos comestibles les gustan o no les gustan a los/las dos?

D **Voy de compras.** Ud. está viviendo con una familia española en Salamanca. Ud. va a ir de compras. Mire la siguiente lista de compras y pregúntele a un miembro de su familia (un[a] compañero[a] de clase) a qué tienda debe ir.

1. camarones
2. pollo
3. queso
4. judías verdes
5. papas
6. torta

E **En el mercado.** Ud. está en una tienda de abarrotes. Pídale al empleado (su pareja) los siguientes productos. Indique la cantidad que Ud. quiere. Luego cambien de papel.

> papas
> Estudiante 1: Quisiera un kilo de papas.
> Estudiante 2: Sí, señor(ita). Un kilo de papas.

1. agua mineral
2. huevos
3. jamón
4. mayonesa
5. mantequilla
6. Coca-Cola
7. crema
8. detergente
9. leche
10. jabón

CAPÍTULO 2 **35**

ESTRUCTURA

Structure Teaching Resources

1. Workbook, *Estructura*
2. Student Tape Manual, *Estructura*
3. Audio Cassette 2B
5. Communication Activities Masters, *Estructura*, A-C
6. Chapter Quizzes, *Estructura*
7. Computer Software, *Estructura*

Bell Ringer Review

Write the following on the board or use BRR Blackline Master 2-3: Write the following:
1. cuatro cosas que hiciste ayer en la escuela
2. cuatro cosas que hiciste ayer después de las clases

El imperfecto y el pretérito

PRESENTATION (page 36)

A. Lead students through steps 1-3.
B. For step 2 draw a time line on the board. Each time you give a verb in the preterite, write an abrupt slash through the time line to indicate completion or termination in the past.
C. As you go over the sentences in step 2, put another time line on the board. Each time you give a verb in the imperfect, draw a long shaded box along it to indicate duration.

ABOUT THE LANGUAGE

La bolsa (grocery bag) is used in most countries. In the Dominican Republic, however, *la funda* is used.

RECYCLING

Other items students learned for carrying groceries are *la canasta* and *el capacho*.

36

ESTRUCTURA

El imperfecto y el pretérito   *Talking About Past Events*

1. The choice of the preterite or the imperfect depends upon whether the speaker is describing a completed action in the past or a continuous, recurring action in the past.

   The preterite is used to express actions or events that began and ended at a definite time in the past.

   Ayer yo fui al mercado.
   Compré cuatro chuletas de cerdo.
   El carnicero me dio las chuletas en una bolsa.

2. The imperfect, in contrast to the preterite, is used to express a habitual, repeated, or continuous action in the past. The moment when the action began or ended is not important.

   Yo iba al mercado todos los días.
   Cada día yo compraba las cosas que necesitaba.
   Siempre volvía a casa con varios paquetes o bolsas.

3. Contrast the following sentences.

Repeated, habitual action	Completed action
Él iba de compras todos los días.	Y él fue al mercado ayer.
Ellos me hablaban cada noche.	Y me hablaron anoche.
Yo lo veía todos los días.	Y lo vi ayer.

36   CAPÍTULO 2

LEARNING FROM PHOTOS

You may wish to ask the following questions about the photo on page 36: ¿Es un mercado moderno o no? ¿Es un mercado al aire libre? El mercado está en México. ¿De qué nacionalidad son las señoras? ¿En qué pone la vendedora las legumbres? ¿Ella le da la bolsa a la señora o tiene la señora su propia bolsa?

Ejercicios

A ¿Una vez o frecuentemente? Contesten.

1. ¿Fue la señora al mercado ayer por la mañana?
   ¿Cuándo fue la señora al mercado?
   ¿Iba la señora al mercado cada mañana?
   ¿Cuándo iba la señora al mercado?
2. El otro día, ¿fue la señora al supermercado en carro?
   ¿Cuándo fue la señora al supermercado en carro?
   ¿Iba en carro todos los días? ¿Lo dejaba en el estacionamiento?
   ¿Cuándo iba la señora en carro? ¿Cuándo lo dejaba en el estacionamiento?
3. ¿Hiciste un viaje el año pasado?
   ¿Cuándo hiciste un viaje?
   ¿Hacías un viaje cada año?
   ¿Cuándo hacías un viaje?
4. ¿Jugaron las muchachas al básquetbol (baloncesto) ayer por la tarde?
   ¿Cuándo jugaron las muchachas al básquetbol?
   ¿Jugaban las muchachas al básquetbol cada tarde?
   ¿Cuándo jugaban ellas al básquetbol?
5. ¿Viste una película anoche?
   ¿Cuándo viste la película?
   ¿Veías una película cada noche?
   ¿Cuándo veías una película?

B Viajes estupendos. Completen.

1. El año pasado mis amigos y yo ___ (hacer) un viaje estupendo.
2. Nosotros ___ (ir) a Guatemala.
3. Yo ___ (tomar) un curso de español en Antigua.
4. Mis amigos ___ (estudiar) el español también pero no ___ (tomar) el curso en la misma escuela que yo.
5. El martes pasado, nosotros ___ (levantarse) temprano.
6. Nosotros ___ (ir) a Chichicastenango.
7. Nosotros ___ (andar) por el mercado de "Chichi".
8. Nosotros ___ (ver) a los indios.
9. Ellos ___ (vender) los productos que ___ (cultivar) o ___ (hacer) y con el dinero que ___ (recibir) por las cosas que ___ (vender), ___ (comprar) las provisiones que ___ (necesitar).

El convento de Santa Clara y la iglesia de San Francisco, Antigua, Guatemala

CAPÍTULO 2 37

PRESENTATION (*page 38*)

Ejercicio D

Before doing Exercise D, ask students if they remember the terms they used for grocery store. Exercise D can be done with books open.

ABOUT THE LANGUAGE

Remind students that *la tienda de abarrotes* is used in Mexico, Central America, and in some areas of South America. *La bodega* and *el colmado* are used in the Caribbean. *La pulpería* is used in certain areas of South America. In Spain, *la tienda de ultramarinos* is used since most canned and packaged items sold there are imported.

ANSWERS

Ejercicio C

Answers will vary.
1. Sí (No), (no) iba a la playa.
2. Sí (No), (no) nadaba mucho.
3. Sí (No), (no) esquiaba en el agua.
4. Sí (No), (no) tomaba el sol.
5. Sí (No), (no) comía muchos mariscos.
6. Sí (No), (no) leía en la playa.
7. Sí (No), (no) salía de noche con mis amigos.
8. Sí (No), (no) íbamos a una discoteca.
9. Sí (No), (no) bailábamos.
10. Sí (No), (no) lo pasábamos bien.
11. Sí (No), (no) fui a la playa el verano pasado.
12. Sí (No), (no) nadé mucho.
13. Sí (No), (no) esquié en el agua.
14. Sí (No), (no) tomé el sol.
15. Sí (No), (no) comí muchos mariscos.
16. Sí (No), (no) leí mucho en la playa.
17. Sí (No), (no) salí de noche con mis amigos.
18. Sí (No), (no) fuimos a una discoteca.
19. Sí (No), (no) bailamos.
20. Sí (No), (no) lo pasamos bien.

Ejercicio D

Answers will vary according to model and cues provided.

38

C El veraneo. Preguntas personales.

1. Durante los veranos, ¿ibas a la playa?
2. ¿Nadabas mucho?
3. ¿Esquiabas en el agua?
4. ¿Tomabas el sol?
5. ¿Comías muchos mariscos?
6. ¿Leías en la playa?
7. ¿Salías de noche con tus amigos?
8. ¿Iban a una discoteca?
9. ¿Bailaban Uds.?
10. ¿Lo pasaban bien?
11. Y el verano pasado, ¿fuiste a la playa?
12. ¿Nadaste mucho?
13. ¿Esquiaste en el agua?
14. ¿Tomaste el sol?
15. ¿Comiste mariscos?
16. ¿Leíste mucho en la playa?
17. ¿Saliste de noche con tus amigos?
18. ¿Fueron Uds. a una discoteca?
19. ¿Bailaron Uds.?
20. ¿Lo pasaron bien?

D De compras. Contesten según el modelo.

   Raúl / pasteles
   Raúl estaba en la pastelería donde compró pasteles.

1. Los señores Colón / una botella de agua mineral
2. Adela / arroz
3. Yo / camarones
4. Los niños / pan
5. Nosotros / un envase de crema
6. Teresa / manzanas y naranjas
7. Mis tías / lechón
8. Don Álvaro / papas y una tajada de jamón
9. Marisela / huevos y queso
10. Rosa María / una caja de jabón en polvo
11. Paco / una lata de atún

Los jóvenes comen pescado en Salinas, Puerto Rico.

38   CAPÍTULO 2

FOR THE NATIVE SPEAKER

An occasional spelling problem may exist with the imperfect tense form of *-ar* verbs. Namely the confusion of *b* and *v*. Students may spell *iva* for *iba*, *estudiava* for *estudiaba*, etc. Have them write this exercise.

Ellos (estar) ___ en casa cuando yo llamé.
Yo los (llamar) ___ para invitarlos a un baile.
Yo no (esperar) ___ que ellos estuvieran allí.
Nosotros (ir) ___ a bailar todos los sábados.
Siempre que yo (llamar) ___, Tere (contestar) ___.

The confusion occurs because *b* and *v* are pronounced the same in most Spanish-speaking countries. In some areas the *b* is pronounced like an English *v*.

Dos acciones en la misma oración *Narrating a Sequence of Events*

1. Many sentences in the past have two verbs which can either be in the same tense or a different tense. Note the following sentences.

    Juan salió y Elena entró.

    In the sentence above, both verbs are in the preterite because they express simple and specific actions or events that had a definite beginning and end in the past.

2. In the sentence below, the two verbs are in the imperfect because they both express continuous actions with no indication of beginning or end.

    Durante las vacaciones Carlos iba a la playa pero yo trabajaba.

3. In the sentence below, the verb in the imperfect *hablaba* describes what was going on. The verb in the preterite *tocó* expresses the action or event that intervened and interrupted the first action.

    Mi mamá hablaba por teléfono cuando Nando tocó a la puerta.

CAPÍTULO 2   39

INDEPENDENT PRACTICE

Assign any of the following:
1. Workbook, *Estructura*
2. Communication Activities Masters, *Estructura*, A
3. Exercises on student pages 37–38

Bell Ringer Review

Write the following on the board or use BRR Blackline Master 2-4: Complete with the preterite.
1. Ayer yo ___ de compras. (ir)
2. Yo ___ al mercado solo(a). Mi hermano no ___. (ir, ir)
3. Yo ___ algunas frutas muy ricas. (comprar)
4. El señor que trabaja en la frutería las ___ en una bolsa. (poner)
5. Cuando yo ___ a casa, ___ una naranja. (volver, comer)
6. Y, ¿quién ___ todas las fresas en seguida? Sí, mi hermanito. (comer)

Dos acciones en la misma oración

PRESENTATION *(page 39)*

A. When explaining the difference between the preterite and the imperfect, you may wish to have students think of a play. Explain that all the stage background, the description, and the scenery are in the imperfect. What the actors and actresses actually do on stage is in the preterite.
B. Give some examples and show the difference between background information and acting. Background: *Él era muy guapo. Había una fiesta. Todo el mundo se divertía. José y Elena bailaban.* Acting: *En ese momento Carlos entró. Dijo "Buenos días" a todo el mundo. Saludó a todos.*
C. Now use two verbs in one sentence to contrast the background information with the actions on stage. For example: *Marisela y Paco bailaban cuando Carlos entró.*

39

Ejercicios

PRESENTATION (page 40)

Ejercicio A

Have students refer to the illustrations on page 40 as they make up their statements.

Ejercicio B

Exercise B can be done first orally with books closed. It can then be written and read in class for additional reinforcement.

ANSWERS

Ejercicio A

1. Ayer Rosaura escribió una carta y Ángel vio una película.
   Mientras Rosaura escribía una carta, Ángel veía una película.
2. Ayer Rosaura hizo unas compras y Ángel preparó la comida.
   Mientras Rosaura hacía unas compras, Ángel preparaba la comida.
3. Ayer Rosaura tomó el metro y Ángel tomó el bus.
   Mientras Rosaura tomaba el metro, Ángel tomaba el bus.
4. Ayer Rosaura jugó al básquetbol y Ángel jugó al vólibol.
   Mientras Rosaura jugaba al básquetbol, Ángel jugaba al vólibol.

Ejercicio B

Answers will vary as shown below.
1. Sí (No), (no) estaba en casa cuando sonó el teléfono.
2. Sí (No), (no) tocaba el piano cuando sonó.
3. Sí (No), (no) contesté al teléfono en cuanto sonó.
4. Sí (No), (no) hablaba por teléfono cuando mi mamá volvió a casa.
5. Sí (No), (no) me preguntó mi mamá con quién hablaba.
6. Hablaba con… cuando mi mamá entró.

Ejercicios

A Ellos lo hicieron y lo hacían. Formen oraciones según el dibujo.

Ayer Rosaura ⎯⎯ y Ángel ⎯⎯ .
Mientras Rosaura ⎯⎯ Ángel ⎯⎯ .

1.
2.
3.
4.

B ¿Qué hacías cuándo…? Contesten.

1. ¿Estabas en casa cuando sonó el teléfono?
2. ¿Tocabas el piano cuando sonó?
3. ¿Contestaste al teléfono en cuanto sonó?
4. ¿Hablabas por teléfono cuando tu mamá volvió a casa?
5. ¿Preguntó tu mamá con quién hablabas?
6. ¿Con quién hablabas cuando tu mamá entró?

ADDITIONAL PRACTICE

Have students say anything they can about the illustrations on page 40.

Los verbos como *querer* y *creer* en el pasado   *Expressing Ideas in the Past*

Since most mental processes involve duration or continuance, verbs that deal with mental activities or conditions are most often expressed in the imperfect tense in the past. The most common of these verbs that you have already learned are:

creer	pensar
desear	preferir
querer	poder
tener ganas	saber

Él sabía lo que preferíamos.
Yo tenía ganas de salir.
Él creía que yo estaba enfermo.

Ejercicios

A **Yo quería.** Preparen una lista de las cosas que *querían* hacer.

Yo...

B **Yo sabía.** Preparen una lista de las cosas que *sabían* hacer cuando eran niños(as).

Yo... cuando...

C **Y yo no podía.** Preparen una lista de las cosas que no *podían* hacer cuando eran niños(as).

Yo no... cuando...

D **Sabía y podía.** Preparen una lista de las cosas que *sabían* hacer y que *podían* hacer.

Yo... y...

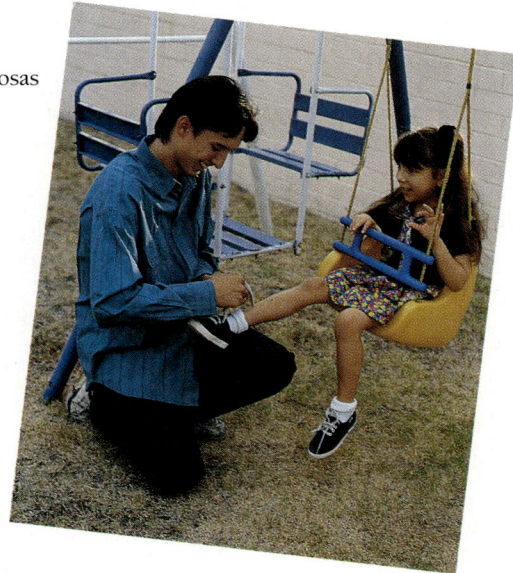

CAPÍTULO 2   41

Bell Ringer Review
Write the following on the board or use BRR Blackline Master 2-5: Your best friend got into trouble. Use preterite forms of these infinitives to tell what happened: **levantarse tarde, no hacer la tarea, hablar mucho en clase, no estudiar para el examen, salir mal en el examen.**

Los verbos como querer y creer *en el pasado*

PRESENTATION *(page 41)*
Guide students through the explanation on page 41. Provide and elicit additional examples.

Ejercicios
PRESENTATION *(page 41)*
You may wish to assign these exercises for homework and go over them the following day in class.

ANSWERS
Ejercicio A
Yo quería (infinitive).

Ejercicio B
Yo sabía (infinitive) **cuando era niño(a).**

Ejercicio C
Yo no podía (infinitive) **cuando era niño(a).**

Ejercicio D
Yo sabía (infinitive) **y podía** (infinitive).

INFORMAL ASSESSMENT
Have students make up as many original sentences as they can using the preterite and the imperfect.

Note The contrast between these two tenses is reintroduced many times in the *Reintegración* section of future chapters.

LEARNING FROM PHOTOS
You may wish to ask the following questions about the photo on page 41: ¿Dónde estaba la niña? ¿Con quién estaba? ¿Se bajó papá? ¿Se bajó para atarle los tenis?

Recycling Students will probably not remember the word for shoelaces. They are *los cordones* or *los pasadores*.

INDEPENDENT PRACTICE
Assign any of the following:
1. Workbook, *Estructura*
2. Communication Activities Masters, *Estructura*, B & C
3. Exercises on student pages 40-41
4. Computer Software, *Estructura*

41

CONVERSACIÓN

Bell Ringer Review

Write the following on the board or use BRR Blackline Master 2-6: Answer the following questions.
1. ¿Qué hiciste esta mañana?
2. ¿A qué hora saliste de casa?
3. ¿Adónde fuiste?
4. ¿Con quién fuiste?

PRESENTATION (page 42)
A. Tell students they will hear a conversation between Carlos and Elena. Have them close their books and listen to the conversation on Cassette 2B.
B. Have students repeat the conversation aloud after you or Cassette 2B.
C. Now have volunteers read the conversation aloud.
D. Allow pairs time to practice.

Ejercicio

ANSWERS
1. Carlos llamó a Elena.
2. La llamó a eso de las nueve.
3. No, ella no estaba en casa.
4. Estaba en el mercado.
5. Fue de compras a las ocho y media.
6. Fue al mercado de Santa Mercedes.
7. Ella compró una cajita de fresas.
8. Estaban a ocho soles el medio kilo.
9. Había una oferta especial.

42

CONVERSACIÓN

Escenas de la vida *Fui de compras*

CARLOS: Te llamé esta mañana y no estabas.
ELENA: ¿A qué hora me llamaste?
CARLOS: Pues, te llamé a eso de las nueve.
ELENA: Salí a las ocho y media para hacer las compras.
CARLOS: ¿Fuiste al mercado de Santa Mercedes?
ELENA: Sí, como siempre. Y me compré una cajita de fresas frescas.
CARLOS: ¿A cuánto estaban las fresas?
ELENA: Había una oferta especial— a ocho soles el medio kilo.

■ **¿Dónde estabas?** Contesten según la conversación.
1. ¿A quién llamó Carlos?
2. ¿A qué hora la llamó?
3. ¿Estaba en casa?
4. ¿Dónde estaba?
5. ¿A qué hora fue de compras?
6. ¿A qué mercado fue?
7. ¿Qué compró?
8. ¿A cuánto estaban las fresas?
9. ¿Qué había?

42   CAPÍTULO 2

COOPERATIVE LEARNING

Have students make up their own conversations based on the one on page 42. They can change *fresas* to anything else they would like to buy.

DID YOU KNOW?

Many markets in Spanish-speaking cities and towns have names of saints.

Comunicación

A **¿En qué puedo servirle?** Trabaje con un(a) compañero(a) de clase. Preparen una lista de comestibles que quieren comprar. Luego decidan quién va a ser el/la comerciante y quién va a ser el/la cliente. Preparen la conversación que van a tener en el mercado o en la tienda de abarrotes.

B **Mi juventud.** Pregúntele a un(a) compañero(a) de clase si él o ella hacía las siguientes cosas cuando era muy joven. Tome apuntes y prepare un informe para la clase.

1. ir muy a menudo al cine
2. tomar una siesta
3. jugar con sus amigos después de las clases
4. pasar la noche con sus abuelos de vez en cuando
5. mirar películas en la televisión
6. ayudar a sus padres con las tareas domésticas

C **Lo que hacía cuando...** Trabaje con un(a) compañero(a) de clase. Uno(a) de Uds. va a decir lo que hacía ayer. El/la otro(a) va a decir algo que ocurrió y que interrumpió lo que Ud. hacía. Luego incluyan las dos acciones en una sola oración.

CAPÍTULO 2 **43**

Comunicación

PRESENTATION (page 43)

These activities enable students to use the vocabulary and structures learned in the chapter in open-ended exchanges. You may wish to assign different ones to different groups or allow students to choose for themselves which ones they wish to do.

ANSWERS
Actividades A-C
Answers will vary.

LEARNING FROM PHOTOS

Have students tell what items are found in a *tienda de abarrotes* like the one on page 43.

INDEPENDENT PRACTICE

Assign any of the following:
1. Workbook, *Un poco más*
2. Exercises and activities on student pages 42-43

LECTURA Y CULTURA

Bell Ringer Review
Write the following on the board or use BRR Blackline Master 2-7: You are planning lunch for a friend. Make a shopping list and note where you are going to buy each item.

READING STRATEGIES
(page 44)

Pre-Reading
Ask students about their families' food-shopping habits. Who does the family shopping? How many times a week? Where do they prefer to shop for groceries? Do they always go to the same store? Why? Do they chat with people who work in the stores?

Reading
A. With books closed, read the selection on page 44 to the class, using as much expression as possible.
B. Now have students open their books. Call on volunteers to read the selection aloud, two or three sentences at a time. After each volunteer reads, ask the class content questions. Here are some possible questions for the first three sentences: *¿Adónde fue la señora Santana a eso de las ocho? En años pasados, ¿quiénes iban a este mismo mercado?*

Post-reading
Assign a silent reading of the selection for independent work.

LECTURA Y CULTURA

DE COMPRAS

Esta mañana a eso de las ocho, la señora Santana salió de su casa en la Ciudad de México y fue de compras. ¿Adónde fue? Pues, fue al mercado de Santa Mercedes. En años pasados su mamá y su abuelita iban a este mismo mercado. ¿Y cuándo iban? ¡Todos los días! Y la señora Santana sigue haciendo sus compras diariamente también. Compra comida muy fresca. Esta mañana, fue de un puesto a otro en el mercado. En cada puesto compró los comestibles que necesitaba. En el puesto de verduras, compró unas legumbres y en el puesto del carnicero compró carne mechada para preparar unos tacos. Puso las compras en la misma canasta que lleva al mercado todos los días. Y hoy, como siempre, ella buscaba las ofertas especiales. ¿Quién no quiere una ganga?

La señora Bravo, igual que la señora Santana, fue de compras esta mañana. Pero ella no fue al mercado de Santa Mercedes en México. Ella fue al mercado de San Miguel en Madrid. Ella también fue de un puesto a otro buscando todo lo que necesitaba y como siempre ponía sus compras en su capacho[1].

A veces la señora Bravo decide no ir al mercado a hacer sus compras. De vez en cuando va a las pequeñas tiendas en su barrio. Por ejemplo, compra la carne en la carnicería, las legumbres en la verdulería, y el pan "de cada día" en la panadería. Y la señora conoce al carnicero, a la verdulera y al panadero. Ellos charlan[2] un poquito antes de hacer los negocios[3].

¿Hay supermercados en España y en Latinoamérica? Sí que hay y se están poniendo más y más populares. Pero mucha gente sigue haciendo sus compras en el mercado o en las pequeñas tiendas especializadas—sobre todo en las grandes ciudades y en los pueblos. Pero en las afueras de las ciudades, en los grandes centros comerciales de los suburbios, hay supermercados modernos con un gran "parking". Los clientes entran en el supermercado, toman un carrito y lo empujan de un departamento a otro. En los supermercados venden productos frescos pero hay también muchos productos congelados o enlatados—en lata o bote.

Y en la caja, un joven o una joven pone todas las compras en bolsas de plástico. En San Juan, por ejemplo, si el cliente quiere, el joven lleva las bolsas al carro y los clientes generosos le dan una propina por el servicio.

[1] capacho *basket*
[2] charlan *chat*
[3] hacer los negocios *getting down to business*

CAPÍTULO 2

CRITICAL THINKING ACTIVITY

(Thinking skills: drawing conclusions)
Read the following to the class or write it on the board or on a transparency. *Explique por qué son más populares los supermercados que las tiendas especializadas en los Estados Unidos.*

Estudio de palabras

¿Cuál es otra palabra? Pareen.

1. todos los días
2. mismo
3. las legumbres
4. un kilo
5. una ganga
6. charlar
7. el parking
8. enlatado
9. la lata
10. los comestibles

a. mil gramos
b. en lata
c. diariamente, cada día
d. el estacionamiento
e. igual
f. las verduras
g. cosas para comer
h. un precio reducido
i. conversar, hablar un poco
j. el bote

Comprensión

A Es cosa de todos los días. Contesten según la lectura.

1. ¿De qué nacionalidad es la señora Santana?
2. ¿Dónde hizo sus compras?
3. ¿Cuándo hace o hacía sus compras?
4. En el mercado, ¿qué compró en cada puesto?
5. ¿Qué llevaba la señora al mercado todos los días?
6. Y hoy, ¿lleva una canasta también?
7. ¿Qué pone en la canasta?
8. ¿Que busca o qué quiere la señora?

B Es igual en Madrid. ¿Sí o no?

1. La señora Bravo es mexicana también.
2. En Madrid no hay mercados como en México.
3. A la señora Bravo, como a todas las madrileñas, le gusta hacer sus compras en el supermercado.
4. Las españolas tienen la costumbre de hacer sus compras en muchas pequeñas tiendas especializadas.
5. La señora Bravo lleva un capacho al mercado.

CAPÍTULO 2 45

Estudio de palabras
ANSWERS
1. c
2. e
3. f
4. a
5. h
6. i
7. d
8. b
9. j
10. g

Comprensión
ANSWERS

Comprensión A
1. Ella es mexicana.
2. Hizo sus compras en el mercado de Santa Mercedes.
3. Hace (hacía) sus compras todos los días.
4. Compró comestibles en cada puesto.
5. Llevaba una canasta (un capacho).
6. Sí, hoy también lleva (llevó) una canasta (un capacho).
7. Pone las compras (los comestibles) en la canasta (el capacho).
8. Ella busca ofertas especiales.

Comprensión B
1. no
2. no
3. no
4. sí
5. sí

LEARNING FROM REALIA

1. Have students look at the ad on page 45 and tell what country it is from. They should be able to guess Spain because it says *tortillas de patatas*.
2. Have students notice how they refer to orange juice. It is *zumo de naranja* in Spain, not *jugo de naranja*. En Puerto Rico it is *jugo de china*.

45

Descubrimiento Cultural

(The Descubrimiento section is optional.)

PRESENTATION *(pages 46-47)*

A. Before reading the selection, have students discuss the following questions in groups:
   1. Bargaining in the markets is a way of life in the Spanish-speaking world. What are the advantages of such a way of doing things? Is shopping in a flea market similar? Support your answer.
   2. What are the advantages and disadvantages of shopping once a week as compared with daily?

B. Hold a question and answer session on the selection in Spanish. If necessary, students can read answers directly from the book.

DESCUBRIMIENTO CULTURAL

En España y en Latinoamérica la gente suele hacer sus compras todos los días. En los Estados Unidos la gente tiende a ir al supermercado una o dos veces a la semana. Compran todo lo que necesitan para una semana entera. Por eso la gente tiende a comprar productos congelados o enlatados. En España y en Latinoamérica la gente suele hacer sus compras en un mercado o en tiendas especializadas pero es algo que poco a poco está cambiando. Los supermercados se están poniendo más y más populares.

En muchos mercados de la América Central y de la América del Sur, venden comestibles en algunos puestos, ropa en otros y electrodomésticos o artesanías en otros. Estos mercados existen sobre todo en México, Guatemala, Ecuador, el Perú y Bolivia, en los países donde hay una gran población indígena—gente de ascendencia india. En las áreas más remotas hay días de mercado, por lo general, uno o dos días por semana. Por ejemplo, el famoso mercado de Chichicastenango en Guatemala es el jueves y el domingo.

En los mercados, la gente regatea. ¿Qué significa "regatea"? Pues, el vendedor le da un precio al cliente y el cliente le dice que "no". Le ofrece un precio más bajo. Luego el vendedor le da o le pone otro precio.

El regateo existe en los mercados—pero en los supermercados, en las tiendas de (por) departamentos y en las tiendas elegantes, no. En estas tiendas hay a veces ofertas especiales—saldos, rebajas, gangas o liquidaciones—pero no hay regateo.

¿Qué es un hipermercado? Pues, es un concepto relativamente nuevo. Un hipermercado es como un gran supermercado, pero no venden solamente comestibles. Venden todo tipo de mercancías: ropa, electrodomésticos, muebles, etc.

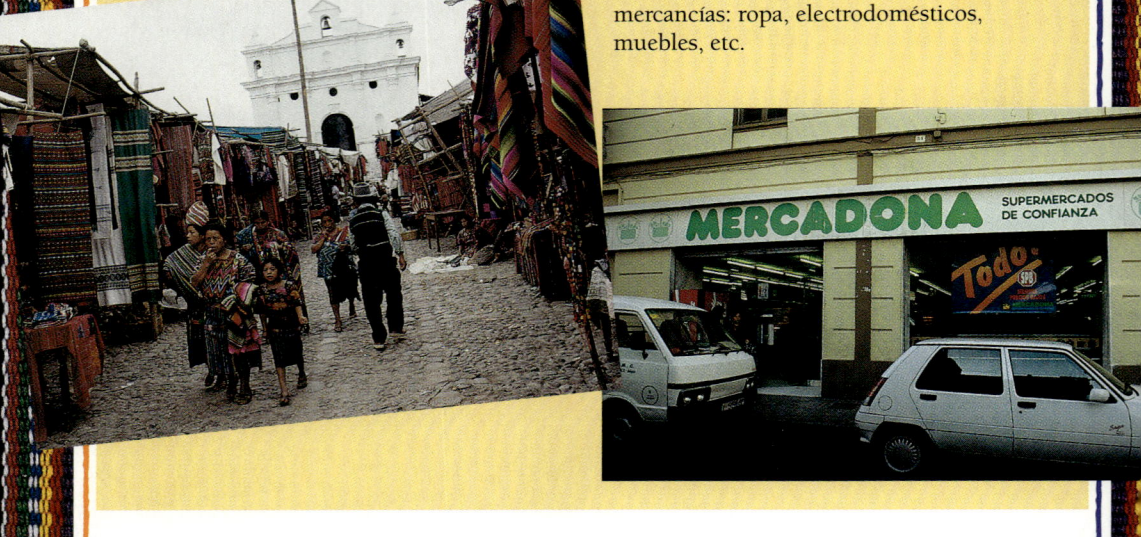

46 CAPÍTULO 2

LEARNING FROM PHOTOS

Ésta es la famosa Iglesia de Santo Tomás en Chichicastenango. Es un centro religioso de los mayas, y en esta iglesia tienen lugar muchas ceremonias que mezclan las creencias católicas y mayas. Mucha gente acude a la iglesia los jueves y los domingos—los días de mercado.

COOPERATIVE LEARNING

Have students work in pairs in order to prepare a conversation about bargaining at an outdoor market. Ask them to use humor and to be as original as possible.

Y AQUÍ EN LOS ESTADOS UNIDOS

En los EE.UU. la gente come comidas típicas de todas partes del mundo. Comemos comida china, japonesa, mexicana, italiana. En las áreas donde vive mucha gente hispana los supermercados tienen secciones dedicadas a comida hispana y llevan productos típicos. Por ejemplo, donde hay mucha gente del Caribe los supermercados venden arroz en grandes sacos de 20 libras o más. Allí se ven frutas y vegetales como los plátanos verdes, guanábanas, yautías y mamey. Y para freír, muchas familias tradicionales todavía usan manteca[1] de cerdo. En el suroeste y otras áreas con grandes poblaciones méxico-americanas los supermercados venden masa harina[2] (de maíz) para hacer tortillas y tamales; tomatillos y una variedad de chiles (pimientos). Y casi todos los hispanos usan el cilantro.

[1] manteca   *lard*
[2] masa harina   *flour*

CAPÍTULO 2   **47**

CRITICAL THINKING ACTIVITY

(Thinking skills: supporting statements with reasons)

Have students debate about the following:
Equipo 1: *Prefiero ir de compras una vez por semana. ¡Basta!*
Equipo 2: *Prefiero ir de compras todos los días. ¿Por qué no?*

LEARNING FROM REALIA

Have students look at the ad for *Continente* on page 47 and learn as many new words as possible.

47

REALIDADES

(The Realidades section is optional.)

PRESENTATION *(pages 48-49)*

A. Allow students to peruse the photos and enjoy them.
B. You may wish to have students read the captions aloud or silently.
C. You may wish to answer the questions in the captions.
D. Have some of your stronger students write a short dialog that might take place in a traditional market between a customer and a merchant.
E. You may wish to ask the following questions about the check out slip from Mercadona (**Realia 5**). *La leche desnatada, ¿tiene crema o no? ¿Tiene cafeína la cola que compró el cliente? ¿Cuál es el monto (total) de la factura? ¿Cuánto dio el cliente? ¿Cuánto le devolvió la empleada? ¿Cómo se llama la empleada?*

REALIDADES

Un hipermercado español **1**. ¿Por qué lo llaman "híper"? ¿Qué se puede comprar allí?

Los pasillos en un supermercado en los EE.UU. **2**. Los productos que se ven son los que prefieren los clientes hispanos. ¿Cuáles son algunos?

Un mercado tradicional en México **3**. ¿Cuáles son los productos que están vendiendo allí?

Cajas de comestibles para un supermercado mexicano **4**. ¿Qué hay en esas cajas?

La cuenta de un supermercado en España **5**. ¿Qué toma esta familia en grandes cantidades? ¿Cuánto tuvieron que pagar en total? ¿Y quién es Mónica Belengue?

INDEPENDENT PRACTICE

Workbook, *Mi autobiografía*

DID YOU KNOW?

En España se vende la leche en cartones que no necesitan refrigeración porque emplean un proceso de "ultrapasteurización" que permite mantener la leche por mucho tiempo sin refrigeración.

49

CULMINACIÓN

RECYCLING
The *Comunicación oral* and *Comunicación escrita* activities allow students to use the vocabulary and grammar from this chapter in open-ended settings. They also provide an opportunity to recycle vocabulary and structures from Chapter 1 and from *Bienvenidos*. Have students do as many of the *actividades* as you wish.

Comunicación oral
PRESENTATION (page 50)
Actividad D
This may be done as a whole-class activity with some students taking the roles of the merchants while others move around visiting the "stands."

ANSWERS
Actividades A–D
Answers will vary.

INFORMAL ASSESSMENT
Activity A may be used to evaluate speaking skills. Use the evaluation criteria given on page 24 of this Teacher's Wraparound Edition.

Comunicación escrita
ANSWERS
Actividades A–C
Answers will vary.

CULMINACIÓN

Comunicación oral

A **¿Dónde compra...?** Entreviste a las siguientes personas (tres compañeros[as] de clase) una señora de 32 años, un muchacho de 17 años y un señor de 65 años que ya no trabaja. Pregúnteles dónde compran lo siguiente. Luego déjele saber a la clase el resultado de su encuesta (*survey*).

1. comida para una semana
2. manzanas importadas
3. una bolsa de patatas fritas
4. verduras muy frescas
5. mucha carne
6. pan
7. leche
8. comida preparada
9. cereales

LOTE COCINA:
1 KG. AZUCAR
+
1 LT. VINAGRE
+
1 KG. SAL =
LOTE 247

B **El regateo.** Trabaje con un(a) compañero(a) de clase. Uds. están en un mercado al aire libre donde venden todo tipo de mercancías, artesanías y comestibles. Uno de Uds. va a ser el/la cliente y el/la otro(a) va a ser el/la comerciante. Preparen la conversación que Uds. dos tienen en el mercado. El/la cliente quiere regatear—no quiere pagar el precio que quiere el/la comerciante.

C **Ayer.** Trabaje con un(a) compañero(a) de clase. Ayer Uds. trataron de hacer muchas cosas. Pero siempre había interrupciones. Preparen una lista de todo lo que hacían y todo lo que intervino e interrumpió lo que hacían.

D **En un mercado en México.** Ud. va de compras a un mercado en México pero no tiene mucho dinero. Haga una lista de alimentos para preparar tres comidas balanceadas. Luego vaya a tres o cuatro puestos diferentes, regatee con los vendedores (sus compañeros de clase) y compre lo que necesita.

Comunicación escrita

A **Fui de compras.** Ud. viajaba por México y fue a un mercado interesante. Escríbale una tarjeta postal a un(a) amigo(a). Descríbale el mercado y todo lo que pasó (ocurrió) en el mercado.

B **Contrastes culturales.** En unos párrafos, contraste cómo se hacen las compras en la mayoría de los países hispanos y cómo se hacen en los EE.UU.

C **¡Gran apertura!** Un supermercado americano quiere abrir sucursales (*branches*) en Europa. Ud. y tres compañeros van a preparar un anuncio para el nuevo supermercado. Incluyan en el anuncio lo que pueden comprar, los precios, las ventas especiales, etc.

50   CAPÍTULO 2

FOR THE NATIVE SPEAKER

Ask students to write a brief essay on the following topic:
En muchos pueblos de España e Hispanoamérica el mercado sirve una función social. Hay quienes dicen que los centros comerciales o los malls sirven una función similar, especialmente para los jóvenes. Escribe un breve ensayo comparando el mercado tradicional con el centro comercial y explica "la función social" de los dos.

Reintegración

A **Cuando era niño(a).** Preguntas personales.

1. ¿Dónde vivías cuando eras pequeño(a)?
2. ¿Quiénes vivían en tu casa?
3. ¿Quién preparaba la comida?
4. ¿Quién era tu maestro(a) favorito(a)?
5. ¿Tenías buenos amigos?
6. ¿Cómo se llamaban tus amigos?
7. ¿Qué programas mirabas en la televisión?
8. ¿Qué te gustaba más que cualquier otra cosa?

B **Ya no, pero antes sí.** Sigan el modelo.

Ya no miro la televisión, *pero antes siempre la miraba.*

1. Ya no juego al fútbol,...
2. Ellos ya no hablan por teléfono,...
3. Papá ya no sube las montañas,...
4. Tú ya no tocas el violín,...
5. Uds. ya no comen carne,...
6. Nosotros ya no vamos a la capital,...
7. Ud. ya no hace la plancha de vela,...

Vocabulario

SUSTANTIVOS

la panadería
la pastelería
la carnicería
la pescadería
la verdulería
la tienda de abarrotes
el supermercado
el hipermercado
el pasillo
el carrito
la caja
el mercado
el puesto
la canasta
la bolsa de plástico
el pan
el pastel
el pescado
el marisco

el atún
las legumbres
las papas
las patatas
la lechuga
el arroz
las habichuelas
los frijoles
las judías verdes
las zanahorias
las frutas
las manzanas
las naranjas
las uvas
las fresas
la piña
la carne
la carne de res
la ternera
el cerdo

el lechón
el jamón
la chuleta
el queso
los huevos
la leche
la crema
la mantequilla
la mayonesa
el detergente
el jabón
el papel higiénico
el paquete
la lata
el bote
la bolsa
la botella
el frasco
el envase
la caja

el rollo
la tajada
la lonja

ADJETIVOS

congelado(a)
líquido(a)
mineral
higiénico(a)

OTRAS PALABRAS Y EXPRESIONES

en polvo
de plástico
¿A cuánto está(n)?
¿Cuánto es?
¿Cuánto cuesta?
¿Cuánto le debo?
¿Algo más?
Nada más.

CAPÍTULO 2   51

CAPÍTULO 3
Scope and Sequence pages 52-75

Topics	Functions	Structure	Culture
Post office

Social and business letters | How to use words and expressions related to postal services

How to talk about future events

How to compare people and things

How to address an envelope in Spanish

How to write a business or personal letter | El futuro de los verbos regulares

El comparativo y el superlativo: formas regulares | Postal service

Letter-writing etiquette

Central post office in Mexico City

Post office in Valencia, Spain

Stamps from Uruguay, Paraguay, and Argentina |

CAPÍTULO 3

Situation Cards

The Situation Cards simulate real-life situations that require students to communicate in Spanish, exactly as though they were in a Spanish-speaking country. The Situation Cards operate on the assumption that the person to whom the message is to be conveyed understands no English. Therefore, students must focus on producing the Spanish vocabulary and structures necessary to negotiate the situations successfully. For additional information, see the Introduction to the Situation Cards in the Situation Cards Envelope.

Communication Transparency

The illustration seen in this Communication Transparency consists of a synthesis of the two vocabulary (Palabras 1&2) presentations found in this chapter. It has been created in order to present this chapter's vocabulary in a new context, and also to recycle vocabulary learned in previous chapters. The Communication Transparency consists of original art. Following are some specific uses:

1. as a cue to stimulate conversation and writing activities
2. for listening comprehension activities
3. to review and reteach vocabulary
4. as a review for chapter and unit tests

CAPÍTULO 3
Print Resources

	Pages
Lesson Plans	
Workbook	
◆ Palabras 1	22-23
◆ Palabras 2	24-25
◆ Estructura	26-27
◆ Un poco más	28-29
◆ Mi autobiografía	30
Communication Activities Masters	
◆ Palabras 1	13-14
◆ Palabras 2	14-15
◆ Estructura	16-17
7 Bell Ringer Reviews	11-12
Chapter Situation Cards A B C D	
Chapter Quizzes	
◆ Palabras 1	12
◆ Palabras 2	13
◆ Estructura	14-15
Testing Program	
◆ Listening Comprehension	9
◆ Reading and Writing	10-14
◆ Proficiency	125
◆ Speaking	143

Nosotros y Nuestro Mundo
- ◆ Nuestro Conocimiento Académico *La cruz y la espada en México*
- ◆ Nuestro Idioma *El tiempo futuro; El comparativo; El superlativo*
- ◆ Nuestra Cultura *Nicaragua*
- ◆ Nuestra Literatura *"Una carta a Dios"* de Gregorio López y Fuentes
- ◆ Nuestra Creatividad
- ◆ Nuestras Diversiones

CAPÍTULO 3
Multimedia Resources

CD-ROM Interactive Textbook Disc 1

Chapter 3 Student Edition
- ◆ Palabras 1
- ◆ Palabras 2
- ◆ Estructura
- ◆ Conversación
- ◆ Lectura y cultura
- ◆ Hispanoparlantes
- ◆ Realidades
- ◆ Culminación
- ◆ Prueba

Audio Cassette Program with Student Tape Manual

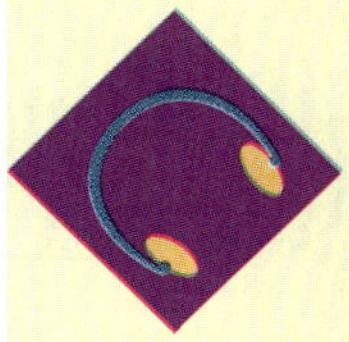

Cassette	Pages
◆ 3A Palabras 1	214
◆ 3A Palabras 2	215
◆ 3A Estructura	215-216
◆ 3A Conversación	216
◆ 3A Segunda parte	216-218

Compact Disc Program with Student Tape Manual

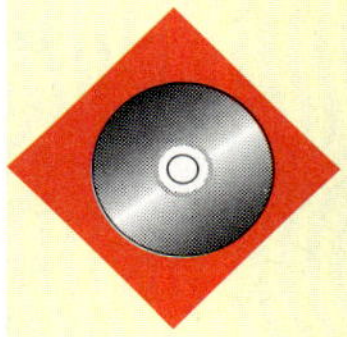

◆ CD 3 Palabras 1	214
◆ CD 3 Palabras 2	215
◆ CD 3 Estructura	215-216
◆ CD 3 Conversación	216
◆ CD 3 Segunda parte	216-218

Overhead Transparencies Binder 
- ◆ Vocabulary 3.1 (A&B); 3.2 (A&B)
- ◆ Communication C-3
- ◆ Maps
- ◆ Fine Art (with Blackline Master Activities)

Video Program 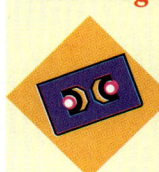
- ◆ Videocassette
- ◆ Video Activities Booklet 7-9
- ◆ Videodisc
- ◆ Video Activities Booklet 7-9

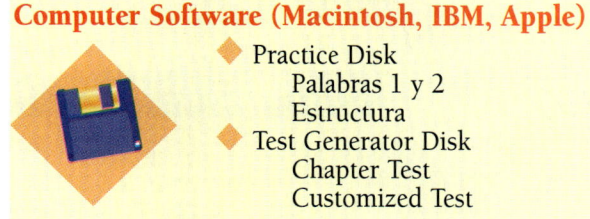

Computer Software (Macintosh, IBM, Apple)
- ◆ Practice Disk
  - Palabras 1 y 2
  - Estructura
- ◆ Test Generator Disk
  - Chapter Test
  - Customized Test

52B

CAPÍTULO 3

CHAPTER OVERVIEW

In this chapter students will learn to communicate with postal employees when sending letters or parcels. They will learn to write social and business letters and address an envelope properly in Spanish. They will also learn to make observations and express opinions using comparative and superlative statements about people and things. The formation and basic uses of the future tense are presented. The cultural focus of Chapter 3 is on the postal systems in some Spanish-speaking countries, the various services they offer and etiquette involved in letter writing.

CHAPTER OBJECTIVES

By the end of this chapter, students will know:
1. vocabulary associated with the postal service and letter writing
2. the formation and use of the comparative
3. the formation and use of the superlative
4. the formation of the future tense of regular verbs

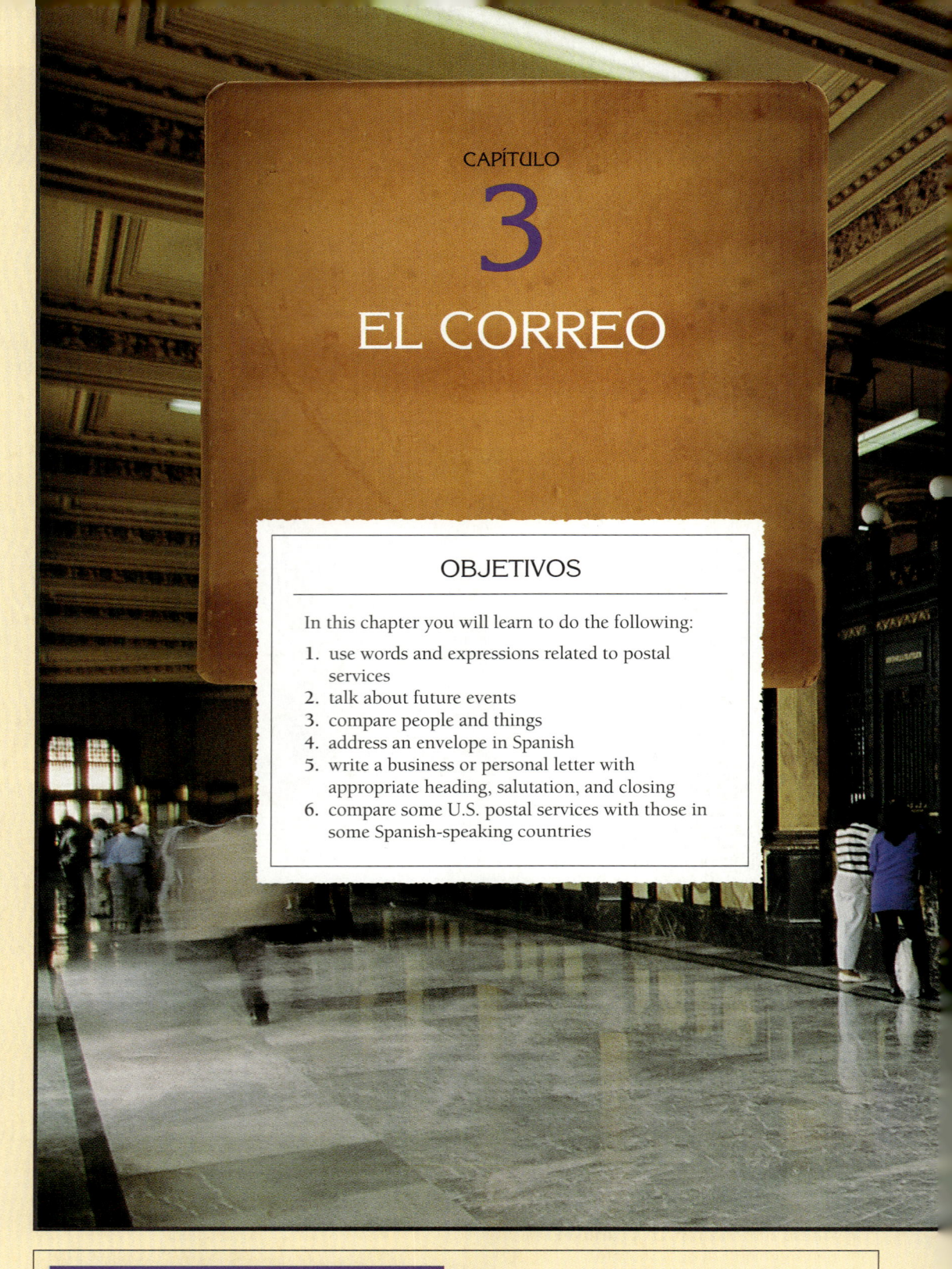

CAPÍTULO 3

EL CORREO

OBJETIVOS

In this chapter you will learn to do the following:
1. use words and expressions related to postal services
2. talk about future events
3. compare people and things
4. address an envelope in Spanish
5. write a business or personal letter with appropriate heading, salutation, and closing
6. compare some U.S. postal services with those in some Spanish-speaking countries

CHAPTER PROJECTS

(optional)
1. Have students make a list of services offered by the U.S. Postal Service and explain these services in Spanish.
2. If you live in an area where foreign language materials are available, have students look for Spanish greeting cards. Prepare a bulletin board using these cards.

CHAPTER 3 RESOURCES

1. Workbook
2. Student Tape Manual
3. Audio Cassette 3A
4. Vocabulary Transparencies
5. Bell Ringer Review Blackline Masters
6. Communication Activities Masters
7. Computer Software: Practice and Test Generator
8. Video Cassette, Chapter 3
9. Video Activities Booklet, Chapter 3
10. Situation Cards
11. Chapter Quizzes
12. Testing Program

Pacing

Chapter 3 will take eight to ten days. Pacing will depend on the length of the class period, the age of the students, and student aptitude. (See the Teacher's Manual for additional suggestions on pacing.)

LEARNING FROM PHOTOS

After presenting the *Palabras 2* vocabulary in this chapter, provide the class with the following information and ask the questions about the photo on pages 52-53. *Es el correo en la ciudad de México. Es un edificio muy bonito, ¿no? ¿Qué opina Ud.? ¿Es nuevo o viejo el correo? ¿Cuántas ventanillas ve Ud.? ¿Hay mucha gente esperando o haciendo cola? ¿Cuáles son algunas diferencias entre este correo y el correo de su ciudad o pueblo?*

VOCABULARIO
PALABRAS 1

Vocabulary Teaching Resources

1. Vocabulary Transparencies, 3.1 (A & B)
2. Audio Cassette 3A
3. Student Tape Manual, *Palabras 1*
4. Workbook, *Palabras 1*
5. Communication Activities Masters, *Palabras 1, A & B*
6. Chapter Quizzes, *Palabras 1*

Bell Ringer Review

Write the following on the board or use BRR Blackline Master 3-1: Write a short note to a friend. Tell him/her what you did last summer.

PRESENTATION (pages 54-55)

A. Have students close their books. Present the new words and phrases using Vocabulary Transparencies 3.1 (A & B).

B. Present one word or phrase at a time. Then build to complete sentences.

Teaching Tip When interspersing questions while introducing material, proceed from the easiest to the most difficult type of question. Begin with yes/no or either/or questions. For example: *¿Es un sobre? ¿Es un sobre o un aerograma?* Save open-ended questions (*¿Qué es esto?*) until students have had a chance to produce or at least hear the new vocabulary several times.

VOCABULARIO

PALABRAS 1

LA CORRESPONDENCIA

la carta 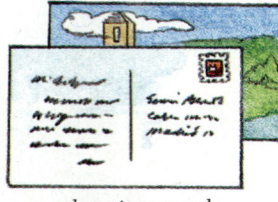
la tarjeta postal 
el aerograma

la estampilla, el sello
el nombre
la calle
la ciudad
el número
la zona postal, el código postal
la dirección
el sobre
el remitente
el destinatario 
el buzón 

54 CAPÍTULO 3

ROLE-PLAY

(Student 1 and Student 2), **levántense, por favor.
Vengan Uds.**
(Student 1) **Ud. es un(a) empleado(a) de correo.**
(Student 2) **Ud. tiene algo que enviar. Vaya Ud. al correo. Diga "buenos días" al (a la) empleado(a).**
(Student 1) **Conteste Ud. Pregúntele al (a la) cliente qué quiere enviar.**
(Student 2) **Dígale lo que quiere enviar. Dígale adónde quiere enviarlo.**
(Student 1) **Dígale cuánto va a costar.**
(Student 2) **Páguele al (a la) empleado(a). Déle el dinero.**
(Student 1) **Déle unos sellos.**
(Student 2) **Mire bien los sellos. Hay un problema. El/la empleado(a) no le dio bastantes sellos. Explíquele el problema al (a la) empleado(a).**

Teresa le escribirá una carta a su amigo.
¿Cuándo la escribirá? Mañana.

Ella enviará la carta mañana también.
Ella echará la carta al buzón.

Su amigo recibirá la carta en unos dos o tres días.

CAPÍTULO 3   55

COGNATE RECOGNITION
Note the following cognates in *Palabras 1*: *postal, certificado, aerograma, ordinario, zona.*

Vocabulary Expansion

Here are some additional words you may give students:
**un telegrama
por avión**

ABOUT THE LANGUAGE
1. In addition to *enviar la carta*, *mandar la carta* is often used.
2. *C/* is the abbreviation for *calle*. *Apto.* and *Dpto.* are abbreviations for *apartamento* and *departamento*, respectively.

ADDITIONAL PRACTICE

¿Cuál es la palabra?
1. lo que se pone en el sobre de una carta
   (*la estampilla, el sello*)
2. Calle San Bernardo 125 (*la dirección*)
3. el que recibe una carta (*el destinatario*)
4. el que envía una carta (*el remitente*)
5. donde se pone una carta para enviarla
   (*el buzón*)

Ejercicios

PRESENTATION *(page 56)*

Ejercicios A and B
A. Exercises A and B can be done with books open.
B. Have students refer to the realia on page 56 as they respond.

ANSWERS

Ejercicio A
1. Es un sello.
2. Es una tarjeta postal.
3. Es el código postal.
4. Es la dirección del destinatario.

Ejercicio B
1. Hay un sello en el sobre.
2. El nombre del remitente es Fernando Rosales Bravo.
3. La dirección de la destinataria es Avda. San Juan de Ulúa 32, Veracruz, 15714.
4. La zona postal es 15714.

Ejercicios

A ¿Qué es? Identifiquen.

1. ¿Es el sobre o el sello?

2. ¿Es una carta o una tarjeta postal?

3. ¿Es el código postal o la clave de área?

4. ¿Es la dirección del remitente o la dirección del destinatario?

B Información en el sobre. Contesten.
1. ¿Cuántos sellos hay en el sobre?
2. ¿Cuál es el nombre del remitente?
3. ¿Cuál es la dirección del destinatario?
4. ¿Cuál es la zona postal?

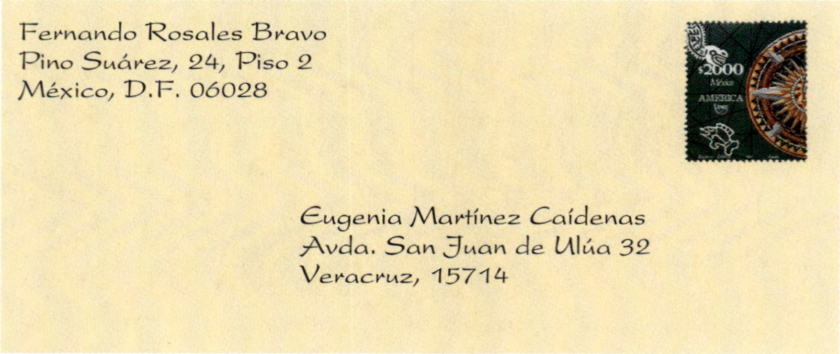

56 CAPÍTULO 3

INDEPENDENT PRACTICE

Assign any of the following:
1. Workbook, *Palabras 1*
2. Communication Activities Masters, *Palabras 1, A & B*
3. Exercises on student pages 56-57 (See suggestions for homework correction in the Teacher's Manual.)

C **Mi dirección.** Preguntas personales.
1. ¿Cuál es el número de tu casa?
2. ¿En qué calle está?
3. ¿Cómo se llama la ciudad o pueblo donde vives?
4. ¿Cuál es tu zona postal?
5. ¿Cuánto cuesta enviar una carta?
6. Y, ¿cuánto cuesta mandar una tarjeta postal?

D **Una carta para su novia.** Contesten según se indica.
1. ¿Escribirá Carlos una carta o una tarjeta postal? (una carta)
2. ¿A quién le escribirá la carta? (a su novia)
3. ¿Cuándo la enviará? (mañana)
4. ¿Dónde la echará? (en el buzón)
5. ¿Cuándo recibirá su novia la carta? (la semana que viene)

CAPÍTULO 3   57

Ejercicios
PRESENTATION (page 57)

Extension of *Ejercicio C*
After completing Exercise C, call on a student to supply all the personal information.

Ejercicio D
Go over Exercise D orally with books open or closed.

Extension of *Ejercicio D*
Have one student retell all the information in Exercise D in his/her own words.

ANSWERS
Ejercicio C
Answers will vary.
1. El número de mi casa es…
2. Está en…
3. La ciudad (el pueblo) donde vivo es…
4. Mi zona postal es…
5. Cuesta… enviar una carta.
6. Cuesta… enviar una tarjeta postal.

Ejercicio D
1. Carlos escribirá una carta.
2. Escribirá una carta a su novia.
3. La enviará mañana.
4. La echará en el buzón.
5. Ella recibirá la carta la semana que viene.

RETEACHING (*Palabras 1*)
Ask the following personal questions in order to review the preterite.
1. ¿Escribiste una carta?
2. ¿A quién escribiste la carta?
3. ¿Pusiste la carta en un sobre?
4. ¿Enviaste la carta? ¿Adónde?

LEARNING FROM PHOTOS
Refer students to the photo at the bottom of page 57 and ask: *¿Qué está leyendo la muchacha? ¿Qué tiene en la mano? ¿Lleva anteojos la muchacha cuando lee? ¿Tiene lentes de contacto o no? ¿Llevas gafas (anteojos) cuando lees? ¿Qué opinas? ¿Está la muchacha en casa o en la oficina? ¿Está leyendo una carta personal o una carta comercial?*

57

VOCABULARIO
PALABRAS 2

Vocabulary Teaching Resources
1. Vocabulary Transparencies 3.2 (*A & B*)
2. Audio Cassette 3A
3. Student Tape Manual, *Palabras 2*
4. Workbook, *Palabras 2*
5. Communication Activities Masters, *Palabras 2, C & D*
6. Chapter Quizzes, *Palabras 2*
7. Computer Software, *Vocabulario*

Bell Ringer Review
Write the following on the board or use BRR Blackline Master 3-2: Answer the following.
1. ¿Te gusta escribir?
2. ¿En qué clase escribes mucho?
3. ¿Qué escribes?
4. Y, ¿qué lees?
5. ¿Les escribes cartas a los (las) amigos(as)?
6. ¿A quiénes escribes?
7. ¿Cuándo les escribes?

PRESENTATION (*pages 58-59*)
A. Have students close their books. Use Vocabulary Transparencies 3.2 (*A & B*) to introduce the new words and expressions.
B. Model each new word or phrase and have students repeat after you or Cassette 3A.
C. After many yes/no and either/or questions, ask open-ended questions. For example: ¿Quién pesará el paquete? ¿Cómo enviará el señor el paquete? ¿Quién reparte (entrega) el correo? ¿Por qué no repartirá (entregará) el correo mañana?

58

VOCABULARIO

PALABRAS 2

EL CORREO

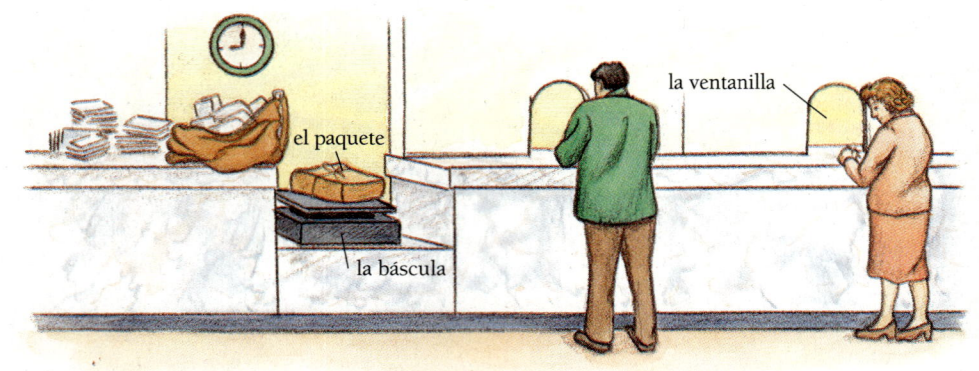

la ventanilla
el paquete
la báscula
la oficina de correos

por correo ordinario 
por correo aéreo 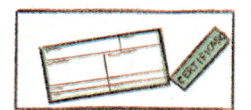
por correo certificado, recomendado

el apartado postal 
la casilla
el cartero

58 CAPÍTULO 3

ADDITIONAL PRACTICE
¿Cuál es la palabra?
1. el aparato que se usa para pesar paquetes, bultos y cartas
(*la báscula*)
2. él que entrega o reparte el correo
(*el cartero*)
3. la manera en que se envía una carta que tiene que llegar rápido
(*por correo aéreo*)

La empleada del correo pesará el paquete.

El señor enviará el paquete por correo ordinario.
Él lo asegurará.
Lo asegurará por 100.000 pesos.

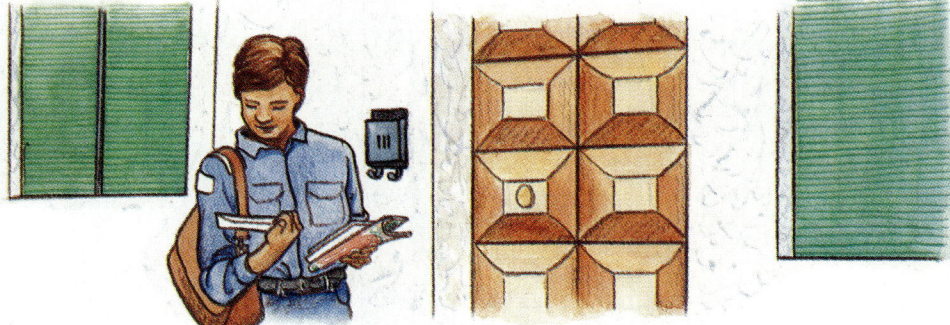

El cartero reparte (entrega) el correo.
Mañana no repartirá (entregará) el correo.
Mañana no hay entrega (reparto).
Mañana es domingo.
Los domingos no hay reparto.

CAPÍTULO 3

PAIRED ACTIVITY
1. The first student plays the role of a person waiting excitedly for the letter carrier to arrive. The second student wants to find out what the other is waiting for. Allow pairs time to prepare their skits. Then have them present their skits to the class.
2. Assign the illustrations on page 58 to one student and those on page 59 to the other. Each student asks the other as many questions as possible about the illustrations on the page assigned to him or her.

INFORMAL ASSESSMENT
Refer to Vocabulary Transparencies 3.2 again. Have individuals make up any statements they can about the illustrations.

ABOUT THE LANGUAGE
1. The word for postmark is *matasellos*. Ask students what they think the literal meaning of *matasellos* is (stamp-killer). Then ask what *papel matamoscas* (fly paper), *matahambre* (a kind of candy—hungry killer), and *matasanos* (old term for a physician—literally killer of well people) might be.

Ejercicios

PRESENTATION (*page 60*)

Ejercicio A
Exercise A can be done with books open or closed.

Ejercicios B and C
The purpose of Exercises B and C is to increase and reinforce the student's "word power" as much and as easily as possible. These exercises can be done with books open.

Variation of *Ejercicio C*
After going over the exercise with books open, have students close their books. Cue words from the second column and have them supply the related verbs. For example: *el recibo-recibir.* Then reverse the process, cueing verbs to elicit noun phrases. This provides practice in developing vocabulary-building techniques.

ANSWERS
Ejercicio A
Answers will vary.

Ejercicio B
1. la oficina de correos
2. entregar
3. el apartado postal
4. por correo recomendado
5. la estampilla
6. despachar

Ejercicio C
1. d
2. f
3. h
4. g
5. a
6. e
7. c
8. b

RETEACHING (*Palabras 2*)
Ask students to describe as completely as possible the man in the illustration on the bottom of page 58.

INFORMAL ASSESSMENT
(*Palabras 2*)
Refer students to the illustrations on pages 58-59. Ask them to make up as many questions as they can. Questions may be directed to the teacher or to classmates.

Ejercicios

A El correo. *Preguntas personales.*

1. ¿Hay un correo cerca de tu casa?
2. Delante del correo, ¿hay buzones?
3. ¿Los buzones están a la izquierda o a la derecha de la entrada?
4. ¿Hay un buzón especial para el correo local y otro para el correo aéreo?
5. ¿Es posible comprar sellos en la ventanilla del correo? ¿Despachan (venden) sellos o estampillas en el correo?
6. ¿Hay también una distribuidora automática de sellos en el correo?
7. Para usar la distribuidora, ¿es necesario introducir monedas en la ranura?
8. ¿Tienes un apartado postal?
9. ¿Qué días de la semana reparte el cartero el correo?

B ¿Cuál es otra palabra? *Expresen las siguientes palabras de otra manera.*

1. la casa de correos
2. repartir
3. la casilla
4. por correo certificado
5. el sello
6. vender

C Una palabra relacionada. *Pareen.*

1. entregar   a. el seguro
2. repartir   b. el remitente
3. enviar   c. el recibo
4. pesar   d. la entrega
5. asegurar   e. la correspondencia
6. corresponder f. el reparto
7. recibir   g. el peso
8. remitir   h. el envío

60   CAPÍTULO 3

LEARNING FROM PHOTOS

Refer students to the photo at the top of page 60 and say: *La señora está en Madrid. ¿Qué esta entregando la señora? ¿Qué es ella? ¿Lleva la cartero el correo en un carrito? ¿Empuja el carrito o tira del carrito? ¿Qué tiene en la mano? ¿Qué lleva la cartero? Describa su uniforme. ¿Qué opina? ¿Es atractivo, el uniforme?*

INDEPENDENT PRACTICE

Assign any of the following:
1. Workbook, *Palabras 2*
2. Communication Activities Masters, *Palabras 2, C & D*
3. Exercises on student pages 60-61
4. Computer Software, *Vocabulario*
(See suggestions for homework correction in the Teacher's Manual.)

Comunicación
Palabras 1 y 2

A **Necesito enviar estas postales.** Ud. está en el correo en Chosica, cerca de Lima. Quiere enviar algunas (tarjetas) postales a casa.

1. Find out how much the postage is.
2. The clerk (your partner) wants to know if you are going to send letters or postcards.
3. Tell him how many stamps you need.

B **Una carta muy importante.** Ud. está en el correo central de Caracas, Venezuela y tiene una carta importante que quiere enviar a los EE.UU.

1. Explain to the clerk (your partner) that you want to send the letter by registered mail.
2. Find out the cost of the postage.
3. Ask when the letter will arrive.

C **El servicio postal.** Una persona define palabras que tienen que ver con el correo y la otra adivina qué palabras son. Cambien de rol.

D **En el correo.** Ud. y un(a) compañero(a) están de vacaciones en Ecuador. Ud. quiere enviar seis tarjetas postales a los EE.UU. Su compañero(a) tiene que enviar un paquete y tres cartas. Pregúntenle al/a la empleado(a) de correo (otro[a] compañero[a] de clase) qué tienen que hacer.

Plaza San Martín, Lima, Perú

Caracas, Venezuela

Monumento que marca por donde pasa el ecuador

CAPÍTULO 3   61

Comunicación
(Palabras 1 and 2)

PRESENTATION (page 61)

These activities allow students to use the chapter vocabulary in open-ended situations. It is not necessary to do all of them. Select those you consider most appropriate.

ANSWERS

Actividades A–D
Answers will vary.

INFORMAL ASSESSMENT
(Palabras 1 and 2)

Have students say anything they can about mailing a letter or parcel.

DID YOU KNOW?

1. *Caracas es una ciudad grandísima y cosmopolita que está creciendo más y más cada día. Se encuentra en un valle largo y estrecho de unos 16 kilómetros. Más de cuatro millones de caraqueños viven aquí— algunos en estos condominios en rascacielos elegantes. Los recién llegados viven en los ranchos en las colinas que rodean la ciudad.*

2. The Equator Monument is just outside Quito, Ecuador, on the way to the lovely market town of Otavalo. The Indians of Otavalo—*los otavaleños*—are world-famous weavers.

61

ESTRUCTURA

El futuro de los verbos regulares — *Expressing Future Events*

1. The future tense is used to tell what will take place in the future. To form the future tense of regular verbs, you add the future endings to the infinitive. Study the following forms.

INFINITIVE	HABLAR	VER	VIVIR	ENDINGS
yo	hablaré	veré	viviré	-é
tú	hablarás	verás	vivirás	-ás
él, ella, Ud.	hablará	verá	vivirá	-á
nosotros(as)	hablaremos	veremos	viviremos	-emos
vosotros(as)	*hablaréis*	*veréis*	*viviréis*	*-éis*
ellos, ellas, Uds.	hablarán	verán	vivirán	-án

2. You have already learned the construction *ir a* + infinitive to express events that will take place in the near future. In everyday conversation, this construction is actually used more frequently than the future tense.

El verano que viene, yo voy a viajar con mi hermano por España.
El verano que viene, viajaré con mi hermano por España.

Vamos a comer en algunos restaurantes típicos.
Comeremos en algunos restaurantes típicos.

Vamos a vivir con una familia española.
Viviremos con una familia española.

Ejercicios

A Él le escribirá. Contesten.

1. ¿Le escribirá Ángel a su novia?
2. ¿Le escribirá en español o en inglés?
3. ¿Cuándo le escribirá?
4. ¿Comprará sellos en el correo?
5. ¿Enviará la carta en el correo?
6. ¿Echará la carta al buzón?
7. ¿Recibirá su novia la carta en algunos días?
8. ¿Ella abrirá la carta en seguida?
9. ¿La leerá?
10. ¿Estará contenta su novia?

B El verano que viene. Preguntas personales.

1. El verano que viene, ¿pasarás algunos días en la playa?
2. ¿Nadarás en el mar, en un lago o en una piscina?
3. ¿Tomarás el sol?
4. ¿Esquiarás en el agua?
5. ¿Comerás pescado y mariscos?
6. ¿Irás a una discoteca con tus amigos?
7. ¿Charlarán Uds.?
8. ¿Bailarán Uds.?
9. ¿Tomarán un refresco?
10. ¿Se divertirán?

C Haré una llamada telefónica. Cambien en el futuro.

1. La voy a llamar por teléfono.
2. Ella va a estar en casa.
3. Ella va a contestar.
4. Nosotros vamos a hablar.
5. Vamos a hablar de la fiesta que vamos a dar.
6. Ella me va a dar una lista de las personas que vamos a invitar.
7. Yo voy a escribir las invitaciones.
8. Yo le voy a leer a Sandra lo que voy a escribir en las invitaciones.
9. Nuestros amigos van a recibir sus invitaciones.
10. Ellos van a estar contentos.
11. ¿Tú vas a recibir una invitación también?
12. ¿Tú vas a ir a la fiesta?

D Ayer, no, pero mañana, sí. Contesten según el modelo.

¿Viste la película ayer?
Ayer no. Pero la veré mañana.

1. ¿Fuiste al cine ayer?
2. ¿Viste la película ayer?
3. ¿Compraste las entradas ayer?
4. ¿Te llamó Teresa ayer?
5. ¿La invitaste al cine?
6. ¿Ella fue?

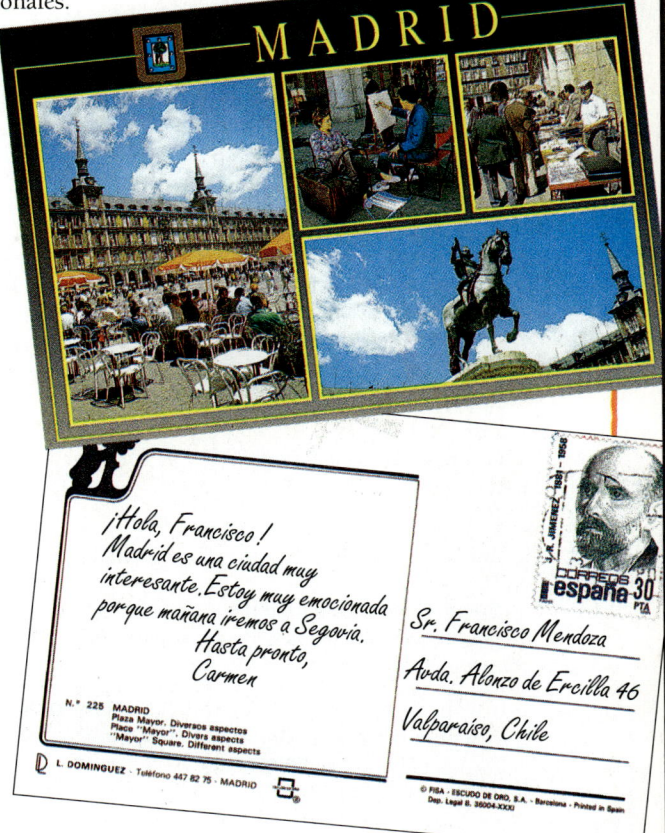

CAPÍTULO 3   63

Ejercicios

PRESENTATION (page 63)

Ejercicio B
Exercise B can be done with books closed or open.

Ejercicio C
Exercise C can be done with books open.

Ejercicio D
Exercise D can be done with books either closed or open.

ANSWERS

Ejercicio B
Answers can be affirmative or negative.
1. Sí, pasaré algunos días en la playa.
2. Nadaré en…
3. Sí, tomaré el sol.
4. Esquiaré en el agua.
5. Sí, comeré pescado y mariscos.
6. Iré a una discoteca con mis amigos.
7. Charlaremos.
8. Bailaremos.
9. Tomaremos un refresco.
10. Nos divertiremos.

Ejercicio C
1. La llamaré por teléfono.
2. Ella estará en casa.
3. Ella contestará.
4. Nosotros hablaremos.
5. Hablaremos de la fiesta que daremos.
6. Ella me dará una lista de las personas que invitaremos.
7. Escribiré las invitaciones.
8. Yo le leeré a Sandra lo que escribiré en las invitaciones.
9. Nuestros amigos recibirán sus invitaciones.
10. Ellos estarán contentos.
11. ¿Recibirás una invitación también?
12. ¿Irás a la fiesta?

Ejercicio D
1. Ayer no. Pero iré al cine mañana.
2. Ayer no. Pero la veré mañana.
3. Ayer no. Pero las compraré mañana.
4. Ayer no. Pero me llamará mañana.
5. Ayer no. Pero la invitaré mañana.
6. Ayer no. Pero irá mañana.

COOPERATIVE LEARNING

Have students work in pairs. One makes a statement in the future, the other asks a question with *ir a*. For example:
E1: *Iré a España.*
E2: *Ah, sí, ¿cuándo vas a ir?*

INDEPENDENT PRACTICE

Assign any of the following:
1. Workbook, *Estructura*
2. Communication Activities Masters, *Estructura*, A
3. Exercises on student pages 62–63
(See suggestions for homework correction in the Teacher's Manual.)

63

Bell Ringer Review

Write the following on the board or use BRR Blackline Master 3-4:
1. ¿Cuál es una pintura que Ud. considera muy bonita?
2. ¿Cuál es su libro favorito?
3. ¿Cuál es una emisión de televisión que Ud. considera muy interesante?
4. ¿Cuál es una cosa que Ud. considera la menos aburrida?

El comparativo y el superlativo
Formas regulares

PRESENTATION (page 64)

A. Have students open their books to page 64. Lead them through steps 1-4 and the examples.
B. Have students make lists of words they know which can be used to describe people.
C. Draw two stick figures on the board and name them. Using their list of adjectives, have students make up sentences comparing the two stick figures.
D. Provide additional examples by comparing objects or students in the room. For example: *Miren. ¿Es Fernando más alto que Alberto? (Sí, es más alto que Alberto.)*
E. Tell students that the superlative is followed by *de* in Spanish. Do not compare it to the "in" in English. When the comparison is made, students tend to get more confused.

El comparativo y el superlativo Comparing People and Things
Formas regulares

1. When we speak or write, we often wish to compare one item or person with another. In order to do so in English, we add *-er* to short adjectives and we use "more" before long adjectives.

   He is nicer than his brother.
   I think he is more intelligent than his brother.

2. This construction is called the comparative. To form the comparative in Spanish, *más* is placed before the adjective or adverb. The word *que* follows.

   Esta carta es más interesante que la otra carta.
   El correo aéreo es (resulta) más caro que el correo ordinario.
   Pero el correo aéreo es más rápido.

3. The superlative is used to express that which is the most. In English *-est* is added to short adjectives and "most" is placed before longer ones.

   He is the nicest person I know.
   I believe she is one of the most intelligent people in the world.

4. In Spanish the superlative is formed by using the appropriate definite article (*el, la, los, las*) plus *más* with the adjective or *el más* with the adverb. The preposition *de* is used with the superlative.

   Este cartero es el (cartero) más simpático de todos (los carteros).
   Esta oficina de correos es la (oficina de correos) más grande de la ciudad.
   Es el correo central.

64 CAPÍTULO 3

LEARNING FROM REALIA	FOR THE NATIVE SPEAKER
Have students identify the three stamps on page 64.	Have students prepare original sentences using the following adjectives: *antipático(a) duro(a), bueno(a), grave, feo(a), hermoso(a), joven, entretenido(a), inteligente, loco(a), exigente, estúpido(a), moderno(a), elegante, fácil, rico(a)*. For example: *Carlos es alto. María es más alta que Carlos. Fernando es el más alto de la clase.*

Ejercicios

A **Más, más y más.** Formen oraciones según el modelo.

rápido   El tren / el bus
El tren es más rápido que el bus.

1. rápido   El tren / el bus
2. rápido   El avión / el tren
3. rápido   El correo aéreo / el correo ordinario
4. caro   El correo aéreo / el correo ordinario
5. alto   Las tarifas aéreas / las tarifas para el bus
6. grande   La Ciudad de México / Nueva York
7. industrial Barcelona / Madrid

El puerto de Barcelona, España

B **Cositas minuciosas.** Contesten según se indica.

1. ¿Cuál es el edificio más alto de los Estados Unidos? (la torre Sears en Chicago)
2. ¿Cuál es el río más largo del mundo? (el Nilo)
3. ¿Cuál es la ciudad más grande del mundo? (México)
4. ¿Cuál es el continente más grande de los siete? (Asia)
5. ¿Cuál es el país más pobre del hemisferio occidental? (Haití)
6. ¿Cuál es el estado más grande de los Estados Unidos? (Alaska)
7. ¿Cuáles son las montañas más altas del mundo? (la cordillera Himalaya)
8. ¿Cuál es el avión comercial más rápido de todos? (el Concorde supersónico)

CAPÍTULO 3   65

DID YOU KNOW?

Barcelona is the largest and most important port in Spain. The port area was extensively remodeled for the summer Olympics of 1992.

INDEPENDENT PRACTICE

Assign any of the following:
1. Workbook, *Estructura*
2. Communication Activities Masters, *Estructura B*
3. Exercises on student page 65
4. Computer Software, *Estructura*

Ejercicios

PRESENTATION (page 65)

Ejercicio A
Have students read the information in their books as they make up the sentences. You may wish to have them prepare this exercise ahead of time before going over it in class.

Ejercicio B
You may wish to have one student read the question. Have another give the cue and then have a third student respond.

ANSWERS

Ejercicio A
1. El tren es más rápido que el bus.
2. El avión es más rápido que el tren.
3. El correo aéreo es más rápido que el correo ordinario.
4. El correo aéreo es más caro que el correo ordinario.
5. Las tarifas aéreas son más altas que las tarifas para el bus.
6. La Ciudad de México es más grande que Nueva York.
7. Barcelona es más industrial que Madrid.

Ejercicio B
1. La torre Sears en Chicago es el edificio más alto de los Estados Unidos.
2. El Nilo es el río más largo del mundo.
3. México es la ciudad más grande del mundo.
4. Asia es el continente más grande de los siete.
5. Haití es el país más pobre del hemisferio occidental.
6. Alaska es el estado más grande de los Estados Unidos.
7. La cordillera Himalaya tiene las montañas más altas del mundo.
8. El Concorde supersónico es el avión comercial más rápido de todos.

65

CONVERSACIÓN

CONVERSACIÓN

Escenas de la vida *En el correo*

ELENA: ¿Cuánto me costará enviar esta tarjeta postal a los Estados Unidos?
EMPLEADA: Por correo aéreo el franqueo es 125 pesetas.
ELENA: ¿Y cuándo llegará la tarjeta?
EMPLEADA: No sé exactamente. Dentro de una semana, probablemente.
ELENA: De acuerdo. Quisiera diez sellos de 125 pesetas, por favor. Estoy segura que escribiré más tarjetas.
EMPLEADA: Aquí tiene Ud. los diez sellos.
ELENA: Gracias. ¿Dónde puedo echar la tarjeta?
EMPLEADA: Al salir del correo, Ud. verá los buzones a mano derecha.
ELENA: Gracias, señora.
EMPLEADA: De nada.

¿Llegará a tiempo? Contesten según la conversación.

1. ¿Dónde está Elena?
2. ¿Qué va a enviar?
3. ¿Cuánto le costará enviar la tarjeta?
4. ¿Llegará mañana la tarjeta?
5. ¿Cuándo llegará?
6. ¿Cuándo recibirán sus amigos la tarjeta?
7. ¿Cuántos sellos quiere Elena?
8. ¿Ella escribirá más tarjetas?
9. ¿Dónde verá los buzones?

66   CAPÍTULO 3

Bell Ringer Review
Write the following on the board or use BRR Blackline Master 3-5: Make a list of all those things you could send in the mail.

PRESENTATION *(page 66)*
A. Have students open their books to page 66 and cover the text with one hand, looking only at the photo. Call on volunteers to tell what they think the conversation is about, based only on what they can see in the photo.
B. Have students listen to the conversation and follow along in their books as you play Cassette 3A.
C. Have the class repeat the conversation after you.
D. Call on two individuals to read the conversation with as much expression as possible.
E. Do the comprehension exercise on this page.

Ejercicio
ANSWERS
1. Elena está en el correo.
2. Ella va a enviar una tarjeta postal.
3. Le costará 125 pesetas.
4. No llegará mañana.
5. La empleada no sabe.
6. Sus amigos recibirán la tarjeta dentro de una semana.
7. Ella quiere diez sellos.
8. Sí, ella escribirá más tarjetas.
9. Ella verá los buzones a mano derecha al salir del correo.

COOPERATIVE LEARNING
Have each team prepare a skit based on a situation in a post office.

Comunicación

A **¿Adónde te puedo escribir?** Ud. está hablando con un amigo que conoció hace poco en la Ciudad de Panamá. Ud. volverá a casa pronto y su nuevo amigo le quiere escribir. Déle la siguiente información.

1. el nombre de su calle o avenida
2. el número de su casa
3. su ciudad o pueblo
4. el código o la zona postal
5. el estado donde Ud. vive

La Ciudad de Panamá, Panamá

B **El verano que viene.** Trabaje con un(a) compañero(a) de clase. Cada uno(a) de Uds. preparará una lista de las cosas que harán el verano que viene. Luego comparen sus listas. Determinen las actividades que harán en común.

C **Año nuevo, vida nueva.** Prepare sus resoluciones para el Año Nuevo. Explique lo que no hace ahora pero que hará el año que viene.

D **En busca de superlativos.** Trabaje con un(a) compañero(a) de clase. Prepare preguntas según el modelo. Su compañero(a) las contestará. Luego cambien de papel.

　　ciudad / bonita / Estados Unidos
　　Estudiante 1: ¿Cuál es la ciudad más bonita de los Estados Unidos?
　　Estudiante 2: En mi opinión, San Antonio es la ciudad más bonita de
　　　　　　　los Estados Unidos.

1. ciudad / bonita / Estados Unidos
2. parque nacional / popular / Estados Unidos
3. deporte / divertido / todos
4. clase / interesante / escuela

CAPÍTULO 3

Comunicación

PRESENTATION (page 67)

These activities allow students to use the chapter vocabulary and grammar in open-ended situations. It is not necessary to do all of them. Select those you consider most appropriate.

ANSWERS

Actividades A–D
　Answers will vary.

LEARNING FROM PHOTOS

Panama City is a very interesting city where great affluence and great poverty live side by side. Because of the Panama Canal, there has always been a strong U.S. influence in Panama. The national currency is the dollar, (called Balboa). Just alongside Panama City is the area in which the *zoneños* have always lived very much in North American style. The relationship between the *panameños* and the *zoneños* has not always been good.

Panama now has sovereign rights to the Canal. All vessels have the right of passage between the Atlantic and the Pacific.

LECTURA Y CULTURA

Bell Ringer Review

Write the following on the board or use BRR Blackline Master 3-6: Write the following information.
1. el nombre de la calle donde vives
2. el número de la casa
3. el nombre de tu pueblo o ciudad
4. tu zona (código) postal

READING STRATEGIES
(page 68)

Pre-Reading

This reading selection differs from others in *A bordo*. It teaches how to address an envelope as well as how to write standard salutations and closings for letters in Spanish.

Reading
A. Have the class follow along as you read the selection aloud, or call on a volunteer with good pronunciation to read it.
B. As each piece of information is given, write an example of it on the board. For example:
el nombre del destinatario:
Mario Benavides
la calle y el número de la casa:
Avenida San Juan 33.

Post-reading

After completing the reading, have students tell what salutations and closings they would use for letters to the following people: *tu mejor amigo(a), tu profesor(a) de español, el director o la directora del colegio, tu tía.*

LECTURA Y CULTURA

ESCRIBIREMOS UNA CARTA

EL SOBRE

—¿Escribiremos una carta en español?
—Sí, mañana en clase. En el sobre indicaremos:

el nombre y la dirección del remitente o de la remitente—Es Ud.

el nombre y la dirección del destinatario o de la destinataria—Es la persona a quien Ud. escribirá y enviará la carta.

Para escribir bien la dirección incluiremos:

el nombre del destinatario
la calle y el número de la casa
el nombre de la ciudad o del pueblo
la zona postal
el nombre del país (Sólo si enviamos la carta de un país, a otro.)

LA CARTA MISMA

Hay dos tipos de cartas. Hay cartas comerciales y hay cartas personales. Una carta comercial emplea fórmulas más formales que una carta personal. Sin embargo, en la parte superior de la hoja escribiremos el lugar y la fecha en una carta comercial y también en una carta personal.

Madrid, 25 de mayo de 19xx

Empezaremos una carta comercial con:

Muy señor mío   Muy distinguido señor
Muy señora mía   Muy distinguida señora

La primera frase será: Acuso recibo de su atenta del 5 del actual.

Su atenta se refiere a la carta y el actual se refiere a este mes.

Terminaremos una carta comercial con: Queda suyo afmo. o S.S.S. (Su seguro servidor).

Empezaremos una carta personal con varias expresiones o fórmulas de saludo. El encabezamiento que usamos dependerá del grado de confianza o intimidad entre nosotros y el/la destinatario(a). Algunas fórmulas son:

Querido amigo   Querida amiga
Querido José   Mi querido José
Querida Teresa   Mi querida Teresa

Y terminaremos la carta con:

Recibe un afectuoso saludo
Con afecto   Un fuerte abrazo

68 CAPÍTULO 3

COOPERATIVE LEARNING

Each team member writes letter salutations or closings on cards (or slips of paper), one item per card. Each member should complete about three such cards. Teams of four mix their cards together in a pile. They take turns drawing one card at a time and saying whether the card item is for a personal or more formal letter. For example: Team member draws *Muy distinguido señor* and says: *Es para una carta a alguien que no conozco muy bien.*

Estudio de palabras

A ¿Qué significa esto? Aquí ven abreviaturas que encontrarán frecuentemente en correspondencia. Pareen.

1. Avda.
2. C/
3. Dpto.
4. Apto.
5. Prov.
6. Sr.
7. Sra.
8. Srta.
9. D.
10. Da.
11. Suyo afmo.
12. S.S.S
13. S.A.

a. Señor
b. Sociedad Anónima (Corporación)
c. Señora
d. Suyo afectísimo
e. Doña
f. Avenida
g. Don
h. Su seguro servidor
i. Departamento
j. Provincia
k. Apartamento
l. Señorita
m. Calle

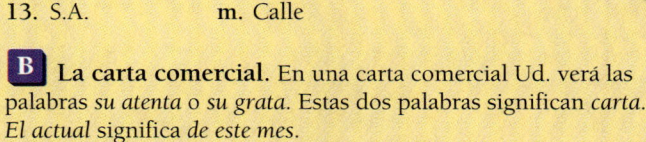

B La carta comercial. En una carta comercial Ud. verá las palabras *su atenta* o *su grata*. Estas dos palabras significan *carta*. *El actual* significa *de este mes*.

Escriba en español: I acknowledge receipt of your letter of the fifteenth of this month.

Comprensión

Una carta. Escriban lo siguiente:

1. la dirección en un sobre como la escriben en muchos países hispanos
2. una fórmula de saludo para un(a) amigo(a)
3. el encabezamiento de una carta comercial
4. una fórmula de conclusión para una carta personal
5. una fórmula de conclusión para una carta comercial

CAPÍTULO 3   69

Estudio de palabras
PRESENTATION (page 69)
Go over the exercises quickly in class with books open.

ANSWERS
Ejercicio A
1. f   8. l
2. m   9. g
3. i   10. e
4. k   11. d
5. j   12. h
6. a   13. b
7. c

Ejercicio B
Acuso recibo de su atenta (grata) del 15 del actual.

Comprensión
PRESENTATION (page 69)
You may have students write the information asked for in this exercise at home first and then share it with the class the following day.

ANSWERS
Answers will vary.
1. Srta. Rosalinda Sánchez, c/ Velázquez, 12, 28009 Madrid, España
2. Querido _____
3. Muy señor mío
4. Recibe un afectuoso saludo
5. Quedo suyo afmo.

RECYCLING
Ask students to look at the postcard on page 63 and tell where Carmen is visiting. Have students write and tell as much as they can about Madrid.

GEOGRAPHY CONNECTION
Have students find *Santiago de Compostela* on the map of Spain on page 452. Tell them that over the centuries, *Santiago de Compostela* has been a famous pilgrimage destination (*peregrinaje*). Some students may want to find out why.

FOR THE NATIVE SPEAKER

Have students write a friendly letter. Remind them that it should contain six parts: *lugar, fecha, saludo, cuerpo de la carta, cierre y firma.* Give them these instructions: *Eres un famoso explorador. Estás en el Amazonas. Le escribes una carta a doña Josefa Garza Restrepo, presidenta del Club de Exploradores. Dile cuándo comenzaste la expedición, quiénes te acompañan,* cuál es el propósito de la expedición, cómo son los habitantes, una cosa interesante (peligrosa) que pasó, cuándo regresarás.

69

Descubrimiento Cultural

(The Descubrimiento section is optional.)

PRESENTATION *(pages 70-71)*

A. You may have students read the selection, or parts of it, aloud in class. Ask questions about content.

B. As an alternative, have students read the entire selection silently. Call on a volunteer or volunteers to summarize in their own words.

ABOUT THE LANGUAGE

Have students look at the photo of the computerized mail distribution system on page 71. Explain that the word "computer" in Latin America is *la computadora*. In Spain, however, it is *el ordenador*. Explain to students that they will hear both *el* and *la* used for machines. Some examples are: *el lavador/la lavadora*; *el copiador/la copiadora*. The reason for this is that some think in terms of *el aparato* (*el aparato lavador*) and others think in terms of *la máquina* (*la máquina lavadora*).

DESCUBRIMIENTO CULTURAL

Un cartero en México, D.F.

En los Estados Unidos es necesario incluir en la dirección el estado en que vive (reside) el destinatario de la carta. En la mayoría de los países hispanos, no es necesario indicar la región o la provincia.

En España y en varios países latinoamericanos el correo tiene bajo su responsabilidad los telégrafos y los teléfonos. A este servicio gubernamental se refiere con el nombre de "Correos y Telecomunicaciones".

70 CAPÍTULO 3

CRITICAL THINKING ACTIVITY

(Thinking skills: making inferences; drawing conclusions)

Read the following to the class or write it on the board or on a transparency.

1. *Generalmente, la gente de los países industriales escribe menos y menos cartas. ¿Por qué? Dé Ud. varias razones.*
2. *¿Es fácil vivir cuando uno no puede depender del correo? Explique.*

LEARNING FROM PHOTOS

Refer students to the photos on student page 70 and ask: *Este cartero mexicano, ¿lleva uniforme o no? ¿Cómo reparte el correo? ¿Dónde lo pone? Esta señora, ¿está en casa o en una oficina? ¿Está haciendo una copia de un documento? ¿Está usando la copiadora?*

En algunos países el departmento o ministerio de Correos y Telecomunicaciones ofrece toda una gama de servicios financieros. El servicio de giros postales[1], por ejemplo, es muy popular en algunos países. Mucha gente paga sus facturas[2] con giros postales.

En algunos países de Latinoamérica, la gente no tiene mucha confianza en el correo. La verdad es que mucha correspondencia se desvía[3] y no llega al destinatario. Por consiguiente, muchas personas se presentan personalmente a la oficina de una compañía para pagar sus facturas. No envían sus pagos por el correo. El uso del fax (facsímil) para mandar mensajes o recados se está poniendo muy popular.

[1] giros postales   *money orders*
[2] facturas   *bills*
[3] se desvía   *gets lost, goes astray*

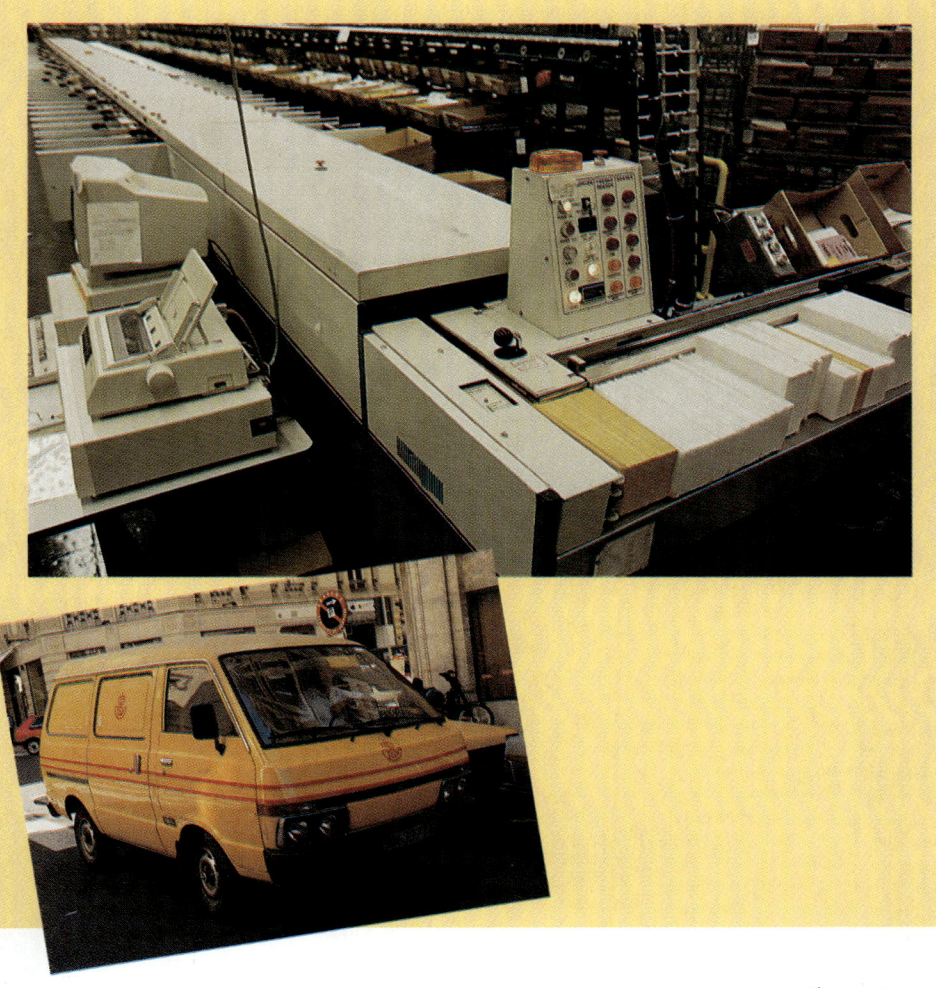

CAPÍTULO 3

DID YOU KNOW?

At a post office in Madrid the *buzón* will have three slots labeled *Madrid*, *Provincias*, and *Extranjero*. How many slots does your post office have for mail?

REALIDADES

(The Realidades section is optional.)

Bell Ringer Review
Write the following on the board or use BRR Blackline Master 3-7: Write four expressions associated with the future.

PRESENTATION *(pages 72-73)*
The purpose of this section is to allow students to enjoy the photographs that bring to life the content of the chapter. You may have students read the captions aloud or silently.

PAIRED ACTIVITY
Have pairs work together to create questions about the photographs. Then combine pairs into groups of four to exchange questions and answers.

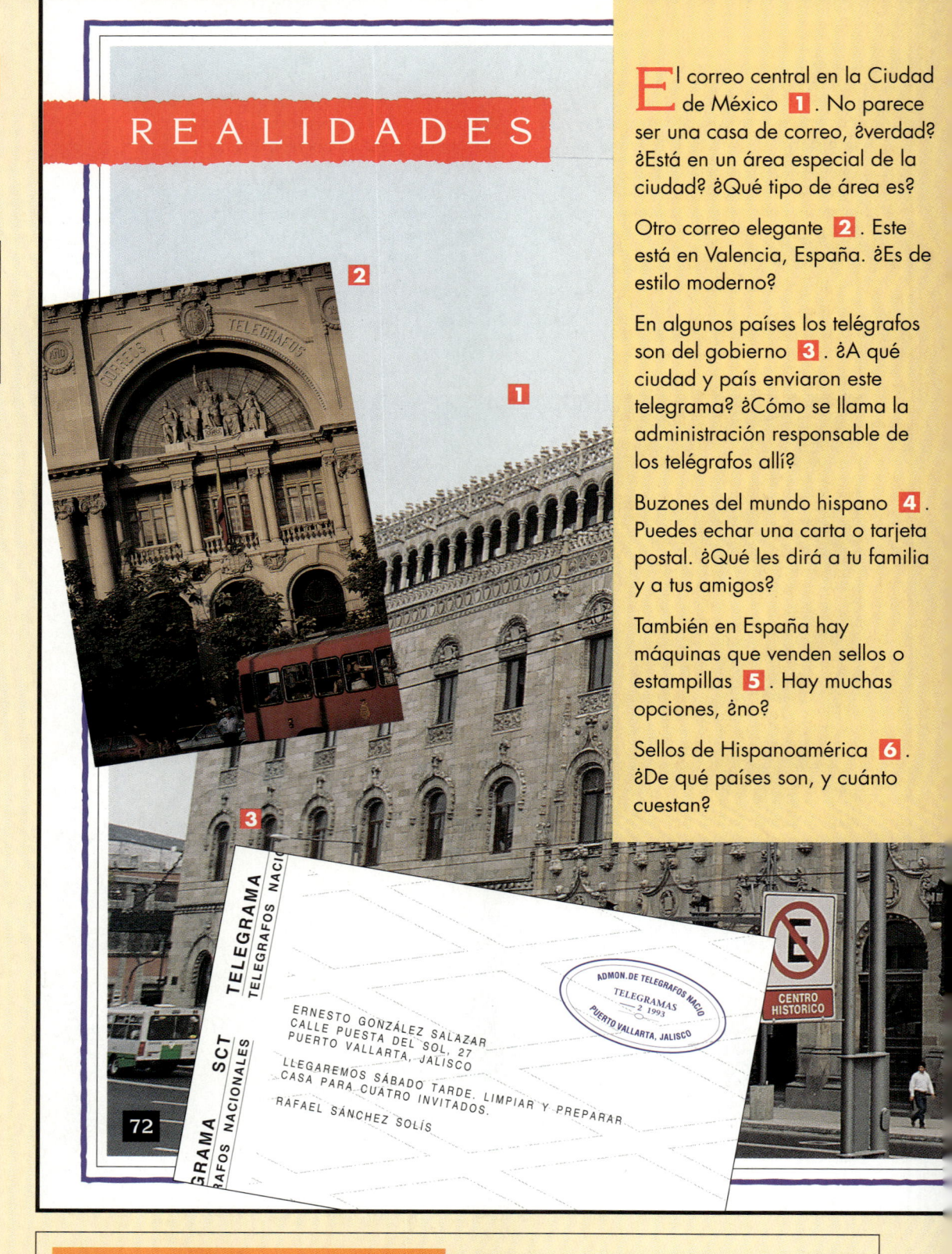

REALIDADES

El correo central en la Ciudad de México **1**. No parece ser una casa de correo, ¿verdad? ¿Está en un área especial de la ciudad? ¿Qué tipo de área es?

Otro correo elegante **2**. Este está en Valencia, España. ¿Es de estilo moderno?

En algunos países los telégrafos son del gobierno **3**. ¿A qué ciudad y país enviaron este telegrama? ¿Cómo se llama la administración responsable de los telégrafos allí?

Buzones del mundo hispano **4**. Puedes echar una carta o tarjeta postal. ¿Qué les dirá a tu familia y a tus amigos?

También en España hay máquinas que venden sellos o estampillas **5**. Hay muchas opciones, ¿no?

Sellos de Hispanoamérica **6**. ¿De qué países son, y cuánto cuestan?

LEARNING FROM REALIA
Refer students to the telegram at the bottom of page 72. Ask who they think the telegram is for. *(la persona que cuida la casa)*

FOR THE NATIVE SPEAKER

Ask students to respond in writing to the following. *El Servicio Postal de los EE.UU. denunció a unas compañías por haber usado un servicio privado como Federal Express para la entrega de correo que no era sumamente urgente. ¿Por qué crees que llevaron a las compañías a la corte? ¿Crees que es justo o no? Defiende tu opinión.*

CULMINACIÓN

Comunicación oral

A **¿Qué sabes del correo?** Ud. está hablando con un amigo o una amiga en Quito, Ecuador. Él o ella quiere saber algo sobre el sistema de correos en los Estados Unidos. Quiere saber si el correo tiene responsabilidad también por las telecomunicaciones. Dígale lo que Ud. sabe del sistema de correos en nuestro país.

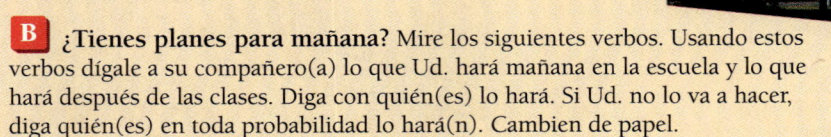

B **¿Tienes planes para mañana?** Mire los siguientes verbos. Usando estos verbos dígale a su compañero(a) lo que Ud. hará mañana en la escuela y lo que hará después de las clases. Diga con quién(es) lo hará. Si Ud. no lo va a hacer, diga quién(es) en toda probabilidad lo hará(n). Cambien de papel.

Quito, E

estudiar
tomar un examen
recibir una nota buena
recibir una nota mala
leer una novela
escribir una composición o una carta
resolver algunos problemas
ir al correo
jugar
hablar

ir a un café
pedir algo
trabajar
tomar un refresco
charlar
volver a casa
comer
mirar la televisión
ver una película
llamar por teléfono

Comunicación escrita

A **Las direcciones.** Prepare los sobres para cartas que Ud. quiere escribir a las siguientes personas.

1. La señora (Sra.) Doña (Da) Clara Álvarez de Toral. Ella vive en el número cuatro de la Costanilla de San Andrés en Madrid, España. La zona postal es la 13.
2. La Srta. Marisol Príncipe. Ella vive en el Condominio Los Flamboyanes en la Avenida Hostos en Ponce, Puerto Rico. El código postal es el 00731.
3. El Sr. D. Rafael Pérez Sanromán. Él vive en el número 426 de Entre Ríos en Buenos Aires.

B **La carta.** Escríbale una carta a un(a) "pen pal" en España. No olvide el encabezamiento, el saludo y la despedida.

C **Una invitación.** Ud. dará una fiesta. Escriba la invitación que les enviará a sus amigos.

74 CAPÍTULO 3

Reintegración

A **En la escuela.** Completen con el presente.

1. Yo ___ mucho en la escuela. (aprender)
2. Nosotros ___ todo lo que nos ___ nuestros profesores. (comprender, decir)
3. En la clase de inglés nosotros ___ que escribir muchas composiciones. (tener)
4. Nosotros ___ con bolígrafo. (escribir)
5. Yo ___ muchos apuntes. (tomar)
6. Yo los ___ en mi bloc. (escribir)
7. En la clase de inglés nosotros ___ mucho. (leer)
8. Yo ___ muchas poesías, y mi amigo ___ muchas novelas. (leer, leer)

B **Mi familia.** Preguntas personales.

1. ¿Tienes una familia grande o pequeña?
2. ¿Cuántos hermanos tienes?
3. ¿Tienen Uds. una casa o un apartamento?
4. ¿Cuántos cuartos tiene tu casa o apartamento?
5. ¿Sales mucho con tus amigos?
6. ¿Adónde van Uds.?
7. De vez en cuando, ¿haces un viaje con tu familia?
8. ¿Adónde vas?

Vocabulario

SUSTANTIVOS
la correspondencia
el correo
la oficina de correos
el empleado de correos
la ventanilla
el buzón
el apartado postal
la casilla
el sello
la estampilla
la tarjeta postal
el aerograma

la carta
el sobre
la dirección
el número
la calle
la zona postal
el código postal
el/la remitente
el/la destinatario(a)
el/la cartero
la entrega
el reparto

VERBOS
corresponder
pesar
asegurar
enviar
echar
repartir

OTRAS PALABRAS Y EXPRESIONES
por correo aéreo
por correo ordinario
por correo certificado
por correo recomendado

CAPÍTULO 3   75

Reintegración

PRESENTATION (*page 75*)

A. These exercises review and recombine material learned earlier with vocabulary and structures from this chapter.
B. Exercises A and B review the present tense of regular verbs.
C. After doing Exercises A and B, you may call on one student to go through the entire exercise. Then have another volunteer summarize the story in his/her own words.

ANSWERS

Ejercicio A
1. Yo aprendo mucho en la escuela.
2. Nosotros comprendemos todo lo que nos dicen nuestros profesores.
3. En la clase de inglés nosotros tenemos que escribir muchas composiciones.
4. Nosotros escribimos con bolígrafo.
5. Yo tomo muchos apuntes.
6. Yo los escribo en mi bloc.
7. En la clase de inglés nosotros leemos mucho.
8. Yo leo muchas poesías, y mi amigo lee muchas novelas.

Ejercicio B
Answers will vary.

Vocabulario

There are approximately 10 cognates in this list.

VIDEO

The video is intended to reinforce the vocabulary, structures, and cultural content in each chapter. It may be used here as a chapter wrap-up activity. See the *Video Activities Booklet* for additional suggestions on its use.

INTRODUCCIÓN (0:10:32)

UNA CARTA (0:12:01)

EL CORREO (0:13:36)

STUDENT PORTFOLIO

Have students keep a Spanish notebook with their best written work from *A bordo* in it. These writings can be based on assignments from the Student Textbook, the Workbook, and Communication Activities Masters. In the Workbook, students will develop an organized autobiography (*Mi autobiografía*) which may also become a part of their portfolio.

INDEPENDENT PRACTICE

1. Exercises on student pages 74-75
2. Workbook, *Mi autobiografía*
3. Chapter 3, Situation Cards

75

CAPÍTULO 4
Repaso Capítulos 1-4 • Scope and Sequence pages 76-111

Topics	Functions	Structure	Culture
Accidents Minor injuries Emergency hospital care	How to talk about common accidents and medical procedures How to report an emergency How to talk about future events How to make comparisons	El futuro de los verbos irregulares El futuro de otros verbos irregulares El comparativo y el superlativo: formas irregulares	Health services in Spanish-speaking countries Hospital de Jesús in Mexico Ambulance team in Madrid Nuestro Mundo: Telecom
Fondo Académico pages 106-111			Las ciencias naturales La sociología La historia

CAPÍTULO 4

Situation Cards

The Situation Cards simulate real-life situations that require students to communicate in Spanish, exactly as though they were in a Spanish-speaking country. The Situation Cards operate on the assumption that the person to whom the message is to be conveyed understands no English. Therefore, students must focus on producing the Spanish vocabulary and structures necessary to negotiate the situations successfully. For additional information, see the Introduction to the Situation Cards in the Situation Cards Envelope.

Communication Transparency

The illustration seen in this Communication Transparency consists of a synthesis of the two vocabulary (Palabras 1&2) presentations found in this chapter. It has been created in order to present this chapter's vocabulary in a new context, and also to recycle vocabulary learned in previous chapters. The Communication Transparency consists of original art. Following are some specific uses:

1. as a cue to stimulate conversation and writing activities
2. for listening comprehension activities
3. to review and reteach vocabulary
4. as a review for chapter and unit tests

CAPÍTULO 4
Print Resources

	Pages
Lesson Plans	
Workbook	
◆ Palabras 1	31-32
◆ Palabras 2	32-33
◆ Estructura	34-36
◆ Un poco más	37-39
◆ Mi autobiografía	40
◆ Self-Test	41-46

Communication Activities Masters
- ◆ Palabras 1 — 18-19
- ◆ Palabras 2 — 20-21
- ◆ Estructura — 22-24

7 Bell Ringer Reviews — 13-15

Chapter Situation Cards A B C D

Chapter Quizzes
- ◆ Palabras 1 — 16
- ◆ Palabras 2 — 17
- ◆ Estructura — 18-20

Testing Program
- ◆ Listening Comprehension — 15
- ◆ Reading and Writing — 16-19
- ◆ Proficiency — 126
- ◆ Speaking — 144

Unit Test: Chapters 1-4
- ◆ Listening Comprehension — 20
- ◆ Reading and Writing — 21-24
- ◆ Speaking — 145
- ◆ Performance Assessment

Nosotros y Nuestro Mundo
- ◆ Nuestro Conocimiento Académico: *La medicina: Cómo prevenir las enfermedades infecciosas*
- ◆ Nuestro Idioma *El futuro de los verbos; Comparativos y superlativos irregulares*
- ◆ Nuestra Cultura *Entrevista con una curandera*
- ◆ Nuestra Literatura *"Casimiro Mendoza"* de Rowena Rivera
- ◆ Nuestra Creatividad
- ◆ Nuestras Diversiones

CAPÍTULO 4
Multimedia Resources

CD-ROM Interactive Textbook Disc 1

Chapter 4 Student Edition
- ◆ Palabras 1
- ◆ Palabras 2
- ◆ Estructura
- ◆ Conversación
- ◆ Lectura y cultura
- ◆ Hispanoparlantes
- ◆ Realidades
- ◆ Culminación
- ◆ Prueba

Review: Chapters 1-4
- ◆ Nuestro Mundo
- ◆ Repaso
- ◆ Fondo Académico
- ◆ Game: El Gran Concurso

Audio Cassette Program with Student Tape Manual

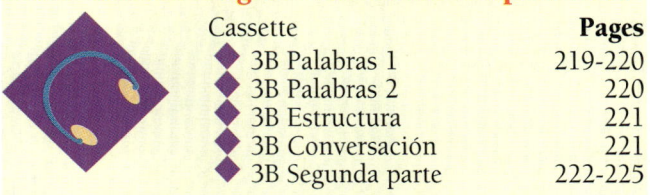

Cassette	Pages
◆ 3B Palabras 1	219-220
◆ 3B Palabras 2	220
◆ 3B Estructura	221
◆ 3B Conversación	221
◆ 3B Segunda parte	222-225

Compact Disc Program with Student Tape Manual

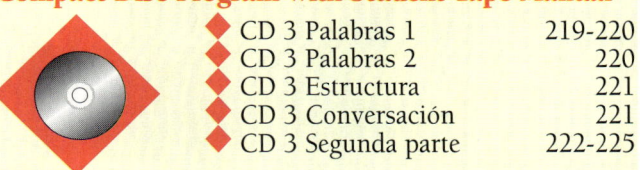

- ◆ CD 3 Palabras 1 — 219-220
- ◆ CD 3 Palabras 2 — 220
- ◆ CD 3 Estructura — 221
- ◆ CD 3 Conversación — 221
- ◆ CD 3 Segunda parte — 222-225

Overhead Transparencies Binder
- ◆ Vocabulary 4.1 (A&B); 4.2 (A&B)
- ◆ Communication C-4
- ◆ Maps
- ◆ Fine Art (with Blackline Master Activities)

Video Program
- ◆ Videocassette
- ◆ Video Activities Booklet — 10-11
- ◆ Videodisc
- ◆ Video Activities Booklet — 10-11

Computer Software (Macintosh, IBM, Apple)
- ◆ Practice Disk
  - Palabras 1 y 2
  - Estructura
- ◆ Test Generator Disk
  - Chapter Test
  - Customized Test

CAPÍTULO 4

CHAPTER OVERVIEW

In this chapter students will learn to describe and report certain accidents and minor injuries and to talk about emergency hospital treatment. They will learn to talk about these and other matters in the future tense. They will expand their knowledge of comparative and superlative constructions in order to make observations and express opinions about people and things. The cultural focus of Chapter 4 is on health services in various Spanish-speaking countries.

CHAPTER OBJECTIVES

By the end of this chapter, students will know:
1. vocabulary associated with minor accidents, injuries, and visits to the doctor
2. vocabulary associated with more serious accidents, illnesses, and emergency hospital care
3. the future tense of irregular verbs
4. the irregular comparatives and superlatives *mejor*, *peor*, *mayor*, and *menor*

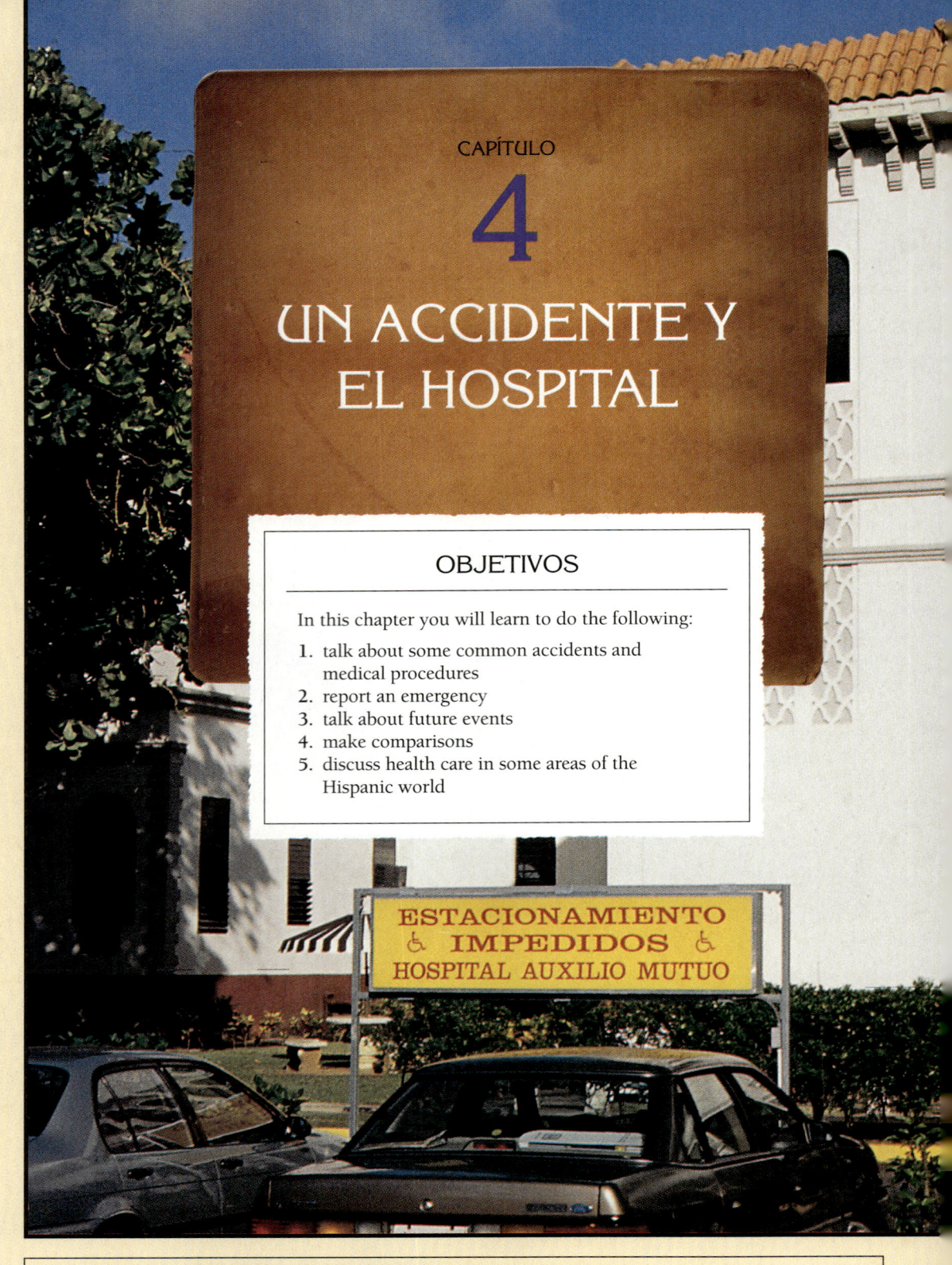

CAPÍTULO 4

UN ACCIDENTE Y EL HOSPITAL

OBJETIVOS

In this chapter you will learn to do the following:

1. talk about some common accidents and medical procedures
2. report an emergency
3. talk about future events
4. make comparisons
5. discuss health care in some areas of the Hispanic world

CHAPTER PROJECTS

(optional)
1. Have students select one of the health problems or injuries they will learn about in this chapter and write a paragraph about it.
2. In *Bienvenidos* some students read about the contributions of Hispanics to the world of medicine. Have those students interested in medicine do a report on one of the following: Miguel Servet, Carlos Juan Finlay y Barres, or Santiago Ramón y Cajal.

CHAPTER 4 RESOURCES

1. Workbook
2. Student Tape Manual
3. Audio Cassette 3B
4. Vocabulary Transparencies
5. Bell Ringer Review Blackline Masters
6. Communication Activities Masters
7. Computer Software: Practice and Test Generator
8. Video Cassette, Chapter 4
9. Video Activities Booklet, Chapter 4
10. Situation Cards
11. Chapter Quizzes
12. Testing Program

Pacing

Chapter 4 will require eight to ten class sessions. Pacing will depend on the length of the class period, the age of the students, and student aptitude. (See the Teacher's Manual for additional suggestions on pacing.)

LEARNING FROM PHOTOS

Refer students to the photo on pages 76-77 and ask: ¿Cómo se llama el hospital? ¿Quiénes pueden estacionar aquí? ¿Qué opina Ud.? ¿Tiene este hospital una afiliación religiosa? ¿Cómo lo sabe? ¿Es bonito el hospital? ¿En qué país cree Ud. que está? (Puerto Rico)

77

VOCABULARIO
PALABRAS 1

Vocabulary Teaching Resources

1. Vocabulary Transparencies, 4.1 (A & B)
2. Audio Cassette 3B
3. Student Tape Manual, *Palabras 1*
4. Workbook, *Palabras 1*
5. Communication Activities Masters, *Palabras 1, A & B*
6. Chapter Quizzes, *Palabras 1*

Bell Ringer Review

Write the following on the board or use BRR Blackline Master 4-1: Write as many words and expressions as you remember related to health or health care.

PRESENTATION (pages 78-79)

A. In addition to Vocabulary Transparencies 4.1 (A & B), you may use gestures or dramatizations to introduce many of these terms. Those which lend themselves to easy dramatization are: *caerse, resbalarse, hacerse daño (lastimarse), torcerse el tobillo,* and *cortarse el dedo.*

B. Refer to yourself or a student model to demonstrate *el hombro, el brazo, el codo, el dedo, la pierna, el tobillo, la muñeca, la rodilla, la frente, la cara, la mejilla,* and *el labio.*

C. Have students repeat the vocabulary after you or Cassette 3B.

D. Call on volunteers to read the sentences from *Palabras 1* with as much natural expression as possible.

E. Refer to the Vocabulary Transparencies and ask questions to elicit the vocabulary. For example: *¿Es la rodilla o la pierna? ¿A Manolo se le rompió el brazo? ¿Tiene una fractura? ¿Tendrá que ir al hospital?*

VOCABULARIO

PALABRAS 1

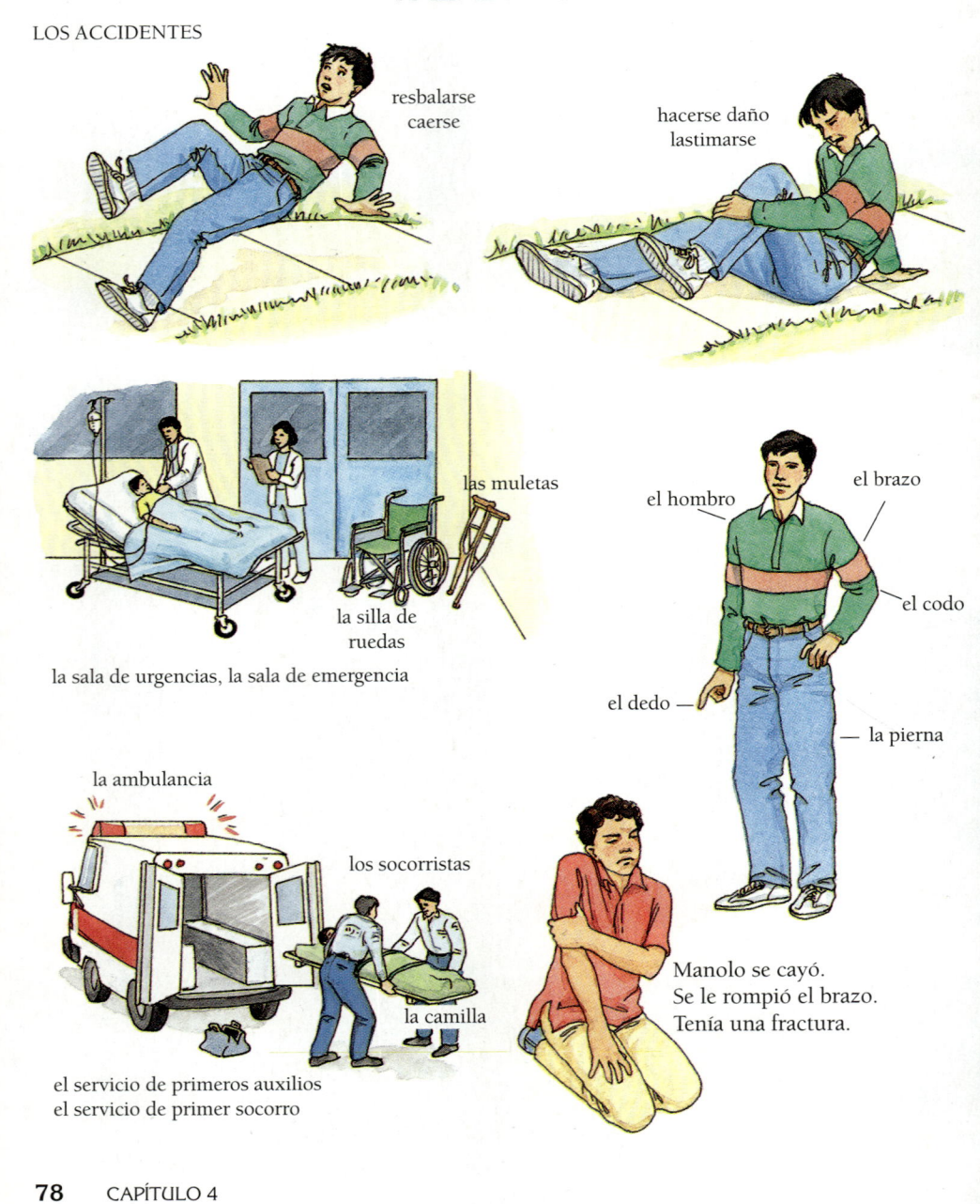

LOS ACCIDENTES

resbalarse
caerse

hacerse daño
lastimarse

las muletas

la silla de ruedas

la sala de urgencias, la sala de emergencia

el hombro
el brazo
el codo
el dedo
la pierna

la ambulancia

los socorristas

la camilla

el servicio de primeros auxilios
el servicio de primer socorro

Manolo se cayó.
Se le rompió el brazo.
Tenía una fractura.

78   CAPÍTULO 4

PANTOMIME 1

_____, levántese.
Venga Ud. aquí, por favor.
Muéstreme el brazo.
Muéstreme el dedo.
Muéstreme el hombro.
Muéstreme el tobillo.
Muéstreme la rodilla.
Muéstreme la muñeca.
Gracias, _____. Siéntese

PANTOMIME 2

_____, levántese.
Venga Ud. acá, por favor.
Vaya Ud. al teléfono.
Descuelgue.
Marque el número.
Hable. Diga lo que pasó.
Gracias, _____. Siéntese.

Elena se resbaló.
Se le torció el tobillo.
Le duele mucho.

la muñeca
la rodilla
el tobillo hinchado

Teresa se lastimó.
Se cortó el dedo.
Tenía una cicatriz.

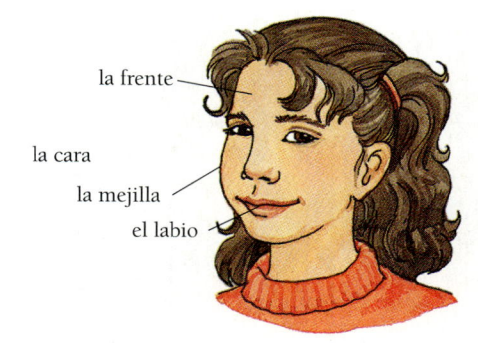

la frente
la cara
la mejilla
el labio

Joselito tuvo un accidente.
Tendrá que ir al hospital.
La ambulancia vendrá.
Lo pondrán en una camilla.

Nota: With expressions such as "to break" or "to sprain," the pronoun *se* is often used along with another pronoun. Rather than try to analyze this construction, just memorize the following expressions.

Se me rompió el brazo.	¿Se te rompió la pierna?	A José se le rompió el dedo.
Se me torció la muñeca.	¿Se te torció el tobillo?	A José se le torció la rodilla.

CAPÍTULO 4 79

PANTOMIME 3

Y ahora _____, venga Ud. aquí, por favor.
Indique lo que le pasó.
Se le rompió el brazo.
Se le torció el tobillo.
Se resbaló.
Se hizo daño.
Gracias, _____.

Note You may interrupt the pantomime to direct additional questions to the class, referring to the student who is miming. For example: *¿Qué le pasó? ¿Qué le duele? ¿Dónde le duele? Muéstreme.*

INFORMAL ASSESSMENT
Call on volunteers to draw human figures on the board. Ask other students to supply labels of as many parts of the body as they

25 cards

Ejercicios

PRESENTATION (page 80)

Ejercicio A

Exercise A can be done with books open as students refer to the illustrations.

Ejercicio B

Exercise B can be done with books open or closed.

Extension of *Ejercicio B*: Speaking

After completing Exercise B, call on a student to retell the story in his/her own words.

ANSWERS

Ejercicio A
1. Es una silla de ruedas.
2. Es la sala de urgencias.
3. Son los socorristas.
4. Son muletas.
5. Se resbaló el joven.
6. Se cayó la joven.

Ejercicio B
1. Sí, José tuvo un accidente.
2. Sí, se cayó.
3. Sí, se lastimó.
4. Sí, tendrá que ir al hospital.
5. Sí, será necesario llamar a los socorristas.
6. Sí, vendrá la ambulancia.
7. Sí, vendrán los socorristas.
8. Sí, examinarán a José.
9. Sí, lo pondrán en una camilla.
10. Sí, lo llevarán al hospital en la ambulancia.

Ejercicios

A ¿Qué es? Identifiquen.

1. ¿Es una silla de ruedas o una camilla?
2. ¿Es la sala de urgencias o el servicio de primeros auxilios? 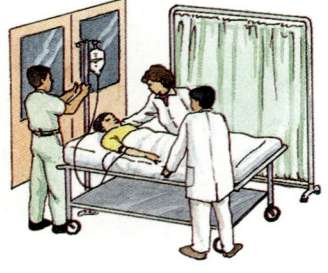
3. ¿Son los médicos o los socorristas? 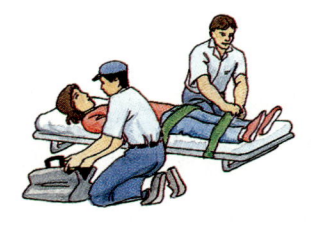
4. ¿Son muletas o camillas? 
5. ¿Se resbaló el joven o se cayó? 
6. ¿Se resbaló la joven o se cayó? 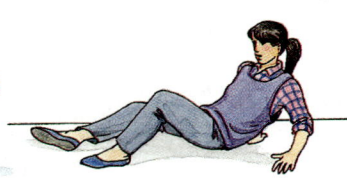

B El accidente de José. Contesten.

1. ¿Tuvo José un accidente?
2. ¿Se cayó?
3. ¿Se lastimó?
4. ¿Tendrá que ir al hospital?
5. ¿Será necesario llamar a los socorristas?
6. ¿Vendrá la ambulancia?
7. ¿Vendrán los socorristas?
8. ¿Examinarán a José?
9. ¿Lo pondrán en una camilla?
10. ¿Lo llevarán al hospital en la ambulancia?

INDEPENDENT PRACTICE

Assign any of the following:
1. Workbook, *Palabras 1*
2. Communication Activities Masters, *Palabras 1*, A & B
3. Exercises on student pages 80-81

C Una serie de accidentes. Describan el dibujo.

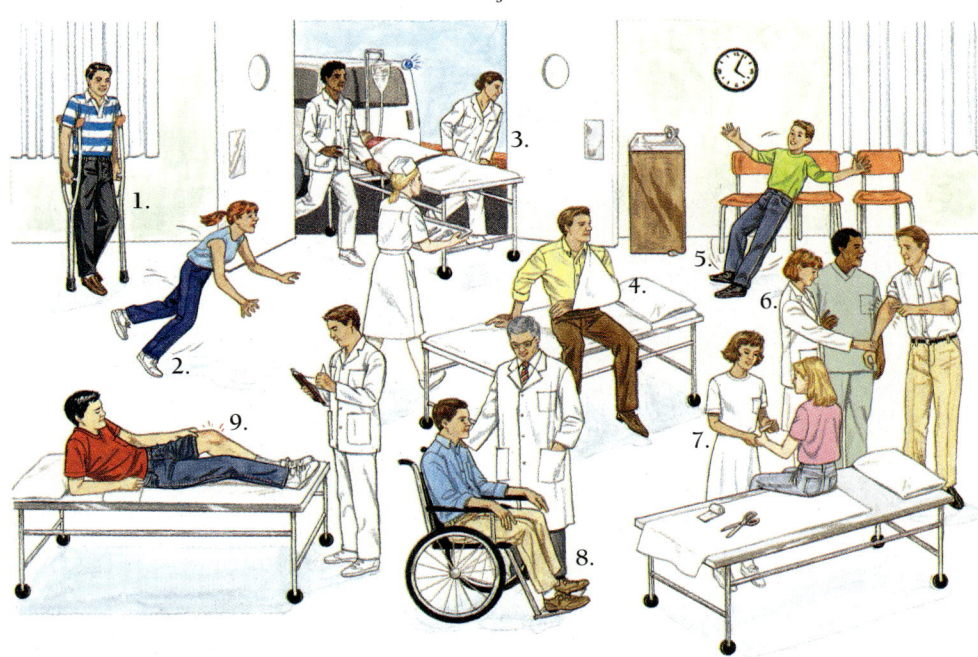

D ¿Cuál es otra palabra? Pareen.
1. Se lastimó.
2. Le duele.
3. el servicio de primeros auxilios
4. la sala de urgencias

a. la sala de emergencia
b. el servicio de primer socorro
c. Le hace mal.
d. Se hizo daño.

CAPÍTULO 4   81

Ejercicios

PRESENTATION (page 81)

Ejercicios C and D
Exercises C and D should be done with books open.

Extension of Ejercicio C
After completing Exercise C, call on a student to retell the story in his/her own words. You may want to ask additional questions to elicit the number of patients, doctors, hospital equipment, time of day, etc., shown in the illustration on page 81.

Ejercicio C
1. Alguien tiene el tobillo vendado y camina con muletas.
2. Alguien se cae.
3. Los socorristas llevan (en camilla) a alguien que tuvo un accidente.
4. Alguien se rompió el brazo.
5. Alguien se resbala.
6. Alguien tiene el codo hinchado.
7. La enfermera pone una venda en un dedo cortado.
8. Alguien está en una silla de ruedas.
9. Se le torció la rodilla.

Ejercicio D
1. d
2. c
3. b
4. a

INFORMAL ASSESSMENT
(Palabras 1)
Check for understanding by referring to the Vocabulary Transparencies and having students say as much as they can about the illustrations.

LEARNING FROM PHOTOS

Refer students to the photo at the bottom of page 81 and ask: ¿Qué estaba jugando el muchacho? ¿Se lastimó? ¿Dónde? ¿Le duele? ¿Cómo lo sabe Ud.? ¿Quién le está dando ayuda? ¿Es el árbitro o el entrenador?

81

VOCABULARIO
PALABRAS 2

Vocabulary Teaching Resources
1. Vocabulary Transparencies 4.2 (*A & B*)
2. Audio Cassette 3B
3. Student Tape Manual, *Palabras 2*
4. Workbook, *Palabras 2*
5. Communication Activities Masters, *Palabras 2, C & D*
6. Chapter Quizzes, *Palabras 2*
7. Computer Software, *Vocabulario*

Bell Ringer Review
Write the following on the board or use BRR Blackline Master 4-2: Choose the correct completion.
1. José abre la boca porque el médico le examina ___.
   a. la cabeza
   b. la cara
   c. la garganta
2. ___ le toma la tensión arterial.
   a. El farmacéutico
   b. La enfermera
   c. La farmacéutica
3. La farmacéutica despacha ___.
   a. medicamentos
   b. recetas
   c. alergias
4. Los medicamentos vienen en forma de ___.
   a. comprimidos
   b. ejercicios
   c. carbohidratos
5. El médico examina a la mayor parte (el número más grande) de sus pacientes en ___.
   a. la sala de urgencias
   b. la farmacia
   c. su consultorio

VOCABULARIO

PALABRAS 2

EN EL HOSPITAL

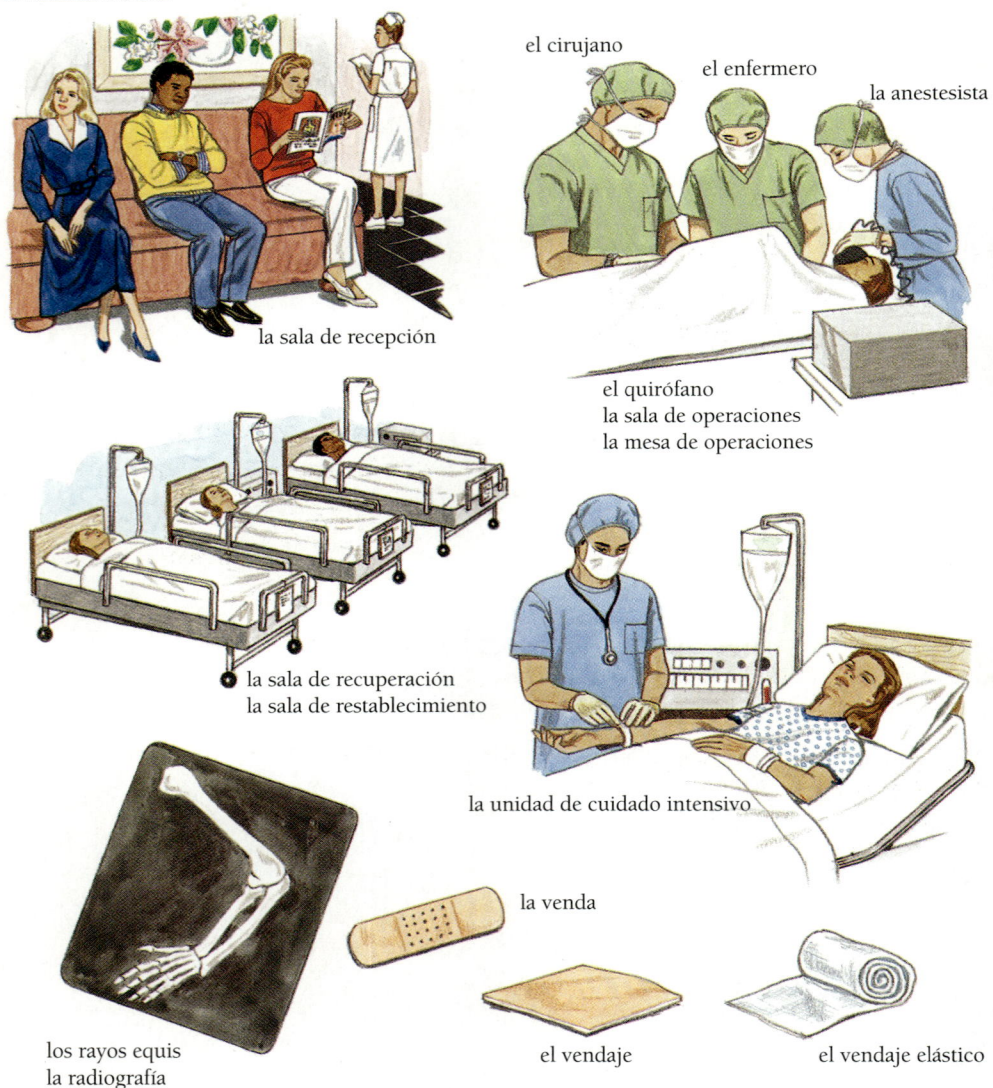

la sala de recepción

el cirujano
el enfermero
la anestesista

el quirófano
la sala de operaciones
la mesa de operaciones

la sala de recuperación
la sala de restablecimiento

la unidad de cuidado intensivo

los rayos equis
la radiografía

la venda

el vendaje

el vendaje elástico

82 CAPÍTULO 4

LEARNING FROM PHOTOS
After presenting the vocabulary in *Palabras 2*, refer students to the photo of the man and the boy at the bottom of page 81. Ask: ¿Qué le pasará al joven? ¿Adónde lo llevarán? ¿Qué le harán?

En la oficina de recepción, el enfermo tendrá que llenar un formulario.

El enfermero le tomará el pulso.

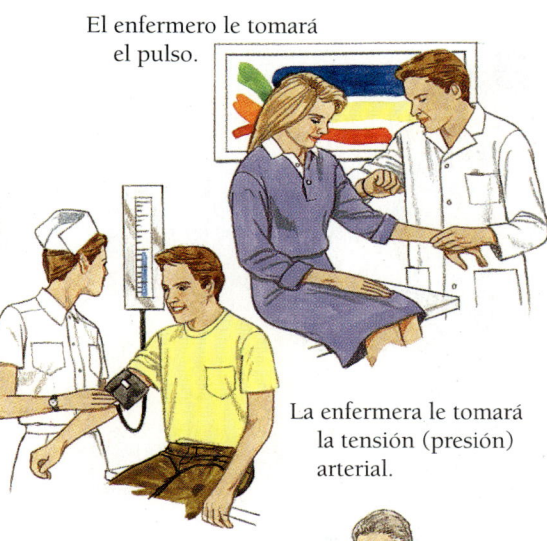

La enfermera le tomará la tensión (presión) arterial.

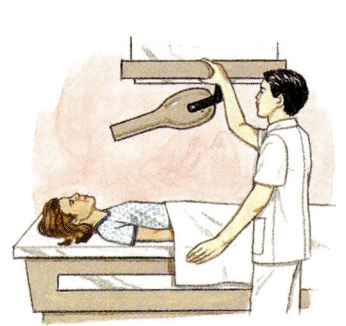

El técnico sacará (tomará) una radiografía (unos rayos equis).

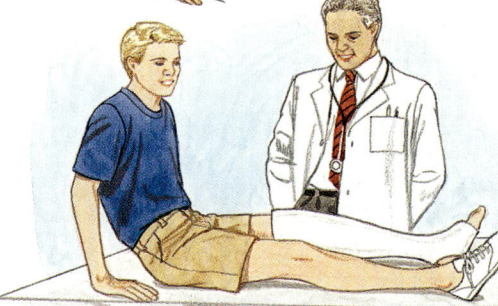

El cirujano ortopédico reducirá la fractura.
Le pondrá la pierna en un yeso.
Le enyesará la pierna.

José no podrá caminar en seguida. Tendrá que andar con muletas.

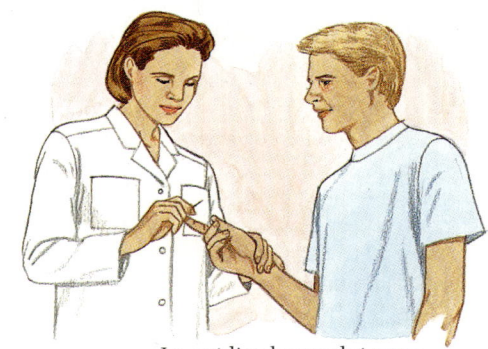

La médica le pondrá unos puntos (unas suturas).

CAPÍTULO 4   83

PRESENTATION (*pages 82–83*)
A. Refer to Vocabulary Transparencies 4.2 (*A & B*). Have students repeat the words, phrases, and sentences after you or Cassette 3B.
B. Practice some of the expressions by putting them into short sentences. For example: (*sacar una radiografía*) *El técnico sacará una radiografía.* (*tomar la tensión arterial*) *La enfermera le tomará la tensión (presión) arterial.*
C. Ask questions such as the following during your presentation: *¿Quién tendrá que llenar un formulario? ¿Quién sacará una radiografía? ¿Qué le pasó? ¿Qué hará el cirujano?*

ABOUT THE LANGUAGE
In a hospital you will see two terms for a ward or unit. For example, you might see *el departamento de radiografía* or *el servicio de radiografía*. You will hear the verb *operar* as well as *hacer una intervención quirúrgica*.

RECYCLING
You may wish to ask students to remember some of the words related to health which they already know: *la fiebre, la gripe, los escalofríos, el catarro, tener dolor de garganta, el estómago, la cabeza.*

COOPERATIVE LEARNING

All members of the team will work together to create as many questions as possible that might appear on a hospital admittance form. They should write one question per card or piece of paper. The teams will exchange their questions. Members will then take turns drawing from the new pile of questions and answering them. Follow up with a class composite hospital admittance form on the board.

Ejercicios

PRESENTATION (*page 84*)

Ejercicios A and B

Exercises A and B can be done with books open.

ANSWERS

Ejercicio A
1. Es la sala de restablecimiento.
2. Son vendas.
3. Es un formulario.
4. Es un yeso.

Ejercicio B
1. Sí
2. Sí
3. No
4. No
5. Sí
6. Sí
7. Sí
8. Sí
9. No
10. Sí
11. No
12. No

Ejercicios

A ¿Qué es? Identifiquen.

1. ¿Es el quirófano o la sala de restablecimiento?
2. ¿Son vendas o radiografías? 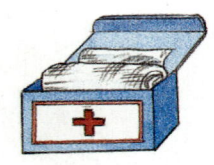
3. ¿Es un formulario o una sutura? 
4. ¿Es un yeso o un punto? 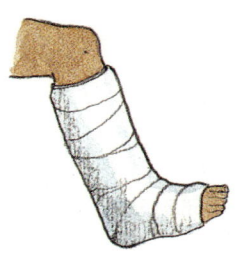

B El hospital. ¿Sí o no?
1. Cuando el enfermo o el paciente va al hospital, llega a la oficina de recepción.
2. Antes de entrar en el hospital, el enfermo o el paciente tiene que llenar o completar un formulario.
3. La enfermera toma la tensión arterial en la cabeza.
4. La enfermera toma la tensión arterial en la muñeca.
5. La enfermera toma el pulso en la muñeca.
6. Los rayos equis son fotografías.
7. El médico especialista en los huesos es el ortopedista.
8. El cirujano opera (hace intervenciones quirúrgicas).
9. El joven tendrá que andar con muletas porque se cortó el dedo.
10. Se cortó la mejilla. Si el médico no le pone suturas, tendrá una cicatriz.
11. Los enfermos que están en una condición seria o grave van a la sala de recuperación.
12. Después de una operación menor, trasladan a los enfermos a la unidad de cuidado intensivo.

84 CAPÍTULO 4

INDEPENDENT PRACTICE

Assign any of the following:
1. Workbook, *Palabras 2*
2. Communication Activities Masters, *Palabras 2, C & D*
3. Exercises on student pages 84–85

C ¿Cuál es otra palabra? Pareen

1. la sala de operaciones
2. la sala de urgencias
3. los rayos equis
4. la sala de recuperación
5. la tensión arterial
6. las suturas
7. lastimarse
8. doler
9. el servicio de primer socorro

a. el servicio de primeros auxilios
b. la presión arterial (sanguínea)
c. los puntos
d. la sala de emergencia
e. hacerse daño
f. la radiografía
g. hacerle mal
h. la sala de restablecimiento
i. el quirófano

Comunicación
Palabras 1 y 2

A **Me lastimé y...** Ud. tuvo varios accidentes. Dígale a un(a) compañero(a) de clase lo que le pasó. Use las expresiones siguientes en su explicación.

1. anteayer / el coche / lastimarse la cara
2. la semana pasada / la discoteca / torcerse el tobillo
3. anoche / la cocina / cortarse el dedo
4. el domingo pasado / la cancha de tenis / resbalarse y torcerse la rodilla
5. durante las vacaciones / la montaña / caerse y romperse la pierna

B **¡Socorro!** Ud. está en la calle Echegaray en Madrid. Ocurre un accidente. No es nada serio pero los accidentados necesitan ayuda. Vaya a un teléfono y llame para pedir ayuda. Explíquele al/a la operador(a) todo lo que pasó y todo lo que Ud. vio.

C **Nos lastimamos.** Ud. y tres compañeros(as) decidieron ir a jugar fútbol. Los cuatro se lastimaron. Uno(a) se resbaló y se le torció el tobillo, otro(a) se cortó el dedo, a otro(a) se le rompió el brazo y Ud. se cayó y se lastimó la muñeca. Uds. van al hospital. Explíquenle al/a la doctor(a) lo que les pasó. El/la doctor(a) les dirá a cada uno de Uds. lo que les tendrá que hacer.

La calle Echegaray, Madrid

CAPÍTULO 4   85

ESTRUCTURA

El futuro de los verbos irregulares

Expressing More Future Actions

Study the following forms of verbs that have an irregular stem in the future tense. Note that the endings are the same as those for the regular verbs.

INFINITIVE	TENER	SALIR	VENIR	ENDINGS
STEM	tendr-	saldr-	vendr-	
yo	tendré	saldré	vendré	-é
tú	tendrás	saldrás	vendrás	-ás
él, ella, Ud.	tendrá	saldrá	vendrá	-á
nosotros(as)	tendremos	saldremos	vendremos	-emos
vosotros(as)	tendréis	saldréis	vendréis	-éis
ellos, ellas, Uds.	tendrán	saldrán	vendrán	-án

INFINITIVE	PONER	SABER	PODER	ENDINGS
STEM	pondr-	sabr-	podr	
yo	pondré	sabré	podré	-é
tú	pondrás	sabrás	podrás	-ás
él, ella, Ud.	pondrá	sabrá	podrá	-á
nosotros(as)	pondremos	sabremos	podremos	-emos
vosotros(as)	pondréis	sabréis	podréis	-éis
ellos, ellas, Uds.	pondrán	sabrán	podrán	-án

86 CAPÍTULO 4

Ejercicios

A **María está enferma.** Contesten según se indica.

1. María está enferma. ¿A quién tendrá que llamar? (al médico)
2. ¿Vendrá el médico a la casa? (no)
3. ¿Adónde tendrá que ir María? (a la consulta del médico)
4. ¿Podrá ir? (sí)
5. ¿Sabrá el médico lo que tiene? (sin duda)

B **Unas vacaciones.** Preguntas personales.

1. ¿Tendrás unas vacaciones este verano?
2. ¿Tendrás que trabajar o podrás ir de vacaciones?
3. ¿Saldrás para la playa o para las montañas?
4. ¿Irás de vacaciones con tus amigos?
5. ¿Saldrán juntos?
6. ¿En qué mes tendrán sus vacaciones?
7. ¿Cuántas semanas podrán Uds. estar fuera de casa?
8. ¿Cuándo sabrás la fecha en que podrás salir?

El futuro de otros verbos irregulares

Expressing More Future Actions

1. Study the future forms of the verbs *decir*, *hacer*, and *querer* that also have an irregular stem.

INFINITIVE	DECIR	HACER	QUERER	ENDINGS
STEM	dir-	har-	querr-	
yo	diré	haré	querré	-é
tú	dirás	harás	querrás	-ás
él, ella, Ud.	dirá	hará	querrá	-á
nosotros(as)	diremos	haremos	querremos	-emos
vosotros(as)	*diréis*	*haréis*	*querréis*	*-éis*
ellos, ellas, Uds.	dirán	harán	querrán	-án

2. The verb *querer* is very seldom used in the future.

CAPÍTULO 4 87

Ejercicios

PRESENTATION (page 88)

Ejercicios A and B

You may wish to assign these exercises as homework first, or you may go over them orally with books open, but without prior preparation.

Ejercicio C

Exercise C can be done orally with books closed.

ANSWERS

Ejercicio A
1. diré, hará
2. dirás, hará, querrá
3. hará
4. haremos
5. tendremos
6. haremos

Ejercicio B
P: dirás, harás
S: podré
P: tendré, harás
S: tendrás, sabré, haré, podré
P: diré, haré
P: iré
S: harás

Ejercicio C
1. Sí, te diré lo que haré.
2. Sí, te diré lo que haré si me dices lo que harás.
3. Sí, lo haremos juntos.
4. Sí, mis hermanos me dirán si lo haremos juntos.
5. Sí, mis hermanos me dirán si ellos lo harán con nosotros.

Ejercicios

A ¿Quieres saber? Completen con el futuro.

1. Yo te ___ lo que él ___ . (decir, hacer)
2. Tú me ___ lo que él ___ o lo que él ___ hacer. (decir, hacer, querer)
3. Tú lo conoces. Si él lo quiere hacer, lo ___ . (hacer)
4. ¿Y qué ___ (nosotros)? (hacer)
5. No sabemos lo que ___ que hacer. (tener)
6. Pero, nosotros ___ lo necesario. (hacer)

B Las vacaciones. Completen con el futuro.

PEPITA: Suso, ¿me ___ (decir) lo que ___ (hacer) durante tus vacaciones?
SUSO: No te ___ (poder) decir nada hasta la semana que viene.
PEPITA: ¿Por qué ___ (tener) que esperar tanto para saber lo que tú ___ (hacer)?
SUSO: Pues, (tú) ___ (tener) que esperar porque yo no ___ (saber) lo que ___ (hacer) ni lo que ___ (poder) hacer hasta entonces.
PEPITA: Pues, yo te ___ (decir) lo que yo ___ (hacer).
SUSO: ¿Qué?
PEPITA: Pues, yo ___ (ir) a España.
SUSO: Tú ___ (hacer) un viaje a España. ¡Qué suerte!

C Entre amigos no hay secretos. Contesten.

1. ¿Me dirás lo que harás?
2. ¿Me dirás lo que harás si te digo lo que yo haré?
3. ¿Lo haremos juntos o no?
4. ¿Tus hermanos te dirán si lo haremos juntos?
5. ¿Y tus hermanos te dirán si ellos lo harán con nosotros?

INSTITUTO DE ACUPUNTURA CHINA
DTRS. TRAN - GUYEN, NATIVOS
SE OBTIENEN EXCELENTES RESULTADOS Y CURACIONES

- REUMA
- DEPRESION PSIQUICA
- INSOMNIO
- ARTROSIS
- CIATICA
- ARTRITIS
- TRATAMIENTO PARA DEJAR DE FUMAR
- ASMA
- OBESIDAD
- ULCERAS GASTRODUODENALES
- CEFALEAS, JAQUECAS
- VARICES

TRATAMIENTO CONTRA TODA CLASE DE DOLORES LOCALES, ETC.
PARA OTRAS ENFERMEDADES CONSULTEN RUEGO PETICION PREVIA DE HORA ☎ 245 30 73

CLINICA: Fco. Silvela, 46-Esc. A, 2.º dcha.

CAPÍTULO 4

COOPERATIVE LEARNING

Have students work in groups of three. One tells something that he/she will do tomorrow. The second student says that he/she won't do it tomorrow because he/she did it yesterday. The third student says he/she will do it tomorrow because he/she does it everyday.

LEARNING FROM REALIA

Refer students to the advertisement at the bottom of page 88 and ask: ¿Qué tratan los médicos del Instituto de Acupuntura China? Según ellos, ¿qué obtienen? Al entrar en el edificio, ¿es necesario tomar cuál escalera? ¿En qué piso está el consultorio? ¿A qué lado?

El comparativo y el superlativo
Formas irregulares
Comparing People and Things

1. The adjectives *bueno* and *malo* have irregular comparative and superlative forms.

ADJETIVO	COMPARATIVO	SUPERLATIVO
bueno	mejor(es)… que	el, la, los, las mejor(es)
malo	peor(es)… que	el, la, los, las peor(es)

Este año, ¿vas a recibir las mejores o las peores notas?
José es el mejor alumno de la clase.
Una fiesta es mejor que un examen.

2. Two other adjectives with irregular forms are *mayor* and *menor*. Although they are not actually the comparative and superlative forms of *joven* and *viejo*, they often refer to age.

Mi hermano es mayor (menor) que Paco.
Teresa es la menor (la mayor) de la clase.

Ejercicio

¿No eres el mayor? Practiquen la conversación.

ROSAURA: Te vi con una muchacha ayer. ¿Quién era?
MARCELO: Era mi hermana mayor, Catalina.
ROSAURA: Yo creía que tú eras el mayor de tus hermanos.
MARCELO: No, no. Todo lo contrario. Yo soy el menor. Mi hermano Santiago es el mayor. Pero no hay duda, yo soy el mejor estudiante de todos.

Contesten según la conversación.

1. ¿Quién es menor, Marcelo o Catalina?
2. ¿Quién es la hermana mayor de Marcelo?
3. ¿Quién es el mayor de los hermanos?
4. ¿Y quién es el menor?
5. ¿Quién es el mejor estudiante de los tres?

En Segovia, España

CAPÍTULO 4   89

Bell Ringer Review
Write the following on the board or use BRR Blackline Master 4-4: Answer the following. Then keep your answers for later.
1. ¿Tienes un amigo muy bueno?
2. ¿Quién es un amigo muy bueno?
3. ¿Cuál es un curso muy bueno?
4. ¿Tienes un pariente que tiene más años que tú?
5. ¿Quién tiene más años que tú?
6. ¿Y quién tiene menos años que tú?

Note Have students rewrite their Bell Ringer Review sentences using *mejor*, *mayor*, or *menor* after you present this point.

El comparativo y el superlativo Formas irregulares
PRESENTATION (page 89)

Have students open their books to page 89. Read the explanatory material aloud, one step at a time. Then call on students to read the adjective forms and the example sentences aloud.

Ejercicio
PRESENTATION (page 89)

Have two students read the conversation aloud to the class. The other students can follow along in their books. Then call on individual students to answer the questions that follow the conversation.

Expansion
Call on one student to retell all the information in his/her own words.

ANSWERS
Ejercicio
1. Marcelo es menor.
2. Catalina
3. Santiago
4. Marcelo
5. Marcelo

LEARNING FROM PHOTOS
1. Refer students to the photo at the bottom of page 89 and ask: *¿Dónde están sentados los jóvenes? ¿Qué están tomando? ¿En qué ciudad están? ¿El café está cerca de qué estructura antigua?*
2. Tell students that this is the famous Roman aqueduct in the city of Segovia, built over 2000 years ago without mortar. It is still in excellent condition.

INDEPENDENT PRACTICE
Assign any of the following:
1. Workbook, *Estructura*
2. Communication Activities Masters, *Estructura*, B & C
3. Exercises on student pages 88-89

89

CONVERSACIÓN

Bell Ringer Review

Write the following on the board or use BRR Blackline Master 4-5: Write the names of three rooms of your house. For each room write one sentence telling what you do there.

PRESENTATION *(page 90)*

A. With books closed, have students listen and repeat as you read the conversation aloud or play Cassette 3B.
B. Open books and call on volunteers to read the conversation in parts with as much expression as possible.
C. Call on indiviual students to answer the questions that follow the conversation.
D. Call on a student to retell the information in the conversation in his/her own words. This activity gives students important practice in going from dialogue to narrative form.

Ejercicio

ANSWERS

1. Catalina está en el hospital.
2. Ella tuvo un accidente.
3. Sí, le tomaron una radiografía.
4. Dentro de poco tendrá los resultados.
5. La médica le dirá lo que tiene que hacer.
6. Sí, la médica lo hará en el hospital.
7. Catalina tiene una fractura.
8. Catalina se le rompió el tobillo.
9. La médica le pondrá el tobillo en un yeso.
10. Ella podrá salir en seguida.
11. Sí, ella se sentirá mejor en casa.

90

CONVERSACIÓN

Escenas de la vida *Una visita al hospital*

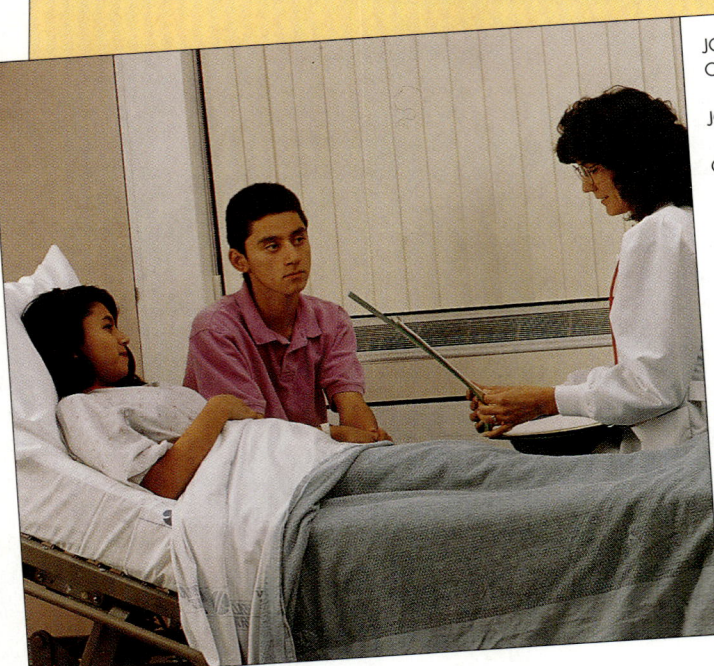

JOSÉ: Catalina, ¿cómo estás?
CATALINA: Ay, ¡qué accidente más tonto tuve yo!
JOSÉ: ¿Tienes los resultados de los rayos equis?
CATALINA: No, la médica los tendrá dentro de poco y me dirá lo que ella tendrá que hacer o lo que yo tendré que hacer. Ah, aquí viene ahora.
CATALINA: ¿Sí, doctora?
DOCTORA: Hola, Catalina. Aquí tengo los resultados de la radiografía. Tú tienes una fractura.
CATALINA: ¿Se me rompió el tobillo?
DOCTORA: Sí, pero no es cosa muy seria. Lo pondré en un yeso y tú podrás salir del hospital en seguida. Te sentirás mejor en casa que aquí, ¿no?
CATALINA: Sí, sí. ¿Tendré que andar con muletas?
DOCTORA: Sí, unos dos o tres días, nada más.

■ **No es nada serio.** Contesten según la conversación.

1. ¿Quién está en el hospital?
2. ¿Está enferma o es que tuvo un accidente?
3. ¿Le tomaron (hicieron) una radiografía?
4. ¿Cuándo tendrá los resultados?
5. ¿Quién le dirá lo que tendrá que hacer?
6. ¿Lo hará en el hospital?
7. ¿Qué tiene Catalina?
8. ¿Qué se le rompió a Catalina?
9. ¿Qué hará la médica?
10. ¿Cuándo podrá Catalina salir del hospital?
11. ¿Se sentirá mejor en casa?

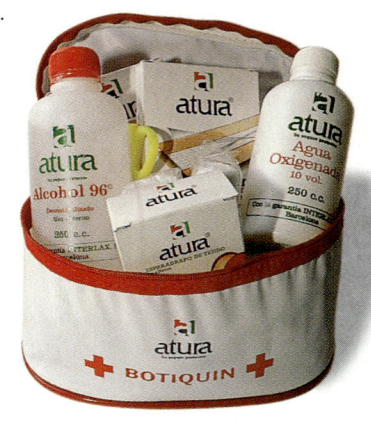

90   CAPÍTULO 4

COOPERATIVE LEARNING

Have team members take turns being "ill." The other members will ask questions to determine the symptoms and to figure out what the "ill" student needs.

Comunicación

A **La pobre Catalina tuvo un accidente.** Llame a un(a) amigo(a) de Catalina por teléfono (un[a] compañero[a] de clase). Dígale que Catalina está en el hospital. El/la amigo(a) quiere saber: qué le pasó; en qué hospital está; cuánto tiempo estará; qué le hará la médica; si puede visitar a Catalina; cuándo saldrá ella del hospital; cuándo estará mejor.

B **Lo que queremos…** Ud. y un(a) compañero(a) de clase prepararán una lista de cosas que harán de adultos. Luego comparen sus listas individuales y determinen los intereses que comparten (tienen en común). Presenten los resultados a la clase.

C **De viaje en Puerto Rico.** Ud. viajaba en Puerto Rico y desgraciadamente tuvo un pequeño accidente, nada serio. Ud. está en la sala de urgencias del Centro Médico en Río Piedras y tiene que dar la siguiente información al/a la recepcionista (su compañero[a] de clase).

1. su nombre
2. su domicilio
3. nombre de sus padres
4. su edad
5. su compañía de seguros
6. un poco sobre su historial médico

D **La buenaventura.** Ud. le dice la buenaventura (fortuna) a un(a) compañero(a) de clase. Su compañero(a) quiere saber todo lo que le pasará en el futuro. Él/ella le hará muchas preguntas. Conteste a todas sus preguntas. Use su imaginación.

E **Este fin de semana.** Con un(a) compañero(a), haga planes para el fin de semana. Discutan sus obligaciones, fiestas, trabajo, estudios, etc.

F **El verano próximo.** Entreviste a un(a) compañero(a) de clase para saber si hará algunas de las cosas siguientes (u otras originales) el verano próximo.

trabajar mucho
vivir en otra ciudad
ir a la playa
leer novelas interesantes
ver películas
visitar otro país
hacer algo diferente que el verano pasado
poder ir a fiestas
salir con los amigos

CAPÍTULO 4

LECTURA Y CULTURA

Bell Ringer Review
Write the following on the board or use BRR Blackline Master 4-6: Answer the following.
1. ¿Cuáles son algunos alimentos que son muy buenos para la salud?
2. ¿Cuáles son algunos alimentos que no son muy buenos para la salud (que son bastante malos para la salud)?

READING STRATEGIES
(page 92)

Note This *Lectura* provides many examples of the preterite and future forms of irregular verbs.

Pre-Reading
Ask if any of your students have ever broken a bone or received some other serious injury. How were they treated?

Reading
A. You may divide the *Lectura* into two segments.
B. Call on volunteers to read aloud about three sentences at a time.
C. Follow each reading with a few questions on content to check comprehension. You may use the questions from *Comprensión*, Exercise A on page 93.

Post-reading
Have students scan the selection and make a list of things that were done to Marcos before his leg was set.

LECTURA Y CULTURA

HOSPITAL DEL SAGRADO CORAZÓN—¡YA VOY!

—Marcos, ¡cuidado! Están haciendo obras[1] allí en la acera[2]. Si no tienes cuidado, te vas a caer. —Él no se caerá. —Ya se cayó.

—¡Ay, qué dolor!

—¿Dónde te duele?

—Aquí. Creo que se me rompió la pierna.

—Te pondré en el sillín[3] de mi moto y te llevaré al hospital del Sagrado Corazón.

—¿Estás loco? No me pondrás en tu moto. No me puedo levantar. El dolor me está matando[4]. ¡Cuánto me duele!

—Pues tendré que llamar al servicio de primeros auxilios.

—¡Ay, bendito! Luego vendrán en la ambulancia con las sirenas y me pondrán en una camilla. ¡Qué escena!

—Pero te darán una inyección para aliviar el dolor. Te sentirás mejor pronto.

—Me estoy poniendo nervioso. ¿Qué me harán en el hospital?

—No tengo idea. Los socorristas te dirán lo que te harán. Llamaré al hospital y luego llamaré a tus padres.

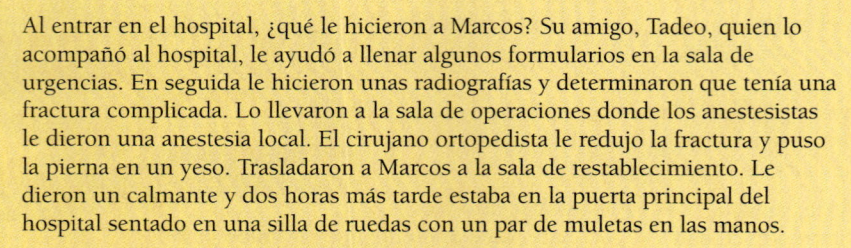

Al entrar en el hospital, ¿qué le hicieron a Marcos? Su amigo, Tadeo, quien lo acompañó al hospital, le ayudó a llenar algunos formularios en la sala de urgencias. En seguida le hicieron unas radiografías y determinaron que tenía una fractura complicada. Lo llevaron a la sala de operaciones donde los anestesistas le dieron una anestesia local. El cirujano ortopedista le redujo la fractura y puso la pierna en un yeso. Trasladaron a Marcos a la sala de restablecimiento. Le dieron un calmante y dos horas más tarde estaba en la puerta principal del hospital sentado en una silla de ruedas con un par de muletas en las manos.

Le dijo su mamá—Volveré en seguida. Voy por el carro.

[1] haciendo obras   *doing repair work*
[2] acera   *sidewalk*
[3] sillín   *seat*
[4] matando   *killing*

92   CAPÍTULO 4

FOR THE NATIVE SPEAKER

In many Hispanic countries medical services are paid by the government. Yet many people who can afford it prefer to get private medical care. Ask students to write a short paper addressing the following issue: *¿Cuáles son algunas ventajas y desventajas del servicio médico totalmente pagado por el gobierno? ¿Para quiénes es un beneficio? ¿Para quiénes no lo es?*

LEARNING FROM PHOTOS

Refer students to the photo on page 92 and ask: *¿Es una bicicleta o una moto? ¿La persona lleva un casco? ¿Es obligatorio llevar un casco cuando uno anda en moto? ¿Tiene un cinturón de seguridad?*

Estudio de palabras

Definiciones. Escojan la definición.

1. operar
2. aliviar
3. la camilla
4. un calmante
5. nervioso
6. completar
7. en seguida
8. la sala de operaciones
9. el cirujano

a. preocupado, agitado
b. el médico que opera
c. el quirófano
d. un analgésico
e. disminuir el dolor
f. hacer una intervención quirúrgica
g. llenar
h. cama para transportar enfermos y heridos
i. inmediatamente

Comprensión

A ¡Pobre Marcos! Contesten según la lectura.

1. ¿Quién se cayó?
2. ¿Por qué se cayó?
3. ¿Dónde le duele?
4. ¿Por qué no puede ir al hospital en la moto de su amigo?
5. ¿A quién llamará su amigo?
6. ¿Por qué habrá una escena?
7. ¿En que vendrán o llegarán los socorristas?
8. ¿Dónde pondrán a Marcos?
9. ¿Qué le darán?
10. ¿Qué aliviará la inyección?
11. Al llegar al hospital, ¿qué llenaron los amigos?
12. ¿Qué le hicieron a Marcos?
13. ¿Qué tenía Marcos?
14. ¿Adónde lo llevaron?

B En la sala de operaciones. Completen.

1. Llevaron a Marcos a la ____.
2. Lo llevaron a la sala de ____ en una ____.
3. ____ redujo la fractura.
4. Luego el cirujano ortopedista le puso un ____.
5. Después trasladaron a Marcos a ____.
6. En la sala de restablecimiento le dieron ____.
7. Marcos salió del hospital en ____.
8. ____ lo llevó a casa.

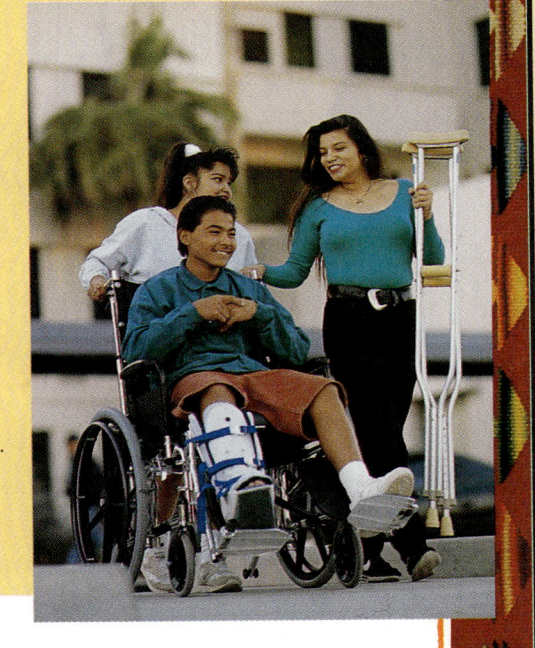

CAPÍTULO 4 93

Estudio de palabras
ANSWERS
1. f
2. e
3. h
4. d
5. a
6. g
7. i
8. c
9. b

Comprensión
ANSWERS
Comprensión A
1. Marcos se cayó.
2. Porque estaban haciendo obras en la acera.
3. Le duele la pierna.
4. No se puede levantar.
5. Su amigo llamará al servicio de primeros auxilios.
6. Porque vendrán en la ambulancia con las sirenas.
7. Ellos vendrán en ambulancia.
8. Pondrán a Marcos en una camilla.
9. Le darán una inyección.
10. Le aliviará el dolor.
11. Los amigos llenaron los formularios.
12. Le hicieron radiografías.
13. Tenía una fractura complicada.
14. Lo llevaron a la sala de operaciones.

Comprensión B
1. sala de urgencias
2. operaciones, camilla
3. El cirujano ortopedista
4. yeso
5. la sala de restablecimiento
6. un calmante
7. una silla de ruedas
8. Su mamá

LEARNING FROM PHOTOS

Refer students to the photo at the bottom of page 93 and ask: *¿Qué opinas? ¿Este muchacho está entrando en el hospital o está saliendo del hospital? ¿Está contento el muchacho? ¿En qué está? ¿Por qué? ¿Qué se lastimó? ¿Quién está empujando la silla de ruedas? ¿Qué tiene en la mano su amiga?*

INDEPENDENT PRACTICE

You may wish to assign the exercises on student page 93.

93

Descubrimiento Cultural

(The Descubrimiento *section is optional.)*

PRESENTATION *(pages 94-95)*

A. It is up to the teacher to decide how to present this section of the chapter. You may have the entire class read it, you may have individuals read it on their own as silent reading, or you may wish to omit it entirely.

B. It is recommended that you let students read this material for the main idea only. It is not necessary that they recall the details.

C. You may wish to compare such things as health services and payment practices in Spanish-speaking countries with those in the U.S.

DESCUBRIMIENTO CULTURAL

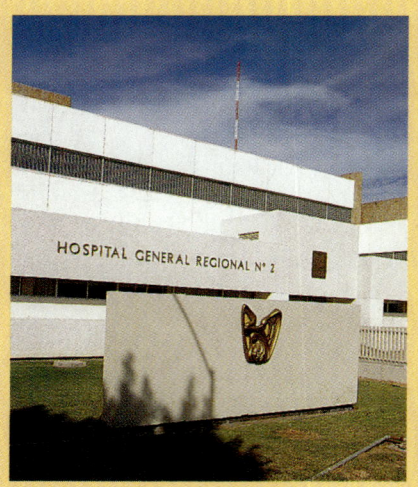

En muchos países hispanos los hospitales están bajo la dirección de un ministerio o departamento del gobierno, el Ministerio de Salud Pública o la Dirección de Sanidad[1], por ejemplo. En general, el cuidado médico en los hospitales es gratis. El seguro social cubre todos los gastos[2] médicos.

La calidad del servicio médico varía de país en país y de región en región. En la mayoría de las grandes ciudades hay hospitales buenos con equipo[3] avanzado y unas instalaciones muy modernas. En las zonas más remotas el equipo es menos avanzado. En las regiones extremadamente remotas, en las montañas y en las selvas tropicales, por ejemplo, hay muy pocos médicos y tampoco hay suficientes hospitales. Es un problema serio porque hay mucha gente que tiene necesidad de mejor asistencia y de mejor cuidado médico.

En todas las ciudades hay grandes hospitales públicos. También existen clínicas privadas. Hay una diferencia entre el significado de la palabra "clínica" en inglés y en español. Una clínica es un hospital privado, a veces el propietario es un médico o grupo de médicos. Las clínicas son para las personas que pueden pagar y que prefieren no ir a un hospital público.

Hay también dispensarios donde tratan a los pacientes que sufren de una herida o de una enfermedad no muy seria. Hoy hay centros médicos dedicados específicamente al tratamiento del SIDA, del alcoholismo y de la adicción a las drogas.

Todos los años, miles de jóvenes de los Estados Unidos van a las universidades de España y de Latinoamérica para estudiar medicina.

Un profesional en el campo de la medicina que existe en los países hispanos pero no en los EE.UU. es el "practicante". El practicante es un diplomado en enfermería. Al practicante se le permite poner inyecciones y practicar curas simples y rutinarias. En caso de heridas o enfermedades graves o complicadas, el practicante manda al paciente a un médico.

En muchas áreas rurales de las Américas las madres todavía dan a luz[4] a sus hijos en casa y no en un hospital. Tradicionalmente las comadronas, unas señoras con mucha experiencia en ayudar a nacer a los niños, cuidaban a las madres. Hoy muchas comadronas son enfermeras especialistas en obstetricia.

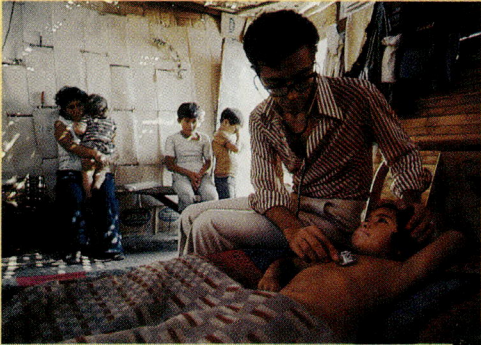

Un practicante

Y AQUÍ EN LOS ESTADOS UNIDOS

En los barrios hispanos de los Estados Unidos mucha gente visita a los herbolarios. Los herbolarios son personas que hacen preparaciones de hierbas para curar una variedad de males o enfermedades. Para cada enfermedad preparan una hierba específica. La gente generalmente hace un tipo de té con las hierbas y lo toma. La palabra "herbolario" se refiere a la persona y a la tienda. Los herbolarios también se llaman "botánicas".

[1] sanidad   *health*
[2] gastos   *expenses*
[3] equipo   *equipment*
[4] dan a luz   *deliver, give birth*

CAPÍTULO 4   **95**

LEARNING FROM PHOTOS

Refer students to the photo on the bottom of page 95 and ask: *¿Por qué el hombre ya no tiene más dolor de cabeza?*

95

REALIDADES

(The Realidades section is optional.)

Bell Ringer Review

Write the following on the board or use BRR Blackline Master 4-7: In your answers, use the following words: *proteínas, fibra, vitaminas, mucha grasa, mucha azúcar*
1. ¿Cuáles son los mejores alimentos para la salud?
2. ¿Cuáles son los peores alimentos para la salud?

PRESENTATION (pages 96-97)

A. The purpose of this section is to have students enjoy the photographs in a relaxed manner in order to gain an appreciation of Hispanic cultures. However, if you would like to do more with the section, have students read the captions and respond to any of the questions embedded in them. You may also wish to have students read and discuss the captions in groups or as a whole-class activity.

REALIDADES

Aquí vemos el patio del Hospital de Jesús en la capital de México **1**. Es uno de los hospitales más viejos de todo México. ¡Qué agradable dar un paseo por este lindo patio! ¿No?

¡Cuidado! Están haciendo obras en esta carretera de México **2**.

Los estudiantes que aquí vemos están charlando delante del departamento de anatomía de la Universidad de Caracas **3**. ¿Van a ser médicos?

Esta ambulancia en Madrid lleva un equipo médico muy avanzado **4**.

Estos socorristas de la Ciudad de México siempre están listos para ayudar en una emergencia **5**.

B. You may wish to ask the following questions regarding the photos and the realia:
Photo 1: ¿Hay hospitales como el Hospital de Jesús en los Estados Unidos? ¿Puedes explicar algunas diferencias?
Photo 2: Refer students to the sign at the bottom of page 97. Explain that this emblem means *Obras, Están haciendo obras* or *Gente trabajando*.
Photo 3: *Describe a los estudiantes de anatomía. ¿Cómo se visten? ¿De qué están hablando?*
Photo 5: *Describe a los socorristas. ¿Qué tipo de trabajo hacen ellos?*

DID YOU KNOW?

En la ambulancia hay una cruz roja. La Cruz Roja es una organización que se fundó en 1864 para ayudar a las víctimas de las guerras y, más tarde, para dar socorro a las víctimas de accidentes. En los países musulmanes, el emblema es una media luna roja, y en el Japón, es un sol rojo.

97

CULMINACIÓN

Comunicación oral

A ¿Qué le pasó? Ud. toma el papel de un(a) médico(a). Un(a) compañero(a) de clase es su paciente. El/la paciente tuvo un accidente. Hágale preguntas sobre el accidente para poder hacerle una diagnosis. Luego descríbale el tratamiento.

B Hubo un accidente. Ud. es un(a) agente de policía y está hablando por teléfono con alguien (un[a] compañero[a] de clase) que le está informando sobre un accidente. Ud. quiere saber lo que pasó, cómo y cuándo ocurrió. Explíquele a su compañero(a) lo que debe hacer y lo que Ud. hará.

C Lo mejor. Trabaje con un(a) compañero(a) de clase. Hablen de otros compañeros. Según Uds., ¿quién o quiénes son los más guapos, serios, inteligentes, divertidos, etc?

Más vale perder un minuto en la vida, que la vida en un minuto. Maneja con cuidado.

Comunicación escrita

A Cuando era niño(a). Escriba una composición de dos o tres párrafos sobre un accidente que tuvo cuando Ud. era niño(a).

B La salud. Ud. ya tiene un vocabulario bastante extenso sobre la salud y los servicios de salud. Prepare un informe escrito sobre los servicios de salud.
1. Prepare una lista de palabras o expresiones relacionadas a este tema.
2. Ponga las palabras y expresiones en oraciones.
3. Luego organice sus oraciones en párrafos.

C Una visita horrible al hospital. Imagínese que Ud. tuvo un pequeño accidente que se convirtió en una experiencia horrible. Desde el momento que llamó a los socorristas hasta el momento que salió del hospital todo anduvo mal. En una carta, descríbale su experiencia a un(a) amigo(a).

> La semana pasada se me torció (rompió)… Caminaba por una acera donde… Cuando llamé a los socorristas, sonaba ocupado…

D ¡Lea las noticias! Imagínese que Ud. es reportero(a) del periódico de su escuela. Ud. vio un accidente que ocurrió en el estacionamiento de los estudiantes. Escriba un artículo para el periódico en el que describe lo que pasó. No se olvide de incluir: qué, quién, cuándo, dónde y cómo.

CAPÍTULO 4

CULMINACIÓN

RECYCLING

The *Comunicación oral* and *Comunicación escrita* activities allow students to use the vocabulary and grammar from this chapter in open-ended settings. They also provide an opportunity to recycle vocabulary and structures from earlier chapters, and from *Bienvenidos*. Have students do as many of the *actividades* as you wish.

Comunicación oral
ANSWERS

Actividades A, B, and C
Answers will vary.

INFORMAL ASSESSMENT

The *Comunicación* activities can be used to evaluate the speaking skills informally. You may assign a grade based on students' ability to communicate in Spanish. Following are some grading suggestions:
5: Complete message conveyed, precise control of structure and vocabulary.
4-3: Complete message conveyed, some structural errors or errors in vocabulary.
2-1: Message partially conveyed, frequent errors.
0: No message conveyed.

Comunicación escrita
ANSWERS

Actividades A-D
Answers will vary.

CRITICAL THINKING ACTIVITY

(*Thinking skills: making inferences; drawing conclusions*)

Have students read the information on page 98, taken from *las páginas amarillas*, and explain in Spanish what it means.

STUDENT PORTFOLIO

Have students keep a Spanish notebook with their best written work from *A bordo* in it. Written assignments that may be included in students' portfolios are the *Actividades escritas* on page 98 and the *Mi autobiografía* section in the Workbook.

Reintegración

A ¿Está enfermo o no? Completen con *ser* o *estar*.

1. Juan ____ de Puerto Rico.
2. Él ____ muy simpático.
3. Él siempre ____ contento.
4. Él ____ muy inteligente y también muy divertido.
5. Hoy el pobre Juan no ____ muy bien.
6. Él ____ un poco enfermo. No se siente bien y tiene fiebre.
7. En este momento él ____ en el consultorio médico.
8. El consultorio ____ en la calle Mendoza.

B En el consultorio. Completen.

1. —¿Te habla el médico?
   —Sí, él ____ habla.
2. —¿Les habla el médico a todos los pacientes?
   —Sí, él ____ habla a todos.
3. —¿Te examina el médico?
   —Sí, él ____ examina.
4. —¿Le explicas tus síntomas al médico?
   —Sí, ____ explico mis síntomas.
5. —¿Te hace una diagnosis el médico?
   —Sí, ____ hace una diagnosis.

Vocabulario

SUSTANTIVOS
el hospital
la sala de recuperación
la sala de operaciones
el quirófano
la mesa de operaciones
la sala de restablecimiento
la unidad de cuidado intensivo
el/la médico(a)
el/la cirujano(a)
el/la ortopedista
el/la enfermero(a)
el/la técnico(a)
el/la anestesista
el/la enfermo(a)
el accidente
la fractura
la cicatriz
la ambulancia
el servicio de primeros auxilios
el servicio de primer socorro
el/la socorrista
la camilla
la silla de ruedas
la muleta
la venda
el vendaje
los rayos equis
la radiografía
la tensión arterial
la presión arterial
el pulso
los puntos
las suturas
el hombro
el brazo
el codo
la muñeca
el dedo
la pierna
el tobillo
la rodilla
la cara
la frente
la mejilla
el labio

ADJETIVOS
ortopédico(a)
hinchado(a)
complicado(a)
elástico(a)
arterial

VERBOS
resbalarse
caerse
lastimarse
hacerse daño
doler(ue)
romperse
torcer(ue)
cortar
enyesar
llenar
caminar

CAPÍTULO 4   99

LEARNING FROM PHOTOS

Have students say all they can about the photo on page 99. You may cue them with questions such as: *¿Dónde están las personas? ¿Qué esperan ellos? ¿Quién será la señora vestida de blanco? ¿Qué le da ella a la señora?*

INDEPENDENT PRACTICE

You may wish to assign any of the following:
1. Exercises on student page 99
2. Workbook, *Mi autobiografía*
3. Chapter 4, Situation Cards

Reintegración

PRESENTATION (page 99)
These exercises recycle health vocabulary from *Bienvenidos*, Chapter 10.

Ejercicio A
Exercise A recycles contrasting uses of *ser* and *estar*.

Ejercicio B
Exercise B recycles indirect object pronouns.

ANSWERS
Ejercicio A
1. es   5. está
2. es   6. está
3. está   7. está
4. es   8. está

Ejercicio B
1. Sí, él me habla.
2. Sí, él les habla a todos.
3. Sí, él me examina.
4. Sí, le explico mis síntomas.
5. Sí, me hace una diagnosis.

Vocabulario

The words and phrases in the *Vocabulario* have been taught for productive use in this chapter. They are summarized here as a resource for both students and teacher. The *Vocabulario* also serves as a convenient resource for the *Culminación* activities. There are approximately 18 cognates in this list.

INFORMAL ASSESSMENT
Have students create original sentences using words from the vocabulary list.

VIDEO
The video is intended to reinforce the vocabulary, structures, and cultural content in each chapter. It may be used here as a chapter wrap-up activity. See the *Video Activities Booklet* for additional suggestions on its use.

INTRODUCCIÓN (0:14:56)

EN LA SALA DE EMERGENCIA (0:16:05)

NUESTRO MUNDO

(optional material)

OVERVIEW

All the readings presented in the *Nuestro Mundo* section are authentic, uncut texts from publications of the Hispanic world. Students should be encouraged to read the text for overall meaning, but not intensively, word for word. Students should find satisfaction in their ability to derive meaning from "real" texts.

PRESENTATION *(page 100)*

A. Have students open their books to page 100 and ask them to study the title. Ask them how many words they know or can figure out. Ask them what the word *Telecom* probably refers to (a company). Someone is against something. Against what? Against *la venta de Telecom* (the sale of Telecom). What kind of business is Telecom probably in? (telecommunications)

B. Have students read the article silently.

C. Ask comprehension questions such as *¿Cuál es el nombre completo de Telecom? ¿Quién es el contralor?* etc.

D. Have students answer the questions orally in class or assign them for independent practice.

ANSWERS

1. Colombian national telecommunications
2. Privatize the telecommunications network
3. He opposes the government's idea of privatization.
4. Joint and private ownership under governmental control
5. A work stoppage
6. It needs to be made into an active and vital enterprise in order to avoid its dissolution within a few years.
7. The government monopoly on telecommunications

NUESTRO MUNDO

The following excerpt is from an article that appeared in EL TIEMPO, Santafé de Bogotá, Colombia. After reading the article, answer the questions that follow.

CONTRALORÍA CONTRA LA VENTA DE TELECOM

La Contraloría General de la República se opone a la privatización de la Empresa Nacional de Telecomunicaciones (Telecom) y propone la creación de una entidad de economía mixta controlada por el Estado. Sin embargo, no comparte el paro realizado por los trabajadores. Según el contralor, Manuel Francisco Becerra Barney, es necesario modificar la estructura de Telecom para hacerla una empresa ágil y evitar que dentro de unos años se derrumbe, pero la solución no es privatizar como propone el gobierno. Dijo que es inconveniente entregar el monopolio estatal de las telecomunicaciones al sector privado.

1. What is Telecom?
2. What is the government attempting to do with Telecom?
3. What does Sr. Becerra oppose?
4. How would you describe *una entidad de economía mixta controlada por el Estado*?
5. What does the phrase *el paro realizado por los trabajadores* probably refer to?
6. Why does Sr. Becerra feel that the structure of Telecom needs to be modified?
7. According to Sr. Becerra, what should not be handed over to the private sector?

DID YOU KNOW?

In most Spanish-speaking countries, the telephone and telegraph system has traditionally been a government monopoly. Recently, however, more and more countries are "privatizing" their systems; selling these utilities to private companies but maintaining control over their operations.

Here is an advertisement that appeared in MÁS, a magazine published in the United States for the Hispanic market.

Como decía mi Papá... el que a buen árbol se arrima, buena sombra le cobija.

Es más que conexiones claras y rápidas...
Es darle prioridad al cliente. Escucharlo en su idioma. Tratarlo con respeto.
Es anticipar sus necesidades y ayudarlo a obtener el mayor provecho de nuestra experiencia en larga distancia.

Servicio AT&T.
Otro beneficio a su favor.
1 800 235-0900.

AT&T
La mejor decisión.

1. The ad opens with an old Spanish proverb. What does the proverb mean?
2. When the ad says "it's more than…" it assumes that two things are taken for granted. What are they?
3. To what is "priority" given?
4. How is the client treated?
5. *Escucharlo en su idioma.* What does that mean, and why might it be important?
6. In what does the company claim to have experience?
7. What does the company anticipate?
8. In the English ads, the company used the phrase "The Right Choice." How have they said that in Spanish?
9. Do you think the appeal of this ad is technical or emotional? Why?

NUESTRO MUNDO

PRESENTATION (*page 101*)
A. Have students open their books to page 101 and ask them to read the advertisement silently, or call on an individual to read aloud each of the features highlighted in the ad.
B. Have students answer the questions orally in class or assign them for independent practice.

ANSWERS
1. He who leans against a good tree finds ample shade.
2. Clear and speedy connections (communications)
3. the client
4. as a number one priority
5. "Listening to one in his/her language"; catering to client's special wants, understanding client's needs
6. long distance communication
7. the client's needs
8. *La mejor decisión*
9. Answers will vary.
   Technical: Spanish-speaking operators, experience in long distance communications; emotional: catering to needs of client, respecting him/her, proverb which appeals to the emotions

REPASO
CAPÍTULOS 1-4

OVERVIEW

This section reviews key grammatical structures and vocabulary from Chapters 1-4. The topics were first presented on the following pages: the imperfect, pages 10-14; the future, pages 62 and 86-87; and the comparative and superlative, pages 64 and 89.

REVIEW RESOURCES
1. Workbook, Self-Test 1
2. Computer Software
3. Testing Program, Unit Test 1-4

Conversación

PRESENTATION (page 102)

A. Have students close their books and listen as you read the conversation.
B. Have students open their books to page 102 and call on two volunteers to read the conversation to the class with as much expression as possible.
C. Have an individual summarize the conversation in his/her own words.

ANSWERS

Ejercicio A
1. En el correo
2. No quedaban sellos.
3. Estaba en el mercado.
4. Hacía las compras.
5. Era sirena de ambulancia.
6. En la carnicería
7. Sufrió un ataque cardíaco.
8. Los socorristas
9. Al hospital
10. Todo el mundo estaba muy triste.
11. Mandarán unas flores.
12. Hoy mismo
13. Nadie; es la persona más simpática de todo el mercado.
14. La Sra. Juana

102

REPASO
CAPÍTULOS 1-4

Conversación   *Estaba en el mercado*

GABRIEL: Teresa, ¿dónde estabas? Llamé hace poco pero nadie contestó.
TERESA: Fui al correo porque tenía que comprar unos sellos. No quedaban sellos para correo aéreo. Volveré mañana. ¿Qué pasa, Gabriel? ¿Dónde estás?
GABRIEL: Pues, te diré. Yo estaba en el mercado y hacía las compras cuando sonó una sirena. Era una ambulancia. Parece que la Sra. Juana, la señora de la carnicería, sufrió un ataque cardíaco. Los socorristas le dieron primeros auxilios y la llevaron al hospital. Todo el mundo estaba muy triste. Le mandaremos unas flores al hospital mañana.
TERESA: ¡Qué lástima! No hay nadie más amable que la Sra. Juana. Ella es la persona más simpática de todo el mercado. Yo iré a visitarla esta semana. Y le enviaré una postal hoy mismo.
GABRIEL: Se cayó la moneda. Tendré que colgar. Hasta luego.

A   La llamada. Contesten.

1. ¿Dónde estaba Teresa cuando Gabriel llamó la primera vez?
2. ¿Por qué tendrá Teresa que volver al correo mañana?
3. ¿Dónde estaba Gabriel cuando oyó la sirena?
4. ¿Qué hacía Gabriel?
5. ¿Qué tipo de sirena era?
6. ¿Dónde trabajaba la señora Juana?
7. ¿Qué le pasó a la señora Juana?
8. ¿Quiénes vinieron en la ambulancia?
9. ¿Adónde la llevaron?
10. ¿Cómo se sentía todo el mundo?
11. ¿Qué mandarán al hospital mañana?
12. ¿Cuándo enviará Teresa una postal?
13. ¿Quién es más simpática que la Sra. Juana?
14. ¿Quién es la persona más amable de todo el mercado?

102   CAPÍTULOS 1-4 REPASO

LEARNING FROM PHOTOS

Have students say as much as they can about the photo on page 102. You may wish to ask questions such as: *¿Dónde está la joven? ¿Qué está comprando? ¿Paga con tarjeta de crédito? ¿Cómo paga?*

B **El correo.** Completen.

Voy al ___(1)___ para comprar sellos y echar unas cartas al ___(2)___ . Tengo que poner la zona ___(3)___ en los sobres. Luego, buscaré una cabina telefónica para hacer una ___(4)___ . Necesito unas ___(5)___ de 25 pesetas porque es un teléfono ___(6)___ , no privado.

Estructura

El imperfecto

1. Review the imperfect tense forms of regular verbs and the verbs *ir* and *ser*, the only irregular verbs in the imperfect tense. Remember that the imperfect tense forms of *-er* and *-ir* verbs are identical.

tomar	tomaba, tomabas, tomaba, tomábamos, *tomabais*, tomaban
comer	comía, comías, comía, comíamos, *comíais*, comían
vivir	vivía, vivías, vivía, vivíamos, *vivíais*, vivían

ir	iba, ibas, iba, íbamos, *ibais*, iban
ser	era, eras, era, éramos, *erais*, eran

2. The imperfect tense is used to express an action in the past that is continuous or repeated. The time when the action was completed is unimportant. The preterite tense is used to express an action completed at a definite time in the past. Often a sentence will contain two types of past action. The action that was going on is expressed by the imperfect tense, and the action that intervened or interrupted that action is expressed by the preterite tense.

   Compraba sellos en el correo cuando vi a Manolo.

A **Cuando éramos niños.** Completen.

Cuando nosotros ___(1)___ (vivir) en la ciudad mi padre ___(2)___ (trabajar) en el correo. Mamá ___(3)___ (tener) un puesto en el mercado. Ella ___(4)___ (vender) legumbres. Mis hermanos y yo ___(5)___ (ir) a la escuela por la mañana. Nosotros ___(6)___ (volver) a casa al mediodía. Yo ___(7)___ (preparar) el almuerzo. Mis hermanos ___(8)___ (tomar) leche, pero yo ___(9)___ (beber) gaseosa con el almuerzo. Por la tarde mi hermano Abel ___(10)___ (ir) al mercado y le ___(11)___ (ayudar) a mamá. Por la noche todos ___(12)___ (estar) juntos en casa. En aquellos tiempos todos nosotros ___(13)___ (ser) muy felices.

CAPÍTULOS 1–4 REPASO **103**

LEARNING FROM REALIA

These stamps from Uruaguay commemorate the 500th anniversary of Columbus' voyage of discovery. You may wish to ask students: *¿De dónde son las tres estampillas? ¿Cuánto vale cada una de las estampillas? ¿Qué conmemoran las estampillas uruguayas? Describan las dos estampillas uruguayas.*

ANSWERS
Ejercicio B
1. correo
2. buzón
3. postal
4. llamada
5. monedas
6. público

Estructura
El imperfecto
PRESENTATION (*page 103*)

A. Have students open their books to page 103. As you lead them through steps 1 and 2, remind them to think of a play or movie. The verbs used to describe the scene or background are in the imperfect.

B. In step 2, use a sweeping horizontal motion of the hand to indicate the imperfect.

ANSWERS
Ejercicio A
1. vivíamos
2. trabajaba
3. tenía
4. vendía
5. íbamos
6. volvíamos
7. preparaba
8. tomaban
9. bebía
10. iba
11. ayudaba
12. estábamos
13. éramos

PRESENTATION (*page 104*)

Ejercicio B

In Exercise B, have students give reasons why verbs are in the imperfect or in the preterite. One way to demonstrate the difference is to ask students which actions began first and continued for some time (the imperfect). Another way is to ask which actions were more sudden, with a clear starting and ending point (the preterite).

ANSWERS

Ejercicio B
1. iba, vio
2. miraba, llamó
3. buscó, hacían
4. estaba, volvió
5. daba, llegó

El futuro

PRESENTATION (*page 104*)

A. Have students open their books to page 104. Lead them through steps 1 and 2. In step 1, stress that the endings are the same for all verbs, but are attached to the entire infinitive.
B. Have students repeat the verb forms after you.

PRESENTATION

Ejercicio C

Exercise C can be done with books open or closed.

ANSWERS

Ejercicio C
1. querrá
2. tendrá
3. podrá
4. haré
5. diré
6. saldrán
7. vendrán
8. sabremos

104

B Un accidente. Completen.
1. Laura ___ al correo cuando ___ el accidente. (ir, ver)
2. Todo el mundo ___ a la víctima pero nadie ___ a la policía. (mirar, llamar)
3. Laura en seguida ___ un teléfono mientras los otros no ___ nada. (buscar, hacer)
4. La víctima todavía ___ en la acera cuando Laura ___ . (estar, volver)
5. Laura le ___ los primeros auxilios a la víctima cuando ___ la ambulancia. (dar, llegar)

El futuro

1. Future time may be expressed in Spanish in various ways. The use of *ir a* + the infinitive is one way, *Voy a estudiar mañana*. Or the true future tense may be used. Review the future tense forms of regular and irregular verbs. Remember, for regular verbs, the future endings are added to the infinitive.

tomar	tomaré, tomarás, tomará, tomaremos, *tomaréis*, tomarán
volver	volveré, volverás, volverá, volveremos, *volveréis*, volverán
vivir	viviré, vivirás, vivirá, viviremos, *viviréis*, vivirán

2. For irregular verbs the regular future tense endings are added to an irregular stem. Review the future stems of irregular verbs.

INFINITIVE	STEM	FUTURE
tener	tendr-	tendré
salir	saldr-	saldré
venir	vendr-	vendré
poner	pondr-	pondré
saber	sabr-	sabré
poder	podr-	podré
decir	dir-	diré
hacer	har-	haré
querer	querr-	querré

C Tendrá que… Cambien en el futuro.
1. Paco va a querer ser médico como su madre.
2. Él va a tener que estudiar más.
3. La universidad no va a poder aceptarlo con malas notas.
4. Yo voy a hacer todo lo posible para ayudar a Paco.
5. Yo le voy a decir lo que tiene que hacer.
6. Primero, Paco y los amigos no van a salir todas las noches.
7. Y los amigos no van a venir a casa a mirar la televisión.
8. Ana y yo vamos a saber cómo hacerle estudiar más.

104 CAPÍTULOS 1–4 REPASO

COOPERATIVE LEARNING

Each team member writes five sentences beginning with *Cuando era niño(a)…* plus an imperfect tense verb phrase. Then each member writes five sentences beginning with *Ayer…* plus a preterite tense verb phrase. Members take turns reading their sentences to each other.

El comparativo y el superlativo

1. To form the comparative the construction *más... que* can be used with an adjective, noun, or adverb.

   Ella es más alta que yo.
   Ella tiene más trabajo que yo.
   Ella camina más rápido que yo.

2. The superlative is formed by using *más* with the appropriate definite article. The superlative is followed by the preposition *de*.

   La Ciudad de México es la ciudad más grande de las Américas.

3. Review the following irregular comparative and superlative forms: the comparative of *bueno(a)* is *mejor*; the superlative is *el* or *la mejor*.

D Es más... que... Contesten según su opinión.

1. ¿Qué enfermedad es más grave que la diabetes?
2. ¿Quiénes estudian más que los socorristas?
3. ¿Cuál es el mejor hospital de esta área?
4. ¿Quién es el médico o la médica más famosa del país?
5. ¿Es más cara la penicilina o la aspirina?
6. ¿Quiénes reciben más dinero, los médicos o los socorristas?
7. En el hospital, ¿quiénes tienen el trabajo más difícil?

Comunicación

A Un accidente. Ud. está caminando por una calle de Santiago de Chile. Alguien se cae en la calle. Llame al servicio de primeros auxilios y explique lo que pasó. Un(a) compañero(a) de clase será el/la operador(a).

B Quiero enviar... Ud. está viajando por México. En Taxco Ud. compró un objeto de plata *(silver)* y quiere mandar el paquete a casa por correo. Prepare una conversación con el/la empleado(a) del correo (un[a] compañero[a] de clase).

CAPÍTULOS 1–4 REPASO

FONDO ACADÉMICO

LAS CIENCIAS NATURALES
(optional material)

OVERVIEW

The three readings in this *Fondo Académico* are related topically to material in Chapters 1, 2 and 4 of *A bordo*. You may have all students read a particular section, or all three sections. Or you may allow students to choose one of the three sections according to their own interests.

These readings may be presented in one of the following ways:
1. As independent reading. Students read the selections and do the post-reading exercises as homework. Homework is handed in. This option is least intrusive on class time and requires a minimum of teacher involvement.
2. As homework with in-class follow-up. The readings and post-reading exercises are assigned as homework. The exercises are reviewed and discussed in class the next day.
3. As an intensive, in-class activity, including pre-reading presentation and exercises, in-class reading and discussion, assignment of the exercises for homework, and a discussion of the assignment in class the following day.

Lectura
Antes de leer

PRESENTATION (pages 106–107)

A. Ask students to list some of the natural sciences. Most of the terms are cognates. For example: *la biología, la patología, la química, la bacteriología*, etc.
B. Have students open their books to page 106 and allow them several minutes to read the *antes de leer* section in their books.

FONDO ACADÉMICO

LAS CIENCIAS NATURALES

Antes de leer

We speak to each other face to face. We talk on the phone. We listen to compact discs and cassettes, radio, and TV. We take sound for granted. Yet sound is one of our foremost means of communication. How does it work? In preparation for reading the following selection, please review how sound is produced, the speed of sound and how the human ear perceives sound.

labels: la oreja, el tímpano, el yunque, el estribo, el ner auditi, el cara, la trompa Eustaqui, el martillo, el lóbulo

Lectura

EL SONIDO

Cuando un objeto vibra rápidamente mueve el aire alrededor. Cuando va en una dirección saca (desplaza) el aire del lugar. Cuando se mueve en la otra dirección, el aire vuelve rápidamente para llenar el espacio[1]. El aire que está al lado del objeto pasa la vibración al aire que está cerca, y este aire sigue pasando la vibración hasta llegar más lejos. Cuando las vibraciones llegan a nuestro oído[2], se llaman ondas sonoras[3], o sonido[4]. Las vibraciones pueden mover las moléculas en el aire o en otro material, sólido o líquido, como el agua o el metal. Pero no hay sonido si no hay un material por donde transmitir las vibraciones.

El sonido se transmite en el aire a unos 330 metros por segundo, pero por un alambre[5] de metal a unos 5.000 metros por segundo. (Esto parece rápido, pero es mucho más lento que la velocidad de la luz. La luz viaja por el aire a 299.700.000 metros por segundo.) Las ondas sonoras viajan más rápidamente por materiales sólidos que por los líquidos o los gases. Mientras más densas las moléculas del material, más rápidamente viaja el sonido.

Los sonidos tienen tres cualidades que nos permiten conocerlos: el tono[6], el timbre[7], y el volumen o la intensidad.

Algunos sonidos son fuertes, y otros son débiles; una sirena y un canario, por ejemplo. Llamamos a esta característica "intensidad". La intensidad depende de la distancia y del material por el que pasa el sonido. El tono se relaciona con la frecuencia de las vibraciones. Un gran número de vibraciones por segundo produce un tono alto o agudo. Un número menor de vibraciones produce un tono bajo o grave.

El timbre es la característica individual de cada sonido independiente del tono o de la intensidad. El saxofón y el clarinete tienen diferentes timbres.

106 FONDO ACADÉMICO

DEVELOPING READING SKILLS

Remind students of the reading tactic of deriving the meaning of unknown words from context. Tell them not to worry if they encounter a word they do not know, to keep reading and to try to guess at the unknown word's meaning from the context surrounding it.

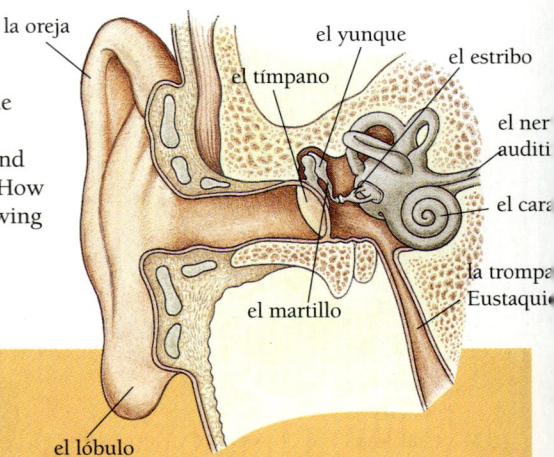

FONDO ACADÉMICO

¿Y cómo oímos los sonidos? El oído humano se divide en tres partes; la oreja u oído externo, el oído medio y el oído interno. Las vibraciones entran por la oreja. Pasan por un canal que las lleva al tímpano[8], una membrana muy sensible[9]. El tímpano transmite las vibraciones a tres huesos muy pequeños que están conectados al tímpano. Desde los huesos las vibraciones llegan al caracol que está lleno de un líquido. Las vibraciones mueven el líquido. Este movimiento activa el nervio auditivo que entonces transmite un mensaje al cerebro.

[1] el espacio *space*
[2] oído *ear*
[3] ondas sonoras *sound waves*
[4] sonido *sound*
[5] alambre *wire*
[6] el tono *pitch*
[7] el timbre *tone*
[8] tímpano *ear drum*
[9] sensible *sensitive*

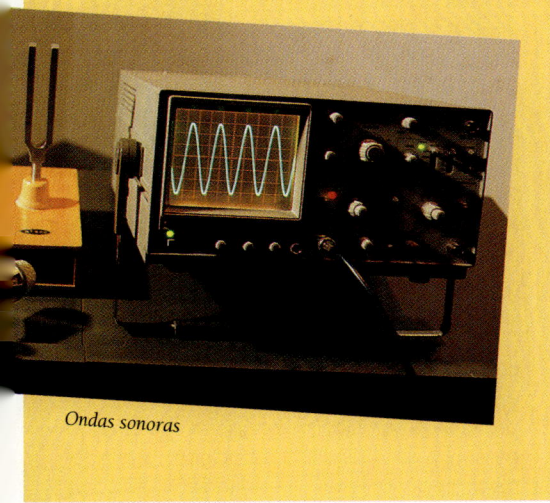

Ondas sonoras

Después de leer

A El sonido. Completen.

1. Cuando un objeto vibra, el aire se ___ .
2. Las vibraciones que oímos se llaman ___ sonoras.
3. Los sonidos se transmiten por un ___ de metal a unos 5.000 metros por segundo.
4. La ___ viaja por el aire mucho más rápidamente que el sonido.
5. La velocidad de los sonidos es mayor por ___ que por gases o líquidos.
6. Las tres cualidades de los sonidos son la ___ , el ___ y el ___ .
7. Un tono bajo se produce con menos ___ que un tono alto.

B El oído. Contesten.

1. ¿En cuántas partes se divide el oído humano?
2. ¿Qué es la oreja?
3. ¿Adónde llegan primero las ondas sonoras?
4. ¿Qué es el tímpano?
5. ¿Qué parte del oído contiene un líquido?
6. ¿Qué lleva los mensajes al cerebro?

C Seguimiento. Contesten.

1. ¿Cómo se llaman en inglés el martillo, el yunque y el estribo?
2. Si la velocidad de los sonidos es mayor cuando la densidad de las moléculas es mayor, ¿viajan más rápidamente o más lentamente los sonidos encima de una montaña o al nivel del mar?
3. Describa la ruta de los sonidos desde la oreja hasta el cerebro.
4. Explique lo que son "ultrasonidos".

FONDO ACADÉMICO **107**

C. You may ask students to list the cognates they find in the reading.

Después de leer

PRESENTATION (page 107)

Ask some simple questions in Spanish about the natural sciences.

ANSWERS

Ejercicio A
1. mueve
2. ondas
3. alambre
4. luz
5. materiales sólidos
6. el tono, el timbre, el volumen (la intensidad)
7. vibraciones por segundo

Ejercicio B
1. tres partes
2. el oído externo
3. por la oreja
4. una membrana sensible
5. el caracol
6. el nervio auditivo

Ejercicio C
1. hammer, anvil, and stirrup
2. encima de una montaña
3. Las vibraciones llegan al caracol, mueven el líquido del caracol que activa el nervio auditivo que transmite un mensaje al cerebro.
4. sonidos de alta frecuencia

ABOUT THE LANGUAGE

1. You may want to remind students that the English word for "ear" is represented by two words in Spanish. *La oreja* is only the outer ear. The middle and inner ears, the actual hearing organ, is *el oído*. An "earache" is *un dolor de oídos*.
2. Some words having to do with hearing are:
   la sordera (deafness)
   el aparato acústico (hearing aid)
   duro de oído (hard of hearing)
   el lenguaje por señas (sign language)

FONDO ACADÉMICO

LA SOCIOLOGÍA

Antes de leer
PRESENTATION (page 108)
A. Have students open their books to page 108 and ask them to look up the words as suggested.
B. Have pairs scan the reading for cognates. There are approximately 55.

Lectura
PRESENTATION (pages 108-109)
A. Have students read the selection aloud or silently.
B. Explain to students that they must use different techniques to guess the meaning of words they are not familiar with. Explain that they should guess the meaning based on the message in the rest of the sentence.

FONDO ACADÉMICO

LA SOCIOLOGÍA

Antes de leer

There is a sociology of medicine. Attitudes toward health and customs regarding health vary among cultures, as do the frequency of different illnesses and the ways in which health care is delivered. In preparation for the following selection please look up and review the following: shamans, *curanderos*, acupuncture.

Lectura

Santiago Ramón y Cajal, médico español

MEDICINA Y SOCIEDAD

La importancia de la salud se nota hasta en los saludos: "¿Cómo estás?" es un saludo en casi todo el Occidente[1]. Ya sabemos que los microbios y los virus causan muchas enfermedades, pero los factores culturales y sociales también influyen mucho en la salud. La incidencia de ciertas enfermedades varía mucho entre diferentes grupos étnicos[2]. No son necesariamente responsables los genes sino también factores tales como la dieta y las costumbres. El cáncer del colon es muy frecuente en los países donde se consume mucha grasa y poca fibra. La incidencia de cáncer del estómago es alta en el Japón, pero baja entre norteamericanos de ascendencia japonesa. Obviamente, la dieta es muy importante. En los EE.UU. se calcula que unos 350.000 personas mueren[3] cada año a causa de enfermedades relacionadas con el tabaco. El cáncer de la piel[4] es más común entre personas de piel muy blanca, las personas que más quieren broncearse en la playa.

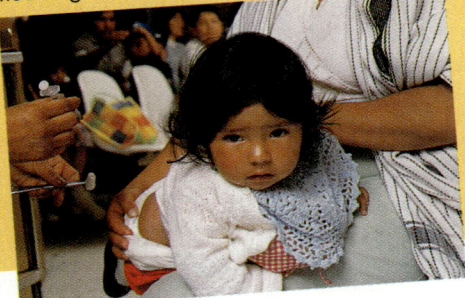

El status social influye mucho en la salud. La esperanza de vida[5] para las personas ricas entre los 65 y 69 años de edad es de 2 a 4 años más que la de los pobres. Muy notable también es la diferencia entre hombres y mujeres. Los hombres, por lo general, gozan de[6] 6 años menos de vida que las mujeres.

La vida moderna impone[7] presiones psicológicas en la gente, el estrés, por ejemplo. El apoyo o el sostén[8] social que proveen la familia, los amigos y las otras personas con quienes interactuamos ayuda mucho en mantener la buena salud física y,

108 FONDO ACADÉMICO

LEARNING FROM PHOTOS

Santiago Ramón y Cajal (1852-1934) fue histólogo y profesor de anatomía en las universidades de Valencia y de Barcelona. Recibió el Premio Nobel de Medicina en 1906 por sus investigaciones acerca de la estructura del sistema nervioso.

FONDO ACADÉMICO

sobre todo, mental.
Todas las sociedades tienen sus "especialistas" para tratar a los enfermos. En las sociedades indígenas había chamanes que curaban a los enfermos por medio de ritos y ceremonias. Hoy todavía existen curanderos en muchos lugares remotos de las Américas. Los curanderos, sin instrucción formal, "curan" con hierbas, pociones y oraciones[9]. En China hay especialistas que se dedican a la acupuntura. La acupuntura se está popularizando en el mundo occidental.

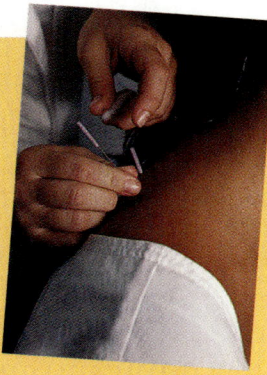

[1] el Occidente *the West*
[2] étnico *ethnic*
[3] mueren *die*
[4] piel *skin*
[5] esperanza de vida *life expectancy*
[6] gozan de *enjoy*
[7] impone *imposes*
[8] el apoyo/el sostén *support*
[9] oraciones *prayers*

Después de leer

A La salud. Contesten.

1. ¿Por qué se menciona el saludo "cómo estás"?
2. ¿Cuáles son las causas de muchas enfermedades?
3. ¿Qué clases de factores influyen en la salud?
4. ¿Entre quiénes varía la incidencia de algunas enfermedades?
5. ¿En qué país es frecuente el cáncer del estómago?

B Seguimiento. Contesten.

1. El artículo dice que "el apoyo o el sostén social que proveen la familia y los amigos ayuda mucho en mantener la buena salud física y, sobre todo, mental". Comente.
2. ¿Cómo influyen la dieta y las costumbres en la salud? Explique.
3. Prepare un informe breve sobre uno de los siguientes temas:
   a. la acupuntura
   b. los chamanes
   c. los curanderos
   d. los efectos del tabaco
   e. la salud y la clase social

Un curandero

FONDO ACADÉMICO

LA HISTORIA

Antes de leer

PRESENTATION *(page 110)*

Note This reading selection will interest students who enjoy history as well as those who have a natural curiosity about the origin of things.

A. Ask students to tell anything they know about Christopher Columbus from their history courses.

B. Write the following on the board and have students look for the information as they read:
1. the difference between the *tortilla mexicana* and the *tortilla española*
2. the history of the potato
3. what the Spaniards brought to the Americas and vice versa
4. what part spices played in the voyages of Columbus

Lectura

PRESENTATION *(pages 110-111)*

Have students open their books to pages 110-111 and ask them to read the selection aloud or silently.

FONDO ACADÉMICO

LA HISTORIA

Antes de leer

The voyage of Columbus resulted in an encounter between the cultures of Europe and those of the indigenous peoples of the Americas. Our very diet is a result of this meeting. Make a list of at least a half dozen foods you think are of American origin and half a dozen brought to the Americas by the Europeans.

Lectura

LOS ALIMENTOS EN LA HISTORIA

Hay tortillas en México y en España, pero lo único que tienen en común es su forma. La tradicional tortilla mexicana es de maíz, la española es de huevo, y en México se llama "omelet". La clásica tortilla a la española es de huevo con patatas, realmente un plato "bicultural" ya que las patatas son de América.

"Bicultural" también es el taco de carne. La carne de res, introducida en México por los españoles, se combina con una tortilla de maíz, invento de los aztecas. El maíz era la comida básica de muchos grupos indígenas antes de la llegada de Colón.

Cristóbal Colón

La patata o papa se cultivaba primero en la región andina. Los conquistadores la introdujeron en Europa. Hoy se conoce en todo el mundo. En Irlanda durante los siglos XVIII y XIX la papa llegó a ser casi un monocultivo. Todos dependían de la papa para comer. El hambre causada por las malas cosechas[1] de papas alrededor de 1850 mató[2] a muchos y causó una tremenda emigración del país. Muchos irlandeses emigraron entonces a los EE.UU., la Argentina, Chile y otros países de las Américas.

Hoy los mexicanos también hacen tortillas de harina[3] de trigo[4]. Los españoles trajeron el trigo de Europa. En las Américas no había trigo. En las Américas tampoco había ganado[5]; ni vacas[6], ni ovejas[7], ni caballos[8]. Los españoles trajeron la uva[9], el azúcar y el café. Y de las Américas llevaron a Europa el chocolate, el tabaco, el tomate, el cacahuete[10] y el pavo[11].

El mismo descubrimiento de América se debe a la comida. Cristóbal Colón buscaba una nueva ruta a Asia. En Asia estaban las especias[12]. Las especias eran necesarias para conservar la comida. En Europa pagaban mucho por las especias que venían por tierra en caravanas en viajes que duraban años. Colón pensaba

110 FONDO ACADÉMICO

CRITICAL THINKING ACTIVITY

(Thinking skills: making inferences; drawing conclusions)

Read the following to the class or write it on the board or on an overhead transparency.

En los tiempos de los incas hubo cientos de variedades de la papa. Hoy solamente se cultivan muy pocas variedades en la mayoría de los países. Algunos científicos creen que esto es peligroso. ¿Por qué? Si no tienes idea, habla con tu profesor(a) de biología.

FONDO ACADÉMICO

llegar a Asia por mar. Como sabemos, Colón nunca llegó a Asia sino a las Américas.

Parte del mural "La almendra del cacao" de Diego Rivera

Muchos siglos antes de Colón los romanos usaban la sal para conservar y dar sabor a la comida. La sal tenía tanta importancia que les pagaban a los legionarios romanos con sal. De allí viene la palabra "salario", o en inglés *salary*.

[1] cosechas *crop*
[2] mató *killed*
[3] harina *flour*
[4] trigo *wheat*
[5] ganado *cattle*
[6] vacas *cows*
[7] ovejas *sheep*
[8] caballos *horses*
[9] uva *grape*
[10] cacahuete *peanut*
[11] pavo *turkey*
[12] especias *spices*

Después de leer

A Escojan.

1. Los europeos comían trigo. ¿Qué comían los aztecas?
   a. arroz   b. maíz   c. uvas
2. ¿Qué forma tiene una tortilla?
   a. la de un cuadro
   b. la de un triángulo
   c. la de un círculo
3. ¿Cuál de los ingredientes del taco tiene su origen en Europa?
   a. la salsa   b. la tortilla   c. la carne
4. ¿Donde se origina la papa?
   a. en los Andes
   b. en España
   c. en Irlanda
5. ¿Cuál fue la causa de la gran emigración de Irlanda?
   a. el hambre
   b. la guerra
   c. las exploraciones
6. ¿Qué buscaba Colón?
   a. un mercado para el ganado europeo
   b. una ruta por mar a Asia
   c. más comercio con las Américas
7. ¿A quiénes les pagaban con sal?
   a. a los conquistadores españoles
   b. a los soldados indios
   c. a los legionarios romanos

B Seguimiento. Contesten.

1. Muchos indios en Norteamérica cazaban bisontes (*bisons*) para su carne. Con la llegada de los españoles, la caza del bizonte se facilitó. Explique por qué.
2. Explique la derivación de la palabra "salario".
3. Dé algunos ejemplos de platos "biculturales".

DID YOU KNOW?

Cristóbal Colón hizo cuatro viajes a las Américas (1492-93; 1493-96; 1498-1500; 1502-04). Busca en la biblioteca una descripción de los cuatro viajes y traza la ruta de cada uno en el mapa.

Después de leer
PRESENTATION *(page 111)*
Go over Exercise A in the *Después de leer* section. Assign Exercise B to more able students.

ANSWERS
Ejercicio A
1. b
2. c
3. c
4. a
5. a
6. b
7. c

Ejercicio B
Answers will vary.
1. Los españoles trajeron caballos y armas de fuego.
2. Viene de la palabra sal, que valía mucho y se usaba como forma de pago.
3. La tortilla española, el taco, el burrito

ABOUT THE LANGUAGE
The Spanish names for the peanut are all derived from original Indian names. In the Caribbean and parts of South America the peanut is *maní*; in México, *cacahuate*; in Spain, *cacahuete*; and in other areas, *cacahué*.

CAPÍTULO 5
Scope and Sequence pages 112–137

Topics	Functions	Structure	Culture
Cars	How to talk about cars and good driving habits	El potencial o condicional: formas regulares	Driving customs in Spanish-speaking countries
Good driving habits	How to buy gas and have your car serviced	El potencial o condicional: formas irregulares	Traffic conditions in large cities
Services at a gas station	How to express conditions	Dos complementos en una oración	Air pollution
	How to refer to people and things already mentioned		"Micro" buses in Buenos Aires
	How to discuss some traffic-related problems		Driving school in Madrid
			Avenida 9 de Julio in Buenos Aires

CAPÍTULO 5

Situation Cards

The Situation Cards simulate real-life situations that require students to communicate in Spanish, exactly as though they were in a Spanish-speaking country. The Situation Cards operate on the assumption that the person to whom the message is to be conveyed understands no English. Therefore, students must focus on producing the Spanish vocabulary and structures necessary to negotiate the situations successfully. For additional information, see the Introduction to the Situation Cards in the Situation Cards Envelope.

Communication Transparency

The illustration seen in this Communication Transparency consists of a synthesis of the two vocabulary (Palabras 1&2) presentations found in this chapter. It has been created in order to present this chapter's vocabulary in a new context, and also to recycle vocabulary learned in previous chapters. The Communication Transparency consists of original art. Following are some specific uses:

1. as a cue to stimulate conversation and writing activities
2. for listening comprehension activities
3. to review and reteach vocabulary
4. as a review for chapter and unit tests

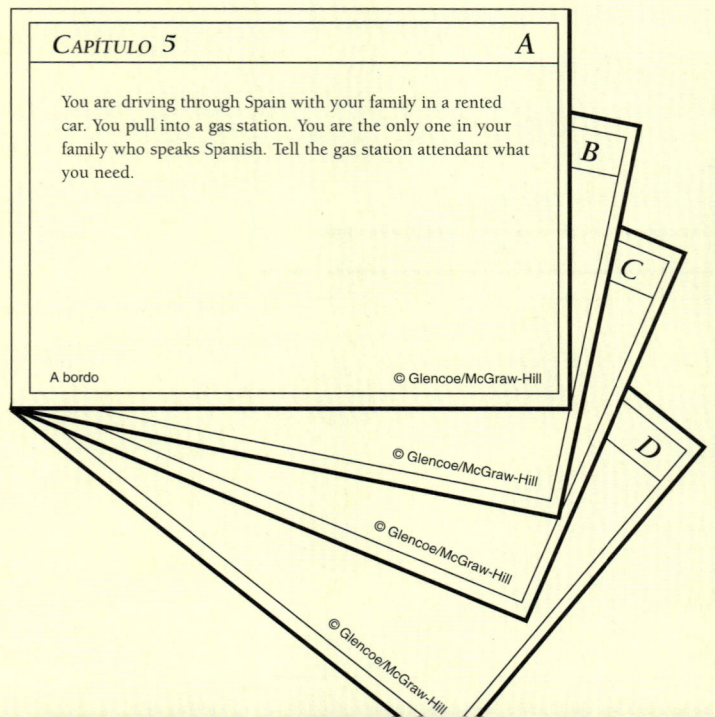

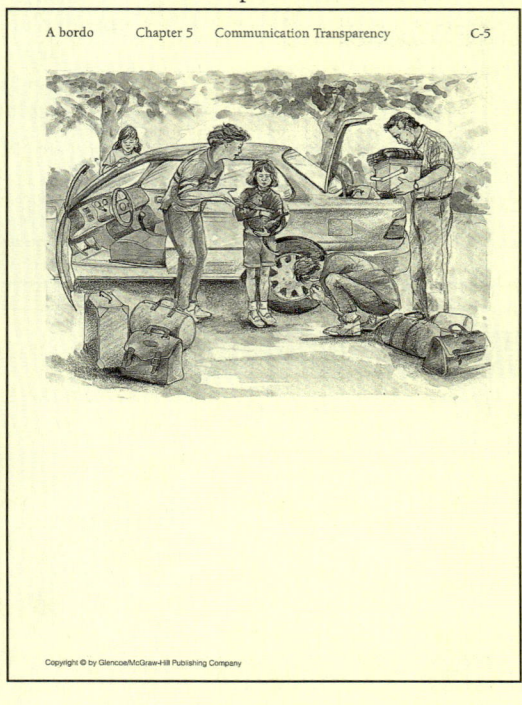

CAPÍTULO 5 A

You are driving through Spain with your family in a rented car. You pull into a gas station. You are the only one in your family who speaks Spanish. Tell the gas station attendant what you need.

A bordo   © Glencoe/McGraw-Hill

112A

CAPÍTULO 5
Print Resources

Lesson Plans

Pages

Workbook
- Palabras 1 — 47-48
- Palabras 2 — 48-50
- Estructura — 51-52
- Un poco más — 53-55
- Mi autobiografía — 56

Communication Activities Masters
- Palabras 1 — 25-26
- Palabras 2 — 27
- Estructura — 28-31

11 Bell Ringer Reviews — 16-18

Chapter Situation Cards A B C D

Chapter Quizzes
- Palabras 1 — 21
- Palabras 2 — 22
- Estructura — 23-25

Testing Program
- Listening Comprehension — 25
- Reading and Writing — 26-29
- Proficiency — 127
- Speaking — 146

Nosotros y Nuestro Mundo
- Nuestro Conocimiento Académico Marketing: el producto y su marca
- Nuestro Idioma El modo potencial o condicional; Dos pronombres en la misma oración
- Nuestra Cultura El Camino Real y las misiones de California
- Nuestra Literatura "El Ford" de Francisco García Pavón
- Nuestra Creatividad
- Nuestras Diversiones

CAPÍTULO 5
Multimedia Resources

CD-ROM Interactive Textbook Disc 2

Chapter 5 Student Edition
- Palabras 1
- Palabras 2
- Estructura
- Conversación
- Lectura y cultura
- Hispanoparlantes
- Realidades
- Culminación
- Prueba

Audio Cassette Program with Student Tape Manual

Cassette — **Pages**
- 4A Palabras 1 — 226
- 4A Palabras 2 — 226-227
- 4A Estructura — 227
- 4A Conversación — 227
- 4A Segunda parte — 228-229

Compact Disc Program with Student Tape Manual
- CD 4 Palabras 1 — 226
- CD 4 Palabras 2 — 226-227
- CD 4 Estructura — 227
- CD 4 Conversación — 227
- CD 4 Segunda parte — 228-229

Overhead Transparencies Binder
- Vocabulary 5.1 (A&B); 5.2 (A&B)
- Communication C-5
- Maps
- Fine Art (with Blackline Master Activities)

Video Program
- Videocassette
- Video Activities Booklet — 12-15
- Videodisc
- Video Activities Booklet — 12-15

Computer Software (Macintosh, IBM, Apple)
- Practice Disk
    - Palabras 1 y 2
    - Estructura
- Test Generator Disk
    - Chapter Test
    - Customized Test

112B

CAPÍTULO 5

CHAPTER OVERVIEW

In this chapter students will learn to talk about cars, good driving habits, rules of the road, and the essentials for communicating at a service station. They will learn the conditional in order to talk about things they would do but for some reason cannot. They will expand their ability to talk about people and things already mentioned through the use of pronouns.

The cultural focus of Chapter 5 is on driving customs in some Spanish-speaking countries, traffic conditions in large cities, and the relationship of the automobile to the problem of air pollution.

CHAPTER OBJECTIVES

By the end of this chapter, students will know:
1. vocabulary associated with automobile types, features, and basic servicing
2. vocabulary associated with driving
3. forms of the conditional with regular verbs
4. forms of the conditional with irregular verbs
5. uses of the conditional and positioning of indirect and direct object pronouns when used together in a single sentence

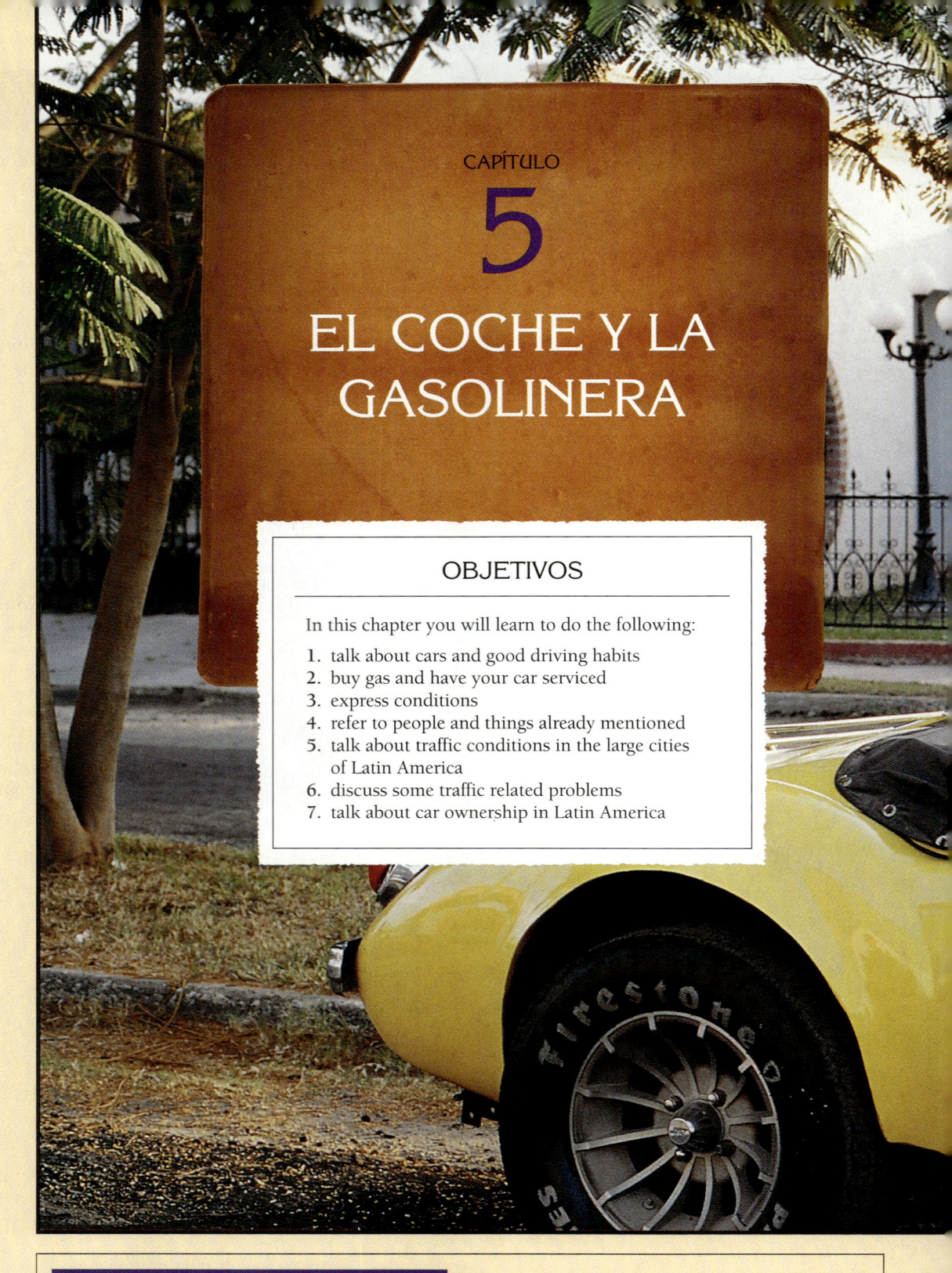

CAPÍTULO 5

EL COCHE Y LA GASOLINERA

OBJETIVOS

In this chapter you will learn to do the following:

1. talk about cars and good driving habits
2. buy gas and have your car serviced
3. express conditions
4. refer to people and things already mentioned
5. talk about traffic conditions in the large cities of Latin America
6. discuss some traffic related problems
7. talk about car ownership in Latin America

CHAPTER PROJECTS

(optional)
1. Borrow a Driver's Education video. View it with students and discuss it with them in Spanish.
2. If road maps of Spanish-speaking countries are available, have groups plan car trips between two points and report on their plans, mentioning stops at gas stations and restaurants along the way.

CHAPTER 5 RESOURCES

1. Workbook
2. Student Tape Manual
3. Audio Cassette 4A
4. Vocabulary Transparencies
5. Bell Ringer Review Blackline Masters
6. Communication Activities Masters
7. Computer Software: Practice and Test Generator
8. Video Cassette, Chapter 5
9. Video Activities Booklet, Chapter 5
10. Situation Cards
11. Chapter Quizzes
12. Testing Program

Pacing

Chapter 5 will require eight to ten class sessions. Pacing will depend on the length of the class period, the age of the students, and student aptitude.

LEARNING FROM PHOTOS

After presenting the *Palabras 1* vocabulary, refer to the photo on pages 112-113. Tell students: *Es una fotografía de jóvenes en Puerto Rico. ¿Qué puedes decir de Puerto Rico? ¿De qué color es el carro? ¿Es un carro deportivo? ¿Es descapotable? ¿Cuántas personas caben en el carro, dos o cuatro? ¿Quién está conduciendo?*

113

VOCABULARIO
PALABRAS 1

Vocabulary Teaching Resources
1. Vocabulary Transparencies, 5.1 (A & B)
2. Audio Cassette 4A
3. Student Tape Manual, *Palabras 1*
4. Workbook, *Palabras 1*
5. Communication Activities Masters, *Palabras 1*, A & B
6. Chapter Quizzes, *Palabras 1*

Bell Ringer Review
Write the following on the board or use BRR Blackline Master 5-1: Write eight words associated with train travel.

PRESENTATION (pages 114-115)

Note More than the usual number of alternate words are offered in this section. All the variants presented in *Palabras 1* are commonly used.

A. Using Vocabulary Transparencies 5.1 (A & B), point to each illustration and have students repeat the corresponding word or phrase two or three times. Dramatize *frenar* and *parar* to clarify meaning.
B. Point to items at random and ask yes/no or either/or questions. After some practice, progress to more open-ended questions, such as *¿Qué es esto?*

BRR
Show picture of a car + ask students to describe it in as many ways as they can.
What about the Bretz car?
BRR Have students fill out a driver's license

114

VOCABULARIO

PALABRAS 1

EL COCHE

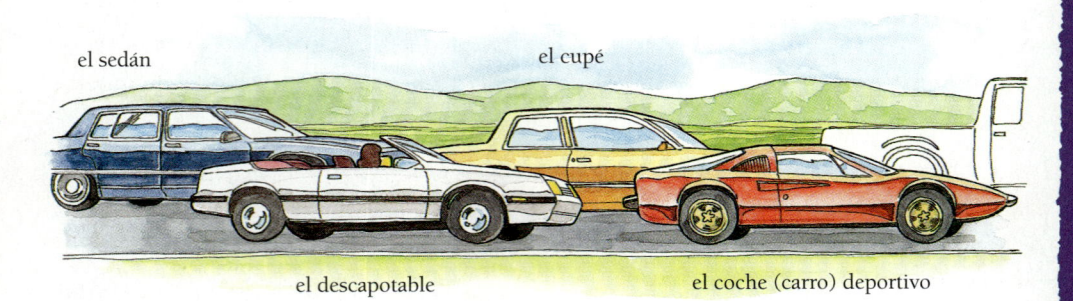

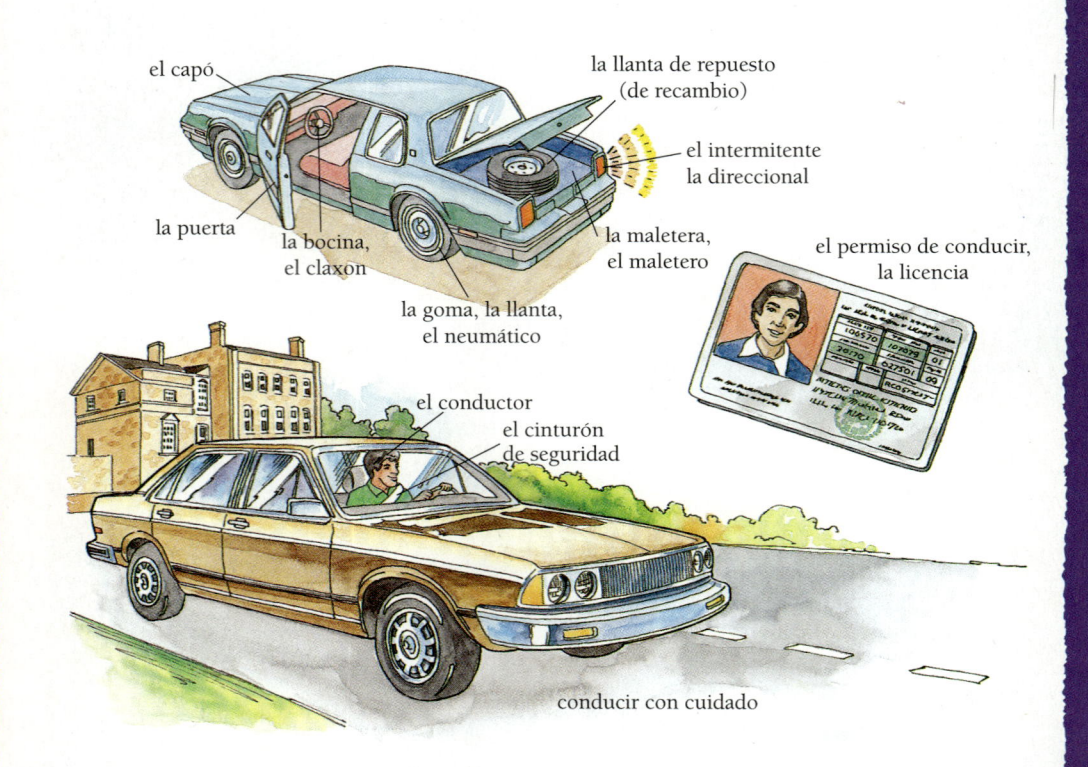

el sedán
el cupé
el descapotable
el coche (carro) deportivo

el capó
la llanta de repuesto (de recambio)
el intermitente
la direccional
la puerta
la bocina, el claxon
la maletera, el maletero
el permiso de conducir, la licencia
la goma, la llanta, el neumático

el conductor
el cinturón de seguridad

conducir con cuidado

114   CAPÍTULO 5

PANTOMIME

(following the Vocabulary presentation)

Getting Ready
Set up a chair in the classroom as a driver's seat. Pieces of paper on the floor can serve as accelerator and brake pedals. Demonstrate the term *el pie*.
_____, levántate, por favor. Ven acá. Es tu coche.
Abre la puerta de tu coche.

Sube.
Siéntate.
Cierra la puerta.
Pon el cinturón de seguridad.
Arranca (prende) el motor.
Pon el pie en el acelerador. Acelera.
Dobla a la derecha.
Párate.
Gracias, _____. Muy bien. Vuelve a tu asiento, por favor.

Design a synonym drill

acelerar
cambiar de velocidad
frenar, poner los frenos
la circulación, el tráfico, el tránsito
adelantar

llegar a un cruce
el cruce
parar el carro
estacionar, aparcar el carro

doblar la esquina
la esquina

Carlos conduciría.
Pero no puede.
¿Por qué? Porque no tiene su permiso de conducir.

Teresa compraría el coche.
Pero no puede.
¿Por qué? Porque no tiene suficiente dinero.

CAPÍTULO 5   **115**

After introducing vocab, use transparencies to stimulate conversation

C. Have students open their books to pages 114-115 and repeat the vocabulary after you or Cassette 4A.
D. Call on volunteers to read the new words and sentences.
E. Show a photo of your own car, or a magazine picture of one, and describe it, using the new vocabulary as much as possible. For example: *Tengo un coche deportivo de color rojo. Es un descapotable americano. Es una marca americana, un Ford. Acelera rapidamente, pero siempre conduzco con cuidado.*

Teaching Tip When an individual cannot respond to a question, try getting the answer from a volunteer by gesturing silently to the class or asking: *¿Quién sabe?* Always have the original student repeat the correct model, and come back to him/her soon with the same item.

RECYCLING

Regular *-ar* verbs are recycled in *Palabras 1* through the introduction of *acelerar, adelantar, cambiar, frenar, parar, llegar, estacionar (aparcar)* and *doblar.* The irregular verb *conducir* is also reintroduced.

ABOUT THE LANGUAGE

1. Another word for "to pass" is *rebasar.*
2. In addition to *estacionar* and *aparcar, parquear* is also used.
3. Noun phrases for "parking lot" are *el estacionamiento, el aparcamiento, el parqueo,* and *el parking.*
4. In addition to *conducir, manejar* is also frequently used.
5. Another common alternate for "tire" is *el caucho.*

Ejercicios

PRESENTATION (page 116)

Ejercicios A and B

Since Exercises A and B involve items pictured on the Vocabulary Transparencies, you may continue to use them as you do these exercises.

ANSWERS

Ejercicio A
1. Es un sedán.
2. Son los frenos.
3. Es el maletero.
4. Es la esquina.
5. Es la goma.

Ejercicio B
1. Sí
2. Sí
3. No
4. No
5. Sí
6. Sí
7. Sí

Try to develop a short PowerPoint for these questions

Ejercicios

A ¿Qué es? Identifiquen.

1. ¿Es un sedán o un cupé?
2. ¿Son los frenos o el acelerador? 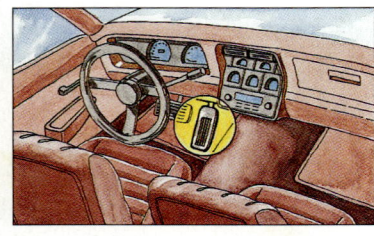
3. ¿Es el maletero o el capó? 
4. ¿Es el cruce o la esquina? 
5. ¿Es el intermitente o la goma? 

B El coche. ¿Sí o no?
1. Un cupé tiene dos puertas.
2. El motor del coche está debajo del capó.
3. La llanta de recambio está en el capó.
4. El conductor pone los intermitentes cuando va a parar el carro.
5. El conductor pone los intermitentes o las direccionales cuando va a doblar.
6. Para parar el carro, es necesario poner los frenos.
7. No es necesario cambiar de velocidad si el carro tiene transmisión automática (cambio automático).

116   CAPÍTULO 5

COOPERATIVE LEARNING

Each member of the team will write down four or five characteristics of their car, or their family car, such as make, model, color, year, or whether old or new. Members will use these lists to describe their cars in Spanish to the rest of the team. Provide a model description first.

Students can ask their teammates Spanish words they can't remember.

AUTOMUNDO MAGAZINE

"La primera revista del automóvil en español en los Estados Unidos"

Aproveche esta oferta única. ¡Suscríbase hoy mismo!

ESPECIAL 10° ANIVERSARIO

C **Nuestro coche.** Preguntas personales.

1. ¿Tienes un coche o tiene tu famila un coche?
2. ¿De qué marca es?
3. ¿Qué modelo es?
4. ¿Es descapotable?
5. ¿Cuántas puertas tiene?
6. ¿Hay una goma de repuesto (recambio) en el maletero?

D **Teresa lo haría, pero no puede.** Contesten según se indica.

1. ¿Compraría Teresa el coche? (sí)
2. ¿Puede comprar el coche? (no)
3. ¿Por qué no puede? (no tiene bastante dinero)
4. ¿Cambiaría Teresa la llanta? (sí)
5. ¿Puede? (no)
6. ¿Por qué no puede? (no tiene llanta de repuesto)
7. ¿Conduciría Lupe? (sí)
8. ¿Puede? (no)
9. ¿Por qué no puede? (dejó su permiso de conducir en casa)
10. ¿Estacionaría Lupe aquí? (no)
11. ¿Por qué no? (está prohibido)

CAPÍTULO 5   117

LEARNING FROM REALIA

Refer students to the advertisement at the top of page 117 and ask: ¿Cuál es el título de la revista? ¿En qué lengua se publica? ¿Dónde se publica?

INDEPENDENT PRACTICE

Assign any of the following:
1. Workbook, *Palabras 1*
2. Communication Activities Masters, *Palabras 1, A & B*
3. Exercises on student pages 116-117

Ejercicios

PRESENTATION (page 117)

Extension of *Ejercicio C*: Listening

After completing Exercise C as a whole-class activity, have students work in pairs. One partner reads the questions in random order. The other listens and responds with book closed. Then partners reverse roles.

Ejercicio D
A. Exercise D introduces the concept that the conditional is used to express what one would do but couldn't because of other circumstances.
B. Exercise D can be done with books open or closed.

ANSWERS
Ejercicio C
Answers will vary.
1. Sí, mi familia tiene un coche. (Yo tengo un coche).
2. El coche es un...
3. Es un...
4. Sí, (No), (no) es descapotable.
5. Tiene... puertas.
6. Sí, tiene una goma de repuesto en el maletero.

Ejercicio D
1. Sí, Teresa compraría el coche.
2. No, no puede comprar el coche.
3. No puede porque no tiene bastante dinero.
4. Sí, Teresa cambiaría la llanta.
5. No, no puede.
6. No puede porque no tiene llanta de repuesto.
7. Sí, Lupe conduciría.
8. No, no puede.
9. No puede porque dejó su permiso de conducir en casa.
10. No, Lupe no estacionaría aquí.
11. Está prohibido estacionar aquí.

INFORMAL ASSESSMENT
(*Palabras 1*)
Check for understanding by having one student read vocabulary items at random from *Palabras 1* while another points to the appropriate illustration on the Vocabulary Transparencies.

VOCABULARIO
PALABRAS 2

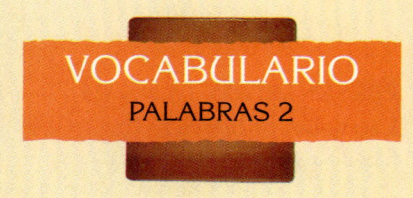

Vocabulary Teaching Resources
1. Vocabulary Transparencies 5.2 (A & B)
2. Audio Cassette 4A
3. Student Tape Manual, *Palabras 2*
4. Workbook, *Palabras 2*
5. Communication Activities Masters, *Palabras 2, C & D*
6. Chapter Quizzes, *Palabras 2*
7. Computer Software, *Vocabulario*

Bell Ringer Review
Write the following on the board or use BRR Blackline Master 5-2: You are at the train station. Complete the following statements and questions.
1. Un boleto para ___, ___.
2. ¿Cuánto cuesta ___?
3. ¿De qué ___ sale el tren?
4. ¿A qué ___ sale?
5. Si sale de aquí a las trece cinco, ¿a qué hora ___ a Córdoba?

PRESENTATION (pages 118-119)
Have students close their books. Show Vocabulary Transparencies 5.2 (A & B). Have students repeat each word or phrase several times after you or Cassette 4A.

ABOUT THE LANGUAGE
Other words for "gasoline" are *bencina*, the usual word in Chile, and *combustible* which is occasionally used in Spain.

VOCABULARIO

PALABRAS 2

LA ESTACIÓN DE SERVICIO

la gasolinera

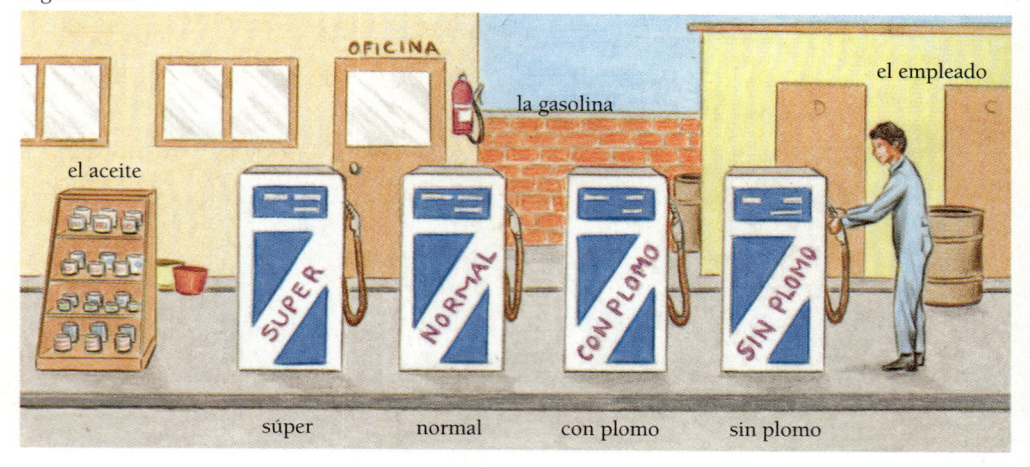

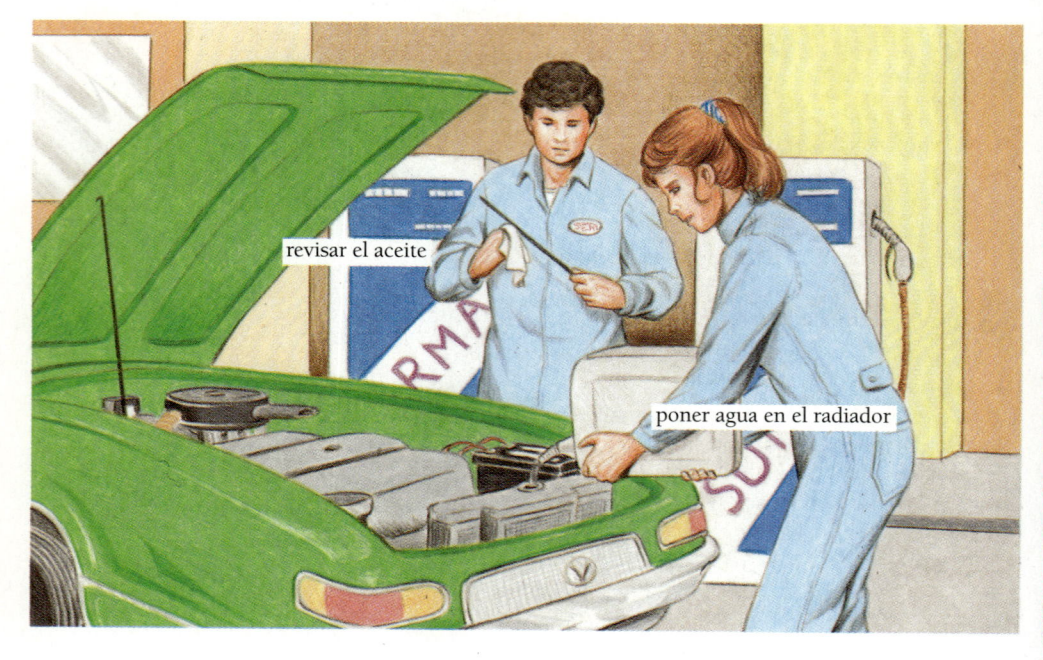

el aceite
la gasolina
el empleado

súper   normal   con plomo   sin plomo

revisar el aceite
poner agua en el radiador

118   CAPÍTULO 5

ADDITIONAL PRACTICE
Ask the following questions about the illustrations on pages 118–119 using the new vocabulary:
¿Dónde están trabajando los jóvenes?
¿Trabajan a tiempo parcial o a tiempo completo?
¿Qué está revisando el muchacho?
¿Qué está poniendo la muchacha en el radiador?
¿Qué está verificando el muchacho?
¿Qué está limpiando la muchacha?
¿En qué está poniendo aire el muchacho?

revisar el agua de la batería

limpiar el parabrisas

el parabrisas

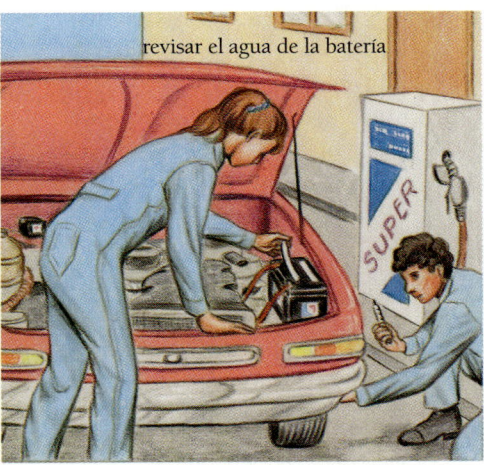

verificar la presión de los neumáticos

poner aire

Favor de llenar el tanque.

¿Súper o normal?

¿Con plomo o sin plomo?

CAPÍTULO 5   119

DID YOU KNOW?

En las gasolineras españolas es necesario pedir específicamente cualquier servicio como revisar el agua, limpiar el parabrisas, etc. Lo único que hacen normalmente es poner gasolina.

Ejercicios

PRESENTATION (page 120)

Ejercicio A
Exercise A can be done with books open.

Extension of *Ejercicio B*
Speaking
After completing Exercise B, call on an individual to summarize the information in his/her own words.

Extension of *Ejercicio C*
Speaking/Listening
After completing Exercise C as a whole-class activity, focus on the listening skill by having students do it again in pairs. One partner reads the questions in random order while the other listens and responds with book closed. Partners can then reverse roles.

ANSWERS
Ejercicio A
1. el motor
2. la batería
3. la gasolina
4. el parabrisas

Ejercicio B
1. c
2. c
3. c
4. a
5. c

Ejercicio C
Answers will vary slightly.
1. ... lleva el coche de mi familia a la gasolinera.
2. Mi carro necesita gasolina normal (súper).
3. Sí, es necesario usar gasolina sin plomo.
4. Sí, a veces es necesario revisar el aceite.
5. Sí, a veces es necesario revisar el agua del radiador.

INFORMAL ASSESSMENT
(*Palabras 2*)
Have students close their books. Check for understanding by referring to Vocabulary Transparencies 5.2 (*A & B*) and allowing students two minutes to write down everything they can remember about them. Call on individuals to report orally on their notes.

Ejercicios

A ¿Qué es? Identifiquen.

1. ¿Es el motor o el tanque de gasolina?
2. ¿Es la batería o el radiador? 
3. ¿Es la gasolina o el aceite? 
4. ¿Es el parabrisas o el intermitente? 

B En la gasolinera. Escojan.
1. En la gasolinera el empleado llena el tanque de ___ .
   a. agua   b. aceite   c. gasolina
2. El empleado revisa ___ .
   a. el agua en los neumáticos   b. el tanque   c. el nivel del aceite
3. El empleado nunca pondría agua en ___ .
   a. la batería   b. el radiador   c. el tanque
4. El empleado podría verificar ___ .
   a. la presión de los neumáticos   b. el aire del radiador   c. el parabrisas
5. El parabrisas está sucio. No puedo ver nada. ¿Me lo ___ Ud., por favor?
   a. llenaría   b. revisaría   c. limpiaría

C Nuestro coche. Preguntas personales.
1. ¿Quién lleva el carro de su familia a la gasolinera?
2. ¿Su carro necesita gasolina normal o súper?
3. ¿Es necesario usar gasolina sin plomo?
4. A veces, ¿es necesario revisar el aceite?
5. A veces, ¿es necesario revisar el agua del radiador?

ADDITIONAL PRACTICE

(*Palabras 2*)
Have students make up original sentences using these words:
la gasolina
el tanque
el parabrisas
el radiador

Comunicación
Palabras 1 y 2

A **En la gasolinera.** Ud. está en una gasolinera en San José, Costa Rica.

1. Tell the attendant (your partner) you need gas.
2. He asks what kind of gas you want.
3. He wants to know how much gas you want.
4. You want the oil and water checked.

B **En Puerto Rico.** Ud. está hablando con un(a) amigo(a) puertorriqueño(a) (un[a] compañero[a] de clase). Él/ella le pide los siguientes informes. Conteste a sus preguntas.

1. if you have a driver's license
2. what state you live in
3. at what age you can get a driver's license
4. if you have to take a test

C **Nuestro auto.** Descríbale a un(a) compañero(a) de clase el coche que tiene la familia de Ud. Luego su compañero(a) le describirá su coche (de él o de ella).

D **Un coche de alquiler**. Ud. está en Cancún, México, y quiere alquilar un coche en una agencia de alquiler. Hágale preguntas al/a la empleado(a) de la agencia (un[a] compañero[a] de clase). Use las siguientes expresiones.

- marcas y modelos de coches
- gasolina
- precio
- transmisión automática
- tarjeta de crédito
- seguro contra accidente

AUTOS PECOS RENT A CAR

ALQUILER DE COCHES

OFICINAS
Tels. 273 30 90 y 274 67 32
C/. Alcalde Sainz de Baranda, 50

C/. Vizcaya, 8 (garage) Tel. 239 71 59

SERVICIO URGENTE: De 22 h. a 7 h.
227 37 42 - 777 55 62

Servicio permanente domingos y festivos incluidos a cualquier hora

CAPÍTULO 5 121

ESTRUCTURA

Structure Teaching Resources

1. Workbook, *Estructura*
2. Student Tape Manual, *Estructura*
3. Audio Cassette 4A
4. Communication Activities Masters, *Estructura*, A-C
5. Chapter Quizzes, *Estructura*
6. Computer Software, *Estructura*

Bell Ringer Review

Write the following on the board or use BRR Blackline Master 5-4: Rewrite the following sentences in the future.

1. Yo voy en tren.
2. Nosotros no conducimos.
3. Felisa compra los boletos.
4. Yo espero aquí con las maletas.
5. El tren llega a las dieciséis.
6. ¿Comen Uds. en el tren?
7. Sí, tomamos el almuerzo en el tren.

El modo potencial o condicional
Formas regulares

PRESENTATION *(page 122)*

A. Have students open their books to page 122. Guide them through steps 1-4.
B. Have them repeat the verb forms after you.
C. Call on individuals to read the example sentences or have the class read them in unison.

Note This grammar concept should not prove difficult for students. They are already familiar with the verb stems from the future tense and with the endings from the imperfect. The uses of the conditional are the same in Spanish and English.

122

ESTRUCTURA

El potencial o condicional *Expressing Conditions*
Formas regulares

1. Study the following forms of regular verbs in the conditional.

INFINITIVE	COMPRAR	VENDER	CONDUCIR	ENDINGS
STEM	comprar-	vender-	conducir-	
yo	compraría	vendería	conduciría	-ía
tú	comprarías	venderías	conducirías	-ías
él, ella, Ud.	compraría	vendería	conduciría	-ía
nosotros(as)	compraríamos	venderíamos	conduciríamos	-íamos
vosotros(as)	*compraríais*	*venderíais*	*conduciríais*	-íais
ellos, ellas, Uds.	comprarían	venderían	conducirían	-ían

2. Note that as with the future, the conditional is formed by adding the appropriate endings to the infinitive. The endings for the conditional are the same as those for the imperfect of *-er* and *-ir* verbs.

3. The uses of the conditional are the same in Spanish and English. The conditional is used to express what would take place under certain circumstances.

> Yo conduciría pero desgraciadamente no tengo mi permiso de conducir.
> Yo compraría el coche pero no tengo suficiente dinero.

4. The conditional is also used to soften requests.

> ¿Me limpiaría Ud. el parabrisas, por favor?
> ¿Me revisaría el aceite, por favor?

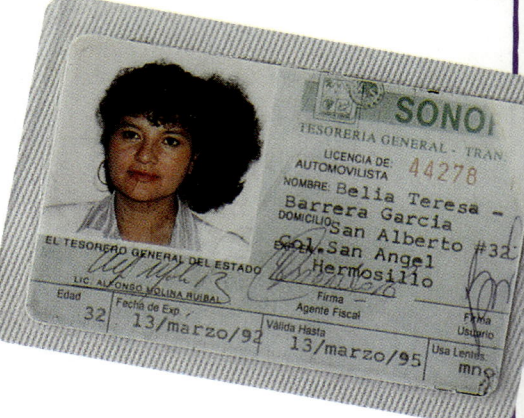

122 CAPÍTULO 5

LEARNING FROM REALIA

Have individuals look at the driver's license at the bottom of page 122 and say at least one sentence about it.

FOR THE NATIVE SPEAKER

Have students create an ad based on the following information. *Motores Moctezuma va a poner en venta un automóvil nuevo. Uds. tienen que preparar la propaganda. Comiencen con un anuncio para el periódico que atraiga compradores. Describan el auto. Denle un nombre atractivo e indiquen al público por qué debe comprarlo.*

Ejercicios

A **Lo que haría yo.** Preguntas personales.

1. ¿Te gustaría comprar un coche?
2. ¿Qué modelo comprarías?
3. ¿Qué color preferirías?
4. ¿Comprarías un coche americano o extranjero?
5. ¿Cuánto pagarías?
6. ¿Preferirías una transmisión automática o manual?

B **Un viaje.** Contesten según se indica.

1. ¿Irían ellos a las montañas o a la playa? (a las montañas)
2. ¿Irían en tren o en coche? (en coche)
3. ¿Quién conduciría? (Teresa)
4. ¿Alquilarían una cabaña o irían a un hotel? (una cabaña)
5. ¿Cuánto tiempo pasarían en las montañas? (unos quince días)
6. ¿Tú irías también? (no)

C **No, no.** Contesten según el modelo.

Ellos piensan ir. ¿Y tú?
No, yo no iría.

1. Ellos piensan llamar. ¿Y tú?
2. Yo pienso escribir. ¿Y Uds.?
3. Carolina piensa visitar a sus primos. ¿Y su hermano?
4. Nosotros pensamos ir. ¿Y Uds.?
5. Ellos piensan viajar en carro. ¿Y Uds.?
6. Teresa piensa conducir. ¿Y tú?

D **Imaginándome millonario(a).** Contesten.

1. ¿Vivirías en la ciudad, en los suburbios o en el campo?
2. ¿Viajarías mucho?
3. ¿Adónde irías?
4. ¿Cómo irías?
5. ¿Con quién irías?
6. ¿Comprarías un coche?
7. ¿Qué tipo de coche comprarías?
8. ¿Trabajarías?

Fiat Tipo.
Nacido para marcar su tiempo.

CAPÍTULO 5 **123**

Ejercicios

PRESENTATION (page 123)

Ejercicios A–D
Exercises A, B, C, and D can be done with books open or closed.

ANSWERS

Ejercicio A
Answers will vary.
1. Sí, me gustaría comprar un coche.
2. Compraría un...
3. Preferiría el color...
4. Compraría un coche extranjero (americano).
5. Pagaría... dólares.
6. Preferiría una transmisión automática (manual).

Ejercicio B
1. Irían a las montañas.
2. Irían en coche.
3. Teresa conduciría.
4. Alquilarían una cabaña.
5. Pasarían unos quince días en las montañas.
6. No, yo no iría.

Ejercicio C
1. No, yo no llamaría.
2. No, nosotros no escribiríamos.
3. No, él no visitaría a sus primos.
4. No, nosotros no iríamos.
5. No, nosotros no viajaríamos en carro.
6. No, yo no conduciría.

Ejercicio D
Answers will vary.
1. Viviría en...
2. Sí, (No, no) viajaría mucho.
3. Iría a...
4. Iría en...
5. Iría con...
6. Sí, compraría un coche.
7. Compraría un...
8. Sí, (No, no) trabajaría.

LEARNING FROM REALIA/PHOTOS

Refer to the advertisement on page 123. Have students scan it for information and give at least one sentence about it.

INDEPENDENT PRACTICE

Assign any of the following:
1. Workbook, *Estructura*
2. Communication Activities Masters, *Estructura, A*
3. Exercises on student pages 122–123

123

Bell Ringer Review

Write the following on the board or use BRR Blackline Master 5-5: Rewrite in the future.
1. Vamos a salir mañana.
2. Te voy a decir a qué hora salimos.
3. Roberto va a querer salir temprano.
4. Vamos a tener que poner el equipaje en la maletera esta noche.
5. Roberto lo va a poner en la maletera.

El modo potencial o condicional
Formas irregulares

PRESENTATION *(page 124)*

Have students open their books to page 124. Lead them through the explanation and have them repeat the verb forms after you.

Ejercicios

PRESENTATION *(page 124)*

Ejercicio A

Exercise A can be done with books open or closed.

ANSWERS

Ejercicio A
1. Dijo que vendría.
2. Dijo que haría el viaje.
3. Dijo que podría pagar el viaje.
4. Dijo que saldría el viernes.
5. Dijo que tendría bastante tiempo.

GEOGRAPHY CONNECTION

The ad on page 124 says that *Distribuidora La Marina Ltda.* is located at the entrance to Bocagrande in Cartagena (Colombia). Bocagrande is a lovely beach resort section of Cartagena. It has beautiful beaches and wonderful seafood restaurants. Cartagena is a city that has a walled citadel, elegant residential areas, and tourist complexes. It has been designated as a "World Cultural Heritage Site" by UNESCO.

El potencial o condicional
Formas irregulares

Expressing More Conditions

The same verbs that are irregular in the future tense are irregular in the conditional. Study the following.

INFINITIVE	FUTURE	CONDITIONAL
tener	tendré	tendría
poner	pondré	pondría
salir	saldré	saldría
poder	podré	podría
saber	sabré	sabría
hacer	haré	haría
decir	diré	diría
querer	querré	querría

Ejercicios

A ¿Él vendrá o no? Contesten según el modelo.

¿Estará Guillermo?
Dijo que estaría.

1. ¿Vendrá Guillermo?
2. ¿Hará el viaje?
3. ¿Podrá pagar el viaje?
4. ¿Saldrá el viernes?
5. ¿Tendrá bastante tiempo?

124 CAPÍTULO 5

LEARNING FROM REALIA

Refer students to the Mobil advertisement at the top of page 124. Ask them what the *Marina Ltda.* is. Ask if they know what *Ltda.* is an abbreviation for *(limitada)*. ("Limited," is the British equivalent of "Incorporated" [Inc.].) In Spanish-speaking countries, it is more common to see *S.A.*, an abbreviation for *Sociedad Anónima*. What does this company sell? Have students look for the Spanish equivalents of the following words: "fuel," "wholesale," and "accessories."

B **Uno sí y el otro no.** Completen con el condicional.
1. Él sabría la dirección pero su hermano no la ___ .
2. Yo te lo diría pero ellos nunca te lo ___ .
3. Nosotros lo haríamos pero ellos no lo ___ nunca.
4. Yo podría ir pero mis amigos no ___ .
5. Uds. lo pondrían en orden pero él no lo ___ .
6. Yo tendría que volver pero tú no ___ .

C **Ahora lo hará pero antes no lo haría.**
Completen con el condicional.
1. Carlos podrá pero antes ___ .
2. Los muchachos vendrán pero antes ___ .
3. Tú lo harás pero antes ___ .
4. Uds. saldrán pero antes ___ .
5. Ud. me lo dirá pero antes ___ .

Una gasolinera en España

CAPÍTULO 5 125

Ejercicios
PRESENTATION
Ejercicios B and C (page 125)
Exercises B and C can be done with books open.

ANSWERS
Ejercicio B
1. sabría
2. dirían
3. harían
4. podrían
5. pondría
6. tendrías

Ejercicio C
1. no podría
2. no vendrían
3. no lo harías
4. no saldrían
5. no lo diría

LEARNING FROM PHOTOS
Refer students to the photo on page 125 and ask: What is the sign *Autolavado* for?

INDEPENDENT PRACTICE
Assign any of the following:
1. Workbook, *Estructura*
2. Communication Activities Masters, *Estructura*, B
3. Exercises on student pages 124-125

> **Bell Ringer Review**
>
> Write the following on the board or use BRR Blackline Master 5-6: Make a list of clothing that you would buy right away if you had enough money.

Dos complementos en una oración: me lo, te lo, nos lo

PRESENTATION *(page 126)*

A. With books open, guide students through steps 1 and 2 on page 126.

B. Call on volunteers to read the example sentences aloud.

C. You may wish to write the example sentences on the board. Circle and box in the objects as is done on page 126. Draw an arrow from the pronoun to the noun it replaces. Have students note that the second pronoun comes after the one that was already there.

Ejercicios

PRESENTATION *(page 126)*

Ejercicios A and B

Exercises A and B can be done with books open or closed.

ANSWERS

Ejercicio A
1. Mamá me lo compró.
2. Mamá me los compró.
3. Mamá me la compró.
4. Mamá me los compró.
5. Mamá me la compró.
6. Mamá me los compró.
7. Mamá me las compró.

Ejercicio B
1. Sí, me la sirvió.
2. Sí, me lo trajo.
3. Sí, me la recomendó.
4. Sí, me las sirvió aparte.
5. Sí, me la dio.

Dos complementos en una oración *me lo, te lo, nos lo*

Referring to People and Things Already Mentioned

1. Sentences can have both a direct and indirect object pronoun. When they do, the indirect object pronoun always precedes the direct object pronoun in Spanish. Both pronouns precede the conjugated form of the verb.

   Elena **me** dio el **regalo**.   Elena **me lo** dio.
   Carlos **nos** preparó **la comida**.   Carlos **nos la** preparó.
   Papá **me** compró **los tenis**.   Papa **me los** compró.
   El profesor **nos** explicó **las reglas**.   El profesor **nos las** explicó.

2. Note that the indirect object *me*, *te*, or *nos* comes before the direct object *lo, la, los, las*.

Ejercicios

A Mamá me lo compró. Contesten según el modelo.

   ¿Quién te compró los jeans?
   Mamá me los compró.

1. ¿Quién te compró el suéter?
2. ¿Quién te compró los tenis?
3. ¿Quién te compró la chaqueta?
4. ¿Quién te compró los zapatos?
5. ¿Quién te compró la raqueta?
6. ¿Quién te compró los anteojos para el sol?
7. ¿Quién te compró las camisas?

B En el restaurante. Contesten con pronombres.

1. ¿Te sirvió la comida el mesero?
2. ¿Te trajo el menú?
3. ¿Te recomendó la especialidad de la casa?
4. ¿Te sirvió las legumbres aparte?
5. ¿Te dio la cuenta?

CAPÍTULO 5

C **¿Quién te compró todo lo que tienes?** Contesten según el modelo.

> Tengo una calculadora.
> ¿Quién te la compró?

1. Tengo discos.
2. Tengo una raqueta de tenis.
3. Tengo un teléfono inalámbrico.
4. Tengo una plancha de vela.
5. Tengo un descapotable.
6. Tengo esquís acuáticos.

D **Él te la escribió.** Empleen dos pronombres en cada oración.

1. Carlos me escribió la carta.
2. Perdón, ¿quién te escribió la carta?
3. Él me envió la carta el otro día.
4. ¿Cuándo te envió la carta?
5. Él me dio las direcciones.
6. ¿Él te dio las direcciones?

E **El profesor nos enseñó mucho.** Empleen dos pronombres en cada oración.

1. El profesor nos enseñó la gramática.
2. Él nos enseñó el vocabulario.
3. Él nos enseñó las palabras.
4. Él nos enseñó los poemas.
5. Él nos explicó la diferencia.
6. Él nos explicó la teoría.
7. Él nos explicó el sistema.
8. Él nos dio la interpretación.

CAPÍTULO 5

DID YOU KNOW?

Gabriela Mistral es una poetisa chilena. Nació en 1889. Fue maestra en varias escuelas primarias y sirvió también de directora de varias escuelas. Ganó el Premio Nóbel de literatura en 1945.

Rubén Darío es un famoso poeta y crítico nicaragüense. Nació en Metapa, Nicaragua en 1867. Se le llama a Darío "el padre del modernismo". Él ejerció una influencia enorme en la literatura contemporánea.

Antonio Machado nació en Sevilla en 1875. Él y su hermano, Manuel, llegaron a ser poetas célebres. Antonio pasó la mayor parte de su vida en ciudades pequeñas de España enseñando francés en institutos de segunda enseñanza. Fue un hombre bastante retirado y modesto.

CONVERSACIÓN

Bell Ringer Review

Write the following on the board or use BRR Blackline Master 5-7: Complete with the verb **trabajar**.
1. Yo ___ tres días a la semana en una gasolinera.
2. Yo no ___ ayer. Mi amiga Teresa ___.
3. Pero yo ___ mañana y ella no ___.
4. Mi padre dice que él ___ siempre cuando era joven.

PRESENTATION *(page 128)*

A. Tell students they are going to hear a conversation between a young woman and a service station attendant.
B. Have students listen with books closed as you read the conversation or play Cassette 4A.
C. Have pairs of students assume the two roles. Allow pairs time to practice the conversation.
D. Call on volunteers to act out the conversation for the class without their books. It is not necessary that the students know the conversation by heart. Allow them to ad lib.

Ejercicio

ANSWERS
1. La señorita está en la gasolinera.
2. Quiere súper, sin plomo.
3. Sí, él revisa el aceite.
4. Sí, lo cambiaría.
5. Porque está un poco sucio.
6. Sí, lo podría cambiar.
7. Tardaría una hora más o menos.
8. No, no puede esperar.
9. Volverá mañana.

128

CONVERSACIÓN

Escenas de la vida *En la gasolinera*

SEÑORITA: Favor de llenar el tanque.
EMPLEADO: Cómo no, señorita. ¿Con normal o súper?
SEÑORITA: Súper, sin plomo. ¿Y me revisaría el aceite, por favor?
EMPLEADO: Sí. Está un poco sucio. Yo lo cambiaría.
SEÑORITA: ¿Me lo podría cambiar ahora?
EMPLEADO: Sí, pero tardaría una hora más o menos.
SEÑORITA: Entonces no puedo ahora. Tengo prisa. Volveré mañana.
EMPLEADO: De acuerdo.

En la gasolinera. Contesten según la conversación.

1. ¿Dónde está la señorita?
2. ¿Qué tipo de gasolina quiere?
3. ¿Revisa el aceite el empleado?
4. ¿Lo cambiaría él?
5. ¿Por qué lo cambiaría?
6. ¿Lo podría cambiar?
7. ¿Cuánto tiempo tardaría?
8. ¿Puede esperar la señorita?
9. ¿Cuándo volverá?

Un carro de energía solar

128   CAPÍTULO 5

CRITICAL THINKING ACTIVITY

(Thinking skills: drawing conclusions; problem solving)

Read the following to the class or put it on the board or on a transparency.
1. Roberto quiere ir a alguna parte. Quiere tomar el coche, pero tiene poca gasolina en el tanque. El tanque está vacío. Roberto cuenta su dinero. No tiene bastante dinero para llenar el tanque. ¿Qué puede hacer?
2. ¿Cuáles son algunas ventajas de un carro de energía solar?

Comunicación

A **Vamos a comprar un carro.** Trabaje con un(a) compañero(a) de clase. Descríbale el carro que le gustaría comprar. Luego él o ella le describirá el carro que a él o a ella le gustaría comprar. Decidan si Uds. comprarían el mismo carro o no.

B **La herencia.** Vamos a imaginar un poquito. Ud. recibió o heredó mucho dinero. Prepare una lista de las cosas que haría con el dinero. Luego, lea su lista y determine las categorías o los tipos de cosas o actividades que a Ud. le interesaría hacer.

C **Hay un problema.** Ud. va a una estación de servicio porque tiene un problema con su carro. Dígale al/a la empleado(a) (un[a] compañero[a] de clase) lo que pasa. El/la empleado(a) le dirá cómo arreglar el carro.

D **¿Harías eso?** Pregúntele a un(a) compañero(a) de clase si él o ella haría las siguientes cosas y cuándo las haría. Luego cambien de papel.

1. comprar un coche de cambio automático
2. estacionar en una zona prohibida
3. conducir sin el permiso de conducir
4. usar el claxon
5. comprar gasolina "súper"
6. comprar un coche viejo

CAPÍTULO 5   129

Bell Ringer Review
Write the following on the board or use BRR Blackline Master 5-8: Rewrite the following sentences using the conditional:
1. Compraré un coche en dos días.
2. Iremos a Managua, Nicaragua.
3. ¿Conducirás el mes que viene?
4. Rosa, Javier y Felipe tomarán el avión.

Comunicación

PRESENTATION *(page 129)*

The *Comunicación* activities allow students to use the chapter vocabulary and grammar in open-ended situations. You may select those you consider most appropriate. You may also allow students to select the activity or activities in which they will take part.

ANSWERS

Actividades A, B, and C
Answers will vary.

Actividad D
Answers to the following questions will vary.
1. ¿Comprarías un coche de cambio automático?
2. ¿Estacionarías en una zona prohibida?
3. ¿Conducirías sin tu permiso de conducir?
4. ¿Usarías el claxon?
5. ¿Comprarías gasolina "súper"?
6. ¿Comprarías un coche viejo?

LEARNING FROM PHOTOS
Refer students to the photo at the top of page 129. Have pairs prepare a conversation between the couple and the car sales representative *(el representante de ventas en una agencia de carros).*

INDEPENDENT PRACTICE
Assign any of the following:
1. Workbook, *Estructura*
2. Communication Activities Masters, *Estructura,* C
3. Exercises on student pages 126, 127, and 129

129

LECTURA Y CULTURA

LOS CARROS EN LATINOAMÉRICA

El año pasado yo estuve en varias ciudades de Latinoamérica. Me gustaría compartir[1] con Uds. algunas cosas que me sorprendieron. Uds. no se pueden imaginar el tráfico que hay en las grandes ciudades.

Yo diría que hay más tráfico en Caracas, Buenos Aires o México que en Chicago o Dallas. Me sorprendió también el estado en que están los carros. Muchos carros que ví en las calles eran viejos, muy viejos. ¿Saben por qué? Pues por varias razones, sobre todo los precios. En la mayoría de los países latinoamericanos los coches son muy caros. El automóvil se considera un lujo. El automóvil en Latinoamérica es para personas con dinero, no es un modo de transporte para el público en general. El pueblo viaja en autobús. Por eso, los gobiernos les imponen impuestos[2] muy altos a los automóviles, especialmente a los carros importados. Un carro de ocasión, es decir, un carro usado de los años 70 costaría unos 10.000 dólares. ¿Cuánto costaría un coche nuevo? Depende, pero por lo general, el comprador de un carro nuevo en Latinoamérica tendría que pagar el doble, o más, de lo que pagaríamos en los Estados Unidos. Por eso, los dueños[3] de los coches los cuidan[4] bien y los reparan frecuentemente. Los mantienen en excelentes condiciones.

Pero no hay duda que estos vehículos viejos causan un problema serio. ¿Cuál es este problema? Es la contaminación del aire. En los Estados Unidos, por ejemplo, existen leyes[5] para la protección del ambiente[6]. Se controlan las emisiones de los carros. Se prohíbe la gasolina con plomo. Pocos países latinoamericanos tienen leyes como éstas. Las emisiones de los buses y camiones[7] con motores diesel y la gasolina con plomo contaminan el aire de bellas ciudades como Santiago de Chile y México. Tan grave es el problema en estas ciudades que el gobierno no permite circular todos los vehículos todos los días. Algunos vehículos circulan los días pares[8], y los otros los días impares.

[1] compartir *share*
[2] impuestos *taxes*
[3] dueños *owners*
[4] cuidan *take care of*
[5] leyes *laws*
[6] ambiente *environment*
[7] camiones *trucks*
[8] pares *even*

Estudio de palabras

A ¿Cuál es la definición? Pareen.

1. la mayoría
2. viejo
3. usado
4. el tráfico
5. de los automóviles
6. el automóvil
7. el carro, el camión
8. el doble
9. reparar
10. causar

a. crear
b. los vehículos
c. dos veces
d. el número más grande
e. el tránsito, la circulación
f. hacer reparaciones
g. antiguo
h. el coche, el carro
i. de ocasión
j. automovilístico

B El verbo y el nombre. Pareen.

1. contaminar
2. costar
3. mantener
4. reparar
5. comprar
6. importar
7. sorprender

a. la reparación
b. el mantenimiento
c. el costo
d. la contaminación
e. la importación
f. la sorpresa
g. la compra, el/la comprador(a)

Comprensión

A ¿Sí o no? Contesten.

1. Hay poco tráfico en las ciudades latinoamericanas porque no hay muchos coches.
2. La mayoría de los coches son nuevos.
3. Los coches cuestan menos en Latinoamérica que en los Estados Unidos.
4. Los vehículos en Latinoamérica causan mucha contaminación del aire en las ciudades.

B Explicación. ¿Por qué mantienen los dueños sus carros en buenas condiciones en Latinoamérica?

C Datos o informes. Indique tres cosas que aprendió sobre las ciudades latinoamericanas en esta lectura.

Versátiles 93. Con ellas, versatilidad es ir rumbo a la diversión y compartir diseño, confort y espacio con quien tú más quieres. Porque Chevrolet Blazer y Suburban tienen el tamaño y el equipamiento que se ajusta a tus deseos y necesidades. Ambas tienen línea de vanguardia, amplia comodidad interior y todo lo que buscas para disfrutar lo mejor con todas las ventajas. Cada una tiene su propia personalidad y además, algo muy familiar. La tecnología en movimiento General Motors. Visita a tu Concesionario.

Versatilidad en dos palabras. Blazer y Suburban.

GENERAL MOTORS MEXICO
Tecnología en Movimiento

Una autopista en Caracas, Venezuela

CAPÍTULO 5   131

Estudio de palabras

ANSWERS

Ejercicio A
1. d
2. g
3. i
4. e
5. j
6. h
7. b
8. c
9. f
10. a

Ejercicio B
1. d
2. c
3. b
4. a
5. g
6. e
7. f

Comprensión

ANSWERS

Comprensión A
1. No
2. No
3. No
4. Sí

Comprensión B
Porque los coches cuestan mucho.

Comprensión C
Answers may include the following.
1. Hay mucha contaminación en las ciudades latinoamericanas.
2. Se prohíbe la gasolina con plomo.
3. El gobierno no permite circular los vehículos todos los días.

GEOGRAPHY CONNECTION

The entire city of Caracas is crisscrossed by highways. It is difficult to get around if one does not know the roads. The new Caracas–La Guaira autopista (a long tunnel) enables one to get to the beaches on the coast in half an hour if there is no traffic.

LEARNING FROM REALIA

Refer students to the automobile advertisement at the top of page 131 and ask: *¿Por qué son tan versátiles estos dos modelos?*

FOR THE NATIVE SPEAKER

Ask students to write a short paper on the following topic. *En algunas ciudades grandes se ha propuesto prohibir el uso de automóviles privados. ¿Qué crees tú? ¿Es buena o mala idea? ¿Por qué? ¿Qué ventajas y desventajas ves con prohibir el uso de automóviles privados?*

131

Bell Ringer Review
Write the following on the board or use BRR Blackline Master 5-10: List some differences between cars in the U.S. and in Latin America.

Descubrimiento Cultural
(The Descubrimiento section is optional.)

PRESENTATION *(pages 132-133)*
A. Have students read the selection silently.
B. Discuss with students the pollution problem in the U.S. and in Hispanic countries.

GEOGRAPHY CONNECTION
La Ciudad de México es la ciudad más grande del mundo con más de 22 millones de habitantes. La Ciudad de México es la ciudad más vieja del continente norteamericano. Tiene más de setecientos años. La Ciudad de México es la ciu-dad más alta del continente norteamericano. Está a una altura de 2.240 metros (7.349 pies). No hay duda que la Ciudad de México es una ciudad de superlativos.

find a video on mexico city?

DESCUBRIMIENTO CULTURAL

Los autobuses son la forma de transporte más popular para el pueblo en los países hispanos. Viajar en bus, bus municipal o privado, resulta muy barato. Pero hay un costo oculto, la contaminación. Para mantener el bajo costo se permite el uso de buses antiguos, mayormente diesel, que emiten enormes cantidades de contaminantes. Los gobiernos necesitan un servicio de transporte barato y por eso no imponen muchas restricciones en los buses.

Muchos gobiernos federales y municipales están tratando de aliviar el problema de la contaminación. Por ejemplo, en la Ciudad de México, los carros con placas o matrículas que tienen un número impar pueden circular en la ciudad ciertos días y los carros que tienen matrícula con número par, los otros días. Es una medida para reducir el tráfico y bajar la cantidad de emisiones de gases tóxicos en el aire.

La Ciudad de México

Una manera de reducir el tráfico es con construir una red de metro. Hoy la Ciudad de México, Caracas y Santiago de Chile tienen nuevas redes excelentes y modernas.

Y AQUÍ EN LOS ESTADOS UNIDOS

Las compañías automovilísticas norteamericanas tienen fábricas en España y en Latinoamérica. La General Motors, la Chrysler y la Ford, todas montan y fabrican vehículos en los países hispanos. Hoy la Ford, por ejemplo, fabrica un modelo, el Festiva, en México para vender en los Estados Unidos. Algunos modelos se introducen en el extranjero y, si tienen buen resultado, después en los EE.UU.

La Respuesta Ecológica
magna SIN
Gasolina sin plomo

Petróleos Mexicanos aporta una respuesta ecológica al problema de la contaminación por combustión en automotores: **MAGNA SIN**, gasolina sin plomo, con calidad y características avaladas por estrictas normas internacionales.

MAGNA SIN es de uso indispensable para los vehículos modelo 1991 que, por ley, vienen equipados con convertidor catalítico; de uso optativo, no indispensable, para los modelos 1986 a 1990.

No es compatible con modelos 1985 y anteriores.

El beneficio ecológico que se deriva de esta nueva gasolina anticontaminante será un logro más de nuestra industria petrolera, siempre preocupada por mejorar la calidad de vida de los mexicanos de hoy y mañana.

Con su Alta Tecnología

PEMEX
Siempre con nosotros

Una estación de ferrocarril en Buenos Aires, Argentina

CAPÍTULO 5   **133**

LEARNING FROM PHOTOS/REALIA

Refer students to the advertisement on page 133 and ask: *¿Cuál es la respuesta ecológica? ¿Qué es Pemex? (Petroméxico)*

REALIDADES

(The Realidades section is optional.)

Bell Ringer Review
Write the following on the board or use BRR Blackline Master 5-11: Write sentences using each of the following words: **el tren, el carro, el metro, el autobús, el taxi.**

PRESENTATION *(pages 134-135)*
The main objective of this section is for students to enjoy the photographs. Here are some additional suggestions for using the *Realidades*.

Pre-reading
Before reading the captions, have students cover them and look only at the photos. Ask them to describe in as much detail as possible what they see. Cue with questions if necessary.

Reading
Have students read the captions on page 134 silently and be prepared to answer the question in caption 3.

Post-reading
Discuss the captions as a class. Ask students (drivers, if possible) what problems they might encounter when driving a car in Latin America for the first time.

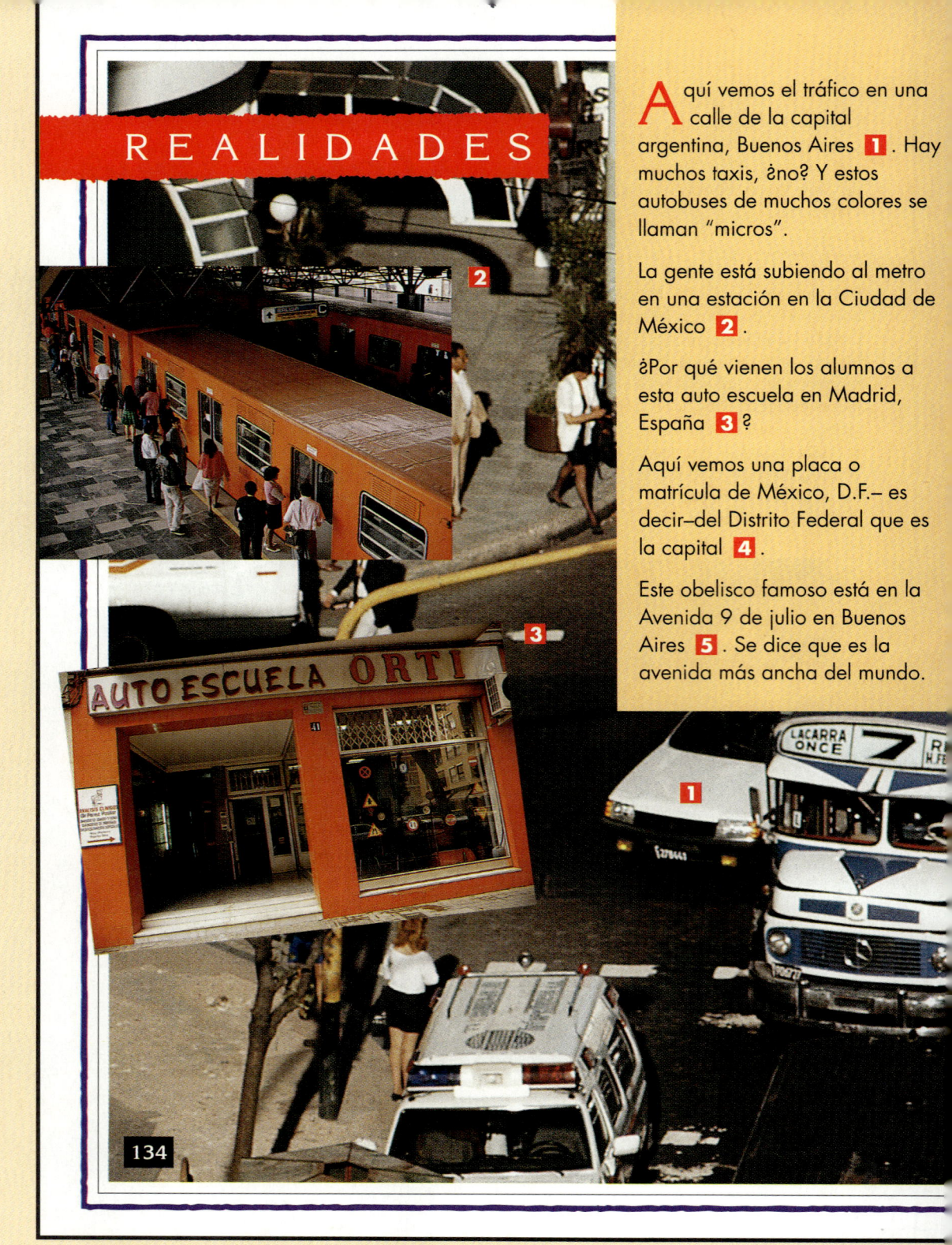

REALIDADES

Aquí vemos el tráfico en una calle de la capital argentina, Buenos Aires **1**. Hay muchos taxis, ¿no? Y estos autobuses de muchos colores se llaman "micros".

La gente está subiendo al metro en una estación en la Ciudad de México **2**.

¿Por qué vienen los alumnos a esta auto escuela en Madrid, España **3**?

Aquí vemos una placa o matrícula de México, D.F.– es decir–del Distrito Federal que es la capital **4**.

Este obelisco famoso está en la Avenida 9 de julio en Buenos Aires **5**. Se dice que es la avenida más ancha del mundo.

LEARNING FROM PHOTOS

Refer students to Photo 1 on page 134 and ask: *¿De qué color son los taxis en Buenos Aires?*

CULMINACIÓN

RECYCLING

The *Comunicación oral* and *Comunicación escrita* activities provide a forum in which students create and answer their own questions and come up with dialogs on their own.

Comunicación oral

ANSWERS
Actividades A, B, and C
Answers will vary.

INFORMAL ASSESSMENT

Activities A and B can be used to evaluate the speaking skills informally. You may assign a grade based on students' ability to communicate in Spanish. Use the evaluation criteria given on page 24 of this Teacher's Wraparound Edition.

Comunicación escrita

ANSWERS
Actividades A and B
Answers will vary.

CULMINACIÓN

Comunicación oral

A ¿Conduces bien o mal? Dígale a un(a) compañero(a) si Ud. hace lo siguiente cuando conduce. Él o ella le dirá si Ud. es buen(a) conductor(a) o no, y por qué o por qué no. Luego cambien de papel.

1. Cuando veo una luz amarilla, acelero.
2. Cuando voy a doblar una esquina, pongo las direccionales.
3. Cuando llego a un cruce, toco la bocina y continúo.
4. Cuando tengo que parar, pongo el pie en el acelerador.
5. Cuando veo a alguien en la calle, pongo los frenos y toco la bocina.

B ¡Qué mala suerte! Ud. no salió bien en el examen que tomó para conseguir su permiso de conducir. Llame a un(a) amigo(a) y explíquele lo que pasó. Dígale por qué Ud. no salió bien. Él o ella le dirá lo que tiene que hacer antes de tomar el examen de nuevo.

C El transporte público. Con un(a) compañero(a) de clase hable de las ventajas (*advantages*) de usar el transporte público para ir al colegio, en vez de usar el coche.

Comunicación escrita

A Por favor... Su coche tiene problemas. Ud. tiene que dejarlo en la estación de servicio pero la estación no está abierta. Escríbale una nota al mecánico explicándole lo que le pasa al coche.

B Un coche nuevo. Imagínese que Ud. tiene un coche nuevo. Escríbale una carta a un(a) amigo(a) describiéndole el viaje que Ud. hará en su coche nuevo.

136 CAPÍTULO 5

LEARNING FROM REALIA

Refer students to the signs on page 136 and ask: *¿Cuál es otra expresión que significa "Gente trabajando"?*
¿Cuál es el rótulo que indica:
a. *Zona escolar*
b. *Vía para doblar a la derecha*
c. *No estacionar*
d. *Tráfico en dos sentidos*

STUDENT PORTFOLIO

Have students keep a Spanish notebook with their best written work from *A bordo* in it. Written assignments that may be included in students' portfolios are the *Actividades escritas* on page 136 and the *Mi autobiografía* section in the Workbook.

Reintegración

A Un viaje. Contesten.
1. ¿Hiciste un viaje?
2. ¿Hizo el mismo viaje tu amigo(a)?
3. ¿Lo hicieron en carro?
4. ¿Adónde fueron?
5. ¿Quién condujo?
6. ¿Pusiste tus maletas en la maletera del carro?
7. Y tu amigo, ¿puso sus maletas en la maletera?
8. Antes de salir, ¿llenaste el tanque de gasolina?
9. ¿A qué gasolinera fuiste?

B Mañana. Contesten.
1. ¿Qué harás mañana?
2. ¿Qué harás durante el verano?
3. ¿Qué harás el año que viene?
4. ¿Qué harás durante el fin de semana?
5. ¿Qué harás durante tus vacaciones?

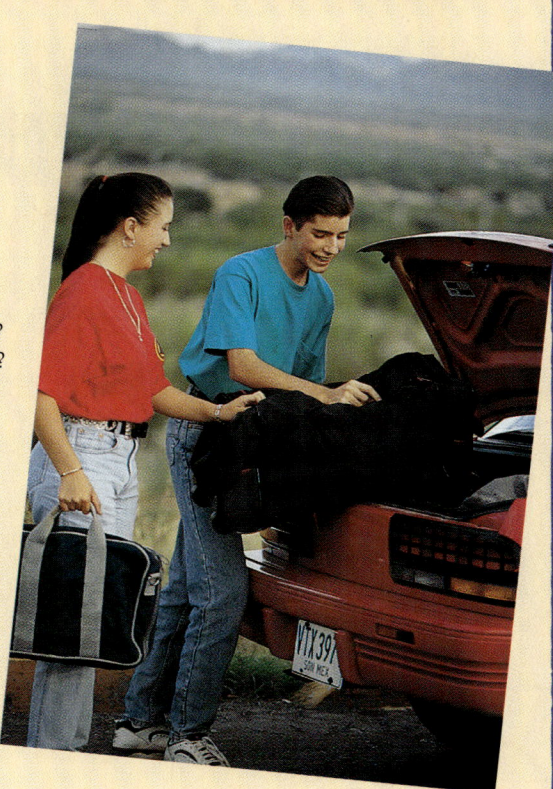

Vocabulario

SUSTANTIVOS
el coche
el carro
el sedán
el cupé
el descapotable
el coche deportivo
la puerta
el capó
la maletera
el maletero
el neumático
la goma
la llanta
la bocina
el claxon
el intermitente
el radiador
la direccional
la batería
el tanque
el parabrisas
el cinturón de seguridad
el freno
el conductor
la licencia
el permiso de conducir
la circulación
el tráfico
el tránsito
el cruce
la gasolinera
la gasolina
el/la empleado(a)
el aceite
la presión
el aire

ADJETIVOS
súper
normal

VERBOS
conducir
acelerar
adelantar
doblar
frenar
parar
estacionar
aparcar
llenar
revisar
verificar
limpiar

OTRAS PALABRAS Y EXPRESIONES
cambiar de velocidad
con cuidado
con plomo
sin plomo
de repuesto
de recambio

CAPÍTULO 5   **137**

LEARNING FROM PHOTOS
Refer students to the photo on page 137. Have them describe it in their own words.

INDEPENDENT PRACTICE
Assign any of the following:
1. Exercises on student page 137
2. Workbook, *Mi autobiografía*
3. Chapter 5, Situation Cards

Reintegración
RECYCLING
Exercise A recycles the preterite of irregular verbs.

ANSWERS
Ejercicio A
Answers will vary.
1. Sí (No), (no) hice un viaje.
2. Sí, (No) mi amigo (no) hizo el mismo viaje.
3. Sí (No), (no) lo hicimos en carro.
4. Fuimos a…
5. Yo conduje (mi amigo condujo).
6. Sí, puse mis maletas en la maletera del carro.
7. Sí, (No,) él (no) puso sus maletas en la maletera del carro.
8. Sí, antes de salir llené el tanque de gasolina.
9. Fui a la gasolinera…

Ejercicio B
Answers will vary, but they should be in the future.

Vocabulario
The words and phrases in the *Vocabulario* have been taught for productive use in this chapter. They are summarized here as a resource for both students and teacher. The *Vocabulario* also serves as a convenient resource for the *Culminación* activities. There are approximately 24 cognates in this list.

VIDEO
The video is intended to reinforce the vocabulary, structures, and cultural content in each chapter. It may be used here as a chapter wrap-up activity. See the *Video Activities Booklet* for additional suggestions on its use.

INTRODUCCIÓN (0:18:46)

LA AUTO ESCUELA (0:20:30)

INTRODUCCIÓN (0:22:49)

LA GASOLINERA (0:23:48)

137

CAPÍTULO 6
Scope and Sequence pages 138-163

Topics	Functions	Structure	Culture
Hotels	How to check in and out of a hotel	Presente perfecto	Hotel accommodations available in Spanish-speaking countries
	How to ask for things you may need when staying in a hotel	Los participios irregulares	Hotel ratings
	How to ask about what you have done recently	Dos complementos con se	Hotel Reina Victoria in Madrid
	How to tell what you do for other people		Hotel Casa Que Canta in Zihuatanejo, México
			Breakfast in Buenos Aires

CAPÍTULO 6

Situation Cards

The Situation Cards simulate real-life situations that require students to communicate in Spanish, exactly as though they were in a Spanish-speaking country. The Situation Cards operate on the assumption that the person to whom the message is to be conveyed understands no English. Therefore, students must focus on producing the Spanish vocabulary and structures necessary to negotiate the situations successfully. For additional information, see the Introduction to the Situation Cards in the Situation Cards Envelope.

Communication Transparency

The illustration seen in this Communication Transparency consists of a synthesis of the two vocabulary (Palabras 1&2) presentations found in this chapter. It has been created in order to present this chapter's vocabulary in a new context, and also to recycle vocabulary learned in previous chapters. The Communication Transparency consists of original art. Following are some specific uses:

1. as a cue to stimulate conversation and writing activities
2. for listening comprehension activities
3. to review and reteach vocabulary
4. as a review for chapter and unit tests

CAPÍTULO 6   A

You have just arrived at a small hotel in Ronda, Spain. Check in at the registration desk.

A bordo   © Glencoe/McGraw-Hill

138A

CAPÍTULO 6
Print Resources

Lesson Plans

	Pages
Workbook	
◆ Palabras 1	57-58
◆ Palabras 2	59-60
◆ Estructura	61-63
◆ Un poco más	64-67
◆ Mi autobiografía 68	

Communication Activities Masters
- ◆ Palabras 1 — 32-33
- ◆ Palabras 2 — 34-37
- ◆ Estructura — 38-39

10 Bell Ringer Reviews — 19-21

Chapter Situation Cards A B C D

Chapter Quizzes
- ◆ Palabras 1 — 26
- ◆ Palabras 2 — 27
- ◆ Estructura — 28-30

Testing Program
- ◆ Listening Comprehension — 30
- ◆ Reading and Writing — 31-34
- ◆ Proficiency — 128
- ◆ Speaking — 147

Nosotros y Nuestro Mundo
- ◆ Nuestro Conocimiento Académico *La industria hotelera*
- ◆ Nuestro Idioma *El presente perfecto*
- ◆ Nuestra Cultura *Mi casa es su casa: la hospitalidad del hispano*
- ◆ Nuestra Literatura *"Una princesa en la Patria de Juárez"* de Leandro J. Cañizares
- ◆ Nuestra Creatividad
- ◆ Nuestras Diversiones

CAPÍTULO 6
Multimedia Resources

CD-ROM Interactive Textbook Disc 2

Chapter 6 Student Edition
- ◆ Palabras 1
- ◆ Palabras 2
- ◆ Estructura
- ◆ Conversación
- ◆ Lectura y cultura
- ◆ Hispanoparlantes
- ◆ Realidades
- ◆ Culminación
- ◆ Prueba

Audio Cassette Program with Student Tape Manual

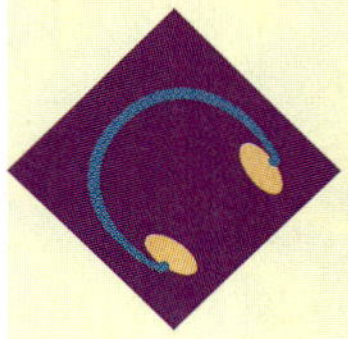

Cassette	Pages
◆ 4B Palabras 1	230
◆ 4B Palabras 2	230
◆ 4B Estructura	231
◆ 4B Conversación	231
◆ 4B Segunda parte	232-233

Compact Disc Program with Student Tape Manual 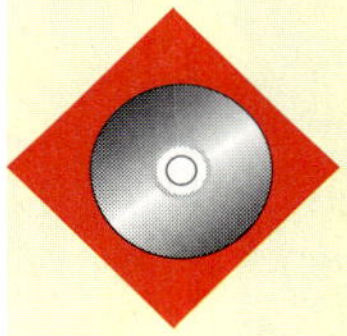
- ◆ CD 4 Palabras 1 — 230
- ◆ CD 4 Palabras 2 — 230
- ◆ CD 4 Estructura — 231
- ◆ CD 4 Conversación — 231
- ◆ CD 4 Segunda parte — 232-233

Overhead Transparencies Binder 
- ◆ Vocabulary 6.1 (A&B); 6.2 (A&B)
- ◆ Communication C-6
- ◆ Maps
- ◆ Fine Art (with Blackline Master Activities)

Video Program 
- ◆ Videocassette
- ◆ Video Activities Booklet — 16-17
- ◆ Videodisc
- ◆ Video Activities Booklet — 16-17

Computer Software (Macintosh, IBM, Apple) 
- ◆ Practice Disk
  - Palabras 1 y 2
  - Estructura
- ◆ Test Generator Disk
  - Chapter Test
  - Customized Test

138B

CAPÍTULO 6

CHAPTER OVERVIEW

In this chapter students will learn to communicate in various situations at hotels, such as making a reservation, checking in, requesting various hotel services, and checking out. They will expand their ability to talk about time relationships by learning formation and basic uses of the present perfect tense. They will also learn the use of *se* when combining direct and indirect object pronouns. The cultural focus of Chapter 6 is on the many types of hotel accommodations available in Spanish-speaking countries.

CHAPTER OBJECTIVES

By the end of this chapter, students will know:
1. vocabulary associated with checking into and out of a hotel
2. vocabulary associated with requesting various hotel services
3. vocabulary associated with basic hotel features and facilities
4. the formation and some basic uses of the present perfect tense
5. the use of the indirect object pronoun *se* in sentences with two object pronouns

Look back into the Internet search or hotels from Sp V H.

CAPÍTULO 6
EL HOTEL

OBJETIVOS

In this chapter you will learn to do the following:

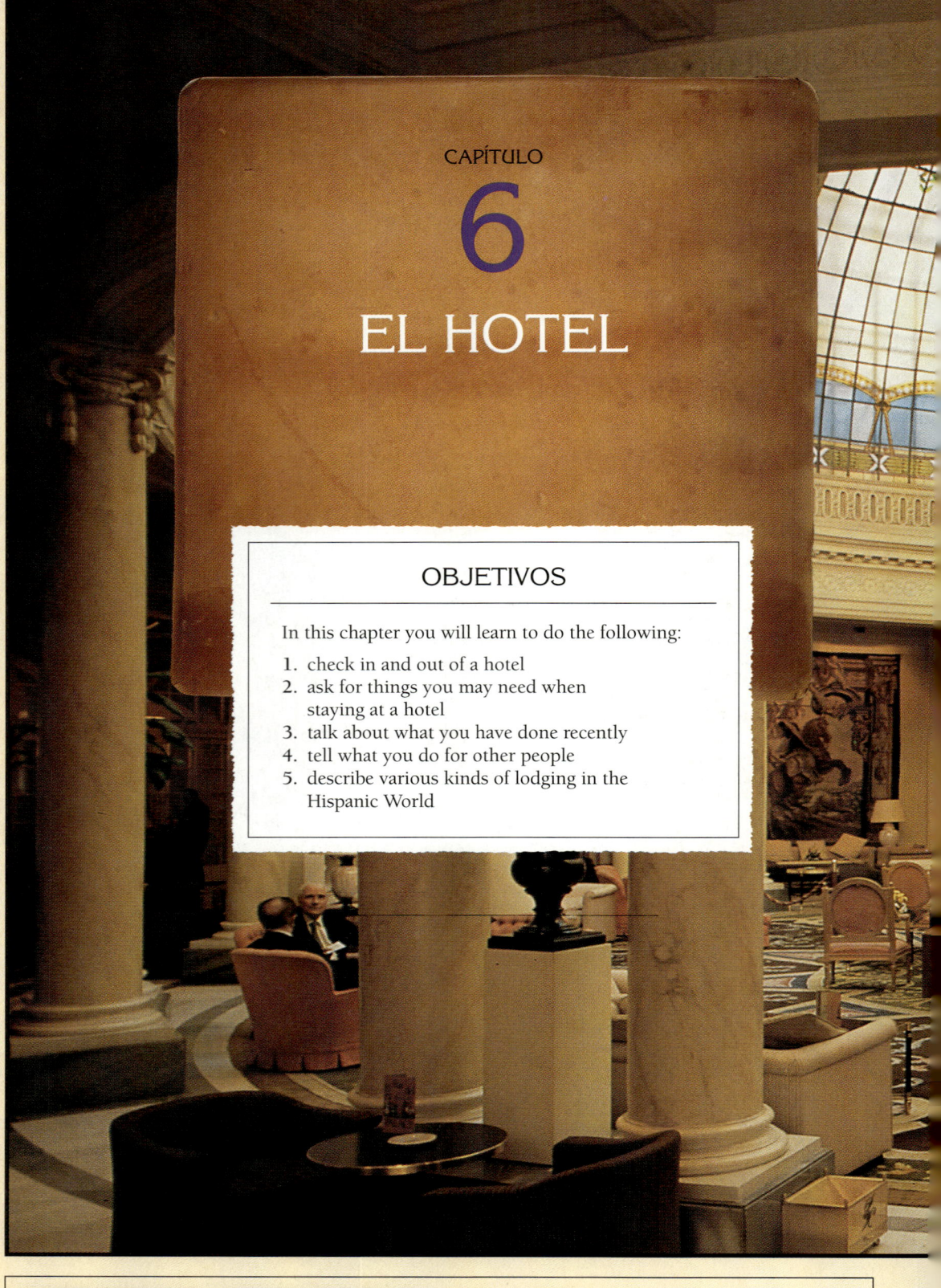

1. check in and out of a hotel
2. ask for things you may need when staying at a hotel
3. talk about what you have done recently
4. tell what you do for other people
5. describe various kinds of lodging in the Hispanic World

CHAPTER PROJECTS

(optional)
1. Have students plan hotel stays in different Hispanic cities. If possible have them collect, or provide them with, pictures and travel brochures of these places.
2. Have groups create their own imaginary hotel and describe it to the class. The class can rate each different hotel as to quality, value-for-price, and cuisine.
3. Invite a native Spanish-speaker or a North American who has travelled in Hispanic countries to share hotel experiences with the class.

CHAPTER 6 RESOURCES

1. Workbook
2. Student Tape Manual
3. Audio Cassette 4B
4. Vocabulary Transparencies
5. Bell Ringer Review Blackline Masters
6. Communication Activities Masters
7. Computer Software: Practice and Test Generator
8. Video Cassette, Chapter 6
9. Video Activities Booklet, Chapter 6
10. Situation Cards
11. Chapter Quizzes
12. Testing Program

Pacing

Chapter 6 will require eight to ten class sessions. Pacing will depend on the length of the class period, the age of the students, and student aptitude.

LEARNING FROM PHOTOS

Refer to the photo on pages 138-139. Tell students: *Éste es el hall del Hotel Palace en la ciudad de Madrid. ¿Qué opinas? ¿Es un hotel lujoso? ¿Tiene cinco estrellas?*

VOCABULARIO
PALABRAS 1

Vocabulary Teaching Resources
1. Vocabulary Transparencies, 6.1 (*A & B*)
2. Audio Cassette 4B
3. Student Tape Manual, *Palabras 1*
4. Workbook, *Palabras 1*
5. Communication Activities Masters, *Palabras 1, A & B*
6. Chapter Quizzes, *Palabras 1*

Bell Ringer Review
Write the following on the board or use BRR Blackline Master 6-1: Write a list of things you have to pack when you go on a trip.

PRESENTATION (pages 140-141)

Note In the vocabulary section, all the present perfect verb forms are in the third person so that students can concentrate on assimilating the vocabulary without worrying about inflections. Students will learn how to manipulate the other forms of the present perfect in the *Estructura* section of this chapter.

A. Have students close their books. Present *Palabras 1* by referring to Vocabulary Transparencies 6.1 (*A & B*). Lead students through the new vocabulary by asking ¿Qué es esto? or ¿Quién es? Model the response and have students repeat after you. For example: ¿Qué es? Es un hotel.
B. Now have students open their books and repeat in unison as you model the entire *Palabras 1* vocabulary, or play Cassette 4B.

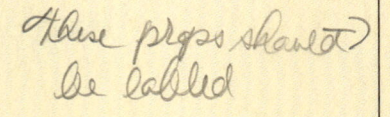

These props should not be labeled

140

VOCABULARIO

PALABRAS 1

EN LA RECEPCIÓN

el recepcionista — la recepcionista — la llegada al hotel
la recepción
el ascensor — el botones, el mozo
la ficha, la tarjeta — el cliente, el huésped — la llave — el equipaje
un cuarto, una habitación
un cuarto sencillo — un cuarto doble

140   CAPÍTULO 6

PANTOMIME 1

(following the Vocabulary presentation)

Getting Ready
Set up places in the classroom in order to create a hotel. As props you might use a room key and a small suitcase.
(Student 1) y (Student 2), **vengan Uds., por favor.**
(Student 1), **llegas al hotel.**
(Student 2), **eres el/la recepcionista.**
(Student 1), **ve a la recepción. Pide una habitación.**
(Student 2), **dále la ficha.**
(Student 1), **llena la ficha. Fírmala.** (**Escribe tu nombre**). **Dále la ficha al/a la recepcionista.**
(Student 2), **dale la llave al/a la cliente.**
(Student 1), **toma tu equipaje. Sube la escalera.**
Gracias, (Student 1) y (Student 2).

La señorita ha llegado al hotel.
Ella ya ha reservado un cuarto.
Ella ha subido a su cuarto.
Ella ha abierto la puerta.
El botones ha subido el equipaje.

la salida del hotel
el cajero
la cuenta, la nota
los gastos
el total, el monto
la caja

El señor ha pedido su nota.
El cajero se la ha dado.

El señor ha abandonado su cuarto.

CAPÍTULO 6   141

PANTOMIME 2

_____, ven acá, por favor.
Tú eres un/una turista. Estás en un hotel, delante de la puerta de tu habitación.
Toma tu llave.
Abre la puerta con la llave.
Toma tu equipaje.
Entra en la habitación.
Pon tu equipaje sobre la cama.
Cierra la puerta.
Mira bien la habitación.
Ve al baño.
Abre la ventana. Mira afuera.
Indica que estás contento(a) con la habitación.
Gracias, _____. Bien hecho.

C. Refer to the Vocabulary Transparencies again. Call on volunteers to read the new words or phrases from their books in random order. Other volunteers will go to the screen and point out the corresponding images.

D. Make true/false statements about the material and have students respond. For example: *La recepción está en el jardín del hotel.* (falso) *La recepción está en el pasillo.* (falso) *El cliente llena la ficha.* (verdad)

Teaching Tip For additional practice in true/false activities, have students correct false statements.

Vocabulary Expansion

You may give students the following expressions that are useful at a hotel:
¿Hay cartas para mí?
¿Hay mensajes para mí?

Ejercicios

PRESENTATION (page 142)

Extension of *Ejercicio A*
Speaking
After completing Exercise A, call on individuals to describe the illustrations to the class.

Ejercicio B
Exercise B prepares students for the present perfect tense presented in the *Estructura* section that follows. Note that in this exercise only the third person form is used, in order to avoid verb manipulation. Students will learn the other verb forms in the *Estructura* section.

Extension of *Ejercicio B*
Listening
After completing Exercise B as a whole-class activity, focus on the listening skill by having students work in pairs. One partner reads the questions in random order while the other listens and answers, with book closed. Then the partners can switch roles.

ANSWERS

Ejercicio A
1. Es la recepción.
2. Es el recepcionista.
3. Es la ficha.
4. Es la llave.
5. La señorita ha llegado al hotel.
6. El mozo ha subido el equipaje.

Ejercicio B
1. Sí, la señorita ha llegado al hotel.
2. Sí, ella tiene una reservación.
3. Ella quiere una habitación sencilla.
4. Sí, la señorita se ha presentado en la recepción.
5. Sí, ha pedido su habitación.
6. Sí, ha llenado la ficha de llegada.
7. Sí, ha ido a su cuarto.
8. Sí, el botones ha subido el equipaje.
9. Sí, la señorita le ha dado una propina.
10. Se la ha dado al botones.

142

Ejercicios

Good pattern for a PowerPoint

A ¿Qué es? Identifiquen.

1. ¿Es la recepción o la caja?
2. ¿Es el recepcionista o el botones? 
3. ¿Es la ficha o la nota? 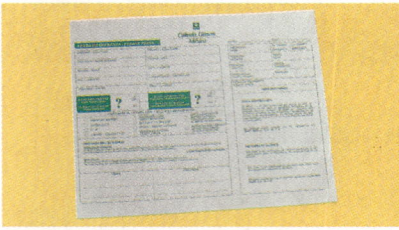
4. ¿Es la llave o la tarjeta de crédito? 
5. ¿La señorita ha llegado al hotel o ha salido del hotel? 
6. ¿El mozo ha subido o ha bajado el equipaje? 

B En la recepción. Contesten. *Tie these questions to trans. from Palabras 1*

1. ¿Ha llegado al hotel la señorita?
2. ¿Tiene ella una reservación?
3. Ella viaja sola. ¿Quiere una habitación doble o sencilla?
4. ¿La señorita se ha presentado en la recepción?
5. ¿Ha pedido su habitación?
6. ¿Ha llenado la ficha de llegada?
7. ¿Ha ido a su cuarto?
8. ¿El botones ha subido el equipaje?
9. ¿La señorita le ha dado una propina?
10. ¿A quién se la ha dado?

142   CAPÍTULO 6

COOPERATIVE LEARNING

Each team assembles a list of hotel events which they can mime. Teams then present their mimes to the class, one event at a time. The class asks questions to determine what they are doing. Chosen team members respond.

Has potential. Teach these "events" as infinitive phrases

C ¿Qué es o quién es? Den la palabra.

1. adonde van los clientes al llegar al hotel
2. adonde van los clientes para pagar su cuenta antes de salir del hotel
3. el que lleva o sube el equipaje a los cuartos de los clientes
4. el que trabaja en la recepción
5. el que trabaja en la caja
6. un cuarto para una sola persona
7. un cuarto para dos personas
8. lo que usa mucha gente para pagar la cuenta o la nota en un hotel
9. lo que abre la puerta

D Una palabra relacionada. Pareen.

1. llegar   a. el pago
2. salir   b. el gasto
3. pagar   c. la reservación
4. gastar   d. la salida
5. recibir   e. la llegada
6. reservar   f. la recepción

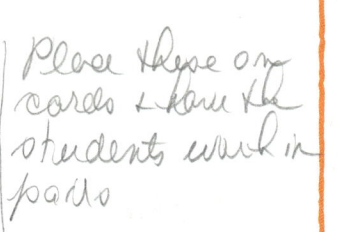

El suite presidencial de un hotel en Querétaro, México

CAPÍTULO 6   143

DID YOU KNOW?

Many hotels in Europe and Latin America still give clients a very large key that is awkward to carry around. The key is left at the reception desk or in some cases with the concierge (*en la conserjería*). In the large chain hotels the computerized card key is sometimes used.

INDEPENDENT PRACTICE

Assign any of the following:
1. Workbook, *Palabras 1*
2. Communication Activities Masters, *Palabras 1, A & B*
3. Exercises on student pages 142–143

Ejercicios
ANSWERS

Ejercicio C
1. a la recepción
2. a la caja
3. el botones (el mozo)
4. el (la) recepcionista
5. el (la) cajero(a)
6. un cuarto sencillo
7. un cuarto doble
8. la tarjeta de crédito
9. la llave

Ejercicio D
1. e
2. d
3. a
4. b
5. f
6. c

INFORMAL ASSESSMENT

(Palabras 1)
Show Vocabulary Transparencies 6.1 (*A & B*) again and have students make up as many questions as they can about the illustrations. This is an important activity because it gives students practice using the interrogative words.

GEOGRAPHY CONNECTION

Querétaro es una ciudad de unas 800.000 habitantes. Es la capital del estado de Querétaro y es un centro industrial importante.

HISTORY CONNECTION

Querétaro ha jugado un papel importantísimo en la historia de México. En esta ciudad nació en 1810 Josefa Ortiz de Domínguez, una gran heroína de la independencia mexicana. Se le llamaba la Corregidora. En 1848 terminó la guerra con los Estados Unidos con la firma del Tratado de Guadalupe Hidalgo en Querétaro y en Querétaro fue firmada la Constitución mexicana en 1917, la misma constitución que rige el Estado hoy.

143

VOCABULARIO
PALABRAS 2

Vocabulary Teaching Resources

1. Vocabulary Transparencies 6.2 (*A & B*)
2. Audio Cassette 4B
3. Student Tape Manual, *Palabras 2*
4. Workbook, *Palabras 2*
5. Communication Activities Masters, *Palabras 2, C & D*
6. Chapter Quizzes, *Palabras 2*
7. Computer Software, *Vocabulario*

Bell Ringer Review

Write the following on the board or use BRR Blackline Master 6-2: Write a list of all the rooms in a typical house.

PRESENTATION (*pages 144–145*)

A. Have students close their books. Model the *Palabras 2* vocabulary using Vocabulary Transparencies 6.2 (*A & B*). Have students repeat the new material after you or Cassette 4B. Have them repeat each word or expression twice.

B. Point to the appropriate illustration and ask questions, beginning with yes/no and either/or and then progressing to more open-ended ones, such as: *¿Qué ha hecho la camarera? ¿Quién ha cambiado las toallas?*

C. Use props such as a pillow, soap, a towel, etc., as cues. Ask students what one needs in order to do various things. For example: *Va a tomar una ducha. Se va a bañar. Se lava el cuerpo. Se seca. Va a dormir. Pone la ropa en el armario.*

VOCABULARIO

PALABRAS 2

EN LA HABITACIÓN

- el aire acondicionado
- el televisor
- la almohada
- la sábana
- la cama

el baño

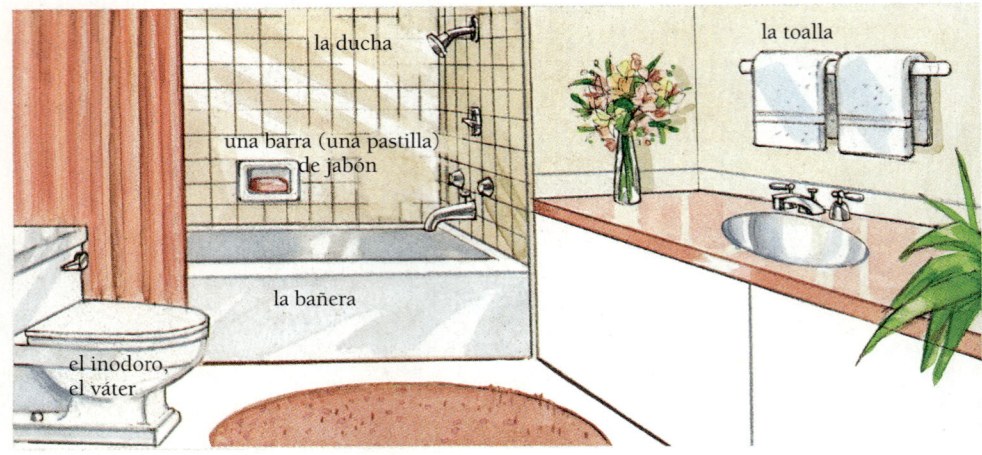

- la ducha
- la toalla
- una barra (una pastilla) de jabón
- la bañera
- el inodoro, el váter

144 CAPÍTULO 6

PANTOMIME

_____, ven acá, por favor.
Estás en un hotel.
Estás en tu cuarto.
Abre la puerta del armario.
Toma una percha.
Cuelga tu abrigo.
Ponlo en el armario.
Cierra la puerta del armario.
Ve al baño.
Mírate en el espejo.
Toma la barra de jabón. Lávate el cuerpo.
Toma una toalla.
Sécate el cuerpo con la toalla.
Gracias, _____. Bien hecho.
Ahora, vuelve a tu asiento, por favor.

el armario

la percha,
el colgador,
el gancho

la camarera

La camarera ha limpiado el cuarto.
Ha hecho (tendido) la cama.

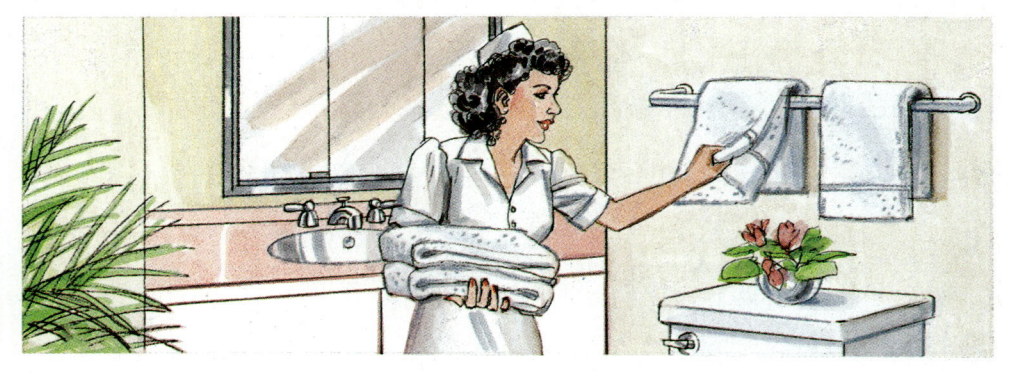

Ha cambiado las toallas.

CAPÍTULO 6

D. When presenting the sentences on page 145, ask questions in order to elicit the desired vocabulary. For example:
¿Quién ha limpiado el cuarto?
¿Qué ha limpiado la camarera?
¿Qué ha tendido la camarera?
¿Quién ha hecho la cama? ¿Qué ha hecho la camarera en el baño?

Teaching Tip When asking questions like the ones above, direct easier questions to the less able students and save difficult ones for more able students.

Vocabulary Expansion

You may wish to give students the following useful expressions:
Quisiera más toallas, por favor.
Otra almohada, por favor.
Necesito otra manta.
No hay jabón.
Necesito un rollo de papel higiénico.

CRITICAL THINKING ACTIVITY

(Thinking skills: making inferences; drawing conclusions)

Read the following to the class or write it on the board or on an overhead transparency.

Los hoteles tienen una hora fija en que sus clientes o huéspedes tienen que abandonar sus cuartos. En algunos hoteles es el mediodía. En otros es a las dos de la tarde— nunca más tarde. ¿Por qué tienen que abandonar los huéspedes sus cuartos para esta hora?

— *Good idea. Type and trans.*

Ejercicios

PRESENTATION (page 146)

Ejercicio A
A. Have students refer to the illustration as they answer.
B. Call on individuals to describe the illustration in their own words.

Ejercicio B
Exercise B can be done with books open.

Extension of *Ejercicio C*
After students give you another word, you may have them use each word in a sentence.

ANSWERS

Ejercicio A
1. Hay una cama en el cuarto.
2. Sí, el cuarto tiene balcón.
3. Sí, tiene baño.
4. Sí, hay una ducha en el cuarto de baño.
6. Hay dos toallas.
7. Hay toallas grandes.
8. La camarera limpia el cuarto.

Ejercicio B
1. La camarera
2. cama
3. cambiado, baño
4. jabón
5. ganchos (perchas, colgadores)
6. aire acondicionado

Ejercicio C
1. la habitación
2. la barra
3. el gancho (el colgador)
4. el monto
5. la cuenta
6. el mozo

INFORMAL ASSESSMENT
(*Palabras 2*)
Check for understanding by having students correct the following statements:
El aire acondicionado está en el baño.
Hay una toalla en la cama.
Hay perchas en la silla.
Hay un inodoro en la habitación.
La camarera ha cambiado el televisor.

146

Ejercicios

A **El cuarto de un hotel.** Contesten según el dibujo.

1. ¿Cuántas camas hay en el cuarto?
2. ¿Tiene balcón el cuarto?
3. ¿Tiene baño el cuarto?
4. ¿Hay una ducha en el cuarto de baño?
5. ¿Cuántas toallas hay?
6. ¿Hay toallas grandes y pequeñas?
7. ¿Quién limpia el cuarto?

B **En el cuarto del hotel.** Completen.

1. ___ ha limpiado el cuarto.
2. Ella ha hecho la ___ .
3. Ella ha ___ las toallas en el ___ .
4. Ella ha traído más barras de ___ .
5. Hay ___ para colgar la ropa en el armario.
6. Hace calor en el cuarto. La señorita ha puesto el ___ ___ .

C **Los sinónimos.** ¿Cuál es otra palabra?

1. el cuarto
2. la pastilla
3. la percha
4. el total
5. la nota
6. el botones

146 CAPÍTULO 6

COOPERATIVE LEARNING

Allow time to prepare. Two team members are having a great time in an expensive hotel. The other two are having a terrible time in a cheap hotel. The four meet at a café and take turns describing their experiences. For example: ¡Nuestra habitación es enorme! ¡Nuestra habitación es como un armario! ¡Las camas son muy cómodas! ¡Nuestras camas son horribles!, etc.

INDEPENDENT PRACTICE

Assign any of the following:
1. Workbook, *Palabras 2*
2. Communication Activities Masters, *Palabras 2, C & D*
3. Exercises on student pages 146–147

Comunicación
Palabras 1 y 2

A **En la pensión.** Ud. ha llegado a la Pensión Costa Azul en Barcelona. Ud. se presenta a la recepción. Hable con el/la recepcionista.

1. Find out if they have a single room.
2. The receptionist wants to know if you have a reservation. You don't.
3. A single room is available. Ask what floor it is on and how much it is.
4. The receptionist asks you if you have luggage.
5. At the end of your stay, ask for your bill and if you can pay with a credit card.

B **Lo que voy a hacer.** Durante su estadía en el hotel, Ud. piensa hacer lo siguiente. Explíquele al/a la recepcionista lo que tiene que tener en el cuarto.

1. Me quiero lavar.
2. Quiero tomar una ducha.
3. Quiero colgar mi ropa en el armario.
4. Está haciendo mucho calor y no me gusta mucho el calor.
5. Quiero tomar un poco de aire fresco sin salir a la calle.
6. Me gustaría ver una película o un partido de fútbol.
7. Quisiera hacer algunas llamadas.
8. Somos cuatro personas.

C **¡Qué hotel!** Ud. ha pasado sus vacaciones en un hotel en San Juan, Puerto Rico. Su compañero(a) de clase quiere saber si le gustó el hotel. Dígale lo que Ud. opina sobre…

1. el servicio de los botones
2. la piscina
3. el baño
4. la cama
5. el restaurante del hotel
6. el desayuno
7. la habitación
8. la vista desde su ventana

El parque Güell, Barcelona, España

CAPÍTULO 6 147

DID YOU KNOW?

Gaudí es el famoso arquitecto, escultor, y herrador catalán. Fue uno de los más importantes exponentes del modernismo. Nació en 1852 y dedicó su vida a la construcción del Templo de la Sagrada Familia en Barcelona, que todavía no ha sido terminado. La vida de Gaudí es triste. Vivió como un recluso. En 1926 fue atropellado (run over) por un tranvía y murió dos días después en el hospital. Nadie sabía quién era. Nadie lo había reconocido. Está enterrado en la cripta de la Sagrada Familia.

ESTRUCTURA

Structure Teaching Resources

1. Workbook, *Estructura*
2. Student Tape Manual, *Estructura*
3. Audio Cassette 4B
4. Communication Activities Masters, *Palabras 2, A-C*
5. Chapter Quizzes, *Estructura*
6. Computer Software, *Estructura*

Bell Ringer Review

Write the following on the board or use BRR Blackline Master 6-4: Complete in the ~~present~~ *preterite.*

1. Nosotros ___ al hotel. (llegar)
2. Nosotros ___ a la recepción. (ir)
3. El recepcionista nos ___ y nos ___ la llave. (hablar, dar)
4. El botones nos ___ con las maletas. (ayudar)
5. Él nos ___ las maletas. (subir)
6. Nosotros ___ en el ascensor. (subir)
7. Yo ___ la puerta con la llave. (abrir)
8. Yo ___ en el hotel pero mis amigos ___ a comer en un restaurante. (comer, salir)

El presente perfecto

PRESENTATION *(pages 148-149)*

A. Have students open their books to page 148. Lead them through steps 1-5.
B. Model the examples and have students repeat them in unison.
C. Write the forms of the verb *haber* on the board.
D. Have students repeat the past participles in step 2 after you.

148

ESTRUCTURA

El presente perfecto
Talking About What You and Others Have Done Recently

1. The present perfect tense in Spanish is formed by using the present tense of the verb *haber* and the past participle. Note the present tense forms of the verb *haber*.

INFINITIVE	HABER
yo	he
tú	has
él, ella, Ud.	ha
nosotros(as)	hemos
vosotros(as)	*habéis*
ellos, ellas, Uds.	han

2. The past participle of regular verbs is formed by adding *-ado* to the infinitive stem of *-ar* verbs and *-ido* to the infinitive stem of *-er* and *-ir* verbs.

hablar	hablado	comer	comido	subir	subido
reservar	reservado	poder	podido	pedir	pedido

3. The present perfect is called a compound tense because it consists of two verb forms: the present tense of the verb *haber* and the past participle of the verb being used.

INFINITIVE	LLEGAR	COMER	SUBIR
yo	he llegado	he comido	he subido
tú	has llegado	has comido	has subido
él, ella, Ud.	ha llegado	ha comido	ha subido
nosotros(as)	hemos llegado	hemos comido	hemos subido
vosotros(as)	*habéis llegado*	*habéis comido*	*habéis subido*
ellos, ellas, Uds.	han llegado	han comido	han subido

148 CAPÍTULO 6

4. The present perfect tense is used to describe a recently completed action. Some time expressions that are used frequently with the present perfect are:

ya	already, yet
todavía no	not yet
jamás	ever, never
nunca	never

alguna vez (handwritten)

Ya has visitado México, ¿verdad?
Sí, he estado dos veces.
Pero todavía no he estado en Taxco.
No he ido nunca a Taxco.

5. In compound tenses the verb *haber* and the participle are never separated.

María ha llegado pero sus amigos no han llegado.
Él ha leído la carta pero su amigo no la ha leído.
Ella se ha levantado pero sus amigos no se han levantado.

Ejercicios

A **En el hotel.** Contesten.

1. ¿Ha llegado Carmen al hotel?
2. ¿Ha ido a la recepción?
3. ¿Se ha presentado en la recepción?
4. ¿Ha llenado la ficha o la tarjeta de recepción?
5. ¿Han llegado sus amigos también?
6. ¿Han subido ellos a su cuarto?
7. Y tú, ¿has estado alguna vez en un hotel?
8. ¿En qué hotel has estado?

La iglesia de Santa Prisca, Taxco, México

CAPÍTULO 6   149

LEARNING FROM PHOTOS

Refer students to the photo on the left at the bottom of page 149 and ask: *¿Adónde están llegando los jóvenes? ¿Qué están llevando? ¿Qué están subiendo?*

E. Put the past participles on the board with *haber* and have students repeat aloud the forms of the present perfect.
F. Have students read the adverbs and the example sentences in step 4 aloud.
G. You may wish to ask questions about the example sentences in step 5. *¿Quién ha llegado? ¿Quiénes no han llegado? ¿Quién ha leído la carta? ¿Quién no la ha leído? ¿Quién se ha levantado? ¿Quiénes no se han levantado?*

Ejercicios

PRESENTATION (page 149)

Ejercicio A
Do Exercise A orally first. Then have students write the answers.

ANSWERS
Ejercicio A
Answers will vary.
1. Sí, Carmen ha llegado al hotel.
2. Sí, ha ido a la recepción.
3. Sí, se ha presentado en la recepción.
4. Sí, ha llenado la ficha de recepción.
5. Sí, sus amigos han llegado también.
6. Sí, han subido a su cuarto.
7. Sí (No), yo (no) he estado en un hotel.
8. Yo he estado en el Hotel…

GEOGRAPHY CONNECTION

Taxco siempre ha sido famoso por sus minas de plata. Es un pueblo bello con casas blancas de estilo colonial y callejuelas empedradas. Está situado en las colinas de la Sierra Madre en el estado de Guerrero. El gobierno mexicano declaró a Taxco un monumento nacional en 1928.

Ejercicios

PRESENTATION (page 150)

Ejercicios B and D
Exercises B and D can be done with books closed.

Extension of Ejercicio B
Exercise B contains a very natural exchange. You may wish to do this with many more verbs. For example: *¿Vas a llamar a José? ¿Vas a telefonear? ¿Vas a dejar un mensaje? ¿Vas a ir a su casa? ¿Vas a hablar con él?*

Ejercicio C
Exercise C can be done with books open.

ANSWERS

Ejercicio B
1. No, porque ya he llamado a María.
2. No, porque ya he ido a la gasolinera.
3. No, porque ya he llenado el tanque.
4. No, porque ya he revisado el aceite.
5. No, porque ya he cambiado la llanta.

Ejercicio C
1. ha llegado
2. Se ha presentado
3. ha ido
4. ha subido
5. hemos llegado
6. Hemos tenido
7. ha habido

Ejercicio D
Answers will vary.
1. Sí (No), (no) he estado alguna vez (nunca) en un país extranjero.
2. Sí (No), (no) he estado en otro estado de los Estados Unidos.
3. Yo he visitado…
4. Sí (No), (no) me han gustado.
5. Sí (No), (no) he viajado en avión.
6. He ido a…
7. He viajado… veces en avión.

150

B **No, ya lo he hecho.** Contesten según el modelo. *Expand*

¿Vas a comer?
No, porque ya he comido.

1. ¿Vas a llamar a María?
2. ¿Vas a ir a la gasolinera?
3. ¿Vas a llenar el tanque?
4. ¿Vas a revisar el aceite?
5. ¿Vas a cambiar la llanta?

C **Ya ha llegado.** Completen con el presente perfecto.

Rosaura ya ___(1)___ (llegar) al hotel. ___(2)___ (presentarse) en la recepción y ___(3)___ (ir) a su cuarto. El mozo le ___(4)___ (subir) las maletas.
Nosotros no ___(5)___ (llegar) todavía. ___(6)___ (tener) un problema. ___(7)___ (haber) mucho tráfico.

D **Mis viajes.** Preguntas personales.

1. ¿Has estado alguna vez en un país extranjero?
2. Si todavía no has estado en un país extranjero, ¿has estado en otro estado de los Estados Unidos?
3. ¿Qué estados o países has visitado?
4. ¿Te han gustado?
5. ¿Ya has viajado en avión?
6. ¿Adónde has ido en avión?
7. Hasta ahora, ¿cuántas veces has viajado en avión?

150 CAPÍTULO 6

FOR THE NATIVE SPEAKER

Students will often try to make "regular" past participles of irregular ones. For example, you may hear *"rompido," "ponido,"* and *"cubrido."* Provide students the following exercise using the past perfect.
1. No European had seen the New World before Columbus.
2. At least no one had returned to Europe or had written about the Americas.

INDEPENDENT PRACTICE

Assign any of the following:
1. Workbook, *Estructura*
2. Communication Activities Masters, *Estructura, A*
3. Exercises on student pages 149-150

Los participios irregulares
Talking About What You and Others Have Done

The following verbs have irregular past participles.

decir	dicho
hacer	hecho
ver	visto
escribir	escrito
abrir	abierto
cubrir	cubierto
morir	muerto
poner	puesto
volver	vuelto
devolver	devuelto

Ejercicios

A **Ella ha hecho una reservación.** Contesten.

1. ¿María ha escrito al hotel?
2. ¿Ella ha hecho una reservación?
3. ¿Ella ha puesto un sello en el sobre?
4. ¿Ella ha vuelto al mismo hotel?
5. ¿Ella ha visto el cuarto?
6. ¿Ella ha abierto la puerta con la llave?
7. ¿Ella ha sacado la ropa de sus maletas?
8. ¿Ella ha puesto su ropa en el armario?
9. ¿Ella ha devuelto la llave a la recepción?

B **Ya lo han hecho.** Contesten según el modelo.

¿Escribirlo?
Pero ya lo han escrito.

1. ¿Escribirlo?
2. ¿Devolverlo?
3. ¿Verlo?
4. ¿Abrirlo?
5. ¿Ponerlo?
6. ¿Decirlo?
7. ¿Hacerlo?

CAPÍTULO 6   **151**

Bell Ringer Review
Write the following on the board or use BRR Blackline Master 6-5: Rewrite in the preterite.
1. Él hace un viaje.
2. Ellos van a México.
3. Yo los veo.
4. Ellos salen el día 20.
5. Y vuelven el día 28.

Los participios irregulares
PRESENTATION *(page 151)*
A. Have students read the past participles aloud.
B. Call on volunteers to write on the board the present perfect tense of two of the verbs.
C. Now have the class repeat these paradigms.

Ejercicios
PRESENTATION *(page 151)*

Ejercicios A and B
A. Go over Exercises A and B by having volunteers do two items each.
B. These exercises can be done orally with books closed.

ANSWERS
Ejercicio A
1. Sí, María ha escrito al hotel.
2. Sí, ella ha hecho una reservación.
3. Sí, ella ha puesto un sello en el sobre.
4. Sí, ella ha vuelto al mismo hotel.
5. Sí, ella ha visto el cuarto.
6. Sí, ella ha abierto la puerta con la llave.
7. Sí, ella ha sacado la ropa de sus maletas.
8. Sí, ella ha puesto su ropa en el armario.
9. Sí, ella ha devuelto la llave a la recepción.

Ejercicio B
1. Pero ya lo han escrito.
2. Pero ya lo han devuelto.
3. Pero ya lo han visto.
4. Pero ya lo han abierto.
5. Pero ya lo han puesto.
6. Pero ya lo han dicho.
7. Pero ya lo han hecho.

LEARNING FROM PHOTOS/REALIA

1. Refer students to the photo on the right on page 150. Have them tell as much as they can about it in their own words.
2. Refer students to the brochure on page 151 and ask: *¿Cómo se llama el hotel? ¿Dónde está?*

Bell Ringer Review

Write the following on the board or use BRR Blackline Master 6-6: Match the following.

1. el disco   a. el esquí
2. las botas   b. la natación
3. la raqueta   c. el golf
4. la bola   d. el patinaje
5. los patines   e. la música
6. el traje de baño f. el tenis

Dos complementos con se

PRESENTATION (page 152)

A. With books opened to page 152, guide students through steps 1-3.

B. You may want to write the sample sentences on the board to reinforce this concept. Draw an arrow from the pronoun to the noun it replaces.

Note Do not wait until all students have mastered this point before going on to new material. Students will need constant practice and reinforcement of the use of *se* throughout their study of Spanish. This is a point that students learn through repeated usage and examples, rather than through explanation.

[Handwritten notes:]
Reteach nouns + use this BRR as a springboard into
Paired practice
Place pictures of familiar objects on cards
Student 1: ¡Me encanta tu libro!
Student 2: ¿De veras? Te lo regalo.

Dos complementos con se

Referring to People and Things Already Mentioned

1. You have already learned that when there are two object pronouns in the same sentence, the indirect object always precedes the direct object.

   Ella **me** ha devuelto **el dinero**.   Ella **me lo** ha devuelto.
   Él **nos** sirvió **la comida**.   Él **nos la** sirvió.

2. When the direct object pronouns *lo, la, los,* or *las* are used with *le* or *les*, both *le* and *les* change to *se*.

   El mesero **les** dio **el menú**.   El mesero **se lo** dio.
   La señora **le** dejó **la propina**.   La señora **se la** dejó.

3. Since *se* can refer to different people, it is frequently clarified by adding a prepositional phrase.

   La señora **le** dio **el regalo** a él.   La señora **se lo** dio a él.
   La señora **le** dio **el regalo** a ella.   La señora **se lo** dio a ella.
   La señora **le** dio **el regalo** a Ud.   La señora **se lo** dio a Ud.
   La señora **les** dio **el regalo** a ellos. La señora **se lo** dio a ellos.
   La señora **les** dio **el regalo** a ellas. La señora **se lo** dio a ellas.
   La señora **les** dio **el regalo** a Uds.   La señora **se lo** dio a Uds.

152 CAPÍTULO 6

FOR THE NATIVE SPEAKER

You may wish to give students this more challenging exercise on double object pronouns. Change the underlined nouns to pronouns.

1. Vamos a entregar <u>los informes</u> a <u>don Anastasio</u>.
2. El cartero trajo <u>los informes</u> para <u>don Anastasio</u>.
3. Felipe está llamando a <u>don Anastasio</u> ahora.
4. Felipe nos dio las <u>postales</u> también.
5. Va a dar<u>nos</u> las otras <u>postales</u> mañana.
6. Clara <u>le</u> está pidiendo <u>los paquetes</u> a Felipe.
7. Él dice que no tiene <u>los paquetes</u>.

Ejercicios

A **¿Quién se lo dio? Su tía se lo dio.** Contesten con pronombres.

1. ¿Quién le dio *el disco* a *Teresa*?
2. ¿Quién le dio *la raqueta* a *Juan*?
3. ¿Quién le dio *los esquís* a *Teresa*?
4. ¿Quién le dio *las botas* a *Juan*?
5. ¿Quién les dio *los boletos* a *Juan y a Teresa*?
6. ¿Quién les dio *las entradas*?

B **Su abuelita se lo compró.** Contesten según el modelo.

> ¿Quién le compró el regalito al niño?
> *Su abuelita se lo compró.*

1. ¿Quién le compró la bicicleta?
2. ¿Quién le compró el pijama?
3. ¿Quién le compró el suéter?
4. ¿Quién le compró los patines?

C **Tomás se la ha escrito, sin duda.**
Expresen con pronombres.

1. Tomás le ha escrito la carta a Lupe.
2. Tomás le ha pedido los sellos a su mamá.
3. Su madre le dio las estampillas.
4. Lupe no le ha contestado la carta.
5. Tomás le ha devuelto los sellos a su mamá.
6. Su amigo le vendió los sellos porque Tomás no pudo ir al correo.

CAPÍTULO 6 153

CONVERSACIÓN

Bell Ringer Review
Write the following on the board or use BRR Blackline Master 6-7: Match the word in the first column with a related word in the second column.
1. reservar   a. recibo
2. confirmar   b. alquiler
3. recibir   c. reservación
4. bañar   d. aparcamiento
5. alquilar   e. confirmación
6. aparcar   f. baño

PRESENTATION (page 154)
A. Tell students they are going to hear a conversation between a hotel receptionist and a guest.
B. Have students open their books to page 154 and follow along as you play Cassette 4B.

PAIRED ACTIVITY
Have pairs of students create hotel-centered skits based on the conversation. Then have them present their skits to the class. They can make any changes they wish.

Ejercicio
ANSWERS
1. La señorita quiere una habitación simple.
2. Ella lo quiere por tres noches.
3. Sí, ella ha hecho una reservación.
4. Sí, ella ha recibido una confirmación.
5. Ella ha hecho la reservación a nombre de Castelar.
6. Le han dado la habitación 503.
7. El mozo le subirá las maletas.

CONVERSACIÓN

Escenas de la vida *En la recepción del hotel*

EL RECEPCIONISTA: ¿Sí, señorita?
LA CLIENTE: Una habitación simple, por favor.
EL RECEPCIONISTA: Sí, señorita. ¿Con baño o sin baño?
LA CLIENTE: Con baño.
EL RECEPCIONISTA: ¿Por cuántas noches?
LA CLIENTE: Tres.
EL RECEPCIONISTA: ¿Ud. ha hecho una reservación?
LA CLIENTE: Sí, y he recibido una confirmación.
EL RECEPCIONISTA: No hay problema. ¿A nombre de quién ha hecho Ud. la reservación?
LA CLIENTE: A nombre de Castelar.
EL RECEPCIONISTA: Aquí tiene Ud. la llave para el 503. ¿Tiene Ud. maletas?
LA CLIENTE: Sí.
EL RECEPCIONISTA: El mozo se las subirá en seguida.

En el hotel. Contesten según la conversación.
1. ¿Quiere la señorita una habitación simple o doble?
2. ¿Por cuántas noches la quiere?
3. ¿Ella ha hecho una reservación?
4. ¿Ha recibido ella una confirmación?
5. ¿A nombre de quién ha hecho ella la reservación?
6. ¿Qué habitación le han dado a la señorita?
7. ¿Quién le subirá las maletas?

Hotel Emperador ★★★★ MADRID

SERVICIOS DEL HOTEL

ALQUILER DE COCHES
Nuestro Conserje le atenderá gustosamente 442

APARCAMIENTO
Muy cerca del Hotel, a 25 mts.

BAR-PIANO
En Planta Noble. Abierto de 11.00 a 24.00 horas. Podrá elegir su música preferida 103

BAR TERRAZA
En planta 10.ª Abierto de Junio a Septiembre de 11.00 a 19.30 horas 403

BOUTIQUE
En el Hall principal del Hotel 803

154 CAPÍTULO 6

LEARNING FROM REALIA
Refer students to the hotel information card at the bottom of page 154 and ask them: ¿Cómo se llama el hotel? ¿Dónde está? ¿Ofrece muchos servicios a sus clientes? Si uno quiere alquilar un coche, ¿con quién debe hablar? ¿Hay aparcamiento en el hotel? ¿Dónde está? ¿Cuántos bares hay? ¿En qué piso está el Bar Terraza? ¿Durante qué meses está abierto? ¿Qué opina Ud.? ¿Es un bar al aire libre? ¿Hay además una piscina? ¿Dónde está la boutique? ¿Qué es una boutique?

Comunicación

A **Una habitación, por favor.** Ud. es el/la cliente que llega a un hotel. Su compañero(a) de clase tomará el papel del/de la recepcionista. Preparen la conversación que Uds. tienen en la recepción.

B **Al salir.** Ud. tomará el papel de un(a) cajero(a) en un hotel. Su compañero(a) de clase es un(a) cliente que está saliendo del hotel. Preparen la conversación que Uds. tienen en la caja del hotel.

C **¿Has… ?** Ud. y un compañero de clase van a preparar una lista de las cosas que ya han hecho hoy. Luego comparen sus listas y determinen cuáles son las cosas que Uds. han hecho. Luego decidan quién ha hecho más.

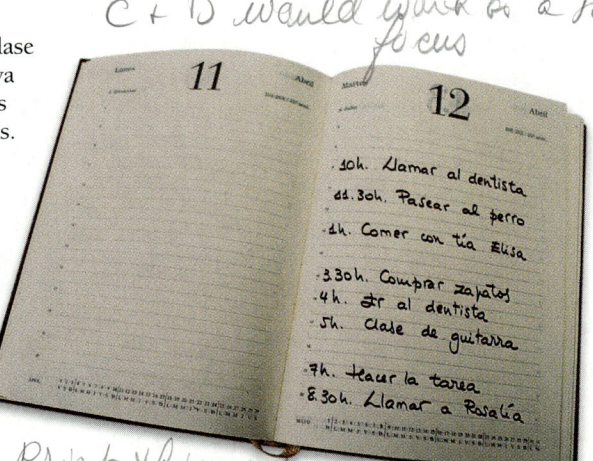

D **Lo que no he hecho nunca.** Prepare una lista de cosas que Ud. no ha hecho nunca pero que quiere hacer.

E **Queremos una habitación.** Con un(a) compañero(a) de clase prepare la siguiente situación. Otro(a) compañero(a) toma apuntes sobre lo que Uds. dicen y luego informa a la clase.

Ud. y dos amigos han llegado al aeropuerto en Tegucigalpa, Honduras. Son las tres de la mañana y Uds. están muy cansados. No tienen una reservación en un hotel. Llame a un hotel. Ud. quiere saber si tienen cuartos disponibles; los precios; dónde está el hotel; qué transporte hay para ir al hotel; y cualquier otra cosa importante.

F **¿Qué prefieres?** Hágale preguntas a un(a) compañero(a) de clase sobre lo que le importa cuando se queda en un hotel. Luego cambien de papel. Use las siguientes expresiones para formar las preguntas.

    clase de hotel
    tipo de habitación
    aire acondicionado
    baño
    balcón
    cerca del centro, la playa
    cómo puede pagar la cuenta

CAPÍTULO 6

Comunicación
PRESENTATION (page 155)

The *Comunicación* activities allow students to use the chapter vocabulary and grammar in open-ended situations. You may select those you consider most appropriate. You may also allow students to select the activity or activities in which they will take part.

ANSWERS
Actividades A–F
Answers will vary.

CRITICAL THINKING ACTIVITY

(Thinking skills: evaluating consequences)

Read the following to the class or write it on the board or on an overhead transparency.

1. *Viajar con mucho dinero en efectivo no es una buena idea. ¿Por qué?*
2. *¿Es una ventaja pagar con una tarjeta de crédito? ¿Por qué?*

LECTURA Y CULTURA

Bell Ringer Review
Write the following on the board or use BRR Blackline Master 6-8: Choose the word you think does not belong.
1. el invitado, el cliente, el propietario. el huésped
2. el lujo, la elegancia, la comodidad, la riqueza, la economía

READING STRATEGIES
(page 156)

Pre-Reading
Show the class several ads and brochures for hotels, preferably from Spanish-speaking countries. Discuss hotel ratings, accommodations, and prices.

Reading
Have students open their books to page 156. Call on volunteers to read a few sentences of the selection at a time. After each reader, ask other students questions on content.

Post-reading
Have students read the *Lectura* at home and complete the *Estudio de palabras* and *Comprensión* exercises that follow.

LECTURA Y CULTURA

LOS HOTELES EN ESPAÑA Y EN LATINOAMÉRICA

La señora Thompson es profesora de español en los Estados Unidos. A ella le encantan la lengua española y las culturas hispanas. Por consiguiente, ella ha viajado mucho a España y a Latinoamérica. Ella se ha alojado[1] o se ha hospedado en muchos tipos de hoteles.

Algunos alumnos de la señora Thompson tienen mucho interés en hacer un viaje a España o a Latinoamérica. Le han preguntado a la Sra. Thompson sobre los hoteles. Ella les ha explicado que hay sin duda hoteles de todas las categorías. Hay hoteles de gran lujo[2] que cuestan mucho y hay también hoteles más modestos que siempre están muy limpios y que resultan más baratos o más económicos. Hay también pensiones. Una pensión es un hotel pequeño o puede ser una casa privada (particular) que por pago aloja a turistas. Una pensión es un tipo de casa de huéspedes[3]. Algunas pensiones son muy buenas y por lo general no son muy caras.

En España y en Puerto Rico hay paradores. Los paradores españoles son del gobierno. En Puerto Rico el gobierno los supervisa. Tienen habitaciones cómodas y ofrecen muchos servicios para los turistas. Tienen restaurantes que suelen servir[4] comidas típicas de la región.

Una casa de huéspedes en México

[1] alojado *stay, lodged*
[2] de gran lujo *deluxe*
[3] casa de huéspedes *guest house, boarding house*
[4] suelen servir *customarily serve*

156   CAPÍTULO 6

CRITICAL THINKING ACTIVITY

(Thinking skills: making inferences)
Read the following to the class or write it on the board or on an overhead transparency.

"Al país que fueres, haz lo que vieres." Éste es un proverbio bien conocido. Explícalo. ¿Qué significa? Ahora, imagínate que estás en algún sitio hispánico. Di lo que vas a hacer para seguir la filosofía del proverbio.

Estudio de palabras

Definiciones. Pareen.

1. se ha alojado
2. tiene interés
3. viajar
4. de todas las clases
5. de gran lujo
6. económico
7. particular
8. cómodo

a. hacer un viaje
b. privado
c. lujoso, elegante
d. confortable
e. se ha hospedado
f. le interesa
g. razonable, no caro
h. de todas las categorías

Comprensión

A De viaje. Contesten.

1. ¿Qué es la Sra. Thompson?
2. ¿Qué le gusta mucho a la señora Thompson?
3. ¿Adónde ha viajado ella?
4. ¿Qué tipos de hoteles hay en España y en Latinoamérica?
5. ¿Qué tipo de comida suelen servir en los comedores o restaurantes de los paradores?

B El hospedaje. Describan.

1. un hotel de lujo
2. una pensión
3. una casa de huéspedes
4. un parador

El Real Monasterio de San Lorenzo de El Escorial, España

CAPÍTULO 6   157

Estudio de palabras
ANSWERS
1. e
2. f
3. a
4. h
5. c
6. g
7. b
8. d

Comprensión
ANSWERS

Comprensión A
1. La señora Thompson es profesora de español.
2. A ella le encantan la lengua española y las culturas hispanas.
3. Ella ha viajado a España y a Latinoamérica.
4. Hay hoteles lujosos, modestos y económicos.
5. Sirven comidas típicas de la región.

Comprensión B
1. Un hotel de lujo es muy elegante y cuesta mucho.
2. Una pensión es un hotel pequeño o una casa privada que aloja a turistas.
3. Una casa de huéspedes también aloja a turistas.
4. Un parador es un tipo de alojamiento que existe en España y Puerto Rico. Un parador tiene habitaciones cómodas y otros servicios.

HISTORY CONNECTION
El monasterio de El Escorial está a 50 kilómetros de Madrid. En este monasterio están sepultados muchos reyes y reinas de España. Felipe II lo hizo construir para conmemorar la muerte de su padre Carlos V y la victoria española en la batalla de San Quintín en 1557.

COOPERATIVE LEARNING

Tell teams the following: *Cada uno de Uds. tiene $1.500 y un mes de vacaciones. Vas a pasar el mes en España. Prepara tu viaje. Después, van a comparar sus itinerarios y decidir quién ha preparado el viaje más interesante y por qué.*

CRITICAL THINKING ACTIVITY

(Thinking skills: making inferences; drawing conclusions)

Read the following to the class or write it on the board or on an overhead transparency.

¿*Preferiría Ud. quedarse en un albergue juvenil o en un hotel? ¿Por qué? Discuta las ventajas y las desventajas de cada uno.*

Bell Ringer Review

Write the following on the board or use BRR Blackline Master 6-9: Use your knowledge from the **Lectura** to list the different types of lodging available in Spanish-speaking countries.

Descubrimiento Cultural

(The Descubrimiento section is optional.)

PRESENTATION (pages 158-159)

A. Before reading the selection, focus on the topic by asking students about their own hotel experiences. Can anyone tell about a stay in a foreign hotel? Has anyone ever stayed in a youth hostel, either in the U.S. or abroad? What was it like?

B. Have students read the selection silently.

DESCUBRIMIENTO CULTURAL

En los Estados Unidos hay muchos moteles. Hay moteles muy grandes que parecen hoteles. Ofrecen casi todos los servicios que ofrece un hotel. En Latinoamérica y en España hay muy pocos moteles.

En España y en otros países europeos, hay albergues para jóvenes[1]. Estos albergues o residencias juveniles ofrecen cuartos limpios y económicos para estudiantes.

Los hoteles en España se clasifican de acuerdo con los servicios que ofrecen, su lugar y categoría, etc. Si un hotel no ofrece comidas, no puede llamarse "hotel". Es una "residencia", aunque puede ofrecer desayunos y servicios de cafetería. El turismo en España siempre ha sido una industria muy importante. Por eso, el Ministerio de Transporte, Turismo y Comunicaciones publica, cada año, una "Guía de Hoteles". Éstas son las categorías:

H = Hotel
HR = Hotel Residencia
HA = Hotel Apartamentos
RA = Residencia Apartamentos
M = Motel
Hs = Hostal
P = Pensión
HsR = Hostal Residencia

En España, las pensiones, como los hoteles, tienen diferentes categorías. Los hoteles pueden llevar de una a cinco estrellas; las pensiones de una a cuatro.

En el pasado, el cliente llegaba a un hotel y se quedaba una semana o más. Pero las cosas han cambiado. El avión ha introducido el turismo rápido. Ahora los clientes pasan una o dos noches en un lugar y salen para otro. Los hoteles han tenido que adaptarse a la vida moderna.

[1] albergues para jóvenes *youth hostels*

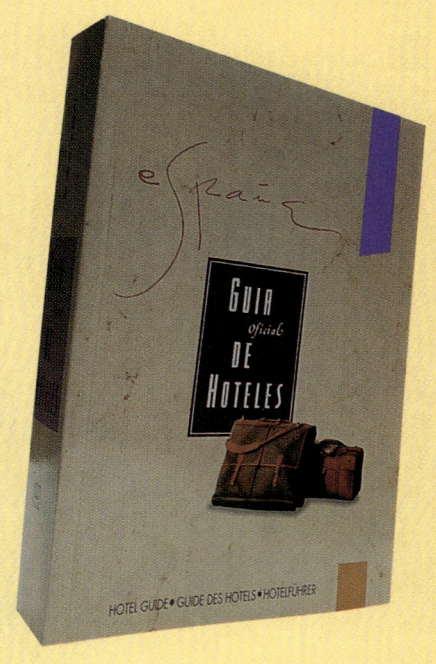

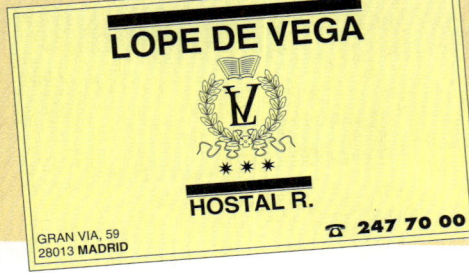

158 CAPÍTULO 6

DID YOU KNOW?

Lope de Vega fue un poeta dramático español. Nació (1562) y murió (1635) en Madrid. Escribió en casi todos los géneros literarios. Pero se conoce más como dramaturgo. Los cuatro famosos dramaturgos del siglo XVII, que se llama también el siglo de oro, son Lope de Vega, Calderón de la Barca, Tirso de Molina y Juan Ruiz de Alarcón.

Y AQUÍ EN LOS ESTADOS UNIDOS

Las grandes cadenas[2] norteamericanas como Hyatt, Marriott, Sheraton y Hilton han comprado o construido hoteles en las capitales y en los lugares de turismo en Latinoamérica y en España. Uno de los primeros hoteles modernos en Madrid, el Hotel Castellana, era norteamericano. Pero también hay cadenas españolas que se han establecido en las dos Américas, incluso en los EE.UU. y en Puerto Rico. Hoteles HUSA (Hoteles Unidos S.A.) y Meliá son algunos. Como la industria hotelera es tan internacional, los empleados tienen que hablar varios idiomas para poder atender a sus clientes. En la recepción de los grandes hoteles en Miami, Houston, Los Ángeles, Nueva York y otras ciudades siempre hay alguien que puede hablar español.

[2]cadenas *chains*

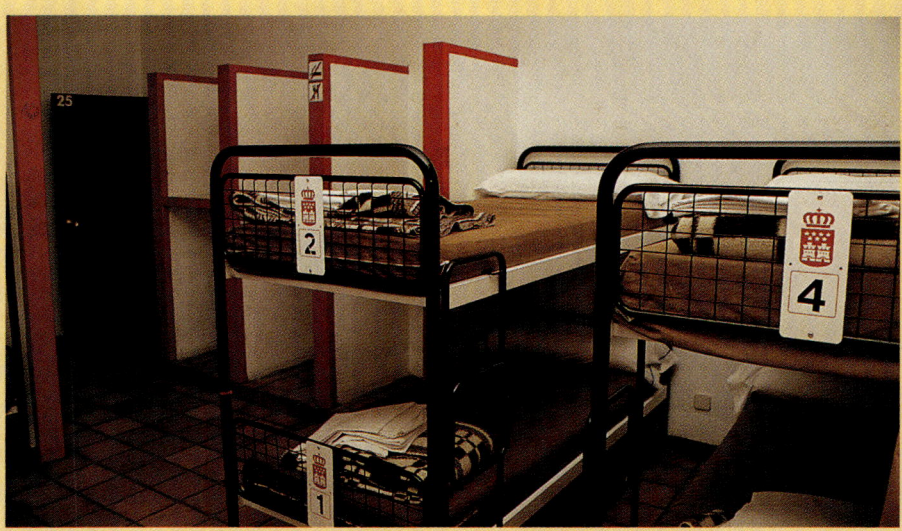

Un hotel Meliá en Puerto Rico

Un albergue juvenil en España

CAPÍTULO 6   **159**

FOR THE NATIVE SPEAKER

Writing Ask students to do one of the following tasks:
1. Tú eres el/la gerente del hotel y necesitas: mozos, maleteros, recepcionistas, camareras, mucamas. Prepara un anuncio clasificado de periódico para cada puesto. Incluye las horas y días de trabajo, experiencia necesaria, beneficios laborales, vacaciones.
2. Tú eres la persona en el periódico que escribe sobre viajes y turismo. Prepara un artículo sobre un hotel que visitaste que no te gustó. Explica el porqué. Debes mencionar: el nombre y sitio del hotel, el tamaño, los precios, una descripción de tu cuarto, el servicio que has recibido, la limpieza o su falta, cualquier otra cosa que no te gustó.

REALIDADES

(The Realidades section is optional.)

Bell Ringer Review

Write the following on the board or use BRR Blackline Master 6-10: Match the word in the first column with a related word in the second column.

1. viajar   a. el costo
2. preguntar   b. el resultado
3. dudar   c. el viaje
4. costar   d. el servicio
5. limpiar   e. la pregunta
6. resultar   f. la limpieza
7. alojar   g. la duda
8. servir   h. el alojamiento

PRESENTATION (pages 160-161)

A. Call on volunteers to read the captions. Answer any questions students may have about them or the photos.

B. Share with students any photos or memorabilia you may have from your own travels in Hispanic countries. Or show a video from your local travel agency or library. You may also want to show photos from resource books.

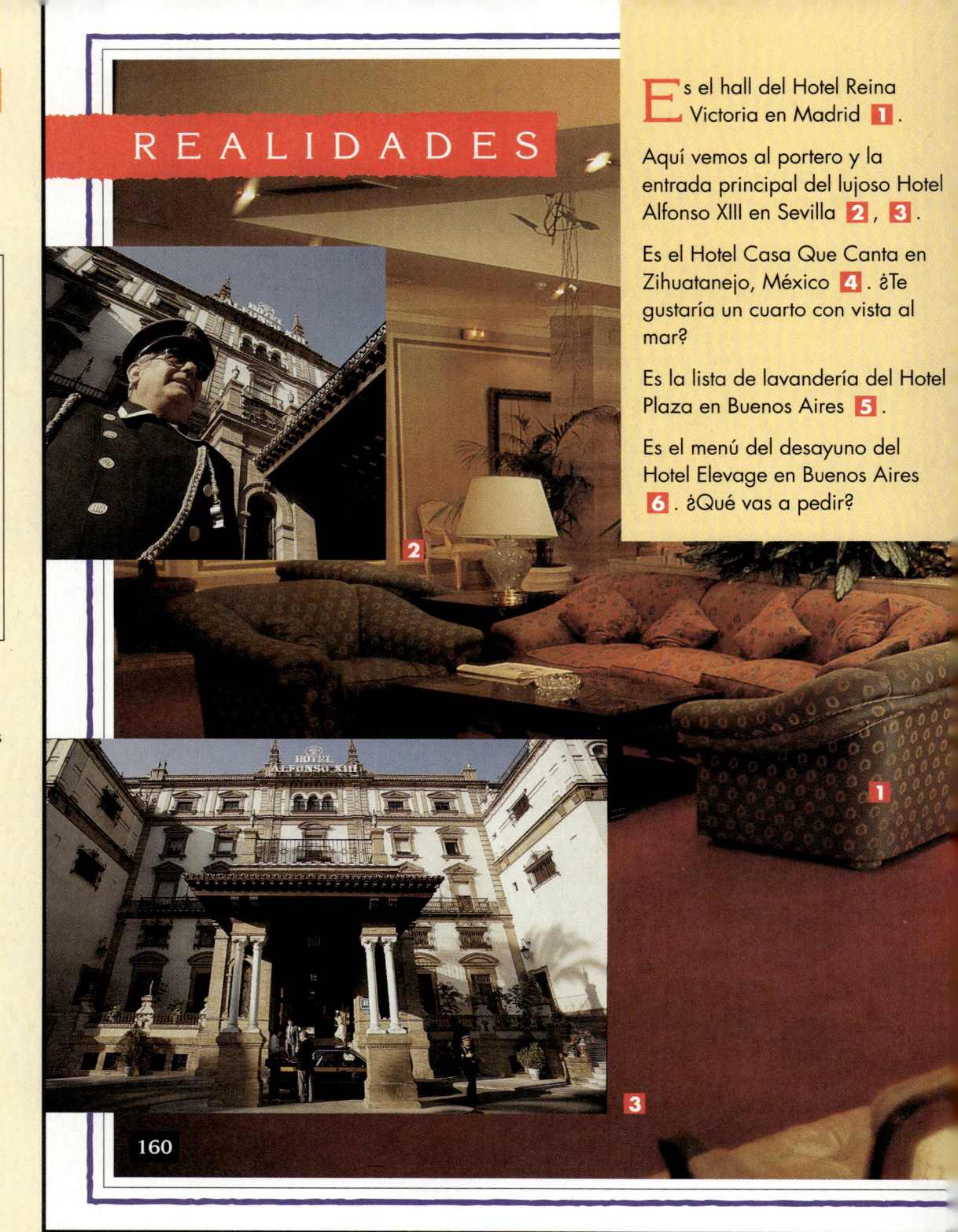

REALIDADES

Es el hall del Hotel Reina Victoria en Madrid **1**.

Aquí vemos al portero y la entrada principal del lujoso Hotel Alfonso XIII en Sevilla **2**, **3**.

Es el Hotel Casa Que Canta en Zihuatanejo, México **4**. ¿Te gustaría un cuarto con vista al mar?

Es la lista de lavandería del Hotel Plaza en Buenos Aires **5**.

Es el menú del desayuno del Hotel Elevage en Buenos Aires **6**. ¿Qué vas a pedir?

ABOUT THE LANGUAGE

Have students scan the *lavandería* list from the Plaza hotel in Buenas Aires. Have them look for some words thay do not recognize that refer to certain articles of clothing. This list does include some interesting Argentinian regionalisms.

remera—man's vest
deshabillé—woman's robe
bombachas—panties
piloto—raincoat
campera—sports coat
pollera—skirt

DID YOU KNOW?

The Hotel Victoria is an old hotel in Plaza Santa Ara. It has some extremely interesting stained-glass windows. It was a long-time favorite of bullfighters and their *aficionados*.

LEARNING FROM REALIA

Have students say all they can about the two pieces of realia on page 161. You may wish to ask questions such as: *En la lista de la lavandería, ¿qué es lo más caro? ¿Qué ofrecen para el desayuno americano? ¿Cuál es más grande, el desayano continental o el americano?*

CULMINACIÓN

Comunicación oral

A El hotel. ¿Se ha alojado o pasado unas vacaciones en un hotel? ¿En qué hotel ha estado? Descríbale el hotel a un(a) compañero(a) de clase. Luego cambien de papel.

B He hecho… Prepare Ud. una lista de cosas interesantes que Ud. ha hecho. Compare su lista con la de un(a) compañero(a). Luego prepare una lista de las cosas que los dos han hecho. Determinen si las van a hacer de nuevo.

C Algo extraordinario. Trabajen en grupos de cuatro. Cada uno de Uds. escribirá algo excepcional que ha hecho. Los otros miembros del grupo le harán preguntas sobre su actividad extraordinaria. Ud. contestará con sí o no. Los otros tendrán que descubrir lo que Ud. ha hecho.

Comunicación escrita

A La reservación. Escríbale una carta a un hotel para hacer una reservación. Incluya todos los detalles e informes necesarios.

B Una confirmación. Escríbale un fax a un hotel confirmando una reservación. Incluya sólo la información más importante.

C La publicidad. Trabajen en grupos de cuatro. Preparen anuncios de publicidad (*advertising*) para un hotel.

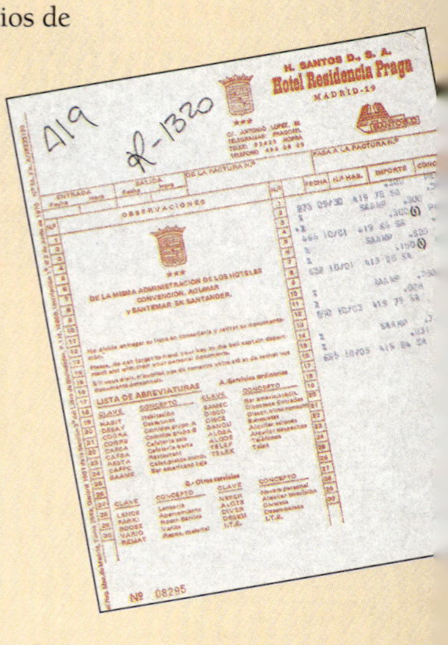

RECYCLING

The *Comunicación oral* and *Comunicación escrita* activities provide opportunities to further practice the present perfect tense and vocabulary within the context of hotels and travel. Material from earlier chapters is recycled.

Comunicación oral
ANSWERS
Actividades A, B, and C
   Answers will vary.

INFORMAL ASSESSMENT

Activity A can be used to evaluate the speaking skill informally. You may assign a grade based on the student's ability to communicate in Spanish. Use the evaluation criteria given on page 24 of this Teacher's Wraparound Edition.

Comunicación escrita
ANSWERS
Actividades A, B, and C
   Answers will vary.

LEARNING FROM REALIA

Have students scan the realia on page 162, looking for expressions they already know and isolating new ones.

STUDENT PORTFOLIO

Written assignments that may be included in students' portfolios are the *Actividades escritas* on page 162 and the *Mi autobiografía* section in the Workbook.

Reintegración

A **¡Qué divertido!** Completen.
1. ¿Cuándo? En el ___ esquiamos y en el ___ nadamos.
2. ¿Dónde? Esquiamos en ___ y nadamos en ___ .
3. Esquiamos cuando hace ___ y nadamos cuando hace ___ .
4. Cuando esquiamos nos ponemos ___ y cuando nadamos nos ponemos ___ .
5. Cuando esquiamos o nadamos, para protegernos del sol nos ponemos ___ .

B **Los deportes.** Identifiquen el deporte.
1. la raqueta, la red, la pelota, la cancha
2. el jardinero, la base, el pícher, el campo
3. el hoyo, la bola, la bolsa
4. el balón, el portero, el gol, el campo
5. el balón, la cesta, driblar

Vocabulario

SUSTANTIVOS
el hotel
la llegada
la salida
la recepción
el/la recepcionista
la reservación
el/la huésped
el/la cliente
la tarjeta
la ficha
el botones
el mozo
el equipaje
el ascensor
la caja
el/la cajero(a)

la cuenta
la nota
el total
el monto
el gasto
la tarjeta de crédito
el cuarto
la habitación
el balcón
el aire acondicionado
el televisor
la cama
la almohada
la sábana
el armario
la percha

el colgador
el gancho
el baño
la bañera
la ducha
el inodoro
el váter
la barra
la pastilla
el jabón
la toalla
la camarera

ADJETIVOS
sencillo(a)
doble

VERBOS
reservar
abrir
limpiar
cambiar

OTRAS PALABRAS Y EXPRESIONES
hacer (tender) la cama
abandonar el cuarto
ya
todavía no
jamás
nunca

CAPÍTULO 6   **163**

Reintegración
RECYCLING
Exercises A and B recycle much of the vocabulary having to do with sports and seasonal activities introduced in *Bienvenidos*.

ANSWERS
Ejercicio A
1. invierno, verano
2. la nieve (el agua), el agua
3. frío, calor
4. los esquís, el traje de baño
5. crema protectora

Ejercicio B
1. el tenis
2. el béisbol
3. el golf
4. el fútbol
5. el baloncesto

Vocabulario
The words and phrases in the *Vocabulario* have been taught for productive use in this chapter. They are summarized here as a resource for both students and teacher. The *Vocabulario* also serves as a convenient resource for the *Culminación* activities. There are approximately 18 cognates in this list.

VIDEO
The video is intended to reinforce the vocabulary, structures, and cultural content in each chapter. It may be used here as a chapter wrap-up activity. See the *Video Activities Booklet* for additional suggestions on its use.

INTRODUCCIÓN   (0:24:41)

EL HOTEL   (0:25:40)

LEARNING FROM PHOTOS
Refer students to the photo on page 163. Have them say as much about the soccer game as they can.

INDEPENDENT PRACTICE
Assign any of the following:
1. Exercises on student page 163
2. Workbook, *Mi autobiografía*
3. Chapter 6, Situation Cards

163

CAPÍTULO 7
Scope and Sequence pages 164-187

Topics	Functions	Structure	Culture
Air travel Airports	How to talk about air travel How to tell about events that were taking place How to compare people and things with the same characteristics	Los tiempos progresivos La comparación de igualdad con adjetivos y adverbios La comparación de igualdad con sustantivos	A flight on a Bolivian airline to La Paz The Andes Mountains Capitán Emilio Carranza Lake Titicaca in Bolivia Jorge Chávez Airport in Lima, Peru

CAPÍTULO 7

Situation Cards

The Situation Cards simulate real-life situations that require students to communicate in Spanish, exactly as though they were in a Spanish-speaking country. The Situation Cards operate on the assumption that the person to whom the message is to be conveyed understands no English. Therefore, students must focus on producing the Spanish vocabulary and structures necessary to negotiate the situations successfully. For additional information, see the Introduction to the Situation Cards in the Situation Cards Envelope.

Communication Transparency

The illustration seen in this Communication Transparency consists of a synthesis of the two vocabulary (Palabras 1&2) presentations found in this chapter. It has been created in order to present this chapter's vocabulary in a new context, and also to recycle vocabulary learned in previous chapters. The Communication Transparency consists of original art. Following are some specific uses:

1. as a cue to stimulate conversation and writing activities
2. for listening comprehension activities
3. to review and reteach vocabulary
4. as a review for chapter and unit tests

CAPÍTULO 7
Print Resources

Lesson Plans

Workbook   Pages
- Palabras 1   69-70
- Palabras 2   71-72
- Estructura   73-75
- Un poco más   76-79
- Mi autobiografía   80

Communication Activities Masters
- Palabras 1   40-42
- Palabras 2   42-43
- Estructura   44-46

7 Bell Ringer Reviews   22-23

Chapter Situation Cards A B C D

Chapter Quizzes
- Palabras 1   31
- Palabras 2   32
- Estructura   33-35

Testing Program
- Listening Comprehension   35
- Reading and Writing   36-39
- Proficiency   129
- Speaking   148

Nosotros y Nuestro Mundo
- Nuestro Conocimiento Académico *Cómo el ser humano llegó a volar*
- Nuestro Idioma *Los tiempos progresivos*
- Nuestra Cultura *La aviación comercial en el mundo hispano*
- Nuestra Literatura: Poesía de María Herrera-Sobek
- Nuestra Creatividad
- Nuestras Diversiones

CAPÍTULO 7
Multimedia Resources

CD-ROM Interactive Textbook Disc 2

Chapter 7 Student Edition
- Palabras 1
- Palabras 2
- Estructura
- Conversación
- Lectura y cultura
- Hispanoparlantes
- Realidades
- Culminación
- Prueba

Audio Cassette Program with Student Tape Manual

Cassette   Pages
- 5A Palabras 1   234-235
- 5A Palabras 2   235-236
- 5A Estructura   236
- 5A Conversación   237
- 5A Segunda parte   237-238

Compact Disc Program with Student Tape Manual
- CD 5 Palabras 1   234-235
- CD 5 Palabras 2   235-236
- CD 5 Estructura   236
- CD 5 Conversación   237
- CD 5 Segunda parte   237-238

Overhead Transparencies Binder
- Vocabulary   7.1 (A&B); 7.2 (A&B)
- Communication C-7
- Maps
- Fine Art (with Blackline Master Activities)

Video Program
- Videocassette
- Video Activities Booklet   18-19
- Videodisc
- Video Activities Booklet   18-19

Computer Software (Macintosh, IBM, Apple)
- Practice Disk
    Palabras 1 y 2
    Estructura
- Test Generator Disk
    Chapter Test
    Customized Test

164B

CAPÍTULO 7

CHAPTER OVERVIEW

In this chapter students will expand their ability to talk about air travel, including boarding, in-flight services, and arrival. They will learn to talk about past events using the past progressive tense, and to make plans for the future using the future progressive tense. They will also learn to make comparisons of equality between people and things. The cultural focus of Chapter 7 is on a typical flight on a Bolivian airline to the Bolivian capital of La Paz. Also discussed is the influence of Latin American geography —especially the Andes Mountains—on air travel there.

CHAPTER OBJECTIVES

By the end of this chapter, students will know:
1. vocabulary associated with the equipment, services, personnel, and procedures a traveler typically encounters when flying with a modern commercial airline
2. vocabulary associated with departure and arrival procedures, the airport itself, and a geographical description of one area in the Andes
3. the past progressive tense
4. the future progressive tense
5. comparisons of equality using nouns, adverbs, and adjectives

CAPÍTULO 7

A BORDO DEL AVIÓN

OBJETIVOS

In this chapter you will learn to do the following:

1. talk about air travel
2. tell about events that were taking place
3. compare people and things with the same characteristics
4. discuss some interesting facts about airports and air travel in the region of the Andes
5. discuss the influence of geography on travel in Latin America

CHAPTER PROJECTS

(optional)

1. Have students visit a travel agency and obtain brochures on Bolivia and other countries in the Andes region of South America. Have them write captions for the brochures in Spanish and design a bulletin board display.
2. Have groups prepare reports on Lake Titicaca, and the Aymará and Quechua peoples.
3. Have individuals or groups prepare reports on different aspects of the history of Andean countries, such as Bolivia, Perú, Chile, or Ecuador.
4. Have groups research modern-day Bolivia, compiling their findings for a class bulletin board display on that country.

CHAPTER 7 RESOURCES

1. Workbook
2. Student Tape Manual
3. Audio Cassette 5A
4. Vocabulary Transparencies
5. Bell Ringer Review Blackline Masters
6. Communication Activities Masters
7. Computer Software: Practice and Test Generator
8. Video Cassette, Chapter 7
9. Video Activities Booklet, Chapter 7
10. Situation Cards
11. Chapter Quizzes
12. Testing Program

Pacing

Chapter 7 will require eight to ten class sessions. Pacing will depend on the length of the class period, the age of the students, and student aptitude.

LEARNING FROM PHOTOS

Refer students to the photo on pages 164-165 and ask: *¿De qué país es este avión? ¿Cómo lo sabes?* (México)

165

VOCABULARIO
PALABRAS 1

Vocabulary Teaching Resources
1. Vocabulary Transparencies, 7.1 (A & B)
2. Audio Cassette 5A
3. Student Tape Manual, *Palabras 1*
4. Workbook, *Palabras 1*
5. Communication Activities Masters, *Palabras 1, A & B*
6. Chapter Quizzes, *Palabras 1*

Bell Ringer Review
Write the following on the board or use BRR Blackline Master 7-1: List all the words and expressions you can remember that have to do with air travel.

PRESENTATION
(pages 166–167)

A. Refer to Vocabulary Transparencies 7.1 (A & B) and have students repeat the new words, phrases, and sentences after you or Cassette 5A.
B. Model the new vocabulary again, moving through the Vocabulary Transparencies at random and calling on volunteers to point to the appropriate image on the screen.
C. Use questioning techniques to present the material on page 167. Begin with simple yes/no and either/or questions.
D. When students have produced the new vocabulary several times, progress to open-ended questions such as: ¿Qué estaba haciendo el asistente de vuelo? ¿Qué les estaba dando a los pasajeros? ¿Qué estaba distribuyendo la asistenta de vuelo? ¿Qué estaban sirviendo los asistentes de vuelo?

VOCABULARIO

PALABRAS 1

DENTRO DEL AVIÓN

la tripulación
la cabina de vuelo (de mando)
la co-piloto
la asistenta de vuelo
el piloto, el comandante
el asistente de vuelo, el sobrecargo

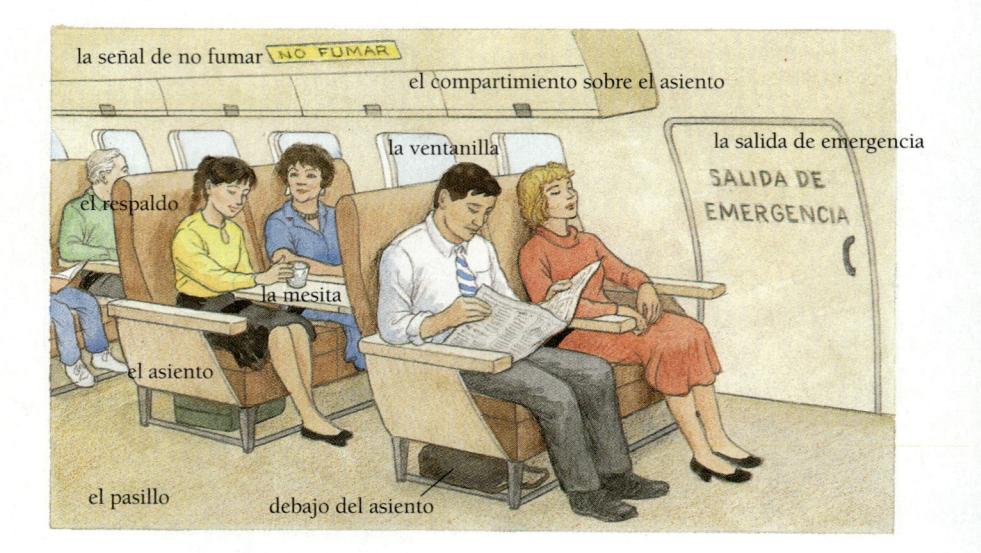

la señal de no fumar — NO FUMAR
el compartimiento sobre el asiento
la ventanilla
la salida de emergencia — SALIDA DE EMERGENCIA
el respaldo
la mesita
el asiento
el pasillo
debajo del asiento

166 CAPÍTULO 7

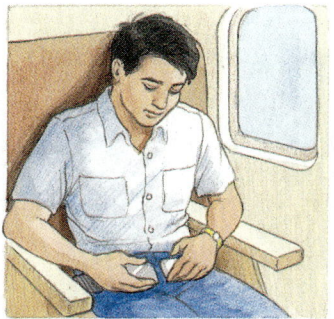

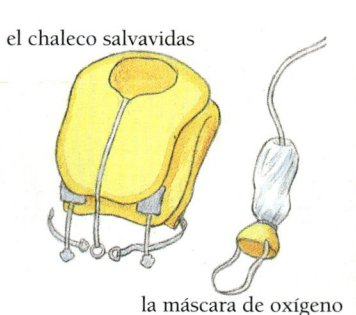

el chaleco salvavidas
la máscara de oxígeno 
abrocharse el cinturón de seguridad
el aseo, el lavabo

presentar una película
los audífonos
los canales de música estereofónica

El asistente de vuelo les estaba dando la bienvenida.
Les estaba dando la bienvenida a bordo.
Les estaba dando la bienvenida a los pasajeros.
Él estaba haciendo algunos anuncios.

La asistenta de vuelo estaba distribuyendo los audífonos.

las bebidas
la comida
el carrito

Los asistentes de vuelo estaban sirviendo la comida.

CAPÍTULO 7 **167**

ABOUT THE LANGUAGE

1. There are several terms for "flight attendant." *El asistente (la asistenta) de vuelo* is becoming more and more common. Other terms are *el/la aeromozo(a)*, and in Spain *la azafata* for a female flight attendant.
2. *El retrete* used to be the Spanish word for "lavatory" in some areas of the world, as well as *el aseo* or *el lavabo*. *El retrete* is becoming less common, however.

FOR THE NATIVE SPEAKER

Hace 40 años los vuelos intercontinentales eran muy raros y sólo para ricos. Hoy hay vuelos baratos entre todos los continentes. ¿Qué influencia ha tenido esto en la manera en que la gente piensa? ¿Nos ha cambiado, o no? ¿Qué opinas?

Ejercicios

PRESENTATION (page 168)

Ejercicios A and B
Exercises A and B are to be done with books open.

ANSWERS

Ejercicio A
1. Es el comandante.
2. Es el cinturón de seguridad.
3. El el asiento.
4. Es la señal de no fumar.
5. Es la cabina de mando.
6. Son los audífonos.

Ejercicio B
1. El piloto dirige el avión.
2. Lo dirige de la cabina de mando.
3. El piloto, el co-piloto y los asistentes de vuelo componen la tripulación.
4. Los asistentes de vuelo sirven a los pasajeros durante el vuelo.
5. Los asistentes de vuelo se responsabilizan de la seguridad de los pasajeros.
6. En caso de una emergencia, los pasajeros salen de las salidas de emergencia.

Ejercicios

A ¿Qué es o quién es? Identifiquen.

1. ¿Es el asistente de vuelo o el comandante?
2. ¿Es el chaleco salvavidas o el cinturón de seguridad? 
3. ¿Es el asiento o la mesita? 
4. ¿Es la máscara de oxígeno o la señal de no fumar? 
5. ¿Es el aseo o la cabina de mando? 
6. ¿Son los audífonos o los canales de música estereofónica? 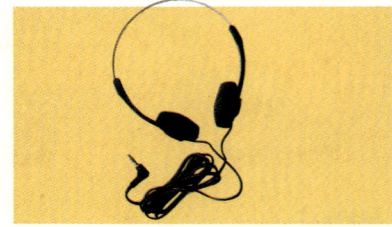

B **A bordo del avión.** Contesten según se indica.
1. ¿Quién dirige el avión? (el piloto)
2. ¿De dónde lo dirige? (de la cabina de vuelo o de la cabina de mando)
3. ¿Quiénes componen la tripulación? (el piloto o el comandante, el co-piloto y los asistentes de vuelo)
4. ¿Quiénes sirven a los pasajeros durante el vuelo? (los asistentes de vuelo)
5. ¿De qué se responsabilizan los asistentes de vuelo? (de la seguridad de los pasajeros)
6. En el caso de una emergencia, ¿de dónde salen los pasajeros? (de las salidas de emergencia)

C Algunas reglas a bordo del avión. Escojan. *Turn into oratory exercise*

1. ¿Qué tienen que abrocharse los pasajeros durante el despegue y el aterrizaje?
   a. el cinturón de seguridad
   b. el respaldo de su asiento
   c. la máscara de oxígeno

2. Si la presión del aire cambia en la cabina durante el vuelo, ¿de qué deben servirse los pasajeros?
   a. del cinturón de seguridad
   b. del chaleco salvavidas
   c. de la máscara de oxígeno

3. Durante el despegue y el aterrizaje, ¿cómo tienen que poner los pasajeros el respaldo de su asiento?
   a. debajo de su asiento
   b. en posición vertical
   c. en el pasillo

4. ¿Dónde tienen que poner los pasajeros su equipaje de mano durante el despegue y el aterrizaje?
   a. en la mesita
   b. en el pasillo
   c. debajo de su asiento o en el compartimiento de equipaje

5. En el caso imprevisto de un aterrizaje de emergencia en el mar, ¿qué tienen que ponerse los pasajeros?
   a. el cinturón de seguridad
   b. el chaleco salvavidas
   c. la salida de emergencia

D ¿Qué va a pasar? Contesten con *Por supuesto* o *Espero que no*.

1. Los pasajeros desembarcarán por la salida de emergencia.
2. Presentarán una película durante el vuelo.
3. Los pasajeros se pondrán el chaleco salvavidas durante el vuelo.
4. Se caerán las máscaras de oxígeno.
5. Los asistentes de vuelo distribuirán los audífonos.
6. El comandante buscará un asiento en la cabina económica.

CAPÍTULO 7   169

PRESENTATION (page 169)

Extension of *Ejercicio C*: Speaking

After completing Exercise C, call on volunteers to give sentences from the unused multiple choice answers.

Ejercicio D
A. Exercise D can be done with books open or closed.
B. When doing the exercise, you may have students read the sentences as questions and then give the appropriate reaction. For example: ¿Los pasajeros desembarcarán por la salida de emergencia? Espero que no.

ANSWERS
Ejercicio C
1. a
2. c
3. b
4. c
5. b

Ejercicio D
1. Espero que no.
2. Por supuesto.
3. Espero que no.
4. Espero que no.
5. Por supuesto.
6. Espero que no.

INDEPENDENT PRACTICE

Assign any of the following:
1. Workbook, *Palabras 1*
2. Communication Activities Masters, *Palabras 1, A & B*
3. Exercises on student pages 168-169

VOCABULARIO
PALABRAS 2

Vocabulary Teaching Resources

1. Vocabulary Transparencies 7.2 (A & B)
2. Audio Cassette 5A
3. Student Tape Manual, *Palabras 2*
4. Workbook, *Palabras 2*
5. Communication Activities Masters, *Palabras 2*, C & D
6. Chapter Quizzes, *Palabras 2*
7. Computer Software, *Vocabulario*

Bell Ringer Review

Write the following on the board or use BRR Blackline Master 7-2: Match the word in the first column with a related word in the second column.

1. controlar   a. el asiento
2. aterrizar   b. el despegue
3. despegar   c. el aterrizaje
4. asistir   d. la comida
5. beber   e. la bebida
6. comer   f. el control
7. salir   g. el vuelo
8. sentar   h. la salida
9. volar   i. el asistente

PRESENTATION *(pages 170-171)*

A. Have students close their books. Model the *Palabras 2* vocabulary using Vocabulary Transparencies 7.2 (A & B). Have students repeat the new material after you or Cassette 5A.

170

VOCABULARIO
PALABRAS 2

EN EL AEROPUERTO

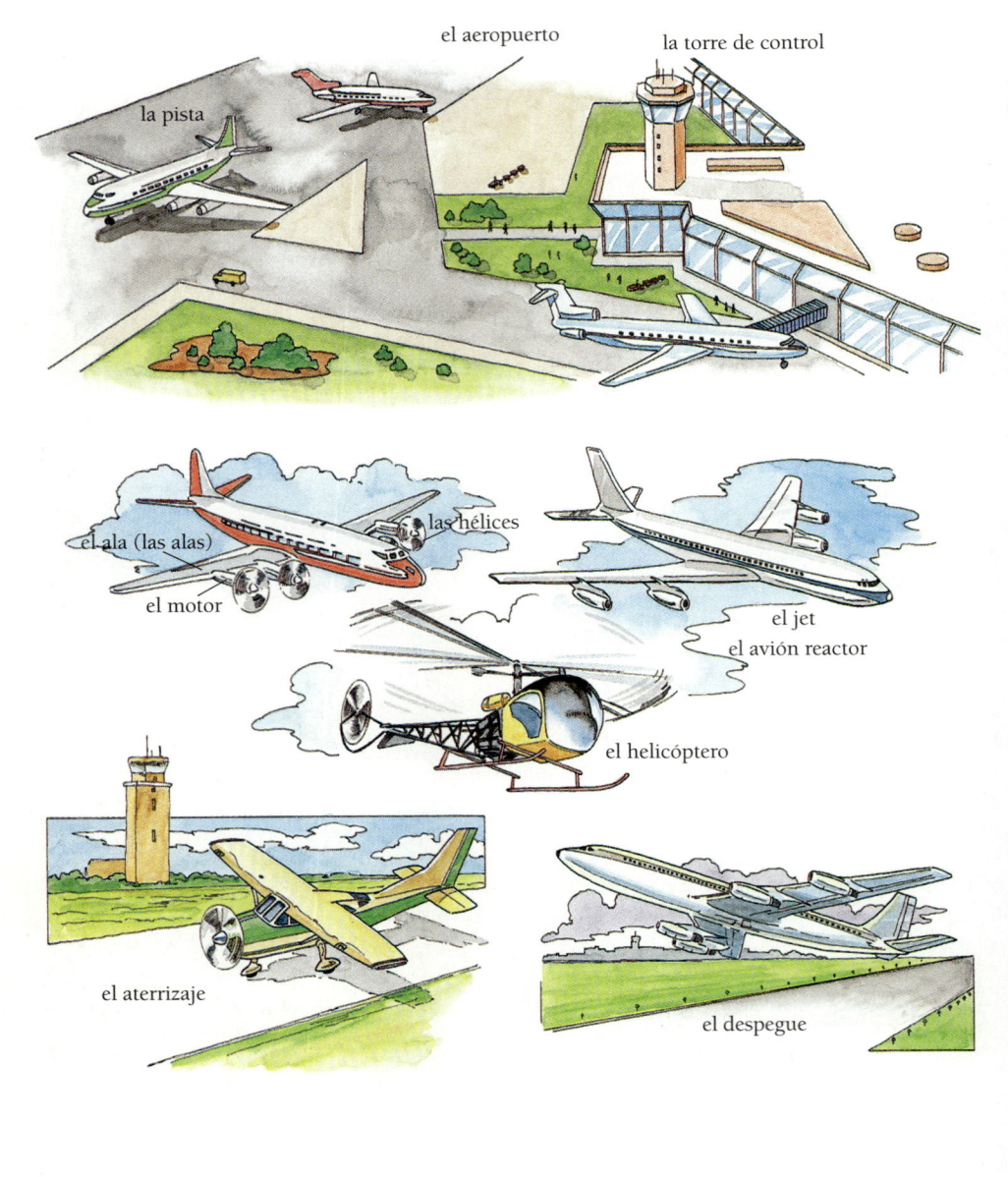

el aeropuerto
la torre de control
la pista
el ala (las alas)
las hélices
el motor
el jet
el avión reactor
el helicóptero
el aterrizaje
el despegue

170 CAPÍTULO 7

PANTOMIME

Have students act out the following:
___ , busca tu asiento.
Pon el equipaje de mano debajo de tu asiento.
Abre el compartimiento de equipaje.
Pon tu equipaje en el compartimiento de equipaje.
Cierra el compartimiento de equipaje.
Siéntate.
Abróchate el cinturón de seguridad.
Pon el respaldo de tu asiento en posición vertical.
El asistente de vuelo llega. Va a darte unos audífonos. Tómalos.
Ponte los audífonos.
Escoge un canal de música.

UN POCO DE GEOGRAFÍA

la altura, la altitud
el pico
la montaña
la cordillera
el altiplano
el valle
la meseta
la llanura
el lago
el nivel del mar

El avión estaba despegando.
No estaba aterrizando.
El avión estaba despegando de la pista.
La pista estaba en la llanura del altiplano.

El avión estaba sobrevolando las montañas.
Los pasajeros estaban viendo los picos y los valles.

CAPÍTULO 7 171

B. Intersperse your presentation of the sentences on page 171 with questions. After yes/no and either/or questions, use open-ended ones, such as: *¿Dónde estaba la pista? ¿Qué estaba sobrevolando el avión? ¿Qué estaban viendo los pasajeros?*
C. Have students open their books and read the new material.
D. You may wish to work Exercises A and B on page 172 into the vocabulary presentation.

RECYCLING
Ask students to recall all the geographical terms they know in Spanish.

ABOUT THE LANGUAGE
Small, single-engine aircrafts such as those shown in the illustrations are usually called *avionetas*.

171

Ejercicios

PRESENTATION (*page 172*)

It is recommended that you go over the exercises on page 172 orally in class before assigning them for independent practice.

Ejercicio A
Exercise A can be done with books open or closed.

Ejercicios B and C
Exercises B and C can be done with books open.

ANSWERS

Ejercicio A
1. Sí
2. No
3. No
4. Sí
5. Sí

Ejercicio B
1. a
2. c
3. a
4. c
5. b
6. c

Ejercicio C
1. Sí, el avión estaba sobrevolando las montañas.
2. Sí, los pasajeros estaban mirando por las ventanillas.
3. Sí, los asistentes de vuelo estaban sirviendo la comida.
4. Sí, una asistenta de vuelo estaba distribuyendo los audífonos.
5. Sí, los asistentes de vuelo estaban empujando el carrito por el pasillo.

Ejercicios

A El aeropuerto. ¿Sí o no?
1. Los aviones despegan de la pista.
2. Los controladores del tráfico aéreo trabajan en la cabina de mando.
3. Un avión reactor tiene hélices.
4. Un avión tiene alas.
5. La torre de control está cerca de la pista.

B ¿Qué es? Escojan.
1. una extensión de tierra que no tiene altos ni bajos
   a. la llanura   b. el pico   c. el valle
2. una gran extensión de terreno elevado (alto) y llano
   a. el pico   b. la montaña   c. la meseta
3. una meseta de mucha extensión y a gran altura
   a. el altiplano   b. el pico   c. el valle
4. espacio de tierra entre montañas
   a. el pico   b. la meseta   c. el valle
5. la parte superior de una montaña o un monte
   a. la llanura   b. el pico   c. el valle
6. grado de elevación donde el mar toca la tierra
   a. la altura   b. la tierra   c. el nivel del mar

C Un vuelo interesante. Contesten según el dibujo.
1. ¿Estaba sobrevolando las montañas el avión?
2. ¿Estaban mirando por las ventanillas los pasajeros?
3. ¿Estaban sirviendo la comida los asistentes de vuelo?
4. ¿Estaba distribuyendo audífonos una asistenta de vuelo?
5. ¿Estaban empujando el carrito por el pasillo los asistentes de vuelo?

CAPÍTULO 7

INDEPENDENT PRACTICE

Assign any of the following:
1. Workbook, *Palabras 2*
2. Communication Activities Masters, *Palabras 2, C & D*
3. Exercises on student pages 172–173

Comunicación
Palabras 1 y 2

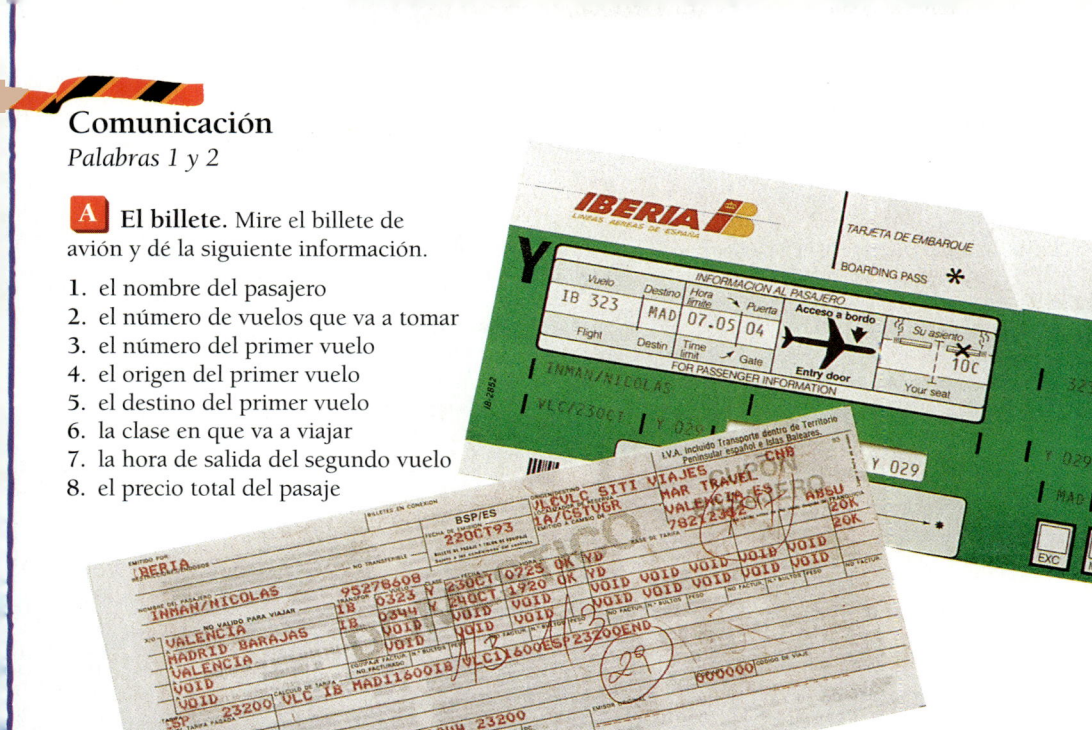

A **El billete.** Mire el billete de avión y dé la siguiente información.

1. el nombre del pasajero
2. el número de vuelos que va a tomar
3. el número del primer vuelo
4. el origen del primer vuelo
5. el destino del primer vuelo
6. la clase en que va a viajar
7. la hora de salida del segundo vuelo
8. el precio total del pasaje

B **En el aeropuerto.** Trabaje con un(a) compañero(a) de clase. Dígale todo lo que tienen que hacer los pasajeros en el aeropuerto antes de abordar el avión. Utilice las siguientes expresiones. Luego, cambien de papel.

    facturar el equipaje
    ir (presentarse) al mostrador de la línea aérea
    recibir (conseguir) una tarjeta de embarque
    pasar por el control de seguridad
    ir a la puerta de salida

C **Voy a viajar a…** Trabaje con un(a) compañero(a) de clase. Imagínese que Ud. va a hacer un viaje fantástico. Dígale a su compañero(a) adónde irá, cómo será su viaje, todo lo que Ud. verá, cómo irá, lo que comprará, etc. Su compañero(a) tomará apuntes y luego le hará preguntas sobre su viaje.

D **Tengo que regresar (volver) a casa.** Ud. está de vacaciones en Tegucigalpa, Honduras y tiene que regresar a casa debido a una emergencia. Un(a) compañero(a) de clase será el/la agente de la línea aérea en el aeropuerto. Preparen la conversación que Uds. tienen para cambiar su boleto.

CAPÍTULO 7 **173**

CRITICAL THINKING ACTIVITY

(Thinking skills: identifying causes)
Read the following to the class or write it on the board or on an overhead transparency. ¿Por qué razones se cancela (se anula) un vuelo?

DID YOU KNOW?

Iberia is the name of the national airline of Spain. It comes from the name of the peninsula Spain occupies, *la Península ibérica. Los iberos* were among the first inhabitants of the peninsula that is today Spain and Portugal.

Comunicación
(Palabras 1 and 2)

PRESENTATION *(page 173)*

A. It is not necessary to have students complete all the activities. Select those which you consider most appropriate. You may wish to have different groups complete different activities.
B. After students have completed Activity B, have them say as much about the trip in their own words as they can.

ANSWERS
Actividades A–D
Answers will vary.

ESTRUCTURA

Los tiempos progresivos
Describing People's Activities

1. You have already learned the present progressive tense, which is used to express an action that is actually in progress. The present progressive is formed by using the present participle and the present tense of the verb *estar*. Review the following forms of the present participle of regular verbs.

hablar	hablando	comer	comiendo	recibir	recibiendo
esperar	esperando	hacer	haciendo	salir	saliendo

Los pasajeros están abordando el avión.
El asistente de vuelo les está dando la bienvenida a bordo.

2. In addition to the present there are other progressive tenses. The imperfect progressive is used to describe what was going on in the past, and the future progressive is used to express what will be going on in the future. The appropriate tense of the verb *estar* is used along with the present participle.

Los asistentes de vuelo estaban anunciando el aterrizaje.
Los pasajeros estaban poniendo el respaldo de sus asientos en posición vertical.
El avión estará aterrizando dentro de poco.
Los pasajeros estarán saliendo por (desembarcando de) la puerta delantera.

174 CAPÍTULO 7

3. The verbs that have a stem change in the preterite have the same stem change in the present participle.

E > I		O > U	
pedir	pidiendo	dormir	durmiendo
servir	sirviendo	morir	muriendo
repetir	repitiendo		
sentir	sintiendo		
decir	diciendo		

4. The following verbs have a *y* in the present participle.

caer	cayendo
leer	leyendo
traer	trayendo
oír	oyendo
distribuir	distribuyendo
construir	construyendo
contribuir	contribuyendo

Ejercicios

A **En el aeropuerto.** Contesten.

1. ¿Estaba haciendo un viaje Clarita?
2. ¿Estaba hablando con la agente en el mostrador de la línea aérea?
3. ¿Estaba facturando su equipaje?
4. ¿Estaba revisando la agente su boleto y su pasaporte?
5. ¿Estaban pasando los otros pasajeros por el control de seguridad?
6. ¿Estaban esperando otros en la puerta de salida?
7. ¿Estaba saliendo el vuelo para Caracas?

B **La llegada.** Contesten según se indica.

1. ¿Estarán llegando pronto los pasajeros? (sí)
2. ¿Estará aterrizando a tiempo el avión? (no, con una demora de veinte minutos)
3. ¿En qué puerta estarán desembarcando los pasajeros? (la puerta 40)
4. ¿Dónde estarán reclamando su equipaje? (en el carrusel B)

CAPÍTULO 7

FOR THE NATIVE SPEAKER

Have students do the following writing exercise to practice the past progressive with verbs that have a *y* in the present participle: *leer, constituir, huir, influir, distribuir, atraer.*

1. *Los asistentes de vuelo ___ unos panfletos al público.*
2. *Todo el mundo ___ los panfletos.*
3. *Parece que los artículos ___ a los lectores y cambiando sus opiniones.*
4. *Los directores se quejaban. Decían que la distribución de panfletos ___ una práctica injusta.*
5. *Y que ___ a mucha gente indeseable.*
6. *Decían que los clientes ___ del local por miedo a un disturbio.*

Ejercicios

PRESENTATION (page 176)
Ejercicios C and D
Exercises C and D can be done with books open.

Ejercicio E
You may have students do Exercise E in pairs. After some practice, call on volunteers to present their sentences to the class.

ANSWERS
Ejercicio C
1. Los asistentes de vuelo estarán dando anuncios.
2. … estarán pasando por la cabina.
3. … estarán distribuyendo audífonos.
4. … estarán dando instrucciones de seguridad.
5. … estarán sirviendo bebidas.
6. … estarán sirviendo una comida.

Ejercicio D
1. Los pasajeros estarán viendo una película.
2. … estarán escuchando música estereofónica.
3. … estarán comiendo.
4. … estarán leyendo la revista de la línea aérea.
5. … estarán durmiendo un poco.

Ejercicio E
Answers will vary.

La comparación de igualdad con adjetivos y adverbios

PRESENTATION (page 176)
Guide students through the topic and have them repeat the sentences in step 2 after you.

C **Durante el vuelo.** Formen oraciones según el modelo.

> los asistentes de vuelo / trabajar
> *Los asistentes de vuelo estarán trabajando.*

1. dar anuncios
2. pasar por la cabina
3. distribuir audífonos
4. dar instrucciones de seguridad
5. servir bebidas
6. servir una comida

D **Durante el vuelo.** Formen oraciones según el modelo.

> los pasajeros / charlar
> *Los pasajeros estarán charlando.*

1. ver una película
2. escuchar música estereofónica
3. comer
4. leer la revista de la línea aérea
5. dormir un poco

E **¿Qué estaban haciendo esta mañana?** Expliquen lo que estaban haciendo los miembros de su familia esta mañana.

1. Mi madre
2. Mi padre
3. Mis hermanos
4. Yo
5. Mis hermanos y yo
6. Y tú

La comparación de igualdad con adjetivos y adverbios
Comparing People and Things

1. In English, to compare things that are the same or equal you use "as… as."
   I am as smart as my brother.

2. In Spanish *tan… como* is used with either an adjective or an adverb.
   Yo soy tan inteligente como mi hermano.
   El tren no viaja tan rápido como el avión.

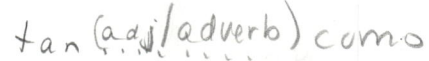

   tan (adj/adverb) como

176   CAPÍTULO 7

Ejercicio

Dos aeropuertos semejantes. Completen.

1. El aeropuerto de Jorge Chávez en Lima es ____ grande ____ el aeropuerto de Ezeiza en Buenos Aires.
2. La terminal del aeropuerto de Jorge Chávez es ____ grande ____ la de Ezeiza.
3. Pero el aeropuerto de Jorge Chávez no está ____ lejos del centro de la ciudad ____ el aeropuerto de Ezeiza.
4. En Buenos Aires hay dos aeropuertos. Uno se llama el aeroparque. El aeroparque no es ____ grande ____ el aeropuerto internacional de Ezeiza.
5. El aeroparque no está ____ lejos de la cuidad ____ Ezeiza.

La comparación de igualdad con sustantivos
Comparing People and Things

1. In English to compare quantities you use "as much... as" or "as many... as."

   He has as much money as I.   *tanto (noun) como*

2. In Spanish, you use *tanto* before the noun and *como* after the noun. *Tanto* is an adjective, therefore, it must agree in gender and number with the noun it modifies.

   Ella tiene tanto dinero como yo.
   Y ella lleva tantas maletas como tú.
   Él tiene tantos blue jeans como Luis.
   Este año hay tanta nieve como el año pasado.

3. Note that *tanto... como* can also be used alone.

   Él viaja tanto como Uds.

Ejercicio

Dos aeropuertos. Contesten.

1. ¿Tiene este aeropuerto tantos vuelos como el otro?
2. ¿Sirve este aeropuerto a tantos pasajeros como el otro?
3. ¿Tiene este aeropuerto tantas pistas como el otro?
4. ¿Tiene este aeropuerto tanto tráfico como el otro?
5. ¿Tiene este avión tantos asientos como el otro?
6. ¿Es este avión tan grande como el otro?
7. ¿Tiene este avión tantas salidas de emergencia como el otro?
8. ¿Es el servicio de esta línea aérea tan bueno como el de la otra línea?

El aeropuerto de Ezeiza, Buenos Aires, Argentina

CONVERSACIÓN

CONVERSACIÓN

Escenas de la vida *A bordo del avión*

RAÚL: ¿Qué estaba diciendo el asistente de vuelo?
MARISA: Estaba anunciando el aterrizaje.
RAÚL: ¿El aterrizaje? ¿Ya estamos llegando?
MARISA: Sí, estaremos aterrizando en algunos momentos. Tienes que poner el respaldo de tu asiento en posición vertical.
RAÚL: Sí, lo sé. ¿Tienes tu cinturón abrochado?
MARISA: Sí. No puedo creer que ya estamos aterrizando en La Paz. ¡Qué paisaje más maravilloso!

El aterrizaje. Contesten según la conversación.
1. ¿Qué estaba anunciando el asistente de vuelo?
2. ¿Cuándo estarán aterrizando?
3. ¿Cómo tienen que poner el respaldo de sus asientos?
4. ¿Qué tienen que abrochar los pasajeros?
5. ¿Adónde están llegando?
6. ¿Cómo es el paisaje?

La Paz, Bolivia

178 CAPÍTULO 7

Bell Ringer Review
Write the following on the board or use BRR Blackline Master 7-5: Indicate whether it's a train trip or a flight.
1. Aquí viene el revisor.
2. Hay asientos (plazas) para ocho personas en cada compartimiento.
3. Los pasajeros se abrochan el cinturón de seguridad.
4. Despega y aterriza.
5. Sale de un andén de la estación de ferrocarril.

PRESENTATION (page 178)
A. Tell students they will hear a conversation between Raúl and Marisa, two passengers on a commercial airliner.
B. Have students close their books and listen as you read the conversation or play Cassette 5A.
C. Now have students open their books. Allow pairs a few minutes to practice reading the conversation.
D. Call on one or two pairs of volunteers to read the conversation to the class with as much expression as possible.

Ejercicio
ANSWERS
1. Estaba anunciando el aterrizaje.
2. Estarán aterrizando en algunos momentos.
3. Tienen que poner el respaldo de su asiento en posición vertical.
4. Tienen que abrochar el cinturón de seguridad.
5. Están llegando a La Paz.
6. El paisaje es maravilloso.

LEARNING FROM PHOTOS
Refer students to the photo at the bottom of page 178. Have students say as much as they can about La Paz.

DID YOU KNOW?
When traveling through Latin America and some other areas of the world, it is necessary to pay an exit airport tax. The amount varies from country to country, but some are as much as $20 to $25 per person.

Comunicación

A **Esta mañana y esta noche.** Trabaje con un(a) compañero(a) de clase. Cada uno(a) preparará una lista de todo lo que estaba haciendo a las ocho esta mañana, y todo lo que estará haciendo a las ocho de la noche. Luego comparen sus listas y determinen si Uds. hacen lo mismo por la mañana o por la noche.

B **Son muy parecidos.** Trabaje con un(a) compañero(a) de clase. Piensen en algunas personas que Uds. conocen que, en su opinión, tienen las mismas características. Comparen a estas dos personas.

C **¿Quién es tan… como…?** Trabaje con un(a) compañero(a) de clase. Pregúntele sus opiniones sobre quiénes o qué tienen las siguientes características. Luego cambien de papel.

    tan rico como
    Estudiante 1: ¿Quién es tan rica
               como Barbra Streisand?
    Estudiante 2: Elizabeth Taylor es tan
               rica como Barbra Streisand.

1. tan grande como
2. tan rápido como
3. tan inteligente como
4. tan alto como
5. tan guapo como
6. tan difícil como
7. tan lejos como
8. tan simpático como
9. tan importante como
10. tan interesante como

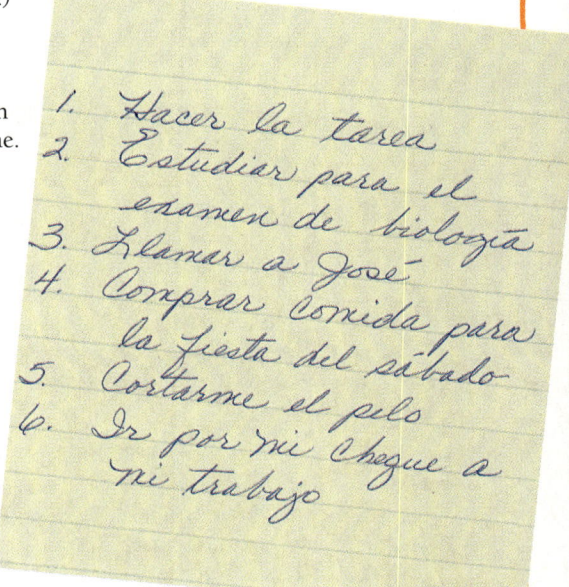

Handwritten note:
1. Hacer la tarea
2. Estudiar para el examen de biología
3. Llamar a José
4. Comprar comida para la fiesta del sábado
5. Cortarme el pelo
6. Ir por mi cheque a mi trabajo

AeroPerú — EL IMPERIO DEL SOL — Descubra Sudamérica — Viajes Fama s.a. de c.v.

CAPÍTULO 7   **179**

LECTURA Y CULTURA

Bell Ringer Review
Write the following on the board or use BRR Blackline Master 7-6: Make up questions about an airplane flight using the following expressions: ¿cuándo? ¿cuánto tiempo? ¿de dónde? ¿a qué hora?

READING STRATEGIES
(page 180)

Pre-Reading
Tell students they are going to learn about an interesting flight taken by Álvaro and a friend to the city of La Paz, Bolivia.

Reading
A. You may break the reading into several parts. Present one paragraph thoroughly, reading it to students as they follow along in their books.
B. Intersperse your reading with your own questions on content. (You may use the questions on page 181.)
C. Have students read every other paragraph silently and follow with more questions.

Post-reading
Call on volunteers to recount the flight in their own words.

LECTURA Y CULTURA

UN VUELO INTERESANTE

Hace poco mi amigo Álvaro y yo estábamos a bordo de un vuelo de la Lloyd Boliviana. Estábamos volando a La Paz, la capital de este país tan interesante y de tanta influencia cultural india. Fue nuestro primer viaje a Bolivia y por eso los anuncios que hizo el comandante nos interesaron mucho.

Vamos a escuchar uno de sus anuncios.

"Señores y señoras. Dentro de poco estaremos aterrizando en el aeropuerto El Alto, el aeropuerto internacional que sirve a La Paz. Se llama "El Alto" porque es el aeropuerto comercial más alto del mundo—a 13.450 pies (4.100 metros) sobre el nivel del mar. Por consiguiente ningún otro aeropuerto del mundo tiene una pista tan larga como la pista de El Alto. La pista mide[1] 4 kilómetros. ¿Por qué es tan larga? Porque a esta altura el aire está muy enrarecido[2] y contiene muy poco oxígeno. Tiene muy poca densidad y no puede sostener el peso del avión para darle fuerza ascensional[3]. Por esta razón el avión tiene que alcanzar una gran velocidad antes de poder despegar. Para alcanzar esta velocidad es necesario tener una pista muy larga".

Durante el vuelo el piloto nos estaba diciendo otras cosas interesantes. Nosotros estábamos a bordo de un jet.

Una vista de La Paz, Bolivia

Pero el piloto nos dijo que los aviones de hélices tenían o tienen que descender después de despegar de El Alto. ¿Tienen que bajar o descender? Sí, porque los aviones de hélices vuelan a una altura de unos 12.000 pies y el aeropuerto está a 13.450 pies. ¿Hay muchos aviones de hélices hoy? Sí, hay, porque en muchas zonas muy remotas los aeropuertos no pueden acomodar los jets.

[1] mide *measures*
[2] enrarecido *thin*
[3] fuerza ascensional *lift*

180 CAPÍTULO 7

CRITICAL THINKING ACTIVITY

(Thinking skills: drawing conclusions based on facts)

Read the following to the class or write it on the board or on an overhead transparency. ¿Por qué es tan apropiado darle el nombre "el Alto" al aeropuerto de La Paz?

Estudio de palabras

A Verbo y sustantivo. Escojan.

1. anunciar
2. medir
3. pesar
4. despegar
5. aterrizar
6. volar

a. el peso
b. la medida
c. el aterrizaje
d. el anuncio
e. el vuelo
f. el despegue

B ¿Cuál es la definición? Escojan.

1. dentro de poco
2. la altura
3. 1.200 metros de largo
4. 1.000 kilos
5. la gran velocidad
6. descender

a. la medida
b. la rapidez
c. en poco tiempo, pronto
d. el peso
e. la altitud
f. bajar

Comprensión

A Un vuelo interesante. Contesten según la lectura.

1. ¿Adónde iban Álvaro y su amigo?
2. ¿Qué les interesaba mucho?
3. ¿Por qué es famoso el aeropuerto El Alto?
4. ¿Qué no contiene el aire a esta altura?
5. ¿Qué tienen que hacer los aviones de hélices después de despegar?

B Informes y datos. Contesten.

1. el nombre del aeropuerto de La Paz
2. la altura del aeropuerto
3. el largo de la pista

C Explicaciones. Contesten.

1. Explique por qué el aeropuerto de La Paz tiene que tener una pista tan larga.
2. Explique por qué los aviones de hélices tienen que bajar o perder altitud después de despegar de La Paz.

Una vendedora en La Paz, Bolivia

CAPÍTULO 7   **181**

Estudio de palabras
ANSWERS
Ejercicio A
1. d
2. b
3. a
4. f
5. c
6. e

Ejercicio B
1. c
2. e
3. a
4. d
5. b
6. f

Comprensión
PRESENTATION *(page 181)*

Comprensión A and B
Exercises A and B deal with factual recall. Exercise B develops the skill of scanning for information as well.

Comprensión C
Exercise C challenges students' critical thinking skills.

ANSWERS
Comprensión A
1. Iban a La Paz.
2. Les interesaban los anuncios que hizo el comandante.
3. Es el aeropuerto comercial más alto del mundo.
4. No contiene mucho oxígeno.
5. Tienen que descender.

Comprensión B
1. El Alto
2. 13.450 pies (4.100 metros)
3. 4 kilómetros

Comprensión C
1. Porque a esta altura el aire está muy enrarecido. Tiene poca densidad y no puede sostener el peso del avión para darle fuerza ascensional.
2. Tienen que bajar porque los aviones de hélices vuelan a una altura de unos 12.000 pies y el aeropuerto está a 13.450 pies.

LEARNING FROM PHOTOS
Refer students to the lower photo on page 181. Ask them: *¿Qué está vendiendo la señora?*

INDEPENDENT PRACTICE
Assign any the following:
1. Workbook, *Un poco más*
2. Exercises on student pages 178, 179, 181

181

Descubrimiento Cultural

(The Descubrimiento *section is optional.)*

PRESENTATION *(pages 182-183)*

A. Before going through the selection with the class, prepare some true/false statements about it and write them on the board.

B. After reading the selection, have students go through your statements. Have them correct the false ones. For example: *El lago Titicaca es el lago navegable más bajo del mundo. (falso) El lago Titicaca es el lago navegable más alto del mundo.*

DESCUBRIMIENTO CULTURAL

El aeropuerto El Alto en La Paz está situado en una llanura del altiplano andino. Aquí siempre hace mucho viento. Antiguamente la ciudad de La Paz estaba situada donde está hoy el aeropuerto. Pero a los conquistadores españoles no les gustaba el viento y por este motivo trasladaron la ciudad a un valle más abajo de la meseta. Hoy en día hay una carretera moderna del aeropuerto a la ciudad. Para ir del aeropuerto a la ciudad el viajero tiene que bajar unos 1.600 pies (485 metros).

Cuando uno desembarca de un avión en La Paz, se siente un poco mareado[1], y a veces tiene dificultad en respirar[2]. Éstos son síntomas típicos del soroche. El soroche es un mal de montaña causado por el enrarecimiento del aire y la falta de oxígeno. En las alturas del altiplano boliviano no hay tanto oxígeno como lo hay al nivel del mar.

La llegada a La Paz es una experiencia maravillosa. La ciudad parece estar en un cráter, en un valle abajo del altiplano. Encima de la ciudad el cielo es claro, limpio y muy azul. Los paceños, los habitantes de La Paz, llaman cariñosamente a su ciudad "El Hueco"[3].

En la carretera del aeropuerto a La Paz uno verá anuncios para los aerodeslizadores o hidrofoils que cruzan el lago Titicaca. Si El Alto es el aeropuerto más alto del mundo, el lago Titicaca es el lago navegable más alto del mundo. El lago Titicaca está entre Bolivia y el Perú. Si a Ud. le interesan los animales, le encantará esta región donde hay ovejas[4], llamas, alpacas, vicuñas y chinchillas. En esta región viven los indios Aymarás y Quechuas.

En el lago Titicaca

Y AQUÍ EN LOS ESTADOS UNIDOS

Todo el mundo conoce el nombre de Charles Lindbergh, "El Águila[5] Solitaria", la primera persona que sobrevoló el Atlántico solo. Pero pocos conocen el nombre del Capitán Emilio Carranza. Lindbergh voló de Wáshington a la Ciudad de México en el mismo avión con el que cruzó el Atlántico. El Presidente de México, Elías Calles, lo invitó. Los mexicanos querían corresponder a este fino gesto.

El 11 de junio de 1928, Emilio Carranza de 22 años de edad, capitán de las

---

DID YOU KNOW?

En el aeropuerto El Alto siempre hay socorristas y médicos presentes para ayudar a los pasajeros que sufren de la altura. Tienen tanques de oxígeno listos para darles oxígeno a los pasajeros que lo necesitan.

Fuerzas Aéreas Mexicanas y sobrino del ex-presidente Venustiano Carranza, salió de México en su avión Excélsior para los Estados Unidos y llegó a Wáshington como héroe. Después de un mes en Norteamérica, era hora de volver a México. El joven aviador despegó del aeropuerto Roosevelt en Nueva York a las 7:05 de la noche, el 12 de julio de 1928. Nunca llegó a México. Una familia que daba un paseo en el campo cerca de Chatsworth, Nueva Jersey, encontró los restos del Excélsior y el cuerpo sin vida del valiente capitán.

Diez mil soldados y marinos norte-americanos marcharon con los restos del héroe mexicano al tren que lo llevaría de la Pennsylvania Station hasta México.

En las escuelas de México hicieron una colecta. Los niños mexicanos dieron sus contribuciones para un monumento en el lugar de la tragedia. Allí está todavía, y cada año, en el aniversario de su muerte, militares y representantes de las dos repúblicas dejan flores en honor de Emilio Carranza.

[1] mareado *dizzy*
[2] respirar *breathing*
[3] hueco *hole*
[4] oveja *sheep*
[5] águila *eagle*

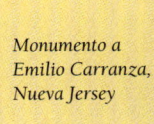

Monumento a Emilio Carranza, Nueva Jersey

Unas mujeres bolivianas

CAPÍTULO 7 **183**

HISTORY CONNECTION

The period from 1911 through the 1920s was one of the most turbulent periods in Mexican history. Francisco I. Madero, Emiliano Zapata, Francisco (Pancho) Villa, and Venustiano Carranza were major players in the Mexican Revolution that began with the overthrow of Porfirio Díaz in 1911. You may wish to assign short biographies of these figures to students as special projects.

FOR THE NATIVE SPEAKER

Have pairs of students compose a letter to a Latin American airline inquiring about possible positions. The letters should request the following information:
1. what positions are available
2. the training needed and where it can be obtained
3. the salary and benefits
4. what jobs require knowledge of English and Spanish

183

REALIDADES

(The Realidades section is optional.)

Bell Ringer Review

Write the following on the board or use BRR Blackline Master 7-7: Answer with *Sí* or *No*.
1. Bolivia es un país montañoso.
2. Los Andes están en el este de la América del Sur.
3. Madrid es la capital de Colombia.
4. Los Pirineos forman una frontera natural entre Francia y España.

PRESENTATION *(pages 184-185)*

Have students read the captions silently and enjoy the photographs. Encourage them to ask questions and express opinions.

REALIDADES

¡Qué vista más fabulosa del lago Titicaca en Bolivia **1**! Es el lago navegable más alto del mundo.

Pasajeros llegando y saliendo del aeropuerto Jorge Chávez que sirve a la capital del Perú, Lima **2**.

Una comida típica que sirven durante un vuelo **3**. ¿Te gusta?

El comandante y el co-piloto en la cabina de mando a bordo de un avión de Viasa, la línea aérea nacional de Venezuela **4**.

184

3

4

185

CULMINACIÓN

RECYCLING

The *Comunicación oral* and *Comunicación escrita* activities encourage students to use all the language they have learned in the chapter and to recombine it with material from previous chapters. It is not necessary to do all the activities with all students. Select the ones you consider most appropriate or allow students to choose the ones they wish to do.

Comunicación oral
ANSWERS
Actividades A, B, and C
  Answers will vary

INFORMAL ASSESSMENT
The *Comunicación oral* activities can be used to assess speaking skills. Use the evaluation criteria given on page 24 of this Teacher's Wraparound Edition.

Comunicación escrita
ANSWERS
Actividades A and B
  Answers will vary.

CULMINACIÓN

Comunicación oral

A **De Dallas a México.** Trabajen en pequeños grupos. Imagínense que un(a) alumno(a) de su grupo estará haciendo su primer viaje en avión. Explíquenle todo lo que tendrá que hacer desde el momento que llega al aeropuerto de Dallas hasta salir del aeropuerto de México.

B **Un viaje en avión.** Mire el horario. Escoja un destino. Luego, hágale preguntas sobre el vuelo a un(a) agente de la compañía aérea (un[a] compañero[a] de clase).

1. Quito / 11:15 / puerta # 14 / 10:45
2. Buenos Aires / 8:00 / puerta # 9 / 7:30
3. Caracas / 12:20 / puerta # 19 / 11:50
4. Madrid / 19:30 / puerta # 38 / 19:00
5. Londres / 18:00 puerta # 35 / 17:00
6. Acapulco / 7:10 / puerta # 3 / 6:40

C **Nuestro estado.** Trabajen en grupos de tres. Tengan una conversación para comparar su estado con algún estado cercano.

Comunicación escrita

A **Un viaje fantástico.** Ud. acaba de volver de un viaje educacional a dos ciudades de Latinoamérica. Escríbale una carta a un(a) amigo(a) comparando las dos ciudades. Puede comparar el tamaño, el tráfico, los precios, los hoteles, los restaurantes y la comida, los museos, los parques, las tiendas, etc.

B **El servicio a bordo.** Imagínese que Ud. ha tomado un vuelo de Nueva York a Madrid. Escríbale una carta a la compañía aérea. En su carta indique si Ud. consideró el servicio bueno o malo. Dé todos los detalles posibles.

186   CAPÍTULO 7

LEARNING FROM REALIA

Refer students to the route map of Mexicana on page 186. Have students identify some of the destinations they would like to visit. Have them tell what they know about some of the cities Mexicana flies to.

Reintegración

A **En el aeropuerto.** Empleen cada palabra en una oración.

1. el mostrador de la línea aérea
2. la tarjeta de embarque
3. el control de seguridad
4. la pantalla de salidas
5. el equipaje de mano
6. facturar el equipaje
7. reclamar el equipaje
8. pasar por la aduana

B **Un viaje en tren.** Completen con el pretérito.

1. La señora ____ un viaje en tren. (hacer)
2. Ella ____ un boleto de ida y vuelta en la ventanilla. (comprar)
3. Los pasajeros ____ al andén. (ir)
4. El mozo ____ y les ____ con su equipaje. (venir, ayudar)
5. El mozo ____ el equipaje en el tren. (poner)

Vocabulario

SUSTANTIVOS
el avión
la tripulación
el asistente de vuelo
la asistenta de vuelo
el sobrecargo
el/la piloto
el/la comandante
la cabina de vuelo (la cabina de mando)
la puerta de salida
la salida de emergencia
el respaldo del asiento
la mesita
la ventanilla
el pasillo
el compartimiento
el cinturón de seguridad
la máscara de oxígeno
el chaleco salvavidas
la señal de no fumar
la bienvenida
el anuncio
el aseo
el lavabo
la bebida
la comida
el carrito
los audífonos
el canal
el aeropuerto
la pista
la torre de control
el avión reactor
el jet
el motor
las hélices
el ala (las alas)
el despegue
el aterrizaje
la geografía
la altura
la altitud
el altiplano
la montaña
la cordillera
el pico
la llanura
la meseta
el valle
el lago
el nivel del mar

ADJETIVOS
estereofónico (a)

VERBOS
distribuir
abrocharse
despegar
aterrizar
sobrevolar

OTRAS PALABRAS Y EXPRESIONES
debajo de
sobre
a bordo
dar la bienvenida

CAPÍTULO 7 **187**

Reintegración

PRESENTATION (*page 187*)

Ejercicio A

Exercise A recycles airline vocabulary presented in *Bienvenidos*, Chapter 8.

Ejercicio B

Exercise B recycles the preterite.

ANSWERS

Ejercicio A
Answers will vary.

Ejercicio B
1. hizo
2. compró
3. fueron
4. vino, ayudó
5. puso

Vocabulario

The words and phrases in the *Vocabulario* have been taught for productive use in this chapter. They are summarized here as a resource for both students and teacher. The *Vocabulario* also serves as a convenient resource for *Culminación* activities. There are approximately 24 cognates in this list.

VIDEO

The video is intended to reinforce the vocabulary, structures, and cultural content in each chapter. It may be used here as a chapter wrap-up activity. See the *Video Activities Booklet* for additional suggestions on its use.

INTRODUCCIÓN (0:28:11)

EL AEROPUERTO (0:29:35)

STUDENT PORTFOLIO

Written assignments that may be included in students' portfolios are the *Actividades escritas* on page 186 and the *Mi autobiografía* section in the Workbook.

INDEPENDENT PRACTICE

Assign any of the following:
1. Exercises on student pages 186-187
2. Workbook, *Mi autobiografía*
3. Chapter 7, Situation Cards

CAPÍTULO 8

Repaso Capítulos 5-8 • Scope and Sequence pages 188-223

Topics	Functions	Structure	Culture
Hairstyles Beauty salon and barber shops	How to use words and expressions related to hairstyles How to explain how you want your hair done when visiting a hairdresser How to refer to people and things already mentioned How to tell what you and others have just done	La colocación de los pronombres de complemento *Acabar de* con infinitivo	Hairstyles in the U.S. vs. hairstyles in parts of the Hispanic world Perfume store in the Zona Rosa, Mexico City Three well-known Spanish soaps: Magno, Heno de Pravia, and Maja *Nuestro Mundo:* Hotel forms in Spain and Latin America
Fondo Académico pages 218-223			Ciencias Naturales: La meteorología Ciencias Sociales: La historia Humanidades: La mitología

CAPÍTULO 8

Situation Cards

The Situation Cards simulate real-life situations that require students to communicate in Spanish, exactly as though they were in a Spanish-speaking country. The Situation Cards operate on the assumption that the person to whom the message is to be conveyed understands no English. Therefore, students must focus on producing the Spanish vocabulary and structures necessary to negotiate the situations successfully. For additional information, see the Introduction to the Situation Cards in the Situation Cards Envelope.

Communication Transparency

The illustration seen in this Communication Transparency consists of a synthesis of the two vocabulary (Palabras 1&2) presentations found in this chapter. It has been created in order to present this chapter's vocabulary in a new context, and also to recycle vocabulary learned in previous chapters. The Communication Transparency consists of original art. Following are some specific uses:

1. as a cue to stimulate conversation and writing activities
2. for listening comprehension activities
3. to review and reteach vocabulary
4. as a review for chapter and unit tests

CAPÍTULO 8   A

You are out of haircare items. Ask a clerk in the supermarket where you can find the items that you need.

CAPÍTULO 8
Print Resources

Pages

Lesson Plans

Workbook
- Palabras 1 — 81-82
- Palabras 2 — 83-84
- Estructura — 85-86
- Un poco más — 87
- Mi autobiografía — 88
- Self-Test — 89-96

Communication Activities Masters
- Palabras 1 — 47-48
- Palabras 2 — 49-50
- Estructura — 51-52

9 Bell Ringer Reviews — 24-25

Chapter Situation Cards A B C D

Chapter Quizzes
- Palabras 1 — 36
- Palabras 2 — 37
- Estructura — 38-39

Testing Program
- Listening Comprehension — 40
- Reading and Writing — 41-45
- Proficiency — 130
- Speaking — 149

Unit Test: Chapters 5-8
- Listening Comprehension — 46
- Reading and Writing — 47-50
- Speaking — 150
- Performance Assessment

Nosotros y Nuestro Mundo
- Nuestro Conocimiento Académico *Historia: Barberos, médicos y cirujanos*
- Nuestro Idioma *El infinitivo*
- Nuestra Cultura *De nuestros nombres y apellidos*
- Nuestra Literatura *"El buen ejemplo"* de Vicente Riva Palacio
- Nuestra Creatividad
- Nuestras Diversiones

CAPÍTULO 8
Multimedia Resources

CD-ROM Interactive Textbook Disc 2

Chapter 8 Student Edition
- Palabras 1
- Palabras 2
- Estructura
- Conversación
- Lectura y cultura
- Hispanoparlantes
- Realidades
- Culminación
- Prueba

Review: Chapters 5-8
- Nuestro mundo
- Repaso
- Fondo Académico
- Game: La Vuelta a España

Audio Cassette Program with Student Tape Manual

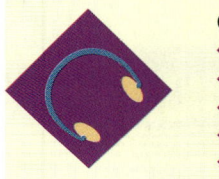

Cassette — **Pages**
- 5B Palabras 1 — 239-240
- 5B Palabras 2 — 240
- 5B Estructura — 240
- 5B Conversación — 241
- 5B Segunda parte — 241-242

Compact Disc Program with Student Tape Manual
- CD 5 Palabras 1 — 239-240
- CD 5 Palabras 2 — 240
- CD 5 Estructura — 240
- CD 5 Conversación — 241
- CD 5 Segunda parte — 241-242

Overhead Transparencies Binder
- Vocabulary 8.1 (A&B); 8.2 (A&B)
- Communication C-8
- Maps
- Fine Art (with Blackline Master Activities)

Video Program
- Videocassette
- Video Activities Booklet — 20-21
- Videodisc
- Video Activities Booklet — 20-21

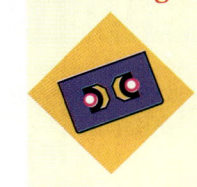

Computer Software (Macintosh, IBM, Apple)
- Practice Disk
    - Palabras 1 y 2
    - Estructura
- Test Generator Disk
    - Chapter Test
    - Customized Test

188B

CAPÍTULO 8

CHAPTER OVERVIEW

In this chapter students will learn the vocabulary associated with various hairstyles and words or expressions they would need at a barber shop or hair styling salon. They will expand their ability to talk about people and places already mentioned by learning to position pronouns in progressive tenses and in relation to infinitives. They will also learn to talk about completed actions using *acabar de* with an infinitive.

The cultural focus of Chapter 8 is on modern hair styling, including contrasting hairstyles in the U.S. with those in parts of the Hispanic world.

CHAPTER OBJECTIVES

By the end of this chapter, students will know:
1. vocabulary associated with features of the head and face
2. vocabulary associated with hairstyles for both sexes
3. the position of object pronouns when used with infinitives and progressive tenses
4. the expression *acabar de* with the infinitive

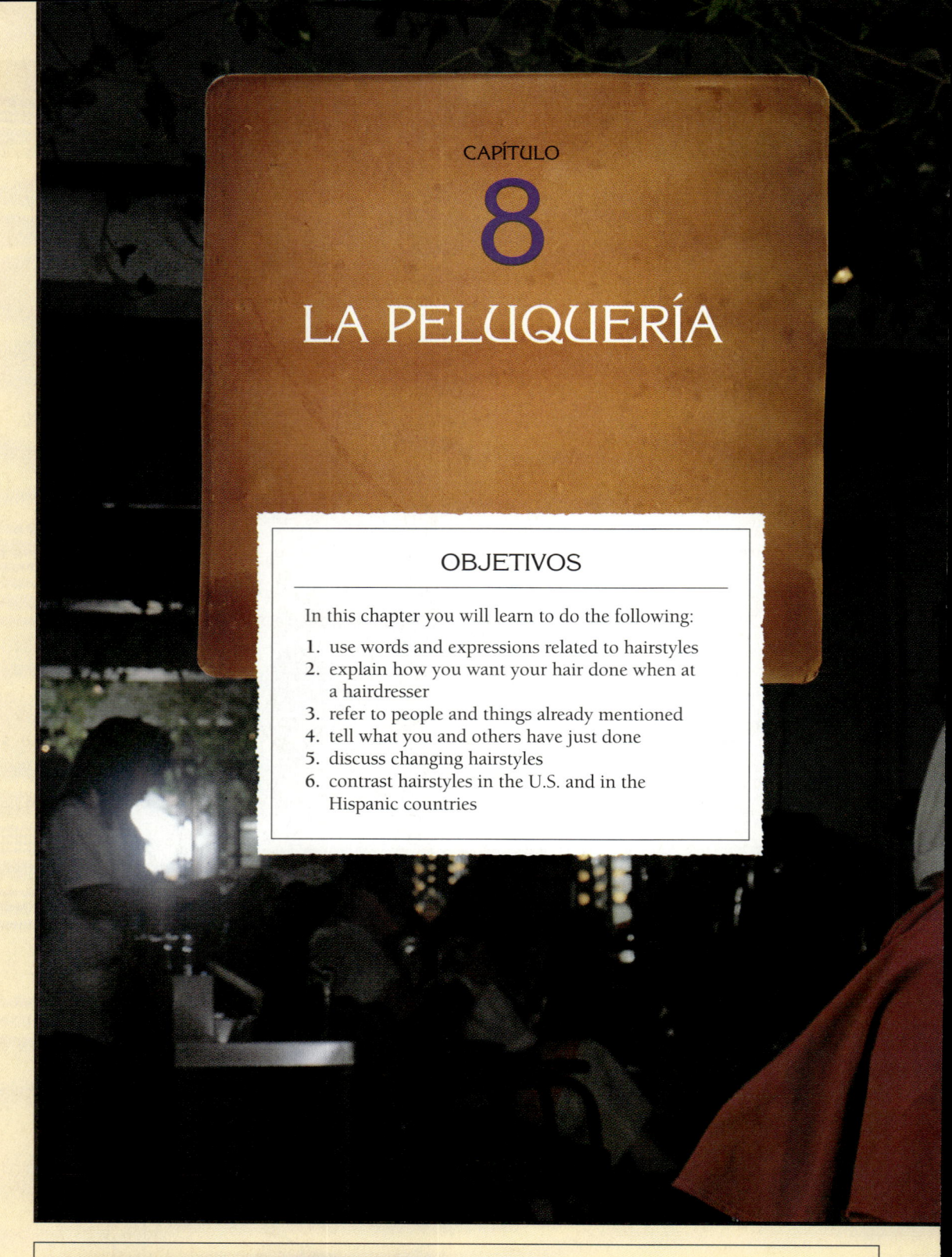

CAPÍTULO 8
LA PELUQUERÍA

OBJETIVOS

In this chapter you will learn to do the following:

1. use words and expressions related to hairstyles
2. explain how you want your hair done when at a hairdresser
3. refer to people and things already mentioned
4. tell what you and others have just done
5. discuss changing hairstyles
6. contrast hairstyles in the U.S. and in the Hispanic countries

CHAPTER PROJECTS

(*optional*)
1. Have students look in North American magazines and newspapers for ads concerning hairstyles and hair products. Discuss trends in this area.
2. Have students bring photos of their favorite celebrities and give oral or written presentations on the celebrities' hairstyles.
3. Have students write letters to their Spanish pen pals, real or imaginary, describing hairstyles which are currently in fashion.

CHAPTER 8 RESOURCES

1. Workbook
2. Student Tape Manual
3. Audio Cassette 5B
4. Vocabulary Transparencies
5. Bell Ringer Review Blackline Masters
6. Communication Activities Masters
7. Computer Software: Practice and Test Generator
8. Video Cassette, Chapter 8
9. Video Activities Booklet, Chapter 8
10. Situation Cards
11. Chapter Quizzes
12. Testing Program

Pacing

Chapter 8 will require eight to ten class sessions. Pacing will depend on the length of the class period, the age of the students, and student aptitude.

LEARNING FROM PHOTOS

After presenting the *Palabras 1* and *Palabras 2* vocabulary, refer students to the photo on pages 188-189. Have students describe in as much detail as possible the hairstyles of both people.

At the end of the chapter, you may return to this photo again and have students prepare a conversation that might take place between the two people.

189

VOCABULARIO
PALABRAS 1

VOCABULARIO

PALABRAS 1

¿CÓMO TE PEINAS?

el pelo, el cabello

el pelo liso, lacio — el pelo rizado — el pelo crespo

el pelo largo — el pelo corto

el pelo rubio — el pelo castaño

la raya

la patilla

el bigote / los bigotes

el pelo negro — el pelo rojo

190 CAPÍTULO 8

Vocabulary Teaching Resources

1. Vocabulary Transparencies, 8.1 (A & B)
2. Audio Cassette 5B
3. Student Tape Manual, *Palabras 1*
4. Workbook, *Palabras 1*
5. Communication Activities Masters, *Palabras 1, A & B*
6. Chapter Quizzes, *Palabras 1*

Bell Ringer Review

Write the following on the board or use BRR Blackline Master 8-1: Make up sentences using the following descriptive words:
alto, bajo, rubio, moreno, guapo, bonito.

PRESENTATION (pages 190-191)

A. With books closed, refer to Vocabulary Transparencies 8.1 (A & B) and have students repeat the new words, phrases, and sentences after you or Cassette 5B.
B. You may want to use students as models of some of the different hair textures, colors, and styles mentioned.
C. Mention various hair features and have students raise their hands if they have that feature. For example: *Levanta la mano si tienes un flequillo, e una cola de caballo. Etc.*

PAIRED ACTIVITY

Each partner draws a person with an unusual hairdo. Partners exchange drawings and describe what they see.

190

ADDITIONAL PRACTICE

(*Palabras 1*)
After presenting the vocabulary on pages 190-191, refer to the Vocabulary Transparencies again. Point to the various hairstyles, textures, and colors at random and have students identify them.

el bucle - rizo de cabello en forma de hélice

el moño

la cola de caballo

los rizos

el peinado afro

la trenza

el flequillo

la onda

el bucle

El señor está peinándose.

La señorita está cepillándose el pelo.

El joven está lavándose el pelo.

CAPÍTULO 8 **191**

FOR THE NATIVE SPEAKER

Have pairs of students create two ads for *Peluquería Unisex 2000*. One ad should be a print ad, the other for the radio. Both ads should include the services provided, such as trims, haircuts, curling, shampooing, coloring, beard and moustache trims, styling, etc. They should also include the address and hours of operation, prices, any specialties, number of hairdressers, and anything else that is special. The radio ads should be presented orally to the class.

191

Ejercicios

PRESENTATION (*pages 192-193*)

Ejercicio A
Exercise A is to be done with books open.

Ejercicio B
Exercise B can be done with books open or closed.

ANSWERS

Ejercicio A
1. Tiene el pelo largo y lacio.
2. Tiene el pelo corto.
3. Tiene el pelo rizado.
4. Tiene el pelo liso (lacio).
5. Tiene el pelo rojo.
6. Tiene el pelo en una cola de caballo.

Ejercicio B
1. femenino
2. femenino
3. unisex
4. femenino
5. unisex
6. masculino
7. unisex
8. masculino

Ejercicios

A ¿Cómo tienen el pelo? Describan los peinados.

1. 2. 3.

4. 5. 6.

B Un peinado masculino o femenino. Escojan.

masculino   femenino   unisex

1. el moño
2. las trenzas
3. la cola de caballo
4. el bucle
5. la raya
6. el bigote
7. los flequillos
8. las patillas

CAPÍTULO 8

FOR THE NATIVE SPEAKER

Discussion *La gente mayor muchas veces se queja de los estilos de pelo de los jóvenes, especialmente de los varones. ¿Qué es lo que les molesta de los estilos de pelo de los jóvenes? ¿Qué preferirían los mayores? ¿Hay algo más en esto que el mero estilo?*

INDEPENDENT PRACTICE

Assign any of the following:
1. Workbook, *Palabras 1*
2. Communication Activities Masters, *Palabras 1, A & B*
3. Exercises on student pages 192-193

C El pelo. *Preguntas personales.*

1. ¿Tienes el pelo liso o rizado?
2. ¿Tienes el pelo rizado o crespo?
3. ¿De qué color es tu pelo?
4. ¿Llevas raya o no?
5. Si llevas raya, ¿la llevas a la derecha, a la izquierda o en el medio?
6. ¿Tienes el pelo largo o corto?

D Mi peinado. *Preguntas personales.*

1. ¿Te peinas frecuentemente?
2. ¿Estás peinándote ahora?
3. ¿Te cepillas el pelo con frecuencia?
4. ¿Te estás cepillando el pelo ahora?
5. ¿Te peinas o te cepillas con más frecuencia?
6. ¿Te lavas el pelo todos los días?
7. ¿Te lavas el pelo mientras estás tomando una ducha?

NUEVO
ELSÈVE YOYOBA

BRILLO Y VITALIDAD PARA TUS CABELLOS.

ELSÈVE
L'ORÉAL

CAPÍTULO 8   193

PRESENTATION
Ejercicios C and D
Exercises C and D can be done with books open or closed.

ANSWERS
Ejercicio C
Answers will vary.
1. Tengo el pelo liso (rizado).
2. Tengo el pelo rizado (crespo).
3. Tengo el pelo rubio (negro, castaño, rojo).
4. Sí, (No, no) llevo raya.
5. Llevo la raya a la derecha (a la izquierda, en el medio).
6. Tengo el pelo largo (corto).

Ejercicio D
Answers will vary.
1. Sí (No), (no) me peino frecuentemente.
2. Sí (No), (no) me estoy peinando ahora.
3. Sí (No), (no) me cepillo el pelo con frecuencia.
4. Sí (No), (no) me estoy cepillando el pelo ahora.
5. Me peino (Me cepillo) con más frecuencia.
6. Sí (No), (no) me lavo el pelo todos los días.
7. Sí (No), (no) me lavo el pelo mientras estoy tomando una ducha.

INFORMAL ASSESSMENT
(Palabras 1)
Have individuals describe their own texture, length, and color of hair.

LEARNING FROM PHOTOS/REALIA

1. Refer students to the photo on page 193. Ask them: *¿Dónde está la muchacha? ¿Cómo tiene el pelo? ¿Se está lavando el pelo? ¿Dónde tiene la toalla?*
2. Refer students to the advertisement on page 193. Ask them: *¿Para qué tipo de producto es la publicidad? Según la publicidad, ¿qué hace Elsève? Elsève es un producto de la compañía L'Oreal. ¿Qué opina Ud.? ¿Es una compañía española, francesa, estadounidense o latinoamericana?*

VOCABULARIO
PALABRAS 2

VOCABULARIO

PALABRAS 2

NECESITO UN CORTE DE PELO

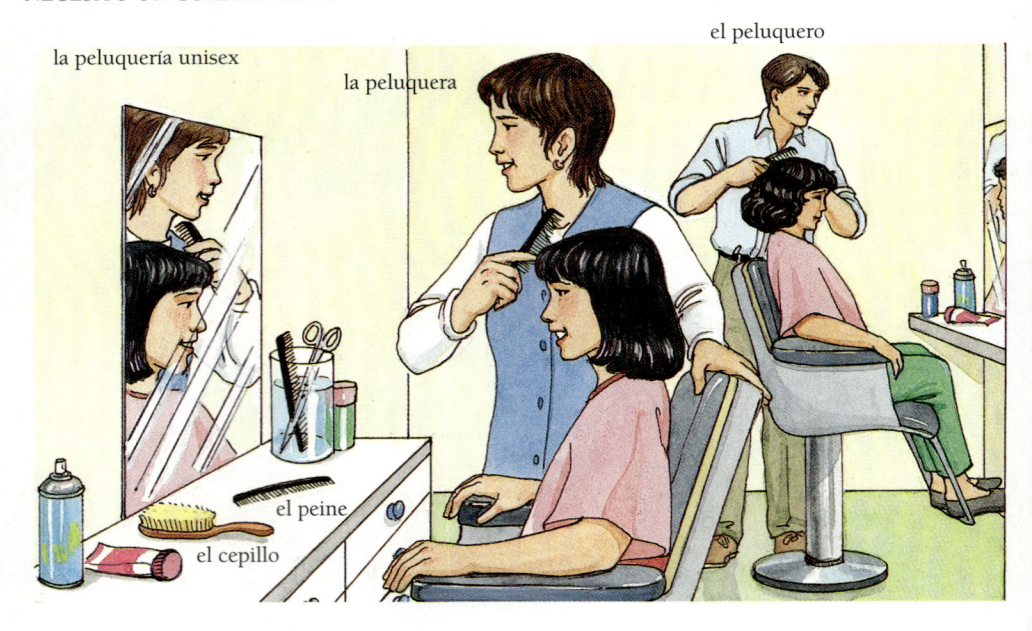

- la peluquería unisex
- la peluquera
- el peluquero
- el peine
- el cepillo
- el secador
- el rizador
- las tijeras
- la navaja
- la maquinilla
- la horquilla
- la laca
- el champú
- el rulo
- la pinza para el cabello

194   CAPÍTULO 8

VOCABULARIO
PALABRAS 2

Vocabulary Teaching Resources

1. Vocabulary Transparencies 8.2 (A & B)
2. Audio Cassette 5B
3. Student Tape Manual, *Palabras 2*
4. Workbook, *Palabras 2*
5. Communication Activities Masters, *Palabras 2, C & D*
6. Chapter Quizzes, *Palabras 2*
7. Computer Software, *Vocabulario*

Bell Ringer Review

Write the following on the board or use BRR Blackline Master 8-2: Make a list of all the parts of the body you know in Spanish.

PRESENTATION *(pages 194–195)*

A. Have students close their books. Model the *Palabras 2* vocabulary using Vocabulary Transparencies 8.2 (A & B). Have students repeat the new material after you or Cassette 5B.
B. Ask questions about the new material. Begin with either/or and yes/no questions, and then progress to open-ended ones. For example: ¿Es el secador o la maquinilla? ¿Es la pinza o la horquilla? ¿Qué es esto?
C. Have students open their books and read the new words, phrases, and sentences.

194

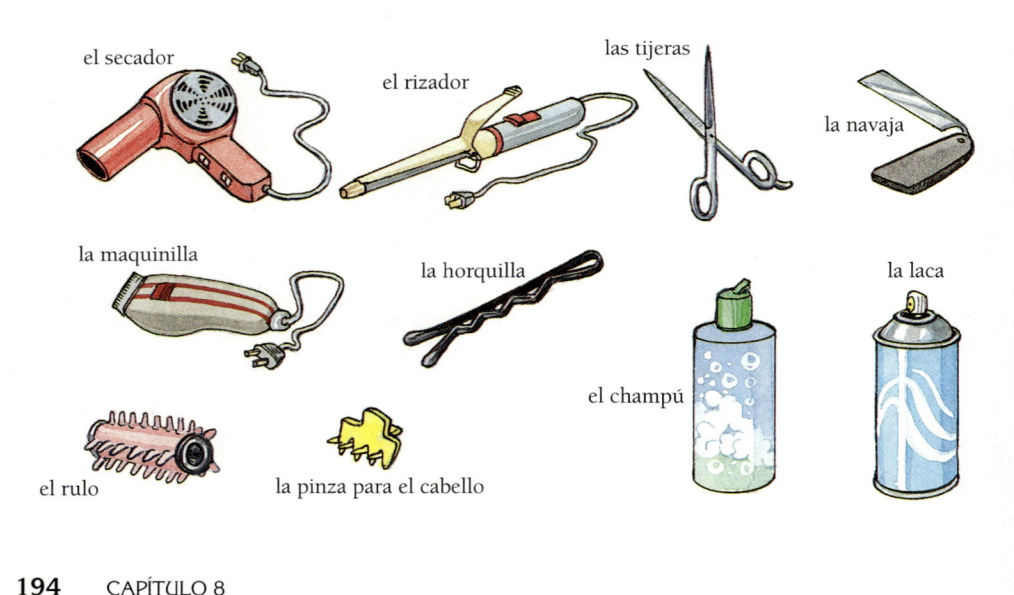

PANTOMIME

Getting Ready
    Write individual actions like the ones below on index cards. Give one card apiece to individuals to mime the action. As each student mimes, ask another to say in Spanish what his/her classmate is doing.
dar un champú a alguien
secar el pelo con un secador
cepillarle el pelo a alguien
cortarse el pelo
peinarse

arriba
al lado
enfrente
atrás
el cuello

el corte de pelo
el peluquero, el barbero

El peluquero está cortándole el pelo.

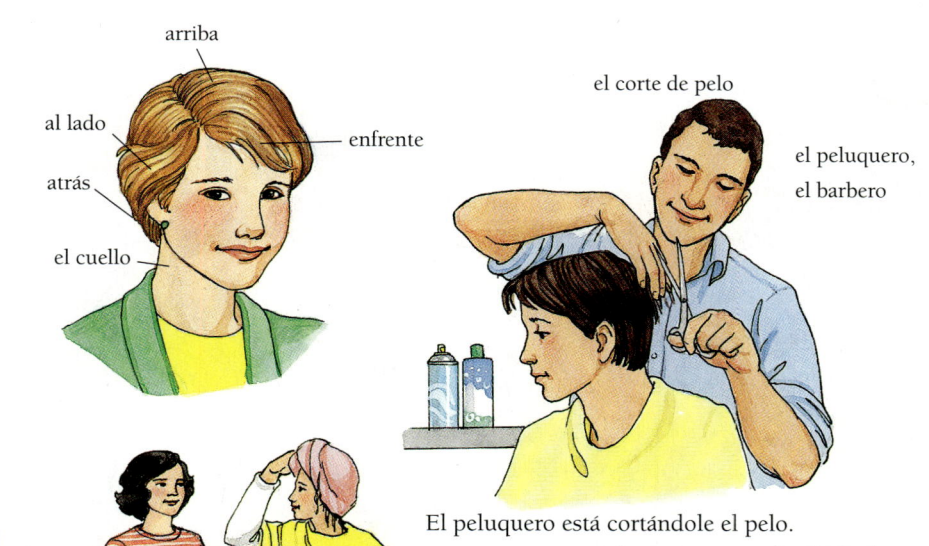

La peluquera acaba de darle un champú.
Acaba de lavarle el pelo (darle un lavado).

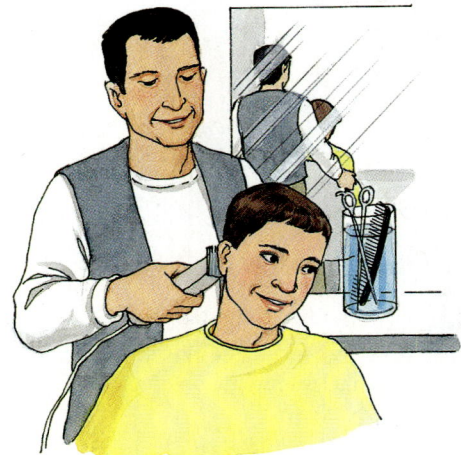

Ahora va a recortarle el pelo.
Va a darle un recorte.

CAPÍTULO 8   **195**

Vocabulary Expansion

You may give students the following names for products:
el rímel (mascara)
el lápiz para los labios
la espuma
el talco
el perfume
el agua de colonia
la crema facial
Then call on individual girls in the class to tell which of these cosmetics they do or don't use.

ADDITIONAL PRACTICE

Ask students the following questions: *¿Cuándo necesitas champú? ¿Cuándo pones laca en los cabellos? ¿Cuándo usas tijeras? ¿Cuándo usas una navaja? ¿Cuándo usas un secador? ¿Cuándo necesitas rulos o un rizador?*

COOPERATIVE LEARNING

1. Have teams of boys discuss and report on their preferred hairstyles for girls. Have teams of girls discuss and report on their preferred hairstyles for boys.
2. Have teams of girls discuss whether they like to do their own hair or go to a salon and why.

195

Ejercicios

PRESENTATION (page 196)

Ejercicios A and B
Exercises A and B can be done with books open.

Ejercicio C
Exercise C can be done with books open or closed.

ANSWERS

Ejercicio A
1. Es el peine.
2. Es el rizador.
3. Es un rulo.
4. Son tijeras.

Ejercicio B
1. Tiene el pelo corto.
2. No tiene bucles.
3. No tiene patillas.
4. Tiene el pelo corto a los lados.

Ejercicio C
Answers will vary.
1. Voy a la peluquería…
2. Sí (No), (no) voy con frecuencia.
3. Prefiero el pelo largo (corto).
4. Sí (No), el peluquero (no) me lava el pelo antes de cortarme el pelo.
5. Cuando me da un corte, usa tijeras (navaja).
6. Me gusta el pelo largo (corto) atrás, en el cuello.

INFORMAL ASSESSMENT
(*Palabras 2*)
Have individuals describe each illustration on page 195 as completely as possible.

Ejercicios

A ¿Qué es? Identifiquen según la foto.

1. ¿Es el peine o el cepillo?
2. ¿Es el secador para el pelo o el rizador?  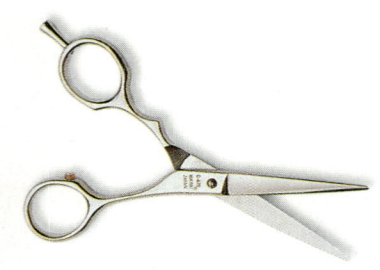
3. ¿Es una horquilla o un rulo?
4. ¿Son tijeras o es una navaja?

B El peinado. Contesten según la foto.
1. Este muchacho, ¿tiene el pelo largo o corto?
2. ¿Tiene bucles enfrente o no?
3. ¿Tiene patillas?
4. ¿Tiene el pelo largo o corto a los lados?

C Mi peinado. Preguntas personales.
1. ¿A qué peluquería vas?
2. ¿Vas con frecuencia (a menudo)?
3. ¿Prefieres el pelo largo o el pelo corto?
4. ¿Te lava el pelo el peluquero antes de cortarte el pelo?
5. Cuando te da un corte, ¿usa tijeras o navaja?
6. ¿Te gusta el pelo largo o corto atrás, en el cuello?

CAPÍTULO 8

INDEPENDENT PRACTICE

Assign any of the following:
1. Workbook, *Palabras 2*
2. Communication Activities Masters, *Palabras 2, C & D*
3. Exercises on student pages 196–197

Comunicación
Palabras 1 y 2

A **El pelo.** Un(a) compañero(a) de clase quiere saber qué peinado prefiere Ud. Déle una descripción completa. Luego cambien de papel.

B **¿Está de moda?** Pregúntele a un(a) compañero(a) de clase si los estilos siguientes están de moda o no.

1. El pelo largo para muchachos
2. El pelo corto para muchachas
3. La onda para muchachas
4. El moño para muchachas
5. La cola de caballo para muchachos
6. El "look" mojado *(wet)* para muchachos
7. El "look" mojado para muchachas
8. Las trenzas para muchachas
9. El afro para gente con pelo crespo
10. El bigote para muchachos

C **¡El pelo de mis sueños!** Escriba un párrafo corto describiendo cómo le gustaría tener el pelo: el color, el largo, el estilo, etc.

CAPÍTULO 8 **197**

Comunicación
(Palabras 1 and 2)

Bell Ringer Review
Write the following on the board or use BRR Blackline Master 8-3: Draw a smiling male face and highlight the following:
el bigote
las patillas
el pelo liso

PRESENTATION (page 197)
It is not necessary that you do all of the *Comunicación* activities. You may select those you consider most appropriate. You may also allow students to select the activities in which they take part.

ANSWERS
Actividades A, B, and C
Answers will vary.

LEARNING FROM REALIA
Refer students to the advertisement at the bottom of page 197. Have students scan the ad and get as much information from it as they can. Ask students to identify and try to figure out what the various products in the ad might be. *(Gel Fijador Extrahúmido; Gel Fijador Extrafuerte; Espuma Moldadora Normal; Espuma Moldadora Extrafuerte; Laca Normal; Laca Extrafuerte; Spray de Moldaje Extrafuerte; Gel Fluido, Crema de Moldaje.)*

ESTRUCTURA

La colocación de los pronombres de complemento

Referring to People or Things Already Mentioned

1. You have already learned that the direct and indirect object pronouns precede the conjugated form of a verb.

   Él me envió la carta.
   ¿Cuándo te la mandó?
   Me la envió el otro día.

   Srta. Norma Marta Ruiz
   Avda. General San Martín, 28
   Montevideo, Uruguay

2. The object pronouns may be attached to either the present participle, *enviando, leyendo, escribiendo,* or the infinitive *enviar, leer, escribir.* They may also precede the helping verb used with the participle or the infinitive.

BEFORE	ATTACHED
Me está escribiendo la carta.	Está escribiéndome la carta. *(present participles)*
¿Cuándo te la va a enviar?	¿Cuándo va a enviártela?
Me la estará enviando hoy.	Estará enviándomela hoy.
Él me va a escribir la carta.	Él va a escribirme la carta. *(infinitive)*
¿Cuándo te la va a enviar?	¿Cuándo va a enviártela?
Me la quiere mandar hoy.	Quiere mandármela hoy.

3. Note that in order to maintain the same stress, a present participle carries a written accent mark when either one or two pronouns are added to it. An infinitive carries a written accent mark only when two pronouns are attached to it.

   diciéndome   decirme
   diciéndomelo   decírmelo

198 CAPÍTULO 8

DID YOU KNOW?

The avenue on the address is *Avda. General San Martín* named for José de San Martín (1778-1850) the hero of Argentine (and Uruguay, since Uruguay was a part of Argentina at the time) independence. Ask students what local streets and avenues are named after historical figures.

Ejercicios

A ¿Qué está haciendo el peluquero? Contesten según el modelo.

> ¿Está recortándote las patillas?
> *Sí, me las está recortando.*
> *Sí, está recortándomelas.*

1. ¿Está enrollándote el pelo?
2. ¿Está cortándote la cola de caballo?
3. ¿Está lavándote el pelo?
4. ¿Está recortándote el bigote?

B En la peluquería. Contesten según el modelo.

> ¿Va a darle el champú?
> *Sí, se lo va a dar.*
> *Sí va a dárselo.*

1. ¿Va a lavarle el pelo?
2. ¿Va a mojarle el pelo?
3. ¿Va a cortarle el pelo?
4. ¿Va a secarle el pelo?

C ¡Yo! Preguntas personales.

1. ¿Estás lavándote el pelo?
2. ¿Vas a lavarte el pelo esta noche?
3. ¿Vas a comprarte el champú?
4. ¿Está cortándote el pelo el peluquero?
5. ¿Va a cortártelo mañana?

D En el cine. Contesten con pronombres.

1. ¿Quiere ver la película Marisol?
2. ¿Va a ver la película?
3. ¿Está comprando las entradas ahora?
4. ¿Está comprando las entradas en la taquilla del cine?
5. ¿Quiere Marisol sentarse en la primera fila?
6. ¿Quiere ver la película de la primera fila?
7. Desde la primera fila, ¿puede ver la película bien?

CAPÍTULO 8 199

PRESENTATION (page 200)

Ejercicio E
Exercise E can be done with books open or closed.

Ejercicio F
Exercise F can be done with books open.

ANSWERS

Ejercicio E
Answers will vary.
1. Yo se las estoy comprando.
   (Yo estoy comprándoselas.)
2. Él me las va a dar.
   (Él va a dármelas.)
3. Yo se las voy a pagar.
   (Voy a pagárselas.)
4. El taquillero me lo está diciendo.
   (El taquillero está diciéndomelo.)
5. Yo se las voy a regalar.
   (Yo voy a regalárselas.)
6. Yo sé que Guillermo la va a invitar al teatro.
   (Yo sé que Guillermo va a invitarla al teatro.)

Ejercicio F
1. No, Susana no está escribiendo la carta.
   (No, Susana no está escribiéndola.)
2. Mañana va a escribírmela.
   (Mañana me la va a escribir.)
3. Sí, está comprándolos ahora.
   (Sí, los está comprando.)
4. No, no está comprándolo.
   (No, no lo está comprando.)
5. Sí, ya lo ha comprado.
6. Mañana va a enviármela.
   (Mañana me la va a enviar.)
7. El cartero va a entregármela.
   (El cartero me la va a entregar.)
8. Sí, la voy a abrir en seguida.
   (Sí, voy a abrirla en seguida.)
9. Voy a leerla con mucho interés.
   (La voy a leer con mucho interés.)
10. Sí, la voy a contestar en seguida.
    (Sí, voy a contestarla en seguida.)
11. Voy a enviársela por correo aéreo.
    (Se la voy a enviar por correo aéreo.)
12. Sí, voy a enviársela en seguida.
    (Sí, se la voy a enviar en seguida.)

200

E **Unas entradas como regalito.** Usen pronombres en la oración.
1. Yo estoy comprando las entradas para Guillermo.
2. El taquillero va a darme las entradas.
3. Yo le voy a pagar las entradas.
4. El taquillero me está diciendo el precio.
5. Yo le voy a regalar las entradas a Guillermo.
6. Yo sé que Guillermo va a invitar a su novia al teatro.

F **Una carta.** Contesten según se indica.
1. ¿Está escribiendo la carta Susana? (no)
2. ¿Cuándo va a escribírtela? (mañana)
3. ¿Está comprando los sellos ahora? (sí)
4. ¿Y está comprando el sobre? (no)
5. ¿Ya lo ha comprado? (sí)
6. ¿Cuándo va a enviarte la carta? (mañana)
7. ¿Quién va a entregarte la carta? (el cartero)
8. ¿La vas a abrir en seguida? (sí)
9. ¿Cómo vas a leer la carta? (con mucho interés)
10. ¿La vas a contestar en seguida? (sí)
11. ¿Cómo vas a enviarle tu carta? (por correo aéreo)
12. ¿Vas a enviársela en seguida? (sí)

200 CAPÍTULO 8

LEARNING FROM REALIA
Refer students to the tickets on page 200. Ask them: *¿Para qué tipo de presentación son las entradas? ¿Cómo se llama la compañía o el grupo que va a bailar? ¿Dónde bailan? ¿Cómo se llama el teatro? ¿Son para el patio o para la galería las entradas? ¿En qué fila están las butacas? ¿Cuáles son los números de las butacas?*

INDEPENDENT PRACTICE
Assign any of the following:
1. Workbook, *Estructura*
2. Communication Activities Masters, *Estructura*, A
3. Exercises on student pages 199–200

Acabar de con el infinitivo

Describing Events That Have Just Taken Place

Acabar de + an infinitive, means "to have just."

> Mi amiga acaba de llegar.
> Y nosotros acabamos de comer.
> Los otros acaban de salir.

Ejercicios

A ¿Acabas de hacerlo o vas a hacerlo?
Preguntas personales. Usen pronombres.

1. ¿Acabas de leer el periódico o vas a leer el periódico?
2. ¿Acabas de escribir la composición o vas a escribir la composición?
3. ¿Acabas de tomar el examen o vas a tomar el examen?
4. ¿Acabas de hacer tus tareas o vas a hacer tus tareas?
5. ¿Acabas de llamar a tu amigo o vas a llamar a tu amigo?

B Hablando personalmente.
Contesten según el modelo.

> ¿Vas a levantarte?
> *No, porque acabo de levantarme.*

1. ¿Vas a lavarte las manos?
2. ¿Vas a cepillarte los dientes?
3. ¿Vas a bañarte?
4. ¿Vas a tomar el desayuno?
5. ¿Vas a salir para la escuela?

C ¿Quién acaba de hacerlo? Contesten según se indica.

1. ¿Quién acaba de salir? (Casandra)
2. ¿Quién acaba de llamar? (el amigo de Casandra)
3. ¿Quién acaba de contestar al teléfono? (yo)
4. ¿Quiénes acaban de hablar? (el amigo de Casandra y yo)

CAPÍTULO 8

Bell Ringer Review
Write the following on the board or use BRR Blackline Master 8-5: Complete with the present perfect. Keep your answers because you will need them later.
1. Él ___. (volver)
2. Yo lo ___. (ver)
3. Él y sus amigos ___ un viaje. (hacer)
4. Ellos ___ un mes en España. (pasar)

Note After completing the *Estructura* exercises, have students redo this Bell Ringer Review using *acabar de*.

Acabar de *con el infinitivo*

PRESENTATION (page 201)

Ask students to open their books to page 201. Guide them through the topic as they follow along in their books. Provide additional examples on the board.

Ejercicios A, B, and C

Exercises A, B, and C can be done with books open.

ANSWERS
Ejercicio A
Answers will vary.
1. Acabo de (voy a) leerlo.
2. Acabo de (voy a) escribirla.
3. Acabo de (voy a) tomarlo.
4. Acabo de (voy a) hacerlas.
5. Acabo de (voy a) llamarlo.

Ejercicio B
1. No, porque acabo de lavarme las manos.
2. No, porque acabo de cepillarme los dientes.
3. No, porque acabo de bañarme.
4. No, porque acabo de tomar el desayuno.
5. No, porque acabo de salir para la escuela.

Ejercicio C
1. Casandra acaba de salir.
2. El amigo de Casandra acaba de llamar.
3. Yo acabo de contestar al teléfono.
4. El amigo de Casandra y yo acabamos de hablar.

INDEPENDENT PRACTICE

Assign any of the following:
1. Workbook, *Estructura*
2. Communication Activities Masters, *Estructura*, B
3. Exercises on student page 201

CONVERSACIÓN

Bell Ringer Review
Write the following on the board or use BRR Blackline Master 8-6: Write four things you always did when you were a child. Remember to use the imperfect.

PRESENTATION (page 202)
A. Tell students they will hear a conversation between a customer and a hairdresser.
B. Have students close their books and listen as you read the conversation or play Cassette 5B.
C. Now have students open their books. Allow pairs time to practice the conversation a few times. Move around the classroom and model correct pronunciation as necessary.
D. Call on a volunteer to summarize the conversation in his/her own words.

Ejercicio
ANSWERS
1. Está en la peluquería.
2. Está hablando con el peluquero.
3. No, no quiere un champú.
4. Porque acaba de lavarse el pelo.
5. Él se lo va a cortar (va a cortárselo).
6. No lo quiere muy corto.
7. Quiere un recorte.
8. No, no quiere laca.
9. Prefiere el "look" natural.

CONVERSACIÓN

Escenas de la vida *En la peluquería*

PELUQUERO: ¿Un champú?
CLIENTE: No, gracias. Acabo de lavarme el pelo.
PELUQUERO: De acuerdo, pero quiero mojarle el pelo antes de cortárselo.
¿Prefiere Ud. el pelo largo o corto?
CLIENTE: Pues, no muy corto. Sólo quiero un recorte.
PELUQUERO: De acuerdo. Voy a quitarle un poco aquí a los lados y enfrente.
¿Quiere Ud. laca?
CLIENTE: No. Me gusta más el "look" natural.

La peluquería. Contesten según la conversación.
1. ¿Dónde está la joven?
2. ¿Con quién está hablando?
3. ¿Quiere un champú?
4. ¿Por qué no?
5. Después de mojarle el pelo, ¿qué hará el peluquero?
6. ¿Cómo quiere el pelo?
7. ¿Qué quiere, un corte o un recorte?
8. ¿Quiere laca?
9. ¿Qué "look" prefiere?

202 CAPÍTULO 8

COOPERATIVE LEARNING

Have teams assume the following roles—two hair stylists, and two clients who are in the stylists' chairs. The two clients are friends. The hair stylists offer suggestions for the clients' hair. The two clients disagree on how each other's hair should be styled. Have each group present its skit to the class.

INDEPENDENT PRACTICE

Assign any of the following:
1. Workbook, *Un poco más*
2. Exercise on student page 202

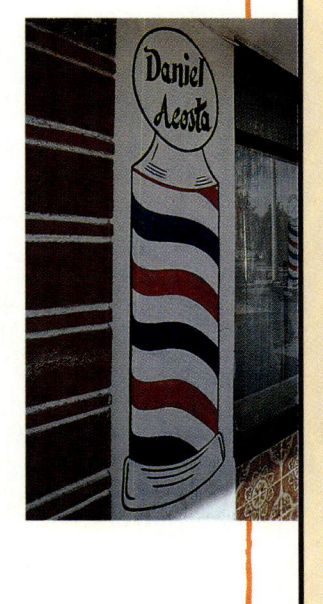

Comunicación

A **Voy a la peluquería.** Ud. tiene el pelo muy largo y decide visitar la peluquería. Hable con el/la peluquero(a) (un[a] compañero[a] de clase).

1. Dígale al/a la peluquero(a) que Ud. quiere un corte de pelo.
2. Él o ella le preguntará qué clase de corte quiere.
3. Él o ella le preguntará si quiere una raya o no, y dónde.
4. Él o ella le preguntará si quiere un corte con tijeras o con maquinilla.

B **Acabamos de…** Trabaje con un(a) compañero(a) de clase. Cada uno(a) preparará una lista de lo que acaba de hacer. Luego comparen sus listas y determinen cuáles de las cosas que los dos acaban de hacer son las mismas.

> Yo acabo de ____ y ____ no acaba de ____ .
> Yo acabo de ____ y ____ acaba de ____ también.
> Nosotros dos acabamos de ____ .

C **Pues acabo de…** Trabaje con un(a) compañero(a) de clase. Dígale algunas cosas que Ud. no va a hacer dentro de poco porque las acaba de hacer.

D **Tiene el pelo corto.** Trabaje con un(a) compañero(a) de clase. Descríbale el pelo y el peinado de otro(a) compañero(a) de clase. Él/ella adivinará a quién está Ud. describiendo. Luego, cambien de papel.

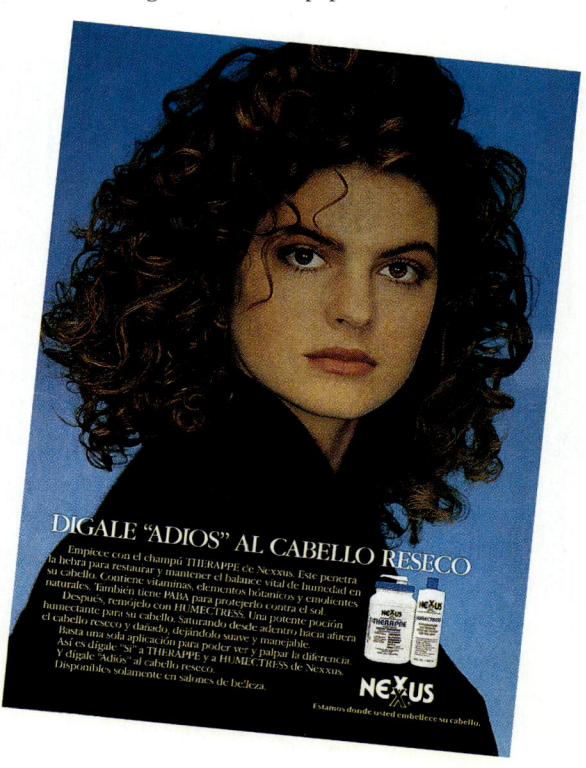

CAPÍTULO 8 203

LECTURA Y CULTURA

Bell Ringer Review

Write the following on the board or use BRR Blackline Master 8-7: Match the word in Column 1 with a related word in Column 2.

1. cortar   a. el lavado
2. lavar   b. el rizo
3. peinar   c. el corte
4. cepillar   d. el recorte
5. recortar   e. el peinado
6. secar   f. el secador
7. rizar   g. el cepillo

READING STRATEGIES
(page 204)

Pre-Reading
A. You may have two students present the reading as a TV interview. Select students who have good pronunciation and have them practice the conversation together a day prior to their classroom presentation.
B. Ask all students to bring in photos of themselves with different hairstyles.

Reading
A. Have the selected pair present their TV interview. Ask comprehension questions of the rest of the class.
B. Open a discussion of changing hairstyles to the whole class, who have now brought their photographs.

Post-reading
Ask students to describe the hairstyles that were "in" last year at your school and elsewhere in the U.S. What styles do they think will be "in" next year?

LECTURA Y CULTURA

NUEVOS PEINADOS EN LATINOAMÉRICA

—Raúl, en este momento, ¿cuál es el último grito de la moda en peinados?

—Francamente no sé cómo responderte. Es difícil, ¿sabes? Los estilos cambian muy de prisa. Este año domina el estilo corto. El "look" es natural, muy informal.

—¡Increíble! El año pasado yo estuve en Chile y todo el mundo tenía el pelo largo.

—Precisamente, como acabo de decirte—la moda cambia rápido. El estilo del momento es el peinado corto o el corte en capas[1], un poco de "gel" o gelatina, quizá—pero laca, no. ¿Y mañana? ¿Quién sabe? Yo tengo una amiga que es peluquera y hace poco estaba diciéndome que cree que dentro de poco el pelo largo va a estar de moda una vez más. ¿Es igual o parecido en los Estados Unidos?

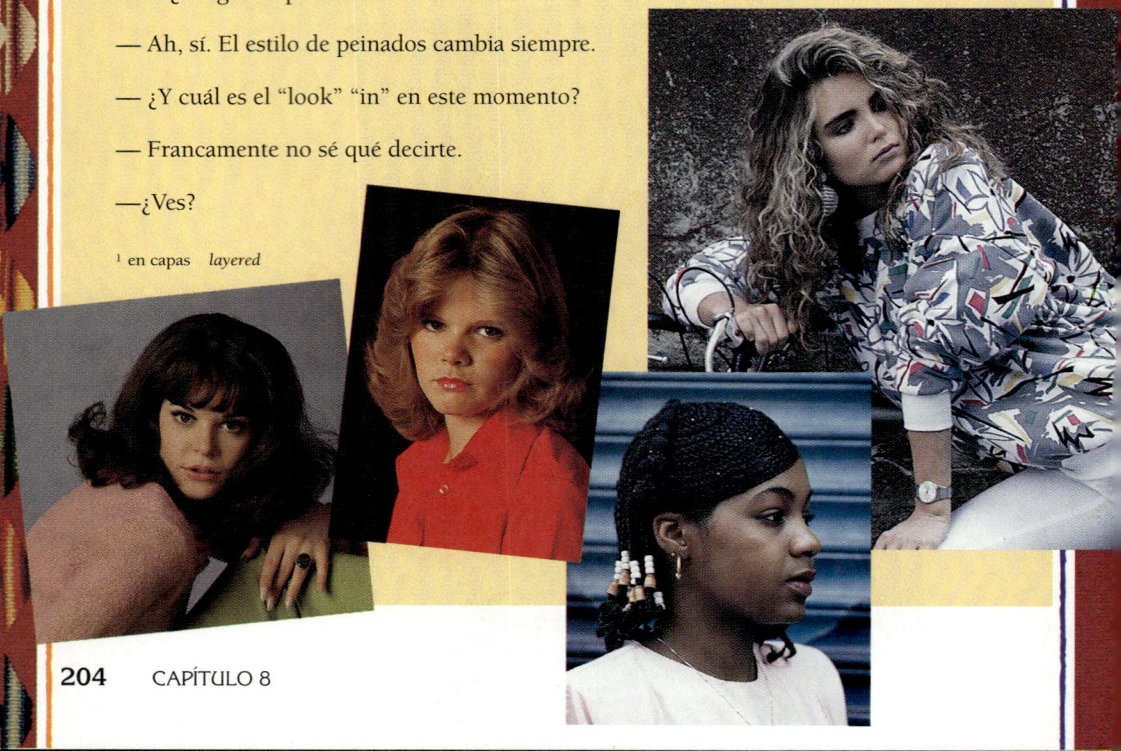

— Ah, sí. El estilo de peinados cambia siempre.

— ¿Y cuál es el "look" "in" en este momento?

— Francamente no sé qué decirte.

—¿Ves?

[1] en capas   *layered*

204   CAPÍTULO 8

LEARNING FROM PHOTOS

Refer to the photos on pages 204-205. Have students describe in as much detail as possible the people in the photos including their hairstyles.

Estudio de palabras

A ¿Cuál es la palabra en español? Escojan.

1. in
2. el gel
3. el look
4. el spray

a. la gelatina
b. la laca
c. de moda, en onda
d. la apariencia

B ¿Cuál es la definición? Escojan.

1. muy de prisa
2. una vez más
3. dentro de poco
4. parecido
5. en este momento
6. contestar

a. en poco tiempo, pronto
b. ahora
c. semejante
d. rápido
e. responder
f. otra vez

Comprensión

Los peinados. ¿Sí o no?

1. En Latinoamérica los estilos de peinados no cambian casi nunca.
2. El pelo corto domina siempre.
3. El "look" informal es muy sofisticado, muy elegante.
4. El "look" informal es más bien natural.
5. En este momento la gente lleva mucha laca.
6. Los peluqueros están diciendo que no volverá de moda el pelo largo.

CAPÍTULO 8

Estudio de palabras
ANSWERS
Ejercicio A
1. c
2. a
3. d
4. b

Ejercicio B
1. d
2. f
3. a
4. c
5. b
6. e

Comprensión
ANSWERS
1. No
2. No
3. No
4. Sí
5. No
6. No

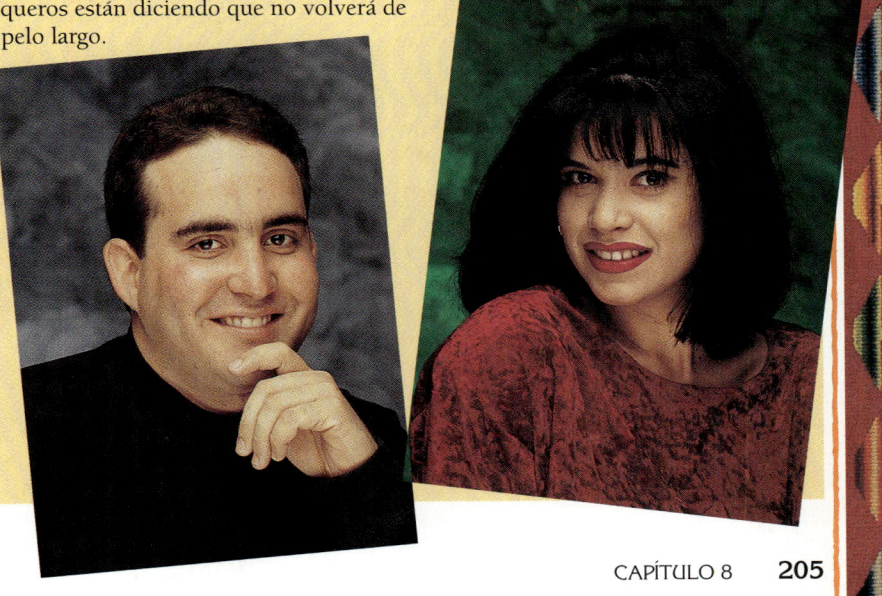

INDEPENDENT PRACTICE

Assign *Estudio de palabras* and *Comprensión* exercises on student page 205.

Bell Ringer Review

Write the following on the board or use BRR Blackline Master 8-8: Answer as you look at page 206.
¿Qué estás leyendo ahora?
¿Qué fotografías estás mirando?
¿Qué estás aprendiendo?

Descubrimiento Cultural

(The Descubrimiento *section is optional.)*

PRESENTATION *(pages 206-207)*

A. Before going through the selection with the class, take a survey. How many students go to a unisex hair stylist? How many go to a barber? How many go to a hairdresser for women?
B. Have students read the selection silently.
C. Have students tell you what they have learned from the selection.

DESCUBRIMIENTO CULTURAL

El pelo y los peinados han tenido siempre gran significado en todas las culturas. En Gran Bretaña los jueces[1] todavía llevan peluca[2]. Algunos militares y religiosos se cortan el pelo *al rape*, dejándose casi nada de pelo en la cabeza. En los países católicos muchos monjes llevan tonsura, una pequeña porción circular de la cabeza afeitada.

En las Américas, entre los indígenas, el peinado, igual que el vestido, frecuentemente identifica al grupo o a la tribu. Y el largo del pelo no tiene nada que ver con el sexo de la persona. En algunos grupos, los hombres llevan el pelo largo, a veces en trenza. En otros grupos, las mujeres se adornan las trenzas con cintas de colores vivos (brillantes). También hay peinados especiales para diferentes ocasiones. Hay peinados para el trabajo, para ir a misa y para ir de paseo[3]. Los adornos en la cabeza son importantes. Por ejemplo, los *caciques*[4] llevan un tipo de adorno y los *curanderos* otro. El arte que nos ha venido de los antiguos incas, aztecas y mayas nos muestra una variedad de peinados y adornos muy elaborados en las cabezas de los dioses. Todavía no sabemos el significado de cada uno.

Y, ¿quién se encarga del cuidado del pelo y la barba? Los peluqueros o barberos, por supuesto. El barbero es un personaje especial en la literatura hispana. El barbero ha tenido fama de independiente y hasta de anarquista. Trabaja por sí solo. No tiene jefes. Conoce todos los secretos del pueblo. Y el hombre que pone el cuello bajo la navaja del barbero pone allí su vida.

En Londres

En Guatemala

Indios otavaleños en el Ecuador

[1] jueces *judges*
[2] peluca *wig*
[3] ir de paseo *to go for a walk*
[4] caciques *chiefs*

206 CAPÍTULO 8

FOR THE NATIVE SPEAKER

Vocabulary enrichment Give students the following list of objects found in beauty parlors and barbershops and ask if they can describe them:
la peluca, el tinte, el cepillo de púas, el peine secapelos eléctrico, la cuchilla para entresacar el cabello, el cepillo de aire caliente, la maquinilla para cortar el pelo, la hoja de afeitar, la navaja de entresacar (aclarar)

Éste ha sido el tema de varios cuentos españoles y latinoamericanos. El barbero español ha sido figura importante en otras literaturas. "Fígaro", el barbero de Sevilla, aparece en la obra del francés Beaumarchais, y en la ópera del mismo nombre del italiano Rossini.

Hablando de los peinados y sus significados, una nota curiosa. Los toreros siempre han llevado coleta. Hoy la coleta es postiza[5], pero antiguamente era de verdad. Todo el mundo sabía quién era torero por la coleta. Cuando un torero se retira de su profesión hay una ceremonia. Al torero se le "corta la coleta". Esta ceremonia también existe al otro lado del mundo, también en conexión con un espectáculo tradicional, como es la corrida de toros. Se trata del Japón, y del "sumo". Los gigantescos atletas del "sumo", que pesan hasta 200 kilos, llevan el pelo en un moño encima de la cabeza. Cuando un "sumo" se retira de su profesión, él también se "corta la coleta".

[5] postiza *false*

Una coleta

CAPÍTULO 8 **207**

OPERA MADRID

Gioachino Rossini
El Barbero de Sevilla

11 y 13 de febrero – 7:30 p.m.

GEOGRAPHY CONNECTION

El mercado que tiene lugar los sábados por la mañana en Otavalo es popularísimo. Los otavaleños son tejedores (weavers) famosos en el mundo entero. Noten que son los otavaleños que llevan el pelo largo en una trenza.

LEARNING FROM PHOTOS

El traje que lleva el torero se llama "traje de luces". El sombrero es una "montera". Los trajes de luces son carísimos porque llevan muchos adornos y todo el trabajo se hace a mano.

LEARNING FROM REALIA

Ask students the following questions: *¿Cómo se llama la ópera? ¿Dónde se está presentando? ¿Cuál es la fecha de la función? ¿A qué hora empieza?*

207

REALIDADES

(The Realidades *section is optional.)*

Bell Ringer Review

Write the following on the board or use BRR Blackline Master 8-9: Make a list of the events for which you like to look really good.

PRESENTATION *(pages 208-209)*

A. Have students read the captions silently and enjoy the photographs. Encourage them to ask questions, express opinions, and discuss the information.

B. In regard to the photos and realia in the *Realidades* section, you may wish to give students the following information:
Realia 3: Spanish soaps are famous for their softness. All soaps are made with fat. Fine soaps from Spain are made with olive oil. These soaps are known internationally as "Castile Soap." *Magno* soap, which is black, is made with a special water and comes from an island off the coast of Galicia.
Photo 4: The Mayas of Guatemala are extraordinary weavers. Each group has its own intricate pattern that distinguishes its parchments from those of other groups.
Photo 6: The word *guagua* is a very interesting word. In the Caribbean Spanish-speaking countries it means "bus." It is also used for "bus" in the *Islas Canarias.* In some Andean countries, namely Perú and Bolivia, *guagua* is the word for "child," almost in the sense of "kid." In the Quechua language a *guagua* is a type of papoose that Indian women use to carry their babies.

REALIDADES

Esta perfumería elegante se encuentra en la Zona Rosa de la Ciudad de México **1**.

El barbero le está dando un corte de pelo a su cliente en una barbería de la Ciudad de México **2**.

Aquí vemos tres pastillas de jabón **3**. ¿De qué marcas son? Magno, Heno de Pravia y Maja son tres marcas españolas muy conocidas por su suavidad.

Unas señoras de ascendencia maya en Guatemala con sus peinados tradicionales **4**.

Una señora indígena de las islas de San Blas, Panamá **5**.

Una boliviana del altiplano de Bolivia con sombrero típico **6**.

208

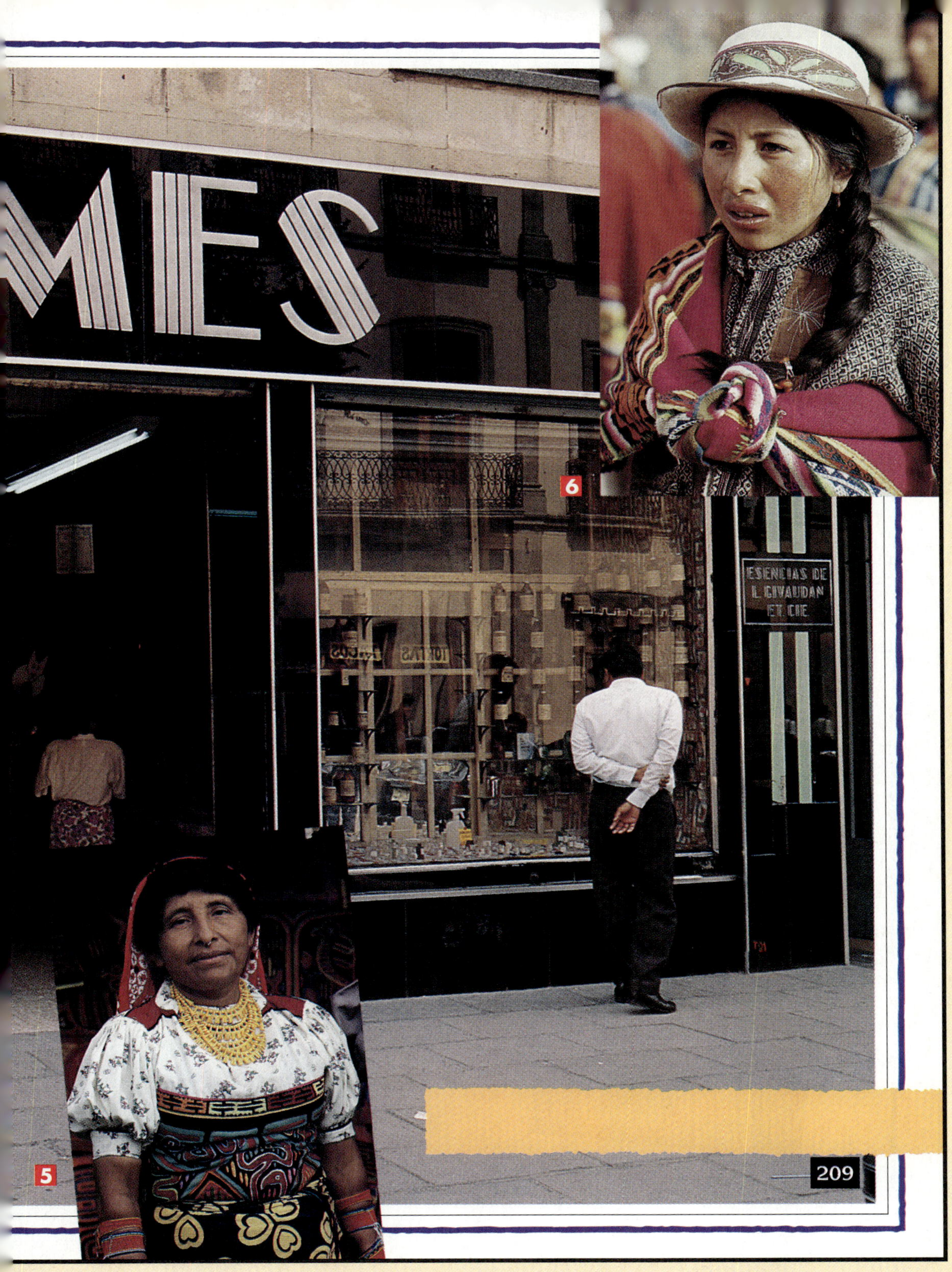
MES
ESENCIAS DE
L. GIVAUDAN
ET CIE
6
5
209

CULMINACIÓN

RECYCLING

The *Comunicación oral* and *Comunicación escrita* activities encourage students to use all the language they have learned in the chapter, and to recombine it with material from previous chapters. It is not necessary to do all the activities with all students. Select the ones you consider most appropriate or allow students to choose the ones they wish to do.

Comunicación oral
ANSWERS
Actividades A and B
Answers will vary.

INFORMAL ASSESSMENT
Activity A can be used to evaluate the speaking skills informally. You may assign a grade based on the student's ability to communicate in Spanish. Use the evaluation criteria given on page 24 of this Teacher's Wraparound Edition.

Comunicación escrita
ANSWERS
Actividad
Answers will vary.

CULMINACIÓN

Comunicación oral

A **Quiero…** Ud. está en una peluquería en un país hispanohablante. Hable con el/la peluquero(a) (su compañero[a]) y dígale cómo Ud. quiere o no quiere el pelo.

B **Los peinados.** En sus propias palabras, describa a un(a) compañero(a) el "look" en peinados que está en onda en este momento en los Estados Unidos. Si hay una gran diferencia entre los peinados masculinos y femeninos, describa estas diferencias.

Comunicación escrita

¡Qué peinados! En un párrafo describa cada uno de los siguientes peinados.

1.
2.
3.
4.

210 CAPÍTULO 8

INDEPENDENT PRACTICE

Assign any of the following:
1. Exercises on student pages 210-211
2. Workbook, *Mi autobiografía*
3. Chapter 8, Situation Cards

Reintegración

A **Un día típico.** Preguntas personales.

1. ¿A qué hora te levantas por la mañana?
2. ¿Se levanta tu hermano(a) a la misma hora?
3. ¿Te lavas la cara y las manos?
4. ¿Te lavas el pelo todos los días?
5. ¿Cuántas veces al día te cepillas los dientes?
6. ¿Qué marca de pasta dentífrica empleas?

B **La escuela primaria.** Preguntas personales.

1. ¿A qué escuela primaria asistías?
2. ¿Quién era tu maestro(a) favorito(a)?
3. ¿Ibas a la escuela a pie o tomabas el autobús?
4. ¿Almorzabas en la cafetería de la escuela o volvías a casa?

Vocabulario

SUSTANTIVOS
el pelo
el cabello
la raya
el moño
la cola de caballo
los rizos
el flequillo
el peinado afro
la onda
el bucle
la patilla
el bigote
la peluquería
el/la peluquero(a)
el/la barbero(a)

el corte de pelo
el recorte
el lavado
el rizado
el peine
el cepillo
el secador
el rizador
las tijeras
la navaja
la maquinilla
la horquilla
el rulo
la pinza para el cabello
el champú
la laca

ADJETIVOS
liso(a)
lacio(a)
rizado(a)
crespo(a)
largo(a)
corto(a)
rubio(a)
castaño(a)
negro(a)
rojo(a)

VERBOS
cortar
recortar
rizar
peinar(se)
cepillar(se)
acabar de

OTRAS PALABRAS Y EXPRESIONES
arriba
en frente
atrás
al lado
en el cuello

CAPÍTULO 8   211

NUESTRO MUNDO

(optional material)

OVERVIEW

All the readings presented in the *Nuestro Mundo* section are authentic, uncut texts from publications of the Hispanic world. Students should be encouraged to read the text for overall meaning, but not intensively, word for word. Students should find satisfaction in their ability to derive meaning from "real" texts. Each reading is related to a theme or themes covered in the previous four chapters.

PRESENTATION *(page 212)*

A. Have students open their books to page 212 and ask them to read the three notices silently.
B. Allow students to answer the questions orally.

Note You may prefer to assign the readings and questions for independent practice.

ANSWERS

1. a
2. c

212

NUESTRO MUNDO

It pays to read the fine print. Here are a number of hotel forms from Spain and Latin America.

HOTEL-RESIDENCIA COVADONGA

No olvide entregar su llave y retirar su documentación.

1. What are they telling you?
   a. Remember to hand in your key and pick up your passport or I.D.
   b. Leave your valuables in the safe before retiring.
   c. Hand in your laundry and laundry list before going to bed.

REGENTE HOTEL

La Administración se hace solamente responsable de los valores depositados en la Caja del Hotel contra recibo.

2. The hotel is responsible only for valuables
   a. held in the cash register
   b. deposited in the bank by hotel staff
   c. left in the hotel safe with a receipt

212   NUESTRO MUNDO

DID YOU KNOW?

In traditional hotels in Spain and Latin America, the room key is attached to a large, heavy disk or block made of metal, plastic, or wood. The purpose is to discourage guests from taking the key with them when they go out. The key should be left with the concierge (*el conserje*), who puts it in the *casillero del correo* or "pigeon holes" along with the guests' mail or messages.

In Spanish hotels, guests are required to leave their passports or national I.D. cards when checking in. This information is made available to the police. Guests can usually retrieve their passports within an hour.

The following note was left for a hotel guest in Santafé de Bogotá, Colombia.

> DE: ANA MARÍA BELLO
> FECHA: 28 Abril
> PARA: D. Manuel Madero Príncipe, hab. 306
>
> Su reserva ha sido confirmada para el 1º de Mayo.
> Bogotá – Miami
> Vuelo 916 Saliendo 11:30 am.
> Favor presentarse al aeropuerto a las 8:30 a.m.
> Su récord localizador es R/RCEYJE
> ¡Feliz viaje!
> A-A American Airlines

1. The note tells the guest that his flight has been ___.
   a. booked   b. cancelled   c. confirmed
2. The passenger's name is ___.
   a. Madero   b. Bello   c. Receyje
3. Flight departure time is ___.
   a. 8:30   b. 9:16   c. 11:30
4. The passenger should get to the airport by ___.
   a. 8:30   b. 9:16   c. 11:30
5. A "récord localizador" is probably ___.
   a. an alarm clock/radio   b. a computer file locater code   c. an aircraft flight recorder
6. The person getting the note is wished a ___.
   a. happy birthday   b. pleasant journey   c. prosperous New Year

NUESTRO MUNDO

ABOUT THE LANGUAGE

1. The abbreviation for ordinal numbers is the cardinal number with a superscript "o" or "a." Thus, *la Quinta Avenida* could be written as *la 5ª Avenida*.
2. In the note on page 213, the months *Abril* and *Mayo* have been capitalized. The names of months can be written with or without an initial capital letter. Lower case is more common.

ANSWERS
1. c
2. a
3. c
4. a
5. b
6. b

REPASO
CAPÍTULOS 5-8

OVERVIEW

This section reviews key grammatical structures and vocabulary from Chapters 5-8. The topics were first presented on the following pages: the conditional, pages 122-124; two object pronouns in the same sentence, page 126; the present perfect, page 148; comparisons of equality, page 177.

REVIEW RESOURCES

1. Workbook, Self-Test 2
2. Computer Software
3. Testing Program, Unit Test 5-8

Conversación

PRESENTATION *(page 214)*

A. Have students close their books and listen as you read the conversation.
B. Have students open their books to page 214 and call on two volunteers to read the conversation to the class with as much expression as possible.
C. Have an individual summarize the conversation in his/her own words.

ABOUT THE LANGUAGE

The bellboy has traditionally been called *el botones* because of the shiny brass buttons on his uniform.

ANSWERS

1. Están en un coche.
2. Las propinas pasan directamente a la cuenta de la compañía. La tripulación no paga.
3. No tiene vuelo mañana.
4. Este hotel cuesta menos.
5. No se paga por estacionar.
6. Iban al Excélsior.

REPASO

CAPÍTULOS 5–8

Conversación

MUJER: Yo estaba pensando en hacer un poco de turismo. Como no tenemos vuelo mañana, me gustaría ir al campo. Por eso alquilé el coche. También me gusta conducir y en el hotel no se paga por estacionar.

HOMBRE: Nos han cambiado de hotel otra vez. Me han dicho que este hotel es tan bueno como el Excélsior y no cuesta tanto como los otros hoteles. Oye, cuando suben el equipaje, ¿tenemos que darle una propina al botones?

MUJER: No. Pasan las propinas directamente a la cuenta de la compañía. La tripulación no paga. He estado en este hotel antes. Los cuartos son grandes y tienen aire acondicionado y televisor. Acabo de ver una gasolinera en la esquina. Vamos a parar. Quiero revisar todo, los frenos, el aceite y las gomas, antes de salir al campo. ¿Quieres ir con nosotros mañana? Hay sitio, este sedán es grande. Estaríamos muy contentos de tenerte con nosotros.

HOMBRE: Con mucho gusto. Pero necesito un recorte. Me queda largo el pelo. Mira, mientras te revisan el coche yo me recortaré en esa peluquería.

MUJER: Uds. los asistentes de vuelo tienen que tratar con el público. En la cabina de mando no tenemos que preocuparnos tanto. Estaré en la gasolinera. Y como hemos aterrizado temprano, en la recepción no nos esperan hasta más tarde.

■ **En el hotel.** Contesten.
1. ¿Dónde están el hombre y la mujer?
2. ¿Por qué no tiene que darle una propina al botones?
3. ¿Por qué alquiló un coche la mujer?
4. ¿Cuál es la razón por el cambio de hoteles?
5. ¿Qué le gusta a la mujer del nuevo hotel?
6. ¿A qué hotel iban antes?
7. ¿Por qué quiere parar la mujer?
8. ¿Qué tipo de coche alquiló la mujer?
9. ¿Qué tiene que hacer el hombre? ¿Por qué?
10. ¿Cuál será la profesión del hombre?
11. ¿Qué será la mujer?
12. ¿Por qué no les esperan hasta más tarde en la recepción del hotel?

COOPERATIVE LEARNING

Using maps, have teams write directions from one point to another. They should not give away the destination but only write the directions to it. Teams exchange maps and directions. The second team must follow the first's directions and to see if they arrive at the correct destination.

LEARNING FROM REALIA

Refer students to the hotel brochure on page 214. Tell them that it is from a small hotel in Santiago, Chile. Ask what they think *un pequeño lujo* means. Above the name of the hotel are the letters M.R., which stand for *Marca Registrada* (trademark). Ask students if they know what that means. Ask: ¿Para qué es el panfleto? ¿Cómo se llama el hotel?

Estructura

El potencial o condicional

The conditional is used in Spanish as in English to express what would take place under certain circumstances. It is formed by adding *-ía, -ías, -ía, -íamos, (-íais)*, or *-ían* to the appropriate stem. The stem for the conditional is the same as for the future. In regular verbs, it is the entire infinitive.

dar	daría, darías, daría, daríamos, *daríais*, darían
ver	vería, verías, vería, veríamos, *veríais*, verían
oír	oiría, oirías, oiría, oiríamos, *oiríais*, oirían

Remember that the same verbs irregular in the future tense are irregular in the conditional.

INFINITIVE	STEM	CONDITIONAL
tener	tendr-	tendría
salir	saldr-	saldría
venir	vendr-	vendría
poner	pondr-	pondría
saber	sabr-	sabría
poder	podr-	podría
decir	dir-	diría
hacer	har-	haría
querer	querr-	querría

A ¿Qué haríamos? Contesten con el condicional.

Ellos van a jugar.
Pues, nosotros no jugaríamos.

1. Ellos van a poder comprar el coche.
2. Ellos van a tener bastante dinero.
3. Ella va a conducir.
4. Ella va a estacionar el coche en la calle.
5. Ellos van a frenar.
6. Ellos van a saber qué hacer.
7. Ella va a poner los intermitentes.
8. Ellos van a revisar el motor cada semana.
9. Ellos van a venir por el camino viejo.

CAPÍTULOS 5–8 REPASO 215

Los complementos

PRESENTATION (page 216)
Have students open their books to page 216. Ask them to read steps 1 and 2 silently. Field any questions they may have.

PRESENTATION
Ejercicio B
If students have difficulty completing Exercise B, you may go back to some of the suggestions given in the appropriate sections of Chapters 5 and 6.

ANSWERS
Ejercicio B
1. Sí, me lo lavó.
2. Sí, se la di.
3. Sí, se lo cortó.
4. Sí, ella se la dio.
5. Sí, nos las dieron.
6. Sí, se la recomendamos.

El presente perfecto de verbos regulares

PRESENTATION (page 216)
A. Write the forms of *haber* on the board.
B. Have students open their books to page 216 and ask them to repeat the past participles in step 1 after you.
C. Have students read the irregular past participles in step 2 aloud.
D. Write the present perfect of two verbs on the board in paradigm order.
E. Have students repeat the paradigms.

Los complementos

1. When both a direct and an indirect object pronoun are used in the same sentence, the indirect object pronoun always precedes the direct object pronoun.

   La Sra. Ruiz me vendió el coche.
   La Sra. Ruiz me lo vendió.

2. The indirect object pronouns *le* and *les* change to *se* when used with the direct object pronouns *lo, los, la, las*. Because *se* can mean *a él, a ella, a Ud., a ellos, a ellas*, or *a Uds.* a prepositional phrase is often added for clarity.

   ¿A quién le regalaste los esquís?
   Yo se los regalé *a ella*.

B ¿Qué hicieron? Contesten que *sí* y usen pronombres.

1. ¿Braulio te lavó el pelo?
2. ¿Y le diste la propina?
3. ¿Y Josefina le cortó el pelo a tu hermana?
4. ¿Y tu hermana también le dio la propina?
5. ¿Y les dieron las gracias a Uds.?
6. ¿Recomendaron Uds. la peluquería a los amigos?

El presente perfecto de verbos regulares

1. Remember, the present perfect tense is used to express an action completed recently. It is formed by combining the present tense of the verb *haber* with the past participle. The past participle is formed by dropping the infinitive ending and adding *-ado* to *-ar* verbs and *-ido* to *-er* and *-ir* verbs.

limpiar	he limpiado, has limpiado, ha limpiado, hemos limpiado, *habéis limpiado*, han limpiado
comer	he comido, has comido, ha comido, hemos comido, *habéis comido*, han comido
subir	he subido, has subido, ha subido, hemos subido, *habéis subido*, han subido

2. These verbs have irregular past participles.

decir	dicho	devolver	devuelto
hacer	hecho	morir	muerto
ver	visto	volver	vuelto
escribir	escrito	cubrir	cubierto
poner	puesto	abrir	abierto

LEARNING FROM REALIA
Have students say all they can about the ad on page 216. You may wish to ask: *¿Para qué es el anuncio? ¿Qué quiere decir "unisex"? ¿Cuál es la profesión del señor Ormazábal? ¿Cuál es la dirección de la peluquería?*

INDEPENDENT PRACTICE
Assign any of the following:
1. Exercises on student pages 214–217
2. Workbook, Self-Test 2

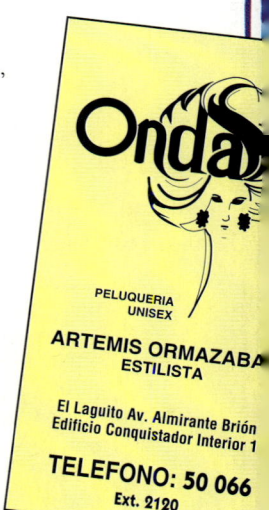

C **Llegaron al hotel.** Contesten con *no* y el presente perfecto.

1. ¿Ya llegaron los Fernández?
2. ¿Ya fueron a recepción?
3. ¿Llenaron la ficha?
4. ¿El mozo les subió el equipaje?
5. ¿El Sr. Fernández ya estacionó el coche?
6. ¿Paco encontró la reservación?

D **En la gasolinera.** Completen con el presente perfecto.

Marisa ___(1)___ (volver) a la gasolinera. Pero ellos no ___(2)___ (abrir) todavía. Nadie le ___(3)___ (decir) a Marisa que los sábados abren tarde. Y, ¿qué ___(4)___ (hacer) ella? Pues ___(5)___ (escribir) una nota y la ___(6)___ (poner) en el parabrisas. Y ___(7)___ (irse) a tomar un café.

Comparativos de igualdad

1. When two things that are equal are compared, the expression "as… as" is used in English. The Spanish equivalent is *tan… como*. *Tan* is always followed by an adjective or adverb.

    José es tan bajo como Roberto.

2. The Spanish equivalent of "as many as" or "as much as" is *tanto… como*. Because *tanto* will usually modify a noun, it must agree with the noun in number and gender.

    Tenemos tantos sellos como ellos.

E **Tengo tantos.** Combinen las frases usando *tan… como* or *tanto… como*.

1. El tren es conveniente. El avión es conveniente.
2. El tren cuesta $200. El avión cuesta $200.
3. El tren tiene 250 asientos. El avión tiene 250 asientos.
4. Las comidas en el tren son buenas. Las comidas en el avión son buenas.
5. Los asientos en el tren son cómodos. Los asientos en el avión son cómodos.

Comunicación

Una reservación. Ud. quiere reservar un cuarto en el Hotel Nacional. Escríbale una carta al hotel. Incluya todos los detalles necesarios.

CAPÍTULOS 5–8 REPASO

FONDO ACADÉMICO

**LAS CIENCIAS:
LA METEOROLOGÍA**
(optional material)

Antes de leer

PRESENTATION (page 218)

A. Have students open their books to page 218 and give a brief definition of the terms put forth in the *Antes de leer* section.
B. Refer students to the illustration in order to provide more technical terms they will need for the reading.
C. Have students scan the selection for cognates.

Lectura

PRESENTATION (pages 218-219)

A. Explain to students that they should try to get the general idea of the selection, but that it is not necessary that they understand every word.
B. Have students read the selection silently.
C. Have pairs prepare lists of all the weather terms they can find in the selection.

FONDO ACADÉMICO

LAS CIENCIAS: LA METEOROLOGÍA

Antes de leer

In the following selection you will review the difference between weather and climate, what causes the seasons, and how climates can change. Please review the following terms in preparation: atmosphere, climate, latitude, altitude, axis, and rotation.

Lectura

EL TIEMPO Y EL CLIMA

El tiempo es la condición diaria de la atmósfera en un lugar específico. El clima es la combinación de condiciones típicas de la atmósfera en una región durante un período de tiempo muy largo. Los vientos, la altura, la latitud y la proximidad de los mares y lagos[1] grandes afectan el clima.

Ya sabemos que la Tierra gira alrededor del Sol en una órbita. La Tierra también da vueltas sobre su eje[2]. La rotación de la Tierra alrededor de su eje causa el día y la noche. El eje de la Tierra está inclinado, y por eso tenemos estaciones del año. Sin esa inclinación y la órbita de la Tierra alrededor del Sol, los días y las noches serían de 12 horas durante todo el año, y no tendríamos estaciones diferentes. Durante el verano los rayos del Sol son más directos que en el invierno. Por eso hace más calor en el verano. Cerca del ecuador[3] (las latitudes entre los grados 23 1/2 norte y 23 1/2 sur) los rayos del Sol llegan en un ángulo[4] de 90 grados durante todo el año. Las latitudes medias se extienden de los 23 1/2 grados a los 66 1/2 grados a los dos lados del ecuador. Como los rayos del Sol son más oblicuos[5], las temperaturas son más moderadas[6]. De las latitudes norte y sur de 66 1/2 grados hasta los polos norte y sur están las zonas más frías del planeta. Esas regiones casi no reciben rayos directos del Sol.

El aire caliente se expande y sube. Tiene baja presión. El aire frío se contrae[7] y baja. Tiene alta presión. Cerca del ecuador el aire se calienta y sube moviendo las capas[8] altas de aire hacia los polos. En los polos el aire se enfría y baja. El aire frío se mueve en dirección de los polos al ecuador, y el aire caliente va

---

CRITICAL THINKING ACTIVITY

(Thinking skills: seeing consequences; problem-solving)

Write the following on the board or on an overhead transparency:

En la Lectura dice que la Tierra da vueltas sobre su eje, y que el eje de la Tierra está inclinado. Vamos a decir que algo cambia el grado de inclinación del eje. ¿Qué pasaría?

LEARNING FROM REALIA

Refer students to the map of the world on page 218. Have them locate and name in Spanish the continents and oceans. Have them also describe where each of the following is located: *el ecuador, el polo norte, el continente de África, el Trópico de Capricornio, la Antártida, el océano Pacífico.*

FONDO ACADÉMICO

del ecuador a los polos. La rotación de la Tierra hace mover los vientos en el hemisferio norte hacia la derecha. En el hemisferio sur se mueven hacia la izquierda. En los dos hemisferios los vientos que van hacia el ecuador soplan[9] de este a oeste. Los vientos que van hacia los polos soplan de oeste a este. Estos vientos traen temperaturas altas a las latitudes medias.

La altura es la elevación sobre el nivel del mar[10]. La altura de una región afecta su temperatura. Mientras más alta la región, más fría. La altura también afecta la precipitación. Cuando un viento caliente pasa por encima de una montaña se enfría, se condensa, forma nubes, y llueve antes de llegar al otro lado. Por eso un lado de la montaña es más verde y húmedo que el otro.

Debido a que el agua absorbe el calor más lentamente que la tierra y lo mantiene por más tiempo, los vientos que pasan sobre el mar traen aire templado a las regiones costeras. En el invierno los continentes se enfrían y en el verano se calientan[11] más rápidamente que los océanos. Por eso las regiones costeras tienen climas más templados.

Los climas cambian a través de largos períodos de tiempo. La destrucción de la vegetación y la contaminación atmosférica pueden causar cambios más rápidos en el clima.

[1] lagos *lakes*
[2] eje *axis*
[3] ecuador *equator*
[4] ángulo *angle*
[5] oblicuos *angled, oblique*
[6] moderadas *moderate*
[7] se contrae *contracts*
[8] capas *layers*
[9] soplan *blow*
[10] nivel del mar *sea level*
[11] se calientan *become warm*

Después de leer

A El tiempo. Contesten.

1. ¿Cuál es la diferencia entre el tiempo y el clima?
2. ¿Cuáles son algunos factores que afectan el clima?
3. ¿Cómo se llama la ruta de la Tierra alrededor del Sol?
4. ¿Sobre qué da vueltas el planeta Tierra?
5. ¿Qué es lo que causa el día y la noche?
6. ¿Durante qué estación del año son más directos los rayos del Sol?
7. ¿Entre qué latitudes hace calor durante todo el año?
8. ¿Cuáles son las latitudes de las zonas templadas?
9. ¿Cuál es el clima entre las latitudes 66 1/2 grados y los polos?
10. ¿Qué tipo de presión tiene el aire caliente?
11. ¿Qué es lo que causa el movimiento de los vientos a la derecha y a la izquierda?
12. ¿Cuál es la relación entre altura y temperatura?
13. ¿Qué puede acelerar los cambios en el clima?

B Seguimiento. Contesten.

1. Explique cómo los vientos afectan el clima.
2. Describa lo que pasa cuando los vientos pasan por las montañas.
3. Prepare un dibujo que enseña la rotación de la Tierra sobre su eje y la órbita de la Tierra alrededor del Sol.
4. Sobre un mapa de las Américas describa el movimiento de los vientos.
5. Explique por qué la gente va a la costa durante el verano.

CRITICAL THINKING ACTIVITY

(*Thinking skills: evaluating information*)
Write the following on the board or on an overhead transparency:
Los pronósticos del tiempo preparados por los expertos frecuentemente no son precisos y contienen errores. ¿Por qué?

Después de leer
PRESENTATION (*page 219*)
Ask students these questions: *¿Qué tiempo hace hoy? Descríbelo con todos los detalles posibles.*

ANSWERS
Ejercicio A
1. El tiempo es la condición diaria de la atmósfera en un lugar específico. El clima es la combinación de condiciones típicas de la atmósfera en una región durante un período de tiempo muy largo.
2. los vientos, la altura, la latitud y la proximidad de los mares y lagos grandes
3. La ruta se llama una órbita.
4. Da vueltas sobre su eje.
5. la rotación de la Tierra
6. Los rayos son más directos en verano.
7. las latitudes entre los grados 23 1/2 norte y 23 1/2 sur
8. las latitudes entre los 23 1/2 grados a los 66 1/2 grados
9. el clima más frío del planeta
10. Tiene baja presión.
11. la rotación de la Tierra
12. Mientras más alta la región, más fría.
13. La destrucción de la vegetación y la contaminación atmosférica pueden causar cambios más rápidos en el clima.

Ejercicio B
1. Los vientos que van hacia los polos soplan de oeste a este. Traen temperaturas altas a las latitudes medias.
2. Cuando un viento caliente pasa por encima de una montaña se enfría, se condensa, forma nubes y llueve antes de llegar al otro lado.
3. Answers will vary.
4. Answers will vary.
5. Los vientos que pasan sobre el mar traen aire templado a las regiones costeras. Hay un clima más templado en la costa hasta en verano.

FONDO ACADÉMICO

LAS CIENCIAS SOCIALES:
LA HISTORIA

Antes de leer
PRESENTATION *(page 220)*
A. Have students open their books to page 220. Ask them to read the *Antes de leer* information.
B. Have students discuss what they already know from their study of American history.
C. Refer students to the map on page 221.

Lectura
PRESENTATION *(pages 220-221)*
A. Have students read the selection silently.
B. Ask comprehension questions such as: *¿Cuándo nació la idea de una carretera panamericana? ¿Cuándo empezó la contrucción?*, etc.

FONDO ACADÉMICO

LAS CIENCIAS SOCIALES: LA HISTORIA

Antes de leer

The jungles and mountains of Latin America have made travel there extremely difficult. In many areas travel by air was far more feasible than overland travel. The idea of a highway from the United States to the end of South America was a dream that took over half a century to become reality. In preparation for the selection, please study the map provided and review the history of the Pan American Highway.

Lectura

LA CARRETERA PANAMERICANA

La idea de una carretera para unir[1] las repúblicas americanas nació en 1923 durante la Conferencia Internacional de los Estados Americanos. En 1929 adoptaron un plan general para la carretera. La construcción empezó en 1930 y tomó más de 30 años para completar.

La carretera cubre unos 27.000 kilómetros. Comienza en Alaska, atraviesa[2] el Canadá y los EE.UU. Pasa por México y Centroamérica hasta llegar a Chile. Otras carreteras que conectan con la Panamericana llegan a Paraguay, la Argentina y Brasil. Algunos países construyeron carreteras secundarias para conectar la Panamericana con áreas antes inaccesibles. Sin contar las carreteras de los EE.UU. que forman, oficialmente, parte de la Carretera Panamericana, la extensión total del sistema es de unos 72.000 kilómetros. La carretera conecta todas las capitales de Centroamérica. La Carretera Simón Bolívar es parte de la Panamericana. Va desde Caracas, Venezuela, por Bogotá, Colombia, a Quito, Ecuador. Desde Quito la Panamericana continúa hacia el sur. Continúa por la costa oeste pasando por Lima y Arequipa, Perú y Antofagasta, Chile, antes de llegar a Santiago. Después de Santiago la carretera vira[3] al este y se extiende unos 1.450 kilómetros hasta Buenos Aires. Hay una ruta alternativa de la Panamericana que comienza en Arequipa, Perú y pasa por La Paz, Bolivia, para llegar a Buenos Aires (unos 3.815 kilómetros). Desde Buenos Aires hay tres rutas que van al este y al norte. Una va a Asunción, Paraguay; otra pasa por Montevideo hasta Porto Alegre, Brasil; la tercera pasa por Curitiba, Brasil, a Río de Janeiro.

CRITICAL THINKING ACTIVITY

(Thinking skills: making inferences)
Write the following on the board or on an overhead transparency.
La Carretera Panamericana conecta, físicamente, las repúblicas del gran continente americano. ¿En qué otras maneras une las Américas?

LEARNING FROM PHOTOS

Refer students to the photo on page 220 and ask them to describe the area shown.

FONDO ACADÉMICO

En la Carretera Panamericana, cerca de todas las grandes ciudades se encuentran gasolineras, hoteles y restaurantes. La carretera pasa por selvas tropicales y montañas altas, hasta de una altura de 4.570 metros. La Carretera Panamericana conecta, físicamente, las repúblicas del gran continente americano.

[1] unir — to unite
[2] atraviesa — it goes through, it passes through
[3] vira — it turns

Después de leer

A La Carretera Panamericana. Completen.

1. Se presentó la idea de una carretera en el año ____.
2. En 1929 se adoptó un ____ general para la carretera.
3. En el norte, la carretera comienza en ____.
4. El largo de la carretera es de unos ____ kilómetros.
5. 72.000 kilómetros es la ____ de la carretera.
6. La sección entre Caracas y Quito se llama Carretera ____.
7. La carretera va por la costa hasta llegar a ____.
8. La ruta alternativa va de ____ a Buenos Aires.
9. Las carreteras que van a Montevideo y Asunción comienzan en ____.
10. El lugar más alto en la carretera es de ____ metros.

B Seguimiento. Contesten.

1. Indique las capitales por las que pasa la Panamericana.
2. Explique por qué tomó tanto tiempo construir la carretera.
3. Explique la razón por el nombre de la sección de la Panamericana entre Caracas y Quito.

FONDO ACADÉMICO 221

Después de leer

PRESENTATION (page 221)

A. Go over the *Después de leer* activities.
B. Say to students: *Nombre tres capitales por las que pasa la Panamericana. ¿Cuántos años tomó para completar? ¿Cuántos kilómetros cubre? ¿Qué se encuentra en la Carretera?*

ANSWERS

Ejercicio A
1. 1923
2. plan
3. Alaska
4. 27.000 kilómetros
5. extensión
6. Simón Bolívar
7. Santiago
8. Arequipa
9. Buenos Aires
10. 4.570

Ejercicio B
Answers will vary.

LEARNING FROM REALIA

Have students trace the route of the *Carretera Panamericana* on a map which shows latitudes and ask them the number of climatic zones through which it passes. Ask: *¿Por cuántas diferentes zonas climáticas pasa la Carretera Panamericana?*

FONDO ACADÉMICO

LAS HUMANIDADES: LA MITOLOGÍA

Antes de leer

The dream of flight dates back to earliest time. Leonardo Da Vinci conceived a kind of flying machine that appeared among his sketches. The following selection is about a myth concerning flight. It is the myth of Daedalus. It comes to us from ancient Greece. Most myths present a moral or lesson. The myth of Daedalus is no exception. As you read consider what the lesson or lessons might be. In preparation, please familiarize yourself with the following figures and terms in Greek mythology:

KING MINOS: A king and lawgiver of ancient Crete. He was the son of Zeus, the chief god of the ancient Greeks.

THE MINOTAUR: A fabulous monster, half bull and half man, he was confined in the Cretan labyrinth and fed with human flesh.

LABYRINTH: An intricate combination of passages in which it is difficult or impossible to reach the exit.

MINERVA: Goddess of wisdom, patroness of the arts and trades.

"El Minotauro" de Pablo Pica

Lectura

DÉDALO

Dédalo era un arquitecto de Atenas, Grecia. El rey Minos le mandó hacer un laberinto. Minos quería meter al Minotauro, un monstruo con cabeza de toro[1] y cuerpo de hombre, en el laberinto. Dédalo perdió el favor de Minos, y el rey lo hizo prisionero y lo metió en una torre[2]. Dédalo pudo escapar de la torre con su hijo, Ícaro. Como la torre estaba en una isla, aunque Dédalo podía salir de la torre, todavía era prisionero. Minos vigilaba[3] e inspeccionaba cuidadosamente todos los barcos que pasaban por la isla. Dijo Dédalo: "Aunque Minos manda[4] en tierra y mar, no puede en el aire. Por allí iré". Así es que Dédalo comenzó a hacerse unas alas para él y para su hijo, Ícaro. Juntó plumas[5], de pequeñas a grandes. Juntó las plumas pequeñas con cera[6], hasta formar unas alas curvas como las de un ave. Por fin Dédalo pudo probar sus alas. Las alas lo levantaron de la tierra. Dédalo le puso las alas a su hijo, Ícaro, y le enseñó a volar. Dédalo le dijo a Ícaro: "Hijo mío, nunca debes volar ni muy alto ni muy bajo. Si vuelas muy bajo la humedad[7] del agua entrará en las plumas y tus alas pesarán[8] demasiado. Si vuelas muy alto el calor del sol afectará la cera y perderás tus alas. Quédate cerca de mí y estarás seguro". Dédalo le dio un beso a su hijo, Ícaro. El último beso que le daría. Dédalo comenzó a volar e Ícaro también. Pasaron las islas

222 FONDO ACADÉMICO

FONDO ACADÉMICO

de Samos y Delos a la izquierda y Lebintos a la derecha. El jóven Ícaro, decidió volar más alto.

—Puedo hacer lo que quiero, puedo volar como los dioses, puedo subir hasta el cielo.

Se separó de su padre y subió hacia el sol. El sol derritió⁹ la cera de las plumas. Las plumas se separaron de las alas. Las alas de Ícaro, sin plumas, ya no podían funcionar. El pobre Ícaro se perdió y se murió en las aguas del mar. Dédalo llegó a Sicilia lejos del rey Minos. Pero llegó solo.

Dédalo tenía un sobrino, Perdiz. Dédalo envidiaba¹⁰ a Perdiz porque era muy talentoso. Trató de matarlo. Lo tiró¹¹ de una torre alta. Pero antes de llegar Perdiz al suelo, la diosa Minerva lo salvó. Ella le cambió en un ave¹². El ave no vuela lejos y vive en la tierra, porque nunca se olvida de lo que pasó. El ave se llama perdiz¹³.

¹ toro	bull
² torre	tower
³ vigilaba	guarded
⁴ manda	rules
⁵ plumas	feathers
⁶ cera	wax
⁷ la humedad	dampness, humidity
⁸ pesarán	will weigh
⁹ derritió	melted
¹⁰ envidiaba	envied
¹¹ tiró	threw
¹² ave	bird
¹³ perdiz	partridge

Después de leer

A **Dédalo.** Contesten.
1. ¿Cuál era la profesión de Dédalo?
2. ¿Quién le mandó hacer un laberinto?
3. ¿Dónde metieron al Minotauro?
4. ¿A quiénes hizo prisioneros en una torre el rey Minos?
5. ¿Por qué no pudo Dédalo salir de la isla?
6. ¿De qué hizo Dédalo las alas?
7. ¿A qué altura le recomendó volar Dédalo a su hijo Ícaro?
8. ¿Adónde llegó Dédalo cuando se escapó de la isla?
9. ¿Qué le pasó a Ícaro?
10. ¿Quién era Perdiz?
11. ¿Por qué quiso Dédalo matar a Perdiz?

B **Seguimiento.** Contesten.
1. Explique la moral o la lección que ofrece el mito.
2. Describa el carácter de Dédalo.
3. Cuente en sus propias palabras la historia de Perdiz.
4. ¿Qué es perdiz en inglés?

FONDO ACADÉMICO **223**

Después de leer
ANSWERS
Ejercicio A
1. Dédalo era arquitecto.
2. El rey Minos le mandó hacer un laberinto.
3. Minos quería meterlo en el laberinto.
4. A Dédalo y a Ícaro.
5. Minos vigilaba todos los barcos que pasaban por la isla.
6. Juntó plumas para hacer las alas.
7. Le recomendó no volar ni muy alto ni muy bajo.
8. Llegó a Sicilia.
9. El sol derritió la cera de las plumas y él se perdió.
10. Perdiz era el sobrino de Dédalo.
11. Le envidiaba.

Ejercicio B
1. El hijo debe prestarle atención al padre y no debe compararse con los dioses.
2. Dédalo era un hombre de carácter fuerte e independiente. Como era un hombre muy inteligente, no quería ser prisionero del rey.
3. Perdiz era el sobrino de Dédalo y él quería ayudar a su tío cuando Dédalo llegó a Sicilia. Pero Dédalo le envidiaba tanto a Perdiz que él trató de matar a su sobrino. La diosa Minerva lo salvó cuando lo cambió en ave.
4. partridge

LEARNING FROM REALIA
Refer students to the map on page 223 and have them trace the route taken by Daedalus on his escape from Minos.

CRITICAL THINKING ACTIVITY
(Thinking skills: identifying causes)
Write the following on the board or on an overhead transparency.

The myth of Daedalus and Icarus is one of the most well known and remembered. Why is this so? What makes the myth so enduring?

CAPÍTULO 9
Scope and Sequence pages 224-249

Topics	Functions	Structure	Culture
Food preparation	How to discuss food and its preparation	El imperativo formal: formas regulares	Variety of foods available in Spanish-speaking countries
Kitchen utensils	How to give commands	El imperativo formal: formas irregulares	The importance of cuisine
Household appliances	How to give information and directions using the passive voice	La voz pasiva con *se*	A recipe for paella
			Fishermen in Valencia
			Sardines from Spain
			Fried plantain
			Meat from Venezuela

CAPÍTULO 9

Situation Cards

The Situation Cards simulate real-life situations that require students to communicate in Spanish, exactly as though they were in a Spanish-speaking country. The Situation Cards operate on the assumption that the person to whom the message is to be conveyed understands no English. Therefore, students must focus on producing the Spanish vocabulary and structures necessary to negotiate the situations successfully. For additional information, see the Introduction to the Situation Cards in the Situation Cards Envelope.

Communication Transparency

The illustration seen in this Communication Transparency consists of a synthesis of the two vocabulary (Palabras 1&2) presentations found in this chapter. It has been created in order to present this chapter's vocabulary in a new context, and also to recycle vocabulary learned in previous chapters. The Communication Transparency consists of original art. Following are some specific uses:

1. as a cue to stimulate conversation and writing activities
2. for listening comprehension activities
3. to review and reteach vocabulary
4. as a review for chapter and unit tests

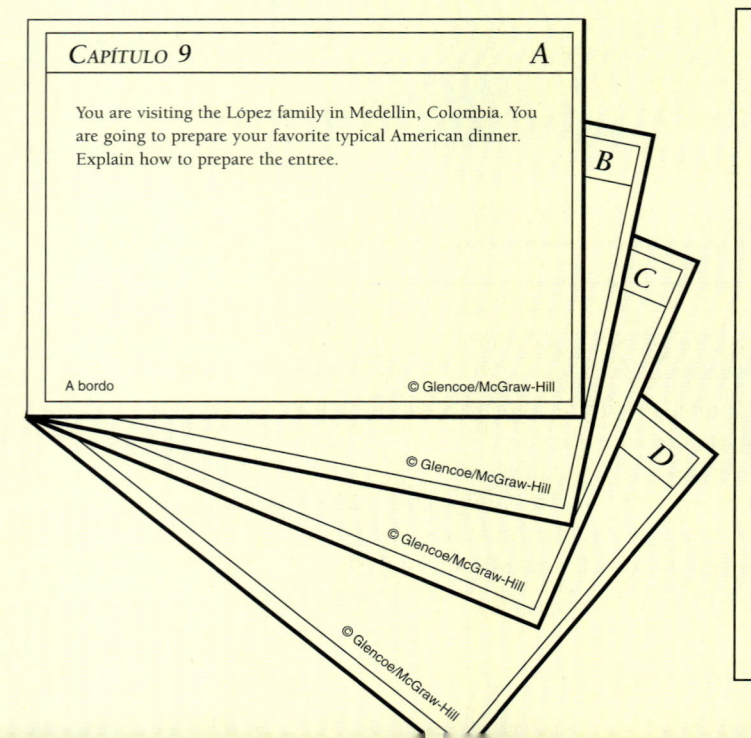

CAPÍTULO 9
Print Resources

Lesson Plans

Workbook
	Pages
◆ Palabras 1	97-98
◆ Palabras 2	99-101
◆ Estructura	102-105
◆ Un poco más	106-108
◆ Mi autobiografía	109

Communication Activities Masters
◆ Palabras 1	53-54
◆ Palabras 2	55-57
◆ Estructura	58-60

10 Bell Ringer Reviews   26-27

Chapter Situation Cards A B C D

Chapter Quizzes
◆ Palabras 1	40
◆ Palabras 2	41
◆ Estructura	42-44

Testing Program
◆ Listening Comprehension	51
◆ Reading and Writing	52-54
◆ Proficiency	131
◆ Speaking	151

Nosotros y Nuestro Mundo
- ◆ Nuestro Conocimiento Académico *La alimentación, clave de la salud*
- ◆ Nuestro Idioma *El indicativo, el subjuntivo, el imperativo; La voz pasiva con el pronombre indefinido se*
- ◆ Nuestra Cultura *El zorro y el loro*
- ◆ Nuestra Literatura *"Cuentos de Jájome"* de Salvador Tío
- ◆ Nuestra Creatividad
- ◆ Nuestras Diversiones

CAPÍTULO 9
Multimedia Resources

CD-ROM Interactive Textbook Disc 3
Chapter 9 Student Edition
- ◆ Palabras 1
- ◆ Palabras 2
- ◆ Estructura
- ◆ Conversación
- ◆ Lectura y cultura
- ◆ Hispanoparlantes
- ◆ Realidades
- ◆ Culminación
- ◆ Prueba

Audio Cassette Program with Student Tape Manual
Cassette	Pages
◆ 6A Palabras 1	243-244
◆ 6A Palabras 2	245
◆ 6A Estructura	246
◆ 6A Conversación	246
◆ 6A Segunda parte	246-248

Compact Disc Program with Student Tape Manual
◆ CD 6 Palabras 1	243-244
◆ CD 6 Palabras 2	245
◆ CD 6 Estructura	246
◆ CD 6 Conversación	246
◆ CD 6 Segunda parte	246-248

Overhead Transparencies Binder
- ◆ Vocabulary   9.1 (A&B); 9.2 (A&B)
- ◆ Communication C-9
- ◆ Maps
- ◆ Fine Art (with Blackline Master Activities)

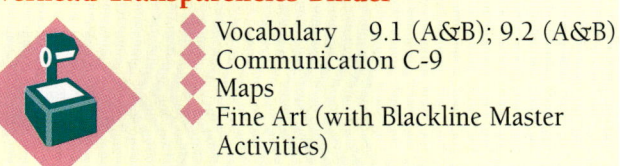

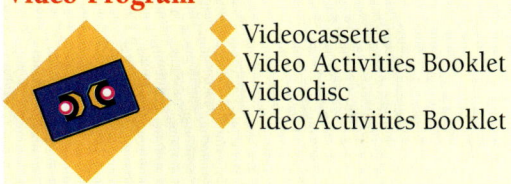

Video Program
◆ Videocassette	
◆ Video Activities Booklet	22-24
◆ Videodisc	
◆ Video Activities Booklet	22-24

Computer Software (Macintosh, IBM, Apple)
- ◆ Practice Disk
  Palabras 1 y 2
  Estructura
- ◆ Test Generator Disk
  Chapter Test
  Customized Test

224B

CAPÍTULO 9

CHAPTER OVERVIEW

In this chapter, students will expand their abilities to talk about food and its preparation. They will learn vocabulary associated with the kitchen, specifically household appliances, cooking equipment, recipe terms, and the names of foods themselves. Students will also increase their communication skills by learning the formal imperative forms and the construction of the passive voice.

The cultural focus of Chapter 9 is on the variety of foods and recipes available in Spanish-speaking countries, and the important role that cuisine plays there.

CHAPTER OBJECTIVES

By the end of this chapter, students will know:
1. vocabulary associated with food and its preparation
2. vocabulary associated with kitchen appliances and cooking equipment
3. the formal imperative forms, regular and irregular
4. the formation and basic use of the passive voice

ABOUT THE LANGUAGE

La cocina has two meanings. The most common is the literal meaning of "kitchen," the place where food is prepared. The second meaning is "cooking" or "cuisine" as in the expression *la cocina española*.

CAPÍTULO 9
LA COCINA

OBJETIVOS

In this chapter you will learn to do the following:

1. talk about food and its preparation
2. give commands
3. give information and directions using the passive voice with *se*
4. discuss the recipe for a good paella
5. identify popular dishes of the Spanish-speaking countries
6. discuss the variety of food available in the Hispanic world

CHAPTER PROJECTS

(optional)
1. Have students make a list of their favorite foods. As they proceed through the chapter, have them observe and jot down differences between Hispanic and North American eating habits.
2. Make a *paella* with the class, using the recipe on page 242.

> ### CHAPTER 9 RESOURCES
>
> 1. Workbook
> 2. Student Tape Manual
> 3. Audio Cassette 6A
> 4. Vocabulary Transparencies
> 5. Bell Ringer Review Blackline Masters
> 6. Communication Activities Masters
> 7. Computer Software: Practice and Test Generator
> 8. Video Cassette, Chapter 9
> 9. Video Activities Booklet, Chapter 9
> 10. Situation Cards
> 11. Chapter Quizzes
> 12. Testing Program

> ### Pacing
> Chapter 9 will require eight to ten class sessions. Pacing will depend on the length of the class period, the age of the students, and student aptitude.

LEARNING FROM PHOTOS

Refer students to the photo spread on pages 224-225 and say: The two large, flat pans in the photo are used for preparing the traditional Spanish *paella*. The pans are usually called *paelleras*. The original name was *paella*, and the recipe actually derived its name from the pan. The man in the photo is the *cocinero* or *jefe de cocina* (chef).

VOCABULARIO
PALABRAS 1

Vocabulary Teaching Resources
1. Vocabulary Transparencies, 9.1 (A & B)
2. Audio Cassette 6A
3. Student Tape Manual, *Palabras 1*
4. Workbook, *Palabras 1*
5. Communication Activities Masters, *Palabras 1*, A & B
6. Chapter Quizzes, *Palabras 1*

Bell Ringer Review
Write the following on the board or use BRR Blackline Master 9-1: Think of the last phone call you made. Tell where you were, whom you called, and what you talked about.

PRESENTATION (pages 226-227)
A. With books closed, refer sudents to Vocabulary Transparencies 9.1 (A & B) and have them repeat the new words, phrases, and sentences after you or Cassette 6A. You may wish to use your own props, such as photos of kitchens or props from your own kitchen.
B. Intersperse the presentation with questions which elicit the new vocabulary.
C. After students have produced the new vocabulary several times, have them open their books to pages 226-227 and call on volunteers to read the new words, phrases, and sentences.

ABOUT THE LANGUAGE
1. Foods are known by a variety of regional names. The names in *Palabras 1* are probably the most common. Here are some alternatives.
   los guisantes: los petit pois
   la toronja: el pomelo

226

VOCABULARIO

PALABRAS 1

¡A COCINAR!

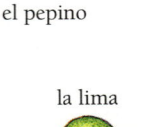

la cocina, el horno de microondas, el congelador, la nevera, la estufa, la hornilla, el hornillo, el horno, el refrigerador

cocinar, revolver, la cazuela, el/la sartén, freír, la parrilla, la olla, hervir, asar

ALGUNOS COMESTIBLES

los guisantes, la coliflor, el pepino, las cebollas, la lima, el limón, las zanahorias, la lechuga, las papas, la toronja, el melocotón

226 CAPÍTULO 9

COOPERATIVE LEARNING
Have half the teams in the class make lists of food items. Have the other half make lists of kitchen items. Teams exchange papers and write sentences using the items on their new lists. When finished, they can check and correct their sentences with the team that drew up the original list.

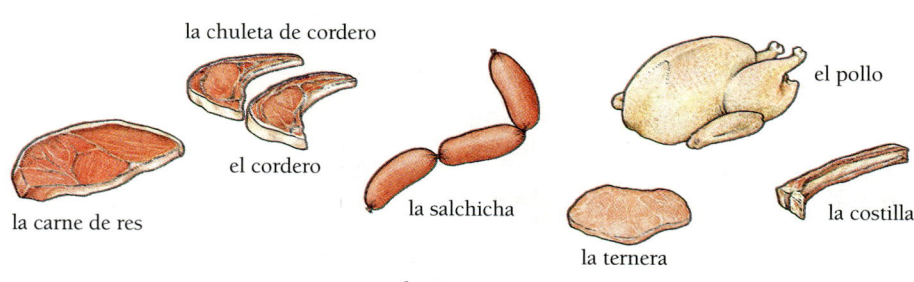

la chuleta de cordero
el pollo
la carne de res
el cordero
la salchicha
la costilla
la ternera
la pimienta
la sal
el azúcar

Señora, ase Ud. la carne en el horno.
Pues, la estoy asando.

Señor, fría Ud. los huevos.
Pues, los estoy friendo.

Señorita, coma Ud. más.
Pues, estoy comiendo más.

CAPÍTULO 9 **227**

---

las papas: las patatas
la carne de res: el bife, la vaca

2. *Salchicha* is the generic term for "sausage." There are many varieties of sausage, the most common being the *chorizo*.

PAIRED ACTIVITY

Each partner makes a list of all the appliances, kitchen items, and food items taught in *Palabras 1*. Reading from his/her list, each partner then asks the other if he/she has the same item. They can also say how they use some of the items. For example: *¿Tienes una olla? Sí. La uso para cocinar las papas*.

CROSS-CULTURAL COMPARISON

Although the pepper shaker is illustrated on student page 227, pepper rarely appears in Hispanic homes or neighborhood restaurants. It will be found in international restaurants, and so we have included it here.

Vocabulary Expansion

You may give students the following additional vocabulary in order to enable them to talk about a typical North American breakfast. Our breakfast habits in the U.S. differ from those of many other countries. It is important that students learn the vocabulary associated with North American customs, since those customs are what people in Hispanic countries would be interested in talking about.

el jugo de naranja
la leche
el chocolate
el cereal
los huevos fritos
los huevos revueltos
un huevo escalfado (poached egg)
un huevo pasado por agua (soft-boiled egg)
el pan tostado
la mermelada
el tocino

Ejercicios

PRESENTATION (*page 228*)

Ejercicios A and B
Exercises A and B are to be done with books open.

Ejercicio C
Exercise C can be done with books open or closed.

ANSWERS

Ejercicio A
1. Es una cocina moderna.
2. La estufa tiene cuatro hornillas.
3. Es una estufa de gas.
4. El refrigerador tiene dos puertas.
5. Sí, la puerta de la izquierda es para el congelador (la congeladora).
6. Sí, un horno de microondas cocina (cuece) rápido.

Ejercicio B
1. sartén
2. asar
3. olla
4. hervir
5. freír (asar)
6. cocinar (freír, hervir, revolver)

Ejercicio C
Answers will vary.
1. Sí (No), (no) me gustan los guisantes.
2. Sí (No), (no) me gusta una ensalada de lechuga y tomates.
3. Sí (No), (no) me gustan las papas fritas.
4. Sí (No), (no) me gustan las toronjas (las naranjas).
5. Me gustan más las legumbres (las frutas).
6. Sí (No), (no) me gusta el pollo.
7. Me gusta más el pollo frito (el pollo asado).
8. Me gusta más la carne (el pescado).

ABOUT THE LANGUAGE
The refrigerator is known by different names. It is *el refrigerador*, *la refrigeradora*, *la nevera*, and *el frigorífico*. Ask students what the word *nevera* might be related to. In Latin America it is not uncommon to hear *el frízer* for the freezer.

228

Ejercicios

A **La cocina.** Contesten según la foto.
1. ¿Es una cocina moderna o anticuada?
2. ¿Cuántas hornillas tiene la estufa?
3. ¿Es una estufa eléctrica o de gas?
4. ¿Cuántas puertas tiene el refrigerador?
5. ¿Es para el congelador (la congeladora) la puerta de la izquierda?
6. ¿Cocina o cuece rápido un horno de microondas?

B **¿Qué necesita el cocinero?** Completen.
1. El cocinero necesita una ___ porque va a freír algo.
2. El cocinero necesita una parrilla porque va a ___ algo.
3. El cocinero necesita una ___ porque va a hervir algo.
4. El cocinero va a ___ el agua.
5. El cocinero va a ___ las chuletas de cerdo.
6. El cocinero va a ___ los huevos.

C **Lo que me gusta y lo que no me gusta.** Preguntas personales.
1. ¿Te gustan los guisantes?
2. ¿Te gusta una ensalada de lechuga y tomates?
3. ¿Te gustan las papas fritas?
4. ¿Te gustan más las toronjas o las naranjas?
5. ¿Te gustan más las legumbres o las frutas?
6. ¿Te gusta el pollo?
7. ¿Te gusta más el pollo frito o el pollo asado?
8. ¿Te gusta más la carne o el pescado?

228 CAPÍTULO 9

D ¿A qué grupo pertenece? Hagan categorías. Escriban en otro papel.

　　　legumbre　　　fruta　　　carne　　　especia

1. la cebolla
2. la toronja
3. la zanahoria
4. el cerdo
5. la papa
6. el cordero
7. el melocotón
8. los guisantes
9. la pimienta

E La cocina. ¿Sí o no?

1. Se puede hervir zanahorias.
2. Se puede asar guisantes.
3. Se puede asar el pollo.
4. Se puede revolver los huevos.
5. Se puede freír la lechuga.
6. Se puede freír la salchicha.
7. Se puede hervir, freír o asar las papas.

CAPÍTULO 9　229

PRESENTATION (page 229)
**Extension of *Ejercicio D*
Writing**
After completing Exercise D, call on volunteers to go to the board and write the items in the exercise with the chosen category beside them. You may also add to the list any additional foods you have taught.

ANSWERS
Ejercicio D
Legumbre
1. la cebolla
3. la zanahoria
5. la papa
8. los guisantes

Fruta
2. la toronja
7. el melcotón

Carne
4. el cerdo
6. el cordero

Especia
9. la pimienta

Ejercicio E
1. Sí
2. No
3. Sí
4. Sí
5. No
6. Sí
7. Sí

LEARNING FROM REALIA
Refer students to the advertisement on page 229. Have them say all they can about it. You might cue them with questions such as: ¿Qué será Publix? ¿Qué producto vende Publix? ¿Quiénes trabajan en Publix?

INDEPENDENT PRACTICE
Assign any of the following:
1. Workbook, *Palabras 1*
2. Communication Activities Masters, *Palabras 1*, A & B
3. Exercises on student pages 228-229

VOCABULARIO
PALABRAS 2

Vocabulary Teaching Resources
1. Vocabulary Transparencies 9.2 (A & B)
2. Audio Cassette 6A
3. Student Tape Manual, *Palabras 2*
4. Workbook, *Palabras 2*
5. Communication Activities Masters, *Palabras 2, C & D*
6. Chapter Quizzes, *Palabras 2*
7. Computer Software, *Vocabulario*

Bell Ringer Review
Write the following on the board or use BRR Blackline Master 9-2: Write the names of the equipment or cookware needed to do each of the following in a kitchen:
1. freír
2. hervir
3. asar
4. congelar

PRESENTATION (pages 230-231)

A. Have students close their books. Model the *Palabras 2* vocabulary using Vocabulary Transparencies 9.2 (A & B). Have students repeat the new material after you or Cassette 6A.

B. Dramatize the meaning of these words: *picar, pelar, limpiar, agregar, retirar, tapar, rebanar, rallar*.

C. When students have produced the new vocabulary several times, have them open their books to pages 230-231 and call on volunteers to read the words, phrases, and sentences. Model pronunciation as necessary.

VOCABULARIO

PALABRAS 2

EN LA COCINA

limpiar
picar
rallar
los pedacitos, los trocitos
pelar
rebanar
las rebanadas
cortar
tapar
agregar

Se quita (retira) del fuego.
Se apaga.

Se pone al fuego.

230   CAPÍTULO 9

PANTOMIME

Use as many props or pictures as possible.

_____, venga Ud. por aquí, por favor.
Vaya Ud. a la cocina.
Saque la carne del refrigerador.
Ase Ud. la carne en el horno.
Pele Ud. las papas.
Ponga Ud. el aceite en la sartén.
Pique Ud. el ajo.
Agregue Ud. las papas y el ajo al aceite.
Fría Ud. las papas y el ajo.
Limpie Ud. la lechuga.
Prepare Ud. la ensalada.
Ponga Ud. la olla al fuego.
Pele las zanahorias y córtelas en rebanadas.
Agregue Ud. las zanahorias.
Gracias. Vuelva Ud. a su asiento.

MÁS COMESTIBLES

- el maíz
- los pimientos
- la papaya
- el coco
- el aguacate
- el ajo
- las cerezas
- el arroz
- las habichuelas negras, los frijoles negros
- la sandía
- el plátano, la banana
- el pescado
- los mariscos
- los camarones, las gambas
- las almejas
- la langosta
- los calamares
- los mejillones
- el aceite

Se limpia la lechuga.

Se pelan las papas.

Se pica el ajo.
Se pican las cebollas.

CAPÍTULO 9   231

ABOUT THE LANGUAGE

1. Here are more alternate names for food items:
   el plátano: la banana, el guineo, el cambur
   los pimientos: los chiles
   la papaya: la fruta bomba
   las habichuelas: los frijoles, los fréjoles
   el aguacate: la palta
   el maíz: el choclo

2. *La langosta* is the spiny lobster with no claws. It is found in the Mediterranean and other warm waters. The "lobster" in the illustration is actually *un bogavante*, called so because it swims in a forward motion, unlike the spiny lobster that, like the crab, moves backward.

3. *Los mariscos* are "seafood." The crab in the illustration is *un cangrejo*. Large sea crabs are *centollos* or *centollas*.

COOPERATIVE LEARNING

Have students work in groups of four. Teams work in round-robin fashion. **E1** gives the name of an appliance or other kitchen item. **E2** asks **E1** if he/she would like to buy it. **E3** asks **E1** what he/she needs it for. **E4** names a new item and the process begins again, this time with **E1** asking the first questions.

DID YOU KNOW?

The squid, *el calamar,* was formerly used solely as bait in the U.S. In Spain and other Mediterranean countries it has long been a favorite food, especially when cut into rings and fried *(calamares fritos)*. Ask students: *¿Cuáles son algunas diferencias entre el pulpo y el calamar?* The octopus *(el pulpo)* is also a popular food.

231

Ejercicios

PRESENTATION (page 232)

Ejercicios A and C
Exercises A and C can be done with books open or closed.

Ejercicio B
Exercise B can be done with books open.

Variation of Ejercicio D
Speaking
When students supply the word, have them use it in an original sentence.

ANSWERS

Ejercicio A
1. Sí
2. No
3. No
4. Sí
5. Sí

Ejercicio B
1. La señora está picando el ajo.
2. La señora está rebanando el pan.
3. La señora está cortando la cebolla.
4. La señora está pelando una papa (patata).
5. La señora está limpiando los camarones (las gambas).

Ejercicio C
1. Sí, se puede hervir o freír el arroz.
2. Sí, se puede rallar la lechuga.
3. Sí, se puede rallar el queso y el coco.
4. Sí, se puede rebanar la sandía.
5. Sí, se puede picar la carne de res.
6. Sí, se puede freír la chuleta.
7. No, no se puede asar el arroz.
8. Sí, se puede tapar la olla.

Ejercicio D
1. los mariscos
2. tapar
3. picar
4. rebanar
5. limpiar
6. tapar
7. quitar

INFORMAL ASSESSMENT
(Palabras 1 and 2)
Check for understanding by having individuals say as much as they can about the illustrations in Vocabulary Transparencies A & B.

232

Ejercicios

A En la cocina. ¿Sí o no?
1. Antes de cocinar, se pone la sartén o la olla al fuego.
2. Antes de empezar a cocinar, se apaga el fuego.
3. Después de cocinar, se limpian y se cortan las legumbres.
4. Es necesario limpiar bien las conchas de las almejas antes de cocinarlas.
5. Antes de hacer la ensalada, se lava la lechuga.

B Preparando la comida. Contesten según el dibujo.

1. ¿Qué está picando la señora?
2. ¿Qué está rebanando la señora? 
3. ¿Qué está cortando la señora? 
4. ¿Qué está pelando la señora? 
5. ¿Qué está limpiando la señora? 

C ¿Qué opinas? ¿Se puede o no?
1. ¿Se puede hervir o freír el arroz?
2. ¿Se puede rallar la lechuga?
3. ¿Se puede rallar el queso o el coco?
4. ¿Se puede rebanar la sandía?
5. ¿Se puede picar la carne de res?
6. ¿Se puede freír la chuleta?
7. ¿Se puede asar el arroz?
8. ¿Se puede tapar la olla?

D Definiciones. ¿Cuál es la palabra?
1. las almejas, los mejillones, la langosta, etc.
2. poner una tapa en una olla
3. cortar en pedacitos muy pequeños
4. cortar en rebanadas
5. lavar
6. lo contrario de destapar
7. retirar

232   CAPÍTULO 9

INDEPENDENT PRACTICE

Assign any of the following:
1. Workbook, *Palabras 2*
2. Communication Activities Masters, *Palabras 2*, C & D
3. Exercises on student page 232

Comunicación
Palabras 1 y 2

A **Lo que me gusta comer.** Haga Ud. una lista de los comestibles que a Ud. le gustan mucho. Luego enséñele la lista a un(a) compañero(a) y pregúntele si a él/ella le gustan las mismas cosas que a Ud.

B **Nuestras comidas favoritas.** Con un(a) compañero(a) hagan una lista de sus comestibles favoritos. Luego decidan a cuál de los dos le gustan más las comidas que son buenas para la salud.

C **Una visita.** Ud. está de visita con la familia Castro. Ellos viven en Medellín, Colombia. Esta noche Ud. les va a preparar una comida típica americana. Los Castro (tres compañeros de clase) quieren saber lo que Ud. piensa cocinar. Explíqueles cómo se prepara cada plato.

D **Una lección gastronómica.** Trabaje con un(a) compañero(a) de clase. Ud. está aprendiendo a cocinar. Su compañero(a) es un(a) cocinero(a) experto(a). Ud. quiere saber cómo se preparan los siguientes comestibles. Pregúntele a su compañero(a). Él/ella le contestará.

| tomate | carne | guisantes |
| arroz | maíz | gambas |

E **Casa en venta.** Su familia está vendiendo su casa. Ud. recibe una llamada telefónica de una persona a quien le interesa comprar la casa. Déle una descripción de la casa especialmente de la cocina.

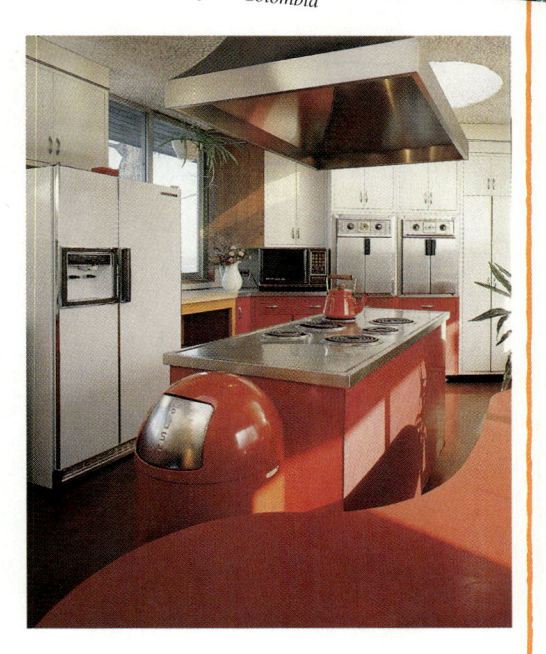

Recogiendo café en Colombia

CAPÍTULO 9   **233**

ESTRUCTURA

El imperativo formal
Formas regulares

Telling Other People What to Do

1. You use the command form of the verb, the imperative, to tell someone what to do. To form the *Ud.* and *Uds.* commands, you drop the "o" from the present tense *yo* form and add the following endings:

INFINITIVE	YO, PRESENT	UD. COMMAND	UDS. COMMAND
hablar	hablø	hable Ud.	hablen Uds.
preparar	preparø	prepare Ud.	preparen Uds.
comer	comø	coma Ud.	coman Uds.
leer	leø	lea Ud.	lean Uds.
abrir	abrø	abra Ud.	abran Uds.

STEM-CHANGING VERBS

INFINITIVE	YO, PRESENT	UD. COMMAND	UDS. COMMAND
pensar	piensø	piense Ud.	piensen Uds.
contar	cuentø	cuente Ud.	cuenten Uds.
volver	vuelvø	vuelva Ud.	vuelvan Uds.
hervir	hiervø	hierva Ud.	hiervan Uds.
pedir	pidø	pida Ud.	pidan Uds.

2. Note that the endings used for the formal commands have the vowel opposite to the vowel usually associated with the conjugation. The *-ar* verbs have *-e* and the *-er* and *-ir* verbs have *-a*.

3. You just add *no* before these commands to make them negative.

prepare Ud.	no prepare Ud.
pida Ud.	no pida Ud.
vuelva Ud.	no vuelva Ud.
preparen Uds.	no preparen Uds.
pidan Uds.	no pidan Uds.
vuelvan Uds.	no vuelvan Uds.

234 CAPÍTULO 9

ESTRUCTURA

Structure Teaching Resources

1. Workbook, *Estructura*
2. Student Tape Manual, *Estructura*
3. Audio Cassette 6A
4. Communication Activities Masters, *Estructura*, A-C
5. Chapter Quizzes, *Estructura*
6. Computer Software, *Estructura*

Bell Ringer Review

Write the following on the board or use BRR Blackline Master 9-4: Make a list of foods you might eat for dinner tonight.

El imperativo formal
Formas regulares

PRESENTATION (pages 234-235)

A. Have students open their books to pages 234-235 and lead them through steps 1-4.
B. Illustrate the difference between singular and plural imperatives by giving a command to an individual and then the same command to a group of students. For example: *María, tome Ud. su libro de español. María y José, tomen Uds. su libro de español.*
C. Practice negative forms by calling out commands and having students change them to the negative. Then reverse the procedure.
D. In step 4, you may wish to explain the reasons for the spelling changes.

Teaching Tip In order to reinforce the uses of formal address, you may wish to assign students temporary names and titles which would require it, such as *Señor Pascal* or *Doña Florencia Matamoros*.

LEARNING FROM PHOTOS

Refer students to the photo on page 234. The objects shown are: *la licuadora* (mixer), *el colador* (colander), and *el rodillo* (roller).

4. Note that the following verbs are regular, but they have a spelling change in the command form.

tocar	toque Ud.	toquen Uds.
picar	pique Ud.	piquen Uds.
jugar	juegue Ud.	jueguen Uds.
pagar	pague Ud.	paguen Uds.
agregar	agregue Ud.	agreguen Uds.
empezar	empiece Ud.	empiecen Uds.

Ejercicios

A ¿Preparo la comida? Contesten según el modelo.

¿Preparo la comida?
Sí, prepare Ud. la comida.

1. ¿Preparo la comida?
2. ¿Limpio la lechuga?
3. ¿Pelo los tomates?
4. ¿Pico el ajo?
5. ¿Hiervo el agua?
6. ¿Frío el pollo?
7. ¿Tapo la sartén?
8. ¿Retiro la sartén del fuego?

B ¿Preparamos la comida? Contesten según el modelo.

¿Preparamos la comida?
*No, no preparen Uds. la comida.
Yo la voy a preparar.*

1. ¿Preparamos la comida?
2. ¿Limpiamos la lechuga?
3. ¿Pelamos los tomates?
4. ¿Picamos el ajo?
5. ¿Hervimos el agua?
6. ¿Freímos el pollo?
7. ¿Tapamos la sartén?
8. ¿Retiramos la sartén del fuego?

CAPÍTULO 9 235

Ejercicios

PRESENTATION (page 236)

Ejercicios C and D
Exercises C and D can be done with books open.

ANSWERS

Ejercicio C
1. Acepte Ud. la carta.
2. Abra Ud. la carta.
3. Lea Ud. la carta.
4. Conteste Ud. la carta.
5. Escriba la carta en inglés.

Ejercicio D
1. … ¡viaje Ud. a España!
2. … ¡pase Ud. un mes en Madrid!
3. … ¡tome Ud. el tren a Toledo!
4. … ¡visite Ud. la capital!
5. … ¡vea Ud. los cuadros de El Greco!
6. … ¡aprenda Ud. el español!
7. … ¡coma Ud. una paella!
8. … ¡beba Ud. horchata!
9. … ¡viva Ud. con una familia española!

HISTORY CONNECTION

The full title for Toledo is *Ciudad Imperial y Coronada*. Moors, Christians, and Jews all contributed to making Toledo one of the leading cities of the time. Toledo was a major source of medieval learning. It had been known as Toletum under the Romans. In 418 the Visigoths replaced the Romans and established their court there until driven out by the Moors in 711. The Moors were driven out in 1085 when Alfonso VI reconquered the city.

This view of Toledo is dominated by the Cathedral, which was built between 1227 and 1493. In addition to the Cathedral, there is the *Sinagoga del Tránsito*, a beautifully preserved 15th-century synagogue.

El imperativo formal Formas irregulares

PRESENTATION (pages 236-237)

Lead students through steps 1 and 2. Have them repeat the command forms after you.

236

C ¿Qué debo hacer con la carta? Contesten con el imperativo.

1. ¿Debo aceptar la carta?
2. ¿Debo abrir la carta?
3. ¿Debo leer la carta?
4. ¿Debo contestar a la carta?
5. ¿Debo escribir la carta en inglés?

D Debe hacer lo que quiere hacer. Contesten según el modelo.

Quiero viajar a España.
Entonces, ¡viaje Ud. a España!

1. Quiero viajar a España.
2. Quiero pasar un mes en Madrid.
3. Quiero tomar el tren a Toledo.
4. Quiero visitar la capital.
5. Quiero ver los cuadros de El Greco.
6. Quiero aprender el español.
7. Quiero comer una paella.
8. Quiero beber horchata.
9. Quiero vivir con una familia española.

Una vista de Toledo, España

El imperativo formal Formas irregulares

Telling Other People What to Do

1. A verb that has an irregularity in the *yo* form of the present tense will keep the same irregularity in the command form since the *yo* form of the present serves as the root for the command. Study the following.

INFINITIVE	YO, PRESENT	UD. COMMAND	UDS. COMMAND
hacer	hago	haga Ud.	hagan Uds.
poner	pongo	ponga Ud.	pongan Uds.
salir	salgo	salga Ud.	salgan Uds.
venir	vengo	venga Ud.	vengan Uds.
decir	digo	diga Ud.	digan Uds.
conducir	conduzco	conduzca Ud.	conduzcan Uds.

236 CAPÍTULO 9

INDEPENDENT PRACTICE

Assign any of the following:
1. Workbook, *Estructura*
2. Communication Activities Masters, *Estructura*, A
3. Exercises on student pages 235-236

2. The following are the only formal commands that are irregular.

ir	vaya Ud.	vayan Uds.
ser	sea Ud.	sean Uds.
saber	sepa Ud.	sepan Uds.
estar	esté Ud.	estén Uds.
dar	dé Ud.	den Uds.

Ejercicios

A **Voy de compras.** Contesten según el modelo.

> Quiero hacer las compras.
> *Pues, haga Ud. las compras.*

1. Quiero hacer las compras.
2. Quiero salir ahora.
3. Quiero ir al mercado de Santa Tecla.
4. Quiero poner mis compras en esta canasta.
5. Quiero ir a pie.
6. No quiero conducir.
7. Quiero ir en carro.

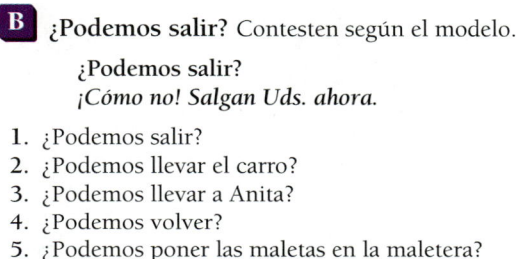

B **¿Podemos salir?** Contesten según el modelo.

> ¿Podemos salir?
> *¡Cómo no! Salgan Uds. ahora.*

1. ¿Podemos salir?
2. ¿Podemos llevar el carro?
3. ¿Podemos llevar a Anita?
4. ¿Podemos volver?
5. ¿Podemos poner las maletas en la maletera?

C **Una llamada telefónica.** Completen con el imperativo.

1. ___ Ud. por teléfono. (llamar)
2. ___ Ud. la llamada. (hacer)
3. ___ la llamada de un teléfono público. (hacer)
4. ___ Ud. a la cabina telefónica. (ir)
5. ___ Ud. el auricular. (descolgar)
6. ___ la moneda en la ranura. (introducir)
7. ___ el tono. (esperar)
8. ___ el número. (marcar)
9. ___ Ud. la contestación. (esperar)
10. ___ Ud. "Aló". (decir)
11. ___ Ud. cortés. (ser)
12. ___ Ud. por Antonio. (preguntar)
13. ___ Ud. con él. (hablar)

CAPÍTULO 9   237

Bell Ringer Review

Write the following on the board or use BRR Blackline Master 9-5: Make a list of things you are not going to do for a while because you have just done them. Write complete sentences and use the expression **acabar de** plus the infinitive.

La voz pasiva con se

PRESENTATION (*page 238*)

A. Lead students through steps 1-3 on page 238.
B. Provide additional examples for step 2 on the board.

Ejercicios

PRESENTATION (*page 238*)

Ejercicios A and B

Exercises A and B can be done with books open or closed.

ANSWERS

Ejercicio A

Answers will vary.
1. Sí, se venden habichuelas en la verdulería.
2. Se venden habichuelas en lata o en bote en el supermercado.
3. Sí, se vende pescado en la pescadería.
4. Sí, se venden bananas en la frutería.
5. Sí, se vende cordero en la carnicería.
6. Sí, se venden pasteles en la pastelería.
7. Sí, se vende leche en la lechería.
8. Sí, también se vende queso en la lechería.

Ejercicio B

1. Se ralla el queso.
2. Se fríen las papas.
3. Se pica el ajo.
4. Se asa la carne en el horno.
5. Se fríen los calamares en aceite.

La voz pasiva con *se*

Talking in General Terms about What Is Done

1. The impersonal passive construction in English is as follows:

   Meat is sold at the butcher shop.

2. In Spanish the pronoun *se* can be used to express the impersonal passive voice. Note that if the subject is singular, the verb is singular. If the subject is plural, the verb is plural.

   Se vende carne en la carnicería.
   Y se venden legumbres en la verdulería.

3. *Se* can also be used to convey the general subject one, they and people.

   Aquí se habla español.   *Spanish is spoken here.*
   One speaks Spanish here.
   They speak Spanish here.
   People speak Spanish here.

Ejercicios

A ¿Dónde se venden? Contesten.

1. ¿Se venden habichuelas en la verdulería?
2. ¿Se venden habichuelas en lata o bote en el supermercado?
3. ¿Se vende pescado en la pescadería?
4. ¿Se venden bananas en la frutería?
5. ¿Se vende cordero en la carnicería?
6. ¿Se venden pasteles en la pastelería?
7. ¿Se vende leche en la lechería?
8. ¿Se vende queso también en la lechería?

B ¿Cuál? Contesten.

1. ¿Se ralla el queso o el tomate?
2. ¿Se fríen las papas o los aguacates?
3. ¿Se pica el ajo o el arroz?
4. ¿Se asa la carne en una sartén o en el horno?
5. ¿Se fríen los calamares en aceite o en maíz?

LEARNING FROM PHOTOS

Refer students to the photo at the bottom of page 238. Ask them what kind of shop this is, and what the fruits and their prices are.

INDEPENDENT PRACTICE

Assign any of the following:
1. Workbook, *Estructura*
2. Communication Activities Masters, *Estructura*, B & C
3. Exercises on student pages 237-239

C ¿Qué se come y dónde? Contesten según se indica.

1. ¿Se comen muchas tortillas en México? (sí)
2. ¿Se come mucho maíz en España? (no)
3. ¿Se come mucha carne de res en la Argentina? (sí)
4. ¿Se bebe mucho vino en Panamá? (no)
5. ¿Se bebe más vino en Chile? (sí)
6. ¿Se comen muchos mariscos en Chile? (sí)
7. ¿Se comen muchas comidas italianas en Uruguay? (sí)
8. ¿Se usa mucho aceite en España? (sí)
9. ¿Se come mucho arroz con habichuelas en Puerto Rico? (sí)
10. ¿Se usan muchas salsas picantes en España? (no)

D ¿Qué idioma se habla dónde? Escojan.

francés español portugués
inglés árabe alemán

1. ¿Qué idioma se habla en el Perú?
2. ¿Qué idioma se habla en el Brasil?
3. ¿Qué idioma se habla en Egipto?
4. ¿Qué idioma se habla en Alemania y en Austria?
5. ¿Qué idioma se habla en Irlanda?
6. ¿Qué idiomas se hablan en Quebec?

CAPÍTULO 9 **239**

PRESENTATION (page 239)

Ejercicios C and D
Exercises C and D can be done with books open.

ANSWERS

Ejercicio C
1. Sí, se comen muchas tortillas en México.
2. No, no se come mucho maíz en España.
3. Sí, se come mucha carne de res en la Argentina.
4. No, no se bebe mucho vino en Panamá.
5. Sí, se bebe más vino en Chile.
6. Sí, se comen muchos mariscos en Chile.
7. Sí, se comen muchas comidas italianas en Uruguay.
8. Sí, se usa mucho aceite en España.
9. Sí, se come mucho arroz con habichuelas en Puerto Rico.
10. No, no se usan muchas salsas picantes en España.

Ejercicio D
1. En el Perú se habla español.
2. En el Brasil se habla portugués.
3. En Egipto se habla árabe.
4. En Alemania y en Austria se habla alemán.
5. En Irlanda se habla inglés.
6. En Quebec se hablan inglés y francés.

LEARNING FROM PHOTOS/REALIA

1. Tell students that in Spain almost all frying is done with oil, preferably olive oil. Spain is one of the world's major producers of olive oil and it also has the lowest per capita consumption of butter in Europe.
2. Have students say all they can about the advertisement at the bottom of page 239. You may wish to ask them: ¿Para qué es el anuncio? ¿Cómo se llama el producto? ¿Qué clase de sopa es? ¿Cuáles son los ingredientes?

CONVERSACIÓN

Bell Ringer Review
Write the following on the board or use BRR Blackline Master 9-6: Choose a favorite dish of yours and write out the instructions for making it.

PRESENTATION (page 240)
A. Tell students they will hear a conversation between Quico and Carlos. Ask them to close their books and listen as you read the conversation or play Cassette 6A.
B. Have students open their books to page 240. Allow pairs time to practice the conversation. Each partner should practice both roles.
C. Call on a volunteer to summarize the conversation in his/her own words.

Ejercicio
ANSWERS
1. A Quico le gusta cocinar.
2. Carlos es un desastre en la cocina.
3. A Quico le gusta preparar la paella.
4. La paella se come en España.
5. La paella es una especialidad de Valencia.
6. Sí (No), (no) me gustaría la paella.

CONVERSACIÓN

Escenas de la vida ¿Yo? ¿En la cocina?

QUICO: Carlos, ¿te gusta cocinar?
CARLOS: A mí, ¿cocinar? De ninguna manera. En la cocina soy un desastre. ¿A ti te gusta?
QUICO: Sí, bastante.
CARLOS: ¿Qué sabes preparar?
QUICO: Muchas cosas, pero mi plato favorito es la paella.
CARLOS: La paella, dices. ¿Qué es?
QUICO: Pues, es una especialidad española—de Valencia. Lleva muchos ingredientes—¡mariscos, arroz!
CARLOS: Se comen muchos mariscos en España, ¿no?
QUICO: Sí, hombre. Y algún día te voy a preparar una buena paella.

Me gusta cocinar. Contesten según la conversación.

1. ¿A quién le gusta cocinar?
2. ¿Quién es un desastre en la cocina?
3. ¿Cuál es el plato que a Quico le gusta mucho preparar?
4. ¿Dónde se come la paella?
5. ¿De qué región de España es la paella una especialidad?
6. ¿Qué opinas? ¿Te gustaría la paella o no?

Una calle en Valencia, España

240 CAPÍTULO 9

LEARNING FROM PHOTOS

1. Refer students to the photo at the top of page 240. Have them say all they can about the young men eating. Cue with questions such as: *¿Qué comidas hay en la mesa? ¿Qué toman ellos?* etc.
2. In regard to the photo at the bottom of page 240, have students describe the street scene in Valencia.

CRITICAL THINKING ACTIVITY

(Thinking skills: making inferences; drawing conclusions)
Read the following to the class or write it on the board or on an overhead transparency.
La paella viene de Valencia. La paella tradicional lleva muchos mariscos. Busca Valencia en el mapa en la página 452. ¿Por qué crees que hay muchos mariscos en la paella?

240

Comunicación

A **En la escuela.** Haga una lista de las cosas que se hacen generalmente en la escuela. Compare su lista con la de un(a) compañero(a) de clase. Dígale a él/ella cuáles son las cosas más importantes de su lista. Su compañero(a) le dirá por qué o por qué no son importantes.

En la escuela se…

B **Personalmente.** Tome Ud. la lista de la Actividad A y dígale a un(a) compañero(a) de clase cuándo Ud. hace cada actividad. Cambien de papel.

C **Comidas populares.** Con un(a) compañero(a) de clase preparen una lista de todos los comestibles que ya han aprendido. Luego decidan cuáles de estos comestibles se comen mucho en los Estados Unidos y cuáles no se comen con mucha frecuencia.

D **En la cocina.** Ud. está dando lecciones de cocina. Explíquele a uno(a) de sus alumnos(as), (un[a] compañero[a] de clase) qué puede hacer con los siguientes comestibles.

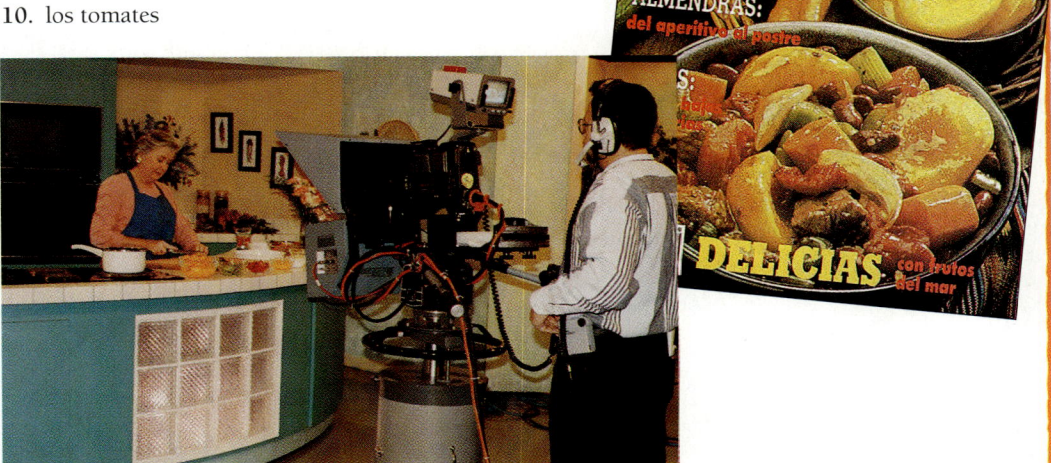

1. las judías verdes
2. los camarones
3. las zanahorias
4. la lechuga
5. el pollo
6. el biftec
7. los calamares
8. las papas
9. las cebollas
10. los tomates

CAPÍTULO 9   241

Bell Ringer Review
Write the following on the board or use BRR Blackline Master 9-7: Your friends are hungry. Let them know what there is to eat in your refrigerator. Start with, **En mi refrigerador hay…**

Comunicación
PRESENTATION (page 241)

Have students do one or all of these activities, allowing them to select those in which they wish to take part.

ANSWERS
Actividades A, B, and C
Answers will vary.

Actividad D
Answers will vary but may resemble the following.
1. Se pueden hervir las judías verdes.
2. Se pueden hervir o freír los camarones.
3. Se tienen que pelar las zanahorias. Se pueden hervir las zanahorias.
4. Se puede picar la lechuga.
5. Se puede asar o se puede freír el pollo.
6. Se puede asar el biftec.
7. Se pueden freír los calamares.
8. Se pueden pelar las papas. Se pueden freír o se pueden cocinar.
9. Se pueden picar las cebollas.
10. Se pueden rebanar o se pueden picar los tomates.

LEARNING FROM REALIA
Refer students to the magazine cover depicted at the bottom of page 241 and have them describe the cover of *Vanidades*. You may wish to ask: *¿Qué artículos hay en este número de la revista?*

COOPERATIVE LEARNING
Have each team create a short TV cooking lesson. The script should be on how to prepare a special dish, the wilder the better. Teams write the script as a group, and then select one or two members to be on camera. You may actually record the cooking lessons on video.

241

LECTURA Y CULTURA

Bell Ringer Review
Write the following on the board or use BRR Blackline Master 9-8: Tell what languages are spoken in the following places. Follow the example: *Acapulco. En Acapulco se habla español.*
1. Lima
2. Nueva York
3. París
4. Brasil
5. Quebec

READING STRATEGIES
(pages 242-243)

Reading
While going through the selection, have students repeat after you the new vocabulary in the recipe.

Post-reading
A. Have students re-read the recipe at home and write the answers to the accompanying exercises.
B. Go over the exercises in class the next day.

LECTURA Y CULTURA

UNA RECETA

Como le dijo Quico a José, la paella es un plato delicioso que es una especialidad de la cocina española. Quien no ha comido una paella no sabe lo que se ha perdido. La paella valenciana lleva muchos ingredientes. Aquí tiene Ud. una receta bastante sencilla para preparar una paella. Decida si a Ud. le gustaría comer esta deliciosa comida.

INGREDIENTES

3 tomates
2 cebollas grandes
2 pimientos (uno verde y uno rojo)
4 dientes[1] de ajo
1/2 kilo de camarones
4 calamares
12 almejas
12 mejillones
langosta (opcional)
1 pollo en partes
3 chorizos
1 paquete de guisantes congelados
1 bote de pimientos morrones
1 1/2 tazas de arroz
3 tazas de consomé de pollo
4 pizcas[2] de azafrán[3]
1/4 taza de aceite de oliva

PREPARACIONES

1. Pique los tomates, los pimientos, las cebollas y el ajo.
2. Lave las almejas y los mejillones en agua fría.
3. Limpie y pele los camarones.
4. Limpie y corte en rebanadas los calamares.
5. Corte en rebanadas los chorizos.
6. Fría o ase el pollo aparte.

COCCIÓN

Se usa una paellera o una olla.

1. Fría ligeramente[4] en el aceite los pimientos y las cebollas picadas.
2. Agregue el ajo y los tomates y fría ligeramente a fuego lento unos dos o tres minutos.
3. Agregue el arroz.
4. Revuelva el arroz con los tomates, las cebollas, los pimientos y el ajo.
5. Agregue el consomé de pollo y llévelo a la ebullición[5].
6. Baje el fuego y agregue los camarones, los calamares, el chorizo, el pollo, las almejas y los mejillones.
7. Agregue el azafrán.
8. Ponga sal y pimienta a su gusto.

[1] dientes *cloves*   [3] azafrán *saffron*   [5] a la ebullición *to a boil*
[2] pizcas *pinches*   [4] ligeramente *lightly*

242   CAPÍTULO 9

DID YOU KNOW?

El azafrán (saffron), a basic ingredient of *paella*, is probably the world's most expensive spice. Only the stigma or pistils of the flower are used. It is estimated that it takes the pistils of 4,000 plants to produce one ounce of saffron powder. Saffron gives the rice of *paella* its distinctive orange-yellow tint.

FOR THE NATIVE SPEAKER

Have students bring a recipe from their home for a traditional Spanish dish. They should be prepared to describe the preparation of the dish in detail.

Si se prepara la paella en una olla, tape la olla y cocine (cueza) a fuego lento encima de la estufa unos 40 minutos. En una paellera, ase la paella en el horno sin tapa o cocine a fuego lento encima de la estufa.

Al final agregue los guisantes y los pimientos y sirva. Ud. notará que el arroz tiene un bonito color amarillo. Es del azafrán.

Estudio de palabras

A ¿Cuál es la palabra? Completen.

1. una ____ para hacer la paella
2. medio ____ de camarones
3. un ____ de guisantes congelados
4. tres ____ de ajo
5. una ____ de sal
6. una ____ de consomé de pollo

Comprensión

A Una paella.

Prepare Ud. una lista de los ingredientes que lleva una paella.

Cultivando azafrán

B La cocción. ¿Sí o no?

1. Se puede asar la paella en la parrilla.
2. La paella lleva muchas papas.
3. Hay muchas especias en una paella.
4. El arroz de una paella se pone amarillo.
5. El chorizo es un tipo de salchicha española.

C ¿Por qué?

Mire Ud. un mapa de España y explique por qué se comen muchos mariscos en España.

CAPÍTULO 9   243

Estudio de palabras
ANSWERS
1. paellera
2. kilo
3. paquete
4. dientes
5. pizca
6. taza

Comprensión
PRESENTATION (page 243)

ANSWERS

Comprensión A
1. Las legumbres que lleva una paella son: tomates, cebollas, pimientos, arroz, ajo y guisantes.
2. Las carnes que lleva una paella son: pollo y chorizos.
3. Los mariscos que lleva una paella son: camarones, calamares, almejas, mejillones y langosta.

Comprensión B
1. No
2. No
3. Sí
4. Sí
5. Sí

Comprensión C
España es una península. Es un país que está rodeado de mares. Por eso se comen muchos mariscos en España.

LEARNING FROM PHOTOS	INDEPENDENT PRACTICE
1. Refer students to the top photo on page 243. The one-piece blue garment the man is wearing is the traditional Spanish working man's outfit. It is called a *mono*. Workers of all kinds wear a *mono*. They are blue and zip up the front. Until recently the standard footwear for workers were *alpargatas,* rope-soled sandals similar to "espadrilles."	Assign the following: 1. Workbook, *Un poco más*

243

Bell Ringer Review

Write the following on the board or use BRR Blackline Master 9-9: Use the following verbs to tell someone how to make a call from a public telephone.

descolgar
introducir
colgar
esperar
marcar
hablar

Descubrimiento Cultural

(The Descubrimiento *section is optional material.)*

PRESENTATION *(pages 244-245)*

Have students read the selection on pages 244-245 aloud as a class, in pairs or groups, or silently.

DESCUBRIMIENTO CULTURAL

Es difícil imaginar lo que sería nuestra dieta sin las contribuciones del Nuevo Mundo. ¿Qué se comería en Europa hoy? O mejor, ¿qué no se comería? Pues sabemos que se comería pollo, pero no se comería pavo[1], porque es nativo de las Américas. ¿Y para beber? ¿Café, té? Pues sí, porque no se originaron en las Américas sino en el Medio Oriente y en Asia. Pero no se podría tomar chocolate, porque el chocolate o "chocolatl" que cultivaban los toltecas y aztecas en México no se encontraba en el Viejo Mundo.

Los tres productos más importantes de la agricultura americana precolombina son el maíz, la papa y el tomate. Los indígenas americanos los cultivaban siglos[2] antes de la llegada de Cristóbal Colón y los españoles. El maíz se cultivaba en la tierra baja, y la papa en el altiplano.

Los incas sabían conservar las papas con un método que las secaba, y también las congelaba. Pronto los españoles reconocieron el valor de esta nueva comida. Las primeras papas llegaron a España en el siglo quince. Desde España pasaron a toda Europa donde hoy son la base de muchas cocinas.

Piense Ud. en una cocina donde nunca aparecería una papa, una mazorca[3] de maíz o un jugoso tomate. ¿Con qué se servirían las famosas hamburguesas? No habría "ketchup" de tomate, ni papas fritas. ¿Y qué harían los italianos sin salsa de tomate para sus espaguetis?

244 CAPÍTULO 9

CRITICAL THINKING ACTIVITY

(Thinking skills: making inferences, drawing conclusions)

Write the following on the board or on a transparency:

La tortilla se hace de maíz y también de trigo. En los tiempos de los aztecas, ¿se podía hacer tortillas de trigo? ¿Por qué o por qué no?

Y AQUÍ EN LOS ESTADOS UNIDOS

¿Sabía Ud. que hubo una época cuando se creía que el tomate era venenoso[4]? Pues, sí. Cuando los españoles llevaron los primeros tomates a Europa, se usaban para adorno nada más. En poco tiempo los españoles y los italianos descubrieron lo deliciosos que eran. Pero los ingleses, no. Ellos creían que la persona que comía un tomate se moriría. Y los colonos ingleses en Norteamérica creían lo mismo hasta el siglo pasado.

[1] pavo *turkey*
[2] siglos *centuries*
[3] mazorca *corn ear*
[4] venenoso *poisonous*

Detalle del mural "El cultivo del maíz" de Diego Rivera

En un mercado al aire libre en Bolivia

Un árbol de cacao

CAPÍTULO 9   **245**

CROSS-CULTURAL CONNECTION

Refer students to the art reproduction at the top of page 245 and tell them that this is a detail of a mural by Diego Rivera (1886-1957), one of the world's foremost muralists. He was closely associated with Picasso and Cézanne when he worked in France. His murals appear in a number of public buildings in Mexico, in the Stock Exchange and Fine Arts buildings in San Francisco, and in locations in Detroit and New York City. Rivera was married to Frida Kahlo, also a famous artist. Rivera often used traditional Indian themes in his work.

LEARNING FROM PHOTOS

1. Refer students to the photo on page 244. Tell them that the woman is preparing tortillas. The tortilla was traditionally made from corn. The corn is still often ground into flour on a quadrangular stone *metate*. Today tortillas are also made from wheat flour.
2. Have students describe the scene in the open-air market in Bolivia in the photo at the bottom of page 245. The woman is wearing a traditional hat. Only the women wear hats of this type, not the men.
3. Tell students that the *Cacao*, in the photo at the bottom of page 245, is the source of chocolate. It is native to the Americas and it served as the basis for many Aztec dishes. Today, in Mexican cuisine, unsweetened chocolate is still used.

REALIDADES

(The Realidades *section is optional material.)*

Bell Ringer Review

Write the following on the board or use BRR Blackline Master 9-10: Make two columns on your paper. Label the left one **fruta** and the right one **legumbre**. Copy each of the following into the appropriate column.
1. el maíz
2. el coco
3. la papaya
4. la sandía
5. el arroz
6. el ajo
7. los pimientos
8. el plátano

PRESENTATION (pages 246-247)

The main objective of the *Realidades* is that students enjoy the photographs and gain a broader appreciation of the cultures of the Hispanic world. Following are some more structured activities which might be applied to the section.

A. Have students cover the captions. Call on volunteers to say as much as they can about each photo. Encourage them to use *creo* or *pienso* to indicate when they are guessing.

B. Call on volunteers to read the captions aloud. Some students may be able to respond to the questions in the captions.

REALIDADES

Los pescadores salen de Valencia en sus barcos **1**. Si tienen suerte volverán con sus barcos llenos de pescado.

El señor recoge tomates en Chihuahua, México **2**. Sus antepasados cultivaban el 'jitomate' hace muchos siglos. ¿Cómo prefieres tú los tomates?

Sardinas de los mares de España **3**. La presentación es bella, ¿verdad? ¿Puedes describirla?

Un plato de ricos tostones o "plátanos a puñetazos" **4**. ¿De qué se hacen los tostones?

Una parrillada en la Argentina **5**. Carne, carne y más carne. Se prepara en el campo al aire libre. Si es la Argentina, ¿qué tipo de carne será?

LEARNING FROM PHOTOS

Have students describe and talk about the photos on student pages 246-247.

GEOGRAPHY CONNECTION

La pampa argentina contiene enormes áreas de pasto (pasture). También es uno de los mayores productores de carne. ¿Hay una conexión? ¿Cuál es?

247

CRITICAL THINKING ACTIVITY

(Thinking skills: making inferences, drawing conclusions)

Read the following to the class or write it on the board or on an overhead transparency.

1. *Entre los países de habla hispana, los que tienen industria pesquera importante son España, Chile y Perú. Explique por qué.*
2. *El límite costal tradicional ha sido de 12 millas. Algunos países, el Perú y Canadá, prefieren un límite mayor. ¿Por qué quieren países como éstos proteger sus costas? Los países consumidores de pescado como el Japón y Taiwán se oponen. ¿Por qué?*

247

CULMINACIÓN

Comunicación oral

A **Un plato favorito.** Hable Ud. con un(a) compañero(a) de clase. Cada uno(a) determinará uno de sus platos favoritos y se lo describirá al otro (a la otra). Su compañero(a) tiene que adivinar qué plato es.

B **Restaurantes étnicos.** ¿Hay restaurantes étnicos, es decir, restaurantes donde preparan y sirven comidas de otras partes del mundo, cerca de donde Ud. vive? Si hay, prepare Ud. una lista de los restaurantes que Ud. conoce y note la nacionalidad de la cocina que sirven. Si Ud. puede, describa un plato de uno de los restaurantes.

C **Gustos y preferencias.** Prepare una lista de diez comestibles. Luego pregúntele a un(a) compañero(a) de clase si le gusta o no cada comestible de su lista. Su compañero(a) contestará con "mucho", "un poco", "no" o "de ninguna manera".

D **¿Te gusta comer?** Mucha gente come sólo para vivir, y mucha gente vive para comer. ¿Cómo se clasificaría Ud.? Explíquele a un(a) compañero(a) por qué.

Comunicación escrita

A **De compras.** Suponga que Ud. va a preparar una comida. Decida lo que Ud. va a cocinar y luego prepare una lista de las compras que tiene que hacer.

B **Una receta.** Escriba la receta de la comida que Ud. va a preparar.

248 CAPÍTULO 9

CULMINACIÓN

RECYCLING

The activities in *Comunicación oral* and *Comunicación escrita* encourage students to use all the language they have learned in the chapter and to recombine it with material from previous chapters. It is not necessary to do all the activities with all students. Select the ones you consider most appropriate or allow students to choose the ones they wish to do.

Comunicación oral
ANSWERS

Actividad A and B
  Answers will vary.

Actividad C
  Answers will vary but may include the following.
  El maíz
  El aceite de oliva
  El arroz
  El ajo
  La papa
  El pan
  Los guisantes
  El queso
  El azúcar
  Los frijoles negros
  El plátano

Actividad D
  Answers will vary.

INFORMAL ASSESSMENT

The *Comunicación oral* can be used to evaluate the speaking skills informally. You may assign a grade based on the student's ability to communicate in Spanish. Use the evaluation criteria given on page 24 of this Teacher's Wraparound Edition.

Comunicación escrita
ANSWERS

Actividades A and B
  Answers will vary.

248

LEARNING FROM REALIA

Refer students to the book covers depicted on page 248. Have them describe and comment on them. Cue with questions such as: ¿Qué tipo de libros son? ¿Qué es "cocina casera"? ¿A qué tipo de comida se dedica el libro de arriba? ¿A qué tipo de comida se dedica el libro de abajo?

FOR THE NATIVE SPEAKER

Have students refer to the tuna cans at the bottom of page 248 and have them respond to the following: *Las latas de atún son de dos tipos. Describa la diferencia entre los dos. Explique las ventajas y desventajas de cada una de las dos preparaciones.*

Reintegración

A **En el restaurante.** Empleen las siguientes palabras en una oración.

1. el restaurante
2. el mesero
3. el menú
4. la especialidad
5. la cuenta
6. la propina

B **La mesa.** Identifiquen según la foto.

C **Siempre, y ayer también.** Completen con el pretérito o el imperfecto.

1. Nosotros siempre ___ en aquel restaurante y ___ allí anoche. (comer)
2. Nosotros siempre ___ al restaurante en carro y ___ en carro anoche. (ir)
3. El mismo mesero siempre nos ___ y él nos ___ anoche. (servir)
4. Yo siempre ___ paella y ___ una paella anoche. (pedir)
5. El mesero siempre me ___ la cuenta y él me la ___ anoche. (dar)
6. Yo siempre ___ y ___ anoche también. (pagar)

Vocabulario

SUSTANTIVOS

la cocina
la estufa
el hornillo
la hornilla
el horno
el horno de microondas
el refrigerador
la nevera
el congelador
el/la sartén
la olla
la cazuela
la tapa
la parrilla
el pedacito
el trocito
la rebanada
los comestibles
los guisantes
las cebollas

las zanahorias
la lechuga
las papas
las habichuelas negras
los frijoles
la coliflor
el maíz
el ajo
el arroz
el pimiento
el aguacate
la lima
el limón
la toronja
el melocotón
el plátano
la banana
la carne de res
el cordero
la ternera

la salchicha
el pollo
la chuleta
la costilla
el pescado
los mariscos
las almejas
los mejillones
los camarones
las gambas
la langosta
los calamares
el aceite
la sal
la pimienta
el azúcar

VERBOS

cocinar
hervir
freír
asar
revolver
agregar
limpiar
pelar
picar
rallar
rebanar
cortar
tapar
apagar

OTRAS PALABRAS Y EXPRESIONES

poner al fuego
retirar del fuego

CAPÍTULO 9 **249**

Reintegración

PRESENTATION (page 249)

Ejercicios A and B
Exercises A and B recycle vocabulary associated with restaurants taught in *Bienvenidos*.

Ejercicio C
Exercise C reviews the contrast of the imperfect and the preterite.

ANSWERS

Ejercicio A
Answers will vary.

Ejercicio B
1. el tenedor
2. la cuchara
3. el cuchillo
4. la servilleta
5. el vaso
6. la cucharita

Ejercicio C
1. comíamos, comimos
2. íbamos, fuimos
3. servía, sirvió
4. pedía, pedí
5. daba, dio
6. pagaba, pagué

Vocabulario

The words and phrases in the *Vocabulario* have been taught for productive use in this chapter. They are summarized here as a resource for both students and teacher. The *Vocabulario* also serves as a convenient resource for *Culminación* activities. There are approximately 12 cognates in this list.

VIDEO
The video is intended to reinforce the vocabulary, structures, and cultural content in each chapter. It may be used here as a chapter wrap-up activity. See the *Video Activities Booklet* for additional suggestions on its use.

INTRODUCCIÓN (0:35:06)

LA COCINA (0:36:37)

INDEPENDENT PRACTICE

Assign any of the following:
1. Exercises on student page 249
2. Workbook, *Mi autobiografía*
3. Chapter 9, Situation Cards

STUDENT PORTFOLIO

Written assignments that may be included in students' portfolios are the *Actividades escritas* on page 248 and the *Mi autobiografía* section in the Workbook.

249

CAPÍTULO 10
Scope and Sequence pages 250-275

Topics	Functions	Structure	Culture
Driving	How to give directions	El imperativo familiar: formas regulares	Driving procedures and etiquette
Giving directions	How to discuss driving	El imperativo de los verbos irregulares	Road signs
	How to use informal commands		1992 Summer Olympics in Barcelona
		El imperativo negativo	
		Los pronombres con el imperativo	A view of the Carretera Panamericana
			La Gran Vía in Madrid
			International traffic signals

CAPÍTULO 10

Situation Cards

The Situation Cards simulate real-life situations that require students to communicate in Spanish, exactly as though they were in a Spanish-speaking country. The Situation Cards operate on the assumption that the person to whom the message is to be conveyed understands no English. Therefore, students must focus on producing the Spanish vocabulary and structures necessary to negotiate the situations successfully. For additional information, see the Introduction to the Situation Cards in the Situation Cards Envelope.

Communication Transparency

The illustration seen in this Communication Transparency consists of a synthesis of the two vocabulary (Palabras 1&2) presentations found in this chapter. It has been created in order to present this chapter's vocabulary in a new context, and also to recycle vocabulary learned in previous chapters. The Communication Transparency consists of original art. Following are some specific uses:

1. as a cue to stimulate conversation and writing activities
2. for listening comprehension activities
3. to review and reteach vocabulary
4. as a review for chapter and unit tests

CAPÍTULO 10   **A**

You rent a car for the day in Madrid. You ask the clerk at the rental agency some questions about the "rules of the road."

CAPÍTULO 10
Print Resources

Lesson Plans

	Pages
Workbook	
◆ Palabras 1	110-111
◆ Palabras 2	111-112
◆ Estructura	113-115
◆ Un poco más	116-117
◆ Mi autobiografía	118

Communication Activities Masters

◆ Palabras 1	61-62
◆ Palabras 2	63-64
◆ Estructura	65-67

11 Bell Ringer Reviews	28-30

Chapter Situation Cards A B C D

Chapter Quizzes

◆ Palabras 1	45
◆ Palabras 2	46
◆ Estructura	47-50

Testing Program

◆ Listening Comprehension	55
◆ Reading and Writing	56-59
◆ Proficiency	132
◆ Speaking	152

Nosotros y Nuestro Mundo

- ◆ Nuestro Conocimiento Académico *La ciencia política*
- ◆ Nuestro Idioma *El imperativo familiar*
- ◆ Nuestra Cultura *La naturaleza y las comunicaciones en Latinoamérica*
- ◆ Nuestra Literatura *"Canción de jinete"* de Federico García Lorca
- ◆ Nuestra Creatividad
- ◆ Nuestras Diversiones

CAPÍTULO 10
Multimedia Resources

CD-ROM Interactive Textbook Disc 3

Chapter 10 Student Edition
- ◆ Palabras 1
- ◆ Palabras 2
- ◆ Estructura
- ◆ Conversación
- ◆ Lectura y cultura
- ◆ Hispanoparlantes
- ◆ Realidades
- ◆ Culminación
- ◆ Prueba

Audio Cassette Program with Student Tape Manual

Cassette	Pages
◆ 6B Palabras 1	249-250
◆ 6B Palabras 2	250
◆ 6B Estructura	250
◆ 6B Conversación	250
◆ 6B Segunda parte	251-252

Compact Disc Program with Student Tape Manual

◆ CD 6 Palabras 1	249-250
◆ CD 6 Palabras 2	250
◆ CD 6 Estructura	250
◆ CD 6 Conversación	250
◆ CD 6 Segunda parte	251-252

Overhead Transparencies Binder

- ◆ Vocabulary 10.1 (A&B); 10.2 (A&B)
- ◆ Communication C-10
- ◆ Maps
- ◆ Fine Art (with Blackline Master Activities)

Video Program

◆ Videocassette	
◆ Video Activities Booklet	25-28
◆ Videodisc	
◆ Video Activities Booklet	25-28

Computer Software (Macintosh, IBM, Apple)

- ◆ Practice Disk
  Palabras 1 y 2
  Estructura
- ◆ Test Generator Disk
  Chapter Test
  Customized Test

250B

CAPÍTULO 10

CHAPTER OVERVIEW

In this chapter, students will expand their ability to ask for and give directions to pedestrians and drivers. They will learn vocabulary related to driving, both on the open road and in the city. They will learn to form and use the familiar imperative, and to position pronouns correctly in the imperative. The cultural focus of Chapter 10 is on driving procedures, customs, and etiquette on the highways in parts of the Hispanic world.

CHAPTER OBJECTIVES

By the end of this chapter, students will know:
1. vocabulary associated with road travel, various traffic situations, and pedestrian traffic
2. how to give and ask for directions and express location
3. the familiar imperative forms of regular and irregular verbs, affirmative and negative constructions
4. the position of object pronouns in the imperative

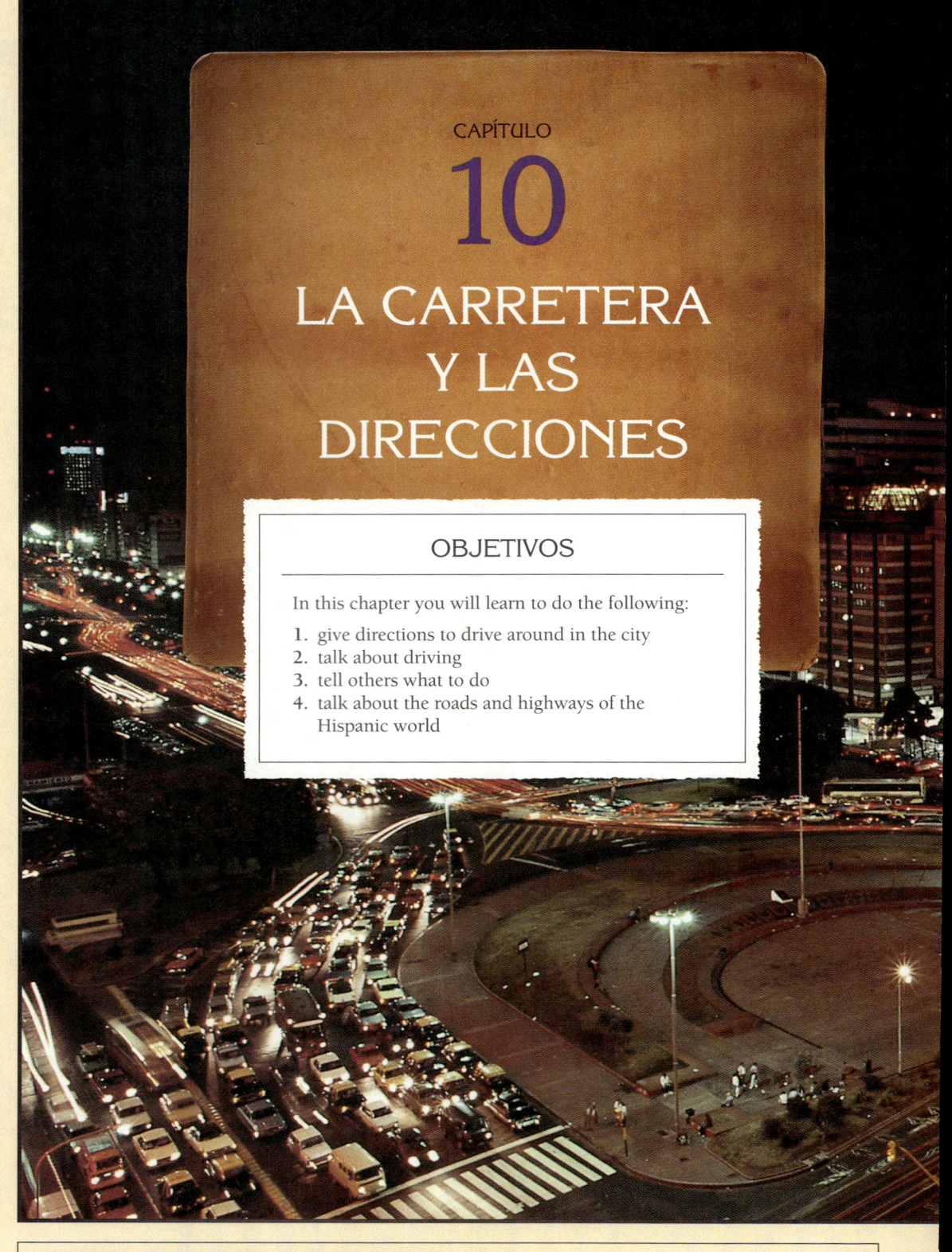

CAPÍTULO 10

LA CARRETERA Y LAS DIRECCIONES

OBJETIVOS

In this chapter you will learn to do the following:

1. give directions to drive around in the city
2. talk about driving
3. tell others what to do
4. talk about the roads and highways of the Hispanic world

CHAPTER PROJECTS

(optional)

1. Obtain a copy of the international pictogram for highways and explain in Spanish what the different symbols refer to (or ask students to explain them). The driver's education instructor in your school may be able to help you obtain such charts.

2. Visit a travel agency and obtain some brochures and information on Uruguay, especially Montevideo and Punta del Este. Have the class create a bulletin board display about these places.

CHAPTER 10 RESOURCES

1. Workbook
2. Student Tape Manual
3. Audio Cassette 6B
4. Vocabulary Transparencies
5. Bell Ringer Review Blackline Masters
6. Communication Activities Masters
7. Computer Software: Practice and Test Generator
8. Video Cassette, Chapter 10
9. Video Activities Booklet, Chapter 10
10. Situation Cards
11. Chapter Quizzes
12. Testing Program

Pacing

Chapter 10 will require eight to ten class sessions. Pacing will depend on the length of the class period, the age of the students, and student aptitude.

LEARNING FROM PHOTOS

Have students say as much as they can about the photo spread on pages 250-251. You may wish to tell them that this scene is of the center of the city of Buenos Aires, Argentina. The monument in the center is *un obelisco*. The pedestrian crosswalks are popularly called *cebras* (zebras). You may say the following: *El cruce de peatones se llama "cebra". La cebra es un animal como el asno o la mula. Vive en África. ¿Por qué dieron el nombre de "cebra" al cruce de peatones?*

251

VOCABULARIO
PALABRAS 1

Vocabulary Teaching Resources

1. Vocabulary Transparencies, 10.1 (A & B)
2. Audio Cassette 6B
3. Student Tape Manual, *Palabras 1*
4. Workbook, *Palabras 1*
5. Communication Activities Masters, *Palabras 1, A & B*
6. Chapter Quizzes, *Palabras 1*

Bell Ringer Review

Write the following on the board or use BRR Blackline Master 10-1: On a piece of paper make two columns. Head the column on the left *el avión* and the one on the right *el coche*. Copy each of the following terms into the correct column.
el compartimiento
el conductor
el chaleco salvavidas
el comandante
el descapotable
el cinturón de seguridad
la cabina
el asistente
el cruce
el aseo
el carrito
el pasillo
el intermitente

PRESENTATION (pages 252–253)

A. With books closed, refer to Vocabulary Transparencies 10.1 (A & B) and have students repeat the new words, phrases, and sentences after you or Cassette 6B.
B. You may use toy cars as props to demonstrate *doblar, estacionar*, etc.

VOCABULARIO

PALABRAS 1

LAS DIRECCIONES

el norte
el oeste   el este
el sur

detrás de
la iglesia
la casa
al lado de
delante de
enfrente de

la manzana
el semáforo
la luz
la esquina
la acera
la cuadra
la calle
la bocacalle, el cruce

252 CAPÍTULO 10

FOR THE NATIVE SPEAKER

Ask students what term for "car" they are familiar with and what terms they recognize for it but do not use. Ask them to discuss where each of these terms is used.

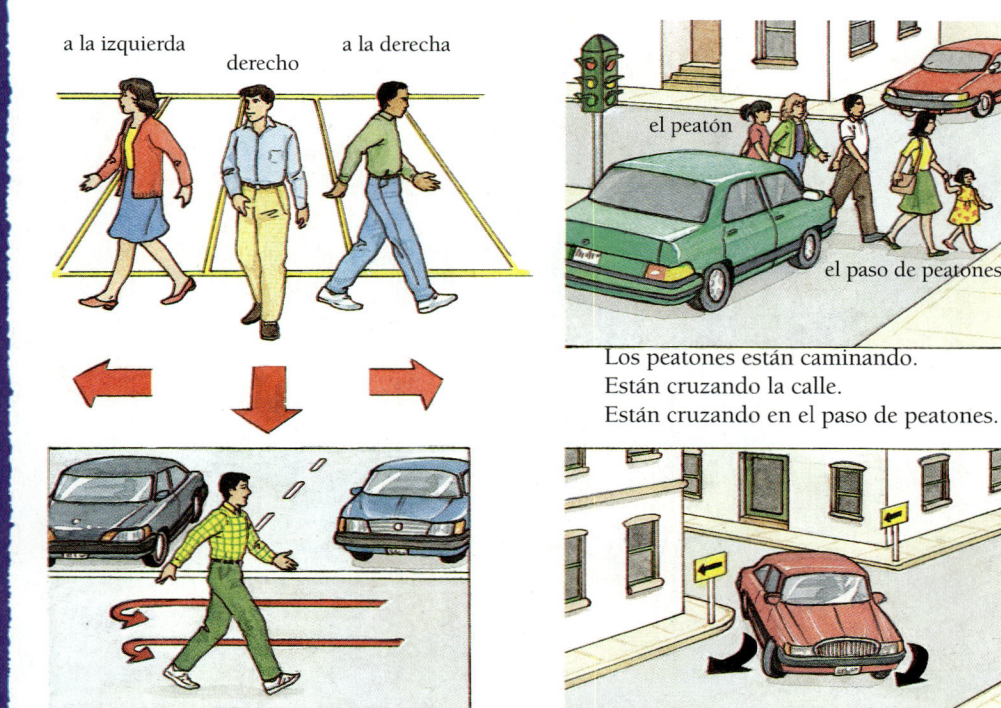

a la izquierda   derecho   a la derecha

el peatón

el paso de peatones

Los peatones están caminando.
Están cruzando la calle.
Están cruzando en el paso de peatones.

El señor dio una vuelta.

Catalina dobló a la derecha.

el parquímetro

La señorita estacionó el coche.

CAPÍTULO 10   **253**

DID YOU KNOW?

In Spain, the usual word for "car" is *coche*, the old word for "coach." In Latin America the most common term is *carro*, the word for "cart" or "wagon." In France an automobile is *une voiture*, also the old word for "coach," while in French Canada the word used until recently was *un char*, the word for "cart" or "wagon." Ask students to comment on this similarity.

C. Use gestures and dramatizations to convey the meanings of *a la derecha*, *a la izquierda*, *derecho*, *al lado de*, *detrás de*, *delante de*, and *en frente de*.

D. After students have had a chance to produce the sentences on page 253 several times, ask questions to elicit the material. For example: *¿Quiénes están cruzando la calle? ¿Dobló Catalina a la derecha o a la izquierda? ¿Qué hizo el señor? ¿Qué están haciendo los peatones?*

ABOUT THE LANGUAGE

1. You may wish to review the vocabulary about the automobile in Chapter 5, page 114.
2. *La manzana* is the square block, bounded on four sides. *La cuadra* can be synonymous with *la manzana*. It also means the distance between two intersecting streets. In Latin America, this is usually between 100 and 150 meters.
3. *La esquina* is the corner where two streets meet. It is the outside corner or angle. An inside corner or angle is usually called *un rincón*.
4. *El norte* also has the figurative meaning of "guide" or "direction."
5. In Spain the word most often used for "to turn" is *doblar*. In Latin America it is usually *virar*. Both terms are understood everywhere.
6. *Estacionar* is the traditional term for "to park." However, *aparcar* is often used, as well as *parquear*, although *parquear* is considered an Americanism.
7. An automobile is a *coche*, *carro*, *automóvil*, *auto*, or *máquina*, depending on the area.

Ejercicios

PRESENTATION (page 254)

Ejercicio A
Exercise A is to be done with books open.

Extension of *Ejercicio B*
Speaking
After completing Exercise B, focus on the speaking skill by having students correct the false statements.

ANSWERS

Ejercicio A
1. El garaje está al lado de la casa.
2. No, el carro no está en el garaje.
3. El carro está en la entrada.
4. Detrás de la casa hay una iglesia.
5. La iglesia está detrás de la casa.

Ejercicio B
1. Sí
2. No
3. Sí
4. No
5. Sí
6. Sí
7. Sí
8. No

GEOGRAPHY CONNECTION

Have students consult the maps on pages 453–454. In Spanish, have them indicate where different countries are in relation to each other. For example: *Chile está al oeste de la Argentina. Guatemala está al sur de México.*

254

Ejercicios

A ¿Dónde está? Contesten según el dibujo.

1. ¿Dónde está el garaje?
2. ¿Está el carro en el garaje?
3. ¿Dónde está el carro?
4. ¿Qué hay detrás de la casa?
5. ¿Dónde está la iglesia?

B Un poco de geografía. ¿Sí o no?

1. Nueva York está al norte de Miami.
2. Chile y la Argentina están en el norte del continente sudamericano.
3. Chile y la Argentina están en el sur de la América del Sur.
4. California está en el este de los Estados Unidos.
5. El océano Pacífico está al oeste de los Estados Unidos.
6. El estado de Massachussetts está en el este.
7. El océano Atlántico está al este de los Estados Unidos.
8. México está al norte de los Estados Unidos.

254   CAPÍTULO 10

LEARNING FROM PHOTOS

Refer students to the compass on page 254 and tell them that the word for "compass" is *la brújula*.

FOR THE NATIVE SPEAKER

Have students write down detailed instructions on how to use a parking meter. They should indicate where the coin goes, what must be turned and in which direction, the time allowed for each coin, the penalty for parking overtime, etc.

C En el centro de la ciudad. Contesten según se indica.

1. ¿Qué hay en el centro de la ciudad? (mucho tráfico)
2. ¿Cuándo se paran los carros? (la luz está roja)
3. ¿Dónde está el semáforo? (en el cruce)
4. ¿Quiénes pueden cruzar la calle cuando se para el tráfico? (los peatones)
5. ¿Dónde deben cruzar? (en el paso de peatones)
6. ¿Dónde hay semáforos? (en las esquinas de los cruces principales)
7. ¿Se puede entrar en esta calle? (no, es de sentido único)
8. ¿Por qué dio la vuelta el señor? (porque iba en sentido contrario)
9. ¿Estacionó la señora el coche? (sí)
10. ¿Dónde introdujo (puso) la moneda? (en la ranura del parquímetro)

D Definiciones. ¿Cuál es la palabra?

1. el semáforo
2. el cruce
3. el tráfico
4. ir a pie
5. estacionar

a. el tránsito
b. caminar
c. la luz del tránsito
d. aparcar
e. la bocacalle

E Lo contrario.

1. seguir derecho
2. la derecha
3. caminar
4. delante de
5. el sur

a. la izquierda
b. el norte
c. detrás de
d. dar la vuelta
e. conducir

La calle Florida en la Argentina

CAPÍTULO 10   255

PRESENTATION (page 255)

Ejercicio C
Exercise C can be done with books open or closed.

Ejercicios D and E
Have students scan the *Palabras 1* vocabulary as they do Exercises D and E.

ANSWERS

Ejercicio C
1. En el centro de la ciudad hay mucho tráfico.
2. Los carros se paran cuando la luz está roja.
3. El semáforo está en el cruce.
4. Los peatones pueden cruzar la calle cuando se para el tráfico.
5. Los peatones deben cruzar en el paso de peatones.
6. Hay semáforos en las esquinas de los cruces principales.
7. No, no se puede entrar en esta calle, es de sentido único.
8. El señor dio la vuelta porque iba en sentido contrario.
9. Sí, la señora estacionó el coche.
10. Ella introdujo (puso) la moneda en la ranura del parquímetro.

Ejercicio D
1. c
2. e
3. a
4. b
5. d

Ejercicio E
1. d
2. a
3. e
4. c
5. b

CRITICAL THINKING ACTIVITY

(Thinking skills: supporting statements with reasons)

Write the following on the board or on a transparency:

La calle en la foto es "peatonal". No se permiten carros. En muchas ciudades hay calles peatonales en los centros comerciales. A algunos comerciantes les gustan las calles peatonales y a otros no. ¿Por qué?

INDEPENDENT PRACTICE

Assign any of the following:
1. Workbook, *Palabras 1*
2. Communication Activities Masters, *Palabras 1*, A & B
3. Exercises on student pages 254–255

255

VOCABULARIO
PALABRAS 2

Vocabulary Teaching Resources
1. Vocabulary Transparencies 10.2 (A & B)
2. Audio Cassette 6B
3. Student Tape Manual, *Palabras 2*
4. Workbook, *Palabras 2*
5. Communication Activities Masters, *Palabras 2, C & D*
6. Chapter Quizzes, *Palabras 2*
7. Computer Software, *Vocabulario*

Bell Ringer Review
Write the following on the board or use BRR Blackline Master 10-2: Write as many words and expressions as you can think of which have to do with giving directions.

PRESENTATION (pages 256-257)

A. Have students close their books. Model the *Palabras 2* vocabulary using Vocabulary Transparencies 10.2 (A & B). Have students repeat the new material after you or Cassette 6B.

B. Intersperse repetitions with yes/no or either/or questions which elicit the new vocabulary. Then progress to more open-ended questions. For example: ¿Cuál es la velocidad máxima? ¿A qué distancia está San Pedro? ¿Dónde debe quedarse Roberto? ¿Qué tiene que pagar? ¿Por qué está prohibido adelantar?

VOCABULARIO

PALABRAS 2

¡MANEJA CON CUIDADO!

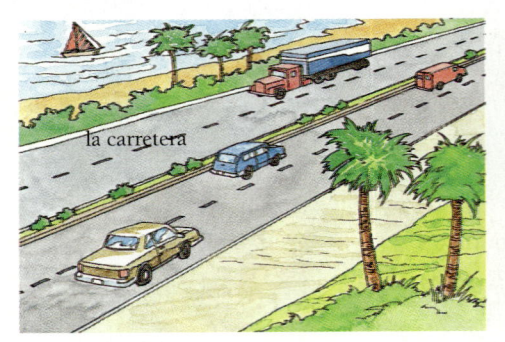

la autopista, la autovía
la salida
la carretera
la garita de peaje
el carril
la entrada

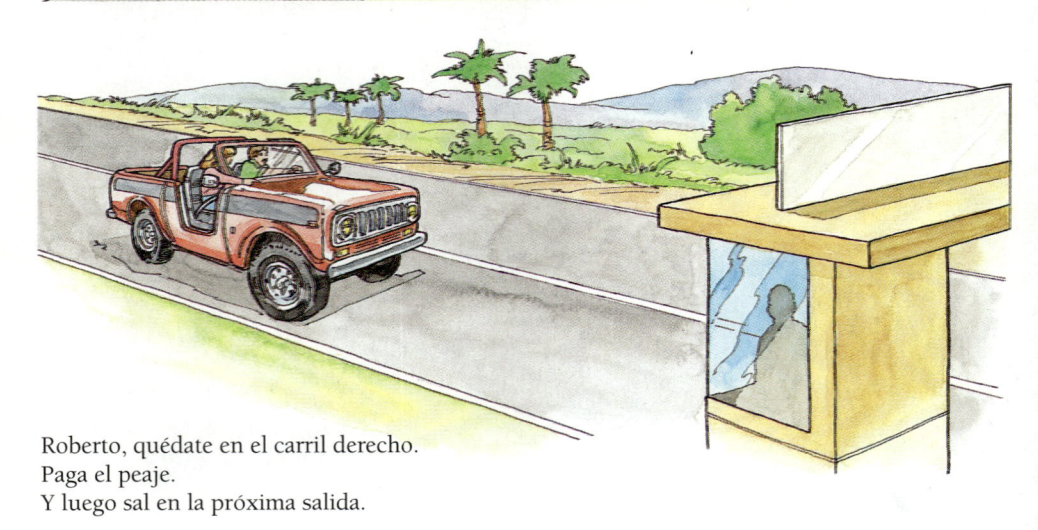

el rótulo
SAN PEDRO 28 KM
80 Km/h
la velocidad máxima

Roberto, quédate en el carril derecho.
Paga el peaje.
Y luego sal en la próxima salida.

256 CAPÍTULO 10

PANTOMIME

Getting Ready
You may wish to set up a chair in front of the class and tell students to pretend that it is the driver's seat in a car. You may use as many additional props as you wish.
___, venga aquí, por favor. Éste es su carro.
Abra la puerta y entre en su carro.
Cierre la puerta.

Encienda el motor.
Ponga el carro en marcha.
Pise el acelerador.
Vaya derecho.
Ahora, pise el freno.
Pare el carro en la garita de peaje.
Pise el acelerador y siga derecho.
Doble a la derecha.
Estacione el carro.
Abra la puerta y salga del carro.
Gracias. Vuelva Ud. a su asiento.

Donde está el rótulo, dobla a la derecha.
Y luego sigue derecho.

Roberto, ¡cuidado!
Está prohibido adelantar.
Hay solamente un carril en cada sentido.

CAPÍTULO 10   257

Vocabulary Expansion

You may wish to ask students the following questions about the two illustrations on page 257: ¿Qué indican los dos rótulos internacionales? (The sign in the top illustration means *sentido [dirección] único[a]*. The one in the bottom illustration means *prohibido adelantar*.)

Teaching Tip You may wish to lead into some of the grammar taught later in this chapter by pointing out the sentences on pages 256-257 which make use of the familiar imperative.

ABOUT THE LANGUAGE

1. You may wish to review vocabulary about the automobile in Chapter 5, page 114.
2. In Spain, drivers learn to *conducir un coche*, while in most of Latin America they learn to *manejar* or *guiar un carro*.
3. The convertible is *el descapotable* in Spain and *el convertible* in much of Latin America.

CROSS-CULTURAL COMPARISON

1. In Puerto Rico, speed limits are posted in *millas por hora*, but distances are given in *kilómetros* and *hectómetros*.
2. Have students convert the distances and speeds shown in the illustrations from the metric to the English system.

COOPERATIVE LEARNING

Have team members practice giving directions to local places in Spanish. Each team then rehearses giving one or two sets of directions and presents them to the class. The class determines what location the directions are for.

CRITICAL THINKING ACTIVITY

(Thinking skills: evaluating consequences; problem-solving)

Write the following on the board or on a transparency:
1. *Explica en español por qué es importante mirar a la derecha y a la izquierda antes de cruzar la calle.*
2. *¿Por qué está prohibido adelantar en algunos casos?*

Ejercicios

PRESENTATION (page 258)

Ejercicio A

Exercise A is to be done with books open.

ANSWERS

Ejercicio A
1. Es una carretera.
2. Es la salida.
3. Tiene dos carriles.
4. Los coches se paran delante de la garita de peaje.
5. Es un rótulo.

CROSS-CULTURAL COMPARISON

In Spain there are different speed limits for different kinds of vehicles. Highway speed limits for passenger cars are usually 100 or 120 kilometers per hour. Seat belts are mandatory only for highway driving, not in the city.

Ejercicios

A ¿Qué es? Contesten según la foto.

1. ¿Es una calle o una carretera?

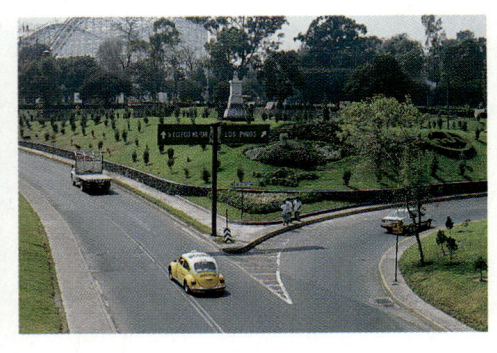

2. ¿Es la salida o la entrada?

3. ¿Tiene dos o cuatro carriles la autopista?

4. ¿Se paran los coches delante de la salida o delante de la garita de peaje?

5. ¿Es un rótulo o un carril?

258   CAPÍTULO 10

CRITICAL THINKING ACTIVITY

(Thinking skills: supporting statements with reasons)

Write the following on the board or on a transparency: *En algunas carreteras hay que pagar peaje. También hay que pagar impuestos al gobierno sobre la gasolina. ¿Cuál es la mejor forma de obtener dinero para las carreteras, y por qué?*

FOR THE NATIVE SPEAKER

Have students prepare a recruitment ad for long distance truck drivers. The name of the company might be *Transportes Continentales*. The ad should indicate the size of the truck, the kinds of cargo to be hauled, hours, salary, and benefits.

B **En la carretera.** Contesten según se indica.
1. ¿Qué vamos a tomar? (la autopista)
2. ¿Qué tenemos que pagar? (el peaje)
3. ¿Dónde lo tenemos que pagar? (en la garita)
4. ¿Cuántos carriles tiene la autopista en cada sentido? (tres)
5. ¿Cuál es la velocidad máxima? (cien kilómetros)
6. ¿Está prohibido adelantar? (no)
7. ¿Está prohibido exceder la velocidad máxima? (sí)

C **Donde vivo yo.** Preguntas personales.
1. ¿Cuál es una autopista cerca de donde tú vives?
2. ¿Es una autopista de peaje?
3. ¿Cuánto es el peaje?
4. ¿Dónde tienes que pagar el peaje? ¿En la salida de la autopista? Si no, ¿a cada cuántos kilómetros hay garitas de peaje?
5. ¿Cuál es el número de la salida más cerca de tu casa?
6. ¿Cuál es la velocidad máxima en la autopista?
7. ¿Cuántos carriles tiene?
8. A la salida, ¿hay un rótulo que indica los pueblos cercanos?

Comunicación
Palabras 1 y 2

A **Cerca de mi casa.** Descríbale a un(a) compañero(a) de clase lo que hay cerca (en los alrededores) de su casa. Dígale dónde están con relación a su casa. Cambien de papel.

B **En la escuela.** Trabaje con un(a) compañero(a) de clase. Él/ella le va a preguntar cómo se puede ir a varios lugares dentro de su escuela o del recinto (*campus*) de su escuela. Ud. va a darle las direcciones.

C **Las autopistas.** Ud. está viajando por el Ecuador. Un(a) amigo(a) ecuatoriano(a) le pregunta cómo son las autopistas donde Ud. vive. Descríbale las autopistas de su estado.

CAPÍTULO 10   259

ESTRUCTURA

El imperativo familiar
Formas regulares

Telling Friends What to Do

1. The *tú* command is used when speaking to a person you know well or to a child. The familiar *tú* form of the command for regular verbs is the same as the *Ud.* form of the verb in the present tense.

UD.	IMPERATIVE (TÚ)
Ud. habla	habla
Ud. come	come
Ud. escribe	escribe

2. The imperative of verbs with a stem change is formed in the same way.

UD.	IMPERATIVE (TÚ)
Ud. cierra	cierra
Ud. pierde	pierde
Ud. vuelve	vuelve
Ud. pide	pide
Ud. fríe	fríe

Ejercicios

A ¿Qué debo hacer? *Contesten según el modelo.*

¿Debo hablar?
Sí, Pepe, habla.

1. ¿Debo hablar?
2. ¿Debo parar?
3. ¿Debo doblar?
4. ¿Debo dar la vuelta?
5. ¿Debo doblar a la derecha?
6. ¿Debo leer lo que hay en el rótulo?
7. ¿Debo seguir derecho?
8. ¿Debo volver?
9. ¿Debo pedir direcciones?

260 CAPÍTULO 10

LEARNING FROM PHOTOS

Refer students to the photo at the bottom of page 260. Have them tell what is happening in it.

INDEPENDENT PRACTICE

Assign any of the following:
1. Workbook, *Estructura*
2. Communication Activities Masters *Estructura*, A
3. Exercises on student pages 260–261

Structure Teaching Resources

1. Workbook, *Estructura*
2. Student Tape Manual, *Estructura*
3. Audio Cassette 6B
5. Communication Activities Masters, *Estructura*, A-D
6. Chapter Quizzes, *Estructura*
7. Computer Software, *Estructura*

Bell Ringer Review

Write the following on the board or use BRR Blackline Master 10-4: Write the opposites of these words and expressions:
1. la izquierda
2. detrás de
3. el este
4. la luz roja

El imperativo familiar
Formas regulares

PRESENTATION (page 260)

A. Have students open their books to page 260. Lead them through steps 1 and 2. Have students repeat the forms.
B. Provide and elicit additional examples.

Ejercicios

PRESENTATION (page 260)

Ejercicio A
Exercise A can be done with books open or closed.

ANSWERS

Ejercicio A
1. … habla.
2. … para.
3. … dobla.
4. … da la vuelta.
5. … dobla a la derecha.
6. … lee lo que hay en el rótulo.
7. … sigue derecho.
8. … vuelve.
9. … pide direcciones.

B ¿Cómo debo ir? *Completen con el imperativo.*

1. Oye, Roberto, ___ a la derecha. (doblar)
2. ___ derecho. (seguir)
3. ___ derecho hasta la tercera bocacalle. (seguir)
4. ___ a la izquierda. (mirar)
5. A mano izquierda, verás la tienda. ___ . (entrar)
6. ___ la escalera. (buscar)
7. ___ al tercer piso. (subir)

C Debes hacer lo que quieres hacer. *Contesten según el modelo.*

Quiero viajar a España.
Entonces, viaja a España.

1. Quiero viajar a España.
2. Quiero pasar un mes en Madrid.
3. Quiero tomar el tren a Toledo.
4. Quiero visitar la capital.
5. Quiero ver los cuadros de El Greco.
6. Quiero aprender el español.
7. Quiero comer una paella.
8. Quiero beber horchata.
9. Quiero vivir con una familia española.

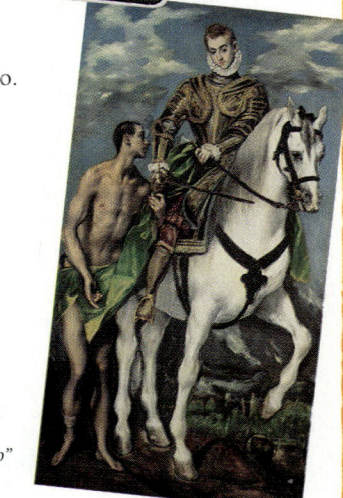

"San Martín y el pordiosero" de El Greco

El imperativo familiar
Formas irregulares

Telling Friends What to Do

The following verbs have irregular forms for the *tú* command. Study the following.

INFINITIVE	IMPERATIVE (TÚ)
decir	di
ir	ve
ser	sé
salir	sal
hacer	haz
tener	ten
venir	ven
poner	pon

CAPÍTULO 10   261

Ejercicios

PRESENTATION (*page 262*)

Ejercicios A and B
Exercises A and B can be done with books open or closed.

Ejercicio C
Exercise C can be done with books open.

ANSWERS

Ejercicio A
1. Sí, ven mañana.
2. Sí, haz el viaje en tren.
3. Sí, sal temprano.
4. Sí, ve en taxi.
5. Sí, di algo al taxista.
6. Sí, pon las maletas en la maletera.

Ejercicio B
1. Pues, haz las compras.
2. Pues, sal ahora.
3. Pues, ve al mercado de Santa Tecla.
4. Pues, pon tus compras en esta canasta.
5. Pues, ve a pie.
6. Pues, conduce.
7. Pues, ve en carro.

Ejercicio C
1. Llama
2. Haz
3. Haz
4. Ve
5. Descuelga
6. Introduce
7. Espera
8. Marca
9. Espera
10. Di
11. Sé
12. Pregunta
13. Habla

262

Ejercicios

A ¿**Debo venir mañana?** Contesten con sí y el imperativo.

1. ¿Debo venir mañana?
2. ¿Debo hacer el viaje en tren?
3. ¿Debo salir temprano?
4. ¿Debo ir en taxi?
5. ¿Debo decir algo al taxista?
6. ¿Debo poner las maletas en la maletera?

B **Voy de compras.** Contesten según el modelo.

Quiero hacer las compras.
Pues, haz las compras.

1. Quiero hacer las compras.
2. Quiero salir ahora.
3. Quiero ir al mercado de Santa Tecla.
4. Quiero poner mis compras en esta canasta.
5. Quiero ir a pie.
6. Quiero conducir.
7. Quiero ir en carro.

C **Una llamada telefónica.** Completen con el imperativo (tú).

1. ____ por teléfono. (llamar)
2. ____ la llamada. (hacer)
3. ____ la llamada de un teléfono público. (hacer)
4. ____ a la cabina telefónica. (ir)
5. ____ el auricular. (descolgar)
6. ____ la moneda en la ranura. (introducir)
7. ____ el tono. (esperar)
8. ____ el número. (marcar)
9. ____ la contestación. (esperar)
10. ____ "Hola". (decir)
11. ____ cortés. (ser)
12. ____ por Antonio. (preguntar)
13. ____ con él. (hablar)

262 CAPÍTULO 10

LEARNING FROM PHOTOS

1. Have students describe the photo at the top of page 262. Point out the juxtaposition of ancient and modern. The *escarabajo* (beetle) taxi is in front of the cathedral in Mexico. Ask students: ¿*Dónde está el maletero de este taxi? ¿Por qué?*
2. Have students say as much as they can about the photo at the bottom.

FOR THE NATIVE SPEAKER

En muchos países hispanos los teléfonos y telégrafos son del gobierno. En los EE.UU. varias compañías telefónicas compiten. ¿Cuáles son las ventajas y desventajas de los dos sistemas? ¿Por qué son tan populares y tan usados los teléfonos públicos en Latinoamérica?

El imperativo negativo

Telling Someone Not to Do Something

1. The negative of the *tú* command is formed the same way as the formal commands (*Ud., Uds.*) You drop the *-o* of the *yo* form of the present tense and add *-es* to *-ar* verbs and *-as* to *-er* and *-ir* verbs.

INFINITIVE	PRESENT (YO)	NEGATIVE COMMMAND (TÚ)
hablar	yo hablø	no hables
comer	yo comø	no comas
abrir	yo abrø	no abras
volver	yo vuelvø	no vuelvas
pedir	yo pidø	no pidas
hacer	yo hagø	no hagas
salir	yo salgø	no salgas

2. The same verbs that are irregular in the formal command are irregular in the negative *tú* command.

ir	no vayas
ser	no seas
saber	no sepas
estar	no estés
dar	no des

Ejercicios

A **No, Pepe. No lo hagas.** Cambien a la forma negativa.

1. ¡Corre, Pepe!
2. ¡Espera, Pepe!
3. ¡Vuelve, Pepe!
4. ¡Come, Pepe!
5. ¡Escribe, Pepe!
6. ¡Baja, Pepe!
7. ¡Haz otro, Pepe!
8. ¡Ven, Pepe!
9. ¡Ten cuidado, Pepe!
10. ¡Sal ahora, Pepe!

CAPÍTULO 10

Bell Ringer Review
Write the following on the board or use BRR Blackline Master 10-5: Write as many words as you can which are associated with hair and hairstyles.

El imperativo negativo
PRESENTATION (*page 263*)
Have students open their books to page 263 and lead them through steps 1 and 2. Then have them repeat the forms after you. Provide and elicit additional examples.

Ejercicios
PRESENTATION (*pages 263-264*)
Ejercicios A and B
You may wish to assign Exercises A and B for independent practice and then go over them in class the following day.

ANSWERS
Ejercicio A
1. ¡No corras, Pepe!
2. ¡No esperes, Pepe!
3. ¡No vuelvas, Pepe!
4. ¡No comas, Pepe!
5. ¡No escribas, Pepe!
6. ¡No bajes, Pepe!
7. ¡No hagas otro, Pepe!
8. ¡No vengas, Pepe!
9. ¡No tengas cuidado, Pepe!
10. ¡No salgas ahora, Pepe!

LEARNING FROM REALIA
Refer students to the road signs on page 263. Ask students: *¿Qué indican los dos rótulos internacionales?*

INDEPENDENT PRACTICE
Assign any of the following:
1. Workbook, *Estructura*
2. Communication Activities Masters, *Estructura*, B & C
3. Exercises on student pages 262-263

ANSWERS

Ejercicio B
1. No, no llames.
2. No, no vayas en carro.
3. No, no vayas a pie.
4. No, no salgas.
5. No, no escribas una carta.
6. No, no vendas el coche.
7. No, no hagas nada.

Bell Ringer Review
Write the following on the board or use BRR Blackline Master 10-6: Tell what you were doing when the following events occurred. Use the past progressive tense.
1. a las doce el 31 de diciembre
2. el 25 de diciembre
3. el día de las gracias
4. el sábado pasado

Los pronombres con el imperativo
PRESENTATION (page 264)

Have students open their books to page 264 and lead them through the presentation. Then have them repeat the forms after you. Provide and elicit additional examples.

Ejercicios
PRESENTATION (page 264)

Ejercicio A
After calling on volunteers to present the conversation with books open, you may have pairs practice it aloud and present it the following day with books closed.

ANSWERS

Ejercicio A
Conversation practice.

264

B ¡Ay, bendito! ¿Lo hago o no lo hago? Contesten según el modelo.

Amigo, ¿hablo o no hablo?
No, no hables.

1. Amigo, ¿llamo o no llamo?
2. ¿Voy en carro o no?
3. ¿Voy a pie o no?
4. ¿Salgo o no?
5. Luego, ¿escribo una carta o no?
6. ¿Vendo el coche o no?
7. ¿Hago algo o no?

Los pronombres con el imperativo   *Telling Friends What to Do*

The object pronouns are attached to the affirmative commands. They precede the negative commands.

FORMAL	
AFFIRMATIVE	NEGATIVE
Levántese Ud.	No se levante Ud.
Míreme Ud.	No me mire Ud.
Escríbale Ud.	No le escriba Ud.
Démelo Ud.	No me lo dé Ud.
Dígaselo Ud.	No se lo diga Ud.

INFORMAL	
AFFIRMATIVE	NEGATIVE
Levántate.	No te levantes.
Mírame.	No me mires.
Escríbele.	No le escribas.
Dámelo.	No me lo des.
Díselo a él.	No se lo digas a él.

Ejercicios

A ¡Qué dormilona es Marisa! Practiquen la conversación.

MAMÁ: Marisa, levántate. Ya es hora.
MARISA: ¡Ay, mamá! Que no. ¡Déjame, por favor!
MAMÁ: Bien. No te levantes. Y no te laves ni te vistas. Quédate en cama.
MARISA: Perdóname, mami. Pero tengo sueño.

264   CAPÍTULO 10

LEARNING FROM PHOTOS

You may wish to have students describe the photo at the bottom of page 264 as thoroughly as possible. Cue with questions such as: ¿Quiénes son las dos personas? ¿Qué hace la muchacha? ¿Dónde está ella? ¿Qué le dice su mamá? ¿Qué hay en las paredes? ¿Qué color le gusta a la muchacha?

B La rutina. Contesten según el modelo.

¿Me levanto?
Sí, levántate.
No, no te levantes.

1. ¿Me levanto?
2. ¿Me lavo?
3. ¿Me lavo el pelo?
4. ¿Me pongo la chaqueta?
5. ¿Me acuesto?

C Sí, dámelas. Contesten según el modelo.

¿Te doy las direcciones?
Sí, dámelas.

1. ¿Te doy las direcciones?
2. ¿Te doy el mapa?
3. ¿Te doy el número de teléfono?
4. ¿Te doy el código?
5. ¿Te doy la zona postal?
6. ¿Te doy las estampillas?
7. ¿Te doy el sobre?

D No, no la escriba Ud. Cambien a la forma negativa.

1. Escríbale.
2. Mándele la carta.
3. Llámelo por teléfono.
4. Déle mis recuerdos.
5. Invítelo a visitarnos.

CAPÍTULO 10 **265**

PRESENTATION
Ejercicios B and C
Exercises B and C can be done with books open or closed.

ANSWERS
Ejercicio B
1. Sí, levántate.
   No, no te levantes.
2. Sí, lávate.
   No, no te laves.
3. Sí, lávatelo.
   No, no te lo laves.
4. Sí, póntela.
   No, no te la pongas.
5. Sí, acuéstate.
   No, no te acuestes.

Ejercicio C
1. Sí, dámelas.
2. Sí, dámelo.
3. Sí, dámelo.
4. Sí, dámelo.
5. Sí, dámela.
6. Sí, dámelas.
7. Sí, dámelo.

Ejercicio D
1. No le escriba Ud.
2. No se la mande Ud.
3. No lo llame Ud. por teléfono.
4. No se los dé Ud.
5. No los invite Ud. a visitarnos.

LEARNING FROM REALIA
Tell students that the map on page 265 shows the major arteries into the city of Santiago, Chile. Ask: ¿Dónde empieza la carretera que va a Viña del Mar? ¿Cerca de qué sección de Santiago está el aeropuerto? ¿En qué dirección quedan los Andes? ¿Qué se puede hacer en Portillo? ¿Qué se puede hacer en Viña del Mar? ¿En qué dirección queda San Bernardo? ¿Dónde se puede esquiar?

INDEPENDENT PRACTICE
Assign any of the following:
1. Workbook, *Estructura*
2. Communication Activities Masters, *Estructura*, D
3. Exercises on student pages 264–265

265

CONVERSACIÓN

Bell Ringer Review
Write the following on the board or use BRR Blackline Master 10-7: Define the following briefly in Spanish:
1. la salida
2. la carretera
3. el rótulo
4. la autopista

PRESENTATION *(page 266)*
A. Tell students they will hear a conversation between Marisa and Catalina in which Marisa asks for directions.
B. Have students close their books and listen as you read the conversation or play Cassette 6B.
C. Have pairs practice reading the conversation with as much expression as possible. Circulate and model pronunciation as necessary.
D. Call on pairs of volunteers to present the conversation to the class. Have a third student act out the directions as they are given.

Ejercicio
ANSWERS
1. Catalina está en la Pensión Rosa.
2. Está cerca del Palacio de Telecomunicaciones.
3. Está a tres cuadras.
4. Debe tomar Quevedo hasta el primer semáforo.
5. Dobla a la derecha.
6. La pensión está a mano izquierda.

266

CONVERSACIÓN

Escenas de la vida ¿Dónde está?

MARISA: Catalina, ¿tú estás en qué pensión?
CATALINA: La Pensión Rosa.
MARISA: Dime dónde está.
CATALINA: Pues, ¿sabes dónde está el Palacio de Telecomunicaciones?
MARISA: Sí, claro.
CATALINA: Pues, está a tres manzanas de allí. En la esquina, donde está Telecomunicaciones, verás Quevedo. Toma Quevedo hasta el primer semáforo. En el semáforo, dobla a la derecha y a mano izquierda verás la pensión.

En la pensión. Contesten según la conversación.
1. ¿En qué pensión está Catalina?
2. ¿Está cerca de qué edificio grande la pensión?
3. ¿A cuántas manzanas del Palacio de Telecomunicaciones está?
4. ¿Hasta dónde debe tomar Quevedo Marisa?
5. ¿Qué hace al llegar al primer semáforo?
6. Y luego, ¿dónde está la pensión?

HOSPEDAJE *Familiar*

266 CAPÍTULO 10

DID YOU KNOW?
Although *pensiones* are rooming houses, many are very elegant. In Spain the *pensiones* also are graded like hotels. Because university dormitories are not as common as in the U.S., many Spanish students live in *pensiones* with *pensión completa*—all their meals.

Comunicación

A **A la escuela.** Roberto Robles es de Oaxaca, México. Él está pasando un mes viviendo con su familia. Mañana él va a visitar su escuela por primera vez. Dígale a Roberto (un[a] compañero[a] de clase) cómo puede ir a su escuela.

Las ruinas de Monte Albán, Oaxaca, México

B **A la capital.** Roberto tiene su permiso de conducir y mañana su papá le va a permitir usar su carro. Roberto quiere ir a visitar la capital de su estado. Explíquele a Roberto (un[a] compañero[a] de clase) cómo puede ir de su pueblo a la capital en carro.

C **Yo no. ¡Tú!** Dígale a un(a) compañero(a) de clase algunas cosas que Ud. cree que él/ella debe hacer. Su compañero(a) no quiere hacer lo que Ud. le dice.

    Estudiante 1: Estudia para el examen de español.
    Estudiante 2: No quiero estudiar. Tú, estudia si quieres.

CAPÍTULO 10   **267**

Bell Ringer Review
Write the following on the board or use BRR Blackline Master 10-8: Complete each sentence with the future tense of the indicated verb.
1. El próximo año mi familia ___ un viaje a México. (hacer)
2. Nosotros ___ en avión. (ir)
3. Mis padres ___ a todos los museos. (ir)
4. Yo ___ de compras. (ir)
5. El viaje ___ fantástico. (ser)

Comunicación
PRESENTATION *(page 267)*
Have students do one or all of these activities, allowing them to select those in which they wish to take part.

ANSWERS
Actividades A, B, and C
Answers will vary.

HISTORY CONNECTION
Monte Albán is near the city of Oaxaca. Long, low buildings with sunken courts and stairways surround an enormous plaza that is 1,000 feet long and 650 feet wide. Great archeological treasures were excavated from the tombs of Monte Albán. The Zapotecs inhabited the area from about 200 B.C. and were driven from the area by the Spaniards in 1521.

LEARNING FROM REALIA
Have students say as much as they can about the I.D. card on page 267.

INDEPENDENT PRACTICE
You may wish to assign the following: Exercises and activities on student pages 266–267

LECTURA Y CULTURA

Bell Ringer Review

Write the following on the board or use BRR Blackline Master 10-9: You are working for the Spanish national airline Iberia and have been assigned to train new flight attendants. Write five things you would tell them. For example: **Indícales las salidas de emergencia a los pasajeros.**

READING STRATEGIES
(page 268)

Pre-Reading
Before reading the selection on page 268, ask some volunteers to do research on Uruguay and in particular Montevideo and Punta del Este.

Reading
A. Go over some paragraphs of the reading selection thoroughly by having volunteers read them aloud. Ask the class your own comprehension questions.
B. Have the class read the paragraphs silently that you did not select, and ask them to make up their own comprehension questions to ask their classmates.

Post-reading
Have students pretend they have just visited Montevideo. Have them write postcards in Spanish describing their experiences.

LECTURA Y CULTURA

LAS DIRECCIONES A MALDONADO

Hablan Felipe y Luisa.

Mañana quiero ir a Maldonado y no sé precisamente dónde está. ¿Me puedes dar direcciones, por favor?

Condominios en Punta del Este, Uruguay

Sí, amigo, ¡cómo no! Es el mismo camino para ir a Punta del Este. Para salir de Montevideo, vas a tomar la Avenida Central. Sigue por la Avenida Central hasta el final. Es una calle de sentido único y no hay muchos semáforos. Al salir de la ciudad, toma la autopista del sur.

En la autopista tienes que pagar un peaje, pero vale la pena[1]. Es mucho más rápido. Tiene varios carriles en cada dirección y no hay tantos embotellamientos[2] como en la (carretera) nacional. La nacional tiene sólo un carril en cada sentido y no sé cuántos semáforos.

Después de pasar por la segunda garita de peaje, quédate en el carril derecho. Sal de la autopista en la primera salida después del peaje. Al salir, sigue derecho hasta la primera bocacalle donde hay un rótulo. El rótulo indica la dirección a Maldonado. En esta primera bocacalle donde está el rótulo, dobla a la izquierda. Sigue hasta el primer semáforo y estarás en el centro mismo de Maldonado. Estaciona con cuidado y no te olvides[3] de poner una moneda en el parquímetro. Si no, te van a clavar[4] con una multa[5].

[1] vale la pena *it's worth it*
[2] embotellamientos *traffic jams, bottlenecks*
[3] no te olvides *don't forget*
[4] clavar *"nail," "stick"*
[5] multa *fine*

Montevideo, Uruguay

268 CAPÍTULO 10

DID YOU KNOW?

Have students locate Uruguay, Montevideo, and Punta del Este on the map of South America on page 453. The only country in South America smaller than Uruguay is Surinam. Uruguay became an independent nation in 1827. Uruguay's population is slightly over three million. Almost half the population lives in the capital, Montevideo, on the estuary of the *Río de la Plata.* Like Argentina, Uruguay has rich agricultural land and a large cattle industry.

Punta del Este boasts magnificent beaches and attracts many tourists, mainly from Argentina.

Estudio de palabras

🟪 **En la carretera.** Pareen.

1. la autopista
2. el carril
3. la bocacalle
4. la garita de peaje
5. el sentido
6. estacionar

a. el cruce
b. aparcar, parquear
c. la autovía
d. la dirección
e. la vía, la banda
f. la cabina de peaje

Comprensión

A **Voy a Maldonado.** Contesten.

1. ¿Adónde quiere ir Felipe?
2. ¿Quién le da las direcciones?
3. ¿Hasta dónde debe ir por la Avenida Central?
4. ¿Por qué es mejor tomar la autopista?
5. ¿Dónde va a salir Felipe de la autopista?
6. Después de salir, ¿qué hay en la primera bocacalle?
7. ¿Por qué debe tener cuidado con el estacionamiento?

B **Detalles.** Busquen los informes en la lectura.

1. el nombre de la calle que Felipe tomará para salir de la ciudad
2. el nombre de la autopista
3. cuántas veces él pagará un peaje
4. el número de carriles en la autopista
5. el número de carriles en la carretera nacional

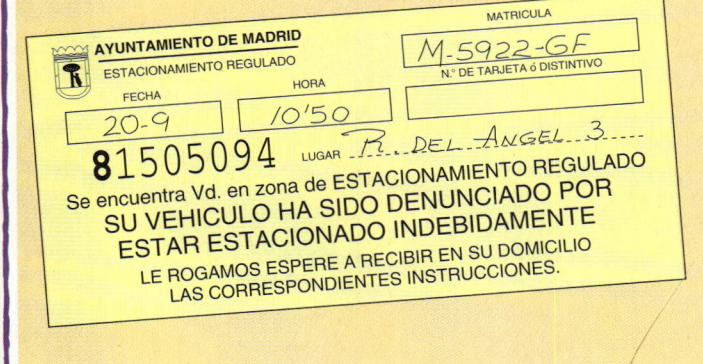

CAPÍTULO 10   **269**

Estudio de palabras
ANSWERS
1. c
2. e
3. a
4. f
5. d
6. b

Comprensión

PRESENTATION *(page 269)*

A. You may wish to intersperse the questions on page 269 with your own as students read the selection.
B. Students can either scan the selection for their answers, or for more of a challenge, have them answer from memory in their own words.

ANSWERS

Comprensión A
1. Felipe quiere ir a Maldonado.
2. Luisa le da las direcciones.
3. Debe ir por la Avenida Central hasta el final.
4. La autopista es mucho más rápido.
5. Va a salir en la primera salida después del peaje.
6. Hay un rótulo en la primera bocacalle.
7. Debe tener cuidado con el estacionamiento porque le pueden clavar con (poner) una multa.

Comprensión B
1. La Avenida Central
2. la autopista del sur
3. dos veces
4. varios carriles en cada dirección
5. un carril en cada sentido

ABOUT THE LANGUAGE
The abbreviation for *usted* on the parking ticket on page 269 is *Vd.*, not *Ud.* Remind students that *usted* is a shortened form of the archaic *Vuestra Merced* (Your Grace). This is why *usted* takes the third person verb form. *Una denuncia* is an accusation or citation. *Denunciar* is to accuse (denounce).

LEARNING FROM REALIA

1. Refer students to the three pieces of realia on page 269. Ask them to identify them. They are: a business card for a Mexican taxi service, a fare card for the Madrid bus system, and a parking ticket from Madrid. The bus fare card is good for multiple trips. It is inserted into a meter and punched.

2. Ask students about the parking ticket. For example: ¿Qué día fue la infracción? ¿A qué hora? ¿Dónde ocurrió? ¿Qué matrícula llevaba el coche?

269

Bell Ringer Review

Write the following on the board or use BRR Blackline Master 10-10: Write three facts about driving in Spain and Latin America.

Descubrimiento Cultural

(The Descubrimiento *section is optional material.)*

PRESENTATION *(page 270-271)*

A. Focus on the topic by comparing the highway systems of the U.S. and Spain.
B. Have students read the selection silently.
C. Have students look at the map of Spain on page 452 and find the cities shown in the photos and/or mentioned in the reading.

DESCUBRIMIENTO CULTURAL

En España, las carreteras tienen clasificaciones. "A" es para una autovía, una autopista de varios carriles en cada sentido. En 1992 eliminaron el peaje en muchas autovías. "N" es para las carreteras nacionales. Hay mucho tráfico en las carreteras nacionales porque no tienen varios carriles en cada sentido y es dificilísimo pasar o adelantar a los camiones. "C" es para los caminos pequeños y pintorescos en el campo.

En 1992 en España celebraron el Quincentenario del viaje de Cristóbal Colón con una exposición internacional, la EXPO '92, en Sevilla. En Barcelona tuvieron lugar los Juegos Olímpicos. Para estos eventos, el gobierno español decidió mejorar y extender el sistema de carreteras. Hoy las autovías van del norte al sur y del este al oeste. Son magníficas carreteras. Algunos detalles interesantes—la velocidad máxima en las autovías—120 kilómetros por hora. Y los niños no pueden sentarse en el asiento delantero. Los niños tienen que estar sentados en el asiento trasero. Es obligatorio abrocharse el cinturón de seguridad en la carretera, pero dentro de la ciudad, no.

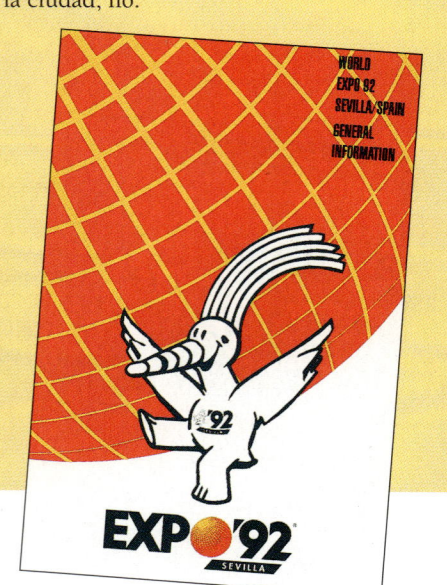

270 CAPÍTULO 10

LEARNING FROM REALIA

1. Refer students to the realia on page 270. You may wish to tell them that in Spain red signs indicate national highways, such as *Nacional 340*. In signs for towns, the larger the letters, the larger the town. Thus Cádiz and Málaga are larger than Torremolinos. The middle sign is outside the airport in Málaga because of the words *Term. Internacional* (International Terminal). Green signs indicate provincial highways. Have students locate all the cities and towns shown on the signs on the map of Spain on page 452.
2. In 1992 there was a World's Fair in Seville called EXPO'92.

Es difícil hablar de las carreteras en Latinoamérica. ¿Por qué? Porque en los alrededores de las grandes ciudades hay carreteras bastante buenas. Pero como ya saben Uds., partes de Latinoamérica son muy grandes. El terreno puede ser muy hostil[1], como por ejemplo, en las junglas o selvas tropicales, en los picos andinos y en los descampados patagónicos. Por eso, el medio de transporte más popular en Latinoamérica es el avión. En las zonas más remotas las carreteras son bastante primitivas y no muy bien marcadas.

[1] hostil   *barren areas*

CAPÍTULO 10   **271**

LEARNING FROM PHOTOS/REALIA

1. Refer students to the photo at the top of page 271. Have them locate Arecibo, Bayamón, and Guaynabo on a map of Puerto Rico. Say: *Este rótulo se encuentra en una carretera de Puerto Rico.*
2. In regard to the Olympic flag on page 271, you may wish to tell students that at the same time that EXPO'92 was being held in Seville, another major event was taking place in Barcelona. Ask students: *¿Qué tuvo lugar en Barcelona en 1992?*

REALIDADES

(The Realidades section is optional material.)

Bell Ringer Review

Write the following on the board or use BRR Blackline Master 10-11: Sketch the inside of an airplane, looking down into it as if the top had been cut off. Label as many parts as you can. Include people you would expect to see on the plane.

PRESENTATION *(pages 272-273)*

A. Have students enjoy the photos and read the captions together.

B. Call on volunteers to read the questions in captions 1, 3, 4, and 5. Call on other volunteers to answer them.

C. After reading the captions, you may wish to share the following information.
Photo 2: *La Gran Vía* is one of the most famous avenues in all of Spain. It has been the subject of songs and *zarzuelas*. After the Spanish Civil War it was renamed *Avenida de José Antonio* after a right-wing political leader. It kept that name until after the death of the dictator Francisco Franco in 1975. With Spain's return to democracy, *La Gran Vía* got its old name back.

REALIDADES

Una vista de la Carretera Panamericana **1**. ¿Cuáles serán esas montañas tan altas?

Estamos en una de las avenidas más famosas de Madrid **2**. Es la Gran Vía.

La agente de policía dirige el tráfico en la Ciudad de México **3**. ¿Qué les está indicando?

Éstas son dos de las señales internacionales para el tráfico en una carretera **4**. ¿Qué les está indicando?

Los conductores de automóviles tienen sus propios clubes y revistas **5**. ¿De qué país es este club, y cómo se llama la revista?

272

LEARNING FROM PHOTOS

Have students discuss the scene of the *Carretera Panamericana*.

CRITICAL THINKING ACTIVITY

(Thinking skills: drawing conclusions)
Write the following on the board or on a transparency:
Las Olimpíadas casi siempre tienen lugar en los países desarrollados y casi nunca en los países pobres. ¿Por qué?

272

FOR THE NATIVE SPEAKER

Un breve ensayo Ask students to prepare a short paper on the following theme: *En Europa y las Américas hay mujeres que sirven de policías. Algunas personas creen que es demasiado peligroso. Otras personas dicen que es justo y beneficioso tener policías mujeres. ¿Qué opinas tú? ¿Es bueno o no? ¿Por qué?*

INDEPENDENT PRACTICE

You may wish to assign the following:
Workbook, *Mi autobiografía*

CULMINACIÓN

RECYCLING

The activities in *Comunicación oral* and *Comunicación escrita* encourage students to use all the language they have learned in the chapter and recombine it with material from previous chapters. It is not necessary to do all the activities with all students. Select the ones you consider most appropriate or allow students to choose the ones they wish to do.

Comunicación oral
ANSWERS

Actividades A and B
  Answers will vary.

INFORMAL ASSESSMENT

Activities A and B can be used to assess speaking skills. Use the evaluation criteria given on page 24 of this Teacher's Wraparound Edition.

Comunicación escrita
ANSWERS

Actividades A and B
  Answers will vary.

CULMINACIÓN

Comunicación oral

A **Del aeropuerto.** Un buen amigo acaba de llegar de México. Está en el aeropuerto donde ha alquilado un carro. Le ha telefoneado para pedir direcciones a su casa. Déle las direcciones.

B **Una receta.** Su mejor amigo(a) le pregunta cómo preparar su comida favorita. Déle la receta.

Comunicación escrita

A **Direcciones.** Imagínese que un buen amigo de Buenos Aires le está visitando. Él quiere ir a ver los lugares interesantes de la ciudad donde Ud. vive. Escríbale las direcciones desde su casa.

El barrio La Boca, Buenos Aires, Argentina

B **No debes…** Sus padres van a salir este fin de semana. Ellos le han escrito una lista en español de ocho cosas que Ud. debe hacer, y ocho cosas que no debe hacer. Escriba lo que dice la lista. Luego compare su lista con la de un(a) compañero(a) de clase. ¿Cuántas cosas son similares?

274 CAPÍTULO 10

LEARNING FROM PHOTOS

Refer students to the photo on page 274. You may wish to tell them that this section of Buenos Aires called *la Boca* has been home to thousands of Italian immigrants to the city. There are more Argentines of Italian descent than of Spanish descent. Argentina, like the U.S., has received enormous populations of immigrants, primarily from Europe.

CRITICAL THINKING ACTIVITY

(Thinking skills: supporting arguments with reasons)

Write the following on the board or on a transparency: *El precio de la gasolina en España y en los países europeos es mucho más alto que en los EE.UU. Es por los altos impuestos que ponen los gobiernos. ¿Qué ventajas hay en subir los impuestos sobre la gasolina, y cuáles son las desventajas?*

Reintegración

A El automóvil. Completen.
1. ___ , ___ y ___ son tipos de automóviles.
2. El motor está debajo del ___ .
3. ___ de repuesto está en ___ .
4. Es necesario tener ___ antes de conducir.
5. Una luz roja indica que el conductor tiene que ___ . Antes es necesario poner los ___ .

B En la gasolinera. Sigan el modelo.

Favor de llenar el tanque.
Llene Ud. el tanque, por favor.

1. Favor de revisar el aceite.
2. Favor de verificar la presión.
3. Favor de poner agua en el radiador.
4. Favor de limpiar el parabrisas.
5. Favor de abrir el capó.

C Y tú también. Escriban las oraciones del Ejercicio B en la forma de *tú*.

Una tienda tejana donde se venden partes de automóviles

Vocabulario

SUSTANTIVOS
la calle
la bocacalle
el cruce
la esquina
el semáforo
la luz
la manzana
la cuadra
la acera
el peatón
el parquímetro
la carretera
la autopista
el peaje
la garita de peaje
la salida
la entrada
el carril
el sentido
el rótulo
la velocidad
el norte
el sur
el este
el oeste

ADJETIVOS
prohibido(a)
máximo(a)

VERBOS
caminar
cruzar
doblar
adelantar
estacionar
parar

OTRAS PALABRAS Y EXPRESIONES
detrás de
delante de
enfrente de
al lado de
a la derecha
a la izquierda
derecho
dar la vuelta

CAPÍTULO 10 275

CAPÍTULO 11
Scope and Sequence pages 276-301

Topics	Functions	Structure	Culture
Social behavior and customs Preferences and opinions	How to discuss good and bad manners How to greet and say good-bye to people properly in a Hispanic setting How to express actions that may or may not take place How to express preferences and opinions	El subjuntivo Formación del subjuntivo El subjuntivo en cláusulas nominales El subjuntivo con expresiones impersonales	Manners, courtesy, and etiquette in Spanish-speaking countries Social behavior in the U.S. vs. Spanish-speaking countries

CAPÍTULO 11

Situation Cards

The Situation Cards simulate real-life situations that require students to communicate in Spanish, exactly as though they were in a Spanish-speaking country. The Situation Cards operate on the assumption that the person to whom the message is to be conveyed understands no English. Therefore, students must focus on producing the Spanish vocabulary and structures necessary to negotiate the situations successfully. For additional information, see the Introduction to the Situation Cards in the Situation Cards Envelope.

Communication Transparency

The illustration seen in this Communication Transparency consists of a synthesis of the two vocabulary (Palabras 1&2) presentations found in this chapter. It has been created in order to present this chapter's vocabulary in a new context, and also to recycle vocabulary learned in previous chapters. The Communication Transparency consists of original art. Following are some specific uses:

1. as a cue to stimulate conversation and writing activities
2. for listening comprehension activities
3. to review and reteach vocabulary
4. as a review for chapter and unit tests

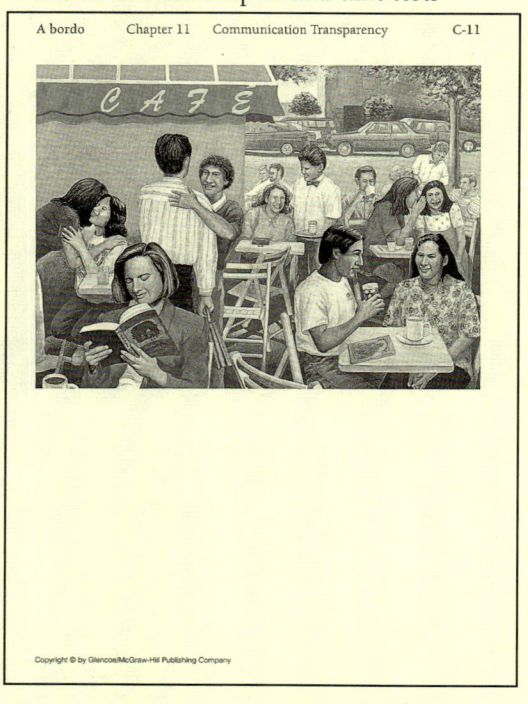

CAPÍTULO 11
Print Resources

Lesson Plans

Workbook   Pages
- Palabras 1   119-120
- Palabras 2   121
- Estructura   122-126
- Un poco más   127
- Mi autobiografía   128

Communication Activities Masters
- Palabras 1   68-69
- Palabras 2   70-71
- Estructura   72-74

11 Bell Ringer Reviews   31-33

Chapter Situation Cards A B C D

Chapter Quizzes
- Palabras 1   51
- Palabras 2   52
- Estructura   53-55

Testing Program
- Listening Comprehension   60
- Reading and Writing   61-64
- Proficiency   133
- Speaking   153

Nosotros y Nuestro Mundo
- Nuestro Conocimiento Académico *Sociología: La socialización y el control social*
- Nuestro Idioma *El subjuntivo*
- Nuestra Cultura *Quedar mal y quedar bien*
- Nuestra Literatura *"La honda"* de Ricardo Piglia
- Nuestra Creatividad
- Nuestras Diversiones

CAPÍTULO 11
Multimedia Resources

CD-ROM Interactive Textbook Disc 3

Chapter 11 Student Edition
- Palabras 1
- Palabras 2
- Estructura
- Conversación
- Lectura y cultura
- Hispanoparlantes
- Realidades
- Culminación
- Prueba

Audio Cassette Program with Student Tape Manual

Cassette   Pages
- 7A Palabras 1   253
- 7A Palabras 2   253
- 7A Estructura   254
- 7A Conversación   255
- 7A Segunda parte   255

Compact Disc Program with Student Tape Manual
- CD 7 Palabras 1   253
- CD 7 Palabras 2   253
- CD 7 Estructura   254
- CD 7 Conversación   255
- CD 7 Segunda parte   255

Overhead Transparencies Binder
- Vocabulary 11.1 (A&B); 11.2 (A&B)
- Communication C-11
- Maps
- Fine Art (with Blackline Master Activities)

Video Program
- Videocassette
- Video Activities Booklet   29-30
- Videodisc
- Video Activities Booklet   29-30

Computer Software (Macintosh, IBM, Apple)
- Practice Disk
    - Palabras 1 y 2
    - Estructura
- Test Generator Disk
    - Chapter Test
    - Customized Test

276B

CAPÍTULO 11

CHAPTER OVERVIEW

In this chapter, students will learn vocabulary associated with desirable and undesirable social behavior as well as some Hispanic social customs. They will learn to express their preferences and opinions and to talk about actions that may or may not take place. The cultural focus of Chapter 11 is on manners, courtesy, and etiquette in many parts of the Hispanic world as contrasted with social behavior or mores in the U.S.

CHAPTER OBJECTIVES

By the end of this chapter, students will know:
1. vocabulary associated with good and bad manners
2. vocabulary associated with some parts of the body
3. vocabulary associated with greeting and leave-taking
4. formation of the present subjunctive with regular and irregular verbs
5. the use of the subjunctive to express desires, preferences, and commands
6. the use of the subjunctive after impersonal expressions

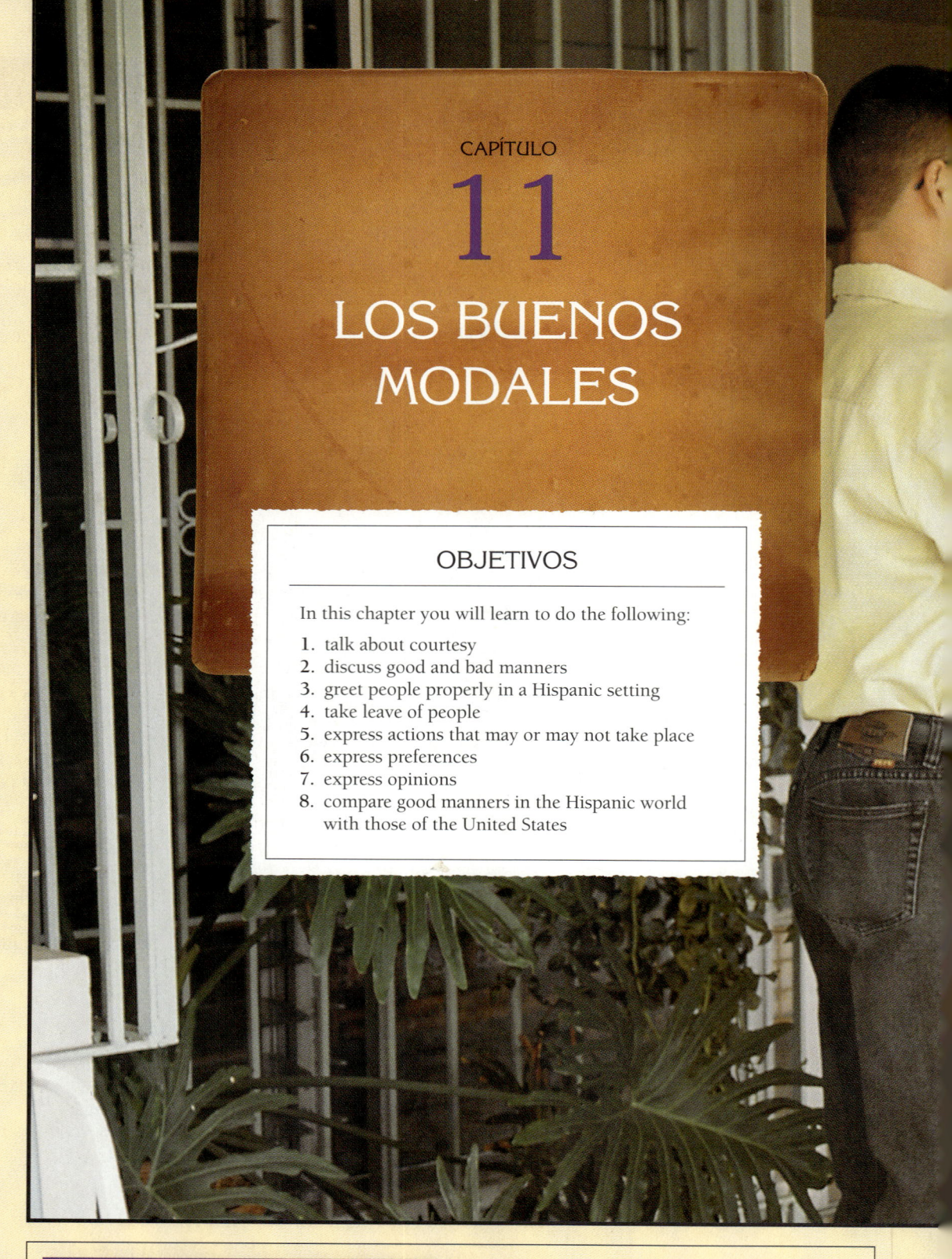

CAPÍTULO 11
LOS BUENOS MODALES

OBJETIVOS

In this chapter you will learn to do the following:

1. talk about courtesy
2. discuss good and bad manners
3. greet people properly in a Hispanic setting
4. take leave of people
5. express actions that may or may not take place
6. express preferences
7. express opinions
8. compare good manners in the Hispanic world with those of the United States

CHAPTER PROJECTS

(optional)
1. Have students prepare in Spanish a list of "do's" and "don'ts" within the range of manners common to the U.S.
2. Have students prepare a report that contrasts Hispanic and North American manners and social customs.
3. Have students prepare a list of formal and informal greetings and leave-takings in Spanish.
4. Have students create a bulletin board display on manners, with drawings and captions depicting good and bad manners.
5. Have students contribute articles to a class booklet entitled *Los Buenos Modales*.

CHAPTER 11 RESOURCES

1. Workbook
2. Student Tape Manual
3. Audio Cassette 7A
4. Vocabulary Transparencies
5. Bell Ringer Review Blackline Masters
6. Communication Activities Masters
7. Computer Software: Practice and Test Generator
8. Video Cassette, Chapter 11
9. Video Activities Booklet, Chapter 11
10. Situation Cards
11. Chapter Quizzes
12. Testing Program

Pacing

Chapter 11 will require eight to ten class sessions. Pacing will depend on the length of the class period, the age of the students, and student aptitude.

LEARNING FROM PHOTOS

Refer students to the photo on pages 276-277. Remind them that everyone, young and old, shakes hands when they meet and when they take leave of each other. Ask where they think the scene takes place. The foliage and dress indicate that the young people are in a tropical climate (Puerto Rico). Have students describe the four people in the photo.

FOR THE NATIVE SPEAKER

Conflicts sometimes arise over what "good and bad manners" are between Hispanic and Anglo cultures. You may ask students: *¿Cuáles son algunas cosas que se consideran malos modales entre los hispanos pero que son aceptables entre los norteamericanos, y vice versa? Cita ejemplos.*

277

VOCABULARIO
PALABRAS 1

Vocabulary Teaching Resources
1. Vocabulary Transparencies, 11.1 (*A & B*)
2. Audio Cassette 7A
3. Student Tape Manual, *Palabras 1*
4. Workbook, *Palabras 1*
5. Communication Activities Masters, *Palabras 1, A & B*
6. Chapter Quizzes, *Palabras 1*

Bell Ringer Review
Write the following on the board or use BRR Blackline Master 11-1: List as many parts of the body as you can remember in Spanish.

PRESENTATION (*pages 278-279*)

A. With books closed, refer to Vocabulary Transparencies 11.1 (*A & B*) and have students repeat the new words, phrases, and sentences after you or Cassette 7A.
B. Dramatize the meaning of *saludar*, *despedirse*, and *confiar un secreto*.
C. Have students open their books to pages 278-279 and call on volunteers to read the material.
D. Ask any questions which elicit the new vocabulary. Examples are: *¿Tiene buenos modales el muchacho? ¿Cómo es? ¿Cómo se comporta? ¿Qué tipo de comportimiento tiene? ¿Es bien o mal educado el muchacho?*

278

VOCABULARIO

PALABRAS 1

¿CÓMO TE COMPORTAS?

Este muchacho tiene buenos modales.
Es cortés.
Se comporta bien.
Tiene buen comportamiento.
Es bien educado.

Y esta niña no tiene buenos modales.
No se comporta bien.
Tiene mal comportamiento.
Es muy mal educada.
Es malcriada.
Es necesario que ella aprenda buenos modales.

una persona menor

una persona mayor

278   CAPÍTULO 11

PANTOMIME

Write the following words or phrases on index cards. Have students draw a card and mime the action. The class asks questions in order to guess what the student is doing.

ser cortés
comportarse bien
comportarse mal
saludar
despedirse
confiar un secreto

saludar

Los amigos se saludan.

despedirse

Los amigos se despiden el uno del otro.

José le confía un secreto a su amiga, Anita.
Él no quiere que nadie sepa su secreto.
Él insiste en que Anita no diga nada a nadie.

ABOUT THE LANGUAGE

1. The word *educado* in the expressions *bien educado(a)* and *mal educado(a)* does not refer to formal education. A person who is *mal educado(a)* is ill-mannered, impolite, rude. A person can be *muy instruido* (well educated) and *mal educado(a)* at the same time. A child who is *malcriado(a)* reflects badly on his/her parents because *malcriado* means literally "poorly raised."

2. *Despedirse* in the reflexive form means "to say good-bye" or "to take leave of" someone. *Despedir* alone, without the reflexive pronoun, can mean "to let go of" or "to fire" an employee.

COOPERATIVE LEARNING

Have teams take sides for a debate. Each team supports one of the following statements.
1. *Los buenos modales son importantes para los adultos solamente.*
2. *Los buenos modales son importantes para todos.*

Ejercicios

PRESENTATION (page 280)

Ejercicios A and B
Exercises A and B are to be done with books open.

Ejercicio C
Exercise C can be done with books open or closed.

ANSWERS

Ejercicio A
1. Los amigos se saludan.
2. Los amigos se despiden.
3. Este niño es bien educado.
4. Este niño es mal educado.
5. Es una persona mayor.
6. Este niño es malcriado.

Ejercicio B
1. c
2. d
3. a
4. b

Ejercicio C
1. Él no tiene buenos modales.
2. Él no tiene buenos modales.
3. Ella tiene buenos modales.
4. Ella no tiene buenos modales.
5. Él no tiene buenos modales.

280

Ejercicios

A ¿Qué hacen? Contesten según el dibujo.

1. ¿Los amigos se saludan o se despiden?
2. ¿Los amigos se saludan o se despiden? 
3. ¿Este niño es bien educado o mal educado? 
4. ¿Este niño es mal educado o bien educado? 
5. ¿Es una persona menor o mayor?  
6. ¿Este niño es cortés o malcriado? 

B Lo contrario. Escojan.
1. saludar   a. malcriado
2. bien educado   b. menor
3. cortés   c. despedirse
4. mayor   d. mal educado

C ¿Buenos modales o no? Decidan.
1. Él siempre habla en voz muy alta.
2. Él se queda sentado cuando alguien se acerca a la mesa.
3. Ella se levanta cuando entra una persona mayor.
4. Ella hace mucho ruido cuando come.
5. Él nunca dice "gracias".

280 CAPÍTULO 11

LEARNING FROM ILLUSTRATIONS

Refer students to the illustration in item number 2 of Exercise A on page 280. Remind them of the differences in gestures among cultures. Hispanic peoples usually wave good-bye with the palm of the hand facing inwards rather than outwards.

INDEPENDENT PRACTICE

Assign any of the following:
1. Workbook, *Palabras 1*
2. Communication Activities Masters, *Palabras 1, A & B*
3. Exercises on student page 280

VOCABULARIO

PALABRAS 2

MODALES Y COSTUMBRES

- los labios
- la mejilla
- la palmadita
- la espalda

CAPÍTULO 11   281

VOCABULARIO
PALABRAS 2

Vocabulary Teaching Resources

1. Vocabulary Transparencies 11.2 (*A & B*)
2. Audio Cassette 7A
3. Student Tape Manual, *Palabras 2*
4. Workbook, *Palabras 2*
5. Communication Activities Masters, *Palabras 2, C & D*
6. Chapter Quizzes, *Palabras 2*
7. Computer Software, *Vocabulario*

Bell Ringer Review

Write the following on the board or use BRR Blackline Master 11-2: Escriba una lista de cinco cosas que Ud. tiene que hacer todos los días en la escuela. Por ejemplo: *saludar a los amigos, hacer tareas.*

PRESENTATION (pages 281-282)

A. Have students close their books. Model the *Palabras 2* vocabulary using Vocabulary Transparencies 11.2 (*A & B*). Have students repeat the material after you or Cassette 7A.
B. Use yourself or a student model to demonstrate *los labios*, *las mejillas*, *la mano*, and *la espalda*.
C. Have students open their books to pages 281-282. Point to an image on the transparencies and have volunteers read the material that corresponds.
D. Have students role-play the actions in the illustrations on page 282.

LEARNING FROM ILLUSTRATIONS

For the illustrations on pages 281-282, have students provide descriptions with as much detail as possible. Remind them that a typical Hispanic handshake consists of one upward and downward motion. The typical North American "multiple-pump" handshake is sometimes considered comical.

281

ABOUT THE LANGUAGE

In many countries people begin to use *tú* with each other very quickly. In the past, and still today in some places, people will use *tú* only after a close friendship has been established. Usually it is the person of greater age or higher status who initiates the change from *usted* to *tú*. This was once called *romper el turrón*, a play on words very similar to "breaking the ice" in English, since *turrón* is a very hard, almond nougat candy that comes in bricks.

El señor Salas se acerca.
La señora Robles se levanta.

La señora Robles le da la mano.
Los señores se estrechan la mano.

un besito

un abrazo

Las dos señoras son muy buenas amigas.
Se dan un besito.

Los dos señores son buenos amigos.
Son amigos íntimos.
Se abrazan.
Se dan unas palmaditas en la espalda.

CAPÍTULO 11

INDEPENDENT PRACTICE

Assign any of the following:
1. Workbook, *Palabras 2*
2. Communication Activities Masters, *Palabras 2, C & D*
3. Exercises on student page 283

Ejercicios

A **Se saludan.** Contesten con *sí* o *no*.

1. ¿La señora Robles está sentada en una oficina?
2. ¿Se acerca el señor Salas?
3. ¿Se levanta la señora Robles?
4. ¿Le da la mano la señora Robles?
5. ¿Se estrechan la mano los dos señores?
6. ¿Se dan un besito?
7. ¿Son buenas amigas las dos señoras?
8. ¿Se dan un besito las dos amigas?
9. ¿Se dan un besito en las mejillas?

B **Buenos modales.** Completen.

1. Los dos señores se ___ la mano.
2. Y las dos señoras se dan ___ también.
3. Las amigas se dan un ___ en las mejillas, no en los labios.
4. Los dos señores se abrazan. Se dan unas ___ en la espalda.

C **Definiciones.** Escojan la palabra.

1. ofrecer una invitación, convidar
   a. confiar   b. invitar
2. acciones, porte, conducta o comportamiento de un individuo
   a. la cortesía   b. los modales
3. hablar a una persona de "tú", no de "Ud."
   a. tutear   b. considerar
4. la conducta, el modo de ser de un individuo
   a. el comportamiento   b. el secreto
5. en confianza
   a. en consideración   b. en secreto
6. emplear una fórmula de cortesía para separarse de una persona
   a. desaparecer   b. despedirse

CAPÍTULO 11

Comunicación
(Palabras 1 and 2)

Bell Ringer Review
Write the following on the board or use BRR Blackline Master 11-3: Write an original sentence telling what the following people are doing right now. Use the present progressive tense.
1. mi madre
2. mi padre
3. yo
4. mi novio(a)
5. mi profesor(a)
6. mi mejor amigo(a)

PRESENTATION (page 284)
You may have students do any number of these activities. You may also allow students to select the activity or activities in which they wish to take part.

ANSWERS
Actividades A–E
  Answers will vary.

Comunicación
Palabras 1 y 2

A **Buenos modales.** Prepare dos listas: una de comportamientos que Ud. considera buenos modales en los Estados Unidos y otra de comportamientos que Ud. considera como falta de buenos modales. Enséñele la lista a un(a) compañero(a) de clase y pregúntele si él o ella está de acuerdo con Ud. Luego díganle a la clase los resultados.

B **Un poco de cortesía.** Es probable que sus padres le digan cosas que Ud. debe hacer para ser cortés. ¿Cuáles son los consejos que le dan o que le han dado sus padres? Dígaselos a dos compañeros de clase. Cambien de papel.

C **Reglamentos escolares.** Escríbale una carta a un(a) amigo(a) donde le deja saber cuáles son los reglamentos de comportamiento o conducta que su profesor(a) de español considera importantes en la clase.

D **¿Cómo se comporta Carlitos?** Escriba una lista de los niños pequeños que Ud. conoce (primos, sobrinos, hermanos, etc.). Luego escriba al lado de cada nombre cómo se comporta cada uno de los niños.

E **¡Qué niño!** Imagínese que ayer por la tarde Ud. y su compañero(a) tuvieron que cuidar a unos niños, pero de familias diferentes. Ud. tuvo suerte porque el niño que cuidó tiene muy buenos modales, pero el niño que cuidó su compañero(a) es completamente lo opuesto. Comparta sus experiencias con su compañero(a).

284 CAPÍTULO 11

LEARNING FROM PHOTOS
Refer students to the photos on page 284 and have them say all they can about them.

DID YOU KNOW?
For many years, metro cars in Madrid had seats reserved for *caballeros mutilados*. These "mutilated gentlemen" were mainly veterans of the Spanish Civil War (1936-1939). Tens of thousands of men were crippled in this war. Those on the winning side (the Fascists) were awarded a small pension. Those on the losing side (the Republicans) were often reduced to begging.

ESTRUCTURA

El subjuntivo
Talking about Actions that May or May Not Take Place

1. All the forms of the verbs you have learned so far have been in the indicative mood. The indicative is used to indicate or express actions that definitely are taking place, did take place or will take place. Let us analyze some statements in the indicative.

   Cuando los amigos de Teresa llegaron, ella se levantó.
   Ella les dio la mano.
   Teresita siempre se levanta cuando llegan sus amigos.
   Ella es muy cortés.

   The above statements express objective, factual, real information. When Teresa's friends arrived she stood up and gave them her hand. Teresa always stands up and extends her hand. She is very courteous. Because of the factual nature of the information in these sentences, they are in the indicative.

2. Now you will learn the subjunctive mood. The subjunctive is used more in Spanish than in English. The subjunctive expresses the opposite of the indicative. The indicative indicates what definitely is. The subjunctive, on the other hand, expresses what may be. Let us analyze some statements in the subjunctive and compare them with statements in the indicative.

   INDICATIVE:
   Carlos se comporta bien. Él es cortés.

   SUBJUNCTIVE:
   Los padres de Carlos quieren que él se comporte bien. Ellos insisten en que él sea cortés.

   The first group of sentences in the indicative points out factual information. The second set of sentences states what Carlos' parents want or insist upon. Note, however, the information is not factual. His parents want him to behave well and they insist that he be polite. In spite of their wishes and insistence, it is not assured that Carlos will act accordingly. It may or may not happen and for this reason the subjunctive must be used in Spanish. Note that the subjunctive appears in a clause introduced by *que*.

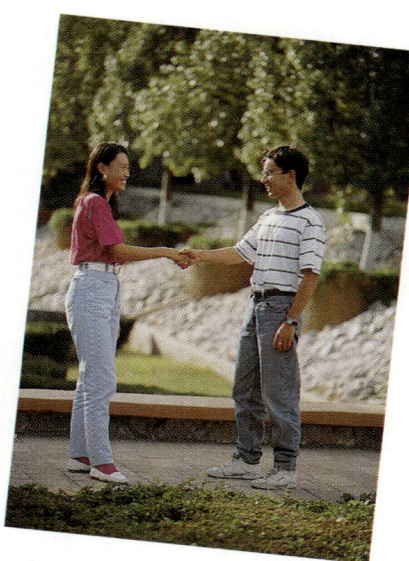

CAPÍTULO 11   **285**

ESTRUCTURA

Structure Teaching Resources
1. Workbook, *Estructura*
2. Student Tape Manual, *Estructura*
3. Audio Cassette 7A
5. Communication Activities Masters, *Estructura*, A-C
6. Chapter Quizzes, *Estructura*
7. Computer Software, *Estructura*

Bell Ringer Review
Write the following on the board or use BRR Blackline Master 11-4: You have just arrived in Barcelona, Spain. What are some gestures or greetings that you may observe? Write them on a piece of paper.

El subjuntivo
PRESENTATION (page 285)

Note The basic concept for students to understand is that the subjunctive is used when we do not know if the action will take place. If we know that it is or will be a reality, the indicative is used. If students understand this, it will not be necessary for them to memorize lists of phrases followed by the subjunctive. You may give students the following simple outline:
INDICATIVE: indicates or points something out; is factual; objective; stands alone; is independent
SUBJUNCTIVE: is subjective, not objective; not factual; cannot stand alone; is dependent on something else

---

INDEPENDENT PRACTICE
You may wish to assign the activities on student page 284.

Formación del subjuntivo

Formación del subjuntivo — *How to Express Desires about the Actions of Others*

1. You are already familiar with the subjunctive form of verbs because of your study of the formal commands. Those forms are the subjunctive.

| hable Ud. | coma Ud. | escriba Ud. | venga Ud. | salga Ud. |
| hablen Uds. | coman Uds. | escriban Uds. | vengan Uds. | salgan Uds. |

2. To form the present tense of the subjunctive drop the final *-o* from the first person singular, *yo*, of the present indicative and add *-e* endings to *-ar* verbs and *-a* endings to *-er* and *-ir* verbs.

PRESENT INDICATIVE	ROOT	PRESENT SUBJUNCTIVE
hablo	habl-	hable
como	com-	coma
escribo	escrib-	escriba
vengo	veng-	venga
salgo	salg-	salga

INFINITIVE	HABLAR	COMER	ABRIR
yo	hable	coma	abra
tú	hables	comas	abras
él, ella, Ud.	hable	coma	abra
nosotros(as)	hablemos	comamos	abramos
vosotros(as)	*habléis*	*comáis*	*abráis*
ellos, ellas, Uds.	hablen	coman	abran

3. Remember that any verb that is irregular in the first person *yo* form of the present tense will maintain that irregularity in the present subjunctive.

INFINITIVE	INDICATIVE (YO)	SUBJUNCTIVE
venir	vengo	venga
tener	tengo	tenga
salir	salgo	salga
poner	pongo	ponga
traer	traigo	traiga
hacer	hago	haga
oír	oigo	oiga
decir	digo	diga
conducir	conduzco	conduzca

286 CAPÍTULO 11

INFINITIVE	VENIR	SALIR
yo	venga	salga
tú	vengas	salgas
él, ella, Ud.	venga	salga
nosotros(as)	vengamos	salgamos
vosotros(as)	vengáis	salgáis
ellos, ellas, Uds.	vengan	salgan

4. The following are the only verbs that do not follow the normal pattern in the present subjunctive.

DAR	ESTAR	IR	SABER	SER
dé	esté	vaya	sepa	sea
des	estés	vayas	sepas	seas
dé	esté	vaya	sepa	sea
demos	estemos	vayamos	sepamos	seamos
deis	estéis	vayáis	sepáis	seáis
den	estén	vayan	sepan	sean

Ejercicio

Los padres de Pepe quieren que él haga muchas cosas. Sigan el modelo.

estudiar
Los padres de Pepe quieren que él estudie.

1. estudiar mucho
2. tomar cinco cursos
3. trabajar duro
4. aprender mucho
5. leer mucho
6. comer bien
7. vivir con ellos
8. recibir buenas notas
9. asistir a la universidad
10. tener éxito
11. salir bien en sus exámenes
12. decir siempre la verdad
13. tener buenos modales
14. ser cortés
15. conducir con cuidado

CAPÍTULO 11   **287**

Ejercicio

PRESENTATION (*page 287*)

This Exercise can be done with books open or closed.

Note The purpose of this exercise is to give students initial practice with one form of the subjunctive. For this reason, the introductory clause *Los padres de Pepe quieren que él…* is constant.

ANSWERS

1. Los padres de Pepe quieren que él estudie mucho.
2. … tome cinco cursos.
3. … trabaje duro.
4. … aprenda mucho.
5. … lea mucho.
6. … coma bien.
7. … viva con ellos.
8. … reciba buenas notas.
9. … asista a la universidad.
10. … tenga éxito.
11. … salga bien en sus exámenes.
12. … diga siempre la verdad.
13. … tenga buenos modales.
14. … sea cortés.
15. … conduzca con cuidado.

LEARNING FROM PHOTOS

Refer students to the photo on page 287 and have them say all they can about it. Tell them the academic gown is known as a *toga*. Ask them why. Also ask: *¿Por qué felicitan al joven? ¿Qué día muy especial es?*

INDEPENDENT PRACTICE

Assign any of the following:
1. Workbook, *Estructura*
2. Communication Activities Masters, *Estructura, A*
3. Exercise on student page 287

287

Bell Ringer Review

Write the following on the board or use BRR Blackline Master 11-5: Your best friend has always been a good influence on you. Use the new vocabulary from Palabras 1 and 2 to describe him/her in at least three sentences.

El subjuntivo en cláusulas nominales

PRESENTATION (page 288)

Have students open their books to page 288 and lead them through the explanation. Have them read the verbs and example sentences aloud.

Note Stress the concept that even though someone wants or insists that something be done, it is not certain that it will take place. It may be helpful for students to relate "subjunctive" to "subjective;" relating to one's own perception of the world, and not necessarily the world as it is. It is in cases of subjectivity that the subjunctive is used.

Ejercicios

PRESENTATION (pages 288-291)

Ejercicios A-F

Exercises A-F can be done with books open or closed.

Ejercicio G

Exercise G is to be done with books open.

ANSWERS

Ejercicio A
1. Sus padres quieren que ellos se comporten bien.
2. … se levanten.
3. … saluden a sus amigos.
4. … tengan buenos modales.
5. … sean corteses.

Ejercicio B
1. Yo prefiero que tú se lo digas.
2. … se lo escribas.
3. … se lo des.
4. … se los envíes.
5. … se lo expliques.

El subjuntivo en cláusulas nominales

Expressing Wishes, Preferences, and Commands

You have learned that the subjunctive is used after the verbs *querer* and *insistir* because even though someone wants or insists that something be done, it may or may not happen. Just as the subjunctive is used after *querer* and *insistir*, it is used for the same reason after the following verbs.

desear	to desire
esperar	to hope
temer	to fear
tener miedo de	to be afraid
preferir	to prefer
mandar	to order

Espero que vengan mis amigos.
Pero temo que lleguen tarde.
Tengo miedo de que no estén para el concierto.
Espero que traten de llegar a tiempo, que hagan un esfuerzo.

Ejercicios

A ¿Qué quieren sus padres? Sigan el modelo.

Sus padres quieren que ——.
Ellos se comportan bien.
Sus padres quieren que ellos se comporten bien.

1. Ellos se comportan bien.
2. Ellos se levantan.
3. Ellos saludan a sus amigos.
4. Ellos tienen buenos modales.
5. Ellos son corteses.

B ¿Qué prefieres? Sigan el modelo.

Yo prefiero que ——.
Tú se lo dices.
Yo prefiero que tú se lo digas.

1. Tú se lo dices.
2. Tú se lo escribes.
3. Tú se lo das.
4. Se lo envías.
5. Se lo explicas.

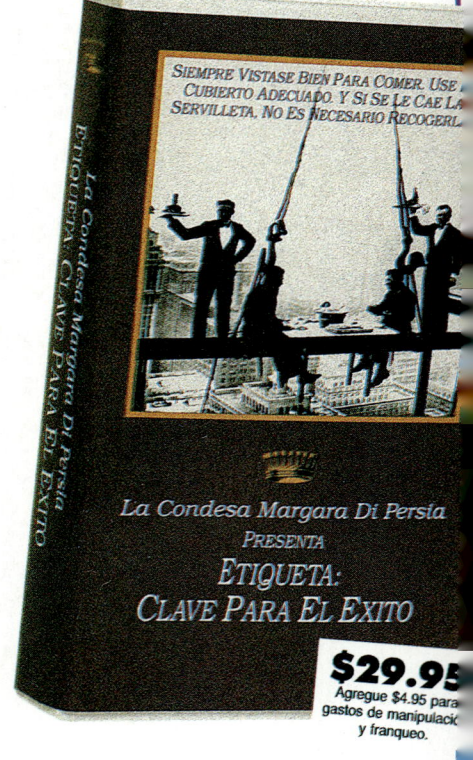

288   CAPÍTULO 11

LEARNING FROM REALIA

1. Tell students that the title to the video on page 288 is *Etiqueta: Clave Para el Éxito*. Spanish has two words for "key." *Llave* is the metal object for opening locks. *Clave* is the figurative "key," something used for solving problems.

2. The ending *-esa* is used to form the feminine for titles of nobility. Ask: *Si el hombre es un conde y la mujer una condesa, ¿qué es la mujer del marqués? (marquesa) ¿del duque? (duquesa) ¿del barón? (baronesa) ¿del príncipe? (princesa).*

3. Challenge students to determine what the three recommendations on the cover of the video say.

C ¿Qué temen ellos? Sigan el modelo.

> Ellos temen que ___ .
> Yo no estoy.
> *Ellos temen que yo no esté.*

1. Yo no estoy.
2. Yo no quiero ir.
3. No voy.
4. Yo no lo hago.
5. No se lo digo al profesor.

D ¿En qué insisten sus padres? Sigan el modelo.

> Sus padres insisten en que ___ .
> Ella estudia mucho.
> *Sus padres insisten en que ella estudie mucho.*

1. Ella estudia mucho.
2. Ella hace sus tareas.
3. Ella recibe buenas notas.
4. Ella es diligente.
5. Ella tiene buenos modales.

E ¡Vamos todos! Contesten.

1. ¿Quieres que yo conduzca?
2. ¿Prefieres que yo vaya en mi carro?
3. ¿Insistes en que todos vayamos juntos?
4. ¿Quieres que Teresa y Pablo vayan también?
5. ¿Prefieres que ellos nos acompañen?
6. ¿Esperas que todos lleguemos a la misma hora?

F Un corte de pelo. Contesten.

1. ¿Quieres que el peluquero te corte el pelo?
2. ¿Quieres que él te dé un champú?
3. ¿Prefieres que él te corte el pelo con navaja o tijeras?
4. ¿Insistes en que él te ponga la raya a la izquierda o a la derecha?
5. ¿Teme el peluquero que tú no le des propina?

CAPÍTULO 11   **289**

ANSWERS

Ejercicio C
1. Ellos temen que yo no esté.
2. … yo no quiera ir.
3. … yo no vaya.
4. … yo no lo haga.
5. … yo no se lo diga al profesor.

Ejercicio D
1. Sus padres insisten en que ella estudie mucho.
2. … haga sus tareas.
3. … reciba buenas notas.
4. … sea diligente.
5. … tenga buenos modales.

Ejercicio E
1. Sí (No), (no) quiero que tú conduzcas.
2. Sí (No), (no) prefiero que tú vayas en tu carro.
3. Sí (No), (no) insisto en que todos vayamos juntos.
4. Sí (No), (no) quiero que Teresa y Pablo vayan también.
5. Sí (No), (no) prefiero que ellos nos acompañen.
6. Sí (No), (no) espero que todos lleguemos a la misma hora.

Ejercicio F
1. Sí (No), (no) quiero que el peluquero me corte el pelo.
2. Sí (No), (no) quiero que me dé un champú.
3. Prefiero que él me corte el pelo con navaja (tijeras).
4. Insisto en que él me ponga la raya a la izquierda (a la derecha).
5. Sí (No), el peluquero (no) teme que yo no le dé propina.

ABOUT THE LANGUAGE
Remind students that "to play an instrument" is *tocar un instrumento*, "to play a game" is *jugar un juego,* and "to play a part" is *hacer un papel. Jugar un papel*, though often said, is considered an anglicism.

LEARNING FROM PHOTOS
Refer students to the photos on page 289 and have them say as much as they can about each of them.

289

ANSWERS

Ejercicio G
1. vayamos
2. veamos
3. sea
4. cambien
5. hagamos
6. vayamos
7. hagamos
8. se queden
9. vaya
10. salgamos
11. miremos
12. veamos

Bell Ringer Review

Write the following on the board or use BRR Blackline Master 11-6: Write logical completions to these sentences:
1. Yo quiero que mis padres…
2. Yo prefiero que el/la profesor(a) de español…
3. Mis padres insisten en que yo…
4. Yo deseo que mi mejor amigo(a)…
5. Mi madre espera que…

El subjuntivo con expresiones impersonales

PRESENTATION *(page 290)*

Have students open their books to page 290 and lead them through the explanation. Then have them read the expressions and example sentences aloud. **Note** You may emphasize here that even though an action is necessary (or important or good), it is not certain that it will occur. Therefore the subjunctive is used.

ABOUT THE LANGUAGE

In Spanish as in English, new terms are being used to describe the elderly. Today's older people are said to be members of *la tercera edad*, an expression similar to the English "senior citizens."

290

G Todos quieren hacer algo distinto. Completen.

Pues, yo no sé lo que vamos a hacer esta noche. Antonio quiere que nosotros ___ (ir) al cine. No sé por qué. Pero insiste en que nosotros ___ (ver) la película que están poniendo ahora en el Metropol. Carlos teme que mañana ___ (ser) el último día. Tiene miedo de que ellos ___ (cambiar) las películas los sábados. ¿Y tú? ¿Qué quieres que nosotros ___ (hacer)? ¿Prefieres que ___ (ir) al cine o que ___ (hacer) otra cosa? ¿Qué me dices? Que Felipe quiere que Uds. ___ (quedarse) en casa. ¿Por qué? Ah, él quiere que todo el grupo ___ (ir) a su casa. Él no quiere que nosotros ___ (salir). Él prefiere que todos ___ (mirar) la televisión y que ___ (ver) el equipo de Barcelona que va a jugar contra Valencia.

El subjuntivo con expresiones impersonales

Expressing Opinions

1. The subjunctive is also used after the following impersonal expressions.

Es imposible	Es bueno
Es posible	Es mejor
Es probable	Es fácil
Es improbable	Es difícil
Es necesario	Es importante

2. Note that all the above expressions take the subjunctive since the action of the verb that follows them may or may not take place.

   Es importante que ellos tengan buenos modales.
   Y es necesario que sean corteses.
   Pero es posible que ellos no tengan buenos modales y que no sean corteses.

290   CAPÍTULO 11

LEARNING FROM PHOTOS

You may wish to ask students the following questions about the photo on page 290: ¿Dónde están los muchachos? ¿Qué están haciendo? ¿Qué ropa llevan los tres? ¿Qué hay en el cuarto?

INDEPENDENT PRACTICE

Assign any of the following:
1. Workbook, *Estructura*
2. Communication Activities Masters, *Estructura*, B
3. Exercises on student pages 288–290

Ejercicios

A **Buenos modales.** Contesten.
1. ¿Es importante que los jóvenes tengan buenos modales?
2. ¿Es necesario que ellos se comporten bien?
3. ¿Es fácil que ellos sean corteses?
4. ¿Es importante que ellos se levanten cuando entra una persona mayor?
5. ¿Es improbable que ellos se den un besito?

B **¿Qué es posible?** Sigan el modelo.

> Es posible que ___ .
> Mañana tenemos examen.
> *Es posible que mañana tengamos examen.*

1. Mañana tenemos examen.
2. El profesor no nos dice nada.
3. Él nos da el examen como una sorpresa.
4. Todos recibimos buenas notas en el examen.
5. El profesor está contento.

C **Esperando a los nietos.** Practiquen la conversación.

ABUELITO: ¿Es posible que ellos lleguen mañana por la mañana?
ABUELITA: Sí, es posible. Pero es improbable.
ABUELITO: Pero es importante que yo sepa.
ABUELITA: Entiendo. Pero dicen que es probable que haga mal tiempo mañana.
ABUELITO: ¿Ah, sí? No lo sabía. ¿Es posible que haga mal tiempo? Entonces es mejor que lleguen tarde. No quiero que tengan un accidente en la carretera.

D **Esperando a los nietos.** Completen según la conversación.

Abuelito está un poco nervioso. Es posible que sus nietos ___ (llegar) mañana por la mañana. Es importante que el abuelito ___ (saber) cuándo van a llegar. Pero es difícil que la abuelita le ___ (decir) la hora de la llegada de los nietos. Es posible que mañana ___ (hacer) muy mal tiempo. Como los nietos vienen en carro será necesario que ellos ___ (conducir) con mucho cuidado. Será necesario que ellos ___ (conducir) despacio si hay mucha nieve. Es mejor que ellos ___ (llegar) un poco tarde. Abuelito no quiere que ellos ___ (tener) un accidente. Es mejor que ___ (llegar) tarde pero sanos y salvos.

CAPÍTULO 11   291

CONVERSACIÓN

CONVERSACIÓN

Escenas de la vida *¿Por qué no nos tuteamos?*

LUPE: Hola, Debbie.
DEBBIE: Hola, Lupe. ¿Cómo está Ud. hoy?
LUPE: Estoy bien, gracias. Y sabes, Debbie, me puedes tutear si quieres.
DEBBIE: ¿Tutear?
LUPE: Sí, me puedes hablar de "tú".
DEBBIE: Ah, decirte ¿cómo estás?, y no ¿cómo está Ud.?
LUPE: Sí, no tenemos que ser tan formalitas. Ahora nos conocemos bién, ¿no crees?
DEBBIE: Sí, y gracias, Lupe.

A ¿Sí o no? Contesten.

1. Debbie y Lupe se conocen bien.
2. Lupe es hispana.
3. Las muchachas siempre se hablaban de "tú".
4. Lupe sugiere que se tuteen.
5. Lupe dice que tienen que ser formalitas.

B ¿Tú o usted? Expliquen.

¿Por qué dice Lupe que ahora las dos muchachas pueden tutearse?

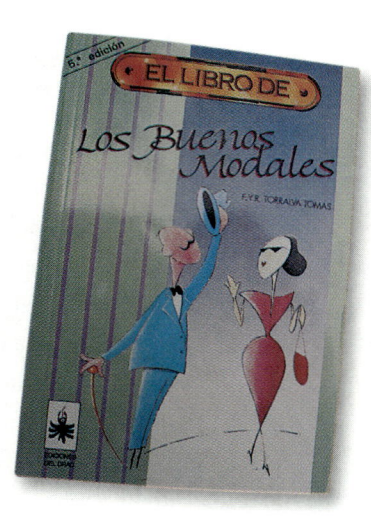

292 CAPÍTULO 11

Bell Ringer Review

Write the following on the board or use BRR Blackline Master 11-7: Complete each sentence with a different verb expressing a wish, preference, or demand.

1. Los estudiantes ___ que los profesores se rían más.
2. Ellos ___ que la comida de la cafetería sea mejor.
3. Ellos ___ que los profesores no les den las tareas el viernes.
4. Los profesores ___ que los estudiantes salgan bien en los exámenes.
5. Ellos ___ que los estudiantes miren la televisión menos.

PRESENTATION (page 292)

A. Tell students they will hear a conversation between Lupe and Debbie, two young women who are working together.
B. Have students close their books and listen as you read the conversation or play Cassette 7A.
C. Have students open their books to page 292. Allow pairs time to practice the conversation. Each partner should practice both roles. Circulate and model pronunciation as necessary.
D. Call on a pair of volunteers to present the conversation to the class with as much expression as possible.

Ejercicios
ANSWERS
Ejercicio A
1. Sí
2. Sí
3. No
4. No
5. Sí
6. No

Ejercicio B
Lupe dice que ahora las dos muchachas se pueden tutear porque se conocen bien.

COOPERATIVE LEARNING

Have teams prepare "orientation guides" for Spanish-speaking exchange students. The guides should focus on North American school etiquette. Teams should brainstorm to come up with recommendations for behavior in such areas as *en la cafetería, en los partidos, en las clases*, and *muchachos y muchachas*. Each recommendation should begin with an impersonal expression. For example: *Es importante que levantes la mano para hablar en clase. No es necesario que te levantes y les des la mano a los compañeros de clase.*

Comunicación

A **Lo que quieren mis padres.** Dígale a un(a) compañero(a) de clase lo que sus padres siempre quieren que Ud. haga. Su compañero(a) le dirá lo que quieren sus padres que él o ella haga. Luego, pongan sus dos listas juntas y decidan cuáles son los mismos consejos que Uds. dos reciben de sus padres. ¿Están de acuerdo Uds. con los consejos que reciben de sus padres? Déjenle saber su opinión a la clase.

B **Mi mejor amigo(a).** Trabaje con un(a) compañero(a) de clase. Cada uno(a) debe preparar una lista de características que Uds. quieren que tenga su mejor amigo(a). Luego comparen sus listas y determinen cuáles son las características que Uds. en común quieren que su mejor amigo(a) tenga. Escriban un párrafo describiendo cómo creen Uds. que debe ser su mejor amigo(a).

C **Buena conducta.** Trabaje con un(a) compañero(a) de clase. Escriban un párrafo en el que describen lo que Uds. consideran ejemplos de buen comportamiento en la escuela.

D **¿Qué crees tú?** Pregúntele a un(a) compañero(a) de clase qué haría él o ella en las siguientes situaciones. Cada respuesta comenzará con "Es importante que…", "Es mejor que…" o "Es recomendable que…". Luego cambien de papel.

1. ver un accidente en la carretera
2. perder una tarjeta de crédito
3. ayudar a un(a) amigo(a) en un examen
4. decir una mentira
5. no entender la tarea de matemáticas

E **Cosas fáciles y difíciles.** Prepare una lista de cosas que es probable que Ud. haga y otra lista de cosas que es difícil que Ud. haga. Luego compare sus listas con las listas de un(a) compañero(a) de clase. Díganle a la clase en qué se parecen las listas.

CAPÍTULO 11   **293**

LECTURA Y CULTURA

Bell Ringer Review

Write the following on the board or use BRR Blackline Master 11-9: Complete the sentences with the present subjunctive form of the verb in parentheses.
1. El director quiere que nosotros ___ mucho. (aprender)
2. El profesor desea que Federico ___ todo lo que dice. (comprender)
3. El director de la escuela quiere que yo ___ a su oficina. (ir)
4. Tus padres quieren que tú ___ buenas notas. (sacar)

READING STRATEGIES
(page 294)

Pre-Reading
Ask students to summarize what they have learned so far about social customs in Hispanic countries.

Reading
A. Have students open their books to page 294 and ask them to read the selection once silently.
B. Go over the selection again, having individuals read four or five sentences aloud.
C. Have students role-play Hispanic leave-takings using the handshake and kisses on the cheeks.

Post-reading
Call on volunteers to summarize in their own words what they have learned about good manners in Hispanic countries.

LECTURA & CULTURA

BUENOS MODALES Y FÓRMULAS DE CORTESÍA

¿Quieres que yo te diga lo que se considera buenos modales en los países hispanos? Bien, pero antes es necesario que tú sepas y reconozcas que es difícil que yo te hable en términos generales. Es importante que te des cuenta[1] de que es posible que existan diferencias en los distintos países. Sin embargo, te daré algunos ejemplos de buenos modales.

Tú estás sentado(a) en un café, en casa o en una oficina. Alguien se acerca. Tú lo conoces. Para ser cortés, es necesario que tú te levantes. Además de levantarte, es importante que tú le des la mano si no quieres que todos te consideren mal educado(a). Aun los jóvenes se dan la mano cuando se encuentran y también cuando se despiden. Es posible que me preguntes si se dan la mano sólo en una situación formal. No, se dan la mano igualmente en situaciones informales. Se le da la mano a un amigo o a un conocido.

¿Un amigo o un conocido? En los países hispanos hay una gran diferencia entre un amigo y un conocido. Un amigo es una persona que conoces muy bien. Es una persona con quien tienes confianza, en quien puedes confiar secretos. Un conocido es una persona que conoces de la escuela, de la oficina, etc., pero no se conocen muy bien. En las culturas hispanas la gente tiene muchos conocidos y pocos amigos. Es justo decir que en los Estados Unidos solemos decir[2] que tenemos muchos "friends" y pocos "acquaintances". En los países hispanos es al revés[3].

Hablando de amigos y conocidos, ¿cómo se saludan y cómo se despiden? Como ya he dicho se les da la mano a conocidos y a amigos. Pero es más común que los amigos se den un besito en cada mejilla. ¿Quiénes se dan un besito en la mejilla? Pues una amiga a otra amiga o un amigo a una amiga. ¿Y dos amigos? Dos amigos se dan un abrazo. Se abrazan dándose unas palmaditas en la espalda.

[1] te des cuenta *you realize*
[2] solemos decir *we usually say*
[3] al revés *the contrary*

294 CAPÍTULO 11

CRITICAL THINKING ACTIVITY

(Thinking skills: making judgements; presenting your side)

Read the following to the class or write it on the board or on an overhead transparency.
¿Está Ud. de acuerdo o no cuando decimos que aquí en los EE.UU. tenemos muchos amigos y pocos conocidos? ¿Cuál es su definición de un amigo?

COOPERATIVE LEARNING

Have teams create scripts for conversations that three young people like the ones in the photo might have. When presenting the conversations, the fourth team member acts as announcer, identifying each of the three characters, giving a brief background for each and setting the scene for the conversation.

Estudio de palabras

A ¿Cuál es el sustantivo? Escojan.

1. considerar
2. existir
3. despedir
4. saludar
5. confiar
6. abrazar
7. besar

a. la despedida
b. la confianza
c. el beso
d. la consideración
e. el abrazo
f. la existencia
g. el saludo

B La cortesía. Completen con un sustantivo.

1. Él confía mucho en ella. Tiene mucha ____ en ella.
2. Los hombres se abrazan. Se dan un ____ el uno al otro.
3. Las amigas se besan en la mejilla. Se dan un ____ en la mejilla.
4. Ellos se despiden por mucho tiempo. A veces las ____ son tristes.

Comprensión

A ¿Sí o no? Contesten.

1. Es fácil que alguien te diga lo que son buenos modales en todos los países hispanos.
2. Los hispanos se quedan sentados cuando se acerca un amigo.
3. Los hispanos se dan la mano sólo en situaciones formales.
4. En las culturas hispanas hay una gran diferencia entre un conocido y un amigo.
5. Las mujeres que son amigas se abrazan cuando se encuentran.

B Los amigos. Contesten.

1. ¿Qué es un amigo?
2. ¿Qué es un conocido?
3. En los países hispanos, ¿cómo suelen despedirse dos amigos?
4. ¿Y dos amigas?

CAPÍTULO 11 **295**

ANSWERS
Estudio de palabras A
1. d
2. f
3. a
4. g
5. b
6. e
7. c

Estudio de palabras B
1. confianza
2. abrazo
3. beso
4. despedidas

Comprensión
ANSWERS
Comprensión A
1. No
2. No
3. No
4. Sí
5. No

Comprensión B
1. Un amigo es una persona que se conoce muy bien.
2. Un conocido es una persona que se conoce de la escuela o de la oficina, pero que no se conoce muy bien.
3. Un amigo y una amiga se dan un besito en la mejilla. Dos amigos se dan un abrazo y unas palmaditas en la espalda.
4. Dos amigas se dan un besito en la mejilla.

COOPERATIVE LEARNING

Have teams prepare composite lists of North American and Hispanic customs. They should mix up the items from both categories. Each team reads through its list to the class. Students classify each item as either *En los países hispanos* or *En los Estados Unidos*.

FOR THE NATIVE SPEAKER

Conversación Have students describe typical school dress in their country of origin. Ask if it is similar to what they see in the photos on page 295 or not. Have them discuss the following topic: *Los jóvenes en todas partes se visten de forma muy similar. ¿Quiere decir esto que todos piensan igual? ¿Qué opinas tú, y por qué?*

Bell Ringer Review

Write the following on the board or use BRR Blackline Master 11-10: Make a list of some common ways for friends to greet each other in the U.S.

Descrubimiento Cultural

(The Descubrimiento *section is optional.*)

PRESENTATION (page 296-297)

Have students open their books to pages 296-297 and ask them to read the selection aloud as a class, in pairs or groups, or silently.

CROSS-CULTURAL COMPARISON

Fast food restaurants have invaded the Spanish-speaking world. North American chains such as McDonald's and Burger King are found almost everywhere. In addition to the chains, there are local versions as well. "Cowboy burgers" and "El Pollo Loco" serve North American style fast food similar to the big chains. The more North American sounding the name, the better. In some countries, "fast food" or "junk food" is called *comida chatarra*, literally "junk-car food."

DESCUBRIMIENTO CULTURAL

Es necesario que todos sepamos que en todas las sociedades hay convenciones de cortesía que uno debe adoptar si no quiere que los otros lo tomen por mal educado. Si Ud. viaja por los países hispanos, hay que tener cuidado con el uso de "tú" y "Ud.". En general, debe dirigirle la palabra con la forma de Ud. a personas mayores como, por ejemplo, a un(a) profesor(a), a un(a) comerciante o a una persona que Ud. no conoce muy bien, a un(a) conocido(a).

Y Ud. puede tutear, hablar de "tú", a un buen amigo, a un pariente si Ud. tiene parientes en un país hispano. Y los jóvenes de la misma edad se tutean casi siempre. Hoy día la gente se tutea más fácilmente que antes pero depende del país. En Puerto Rico, por ejemplo, en seguida se tutea. En México es mejor que espere hasta que la otra persona le tutee. Cuando alguien le tutea, es como una invitación. La persona quiere que Ud. la tutee también.

296 CAPÍTULO 11

LEARNING FROM PHOTOS

Refer students to the photo on page 296 and ask: *¿Cuál de las personas es la mayor? ¿Quién será ella? ¿Cuántas generaciones están representadas en la foto? ¿Dónde están estas personas? ¿A quién prestan mucha atención?*

Hay que tener cuidado con el uso de la palabra "invitar". Si Ud. invita a una persona a tomar algo en un café o en un restaurante diciendo "José, te invito a…" significa que Ud. va a pagar. José no va a pagar y tampoco van a compartir (dividir) la cuenta. Hablando de un café o de un restaurante, si Ud. pasa por delante de una persona que está comiendo, es aconsejable que le diga "Buen provecho". Significa que Ud. quiere que la persona guste de lo que está comiendo. La gente sigue diciendo "buen provecho" pero es una costumbre que poco a poco está desapareciendo en algunos lugares.

En cuanto a las costumbres o convenciones de cortesía, si Ud. se encuentra en un país extranjero, es importante que se fije en[1] lo que hacen los otros. Hay un refrán español que dice: "A tierra que vayas, haz lo que veas". Es decir que todo no es lo mismo en todas partes. Y como decimos en inglés, "Cuando en Roma, haz (haga) lo que hacen los romanos".

[1] se fije en *take note of*

CAPÍTULO 11 **297**

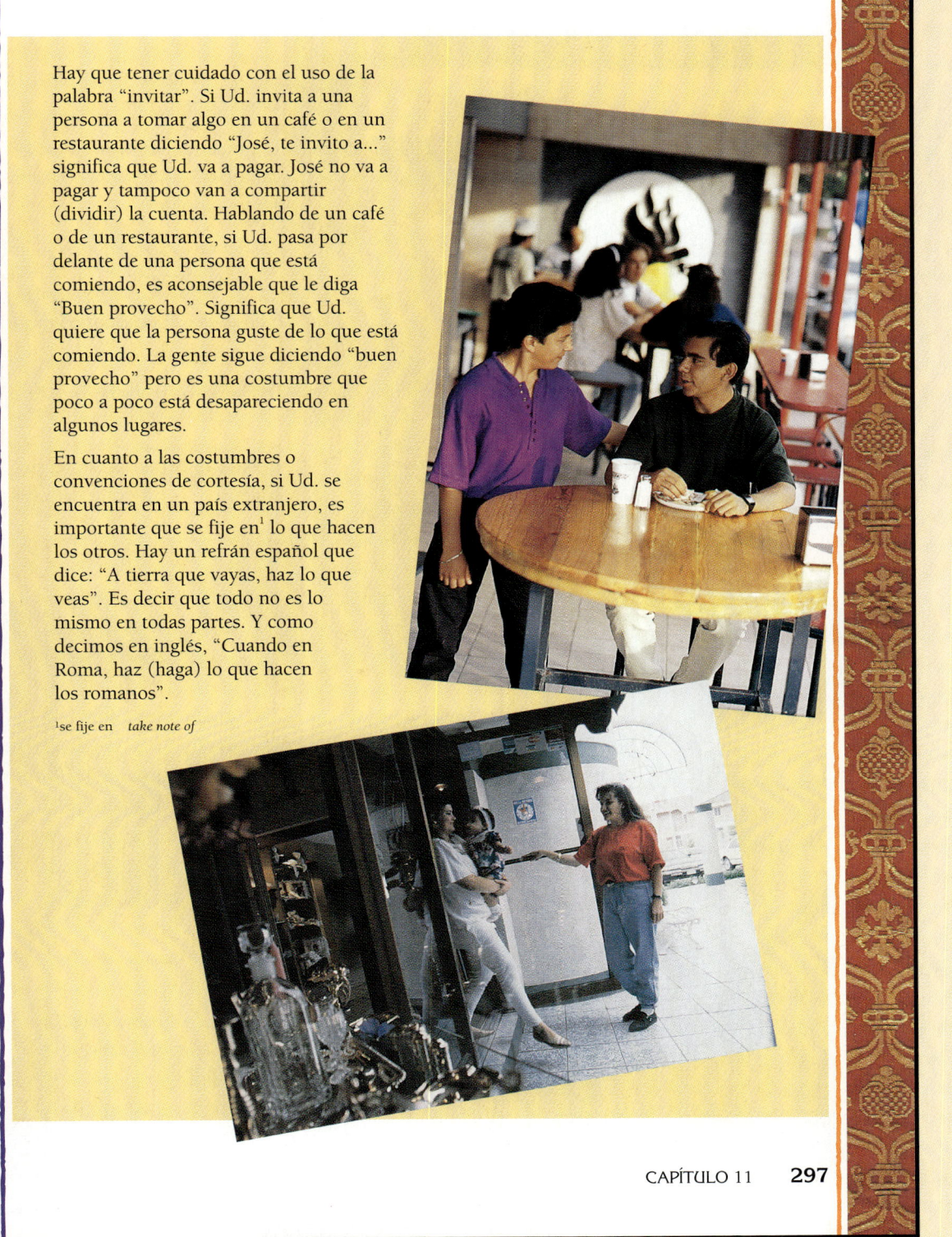

FOR THE NATIVE SPEAKER

Conversación A los jóvenes les gusta la comida rápida—las hamburguesas y papas fritas. Mucha gente cree que así se van a perder las comidas típicas de cada región; que nadie va a molestarse en preparar esos platos tradicionales. ¿Qué crees? ¿Tienen razón o no? ¿Por qué?

PAIRED ACTIVITY
Have students play the roles of the two men in the upper photo on page 297, and the two women in the photo at the bottom. Ask them to use polite expressions.

REALIDADES

(The Realidades section is optional material.)

Bell Ringer Review
Write the following on the board or use BRR Blackline Master 11-11: Make a list of things that your parents have stressed that you do to be polite and courteous.

PRESENTATION *(pages 298-299)*

A. Allow students time to look at the photographs on pages 298-299 and discuss them among themselves. Invite them to share their questions and comments.

B. Have students describe the people and comment on the relationships they think they see. You may wish to ask questions such as: ¿En cuál de las fotos se saludan más formalmente? ¿Son muy buenos amigos o solamente conocidos? ¿Dónde están la niña y su abuelo? ¿Dónde le da el niño el besito a su abuela?

REALIDADES

La chica habla con su abuelo **1**. No es malcriada. Tiene buen comportamiento.

Los muchachos son buenos amigos **2**. Se dan palmaditas en la espalda.

Los jóvenes son amigos íntimos **3**. Se abrazan.

Este joven tiene buenos modales **4**. Es cortés.

Los señores se estrechan la mano **5**.

El niño le da un besito a su abuela **6**. Se comporta bien.

INDEPENDENT PRACTICE

Assign the following:
Workbook, *Un poco más*

299

CULMINACIÓN

RECYCLING

The activities in *Comunicación oral* and *Comunicación escrita* encourage students to use all the language they have learned in the chapter and recombine it with material from previous chapters.

Comunicación oral
ANSWERS
Actividades A, B, and C
   Answers will vary.

INFORMAL ASSESSMENT
   Activities A, B, and C can be used to assess speaking skills. Use the evaluation criteria given on page 24 of this Teacher's Wraparound Edition.

Comunicación escrita
ANSWERS
Actividades A, B, and C
   Answers will vary.

CULMINACIÓN

Comunicación oral

A **Saludos.** Mire las siguientes fotografías. Salude a cada persona apropiadamente. Ud. no quiere ser descortés. Mire las fotografías una vez más. Despídase de cada persona apropiadamente.

B **Convenciones de cortesía.** Trabaje con un(a) compañero(a) de clase. Imagínese que Ud. es de un país hispanohablante de la América del Sur. Hágale preguntas a su compañero(a) americano(a) sobre las convenciones de cortesía en los Estados Unidos. Su compañero(a) se las contestará.

C **Las profesiones.** Haga una lista de profesiones. Escriba varias oraciones describiendo las características que necesita una persona en cada una de las profesiones. Luego léale las oraciones a un(a) compañero(a) de clase. Su compañero(a) tiene que adivinar cuál es cada profesión. Cambien de papel.

Estudiante 1: Es importante que sepa explicar bien.
              Es bueno que sea simpático.
              Es necesario que tenga buena disciplina.
Estudiante 2: Es un profesor.

Comunicación escrita

A **La etiqueta.** Escriba un párrafo para un libro de etiqueta explicando algunas convenciones de cortesía y algunos ejemplos de buenos modales.

B **Los buenos modales.** Ud. está viajando por un país hispano. Escríbale una carta a un(a) amigo(a). En la carta descríbale algunas costumbres o convenciones de cortesía que Ud. ha notado (en que Ud. se ha fijado) en Latinoamérica que son distintas o diferentes de nuestras convenciones.

C **Los reglamentos.** Escríbale una nota a un(a) amigo(a) donde le dice cómo tiene que prepararse para el examen de español.

   Es bueno que… y después es mejor que…

300 CAPÍTULO 11

FOR THE NATIVE SPEAKER

A major cause of conflict between people of different cultures is the contrast in customs of courtesy. Your students are probably very sensitive to these differences. Ask them to comment on the following:
   ¿Cuándo y a quién dan la mano? ¿Cómo saludan a los tíos, primos y abuelos? ¿Cómo saluda la madre a sus amigas? ¿Qué se sirve a los invitados? ¿Con quiénes usan tú o usted los padres? Si varias personas hablan a la vez o si cada persona espera su turno. Si han notado diferencias entre las dos culturas en situaciones como la cola para comprar boletos; el manejar un automóvil; el trato de los niños; y el trato con los ancianos.

Reintegración

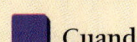

Cuando yo era joven. Completen con el pretérito o el imperfecto.
1. Cuando María ___ joven, siempre ___ bien. (ser, comportarse)
2. Sus padres la ___ y ella los ___ . (adorar, adorar)
3. Ellos le ___ mucho cariño. (tener)
4. Cuando María ___ su cumpleaños, sus padres siempre ___ una fiesta en su honor y le ___ regalos. (celebrar, dar, comprar)
5. Sus abuelos y todos los otros parientes de María siempre ___ a su fiesta de cumpleaños. Siempre ___ . (venir, asistir)
6. Un año su abuelito ___ a la fiesta con un regalo excepcional. (venir)
7. María ___ cinco años. (tener)
8. Y su abuelito le ___ una mascota, un perrito. (dar)
9. El perrito ___ adorable. A María le ___ mucho y ella ___ muy contenta. (ser, gustar, estar)
10. María ___ a su abuelito, ___ en sus piernas y le ___ un besito. (correr, sentarse, dar)

Vocabulario

SUSTANTIVOS
los modales
la cortesía
el comportamiento
el besito
el abrazo
la palmadita
la espalda
la mejilla

ADJETIVOS
cortés
descortés
educado(a)
malcriado(a)
íntimo(a)
menor
mayor

VERBOS
comportarse
saludar
tutear
despedirse
confiar
acercarse
desear
esperar
temer
tener miedo
preferir
mandar

OTRAS PALABRAS Y EXPRESIONES
el uno del otro
dar la mano
estrechar la mano
dar palmaditas
es bueno
es mejor
es fácil
es difícil
es importante
es necesario
es probable
es improbable
es posible
es imposible

CAPÍTULO 11   **301**

CAPÍTULO 12

Repaso Capítulos 9-12 • Scope and Sequence pages 302-339

Topics	Functions	Structure	Culture
Holidays Family celebrations	How to talk about family celebrations How to discuss some important holidays How to give advice and make suggestions to others How to express doubt, uncertainty, or disbelief How to express emotional reactions to the actions of others	El subjuntivo de los verbos de cambio radical El subjuntivo con verbos como *pedir* y *aconsejar* El subjuntivo con expresiones de duda El subjuntivo con expresiones de emoción	Hispanic customs, holidays, and celebrations Tamales, a traditional Christmas food in Mexico Holy Week in Antigua, Guatemala Sweets served in Mexico on All Saint's Day Nuestro Mundo: Kamikaze driver in Guadalajara
Fondo Académico pages 334-339			Las Ciencias Naturales Las Ciencias Sociales Las humanidades

CAPÍTULO 12

Situation Cards

The Situation Cards simulate real-life situations that require students to communicate in Spanish, exactly as though they were in a Spanish-speaking country. The Situation Cards operate on the assumption that the person to whom the message is to be conveyed understands no English. Therefore, students must focus on producing the Spanish vocabulary and structures necessary to negotiate the situations successfully. For additional information, see the Introduction to the Situation Cards in the Situation Cards Envelope.

Communication Transparency

The illustration seen in this Communication Transparency consists of a synthesis of the two vocabulary (Palabras 1&2) presentations found in this chapter. It has been created in order to present this chapter's vocabulary in a new context, and also to recycle vocabulary learned in previous chapters. The Communication Transparency consists of original art. Following are some specific uses:

1. as a cue to stimulate conversation and writing activities
2. for listening comprehension activities
3. to review and reteach vocabulary
4. as a review for chapter and unit tests

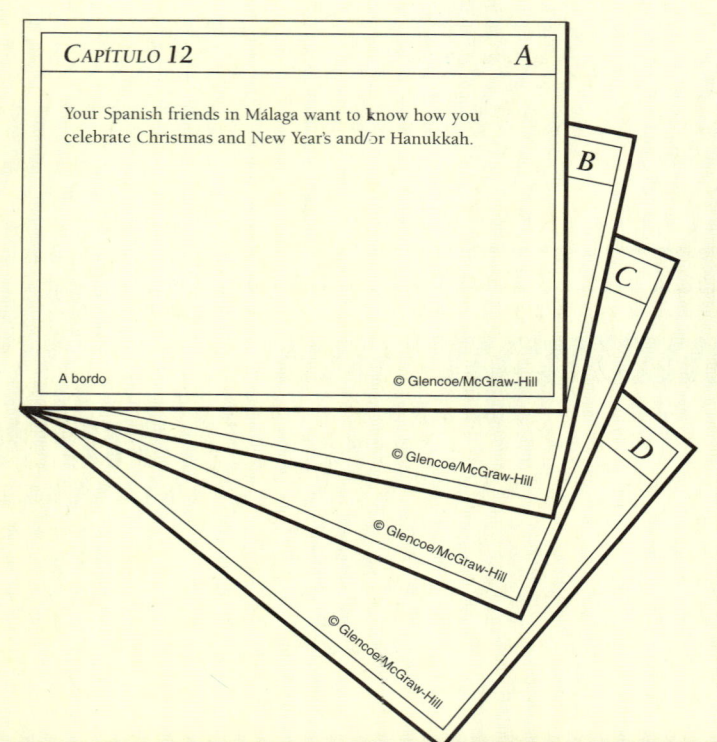

CAPÍTULO 12
Print Resources

Lesson Plans

Pages

Workbook
- Palabras 1 — 129-130
- Palabras 2 — 130-132
- Estructura — 133-136
- Un poco más — 137
- Mi autobiografía — 138
- Self-Test — 139-146

Communication Activities Masters
- Palabras 1 — 75-77
- Palabras 2 — 78
- Estructura — 79-82

9 Bell Ringer Reviews — 34-36

Chapter Situation Cards A B C D

Chapter Quizzes
- Palabras 1 — 56
- Palabras 2 — 57
- Estructura — 58-61

Testing Program
- Listening Comprehension — 65
- Reading and Writing — 66-69
- Proficiency — 134
- Speaking — 154

Unit Test: Chapters 9-12
- Listening Comprehension — 70
- Reading and Writing — 71-74
- Speaking — 155
- Performance Assessment

Nosotros y Nuestro Mundo
- Nuestro Conocimiento Académico *Antropología*
- Nuestro Idioma *El subjuntivo de los verbos de cambio radical*
- Nuestra Cultura *"Fiesta de Reyes"* de José Alegría Santos
- Nuestra Literatura *"Una escena de Nochebuena"* de Manuel Gutiérrez Nájera
- Nuestra Creatividad
- Nuestras Diversiones

CAPÍTULO 12
Multimedia Resources

CD-ROM Interactive Textbook Disc 3

Chapter 12 Student Edition
- Palabras 1
- Palabras 2
- Estructura
- Conversación
- Lectura y cultura
- Hispanoparlantes
- Realidades
- Culminación
- Prueba

Review: Chapters 9-12
- Nuestro mundo
- Repaso
- Fondo Académico
- Game: El Gran Concurso

Audio Cassette Program with Student Tape Manual

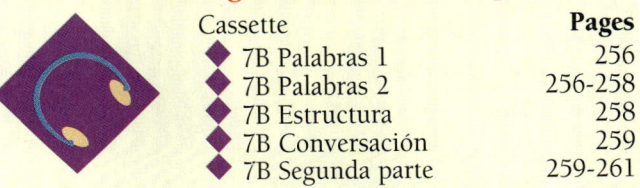

Cassette — Pages
- 7B Palabras 1 — 256
- 7B Palabras 2 — 256-258
- 7B Estructura — 258
- 7B Conversación — 259
- 7B Segunda parte — 259-261

Compact Disc Program with Student Tape Manual
- CD 7 Palabras 1 — 256
- CD 7 Palabras 2 — 256-258
- CD 7 Estructura — 258
- CD 7 Conversación — 259
- CD 7 Segunda parte — 259-261

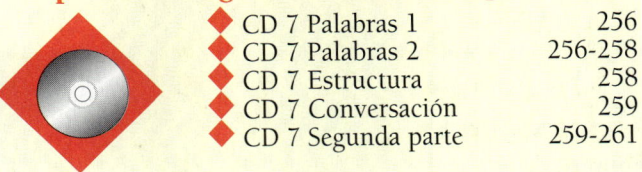

Overhead Transparencies Binder
- Vocabulary 12.1 (A&B); 12.2 (A&B)
- Communication C-12
- Maps
- Fine Art (with Blackline Master Activities)

Video Program
- Videocassette
- Video Activities Booklet — 31-32
- Videodisc
- Video Activities Booklet — 31-32

Computer Software (Macintosh, IBM, Apple)
- Practice Disk
    - Palabras 1 y 2
    - Estructura
- Test Generator Disk
    - Chapter Test
    - Customized Test

302B

CAPÍTULO 12

CHAPTER OVERVIEW

In this chapter, students will learn to describe and discuss several important holidays and family celebrations. They will learn some additional uses of the subjunctive, such as giving advice and making suggestions, using expressions of doubt and uncertainty, and expressing emotional reactions. The cultural focus of Chapter 12 is on important holiday celebrations, both religious and secular, in the Hispanic world.

CHAPTER OBJECTIVES

By the end of this chapter, students will know:
1. vocabulary associated with holidays and celebrations
2. the forms of the present subjunctive for radical changing verbs
3. the use of the subjunctive when giving advice and making suggestions
4. the use of the subjunctive when talking about actions that may or may not take place
5. the use of the subjunctive when expressing emotional reactions
6. the use of the subjunctive when expressing doubt or uncertainty

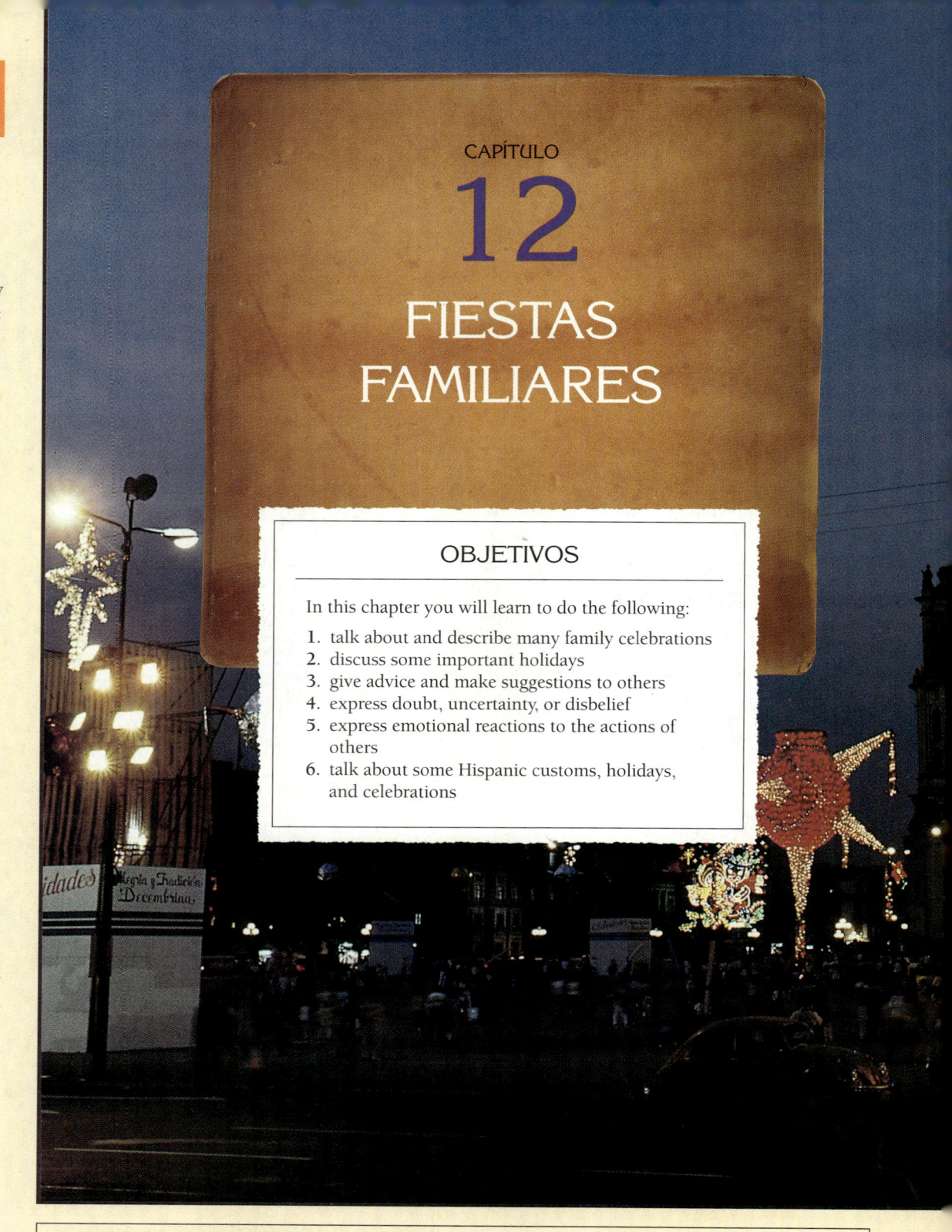

CAPÍTULO 12
FIESTAS FAMILIARES

OBJETIVOS

In this chapter you will learn to do the following:
1. talk about and describe many family celebrations
2. discuss some important holidays
3. give advice and make suggestions to others
4. express doubt, uncertainty, or disbelief
5. express emotional reactions to the actions of others
6. talk about some Hispanic customs, holidays, and celebrations

CHAPTER PROJECTS

(optional)
1. Have students prepare original greeting cards in Spanish for various holidays and occasions. Create a bulletin board display of the class's cards.
2. Have students select a holiday such as Christmas that is celebrated in both the Hispanic world and the U.S., and prepare a report comparing/contrasting the ways in which the holiday is celebrated in the two different cultures.
3. Have students prepare a report on either *el dos de noviembre* or *el seis de enero*.
4. Have students look for *tamales* in their local market and hold a party with *tamales* among the foods. If your school has a home economics department, you may have the class make their own *tamales*.

CHAPTER 12 RESOURCES

1. Workbook
2. Student Tape Manual
3. Audio Cassette 7B
4. Vocabulary Transparencies
5. Bell Ringer Review Blackline Masters
6. Communication Activities Masters
7. Computer Software: Practice and Test Generator
8. Video Cassette, Chapter 12
9. Video Activities Booklet, Chapter 12
10. Situation Cards
11. Chapter Quizzes
12. Testing Program

Pacing

Chapter 12 will require eight to ten class sessions. Pacing will depend on the length of the class period, the age of the students, and student aptitude.

GEOGRAPHY CONNECTION

The scene in the photo spread on pages 302-303 is the *Zócalo* in Mexico City. It is the largest paved square in the Western Hemisphere. Also known as the *Plaza de la Constitución*, it was constructed upon the same site as the main temple of Tenochtitlan, the ancient city of the Aztecs. The Spaniards built convents, mansions, and public buildings around the plaza. The majority of them are still standing. The Mexican government has designated the *Zócalo* as a national monument, and the *Zócalo*, together with the surrounding area, a *centro histórico*.

LEARNING FROM PHOTOS

Tell students that the scene on pages 302-303 is of Christmas in downtown Mexico City. The sign on the left reads *Alegría y Tradición Decembrina*. Ask students what this means. Also ask what holidays might be included in *alegría y tradición decembrina*. Have students say as much as they can about the photo.

VOCABULARIO
PALABRAS 1

Vocabulary Teaching Resources
1. Vocabulary Transparencies, 12.1 (A & B)
2. Audio Cassette 7B
3. Student Tape Manual, Palabras 1
4. Workbook pages Palabras 1
5. Communication Activities Masters, Palabras 1, A & B
6. Chapter Quizzes, Palabras 1

Bell Ringer Review
Write the following on the board or use BRR Blackline Master 12-1: Complete each sentence with the correct form of the conditional tense of the verb in parentheses.
1. ¿Qué ____ tú en esta situación? (hacer)
2. ¿____ Ud. ayudarme? (Poder)
3. Me ____ hacer un viaje a España. (gustar)
4. Yo ____ estudiar francés. (preferir)

PRESENTATION (pages 304–305)
A. With books closed, refer to Vocabulary Transparencies 12.1 (A & B) and have students repeat the new words, phrases, and sentences after you or Cassette 7B.
B. Have students open their books to pages 304–305 and call on volunteers to read the new words, phrases, and sentences.

CROSS-CULTURAL COMPARISON
Ask students: *Si el calendario es un calendario hispano, ¿qué día de la semana es el 4 de mayo?* (viernes)

VOCABULARIO

PALABRAS 1

¡FELIZ CUMPLEAÑOS!

el nacimiento

El niño nació el cuatro de mayo.
El cuatro de mayo es el día de su nacimiento.
Se celebrará su cumpleaños el cuatro de mayo.

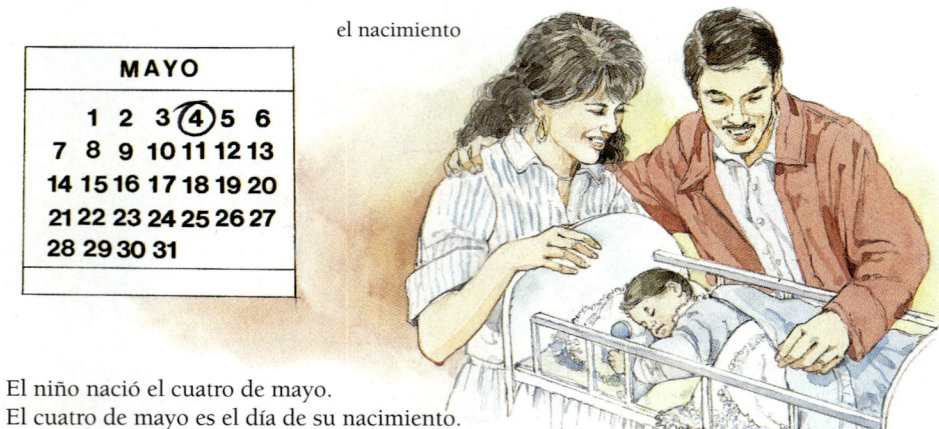

la iglesia   el bautizo   el padrino
                              la madrina

el cura

el niño

El cura bautiza al niño.
Los padres les piden a sus amigos que sean padrino y madrina.

304   CAPÍTULO 12

la vela
la torta
el pastel
el bizcocho
el salón del hotel

Rosalía cumple quince años.
Ella es quinceañera.
Sus padres le dan una fiesta.
La quinceañera se viste de gala.
Se reúne toda la familia.

el cementerio, el camposanto
la tumba
las flores

Los muertos o los difuntos son los que ya no viven, que han muerto.
Los difuntos están enterrados en las tumbas.

CAPÍTULO 12 **305**

DID YOU KNOW?

The cemetery in the illustration on page 305 is similar to a North American cemetery. Traditional village cemeteries in Spain consist of *nichos* in a wall, above ground, one on top of another. A family may retain one or more *nichos* for generations. Every few decades the bones may be removed to make room for another "tenant."

ABOUT THE LANGUAGE

1. The name for a baptismal font like the one shown on page 304 is *la pila de bautismo*. "Holy water" is *agua bendita*.
2. As shown on page 305, "cake" has a number of names in Spanish. In many areas it is called *"queik"* or *"queik de cumpleaños"*.
3. Other words for the clergy (*el clero*) are:
   priest: *cura, sacerdote* (Roman Catholic)
   minister: *ministro* (Protestant)
   rabbi: *rabino* (Jewish)
   imam: *imán* (Muslin)

305

Ejercicios

PRESENTATION (page 306)

Ejercicio A

Exercise A can be done with books open or closed.

Ejercicio B

Exercise B is to be done with books open.

ANSWERS

Ejercicio A
1. El niño nació el 4 de mayo.
2. Lo bautizaron en junio.
3. El cura lo bautizó.
4. Lo bautizó en la iglesia.
5. El señor Villabuena era el padrino.
6. Su esposa (la señora Villabuena) era la madrina.
7. Sí, los padres están contentos que sus amigos sirvan de padrinos.
8. Después de la ceremonia en la iglesia, hay una fiesta familiar en casa.

Ejercicio B
1. La muchacha tiene quince años.
2. Sus padres le dan una fiesta.
3. Se reúnen sus amigos y sus parientes.
4. Le dan (traen) regalos a la muchacha.
5. La recepción tiene lugar en (un salón de baile de) un hotel.
6. Sí, todos comen una rebanada (tajada) de torta.
7. Hay quince velas en la torta.
8. La quinceañera se viste de gala.

306

Ejercicios

A **El bautizo.** Contesten según se indica.

1. ¿Qué día nació el niño? (el 4 de mayo)
2. ¿Cuándo lo bautizaron? (en junio)
3. ¿Quién lo bautizó? (el cura)
4. ¿Dónde lo bautizó? (en la iglesia)
5. ¿Quién era el padrino? (el señor Villabuena)
6. ¿Y quién era la madrina? (su esposa)
7. ¿Están contentos los padres que sus amigos sirvan de padrinos? (sí)
8. ¿Qué hay después de la ceremonia en la iglesia? (una fiesta familiar en casa)

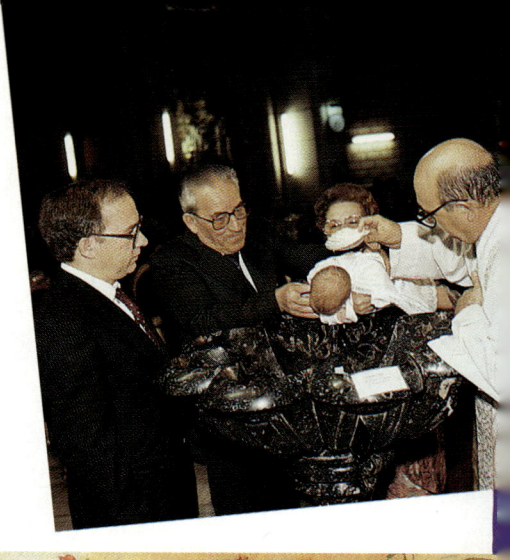

B **La quinceañera.** Contesten según el dibujo.

1. ¿Cuántos años tiene la muchacha?
2. ¿Qué le dan sus padres?
3. ¿Quiénes se reúnen?
4. ¿Qué le dan (traen) a la muchacha?
5. ¿Dónde tiene lugar la recepción?
6. ¿Comen todos una rebanada (tajada) de torta?
7. ¿Cuántas velas hay en la torta?
8. ¿Cómo se viste la quinceañera?

306   CAPÍTULO 12

LEARNING FROM PHOTOS

Refer students to the photo at the top of page 306. Have them tell what is happening in it, including who each person is. The *padrinos* are much older than the parents. Who might the *padrinos* be?

C El cumpleaños. *Completen.*

1. El día que nace un niño o una niña es el día de su ___ .
2. En el futuro celebrarán su ___ en esta fecha.
3. El ___ es una ceremonia religiosa.
4. En la iglesia católica y en algunas otras iglesias cristianas el bautismo tiene lugar en la ___ .
5. Una muchacha que ___ quince años es una quinceañera.

D Preguntas. *Formen preguntas.*

1. El niño nació *el cuatro de mayo.*
2. *El cura* lo bautizó.
3. *Los padrinos* asistieron al bautizo.
4. El cura bautizó al niño *en la iglesia.*
5. Los padrinos estaban *contentos.*

E El camposanto. *Contesten según se indica.*

1. ¿Quiénes están enterrados en el cementerio? (los muertos)
2. ¿Cuál es otra palabra que significa "el muerto"? (el difunto)
3. ¿Dónde están enterrados los difuntos? (en el camposanto)
4. ¿Cuál es otra palabra que significa "el camposanto"? (el cementerio)
5. ¿Qué ponen los parientes de los difuntos en las tumbas? (flores)

Celebración del día de los Muertos en México

CAPÍTULO 12 307

DID YOU KNOW?

On November 2, *El día de los Muertos* (All Souls Day), is celebrated in most Hispanic countries. People visit the cemeteries. In parts of Mexico people bring offerings of food and drink to the dead. Cakes and candies in the form of skulls and skeletons are prepared for the occasion. The visit with the dead is an all-day outing.

INDEPENDENT PRACTICE

Assign any of the following:
1. Workbook, *Palabras 1*
2. Communication Activities Masters, *Palabras 1, A & B*
3. Exercises on student pages 306-307

Ejercicios
PRESENTATION (*page 307*)

Ejercicios C, D, and E
Exercise C, D, and E can be done with books open.

ANSWERS

Ejercicio C
1. nacimiento
2. cumpleaños
3. bautizo
4. iglesia
5. cumple

Ejercicio D
1. ¿Cuándo nació el niño?
2. ¿Quién lo bautizó?
3. ¿Quiénes asistieron al bautizo?
4. ¿Dónde bautizó el cura al niño?
5. ¿Cómo estaban los padrinos?

Ejercicio E
1. Los muertos están enterrados en el cementerio.
2. "El difunto" es otra palabra que significa "el muerto".
3. Los difuntos están enterrados en el camposanto.
4. "El cementerio" es otra palabra que significa "camposanto".
5. Los parientes de los difuntos ponen flores en las tumbas "el".

307

VOCABULARIO
PALABRAS 2

Vocabulary Teaching Resources
1. Vocabulary Transparencies 12.2 (A & B)
2. Audio Cassette 7B
3. Student Tape Manual, *Palabras 2*
4. Workbook, *Palabras 2*
5. Communication Activities Masters, *Palabras 2, C & D*
6. Chapter Quizzes, *Palabras 2*
7. Computer Software, *Vocabulario*

Bell Ringer Review
Write the following on the board or use BRR Blackline Master 12-2: Divide a piece of paper into two columns. Head one column cortés *and the other* descortés. *Copy each of the following into the appropriate column.*
1. llegar a una cita a tiempo
2. empujar
3. ofrecer tu asiento a un anciano en el bus
4. comer con la boca cerrada
5. hablar con la boca llena
6. estrecharle la mano a alguien
7. tutear a un vendedor

PRESENTATION (pages 308-309)
A. Have students close their books. Model the *Palabras 2* vocabulary using Vocabulary Transparencies 12.2 (A & B). Have students repeat the new material after you or Cassette 7B.

308

VOCABULARIO

PALABRAS 2

¡FELIZ NAVIDAD Y PRÓSPERO AÑO NUEVO!

la Navidad

el árbol de Navidad

los camellos

los Reyes Magos

los regalos de Navidad, los aguinaldos

la Misa

La Navidad es el 25 de diciembre.
El 24 es la víspera de la Navidad, o Nochebuena.
La misa del gallo tiene lugar a la medianoche de la víspera de Navidad.

308   CAPÍTULO 12

PANTOMIME
Have students mime the following actions:
Abre tu regalo de Navidad.
Canta un villancico (Christmas carol).
Pon paja en tus zapatos.
Enciende una vela del candelabro.

DID YOU KNOW?
Los Reyes Magos son Gaspar, Melchor y Baltasar. La tradición es que le trajeron al Niño Jesús regalos de oro, incienso y mirra. La tradición también dice que el rey Baltasar era africano.

Los Reyes Magos van a llegar.
Traen regalos (aguinaldos).
Los niños ponen paja en sus zapatos.

la paja

Los padres les aconsejan a los niños que sean buenos.
Les dicen que se comporten bien.
Los niños quieren que los Reyes les traigan aguinaldos.

la menora
la vela
el brazo
el candelabro

DICIEMBRE

					1	2
3	4	5	6	7	8	9
10	11	12	13	14	15	16
17	18	19	20	21	22	23
24/31	25	26	27	28	29	30

Hanuka es la fiesta de las luces.
Es una fiesta hebrea (de los judíos).
La fiesta dura ocho días.
La menora es un candelabro de siete brazos.
La menora para la fiesta de luces tiene nueve brazos.
Durante la fiesta los niños encienden las velas del candelabro.

CAPÍTULO 12

DID YOU KNOW?

1. Service workers of all kinds expect an *aguinaldo* (a money gift) at Christmas time. People receive Christmas greetings from the plumber, the mail carrier, the trash collector, etc. An envelope with a cash *aguinaldo* is the expected return greeting.

2. There are sizable Jewish populations in several countries in Latin America, Mexico, Panamá, and Argentina in particular.

B. After some practice, use questions such as the following to elicit the vocabulary: ¿Qué traen los Reyes Magos? ¿Qué ponen los niños en sus zapatos? ¿Qué es Hanuka? ¿Cuánto tiempo dura la fiesta de Hanuka? ¿Qué es la menora? ¿Cuándo tiene lugar la misa del gallo? ¿Quiénes quieren que los Reyes les traigan aguinaldos?

Vocabulary Expansion

You may give students the names of a few Christmas carols in Spanish:
Noche de Paz (Silent Night)
Campana sobre Campana (Bells Over Bethlehem)
Navidad (Deck the Halls)
Paz en la Tierra (Joy to the World)

ABOUT THE LANGUAGE

La misa del gallo, on page 308, can be either midnight Mass or a Mass at dawn. The name comes from the cock's crow, *el canto del gallo*, which is always associated with the sunrise.

Ejercicios

PRESENTATION (page 310)

Ejercicios A–D
Exercises A–D can be done with books open or closed.

Extension of *Ejercicio A*
Speaking
After completing Exercise A, have a volunteer give a description of Christmas in his/her own words.

Extension of *Ejercicio C*
Writing
After completing Exercise C, have students correct the false statements in writing.

Extension of *Ejercicio D*
Speaking
After completing Exercise D, have a volunteer describe Hanukkah in his/her own words.

ANSWERS

Ejercicio A
1. La Navidad es el 25 de diciembre.
2. El 24 de diciembre es la víspera de la Navidad.
3. En la iglesia católica, la misa del gallo tiene lugar el 24 de diciembre (Nochebuena).
4. En los Estados Unidos, los niños (y otros) reciben sus aguinaldos (regalos) el 25 de diciembre.
5. En los Estados Unidos, San Nicolás trae los aguinaldos.
6. En los Estados Unidos, las familias cristianas decoran el árbol de Navidad.

Ejercicio B
1. el veinticinco de diciembre
2. la misa del gallo
3. el camello
4. un aguinaldo

Ejercicio C
1. Sí
2. No
3. Sí
4. Sí
5. No

Ejercicio D
1. Hanuka es la fiesta de las luces.
2. Los judíos celebran Hanuka.
3. La fiesta dura ocho días.

310

Ejercicios

A La Navidad. Contesten.
1. ¿Cuál es la fecha de la Navidad?
2. ¿Cuál es la fecha de la víspera de la Navidad?
3. En la iglesia católica, ¿cuándo tiene lugar la misa del gallo?
4. En los Estados Unidos, ¿cuándo reciben los niños (y otros) aguinaldos?
5. ¿Quién les trae los aguinaldos, San Nicolás (*Santa Claus*) o los Reyes?
6. Para la Navidad, ¿qué decoran las familias cristianas en los Estados Unidos?

B Definiciones. ¿Qué es?
1. el día que nació el niño Jesús
2. la misa que tiene lugar la medianoche de la víspera de la Navidad
3. un animal que sobrevive bien en el desierto
4. un regalo de Navidad

C Algunas costumbres navideñas.
¿Sí o no?
1. Los padres siempre les aconsejan a los niños que se comporten bien.
2. Los niños que son malos reciben aguinaldos.
3. La celebración de la Navidad es una costumbre cristiana.
4. El árbol de Navidad es una costumbre religiosa.
5. Los camellos llevan zapatos llenos de paja.

D Hanuka. Contesten según se indica.
1. ¿Qué es Hanuka? (la fiesta de las luces)
2. ¿Quiénes celebran Hanuka? (los judíos)
3. ¿Cuánto tiempo dura la fiesta? (ocho días)
4. ¿Cómo se llama el candelabro que se usa durante la fiesta de las luces? (la menora)
5. ¿Cuántos brazos tiene? (nueve)
6. ¿Quiénes encienden las velas? (los niños)
7. ¿Cuántas velas encienden cada noche de la fiesta? (una)

310   CAPÍTULO 12

DID YOU KNOW?

The Christmas tree is not part of the Hispanic tradition. However, it is often found in Hispanic homes today, along with Santa Claus. The traditional Christmas display is the *nacimiento* or creche. The *nacimientos* come in infinite varieties. Some consist of primitive wood carvings. Some are made of finest porcelain. The simplest have the baby Jesus with Mary and Joseph. More elaborate *nacimientos* have the *Reyes Magos*, shepherds with their sheep, and a stable full of animals.

Comunicación
Palabras 1 y 2

A **La Navidad.** En los Estados Unidos las familias cristianas celebran la Navidad. Para ellas es una fiesta importante. Describa algunas costumbres navideñas tradicionales de los Estados Unidos.

B **Fiestas tradicionales.** Dígale a un(a) compañero(a) de clase todo lo que sabe sobre alguna fiesta tradicional, religiosa o cultural. Incluya información sobre el origen de la celebración, así como detalles de las ceremonias y las comidas tradicionales de la fiesta.

C **La familia.** Con un(a) compañero(a) de clase, prepare una conversación sobre fiestas familiares. Ud. hará las preguntas y su compañero(a) las contestará. Luego cambien de papel. Pregúntele:

1. si celebran la Navidad, Hanuka u otra ocasión religiosa
2. cómo celebran esos días
3. si cambian regalos entre todos o si se los dan sólo a los niños
4. si celebran el cumpleaños de cada miembro de la familia
5. cómo celebraron su último *(last)* cumpleaños
6. cuándo su familia tiene una reunión anual u otra ocasión cuando se reúnen todos

D **En las fiestas familiares.** Explíquele a un(a) compañero(a) de clase las fechas que celebran Ud. y su familia. Déjele saber por qué esas fechas son importantes. Dígale como las celebran. Cambien de papel.

CAPÍTULO 12 311

---

4. La menora es el candelabro que se usa durante la fiesta de las luces.
5. Tiene nueve brazos.
6. Los niños encienden las velas.
7. Encienden una vela cada noche de la fiesta.

Comunicación
(Palabras 1 and 2)

Bell Ringer Review
Write the following on the board or use BRR Blackline Master 12-3: Complete the following impersonal expressions with a subjunctive clause:
1. Es necesario que…
2. Es importante que…
3. Es posible que…
4. Es mejor que…

PRESENTATION *(page 311)*
A. You may have students do any number of these activities. You may also allow students to select the activity(ies) in which they would like to take part.
B. After completing the activities, have each student prepare and present a description of one of his/her family holiday celebrations.

ANSWERS
Actividades A and B
Answers will vary.

Actividad C
Questions and answers will vary.

Actividad D
Answers will vary.

ABOUT THE LANGUAGE
In Spanish people often refer to *las Navidades*. The expression refers to the traditional twelve days of Christmas, commencing on the 25th of December and ending on the Epiphany, the 6th of January.

CRITICAL THINKING ACTIVITY
(Thinking skills: identifying causes; comparing and contrasting)

Read the following to the class or write it on the board or on an overhead transparency.

El árbol de Navidad y Santa Claus no son parte de la tradición hispana. Pero hoy aparecen en muchas partes del mundo hispano durante las Navidades. ¿Cómo explicas esto?

INDEPENDENT PRACTICE
Assign any of the following:
1. Workbook, *Palabras 2*
2. Communication Activities Masters, *Palabras 2, C & D*
3. Exercises and activities on student pages 310-311

ESTRUCTURA

Structure Teaching Resources

1. Workbook, *Estructura*
2. Student Tape Manual, *Estructura*
3. Audio Cassette 7B
4. Communication Activities Masters, *Estructura*, A-D
5. Chapter Quizzes, *Estructura*
6. Computer Software, *Estructura*

Bell Ringer Review

Write the following on the board or use BRR Blackline Master 12-4: Make a list of things you have done so far today using the present perfect tense.

El subjuntivo de los verbos de cambio radical

PRESENTATION *(page 312)*

A. Have students open their books to page 312 and lead them through steps 1 and 2.
B. Write the forms of one or two of the verbs on the board.
C. Have students repeat the verb forms.
D. With books closed, call on volunteers to write conjugations of other verbs, following the model(s) which you have provided. Have the class repeat these forms.

ESTRUCTURA

El subjuntivo de los verbos de cambio radical

Expressing More Actions that May or May Not Take Place

1. Verbs that have a stem change in the present indicative also have a stem change in the present subjunctive. Observe the following.

(O > UE)		(E > IE)	
ENCONTRAR	**PODER**	**CERRAR**	**PERDER**
encuentre	pueda	cierre	pierda
encuentres	puedas	cierres	pierdas
encuentre	pueda	cierre	pierda
encontremos	podamos	cerremos	perdamos
encontréis	*podáis*	*cerréis*	*perdáis*
encuentren	puedan	cierren	pierdan

Verbs that follow the same e > ie pattern are *sentarse, comenzar, empezar,* and *pensar.* Verbs that follow the o >ue pattern are *acostarse, encontrar(se), recordar,* and *volver. Jugar* also changes to -ue.

2. Note that the verbs *dormir* and *sentir* have a stem change in every form of the present subjunctive. Verbs like *pedir* have an -i in all forms of the present subjunctive.

O > UE, U	E > IE, I	E > I
DORMIR	**SENTIR**	**PEDIR**
duerma	sienta	pida
duermas	sientas	pidas
duerma	sienta	pida
durmamos	sintamos	pidamos
durmáis	*sintáis*	*pidáis*
duerman	sientan	pidan

Morir is conjugated like *dormir,* and *preferir* is conjugated like *sentir. Repetir, freír, seguir,* and *servir* are conjugated like *pedir.*

312 CAPÍTULO 12

FOR THE NATIVE SPEAKER

Have students study the following sentences. Ask them to indicate the mood for each verb: indicative, subjunctive, conditional, or imperative. If the verb is indicative, have them determine the tense, as well.

1. *Ramón, ¡no hables más!*
2. *Nadie te escuchará.*
3. *Todos dicen que tú hablas demasiado.*
4. *Yo espero que te calles.*
5. *¿Ves? Mientras te hablamos tú estás hablando.*
6. *Es imposible que tú aprendas nada.*
7. *Dudo que cambies.*
8. *Insistimos en que guardes silencio.*
9. *¡No vuelvas a decir nada!*

Ejercicio

Yo quiero. Sigan el modelo.

Yo quiero ____ .
Él vuelve mañana.
Yo quiero que él vuelva mañana.

1. Él vuelve mañana.
2. Él nos encuentra delante del restaurante.
3. Él se sienta a nuestra mesa.
4. Él pide algo bueno.
5. Él me recomienda un plato.
6. El mesero nos sirve ahora.

El subjuntivo con verbos como *pedir* y *aconsejar*

Giving Advice and Making Suggestions

1. The following verbs are followed by the subjunctive because even though one asks, advises, or tells someone to do something, it is not certain the person will do it. It may or may not happen.

pedir	to ask
rogar	to beg, plead
sugerir	to suggest
aconsejar	to advise
exigir	to demand
decir	to tell (someone to do something)
escribir	to write (someone to do something)

   Ellos le sugieren que termine con su trabajo en seguida.
   Él me recomienda que lo haga.
   Él nos aconseja que salgamos ahora.

2. Note too that an indirect object pronoun, *me, le,* etc., accompanies the above verbs. The indirect object pronoun serves as the subject of the dependent clause.

   Él me pide que (yo) vaya y yo le pido que (él) vaya.

3. The verbs *decir* and *escribir* are followed by the subjunctive only when they imply a command. If someone tells or writes about an event, the subjunctive is not used. Observe the following:

   Yo le digo que vaya.
   Yo le digo que el tren está llegando.
   Yo le escribo a mi abuela que la voy a visitar.
   Mi abuela me escribe que estudie.

CAPÍTULO 12

Ejercicios

PRESENTATION (page 314)

Ejercicios A and B
Exercises A and B can be done with books open or closed.

Variation of Ejercicio C
Paired Activity
Have pairs complete Exercise C. One partner reads the questions and the other responds with his/her book closed. Then partners can reverse roles.

ANSWERS

Ejercicio A
1. Mi primo me escribe que vaya a la fiesta.
2. … que tome el tren.
3. … que llegue un día antes de la fiesta.
4. … que no vaya a un hotel.
5. … que me quede en casa de mis tíos.

Ejercicio B
1. El profesor nos aconseja que lleguemos a clase a tiempo.
2. … nos sentemos en seguida.
3. … no digamos nada a nadie, que nos callemos.
4. … contestemos (a) sus preguntas.
5. … hagamos preguntas si no comprendemos.
6. … estudiemos.
7. … hagamos nuestras tareas con cuidado.
8. … escribamos claramente.

Ejercicio C
1. Sí, mis padres me aconsejan que sea bueno(a).
2. … me comporte bien.
3. Sí (No), mis padres (no) me piden que ayude con las tareas domésticas.
4. Sí, mis padres me piden que les diga adónde voy y con quiénes.
5. … sugieren que haga mis tareas antes de poner la televisión.
6. Sí (No), mis padres (no) me dicen que me acueste antes de las diez y media.

314

Ejercicios

A ¿Qué te escribe tu primo? Sigan el modelo.

> Mi primo me escribe.
> ir a la fiesta
> *Mi primo me escribe que vaya a la fiesta.*

1. ir a la fiesta
2. tomar el tren
3. llegar un día antes de la fiesta
4. no ir a un hotel
5. quedarse en casa de mis tíos

B El profesor nos aconseja. Sigan el modelo.

> El profesor nos aconseja.
> Llegamos a clase a tiempo.
> *El profesor nos aconseja que lleguemos a clase a tiempo.*

1. Llegamos a clase a tiempo.
2. Nos sentamos en seguida.
3. No decimos nada a nadie. Nos callamos.
4. Contestamos a sus preguntas.
5. Hacemos preguntas si no comprendemos.
6. Estudiamos.
7. Hacemos nuestras tareas con cuidado.
8. Escribimos claramente.

C Mis padres. Contesten.

1. ¿Tus padres te aconsejan que seas bueno?
2. ¿Tus padres te aconsejan que te comportes bien?
3. ¿Tus padres te piden que ayudes con las tareas domésticas?
4. ¿Tus padres te piden que les digas adónde vas y con quiénes?
5. ¿Tus padres te sugieren que hagas tus tareas antes de poner la televisión?
6. ¿Tus padres te dicen que te acuestes antes de las diez y media?

314 CAPÍTULO 12

LEARNING FROM PHOTOS
Refer students to the photo at the top of page 314 and ask: *¿Dónde están las tres personas? ¿Qué son ellos? ¿Qué puedes decir de la ropa que ellos llevan?* (The students are wearing uniforms.)

INDEPENDENT PRACTICE
Assign any of the following:
1. Workbook, *Estructura*
2. Communication Activities Masters, *Estructura, A & B*
3. Exercises on student pages 313–314

El subjuntivo con expresiones de duda

Expressing Doubt or Uncertainty

1. The subjunctive is always used after any expression that implies doubt.

    Yo dudo que ellos lleguen hoy.
    Y Elena no cree que vengan mañana tampoco.

2. Note, however, that if the statement implies certainty rather than doubt, the indicative, not the subjunctive, is used.

    Yo no dudo que ellos van a llegar.
    Y creo que llegarán hoy.

3. Note also that after an expression that implies certainty, the future is often used. Review the following expressions of doubt and certainty.

SUBJUNCTIVE	INDICATIVE
dudar	no dudar
es dudoso	no es dudoso
no estar seguro(a)	estar seguro(a)
no creer	creer
no es cierto	es cierto

Ejercicios

A ¿Lo crees o no lo crees? Comiencen la oración con *creo* o *no creo*.

1. El mundo es redondo.
2. Hace calor en la Antártida.
3. Los coches contaminan el aire.
4. Los aviones vuelan a una altura de un millón de metros.
5. Los trenes son mucho más rápidos que los aviones.

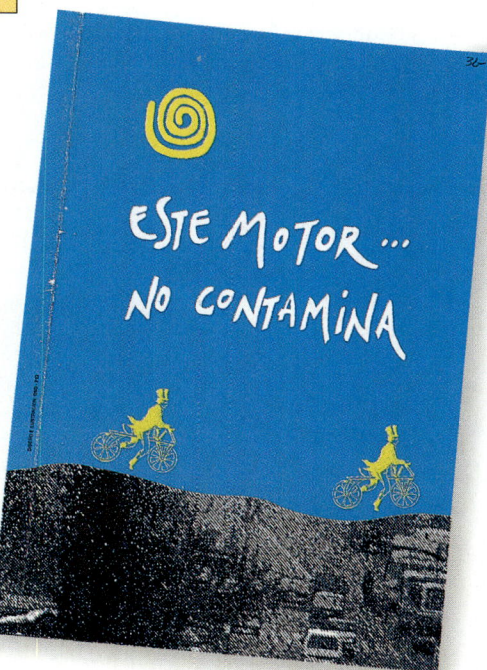

CAPÍTULO 12

LEARNING FROM REALIA

Have students give their interpretation of the saying *Este motor no cantamina* on the cover of the book on page 315.

CRITICAL THINKING ACTIVITY

(*Thinking skills: drawing conclusions; comparing and contrasting*)
Read the following to the class or write it on the board or on an overhead transparency.
    En algunas ciudades en otros países, mucha gente va al trabajo, a la escuela o a la universidad en bicicleta. ¿Es buena idea o no? ¿Por qué o por qué no? ¿Se podría hacer lo mismo en las grandes ciudades de los EE.UU.? ¿Qué problemas habría?

Bell Ringer Review

Write the following on the board or use BRR Blackline Master 12-6: Write the opposite of the following words and expressions:
cortés
bien educado
comportarse bien
saludar

El subjuntivo con expresiones de duda

PRESENTATION (*page 315*)

A. Have students open their books to page 315 and lead them through steps 1-3.
B. Have students repeat the sample sentences in steps 1 and 2.

Ejercicios

PRESENTATION (*page 315*)

Ejercicio A
Exercise A can be done with books open or closed.

ANSWERS

Ejercicio A
Answers will vary.
1. Creo que el mundo es redondo.
2. No creo que haga calor en la Antártida.
3. Creo que los coches contaminan el aire.
4. No creo que los aviones vuelen a una altura de un millón de metros.
5. No creo que los trenes sean mucho más rápidos que los aviones.

ABOUT THE LANGUAGE

The girl in the photo at the bottom of page 314 *está fregando el suelo*. The word for "mop" is *fregona*, which also used to mean the person who cleaned the floor, usually on hands and knees. Because so many floors are tile, this was often a daily, burdensome chore. Occasionally one may hear *el mapo* for "mop." Ask native speakers how they say "mop the floor."

PRESENTATION (page 316)

ANSWERS

Ejercicio B

Answers will vary.
1. Creo que mi mejor amigo(a) va a recibir una "A" en todos sus cursos. (Dudo que mi mejor amigo[a] reciba una "A" en todos sus cursos.)
2. Creo que mi mejor amigo(a) va a asistir a la universidad. (Dudo que mi mejor amigo[a] asista a la universidad.)
3. Creo que mi mejor amigo(a) va a ser médico(a). (Dudo que mi mejor amigo[a] sea médico[a].)
4. Creo que mi mejor amigo(a) va a tener una familia grande. (Dudo que mi mejor amigo[a] tenga una familia grande.)

Ejercicio C
1. invita
2. sea
3. es
4. dé
5. va
6. alquile
7. recibe

El subjuntivo con expresiones de emoción

PRESENTATION (page 316)

A. Have students open their books to page 316 and lead them through steps 1 and 2.
B. Call on volunteers to read the sample sentences aloud.

Note The use of the subjunctive after these expressions does not fit the general rule that it be used when it is uncertain whether or not an event will take place. Emphasize here that the subjunctive is used due to the subjective nature of the statements, as explained in step 1.

316

B Mi mejor amigo(a). Contesten con *creo* o *dudo*.

1. ¿Tu mejor amigo(a) va a recibir una "A" en todos sus cursos?
2. ¿Va a asistir a la universidad?
3. ¿Va a ser médico(a)?
4. ¿Va a tener una familia grande?

C Una fiesta. Completen.

1. Yo creo que él nos ___ . (invitar)
2. Dudo que la fiesta ___ el domingo. (ser)
3. Estoy seguro(a) que ___ el sábado. (ser)
4. Yo dudo que él ___ la fiesta en casa. (dar)
5. Yo creo que ___ a dar la fiesta en un hotel. (ir)
6. Yo lo dudo. Dudo que él ___ un salón en un hotel. (alquilar)
7. Es cierto que él ___ muchos regalos. (recibir)

Una fiesta en San Juan, Puerto Rico

El subjuntivo con expresiones de emoción
Expressing Emotional Reactions to the Actions of Others

1. The subjunctive is required in the dependent clause after any expression or verb that expresses an emotion. The subjunctive is used because it is a subjective opinion. One may be happy over the fact, but someone else may be sad.

    Me alegro de que él lo sepa.
    Te alegras, ¿de veras? Yo no. Yo estoy triste que él lo sepa.

    ¿Sientes que él vaya?
    Yo no. Estoy contento que él vaya.

2. The following are verbs and expressions that are used to convey emotions.

    alegrarse de
    estar alegre
    estar contento(a)
    estar triste
    sentir
    ser una lástima
    sorprender

316   CAPÍTULO 12

LEARNING FROM PHOTOS

1. Ask students to compare the party in the photo at the top of page 316 to a typical one they might go to. Cue with questions such as: *¿Ves algunas diferencias o no? Si ves algunas diferencias, ¿cuáles son? ¿Qué están haciendo los muchachos en San Juan, y qué hacen Uds.?*

2. You may wish to ask the following questions about the photo at the bottom of page 316: *¿Qué están celebrando? ¿Para quién es la fiesta? ¿Quiénes están allí? ¿Qué van a comer ellos? ¿Qué dirá en el pastel?*

Ejercicios

A **Me alegro.** Sigan el modelo.

>Él lo sabe.
>Me alegro de que él lo sepa y mi hermano siente que él lo sepa.

1. Él lo sabe.
2. Él viene.
3. Él tiene las noticias.
4. Él nos dice lo que está pasando.
5. Él no guarda secretos.

B **Una fiesta.** Contesten.

1. ¿Te alegras de que yo vaya a la fiesta?
2. ¿Te alegras de que esté Ramón también?
3. ¿Sientes que no vaya su hermana?
4. ¿Te sorprende que ella no esté?
5. ¿Pero estás contento(a) que ella se encuentre mejor?

C **El pobre Luis.** Completen.

1. Estoy triste que Luis no ___ . (venir)
2. Me sorprende que él ___ enfermo. (estar)
3. Siento que él ___ en el hospital. (estar)
4. Estoy contento que su condición se ___ . (mejorar)
5. Es una lástima que él ___ que guardar cama. (tener)

CAPÍTULO 12 317

Ejercicios

PRESENTATION (page 317)

Ejercicios A and B
Exercises A and B can be done with books open or closed.

Ejercicios C
Exercise C can be done with books open.

ANSWERS

Ejercicio A
1. Me alegro de que él lo sepa y mi hermano siente que él lo sepa.
2. Me alegro de que él venga y mi hermano siente que él venga.
3. Me alegro de que él tenga las noticias y mi hermano siente que él tenga las noticias.
4. Me alegro de que él nos diga lo que está pasando y mi hermano siente que él nos diga lo que está pasando.
5. Me alegro de que él no guarde secretos y mi hermano siente que él no guarde secretos.

Ejercicio B
1. Sí (No), (No) me alegro de que tú vayas a la fiesta.
2. Sí (No), (No) me alegro de que esté Ramón también.
3. Sí (No), (No) siento que no vaya su hermana.
4. Sí (No), (No) me sorprende que ella no esté.
5. Sí (No), (No) estoy contento(a) que ella se encuentre mejor.

Ejercicio C
1. venga
2. esté
3. esté
4. mejore

COOPERATIVE LEARNING

Have teams create conversations for the three people in the photo at the bottom of page 317. A fourth team member can act as announcer, giving a brief background for the characters and setting the scene. Have teams present their conversations to the class.

INDEPENDENT PRACTICE

Assign any of the following:
1. Workbook, *Estructura*
2. Communication Activities Masters, *Estructura*, C & D
3. Exercises on student pages 315-317

CONVERSACIÓN

Bell Ringer Review

Write the following on the board or use BRR Blackline Master 12-7: Complete the following sentences:
1. Tengo miedo de que…
2. Lucía está triste de que…
3. ¿Te sorprende que…?
4. Estoy contento(a) que…
5. Siento que…

PRESENTATION (page 318)

A. Tell students they will hear a conversation between Chefa and Lupe.
B. Have students close their books and listen as you read the conversation or play Cassette 7B.
C. Have students open their books to page 318. Allow pairs time to practice the conversation.
D. Call on a volunteer pair to read the conversation to the class with as much expression as possible.

Ejercicio

ANSWERS
1. El cumpleaños de Lupe es el diez de julio.
2. Ella va a cumplir dieciséis años.
3. Sí, habrá una fiesta en honor de su cumpleaños.
4. Va a invitar a toda su familia.
5. Porque ella tiene una familia muy grande.

318

CONVERSACIÓN

Escenas de la vida *El cumpleaños de Lupe*

CHEFA: Lupe, ¿cuándo es tu cumpleaños?
LUPE: El día diez de julio.
CHEFA: ¿Cuántos años vas a cumplir?
LUPE: Dieciséis.
CHEFA: ¿Vas a tener una fiesta?
LUPE: ¡Claro! Creo que voy a invitar a toda mi familia.
CHEFA: ¿Tienes una familia grande?
LUPE: Sí, somos muchos. Y me alegro de que seamos muchos.
CHEFA: Yo sé por qué. No hay duda que recibirás muchos regalos.

La fiesta. Contesten según la conversación.
1. ¿Cuándo es el cumpleaños de Lupe?
2. ¿Cuántos años va a cumplir?
3. ¿Habrá una fiesta en honor de su cumpleaños?
4. ¿A quiénes va a invitar?
5. ¿Por qué sabe Lupe que ella va a recibir muchos regalos?

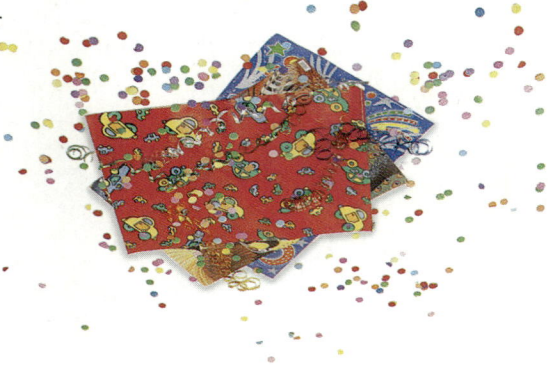

318 CAPÍTULO 12

FOR THE NATIVE SPEAKER

Have students prepare a brief essay on the following theme: *Las familias hoy día tienden a ser mucho más pequeñas que en el pasado. La familia nuclear, los padres y uno o dos hijos, se está haciendo la norma. ¿Qué ventajas y desventajas ves en la familia pequeña? ¿Existen ventajas en una familia numerosa? ¿Cuáles son?*

Comunicación

A **Consejero.** Aconseje a un(a) amigo(a) sobre lo que debe hacer en cada una de las siguientes situaciones. Luego cambien de papel.

>si Mamá está triste
>Estudiante 1: ¿Qué debo hacer si Mamá está triste?
>Estudiante 2: Te aconsejo que le des un besito.

1. si Mamá está triste
2. si recibo mala nota en un examen
3. si mi amigo(a) se enfada conmigo
4. si pierdo las llaves de mi casa
5. si mi hermano(a) me rompe un disco
6. si olvido el cumpleaños de mi madre/padre
7. si rompo un vaso de cristal

B **Mi horóscopo.** Aquí tiene Ud. su horóscopo. Dígale a un(a) compañero(a) de clase lo que dice. Él o ella le indicará si lo cree o si lo duda y le dirá las razones por su respuesta. Luego cambien de papel.

1. Me voy a enamorar.
2. Voy a perder mucho dinero.
3. Voy a recibir buenas noticias.
4. Voy a recibir malas noticias.
5. Voy a ganar la lotería.

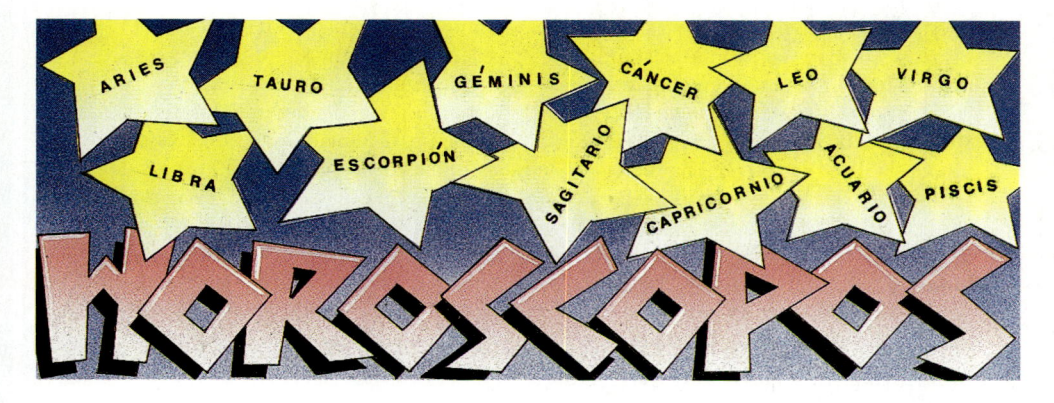

C **¿Pasará o no?** Con un(a) compañero(a) de clase determinen las cosas o los eventos que Uds. creen que van a pasar u ocurrir en su vida y cosas que no creen que pasen ni ocurran. Luego comparen Uds. sus dos listas para determinar lo que Uds. tienen en común.

D **Algunas emociones.** Prepare Ud. una lista de cosas que le ponen contento(a) y cosas que le ponen triste.

>Estoy contento(a) que…
>Y estoy triste que…

LECTURA Y CULTURA

Bell Ringer Review

Write the following on the board or use BRR Blackline Master 12-8: Complete the sentences with the correct form and tense of the verb in parentheses.
1. Esta mañana yo _____ el autobús para ir a la escuela. (tomar)
2. Se _____ los frenos para parar el carro. (poner)
3. Cuando era joven, yo _____ tomar el tren. (preferir)
4. Por más dinero, yo _____ alquilar un coche. (poder)
5. Mañana, yo _____ otra vez en la parada del autobús. (estar)

READING STRATEGIES

(page 320)

Note It is recommended that you present the *Lectura y Cultura* as thoroughly as you feel is necessary based on the interests of your students.

Pre-Reading
Tell students they are going to read about several important celebrations in the lives of many Hispanic people.

Reading
A. Have students open their books to page 320 and ask them to read the selection once silently.
B. Call on individuals to read about half a paragraph aloud at a time. Ask comprehension questions about the portion read and call on other students to answer them.

Post-reading
Call on volunteers to summarize in their own words what was read.

LECTURA Y CULTURA

DESDE EL NACIMIENTO HASTA LA MUERTE

No hay duda que se considera a la familia el núcleo principal de las sociedades hispanas. La familia es sumamente importante y también son importantes las fiestas y celebraciones familiares. Durante estas festividades se reúne toda la familia—hasta los parientes lejanos[1].

Poco después del nacimiento de un niño, un nuevo miembro de la familia, tiene lugar el bautizo. Llevan al niño a la iglesia donde recibe el sacramento del bautismo. (La religión predominante en los países hispanos es el catolicismo, aunque hoy en día están en aumento las iglesias pentacosteses y evangélicas.) Después de la ceremonia en la iglesia hay una fiesta donde se ofrecen comida y refrescos en la casa de los padres. Para el bautizo del niño los padres escogen[2] a un padrino y a una madrina. Es una decisión importante porque el padrino y la madrina van a formar parte de la familia. Y es posible que ellos tengan que sustituir a los padres naturales.

La Navidad, o las Navidades, duran desde la Navidad, el 25 de diciembre, hasta Reyes, el 6 de enero. Muchas familias van a la misa del gallo, a la medianoche el día 24 de diciembre, la Nochebuena. En cada país se preparan platos especiales para Navidad. En España, el pavo[3] es tradicional; en el Caribe, el lechón y postres típicos. En muchas partes del mundo hispano, los niños no reciben sus regalos el 25 de diciembre. Los reciben el 6 de enero, el día de los Reyes. Es el día en que llegaron los Reyes Magos a Belén con regalos para el niño Jesús. Para la visita de los Reyes, los niños ponen sus zapatos en la puerta de la casa. En los zapatos ponen paja para los camellos. No quieren que los camellos pasen hambre. Los padres les aconsejan a los hijos que sean buenos y que se comporten bien para que los Reyes les dejen regalos en los zapatos.

Tampoco se puede olvidar[4] a los parientes que ya no están con nosotros, porque se han muerto. El 2 de noviembre es el día de los Difuntos. Todos van al cementerio a poner flores en las tumbas de los miembros difuntos de la familia. En México y en el Perú, dos países con grandes poblaciones indígenas, los indios se visten de sus mejores ropas y van al cementerio con canastas llenas de comida. Ponen flores, velas y canastas de comida en las tumbas. Cantan a los parientes que ya están en el paraíso[5]. Ofrecen comida a los difuntos y después ellos comen y se divierten. Es una fiesta alegre, no triste, en honor de los parientes muertos. Comen pasteles y bizcochos en forma de esqueletos.

[1] parientes lejanos *distant relatives*
[2] escogen *choose*
[3] el pavo *turkey*
[4] olvidar *forget*
[5] paraíso *paradise*

CAPÍTULO 12

COOPERATIVE LEARNING

Have each team develop a proposal for a national holiday. They may choose the event or person they wish to celebrate. In their proposal, they should present the reasons for their selection. They might begin their proposal with: *Nosotros queremos que se celebre…*

Estudio de palabras

¿Cuál es el sustantivo? Escojan.

1. reunir
2. comer
3. decidir
4. nacer
5. morir
6. creer
7. llegar
8. aconsejar
9. comportarse

a. el consejo
b. la creencia
c. el comportamiento
d. la reunión
e. la llegada
f. la comida
g. la muerte
h. la decisión
i. el nacimiento

Comprensión

A ¿Cuándo son las fiestas? Contesten.

1. ¿Cuándo es o cuándo tiene lugar el bautizo?
2. ¿Dónde tiene lugar el bautizo?
3. ¿Cuál es la fecha de la Navidad?
4. ¿Cuándo tiene lugar la misa del gallo?
5. ¿Qué es el 6 de enero?
6. ¿Cuándo reciben los niños hispanos sus regalos?
7. ¿Quiénes se los traen?
8. ¿Dónde los ponen?
9. ¿Y qué ponen los niños en los zapatos? ¿Por qué?
10. ¿Cuándo van todos al cementerio?
11. ¿Qué ponen en las tumbas de los parientes muertos?

B Datos de interés. Den la información.

1. la religión predominante en los países hispanos
2. un sacramento de la iglesia católica
3. religiones en aumento en los países hispanos
4. dos países que tienen una gran población indígena

C Explicaciones. Contesten.

1. Explique por qué el 6 de enero es el día de los Reyes y por qué los niños reciben sus aguinaldos ese día.
2. Explique lo que hacen los indios el día de los Difuntos y por qué.

CAPÍTULO 12   321

Estudio de palabras
ANSWERS
1. d   4. i   7. e
2. f   5. g   8. a
3. h   6. b   9. c

Comprensión
PRESENTATION (page 321)

Comprensión A
Exercise A deals with factual recall.

Comprensión B
Exercise B has students scan for information.

Comprensión C
Exercise C has students explain and summarize two celebrations.

ANSWERS

Comprensión A
1. El bautizo tiene lugar poco después que nace un niño.
2. El bautizo tiene lugar en la iglesia.
3. La Navidad es el 25 de diciembre.
4. La misa del gallo tiene lugar el 24 de diciembre.
5. El 6 de enero es el día de los Reyes Magos.
6. Los niños hispanos reciben sus regalos el 6 de enero.
7. Los Reyes Magos se los traen.
8. Los ponen en los zapatos de los niños.
9. Los niños ponen paja en los zapatos para que los camellos (de los Reyes) no pasen hambre.
10. Van al cementerio el 2 de noviembre, el día de los Difuntos.
11. Ponen flores en las tumbas.

Comprensión B
1. La religión católica es la religión predominante en los países hispanos.
2. El bautizo es un sacramento de la iglesia católica.
3. Las iglesias pentecostesas y evangélicas están en aumento en los países hispanos.
4. México y el Perú son dos países que tienen una gran población indígena.

Comprensión C
Answers will vary.

LEARNING FROM PHOTOS

Have students describe the photo on page 321 as completely as possible. You may wish to ask questions such as: *¿Dónde están los zapatos? ¿Son zapatos de adulto o de niño? ¿Quién los puso allí? ¿Por qué los puso allí? ¿Qué hay en los zapatos? ¿Quiénes o qué van a comer la paja? ¿Qué día es, probablemente?*

INDEPENDENT PRACTICE

Assign any of the following:
1. Workbook, *Un poco más*
2. Exercises on student page 321

321

Descubrimiento Cultural

(The Descubrimiento section is optional material.)

PRESENTATION *(pages 322-323)*

You may choose sections of this *Descubrimiento* which you think will be of particular interest to your students. Or you may allow different students to read different sections.

Note The first paragraph deals with the celebration of Roman Catholic Baptism, the second with Hanukkah, and the third with Roman Catholic Holy Week.

GEOGRAPHY CONNECTION

Seville is the capital of the province of Seville, and the major city of the region of *Andalucía.* During the period of discovery and colonization of the Americas, *la Casa de Contratación* was established by King Ferdinand and Queen Isabella in Seville (1503) to take care of all commercial dealings in the New World.

The photo on page 322 is of *Semana Santa* (Holy Week) in Seville. Processions are held during Holy Week in most Spanish cities and towns, but those of Seville are the most renowned. The large float shown is carried by dozens of men whose feet can be seen beneath the cloth. The floats weigh tons and the men have to stop often to rest. The *cofradías* are groups of people who sponsor the float and march behind it. The floats depict scenes from the crucifixion of Christ.

DESCUBRIMIENTO CULTURAL

La selección de los padrinos es una decisión importante porque es posible que estas personas tengan que asumir la obligación de criar y mantener a sus ahijados en el caso de la muerte de los padres naturales. Por eso una familia pobre trata de encontrar a una persona de importancia y de suficientes recursos económicos para que sea padrino o madrina de su hijo. El padrino o la madrina de un niño de la clase alta debe saber manejar la herencia del ahijado si es necesario. Ser padrino o madrina es una obligación importante, y como ya saben Uds., estas personas se consideran parte de la familia de su ahijado o ahijada.

Los adherentes de la religión judía, los judíos, no celebran la Navidad. En diciembre los judíos celebran Hanuka o el festival de las luces. Este festival empieza el 25 del mes hebreo de Kislen y dura ocho días, hasta el 2 de Tevet. Hanuka conmemora la rededicación del Templo de los Macabeos después de su victoria contra los sirios bajo el rey Antíoco IV. Cada noche, los miembros de la familia judía encienden una vela en la menora.

Hay una fiesta cristiana que coincide con una fiesta judía por muy claras razones históricas. Se trata de la Pascua. Para los cristianos la Pascua o Pascua Florida, conmemora la resurrección de Jesucristo. Pero la palabra "pascua" viene del hebreo "pesah" que es la fiesta más solemne de los judíos porque conmemora la libertad del cautiverio en Egipto. La Semana Santa de los cristianos tiene lugar durante la misma época del año que la Pascua judía. Jesucristo estuvo en Jerusalén para la Pascua cuando murió. La Semana Santa, en los países hispanos, es notable por las procesiones y ceremonias religiosas. Las procesiones de Semana Santa en Sevilla tienen fama mundial.

Semana Santa en Sevilla, España

CAPÍTULO 12

Y AQUÍ EN LOS ESTADOS UNIDOS

En 1492 los Reyes Católicos expulsaron a los árabes y a los judíos de España. Algunos judíos fueron a Holanda, y de Holanda a Angloamérica. Otros salieron para el Nuevo Mundo con los colonizadores españoles. Muchos, para evitar la persecución, decían que eran cristianos, pero seguían practicando su religión.

En 1992, unos antropólogos norteamericanos, haciendo unas investigaciones en Nuevo México, encontraron familias "católicas" que, sin saber por qué, seguían unas tradiciones familiares muy curiosas durante la Pascua Florida. Iban a un lugar escondido[1], y allí encendían un candelabro de nueve brazos, y comían unos platos especiales. Cuando se les preguntó si eran judíos, contestaron que no, que eran católicos. ¿Por qué la comida escondida y el candelabro de nueve brazos? No sabían qué contestar, excepto que era "una tradición familiar".

[1] escondido *hidden*

Un convento en Nuevo México iluminado por luminarias para la Navidad

CAPÍTULO 12   **323**

HISTORY CONNECTION

The first Spanish settlement in New Mexico was in 1598, although there had been explorations under Coronado and Cabeza de Vaca as early as 1528. Santa Fe became the Spanish capital of *el reino y las provincias de Nuevo México* in 1610. A number of important missions were founded in New Mexico in the 16th and 17th centuries.

LEARNING FROM PHOTOS

Refer students to the photo at the top of page 323 and say: *La muchacha está encendiendo las velas de la menora. ¿De qué religión es la familia? ¿Qué día están celebrando?* Bottom photo: *Las luminarias son luces que se ponen en ventanas, balcones, torres y calles durante las fiestas públicas.*

323

REALIDADES

(The Realidades section is optional.)

Bell Ringer Review

Write the following on the board or use BRR Blackline Master 12-9: Put the following scrambled conversation into a logical order.
1. ¿De parte de quién?
2. ¿Puedo dejarle un mensaje?
3. ¿Está el señor Salas, por favor?
4. ¡Hola!
5. De acuerdo.
6. De Roberto Díaz.
7. Lo siento, pero no está.
8. Un momento. Favor de no colgar.

PRESENTATION *(pages 324-325)*

A. Allow students time to look at the photographs on pages 324-325 and to discuss them among themselves. Invite them to share their questions and comments.

B. Refer to **Photo 5** and say: *Las posadas son una costumbre tradicional de Navidad en México y el sudoeste de los EE.UU. La gente va de casa en casa como San José y la Virgen María, buscando "posada", un lugar en dónde dormir. Después de pedir varias veces, pueden entrar, y la gente de la casa les ofrece algo de comer o beber.*

REALIDADES

Las comidas especiales para la Navidad son tradicionales **1**. Una familia mexicana come los tradicionales tamales. ¡Qué ricos son!

Semana Santa en Antigua, Guatemala **2**. El suelo se cubre de flores. Es una alfombra preciosa.

Los padrinos llevan al bebé en sus brazos **3**. ¿Qué acaban de celebrar?

Estos dulces se preparan para el día de los Difuntos en México **4**. ¿Qué forma tienen los dulces? ¿Por qué?

Es la Navidad. Aquí ves las "posadas" que son tradicionales en el suroeste de los EE.UU. **5**.

324

CROSS-CULTURAL COMPARISON

The *posadas* at Christmas time have people going from house to house, visiting their neighbors as part of a traditional Christmas ceremony. Ask students if they see any similarity between *las posadas* and any English or American Christmas tradition. Tell students: *En las posadas, las personas van de casa en casa "pidiendo posada". ¿Tienen los norteamericanos alguna tradición similar?*

FOR THE NATIVE SPEAKER

Have students write a description of their own family traditions for *el día de los Difuntos* or *el día de Todos los Santos*.

CULMINACIÓN

RECYCLING

The activities in *Comunicación oral* and *Comunicación escrita* encourage students to use all the language they have learned in the chapter and to recombine it with material from previous chapters. It is not necessary to do all the activities with all students. Select the ones you consider most appropriate or allow students to choose the ones they wish to do.

Comunicación oral
ANSWERS
Actividad A
 Answers will vary according to the model.
Actividad B
 Answers will vary.

INFORMAL ASSESSMENT
Activities A and B can be used to assess speaking skills. Use the evaluation criteria given on page 24 of this Teacher's Wraparound Edition.

Comunicación escrita
ANSWERS
Actividades A and B
 Answers will vary.

CULMINACIÓN

Comunicación oral

A **Un cumpleaños especial.** Haga una lista de los regalos que le gustaría dar a cada miembro de su familia y a sus amigos para su cumpleaños. Enséñele la lista a un(a) compañero(a) de clase. Él o ella le dirá que compre otra cosa. Cambien de papel.

> Estudiante 1: A mi mamá le voy a dar (regalar) un vestido.
> Estudiante 2: No creo que le guste un vestido. Es mejor que le des (regales) una blusa.

B **Quince o dieciséis.** Haga Ud. algunas comparaciones culturales. Trabaje con un(a) compañero(a) de clase. Uno(a) de Uds. describirá lo que es el "sweet sixteen". El otro o la otra describirá la fiesta de la quinceañera. Luego hagan algunas comparaciones entre las dos fiestas.

Comunicación escrita

A **Una carta.** Escriba una carta a una persona en un país hispano. Explíquele cuál es su día de fiesta o celebración favorita. Descríbasela y explíquele por qué le gusta tanto y por qué es su favorita.

B **Otra carta.** Ud acaba de recibir una carta de un buen amigo en Paraguay. Le ha escrito muchas noticias. Contéstele usando las siguientes expresiones.

1. Me alegro de que…
2. Pero, siento que…
3. Me sorprende que…
4. No puedo creer que…
5. Es fantástico que…
6. Espero que…

326 CAPÍTULO 12

COOPERATIVE LEARNING

Refer to the ads on pages 326-327. Have teams choose either "Fiesta Planners" or *el Palacio de Hierro*, and create a radio ad for their choice. They should completely script the ad. Have them select one or more of their group to give the ad "on the air" to the entire class. You may wish to actually record the ads. Encourage students to be creative!

Reintegración

A **Regalos.** Contesten.

1. ¿Qué compraste para tu padre o para tu madre? ¿Por qué se lo/la compraste? ¿Para cuándo o qué ocasión? ¿Dónde lo/la compraste?
2. ¿Qué compraste para un(a) hermano(a)? ¿Por qué se lo/la compraste? ¿Para cuándo o qué ocasión? ¿Dónde lo/la compraste?
3. ¿Qué compraste para un(a) amigo(a)? ¿Por qué se lo/la compraste? ¿Para cuándo o qué ocasión? ¿Dónde lo/la compraste?

B **Cuestión de gustos.** Sigan el modelo.

Juan quiere estos zapatos.
Le gustan.

1. Yo quiero esta mochila.
2. Ella quiere estos esquís.
3. Yo quiero esta raqueta.
4. Ellos quieren esta calculadora.
5. Quieres estas cintas.
6. Queremos este disco.
7. Quiero esta camisa.
8. Elena quiere estos tenis.

Vocabulario

SUSTANTIVOS
el nacimiento
el/la niño(a)
el bautizo
la iglesia
el cura
la madrina
el padrino
el cumpleaños
la quinceañera
el/la muerto(a)
el/la difunto(a)
el cementerio
el camposanto
la tumba
las flores
la torta
el pastel
el bizcocho
el salón del hotel

la Navidad
el árbol de Navidad
el zapato
la paja
los Reyes Magos
el camello
el regalo de Navidad
el aguinaldo
la misa
la misa del gallo
la víspera
la Nochebuena
la fiesta de las luces
el judío
la menora
el candelabro
el brazo
la vela

ADJETIVOS
hebreo(a)

VERBOS
nacer
bautizar
cumplir (años)
alegrarse de
vivir
morir
enterrar
sentir
reunirse
encender
rogar
sugerir
aconsejar
exigir
dudar
creer

OTRAS PALABRAS Y EXPRESIONES
estar seguro(a)
estar alegre
estar triste
ser una lástima

CAPÍTULO 12 **327**

NUESTRO MUNDO

(optional material)

OVERVIEW

All the readings presented in the *Nuestro Mundo* section are authentic, uncut texts from publications of the Hispanic world. Students should be encouraged to read the text for overall meaning, but not intensively, word for word. Students should find satisfaction in their ability to derive meaning from "real" texts. Each reading is related to a theme or themes covered in the previous four chapters.

PRESENTATION *(page 328)*

A. Ask students if they have ever heard the term "kamikaze" and what they think it means.
B. Have students open their books to page 328 and ask them to read the article silently.

Ejercicios

PRESENTATION *(page 328)*

A. Have students jot down the answers to the multiple choice questions.
B. Do Exercise B as the basis for an oral discussion.

Note You may prefer to assign the readings and questions for independent practice.

ANSWERS

Ejercicio A
1. b
2. b
3. b

Ejercicio B
1. The driver was going the wrong way on the highway.
2. Approximately 1 gram per liter of blood.
3. He was headed for Barcelona, but in the lane that goes to Madrid.
4. Rodríguez Caballero is a "kamikaze" because he was drinking and driving and going the wrong way.

328

NUESTRO MUNDO

The highway is often a dangerous place. This article is from the Spanish newspaper EL INDEPENDIENTE. "Kamikaze" pilots in World War II would deliberately fly their bomb-loaded planes into enemy ships. Spain has a number of highways designated National I, II, etc.

DETENIDO UN "KAMIKAZE" EN GUADALAJARA

Fernando Rodríguez Caballero, un presunto conductor "kamikaze", fue detenido el pasado domingo en Taracena (Guadalajara), después de viajar en un Audi 80, matrícula CS 5818 W, 17 kilómetros en dirección contraria por la N-II. El detenido, de 37 años, ha sido acusado del crimen de conducción temeraria. Rodríguez Caballero dio un índice de alcoholemia de dos gramos por litro de sangre, más del doble de lo permitido. El conductor entró en la autopista en Azuqueca. De allí se dirigió a Barcelona, pero por el carril que lleva a Madrid.

A **El conductor.** Escojan.

1. This incident took place on a ___ .
   a. Saturday b. Sunday c. Monday
2. The driver's age is ___ .
   a. 17 b. 37 c. 80
3. He was headed towards ___ .
   a. Azuqueca b. Barcelona c. Madrid

B **¡Qué mal maneja!** Answer.

1. Explain in your own words why the driver was stopped.
2. What is the legal blood alcohol limit in Spain?
3. What does the following sentence mean?
   Se dirigió a Barcelona, pero por el carril que lleva a Madrid.
4. Why do you think they call Rodríguez Caballero a "kamikaze"?

328   NUESTRO MUNDO

DID YOU KNOW?

Kamikaze is the Japanese word for "Divine Wind." It refers to the typhoon that destroyed the fleet of Kublai Khan when he tried to invade Japan in 1281. During World War II, many of Japan's kamikaze suicide pilots were teenagers.

The following announcements appeared in the social pages of EL DIARIO DE HOY, San Salvador, El Salvador.

CUMPLEAÑOS
En ocasión de encontrarse celebrando su cumpleaños la señorita **Claudia Elizabeth Galdámez**, será agasajada en ambiente familiar por sus padres.

LLUVIA DE REGALOS
Por la próxima visita de la cigüeña, **doña Cecilia de Lemus** fue agasajada con un té y regalos para bebé, ofrecido por un grupo de amigas, las oferentes colmaron de finas atenciones a la futura mamá.

COMUNIÓN
Este día, en la Iglesia María Auxiliadora de la ciudad de Santa Tecla, recibirá el sacramento de la comunión **Rolando Mauricio Mixco Chacón**. Después de la ceremonia será agasajado con un desayuno.

ANIVERSARIO DE BODAS
Conmemorando su aniversario de boda se encuentran el Ing. **Arnaldo Hirlemann Polh** y **doña Marina Zepeda de Hirlemann**, quienes serán objeto de cariñosas felicitaciones.

PRÓXIMAS NUPCIAS
Por su próximo matrimonio el Ing. **Carlos Salgado Lemus** y la Arq. **Claudia Lorena Cruz Solís** fueron agasajados con un cóctail ofrecido por doña Doris Valiente de Moncada.

MISA
Este día, a las once de la mañana se oficiará una misa de fin de novenario por el alma de la señora doña **Marina Palomo de Martínez**. La familia estará recibiendo el pésame de sus numerosas relaciones sociales.

PRÓXIMO ENLACE
Por su próxima boda, la señorita **Elyen Angélica Diermissen** fue agasajada con un té para la feliz novia y demás invitadas.

La crónica social. Contesten.

1. A professional couple was given an engagement party. Who are they, and what are their professions?
2. Whose parents are giving her a birthday party?
3. What are the Hirlemann's celebrating?
4. There is a religious observance for someone who died. Who is it?
5. What are they doing for Cecilia de Lemus? Why? What kind of bird might a *cigüeña* be?
6. Who is having a First Communion, and what will happen after the ceremony?
7. What will Srta. Diermissen be doing soon? What did her friends do for her?

E.P.D.
LA SEÑORA

Doña Marina Palomo de Martínez
HA FALLECIDO

DESPUES DE RECIBIR LOS SANTOS SACRAMENTOS Y LA BENDICIÓN PAPAL

Dispuesto su entierro para el miércoles, día 2 de septiembre a las 10:00 a.m. Los que suscriben: sus hermanos y sobrinos en su nombre y en el de los demás familiares ruegan a las personas de su amistad se sirvan concurrir a la Funeraria Rivero, sita en la Calle Independencia, para desde allí acompañar el cadáver hasta el Cementerio San Felipe, previa Misa en la Iglesia Sam Ramón, favor que agradecerán eternamente

San Salvador 2 de septiembre

Antonio Martínez, José Ignacio Martínez Palomo, Eugenia Martínez de Rosas, Elena Suárez Martínez, Inés Palomo de García, Luis Antonio Palomo Serrano, Dra. Ana Palomo de Suárez

NUESTRO MUNDO

REPASO
CAPÍTULOS 9–12

OVERVIEW
This section reviews key grammatical structures and vocabulary from Chapters 9-12. The topics were first presented on the following pages: the passive voice with *se*, 238; the present subjunctive, pages 285-288, 290, 312-313, and 315-316.

REVIEW RESOURCES
1. Workbook, Self-Test 3
2. Computer Software
3. Testing Program, Unit Test 9-12

Conversación
PRESENTATION (*page 330*)

With books open, break the conversation into three parts and have three pairs of students assume roles and read it aloud.

REPASO
CAPÍTULOS 9–12

Conversación

FERNANDO: Tengo miedo de que lleguemos tarde. Es importante que los padrinos estén allí a tiempo para la fiesta de la quinceañera.

ELENA: Cálmate, hombre. Te digo que no te preocupes. No voy a exceder la velocidad máxima. Seguimos derecho dos o tres kilómetros más. Es la próxima salida de la autopista. Salimos, doblamos a la izquierda en el cruce y tomamos la Nacional Cuatro Norte. La iglesia está detrás del estadio.

FERNANDO: Espero que tu hermana nos prepare una de esas comidas fabulosas. ¡Carne asada, pescado frito, ensalada de mariscos! La puedo oír —Vengan todos a comer. No sean tímidos. Pruébenlo todo. —¡Qué alegría! ¡En casa de tu hermana sí que se come bien!

ELENA: No quiero que te hagas el cerdo[1]. Ya estás demasiado gordo[2]. Después de la ceremonia iremos a casa de Lupe y Rafael para la recepción. Acuérdate de darle la mano al cura. Y saluda a Rafael. Sé cortés con él. No seas mal educado.

FERNANDO: Dudo que pueda ser cortés con ése, pero por ti y por nuestra sobrina quinceañera haré lo posible.

ELENA: Gracias. ¡Qué amable! Oye, quiero que vayamos al camposanto mañana. Busca un lugar donde se venden flores para ponerlas en la tumba de mis abuelos.

FERNANDO: Sí, sí. Eloísa, mira el rótulo. Es la salida nuestra.

[1] cerdo *pig*
[2] gordo *fat*

LEARNING FROM PHOTOS

Have students describe the photo on page 330 in as much detail as they can. You may wish to ask them the following questions: *¿Hay mucho tráfico en la carretera? ¿Qué tipo de vehículo es? ¿Quién está manejando? ¿Qué tiempo hace?*

Vamos a la fiesta. Escojan.

1. Las dos personas probablemente son ___ .
   a. un matrimonio   b. unas quinceañeras   c. curas

2. Ellos están en ___ .
   a. el estadio   b. la iglesia   c. la autopista

3. El hombre tiene miedo de ___ .
   a. comer mucho   b. llegar tarde   c. ir muy rápido

4. El estadio está en frente ___ .
   a. de la casa de la hermana   b. de la iglesia   c. del cruce

5. La Nacional Cuatro es ___ .
   a. una carretera   b. un estadio   c. un restaurante

6. Parece que al hombre le gusta mucho ___ .
   a. conducir   b. cocinar   c. comer

7. El hombre y la mujer son los ___ de la quinceañera.
   a. padres   b. abuelos   c. tíos

8. Y también son sus ___ .
   a. padrinos   b. curas   c. hermanos

9. Parece que al señor no le gusta ___ .
   a. Rafael   b. Lupe   c. Eloísa

10. Mañana los señores van ___ .
    a. al estadio   b. al cementerio   c. a la iglesia

Estructura

La voz pasiva con *se*

The true passive voice "Spanish is spoken," is less frequent in Spanish than in English. The construction *se* with the third person singular or plural of the verb is more common.

   Se vende carne allí.
   Se sirven comidas a los pobres.

A **Una paella.** Completen con la voz pasiva.

1. ___ la paella con arroz y mariscos. (preparar)
2. Primero ___ los camarones. (pelar)
3. ___ las almejas y los mejillones. (limpiar)
4. ___ y ___ unos chorizos. (cortar, freír)
5. ___ agregar pollo u otra carne. (poder)
6. La paella ___ bien caliente. (servir)

CAPÍTULOS 9–12 REPASO   331

El subjuntivo
Verbos regulares e irregulares

PRESENTATION (*page 332*)

A. Lead students through steps 1-2 on page 332 and have them repeat the verb forms aloud.

B. Now lead students through steps 3-5. Emphasize once again that these expressions are followed by the subjunctive because it is not certain that the action expressed by the subjunctive verb will take place.

El subjuntivo—verbos regulares e irregulares

1. Review the forms of the present subjunctive.

hablar	hable, hables, hable, hablemos, *habléis*, hablen
comer	coma, comas, coma, comamos, *comáis*, coman
subir	suba, subas, suba, subamos, *subáis*, suban
hacer	haga, hagas, haga, hagamos, *hagáis*, hagan
poner	ponga, pongas, ponga, pongamos, *pongáis*, pongan
traer	traiga, traigas, traiga, traigamos, *traigáis*, traigan
conocer	conozca, conozcas, conozca, conozcamos, *conozcáis*, conozcan
oír	oiga, oigas, oiga, oigamos, *oigáis*, oigan
decir	diga, digas, diga, digamos, *digáis*, digan

Remember, like the commands, the subjunctive is formed from the first person *yo* form of the present tense.

2. The following verbs do not follow that pattern.

dar	dé, des dé, demos *deis*, den
estar	esté estés, esté, estemos, *estéis*, estén
ir	vaya, vayas, vaya, vayamos, *vayáis*, vayan
saber	sepa, sepas, sepa, sepamos, *sepáis*, sepan
ser	sea, seas, sea, seamos, *seáis*, sean

3. The following verbs and expressions are followed by the subjunctive since it cannot be determined whether the action expressed in the dependent clause will actually be carried out.

querer	tener miedo de	preferir
desear	prohibir	mandar
temer	esperar	insistir

4. When a clause is introduced by a statement of doubt, the subjunctive must be used. When the statement implies certainty, however, the indicative is used.

Dudo que él venga.   No dudo que él vendrá.
Es dudoso que él lo sepa.   Es cierto que él lo sabe.
No creo que él esté enfermo. Creo que él está enfermo.

5. The subjunctive is used after many impersonal expressions.

es posible	es difícil	es probable
es bueno	es importante	es mejor
es mejor	es necesario	es fácil
es imposible		

CAPÍTULOS 9–12 REPASO

B **Su padre quiere que…** Completen con el presente de subjuntivo.
1. Su padre quiere que Joselito ___ bien. (portarse)
2. Él no quiere que el niño ___ ruido. (hacer)
3. Insiste en que ___ bien educado. (ser)
4. Los padres quieren que sus hijos ___ bien. (comportarse)
5. Joselito teme que sus padres no ___ contentos con él. (estar)
6. Le mandan que ___ a los mayores. (saludar)
7. Y que les ___ la mano. (dar)

C **La mamá de Sara.** Cambien la oración según el modelo.

Sara va de compras / mamá quiere
Mamá quiere que Sara vaya de compras.

1. Sara sale en seguida / mamá prefiere
2. Sara lleva bastante dinero / mamá insiste en
3. Sara no tiene cuidado / mamá teme
4. Sara hace las compras en el centro / mamá espera
5. Sara pierde el dinero / mamá tiene miedo

D **Luis va a venir.** Completen.

No creo que Luis ___(venir) hoy. Pero estoy seguro que él ___(estar) aquí mañana. Martín duda que Luis ___(saber) cómo venir. Yo no estoy seguro tampoco de que él ___(conocer) la ruta al pueblo. Espero que él ___(llamar) si se pierde. Temo que él ___(salir) sin un mapa bueno. De todos modos, me alegro que él ___(venir) a estar con nosotros.

E **Una conversación.** Completen con el subjuntivo.

MARTÍN: Ellos vienen, ¿no?
ROSA: No, es imposible que ___. (venir)
MARTÍN: Ay, pero yo quiero que ellos ___ aquí la semana que viene. (estar)
ROSA: Es dudoso que ___ tan pronto. (llegar)
MARTÍN: Pues yo les escribiré que ___ el primer avión. (tomar)
ROSA: Y yo temo que no ___ el viaje. (hacer)

Comunicación

¿Cómo se prepara? Un estudiante de Uruguay quiere saber cómo preparar un plato típico norteamericano. Escoja uno y explíquele cómo se prepara. Déle la receta.

CAPÍTULOS 9–12 REPASO

FONDO ACADÉMICO

LAS CIENCIAS NATURALES
(optional material)

OVERVIEW

The three readings in this section deal with nutrition, the religious tradition in Spain and the Americas, and the importance of food as described in a literary selection by Juan Antonio de Zunzunegui.

Antes de leer

PRESENTATION (page 334)

A. Have students open their books to page 334 and ask them to read the *Antes de leer* section silently. On the board write the names of the three types of foods from the reading. Individually or in groups, have students make a list in Spanish of all the foods they have learned to identify in Chapter 9. Then have them give you the names of the foods and indicate in which category they belong as you write them on the board.

B. Have students quickly scan the reading selection for cognates.

C. Show students pictures of foods from Hispanic advertisements which describe the content or benefits of the particular food product. You may use food packages labeled in both Spanish and English which provide nutritional information.

Lectura

PRESENTATION (pages 334–335)

If you are doing the selection intensively, ask comprehension questions like these after the reading: ¿Para qué necesita el cuerpo humano alimentos formativos? ¿Qué nos dan los alimentos energéticos? ¿Qué regulan los alimentos reguladores?

FONDO ACADÉMICO

LAS CIENCIAS NATURALES

Antes de leer

Living organisms need nutrients in order to exist. Green plants can produce their own food from the energy they receive from sunlight. Plants are producers. All animals are consumers. They derive their nutrients from plants or from other animals. In the following selection you will learn about the basic types of nutrients. You will learn which nutrients form cells, which provide energy and which regulate the functions of the body.

Lectura

LA NUTRICIÓN

Los alimentos que consumimos son de tres tipos: formativos, energéticos y reguladores. Los alimentos formativos son los que forman materia viva, las nuevas células. Los alimentos energéticos nos dan energía. Los alimentos reguladores regulan el funcionamiento del organismo humano.

El cuerpo humano necesita alimentos formativos para la creación de células. Las células que forman el cuerpo humano no son eternas. Cada segundo millones de células mueren, pero nuevas células toman su lugar. Las proteínas forman parte de las células. Y las proteínas se forman de aminoácidos. Hay 21 aminoácidos diferentes. El cuerpo humano no puede usar directamente las proteínas animales y vegetales que comemos. Tiene que cambiar su forma. Entonces el cuerpo descompone las proteínas en aminoácidos. Después el cuerpo reconstruye los aminoácidos en proteínas de una forma que podemos usar.

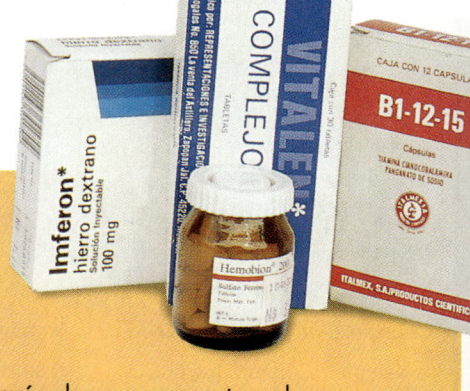

Algunos comestibles formativos son los huevos, la leche, el pescado, la carne y las habichuelas o frijoles.

Los alimentos energéticos nos dan la energía para mantener constante la temperatura del cuerpo, la respiración y los latidos o pulsaciones del corazón[1]. Y, obviamente, necesitamos energía para todas nuestras actividades. Si somos muy activos necesitamos más alimentos energéticos. Estos alimentos son los glúcidos (hidratos de carbono[2]) y las grasas.

Algunos comestibles energéticos son las papas, el pan, el maíz[3], el azúcar, el aceite de oliva y la mantequilla[4].

334 FONDO ACADÉMICO

COOPERATIVE LEARNING

A. Have teams list the foods on the school cafeteria menu. They should divide the foods into the six categories. Ask what, if anything, should or should not be there.

B. Divide the class into six teams, one for each of the food categories. Each team prepares a list of their favorite and least favorite foods within the category.

FONDO ACADÉMICO

Los alimentos reguladores son los que controlan o regulan las funciones del cuerpo. Las vitaminas, los minerales como el calcio, el sodio y el hierro[5] y el agua son alimentos reguladores. Se encuentran en comestibles como la lechuga y otras verduras, los tomates, los mariscos, las frutas, la leche y los productos de la leche como el queso y el yogur y, obviamente, en la sal y el agua.

Una dieta que incluye comestibles de los grupos básicos provee todos los alimentos que necesitamos. Los grupos son: las carnes y las legumbres; las frutas y verduras; los productos lácteos (de la leche); y el pan y los cereales y las grasas y dulces.

[1] los latidos del corazón *heartbeats*
[2] hidratos de carbono *carbohydrates*
[3] el maíz *corn*
[4] la mantequilla *butter*
[5] el hierro *iron*

Después de leer

A ¿En qué grupo están? Escojan.

las carnes y legumbres
los productos lácteos
las frutas y verduras
el pan y los cereales

1. las papas
2. la salchicha
3. las zanahorias
4. la toronja
5. el pescado
6. el arroz
7. la piña
8. la tarta
9. el helado
10. los huevos
11. el maíz
12. los camarones

B Más sobre los alimentos. Contesten.

1. ¿Cuáles son tres alimentos reguladores?
2. ¿Cuál es una función vital que requiere energía?
3. ¿Dónde se encuentran los aminoácidos?
4. ¿Qué tipo de alimento son los hidratos de carbono y las grasas?
5. ¿Por qué son necesarios los alimentos formativos?
6. ¿Cuántos aminoácidos hay?

C Seguimiento. Contesten.

1. Explique lo que pasa con las proteínas que comemos.
2. Los vegetarianos no comen carne. Explique cómo ellos pueden alimentarse de los grupos básicos.
3. Dé Ud. algunos ejemplos de alimentos que son al mismo tiempo energéticos y también reguladores.
4. Indique en qué grupo básico están los diferentes ingredientes de una paella.

FONDO ACADÉMICO 335

DID YOU KNOW?

Most major U.S. pharmaceutical companies have branches in Spain and Latin America where they produce the same medicines as in the U.S., usually for sale at prices much lower than in the U.S. Puerto Rico is one of the major U.S. producers of pharmaceuticals. Many U.S. companies have their major manufacturing operations on the island.

Después de leer
PRESENTATION (page 335)
Ejercicios A, B, and C
Students can prepare the answers to Exercises A, B, and C on their own. Then go over them in class.

ANSWERS
Ejercicio A
1. las frutas y verduras
2. las carnes
3. las frutas y verduras
4. las frutas y verduras
5. las carnes
6. el pan y los cereales
7. las frutas y verduras
8. el pan y los cereales
9. los productos lácteos
10. las carnes y legumbres
11. el pan y los cereales
12. las carnes

Ejercicio B
1. las vitaminas, los minerales y el agua
2. mantener constante la temperatura del cuerpo
3. en las células
4. los glúcidos
5. para la creación de células
6. Hay 21 aminoácidos.

Ejercicio C
Answers will vary but may resemble the following.
1. El cuerpo tiene que cambiar su forma.
2. Ellos pueden comer de los cuatro grupos básicos sin comer carne. El grupo de la carne incluye legumbres.
3. Las papas y el maíz son alimentos energéticos y también reguladores.
4. Una paella lleva carne, mariscos, vegetales, arroz y aceite de oliva. Los ingredientes pertenecen a tres de los grupos básicos.

FONDO ACADÉMICO

LAS CIENCIAS SOCIALES

Antes de leer
PRESENTATION (page 336)

Note This selection may especially interest those students who enjoy the study of religions.
A. Have students open their books to page 336 and ask them to do the review activity in the *Antes de leer* section.
B. Have students scan the reading for cognates.

Lectura
PRESENTATION (pages 336-337)

Note Most students are already familiar with much of the information in the selection after having studied Spanish for one year.
A. Have students read the selection aloud or silently.
B. Have students look for answers to *Después de leer* Exercise A as they read.

HISTORY CONNECTION

The Spanish Jews are Sephardim. The Sephardim are one of the two major divisions of the Jewish people, the other being the Ashkenazim, who lived in Germanic lands. The Sephardim lived on the Iberian Peninsula until 1492. The language of the Sephardim is *Ladino,* which contains many characteristics of medieval Castilian combined with Hebrew, Turkish, Arabic, and other languages.

El Cid conquered the Moorish kingdom of Valencia in 1094 and ruled there until 1102. His exploits are the subject of the 12th century *Cantar del mío Cid* and subsequent poetic and dramatic works. The name *El Cid* comes from the Arabic *Sidi,* meaning "lord" or "sir."

FONDO ACADÉMICO

LAS CIENCIAS SOCIALES

Antes de leer

The religious traditions of Western Europe and, consequently, of Spain and the Americas, are primarily Judeo-Christian. Of course, there are other great world religions, Islam, Hinduism, and Buddhism among others. Spain was Christianized during Roman times. Later it was invaded and conquered by Islamic Arabs. In Islamic Spain the Jews lived at peace for hundreds of years with both Christians and Muslims. In preparation for the following selection please review, briefly, the history of Judaism, Christianity, and Islam.

Lectura

ESPAÑA Y LAS GENTES DEL LIBRO

Los romanos le dieron a España su lengua y su religión. Y España hizo lo mismo con sus colonias en el Nuevo Mundo.

En el año 711 los árabes invadieron a España y trajeron con ellos su religión, Islám, la religión de Mahoma (570-632). Los mahometanos creen que Mahoma es un profeta. También consideran profetas a Abrahán y Jesucristo. Los mahometanos, igual que los judíos y los cristianos, son

Maimónides (1135-1204)

monoteístas. Ellos creen en un solo dios, Alá. El libro sagrado de Islám es el Corán[1].

Los judíos estuvieron en España desde los tiempos de los romanos. Vivían tranquilamente en la España musulmana. El gran filósofo judío, Maimónides (Moisés ben Maimón) nació en Córdoba. Era sefardí. Los sefardíes son judíos españoles.

Desde 711 hasta 1492 hubo luchas[2] intermitentes entre cristianos y musulmanes. En 1492 los Reyes Católicos, Fernando e Isabel, conquistaron la última parte de España en manos de los árabes, el reino de Granada. En 1492 los reyes expulsaron a los musulmanes y a los judíos de España. En un solo año España perdió algunos de sus mejores artesanos, agricultores, comerciantes[3], científicos y pensadores[4]. Los árabes volvieron al norte de África. Los

336 FONDO ACADÉMICO

DID YOU KNOW?

An impressive heroic statue of the Cid can be found in New York City at the Museum of the Hispanic Society of America.

FONDO ACADÉMICO

sefardíes se fueron a Turquía, Portugal, Holanda y África. Algunos sefardíes vinieron a Nueva Amsterdam (Nueva York) con los holandeses en el siglo XVI.

Los islamitas consideran a los judíos y a los cristianos "gentes del libro" porque todos—islamitas, judíos y cristianos—creen en un solo dios y aceptan el Antiguo Testamento, la Biblia, o "el libro".

Hoy en Latinoamérica las "gentes del libro" son: 395.554.500 cristianos, de los cuales 371.863.600 son católicos; 990.000 judíos y 645.000 islamitas.

[1] el Corán Koran
[2] luchas battles
[3] comerciantes merchants
[4] pensadores thinkers

La Gran Mezquita de Córdoba

Después de leer

A **Los árabes.** Completen.

1. Los ___ trajeron el cristianismo a España.
2. Las colonias españolas en América recibieron su ___ y su religión de España.
3. La religión de la mayoría de los árabes es ___.
4. El gran profeta de Islám es ___.
5. A los que creen en un solo dios se les llama ___.
6. El gran filósofo sefardí era ___.
7. Después de su expulsión de España, los árabes fueron al ___.
8. Algunos sefardíes fueron a Norteamérica con los ___.
9. El último lugar en España en manos de los árabes era ___.
10. La religión que predomina numéricamente en Latinoamérica es ___.

B **Seguimiento.** Contesten.

1. Indique un resultado de la expulsión de los árabes y los judíos de España.
2. Explique lo que quiere decir "gentes del libro".
3. Indique cuáles son los libros sagrados de los judíos, los cristianos y los islamitas.

Rodrigo Díaz de Vivar, "El Cid Campeador" (1043-1099)

FONDO ACADÉMICO 337

LEARNING FROM PHOTOS

La gran Mezquita de Córdoba o Mezquita de Abd er-Rahmán tiene más de mil años. En su época, solamente la Mezquita de La Meca era más grande. Hace más de 750 años los cristianos construyeron una catedral dentro de la Mezquita.

DID YOU KNOW?

Córdoba fue la capital de "al Andalus", la España musulmana, desde 756 hasta 1031.

Después de leer
PRESENTATION (page 337)
Go over the *Después de leer* activities.

ANSWERS
Ejercicio A
1. romanos
2. lengua
3. el islamismo
4. Mahoma
5. "gentes del libro"
6. Maimónides
7. al norte de África
8. holandeses
9. Granada
10. el catolicismo

Ejercicio B
Answers will vary but may resemble the following.
1. España perdió algunos de sus mejores artesanos, agricultores, comerciantes, científicos y pensadores.
2. Los cristianos, los islamitas y los judíos son "gentes del libro" porque creen en un solo Dios y aceptan la Biblia.
3. El libro sagrado de los cristianos es la Biblia, el libro sagrado de los islamitas es el Corán y el libro sagrado de los judíos es el Antiguo Testamento de la Biblia.

FONDO ACADÉMICO

LAS HUMANIDADES

Antes de leer

PRESENTATION (page 338)

A. Have students open their books to page 338 and ask them to read the information in the *Antes de leer* section.
B. Have students scan the reading for cognates.

Lectura

PRESENTATION (pages 338-339)

Have students read the selection silently.

FONDO ACADÉMICO

LAS HUMANIDADES

Antes de leer

Food has played a prominent role in many literary works. The witches in *Macbeth* create a lovely pot of "Fillet of a fenny snake… eye of newt, and toe of frog, wool of bat, and tongue of dog… lizard's leg, and owlet's wing." In Hemingway's *Old Man and the Sea* Santiago, the aged fisherman, dreams of how his great fish will taste. The Christmas dinner in *Oliver Twist* and the lovely smells emanating from the chocolate factory in *Willy Wonka and the Chocolate Factory* are artfully described.

Of all the regions of Spain, the one where food is most important is the Basque country. Basque men join eating clubs where monumental quantities of food are bought, prepared, and consumed by the members. The following selection ends with a brief excerpt from the novel *La quiebra*, by the Basque author Juan Antonio de Zunzunegui.

Lectura

JUAN ANTONIO DE ZUNZUNEGUI— NOTA BIOGRÁFICA

Zunzunegui nació en Bilbao en 1902 y murió en Madrid en 1982. Escribió con un estilo realista. Sus descripciones de personas son excelentes. Sus novelas y cuentos tienen como escenario a Bilbao, el puerto, el pueblo y las costumbres. Dice Zunzunegui de su arte:

—Al verdadero novelista se le ve en el diálogo. Pues hablando es cómo se muestran las personas y en el diálogo es donde se dibujan los caracteres.

Zunzunegui describe una comida en su tierra. Los invitados son gente del pueblo. Chomín trabaja en la construcción. Otro es carpintero, otro es albañil[1]. Vienen de diferentes partes de España. Cruz, es andaluz, de Huelva. Otro es de Navarra. Comen un pescado en salsa roja. Todos tienen apetito: comen muy contentos, y toman demasiado vino. Anabitarte empieza a hablar de las regiones y de las comidas. Él dice que donde se come peor es en el sur, en Andalucía, donde todo se fríe. Él dice que los andaluces comen cualquier cosa.

De cómo la comida es lo que más nos distingue[2] a los españoles, de la novela *La quiebra*, de Juan Antonio de Zunzunegui.

—Está visto que es la comida lo que más nos distingue a los hombres de España— dijo Fermín.

Chomín comía y bebía sin decir palabra.

—Sí, a la gente no es necesario preguntarle de dónde es ni cómo piensa, sino cómo come…—opinó Anabitarte—. Mejor que dividir a España en cuarenta y nueve provincias, sería partirla[3] así: tierras donde se fríe, tierras donde se asa y tierras

338 FONDO ACADÉMICO

DID YOU KNOW?

The traditional regions and provinces at the time Zunzunegui wrote *La quiebra* have been reorganized. Today there are *autonomías* and *comunidades*, not all of which conform to the old arrangement.

FONDO ACADÉMICO

donde se guisa[4], o de otra forma: gentes de sartén, gentes de parrilla y gentes de cazuela…, y nada más.

—Tierras donde se fríe—continuó Anabitarte—; no hay necesidad de señalar cuales son.

—¡Tierras del aceite, claro!—interrumpió Chomín.

—Más al norte, en el centro de España—continuó Anabitarte—, están las tierras donde se asa. Tierras altas, frías, de heladas[5] y nieves. Aquí están las gentes de parrilla, que asan el ganado y la caza. Aquí entran los hombres de ambas[6] Castillas. Ya al Norte, vienen las tierras donde se guisa; gentes de cazuela, gentes de salsa; éstos somos nosotros. Se guisa en Bilbao, en Gijón, en San Sebastián, en Vigo, en la Coruña. La salsa en la cocina es la invención del hombre; la salsa es el progreso, la salsa es la civilización.

[1] albañil *mason*
[2] distingue *identifies*
[3] partirla *divide it*
[4] guisa *stews*
[5] heladas *frost*
[6] ambas *both*

Después de leer

A **Los invitados.** Escojan.

1. Los invitados son trabajadores/profesionales.
2. Huelva está en Andalucía/Navarra.
3. El plato principal es de carne/pescado.
4. Ellos toman demasiado café/vino.
5. Cruz/Anabitarte dice que se come mal en Andalucía.
6. Cuando comía, Chomín hablaba/no hablaba.
7. En España había 49 platos/provincias.
8. Las tierras donde se fríen son las tierras de la salsa/del aceite.
9. Según Anabitarte, se puede determinar de qué parte de España es una persona si se sabe lo que come/piensa.

B **Seguimiento.** Contesten.

1. Explique cómo Anabitarte cree que España debe dividirse.
2. Busque las siguientes ciudades en el mapa: Bilbao, Gijón, San Sebastián, Vigo y la Coruña e indique en qué regiones están.
3. Explique las tres "regiones" de España según Anabitarte.
4. Indique la región que Anabitarte considera la mejor, y diga por qué.
5. En un mapa de España indique las tres regiones de Anabitarte.
6. Parece que hay algún prejuicio (*prejudice*) contra una de las regiones, ¿cuál es?
7. Explique lo que dice Zunzunegui del diálogo.

FONDO ACADÉMICO **339**

CAPÍTULO 13
Scope and Sequence pages 340-363

Topics	Functions	Structure	Culture
Caring for clothing	How to talk about camping	El infinitivo o el subjuntivo	Camping and hiking in Spain and South America
Camping and backpacking	How to describe nature walks	Repaso del pretérito de los verbos irregulares	Guadalquivir River in Sevilla
	How to take your clothes to a laundry or dry cleaner when in a Spanish-speaking country		Camino Inca in Machu Picchu
	How to express wishes, preferences, and demands concerning oneself and others		Strait of Magellan

CAPÍTULO 13

Situation Cards

The Situation Cards simulate real-life situations that require students to communicate in Spanish, exactly as though they were in a Spanish-speaking country. The Situation Cards operate on the assumption that the person to whom the message is to be conveyed understands no English. Therefore, students must focus on producing the Spanish vocabulary and structures necessary to negotiate the situations successfully. For additional information, see the Introduction to the Situation Cards in the Situation Cards Envelope.

Communication Transparency

The illustration seen in this Communication Transparency consists of a synthesis of the two vocabulary (Palabras 1&2) presentations found in this chapter. It has been created in order to present this chapter's vocabulary in a new context, and also to recycle vocabulary learned in previous chapters. The Communication Transparency consists of original art. Following are some specific uses:

1. as a cue to stimulate conversation and writing activities
2. for listening comprehension activities
3. to review and reteach vocabulary
4. as a review for chapter and unit tests

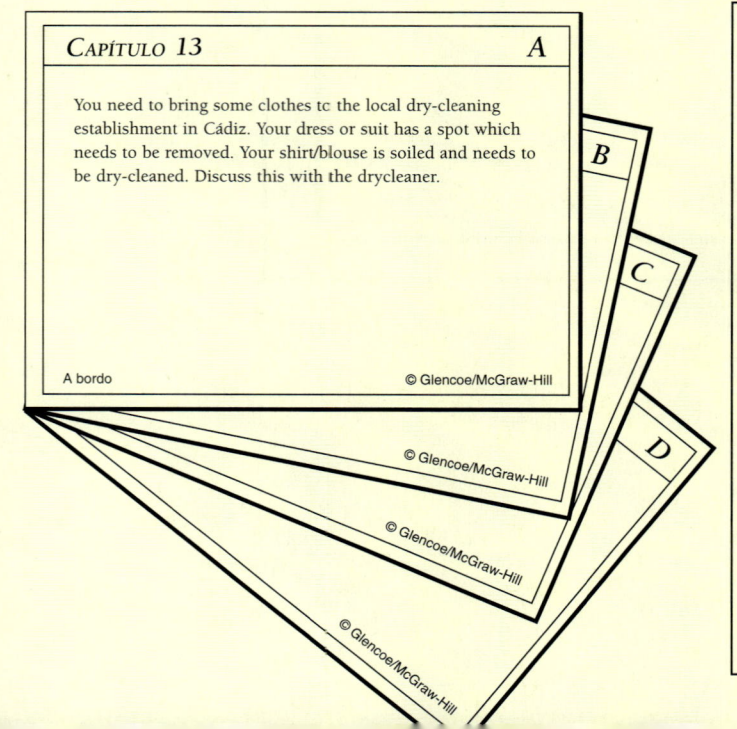

CAPÍTULO 13
Print Resources

Lesson Plans

Workbook
	Pages
◆ Palabras 1	147
◆ Palabras 2	148-149
◆ Estructura	150-151
◆ Un poco más	152-155
◆ Mi autobiografía	156

Communication Activities Masters
◆ Palabras 1	83-85
◆ Palabras 2	85-88
◆ Estructura	89-90

9 Bell Ringer Reviews   37-38

Chapter Situation Cards A B C D

Chapter Quizzes
◆ Palabras 1	62
◆ Palabras 2	63
◆ Estructura	64-65

Testing Program
◆ Listening Comprehension	75
◆ Reading and Writing	76-79
◆ Proficiency	135
◆ Speaking	156

Nosotros y Nuestro Mundo
- ◆ Nuestro Conocimiento Académico *La ecología*
- ◆ Nuestro Idioma *Infinitivo o subjuntivo; El pretérito*
- ◆ Nuestra Cultura *Las Galápagos*
- ◆ Nuestra Literatura *"El progreso suicida"* de Arturo Uslar Pietri
- ◆ Nuestra Creatividad
- ◆ Nuestras Diversiones

CAPÍTULO 13
Multimedia Resources

CD-ROM Interactive Textbook Disc 4
Chapter 13 Student Edition
- ◆ Palabras 1
- ◆ Palabras 2
- ◆ Estructura
- ◆ Conversación
- ◆ Lectura y cultura
- ◆ Hispanoparlantes
- ◆ Realidades
- ◆ Culminación
- ◆ Prueba

Audio Cassette Program with Student Tape Manual
Cassette	Pages
◆ 8A Palabras 1	262-263
◆ 8A Palabras 2	263-264
◆ 8A Estructura	264
◆ 8A Conversación	264
◆ 8A Segunda parte	265-266

Compact Disc Program with Student Tape Manual
◆ CD 8 Palabras 1	262-263
◆ CD 8 Palabras 2	263-264
◆ CD 8 Estructura	264
◆ CD 8 Conversación	264
◆ CD 8 Segunda parte	265-266

Overhead Transparencies Binder
- ◆ Vocabulary 13.1 (A&B); 13.2 (A&B)
- ◆ Communication C-13
- ◆ Maps
- ◆ Fine Art (with Blackline Master Activities)

Video Program
◆ Videocassette	
◆ Video Activities Booklet	33-34
◆ Videodisc	
◆ Video Activities Booklet	33-34

Computer Software (Macintosh, IBM, Apple)
- ◆ Practice Disk
  - Palabras 1 y 2
  - Estructura
- ◆ Test Generator Disk
  - Chapter Test
  - Customized Test

CAPÍTULO 13

CHAPTER OVERVIEW

In this chapter, students will learn the vocabulary needed to discuss clothing and its care, including using the laundromat, and requesting services at a dry cleaning establishment. They will also learn to talk about camping and backpacking. Further uses of the subjunctive are presented, along with a review of irregular verbs in the preterite. The cultural focus of Chapter 13 is on areas of Spain and Latin America of interest to campers and backpackers.

CHAPTER OBJECTIVES

By the end of this chapter, students will know:
1. vocabulary associated with doing the laundry or having it done, including visiting dry cleaners or laundromats
2. vocabulary associated with camping and nature
3. use of the subjunctive versus the infinitive when expressing wishes and preferences
4. formation and use of the preterite with irregular verbs (review)

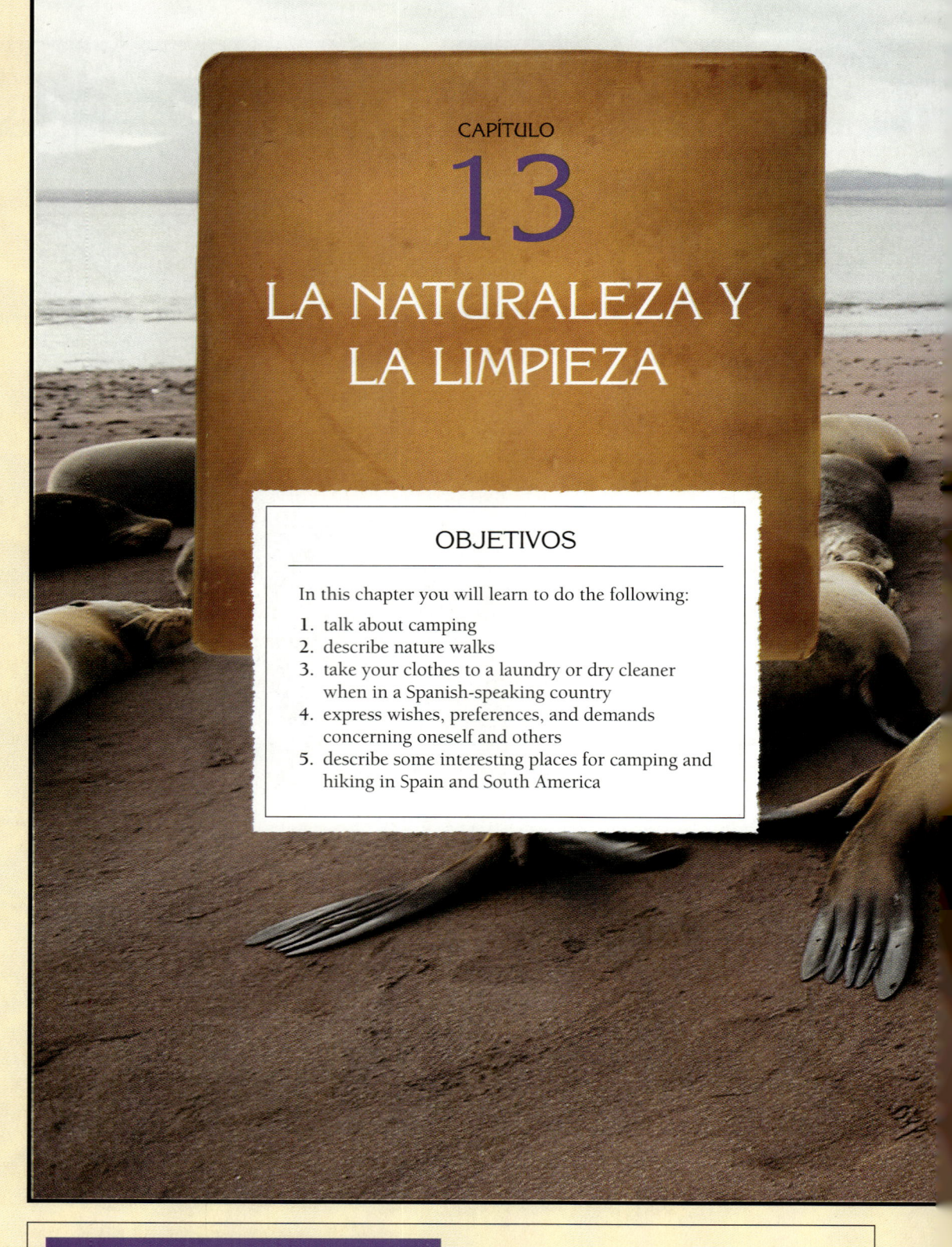

CAPÍTULO 13

LA NATURALEZA Y LA LIMPIEZA

OBJETIVOS

In this chapter you will learn to do the following:
1. talk about camping
2. describe nature walks
3. take your clothes to a laundry or dry cleaner when in a Spanish-speaking country
4. express wishes, preferences, and demands concerning oneself and others
5. describe some interesting places for camping and hiking in Spain and South America

CHAPTER PROJECTS

(optional)
1. Have students prepare a simple manual in Spanish on how to use a washing machine and dryer.
2. Have students prepare and present a report on the *Coto Doñana* in the South of Spain.
3. Have students prepare and present a report on Machu Picchu.

CHAPTER 13 RESOURCES

1. Workbook
2. Student Tape Manual
3. Audio Cassette 8A
4. Vocabulary Transparencies
5. Bell Ringer Review Blackline Masters
6. Communication Activities Masters
7. Computer Software: Practice and Test Generator
8. Video Cassette, Chapter 13
9. Video Activities Booklet, Chapter 13
10. Situation Cards
11. Chapter Quizzes
12. Testing Program

Pacing

Chapter 13 will require eight to ten class sessions. Pacing will depend on the length of the class period, the age of the students, and student aptitude.

LEARNING FROM PHOTOS

In regard to the spread on pages 340-341, you may wish to ask the following questions, after having completed the chapter: ¿Dónde está la península de Valdés? Búscala en el mapa de la Argentina. ¿En qué mar está? ¿Estos lobos de mar son del norte o del sur? You may also wish to tell students the following: Estos animales se dividen en tres grupos: los del norte, los de aguas templadas, y los antárticos. Estos "lobos de mar" son del último grupo. Están en la península de Valdés en la Argentina. Estos animales llevan varios nombres, dependiendo de su tamaño etc. Todos son de la familia "phocidae", el nombre científico en latín.

341

VOCABULARIO
PALABRAS 1

Vocabulary Teaching Resources
1. Vocabulary Transparencies, 13.1 (A & B)
2. Audio Cassette 8A
3. Student Tape Manual, *Palabras 1*
4. Workbook, *Palabras 1*
5. Communication Activities Masters, *Palabras 1, A & B*
6. Chapter Quizzes, *Palabras 1*

Bell Ringer Review
Write the following on the board or use BRR Blackline Master 13-1: Make a list of all the words you can remember having to do with clothing.

PRESENTATION (pages 342-343)
A. With books closed, refer to Vocabulary Transparencies 13.1 (A & B) and have students repeat the new words, phrases, and sentences after you or Cassette 8A. Intersperse repetitions with questions that elicit the new vocabulary.
B. Have students open their books to pages 342-343 and call on volunteers to read the new words, phrases, and sentences.

VOCABULARIO
PALABRAS 1

POR EL SENDERO

la senda, el sendero

la hamaca

el camping

la tienda de campaña, la carpa

el saco para dormir

la mochila

el hornillo

la caravana, la casa-remolque

342 CAPÍTULO 13

DID YOU KNOW?
Camping is very popular throughout Europe. Spain is one of the favorite destinations and receives many thousands of campers from the rest of Europe every year. Campsites are especially popular on the coasts, where the beaches are a particular attraction. Some campsites are quite elegant.

la caminata

Los jóvenes dieron una caminata.
Dieron una caminata por el parque nacional.

El joven puso su ropa en una mochila.

Las amigas levantaron una tienda (una carpa).

Rosaura quiere comer.
Pero ella no quiere preparar la comida.
Quiere que Felipe la prepare.
Le dice que prepare la comida en el hornillo.

CAPÍTULO 13

PAIRED ACTIVITY
Once the class has thoroughly practiced the new vocabulary, have pairs make up conversations between two people on a camping expedition.

ABOUT THE LANGUAGE
Dar una caminata is "to take a hike." However, those who are serious mountain climbers are called *alpinistas*. Their sport is *el alpinismo*. You may wish to ask students the derivation of *alpinismo* (*los Alpes*/the Alps, where the sport began).

INFORMAL ASSESSMENT
In order to check comprehension show Vocabulary Transparencies 13.1 (*A & B*) again and do the following:
1. Have students identify items at random.
2. Have students make up sentences about the illustrations.

Ejercicios

PRESENTATION (page 344)

Ejercicio A
Exercise A can be done with books open.

ANSWERS

Ejercicio A
1. Los jóvenes dieron una caminata.
2. La senda iba por las montañas.
3. Llevaron su ropa en una mochila.
4. Prepararon la comida en el hornillo.
5. Durmieron en un saco para dormir.
6. La familia viajó en una caravana.

Ejercicios

A De camping. Contesten según el dibujo.

1. ¿Los jóvenes dieron un paseo o una caminata?
2. ¿Iba la senda por las montañas o por la playa?
3. ¿Llevaron ellos su ropa en una maleta o en una mochila?

4. ¿Prepararon la comida en el hornillo o en la estufa?
5. ¿Durmieron en un saco para dormir o en una hamaca?
6. ¿Viajó la familia en un camper o en una caravana?

344   CAPÍTULO 13

INDEPENDENT PRACTICE

Assign any of the following:
1. Workbook, *Palabras 1*
2. Communication Activities Masters, *Palabras 1, A & B*
3. Exercises on student pages 344–345

B **De camping.** Preguntas personales.

1. ¿Te gusta el camping?
2. ¿Vas de camping de vez en cuando?
3. ¿Hay campamentos cerca de donde tú vives?
4. ¿Tienen caravanas muchas familias?
5. ¿Tiene tu familia una caravana?
6. ¿A ti te gustan las caminatas?
7. ¿Dónde puedes dar una caminata donde tú vives?
8. Si vas de camping, ¿prefieres dormir en un saco para dormir o en una hamaca?

C **En el campamento.** Escojan el verbo para completar la oración.

dieron	levantaron	llevaron
durmieron	anduvieron	fueron
cocinaron		

1. Los amigos ___ de camping.
2. ___ una caminata por las montañas.
3. ___ una tienda en el campamento.
4. ___ en un hornillo.
5. ___ en un saco para dormir.
6. ___ su ropa en una mochila.
7. ___ por unas sendas pintorescas en el parque.

Un parque nacional en Costa Rica

Un camping en España

CAPÍTULO 13   **345**

PRESENTATION (page 345)
Ejercicio B
Exercise B can be done with books open or closed.

Extension of *Ejercicio B*
Writing
After completing Exercise B, have students write summaries of the information in the exercise in their own words.

Ejercicio C
Exercise C can be done with books open.

ANSWERS
Ejercicio B
Answers will vary.
1. Sí (No), (no) me gusta el camping.
2. Sí (No), (no) voy de camping de vez en cuando (nunca).
3. Sí (No), (no) hay campamentos cerca de donde yo vivo.
4. Sí (No), muchas familias (no) tienen caravanas.
5. Sí (No), mi familia (no) tiene caravana.
6. Sí (No), a mí (no) me gustan las caminatas.
7. Puedo dar una caminata en…
8. Prefiero dormir en un saco para dormir (en una hamaca).

Ejercicio C
1. fueron
2. dieron
3. levantaron
4. cocinaron
5. durmieron
6. llevaron
7. anduvieron

LEARNING FROM PHOTOS

1. You may wish to tell students that Costa Rica has a number of historical and archeological national parks. The government has made a dramatic effort to protect the flora and fauna of the region. The *Tortuguero* national park on the Caribbean is helping to save a number of endangered sea turtle species.

2. You may wish to ask the following questions about the photo at the bottom of page 345: ¿Cómo se llama el camping? El nombre quiere decir "Colina Verde". ¿Es español el nombre? (The name is *Catalán*.) Está en España, ¿qué lengua será? ¿Cuál es la velocidad máxima para los carros en el camping? ¿Qué tienen que hacer las personas que visitan?

345

VOCABULARIO
PALABRAS 2

TENGO QUE LAVAR MI ROPA

arrugada

sucia

manchada

una mancha

José sacó su ropa de la mochila.
¡Qué sucia estaba!
¡Qué arrugada estaba!

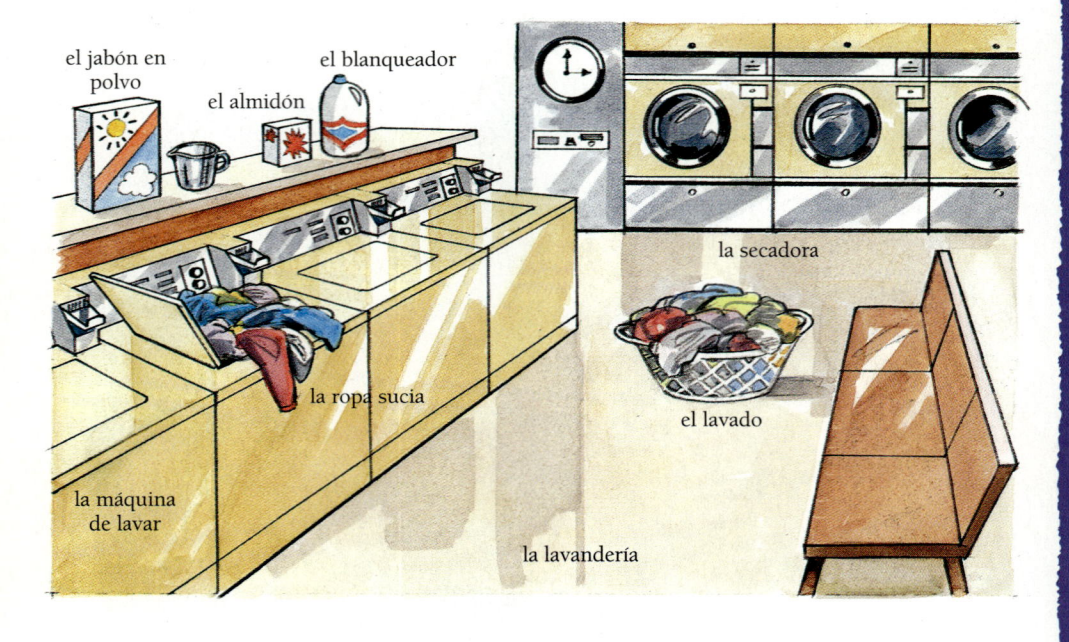

el jabón en polvo

el almidón

el blanqueador

la secadora

la ropa sucia

el lavado

la máquina de lavar

la lavandería

Sidebar (Teacher's Edition)

VOCABULARIO PALABRAS 2

Vocabulary Teaching Resources
1. Vocabulary Transparencies 13.2 (A & B)
2. Audio Cassette 8A
3. Student Tape Manual, *Palabras 2*
4. Workbook, *Palabras 2*
5. Communication Activities Masters, *Palabras 2, C & D*
6. Chapter Quizzes, *Palabras 2*
7. Computer Software, *Vocabulario*

Bell Ringer Review
Write the following on the board or use BRR Blackline Master 13-2: Make a list of words and expressions you might need when shopping for clothes.

PRESENTATION (pages 346-347)

A. Have students close their books. Model the *Palabras 2* vocabulary using Vocabulary Transparencies 13.2 (A & B). Have students repeat the material after you or Cassette 8A.

B. After some practice, use questions such as the following to elicit the vocabulary: ¿Qué sacó José de la mochila? ¿Cómo estaba la ropa? ¿Dónde puso la ropa? Después de lavar la ropa, ¿dónde la puso? ¿Qué le aconseja la empleada al señor? ¿Por qué? ¿Qué recomienda ella?

PANTOMIME

Getting Ready
You may wish to use as many props as possible, or you may use pictures of items for students to perform this pantomime.

_____, saca la ropa de tu mochila.
Mírala. ¡Qué sucia está!
Pon la ropa en la mochila.
Ve a la lavandería.
Saca la ropa de la mochila otra vez.
Pon el lavado en la máquina de lavar.
Añade el jabón en polvo.
Abre la botella de blanqueador.
Pon una tapa de blanqueador en la máquina de lavar.
Prende la máquina.
¡Ya está! Saca la ropa limpia de la máquina.

José fue a la lavandería.
Llevó su ropa sucia a la lavandería.
Lavó su ropa.

la plancha

El joven planchó su camisa.

la limpieza en seco

encogerse

la tintorería

Señor, le aconsejo que no lave este suéter.
Es de lana.
Se va a encoger.
Le recomiendo (sugiero, aconsejo) que lo limpie en seco.

CAPÍTULO 13   **347**

ABOUT THE LANGUAGE

The dryer is called a *secadora,* but in some places it is called a *secador.* The gender of a number of common objects changes from place to place. Students already learned about *bolso* (Spain) and *bolsa* (Latin America). Other examples are:

maletero/maleta
refrigerador/refrigeradora
el radio/la radio
el computador/la computadora

COOPERATIVE LEARNING

Have students work in small groups to make up a conversation between the two people in the last illustration.

Ejercicios

PRESENTATION (page 348)

Ejercicio A
Exercise A can be done with books open or closed.

Ejercicios B and C
Exercises B and C are to be done with books open.

ANSWERS

Ejercicio A
1. José sacó su ropa de la mochila.
2. La ropa estaba sucia.
3. José fue a la lavandería.
4. Llevó el lavado a la lavandería.
5. Lavó la ropa en la máquina de lavar.
6. Puso dos paquetes de detergente en la máquina.
7. Secó la ropa en la secadora.
8. No, no planchó la ropa.

Ejercicio B
1. lavar
2. limpiar en seco
3. planchar
4. lavandería
5. tintorería
6. máquina de lavar, secadora

Ejercicio C
1. c
2. e
3. g
4. a
5. f
6. d
7. b

Ejercicios

A ¡Qué ropa más sucia! Contesten según se indica.

1. ¿De dónde sacó José su ropa? (de la mochila)
2. ¿Cómo estaba? (sucia)
3. ¿Adónde fue José? (a la lavandería)
4. ¿Qué llevó a la lavandería? (el lavado)
5. ¿Dónde lavó la ropa? (en la máquina de lavar)
6. ¿Qué puso en la máquina? (dos paquetes de detergente)
7. ¿Dónde secó la ropa? (en la secadora)
8. ¿Planchó la ropa? (no)

B La ropa. Completen.

1. Esta camisa está manchada. La tengo que ____ .
2. Este suéter está sucio. Lo tengo que ____ .
3. Este pantalón está arrugado. Lo tengo que ____ .
4. Me van a lavar la ropa sucia en la ____ .
5. Y me van a limpiar en seco la chaqueta en la ____ .
6. Lavo la ropa en la ____ y luego la seco en la ____ .

C Palabras relacionadas. Pareen.

1. lavar   a. la recomendación
2. planchar   b. el consejo
3. caminar   c. el lavado
4. recomendar   d. la limpieza
5. sugerir   e. el planchado
6. limpiar   f. la sugerencia
7. aconsejar   g. la caminata

348   CAPÍTULO 13

LEARNING FROM PHOTOS

Have students say all they can about the photo at the top of page 348.

LEARNING FROM REALIA

You may wish to ask the following questions about the detergent packages on page 348: ¿Qué clase de productos son éstos? ¿Para qué se usan? ¿Cuántas veces puedes lavar la ropa con el paquete de ARIEL? ¿Qué quiere decir "limonado" en el paquete de RÁPIDO?

Comunicación
Palabras 1 y 2

A **De camping.** Ud. y un(a) compañero(a) van a hacer una excursión. Van de camping. Piensan dar unas caminatas. Preparen una lista de la ropa que van a poner en su mochila.

B **En un hotel o en un camping.** Con un(a) compañero(a) de clase, preparen una lista de cosas o actividades que pueden hacer los clientes de un hotel. Luego preparen una lista de las cosas que pueden hacer los viajeros que van de camping. Entonces decidan lo que Uds. preferirían hacer—quedarse en un hotel o ir de camping. Expliquen por qué. Si no están de acuerdo, expliquen sus diferencias de opinión.

C **En una lavandería.** Imagínese que Ud. está trabajando a tiempo parcial en una lavandería en un barrio donde vive mucha gente de ascendencia hispana. Explíquele a un(a) cliente cómo usar la máquina de lavar. Use las siguientes expresiones.

1. esperar media hora
2. prender *(start)* la máquina
3. escoger la temperatura
4. poner blanqueador
5. poner detergente
6. poner la ropa sucia
7. introducir monedas
8. sacar el lavado

CAPÍTULO 13

Comunicación
(*Palabras 1* and *2*)

PRESENTATION (page 349)
You may have students do any number of these activities. You may also allow students to select the activity or activities in which they wish to take part.

RECYCLING
You may quickly review the vocabulary from Chapter 16 of *Bienvenidos*, which deals with camping.

ANSWERS
Actividades A, B, **and** *C*
Answers will vary

LEARNING FROM PHOTOS
Refer students to the two photos on page 349. Ask them to describe and compare the swimming scenes in both photos. Cue with questions such as: *En la foto de arriba, ¿dónde nadan las personas? ¿Dónde están en la foto de abajo? ¿Están en el campo o en la ciudad? ¿Dónde preferirías tú nadar, en el sitio de arriba o el de abajo? ¿Por qué?*

INDEPENDENT PRACTICE
Assign any of the following:
1. Workbook, *Palabras 2*
2. Communication Activities Masters, *Palabras 2, C & D*
3. Exercises and activities on student pages 348-349

ESTRUCTURA

El infinitivo o el subjuntivo

Expressing Your Wishes and Preferences and Those of Others

1. With any verbs or expressions that require the subjunctive, the subjunctive is used only when there is a change of subject. That is to say the subjunctive is used when the subject of the main clause is different from the subject of the dependent clause that follows *que*.

MAIN		DEPENDENT
Yo quiero	que	Juan nos acompañe.
Él prefiere	que	vayamos juntos.
Pues, es necesario	que	decidamos lo que vamos a hacer.

2. If there is no change of subject, the infinitive is used.

> Juan quiere acompañarnos.
> Él prefiere no salir.
> Es necesario decidir.

Ejercicios

A **Estoy de acuerdo.** Contesten según el modelo.

> Ellos quieren que tú vayas.
> *Pues, no hay problema. Quiero ir.*

1. Ellos quieren que tú hagas el viaje.
2. Ellos quieren que tú vayas con ellos.
3. Ellos quieren que tú conduzcas.
4. Ellos quieren que tú tomes la autopista.
5. Ellos quieren que tú vuelvas con ellos también.

B **El lavado.** Contesten.

1. ¿Quieres lavar la ropa sucia?
2. ¿O prefieres que yo te la lave?
3. ¿Quieres ir a la lavandería?
4. ¿O quieres que yo vaya a la lavandería?
5. ¿Es posible lavar el suéter o es necesario limpiarlo en seco?
6. ¿Quieres que yo lo lleve a la tintorería?

C **Juan quiere pero yo prefiero.** Completen según el modelo.

> ir al museo/ir al cine
> *Juan quiere que yo vaya al museo pero yo prefiero ir al cine.*

1. ir en autobús/ir en tren
2. ir a un hotel/ir de camping
3. nadar/esquiar en el agua
4. esquiar/patinar
5. cocinar/comer en un restaurante

D **Un pequeño conflicto.** Completen.

Pilar quiere ___(mirar)___ la televisión pero Tomás prefiere que todos ___(salir)___ de casa. Él desea ___(estudiar)___ y no quiere que nadie ___(hacer)___ ruido. Él le pide a Pilar que no ___(poner)___ la tele. Y Pilar no quiere ___(perder)___ el campeonato de tenis en la tele. Ella insiste en que Tomás ___(ir)___ a otro cuarto a estudiar, pero Tomás no quiere ___(ir)___ a otro cuarto. Quiere ___(quedarse)___ donde está.

CAPÍTULO 13   351

Bell Ringer Review

Write the following on the board or use BRR Blackline Master 13-4: Complete with the present tense. Then keep your paper.
1. Yo ____ un viaje. (hacer)
2. Yo ____ a España. (ir)
3. Nosotros ____ en el aeropuerto. (estar)
4. Mi amigo, Juan, ____ conmigo. (venir)
5. Nosotros ____ por toda España. (andar)
6. Yo ____. (conducir)

Repaso del pretérito de los verbos irregulares
PRESENTATION *(page 352)*

Note This segment reviews the forms of irregular verbs in the preterite in a convenient, condensed chart format. They are reviewed in order to prepare students for the introduction of the imperfect subjunctive in the next chapter.

A. Have students open their books to page 352 and ask them to repeat the verb forms in unison.

Ejercicios
PRESENTATION *(page 352)*

Ejercicio A
Exercise A can be done with books closed.

ANSWERS
Ejercicio A
Answers will vary.
1. Sí (No), (no) fui al mercado.
2. Sí (No), (no) anduve por todo el mercado.
3. Sí (No), (no) fui de un puesto a otro.
4. Sí (No), (no) pude comprar frutas frescas.
5. Sí (No), (no) hice muchas compras.
6. Puse las compras en una bolsa (en una canasta).

Repaso del pretérito de los verbos irregulares

Telling What You and Others Did in the Past: A Review

Review the forms of the preterite of the following irregular verbs.

estar	estuve, estuviste, estuvo, estuvimos, *estuvisteis*, estuvieron
tener	tuve, tuviste, tuvo, tuvimos, *tuvisteis*, tuvieron
andar	anduve, anduviste, anduvo, anduvimos, *anduvisteis*, anduvieron
poner	puse, pusiste, puso, pusimos, *pusisteis*, pusieron
poder	pude, pudiste, pudo, pudimos, *pudisteis*, pudieron
saber	supe, supiste, supo, supimos, *supisteis*, supieron
querer	quise, quisiste, quiso, quisimos, *quisisteis*, quisieron
hacer	hice, hiciste, hizo, hicimos, *hicisteis*, hicieron
venir	vine, viniste, vino, vinimos, *vinisteis*, vinieron
decir	dije, dijiste, dijo, dijimos, *dijisteis*, dijeron
traer	traje, trajiste, trajo, trajimos, *trajisteis*, trajeron
conducir	conduje, condujiste, condujo, condujimos, *condujisteis*, condujeron
ir	fui, fuiste, fue, fuimos, *fuisteis*, fueron

Ejercicios

A Al mercado. Contesten.

1. ¿Fuiste al mercado?
2. ¿Anduviste por todo el mercado?
3. ¿Fuiste de un puesto a otro?
4. ¿No pudiste comprar frutas frescas?
5. ¿Hiciste muchas compras?
6. ¿Pusiste tus compras en una bolsa o en una canasta?

Un mercado en México

LEARNING FROM PHOTOS

Give students the following information about the photo on page 352: El mercado en la foto es típico de los mercados en los pueblos de Latinoamérica en las zonas tropicales. Tienen techo para protección contra la lluvia, pero no tienen paredes porque no hace mucho frío. Los mercados son del municipio. Los vendedores pagan al municipio para vender sus productos allí.

ADDITIONAL PRACTICE

Have students take the sentences from the **Bell Ringer Review** above and ask them to rewrite them in the preterite.

B Hoy y ayer también. Cambien al pretérito.

1. Ella va.
2. Ella no puede.
3. Ella lo sabe.
4. Ella no quiere.
5. Ella lo dice.
6. Ella conduce.
7. Ella lo trae.
8. Ella no lo hace.

C Hoy y ayer también. Cambien *ella* en *ellos* en el Ejercicio B.

D Un picnic. Completen.

Ayer nosotros ___ (hacer) un picnic. ¿Me preguntas adónde (nosotros) ___ (ir)? Pues, ___ (ir) al parque Florida. No solamente una persona ___ (traer) la comida. Todos nosotros ___ (traer) algo. ¿Qué ___ (hacer) yo? Pues, yo ___ (hacer) empanadas. Estaban muy buenas, muy ricas y todos mis amigos ___ (pedir) más. Todos ___ (repetir).

Un parque en Buenos Aires, Argentina

CAPÍTULO 13 353

Ejercicios

PRESENTATION (page 353)

Ejercicios B and C
Exercises B and C can be done with books closed.

Ejercicio D
Exercise D is to be done with books open.

ANSWERS

Ejercicio B
1. Ella fue.
2. Ella no pudo.
3. Ella lo supo.
4. Ello no quiso.
5. Ella lo dijo.
6. Ella condujo.
7. Ella lo trajo.
8. Ella no lo hizo.

Ejercicio C
1. Ellos fueron.
2. Ellos no pudieron.
3. Ellos lo supieron.
4. Ellos no quisieron.
5. Ellos lo dijeron.
6. Ellos condujeron.
7. Ellos lo trajeron.
8. Ellos no lo hicieron.

Ejercicio D
1. hicimos
2. fuimos
3. fuimos
4. trajo
5. trajimos
6. hice
7. hice
8. pidieron
9. repitieron

LEARNING FROM PHOTOS

Have students describe the scenes in the two photos on page 353 as completely as they can. You may wish to ask: *¿Qué hacen los jóvenes en la foto a la derecha?*

CRITICAL THINKING ACTIVITY

(Thinking skills: comparing and contrasting; evaluating facts; identifying causes)

Read the following to the class or write it on the board or on an overhead transparency.

¿El parque en Buenos Aires se parece a parques en los EE.UU.? ¿Cómo? ¿La vegetación nos dice algo de la posición geográfica? ¿Está el parque en una zona tropical? ¿Cómo sabes que no es tropical? ¿Qué tipo de clima será? ¿Por qué?

353

CONVERSACIÓN

Bell Ringer Review
Write the following on the board or use BRR Blackline Master 13-5: Write all the words and phrases you can remember dealing with camping.

PRESENTATION (page 354)

A. Tell students they will hear a conversation between Antonio and an employee at a laundromat.
B. Have students close their books and listen as you read the conversation or play Cassette 8A.
C. Now have students open their books to page 354. Read or play the conversation a second time and have students read aloud along with you or the cassette.
D. Allow pairs time to practice the conversation. Then call on a volunteer pair to present it to the class.

Ejercicio
ANSWERS

1. Antonio lleva una camisa.
2. Quiere que el señor la lave y la planche.
3. No quiere almidón.
4. La mancha está en la manga.
5. Antonio no sabe de qué es la mancha.
6. No quiere prometer quitar la mancha.
7. La quiere para mañana.

354

CONVERSACIÓN

Escenas de la vida *En la lavandería*

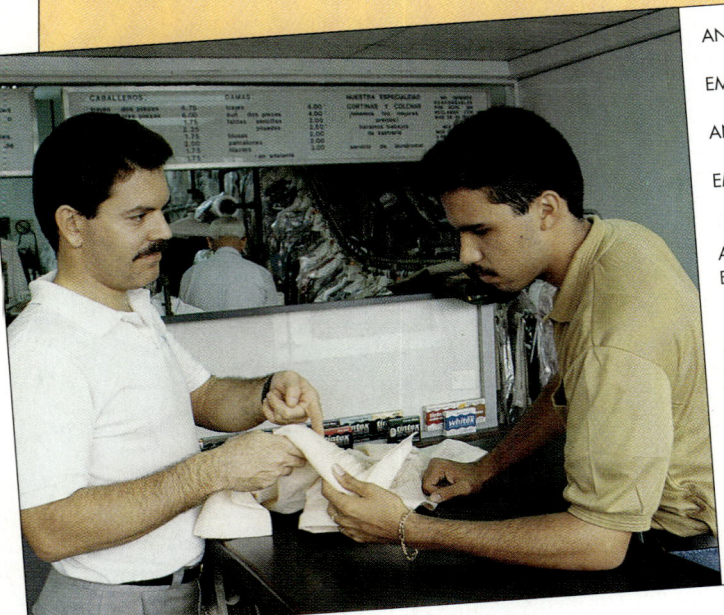

ANTONIO: ¿Me puede lavar y planchar esta camisa, por favor?
EMPLEADO: Sí, señor. ¿Quiere Ud. almidón o no?
ANTONIO: No, sin almidón, por favor.
EMPLEADO: ¿Ve Ud. que aquí hay una mancha en la manga? ¿De qué es? ¿Sabe Ud.?
ANTONIO: No, no sé.
EMPLEADO: Pues, trataré de quitársela pero no quiero prometerle.
ANTONIO: De acuerdo.
EMPLEADO: ¿Para cuándo quiere Ud. la camisa?
ANTONIO: La necesito para mañana.
EMPLEADO: Muy bien.

La lavandería. Contesten según la conversación.

1. ¿Qué lleva Antonio a la lavandería?
2. ¿Qué quiere que el señor haga con la camisa?
3. ¿Quiere almidón o no?
4. ¿Dónde está manchada la camisa?
5. ¿De qué es la mancha?
6. ¿Promete el señor quitar la mancha?
7. ¿Para cuándo quiere Antonio la camisa?

TINTORERÍA POPOCATEPETL
PLAZA POPOCATEPETL
COL. HIPODROMO CONDESA Nº 35

5-14-95-12
SERVICIO A DOMICILIO
55 AÑOS DE EXPERIENCIA
ACABADO A MANO
LA MEJOR CALIDAD Y SERVICIO

354 CAPÍTULO 13

LEARNING FROM PHOTOS/REALIA

1. Refer students to the photo on page 354 and ask: *Hay tres listas en la pared, ¿cuáles son? ¿Qué indica cada lista? Hay dos productos en el mostrador, "whitex" y "tintex", ¿para qué se usarán esos productos?*
2. In regard to the ad, ask: *¿En qué país está la tintorería? ¿Cómo lo sabes? ¿Qué es Popocatépetl? ¿Qué servicio ofrece la tintorería? ¿Qué quiere decir "servicio a domicilio"? Y, ¿"acabado a mano"? ¿Cuál es la dirección de la tintorería?*

Comunicación

A **Consejos.** Trabaje con un(a) compañero(a) de clase. Ud. le va a aconsejar que haga cinco cosas. Él o ella le va a decir si lo quiere hacer o no. Si no lo quiere hacer, le dirá que lo haga Ud.

B **Sugerencias.** Un(a) compañero(a) de clase le va a decir algunas cosas que no quiere hacer. Cada vez que él o ella le dice algo que no quiere hacer, Ud. le va a sugerir que haga algo diferente.

C **En la tintorería.** Ud. tiene una chaqueta que está sucia y arrugada. Hay también una mancha en la chaqueta y le falta un botón. Con un(a) compañero(a) de clase, preparen Uds. un diálogo que tiene lugar en la tintorería.

D **Favores muy grandes.** Dígale a un(a) compañero(a) de clase que haga lo siguiente. Su compañero(a) le dirá si puede hacerlo o no.

> quitarme la mancha de la camisa.
> Estudiante 1: Deseo que me quites la mancha de la camisa.
> Estudiante 2: Lo intentaré. No creo que sea posible.

1. quitarme la mancha de la camisa
2. plancharme los pantalones
3. lavarme los calcetines
4. llevar mi chaqueta a la tintorería
5. poner mi traje de baño en la secadora
6. lavarme la ropa sucia

CAPÍTULO 13   355

Bell Ringer Review

Write the following on the board or use BRR Blackline Master 13-6: Make one complete sentence out of each of the following groups of words:
1. Yo/querer/tener éxito
2. Yo/querer/Teresa/tener éxito
3. Papá/preferir/quedarse en casa
4. Papá/preferir/nosotros/quedarse en casa
5. María/querer/volver pronto
6. Mamá/querer/nosotros/volver pronto

Comunicación

PRESENTATION (page 355)

These activities encourage students to reincorporate previously learned vocabulary and structures and use them on their own. You may select those activities that you consider most appropriate, or you may allow students to select the ones in which they participate.

ANSWERS

Actividades A, B, and C
Answers will vary.

Actividad D
Answers will vary according to the model.

INDEPENDENT PRACTICE

Assign any of the following:
1. Workbook, *Estructura*
2. Communication Activities Masters, *Estructura*, B
3. Exercises on student pages 352–354

LEARNING FROM PHOTOS

You may wish to use the buttons on page 355 for an exercise on location and description. Have students make up questions in order to locate specific buttons and ask them of their partners. For example: *Este botón es blanco. Está a la izquierda y debajo del botón azul en forma de corazón. ¿Cuál es?* When a partner is stumped, roles are exchanged.

355

LECTURA Y CULTURA

Bell Ringer Review
Write the following on the board or use BRR Blackline Master 13-7: Write a list of any geographical terms you remember.

READING STRATEGIES
(page 356)

Pre-Reading
Refer students to the map of Spain on page 452. Point out the *Coto Doñana* area and the Guadalquivir River.

Reading
Have students open their books to page 356 and ask volunteers to read aloud four or five sentences of the selection at a time. After each person reads, ask the class your own content questions, or use the *Comprensión* questions on page 357.

Post-reading
Ask students to tell about their own camping experiences in Spanish.

HISTORY CONNECTION
Coto Doñana was the private hunting preserve of Spanish kings until early in this century. King Alfonso XIII (1886-1941), an avid hunter, was a frequent visitor.

LECTURA Y CULTURA

ISABEL LA NATURALISTA

A Isabel Dávila le encanta la naturaleza. Le interesan mucho la ecología y la protección ambiental.

Recientemente Isabel y algunos amigos fueron de camping en el sur de España. Dieron una caminata por el Coto Doñana. Es una gran extensión de tierra donde desemboca[1] el río Guadalquivir en el océano Atlántico. ¿Por qué le interesó tanto a Isabel esta región? Le interesó porque es un tesoro ecológico. La Reserva del Coto Doñana se divide en tres partes y cada parte es un ecosistema. Primero hay dunas. Los vientos del Atlántico soplan[2] sobre las arenas y forman dunas. El segundo ecosistema es un área baja y pantanosa[3] donde entran frecuentemente las aguas del mar. El tercer ecosistema es el de los matorrales[4] o cotos.

El Coto Doñana

El río Guadalquivir, España

En estos tres ecosistemas viven una gran variedad de aves[5], mamíferos y reptiles. Y aquí descansan las aves durante su migración del norte de Europa a África. La posible destrucción de este tesoro ecológico afectaría la ecología de Europa y gran parte de África. Hace poco un fuego[6] destruyó una parte de esta reserva biológica. ¿Cuál fue la causa del fuego o incendio? El descuido de algunos turistas que estaban de excursión en la región.

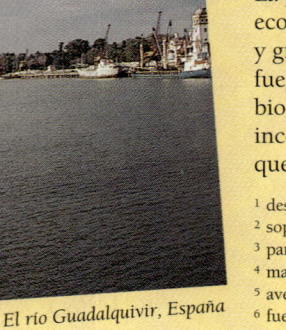

[1] desemboca *empties*
[2] soplan *blow*
[3] pantanosa *swampy, marshy*
[4] matorrales *underbrush, thicket*
[5] aves *birds*
[6] fuego *fire*

356 CAPÍTULO 13

DID YOU KNOW?

1. The importance of *Coto Doñana* has been recognized by the European Community. The Community has collaborated in maintaining the *Coto* as a wildlife sanctuary for migratory birds as well as rare native species. Two rare species of eagle, *el águila real* and *el águila imperial* are found there, as well as the *lince* (lynx), among other rare fauna.

2. Francisco de Goya painted a famous portrait of the Duchess of Alba at *Coto Doñana*. The painting hangs in the Museum of the Hispanic Society of America in New York City. Ask students to try to find a reproduction of the painting.

3. Honduras is one of the world's major producers of timber, especially of valuable hardwoods such as mahogany.

Estudio de palabras

A **La naturaleza.** ¿Cuál es la palabra?

1. no hace mucho tiempo
2. del ambiente
3. de la ecología
4. un monte de arena en los desiertos o en las playas
5. animales vertebrados, las hembras producen leche
6. cocodrilos, iguanas, víboras, cobras, boas, etc.
7. animal de sangre caliente que tiene pico, plumas y alas y puede volar
8. un incendio

B **Palabras relacionadas.** Pareen.

1. la protección
2. la caminata
3. la extensión
4. la desembocadura
5. el interés
6. la migración
7. el descanso
8. la destrucción

a. extender
b. interesar
c. descansar
d. proteger
e. destruir
f. desembocar
g. caminar
h. migrar

Comprensión

A **El Coto Doñana.** Contesten.

1. ¿Cuáles son algunas cosas que le interesan a Isabel Dávila?
2. ¿Dónde fueron de camping Isabel y sus amigos?
3. ¿Por qué le interesó a Isabel el Coto Doñana?
4. ¿Qué viven en los tres ecosistemas del Coto Doñana?
5. ¿Cuándo descansan las aves en la reserva?
6. ¿Qué destruyó una parte de la reserva?
7. ¿Quiénes causaron el fuego?

B **Informes.** Busquen dónde dice lo siguiente.

1. lo que es el Coto Doñana y dónde está
2. el número de ecosistemas en el Coto Doñana
3. lo que hay en cada uno de los ecosistemas
4. un río en el sur de España
5. el mar en que desemboca este río

Un incendio forestal en Honduras

CAPÍTULO 13   357

CRITICAL THINKING ACTIVITY

(Thinking skills: making inferences)
Read the following to the class or write it on the board or on a transparency.
¿Qué tipo de persona tendría interés en las regiones descritas en la Lectura?

INDEPENDENT PRACTICE

Assign any of the following:
1. Workbook, *Un poco más*
2. Exercises on page 357

Estudio de palabras

PRESENTATION (page 357)

Ejercicios A and B
Allow students to scan the selection for answers to Exercises A and B.

ANSWERS

Ejercicio A
1. recientemente
2. ambiental
3. ecológico
4. duna
5. mamífero
6. reptiles
7. ave
8. fuego

Ejercicio B
1. d
2. g
3. a
4. f
5. b
6. h
7. c
8. e

Comprensión

PRESENTATION (page 357)

Comprensión B
Students may need to scan the selection for the answers to Exercise B.

ANSWERS

Comprensión A
1. Le interesan la ecología y la protección ambiental.
2. Fueron de camping en el sur de España.
3. El Coto Doñana le interesó porque es un tesoro ecológico.
4. En los tres ecosistemas viven una gran variedad de aves, mamíferos y reptiles.
5. Las aves descansan durante su migración del norte de Europa a África.
6. Un fuego destruyó una parte de la reserva.
7. Unos turistas descuidados causaron el fuego.

Comprensión B
1. Paragraph 2, lines 4-6
2. Paragraph 2, lines 9-10
3. Paragraph 2, lines 11-17
4. Paragraph 2, line 5
5. Paragraph 2, line 6

Bell Ringer Review

Write the following on the board or use BRR Blackline Master 13-8: What did you do this morning before you left for school? Write five sentences. For example:
Me desperté a las siete.

Descubrimiento Cultural

(*The* Descubrimiento *section is optional.*)

PRESENTATION (pages 358-359)

A. Refer students to a map of the areas discussed in the reading.
B. Have students open their books to pages 358-359 and read the selection silently.

DESCUBRIMIENTO CULTURAL

Una calle en Cuzco

¿A ti te gustan las caminatas? Pues, debes dar una caminata por el camino de los incas, una de las más interesantes caminatas del mundo. Es el camino que usaban los incas para llegar a Machu Picchu. El camino se encuentra por encima del fondo de un valle andino. Para llegar al camino puedes tomar el tren de Cuzco. En vez de continuar hasta Machu Picchu, bajas en el kilómetro 88 y allí empiezas tu caminata por el camino. ¿En cuántas horas vas a llegar a Machu Picchu? No es cuestión de horas. Es cuestión de días. Te tomará entre tres y seis días. Depende de tu manera de caminar. No olvides de llevar una carpa y un hornillo. Pero si decides dar una caminata por este camino famoso, tienes que ser aventurero. Hoy en día hay que tener mucho cuidado por dos motivos o razones. Si sales de los senderos y circulas por los matorrales, debes tener cuidado con las víboras[1]. También hay que preocuparse de los guerrilleros—que son miembros de un grupo revolucionario radical que quieren derrocar[2] al gobierno peruano. Estos guerrilleros han cometido muchos actos terroristas.

Si te interesan los animales debes ir a la península Valdés en la Argentina. Aquí es donde pasan el verano los famosos pingüinos magallánicos. En marzo salen de la península Valdés a pasar el invierno en la Antártida. Aquí hay también adorables lobos del mar y elefantes marinos. Por lo general, estos animales grandes no son peligrosos. ¡Pero cuidado! No bloquees su camino al mar.

En todos los idiomas hay palabras o sonidos para imitar los sonidos que hacen los animales. En inglés los perros dicen "bow-wow" o "woof-woof", los gallos dicen "cockadoodledoo", las gallinas, "cluck-cluck" y los pajaritos, "tweet-tweet". "Baa-baa" dice la oveja. Pero los animales españoles y latinoamericanos no van a "hablar inglés", ¿verdad? ¿Qué dicen ellos, pues?

El camino inca

358 CAPÍTULO 13

FOR THE NATIVE SPEAKER

Ask students to prepare the following: *Estás en una universidad hispana. Tienes que reclutar estudiantes para colaborar en un proyecto de repoblación forestal. Prepara una hoja que explica la importancia ecológica del proyecto y lo que tendrán que hacer los voluntarios.*

Nuestro mejor amigo, el señor perro, dice "jau-jau" o "guau-guau". El gallo, cuando nos despierta por la mañana, canta "quiquiriquí" y la señora gallina, "clo-clo". El pajarito hispano canta dulcemente "pío-pío", y la oveja castellana dice "bé".

Curiosos son dos animales que hablan un idioma multinacional.
El pato inglés puede decir "quack-quack", pero su primo chileno le entiende perfectamente porque él dice "cuá-cuá". Y la elegante felina, doña gata, se entiende en Londres, Nueva York, París y Buenos Aires cuando dice "miau".

[1] víboras   snakes
[2] derrocar   overthrow

Un glaciar en la Antártida

Lobos del mar en la península Valdés, Argentina

CAPÍTULO 13   **359**

HISTORY CONNECTION

Cuzco was the center of Inca civilization. The Incas dominated western South America from Quito, Ecuador to the Río Maule in Chile, until the Spanish conquest in 1532. According to tradition, Cuzco was founded by Manco Cápac I, *hijo del Sol*, early in the 13th century. *El camino inca* leads from Cuzco to the fortress city of Machu Picchu, high in the Andes.

DID YOU KNOW?

La Antártida es el quinto más grande de los continentes, con una superficie de 14.245.000 kilómetros cuadrados. El capitán inglés James Cook la descubrió en 1772-75. Hoy varios países tienen centros científicos en la Antártida. Los países son los EE.UU., Nueva Zelanda, Australia, Francia, la Argentina, Japón, Rusia, el Reino Unido y Sudáfrica.

REALIDADES

(The Realidades section is optional.)

Bell Ringer Review
Write the following on the board or use BRR Blackline Master 13-9: Choose the correct completion for each sentence:
1. Alano está cierto que tú (vas, vayas) a ganar el partido.
2. Estamos contentos que Josefina (viene, venga) a la fiesta.
3. Yo creo que Raquel (sabe, sepa) preparar una paella.
4. No creo que ella (sabe, sepa) utilizar una parrilla.
5. Espero que tú (sacas, saques) buenas notas.

PRESENTATION *(pages 360-361)*
Allow students time to look at the photographs and discuss them among themselves. Invite them to share their questions and comments.

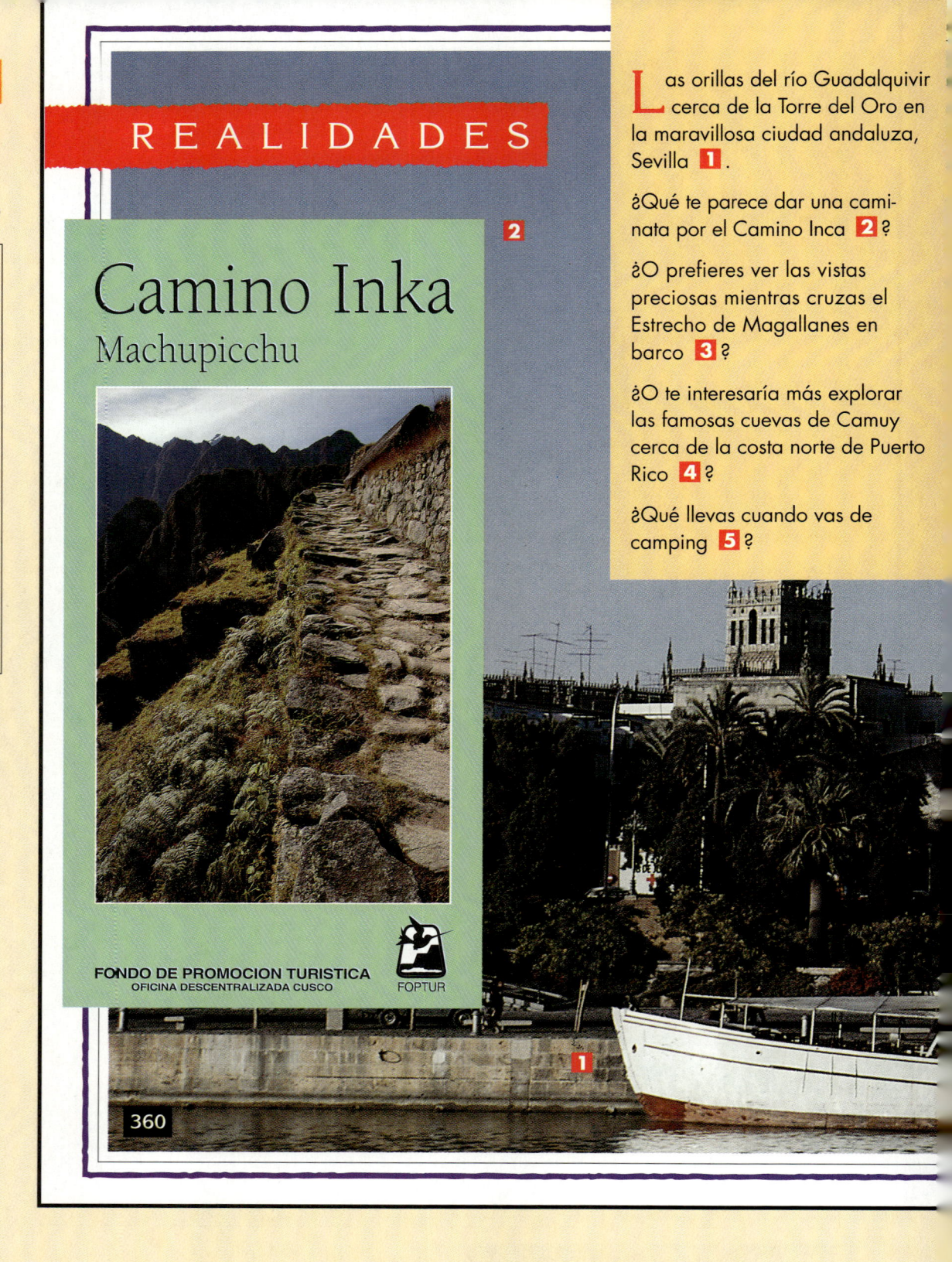

REALIDADES

Camino Inka
Machupicchu

FONDO DE PROMOCION TURISTICA
OFICINA DESCENTRALIZADA CUSCO
FOPTUR

Las orillas del río Guadalquivir cerca de la Torre del Oro en la maravillosa ciudad andaluza, Sevilla **1**.

¿Qué te parece dar una caminata por el Camino Inca **2**?

¿O prefieres ver las vistas preciosas mientras cruzas el Estrecho de Magallanes en barco **3**?

¿O te interesaría más explorar las famosas cuevas de Camuy cerca de la costa norte de Puerto Rico **4**?

¿Qué llevas cuando vas de camping **5**?

HISTORY CONNECTION

Photo 1: *La Torre del Oro (1220) era el lugar donde se guardaba el oro que venía a España desde las Américas. La torre está a orillas del Guadalquivir en Sevilla. Aunque Sevilla no está en la costa, todavía es un puerto, porque los barcos pueden subir por el río Guadalquivir.*

Photo 2: The "lost city" of Machu Picchu was found again in 1911 during an exploration by the North American Hiram Bingham. Machu Picchu lies about 80 kilometers northwest of Cuzco, 600 meters above the Río Urubamba. The city contains 13 square kilometers of terrace and construction, and over 3,000 steps joining different levels. It is considered by many to be the most important ruin in the Americas. Some historians think that Machu Picchu was the Inca capital prior to Cuzco.

GEOGRAPHY CONNECTION

Photo 3: *El Estrecho de Magallanes* or Strait of Magellan separates South America from Tierra del Fuego. It is 530 kilometers long and 4 to 24 kilometers wide. It was discovered by Fernando Magallanes (Ferdinand Magellan) in 1520. It was the sea route around South America until the opening of the Panama Canal. Have students locate the Strait of Magellan on a map.

Photo 4: The Camuy River disappears into the "Hoyo Azul" or "Blue Hole" near Lares, Puerto Rico. The river runs underground through a massive network of caves. A part of the network has been developed into the Río Camuy Cave Park. At some point the river flows hundreds of feet below the surface.

CULMINACIÓN

Comunicación oral

A **¿Quieres que…?** Ud. llama a un(a) amigo(a) (un[a] compañero[a] de clase) y le pregunta si quiere hacer las cosas o ir a los lugares indicados. Su amigo(a) le dice que no, que prefiere que Uds. vayan a otro lugar o que hagan algo diferente. Ud. le contesta diciendo que Ud. no quiere hacer eso, y ofrece otra opción.

1. ir al cine
2. jugar al tenis
3. visitar a *(name a friend)*
4. escuchar mi nuevo disco de *(name an album)*
5. ir al supermercado
6. jugar a las cartas

B **Una encuesta.** Con un(a) compañero(a) de clase escriban diez preguntas para una encuesta sobre la opinión de los estudiantes sobre el camping. Hágales las preguntas a cuatro estudiantes, y luego déle los resultados a la clase.

   Estudiante 1: ¿Te gusta ir de camping?
   Estudiante 2: Mucho / De vez en cuando / Nunca

Comunicación escrita

A **Lo que necesito.** Ud. va de camping por dos semanas en una región montañosa, donde también hay un lago. Escriba una lista de la ropa, cosas personales y equipo de camping que necesita llevar. Luego compare su lista con la de su compañero(a) de clase.

   Ropa   Cosas Personales   Equipo De Camping

B **Mis vacaciones de primavera.** Imagínese que Ud. acaba de regresar a la escuela después de pasar sus vacaciones de primavera en un campamento de jóvenes que está en la orilla del mar. Escriba una lista de diez cosas interesantes que Ud. hizo mientras estuvo en el campamento.

362 CAPÍTULO 13

Reintegración

A **Lo que yo quiero.** Comiencen la oración con *Yo quiero que…*

1. Sacas tu ropa sucia de la mochila.
2. Vas a la lavandería.
3. Lavas tu ropa sucia.
4. La lavas en agua caliente.
5. Pones el lavado en la máquina de lavar.
6. Echas dos tazas de jabón en polvo.
7. Pones también una tapa de blanqueador.
8. Sacas el lavado de la secadora.

B **¿Dónde lo puedes lavar?** Escojan.

      En la lavandería   En la tintorería

1. una camisa
2. un suéter de lana
3. un traje de baño
4. los calcetines
5. una chaqueta
6. un pantalón de lana
7. un pantalón de denim
8. la ropa interior

Vocabulario

SUSTANTIVOS
el camping
la caravana
la casa-remolque
la tienda de campaña
la carpa
el saco para dormir
la hamaca
el hornillo
la caminata
la senda
el sendero
la lavandería
la ropa
el lavado
la máquina de lavar
la secadora
el jabón en polvo
el blanqueador
el almidón
la tintorería
la limpieza en seco
la plancha
el suéter

ADJETIVOS
sucio(a)
arrugado(a)
manchado(a)

VERBOS
planchar
encoger

OTRAS PALABRAS Y EXPRESIONES
limpiar en seco

CAPÍTULO 13   **363**

CAPÍTULO 14
Scope and Sequence pages 364-387

Topics	Functions	Structure	Culture
Money Banking and financial transactions	How to exchange money in Spanish-speaking countries How to conduct banking transactions How to discuss financial matters How to express emotions, wishes, and preferences in the past How to talk about conditions	El imperfecto del subjuntivo Usos del imperfecto del subjuntivo Cláusulas con si	Cost of education in the U.S. and Hispanic countries Money machine in Mexico Bolsa de Valores in Buenos Aires Credit card from Cafetero de Colombia Bank

CAPÍTULO 14

Situation Cards
The Situation Cards simulate real-life situations that require students to communicate in Spanish, exactly as though they were in a Spanish-speaking country. The Situation Cards operate on the assumption that the person to whom the message is to be conveyed understands no English. Therefore, students must focus on producing the Spanish vocabulary and structures necessary to negotiate the situations successfully. For additional information, see the Introduction to the Situation Cards in the Situation Cards Envelope.

Communication Transparency
The illustration seen in this Communication Transparency consists of a synthesis of the two vocabulary (Palabras 1&2) presentations found in this chapter. It has been created in order to present this chapter's vocabulary in a new context, and also to recycle vocabulary learned in previous chapters. The Communication Transparency consists of original art. Following are some specific uses:

1. as a cue to stimulate conversation and writing activities
2. for listening comprehension activities
3. to review and reteach vocabulary
4. as a review for chapter and unit tests

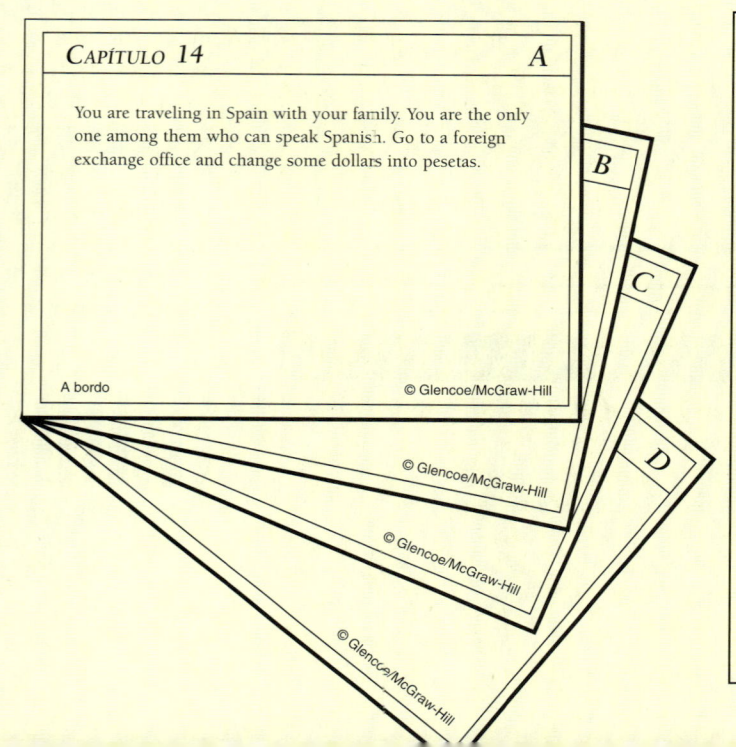

CAPÍTULO 14
Print Resources

Lesson Plans

Workbook   Pages
- Palabras 1   157-158
- Palabras 2   159
- Estructura   160-163
- Un poco más   164-166
- Mi autobiografía   167

Communication Activities Masters
- Palabras 1   91-93
- Palabras 2   94-95
- Estructura   96-97

8 Bell Ringer Reviews   39-40

Chapter Situation Cards A B C D

Chapter Quizzes
- Palabras 1   66
- Palabras 2   67
- Estructura   68-69

Testing Program
- Listening Comprehension   80
- Reading and Writing   81-83
- Proficiency   136
- Speaking   157

Nosotros y Nuestro Mundo
- Nuestro Conocimiento Académico *Economía: El dinero y la banca*
- Nuestro Idioma *El imperfecto del subjuntivo; Cláusulas con si*
- Nuestra Cultura *Los inmigrantes*
- Nuestra Literatura *"El voto"* de Emilio Pardo Bazán
- Nuestra Creatividad
- Nuestras Diversiones

CAPÍTULO 14
Multimedia Resources

CD-ROM Interactive Textbook Disc 4

Chapter 14 Student Edition
- Palabras 1
- Palabras 2
- Estructura
- Conversación
- Lectura y cultura
- Hispanoparlantes
- Realidades
- Culminación
- Prueba

Audio Cassette Program with Student Tape Manual

Cassette   Pages
- 8B Palabras 1   267-268
- 8B Palabras 2   268-269
- 8B Estructura   269
- 8B Conversación   270
- 8B Segunda parte   270-272

Compact Disc Program with Student Tape Manual
- CD 8 Palabras 1   267-268
- CD 8 Palabras 2   268-269
- CD 8 Estructura   269
- CD 8 Conversación   270
- CD 8 Segunda parte   270-272

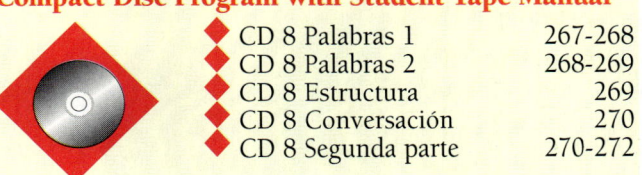

Overhead Transparencies Binder
- Vocabulary 14.1 (A&B); 14.2 (A&B)
- Communication C-14
- Maps
- Fine Art (with Blackline Master Activities)

Video Program
- Videocassette
- Video Activities Booklet   35-37
- Videodisc
- Video Activities Booklet   35-37

Computer Software (Macintosh, IBM, Apple)
- Practice Disk
  - Palabras 1 y 2
  - Estructura
- Test Generator Disk
  - Chapter Test
  - Customized Test

364B

CAPÍTULO 14

CHAPTER OVERVIEW

In this chapter, students will learn to communicate in situations involving changing money, and carrying out simple financial and banking transactions. Vocabulary presented includes activities associated with currency exchange, savings accounts, and checks. Forms and uses of the imperfect tense of the subjunctive are also taught. The cultural focus of Chapter 14 is on the cost of education in the Hispanic world as contrasted with that in the U.S.

CHAPTER OBJECTIVES

By the end of this chapter, students will know:
1. vocabulary associated with the exchange of money in the Hispanic world
2. vocabulary associated with a variety of banking transactions
3. the forms and uses of the imperfect subjunctive
4. the use of the subjunctive in *si* clauses

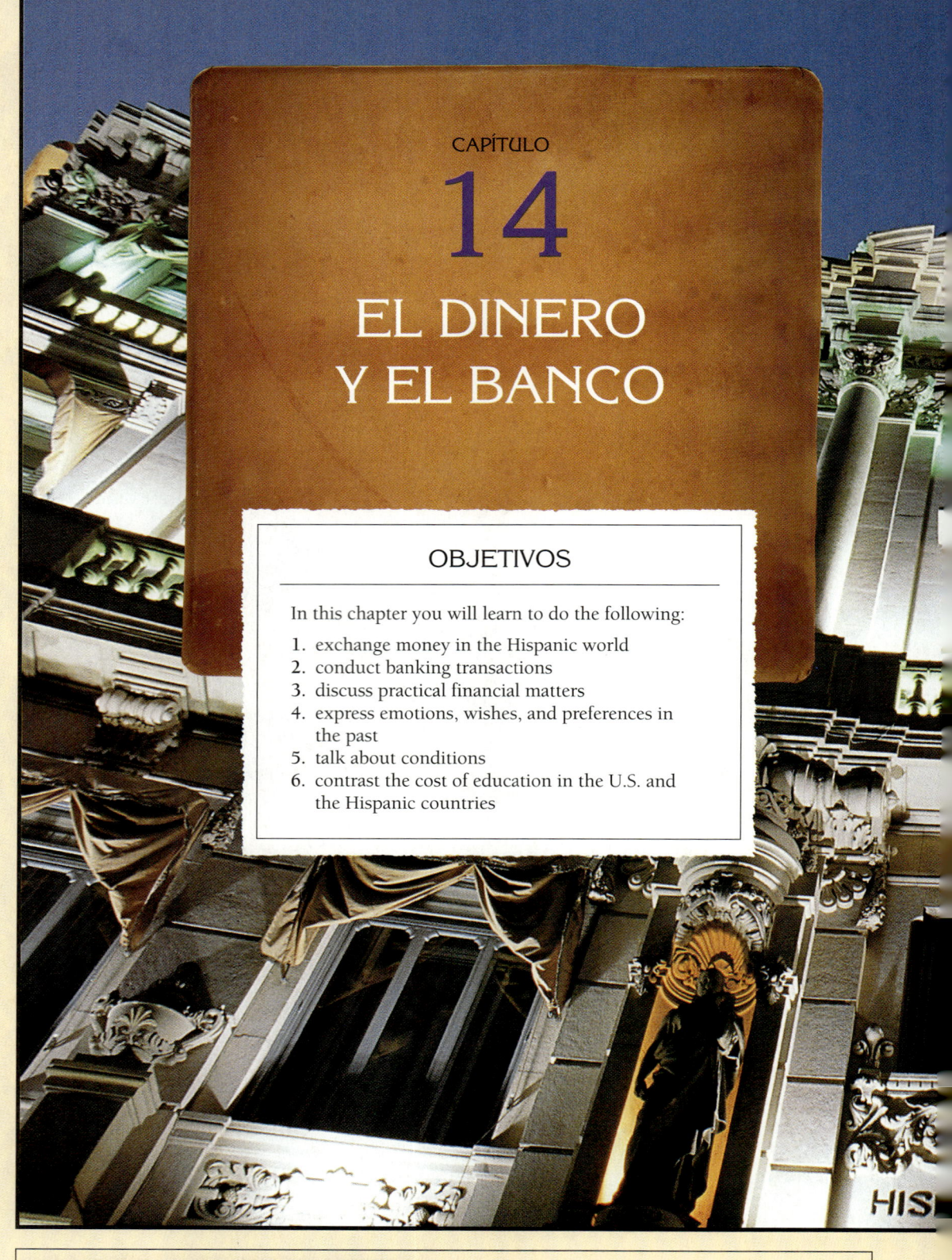

CAPÍTULO 14

EL DINERO Y EL BANCO

OBJETIVOS

In this chapter you will learn to do the following:

1. exchange money in the Hispanic world
2. conduct banking transactions
3. discuss practical financial matters
4. express emotions, wishes, and preferences in the past
5. talk about conditions
6. contrast the cost of education in the U.S. and the Hispanic countries

CHAPTER PROJECTS

(optional)
1. Check the newspaper for exchange rates of the Spanish *peseta* and the Mexican *peso*. Have students keep track of the rates throughout the chapter.
2. Have students draw up a personal budget and keep a diary of their expenditures throughout the chapter. At chapter's end, have them write or tell what they have learned about themselves from doing this.
3. If available, pass around money from Hispanic countries. If this is not available, show students photos of foreign money, including those on student pages 381-382.

CHAPTER 14 RESOURCES

1. Workbook
2. Student Tape Manual
3. Audio Cassette 8B
4. Vocabulary Transparencies
5. Bell Ringer Review Blackline Masters
6. Communication Activities Masters
7. Computer Software: Practice and Test Generator
8. Video Cassette, Chapter 14
9. Video Activities Booklet, Chapter 14
10. Situation Cards
11. Chapter Quizzes
12. Testing Program

Pacing

Chapter 14 will require eight to ten class sessions. Pacing will depend on the length of the class period, the age of the students, and student aptitude.

ABOUT THE LANGUAGE

The word *banco* also means "bench." The origin of *banco* is the Latin word with the same meaning. In Roman times money transactions were carried out on a bench (*banco*). In modern Spanish *el banco* is the physical bank, the building. *La banca* is the banking industry.

LEARNING FROM PHOTOS

Refer students to the photo on pages 364-365. You may wish to tell them that the *Banco Hispano Americano* is located on the *Calle de Alcalá* in Madrid. Many of the great banks of Spain are located on *Alcalá* in magnificent, palatial buildings constructed mostly in the early 20th century.

365

VOCABULARIO
PALABRAS 1

Vocabulary Teaching Resources

1. Vocabulary Transparencies, 14.1 (*A & B*)
2. Audio Cassette 8B
3. Student Tape Manual, *Palabras 1*
4. Workbook, *Palabras 1*
5. Communication Activities Masters, *Palabras 1, A & B*
6. Chapter Quizzes, *Palabras 1*

Bell Ringer Review

Write the following on the board or use BRR Blackline Master 14-1: List at least five ways in which you spend money in any given week.

PRESENTATION (pages 366-367)

A. With books closed, refer to Vocabulary Transparencies 14.1 (*A & B*) and have students repeat the new words, phrases, and sentences after you or Cassette 8B.

B. Point to items on the screen randomly and have students repeat the vocabulary after you.

C. After some practice, ask *¿Qué es esto?* as you point to the items and call on volunteers to respond.

D. Have students open their books to pages 366-367. Ask for volunteers to read the words, phrases, and sentences. Ask questions such as: *¿Qué quisiera la mujer? ¿Qué preferiría ella? ¿A cuánto está el cambio?*, etc.

E. Pass around bills or coins from Spanish-speaking countries that you or your students have brought in.

VOCABULARIO

PALABRAS 1

¿NECESITAS DINERO?

el banco
el cajero
la ventanilla
la caja
el empleado del banco
el dinero
las monedas
los billetes
el dinero en efectivo
el cheque
el cheque de viajero

366 CAPÍTULO 14

PANTOMIME 1

Getting Ready
Set up a mock bank counter.
_____, ven acá, por favor.
Espero que tengas dinero, a lo menos, un poco. ¿No? (If the student has no money, lend some to him/her.)
Bueno. Muéstrame tu bolsillo.
Muéstrame un billete.
Muéstrame una moneda.
Pon tu dinero en tu billetera.
Pon tu billetera en tu bolsillo.
Muy bien, _____, y gracias. Vuelve a tu asiento, por favor.

BANCO NACIONAL

una oficina de cambio

el cambista

cambiar dinero

el tipo de cambio,
la tasa de cambio

Quisiera que Ud. me cambiara este cheque de viajero.
Preferiría que Ud. me diera billetes pequeños.

¿Cuál es el tipo de cambio?

El cambio está a 130 pesos el dólar.

El tipo (la tasa) de cambio fluctúa.

CAPÍTULO 14   367

Vocabulary Expansion

You may give students the following additional vocabulary in order to talk about money and banking:
la tasa de interés
los servicios bancarios
cobrar interés
los préstamos
las hipotecas
la transacción

LEARNING FROM ILLUSTRATIONS

Refer students to the illustrations on page 367. Have them find the current exchange rate for each of the currencies listed in them. This will provide a review of the names of countries and adjectives of nationality. The exchange rates appear in most major newspapers. Also, ask questions about the lists, such as: ¿Cuál es la moneda alemana? ¿Dónde usan marcos?, etc.

367

Ejercicios

PRESENTATION (page 368)

Extension of Ejercicio C
Speaking
After completing Exercise C, have a volunteer retell the information in his/her own words.

ANSWERS

Ejercicio A
1. Sí, es un cheque de un banco mexicano.
2. Son pesetas españolas.
3. Hay cuatro billetes.
4. No, no hay billetes de cien pesetas.
5. El tipo de cambio es…

Ejercicio B
1. billetes
2. billetes
3. dólar
4. monedas

Ejercicio C
1. Sarita está haciendo un viaje.
2. Ella está en España.
3. La peseta es la moneda española.
4. No, Sarita no tiene pesetas.
5. Ella tiene dólares.
6. Ella tiene que cambiar el dinero.
7. Ella va a cambiar cincuenta dólares.
8. Ella va al banco.
9. El tipo de cambio es cien pesetas al dólar.
10. Sarita va a recibir cinco mil pesetas.

RETEACHING (*Palabras 1*)

A. Using Vocabulary Transparencies 14.1 (*A & B*), designate the various illustrations at random and have individuals say as much as they can about each one.

B. Place some props and pictures representing the *Palabras 1* vocabulary in a bag. Have an individual draw one item or picture and say as much about it as he/she can.

368

Ejercicios

A **Dinero y más dinero.** Contesten según las fotos.

1. ¿Es un cheque de un banco mexicano?
2. ¿Son pesetas españolas o pesos mexicanos?
3. ¿Cuántos billetes hay?
4. ¿Hay billetes de 1000 pesetas?
5. ¿Cuál es el tipo de cambio?

B **La moneda estadounidense.** Completen.

La moneda de los Estados Unidos es el dólar. Hay ___(1)___ de 1, 5, 10, 20, 50 y 100 dólares. Hay algunos ___(2)___ de 2 dólares, pero no muchos. El ___(3)___ estadounidense se divide en 100 centavos. Hay ___(4)___ de 1, 5, 10, 25 y 50 centavos.

C **Asuntos financieros.** Contesten según se indica.

1. ¿Quién está haciendo un viaje? (Sarita)
2. ¿Dónde está? (en España)
3. ¿Cuál es la moneda española? (la peseta)
4. ¿Tiene Sarita pesetas? (no)
5. ¿Qué tiene? (dólares)
6. ¿Qué tiene que hacer? (cambiar dinero)
7. ¿Cuánto va a cambiar? (cincuenta dólares)
8. ¿Adónde va? (al banco)
9. ¿Cuál es el tipo de cambio? (cien pesetas al dólar)
10. ¿Cuántas pesetas va a recibir Sarita? (cinco mil)

368   CAPÍTULO 14

CRITICAL THINKING ACTIVITY

(*Thinking skills: identifying causes*)
Read the following to the class or write it on the board or on an overhead transparency.

En muchos países, especialmente en los países donde hay mucho analfabetismo (falta de habilidad para leer), los billetes de banco son de diferentes tamaños. Los que valen más son más grandes. También son de diferentes colores dependiendo del valor. ¿Cuál será la razón por tener billetes de diferentes tamaños y colores?

INDEPENDENT PRACTICE

Assign any of the following:
1. Workbook, *Palabras 1*
2. Communication Activities Masters, *Palabras 1, A & B*
3. Exercises on student page 368

VOCABULARIO

PALABRAS 2

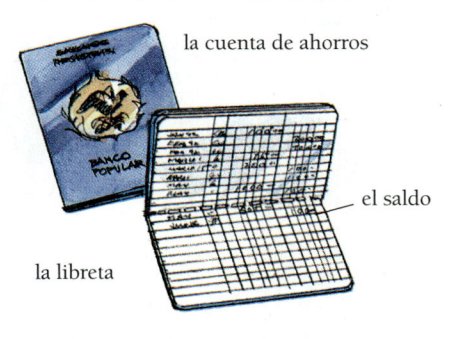

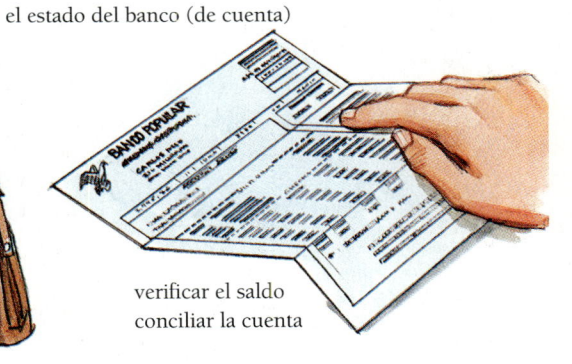

¿TIENE UD. UNA CUENTA EN ESTE BANCO?

la cuenta de ahorros

la cuenta corriente

el saldo

la libreta

la chequera, el talonario

firmar el cheque

endosar el cheque

el estado del banco (de cuenta)

cobrar el cheque

verificar el saldo
conciliar la cuenta

CAPÍTULO 14 369

VOCABULARIO
PALABRAS 2

Vocabulary Teaching Resources

1. Vocabulary Transparencies 14.2 (A & B)
2. Audio Cassette 8B
3. Student Tape Manual, *Palabras 2*
4. Workbook, *Palabras 2*
5. Communication Activities Masters, *Palabras 2, C & D*
6. Chapter Quizzes, *Palabras 2*
7. Computer Software, *Vocabulario*

Bell Ringer Review
Write the following on the board or use BRR Blackline Master 14-2: In Spanish, write down at least three different ways you can earn some extra money.

PRESENTATION (pages 369-370)

A. Have students close their books. Model the *Palabras 2* vocabulary using Vocabulary Transparencies 14.2 (A & B). Have students repeat the new material after you or Cassette 8B.

B. Intersperse repetitions with questions which elicit the new vocabulary. For example (referring to the bottom illustrations on student page 370): ¿Qué era necesario? ¿Qué quería hacer la señora? ¿Qué quería el cajero? ¿Qué quería mamá?

ROLE-PLAY

Getting Ready
This is a paired activity. Have students use their own money or supply play money. Demonstrate *vacío*.

_____ y _____, vengan Uds. aquí, por favor.
_____, tú no tienes dinero.
Muestra tus bolsillos vacíos a _____.
Pídele dinero.
_____, saca tu billetera.
Saca unos billetes.
Dale los billetes a _____.
_____, pon los billetes en tu bolsillo.
Estás contento(a).
Dile gracias a _____.
Dale la mano.

369

ABOUT THE LANGUAGE

The verb *cobrar* has a number of meanings: *cobrar un cheque* is "to cash a check," *cobrar un sueldo* is "to receive one's pay," and *cobrar mucho por el producto* is "to charge a lot for the product."

hacer un depósito
depositar (ingresar) dinero

llenar un formulario de retiro

sacar (retirar) dinero de la cuenta

Era necesario que la señora firmara el cheque.
La señora quería cobrar el cheque.
El cajero quería que ella endosara el cheque.

Mamá me pidió que fuera al banco.
Quería que yo hiciera un depósito.
Quería que yo ingresara 100 dólares en su cuenta de ahorros.

CAPÍTULO 14

COOPERATIVE LEARNING

Have teams create and present skits based on bank conversations like the ones on page 370.

Ejercicios

A **El banco.** Preguntas personales.

1. ¿Te gusta ahorrar dinero?
2. ¿Tienes una cuenta de ahorros?
3. ¿Haces muchos depósitos en tu cuenta de ahorros?
4. ¿Cuál es el saldo de tu cuenta?
5. ¿Cuál es el tipo (la tasa) de interés? ¿Sabes?
6. ¿Tienes una libreta o un certificado de depósito?
7. ¿Tienes una cuenta corriente?
8. ¿Tienen tus padres una cuenta corriente?
9. ¿Pagan ellos sus cuentas o facturas con cheque?
10. ¿Prefieren pagar sus facturas con cheque o en efectivo?

B **Finanzas.** Completen.

1. Una ___ o un ___ tiene una cantidad de cheques.
2. Un cheque no es válido si la persona que escribe el cheque no lo ___ .
3. Es necesario tener una cuenta ___ en el banco si uno quiere escribir cheques.
4. El banco manda (envía) un ___ a sus clientes cada mes (mensualmente).
5. El cliente tiene que verificar el ___ en el estado del banco y el ___ que tiene en su chequera.

C **Ahorros para el futuro.** Escojan.

1. Roberto quiere tener dinero para el futuro. Debe abrir ___ .
   a. una cuenta corriente   b. una cuenta de ahorros   c. un banco
2. Si Roberto quiere ahorrar mucho dinero, tendrá que ___ .
   a. retirar mucho dinero   b. ingresar muchos fondos   c. cobrar muchos cheques
3. Roberto no paga siempre con dinero en efectivo o tarjeta de crédito. Él paga con ___ .
   a. billetes   b. libretas   c. cheques
4. Roberto no tiene más cheques. Necesita ___ .
   a. otra cuenta   b. otro talonario   c. otro estado
5. No se puede escribir otro cheque si no hay ___ en la cuenta corriente.
   a. fondos   b. cheques   c. depósitos

DID YOU KNOW?

In Spain and other Spanish-speaking countries, the postal service sponsors savings programs much like a savings bank. In Spain it is called *La Caja Postal*. In the U.S., there used to be a postal savings system (1911-1966). These systems were established by the government to encourage saving.

Comunicación
(Palabras 1 and 2)

Bell Ringer Review
Write the following on the board or use BRR Blackline Master 14-3: Write down several reasons why it is a good idea to have a savings account.

PRESENTATION *(page 372)*
You may have students do any number of these activities. You may also allow students to select the activity or activities in which they would like to take part.

ANSWERS
Actividades A–D
Answers will vary.

Comunicación
Palabras 1 y 2

A **Necesito cambiar dinero.** Ud. está viajando por un país hispano y tiene que cambiar dinero. Ud. va al banco y habla con el empleado del banco.

Dígale:
- a. cuánto dinero Ud. quiere cambiar
- b. si va a cambiar dinero en efectivo o cheques de viajero
- c. que Ud. no quiere sólo billetes grandes

Pregúntele:
- a. cuál es el tipo de cambio
- b. si necesita ver su pasaporte
- c. si Ud. tiene que pasar a la caja para cobrar su dinero

B **Vacaciones y gastos pagados.** Ud. acaba de ganarse unas vacaciones a Europa, incluso 500 dólares para sus gastos personales en cada país. Use la tabla de tipos de cambio que se da a continuación para saber a cuánto equivalen los 500 dólares en la moneda de cada país.

1 dólar equivale a 1.7 marcos alemanes
Entonces, en Alemania, tendré 850 marcos alemanes.

UN DOLAR EQUIVALE A...	
1. 130 pesetas españolas	5. 1625 liras italianas
2. 1.7 marcos alemanes	6. 170 escudos portugueses
3. 5.8 francos franceses	7. 1.5 francos suizos
4. .66 libras esterlinas (inglesas)	8. 1300 chelines austriacos

C **Un poco de matemáticas.** Practique un poco de matemáticas con un(a) compañero(a) de clase. Pregúntele cuánto equivale cierta cantidad de dólares (cualquier cantidad) con relación a los tipos de cambio que se dan en la Actividad B. Busque en un periódico los tipos de cambio de las monedas de algunos países latinoamericanos con relación al dólar e inclúyalos en esta actividad.

D **Una cuenta bancaria.** Ud. está interesado en abrir una cuenta en un banco. Hable con el empleado del banco (un[a] compañero[a] de clase) para obtener la información necesaria. Pregúntele qué tipo de cuenta paga más intereses (cuenta corriente o cuenta de ahorros); cuál es la tasa de interés que pagan; si el banco da gratis los talonarios de cheques; y si se puede pagar la cuenta de la electricidad directamente por medio del banco. Finalmente, pregúntele a qué hora se abre y se cierra el banco todos los días.

372 CAPÍTULO 14

FOR THE NATIVE SPEAKER
If possible, have students bring in a bank note from their country of origin. Have them tell the class who or what appears on the bill and what the importance of that person or object is. An example would be the *quetzal* of Guatemala.

INDEPENDENT PRACTICE
Assign any of the following:
1. Workbook, *Palabras 2*
2. Communication Activities Masters, *Palabras 2, C & D*
3. Exercises and activities on student pages 371–372

ESTRUCTURA

El imperfecto del subjuntivo

Speaking about the Past Using the Subjunctive

The imperfect subjunctive of all verbs is formed by dropping the ending *-on* of the *ellos(as)* form of the preterite tense.

PRETERITE	STEM	IMPERFECT SUBJUNCTIVE
hablaron	hablar-	hablara
vendieron	vendier-	vendiera
abrieron	abrier-	abriera
estuvieron	estuvier-	estuviera
pusieron	pusier-	pusiera
dijeron	dijer-	dijera

El Banco de Bilbao, Madrid, España

To this root the following endings are added.

INFINITIVE	HABLAR	COMER	ABRIR	ENDINGS
STEM	HABLAR-	COMIER-	ABRIER-	
yo	hablara	comiera	abriera	-a
tú	hablaras	comieras	abrieras	-as
él, ella, Ud.	hablara	comiera	abriera	-a
nosotros(as)	habláramos	comiéramos	abriéramos	-amos
vosotros(as)	hablarais	comierais	abrierais	-ais
ellos, ellas, Uds.	hablaran	comieran	abrieran	-an

Stem-changing verbs

INFINITIVE	PRETERITE (ELLOS)	STEM	IMPERFECT SUBJUNCTIVE
pedir	pidieron	pidier-	pidiera
servir	sirvieron	sirvier-	sirviera
dormir	durmieron	durmier-	durmiera

CAPÍTULO 14   373

> **Bell Ringer Review**
>
> *Write the following on the board or use BRR Blackline Master 14-5:* Make a list of activities you will do tomorrow as part of your daily routine.

Usos del imperfecto del subjuntivo

PRESENTATION (page 374)

A. Ask students to open their books to page 374. Lead them through steps 1-2.
B. Call on volunteers to read the sample sentences in each step aloud.

Irregular verbs

INFINITIVE	PRETERITE (ELLOS)	STEM	IMPERFECT SUBJUNCTIVE
andar	anduvier*on*	anduvier-	anduviera
estar	estuvier*on*	estuvier-	estuviera
tener	tuvier*on*	tuvier-	tuviera
poder	pudier*on*	pudier-	pudiera
poner	pusier*on*	pusier-	pusiera
saber	supier*on*	supier-	supiera
querer	quisier*on*	quisier-	quisiera
venir	vinier*on*	vinier-	viniera
hacer	hicier*on*	hicier-	hiciera
leer	leyer*on*	leyer-	leyera
oír	oyer*on*	oyer-	oyera
decir	dijer*on*	dijer-	dijera
conducir	condujer*on*	condujer-	condujera
traer	trajer*on*	trajer-	trajera
ir	fuer*on*	fuer-	fuera
ser	fuer*on*	fuer-	fuera

Usos del imperfecto del subjuntivo
Speaking about the Past Using the Subjunctive

1. The same rules that govern the use of the present subjunctive govern the use of the past subjunctive. The tense of the verb of the main clause determines whether the present or imperfect subjunctive is to be used in the dependent clause. If the verb of the main clause is in the present or the future, the present subjunctive is used in the dependent clause.

   > Quiero que él me cobre el cheque.
   > Él nos pide que abramos una cuenta en el banco.
   > Ellos insistirán en que paguemos la factura en dólares.
   > Será necesario que tengas el cambio exacto.

2. When the verb of the main clause is in the preterite, imperfect, or conditional, the verb of the dependent clause must be in the imperfect subjunctive.

   > Yo quería que él me cobrara el cheque.
   > Él nos pidió que abriéramos una cuenta en el banco.
   > Ellos insistirían en que pagáramos la factura en dólares.
   > Sería necesario que tuvieras el cambio exacto.

374 CAPÍTULO 14

FOR THE NATIVE SPEAKER

Fill in the blanks with the appropriate form of the verb in parentheses.

1. El gobierno temía que los banqueros (especular) _____ sobre el valor de la moneda.
2. Los alcistas esperaban que (subir) _____ y los bajistas que (caer) _____.
3. Algunos preferían que el gobierno (emitir) _____ más billetes.
4. Así harían que (circular) _____ más dinero.
5. Los que debían mucho dinero deseaban que los bancos (negociar) _____ con ellos.
6. Los cambistas no querían que se (descontar) _____ la moneda.
7. No querían que los bancos les (abonar) _____ sólo una parte de sus obligaciones.
8. Los accionistas les decían a sus clientes que (cargar) _____ todas sus compras a sus tarjetas de crédito.

Ejercicios

A **En el banco.** Contesten.

1. ¿Quería el cliente que el cajero le cobrara el cheque?
2. ¿Quería el cajero que el cliente endosara el cheque?
3. ¿Quería el cajero que el cliente presentara alguna identificación?
4. ¿Quería el cliente que el cajero le diera billetes pequeños?
5. ¿Quería el cajero que el cliente pasara a la caja para cobrar su dinero?

B **Los padres de Susana querían que…** Sigan el modelo.

estudiar
Los padres de Susana querían que ella estudiara.

1. estudiar mucho
2. tomar cinco cursos
3. trabajar duro
4. aprender mucho
5. leer mucho
6. comer bien
7. vivir con ellos
8. recibir buenas notas
9. asistir a la universidad
10. tener éxito
11. salir bien en sus exámenes
12. decir siempre la verdad
13. ser cortés
14. conducir con cuidado

C **¿Qué preferirías?** Sigan el modelo.

Yo preferiría que _____ .
Tú se lo dices.
Yo preferiría que tú se lo dijeras.

1. Tú se lo dices.
2. Tú se lo escribes.
3. Tú se lo das.
4. Se lo envías.
5. Se lo explicas.

D **¿Qué temían ellos?** Sigan el modelo.

Ellos temían que _____ .
Yo no estoy.
Ellos temían que yo no estuviera.

1. Yo no estoy.
2. Yo no quiero ir.
3. No voy.
4. Yo no lo hago.
5. Yo no se lo digo a nadie.

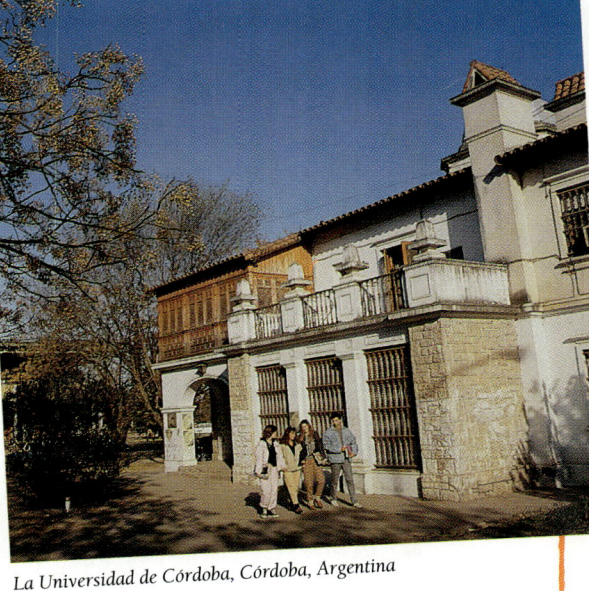

La Universidad de Córdoba, Córdoba, Argentina

CAPÍTULO 14 **375**

Ejercicios

PRESENTATION (*page 376*)

Ejercicio E
Exercise E can be done with books open or closed.

Ejercicios F and G
Exercises F and G can be done with books open.

ANSWERS

Ejercicio E
1. Sus padres insistieron en que ella estudiara mucho.
2. ... hiciera sus tareas.
3. ... recibiera buenas notas.
4. ... fuera diligente.

Ejercicio F
1. ... cambiara
2. ... hablaras
3. ... tuviera
4. ... hiciera
5. ... pusieran

Ejercicio G
1. fuéramos
2. viéramos
3. fuera
4. cambiaran
5. hiciéramos
6. fuéramos
7. hiciéramos
8. nos quedáramos
9. saliéramos
10. miráramos
11. viéramos

E ¿En qué insistieron sus padres? Sigan el modelo.

Sus padres insistieron en que ___ .
Ella estudia mucho.
Sus padres insistieron en que ella estudiara mucho.

1. Ella estudia mucho.
2. Ella hace sus tareas.
3. Ella recibe buenas notas.
4. Ella es diligente.

F Ella sabe mucho de finanzas. Completen.

1. Ella quiere que yo cambie el dinero.
   Ella quería que yo ___ el dinero.
2. Ella te pide que hables con el empleado del banco.
   Ella te pidió que ___ con el empleado del banco.
3. Ella me aconseja que tenga cheques de viajero.
   Ella me aconsejó que ___ cheques de viajero.
4. Ella insiste en que el banco le haga cambio.
   Ella insistió en que el banco le ___ cambio.
5. Ella les dice que pongan su dinero en el banco.
   Ella les dijo que ___ su dinero en el banco.

G ¿Qué íbamos a hacer anoche? Completen.

Yo no sabía lo que íbamos a hacer anoche. Antonio quería que nosotros ___ (ir) al cine. No sé por
                                            1
qué. Pero él insistió en que nosotros ___ (ver) la
                                        2
película que estaban poniendo en el Metropol.
Antonio temía que ayer ___ (ser) el último día.
                        3
Tenía miedo de que ellos ___ (cambiar) las
                          4
películas los sábados. Y tú, ¿qué querías que nosotros ___ (hacer)? ¿Preferías
                                                        5
que ___ (ir) al cine o que ___ (hacer) otra cosa? Felipe quería que
     6   7
nosotros ___ (quedarse) en casa. ¿Por qué? Ah, él no quería que ___ (salir). Él
          8   9
prefería que todos ___ (mirar) la televisión para que ___ (ver) el campeonato
                    10   11
entre Barcelona y Valencia.

376 CAPÍTULO 14

LEARNING FROM REALIA

You may wish to ask the following questions about the advertisement on page 376: *¿Para qué se puede usar la tarjeta Visa? ¿Qué es un "cajero automático" en inglés? ¿En cuántos sitios en Europa hay cajeros automáticos de Visa?*

INDEPENDENT PRACTICE

Assign any of the following:
1. Workbook, *Estructura*
2. Communication Activities Masters, *Estructura*, A–C
3. Exercises on student pages 375-377

Cláusulas con si

Expressing Conditions

1. *Si* clauses (if clauses) have a fixed sequence of tenses. Observe the following sentences.

   Si yo tengo bastante dinero, iré a Puerto Rico.
   Si voy a Puerto Rico, visitaré el Morro.
   Si yo tuviera bastante dinero, iría a Puerto Rico.
   Si fuera a Puerto Rico, visitaría el Morro.

2. Note the sequence of tenses for *si* clauses:

SI CLAUSE	MAIN CLAUSE
Present Indicative	Future
Imperfect Subjunctive	Conditional

Ejercicios

A Si tengo dinero, iré a España. Contesten.

1. Si recibes mucho dinero, ¿lo pondrás en el banco o no?
2. Si alguien te da mil dólares, ¿harás un viaje a España?
3. Si vas a España, ¿tendrás que cambiar tus dólares en pesetas?
4. Si estás en España, ¿cambiarás tu dinero en el banco o en el hotel?
5. Si vas a España, ¿irás a Sevilla?
6. Si vas a Sevilla, ¿visitarás el famoso Alcázar de Sevilla?
7. Si haces el viaje a España, ¿irás en avión?

B Lo que haría si pudiera. Contesten.

1. Si recibieras mucho dinero, ¿lo pondrías en el banco o no?
2. Si alguien te diera mil dólares, ¿harías un viaje a España?
3. Si fueras a España, ¿tendrías que cambiar tus dólares en pesetas?
4. Si estuvieras en España, ¿cambiarías tu dinero en el banco o en el hotel?
5. Si fueras a España, ¿irías a Sevilla?
6. Si fueras a Sevilla, ¿visitarías el famoso Alcázar de Sevilla?
7. Si hicieras un viaje a España, ¿irías en avión?

El Alcázar de Sevilla, España

CAPÍTULO 14   **377**

CONVERSACIÓN

Bell Ringer Review

Write the following on the board or use BRR Blackline Master 14-6: Complete the sentences:
1. El profesor de español no está seguro que…
2. Mis amigos no creen que…
3. Él no está seguro que…
4. Me sorprende que…

PRESENTATION *(page 378)*

A. Tell students they will hear a conversation between a customer in a bank and a teller.
B. Have students close their books and listen as you read the conversation on page 378 or play Cassette 8B.
C. Divide the class into two groups, each of which assumes the role of one of the women in the conversation. Have each group repeat its part of the conversation in unison after you or the cassette.
D. Choose a volunteer from each group to present the conversation to the class.
E. Supply substitutions for the amount of money exchanged and the rate of exchange. Call on pairs to present the conversation making these substitutions.

Ejercicio

ANSWERS
1. veinte dólares
2. el banco
3. el tipo de cambio hoy
4. cheque de viajero
5. a quinientos pesos el dólar
6. firmar el cheque
7. le dé billetes pequeños

378

CONVERSACIÓN

Escenas de la vida *En el banco*

SEÑORITA: Quisiera cambiar dos cientos dólares, por favor.
EMPLEADA: Sí, señorita.
SEÑORITA: ¿Cuál es el tipo de cambio hoy?
EMPLEADA: ¿Tiene Ud. dinero en efectivo o un cheque de viajero?
SEÑORITA: Un cheque de viajero.
EMPLEADA: Está a ciento veinticinco pesetas el dólar.
SEÑORITA: De acuerdo.
EMPLEADA: Por favor firme el cheque aquí. Y su pasaporte, por favor.
SEÑORITA: Aquí lo tiene Ud. Quisiera que Ud. me diera billetes pequeños, por favor.

El banco. Completen según la conversación.
1. La señorita quiere cambiar ___.
2. Va a cambiar el dinero en ___.
3. Quiere saber ___.
4. Ella tiene ___.
5. El cambio está ___.
6. La señorita tiene que ___.
7. Ella insiste en que la empleada del banco ___.

378 CAPÍTULO 14

LEARNING FROM PHOTOS

Have students say all they can about the photo on page 378. You may wish to ask questions such as: ¿Dónde están las mujeres? Describe a la empleada. ¿Cómo es ella? ¿Cómo es la cliente? ¿Qué está haciendo la cliente?

LEARNING FROM REALIA

Refer students to the currency exchange slip on page 378 and ask: ¿Para qué tipo de transacción es el documento? ¿Qué clase de divisa está cambiando el cliente? ¿Cuál es el tipo de cambio? ¿Cuántos dólares está cambiando el cliente? ¿Cuántas pesetas recibe? ¿Cuánto es la comisión que recibe el banco? ¿Cómo se llama el banco?

Comunicación

A **En el banco.** Trabaje con un(a) compañero(a) de clase. Ud. es el/la cliente, y su compañero(a) de clase es el/la empleado(a) del banco. Ud. quiere cambiar cien dólares. Preparen una conversación en el banco.

B **Cuando era joven.** Prepare Ud. una lista de las cosas que sus padres siempre querían que Ud. hiciera cuando era niño(a). Decida lo que Ud. creía que era importante que hiciera y lo que francamente no era tan necesario que hiciera.

C **El profesor exigente.** Ud. y un(a) compañero(a) de clase van a escoger a un(a) profesor(a) con quien Uds. estudiaron el año pasado (profesores distintos). Cada uno de Uds. va a decir lo que su profesor(a) insistió en que Uds. hicieran. Luego comparen sus listas y decidan cuáles son las cosas que los dos profesores exigían que Uds. hicieran. Decidan cuál era el profesor más exigente y por qué.

D **¿Qué harías si…?** Trabaje con un(a) compañero(a) de clase. Pregúntele lo que haría en cada una de las siguientes circunstancias. Luego cambien de papel. ¡Sean originales e imaginativos!

1. si ganaras un viaje a cualquier parte del mundo
2. si te olvidaras de llevar tu boleto en el tren
3. si pudieras pasar un mes de vacaciones en tu lugar favorito
4. si perdieras todas las cosas de tu casa
5. si recibieras un millón de dólares

CAPÍTULO 14 379

LECTURA Y CULTURA

Bell Ringer Review

Write the following on the board or use BRR Blackline Master 14-7: Complete the sentence with the indicative or subjunctive, whichever is appropriate, of the verbs in parentheses:
1. No creo que nosotros ____ a las montañas este año. (ir)
2. Es cierto que tú ____ viajar el año que viene. (querer)
3. Estoy seguro que esta región ____ muy hermosa. (ser)
4. Me sorprende que mis padres no me ____ visitarte. (permitir)
5. Dudo que él ____ bastante dinero. (tener)

READING STRATEGIES
(page 380)

Pre-Reading
Survey students to find out who works part-time, and who plans to work while attending college.

Reading
A. Allow students five minutes to read the selection on page 380 silently. Encourage them to read for main ideas and important details only, not to use dictionaries, and to read on when they encounter difficult places. Tell them they will have a chance to re-read the selection.
B. Now call on volunteers to re-read the *Lectura* aloud. Stop occasionally to ask comprehension questions.

Post-reading
Call on more able students to contrast the costs of secondary school and college in Hispanic countries with those costs in the U.S.

380

LECTURA Y CULTURA

EL DINERO ES ORO[1]

Hay un refrán español que dice que "el dinero vaya y venga y con sus frutos nos mantenga". Y es verdad. El dinero es algo que necesitamos para vivir. En los Estados Unidos, los padres se preocupan[2] del dinero que necesitan para darles una buena educación a sus hijos. Siempre están tratando de ahorrar dinero para poder pagar los gastos[3] universitarios que son muy altos. Los padres saben que tendrán que ingresar muchos fondos en su cuenta corriente para pagar la matrícula (la inscripción) y la pensión[4] de sus hijos.

En España y en Latinoamérica los padres se preocupan igualmente del dinero que necesitan para mandar a sus hijos a la escuela. Pero note, hemos dicho a la escuela, no a la universidad. En los países hispanos, las grandes universidades son del estado y son gratis. Pero la gran mayoría de las familias de la clase media envían a sus hijos a escuelas privadas, academias o colegios. Por consiguiente, es la educación preuniversitaria que les cuesta mucho. Por lo general los padres tienen que pagar la matrícula y los otros gastos mensualmente. Y claro que ellos pagan sus gastos en la moneda nacional—la peseta en España, el peso en México y el bolívar en Venezuela.

Sería importante que Ud. supiera algo sobre la economía si Ud. pensara viajar al extranjero. Cada moneda tiene su propio valor con relación a las otras divisas del mundo. Por ejemplo, en un momento dado el dólar estadounidense puede valer[5] 100 pesetas españolas y 400 pesos chilenos. Pero el tipo de cambio no es constante. Cambia cada día. Algunos países latinoamericanos tienen una economía bastante estable y el valor de su moneda no fluctúa mucho. Pero otros países tienen economías menos estables y la gente habla de la hiperinflación. Hasta recientemente, existía la hiperinflación en la Argentina, por ejemplo. Lo que costaba cien australes hoy, costaba doscientos mañana. Hoy el dólar estaba a 2.000 y mañana a 2.200. Cuando existe la hiperinflación nadie quiere ahorrar dinero. El dinero no tiene valor. No es nada más que papel. La gente lo gasta inmediatamente porque saben que lo que cuesta cien hoy costará el doble dentro de poco. Y si no gastan el dinero lo convierten en una moneda firme. Compran dólares, yenes japoneses, francos suizos o libras esterlinas. En la Argentina ha habido muchos cambios económicos y ha bajado la inflación. El gobierno argentino cambió una vez más el austral en el peso argentino. El nuevo peso empezó a la par con el dólar. Suprimieron cinco ceros al viejo austral.

[1] oro   *gold*
[2] se preocupan   *worry about*
[3] gastos   *expenses*
[4] pensión   *room and board*
[5] valer   *be worth*

380   CAPÍTULO 14

CRITICAL THINKING ACTIVITY

(Thinking skills: supporting statements with reasons)

Read the following to the class or write it on the board or on an overhead transparency:
1. *En tu opinión, ¿es importante ahorrar dinero? ¿Por qué?*
2. *¿Es importante o no hacerse rico(a)? ¿Por qué?*

Estudio de palabras

Definiciones. Escojan.

1. el colegio
2. firme
3. mensualmente
4. la mayoría
5. suprimir
6. preocuparse
7. convertir
8. gratis
9. preuniversitario

a. el porcentaje más alto
b. ponerse nervioso
c. una escuela secundaria
d. que no cuesta nada
e. omitir
f. cambiar en
g. cada mes
h. antes de la universidad
i. estable

Comprensión

A Problemas económicos. Contesten.

1. ¿Qué problema financiero preocupa a los padres en los EE.UU.?
2. ¿Qué problema financiero preocupa a los padres en España y en Latinoamérica?
3. ¿Con qué paga la gente sus gastos?
4. ¿Por qué no se ahorra dinero cuando hay hiperinflación?

B La economía. ¿Sí o no?

1. Todos los países latinoamericanos tienen una economía estable.
2. Todos los países latinomericanos tienen la misma moneda nacional.
3. Todas las monedas latinoamericanas tienen el mismo tipo de cambio con el dólar.
4. La hiperinflación existe cuando los precios no cambian mucho y el valor de la moneda no fluctúa radicalmente.

C Informes. ¿Cuál es?

1. la moneda estadounidense
2. la moneda española
3. la moneda mexicana
4. la moneda japonesa
5. la moneda suiza
6. la moneda de Gran Bretaña
7. la moneda venezolana

D Diferencias. Contesten.

¿Cuál es la gran diferencia que hay entre los sistemas de educación en los Estados Unidos y España y Latinoamérica?

CAPÍTULO 14 381

Estudio de palabras
ANSWERS
1. c
2. i
3. g
4. a
5. e
6. b
7. f
8. d
9. h

Comprensión
ANSWERS

Comprensión A
1. Ellos se preocupan del dinero que necesitan para darles una buena educación a sus hijos.
2. En España y en Latinoamérica los padres se preocupan de la educación preuniversitaria de los hijos.
3. La gente paga sus gastos en moneda nacional.
4. La gente no quiere ahorrar cuando hay hiperinflación porque el dinero no tiene valor.

Comprensión B
1. No
2. No
3. No
4. No

Comprensión C
1. el dólar
2. la peseta
3. el peso
4. el yen
5. el franco suizo
6. la libra esterlina
7. el bolívar

Comprensión D
  En España y en Latinoamérica las grandes universidades son del estado y son gratis.

FOR THE NATIVE SPEAKER

Algunas monedas tienen un alto valor respecto a otras divisas. Durante los años 80 y 90, el marco alemán y el yen japonés tenían un valor muy superior a otras divisas. ¿Qué desventaja existe con una moneda con un valor muy alto?

INDEPENDENT PRACTICE

Assign any of the following:
1. Workbook, *Un poco más*
2. Exercises on student page 381

381

Descubrimiento Cultural

(The Descubrimiento section is optional.)

PRESENTATION *(pages 382-383)*

A. Before reading, focus on the topic by sharing with students the list of exchange rates taken from a major newspaper. You may distribute photocopies of the list and discuss it with the class.

B. Have students open their books to pages 382-383. Ask them to read the selection silently.

DESCUBRIMIENTO CULTURAL

Ya sabemos que la peseta es la moneda nacional de España y que muchos países de Latinoamérica como México, Colombia, Chile y la Argentina tienen el peso como moneda nacional. Pero las monedas de algunos países llevan nombres interesantes.

La moneda de Guatemala es el quetzal. El quetzal es un ave bonita de plumaje suave, de color verde y rojo, con una cola[1] larga. El quetzal se considera un ave sagrada en Guatemala. En la civilización azteca y maya el quetzal era el ave del paraíso.

La tradicional moneda peruana era el sol. Debido a la hiperinflación el gobierno introdujo una nueva moneda–el inti. Hace algunos años, la hiperinflación de nuevo obligó al cambio. ¿Qué moneda introdujeron entonces? El sol. El nuevo sol tiene el valor de miles de antiguos intis. Entre los antiguos peruanos, los incas, cuya lengua es el quechua, el inti es el sol.

En Venezuela la gente paga sus deudas con bolívares. El bolívar lleva el nombre de Simón Bolívar. Él nació en Caracas en 1783. Recibió su educación en España y en los Estados Unidos. Volvió a Venezuela en 1810 donde tomó parte en la rebelión de la colonia contra la dominación española. Entró triunfante en Caracas en 1813 y fue recibido con el nombre de El Libertador. Continuó luchando contra los españoles en Colombia, Venezuela, Ecuador y el Perú.

¿Han oído hablar de Balboa—Vasco Núñez de Balboa? Pues, él nació en Badajoz, España, en 1475. Atravesó el

La Santa María, réplica de la carabela de Colón, Barcelona, España

382 CAPÍTULO 14

LEARNING FROM REALIA

Refer students to the advertisement for coins on page 382. Have them study the ad and ask: *¿Para qué ocasión emitieron las monedas? ¿Cuántos años representa un "quinto centenario"? ¿Qué representa la abreviatura "PTAS."? Algunas monedas son de 20.000 pesetas, otras de 5.000. ¿Cuál es la diferencia entre las dos monedas? ¿Qué querrá decir "de curso legal"? ¿Cómo se dice eso en inglés?*

istmo de Panamá en 1513 y descubrió el océano Pacífico. Hizo un viaje de exploración por la costa occidental de la América del Sur hasta el Perú, donde fue decapitado por orden de su suegro (el padre de su esposa) en 1517. Y, ¿en qué país es el balboa la moneda nacional? En Panamá, donde el dólar circula libremente. El "balboa" es un "dólar". Hay monedas panameñas, pero los billetes son billetes de dólar.

En Costa Rica y el Salvador la gente usa el colón. El colón lleva el nombre del famoso descubridor del Nuevo Mundo, el genovés Cristóbal Colón, que en 1492 salió del puerto de Palos en el sur de España con tres carabelas—la Pinta, la Niña y la Santa María—rumbo a[2] las Indias. Pero en vez de llegar a las Indias, llegó a las Américas.

[1] cola   *tail*
[2] rumbo a   *towards, in direction of*

La estatua de Simón Bolívar en la plaza Bolívar, Caracas, Venezuela

Vasco Núñez de Balboa descubriendo el océano Pacífico

CAPÍTULO 14   **383**

INTERDISCIPLINARY CONNECTION

Ask students to read the poem "On First Looking into Chapman's Homer" by the English poet John Keats. Ask them if they can find the historical error in the last stanza.

ADDITIONAL PRACTICE

Set up a mock bank with students playing the roles of bank personnel at a new accounts window and a currency exchange desk. Distribute play money, photocopied checks, traveler's checks, and any other appropriate forms you can get from a local bank. Have other students act as customers engaging in various bank transactions studied in this chapter.

DID YOU KNOW?

Spanish children used to learn this rhyme:
*Por Castilla y con Pinzón
Nuevas tierras halló Colón.*
Ask students what they think the rhyme means. Pinzón was one of Columbus' co-captains.

383

REALIDADES

(The Realidades section is optional.)

Bell Ringer Review
Write the following on the board or use BRR Blackline Master 14-8: Write five original sentences. Use your imagination. *¿Qué harías si ganaras la lotería?*

PRESENTATION *(pages 384-385)*

The object of this section is for students to enjoy the photographs. However, if you would like to apply more structured activities to it, here are some suggestions.

A. Ask students what they know about current economic changes taking place in Europe, such as the formation of the new European Economic Community.

B. Ask volunteers to read the captions on the photos. Hold a class discussion on the captions and photographs.

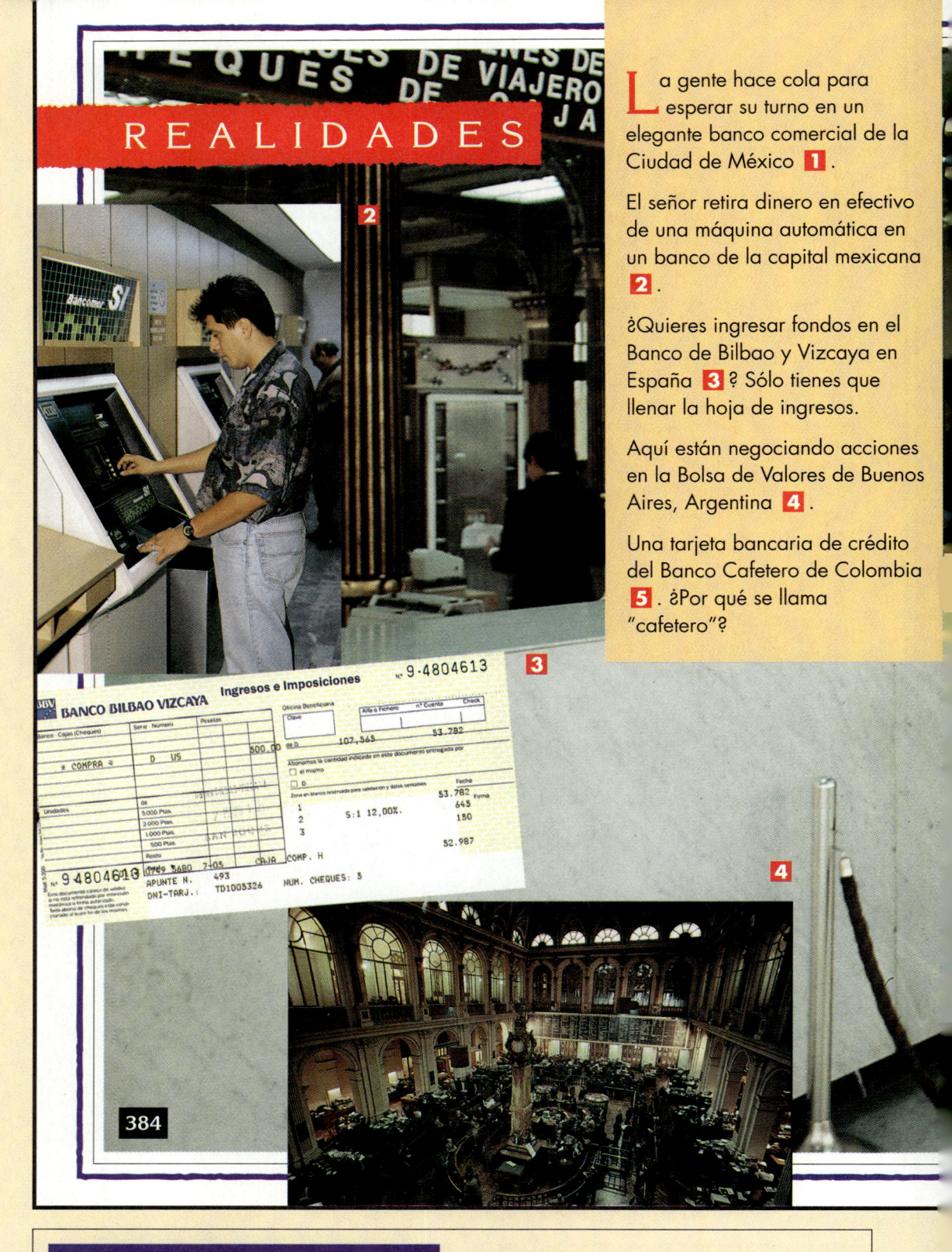

REALIDADES

La gente hace cola para esperar su turno en un elegante banco comercial de la Ciudad de México **1**.

El señor retira dinero en efectivo de una máquina automática en un banco de la capital mexicana **2**.

¿Quieres ingresar fondos en el Banco de Bilbao y Vizcaya en España **3**? Sólo tienes que llenar la hoja de ingresos.

Aquí están negociando acciones en la Bolsa de Valores de Buenos Aires, Argentina **4**.

Una tarjeta bancaria de crédito del Banco Cafetero de Colombia **5**. ¿Por qué se llama "cafetero"?

CRITICAL THINKING ACTIVITY

(Thinking skills: supporting statements with reasons)

Read the following to the class or write it on the board or on an overhead transparency:

¿Cómo prefieres pagar: en efectivo, con una tarjeta de crédito, con un cheque o con un cheque de viajero? Explica por qué.

FOR THE NATIVE SPEAKER

Ask students to find out the following information: *En las bolsas de valores negocian dos tipos de acciones: acciones comunes y acciones preferentes. Busca información en la biblioteca (bajo "economía") sobre los dos tipos de acciones y después explica la diferencia a la clase.*

385

CULMINACIÓN

RECYCLING

The activities in *Comunicación oral* and *Comunicación escrita* sections encourage students to use all the language they have learned in the chapter and to recombine it with material from previous chapters. It is not necessary to do all the activities with all students. Select the ones you consider most appropriate or allow students to choose the ones they wish to do.

Comunicación oral
ANSWERS
Actividad A
  El día de la comida, la comida valía quince dólares.
  Cuando pagó la cuenta, la comida valía veintiún dólares con ochenta y un centavos. Ud. perdió seis dólares con ochenta y un centavos.

Actividades B and C
  Answers will vary.

INFORMAL ASSESSMENT
Activities A, B, and C can be used to assess speaking skills. Use the evaluation criteria given on page 24 of this Teacher's Wraparound Edition.

PAIRED ACTIVITY
Have pairs find the current exchange rate in the newspaper. Each partner takes a turn as a tourist from Spain or a country in Latin America and exchanges whatever amount he/she wishes from the national currency into U.S. dollars. The other partner is the money changer. Students should be sure that exchanges are accurate.

Comunicación escrita
ANSWERS
Actividades A, B, and C
  Answers will vary.

386

CULMINACIÓN

Comunicación oral

A **¿Pagó más o pagó menos?** Ud. estaba viajando por un país latinoamericano. Ud. fue a un restaurante y pagó su cuenta con una tarjeta de crédito. La comida le costó 1.200 pesos. Ud. fue al restaurante el 10 de agosto y el cambio estaba a 80 pesos el dólar. ¿Cuánto le costó la comida?

Pero Ud. no pagó la factura de su tarjeta de crédito el 10 de agosto. La compañía de crédito registró la transacción el 22 de agosto. Entre el día 10 y el 22, habían revaluado el peso y aquel día el tipo de cambio subió a 55 pesos el dólar. ¿Cuánto le costó la comida en dólares? ¿Cuánto perdió o ganó Ud.?

B **Un hermanito travieso.** Ud. le dice a un(a) compañero(a) de clase que su hermanito acaba de hacer las siguientes cosas. Su compañero(a) de clase demuestra su disgusto y replica que le había dicho que no lo hiciera.

1. romper el estéreo
2. manchar la alfombra con jugo de tomate
3. sacar toda tu ropa del armario
4. escribir en los libros y revistas
5. acostarse muy tarde

C **Las quejas.** Dígale a su compañero(a) las cosas que le gustaría a Ud. que hiciera el presidente por el país. También dé una razón por qué el presidente debe hacerlas. Cambien de papel e informen a la clase.

Comunicación escrita

A **Escritor publicitario.** Escriba un anuncio comercial para un banco. Incluya información sobre la tasa de interés que paga, tipos de cuentas y servicios bancarios que presta. Anuncie que el banco cobra intereses muy bajos por préstamos *(loans)* e hipotecas *(mortgages)*. Podría anunciar también que el banco ofrece regalos especiales a los clientes que abren una nueva cuenta con cierta cantidad mínima.

B **Un anuncio comercial.** Trabaje con un(a) compañero(a) de clase. Usen la información de la Actividad A para crear un anuncio comercial para la televisión. Escriban un guión *(script)* y ensayen el anuncio. Luego lo pueden presentar a la clase o a un grupo de compañeros de clase.

386 CAPÍTULO 14

DID YOU KNOW?

The Spanish language is called either *español* or *castellano*. Spanish is the language that was spoken in *Castilla*. There were two other Latin-derived languages on the Iberian Peninsula: Castilian in the center, Galaico/Portuguese in the west and Catalan/Provençale in the east. In Spain, Castilian came to predominate, but the other languages, and Basque as well, still thrive. The ad on page 387 is written in *gallego* or Galician, the variant of Portuguese spoken in northwestern Spain. Have students try to translate the title of the ad into *castellano*. (The rest of the ad is in *castellano*.)

C **Hay que ahorrar, pero…** Escriba cinco razones por qué se debe ahorrar dinero. Luego escriba dos circunstancias bajo las que no es razonable o posible ahorrar.

Reintegración

A **En el hotel.** Completen.

1. Mucha gente come en el ___ del hotel.
2. Después de comer los clientes piden la ___ . Se la pagan al mesero o la pagan en la ___ .
3. Aun si el servicio está incluido, los clientes le dejan una ___ al mesero, sobre todo si les ha dado buen servicio.
4. Al salir de un hotel, los clientes abandonan el cuarto y luego pasan a la ___ .
5. Ellos le piden su ___ al cajero.
6. La cuenta o ___ contiene una lista de todos los ___ del cliente.
7. El cliente mira la cuenta para verificar el ___ .
8. Muchos clientes pagan con una ___ . Los clientes pueden pagar con ___ o ___ , pero la mayoría de los hoteles no aceptan ___ personales.

B **No en el pasado.** Sigan el modelo.

> Él preferiría que yo fuera al banco.
> Él prefiere que yo vaya al banco.

1. Él preferiría que yo hablara con el cajero.
2. Él quería que yo hiciera un depósito.
3. Me aconsejó que no retirara dinero de la cuenta.
4. Yo quería que él me cambiara el dinero.
5. Yo le pedí al cambista que me diera billetes pequeños.
6. Él me pidió que llenara un formulario y que firmara el cheque de viajero.

Vocabulario

SUSTANTIVOS
el banco
la caja
la ventanilla
el/la cajero(a)
el/la empleado(a) del banco
el dinero
el dinero en efectivo
el billete
la moneda
el cheque
el cheque de viajero
el cambio
la oficina de cambio
el/la cambista
el tipo de cambio
la tasa de cambio
la cuenta
la cuenta de ahorros
la libreta
el depósito
el ingreso
el retiro
el formulario de retiro
la cuenta corriente
el talonario
la chequera
el estado de banco
  (de cuenta)
el saldo

VERBOS
firmar
endosar
cobrar
depositar
ingresar
retirar
sacar
cambiar

verificar
conciliar
llenar

OTRAS PALABRAS Y EXPRESIONES
¿Cuál es el tipo de cambio?

CAPÍTULO 14   **387**

CAPÍTULO 15
Scope and Sequence pages 388-413

Topics	Functions	Structure	Culture
Dating and wedding customs	How to discuss dating customs in Spanish-speaking countries How to describe a typical wedding ceremony How to talk about actions that may or may not take place	El subjuntivo en cláusulas adverbiales El subjuntivo con *aunque* El subjuntivo con cláusulas adverbiales de tiempo	Dating, courtship, and marriage in Spanish-speaking countries A wedding in Buenos Aires A Jewish wedding

CAPÍTULO 15

Situation Cards

The Situation Cards simulate real-life situations that require students to communicate in Spanish, exactly as though they were in a Spanish-speaking country. The Situation Cards operate on the assumption that the person to whom the message is to be conveyed understands no English. Therefore, students must focus on producing the Spanish vocabulary and structures necessary to negotiate the situations successfully. For additional information, see the Introduction to the Situation Cards in the Situation Cards Envelope.

Communication Transparency

The illustration seen in this Communication Transparency consists of a synthesis of the two vocabulary (Palabras 1&2) presentations found in this chapter. It has been created in order to present this chapter's vocabulary in a new context, and also to recycle vocabulary learned in previous chapters. The Communication Transparency consists of original art. Following are some specific uses:

1. as a cue to stimulate conversation and writing activities
2. for listening comprehension activities
3. to review and reteach vocabulary
4. as a review for chapter and unit tests

CAPÍTULO 15
Print Resources

Lesson Plans

Workbook
	Pages
◆ Palabras 1	168
◆ Palabras 2	169-170
◆ Estructura	171-175
◆ Un poco más	176-177
◆ Mi autobiografía	178

Communication Activities Masters
◆ Palabras 1	98-99
◆ Palabras 2	100-101
◆ Estructura	102-105

9 Bell Ringer Reviews
41-42

Chapter Situation Cards A B C D

Chapter Quizzes
◆ Palabras 1	70
◆ Palabras 2	71
◆ Estructura	72-74

Testing Program
◆ Listening Comprehension	84
◆ Reading and Writing	85-88
◆ Proficiency	137
◆ Speaking	158

Nosotros y Nuestro Mundo
- ◆ Nuestro Conocimiento Académico *Sociología: Endogamia y exogamia*
- ◆ Nuestro Idioma *Cláusulas adverbiales con aunque; Cláusulas adverbiales de tiempo*
- ◆ Nuestra Cultura "*Gente conmigo*"
- ◆ Nuestra Literatura "*Bodas*" de Pablo Neruda
- ◆ Nuestra Creatividad
- ◆ Nuestras Diversiones

CAPÍTULO 15
Multimedia Resources

CD-ROM Interactive Textbook Disc 4
Chapter 15 Student Edition
- ◆ Palabras 1
- ◆ Palabras 2
- ◆ Estructura
- ◆ Conversación
- ◆ Lectura y cultura
- ◆ Hispanoparlantes
- ◆ Realidades
- ◆ Culminación
- ◆ Prueba

Audio Cassette Program with Student Tape Manual
Cassette	Pages
◆ 9A Palabras 1	273-274
◆ 9A Palabras 2	274-275
◆ 9A Estructura	275-276
◆ 9A Conversación	276
◆ 9A Segunda parte	277-278

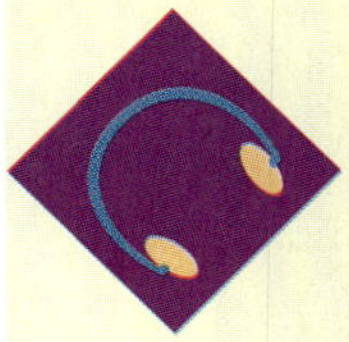

Compact Disc Program with Student Tape Manual
◆ CD 9 Palabras 1	273-274
◆ CD 9 Palabras 2	274-275
◆ CD 9 Estructura	275-276
◆ CD 9 Conversación	276
◆ CD 9 Segunda parte	277-278

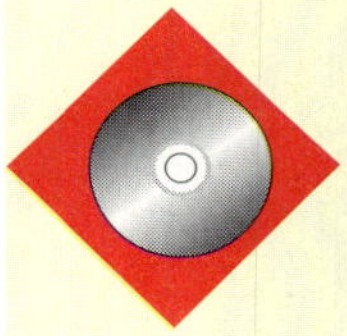

Overhead Transparencies Binder
- ◆ Vocabulary 15.1 (A&B); 15.2 (A&B)
- ◆ Communication C-15
- ◆ Maps
- ◆ Fine Art (with Blackline Master Activities)

Video Program
- ◆ Videocassette
- ◆ Video Activities Booklet 38-40
- ◆ Videodisc
- ◆ Video Activities Booklet 38-40

Computer Software (Macintosh, IBM, Apple)
- ◆ Practice Disk
   Palabras 1 y 2
   Estructura
- ◆ Test Generator Disk
   Chapter Test
   Customized Test

388B

CAPÍTULO 15

CHAPTER OVERVIEW
In this chapter, students will learn to describe and discuss dating and wedding customs in Spanish-speaking countries. Additional uses of the subjunctive are presented. The cultural focus of Chapter 15 is on dating, courtship, and marriage in Hispanic countries.

CHAPTER OBJECTIVES
By the end of this chapter, students will know:
1. vocabulary associated with dating
2. vocabulary associated with engagements
3. vocabulary associated with weddings
4. the use of the subjunctive in various kinds of adverbial clauses

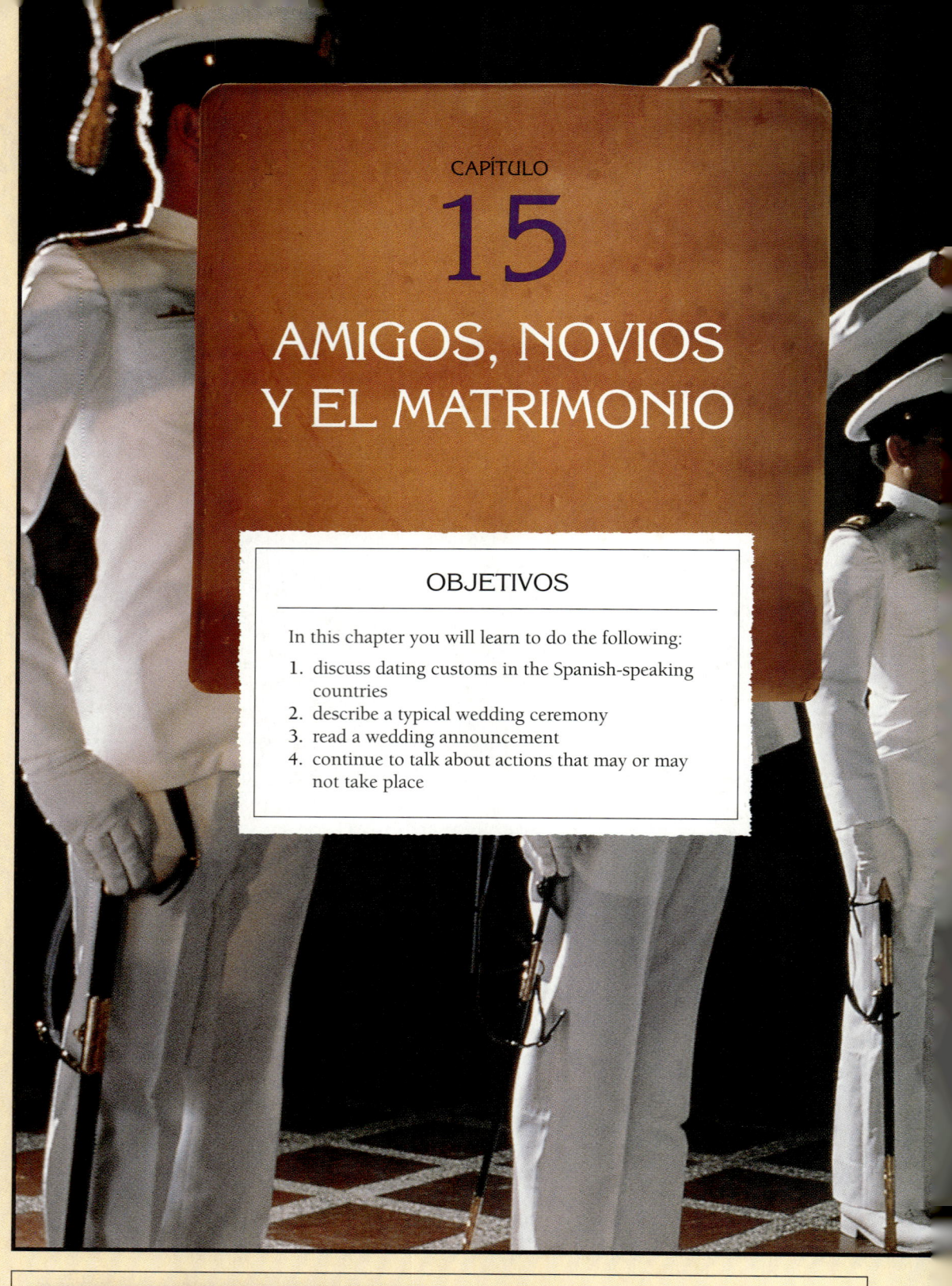

CAPÍTULO 15
AMIGOS, NOVIOS Y EL MATRIMONIO

OBJETIVOS

In this chapter you will learn to do the following:
1. discuss dating customs in the Spanish-speaking countries
2. describe a typical wedding ceremony
3. read a wedding announcement
4. continue to talk about actions that may or may not take place

CHAPTER PROJECTS
(optional)
1. Have students prepare wedding announcements and/or wedding invitations.
2. Have students prepare an advertisement for engagement and wedding rings.
3. Have students visit a travel agency and collect brochures relating to honeymoon places. Then have them write captions in Spanish and use the materials to create a bulletin board display.

CHAPTER 15 RESOURCES

1. Workbook
2. Student Tape Manual
3. Audio Cassette 9A
4. Vocabulary Transparencies
5. Bell Ringer Review Blackline Masters
6. Communication Activities Masters
7. Computer Software: Practice and Test Generator
8. Video Cassette, Chapter 15
9. Video Activities Booklet, Chapter 15
10. Situation Cards
11. Chapter Quizzes
12. Testing Program

Pacing

Chapter 15 will require eight to ten class sessions. Pacing will depend on the length of the class period, the age of the students, and student aptitude.

LEARNING FROM PHOTOS

Have students say all they can about the photo on pages 388-389. Cue with questions such as: ¿Qué están celebrando? ¿Cómo se viste la novia? ¿Qué profesión tiene el novio? El joven saluda a sus compañeros. ¿Qué tipo de saludo es?

389

VOCABULARIO
PALABRAS 1

Vocabulary Teaching Resources

1. Vocabulary Transparencies, 15.1 (A & B)
2. Audio Cassette 9A
3. Student Tape Manual, *Palabras 1*
4. Workbook, *Palabras 1*
5. Communication Activities Masters, *Palabras 1, A & B*
6. Chapter Quizzes, *Palabras 1*

Bell Ringer Review

Write the following on the board or use BRR Blackline Master 15-1: Name five occasions for celebration in the Hispanic family.

PRESENTATION (pages 390-391)

A. With books closed, refer to Vocabulary Transparencies 15.1 (A & B) and have students repeat the new words, phrases, and sentences after you or Cassette 9A.

B. Have students open their books and read the new words, phrases, and sentences.

VOCABULARIO

PALABRAS 1

EL COMPROMISO

la pareja

la sortija de compromiso

el anillo de boda

la dueña

los novios

390 CAPÍTULO 15

ADDITIONAL PRACTICE

Show Vocabulary Transparencies 15.1 (A & B) and have students describe each illustration saying as much as they can. This acitivity can also serve as an informal assessment.

Te quiero, José.
Te quiero a ti también, Elena.

La pareja tiene una cita.
Salen juntos.
Son novios.

Se están enamorando.
Se quieren mucho.

Se comprometen.
Anuncian su compromiso.

Los padres de los novios se conocen antes de que los jóvenes se casen.
Se conocen antes de que tenga lugar el enlace nupcial.

el marido y la mujer
el esposo y la esposa
el matrimonio

CAPÍTULO 15

ABOUT THE LANGUAGE

Un anillo is literally "a ring." *Un anillo de boda* is "a wedding band." *Una sortija* is a ring with stones or other adornment. Engagement rings can also be *anillos de compromiso*. Wedding rings are sometimes called *arras* or *alianzas*. *Las arras* used to be thirteen gold coins that were given by the groom to the bride in exchange for her dowry (*la dote*).

DID YOU KNOW?

Until recent years, it was customary in Hispanic countries for a dowry to accompany the bride. The value of the dowry corresponded to the status of the bride's family. Affluent families would provide a dowry of lands, money, or investments. Farm families' dowries consisted of livestock or acreage. Poorer families might provide little more than clothing and linens. The custom of the dowry has virtually disappeared except in some rural areas.

Ejercicios

PRESENTATION (page 392)

Ejercicio A
Exercise A can be done with books open or closed.

Extension of Ejercicio A
Speaking
After completing Exercise A, call on a volunteer to read the entire exercise as a story.

Ejercicio B
Exercise B is to be done with books open.

ANSWERS

Ejercicio A
1. Sí, José y Elena se conocen.
2. Sí, salen juntos cada fin de semana.
3. Sí, los jóvenes se están enamorando.
4. Sí, José quiere mucho a Elena.
5. Sí, Elena quiere a José.
6. Sí, la pareja se quiere mucho.
7. Sí, se van a comprometer.
8. Sí, van a anunciar el compromiso el mes que viene.

Ejercicio B
1. a
2. b
3. b
4. a
5. b

Ejercicios

A Una pareja romántica. Contesten.

1. ¿Se conocen José y Elena?
2. ¿Salen juntos cada fin de semana?
3. ¿Se están enamorando los jóvenes?
4. ¿José quiere mucho a Elena?
5. ¿Y Elena quiere a José?
6. ¿Se quiere mucho la pareja?
7. ¿Se van a comprometer?
8. ¿Van a anunciar el compromiso el mes que viene?

B Los enamorados. Escojan.

1. Los novios son ___ .
   a. una pareja   b. una cita
2. El novio le da a la novia ___ cuando se comprometen.
   a. un anillo de boda   b. una sortija
3. La ___ es una chaperona.
   a. esposa   b. dueña
4. El marido y la mujer son ___ .
   a. un matrimonio   b. comprometidos
5. No van a seguir saliendo juntos a menos que ___ .
   a. se conozcan   b. se enamoren

392   CAPÍTULO 15

LA POPULARIDAD ETERNA DE LOS DIAMANTES DE COMPROMISO

LEARNING FROM PHOTOS/REALIA

1. Have students comment on the advertisement on page 392. You may wish to ask the following questions: ¿Para qué es el anuncio? ¿Para quiénes es el anuncio? ¿Qué llevan la mayoría de los anillos de compromiso? ¿Qué es un "solitario"?
2. In regard to the wedding photo and invitation on page 393, have students say all they can about them. Cue with questions such as: ¿Cómo se llaman los novios? ¿Cuál será el nombre completo de "Salva"? ¿Cuáles son los apellidos de las familias? ¿Dónde será la ceremonia? ¿Qué van a tener después de la ceremonia? ¿Dónde?

C El amor y el matrimonio. ¿Sí o no?

1. Los novios no serán un matrimonio hasta que se casen.
2. En Latinoamérica los jóvenes se casan antes de que sus padres se conozcan.
3. Los jóvenes se casan antes de enamorarse.
4. El enlace matrimonial (nupcial) tiene lugar el día del casamiento.
5. Los enamorados se quieren.

D Palabras relacionadas. Escojan.

1. comprometerse
2. casarse
3. enamorarse
4. conocer
5. anunciar
6. enlazar

a. los casados, el casamiento
b. el conocimiento
c. el enlace
d. el anuncio
e. el/la comprometido(a), el compromiso
f. el/la enamorado(a)

CAPÍTULO 15   **393**

Ejercicios

PRESENTATION *(page 393)*

Ejercicios C and D
Exercises C and D are to be done with books open.

Extension of *Ejercicio C*
After completing Exercise C, have students correct the false statements.

ANSWERS
Ejercicio C
1. Sí
2. No
3. No
4. Sí
5. Sí

Ejercicio D
1. e
2. a
3. f
4. b
5. d
6. c

DID YOU KNOW?

You may wish to tell students that the custom of the *dueña* has disappeared. Traditionally the role of the *dueña* was played by a widowed or single female relative, usually the sister of one of the parents, who lived with the family.

INDEPENDENT PRACTICE

Assign any of the following:
1. Workbook, *Palabras 1*
2. Communication Activities Masters, *Palabras 1, A & B*
3. Exercises on student page 392-393

393

VOCABULARIO
PALABRAS 2

Vocabulary Teaching Resources
1. Vocabulary Transparencies 15.2 (*A & B*)
2. Audio Cassette 9A
3. Student Tape Manual, *Palabras 2*
4. Workbook, *Palabras 2*
5. Communication Activities Masters, *Palabras 2, C & D*
6. Chapter Quizzes, *Palabras 2*
7. Computer Software, *Vocabulario*

Bell Ringer Review
Write the following on the board or use BRR Blackline Master 15-2: Write as many terms for members of the family as you can remember.

PRESENTATION (pages 394-395)

A. Have students close their books. Model the *Palabras 2* vocabulary using Vocabulary Transparencies 15.2 (*A & B*). Have students repeat the new material after you or Cassette 9A.
B. Call individuals to the screen and have them point to the appropriate illustration as you say: *Son las damas de honor. Es el padrino.*
C. Have students open their books to pages 394-395 and ask them to read the words, phrases, and sentences aloud.
D. Ask questions to elicit the new vocabulary. For example: *¿Quiénes se casan? ¿Qué intercambian los novios? ¿Quiénes dan la recepción? ¿Quiénes reciben a los invitados? ¿Qué les dan los invitados a los novios? ¿Quién hace un brindis? ¿Para qué les brindó? ¿Quiénes salen para su viaje de novios? ¿Dónde van a pasar su luna de miel?*

394

VOCABULARIO
PALABRAS 2

LA CEREMONIA

la boda — la iglesia — el altar

el matrimonio

la madrina — el padrino

los pajes de honor — las damas de honor

394 CAPÍTULO 15

PANTOMIME

Have students mime the following actions:
Intercambien Uds. anillos de boda.
Reciban Uds. a los invitados.
Den Uds. la enhorabuena.
Hagan Uds. un brindis.
Salgan Uds. para su viaje de novios.

Los novios se casan.
Durante la ceremonia intercambian anillos de boda.

la recepción

el banquete

Los padres de la novia dan una recepción.
Los novios reciben a los invitados.
Los invitados les dan la enhorabuena. ¡Felicitaciones!

El padrino hace un brindis.
Brindó por los novios.
Les brindó para que tuvieran mucha felicidad y muy buena suerte.

Los recién casados salen para su viaje de novios.
Van a pasar su luna de miel en Europa.

CAPÍTULO 15

E. When presenting the wedding vocabulary, you may have students stage a mock wedding ceremony.

Vocabulary Expansion

You may provide students with the following additional vocabulary in order to talk about weddings:
el ramo de novia (bouquet)
el velo (veil)
el smoking (tuxedo)
el frac/el traje de etiqueta (tails)
el traje de novia (wedding gown)

ABOUT THE LANGUAGE

"The honeymoon" is literally *la luna de miel*. It refers to the period of time immediately after the wedding. The *viaje de novios* is the traditional honeymoon trip.

Ejercicios

PRESENTATION (page 396)

Ejercicios A and B
Exercises A and B are to be done with books open.

ANSWERS

Ejercicio A
1. dos pajes
2. la madrina
3. los novios
4. el padrino
5. dos damas de honor

Ejercicio B
1. la iglesia
2. el anillo de boda
3. los pajes
4. las damas de honor
5. la sortija de compromiso
6. el padrino
7. la madrina
8. la recepción
9. el brindis
10. el viaje de novios

Ejercicios

A ¿Quién es? Identifiquen según el dibujo.

1.   2.   3.   4.   5.

B ¿Qué es o quién es? Identifiquen.
1. El lugar donde tiene lugar la mayoría de las ceremonias nupciales religiosas.
2. Es de oro. Durante la boda el novio se lo pone en el dedo de la novia y viceversa.
3. Son los amigos del novio. Asisten a la boda y toman parte en la ceremonia.
4. Estas mujeres desfilan con la novia y le sirven durante la ceremonia. Son amigas o parientes.
5. Es de oro y frecuentemente tiene diamantes. El novio se la da a la novia cuando se comprometen.
6. En la boda este señor está siempre al lado del novio. Es su hombre de confianza.
7. Esta señorita o señora es para la novia lo que es el hombre de confianza para el novio.
8. Lo que dan los padres de la novia después de la ceremonia nupcial.
9. Lo que hace el padrino durante la recepción.
10. El viaje que hacen los recién casados.

396 CAPÍTULO 15

LEARNING FROM REALIA

Have students say all they can about the advertisement on page 397. Ask questions such as: *¿Para qué es el anuncio? ¿Cómo se llama el hotel? ¿Para quiénes en especial es el anuncio?*

C Las bodas. Contesten.
1. ¿Dónde tiene lugar la ceremonia nupcial religiosa?
2. En los Estados Unidos, ¿es necesario tener una ceremonia civil y otra religiosa?
3. ¿Quiénes acompañan a los novios durante la ceremonia?
4. ¿Qué intercambian los novios?
5. ¿Qué dan los padres de la novia después de la ceremonia?
6. ¿Qué les dan los invitados a los recién casados?

Comunicación
Palabras 1 y 2

A Mis opiniones. Conteste a las siguientes preguntas personales. Si quiere divertirse, puede dar respuestas falsas.
1. ¿Sales siempre con el/la mismo(a) muchacho(a)?
2. ¿Tienes novio(a)?
3. ¿Van Uds. a la misma escuela?
4. ¿Hace cuánto tiempo que Uds. salen juntos?
5. ¿Conoces a sus padres?
6. ¿Adónde van cuando tienen cita?
7. ¿Quién paga?
8. ¿Cuántos años quieres tener cuando te cases?
9. ¿Cuántos hijos quieres tener?
10. ¿Quieres casarte con una persona menor o mayor que tú?

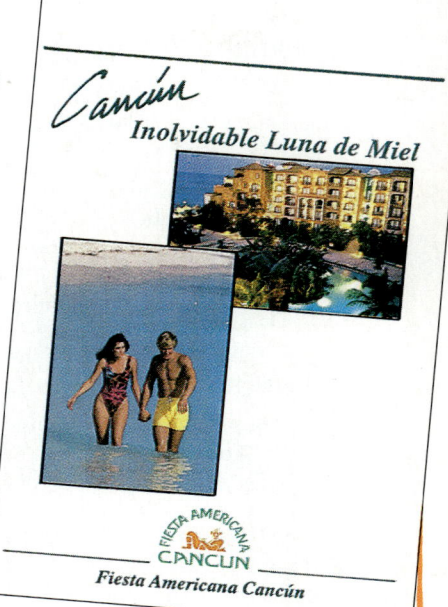

B El novio o la novia ideal. Prepare una lista de las características que Ud. quiere en un(a) novio(a). Luego compare su lista con la de un(a) compañero(a) de clase. Decidan si Uds. podrían tener el/la mismo(a) novio(a).

C No te cases. Escríbale una carta a un(a) amigo(a) donde le explica por qué no es conveniente casarse muy joven.

D En la agencia de viajes. Ud. es el/la cliente y un(a) compañero(a) de clase es un(a) agente de viajes. Ud. está en su oficina para hacer reservaciones para su viaje de novios. Preparen la conversación que Uds. tienen.

E El/la más popular. Ud. está entrevistando al/a la muchacho(a) más popular de su escuela (un[a] compañero[a] de clase). Pregúntele si en este momento tiene novio(a), si ha tenido muchos(as) novios(as), si prefiere salir en pareja o con un grupo de amigos, si sale entre semana o solamente los fines de semana, y por qué cree que es el/la muchacho(a) más popular de la escuela.

CAPÍTULO 15   397

ESTRUCTURA

Structure Teaching Resources
1. Workbook, *Estructura*
2. Student Tape Manual, *Estructura*
3. Audio Cassette 9A
4. Communication Activities Masters, *Estructura*, A-C
5. Chapter Quizzes, *Estructura*
6. Computer Software, *Estructura*

Bell Ringer Review
Write the following on the board or use BRR Blackline Master 15-4: ¿Por qué irías a los lugares siguientes?:
1. un balneario
2. una estación de esquí
3. el campo
4. un camping
5. una ciudad

El subjuntivo en cláusulas adverbiales

PRESENTATION (page 398)
A. Have students open their books to page 398. Lead them through steps 1-3.
B. Call on volunteers to read the expressions in step 1 aloud.
C. Have students read the sample sentences in step 3 aloud.

PAIRED ACTIVITY
Have pairs invent conversations which might take place between the two young people in the photo at the top of page 399.

ESTRUCTURA

El subjuntivo en cláusulas adverbiales
Using the Subjunctive After Certain Conjunctions

1. The subjunctive is used after the following expressions.

para que	so that
de manera que	so that
de modo que	so that
con tal de que	provided that
sin que	without, unless
a menos que	unless

2. Note the logic in the use of the subjunctive. The subjunctive is used because the information in the clause is not definite.

   El profesor habla claramente para que (de manera que) sus alumnos comprendan.
   The teacher speaks clearly so that his students may understand.

   Even though the teacher tries his/her best to explain the lesson clearly so that all students will understand, there still exists the possibility that some do not understand.

3. Note that the tense of the verb in the main clause determines the tense of the subjunctive in the dependent clause.

MAIN	DEPENDENT
Present Future	Present subjunctive
Preterite Imperfect Conditional	Imperfect subjunctive

   Él irá con tal de que Ud. vaya.
   Él iría con tal de que Ud. fuera.
   Él lo hace para que Ud. no tenga que hacerlo.
   Él lo hizo para que Ud. no tuviera que hacerlo.

398   CAPÍTULO 15

FOR THE NATIVE SPEAKER
Have students do the following exercise. *Hay que unir las dos oraciones usando la palabra o frase indicada y cambiando el verbo si es necesario.*
1. Todos vamos a asistir. No hay sitio. (a menos que)
2. Iría. Tú me acompañabas. (con tal de que)
3. No lo llamaron. No se incomodó. (para que)
4. Creen que lo pueden hacer. Nos quejamos. (sin que)
5. Te lo digo. Sabes lo que pasa. (para que)
6. Llevaría a Teresa. No quería ir. (a menos que)
7. Ellos te pagarán. Les das un recibo. (con tal de que)
8. Tratamos de explicárselo. Él se ofendió. (sin que)

Ejercicios

A **Todo para que yo comprenda.** Contesten.

1. ¿Él te lee la carta en español para que tú la comprendas?
2. ¿Él te habla despacio de manera que tú sepas lo que está diciendo?
3. ¿Él hablará más despacio con tal de que tú le digas que lo haga?

B **Todo para que yo comprendiera.** Contesten.

1. ¿Él te leyó la carta en español para que tú la comprendieras?
2. ¿Él te habló despacio para que supieras lo que estaba diciendo?
3. ¿Tú comprendiste sin que él tradujera?
4. ¿Él hablaría más despacio con tal de que tú le dijeras que lo hiciera?

C **No lo haré solo.** Contesten según el modelo.

> ¿Lo harás?
> Sí, lo haré con tal de que tú lo hagas también.

1. ¿Harás el viaje?
2. ¿Irás?
3. ¿Tomarás el avión?
4. ¿Te quedarás en un hotel de lujo?
5. ¿Esquiarás en el agua?

D **No lo haría.** Contesten según el modelo.

> ¿Lo harías?
> No, no lo haría sin que ellos lo hicieran.

1. ¿Irías al partido?
2. ¿Comprarías las entradas?
3. ¿Te sentarías en la primera fila?
4. ¿Mirarías el partido en la televisión?

Un partido de béisbol en Caracas, Venezuela

CAPÍTULO 15   399

Bell Ringer Review
Write the following on the board or use BRR Blackline Master 15-5: ¿Que hace Ud. cuando...
1. ... hace buen tiempo?
2. ... hace mal tiempo?
3. ... hace calor?
4. ... hace frío?

El subjuntivo con aunque

PRESENTATION *(page 400)*

A. Have students open their books to page 400. Lead them through steps 1-2.
B. Have volunteers read the sample sentences aloud.

Ejercicios

PRESENTATION *(page 400)*

Ejercicios A and B
  Exercises A and B can be done with books open or closed. Exercise B contrasts the use of the subjunctive with that of the indicative.

ANSWERS

Ejercicio A
1. Sí, iría a la playa aunque hiciera muy mal tiempo.
2. Sí, nadaría aunque estuviera fría el agua.
3. Sí, me metería en el agua aunque no tuviera traje de baño.
4. Sí, me sentaría en la playa aunque no hubiera sol.

Ejercicio B
1. Sí, iré a la playa aunque hace tan mal tiempo.
2. Sí, iré a la playa aunque llueva.
3. Sí, nadaré aunque el agua esté muy fría.
4. Sí, nadaré aunque el agua está tan fría.
5. Sí, nadaré aunque no tengo traje de baño.
6. Sí, me sentaré en la playa aunque no hay sol.

400

El subjuntivo con *aunque*   *Using the Subjunctive With Aunque*

1. *Aunque* ("although, even though") can be followed by either the subjunctive or the indicative depending upon the meaning.

   Ellos saldrán aunque llueva.
   Ellos saldrán aunque llueve.

   The first sentence uses the subjunctive because they will go out even if it rains and it is not sure that it will rain. The second sentence uses the indicative. The meaning here is that they will go out even though it is raining and it is a fact that it is raining. Since it is a fact, there is no reason to use the subjunctive.

2. Note that the tense of the verb in the main clause determines whether the present or imperfect subjunctive is used.

   Se casarán aunque no tengan mucho dinero.
   Se casarían aunque no tuvieran mucho dinero.

A Te gusta mucho la playa. Contesten con *sí*.
1. ¿Irías a la playa aunque hiciera muy mal tiempo?
2. ¿Nadarías aunque estuviera fría el agua?
3. ¿Te meterías en el agua aunque no tuvieras traje de baño?
4. ¿Te sentarías en la playa aunque no hubiera sol?

B ¿Estás seguro(a) que irás? Contesten con *sí*.
1. ¡Qué mal tiempo está haciendo! ¿Irás a la playa aunque hace tan mal tiempo?
2. Creo que va a llover. ¿Irás a la playa aunque llueva?
3. Es posible que el agua esté fría. ¿Nadarás aunque esté muy fría?
4. Aquí el agua siempre está fría. ¿Nadarás aunque está tan fría?
5. Pero no tienes traje de baño. ¿Nadarás aunque no lo tienes?
6. Está completamente nublado. ¿Te sentarás en la playa aunque no hay sol?

400   CAPÍTULO 15

INDEPENDENT PRACTICE

Assign any of the following:
1. Workbook, *Estructura*
2. Communication Activities Masters, *Estructura*, B
3. Exercises on student pages 400–401

C No importa. Escojan.

1. Ayer ellos fueron a la playa aunque ____ muy mal tiempo.
   a. hacía   b. hiciera

2. A Carlos no le importa. Él nadaría aunque el agua ____ a cinco grados.
   a. estaba   b. estuviera

3. Él está loco. Se metió en el agua aunque no ____ traje de baño.
   a. tenía   b. tuviera

4. Él me dijo que no sabía la temperatura del agua pero que nadaría aunque ____ muy fría.
   a. estaba   b. estuviera

El subjuntivo con cláusulas adverbiales de tiempo

Using the Subjunctive With Time Expressions

1. Study the following adverbial time expressions.

cuando	when
en cuanto	as soon as
tan pronto como	as soon as
hasta que	until
después de que	after

2. Observe the following sentences.

   Yo lo veré cuando llegue.
   Le hablaré tan pronto como lo vea.

   Yo lo vi cuando llegó.
   Le hablé tan pronto como lo vi.
   Le saludé en cuanto bajó del tren.

   Note that in the first set of sentences the subjunctive was used. Since the action of each sentence is in the future, the action in the time clause has not yet occurred and it cannot be assured that it will occur. It may take place and it may not. For this reason the subjunctive must be used.

   In the second set of sentences the indicative was used because the action of each sentence is in the past, the event already took place. The indicative is used because the verb states what in reality happened.

3. The adverbial conjunction of time *antes de que* is an exception. It is always followed by the subjunctive, even in the past.

   Él saldrá antes de que los otros vuelvan.
   Él salió antes de que los otros volvieran.

CAPÍTULO 15   **401**

PRESENTATION (page 401)

Ejercicio C
Exercise C is to be done with books open.

Ejercicio C
1. a
2. b
3. a
4. b

El subjuntivo con cláusulas adverbiales de tiempo

PRESENTATION *(page 401)*
A. Have students open their books to page 401. Lead them through topics 1-3.
B. Call on volunteers to read the sample sentences and time expressions aloud.

FOR THE NATIVE SPEAKER

Have a group of students develop a short story based on the photograph on page 401. Say: *Usando la foto como inspiración, escriban ustedes un cuento corto. En el cuento deben indicar quiénes son las dos personas, qué relación existe entre ellos, la razón por la que están en la estación de ferrocarril, cuál es el problema, si es que hay uno, etc.*

Ejercicios

PRESENTATION (page 402)

Ejercicios A and B
Exercises A and B can be done with books open or closed.

ANSWERS

Ejercicio A
Answers will vary.
1. Sí, (No, no) veré a mi primo una vez más antes de que se case.
2. Sí, felicitaré a los novios en cuanto salgan de la iglesia.
3. Sí, les llevaré un regalo cuando vaya a la recepción.
4. Sí, (No, no) los veré después de que regresen (vuelvan) de su luna de miel.

Ejercicio B
Answers will vary.
1. Sí, (No, no) vi a mi primo antes de que se casara.
2. Sí, les di la enhorabuena a los novios en cuanto salieron de la iglesia.
3. Sí les llevé un regalo cuando fui a la recepción.
4. Sí, (No, no) los vi cuando regresaron (volvieron) de su luna de miel.

Ejercicios

A La boda de mi primo. Contesten.
1. ¿Verás a tu primo una vez más antes de que se case?
2. ¿Felicitarás a los novios en cuanto salgan de la iglesia?
3. ¿Les llevarás un regalo cuando vayas a la recepción?
4. ¿Los verás después de que regresen (vuelvan) de su luna de miel?

Pedro Ruiz Alarcón   Anastasio Pérez Tomé
Ester Muñyoz Carrión   Hilda Aparicio Yábar

Tienen el gusto de participarles el enlace de sus hijos

Mónica y Enrique

é invitarles a la ceremonia religiosa, que se realizará
el día 30 de Junio a las 3 p.m. en la Iglesia de La Merced

Lima   Junio de 1994

B La boda de mi primo. Contesten.
1. ¿Viste a tu primo antes de que se casara?
2. ¿Les diste la enhorabuena a los novios en cuanto salieron de la iglesia?
3. ¿Les llevaste un regalo cuando fuiste a la recepción?
4. ¿Los viste cuando regresaron (volvieron) de su luna de miel?

Una boda en Chincheros, Perú

CAPÍTULO 15

LEARNING FROM REALIA

1. Have students describe the advertisement at the top of page 402. Cue with questions such as: ¿Cómo se llama la compañía del anuncio? ¿Cuál es el producto de la compañía? ¿De qué ciudad y país viene el anuncio? ¿Cómo puede una persona comunicarse con Orly?
2. Have students say everything they can about the wedding invitation on page 402.

You may wish to ask questions such as: ¿Qué es esta tarjeta? ¿Quiénes son los novios? ¿Cuál es la fecha de la boda? ¿Quiénes son las personas que aparecen en la parte de arriba? ¿Cuándo y dónde es la boda?

C ¿Cuándo irás? Completen con el verbo indicado.

Iré tan pronto como ellos me ___ .

1. pagar
2. llamar
3. invitar
4. escribir
5. avisar
6. ver

D ¿Cuándo fuiste? Completen con el verbo indicado.

Yo fui en cuanto ellos me ___ .

1. pagar
2. llamar
3. invitar
4. escribir
5. avisar
6. ver

E Las bodas. Completen.

1. Los invitados llegarán a la iglesia antes de que ___ los novios. (llegar)
2. Ellos entrarán en la iglesia antes de que ___ los novios. (entrar)
3. Los invitados se sentaron antes de que ___ la marcha nupcial. (empezar)
4. El cura les dio la bendición antes de que ___ la ceremonia. (terminar)
5. Los novios no se levantaron para salir antes de que ___ el órgano. (sonar)

CAPÍTULO 15

Ejercicios

PRESENTATION (page 403)

Ejercicios C, D, and E

Exercises C, D, and E can be done with books open or closed.

Extension of Ejercicio E
Speaking

After completing Exercise E, call on one volunteer to read the entire exercise as a story.

ANSWERS

Ejercicio C
1. paguen
2. llamen
3. inviten
4. escriban
5. avisen
6. vean

Ejercicio D
1. pagaron
2. llamaron
3. invitaron
4. escribieron
5. avisaron
6. vieron

Ejercicio E
1. lleguen
2. entren
3. empezara
4. terminara
5. sonara

LEARNING FROM REALIA AND PHOTOS

1. Refer students to the two photos of weddings on pages 402-403. Have students describe them in as much detail as possible. Then have them compare and contrast the two weddings shown. Cue with questions such as: ¿Cuáles son algunas diferencias que notan ustedes entre las dos bodas?

2. Ask students to comment on the ad on page 403. Ask questions such as: ¿Qué clase de arras son éstas? ¿Cómo "personalizan" las arras?

CONVERSACIÓN

Bell Ringer Review

Write the following on the board or use BRR Blackline Master 15-6: Fill in the blanks with a reflexive pronun or an "X" if no pronoun is needed.
1. Mi madre ____ despierta a las seis.
2. En seguida ____ despierta a mi padre.
3. Ellos ____ preparan el desayuno.
4. Yo ____ preparo en mi cuarto.
5. Entonces yo ____ preparo nuestros sándwiches para el almuerzo.

PRESENTATION (page 404)

A. Tell students they will hear a conversation between Marcos and Elena, two young people who work together.
B. Have students close their books and listen as you read the conversation or play Cassette 9A.
C. Have students open their books to page 404 and ask them to repeat the conversation chorally after you or the cassette.
D. Call on a pair of volunteers to read the conversation with as much expression as possible.

ANSWERS

Ejercicio A
1. Elena tiene una cita con Pepe.
2. Tiene una cita con Pepe el viernes.
3. Sí, están saliendo mucho.
4. Marcos cree que están saliendo mucho.
5. No, no es nada serio.
6. Elena dice que son buenos amigos, nada más.

Ejercicio B
Marcos se refiere a la amistad (relación amistosa) entre Elena y Pepe.

404

CONVERSACIÓN

Escenas de la vida ¿Te estás enamorando?

MARCOS: ¿Qué haces el viernes, Elena?
ELENA: ¿El viernes? Tengo una cita con Pepe.
MARCOS: Estás saliendo mucho con Pepe, ¿no? ¿Se está poniendo serio esto?
ELENA: No, no es nada serio. Somos muy buenos amigos, nada más.

A **Está enamorada.** Contesten según la conversación.
1. ¿Con quién tiene una cita Elena?
2. ¿Cuándo tiene una cita con Pepe?
3. ¿Están saliendo mucho los dos?
4. ¿Quién cree que están saliendo mucho?
5. ¿Se está poniendo seria la cosa?
6. ¿Qué dice Elena?

B **La cita.** ¿A qué se refiere Marcos con la palabra "esto"?

404 CAPÍTULO 15

INDEPENDENT PRACTICE

Assign any of the following:
1. Workbook, *Estructura*
2. Communication Activities Masters, *Estructura, C*
3. Exercises on student pages 402–405

ADDITIONAL PRACTICE

Have pairs create original conversations based on the photo on page 404 and present them to the class. The more creative their conversation, the better.

Comunicación

A **Agente de atletas profesionales.** Ud está negociando un contrato para una famosa tenista norteamericana para jugar en Latinoamérica. Dígale al empresario que ella no jugará a menos que…

B **Papá, quiero casarme.** Su amigo(a) quiere casarse. Dígale que sus padres no se opondrían al casamiento con tal que…

C **Quiero que todo salga bien.** Ud. tiene que organizar la recepción para una prima que se casa. Su compañero es el dueño del restaurante. Dígale todo lo que Ud. quiere que ellos hagan.

D **Me quiero casar.** Imagínese que Ud. es una persona famosa que recibió una propuesta de matrimonio de parte de un(a) admirador(a) secreto(a). Escríbale una nota diciéndole que Ud. no se casaría aunque…

E **Te lo hacen muy difícil.** Los gobiernos imponen reglamentos para las personas que van a casarse. Con un grupo, prepare una lista de reglamentos. Por ejemplo: Los novios no pueden casarse sin que tengan un millón de dólares. Preparen tantos reglamentos como puedan. Mientras más raros, ¡mejor!

F **Sí, hazlo, pero antes de que lo hagas…** Dígale a un(a) compañero(a) de clase que Ud. tiene que hacer lo siguiente. Su compañero(a) le dirá que haga otra cosa primero.

Antes de que te acuestes, quiero que estudies.

1. poner la televisión
2. preparar el desayuno
3. llevar el perro de paseo
4. lavar el coche
5. tomar un baño

Arantxa Sánchez-Vicario, tenista española

LECTURA Y CULTURA

EL AMOR ES UNA COSA DIVINA

Como dice el refrán español, "el amor es una cosa divina". Pero antes de que haya amor es necesario que los dos individuos se conozcan. Aquí tenemos la historia de Mónica y Ángel. Ellos son de Medellín, Colombia, y se conocieron en la universidad. En cuanto Ángel vio a Mónica supo que esta muchacha le interesaba. Y Mónica encontró a Ángel un buen mozo[1]. Los dos empezaron a salir juntos, y después de salir dos o tres veces, Mónica invitó a Ángel a su casa de manera que sus padres lo conocieran. Y dentro de poco Ángel invitó a Mónica a su casa para que ella y sus padres se conocieran. Los padres hispanos quieren saber con quién están saliendo sus hijos. Hoy en día los jóvenes salen solos. Ya no hay dueñas como en tiempos pasados, pero es de rigor[2] que los padres sepan con quién están saliendo. Los padres les aconsejan a los jóvenes que se conozcan bien antes de que se casen y que esperen hasta que estén seguros que quieren pasar la vida juntos. Mónica y Ángel saben que el matrimonio es una decisión importante y seria. En los países hispanos todavía hay pocos divorcios y en algunos países el divorcio está prohibido.

Ángel y Mónica seguían saliendo juntos y cada mes se querían más. Sabían que querían casarse. Ángel fue a la casa de Mónica y le pidió al padre la mano de su hija. Poco después los padres anunciaron el compromiso de sus hijos. Hubo un cóctel[3] elegante en el que fijaron la fecha para sus bodas, y todos los parientes de las dos familias y los amigos íntimos festejaron a los nuevos comprometidos. Estas fiestas y reuniones familiares son muy importantes porque el matrimonio es el enlace de las dos familias y durante las fiestas antenupciales las dos familias van conociéndose.

Se casaron un año después. El día de la boda hay generalmente dos ceremonias— la civil y la religiosa. Los novios van a la iglesia acompañados del padrino y de la madrina, de sus pajes de honor y de sus damas de honor. Mónica le pidió a su madre que le sirviera de madrina y Ángel le pidió a su padre que fuera su padrino. Después de la ceremonia Ángel y Mónica salieron de la iglesia como esposo y esposa y fueron a una recepción en donde sus familiares y sus amigos íntimos les dieron la enhorabuena.

Al terminar la recepción, Ángel y Mónica salieron para su viaje de novios. Fueron a Europa a pasar su luna de miel.

[1] buen mozo *nice looking young man*
[2] de rigor *essential*
[3] cóctel *party*

Estudio de palabras

A **Definiciones.** Pareen.

1. el refrán
2. buen mozo
3. la dueña
4. rogar
5. seguro
6. un cóctel
7. los parientes
8. el marido

a. (joven) guapo
b. el esposo
c. el proverbio
d. cierto
e. miembros de la familia
f. la chaperona
g. una fiesta
h. pedir

Comprensión

A **Los novios.** Contesten.

1. ¿De dónde son Mónica y Ángel?
2. ¿Dónde se conocieron?
3. ¿Qué hizo Ángel cuando supo que él y Mónica iban a comprometerse?
4. ¿Qué hubo para anunciar su compromiso?
5. ¿Para qué sirven las fiestas antenupciales?

B **La pareja.** Completen.

1. Antes de que una pareja se enamore, es necesario que ———.
2. Los padres hispanos insisten en que sepan ———.
3. El día de la boda hay ———.
4. Durante la recepción los invitados les ———.

C **El matrimonio.** ¿Sí o no?

1. Los padres no conocieron a los novios de sus hijos hasta mucho después de que comenzaron a salir juntos.
2. Los jóvenes no pueden salir sin ser acompañados de una dueña.
3. Les dan fiestas a los novios para que los parientes puedan ir conociéndose antes de las bodas.
4. Las parejas hispanas suelen casarse algunos días después de anunciar su compromiso.
5. Los novios hispanos siempre escogen a un(a) amigo(a) íntimo(a) para su padrino o madrina.

CAPÍTULO 15   407

Post-reading
Call on volunteers to summarize what was read in their own words.

Estudio de palabras
ANSWERS

1. c
2. a
3. f
4. h
5. d
6. g
7. e
8. b

Comprensión
PRESENTATION (page 407)

Ejercicio A
Exercise A deals with factual recall.

Ejercicios B and C
Exercises B and C have students read for information.

ANSWERS

Comprensión A
1. Ellos son de Medellín, Colombia.
2. Ellos se conocieron en la universidad.
3. Angel fue a la casa de Mónica y le pidió al padre la mano de su hija.
4. Hubo un cóctel elegante.
5. Las fiestas antenupciales sirven para que las dos familias se conozcan.

Comprensión B
1. se conozca
2. con quién andan sus hijos
3. dos ceremonias, la civil y la religiosa
4. dan la enhorabuena

Comprensión C
1. No
2. No
3. Sí
4. No
5. No

HISTORY CONNECTION
The requirement of a double ceremony, one religious and one civil, is a result of anticlericalism at the turn of the century and the movement to separate church and state. In Mexico, for example, priests were not allowed to wear clerical garb in the street. Only civil marriages were officially recognized.

407

INDEPENDENT PRACTICE

Assign any of the following:
1. Workbook, *Un poco más*
2. Exercises on student page 407

Bell Ringer Review

Write the following on the board or use BRR Blackline Master 15-8: Imagine you are planning to open savings and checking accounts in a new bank. What are some words you would need to know?

Descubrimiento Cultural

(The Descubrimiento section is optional.)

PRESENTATION *(pages 408-409)*

Have students open their books to pages 408-409 and ask them to read the selection aloud as a class, in pairs or groups, or silently.

CROSS-CULTURAL COMPARISON

In remote areas of Latin America, where a priest might not come by for years, a common sight would be the wedding of a couple and the simultaneous baptizing of two or three of their children, taking advantage of the priest's visit to formalize a relationship that had begun some years before.

DESCUBRIMIENTO CULTURAL

Los términos "novio" y "novia" tienen y han tenido varios significados a través del tiempo. Según el diccionario, "novio/novia" es:

1. una persona recién casada
2. la persona que está próxima a casarse
3. la persona que mantiene relaciones amorosas en expectativa de futuro matrimonio

Ahora bien, existen otros términos más específicos para estos diferentes estados. Por ejemplo, "el pretendiente" es el hombre que "pretende" o tiene la intención de casarse. No se han formalizado las relaciones, necesariamente, pero todo el mundo sabe que la intención del joven es casarse. La "prometida" o el "prometido" es la persona que con cierta formalidad ha hecho y recibido promesa de casamiento. Y el "desposado" o la "desposada" es la persona recién casada. Los religiosos, algunos oficiales del gobierno, y los capitanes de barcos están autorizados para "desposar" a los que se presentan para casarse.

Antiguamente, cuando una persona tenía novio, se esperaba que los dos se casaran. Por eso, se evitaba que una pareja saliera sola. La legendaria "dueña", casi siempre una tía soltera[1] o viuda[2], acompañaba a los jóvenes a los bailes o los paseos[3]. En los paseos por la plaza del pueblo, los muchachos iban en una dirección y las muchachas en la otra. Cuando pasaban, se miraban, y más de un amor comenzó en el paseo. Más tarde, sin una dueña, se les permitía salir a los jóvenes, pero siempre en grupo, nunca solos.

Hoy, los "novios" son de varias categorías. En muchas partes del mundo hispano, un "novio" o una "novia" es más o menos como el *boyfriend* o *girlfriend* de Norteamérica. Pero también hay "novios formales". Los "novios formales" son mucho más que un simple *boyfriend* o *girlfriend*. Los novios formales son "prometidos".

408 CAPÍTULO 15

CRITICAL THINKING ACTIVITY

(Thinking skills: supporting arguments with reasons; presenting your side)

Read the following to the class or write it on the board or on an overhead transparency.

Las bodas lujosas y elegantes, y muy caras, están otra vez de moda. Algunos dicen que esto representa un deseo de volver al formalismo y tradición del pasado. Otros dicen que es cuestión de "status" social. ¿Qué opinas tú? ¿Quiénes deben determinar el tipo de boda que tienen los novios, los novios o los padres de los novios? ¿Por qué?

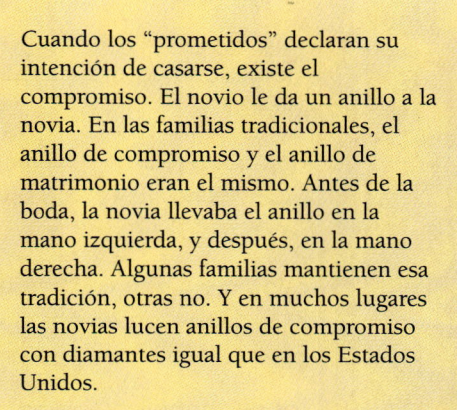

Cuando los "prometidos" declaran su intención de casarse, existe el compromiso. El novio le da un anillo a la novia. En las familias tradicionales, el anillo de compromiso y el anillo de matrimonio eran el mismo. Antes de la boda, la novia llevaba el anillo en la mano izquierda, y después, en la mano derecha. Algunas familias mantienen esa tradición, otras no. Y en muchos lugares las novias lucen anillos de compromiso con diamantes igual que en los Estados Unidos.

[1] soltera   *unmarried older woman*
[2] viuda   *widow*
[3] paseos   *walks*

CAPÍTULO 15   **409**

REALIDADES

(The Realidades section is optional.)

Bell Ringer Review

Write the following on the board or use BRR Blackline Master 15-9: Write down a suggestion you might make to a friend who is going with you to each of the following places. Use the *tú* form of the imperative.
1. al restaurante o al café
2. a la clase
3. a la peluquería
4. al hotel

PRESENTATION (pages 410–411)

A. Allow students time to enjoy the photos and discuss them among themselves. Answer any comments and address any questions they may have.

B. In regard to the photos in the *Realidades* section you may wish to ask the following questions:

Photo 1: *Describe la iglesia en la foto.*

Photo 2: *¿Dónde tiene lugar esta boda? ¿De qué religión son los novios? ¿Cuál de las personas es el rabino?*

Photo 3: *¿Qué están diciendo estos dos jóvenes?*

Photo 4: *Describe los trajes de los novios.*

Photo 5: *Explica la costumbre de tirar el ramo.*

REALIDADES

Una boda muy elegante en Buenos Aires, Argentina **1**. ¿Te gustaría casarte en esta iglesia?

Una boda judía **2**. ¿Dónde están los novios? ¿Qué lleva el novio en la cabeza?

Esta pareja está enamorada **3**. Ellos dan un paseo por el parque. ¿Cuándo se casarán?

Los novios bailan **4**. Son muy felices. Los invitados les han dado la enhorabuena.

La novia tira su ramo de flores **5**. ¿Quién será la próxima en casarse?

411

CULMINACIÓN

RECYCLING

The activities in *Comunicación oral* and *Comunicación escrita* encourage students to use all the language they have learned in the chapter and to recombine it with material from previous chapters. It is not necessary to do all the activities with all students. Select the ones you consider most appropriate or allow students to choose the ones they wish to do.

Comunicación oral
ANSWERS

Actividades A, B, and C
  Answers will vary.

INFORMAL ASSESSMENT

Activities A and B can be used to assess speaking skills. Use the evaluation criteria given on page 24 of this Teacher's Wraparound Edition.

Comunicación escrita
ANSWERS

Actividades A–D
  Answers will vary.

CULMINACIÓN

Comunicación oral

A **Mi novio(a) ideal.** Describa a su novio(a) ideal. ¿Cómo será esta persona? Describa sus características físicas, su personalidad, sus intereses, sus gustos, su condición económica, etc.

B **Una ceremonia nupcial.** Ud. está hablando con un amigo de Chile. Él quiere saber algo sobre las bodas en los Estados Unidos. Descríbale una ceremonia nupcial a la que Ud. ha asistido.

C **¿Te casarías con un millonario?** Haga una lista de personas famosas. Pregúntele a un(a) compañero(a) de clase si se casaría con esa persona.

Comunicación escrita

A **Una invitación.** Prepare Ud. una invitación a una boda.

B **Notas sociales.** Ud. está haciendo planes para su casamiento. Su familia es bien conocida en su comunidad. El periódico local ha pedido información sobre la boda para publicar un artículo en la sección social. Escríbales la información, incluyendo la fecha y la hora del casamiento, dónde va a tener lugar, los nombres del padrino, la madrina y de las damas y pajes de honor, el lugar de la recepción y el número de invitados.

C **El evento social del año.** Escriba un reporte para un periódico sobre la boda más espectacular que Ud. pueda imaginar. Dé la mayor cantidad posible de detalles.

D **¡Ay, Dios! ¡Qué desastre!** Una recepción de bodas, a la que Ud. asistió recientemente, resultó ser un completo desastre. Escriba una carta a un(a) amigo(a) describiéndole todo lo que pasó. Use mucho humor y creatividad.

412 CAPÍTULO 15

FOR THE NATIVE SPEAKER

Conversación En la Lectura, Mónica y Ángel se casaron un año después del compromiso. En algunas sociedades los noviazgos duran varios años, en otras los novios se casan después de conocerse sólo algunos meses. ¿Qué crees? ¿Cuáles son las ventajas y desventajas de ser novios por mucho tiempo o sólo unos meses? ¿Cuál es un período de tiempo ideal? ¿Por qué?

LEARNING FROM PHOTOS

Have students tell all they can in their own words about the Berríos-García wedding on page 412.

Reintegración

A **La familia.** Identifiquen.

1. el hermano de mi madre
2. la hermana de mi padre
3. el padre de mi padre
4. la madre de mi padre
5. otro hijo de mis padres
6. los hijos de mis tíos

B **Mi casa.** Describa lo que para Ud. sería una casa ideal.

C **Un viaje.** Preguntas personales.

1. Si ganaras la lotería, ¿harías un viaje?
2. ¿Adónde irías?
3. ¿Quién te acompañaría?
4. ¿Cómo viajarían?
5. ¿Qué harían Uds. durante el viaje?
6. ¿Qué verían y qué visitarían?

D **Otro viaje.** En el Ejercicio C, cambien "si ganaras" la lotería en "si ganas" la lotería. Hagan los cambios necesarios en las preguntas y contéstenlas.

Vocabulario

SUSTANTIVOS
los novios
los enamorados
la pareja
la cita
la dueña
el compromiso
el/la comprometido(a)
la sortija de compromiso
el matrimonio
el anillo de boda
el esposo
la esposa
el marido
la mujer
el enlace
la boda
la ceremonia
el altar
la iglesia
el padrino
la madrina
el paje de honor
la dama de honor
la recepción
el cóctel
el banquete
el/la invitado(a)
el brindis
la felicidad
la suerte
el/la recién casado(a)
el viaje de novios
la luna de miel

ADJETIVOS
nupcial

VERBOS
enamorarse
querer a
comprometerse
casarse
anunciar
intercambiar
brindar

OTRAS PALABRAS Y EXPRESIONES
para que
de manera que
de modo que
con tal que
sin que
a menos que
aunque
cuando
en cuanto
tan pronto como
hasta que
después de que
antes de que

CAPÍTULO 15   **413**

STUDENT PORTFOLIO

Written assignments that may be included in students' portfolios are the *Actividades escritas* on page 412 and the *Mi autobiografía* section in the Workbook.

INDEPENDENT PRACTICE

Assign any of the following:
1. Exercises on student page 413
2. Workbook, *Mi autobiografía*
3. Chapter 15, Situation Cards

Reintegración

PRESENTATION (page 413)

Ejercicio A
Exercise A recycles family vocabulary.

Ejercicio B
Exercise B recycles vocabulary associated with the home.

Ejercicio C
Exercise C reviews the conditional mood with *si* clauses.

Ejercicio D
Exercise D reviews the future tense with *si* clauses.

ANSWERS

Ejercicio A
1. mi tío
2. mi tía
3. mi abuelo
4. mi abuela
5. mi hermano
6. mis primos

Ejercicios B and C
Answers will vary.

Ejercicio D
1. Si gano la lotería, (no) haré un viaje.
2. Iré a…
3. Me acompañará…
4. Viajaremos…
5. Visitaremos…
6. Veremos…

PAIRED ACTIVITY
Have pairs create classified advertisements designed to sell the house in the photo on page 413. Ads must at least describe the house as it appears in the photo. Students should then use their imaginations from that point.

Vocabulario

There are approximately 13 cognates in this list.

VIDEO
The video is intended to reinforce the vocabulary, structures, and cultural content in each chapter. It may be used here as a chapter wrap-up activity. See the *Video Activities Booklet* for additional suggestions on its use.

AMIGOS, NOVIOS Y EL MATRIMONIO   (0:58:58)

CAPÍTULO 16
Repaso Capítulos 13-16 • Scope and Sequence pages 414-447

Topics	Functions	Structure	Culture
Professions and trades Job interviews and résumés Fondo Académico pages 442-447	How to talk about professions and occupations How to interview for a job How to discuss work qualifications How to introduce statements with "perhaps" or "maybe"	El subjuntivo en cláusulas relativas El subjuntivo con *ojalá*, *tal vez* y *quizá(s)*	The importance of the Spanish language in the business world A photographer in Puerto Rico Classified announcement in a Mexican newspaper Nuestro Mundo: Medications from Mexico and Spain Las Ciencias Las Ciencias Sociales: La economía Las humanidades: Las bellas artes

CAPÍTULO 16

Situation Cards

The Situation Cards simulate real-life situations that require students to communicate in Spanish, exactly as though they were in a Spanish-speaking country. The Situation Cards operate on the assumption that the person to whom the message is to be conveyed understands no English. Therefore, students must focus on producing the Spanish vocabulary and structures necessary to negotiate the situations successfully. For additional information, see the Introduction to the Situation Cards in the Situation Cards Envelope.

Communication Transparency

The illustration seen in this Communication Transparency consists of a synthesis of the two vocabulary (Palabras 1&2) presentations found in this chapter. It has been created in order to present this chapter's vocabulary in a new context, and also to recycle vocabulary learned in previous chapters. The Communication Transparency consists of original art. Following are some specific uses:

1. as a cue to stimulate conversation and writing activities
2. for listening comprehension activities
3. to review and reteach vocabulary
4. as a review for chapter and unit tests

CAPÍTULO 16
Print Resources

Lesson Plans

Pages

Workbook
- Palabras 1 — 179
- Palabras 2 — 180
- Estructura — 181-182
- Un poco más — 183-185
- Mi autobiografía — 186
- Self-Test — 187-191

Communication Activities Masters
- Palabras 1 — 106-107
- Palabras 2 — 108
- Estructura — 109-110

9 Bell Ringer Reviews — 43-44

Chapter Situation Cards A B C D

Chapter Quizzes
- Palabras 1 — 75
- Palabras 2 — 76
- Estructura — 77-78

Testing Program
- Listening Comprehension — 89
- Reading and Writing — 90-93
- Proficiency — 138
- Speaking — 159

Unit Test: Chapters 13-16
- Listening Comprehension — 94
- Reading and Writing — 95-97
- Speaking — 160
- Performance Assessment

Nosotros y Nuestro Mundo
- Nuestro Conocimiento Académico *Los estudios y el trabajo*
- Nuestro Idioma *Sobre los afijos*
- Nuestra Cultura *Oficios*
- Nuestra Literatura *"Pataruco"* de Rómulo Gallegos
- Nuestra Creatividad
- Nuestras Diversiones

CAPÍTULO 16
Multimedia Resources

CD-ROM Interactive Textbook Disc 4

Chapter 16 Student Edition
- Palabras 1
- Palabras 2
- Estructura
- Conversación
- Lectura y cultura
- Hispanoparlantes
- Realidades
- Culminación
- Prueba

Review: Chapters 13-16
- Nuestro mundo
- Repaso
- Fondo Académico
- Game: La Vuelta a España

Audio Cassette Program with Student Tape Manual

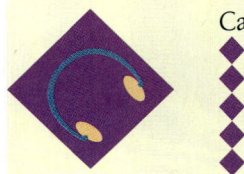

Cassette	Pages
9B Palabras 1	279-280
9B Palabras 2	280-281
9B Estructura	281
9B Conversación	281
9B Segunda parte	282-284

Compact Disc Program with Student Tape Manual
- CD 9 Palabras 1 — 279-280
- CD 9 Palabras 2 — 280-281
- CD 9 Estructura — 281
- CD 9 Conversación — 281
- CD 9 Segunda parte — 282-284

Overhead Transparencies Binder
- Vocabulary 16.1 (A&B); 16.2 (A&B)
- Communication C-16
- Maps
- Fine Art (with Blackline Master Activities)

Video Program
- Videocassette
- Video Activities Booklet — 41-42
- Videodisc
- Video Activities Booklet — 41-42

Computer Software (Macintosh, IBM, Apple)
- Practice Disk
  - Palabras 1 y 2
  - Estructura
- Test Generator Disk
  - Chapter Test
  - Customized Test

CAPÍTULO 16

CHAPTER OVERVIEW

In this chapter, students will learn to identify and discuss professions and trades. They will learn how their knowledge of Spanish can help them in their future careers. They will also learn language related to conducting themselves at job interviews and developing résumés. The cultural focus of Chapter 16 is on jobs and the importance of the Spanish language in the business world.

CHAPTER OBJECTIVES

By the end of this chapter, students will know:
1. vocabulary associated with professions and trades
2. vocabulary associated with job hunting and the workplace
3. the use of the subjunctive in relative clauses
4. the use of the subjunctive after expressions like *ojalá, tal vez,* and *quizá(s)*

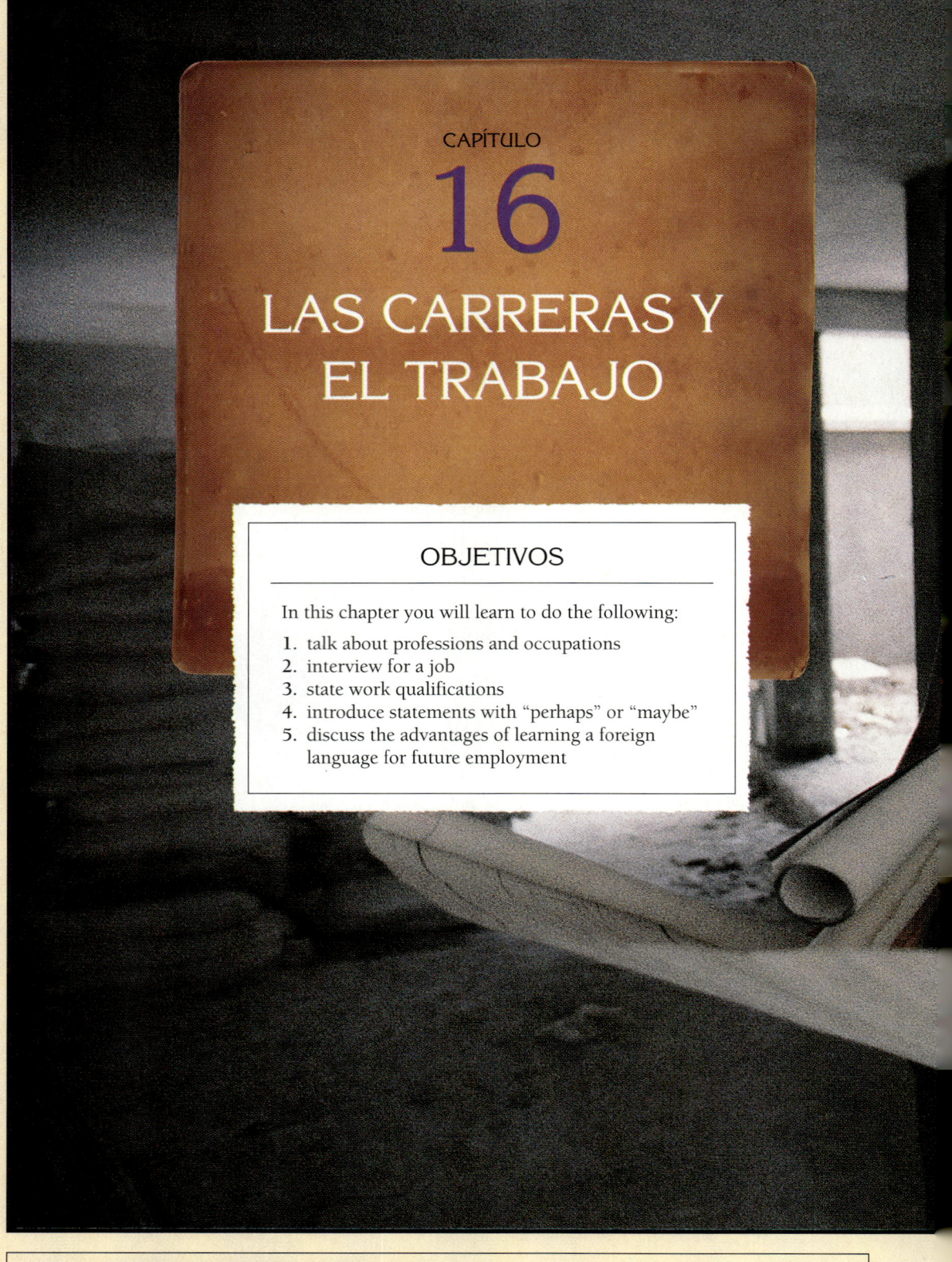

CAPÍTULO 16
LAS CARRERAS Y EL TRABAJO

OBJETIVOS

In this chapter you will learn to do the following:

1. talk about professions and occupations
2. interview for a job
3. state work qualifications
4. introduce statements with "perhaps" or "maybe"
5. discuss the advantages of learning a foreign language for future employment

CHAPTER PROJECTS

(optional)
1. Have students prepare a report on what they think they would like to do when they complete their education, and how Spanish might help them in their careers.
2. Have students fill out a job application. They might refer to the one in Spanish on page 425.
3. Have students prepare their *curriculum vitae* in Spanish.

CHAPTER 16 RESOURCES

1. Workbook
2. Student Tape Manual
3. Audio Cassette 9B
4. Vocabulary Transparencies
5. Bell Ringer Review Blackline Masters
6. Communication Activities Masters
7. Computer Software: Practice and Test Generator
8. Video Cassette, Chapter 16
9. Video Activities Booklet, Chapter 16
10. Situation Cards
11. Chapter Quizzes
12. Testing Program

Pacing

Chapter 16 will require eight to ten class sessions. Pacing will depend on the length of the class period, the age of the students, and student aptitude.

ABOUT THE LANGUAGE

1. You may wish to tell students that the woman in the photo on pages 414-415 is *una arquitecta*. Although the names of most professions have both masculine and feminine forms (*la ingeniera, la doctora, la farmacéutica*), some change only in the article: *el/la cartero* ("letter carrier"—*la cartera* is a "wallet"), *el/la contable, el/la juez,* and all those that end in *-a*: *el/la anestesista, el/la electricista, el/la artista,* etc.
2. Both people in the photo are wearing *un casco*.

VOCABULARIO
PALABRAS 1

Vocabulary Teaching Resources
1. Vocabulary Transparencies, 16.1 (*A & B*)
2. Audio Cassette 9B
3. Student Tape Manual, *Palabras 1*
4. Workbook, *Palabras 1*
5. Communication Activities Masters, *Palabras 1, A & B*
6. Chapter Quizzes, *Palabras 1*

Bell Ringer Review
Write the following on the board or use BRR Blackline Master 16-1: Make a list of the trades and professions you know in Spanish.

PRESENTATION (*pages 416-417*)

A. With books closed, refer to Vocabulary Transparencies 16.1 (*A & B*) and have students repeat the new words, phrases, and sentences after you or Cassette 9B.

B. Have students open their books to pages 416-417 and ask them to read the new words, phrases, and sentences.

C. Call on volunteers to designate various illustrations at random and name the professions.

VOCABULARIO

PALABRAS 1

EL TRABAJO O EL OFICIO

la escuela
el profesor

el consejero de orientación
el orientador

la directora

la oficina

el secretario

la contable

el programador de informática

la fábrica

la tienda

la tienda por departamentos

los obreros
los trabajadores

el comerciante
el mercader

la empleada
la dependiente

416 CAPÍTULO 16

PANTOMIME

Write the following sentences on cards, one to a card, and distribute them for students to mime the actions. Have the rest of the class guess what profession each individual is miming.

Tú eres artista.
Tú eres juez.
Tú eres escultor(a).
Tú eres secretario(a).
Tú eres profesor(a).
Tú eres programador(a) de informática.

el hospital
la médica
la enfermera
el técnico

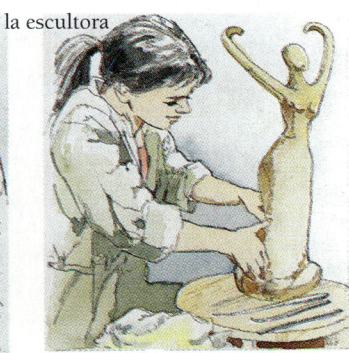

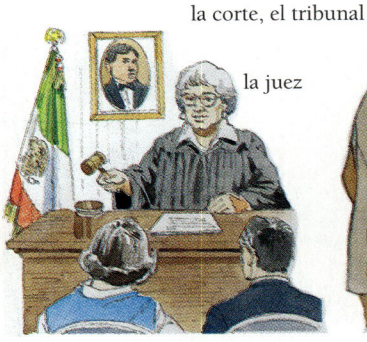

el taller
el artesano
el artista
el pintor
la escultora

la alcaldía, el ayuntamiento
el funcionario
la corte, el tribunal
la juez
el abogado

Nota: Aquí tiene Ud. más profesiones que ya conoce.

el cajero	el peluquero
el mozo	el recepcionista
el botones	el agente
el piloto	el policía
el controlador	el operador
el revisor	el mecánico
el cartero	

CAPÍTULO 16

ABOUT THE LANGUAGE

1. *Programadores* work with *ordenadores* in Spain, *computadoras* in Latin America, but their field (computer science) is called *la informática*.
2. *La fábrica* is the most common word for "factory." *Factoría* is also used and is not an Anglicism. *Manufactura* also exists but is less frequent.

LEARNING FROM ILLUSTRATIONS

You may wish to ask the following questions about the illustrations at the bottom of page 417: *Miren la bandera. ¿Qué bandera es? Entonces, ¿en qué país están estas personas? Describan la bandera.*

Ejercicios

PRESENTATION (*pages 418-419*)

Ejercicio A
   Exercise A is to be done with books open.

Ejercicios B and C
   Exercises B and C recycle vocabulary related to work and professions taught in earlier chapters of *A bordo* as well as in *Bienvenidos*.

Ejercicio D
   Exercise D can be done with books open or closed.

ANSWERS

Ejercicio A
1. Es una oficina.
2. Es una farmacia.
3. Es una fábrica.
4. Es la consulta del médico.
5. Es la alcaldía.
6. Es el garaje.

Ejercicio B
1. Los obreros trabajan en la fábrica.
2. Los funcionarios trabajan en la alcaldía.
3. Los/las enfermeros(as) y los/las técnicos(as) trabajan en el hospital.
4. El mozo, el botones y el/la recepcionista trabajan en el hotel.
5. La tripulación trabaja a bordo del avión.
6. Los profesores y el/la director(a) trabajan en la escuela.
7. El farmacéutico trabaja en la farmacia.
8. El/la contable trabaja en el banco.
9. Los empleados trabajan en el correo.
10. El médico y el/la enfermero(a) trabajan en la consulta del médico.

ABOUT THE LANGUAGE
   Lawyers' offices are *bufetes*, doctors' offices are *consultas* or *consultorios*, and all others are simply *oficinas*.

418

Ejercicios

A Los lugares de trabajo. Contesten según el dibujo.

1. ¿Es una escuela o una oficina?
2. ¿Es un hospital o una farmacia? 
3. ¿Es una oficina o una fábrica? 
4. ¿Es la corte o la consulta del médico? 
5. ¿Es la alcaldía o la iglesia? 
6. ¿Es el garaje o el bufete del abogado? 

B ¿Quién trabaja dónde? Contesten.
1. ¿Quién trabaja en la fábrica?
2. ¿Quién trabaja en la alcaldía?
3. ¿Quién trabaja en el hospital?
4. ¿Quién trabaja en el hotel?
5. ¿Quién trabaja a bordo del avión?
6. ¿Quién trabaja en la escuela?
7. ¿Quién trabaja en la farmacia?
8. ¿Quién trabaja en el banco?
9. ¿Quién trabaja en el correo?
10. ¿Quién trabaja en la consulta del médico?

418   CAPÍTULO 16

CRITICAL THINKING ACTIVITY

(*Thinking skills: making inferences, drawing conclusions*)

   Write the following on the board or on an overhead transparency.
   La dentista y el técnico de laboratorio llevan máscara. El uso de máscara en las consultas de los dentistas y en los laboratorios es reciente. ¿Por qué llevan máscara? ¿Por qué no llevaban máscara antes?

C ¿Quién hace este trabajo? Identifiquen.

1. Ayuda al médico en el hospital.
2. Trabaja en el laboratorio anatómico.
3. Prepara las recetas que escribe el médico.
4. Ayuda a las personas a defenderse en la corte.
5. Vende mercancías.
6. Prepara cuentas y estados financieros.
7. Da cortes de pelo.
8. Dirige la circulación (el tránsito, el tráfico).
9. Reparte el correo.
10. Registra a los clientes (huéspedes) cuando llegan al hotel.

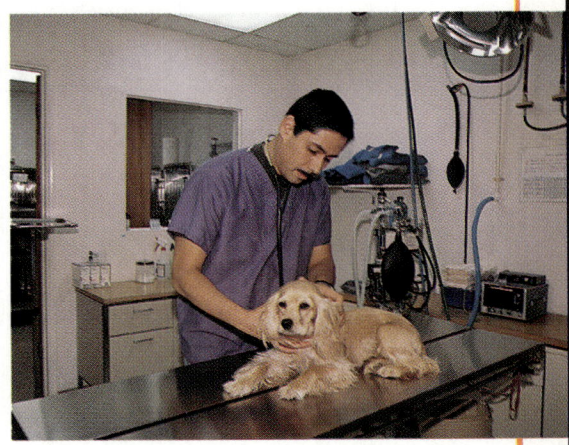

D Una carrera que me interesaría. Contesten según el modelo.

agente de policía
Sí, me gustaría ser agente de policía. Me interesaría.
No, no me gustaría ser agente de policía. No me interesaría.

1. médico
2. director de una gran empresa (compañía)
3. industrial
4. abogado
5. farmacéutico
6. dentista
7. piloto
8. contable
9. funcionario en una agencia del gobierno
10. veterinario

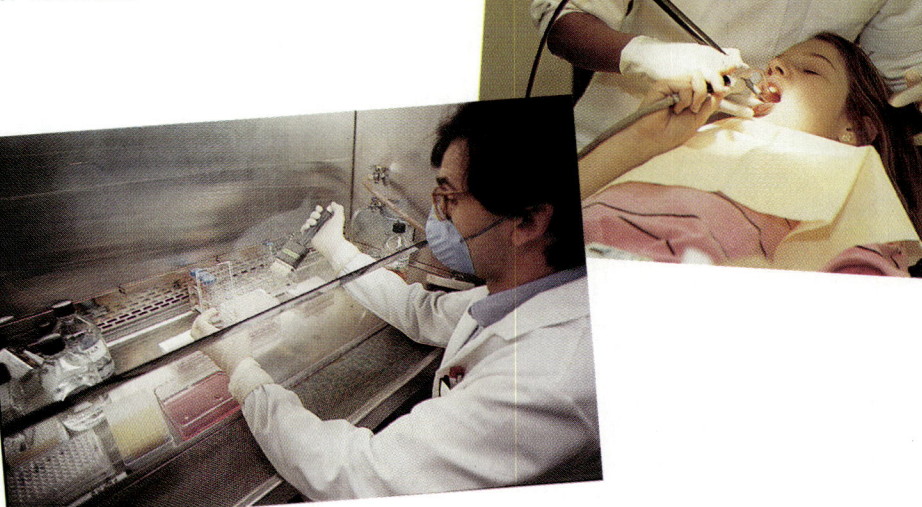

CAPÍTULO 16

VOCABULARIO
PALABRAS 2

Vocabulary Teaching Resources

1. Vocabulary Transparencies 16.2 (*A & B*)
2. Audio Cassette 9B
3. Student Tape Manual, *Palabras 2*
4. Workbook, *Palabras 2*
5. Communication Activities Masters, *Palabras 2, C & D*
6. Chapter Quizzes, *Palabras 2*
7. Computer Software, *Vocabulario*

Bell Ringer Review

Write the following on the board or use BRR Blackline Master 16-2: Where would you find the following people?
1. el cajero
2. el piloto
3. el juez
4. el cartero
5. el botones
6. el mozo
7. el artesano
8. el médico
9. el obrero

PRESENTATION (pages 420-421)

A. Have students close their books. Model the *Palabras 2* vocabulary using Vocabulary Transparencies 16.2 (*A & B*). Have students repeat the new material after you or Cassette 9B.
B. Intersperse your presentation with questions in order to elicit the vocabulary. For example: *¿Qué quiere decir la población activa? ¿Quién es un desempleado? ¿Dónde trabajan los técnicos especialistas? ¿Cómo se llaman los que trabajan en la agricultura?*
C. Call on volunteers to read the new words aloud.

420

VOCABULARIO

PALABRAS 2

EN BUSCA DE EMPLEO

el aspirante
el candidato

una solicitud de empleo
un historial (currículo) profesional

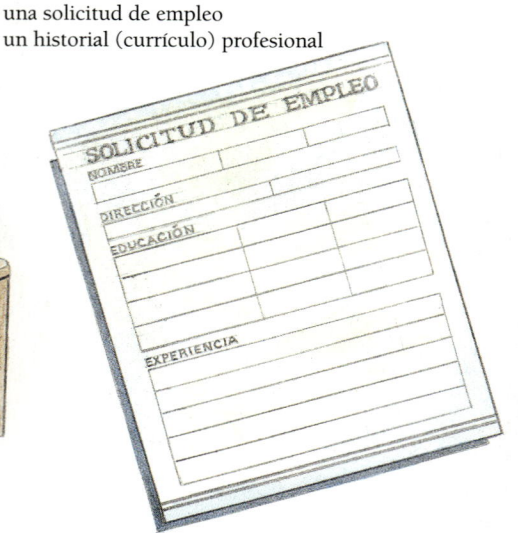

el departamento (servicio) de personal,
el servicio de recursos humanos

La señorita está libre.
No tiene trabajo. Está desempleada (desocupada).
Puede comenzar a trabajar en seguida.
Quizá empiece a trabajar mañana. Puede ser.

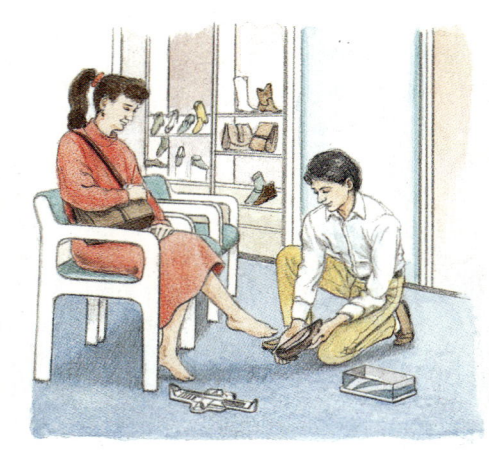

Él no trabaja a tiempo completo. (cuarenta horas por semana)
Él trabaja a tiempo parcial. (unas veinte horas por semana)

420   CAPÍTULO 16

la electricista

el plomero, el fontanero

el carpintero

Las profesiones son los trabajos que requieren un título universitario en campos como la medicina, arquitectura, farmacia, economía, pedagogía, etc.

Los oficios son los trabajos de especialistas como electricistas, fontaneros (plomeros), carpinteros, etc.

Los que trabajan en la agricultura y labran la tierra son labradores.

Los que se dedican a la compra y venta son comerciantes.

Y hay técnicos especialistas que trabajan en laboratorios y en campos como la energía nuclear, la informática, etc.

Nota:
la población activa   la gente que trabaja o que ejerce una profesión
el desempleado   una persona que no tiene trabajo y lo busca

CAPÍTULO 16   421

Ejercicios

PRESENTATION (page 422)

Ejercicios A, B, and C
Exercises A, B, and C can be done with books closed or open.

Extension of Ejercicio A
After completing Exercise A, call on a volunteer to retell the story in his/her own words.

ANSWERS

Ejercicio A
1. Sí, Juana busca trabajo.
2. Ella lee un anuncio en el periódico.
3. La Compañía Austral está buscando (reclutando) candidatos.
4. Juana va al servicio (departamento) de personal.
5. Ella llena una solicitud de empleo.
6. Ella le da su historial profesional a la recepcionista.
7. Sí, ella tiene referencias en su historial.
8. Ella tiene su título universitario en informática.
9. Sí, ella va a tener una entrevista.
10. Ella puede empezar a trabajar inmediatamente.

Ejercicio B
Answers will vary.
1. Sí, (No, no) trabajo.
2. Trabajo en…
3. Trabajo a tiempo parcial (tiempo completo).
4. Sí, (No, no) estoy desempleado(a).
5. Sí, (No, no) tengo un salario.
6. Es un salario bueno (módico).

Ejercicio C
Answers will vary.

Ejercicios

A **Ella solicita trabajo.** Contesten según se indica.
1. ¿Juana busca trabajo? (sí)
2. ¿Qué lee? (un anuncio en el periódico)
3. ¿Qué compañía está buscando (reclutando) candidatos? (Austral)
4. ¿Adónde va Juana? (al servicio o departamento de personal)
5. ¿Qué llena ella? (una solicitud de empleo)
6. ¿Qué le da a la recepcionista en el servicio de personal? (su historial profesional)
7. ¿Ella tiene referencias en su historial? (sí)
8. ¿En qué tiene su título universitario Juana? (en informática)
9. ¿Ella va a tener una entrevista? (sí)
10. ¿Cuándo puede empezar a trabajar? (inmediatamente)

B **Mi trabajo.** Preguntas personales.
1. ¿Trabajas?
2. ¿Dónde?
3. ¿Trabajas a tiempo completo o a tiempo parcial?
4. ¿Estás desempleado(a)?
5. ¿Tienes un salario?
6. ¿Es un salario bueno o módico?

C **¿Qué campo te interesa?**
Contesten con *sí* o *no*.
1. la arquitectura
2. las ciencias naturales
3. la ciencia política
4. la medicina
5. la pedagogía
6. la criminología
7. las finanzas y la contabilidad
8. la informática
9. la publicidad
10. el marketing, el mercadeo
11. la sociología
12. el turismo

422 CAPÍTULO 16

LEARNING FROM REALIA

1. Refer students to the ad on page 422 and have them say all they can about it. You may ask: *¿En qué ciudad, y en qué parte de la ciudad, está el centro? ¿Para qué profesiones prepara el centro?*
2. Have students look for the Spanish equivalents for "graphic design," "dental surgeon," "business administration," and "marketing."
3. Have students say in their own words what the motto means: *Recibimos a sus hijos en preescolar y los entregamos profesionistas.*

Comunicación
Palabras 1 y 2

A **Te recomiendo que…** Imagínese que Ud. es consejero(a) de orientación en su escuela. Ud. está dándoles entrevistas a sus alumnos. ¿Qué profesiones u oficios recomendaría Ud. a los alumnos a quienes les interesan los siguientes campos?

las matemáticas	el comercio
la biología	los deportes
la literatura	las artes
los idiomas	

B **Adivina lo que hago en mi trabajo.** Piense en un trabajo o profesión y dígale a su compañero(a) de clase dónde trabaja Ud. Su compañero(a) tiene que adivinar lo que Ud. hace. Si no acierta la primera vez, continúe dándole más pistas hasta que su compañero(a) adivine correctamente. Luego cambien de papel, alternándose hasta que adivinen tres veces cada uno.

C **La entrevista.** Imagínese que Ud. es un(a) consejero(a) en una agencia de empleos. Un(a) compañero(a) de clase es un(a) aspirante. Entreviste al/a la aspirante. Pregúntele acerca de sus estudios, experiencia, aptitudes personales, talentos artísticos y buen sentido para los negocios (*business*). Después de la entrevista recomiéndele un puesto al/a la aspirante.

Tengo un trabajo…

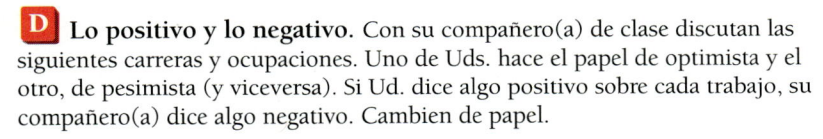

D **Lo positivo y lo negativo.** Con su compañero(a) de clase discutan las siguientes carreras y ocupaciones. Uno de Uds. hace el papel de optimista y el otro, de pesimista (y viceversa). Si Ud. dice algo positivo sobre cada trabajo, su compañero(a) dice algo negativo. Cambien de papel.

1. mecánico
2. agente de viajes
3. abogado
4. profesor
5. músico
6. técnico de computadoras
7. artista
8. cocinero

CAPÍTULO 16   **423**

ESTRUCTURA

El subjuntivo en cláusulas relativas
Describing Indefinite Persons or Things

A grouping of words that modifies a noun is called a relative clause. A relative clause can modify or describe a noun that refers to a specific, definite person or thing, or an indefinite person or thing. When the clause describes a definite person or thing, the verb in the clause is in the indicative. If, however, it modifies an indefinite person or thing, the verb is in the subjunctive. Note too that the *a personal* is omitted when the object is indefinite.

Conocemos a una secretaria que habla bien el español.
Buscamos una secretaria que hable bien el español.

Ejercicios

A Hay que tener ciertas cualificaciones. Completen.

1. La compañía Vensa está buscando alguien que ____ (tener) experiencia, que ____ (conocer) bien el español y el inglés y que ____ (poder) viajar.
2. El director del servicio de personal me dijo que necesitan alguien que ____ (estar) libre inmediatamente.
3. Han entrevistado a dos candidatos. Hay un candidato que ____ (tener) experiencia, que ____ (querer) y ____ (poder) trabajar en seguida.
4. Desgraciadamente él no habla inglés y la compañía sigue buscando alguien que ____ (hablar) inglés y que ____ (conocer) el mercado norteamericano.

B Están buscando empleados. Contesten.

1. ¿Está buscando un representante la compañía Vensa?
2. ¿Están ofreciendo un puesto que paga bien?
3. ¿Buscan alguien que tenga experiencia en ventas?
4. ¿Quieren alguien que pueda viajar?
5. ¿Necesitan una persona que conozca más de un idioma?
6. ¿Están buscando un candidato que esté libre inmediatamente?

CAPÍTULO 16

El subjuntivo con *ojalá, tal vez, quizá(s)*

Introducing Statements With Perhaps or Maybe

1. The expressions *ojalá (que)*, "would that, I wish," and *quizá(s)*, "perhaps," are always followed by the subjunctive.

    ¡Ojalá que encontrara trabajo!
    ¡Ojalá que le den una entrevista!
    ¡Quizás lo llamen mañana!

2. The expression *tal vez*, "perhaps, maybe," can be followed by either the subjunctive or the future of the indicative.

    ¡Tal vez venga!
    ¡Tal vez vendrá!

Ejercicios

A ¡Ojalá que tenga trabajo! Contesten según el modelo.

> ¿Va a buscar trabajo Eduardo?
> *¡Ojalá que busque trabajo!*

1. ¿Va a buscar trabajo Eduardo?
2. ¿Va a leer los anuncios en el periódico?
3. ¿Va a preparar su historial profesional?
4. ¿Va a mandar su historial profesional a varias compañías?
5. ¿Va a tener una entrevista?
6. ¿Va a encontrar un puesto?

B No sé. ¡Quizá! Contesten según el modelo.

> ¿Va a venir Sandra?
> *No sé. ¡Quizá venga!*

1. ¿Va a venir Sandra?
2. ¿Va a llegar mañana?
3. ¿Va a pasar algunos días aquí?
4. ¿Va a volver a vivir aquí?
5. ¿Va a buscar trabajo aquí?

CAPÍTULO 16   425

CONVERSACIÓN

CONVERSACIÓN

Bell Ringer Review
Write the following on the board or use BRR Blackline Master 16-6: Name five articles of clothing a young man would wear for a job interview. Do the same for a young woman.

PRESENTATION *(page 426)*

A. Tell students they will hear a conversation between a woman and a young applicant for employment.
B. Have students close their books and listen as you read the conversation or play Cassette 9B.
C. Have students open their books to page 425 and call on a pair of volunteers to read the conversation with as much expression as possible.
D. Go over the *Comprensión* exercise.
E. Call on a volunteer to retell the story of the conversation in his/her own words.

PAIRED ACTIVITY
Have pairs prepare job interview skits. One partner is the applicant and the other is the interviewer. Allow them time to practice and have them present their skits to the class.

Ejercicio

ANSWERS

1. Sí, Carolina es alumna.
2. Sí, ella va a continuar con sus estudios.
3. Sí, ella asistirá a la universidad.
4. Sí, recibirá su título.
5. Piensa especializarse en marketing.
6. Le gustaría trabajar con una empresa multinacional.
7. Porque ella quiere ver el mundo.
8. Porque es necesario para el trabajo que quiere.

426

Escenas de la vida *Me interesa el mercadeo*

SEÑORA: ¿Es Ud. alumna?
CAROLINA: Sí, soy alumna.
SEÑORA: ¿Ud. piensa asistir a la universidad?
CAROLINA: Sí.
SEÑORA: ¿Qué va a estudiar? ¿Qué campos le interesan?
CAROLINA: Quizás me especialice en marketing. Y después, quisiera trabajar en una empresa multinacional.
SEÑORA: ¿Le gustaría viajar?
CAROLINA: Mucho. ¡Ojalá que pudiera ver el mundo!
SEÑORA: Entonces, debe seguir con sus estudios de español.

El mercadeo. Contesten según la conversación.

1. ¿Carolina es alumna?
2. ¿Ella va a continuar con sus estudios?
3. ¿Ella asistirá a la universidad?
4. ¿Recibirá su título?
5. ¿En qué piensa especializarse?
6. ¿Con qué tipo de compañía le gustaría trabajar?
7. ¿Por qué?
8. ¿Por qué debe seguir con sus estudios de español?

426 CAPÍTULO 16

LEARNING FROM PHOTOS/REALIA

1. Refer students to the photo on page 426 and have them say as much as they can about the two people in it.
2. Have students consult the university brochure and identify the area in which the specific fields are found. Cue with questions such as: *¿En qué área está la pedagogía? ¿… la ecología?*

DID YOU KNOW?

The *Bachillerato* is approximately equivalent to a U.S. high school diploma. The *Licenciatura* is usually equivalent to a Bachelor Degree in the U.S. The *Maestría* is similar to a U.S. Master's Degree.

Comunicación

A **El trabajo ideal.** Piense en lo que Ud. consideraría un trabajo ideal—algo que a Ud. le gustaría hacer, que le interesaría mucho. Mencione todos sus deseos usando "¡Ojalá!"

B **Posibles carreras.** Trabaje Ud. con un(a) compañero(a) de clase. Cada uno(a) de Uds. preparará una lista de las cosas que le interesan y de las materias o asignaturas que prefieren en la escuela. Luego miren sus listas. Determinen los intereses que tienen en común y los que son muy diferentes. Sugiérale a su compañero(a) algunas profesiones que posiblemente le interesarían. Su compañero(a) le hará a Ud. algunas sugerencias también.

C **Entrevista de candidatos.** Imagínese que Ud. es un oficial de recursos humanos que tiene que entrevistar a varios alumnos de nivel secundario para el puesto de consejero orientador en un campamento de niños. Prepare una lista de las preguntas que hará durante las entrevistas. Después, use estas preguntas entrevistando al primer candidato (su compañero[a] de clase). Luego cambien de papel.

Roberto C. Goizueta, presidente de Coca-Cola

Franklin Chang Díaz, astronauta

Isabel Allende, escritora chilena

CAPÍTULO 16 **427**

FOR THE NATIVE SPEAKER

Give students the following assignment. *Escoge a una de las tres personas en las fotos. Ve a la biblioteca y prepara una breve biografía en español. Revisa la biografía y asegúrate de que no hay errores antes de entregarla.*

INDEPENDENT PRACTICE

Assign any of the following:
1. Workbook, *Un poco más*
2. Exercise and activities on student pages 426–427

Comunicación

PRESENTATION (page 427)

These activities encourage students to reincorporate previously learned vocabulary and structures and use them on their own. You may select those activities that you consider most appropriate, or you may allow students to select the ones in which they would like to participate.

ANSWERS

Actividades A, B, and C
Answers will vary.

LECTURA Y CULTURA

Bell Ringer Review
Write the following on the board or use BRR Blackline Master 16-7: Complete the sentences:
1. Me encanta la clase de español aunque...
2. No miro la televisión a menos que...
3. Me gustaría hacer un viaje con tal de que...
4. No saldré este fin de semana sin que...

READING STRATEGIES
(page 428)
Pre-Reading
Ask students how they think their knowledge of Spanish will help them in their careers.

Reading
A. Have students open their books to page 428 and ask them to read the selection once silently.
B. Call on individuals to read one paragraph each. Ask content questions about each paragraph.

Post-reading
Ask students to summarize in their own words what they have learned from the reading.

LECTURA Y CULTURA

EL ESPAÑOL Y SU CARRERA

¿Cree Ud. que el español le será útil en su carrera? Quizá diga que Ud. no sabe. Tal vez tenga Ud. razón por no saber precisamente lo que Ud. hará ni dónde trabajará cuando tenga su título universitario. Pero no hay duda que el conocimiento de un idioma extranjero como el español será un gran beneficio.

Hoy en día el comercio internacional es de suma importancia. No es suficiente exportar nuestros productos al extranjero. Hay que tener una presencia real en muchos países. Así, muchas grandes empresas norteamericanas han llegado a ser multinacionales. Quiere decir que tienen instalaciones o sucursales[1] y filiales en el extranjero. Por esta razón es posible que Ud. trabaje con una compañía norteamericana pero que su oficina esté en un país hispanohablante. Una gran parte de los ingresos[2] de las empresas multinacionales vienen de sus inversiones[3] en el extranjero.

Acuérdese[4] que el español en sí no es una carrera. Pero, el español con otra especialización le da a uno una ventaja de valor incalculable. Si Ud. conoce la contabilidad, la medicina o el marketing, por ejemplo, y además tiene un buen conocimiento del español, podrá trabajar con una empresa multinacional. Con el español y su otra especialización, Ud. podrá encontrar un trabajo que le pague bien, le sea interesante y le permita viajar y conocer el mundo. ¡Ojalá! ¿No?

[1] sucursales *branches*
[2] ingresos *income*
[3] inversiones *investments*
[4] acuérdese *remember*

CAPÍTULO 16

CRITICAL THINKING ACTIVITY

(Thinking skills: communicating; classifying information)

Write the following on the board or on an overhead transparency.
1. *Haz una lista de ventajas que tiene una persona que habla varias lenguas.*
2. *Clasifica estas ventajas en las siguientes categorías: ventajas culturales, ventajas económicas, ventajas comerciales.*

Estudio de palabras

El nombre y el verbo. Pareen.

1. trabajar
2. invertir
3. conocer
4. pagar
5. beneficiar
6. especializarse
7. viajar
8. exportar
9. producir
10. ingresar

a. el pago
b. el viaje
c. el trabajo
d. la exportación
e. la inversión
f. la especialización
g. el conocimiento
h. el producto
i. el beneficio
j. los ingresos

Una fábrica de Ford, México

Comprensión

A El español. Contesten.

1. ¿Cree Ud. que el español le será útil en su carrera?
2. ¿Ha escogido Ud. una carrera que quisiera seguir? Si Ud. contesta que sí, ¿cuál es?
3. Hoy en día, ¿qué es muy importante?
4. ¿Cuál es una ventaja de valor incalculable?

B El comercio y las lenguas. ¿Sí o no?

1. El único comercio internacional es la exportación de bienes (productos).
2. Es posible tener un puesto con una empresa norteamericana y trabajar en el extranjero.
3. Muchas empresas multinacionales tienen instalaciones y sucursales en países extranjeros.
4. El español en sí es una carrera excelente.
5. El conocimiento de un idioma como el español le podrá beneficiar en muchas carreras diferentes.

Una fábrica de la empresa Hewlett Packard, Barcelona, España

CAPÍTULO 16 429

Estudio de palabras
ANSWERS
1. c
2. e
3. g
4. a
5. i
6. f
7. b
8. d
9. h
10. j

Comprensión
ANSWERS

Comprensión A
Answers will vary.
1. Sí, (No,) el español (no) me será útil en mi carrera.
2. Sí, quisiera seguir la carrera de…
   No, no he escogido la carrera.
3. Hoy en día (el comercio internacional) es muy importante.
4. El español es una ventaja de valor incalculable.

Comprensión B
1. No
2. Sí
3. Sí
4. No
5. Sí

LEARNING FROM PHOTOS

Refer students to the photos on pages 428-429 and ask: ¿A qué se dedica la IBM? ¿Qué tipo de producto fabrican ellos? ¿Para qué se usan esos productos? ¿Cuál de las tres compañías es la más antigua? ¿Qué fabrica la Ford? ¿La planta en la foto fabrica automóviles? ¿Qué quiere decir "ensamble"? ¿Qué productos fabrica la Hewlett Packard?

INDEPENDENT PRACTICE

Assign the exercises on student page 429.

Bell Ringer Review

Write the following on the board or use BRR Blackline Master 16-8: Choose the correct verb form in the following sentences:
1. La compañía está buscando alguien que (tiene/tenga) experiencia.
2. Conocemos a una secretaria que (habla/hable) bien el español.
3. Están ofreciendo un puesto que (paga/pague) bien.
4. Ojalá que me (llaman/llamen) mañana.

Descubrimiento Cultural

(The Descubrimiento section is optional.)

PRESENTATION *(pages 430–431)*

Have students open their books to pages 430–431 and ask them to read the selection silently. Ask if they can think of any other Spanish companies that do business in the United States.

DESCUBRIMIENTO CULTURAL

Desde hace ya mucho tiempo se habla de la presencia de empresas norteamericanas en el extranjero. En todas las grandes ciudades de España y Latinoamérica se veía anuncios para IBM de México, Ford de España o Xerox Venezolano. Tanto que en México había un chiste que decía:—si dice "de México" es porque no lo es.

Hoy, no solamente las empresas o compañías norteamericanas son multinacionales. Cada día vemos más y más empresas japonesas, europeas y latinoamericanas con sucursales y filiales en los Estados Unidos. La famosa casa de porcelanas Lladró tiene una sucursal en la Calle 57 de Nueva York. Las cadenas españolas HUSA y Meliá tienen hoteles en ciudades norteamericanas. La línea aérea Iberia pensaba utilizar Miami como centro para vuelos a Latinoamérica. Importantes periódicos y revistas de Nueva York tienen dueños británicos. Los japoneses fabrican automóviles en Tennessee y Kentucky. Las acciones de las compañías telefónicas de México y España se negocian[1] en Wall Street.

Así es posible que algún día Ud. trabaje con una empresa española o latinoamericana sin tener que salir de los Estados Unidos.

[1] se negocian *are traded*

Una sucursal de la empresa Xerox, Caracas, Venezuela

Una fábrica en Córdoba, Argentina

430 CAPÍTULO 16

LEARNING FROM PHOTOS

Refer students to the photos on page 430. Ask them to compare the kind of work done in the two locations. Cue with questions such as: *¿Qué tipo de trabajo hacen las personas en el edificio de la Xerox? ¿Es trabajo de fábrica o de oficina? ¿Allí hay más obreros o secretarios? ¿Qué tipo de trabajo están haciendo en Córdoba, Argentina? ¿Qué son los señores que están en la foto?*

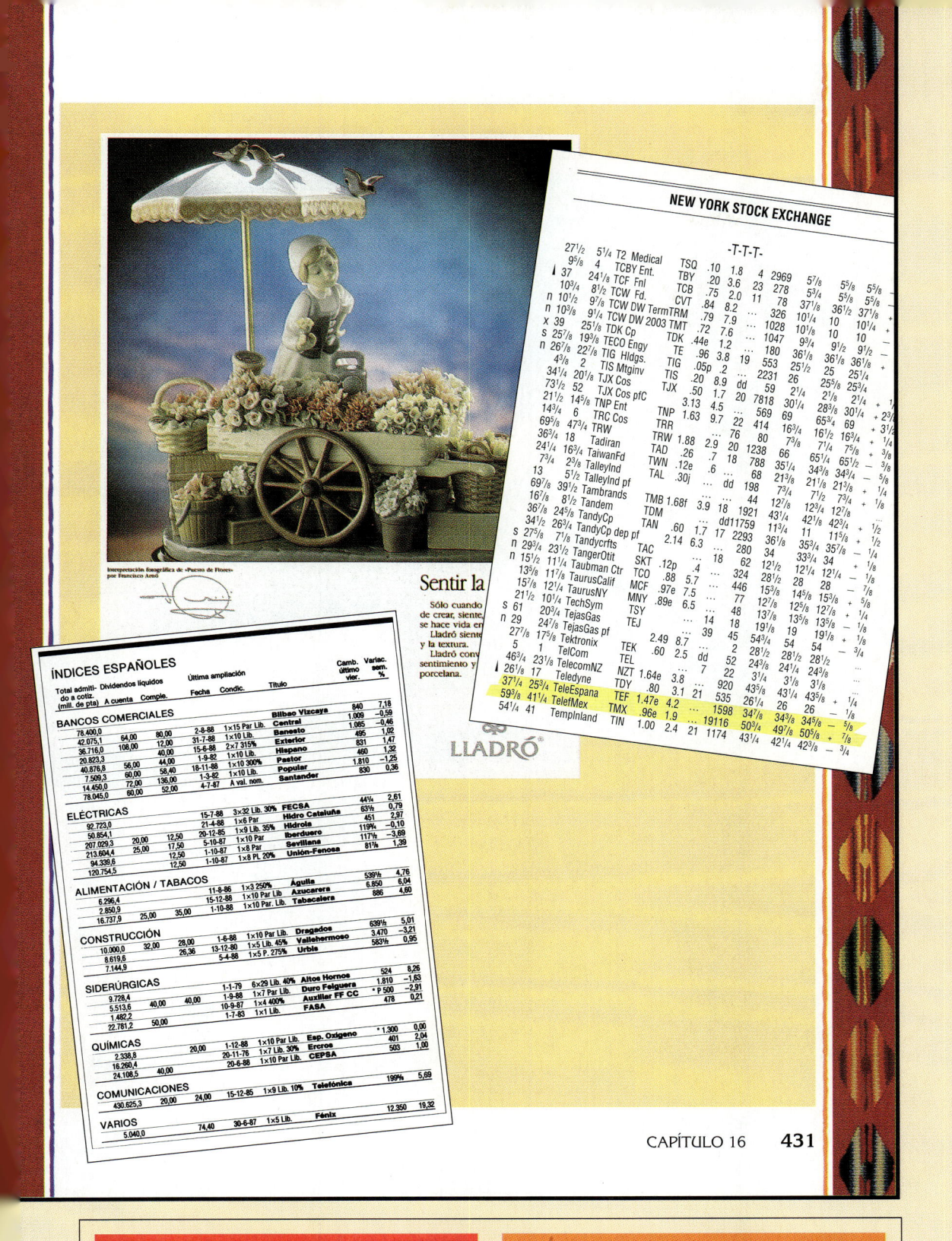

FOR THE NATIVE SPEAKER

Have students describe the categories shown in the Spanish Stock Exchange report and explain them. *Bancos Comerciales, Eléctricas, Alimentación/Tabacos, Construcción, Siderúrgicas, Químicas, Comunicaciones, Varios.* Ask: *¿Qué tipos de compañías están en cada categoría? Indica cuál sería una compañía norteamericana que figuraría en cada categoría.*

LEARNING FROM REALIA

You may wish to ask the following questions about the stock market reports on page 431: *¿Cuál es una compañía española que negocia en la Bolsa de Nueva York? ¿Cuál es una compañía mexicana? ¿En qué industria están las dos compañías? ¿Cuáles valen más, las acciones de la telefónica española o la mexicana?*

CAPÍTULO 16 **431**

REALIDADES

(The Realidades *section is optional.)*

Bell Ringer Review
Write the following on the board or use BRR Blackline Master 16-9: Imagine you are a doctor. Write five sentences telling what you did yesterday.

PRESENTATION *(pages 432-433)*
Allow students time to enjoy the photos and discuss them among themselves. Answer any comments and address any questions they may have.

REALIDADES

La fotógrafa está tomando fotografías de un arroyo en las montañas del centro de Puerto Rico **1**.

Un carpintero construyendo una casa en el norte de México **2**.

Un anuncio clasificado que apareció en un periódico mexicano **3**.

Un camarógrafo en una estación de televisión en la Ciudad de México **4**.

Una señora de ascendencia hispana que trabaja de bombera en Arizona **5**.

CRITICAL THINKING ACTIVITY
(Thinking skills: evaluating facts; weighing arguments)
Write the following on the board or on an overhead transparency:
Las grandes empresas multinacionales tienen filiales o sucursales en muchos países. Varias compañías extranjeras han establecido fábricas en los EE.UU. ¿Se debe permitir que compañías extranjeras establezcan fábricas en los EE.UU. o no? ¿Cuáles son las ventajas y desventajas?

—AAA—
EMPRESA LÍDER EN EL RAMO DE CONFITERÍA SOLICITA

DISEÑADOR GRÁFICO

Requisitos:
- ★ Edad máxima 26 años
- ★ Sexo indistinto
- ★ Presentar carpeta de trabajo
- ★ Solicitud elaborada con fotografía reciente
- ★ Sin problemas de horario
- ★ Experiencia no necesaria

Ofrecemos:
- ☆ Sueldo según aptitudes
- ☆ Prestaciones de ley
- ☆ Proyección dentro de la empresa
- ☆ Agradable ambiente de trabajo

Interesados presentar currículum vitae en **LUZ SAVIÑON No. 13, Desp. 505, Col. Del Valle,** horario de 9:00 a 18:00 horas, con el **Lic. ALEJANDRO GONZALEZ VILLANUEVA** y/o **Srta. MARY CARMEN MARTÍNEZ**

HISTORY CONNECTION

The Spanish explorer Cabeza de Vaca reached Arizona around 1536. Coronado crossed Arizona as far west as the Grand Canyon in 1540 in search of the legendary seven cities of gold. Father Eusebio Kino founded a number of missions near present-day Nogales and Tucson in the 17th century. Arizona was under Mexican control from the end of the War of Indèpendence from Spain in 1821 to 1848. After the Mexican-American War (1846-1848), under the Treaty of Guadalupe Hidalgo, Mexico relinquished control of the area now comprising Arizona and New Mexico.

Arizona has a large Hispanic population, about twenty percent of the total.

LEARNING FROM PHOTOS

Refer students to the *Realidades* photos. Have them describe each of the people in them.

CULMINACIÓN

RECYCLING

The activities in *Comunicación oral* and *Comunicación escrita* encourage students to use all the language they have learned in the chapter and to recombine it with material from previous chapters. It is not necessary to do all the activities with all students. Select the ones you consider most appropriate or allow students to choose the ones they wish to do.

Comunicación oral
ANSWERS
Actividades A, B, and C
Answers will vary.

INFORMAL ASSESSMENT

Activities A, B, and C can be used to assess speaking skills. Use the evaluation criteria given on page 24 of this Teacher's Wraparound Edition.

Comunicación escrita
ANSWERS
Actividades A-D
Answers will vary.

CULMINACIÓN

Comunicación oral

A **¿Qué te interesa?** Hable Ud. con un(a) compañero(a). Discutan las cosas que les interesan y las cosas que les aburren. Después de la conversación, decidan cuáles son algunas profesiones que les interesarían y cuáles no les interesarían, y diga por qué.

B **Puestos deseables.** Ud. está hablando con un amigo latinoamericano. Él quiere saber cuáles son las profesiones u oficios más populares en los EE.UU. Contéstele.

C **La importancia del español.** A Ud. se le ha encargado la tarea de animar a los estudiantes de primer año de español a que continúen aprendiendo español hasta su último año en la escuela. Con un(a) compañero(a) de clase preparen una lista de razones importantes, personales y profesionales, para que los estudiantes norteamericanos aprendan español. Luego, preparen y presenten una conversación para animar a los estudiantes de su clase a que continúen estudiando español. Traten de ser creativos y utilicen su sentido de humor, si así lo desean, de modo que el mensaje se presente con claridad.

Comunicación escrita

A **Mi currículo profesional.** Prepare Ud. su historial profesional en español.

B **Quisiera estudiar para...** Escriba uno o dos párrafos en los que Ud. indica lo que Ud. quisiera hacer, es decir, la carrera que a Ud. le gustaría tener. Indique por qué.

C **¿Necesita trabajo?** Imagínese que Ud. trabaja para una agencia de empleos. Escriba varios anuncios breves para los siguientes puestos. Indique los requisitos y cualidades que los patrones buscan en los solicitantes.

1. mecánico de coches
2. camarero(a) para un restaurante español
3. enfermero(a)
4. dependiente de una tienda de modas

D **¡Muchas gracias por todo!** Imagínese que Ud. acaba de obtener un puesto maravilloso. Escríbale una carta a su maestro(a) favorito(a) dándole las gracias por todo el apoyo *(support)* que le dio. Cuéntele de su nuevo puesto, lo que va a hacer, cuánto paga, las tareas que tiene que hacer, etc.

434 CAPÍTULO 16

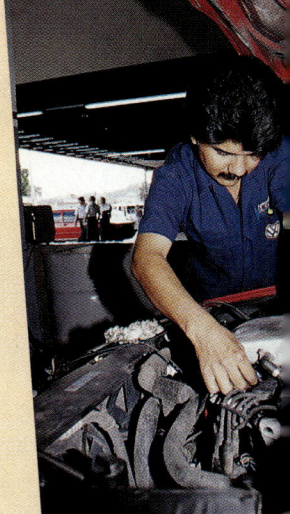

STUDENT PORTFOLIO

Written assignments that may be included in students' portfolios are the *Actividades escritas* on page 434 and the *Mi autobiografía* section in the Workbook.

Reintegración

Todos los tiempos. Completen con *hacer, ir* o *decir*.

1. Ellos ____ un viaje hoy (hacer)
2. Ellos ____ un viaje ayer. (hacer)
3. Ellos ____ muchos viajes cuando eran jóvenes. (hacer)
4. Ellos ____ un viaje mañana. (hacer)
5. Nosotros ____ a España cada año. (ir)
6. Nosotros ____ a España el año pasado. (ir)
7. Nosotros siempre ____ a España cuando nuestros primos vivían allí. (ir)
8. Nosotros ____ a España el año que viene. (ir)
9. Yo se lo ____ a él ahora. (decir)
10. Yo se lo ____ a él ayer. (decir)
11. Yo siempre le ____ la misma cosa. (decir)
12. Yo se lo ____ mil veces si fuera necesario. (decir)

Un edificio de apartamentos diseñado por el arquitecto español Antonio Gaudí, Barcelona, España

Vocabulario

SUSTANTIVOS

el trabajo
la profesión
el oficio
el/la director(a)
el/la secretario(a)
el/la contable
el/la programador(a)
el/la consejero(a) de orientación
el/la orientador(a)
el/la comerciante
el/la mercader
el/la empleado(a)
el/la dependiente
el/la médico(a)
el/la enfermero(a)
el/la técnico(a)
el/la artesano(a)
el/la artista
el/la pintor(a)
el/la escultor(a)

el/la funcionario(a)
el/la juez
el/la abogado(a)
el/la electricista
el/la plomero(a)
el/la fontanero(a)
el/la carpintero(a)
el/la desempleado(a)
el desempleo

la oficina
la fábrica
el taller
el laboratorio
la alcaldía
el ayuntamiento
la corte
el tribunal
el campo
la agricultura
la compra y venta

la informática
la energía nuclear
la arquitectura
la pedagogía

el departamento (servicio) de personal
el departamento de recursos humanos
el/la candidato(a)
el/la aspirante
la solicitud de empleo
el historial profesional
el currículo profesional
el título

ADJETIVOS

libre
desocupado(a)
desempleado(a)

universitario(a)
especialista
nuclear

VERBOS

ejercer (una profesión)
requerir
labrar (la tierra)
solicitar (trabajo)

OTRAS PALABRAS Y EXPRESIONES

en seguida
a tiempo completo
a tiempo parcial
la población activa
ojalá (que)
tal vez
quizá(s)

CAPÍTULO 16   435

NUESTRO MUNDO

OVERVIEW

All the readings presented in the *Nuestro Mundo* section are authentic, uncut texts from publications of the Hispanic world. Students should be encouraged to read the text for overall meaning, but not intensively, word for word. Students should find satisfaction in their ability to derive meaning from "real" texts. Each reading is related to a theme or themes covered in the previous four chapters.

PRESENTATION (pages 436-437)

A. Ask students what they would expect to find on a medicine label.
B. Have students open their books to pages 436-437 and ask them to read the information taken from the labels for the two medications.

NUESTRO MUNDO

Here are labels for two medications.

This one is from Mexico.

NAXEN

DOSIS: La que el médico señale.

VÍA DE ADMINISTRACIÓN: Oral

Su venta requiere receta médica.

Consérvese en lugar fresco y seco.

Protéjase de la luz.

No se deje al alcance de los niños.

No se administre en el embarazo y lactancia, ni en niños menores de 12 años.

FÓRMULA: Cada tableta contiene: Naproxén** 500 mg

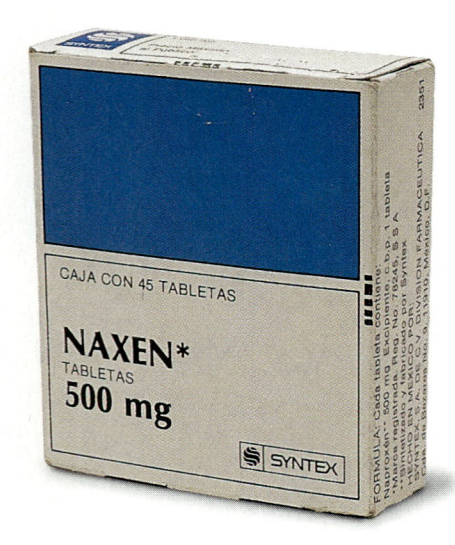

436 NUESTRO MUNDO

DID YOU KNOW?

Medications such as NAXEN, sold in the U.S. as Naprosyn, require a doctor's prescription in the U.S., but are sold "over the counter" in Spain and Latin America. There, it is very common for pharmacists to listen to symptoms and suggest medications.

This one is from Spain.

CORTAL

Alivia los dolores de cabeza, dolores musculares, neuralgia, los malestares de resfriados y baja la fiebre.

DOSIS: Adultos de 1 a 2 tabletas con agua. Repítase 1 tableta cada 3 o 4 horas si fuera necesario. Niños de 6 a 12 años, la mitad de las dosis para adultos. Para niños menores de 6 años, consúltese al médico.

FÓRMULA: cada tableta contiene: aspirina, 500 mg.; cafeína, 30 mg.

ADVERTENCIA: MANTENGA ÉSTE Y TODO MEDICAMENTO FUERA DEL ALCANCE DE LOS NIÑOS. EN CASO DE DOSIS EXCESIVA ACCIDENTAL, LLÁMESE AL MÉDICO INMEDIATAMENTE.

■ **Los medicamentos.** Now answer the following questions based on the information on the two labels.

1. Which of the medications would you probably take for a headache?
2. Which of the two medications always requires a doctor's prescription?
3. Both medications give the same warning. What is it?
4. Both medications are administered the same way. How?
5. Both contain the same amount of medication. How much is it?
6. Who should NOT take the medication *Naxen*?
7. With regard to *Cortal*, when should a doctor be notified?
8. What are the two ingredients of *Cortal*?
9. What is the price given for *Cortal*?
10. Which of the two medications probably has more serious side effects?

NUESTRO MUNDO 437

PAIRED ACTIVITY

CORTAL is a very popular headache remedy. Have pairs create a jingle for CORTAL and sing it to the class.

Ejercicio

PRESENTATION (*page 437*)

As you ask each question, have students indicate the place in the text that provided the information for their anwer.

ANSWERS

1. Cortal
2. Naxen
3. Keep out of reach of children.
4. Orally (by mouth)
5. 500 mg
6. Pregnant or nursing women
7. In case of an excessive accidental dose
8. Aspirin and caffeine
9. Free sample
10. Naxen

CRITICAL THINKING ACTIVITY

(*Thinking skills: making inferences; drawing conclusions*)

Write the following on the board or on an overhead transparency:

Compara las dosis para los dos medicamentos. ¿Qué diferencia hay entre las dos? ¿Qué nos puede indicar la diferencia?

REPASO
CAPÍTULOS 13–16

Conversación

MERCE: Hola, Manuel. ¿Adónde vas tan de prisa?

MANUEL: A la tintorería y después al banco antes de que cierren. Les pedí que limpiaran, plancharan y le quitaran unas manchas a mi uniforme de gala. Ojalá que puedan. Espero llegar a tiempo al banco. Tengo que cobrar un cheque. Mañana se casa mi hermana, y yo soy uno de los pajes.

MERCE: Ella se casa con Daniel, el hijo del abogado Ferraz, ¿verdad? El hombre tiene cuentas en todos los bancos. Tan pronto como se muera el viejo, se hará rico Danielito.

MANUEL: ¡Qué cosas dices, mujer! Y si no tuviera un céntimo, Sara todavía se casaría con él. Están enamorados, ¿no comprendes?

MERCE: Me callaré entonces, para que no te enfades, capitán. Oye, ¿te dije que tengo un puesto nuevo? Soy administradora con Teleuropa S.A.

MANUEL: ¿La multinacional? ¡Enhorabuena, Merce! Quizás te hagas millonaria igual que el viejo Ferraz.

MERCE: Si me hiciera millonaria, ¿te casarías conmigo?

MANUEL: Merce, contigo me casaría aunque fueras la mujer más pobre del mundo.

MERCE: Anda, guapo. Muchas gracias, pero busco un hombre que siempre diga la verdad. Hasta luego.

Los mandados. Contesten.

1. ¿Qué quiere Manuel que le hagan en la tintorería?
2. ¿Por qué tiene tanta prisa?
3. ¿Qué va a pasar mañana?
4. ¿Cuál será la profesión de Manuel?
5. ¿Por qué tiene que ir al banco?
6. ¿Con quién se casa Sara?
7. ¿Cuál es la profesión del padre del novio de Sara?
8. Según Merce, ¿que pasaría si se muriera el Sr. Ferraz?
9. ¿Por qué se casarían los novios aunque fuera pobre Daniel?
10. ¿Por qué no dice más Merce?
11. ¿Cuál es la nueva profesión de Merce?
12. ¿Qué le dice Manuel?
13. ¿Qué le pregunta Merce?
14. ¿Por qué no se casaría Merce con Manuel?

Estructura

El subjuntivo y el infinitivo

Remember, the subjunctive is used when there is a change of subject from the main clause to the dependent clause. If the subject of both clauses is the same, then the infinitive is used.

CHANGE OF SUBJECT	NO CHANGE OF SUBJECT
Yo quiero que tú comas.	Yo quiero comer.

A Quieren que... Contesten con *no* según el modelo.

Ella quiere que Luis juegue.
Pues, él no quiere jugar.

1. El profesor quiere que tú escribas.
2. Nosotros queremos que Uds. se vayan.
3. El director quiere que Rodríguez trabaje esta noche.
4. Mamá quiere que yo lave los platos.
5. Jorge quiere que Elena conduzca.

El imperfecto del subjuntivo

1. In order to form the imperfect subjunctive of all verbs, the ending of the third person plural of the preterite indicative -*on* is dropped and the appropriate imperfect subjunctive endings are added. Review the forms of the imperfect subjunctive.

hablar	hablara, hablaras, hablara, habláramos, *hablarais*, hablaran
comer	comiera, comieras, comiera, comiéramos, *comierais*, comieran
escribir	escribiera, escribieras, escribiera, escribiéramos, *escribierais*, escribieran

pedir	pidiera, pidieras, pidiera, pidiéramos, *pidierais*, pidieran
saber	supiera, supieras, supiera, supiéramos, *supierais*, supieran
venir	viniera, vinieras, viniera, viniéramos, *vinierais*, vinieran
oír	oyera, oyeras, oyera, oyéramos, *oyerais*, oyeran
decir	dijera, dijeras, dijera, dijéramos, *dijerais*, dijeran
ir/ser	fuera, fueras, fuera, fuéramos, *fuerais*, fueran

2. The past subjunctive functions as does the present subjunctive. If the verb of the main clause is present or future, the present subjunctive is used in the dependent clause. If the verb of the main clause is in the preterite, imperfect, or conditional, the verb of the dependent clause will be in the past subjunctive.

CAPÍTULOS 13–16 REPASO

---

9. Se casarían porque están enamorados.
10. Para que no se enfade Manuel.
11. Es administradora con Teleuropa S.A.
12. ¡Enhorabuena! Quizás te hagas millonaria.
13. Si me hiciera millonaria, ¿te casarías conmigo?
14. Por que ella busca un hombre que siempre diga la verdad.

Estructura

El subjuntivo y el infinitivo

PRESENTATION (page 439)

Note This section reviews the use of the subjunctive when there is a change of subject, as contrasted with the use of the infinitive when the subject is the same.

Have students open their books to page 439. Ask them to read the explanation silently.

PRESENTATION

Ejercicio A

Have a pair of students do the exercise with books open. Have one student make the statement and have the other respond.

ANSWERS

Ejercicio A

1. Pues, yo no quiero escribir.
2. Pues, nosotros no queremos ir.
3. Pues, Rodríguez no quiere trabajar esta noche.
4. Pues, yo no quiero lavar los platos.
5. Pues, Elena no quiere conducir.

El imperfecto del subjuntivo

PRESENTATION (page 439)

A. Lead students through steps 1 and 2.
B. Then have students repeat the verb forms in step 1.

LEARNING FROM PHOTOS

Have students say all they can about the photo on page 439. You may wish to cue them with questions such as the following: *¿Dónde está la muchacha? ¿Qué hace ella? ¿Qué hay en la botella? ¿Qué lleva ella en las manos?*

PRESENTATION (page 440)

Ejercicios B and *C*

Exercises B and C are to be done with books open.

ANSWERS

Ejercicio B
1. No, aunque yo quería que ganaran.
2. ... recibieran el cheque.
3. ... vendiera el coche.
4. ... estuviera contenta.
5. ... dijera la verdad.
6. ... tú lo hicieras bien.

Ejercicio C
1. trabajáramos
2. permitiera
3. tuviera
4. hiciéramos
5. pagara

El subjuntivo en cláusulas adverbiales

PRESENTATION (page 440)

Have students open their books to page 440 and ask them to read the explanation silently and to repeat the conjunctions after you.

PRESENTATION (page 440)

Ejercicio D

Allow students time to prepare Exercise D before going over it together in class.

ANSWERS

Ejercicio D
1. acompañara
2. dieran
3. paguen
4. pudiéramos
5. viaje

B ¿Quién ganó? Contesten según el modelo.

¿Roberto vino ayer?
No, aunque yo quería que viniera.

1. ¿Los "Osos" ganaron?
2. ¿Uds. recibieron el cheque?
3. ¿Francisco vendió el coche?
4. ¿La maestra estuvo contenta?
5. ¿Ernesto dijo la verdad?
6. ¿Tú lo hiciste bien?

C El trabajo. Completen.

1. El jefe quería que nosotros ___ el domingo. (trabajar)
2. Le pedimos que nos ___ trabajar el sábado. (permitir)
3. Yo le dije que ___ confianza en nosotros. (tener)
4. Era importante que ___ un trabajo perfecto. (hacer)
5. Sería bueno si el jefe nos ___ más. (pagar)

El subjuntivo en cláusulas adverbiales

Review the conjunctions that are followed by the subjunctive in the dependent clause:

para que	so that
de manera que	so that
de modo que	so that
con tal que	provided that
sin que	without, unless
a menos que	unless

Remember that *aunque* can be followed by either the subjunctive or the indicative. If there is a doubt expressed in the verb following *aunque,* the subjunctive is used. If there is no doubt, the indicative is used.

D Vamos a la capital. Completen.

Yo le dije a Rita que no iría a la capital sin que ella me ___ (acompañar).
                                                              1
Ella dijo que sí, con tal que sus padres le ___ (dar) el dinero para el viaje.
                                             2
A menos que ellos le ___ (pagar) el viaje, ella no podrá ir. Papá me dio unos
                      3
10.000 pesos para que nosotros ___ (poder) alquilar un carro. Pero, a menos
                                4
que ___ (viajar) Rita conmigo, yo no iré.
     5

440 CAPÍTULOS 13–16 REPASO

LEARNING FROM REALIA

Refer students to the advertisement on page 440 and have them say all they can about it. Cue with questions such as: *¿Ellos venden o alquilan carros? ¿Dónde tienen oficinas?*

El subjuntivo en cláusulas adverbiales de tiempo

1. Review the following adverbial expressions of time:

cuando	when
en cuanto	as soon as
tan pronto como	as soon as
hasta que	until
después de que	after

2. Remember, the subjunctive is used with these expressions when the action is to occur in the future. If the action has already occurred, then the indicative is used.

   Yo le hablaré tan pronto como llegue.
   Yo le hablé tan pronto como llegó.

3. The expression *antes de que* always takes the subjunctive, whether in past, present, or future.

E **El baile.** Completen.
1. Nosotros saldremos en cuanto nos ___ (servir) el café.
2. Pero tan pronto como ___ (sonar) la música, todos nos pusimos de pie.
3. Ya te dije, cuando tú y yo ___ (tener) una oportunidad, nos escaparemos.
4. Podremos salir después de que ___ (terminar) este baile.
5. Pero hasta que no se ___ (acabar) estaremos aquí.
6. Me mataré antes de que ___ (ir) a otra boda.
7. Te digo que no asistiré a otra boda hasta que ___ (casarse) nuestra hija.

Comunicación

A **Su amigo.** Su amigo mexicano se va a casar. Llame al periódico Excélsior y déles los detalles de la boda: nombres, fecha, lugar, hora, padrino, madrina, etc.

B **Una doctora muy famosa.** El periódico de su escuela le ha encargado a Ud. para que entreviste a una famosa doctora venezolana. Pregúntele sobre sus estudios, dónde trabaja, qué es lo que más le gusta de su trabajo, etc. Un(a) compañero(a) de clase hará el papel de la doctora.

EXCELSIOR
EL PERIODICO DE LA VIDA NACIONAL

Registrado Como Artículo de Segunda Clase en la Administración de Correos, el 18 de Marzo de 1917

CAPÍTULOS 13–16 REPASO

FONDO ACADÉMICO

LAS CIENCIAS: LA ECOLOGÍA
(optional material)

OVERVIEW

The three readings in this section deal with ecology, economics, and the Spanish artist Pablo Picasso.

Antes de leer

PRESENTATION (page 442)

A. Have students answer the questions in the *Antes de leer* section.
B. Provide students with a list of cognates in the selection or have them scan the selection and find them for themselves.

Lectura

PRESENTATION (pages 442-443)

A. Allow students 2-3 minutes to read each paragraph silently. Then ask what the paragraph is about.
B. Divide the class into four groups. Each group discusses one topic within the selection and reports on it to the rest of the class. You might divide the selection this way:
 1. coyotes in the U.S.
 2. car emissions
 3. Chernobyl and Bhopal
 4. overpopulation.

ABOUT THE LANGUAGE

The *coyote* gets its name from the Aztecs. They gave it the name *coyotl*.

442

FONDO ACADÉMICO

LAS CIENCIAS

El emblema de Madrid

Antes de leer

Recent years have witnessed a growing concern for the ecology. The very word is of relatively recent origin. In 1878 the German biologist Ernest Heinrich Haeckel coined the term to describe the relationship between animals and their organic and inorganic environments. In the following selection look for responses to these questions: What causes deserts?; Why have some species of animals disappeared?; What are some effects of overpopulation?; How do predators help humankind?

Lectura

EL HOMBRE, ¿ENEMIGO DE LA NATURALEZA?

El emblema de Madrid es el oso[1] y el madroño. Todavía se ven algunos madroños, un tipo de árbol, en Madrid. Pero los únicos osos están en el zoológico. No es solamente que el hombre los matara, sino que también destruyó su habitat. Para construir sus casas y plantar[2] sus cosechas[3] el hombre limpió la tierra de vegetación. Los bosques desaparecieron. Sin árboles, las lluvias y los vientos erosionaban la tierra y en poco tiempo la tierra misma estaba tan seca y gastada[4] que ya no era productiva. Las plantas evitan la erosión. Las plantas conservan el agua de la lluvia, proveen nutrimentos a la tierra y ayudan a conservar la humedad. Sin vegetación la tierra se convierte en desierto.

Existe un equilibrio[5] precario entre todos los seres vivientes[6], plantas y animales. Un ejemplo. En los EE.UU. muchos rancheros consideran enemigos a los coyotes porque de vez en cuando se comen una vaca o una oveja. Pero los coyotes se alimentan mayormente de ratones[7] y conejos[8]. Sin los coyotes, los conejos y ratones se multiplicarían rápidamente y se comerían grandes cantidades de la hierba[9] que necesita el ganado. Así, perderían los rancheros.

El aire, la tierra y el agua son tres elementos necesarios para la vida, pero los seguimos contaminando. Algunas sustancias químicas que llegan a los ríos desde las fábricas directamente o por lluvia ácida matan las plantas y los peces[10]. Los detergentes y las aguas negras[11] hacen multiplicar microorganismos que acaban con el oxígeno del agua. Sin oxígeno, las plantas, los peces y otros animales acuáticos mueren. Hay ríos "muertos"

442   FONDO ACADÉMICO

LEARNING FROM REALIA

The shield of Madrid depicts a bear and a *madroño* tree. Shields or coats of arms date back to the Middle Ages. In Spain, *blasón* is the word for the art of heraldry. Cities, states, families, and universities all have coats of arms. Have students find the coat of arms or shield of their state or city, and describe it in detail, in Spanish.

FONDO ACADÉMICO

donde no vive nada. En algunas zonas la contaminación del aire, causada por las emisiones de vehículos y fábricas, es tan grave que mucha gente se enferma y muere. La Ciudad de México es un ejemplo. La contaminación del aire hizo que el gobierno limitara el uso de automóviles en la ciudad. Y no podemos olvidarnos del desastre de Chernobil (1986), cuando el reactor atómico se destruyó por fusión emitiendo cantidades de material radiactivo al aire; y la tragedia de Bhopal en la India (1984), donde un accidente en una fábrica química contaminó el aire de gases tóxicos que mataron a más de 2.000 e hicieron daño a unos 150.000. La población humana está creciendo aceleradamente. En México unos 34 niños nacen al año por cada 1.000 personas; en España 12, y en los EE.UU. 16. La superpoblación resulta en una demanda excesiva de energía, de tierra, de vivienda[12] y de varios recursos naturales[13]. Perdemos para siempre bosques y acuíferos. Queremos satisfacer las necesidades de la humanidad sin destruir la naturaleza y la calidad de vida. No será fácil.

[1] el oso *bear*
[2] plantar *to plant*
[3] cosechas *crops*
[4] gastada *barren*
[5] equilibrio *balance*
[6] los seres vivientes *living beings*
[7] ratones *mice*
[8] conejos *rabbits*
[9] la hierba *grass*
[10] los peces *fish*
[11] las aguas negras *sewage*
[12] vivienda *housing*
[13] recursos naturales *natural resources*

Después de leer

A ¿Por qué? Contesten.

1. ¿Cómo ayudan los coyotes a los rancheros?
2. ¿Qué ocurre cuando echan grandes cantidades de detergentes y aguas negras a los ríos?
3. ¿Cómo y por qué "mueren" los ríos?
4. ¿Cuáles son algunos problemas que causa la superpoblación?
5. ¿Por qué quieren algunos rancheros eliminar a los coyotes?

B Seguimiento. Contesten.

1. Explique por qué desaparecen algunas especies de animales.
2. Explique como se forman los desiertos.
3. ¿Qué es la "lluvia ácida"?
4. El acidente nuclear afectó plantas y animales en otras partes de Europa lejos de Chernobil. Explique por qué.
5. Infórmese sobre el desastre de Bhopal y escriba un breve informe en español.

FONDO ACADÉMICO 443

FONDO ACADÉMICO

LAS CIENCIAS SOCIALES: LA ECONOMÍA

Antes de leer

PRESENTATION (page 444)

A. Allow students time to read the *Antes de leer* material silently and review the terms it contains.

B. Have pairs of students compile lists of cognates from the reading selection.

Lectura

PRESENTATION (pages 444-445)

Have students read the selection aloud or silently.

FONDO ACADÉMICO

LAS CIENCIAS SOCIALES: LA ECONOMÍA

Antes de leer

The British economist Robert Malthus (1766-1834) called economics "the dismal science." Dismal or not, a knowledge of economic principles is essential to survival in the modern world. The following selection provides a brief explanation of economics. Please review the following terms in preparation: capital, natural resources, human resources, raw material, real property, opportunity costs.

Lectura

LA ECONOMÍA

Hay varias definiciones de economía. Es el estudio de las decisiones que se toman en la producción, distribución y consumo[1] de bienes[2] y servicios. Es el estudio de las maneras en que las sociedades deciden lo que se va a producir, cómo se va a producir y para quién. Y es el estudio del uso y control de recursos limitados para satisfacer las necesidades y los deseos humanos.

Las necesidades materiales de individuos e instituciones no tienen límite. Hay artículos de primera necesidad como la comida y la ropa. Hay bienes y servicios que no son de primera necesidad, pero son importantes para algunas personas: los diamantes, los perfumes, los viajes de turismo. Los recursos económicos sí tienen límite. Los recursos son escasos[3]. Los recursos económicos son el total de recursos naturales, humanos y fabricados que se usan en la producción de bienes y la provisión de servicios.

Los recursos se dividen en dos categorías: los recursos de propiedad[4] —bienes raíces[5], materia prima[6] y capital— y los recursos humanos. Debido a que los recursos productivos son escasos, es imposible dar a la sociedad todos los bienes y servicios que desea. La escasez de recursos nos obliga a escoger entre los diferentes bienes y servicios.

Si usamos los recursos para una cosa, perdemos la oportunidad de usar esos recursos para otra cosa. Este sacrificio se llama "el costo de oportunidad". Si decides ir al cine en lugar de estudiar para un examen, estás sacrificando la oportunidad de estudiar. Es el costo de oportunidad de ir al cine.

Los economistas tratan de contestar preguntas como: ¿Por qué sufrimos

444 FONDO ACADÉMICO

CRITICAL THINKING ACTIVITY

(Thinking skills: seeing relationships; evaluating sources of ideas)

Write the following on the board or on a transparency:

Malthus decía que mientras la población crecía geométricamente, las fuentes de comestibles crecían aritméticamente. Ésta es la "teoría de Malthus". Explique lo que quiere decir la teoría y, si fuera verdad, ¿cuál sería el resultado?

444

FONDO ACADÉMICO

períodos de desempleo? ¿Cuál es el efecto del déficit público en la inflación y en el desempleo? ¿Cómo afecta el valor del dólar a la economía de los EE.UU.?

[1] consumo *consumption*
[2] bienes *goods*
[3] escasos *scarce*
[4] propiedad *property*
[5] bienes raíces *real estate*
[6] materia prima *raw material*

La Bolsa de Valores, Argentina

Después de leer

A ¿Qué es? Escojan.

recurso de propiedad
recurso humano

1. una fábrica
2. el carbón
3. una ingeniera
4. el dinero
5. los obreros
6. una máquina

B La economía. Contesten.

1. ¿Cuáles son algunos bienes de primera necesidad?
2. ¿Cuáles son dos bienes que no son de primera necesidad?
3. ¿Qué son escasos?
4. ¿Cuáles son las dos categorías de recursos?
5. ¿Por qué hay que escoger entre diferentes bienes y servicios?

C Seguimiento. Contesten.

1. Malthus tenía una teoría económica muy famosa. Busque la teoría y escriba un resumen breve de la teoría en español.
2. Dé un ejemplo original de un "costo de oportunidad".
3. Dé las tres definiciones de "economía".
4. Diga cuál de los dos tipos de recursos —recursos de propiedad y recursos humanos— Ud. considera más importantes y explique por qué.

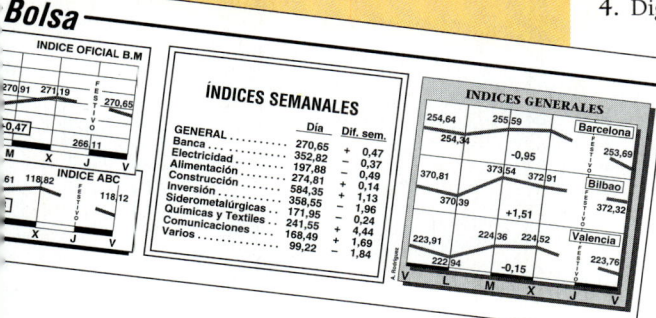

FONDO ACADÉMICO **445**

Después de leer

PRESENTATION (page 445)

Ejercicios A, B, and C

Have the students scan the *Lectura* for the answers to the exercises.

ANSWERS

Ejercicio A
1. recurso de propiedad
2. recurso de propiedad
3. recurso humano
4. recurso de propiedad
5. recurso humano
6. recurso de propiedad

Ejercicio B
1. La comida y la ropa son bienes de primera necesidad.
2. Dos bienes que no son de primera necesidad son los diamantes y los perfumes.
3. Los recursos son escasos.
4. Las dos categorías de recursos son: los recursos de propiedad y los recursos humanos.
5. La escasez de recursos nos obliga a escoger entre los diferentes bienes y servicios.

Ejercicio C
1. Answers will vary.
2. Answers may resemble the following model. Tengo la oportunidad de trabajar o ir de viaje durante el verano. Si escojo el viaje, tengo que sacrificar la oportunidad de trabajar y ganar dinero.
3. La economía es el estudio de las decisiones que se toman en la producción, distribución y consumo de bienes y servicios. Es el estudio de las maneras en que las sociedades deciden lo que se va a producir. Es el estudio del uso y control de recursos limitados para satisfacer las necesidades y los deseos humanos.
4. Answers will vary.

445

FONDO ACADÉMICO

LAS HUMANIDADES: LAS BELLAS ARTES

Antes de leer

PRESENTATION (page 446)

Allow students some time to study the photo and art on pages 446-447.

Lectura

PRESENTATION (page 446)

Have students read the selection silently.

FONDO ACADÉMICO

LAS HUMANIDADES: LAS BELLAS ARTES

Antes de leer

The work people do has often been a source of artistic expression. In the work of the Spanish artist Pablo Picasso, for example, bullfighters and circus performers appear again and again. Picasso began painting in the 19th century and continued until his death in 1973. He went through various styles, from realism to cubism. Here are four paintings by Picasso that depict members of different professions or callings. Please study the pictures.

Las profesiones en cuatro obras de Picasso.

Pablo Picasso (1881-1973)

a.

b.

446 FONDO ACADÉMICO

LEARNING FROM REALIA

Refer to the four paintings reproduced on pages 446-447. Have students describe each of them. Ask them to respond emotionally to the works as well. Cue with questions such as the following:

a. ¿Cómo te sientes al ver el cuadro del actor? ¿Dónde está el público? ¿Por qué no pone Picasso el público en el cuadro?

b. Mira el cuadro de "El peinado". ¿Cómo es la señora? ¿Qué se le ve a la señora que la peina? ¿Por qué sólo se le ven las manos?

c. Mira la "Familia de saltimbanquis". Describe su actitud. ¿Qué expresión parecen tener todos en la cara? ¿Por qué será?

d. El cuadro de "Los músicos" es uno de los más famosos de Picasso. ¿Cómo se sabe que son músicos? ¿Qué otros pintores eran cubistas? ¿Qué querían decirnos con ese estilo?

446

FONDO ACADÉMICO

Después de leer

A Las obras. Contesten.

1. ¿Cuál de las obras es cubista?
2. ¿Qué oficios o profesiones representan?
3. ¿Cuál de los cuadros es de un actor?
4. ¿En qué cuadro aparecen artistas del circo?
5. Picasso pintó tres de los cuadros durante un período de dos o tres años. ¿Cuál de los cuadros pintó Picasso quince años más tarde? ¿Qué lo indica?

B El título. Pareen el título con el cuadro.

1. ____ La familia de saltimbanques (acróbatas)
2. ____ El peinado
3. ____ Tres músicos
4. ____ El actor

C Seguimiento. Contesten

1. Indique cuál de las obras Ud. considera la menos realista y por qué.
2. Tres de los oficios o profesiones que se representan en los cuadros tienen algo en común. ¿Qué? Comenten.
3. Los historiadores del arte hablan del "período rosa" y del "período azul" en la obra de Picasso. ¿Cuál de los cuadros es de cada uno de los dos períodos?

c.

d.

FONDO ACADÉMICO **447**

DID YOU KNOW?

El cuadro "Los tres músicos" es una obra cubista. El cubismo fue un movimiento artístico que comenzó en París alrededor de 1907. Pablo Picasso fue uno de los más importantes pintores cubistas. Otros fueron el español Juan Gris y el francés Georges Braque. El movimiento duró hasta poco después de la Primera Guerra Mundial.

Después de leer

PRESENTATION (page 447)

A. After completing the *Después de leer* activities, have students prepare their own lists of painters, authors, and other artists whom they particularly like.

B. Ask students: *¿Quiénes son algunos artistas españoles y mexicanos?*

ANSWERS

Ejercicio A
1. d
2. actor, peluquera, saltimbanqui, músico
3. a
4. c
5. Los músicos. El estilo ha cambiado mucho.

Ejercicio B
1. c
2. b
3. d
4. a

Ejercicio C
Answers will vary.

447

APÉNDICES

449

MAPAS

ESPAÑA

Mar Cantábrico
Golfo de Vizcaya
Océano Atlántico
Mar Mediterráneo

FRANCIA
ANDORRA
PORTUGAL
ARGELIA
MARRUECOS

ISLAS BALEARES
- Menorca
- Mallorca
- Palma de Mallorca
- Ibiza
- Formentera

Ciudades y puntos:
- Santiago de Compostela
- Oviedo
- Santander
- Bilbao
- San Sebastián
- Pamplona
- León
- Burgos
- Zaragoza
- Barcelona
- Valladolid
- Salamanca
- Segovia
- Ávila
- Madrid
- Toledo
- Valencia
- Alicante
- Murcia
- Córdoba
- Sevilla
- Granada
- Málaga
- Jerez de la Frontera
- Cádiz
- Tánger
- Gibraltar (R.U.)
- Ceuta (Esp.)
- Peñón de Vélez de la Gomera (Esp.)
- Peñón de Alhucemas (Esp.)
- Melilla (Esp.)
- Islas Chafarinas (Esp.)
- Lisboa

Relieve:
- CORDILLERA CANTÁBRICA
- PIRINEOS
- SIERRA DE GUADARRAMA
- SIERRA MORENA
- SIERRA NEVADA

Ríos: Ebro, Duero, Tajo, Guadiana, Guadalquivir

ISLAS CANARIAS
- La Palma
- Santa Cruz de Tenerife
- Tenerife
- Gomera
- Gran (Canaria)
- Las Palmas
- Lanzarote
- Fuerteventura

452

LA AMÉRICA DEL SUR

MÉXICO, LA AMÉRICA CENTRAL Y EL CARIBE

VERBOS

A. Verbos regulares

INFINITIVO	hablar *to speak*	comer *to eat*	vivir *to live*
PRESENTE PROGRESIVO[1]	estar hablando	estar comiendo	estar viviendo
PRESENTE	yo hablo tú hablas él, ella, Ud. habla nosotros(as) hablamos *vosotros(as) habláis* ellos, ellas, Uds. hablan	yo como tú comes él, ella, Ud. come nosotros(as) comemos *vosotros(as) coméis* ellos, ellas, Uds. comen	yo vivo tú vives él, ella, Ud. vive nosotros(as) vivimos *vosotros(as) vivís* ellos, ellas, Uds. viven
PRETÉRITO	yo hablé tú hablaste él, ella, Ud. habló nosotros(as) hablamos *vosotros(as) hablasteis* ellos, ellas, Uds. hablaron	yo comí tú comiste él, ella, Ud. comió nosotros(as) comimos *vosotros(as) comisteis* ellos, ellas, Uds. comieron	yo viví tú viviste él, ella, Ud. vivió nosotros(as) vivimos *vosotros(as) vivisteis* ellos, ellas, Uds. vivieron
IMPERFECTO	yo hablaba tú hablabas él, ella, Ud. hablaba nosotros(as) hablábamos *vosotros(as) hablabais* ellos, ellas, Uds. hablaban	yo comía tú comías él, ella, Ud. comía nosotros(as) comíamos *vosotros(as) comíais* ellos, ellas, Uds. comían	yo vivía tú vivías él, ella, Ud. vivía nosotros(as) vivíamos *vosotros(as) vivíais* ellos, ellas, Uds. vivían
FUTURO	yo hablaré tú hablarás él, ella, Ud. hablará nosotros(as) hablaremos *vosotros(as) hablaréis* ellos, ellas, Uds. hablarán	yo comeré tú comerás él, ella, Ud. comerá nosotros(as) comeremos *vosotros(as) comeréis* ellos, ellas, Uds. comerán	yo viviré tú vivirás él, ella, Ud. vivirá nosotros(as) viviremos *vosotros(as) viviréis* ellos, ellas, Uds. vivirán
POTENCIAL	yo hablaría tú hablarías él, ella, Ud. hablaría nosotros(as) hablaríamos *vosotros(as) hablaríais* ellos, ellas, Uds. hablarían	yo comería tú comerías él, ella, Ud. comería nosotros(as) comeríamos *vosotros(as) comeríais* ellos, ellas, Uds. comerían	yo viviría tú vivirías él, ella, Ud. viviría nosotros(as) viviríamos *vosotros(as) viviríais* ellos, ellas, Uds. vivirían

[1]Verbos con gerundio irregular: *caer: cayendo, construir: construyendo, contribuir: contribuyendo, distribuir: distribuyendo*

A. Verbos regulares

INFINITIVO	hablar *to speak*	comer *to eat*	vivir *to live*
PRESENTE PERFECTO[2]	yo he hablado tú has hablado él, ella, Ud. ha hablado nosotros(as) hemos hablado *vosotros(as) habéis hablado* ellos, ellas, Uds. han hablado	yo he comido tú has comido él, ella, Ud. ha comido nosotros(as) hemos comido *vosotros(as) habéis comido* ellos, ellas, Uds. han comido	yo he vivido tú has vivido él, ella, Ud. ha vivido nosotros(as) hemos vivido *vosotros(as) habéis vivido* ellos, ellas, Uds. han vivido
SUBJUNTIVO PRESENTE	yo hable tú hables él, ella, Ud. hable nosotros(as) hablemos *vosotros(as) habléis* ellos, ellas, Uds. hablen	yo coma tú comas él, ella, Ud. coma nosotros(as) comamos *vosotros(as) comáis* ellos, ellas, Uds. coman	yo viva tú vivas él, ella, Ud. viva nosotros(as) vivamos *vosotros(as) viváis* ellos, ellas, Uds. vivan
SUBJUNTIVO IMPERFECTO	yo hablara tú hablaras él, ella, Ud. hablara nosotros(as) habláramos *vosotros(as) hablarais* ellos, ellas, Uds. hablaran	yo comiera tú comieras él, ella, Ud. comiera nosotros(as) comiéramos *vosotros(as) comierais* ellos, ellas, Uds. comieran	yo viviera tú vivieras él, ella, Ud. viviera nosotros(as) viviéramos *vosotros(as) vivierais* ellos, ellas, Uds. vivieran
IMPERATIVO FORMAL	hable (Ud.) hablen (Uds.)	coma (Ud.) coman (Uds.)	viva (Ud.) vivan (Uds.)
IMPERATIVO FAMILIAR	habla (tú)	come (tú)	vive (tú)

[2]Verbos con participio pasado irregular: *abrir: abierto, cubrir: cubierto, devolver: devuelto, escribir: escrito, freír: frito, morir: muerto, ver: visto*

VERBOS

B. Verbos con cambio radical

INFINITIVO	preferir[3] (e>ie) *to prefer*	volver[4] (o>ue) *to return*	pedir[5] (e>i) *to ask for*
PRESENTE PROGRESIVO	estar prefiriendo	estar volviendo	estar pidiendo
PRESENTE	yo prefiero tú prefieres él, ella, Ud. prefiere nosotros(as) preferimos *vosotros(as) preferís* ellos, ellas, Uds. prefieren	yo vuelvo tú vuelves él, ella, Ud. vuelve nosotros(as) volvemos *vosotros(as) volvéis* ellos, ellas, Uds. vuelven	yo pido tú pides él, ella, Ud. pide nosotros(as) pedimos *vosotros(as) pedís* ellos, ellas, Uds. piden
PRETÉRITO	yo preferí tú preferiste él, ella, Ud. prefirió nosotros(as) preferimos *vosotros(as) preferisteis* ellos, ellas, Uds. prefirieron	yo volví tú volviste él, ella, Ud. volvió nosotros(as) volvimos *vosotros(as) volvisteis* ellos, ellas, Uds. volvieron	yo pedí tú pediste él, ella, Ud. pidió nosotros(as) pedimos *vosotros(as) pedisteis* ellos, ellas, Uds. pidieron
IMPERFECTO	yo prefería tú preferías él, ella, Ud. prefería nosotros(as) preferíamos *vosotros(as) preferíais* ellos, ellas, Uds. preferían	yo volvía tú volvías él, ella, Ud. volvía nosotros(as) volvíamos *vosotros(as) volvíais* ellos, ellas, Uds. volvían	yo pedía tú pedías él, ella, Ud. pedía nosotros(as) pedíamos *vosotros(as) pedíais* ellos, ellas, Uds. pedían
FUTURO	yo preferiré tú preferirás él, ella, Ud. preferirá nosotros(as) preferiremos *vosotros(as) preferiréis* ellos, ellas, Uds. preferirán	yo volveré tú volverás él, ella, Ud. volverá nosotros(as) volveremos *vosotros(as) volveréis* ellos, ellas, Uds. volverán	yo pediré tú pedirás él, ella, Ud. pedirá nosotros(as) pediremos *vosotros(as) pediréis* ellos, ellas, Uds. pedirán
POTENCIAL	yo preferiría tú preferirías él, ella, Ud. preferiría nosotros(as) preferiríamos *vosotros(as) preferiríais* ellos, ellas, Uds. preferirían	yo volvería tú volverías él, ella, Ud. volvería nosotros(as) volveríamos *vosotros(as) volveríais* ellos, ellas, Uds. volverían	yo pediría tú pedirías él, ella, Ud. pediría nosotros(as) pediríamos *vosotros(as) pediríais* ellos, ellas, Uds. pedirían

[3]Verbos similares: *sugerir: sugiriendo*

[4]Verbos similares: *morir: muriendo, jugar*

[5]Verbos similares: *freír: friendo, pedir: pidiendo, repetir: repitiendo, seguir: siguiendo, sentir: sintiendo, servir: sirviendo*

B. Verbos con cambio radical

INFINITIVO	preferir[3] (e>ie) *to prefer*	volver[4] (o>ue) *to return*	pedir[5] (e>i) *to ask for*
PRESENTE PERFECTO	yo he preferido tú has preferido él, ella, Ud. ha preferido nosotros(as) hemos preferido *vosotros(as) habéis preferido* ellos, ellas, Uds. han preferido	yo he vuelto tú has vuelto él, ella, Ud. ha vuelto nosotros(as) hemos vuelto *vosotros(as) habéis vuelto* ellos, ellas, Uds. han vuelto	yo he pedido tú has pedido él, ella, Ud. ha pedido nosotros(as) hemos pedido *vosotros(as) habéis pedido* ellos, ellas, Uds. han pedido
SUBJUNTIVO PRESENTE	yo prefiera tú prefieras él, ella, Ud. prefiera nosotros(as) prefiramos *vosotros(as) prefiráis* ellos, ellas, Uds. prefieran	yo vuelva tú vuelvas él, ella, Ud. vuelva nosotros(as) volvamos *vosotros(as) volváis* ellos, ellas, Uds. vuelvan	yo pida tú pidas él, ella, Ud. pida nosotros(as) pidamos *vosotros(as) pedáis* ellos, ellas, Uds. pidan
SUBJUNTIVO IMPERFECTO	yo prefiriera tú prefirieras él, ella, Ud. prefiriera nosotros(as) prefiriéramos *vosotros(as) prefirierais* ellos, ellas, Uds. prefirieran	yo volviera tú volvieras él, ella, Ud. volviera nosotros(as) volviéramos *vosotros(as) volvierais* ellos, ellas, Uds. volvieran	yo pidiera tú pidieras él, ella, Ud. pidiera nosotros(as) pidiéramos *vosotros(as) pidierais* ellos, ellas, Uds. pidieran
IMPERATIVO FORMAL	prefiera (Ud.) prefieran (Uds.)	vuelva (Ud.) vuelvan (Uds.)	pida (Ud.) pidan (Uds.)
IMPERATIVO FAMILIAR	prefiere (tú)	vuelve (tú)	pide (tú)

[3]Verbos similares: *sugerir: sugiriendo*

[4]Verbos similares: *morir: muriendo, jugar*

[5]Verbos similares: *freír: friendo, pedir: pidiendo, repetir: repitiendo, seguir: siguiendo, sentir: sintiendo, servir: sirviendo*

VERBOS **459**

C. Verbos irregulares

INFINITIVO	**andar** *to walk*	**conocer** *to know*	**dar** *to give*
PRESENTE PROGRESIVO	estar andando	estar conociendo	estar dando
PRESENTE	yo ando tú andas él, ella, Ud. anda nosotros(as) andamos *vosotros(as) andáis* ellos, ellas, Uds. andan	yo conozco tú conoces él, ella, Ud. conoce nosotros(as) conocemos *vosotros(as) conocéis* ellos, ellas, Uds. conocen	yo doy tú das él, ella, Ud. da nosotros(as) damos *vosotros(as) dais* ellos, ellas, Uds. dan
PRETÉRITO	yo anduve tú anduviste él, ella, Ud. anduvo nosotros(as) anduvimos *vosotros(as) anduvisteis* ellos, ellas, Uds. anduvieron	yo conocí tú conociste él, ella, Ud. conoció nosotros(as) conocimos *vosotros(as) conocisteis* ellos, ellas, Uds. conocieron	yo di tú diste él, ella, Ud. dio nosotros(as) dimos *vosotros(as) disteis* ellos, ellas, Uds. dieron
IMPERFECTO	yo andaba tú andabas él, ella, Ud. andaba nosotros(as) andábamos *vosotros(as) andabais* ellos, ellas, Uds. andaban	yo conocía tú conocías él, ella, Ud. conocía nosotros(as) conocíamos *vosotros(as) conocíais* ellos, ellas, Uds. conocían	yo daba tú dabas él, ella, Ud. daba nosotros(as) dábamos *vosotros(as) dabais* ellos, ellas, Uds. daban
FUTURO	yo andaré tú andarás él, ella, Ud. andará nosotros(as) andaremos *vosotros(as) andaréis* ellos, ellas, Uds. andarán	yo conoceré tú conocerás él, ella, Ud. conocerá nosotros(as) conoceremos *vosotros(as) conoceréis* ellos, ellas, Uds. conocerán	yo daré tú darás él, ella, Ud. dará nosotros(as) daremos *vosotros(as) daréis* ellos, ellas, Uds. darán
POTENCIAL	yo andaría tú andarías él, ella, Ud. andaría nosotros(as) andaríamos *vosotros(as) andaríais* ellos, ellas, Uds. andarían	yo conocería tú conocerías él, ella, Ud. conocería nosotros(as) conoceríamos *vosotros(as) conoceríais* ellos, ellas, Uds. conocerían	yo daría tú darías él, ella, Ud. daría nosotros(as) daríamos *vosotros(as) daríais* ellos, ellas, Uds. darían

C. Verbos irregulares

INFINITIVO	**andar** *to walk*	**conocer** *to know*	**dar** *to give*
PRESENTE PERFECTO	yo he andado tú has andado él, ella, Ud. ha andado nosotros(as) hemos andado *vosotros(as) habéis andado* ellos, ellas, Uds. han andado	yo he conocido tú has conocido él, ella, Ud. ha conocido nosotros(as) hemos conocido *vosotros(as) habéis conocido* ellos, ellas, Uds. han conocido	yo he dado tú has dado él, ella, Ud. ha dado nosotros(as) hemos dado *vosotros(as) habéis dado* ellos, ellas, Uds. han dado
SUBJUNTIVO PRESENTE	yo ande tú andes él, ella, Ud. ande nosotros(as) andemos *vosotros(as) andéis* ellos, ellas, Uds. anden	yo conozca tú conozcas él, ella, Ud. conozca nosotros(as) conozcamos *vosotros(as) conozcáis* ellos, ellas, Uds. conozcan	yo dé tú des él, ella, Ud. dé nosotros(as) demos *vosotros(as) deis* ellos, ellas, Uds. den
SUBJUNTIVO IMPERFECTO	yo anduviera tú anduvieras él, ella, Ud. anduviera nosotros(as) anduviéramos *vosotros(as) anduvierais* ellos, ellas, Uds. anduvieran	yo conociera tú conocieras él, ella, Ud. conociera nosotros(as) conociéramos *vosotros(as) conocierais* ellos, ellas, Uds. conocieran	yo diera tú dieras él, ella, Ud. diera nosotros(as) diéramos *vosotros(as) dierais* ellos, ellas, Uds. dieran
IMPERATIVO FORMAL	ande (Ud.) anden (Uds.)	conozca (Ud.) conozcan (Uds.)	dé (Ud.) den (Uds.)
IMPERATIVO FAMILIAR	anda (tú)	conoce (tú)	da (tú)

C. Verbos irregulares

INFINITIVO	**decir** *to say, to tell*	**empezar** *to begin*	**estar** *to be*
PRESENTE PROGRESIVO	estar diciendo	estar empezando	
PRESENTE	yo digo tú dices él, ella, Ud. dice nosotros(as) decimos *vosotros(as) decís* ellos, ellas, Uds. dicen	yo empiezo tú empiezas él, ella, Ud. empieza nosotros(as) empezamos *vosotros(as) empezáis* ellos, ellas, Uds. empiezan	yo estoy tú estás él, ella, Ud. está nosotros(as) estamos *vosotros(as) estáis* ellos, ellas, Uds. están
PRETÉRITO	yo dije tú dijiste él, ella, Ud. dijo nosotros(as) dijimos *vosotros(as) dijisteis* ellos, ellas, Uds. dijeron	yo empecé tú empezaste él, ella, Ud. empezó nosotros(as) empezamos *vosotros(as) empezasteis* ellos, ellas, Uds. empezaron	yo estuve tú estuviste él, ella, Ud. estuvo nosotros(as) estuvimos *vosotros(as) estuvisteis* ellos, ellas, Uds. estuvieron
IMPERFECTO	yo decía tú decías él, ella, Ud. decía nosotros(as) decíamos *vosotros(as) decíais* ellos, ellas, Uds. decían	yo empezaba tú empezabas él, ella, Ud. empezaba nosotros(as) empezábamos *vosotros(as) empezabais* ellos, ellas, Uds. empezaban	yo estaba tú estabas él, ella, Ud. estaba nosotros(as) estábamos *vosotros(as) estabais* ellos, ellas, Uds. estaban
FUTURO	yo diré tú dirás él, ella, Ud. dirá nosotros(as) diremos *vosotros(as) diréis* ellos, ellas, Uds. dirán	yo empezaré tú empezarás él, ella, Ud. empezará nosotros(as) empezaremos *vosotros(as) empezaréis* ellos, ellas, Uds. empezarán	yo estaré tú estarás él, ella, Ud. estará nosotros(as) estaremos *vosotros(as) estaréis* ellos, ellas, Uds. estarán
POTENCIAL	yo diría tú dirías él, ella, Ud. diría nosotros(as) diríamos *vosotros(as) diríais* ellos, ellas, Uds. dirían	yo empezaría tú empezarías él, ella, Ud. empezaría nosotros(as) empezaríamos *vosotros(as) empezaríais* ellos, ellas, Uds. empezarían	yo estaría tú estarías él, ella, Ud. estaría nosotros(as) estaríamos *vosotros(as) estaríais* ellos, ellas, Uds. estarían

C. Verbos irregulares

INFINITIVO	decir *to say, to tell*	empezar *to begin*	estar *to be*
PRESENTE PERFECTO	yo he dicho tú has dicho él, ella, Ud. ha dicho nosotros(as) hemos dicho *vosotros(as) habéis dicho* ellos, ellas, Uds. han dicho	yo he empezado tú has empezado él, ella, Ud. ha empezado nosotros(as) hemos empezado *vosotros(as) habéis empezado* ellos, ellas, Uds. han empezado	yo he estado tú has estado él, ella, Ud. ha estado nosotros(as) hemos estado *vosotros(as) habéis estado* ellos, ellas, Uds. han estado
SUBJUNTIVO PRESENTE	yo diga tú digas él, ella, Ud. diga nosotros(as) digamos *vosotros(as) digáis* ellos, ellas, Uds. digan	yo empiece tú empieces él, ella, Ud. empiece nosotros(as) empecemos *vosotros(as) empecéis* ellos, ellas, Uds. empiecen	yo esté tú estés él, ella, Ud. esté nosotros(as) estemos *vosotros(as) estéis* ellos, ellas, Uds. estén
SUBJUNTIVO IMPERFECTO	yo dijera tú dijeras él, ella, Ud. dijera nosotros(as) dijéramos *vosotros(as) dijerais* ellos, ellas, Uds. dijeran	yo empezara tú empezaras él, ella, Ud. empezara nosotros(as) empezáramos *vosotros(as) empezarais* ellos, ellas, Uds. empezaran	yo estuviera tú estuvieras él, ella, Ud. estuviera nosotros(as) estuviéramos *vosotros(as) estuvierais* ellos, ellas, Uds. estuvieran
IMPERATIVO FORMAL	diga (Ud.) digan (Uds.)	empiece (Ud.) empiecen (Uds.)	esté (Ud.) estén (Uds.)
IMPERATIVO FAMILIAR	di (tú)	empieza (tú)	está (tú)

C. Verbos irregulares

INFINITIVO	**hacer** *to do*	**ir** *to go*	**leer** *to read*
PRESENTE PROGRESIVO	estar haciendo	estar yendo	estar leyendo
PRESENTE	yo hago tú haces él, ella, Ud. hace nosotros(as) hacemos *vosotros(as) hacéis* ellos, ellas, Uds. hacen	yo voy tú vas él, ella, Ud. va nosotros(as) vamos *vosotros(as) vais* ellos, ellas, Uds. van	yo leo tú lees él, ella, Ud. lee nosotros(as) leemos *vosotros(as) leéis* ellos, ellas, Uds. leen
PRETÉRITO	yo hice tú hiciste él, ella, Ud. hizo nosotros(as) hicimos *vosotros(as) hicisteis* ellos, ellas, Uds. hicieron	yo fui tú fuiste él, ella, Ud. fue nosotros(as) fuimos *vosotros(as) fuisteis* ellos, ellas, Uds. fueron	yo leí tú leíste él, ella, Ud. leyó nosotros(as) leímos *vosotros(as) leísteis* ellos, ellas, Uds. leyeron
IMPERFECTO	yo hacía tú hacías él, ella, Ud. hacía nosotros(as) hacíamos *vosotros(as) hacíais* ellos, ellas, Uds. hacían	yo iba tú ibas él, ella, Ud. iba nosotros(as) íbamos *vosotros(as) ibais* ellos, ellas, Uds. iban	yo leía tú leías él, ella, Ud. leía nosotros(as) leíamos *vosotros(as) leíais* ellos, ellas, Uds. leían
FUTURO	yo haré tú harás él, ella, Ud. hará nosotros(as) haremos *vosotros(as) haréis* ellos, ellas, Uds. harán	yo iré tú irás él, ella, Ud. irá nosotros(as) iremos *vosotros(as) iréis* ellos, ellas, Uds. irán	yo leeré tú leerás él, ella, Ud. leerá nosotros(as) leeremos *vosotros(as) leeréis* ellos, ellas, Uds. leerán
POTENCIAL	yo haría tú harías él, ella, Ud. haría nosotros(as) haríamos *vosotros(as) haríais* ellos, ellas, Uds. harían	yo iría tú irías él, ella, Ud. iría nosotros(as) iríamos *vosotros(as) iríais* ellos, ellas, Uds. irían	yo leería tú leerías él, ella, Ud. leería nosotros(as) leeríamos *vosotros(as) leeríais* ellos, ellas, Uds. leerían

C. Verbos irregulares

INFINITIVO	hacer *to do*	ir *to go*	leer *to read*
PRESENTE PERFECTO	yo he hecho tú has hecho él, ella, Ud. ha hecho nosotros(as) hemos hecho *vosotros(as) habéis hecho* ellos, ellas, Uds. han hecho	yo he ido tú has ido él, ella, Ud. ha ido nosotros(as) hemos ido *vosotros(as) habéis ido* ellos, ellas, Uds. han ido	yo he leído tú has leído él, ella, Ud. ha leído nosotros(as) hemos leído *vosotros(as) habéis leído* ellos, ellas, Uds. han leído
SUBJUNTIVO PRESENTE	yo haga tú hagas él, ella, Ud. haga nosotros(as) hagamos *vosotros(as) hagáis* ellos, ellas, Uds. hagan	yo vaya tú vayas él, ella, Ud. vaya nosotros(as) vayamos *vosotros(as) vayáis* ellos, ellas, Uds. vayan	yo lea tú leas él, ella, Ud. lea nosotros(as) leamos *vosotros(as) leáis* ellos, ellas, Uds. lean
SUBJUNTIVO IMPERFECTO	yo hiciera tú hicieras él, ella, Ud. hiciera nosotros(as) hiciéramos *vosotros(as) hicierais* ellos, ellas, Uds. hicieran	yo fuera tú fueras él, ella, Ud. fuera nosotros(as) fuéramos *vosotros(as) fuerais* ellos, ellas, Uds. fueran	yo leyera tú leyeras él, ella, Ud. leyera nosotros(as) leyéramos *vosotros(as) leyerais* ellos, ellas, Uds. leyeran
IMPERATIVO FORMAL	haga (Ud.) hagan (Uds.)	vaya (Ud.) vayan (Uds.)	lea (Ud.) lean (Uds.)
IMPERATIVO FAMILIAR	haz (tú)	ve (tú)	lee (tú)

VERBOS

C. Verbos irregulares

INFINITIVO	**oír** *to hear*	**poder** *to be able*	**poner** *to put*
PRESENTE PROGRESIVO	estar oyendo		estar poniendo
PRESENTE	yo oigo tú oyes él, ella, Ud. oye nosotros(as) oímos *vosotros(as) oís* ellos, ellas, Uds. oyen	yo puedo tú puedes él, ella, Ud. puede nosotros(as) podemos *vosotros(as) podéis* ellos, ellas, Uds. pueden	yo pongo tú pones él, ella, Ud. pone nosotros(as) ponemos *vosotros(as) ponéis* ellos, ellas, Uds. ponen
PRETÉRITO	yo oí tú oíste él, ella, Ud. oyó nosotros(as) oímos *vosotros(as) oísteis* ellos, ellas, Uds. oyeron	yo pude tú pudiste él, ella, Ud. pudo nosotros(as) pudimos *vosotros(as) pudisteis* ellos, ellas, Uds. pudieron	yo puse tú pusiste él, ella, Ud. puso nosotros(as) pusimos *vosotros(as) pusisteis* ellos, ellas, Uds. pusieron
IMPERFECTO	yo oía tú oías él, ella, Ud. oía nosotros(as) oíamos *vosotros(as) oíais* ellos, ellas, Uds. oían	yo podía tú podías él, ella, Ud. podía nosotros(as) podíamos *vosotros(as) podíais* ellos, ellas, Uds. podían	yo ponía tú ponías él, ella, Ud. ponía nosotros(as) poníamos *vosotros(as) poníais* ellos, ellas, Uds. ponían
FUTURO	yo oiré tú oirás él, ella, Ud. oirá nosotros(as) oiremos *vosotros(as) oiréis* ellos, ellas, Uds. oirán	yo podré tú podrás él, ella, Ud. podrá nosotros(as) podremos *vosotros(as) podréis* ellos, ellas, Uds. podrán	yo pondré tú pondrás él, ella, Ud. pondrá nosotros(as) pondremos *vosotros(as) pondréis* ellos, ellas, Uds. pondrán
POTENCIAL	yo oiría tú oirías él, ella, Ud. oiría nosotros(as) oiríamos *vosotros(as) oiríais* ellos, ellas, Uds. oirían	yo podría tú podrías él, ella, Ud. podría nosotros(as) podríamos *vosotros(as) podríais* ellos, ellas, Uds. podrían	yo pondría tú pondrías él, ella, Ud. pondría nosotros(as) pondríamos *vosotros(as) pondríais* ellos, ellas, Uds. pondrían

C. Verbos irregulares

INFINITIVO	oír *to hear*	poder *to be able*	poner *to put*
PRESENTE PERFECTO	yo he oído tú has oído él, ella, Ud. ha oído nosotros(as) hemos oído *vosotros(as) habéis oído* ellos, ellas, Uds. han oído	yo he podido tú has podido él, ella, Ud. ha podido nosotros(as) hemos podido *vosotros(as) habéis podido* ellos, ellas, Uds. han podido	yo he puesto tú has puesto él, ella, Ud. ha puesto nosotros(as) hemos puesto *vosotros(as) habéis puesto* ellos, ellas, Uds. han puesto
SUBJUNTIVO PRESENTE	yo oiga tú oigas él, ella, Ud. oiga nosotros(as) oigamos *vosotros(as) oigáis* ellos, ellas, Uds. oigan	yo pueda tú puedas él, ella, Ud. pueda nosotros(as) podamos *vosotros(as) podáis* ellos, ellas, Uds. puedan	yo ponga tú pongas él, ella, Ud. ponga nosotros(as) pongamos *vosotros(as) pongáis* ellos, ellas, Uds. pongan
SUBJUNTIVO IMPERFECTO	yo oyera tú oyeras él, ella, Ud. oyera nosotros(as) oyéramos *vosotros(as) oyerais* ellos, ellas, Uds. oyeran	yo pudiera tú pudieras él, ella, Ud. pudiera nosotros(as) pudiéramos *vosotros(as) pudierais* ellos, ellas, Uds. pudieran	yo pusiera tú pusieras él, ella, Ud. pusiera nosotros(as) pusiéramos *vosotros(as) pusierais* ellos, ellas, Uds. pusieran
IMPERATIVO FORMAL	oiga (Ud.) oigan (Uds.)	pueda (Ud.) puedan (Uds.)	ponga (Ud.) pongan (Uds.)
IMPERATIVO FAMILIAR	oye (tú)	puede (tú)	pon (tú)

C. Verbos irregulares

INFINITIVO	**querer** *to want*	**saber** *to know*	**salir** *to leave*
PRESENTE PROGRESIVO	estar queriendo	estar sabiendo	estar saliendo
PRESENTE	yo quiero tú quieres él, ella, Ud. quiere nosotros(as) queremos *vosotros(as) queréis* ellos, ellas, Uds. quieren	yo sé tú sabes él, ella, Ud. sabe nosotros(as) sabemos *vosotros(as) sabéis* ellos, ellas, Uds. saben	yo salgo tú sales él, ella, Ud. sale nosotros(as) salimos *vosotros(as) salís* ellos, ellas, Uds. salen
PRETÉRITO	yo quise tú quisiste él, ella, Ud. quiso nosotros(as) quisimos *vosotros(as) quisisteis* ellos, ellas, Uds. quisieron	yo supe tú supiste él, ella, Ud. supo nosotros(as) supimos *vosotros(as) supisteis* ellos, ellas, Uds. supieron	yo salí tú saliste él, ella, Ud. salió nosotros(as) salimos *vosotros(as) salisteis* ellos, ellas, Uds. salieron
IMPERFECTO	yo quería tú querías él, ella, Ud. quería nosotros(as) queríamos *vosotros(as) queríais* ellos, ellas, Uds. querían	yo sabía tú sabías él, ella, Ud. sabía nosotros(as) sabíamos *vosotros(as) sabíais* ellos, ellas, Uds. sabían	yo salía tú salías él, ella, Ud. salía nosotros(as) salíamos *vosotros(as) salíais* ellos, ellas, Uds. salían
FUTURO	yo querré tú querrás él, ella, Ud. querrá nosotros(as) querremos *vosotros(as) querréis* ellos, ellas, Uds. querrán	yo sabré tú sabrás él, ella, Ud. sabrá nosotros(as) sabremos *vosotros(as) sabréis* ellos, ellas, Uds. sabrán	yo saldré tú saldrás él, ella, Ud. saldrá nosotros(as) saldremos *vosotros(as) saldréis* ellos, ellas, Uds. saldrán
POTENCIAL	yo querría tú querrías él, ella, Ud. querría nosotros(as) querríamos *vosotros(as) querríais* ellos, ellas, Uds. querrían	yo sabría tú sabrías él, ella, Ud. sabría nosotros(as) sabríamos *vosotros(as) sabríais* ellos, ellas, Uds. sabrían	yo saldría tú saldrías él, ella, Ud. saldría nosotros(as) saldríamos *vosotros(as) saldríais* ellos, ellas, Uds. saldrían

VERBOS

C. Verbos irregulares

INFINITIVO	querer *to want*	saber *to know*	salir *to leave*
PRESENTE PERFECTO	yo he querido tú has querido él, ella, Ud. ha querido nosotros(as) hemos querido *vosotros(as) habéis querido* ellos, ellas, Uds. han querido	yo he sabido tú has sabido él, ella, Ud. ha sabido nosotros(as) hemos sabido *vosotros(as) habéis sabido* ellos, ellas, Uds. han sabido	yo he salido tú has salido él, ella, Ud. ha salido nosotros(as) hemos salido *vosotros(as) habéis salido* ellos, ellas, Uds. han salido
SUBJUNTIVO PRESENTE	yo quiera tú quieras él, ella, Ud. quiera nosotros(as) queramos *vosotros(as) queráis* ellos, ellas, Uds. quieran	yo sepa tú sepas él, ella, Ud. sepa nosotros(as) sepamos *vosotros(as) sepáis* ellos, ellas, Uds. sepan	yo salga tú salgas él, ella, Ud. salga nosotros(as) salgamos *vosotros(as) salgáis* ellos, ellas, Uds. salgan
SUBJUNTIVO IMPERFECTO	yo quisiera tú quisieras él, ella, Ud. quisiera nosotros(as) quisiéramos *vosotros(as) quisierais* ellos, ellas, Uds. quisieran	yo supiera tú supieras él, ella, Ud. supiera nosotros(as) supiéramos *vosotros(as) supierais* ellos, ellas, Uds. supieran	yo saliera tú salieras él, ella, Ud. saliera nosotros(as) saliéramos *vosotros(as) salierais* ellos, ellas, Uds. salieran
IMPERATIVO FORMAL	quiera (Ud.) quieran (Uds.)	sepa (Ud.) sepan (Uds.)	salga (Ud.) salgan (Uds.)
IMPERATIVO FAMILIAR	quiere (tú)	sabe (tú)	sal (tú)

C. Verbos irregulares

INFINITIVO	ser *to be*	tener *to have*	traer *to bring*
PRESENTE PROGRESIVO	estar siendo	estar teniendo	estar trayendo
PRESENTE	yo soy tú eres él, ella, Ud. es nosotros(as) somos *vosotros(as) sois* ellos, ellas, Uds. son	yo tengo tú tienes él, ella, Ud. tiene nosotros(as) tenemos *vosotros(as) tenéis* ellos, ellas, Uds. tienen	yo traigo tú traes él, ella, Ud. trae nosotros(as) traemos *vosotros(as) traéis* ellos, ellas, Uds. traen
PRETÉRITO	yo fui tú fuiste él, ella, Ud. fue nosotros(as) fuimos *vosotros(as) fuisteis* ellos, ellas, Uds. fueron	yo tuve tú tuviste él, ella, Ud. tuvo nosotros(as) tuvimos *vosotros(as) tuvisteis* ellos, ellas, Uds. tuvieron	yo traje tú trajiste él, ella, Ud. trajo nosotros(as) trajimos *vosotros(as) trajisteis* ellos, ellas, Uds. trajeron
IMPERFECTO	yo era tú eras él, ella, Ud. era nosotros(as) éramos *vosotros(as) erais* ellos, ellas, Uds. eran	yo tenía tú tenías él, ella, Ud. tenía nosotros(as) teníamos *vosotros(as) teníais* ellos, ellas, Uds. tenían	yo traía tú traías él, ella, Ud. traía nosotros(as) traíamos *vosotros(as) traíais* ellos, ellas, Uds. traían
FUTURO	yo seré tú serás él, ella, Ud. será nosotros(as) seremos *vosotros(as) seréis* ellos, ellas, Uds. serán	yo tendré tú tendrás él, ella, Ud. tendrá nosotros(as) tendremos *vosotros(as) tendréis* ellos, ellas, Uds. tendrán	yo traeré tú traerás él, ella, Ud. traerá nosotros(as) traeremos *vosotros(as) traeréis* ellos, ellas, Uds. traerán
POTENCIAL	yo sería tú serías él, ella, Ud. sería nosotros(as) seríamos *vosotros(as) seríais* ellos, ellas, Uds. serían	yo tendría tú tendrías él, ella, Ud. tendría nosotros(as) tendríamos *vosotros(as) tendríais* ellos, ellas, Uds. tendrían	yo traería tú traerías él, ella, Ud. traería nosotros(as) traeríamos *vosotros(as) traeríais* ellos, ellas, Uds. traerían

C. Verbos irregulares

INFINITIVO	ser *to be*	tener *to have*	traer *to bring*
PRESENTE PERFECTO	yo he sido tú has sido él, ella, Ud. ha sido nosotros(as) hemos sido *vosotros(as) habéis sido* ellos, ellas, Uds. han sido	yo he tenido tú has tenido él, ella, Ud. ha tenido nosotros(as) hemos tenido *vosotros(as) habéis tenido* ellos, ellas, Uds. han tenido	yo he traído tú has traído él, ella, Ud. ha traído nosotros(as) hemos traído *vosotros(as) habéis traído* ellos, ellas, Uds. han traído
SUBJUNTIVO PRESENTE	yo sea tú seas él, ella, Ud. sea nosotros(as) seamos *vosotros(as) seáis* ellos, ellas, Uds. sean	yo tenga tú tengas él, ella, Ud. tenga nosotros(as) tengamos *vosotros(as) tengáis* ellos, ellas, Uds. tengan	yo traiga tú traigas él, ella, Ud. traiga nosotros(as) traigamos *vosotros(as) traigáis* ellos, ellas, Uds. traigan
SUBJUNTIVO IMPERFECTO	yo fuera tú fueras él, ella, Ud. fuera nosotros(as) fuéramos *vosotros(as) fuerais* ellos, ellas, Uds. fueran	yo tuviera tú tuvieras él, ella, Ud. tuviera nosotros(as) tuviéramos *vosotros(as) tuvierais* ellos, ellas, Uds. tuvieran	yo trajera tú trajeras él, ella, Ud. trajera nosotros(as) trajéramos *vosotros(as) trajerais* ellos, ellas, Uds. trajeran
IMPERATIVO FORMAL	sea (Ud.) sean (Uds.)	tenga (Ud.) tengan (Uds.)	traiga (Ud.) traigan (Uds.)
IMPERATIVO FAMILIAR	sé (tú)	ten (tú)	trae (tú)

VERBOS

C. Verbos irregulares

INFINITIVO	**venir** *to come*	**ver** *to see*	
PRESENTE PROGRESIVO	estar viniendo	estar viendo	
PRESENTE	yo vengo tú vienes él, ella, Ud. viene nosotros(as) venimos *vosotros(as) venís* ellos, ellas, Uds. vienen	yo veo tú ves él, ella, Ud. ve nosotros(as) vemos *vosotros(as) veis* ellos, ellas, Uds. ven	
PRETÉRITO	yo vine tú viniste él, ella, Ud. vino nosotros(as) vinimos *vosotros(as) vinisteis* ellos, ellas, Uds. vinieron	yo vi tú viste él, ella, Ud. vio nosotros(as) vimos *vosotros(as) visteis* ellos, ellas, Uds. vieron	
IMPERFECTO	yo venía tú venías él, ella, Ud. venía nosotros(as) veníamos *vosotros(as) veníais* ellos, ellas, Uds. venían	yo veía tú veías él, ella, Ud. veía nosotros(as) veíamos *vosotros(as) veíais* ellos, ellas, Uds. veían	
FUTURO	yo vendré tú vendrás él, ella, Ud. vendrá nosotros(as) vendremos *vosotros(as) vendréis* ellos, ellas, Uds. vendrán	yo veré tú verás él, ella, Ud. verá nosotros(as) veremos *vosotros(as) veréis* ellos, ellas, Uds. verán	
POTENCIAL	yo vendría tú vendrías él, ella, Ud. vendría nosotros(as) vendríamos *vosotros(as) vendríais* ellos, ellas, Uds. vendrían	yo vería tú verías él, ella, Ud. vería nosotros(as) veríamos *vosotros(as) veríais* ellos, ellas, Uds. verían	

C. Verbos irregulares

INFINITIVO	venir *to come*	ver *to see*	
PRESENTE PERFECTO	yo he venido tú has venido él, ella, Ud. ha venido nosotros(as) hemos venido *vosotros(as) habéis venido* ellos, ellas, Uds. han venido	yo he visto tú has visto él, ella, Ud. ha visto nosotros(as) hemos visto *vosotros(as) habéis visto* ellos, ellas, Uds. han visto	
SUBJUNTIVO PRESENTE	yo venga tú vengas él, ella, Ud. venga nosotros(as) vengamos *vosotros(as) vengáis* ellos, ellas, Uds. vengan	yo vea tú veas él, ella, Ud. vea nosotros(as) veamos *vosotros(as) veáis* ellos, ellas, Uds. vean	
SUBJUNTIVO IMPERFECTO	yo viniera tú vinieras él, ella, Ud. viniera nosotros(as) viniéramos *vosotros(as) vinierais* ellos, ellas, Uds. vinieran	yo viera tú vieras él, ella, Ud. viera nosotros(as) viéramos *vosotros(as) vierais* ellos, ellas, Uds. vieran	
IMPERATIVO FORMAL	venga (Ud.) vengan (Uds.)	vea (Ud.) vean (Uds.)	
IMPERATIVO FAMILIAR	ven (tú)	ve (tú)	

VERBOS

D. Verbos reflexivos

INFINITIVO	**lavarse** *to wash oneself*		
PRESENTE PROGRESIVO	estar lavándose		
PRESENTE	yo me lavo tú te lavas él, ella, Ud. se lava nosotros(as) nos lavamos *vosotros(as) os laváis* ellos, ellas, Uds. se lavan		
PRETÉRITO	yo me lavé tú te lavaste él, ella, Ud. se lavó nosotros(as) nos lavamos *vosotros(as) os lavasteis* ellos, ellas, Uds. se lavaron		
IMPERFECTO	yo me lavaba tú te lavabas él, ella, Ud. se lavaba nosotros(as) nos lavábamos *vosotros(as) os lavabais* ellos, ellas, Uds. se lavaban		
FUTURO	yo me lavaré tú te lavarás él, ella, Ud. se lavará nosotros(as) nos lavaremos *vosotros(as) os lavaréis* ellos, ellas, Uds. se lavarán		
POTENCIAL	yo me lavaría tú te lavarías él, ella, Ud. se lavaría nosotros(as) nos lavaríamos *vosotros(as) os lavaríais* ellos, ellas, Uds. se lavarían		

D. Verbos reflexivos

INFINITIVO	**lavarse** *to wash oneself*		
PRESENTE PERFECTO	yo me he lavado tú te has lavado él, ella, Ud. se ha lavado nosotros(as) nos hemos lavado *vosotros(as) os habéis lavado* ellos, ellas, Uds. se han lavado		
SUBJUNTIVO PRESENTE	yo me lave tú te laves él, ella, Ud. se lave nosotros(as) nos lavemos *vosotros(as) os lavéis* ellos, ellas, Uds. se laven		
SUBJUNTIVO IMPERFECTO	yo me lavara tú te lavaras él, ella, Ud. se lavara nosotros(as) nos laváramos *vosotros(as) os lavarais* ellos, ellas, Uds. se lavaran		
IMPERATIVO FORMAL	lávese (Ud.) lávense (Uds.)		
IMPERATIVO FAMILIAR	lávate (tú)		

VERBOS

E. Verbos reflexivos con cambio radical

INFINITIVO	acostarse (o>ue) *to go to bed*	despertarse (e>ie) *to wake up*	dormirse (o>ue, u) *to fall asleep*
PRESENTE PROGRESIVO	estar acostándose	estar despertándose	estar durmiéndose
PRESENTE	yo me acuesto tú te acuestas él, ella, Ud. se acuesta nosotros(as) nos acostamos *vosotros(as) os acostáis* ellos, ellas, Uds. se acuestan	yo me despierto tú te despiertas él, ella, Ud. se despierta nosotros(as) nos despertamos *vosotros(as) os despertáis* ellos, ellas, Uds. se despiertan	yo me duermo tú te duermes él, ella, Ud. se duerme nosotros(as) nos dormimos *vosotros(as) os dormís* ellos, ellas, Uds. se duermen
PRETÉRITO	yo me acosté tú te acostaste él, ella, Ud. se acostó nosotros(as) nos acostamos *vosotros(as) os acostasteis* ellos, ellas, Uds. se acostaron	yo me desperté tú te despertaste él, ella, Ud. se despertó nosotros(as) nos despertamos *vosotros(as) os despertasteis* ellos, ellas, Uds. se despertaron	yo me dormí tú te dormiste él, ella, Ud. se durmió nosotros(as) nos dormimos *vosotros(as) os dormisteis* ellos, ellas, Uds. se durmieron
IMPERFECTO	yo me acostaba tú te acostabas él, ella, Ud. se acostaba nosotros(as) nos acostábamos *vosotros(as) os acostabais* ellos, ellas, Uds. se acostaban	yo me despertaba tú te despertabas él, ella, Ud. se despertaba nosotros(as) nos despertábamos *vosotros(as) os despertabais* ellos, ellas, Uds. se despertaban	yo me dormía tú te dormías él, ella, Ud. se dormía nosotros(as) nos dormíamos *vosotros(as) os dormíais* ellos, ellas, Uds. se dormían
FUTURO	yo me acostaré tú te acostarás él, ella, Ud. se acostará nosotros(as) nos acostaremos *vosotros(as) os acostaréis* ellos, ellas, Uds. se acostarán	yo me despertaré tú te despertarás él, ella, Ud. se despertará nosotros(as) nos despertaremos *vosotros(as) os despertaréis* ellos, ellas, Uds. se despertarán	yo me dormiré tú te dormirás él, ella, Ud. se dormirá nosotros(as) nos dormiremos *vosotros(as) os dormiréis* ellos, ellas, Uds. se dormirán
POTENCIAL	yo me acostaría tú te acostarías él, ella, Ud. se acostaría nosotros(as) nos acostaríamos *vosotros(as) os acostaríais* ellos, ellas, Uds. se acostarían	yo me despertaría tú te despertarías él, ella, Ud. se despertaría nosotros(as) nos despertaríamos *vosotros(as) os despertaríais* ellos, ellas, Uds. se despertarían	yo me dormiría tú te dormirías él, ella, Ud. se dormiría nosotros(as) nos dormiríamos *vosotros(as) os dormiríais* ellos, ellas, Uds. se dormirían

E. Verbos reflexivos con cambio radical

INFINITIVO	acostarse (o>ue) *to go to bed*	despertarse (e>ie) *to wake up*	dormirse (o>ue, u) *to fall asleep*
PRESENTE PERFECTO	yo me he acostado tú te has acostado él, ella, Ud. se ha acostado nosotros(as) nos hemos acostado *vosotros(as) os habéis acostado* ellos, ellas, Uds. se han acostado	yo me he despertado tú te has despertado él, ella, Ud. se ha despertado nosotros(as) nos hemos despertado *vosotros(as) os habéis despertado* ellos, ellas, Uds. se han despertado	yo me he dormido tú te has dormido él, ella, Ud. se ha dormido nosotros(as) nos hemos dormido *vosotros(as) os habéis dormido* ellos, ellas, Uds. se han dormido
SUBJUNTIVO PRESENTE	yo me acueste tú te acuestes él, ella, Ud. se acueste nosotros(as) nos acostemos *vosotros(as) os acostéis* ellos, ellas, Uds. se acuesten	yo me despierte tú te despiertes él, ella, Ud. se despierte nosotros(as) nos despertemos *vosotros(as) os despertéis* ellos, ellas, Uds. se despierten	yo me duerma tú te duermas él, ella, Ud. se duerma nosotros(as) nos durmamos *vosotros(as) os durmáis* ellos, ellas, Uds. se duerman
SUBJUNTIVO IMPERFECTO	yo me acostara tú te acostaras él, ella, Ud. se acostara nosotros(as) nos acostáramos *vosotros(as) os acostarais* ellos, ellas, Uds. se acostaran	yo me despertara tú te despertaras él, ella, Ud. se despertara nosotros(as) nos despertáramos *vosotros(as) os despertarais* ellos, ellas, Uds. se despertaran	yo me durmiera tú te durmieras él, ella, Ud. se durmiera nosotros(as) nos durmiéramos *vosotros(as) os durmierais* ellos, ellas, Uds. se durmieran
IMPERATIVO FORMAL	acuéstese (Ud.) acuéstense (Uds.)	despiértese (Ud.) despiértense (Uds.)	duérmase (Ud.) duérmanse (Uds.)
IMPERATIVO FAMILIAR	acuéstate (tú)	despiértate (tú)	duérmete (tú)

E. Verbos reflexivos con cambio radical

INFINITIVO	divertirse (e>ie, i) *to enjoy oneself*	sentarse (e>ie) *to sit down*	vestirse (e>i, i) *to dress oneself*
PRESENTE PROGRESIVO	estar divirtiéndose	estar sentándose	estar vistiéndose
PRESENTE	yo me divierto tú te diviertes él, ella, Ud. se divierte nosotros(as) nos divertimos *vosotros(as) os divertís* ellos, ellas, Uds. se divierten	yo me siento tú te sientas él, ella, Ud. se sienta nosotros(as) nos sentamos *vosotros(as) os sentáis* ellos, ellas, Uds. se sientan	yo me visto tú te vistes él, ella, Ud. se viste nosotros(as) nos vestimos *vosotros(as) os vestís* ellos, ellas, Uds. se visten
PRETÉRITO	yo me divertí tú te divertiste él, ella, Ud. se divirtió nosotros(as) nos divertimos *vosotros(as) os divertisteis* ellos, ellas, Uds. se divirtieron	yo me senté tú te sentaste él, ella, Ud. se sentó nosotros(as) nos sentamos *vosotros(as) os sentasteis* ellos, ellas, Uds. se sentaron	yo me vestí tú te vestiste él, ella, Ud. se vistió nosotros(as) nos vestimos *vosotros(as) os vestisteis* ellos, ellas, Uds. se vistieron
IMPERFECTO	yo me divertía tú te divertías él, ella, Ud. se divertía nosotros(as) nos divertíamos *vosotros(as) os divertíais* ellos, ellas, Uds. se divertían	yo me sentaba tú te sentabas él, ella, Ud. se sentaba nosotros(as) nos sentábamos *vosotros(as) os sentabais* ellos, ellas, Uds. se sentaban	yo me vestía tú te vestías él, ella, Ud. se vestía nosotros(as) nos vestíamos *vosotros(as) os vestíais* ellos, ellas, Uds. se vestían
FUTURO	yo me divertiré tú te divertirás él, ella, Ud. se divertirá nosotros(as) nos divertiremos *vosotros(as) os divertiréis* ellos, ellas, Uds. se divertirán	yo me sentaré tú te sentarás él, ella, Ud. se sentará nosotros(as) nos sentaremos *vosotros(as) os sentaréis* ellos, ellas, Uds. se sentarán	yo me vestiré tú te vestirás él, ella, Ud. se vestirá nosotros(as) nos vestiremos *vosotros(as) os vestiréis* ellos, ellas, Uds. se vestirán
POTENCIAL	yo me divertiría tú te divertirías él, ella, Ud. se divertiría nosotros(as) nos divertiríamos *vosotros(as) os divertiríais* ellos, ellas, Uds. se divertirían	yo me sentaría tú te sentarías él, ella, Ud. se sentaría nosotros(as) nos sentaríamos *vosotros(as) os sentaríais* ellos, ellas, Uds. se sentarían	yo me vestiría tú te vestirías él, ella, Ud. se vestiría nosotros(as) nos vestiríamos *vosotros(as) os vestiríais* ellos, ellas, Uds. se vestirían

E. Verbos reflexivos con cambio radical

INFINITIVO	divertirse (e>ie, i) *to enjoy oneself*	sentarse (e>ie) *to sit down*	vestirse (e>i, i) *to dress oneself*
PRESENTE PERFECTO	yo me he divertido tú te has divertido él, ella, Ud. se ha divertido nosotros(as) nos hemos divertido *vosotros(as) os habéis divertido* ellos, ellas, Uds. se han divertido	yo me he sentado tú te has sentado él, ella, Ud. se ha sentado nosotros(as) nos hemos sentado *vosotros(as) os habéis sentado* ellos, ellas, Uds. se han sentado	yo me he vestido tú te has vestido él, ella, Ud. se ha vestido nosotros(as) nos hemos vestido *vosotros(as) os habéis vestido* ellos, ellas, Uds. se han vestido
SUBJUNTIVO PRESENTE	yo me divierta tú te diviertas él, ella, Ud. se divierta nosotros(as) nos divirtamos *vosotros(as) os divirtáis* ellos, ellas, Uds. se diviertan	yo me siente tú te sientes él, ella, Ud. se siente nosotros(as) nos sentemos *vosotros(as) os sentéis* ellos, ellas, Uds. se sienten	yo me vista tú te vistas él, ella, Ud. se vista nosotros(as) nos vistamos *vosotros(as) os vistáis* ellos, ellas, Uds. se vistan
SUBJUNTIVO IMPERFECTO	yo me divirtiera tú te divirtieras él, ella, Ud. se divirtiera nosotros(as) nos divirtiéramos *vosotros(as) os divirtierais* ellos, ellas, Uds. se divirtieran	yo me sentara tú te sentaras él, ella, Ud. se sentara nosotros(as) nos sentáramos *vosotros(as) os sentarais* ellos, ellas, Uds. se sentaran	yo me vistiera tú te vistieras él, ella, Ud. se vistiera nosotros(as) nos vistiéramos *vosotros(as) os vistierais* ellos, ellas, Uds. se vistieran
IMPERATIVO FORMAL	diviértase (Ud.) diviértanse (Uds.)	siéntese (Ud.) siéntense (Uds.)	vístase (Ud.) vístanse (Uds.)
IMPERATIVO FAMILIAR	diviértete (tú)	siéntate (tú)	vístete (tú)

480

VOCABULARIO ESPAÑOL-INGLÉS

The *Vocabulario español-inglés* contains all productive and receptive vocabulary from Levels 1 and 2.

The numbers following each entry indicate the chapter and vocabulary section in which the word is introduced. For example, **3.2** means that the word first appeared in Level 2, *Capítulo 3, Palabras 2*. Numbers preceded by I indicate vocabulary introduced in Level I; I-BV refers to the introductory *Bienvenidos* lesson.

Words without chapter references indicate receptive vocabulary (not taught in the *Palabras* sections) in *A bordo*.

The following abbreviations are used in this glossary.

adj.	adjective
adv.	adverb
conj.	conjunction
dem. adj.	demonstrative adjective
dem. pron.	demonstrative pronoun
dir. obj.	direct object
f.	feminine
fam.	familiar
form.	formal
ind. obj.	indirect object
inf.	infinitive
inform.	informal
interr.	interrogative
interr. adj.	interrogative adjective
interr. pron.	interrogative pronoun
inv.	invariable
irreg.	irregular
m.	masculine
n.	noun
past. part.	past participle
pl.	plural
poss. adj.	possessive adjective
prep.	preposition
pron.	pronoun
sing.	singular
subj.	subject
subjunc.	subjunctive

A

a to, at
  a bordo on board, 7.1
  a eso de about, around
  a menudo often, 1
abajo down; below
abandonar to leave, 6.1
el/la abogado(a) lawyer, 16.1
el/la abonado(a) subscriber
abordar to get on, board, I-8.1
  el pase de abordar boarding pass, I-8.1
abotonar to button
abrazar(c) to embrace, hug, 11.2
el abrazo hug, 11.2
la abreviatura abbreviation
el abrigo overcoat, I-13.1
abril April, I-BV
abrir to open, I-8.2
abrocharse to fasten, 7.1
absorber to absorb
el/la abuelo(a) grandfather, grandmother I-6.1
  los abuelos grandparents, I-6.1
abundante abundant
aburrido(a) boring, I-1.1
aburrir to bore, I-13
el abuso abuse
acabar de to have just (done something), 8.2
la academia academy
académico(a) academic
acampar to camp, I-16.2
el accidente accident, 4.1
las acciones stock
el aceite oil, I-15.2
aceleradamente quickly
acelerar to accelerate, 5.1
aceptar accept
la acera sidewalk, 10.1
acercarse(qu) to approach, 11.2
acomodar to accommodate
acompañado(a) accompanied
acompañar to accompany
aconsejable advisable
aconsejar to advise, 12.2
acordarse (ue) to remember
acostarse (ue) to go to bed, I-16.1
la actividad activity, 5.2
activo(a) active, 16.2
el acto act
el actor actor, I-12.2
la actriz actress, I-12.2
actual present, current
la actualidad present time
actualmente at the present time
acuático(a): el esquí acuático water skiing, I-11.1
acudir to go; to attend
el acueducto aqueduct
acuerdo: de acuerdo according to; OK, all right
acuífero(a) aquiferous, water-bearing
acusar to accuse; to acknowledge (receipt of a letter)
adaptar to adapt
adecuado(a) adequate
adelantar to overtake, 5.1
además (de) besides
el/la adherente adherent
la adicción addiction
adiós good-bye, I-BV
la adivinanza riddle, puzzle
adivinar to guess
el/la adolescente adolescent
¿adónde? (to) where?, I-4
adoptar to adopt
adorable adorable
adorar to adore, 1.2
adornar to adorn
el adorno ornament
la aduana customs, I-8.2
la advertencia warning
aéreo(a) air
  la línea aérea airline
  por correo aéreo by air mail, 3.2
aeróbico(a) aerobic, I-10.2
el aerodeslizador hydrofoil
el aerograma aerogram, 3.1
el aeropuerto airport, I-8.1
afectar to affect
el afecto affection, fondness
afectuoso(a) affectionate
afeitarse to shave, I-16.1
  la crema de afeitar shaving cream, I-16.2
las afueras outskirts, I-5.1
agasajar to entertain splendidly
la agencia de viajes travel agency
el/la agente agent, I-8.1
ágil agile
la aglomeración collection
agonizante dying
agosto August (m.), I-BV
agotador(a) exhausting
agradable pleasant
agregar(gu) to add, 9.2
el/la agricultor(a) farmer
la agricultura agriculture, 16.2
el agua (f.) water, 5.2
  el agua de colonia cologne
  el agua mineral mineral water, 2.2
las aguas negras sewage
el aguacate avocado, 9.2
agudo(a) sharp
el águila (f.) eagle
el aguinaldo Christmas present, 12.2
el/la ahijado(a) godchild
ahora now, I-BV
ahorrar to save, 14.2
los ahorros savings
el aire air, 5.2
  al aire libre outdoors, I-9.2
  el aire acondicionado air conditioning, 6.2
aislado(a) isolated
el ajo garlic, 9.2
al (a + el) to the, at the
el ala (f.) wing(s), 7.2
el alambre wire
el/la albañil mason
la alberca swimming pool, I-11.2
el albergue juvenil youth hostel, I-16.2
la alcaldía city hall, 16.1
el alcance reach
alcanzar (c) reach
el alcohol alcohol
la alcoholemia blood alcohol level
el alcoholismo alchoholism
alegrarse de to be glad about, 12
alegre happy, 1.2
alemán (alemana) German
la alergia allergy, I-10.2
el alga (f.) seaweed
el álgebra (f.) algebra, I-2.2
algo something, I-9.1
  ¿Algo más? Something more?, 2.2
alguien somebody, I-13
algún, alguno(a) some, any, 2.1
la alimentación food

VOCABULARIO ESPAÑOL-INGLÉS   **483**

alimentar to feed
alimentario(a) nourishing
el **alimento** food
aliviar to alleviate
allá there
allí there
el **alma** (f.) soul
el **almacén** department store
la **almeja** clam, 9.2
el **almidón** starch, 13.2
la **almohada** pillow, 6.2
el **almuerzo** lunch, I-5.2
alojar to lodge, stay
alquilar to rent, I-11.1
el **alquiler** rent
alrededor (de) around, I-6.2
los **alrededores** outskirts
el **altar** altar, 15.2
la **alteración** alteration
alternativo(a) alternate
el **altiplano** plateau, 7.2
la **altitud** altitude, 7.2
alto(a) tall, I-1.1; high, I-3.2
la **altura** height; altitude, 7.2
el/la **alumno(a)** student, I-1.1
amable kind, I-2.1
amarillo(a) yellow, I-13.2
Amazonas: el río Amazonas Amazon River
amazónico(a) Amazon, Amazonian
ambiental environmental
el **ambiente** environment
ambos(as) both
la **ambulancia** ambulance, 4.1
la **ameba** amoeba
la **América del Sur** South America, I-8.1
americano(a) American, I-1.2
el/la **amigo(a)** friend, I-1.1
el **aminoácido** amino acid
el **amor** love
amoroso(a) amorous
amplio(a) large, roomy
el **análisis** analysis
analizar(c) to analyze
anaranjado(a) orange (color), I-13.2
el/la **anarquista** anarquist
el/la **anatomista** anatomist
ancho(a) wide, I-13.2
la **anchura** width
andar (irreg.) to walk, 4.2
andar en monopatín to skateboard
el **andén** railway platform, I-14.1

andino(a) Andean
la **anestesia** anesthesia
la **anestesia local** local anesthesia
el/la **anestesista** anesthetist, 4.2
el **ángulo** angle
el **anillo** ring, 15.1
el **anillo de boda** wedding ring, 15.1
el **animal** animal
el **aniversario** anniversary
anoche last night, I-11.2
anónimo(a) anonymous
el **anorak** anorak, I-9.1
anotar una carrera to score a run (baseball)
antártico(a) antarctic
la **Antártida** Antarctic
anteayer the day before yesterday, I-11.2
antenupcial prenuptial
los **anteojos de (para el) sol** sunglasses, I-11.1
antes de que before, 15.1
los **antibióticos** antibiotics
anticipar to anticipate
antiguo(a) ancient, old
antipático(a) unpleasant (person), I-1.1
la **antropología** anthropology
el/la **antropólogo(a)** anthropologist
anunciar to announce, 15.1
el **anuncio** advertisement, announcement, 7.1
el **año** year, I-11.2
el **año pasado** last year, I-11.2
este año this year, I-11.2
hace muchos años it's been many years
¡Próspero año nuevo! Happy New Year!, 12.2
apagar (gu) to turn off, 9.2
el **aparato** apparatus
aparcar (qu) to park, 5.1
aparecer (zc) to appear
el **apartado postal** post office box, 3.2
el **apartamento** apartment, I-5.1
aparte separate
el **apellido** last name
el **apetito** appetite
el **apio** celery
aplaudir to applaud, I-12.2
el **aplauso** applause
el **apodo** nickname

el **apoyo** support
aprender to learn, I-5.2
el **aprendizaje** learning
apretar (ie) to pinch, I-13.2
Me aprieta(n). It (They) pinch(es) me., I-13.2; It's tight on me.
aprobado(a) passing (grade)
aproximadamente approximately
los **apuntes** notes, I-3.2
tomar apuntes to take notes, I-3.2
aquel, aquella that, I-9.2
aquí here
el/la **árabe** Arab
el/la **árbitro(a)** referee, I-7.1
el **árbol** tree, I-6.2
el **árbol de Navidad** Christmas tree, 12.2
el **árbol genealógico** family tree
el **área** (f.) area
la **arena** sand, I-11.1
argentino(a) Argentinian, I-2.1
la **aritmética** arithmetic, I-2.2
armar una tienda to put up a tent, I-16.2
el **armario** closet, 6.2
el **aro** hoop, I-7.2
arqueológico(a) archeological
la **arquitectura** architecture, 16.2
las **arras** thirteen coins given by bridegroom to bride at a wedding ceremony
arreglar to fix
arriba above, 8.2
arrimar to put or place near
el **arroz** rice, I-15.2
arrugado(a) wrinkled, 13.2
el **arte** (f.) art, I-2.2
las **bellas artes** fine arts
el **artefacto** artifact
arterial arterial, 4.2
la **artesanía** handicraft
el/la **artesano(a)** artisan, 16.1
el **artículo** article
el **artículo de tocador** toiletry item
el/la **artista** artist, I-12.2
artístico(a): el patinaje artístico figure skating, I-12
asar to broil, 9.1
la **ascendencia** ancestry
el **ascensor** elevator, I-5.1
asegurar to insure, 3.2

484   VOCABULARIO ESPAÑOL-INGLÉS

el **aseo** lavatory, **7.1**
así thus
el **asiento** seat, I-8.1
    el **número del asiento** seat number, I-8.1
la **asignatura** subject, I-2.2
la **asistencia** assistance; attendance
el **asistente (la asistenta) de vuelo** flight attendant, I-8.2
asistir to attend; to assist, I-5.2
el **asombro** amazement
el/la **aspirante** candidate, **16.2**
asumir to assume
el **asunto** subject
atacar (qu) to attack
el **ataque** attack
la **atención** attention, kindness
atender (ie) to attend to, take care of
atento(a) polite, courteous
el **aterrizaje** landing, **7.2**
aterrizar (c) to land, I-8.2
Atlántico: océano Atlántico Atlantic Ocean
el/la **atleta** athlete
la **atmósfera** atmosphere
atómico(a) atomic
atractivo(a) attractive, I-1.2
atrapar to catch, I-7.2
atrás behind, **8.2**
atravesar (ie) to cross; to go through
el **atún** tuna, **2.2**
los **audífonos** earphones, **7.1**
auditivo(a) auditive
el **aumento** increase
    en aumento on the increase
aun even
aunque although, **15**
el **auricular** receiver (of telephone), **1.1**
austral southern
el **autobús** bus, I-3.1
    perder el autobús to miss the bus, I-12.1
automáticamente automatically
automático(a) automatic, **1.1**
el **automóvil** car
la **autopista** super highway, **10.2**
el/la **autor(a)** author, I-12.2
autorizado(a) authorized
la **autovía** super highway, **10.2**
avanzado(a) advanced

el **ave** (f.) bird
la **avenida** avenue, I-5.1
el/la **aventurero(a)** adventurer
el/la **aviador(a)** aviator
el **avión** airplane, I-8.1
    en avión by plane, I-8.1
    el **avión reactor** jet, **7.2**
la **avioneta** small airplane
el **aviso** warning
ayer yesterday, I-11.1
    ayer por la mañana yesterday morning, I-11.2
    ayer por la tarde yesterday afternoon, I-11.2
la **ayuda** help
ayudar to help
el **ayuntamiento** city hall, **16.1**
el **azafrán** saffron
el **azúcar** sugar, **9.1**
azul blue, I-13.2
    azul marino navy blue

B

la **bacteria** bacterium
bailar to dance, I-4.2
el **baile** dance
bajar to go down, I-9.1
    bajar del tren to get off the train, I-14.2
bajo below (prep.), I-9.1
    bajo cero below zero, I-9.1
bajo(a) short (person), I-1.1; low, I-3.2
el **balcón** balcony, I-6.2
la **ballena** whale
el **balneario** beach resort, I-11.1
el **balón** ball, I-7.1
el **baloncesto** basketball, I-7.2
la **banana** banana, **9.2**
bancario(a) banking
el **banco** bench, I-BV; bank, **14.2**
    el **estado de banco (de cuenta)** bank statement, **14.2**
la **banda** (music) band
la **bandera** flag
el **banquete** banquet, **15.2**
el **bañador** bathing suit, I-11.1
bañarse to go for a swim, I-16.2; to take a bath
la **bañera** bathtub, **6.2**
el **baño** bathroom, **6.2**
    el **cuarto de baño** bathroom, I-5.1

el **traje de baño** bathing suit, I-11.1
barato(a) cheap, I-13.1
la **barba** beard
el/la **barbero(a)** barber, **8.2**
el **barco** boat
el **barquito** small boat, I-11.1
la **barra** bar (of soap), I-16.2
el **barrio** neighborhood
basar to base
    basarse to be based
la **báscula** scale, I-8.1
la **base** base, I-7.2
básico(a) basic
el **básquetbol** basketball, I-7.2
bastante rather, quite, I-1.1
el **bastón** pole, I-9.1; club (golf), I-11.2
la **batalla** battle
el **bate** bat, I-7.2
el/la **bateador(a)** batter (baseball), I-7.2
batear to hit (baseball), I-7.2
la **batería** battery, **5.2**
bautizar to baptize, **12.1**
el **bautizo** baptism, **12.1**
el/la **bebé** baby
beber to drink, I-5.2
la **bebida** drink, **7.1**
el **béisbol** baseball, I-7.2
belga Belgian
la **belleza** beauty
bello(a) beautiful
    las **bellas artes** fine arts
bendito: ¡Ay, bendito! Dear Lord!
el **beneficio** benefit
el **beso (besito)** kiss, **11.2**
la **biblioteca** library, I-4.1
la **bicicleta** bicycle, I-6.2
bien fine, well, I-BV
    bien cocido (hecho) well done (meat), I-15.2
los **bienes** goods
    los **bienes raíces** real estate
la **bienvenida** welcome, **7.1**
el **biftec** steak, I-15.2
el **bigote** mustache, **8.1**
bilingüe bilingual
la **bilis** bile
el **billete** ticket, I-8.1; bill (money), **14.1**
    el **billete de ida y vuelta** round-trip ticket, I-14.1
    el **billete sencillo** one-way ticket, I-14.1

VOCABULARIO ESPAÑOL-INGLÉS

biográfico(a) biographical
la biología biology, I-2.2
biológico(a) biological
el/la biólogo(a) biologist
el bizcocho cookie, 12.1
blanco(a) white, I-13.2
el blanqueador bleach, 13.2
el bloc writing pad, I-3.2
bloquear to block, I-7.1
el blue jean blue jeans, I-13.1
la blusa blouse, I-13.1
   la blusa de cuello sin espalda halter, 13
el blusón jacket, I-13.1
la boca mouth, I-10.2
la bocacalle intersection, 10.1
el bocadillo sandwich, I-5.2
la bocina receiver (of telephone), 1.1; horn, 5.1
la boda wedding, 15.2
   el anillo de boda wedding ring, 15.1
la bola (golf)ball, I-11.2
la boletería ticket window, I-9.1
el boleto ticket, I-8.1
el bolígrafo ballpoint pen, I-BV
la bolsa bag, 2.2
   la bolsa de plástico plastic bag, 2.2
bonito(a) pretty, I-6.2
borde: al borde de on the brink of
bordo: a bordo de aboard, on board
el bosque forest, I-16.2
la bota boot, I-9.1
la botánica botany; herbalist's shop
el bote can, 2.2
la botella bottle, 2.2
el botiquín medical kit, first-aid kit, I-16.2
el botón button, I-13.2
   de (a) botones push button, 1.1
los botones bellhop, 6.1
brasileño(a) Brazilian
el brazo arm, 4.1; branch (of candelabra), 12.2
brillante bright, shining
brillar to shine, I-11.1
brincar to bounce
brindar to toast (to one's health), 15.2
el brindis toast (to one's health), 15.2

británico(a) British
bronceador: la crema bronceadora suntan lotion, I-11.1
broncearse to get a tan
bucear to skindive, I-11.1
el buceo skindiving, I-11.1
el bucle curl, 8.1
la buenaventura fortune (as told by a fortune teller)
bueno(a) good, I-1.2
   Buenas noches. Good evening., Good night., I-BV
   Buenas tardes. Good afternoon., I-BV
   Buenos días. Hello, good morning., I-BV
el burro donkey
el bus bus, I-3.1
la busca search, 16.2
   en busca de in search of, 16.2
buscar to look for, 16.2
la butaca orchestra seat, I-12.1
el buzón mailbox, 3.1

C

el caballero man, gentleman, I-13.1
el caballo horse
el cabello hair, 8.1
la cabeza head, I-7.1
   el dolor de cabeza headache, I-10.1
la cabina booth
   la cabina de mando (vuelo) cockpit, 7.1
   la cabina telefónica telephone booth, 1.1
cabotaje: de cabotaje domestic, I-8
el cacahuete peanut
el cacique chief
cada each, 10.2
la cadena chain
caerse (irreg.) to fall, 4.1
el café coffee, I-5.2; café
la cafetería cafeteria
la caja cash register, I-13.1; box, checkstand, 2.2; cashier desk, 6.1
el/la cajero(a) cashier, 6.1; teller, 14.1
el calamar squid, 9.2
los calcetines socks, I-13.1

el calcio calcium
la calculadora calculator, I-BV
el calendario calendar
calentarse (ie) to warm, become warm
la calidad quality
caliente warm
la calificación grade, I-3.2
la calistenia calisthenics
la calle street, I-5.1
la callejuela side street; alley
el calmante sedative
el calor heat, I-11.1
   Hace calor. It's hot., I-11.1
la caloría calorie, I-10.2
la cama bed, I-10.1
la cámara: de cámara court, royal
la camarera maid, 6.2
el camarón shrimp, prawn, 2.1
cambiar to change, exchange, 6.2
   cambiar de velocidad to shift gears, 5.1
el cambio change; exchange rate, 14.1
el/la cambista broker, 14.1
el camello camel, 12.2
la camilla stretcher, 4.1
caminar to walk, 4.2
la caminata hike, I-16.2
   dar una caminata to take a hike, I-16.2
el camino road, trail, path
el camión truck
la camisa shirt, I-13.1
   la camisa de deporte sports shirt
la camiseta undershirt, I-13.1
el campamento camp, I-16.2
la campaña campaign
   la tienda de campaña tent, 13.1
el campeonato championship
el camping camping, campgrounds, I-16.2
   ir de camping to go camping
el campo country, I-5.1; field, I-7.1
   el campo de fútbol soccer field, I-7.1
el camposanto cemetery, 12.1
canadiense (canadiensa) Canadian
el canal channel, 7.1

VOCABULARIO ESPAÑOL-INGLÉS

el **canario** canary
la **canasta** basket, 2.2
el **canasto** basket, I-7.2
el **cáncer** cancer
la **cancha** court (sports), I-7.2
    la **cancha de tenis** tennis court, I-11.2
la **canción** song
el **candelabro** candelabra, 12.2
el/la **candidato(a)** candidate, 16.2
    cansado(a) tired, I-10.1
el/la **cantante** singer
    cantar to sing, I-4.2
la **cantidad** quantity
la **cantimplora** canteen, I-16.2
la **cantina** lunchroom
el **cañón** canyon
el **capacho** basket
la **capa** layer
    en capas layered
la **capital** capital
el **capó** hood, 5.1
    capturar to capture
la **cara** face, I-16.1
la **carabela** caravel
el **caracol** cochlea (internal ear)
el **carácter** character
la **característica** characteristic
la **caravana** trailer, 13.1; caravan
el **carbohidrato** carbohydrate, I-10.2
    cardíaco(a) heart
el **Caribe** Caribbean
la **caridad** charity
    cariñosamente affectionately
    cariñoso(a) affectionate
la **carne** meat, I-5.2
    la **carne de res** beef, 2.1
la **carnicería** butcher shop, 2.1
el/la **carnicero(a)** butcher
    carnívoro(a) carnivorous
    caro(a) expensive, I-13.1
la **carpa** tent, I-16.2
el/la **carpintero(a)** carpenter, 16.2
la **carrera** career
la **carretera** highway, 10.2
el **carril** lane (of highway), 10.2
el **carrito** cart, 2.1; shopping cart
el **carro** car, I-3.1
la **carta** letter, I-5.2
    la **carta de memoria** memory chart
el/la **cartero** mail carrier, 3.2
la **casa** house, I-4.1
    la **casa de huéspedes** guest house

la **casa particular** private house
    en casa at home
    ir a casa to go home, I-4.1
la **casa-remolque** trailer, 13.1
el **casamiento** marriage, wedding
    casarse to get married, 15.1
    casi almost
    casi crudo rare (meat), I-15.2
la **casilla** post office box, 3.2
el **casino** casino
el **caso** case
    castaño(a) brown, 8.1
el **castigo** punishment
    castizo(a) real, legitimate, genuine
el **catálogo** catalogue
el **catarro** cold (medical), I-10.1
    tener catarro to have a cold, I-10.1
el/la **cátcher** catcher, I-7.2
    cate failing (grade)
la **catedral** cathedral
la **categoría** category
el **catolicismo** Catholicism
    católico(a) Catholic
la **causa** cause
    a causa de because of
    causar to cause
el **cautiverio** captivity
    cautivo(a) captured
la **caza** (wild) game
    cazar to hunt
la **cazuela** pot, 9.1
la **cebolla** onion, 9.1
la **celebración** celebration
    celebrar to celebrate, 12.1
la **célula** cell
    celular cellular, 1.1
el **cementerio** cemetery, 12.1
la **cena** dinner, I-5.2
    cenar to dine
el **centígrado** centigrade, I-9.1
el **centro** center
    el **centro comercial** shopping center, I-4.1
    Centroamérica Central America
    cepillarse to brush one's hair, I-16.1
el **cepillo** brush, I-16.2
la **cera** wax
    cerca de near
las **cercanías** outskirts

el **cerdo** pig, pork, 2.1
el **cereal** cereal
la **ceremonia** ceremony, 15.2
la **cereza** cherry, 9.2
    cero zero, I-BV
el **cesto** basket, I-7.2
la **chabola** shack
el **chaleco salvavidas** life vest, 7.1
el **chaman** shaman
el **champú** shampoo, I-16.2
    chao good-bye, I-BV
la **chaqueta** jacket, I-13.1
    charlar to chat
el **cheque** check, 14.1
    el **cheque de viajero** traveler's check, 14.1
la **chequera** checkbook, 14.2
el/la **chico(a)** boy (girl)
el **chimpancé** chimpanzee
    chino(a) Chinese
el **chiste** joke
el **chocolate** chocolate
el **chorizo** pork and garlic sausage
la **choza** shack
la **chuleta** chop, 2.1
el **churro** a type of doughnut
la **cicatriz** scar, 4.1
el **ciclomotor** motorbike, I-6.2
el **cielo** sky, I-11.1
    cien(to) one hundred, I-BV
la **ciencia** science, I-2.2
    la **ciencia política** political science
    las **ciencias naturales** natural sciences
    las **ciencias sociales** social sciences, I-2.2
    de ciencia ficción science fiction (book, movie, etc.)
el/la **científico** scientist
    científico(a) scientific (adj.)
    cierto(a) certain
la **cigüeña** stork
    cinco five, I-BV
    cincuenta fifty, I-BV
el **cine** movie theater, I-12.1
    cinematográfico(a) cinematographic
la **cinta** tape, I-4.1; ribbon
el **cinturón** belt, I-13.1
    el **cinturón de seguridad** seat belt, 5.1
la **circulación** circulation; traffic, 5.1

VOCABULARIO ESPAÑOL-INGLÉS   **487**

circular to circulate, travel; circular (adj.)
el círculo circle
el/la cirujano(a) surgeon, 4.2
la cirugía surgery
la cita date, 15.1
la ciudad city, I-5.1
el/la ciudadano(a) citizen
civil civil
la civilización civilization
el clarinete clarinet
claro (que sí) of course (adv.)
claro(a) clear (adj.)
la clase class, I-2.1; type
   la clase alta upper class
   la clase media middle class
clásico(a) classical, I-4
la clasificación classification
clasificar to classify
clavar to nail, stick
la clave de área area code, 1.1
el claxon horn, 5.1
el/la cliente client, customer, I-5.2
el clima climate
climático(a) climatic
la clínica clinic, I-10.2; private hospital
cobijar to cover
cobrar to cash, 14.2
la cocción cooking
el coche car, I-3.1; train car, I-14.2
   el coche deportivo sports car, 5.1
el coche-cama sleeping car, I-14.2
el coche-comedor dining car, I-14.2
cocido(a) cooked, I-15.2
   bien cocido (hecho) well done (meat), I-15.2
la cocina cooking; kitchen, I-4.1
cocinar to cook, 9.1
el/la cocinero(a) cook, I-15.1
el coco coconut, 9.2
el cóctel cocktail, 15
el código de area area code
el código postal zip code, 3.1
el codo elbow, 4.1
coeducacional coeducational
coincidir to coincide
la cola line (of people), I-12.1; tail
   la cola de caballo pony tail, 8.1
   hacer cola to wait in line

la colección collection
la colecta collection
el colegio high school, I-1.1
la coleta pigtail, queue
el colgador clothes hanger, 6.2
colgar (ue) to hang up, 1
la coliflor cauliflower, 9.1
la colina hill, I-16.2
colmar to lavish, heap
colombiano(a) Colombian, 1
el colón colon
la colonia colony
el/la colonizador(a) colonist
el/la colono colonist
el color color, I-13.2
   de color crema, vino, café, oliva, marrón, turquesa cream-, wine-, coffee-, olive-, brown-, turquoise-colored, I-13.2
la comadrona midwife
el/la comandante captain, I-8.2
la combinación combination
combinar to combine
la comedia comedy
el comedor dining room, I-5.1
el comentario commentary
comenzar (ie)(c) to begin, 7
comer to eat, I-5.2
comercial of or pertaining to business
el/la comerciante businessman(woman); merchant, 16.1
el comercio business
el comestible food, 2.1
cometer to commit
la comida meal, I-5.2
   la comida rápida fast food
como as, like
¿cómo? what?; how?, I-1.1
   ¿Cómo estás? How are you?
cómodo(a) comfortable
la compañía company
el/la compañero(a) friend, companion
la comparación comparison
comparar to compare
el compartamiento compartment, I-14.2
compartir to share
la competencia competition
competir to compete
completamente completely
completar to complete

completo: a tiempo completo full-time, 16.2
complicado(a) complicated
el comportamiento behavior, 11.1
comportarse to behave, 11.1
la compra y venta trade, 16.2
el/la comprador(a) buyer
comprar to buy, I-5.2
compras: de compras shopping, I-13.1
comprender to understand, I-5.2
el comprimido pill, I-10.2
comprometerse to get engaged, 15.1
el/la comprometido(a) fiancé(e), 15
el compromiso engagement, 15.1
   la sortija de compromiso engagement ring, 15.1
el compuesto compound
la computadora computer, I-BV
común common
la comunicación communication
comunicar to communicate
la comunidad community
la comunión communion
con with
   con cuidado carefully, 5.1
   con frecuencia frequently, 1
   con retraso late, I-14.2
   con tal que provided that, 15
   con una demora late, I-14.2
el concepto concept
el concierto concert, I-12.2
conciliar to reconcile, 14.2
el concurso contest
condensar to condense
el condominio condominium
la conducción driving
conducir (zc) to drive, 5.1
la conducta conduct
el/la conductor(a) driver, 5.1
conectar to connect
el conejo rabbit
la conexión connection
la conferencia conference
la confianza confidence, trust
confiar to confide, 11.1
la confirmación confirmation
confrontar to confront
congelado(a) frozen, 2.2

488 VOCABULARIO ESPAÑOL-INGLÉS

el **congelador** freezer, **9.1**
conmemorar to commemorate
conocer (zc) to know (a person), **I-9.1**
el/la **conocido(a)** acquaintance
el **conocimiento** knowledge
la **conquista** conquest
conquistar to conquer
el/la **consejero(a) de orientación** counselor, **16.1**
el **consejo** advice
conservar to conserve, preserve
el **consomé** consommé
considerar to consider
constante constant
la **construcción** construction
construir (y) to build, construct
la **consulta del médico** doctor's office, **I-10.2**
el **consultorio del médico** doctor's office, **I-10.2**
el/la **consumidor(a)** consumer
consumir to consume
el **consumo** consumption
la **contabilidad** accounting
el/la **contable** accountant, **16.1**
la **contaminación** contamination
el **contaminante** contaminant
contaminar to contaminate
contemporáneo(a) contemporary
contener (irreg.) to contain
contento(a) happy, **I-10.1**
la **contestación** answer
el **contestador automático** answering machine, **1.1**
contestar to answer, **1.2**
el **continente** continent
continuar to continue
contra against
el/la **contralor** comptroller
la **contraloría** comptrollership
contraer to contract
contrario(a) opposite, **I-7**
  lo contrario the opposite
la **contribución** contribution
el **control** inspection, **I-8.1**
  el **control de pasaportes** passport inspection, **I-8.2**
  el **control de seguridad** security inspection, **I-8.1**
controlado(a) controlled

el/la **controlador(a)** controller, **16.1**
controlar to control
la **convención** convention; agreement
el **convento** convent
la **conversación** conversation, **1.2**
convertir (ie, i) to convert
la **copa** cup
  la Copa Mundial World Cup
el/la **co-piloto** copilot, **I-8.2**
el **Corán** Koran
el **corazón** heart
  el **latido del corazón** heartbeat
la **corbata** necktie, **I-13.1**
el **cordero** lamb, **9.1**
la **cordillera** mountain range, **7.2**
corregir (j) to correct
el **correo** mail, **3.2**
  por correo aéreo by air mail, **3.2**
  por correo certificado certified mail, **3.2**
  por correo ordinario regular mail, **3.2**
  por correo recomendado certified mail, **3.2**
correr to run, **I-7.2**
la **correspondencia** correspondence, **3.1**
corresponder to correspond
la **corrida de toros** bullfight
cortar to cut, **4.1**
la **corte** court, **16.1**
el **corte de pelo** haircut, **8.2**
cortés courteous, **11.1**
la **cortesía** courtesy, **11**
corto(a) short, **I-13.2**
  el **pantalón corto** shorts
la **cosa** thing
la **cosecha** crop
los **cosméticos** cosmetics
la **costa** coast
  costal coastal
costar (ue) to cost, **I-13.1**
la **costilla** rib, **9.1**
la **costumbre** custom, **11.2**
el **cráter** crater
la **creación** creation
creer (y) to believe, **12**
la **crema: la crema bronceadora** suntan lotion, **I-11.1**

la **crema de afeitar** shaving cream, **I-16.2**
la **crema protectora** sunblock, **I-11.1**
la **cremallera** zipper, **I-13.2**
crespo(a) curly, **8.1**
criar to raise
el **crimen** crime
cristalino(a) crystalline, transparent
cristiano(a) Christian
el **cruce** intersection, **5.1**
crudo(a) raw, **I-15.2**
  casi crudo rare (meat), **I-15.2**
cruel cruel
cruzar (c) to cross, **10.1**
el **cuaderno** notebook, **I-BV**
la **cuadra** (city) block, **10.1**
cuadrado(a) square
el **cuadrante** quadrant
el **cuadro** painting, picture, **I-12.2**
cuadros: a cuadros plaid, **I-13.2**
¿cuál? what?, which?, **I-BV**
  ¿Cuál es la fecha de hoy? What is today's date?, **I-BV**
la **cualidad** quality
la **cualificación** qualification
cualquier any
cuando when, **15**
¿cuándo? when?, **I-3.1**
cuanto as
  en cuanto as soon as, **1.2**
  en cuanto a as to
¿cuánto(a)? how much?, **I-BV**
  ¿A cuánto está(n)? How much is it? (are they), **2.2**
  ¿Cuánto cuesta? How much does it cost?, **I-13.1**
  ¿Cuánto es? How much is it?, **I-BV**
  ¿Cuánto le debo? How much do I owe you?, **2.2**
cuarenta forty, **I-BV**
cuarto(a) fourth, **I-5.1**
el **cuarto** room, **I-5.1**; quart; fourth
  el **cuarto de baño** bathroom, **I-5.1**
  el **cuarto de dormir** bedroom, **I-5.1**
  el **cuarto doble** double room, **6.1**

VOCABULARIO ESPAÑOL-INGLÉS **489**

el **cuarto sencillo** single room, 6.1
menos **cuarto** a quarter to the hour
y **cuarto** a quarter past the hour
cuatro four, I-BV
cubano(a) Cuban
cubierto(a) covered, I-9.2
cubrir to cover
la **cuchara** spoon, I-15.1
la **cucharita** teaspoon, I-15.1
la **cuchilla** blade, I-9.2
el **cuchillo** knife, I-15.1
el **cuello** neck, 8.2
la **cuenta** bill, I-12.2; account, 14.2
la **cuenta corriente** checking account, 14.2
la **cuenta de ahorros** savings account, 14.2
el **cuento** story
el **cuentagotas** eyedropper
el **cuerpo** body
la **cuesta** slope, I-9.1
la **cuestión** question
el **cuidado** care
con **cuidado** carefully, 5.1
¡**cuidado**! be careful!, 10.2
cuidar to take care of
cultivar to grow
la **cultura** culture
el **cumpleaños** birthday, I-6.2
Feliz cumpleaños. Happy birthday., 12.1
cumplir to be (so many years) old, 12.1
cumplir años to have one's birthday, 12.1
el **cupé** coupe, 5.1
el **cura** priest, 12.1
la **cura** cure, treatment
el/la **curandero(a)** faith healer
curar to cure
curioso(a) curious
el **currículo profesional** curriculum vitae, 16.2
el **curso** course, I-2.1
curvo(a) curved

D

la **dama** woman, lady, I-13.1
la **dama de honor** bridesmaid, 15.2

dar (irreg.) to give, I-4.2
dar a luz to deliver, give birth
dar la bienvenida to welcome, 7.1
dar la vuelta to turn around, 10.1
dar palmaditas to slap gently, 11.2
dar una caminata to take a hike, I-16.2
dar una representación to put on a performance, I-12.2
dar vuelta to go around
darse cuenta to realize
dar(se) la mano to offer one's hand, 11.2; to shake hands
dar(se) prisa to rush, hurry
el **dátil** date (fruit)
el **dato** fact
de of, from, for, I-1.1
de equipo (adj.) team, I-7
de jazz (adj.) jazz, I-4
De nada. You're welcome., I-BV
de nuevo again
de rock (adj.) rock, I-4
de vez en cuando now and then
debajo de under, 7.1
deber to owe; + infinitive, should, ought
debido a due to
débil weak
decapitar to decapitate
decidir to decide
decimal decimal
décimo(a) tenth, I-5.1
decir (irreg.) to say, tell, I-9
la **decisión** decision
declarar to declare
dedicado(a) dedicated
dedicar(se) to dedicate (oneself), 16.2
el **dedo** finger, 4.1
el **dedo pequeño** little finger
el **déficit** deficit
la **definición** definition
dejar to leave (something behind), I-12.2; to allow
dejar una propina to leave a tip, I-12.2
del (de + el) from the, of the

delante de in front of, 10.1
delantero(a) front
delicioso(a) delicious, I-15.2
la **demanda** demand
demasiado too, too much, I-13.2
la **demografía** demography
la **demora** delay, I-14.2
con una demora late, I-14.2
la **densidad** density
denso(a) thick
dentro de in, 7.1; inside (adv.); within
dentro de poco soon
el **departamento (servicio) de personal** human resources department, 16.2
el **departamento de recursos humanos** human resources department, 16.2
depender (ie) to depend
el/la **dependiente** salesperson, I-13.1; clerk, 16.1
los **deportes** sport, I-2.2
deportivo(a) related to sports
depositar to deposit, 14.2
el **depósito** deposit, 14.2
depredador(a) plunderer
la **derecha** right, I-5.1
a la derecha to the right, I-5.1
derecho(a) straight, 10.1; right, right-hand
derretir to melt
derrocar to overthrow
derrotar to defeat
derrumbar to fail
desaparecer (zc) to disappear
desaprobado(a) failing
el **desastre** disaster
desayunarse to eat breakfast, I-16.1
el **desayuno** breakfast, I-5.2
el **descampado** open country
el **descanso** rest
el **descapotable** convertible, 5.1
descender (ie) to descend
el/la **descendiente** descendent
descolgar (ue) to pick up (the telephone), 1.1
descomponer to decompose
descortés discourteous, 11
describir to describe
la **descripción** description
el/la **descubridor(a)** discoverer
el **descubrimiento** discovery

descubrir to discover
el descuido carelessness
desde from; since
desear to wish, want, 11
desembocar to empty
desempleado(a) unemployed (adj.), 16.2
el/la desempleado(a) unemployed person, 16.2
el desempleo unemployment
desgraciadamente unfortunately
el desierto desert
desocupado(a) unemployed, 16.2
el desodorante deodorant, I-16.2
despachar to sell, dispense, I-10.2
despedirse (i, i) to say goodbye, 11.1
despegar (gu) to take off (airplane), I-8.2
el despegue the takeoff, 7.2
despertarse (ie) to wake up, I-16.1
desplazar to displace
el/la desposado(a) newlywed
desposar to wed, marry
después de (que) after, I-4.1
el/la destinatario(a) receiver, 3.1
el destino destination, I-8.1
    con destino a to
la destrucción destruction
desviarse to get lost, go astray
el detalle detail
detener (irreg.) to stop
el detergente detergent, 2.2
determinar to determine
detrás de behind, 10.1
la deuda debt
devolver (ue) to return, I-7.2
el día day, I-BV
    el Día de los Difuntos Day of the Dead
    el día de los Reyes Day of the Three Kings
la diagnosis diagnosis, I-10.2
el diálogo dialogue
el diamante diamond
diariamente daily
diario(a) daily; diary
dibujar to sketch
el dibujo drawing
el diccionario dictionary
diciembre December, I-BV

el diente tooth, I-16.1; clove
la dieta diet, I-10.2
diez ten, I-BV
la diferencia difference
diferente different
difícil difficult, I-2.1
el/la difunto(a) dead person, 12.1
    el Día de los Difuntos Day of the Dead
dinámico(a) dynamic
el dinero money, 14.1
    el dinero en efectivo cash, 14.1
el/la dios(a) god (goddess)
el/la diplomado(a) graduate
la dirección address, 3.1; direction, 10.1
la direccional turn signal, 5.1
directamente directly
el directivo board of directors, management
directo(a) direct
el/la director(a) conductor, I-12.2; director; principal, 16.1
dirigir to direct
discar to dial, 1
la disciplina subject, I-2.2
el disco record, I-4.1; dial (of telephone), 1.1
la discoteca discotheque
la disección dissection
el/la diseñador(a) designer
diseñar to design
disfrutar to enjoy
el dispensario dispensary
la distancia distance
distinguido(a) distinguished
distinguir to identify
distinto(a) distinct
la distribución distribution
distribuir (y) to distribute, 7.1
el distrito district
la diversión amusement
divertido(a) fun, I-1.1
divertirse (ie, i) to enjoy oneself, I-16.2
dividir to divide
divino(a) divine
la divisa foreign currency
el divorcio divorce
doblado(a) dubbed
doblar to turn, 5.1
doble double, 6.1
la documentación documentation

el dólar dollar
doler (ue) to hurt, ache, I-10.2
    Me duele_____.
    My (part of body) hurts., I-10
el dolor ache, pain, I-10.1
    el dolor de cabeza headache, I-10.1
    el dolor de estómago stomachache, I-10.1
    el dolor de garganta sore throat, I-10.1
la dominación domination
dominante dominant
dominar to dominate
el domingo Sunday, I-BV
dominicano(a) Dominican
el dominio power
¿dónde? where?, I-1.2
dormir (ue, u) to sleep, I-7
    dormirse (ue, u) to fall asleep, I-16.1
el dormitorio bedroom, I-5.1
dos two, I-BV
la dosis dose, I-10.2
dramáticamente dramatically
dramático(a) dramatic
driblar con to dribble (sports), I-7.2
la droga drug, I-10.2
la drogadicción drug addiction
la droguería drugstore
la ducha shower, I-16.2
    tomar una ducha to take a shower, I-16.2
la duda doubt
    no hay duda there is no doubt
dudar to doubt, 12
la dueña chaperone, 15.1
    duele: Me duele_____.
    My (part of body) hurts., I-10
el/la dueño(a) owner
la duna dune
durante during, I-4.2
durar to last, 12.2
duro(a) hard

E

e and (used instead of y before words beginning with i or hi)

VOCABULARIO ESPAÑOL-INGLÉS **491**

la **ebullición** boiling
    a la ebullición to a boil
echar to throw, **3.1**
    echar una siesta to take a nap, I-11.1
la **ecología** ecology
ecológico(a) ecologic
la **economía** economy; economics, **16.2**
    la economía doméstica home economics, I-2.2
económico(a) economical
el **ecosistema** ecosystem
el **ecuador** equator
ecuatorial equatorial
ecuatoriano(a) Ecuadorean
la **edad** age
    la Edad Media Middle Ages
el **edificio** building, I-5.1
la **educación** education
    la educación cívica social studies, I-2.2
    la educación física physical education, I-2.2
educacional educational
educado(a) well-mannered, polite, **11.1**
educar to educate
el **efecto** effect
el **eje** axis
el **ejemplo** example
    por ejemplo for example
ejercer (una profesión) to practice (a profession), **16.2**
el **ejercicio** exercise, I-10.2
    el ejercicio aeróbico aerobic exercise, I-10.2
    el ejercicio físico physical exercise, I-10.2
el the (m. sing.), I-1.1
él he; (to, for) him, I-1.1
elaborado(a) elaborate
elástico(a) elastic, **4.2**
el/la **electricista** electrician, **16.2**
el **electrodoméstico** domestic appliance
el **elefante** elephant
    el elefante marino walrus
elegante elegant
el **elemento** element
la **elevación** elevation
eliminar to eliminate
ella she; (to, for) her, I-1.2
ellos(as) they; (to, for) them
el **embarazo** pregnancy
el **embarque** boarding, **8**

el **emblema** emblem
el **embotellamiento** traffic jam, bottleneck
el/la **emigrante** emigrant
emigrar to emigrate
la **emisión** emission
    la emisión deportiva sports broadcast, I-5.2
emitir to emit
la **emoción** emotion; excitement
empatado(a) tied, **7**
empezar (ie) (c) to begin, I-7.1
el/la **empleado(a)** employee, **3.2**; attendant, **5.2**
    el/la empleado(a) de correo postal employee, **3.2**
    el/la empleado(a) del banco bank clerk, **14.1**
emplear to employ; to use
el **empleo** job, **16.2**
    la solicitud de empleo job application, **16.2**
la **empresa** business; company
empujar to push, **2.1**
en in, I-1.1
    en autobús by bus, I-3.1
    en avión by plane, I-8
    en carro (coche) by car, I-3.1
    en cuanto as soon as, **1.2**
    en cuanto a as to
    en este momento right now, I-8.1
    en seguida right away, **1.2**
    en todas partes everywhere
el/la **enamorado(a)** sweetheart, **15**
enamorarse to fall in love, **15.1**
el **encabezamiento** heading
encantar to love, I-13
encargarse to take charge of
encender (ie) to light, **12.2**
encestar to make a basket, I-7.2
encima above; overhead
    por encima de above, over
encogerse to shrink, **13.2**
encontrar (ue) to find
    encontrarse (ue) to meet
endosar to endorse, **14.2**
el/la **enemigo(a)** enemy
energético(a) energetic
la **energía** energy, **16.2**
    la energía nuclear nuclear energy, **16.2**
enero January, I-BV
enfadar to annoy, anger, I-13

la **enfermedad** sickness
el/la **enfermero(a)** nurse, I-10.2
enfermo(a) sick, I-10.1
el/la **enfermo(a)** sick person, I-10.2
enfrente de in front of, **8.2**; opposite, **10.1**
enfriarse to become cold
la **enhorabuena** congratulations, **15.2**
el **enlace** union
    el enlace nupcial wedding, **15.1**
enlatado(a) canned
enlazar to join, connect
enojar to annoy, anger, I-13
enorme enormous
enrarecido(a) thin (air)
el **enrarecimiento** thinning (of the air)
la **ensalada** salad, I-5.2
en seguida at once, immediately, I-16
la **enseñanza** teaching
enseñar to teach, I-3.2
entero(a) whole
enterrar (ie) to bury, **12.1**
la **entidad** entity
el **entierro** burial
la **entrada** entrance, I-6.2; inning, I-7.2; admission ticket, I-12.2
entrar to enter, I-3.1
    entrar en escena to come on stage, I-12.2
entre between, among
la **entrega** delivery, **3.2**
entregar to deliver, **3.2**
el **entremés** appetizer
la **entrevista** interview
el **envase** container, **2.2**
enviar to send, **3.1**
envidiar to envy
enyesar to put in a plaster cast, **4.2**
épico(a) epic
el **época** epoch, age
el **equilibrio** equilibrium, balance
el **equipaje** baggage, luggage, I-8.1
    el equipaje de mano hand (carry-on) luggage, I-8.1
    el reclamo de equipaje baggage claim, I-8.2
el **equipo** team, I-7.1; equipment

equivalente equivalent
equivocado(a) wrong, **1.1**
eres you (sing. fam.) are
erosionar to erode
es he/she/it is, I-1.1
la **escalera** stairway, I-5.1
los **escalofríos** chills, I-10.1
escandinavo(a) Scandinavian
escaparse to escape
el **escaparate** shop window, I-13.1
escaso(a) scarce
la **escena** scene; stage, I-12.2
    entrar en escena to come on stage, I-12.2
el **escenario** stage, scenery
escoger (j) to choose
escolar of or pertaining to school, I-3.1
escondido(a) hidden
escribir to write, I-5.2
escrito(a) written
escuchar to listen, I-4.1
la **escuela** school, I-1.1
    la **escuela intermedia** intermediate school
    la **escuela primaria** elementary school
    la **escuela secundaria** high school, I-1.1
    la **escuela superior** high school
    la **escuela vocacional** vocational school
el/la **escultor(a)** sculptor, I-12.2
la **escultura** sculpture
eso: a eso de about, I-3.1
el **espacio** space
la **espalda** back, **11.2**
España Spain
español(a) Spanish, I-2.2
el **español** Spanish (language), I-2.2
el **espagueti** spagetti
la **especia** spice
la **especialidad** specialty
especialista specialist (adj.), **16.2**
el/la **especialista** specialist, **16.2**
la **especialización** specialization
especializado(a) specialized
especialmente especially
específicamente specifically
específico(a) specific
espectacular spectacular

el **espectáculo** show, performance, I-12.2
el/la **espectador(a)** spectator, I-7
el **espejo** mirror, I-16.1
la **esperanza** hope
    la **esperanza de vida** life expectancy
esperar to wait for, I-14
la **espinaca** spinach
las **esposas** handcuffs
el/la **esposo(a)** husband (wife), I-6.1
el **esquí** ski, I-9.1; skiing, I-9.1
    el **esquí acuático** water skiing, I-11.1
    el **esquí alpino** downhill skiing, I-9.1
    el **esquí de descenso** downhill skiing, I-9.1
    el **esquí de fondo** cross-country skiing, I-9.1
    el **esquí nórdico** cross-country skiing, I-9.1
el/la **esquiador(a)** skier, I-9.1
esquiar to ski, I-9.1
    esquiar en el agua to waterski, I-11.1
la **esquina** corner, **5.1**
    ¿Está (el nombre de una persona)? May I talk to (name of person)?, **1.1**
estable stable
establecer (zc) to establish
la **estación** season; station, I-12.1
    la **estación de esquí** ski resort, I-9.1
    la **estación de ferrocarril** train station, I-14.1
    la **estación de servicio** service station, **5.2**
estacionar to park, **5.1**
el **estadio** stadium, I-7.1
el **estado** state
    el **estado de banco (de cuenta)** bank statement, **14.2**
    el **estado libre asociado** commonwealth
los **Estados Unidos** United States
estadounidense from the United States
la **estampilla** stamp, **3.1**
están they/you (pl. form.) are, I-4.1
    Están hablando. They

are speaking., **1.1**
el **estanco** tobacco store
estar (irreg.) to be, I-4.1
    estar enfermo(a) to be sick
    estar en onda to be in vogue
estás you (sing. fam.) are
estatal of the state
la **estatua** statue, I-12.2
el **este** east, **10.1**
este(a) this, I-9
estereofónico(a) stereophonic, **7.1**
esterlino(a) sterling
el **estilo** style
el **estómago** stomach, I-10.1
    el **dolor de estómago** stomachache, I-10.1
estornudar to sneeze, I-10.1
éstos(as) these (ones)
estoy I am
estrechar la mano to shake hands, **11.2**
estrecho(a) tight, I-13.2; narrow
la **estrella** star
el **estrés** stress
la **estructura** structure
el/la **estudiante** student
estudiantil (adj.) student
estudiar to study, I-3.2
el **estudio** study
la **estufa** stove, **9.1**
estupendo(a) terrific
eterno(a) eternal
la **etnicidad** ethnicity
étnico(a) ethnic
el **eucalipto** eucalyptus tree
la **Europa** Europe, **15.2**
europeo(a) European
la **evaluación** evaluation
evangelista Evangelistic
el **evento** event
evitar to avoid
exacto(a) exact
el **examen** examination, I-3.2
examinar to examine, I-10.2
excelente excellent
la **excepción** exception
excesivo(a) excessive
el **exceso** excess
exclusivamente exclusively
la **excursión** excursion
exigente demanding
exigir to demand, **12**
existir to exist

VOCABULARIO ESPAÑOL-INGLÉS   **493**

exótico(a) exotic
expandir to expand
la expectativa expectation
el experimento experiment
experto(a) expert, I-9.1
explicar (qu) to explain
la exploración exploration
el/la explorador(a) explorer
exponer to explain, expound
exportar to export
la exposición exhibition, I-12.2
la expresión expression
expulsar to expel
extender (ie) to extend
la extensión extension
externo(a) external
extranjero(a) foreign
el extranjero abroad
extraordinario(a) extraordinary
extremadamente extremely
extremo(a) extreme

F

la fábrica factory, 16.1
fabricar to make
fabuloso(a) fabulous
fácil easy, I-2.1
fácilmente easily
la factura bill
facturar to check (luggage), I-8.1
facultativo(a) optional
la falda skirt, I-13.1
falso(a) false
la falta lack
faltar to lack
la fama fame
la familia family, I-5.1
familiar of the family (adj.)
famoso(a) famous
fanfarrón(a) boastful, I-9.1
fantástico(a) fantastic, I-1.2
el/la farmacéutico(a) pharmacist, I-10.2
la farmacia pharmacy, I-10.2
el faro headlight
fascinante fascinating
fascinar to fascinate
el favor favor
el fax fax
febrero February, I-BV
la fecha date, I-BV

¿Cuál es la fecha de hoy? What is today's date?, I-BV
la felicidad happiness, 15.2
¡Felicitaciones! Congratulations! 15.2
feliz happy, 12.1
Feliz cumpleaños. Happy birthday., 12.1
Feliz Navidad. Merry Christmas., 12.2
femenino(a) feminine
el fenómeno phenomenon
la feria fair
el ferrocarril railway, railroad, I-14.1
festejar to celebrate
la festividad festivity
la fibra fiber, I-10.2
la ficha token; registration card, 6.1
la fiebre fever, I-10.1
la fiesta party, I-4.2
la fiesta de las luces Festival of Lights, 12.2
fijar to fix
fijarse en to take note of
la fila row, I-8; line, I-12.1
la filial branch office
el film(e) film, I-12.1
el/la filósofo(a) philosopher
el fin end
el fin de semana weekend
en fin finally
el final end
financiero(a) financial
la finanza finance
fino(a) fine
el fiordo fjord
firmar to sign, 14.2
firme firm, stable
la física physics, I-2.2
físicamente physically
el/la físico physicist
físico(a) physical, I-10.2
la fisiología physiology
flamenco(a) Flemish; flamenco
el flequillo bangs, 8.1
la flexibilidad flexibility
la flor flower, I-6.2
fluctuar to fluctuate, 14.1
el fondo bottom; fund
el/la fontanero(a) plumber, 16.2
la formación formation
formal formal

la formalidad formality
formalizar to formalize
formar to form, make
formativo(a) formative
la fórmula method, pattern
la formulación formation, formulation
el formulario form, 4.2
el formulario de retiro withdrawal slip, 14.2
la foto photo
la fractura fracture, 4.1
francamente frankly
francés (francesa) French, I-2.2
el franco Franc
el franqueo postage
el frasco jar, 2.2
la frase sentence; phrase
la frecuencia frequency
con frecuencia frequently
frecuentar to frequent
frecuentemente frequently
freír (i, i) to fry, I-15.1
frenar to brake, 5.1
el freno brake, 5.1
la frente forehead, 4.1
frente a facing, opposite
la fresa strawberry, 2.1
fresco(a) fresh, cool
Hace fresco. It's cool.
el frijol bean, I-15.2
el frío cold (weather), I-9.1
Hace frío. It's cold., I-9.1
frito(a) fried
la frontera border
la fruta fruit, I-15.2
el fuego fire, 9.2
fuerte strong
la fuerza aérea air force
la fuerza ascensional lift
la función function
el funcionamiento functioning
funcionar to function
el/la funcionario(a) city hall employee, 16.1
el/la fundador(a) founder
fundir to found
la fusión fusion
el fútbol soccer, I-7.1
el campo de fútbol soccer field, I-7.1
el futuro future

494 VOCABULARIO ESPAÑOL-INGLÉS

G

la **gabardina** raincoat, I-13.1
las **gafas** glasses, goggles, I-9.1
gallego(a) Galician
la **gallina** hen
el **gallo** rooster
el **galón** gallon
la **gama** range
la **gamba** shrimp, 9.2
el **ganado** cattle
el/la **ganador(a)** winner
ganar to win, I-7.1; to earn
el **gancho** clothes hanger, 6.2
la **ganga** bargain
el **garaje** garage, I-6.2
la **garganta** throat, I-10.1
 el **dolor de garganta** sore throat, I-10.1
la **garita de peaje** toll booth, 10.2
gas: con gas carbonated
la **gaseosa** soft drink, soda, I-5.2
la **gasolina** gas, 5.2
la **gasolinera** gas station, 5.2
gastado(a) spent, barren
el **gasto** expense; charge, 6.1
el/la **gato(a)** cat, I-6.1; jack
gastronómico(a) gastronomic
la **gelatina** gelatin
la **generación** generation
general: por lo general in general
generalizar to generalize
generalmente generally
el **género** kind, sort, genre
generoso(a) generous
genovés(a) Genovese
la **gente** people, 16.2
la **geografía** geography, I-2.2
geográfico(a) geographic
la **geometría** geometry, I-2.2
el **gesto** gesture
gigantesco(a) gigantic, huge
el **gimnasio** gymnasium
girar to rotate
el **giro postal** money order
el **glaciar** glacier
el **gobierno** government
el **gol** goal (soccer), I-7.1
 meter un gol to score a goal, I-7.1
el **golf** golf, I-11.2
 el **campo de golf** golf course, I-11.2
 el **juego de golf** golf game, I-11.2

la **bolsa de golf** golf bag, I-11.2
golpear to hit, I-11.2
la **goma** eraser, I-BV; tire, 5.1
el **gorro** cap, I-9.1
gozar to enjoy
gracias thank you, I-BV
el **grado** degree, I-9.1
el **gramo** gram
gran, grande big, I-2.1
 las **Grandes Ligas** Major Leagues
la **grasa** grease
gratis free
grato(a) agreeable, pleasant
grave serious, grave
el **green** green (golf), I-11.2
griego(a) Greek
la **gripe** flu, cold, I-10.1
gris grey, I-13.2
gritar to shout
el **grito** shout, cry
el **grupo** group
el **guante** glove, I-7.2
guardar to guard, I-7
 guardar cama to stay in bed, I-10.1
guatemalteco(a) Guatemalan
gubernamental governmental
la **guerra** war
guerrero(a) war-like
el/la **guerrillero(a)** guerrilla
la **guía telefónica** telephone book, 1.1
el **guisante** pea, 9.1
guisar to stew
la **guitarra** guitar, I-4.2
gustar to like, enjoy, I-13.1

H

haber to have (auxiliary verb)
la **habichuela** bean, I-15.2
 la **habichuela negra** black bean, 9.2
la **habitación** room, I-5.1
el/la **habitante** inhabitant
habla: de habla española Spanish-speaking
hablar to speak, I-3.1
hace:
 Hace calor. It's hot., I-11.1
 Hace frío. It's cold., I-9.1

hace mucho tiempo a long time ago
Hace muchos años que For many years
hace poco a short time ago
Hace sol. It's sunny., I-11.1
hacer (irreg.) to do; to make, I-8.1
 hacer cola to line up
 hacer un viaje to take a trip, I-8.1
 hacer juego con to go with, I-13.2
 hacer la cama to make the bed, 6.2
 hacer la maleta to pack one's suitcase, I-8
 hacer los negocios to get down to business
 hacer obras to do repair work
 hacer una llamada to make a call, 1.1
 hacerse daño to hurt oneself, 4.1
hacia toward
el **hallazgo** finding
la **hamaca** hammock, I-11.1
la **hambre** hunger, I-15.1
 pasar hambre to go hungry
 tener hambre to be hungry, I-15.1
la **hamburguesa** hamburger
Hanuka Hanukkah, 12.2
la **harina** flour
hasta (que) until, I-BV; up to
 Hasta la vista. See you later.
 Hasta luego. See you later., I-BV
 Hasta mañana. See you tomorrow., I-BV
 Hasta pronto. See you soon., I-BV
hay there is, there are, I-5.1
 Hay (Hace) sol. It's sunny., I-11.1
hebreo(a) Hebrew, 12.2
la **helada** frost
el **helado** ice cream, I-5.2
las **hélices** propellers, 7.2
el **helicóptero** helicopter, 7.2
el **hemisferio** hemisphere
herbívoro(a) herbivorous
el/la **herbolario(a)** herbalist
heredar to inherit

VOCABULARIO ESPAÑOL-INGLÉS

la **herencia** inheritance
la **herida** wound
el/la **hermanastro(a)** stepbrother (stepsister)
el/la **hermano(a)** brother (sister), I-2.1
el **héroe** hero
hervir (ie) to boil, 9.1
la **hibridación** hybridization
el **hidrato de carbono** carbohydrate
el **hidrofoil** hydrofoil
el **hielo: el patinaje sobre hielo** ice skating, I-9.2
la **hierba** herb; grass
el **hierro** iron
higiénico(a) sanitary, 2.2
    el **papel higiénico** toilet paper, I-16.2
el/la **hijastro(a)** stepson (stepdaughter)
el/la **hijo(a)** son (daughter), I-6.1
    los **hijos** children (sons and daughters), I-6.1
hinchado(a) swollen, 4.1
la **hiperinflación** hyperinflation
el **hipermercado** supermarket, 2.1
el **hipopótamo** hippopotamus
hispánico(a) Hispanic (adj.)
hispano(a) Hispanic (person)
hispanohablante Spanish-speaking
la **historia** history, I-2.2; story
el/la **historiador(a)** historian
el **historial profesional** curriculum vitae, 16.2
histórico(a) historic
el **hit** hit (baseball), I-7.2
la **hoja** sheet, I-BV; blade, I-9.2
    la **hoja de papel** sheet of paper, I-BV
hola hello, I-BV
holandés (holandesa) Dutch
el **hombre** man
el **hombro** shoulder, 4.1
honesto(a) honest, I-1.2
el **honor** honor
la **hora** hour; time
el **horario** schedule, I-14.1
el **hornillo** portable stove, I-16.2
el/la **hornillo(a)** (stove) burner, 9.1
el **horno** oven, 9.1
    el **horno de microondas** microwave oven, 9.1

el **horóscopo** horoscope
la **horquilla** bobby pin, 8.2
hospedar to lodge, stay
el **hospital** hospital, I-10.2
hostil hostile
el **hotel** hotel, 6.1
hotelero(a) hotelkeeper
hoy today, I-11.2
    ¿Cuál es la fecha de hoy? What is today's date?, I-BV
    hoy día nowadays; today
    hoy en día nowadays
el **hoyo** hole, I-11.2
el **hueco** hole
el **hueso** bone
el/la **huésped** guest, 6.1
el **huevo** egg, I-15.2
    los **huevos duros** poached eggs
    los **huevos pasados por agua** softboiled eggs
    los **huevos revueltos** scrambled eggs
las **humanidades** humanities
el/la **humanista** humanist
humano(a) human, 16.2
la **humedad** dampness
humilde humble
el **humor: de buen humor** in a good mood, I-10
    de mal humor in a bad mood, I-10
el **huso horario** time zone

I

la **idea** idea
idéntico(a) identical
la **identidad** identity
identificar to identify
el **idioma** language
el **ídolo** idol
la **iglesia** church, 10.1
igual equal
imaginar to imagine
imitar to imitate
impar odd
el **imperio** empire
imponer to impose
importado(a) imported
la **importancia** importance
importante important, 11
importar to be important
imposible impossible, 11

impresionado(a) impressed
impresionante amazing, impressive
improbable improbable, 11
el **impuesto** tax
inaccesible inaccessible
inalámbrico(a) cordless, 1.1
incalculable incalculable
incainco(a) Inca (adj.)
el **incendio** fire
inclinado(a) slanted
incluir (y) to include
incluso including
inconveniente inconvenient
increíble incredible
independiente independent
indicar (qu) to indicate
el **índice** ratio; index
indígena native (adj.)
indio(a) Indian
individual individual (adj.), I-7
el/la **individuo** individual (person)
la **industria** industry
industrializado(a) industrialized
el/la **infante** infant
inferior inferior; lower
el **infierno** hell
la **inflación** inflation
la **influencia** influence
la **información** information
informal informal
informar to inform
la **informática** computer sciences, 16.1
el **informe** report
el **inglés** English (language), I-2.2
inglés (inglesa) English (adj.)
el **ingrediente** ingredient
ingresar to deposit, 14.2
el **ingreso** deposit, income
inhóspito(a) inhospitable
inmediatamente immediately
inmenso(a) immense
el **inodoro** toilet, 6.2
el/la **inquilino(a)** tenant
la **inscripción** enrollment
insistir to insist, 11.1
inspeccionar to inspect, I-8.2
inspirar to inspire
la **instalación** installation
instalarse to establish oneself
la **institución** institution
el **instituto** institute

las **instrucciones** instructions, I-5.2
el **instrumento** instrument
insuficiente insufficient
el **insulto** insult
íntegro(a) integral
inteligente intelligent, I-2.1
la **intención** intention
la **intensidad** intensity
intensivo(a) intensive, 4.2
interactuar to interact
intercambiar to exchange, 15.2
intercambio exchange
el **interés** interest
interesante interesting, I-2.1
interesar to interest, I-13.1
el/la **interlocutor(a)** caller, 1.1
intermitente intermittent (adj.)
el **intermitente** turn signal, 5.1
internacional international
interno(a) internal
el/la **intérprete** interpreter
interrogativo(a) interrogative
interrumpir to interrupt
interurbano(a) interurban
intervenir to intervene
la **intimidad** intimacy
íntimo(a) close, intimate, 11.2
introducir (zc) to insert, 1.1; to introduce
invadir to invade
la **invención** invention
la **inversión** investment
la **investigación** investigation
el **invierno** winter, I-9.1
la **invitación** invitation, I-5.2
el/la **invitado(a)** guest, 15.2
invitar to invite, I-4.2
la **inyección** injection, shot
ir (irreg.) to go, I-4.1
  ir a (+ inf.) to be going to, I-6
  ir de camping to go camping
  ir de compras to go shopping
  ir de paseo to go for a walk
irlandés (irlandesa) Irish
la **isla** island
el **istmo** isthmus
el **italiano** Italian (language), I-2.2
la **izquierda** left, I-5.1
  a la izquierda to the left, I-5.1

J

el **jabón** soap, I-16.2
  el **jabón en polvo** powdered soap, 2.2
jamás never, 6
el **jamón** ham, I-15.2
japonés (japonesa) Japanese
el **jardín** garden, I-6.2
el/la **jardinero(a)** outfielder (baseball), I-7.2
el/la **jefe(a)** leader, chief
el **jersey** sweater, I-13.1
el **jet** jet, 7.2
el **jonrón** home run, I-7.2
joven young (adj.), I-6.1
el/la **joven** young person, 15.1
las **joyas** jewelry
la **judía verde** string bean, 2.1
el/la **judío(a)** Jew, 12.2
el **juego** game
  hacer juego con to go with, match, I-13.2
el **jueves** Thursday, I-BV
el/la **juez** judge, 16.1
el/la **jugador(a)** player, I-7.1
jugar (ue) to play, I-7.1
el **jugo** juice
jugoso(a) juicy
julio July, I-BV
la **jungla** jungle
junio June, I-BV
junto(a) together, 15.1
el **juramento** oath
justo(a) fair, reasonable

K

el **kilo(gramo)** kilogram, 2.2
el **kilómetro** kilometer

L

la the (f. sing.), I-1.1
el **laberinto** labyrinth
el **labio** lip, 4.1
el **laboratorio** laboratory, 16.2
el/la **labrador(a)** farm worker, 16.2
labrar (la tierra) to farm (the land), 16.2
la **laca** hair spray, 8.2
lacio(a) straight (hair), 8.1
la **lactancia** nursing period
lado: al lado de to the side of, 8.2
el **lago** lake, 7.2
la **lana** wool, 13.2
la **langosta** lobster, 2.1
la **lanza** spear
el/la **lanzador(a)** pitcher, I-7.2
lanzar to throw, I-7.1
el **lápiz** pencil, I-5.2
largo(a) long, I-13.2
  a lo largo de along
las the (f. pl.)
la **lástima** pity, 12
  ser una lástima to be a pity, 12
lastimarse to get hurt, 4.1
la **lata** can, 2.2
el **latido** beat
  el **latido del corazón** heartbeat
la **Latinoamérica** Latin America
latinoamericano(a) Latin American
la **latitud** latitude
el **latín** Latin, I-2.2
el **lavabo** lavatory, 7.1
el **lavado** wash, 8.2; laundry, 13.2
la **lavandería** laundromat, 13.2
lavar to wash, 13.2
  lavarse to wash oneself, I-16.1
le him, her, you (form.) (pron.)
la **lección** lesson, I-3.2
la **leche** milk, I-5.2
el **lechón** roast suckling pig, 2.1
la **lechuga** lettuce, I-15.2
la **lectura** reading
leer (y) to read, I-5.2
legendario(a) legendary
la **legumbre** vegetable, I-15.2
lejano(a) distant
la **lengua** language, I-2.2; tongue
  la **lengua materna** native language
lento(a) slow
les them, you (form.) (pron.)
levantar to raise, 13.1
  levantarse to get up, I-16.1
la **ley** law
la **leyenda** legend
la **libertad** freedom

VOCABULARIO ESPAÑOL-INGLÉS

el/la **libertador(a)** liberator
la **libra** pound
libre free, I-14.2
la **libreta** notebook, I-3.2; passbook, **14.2**
el **libro** book, I-BV
la **licencia** driver's license, **5.1**
el **liceo** primary school (in México); high school (in most places)
ligeramente lightly
ligero(a) light
la **lima** lime, **9.1**
limitar to limit
el **límite** limit; boundary
el **limón** lemon, **9.1**
la **limonada** lemonade, I-BV
el **limpiaparabrisas** windshield wiper
limpiar to clean, **5.2**
  limpiar en seco to dry clean, **13.2**
la **limpieza en seco** dry cleaning, **13.2**
limpio(a) clean
la **línea** line, **1.1**
  La línea está ocupada. The line is busy., **1.1**
  la línea aérea airline, I-8.1
la **linfa** lymph
la **linterna** flashlight, I-16.2
la **liquidación** sale
el **líquido** liquid
líquido(a) liquid (adj.), **2.2**
liso(a) straight (hair), **8.1**; smooth
la **lista** list
la **litera** berth, I-14.2
la **literatura** literature
el **litro** liter
la **llamada** call, **1.1**
  llamar por teléfono to call by telephone, **1.1**
  llamarse to be called, named, I-16.1
la **llanta** tire, **5.1**
la **llanura** plain, **7.2**
la **llave** key, **6.1**
la **llegada** arrival, I-8.1
  el tablero de llegadas y salidas arrival and departure board, I-8.1
llegar to arrive, I-3.1
llenar to fill (out), **4.2**
llevar to carry, I-3.2; to wear
llover(ue) to rain, I-11.1

Llueve. It's raining., I-11.1
el **lobo de mar** sea lion
la **localidad** seat (in theater), I-12.1
loco(a) crazy
la **longitud** longitude
la **lonja** slice, **2.2**
los the (m. pl.)
la **lucha** fight, battle
luchar to fight
lucir (zc) to display
luego then, **10.2**
  Hasta luego. See you later, I-BV
el **lugar** place, **12.2**
  tener lugar to take place, **12.2**
el **lujo** luxury
  de (gran) lujo deluxe
la **luna de miel** honeymoon, **15.2**
el **lunes** Monday, I-BV
la **luz** light, **10.1**

M

la **madera** wood
la **madre** mother, I-6.1
el/la **madrileño(a)** native of Madrid
la **madrina** godmother, **12.1**; maid of honor, **15.2**
el **madroño** madrone tree
el/la **maestro(a)** master, teacher
magallánico(a) Magellanic
magnífico(a) magnificent
el/la **mahometano(a)** Muslim
el **maíz** corn, **9.2**
el **mal** illness, ailment
malcriado(a) bad-mannered, spoiled, **11.1**
el **malestar** malaise
la **maleta** suitcase, I-8.1
  hacer la maleta to pack one's suitcase, I-8
el/la **maletero(a)** trunk (of car), I-8.1; porter, I-14.1
malo(a) bad, I-1
la **mamá** mother, I-5.2
el **mamífero** mammal
la **mancha** stain, **13.2**
manchado(a) stained, **13.2**
mandar to send, **11**; to rule
manejar to drive, **10.2**; to manage
manera way, manner, I-1.1
  de manera que so that, **15**

de ninguna manera by no means, I-1.1
la **manga** sleeve, I-13.2
el **mango** handle, I-11.2
la **manía** mania
la **mano** hand, I-7.1
  dar la mano to offer one's hand, **11.2**
  el equipaje de mano hand (carry-on) luggage, I-8.1
  estrechar la mano to shake hands, **11.2**
la **mansión** mansion
la **manteca** lard
la **mantequilla** butter, **2.1**
el **mantel** tablecloth, I-15.1
mantener to maintain
el **mantenimiento** maintenance
la **manzana** apple, **2.1**; (city) block, **10.1**
la **mañana** morning, I-2
  esta mañana this morning, I-11.2
mañana tomorrow (adv.), **3.1**
el **mapa** map
la **máquina de lavar** washing machine, **13.2**
la **maquinilla** electric hair clipper, **8.2**
el **mar** sea, I-11.1
  El Mar Caribe Caribbean Sea
maravilloso(a) wonderful
marcado(a) marked
marcar to score (sports), I-7.1; to dial, **1.1**
mareado(a) dizzy
el **marido** husband, I-6.1
el **marisco** shellfish, I-15.2
marrón brown, I-13.2
el **martes** Tuesday, I-BV
marzo March, I-BV
más more, most, **9.1**
la **masa** mass
  la masa harina flour
la **máscara de oxígeno** oxygen mask, **7.1**
masculino(a) masculine
matar to kill
las **matemáticas** mathematics, I-2.2
la **materia** subject matter, I-2.2; matter
  la materia prima raw material
el **material** material
materno(a) maternal

498 VOCABULARIO ESPAÑOL-INGLÉS

la **lengua materna** native language
los **matorrales** underbrush, thickets
la **matrícula** registration
el **matrimonio** wedding, **15.2** marriage; married couple, bride and groom, **15.1**
máximo(a) maximum, **10.2**
el/la **maya** Maya, Mayan
mayo May, I-BV
la **mayonesa** mayonnaise, **2.2**
mayor great, greater, greatest; older, **11.1**
la **mayoría** majority
mayormente principally, mainly
la **mazorca** corn ear
me (to, for) me
el/la **mecánico** mechanic, **16.1**
la **mecha** lock (of hair), **8.1**
mechado(a) shredded
la **medianoche** midnight, I-2
el **medicamento** medication, I-10.2
la **medicina** medicine, I-10
médico(a) medical
el/la **médico(a)** doctor, I-10.2
la **medida** measurement; method
medieval medieval
el **medio** mean, way
medio(a) middle (adj.); half
 a término medio medium (meat), I-15.2
 la clase media middle class
 y media half past the hour
las **medias** pantihose, stockings, I-13.1
el **mediodía** midday, noon, I-2
medir (i, i) to measure
la **mejilla** cheek, **4.1**
el **mejillón** mussel, **9.2**
mejor better, **11**
mejorar to improve
el **melocotón** peach, **9.1**
la **membrana** membrane
la **memoria** memory
 la carta de memoria memory chart
menor younger, **11.1**
la **menora** menorah, **12.2**
menos less
 a menos que unless, **15**
 menos cuarto a quarter to (the hour), I-2
 menos de less than
el **mensaje** message
mensualmente monthly
mental mental
el **menú** menu, I-12.2
el/la **mercader** merchant, **16.1**
el **mercado** market, **2.1**
la **mercancía** merchandise
el **meridiano** meridian
la **merienda** snack, I-4.1
la **mermelada** marmalade
el **mes** month
la **mesa** table, I-12.2
 la mesa de operaciones operating table, **4.2**
el/la **mesero(a)** waiter (waitress), I-12.2
la **meseta** plateau, **7.2**
la **mesita** tray table, **7.1**
el **metal** metal
la **meteorología** meteorology
meter to put in, I-7.1
 meter en el cesto to make a basket, I-7.2
 meter un gol to score a goal, I-7.1
el **método** method
métrico(a) metric
el **metro** meter; subway, I-12.1
mexicano(a) Mexican, I-1.1
mezclar to mix
mi my
mí me
el **microbio** microbe
microscópico(a) microscopic
el **microscopio** microscope
el/la **miembro** member
mientras while, **2.2**
el **miércoles** Wednesday, I-BV
la **migración** migration
mil (one) thousand, I-BV
el **militar** soldier
la **milla** mile
el **millón (de)** million
el/la **millonario(a)** millionaire
mineral mineral, **2.2**
el **ministerio** minestry
el **minuto** minute
mirar to look at, I-3.2
 mirarse to look at oneself, I-16.1
la **misa** Mass, **12.2**
 la misa del gallo midnight Mass, **12.2**
mismo(a) same; myself, yourself, him/her/itself, ourselves, yourselves, themselves
 lo mismo the same
la **mitad** half
la **mitología** mythology
mixto(a) mixed
la **mochila** bookbag, knapsack, I-BV
la **moda** style
 de moda in style
los **modales** manners, **11.1**
el **modelo** model
moderado(a) moderate
moderno(a) modern
modesto(a) modest
modificar to modify
el/la **modisto(a)** designer (clothes)
modo: de modo que so that, **15**
la **molécula** molecule
molestar to bother, I-13
el **momento** moment
 en este momento right now, I-8.1
 Un momento, por favor. One moment, please., **1.1**
la **moneda** coin, **1.1**
el **monje** monk
el **monocultivo** monoculture
el **monopatín** skateboard
 andar en monopatín to skateboard, I-9.2
el **monopolio** monopoly
el/la **monoteísta** monotheist
el **monstruo** monster
la **montaña** mountain, I-9.1
montañoso(a) mountainous
montar to assemble
el **monto** total, **6.1**
el **monumento** monument
el **moño** bun, chignon, **8.1**
moreno(a) dark, I-1.1
morir (ue, u) to die, I-15
el **morrón** large, red, sweet pepper
el **mostrador** counter, I-8.1
mostrar (ue) to show
el **motel** motel
el **motivo** motive, reason
el **moto** motorcycle
el **motor** motor, engine, **7.2**
la **motricidad** motor function
mover (ue) to move

VOCABULARIO ESPAÑOL-INGLÉS

el/la **mozo(a)** porter, I-14.1; bellhop, **6.1**; young person
el/la **muchacho(a)** boy (girl), I-BV
mucho(a) a lot; many, I-5
  Mucho Gusto. Nice to meet you., I-BV
el **mueble** piece of furniture
el/la **muerto(a)** dead person, **12.1**
la **mujer** wife, I-6.1
la **muleta** crutch, **4.1**
la **multa** fine
multinacional multinational
múltiple multiple
multiplicar to multiply
mundial worldwide
  la Copa Mundial World Cup
  la Serie Mundial World Series
el **mundo** world
  el Nuevo Mundo New World
la **muñeca** wrist, **4.1**
el **mural** mural, I-12.2
muscular muscular
el **museo** museum, I-12.2
la **música** music, I-2.2
musical musical, I-12.2
el/la **músico** musician, I-12.2
musulmán (musulmana) Muslim
muy very, I-1.1

N

nacer (zc) to be born, **12.1**
el **nacimiento** birth, **12.1**
nacional national, **13.1**
la **nacionalidad** nationality, I-1
nada nothing, I-13.1
nadar to swim, I-11.1
nadie no one, nobody, I-13
la **naranja** orange, **2.1**
los **narcóticos** narcotics
natural natural
la **naturaleza** nature
el/la **naturalista** naturalist
la **navaja** razor, I-16.1
navegable navegable
la **Navidad** Christmas, **12.2**
  el regalo de Navidad Christmas present, **12.2**
  Feliz Navidad Merry Christmas, **12.2**

  la víspera de Navidad Christmas Eve, **12.2**
necesariamente necessarily
necesario(a) necessary, **11.1**
la **necesidad** necessity
necesitar to need, **8.2**
negativo(a) negative
negociarse to trade
negro(a) black, I-13.2
el **nervio** nerve
nervioso(a) nervous, I-10.1
el **neumático** tire, **5.1**
la **nevada** snowfall, I-9.1
  nevar (ie) to snow, I-9.1
  Nieva. It's snowing., I-9
la **nevera** refrigerator, **9.1**
ni... ni neither... nor
  Ni yo tampoco. Me neither., I-13
nicaragüense Nicaraguan
el/la **nieto(a)** grandchild, I-6.1
  los nietos grandchildren, I-6.1
la **nieve** snow, I-9.1
ninguna: de ninguna manera by no means, I-1.1
el/la **niño(a)** boy (girl), **1.2**
el **nivel** level, **7.2**
  el nivel del mar sea level, **7.2**
no no
  No hay de qué. You're welcome., I-BV
el **noble** noble
nocturno(a) (adj.) night
la **noche** night
  esta noche tonight, I-11.2
la **Nochebuena** Christmas Eve, **12.2**
el **nombre** name, **3.1**
  normal regular (gas), **5.2**
el **norte** north, **10.1**
norteamericano(a) North American
la **Noruega** Norway
nos us (pron.)
nosotros(as) we, I-2.2
la **nota** grade, I-3.2; bill, **6.1**; note
notable outstanding; notable
notar to note
las **noticias** news, I-5.2
la **novela** novel, I-5.2
el/la **novelista** novelist
el **novenario** nine days of mourning

noveno(a) ninth, I-5.1
noventa ninety, I-BV
noviembre November, I-BV
el/la **novio(a)** fiancé(e), boyfriend (girlfriend), **15.1**
la **nube** cloud, I-11.1
nublado(a) cloudy, I-11.1
  Está nublado. It's cloudy., I-11.1
nuclear nuclear, **16.2**
  la energía nuclear nuclear energy, **16.2**
el **núcleo** nucleus
nuestro(a) our
nueve nine, I-BV
nuevo(a) new, I-6.2
el **número** number, I-8.1
  el número de teléfono telephone number, **1.1**
  el número del asiento seat number, I-8.1
  el número del vuelo flight number, I-8.1
numeroso(a) numerous
nunca never, I-13.1
la **nutrición** nutrition
el **nutrimento** nutriment

O

o or
el **objetivo** objective
el **objeto** object
oblicuo(a) angled, oblique
la **obligación** obligation
obligar to force
obligatorio(a) mandatory
la **obra** work, I-12.2
obrar to work
el/la **obrero(a)** worker, **16.1**
observar to observe
la **obstetricia** obstetrics
obtener to obtain
obviamente obviously
obvio(a) obvious
la **ocasión** occasion
  de ocasión secondhand
occidental western
el **Occidente** West
el **océano** ocean
  el océano Atlántico Atlantic Ocean
  el océano Pacífico Pacific Ocean
ochenta eighty, I-BV

ocho eight, I-BV
octavo(a) eighth, I-5.1
octubre October, I-BV
oculto(a) hidden
ocupado(a) occupied, I-14.2; busy, 1.1
   el tono de ocupado busy tone, 1.1
   La línea está ocupada. The line is busy., 1.1
   Suena ocupado. It is busy., 1.1
ocupar to occupy
el oeste west, 10.1
   del oeste Western (movie)
el/la oferente offerer
la oferta offer
oficialmente officially
oficiar to officiate, celebrate
la oficina office, 16.1
   la oficina de cambio exchange office, 14.1
   la oficina de correos post office, 3.2
   la oficina de recepción (hospital) admitting office, 4.2
el oficio trade, 16.1
ofrecer (zc) to offer
el oído ear
oír (y) to hear
ojalá (que) I hope (that), 16
la ola wave, I-11.1
olímpico(a) Olympic
oliva olive colored
la olla pot, 9.1
olvidar to forget
   no te olvides don't forget
omnívoro(a) omnivorous
la onda wave, 8.1
   las ondas sonoras sound waves
la onza ounce
la opción option
opciónal optional
la ópera opera
el/la operador(a) operator, 16.1
la opereta operetta
opinar to think; to express an opinion
oponer to oppose
la oportunidad opportunity
oprimir to push
la oración sentence; prayer
el orangután orangutan
la órbita orbit

el orden order
el ordenador computer
la oreja ear
orgánico(a) organic
el organismo organism
el/la orientador(a) counselor, 16.1
oriental eastern
el origen origin
original original
originar to originate
originario(a) originating; native, descendant
la orilla bank (of a river), I-16.2
el oro gold
la orquesta orchestra, I-12.2
ortopédico(a) orthopedic, 4.2
el/la ortopedista orthopedist, 4.2
el oso bear
el otoño autumn, I-7.1
otro(a) other, I-2.2
   el uno del otro each other, 11.1
el out out (baseball), I-7.2
la ovación ovation
ovalado(a) oval
la oveja sheep
el oxígeno oxygen, 7.1
oye listen

P

el padre father, I-6.1
   los padres parents, I-6.1
el padrino godfather, 12.1; best man, 15.2
   los padrinos godparents
la paella Valencian rice dish with meat, chicken, or fish and vegetables
la paellera paella pan
pagar to pay, I-13.1
el pago pay; payment
el país country
el paisaje countryside
la paja straw, 12.2
el pájaro bird
el paje de honor usher, 15.2
la palabra word
el palacio palace
la palmadita slap, 11.2
   dar palmaditas to slap gently, 11.2
la palmera palm tree
el palo (golf) club, I-11.2
el pan bread, I-15.2

el pan tostado toast
la panadería bakery, 2.1
el/la panadero(a) baker
panameño(a) Panamanian
el panqueque pancake
la pantalla screen, I-8.1
el pantalón corto shorts
   los pantalones pants, I-13.1
pantanoso(a) swampy, marshy
la papa potato, I-5.2
   las papas fritas French fries
el papá father, I-5.2
la papaya papaya, 9.2
el papel paper, I-BV
   la hoja de papel sheet of paper, I-BV
   el papel higiénico toilet paper, I-16.2
el paquete package, 2.2
par equal (adj.)
el par pair
para for; to
   para que in order that, so that, 15.2
el parabrisas windshield, 5.2
el parachoques bumper
la parada stop, I-14.2
el parador inn
el paraíso paradise
el paramecio paramecium
parar to stop, I-7.1
el parasol parasol, I-11.1
parcial: a tiempo parcial part-time, 16.2
parear to pair, match
parecer (zc) to seem; to resemble
parecido(a) similar
la pareja couple, 15.1
el/la pariente relative
los parientes lejanos distant relatives
el paro stop, stoppage
el parque park, I-6.2
el parquímetro parking meter, 10.1
la parrilla grill, 9.1
la parte part
   ¿De parte de quién? Who is calling?, 1.1
particular private; particular, I-5.1
el partido game, I-7.1
partir to divide
el pasado past
pasado(a) last, gone by (adj.)

VOCABULARIO ESPAÑOL-INGLÉS

el año pasado last year
el/la pasajero(a) passenger, I-8.1
el pasaporte passport, I-8.2
    el control de pasaportes passport inspection, I-8.2
pasar to pass, I-7.2; to spend, 15.2; to happen
    pasar hambre to go hungry
el pasatiempo pastime, hobby
la Pascua Easter
el pase de abordar boarding pass, I-8.1
el paseo stroll, walk
el pasillo corridor, I-14.2; aisle, 2.1
el paso de peatones crosswalk, 10.1
la pasta dentífrica toothpaste, I-16.2
el pastel pie, 2.1; pastry, 12.1
la pastelería pastry shop, 2.1
la pastilla pill, I-10.2; bar (of soap), I-16.2
el/la pastor(a) shepherd
    el pastor vasco Basque shepherd
la patata potato, 2.1
paterno(a) paternal
la patilla sideburn, 8.1
el patín skate, I-9.2
el patinadero skating rink, I-9.2
el/la patinador(a) skater, I-9.2
el patinaje skating, I-9.2
    el patinaje artístico figure skating, I-9.2
    el patinaje sobre hielo ice-skating, I-9.2
    el patinaje sobre ruedas roller skating, I-9.2
    la pista de patinaje skating rink, I-9.2
patinar to skate, I-9
el patio patio, courtyard
la patología pathology
la patria homeland, native land
el/la patrón (patrona) patron
el pavo turkey
el peaje toll, 10.2
el peatón pedestrian, 10.1
el pecho chest, I-10.2
el pedacito little piece, 9.2
la pedagogía education, 16.2
pedir (i, i) to ask for, I-15.1
el peinado hairdo
    el peinado afro afro hairstyle, 8.1

peinarse to comb one's hair, I-16.1
el peine comb, I-16.2
pelar to peel, 9.2
la película movie, film, I-5.2
    dar una película to show a movie
el peligro danger
peligroso(a) dangerous
el pelo hair, I-16.1
    tomar el pelo a alguien to pull someone's leg
la pelota ball, I-7.2
la peluca wig
la peluquería hair salon, 8.2
el/la peluquero(a) hair stylist, 8.2
la península peninsula
el/la pensador(a) thinker
pensar to think
la pensión boarding house, I-16.2; small hotel; room and board
pentecostal Pentecostal
peor worse
el pepino cucumber, 9.1
pequeño(a) small, I-2.1
la pera pear
la percepción perception
la percha clothes hanger, 6.2
perder (ie) to lose, I-7.1
    perder el autobús to miss the bus, I-12.1
el perdiz partridge
perdón excuse me
el peregrinaje pilgrimage
el perfume perfume
la perfumería perfume shop
el periódico newspaper, I-5.2
el período period; space of time
perjudicial harmful
permanente permanent
el permiso de conducir driver's license, 5.1
permitido(a) permitted
permitir to permit
pero but
el/la perro(a) dog, I-6.1
la persecución persecution
la persona person, 11.1
el personaje character
personal personal
personalmente personally
pertenecer (zc) to belong
peruano(a) Peruvian
el pésame condolences
pesar to weigh, 3.2

la pescadería fish market, 2.1
el pescado fish (when caught), I-15.2
el/la pescador(a) fisherman(woman)
pescar to fish
el peso weight; monetary unit of several Latin American Countries
el pez fish (alive)
el/la pianista pianist
el piano piano, I-4.2
picar to dice, 9.2
el/la pícher pitcher (sports), I-7.2
el pico peak, 7.2
el pie foot, I-7.1
    a pie on foot, I-3.1
    de pie standing
la piel skin
la pierna leg, 4.1
la píldora pill, I-10.2
el/la piloto pilot, I-8.2
la pimienta pepper, I-15.1
el pimiento bell pepper, 9.2
el pinar pine grove
el pingüino penguin
el pino pine tree
la pinta pint
pintar to paint
el/la pintor(a) painter, 16.1
pintoresco(a) picturesque
la pintura painting
la pinza para el cabello hair clip, 8.2
la piña pineapple, 2.1
la piscina swimming pool, I-11.2
el piso floor, I-5.1
la pista ski trail, I-9.1; runway, 7.2
    la pista de patinaje skating rink, I-9.2
la pizarra chalkboard, I-BV
el pizarrón chalkboard, I-3.2
la pizca pinch
la placa license plate
el plan plan
la plancha iron, 13.2
    la plancha de vela windsurf board, I-11.1
planchar to iron, 13.2
el planeta planet
la planta floor; plant, I-6.2
    la planta baja ground floor, I-5.1
plantar to plant

502   VOCABULARIO ESPAÑOL-INGLÉS

plástico(a) plastic
 de plástico plastic, 2.2
 la bolsa de plástico plastic bag, 2.2
la plata silver
el plátano plantain; banana, 9.2
el platillo home plate (baseball), I-7.2; saucer, I-15.1
el platino platinum
el plato plate, dish, I-15.1
la playa beach, I-11.1
 playero(a) beach (adj.), I-11.1
 la toalla playera beach towel, I-11.1
plegable folding, I-11.1
el/la plomero(a) plumber, 16.2
 plomo lead, 5.2
 con plomo leaded, 5.2; sin plomo unleaded, 5.2
la pluma feather
el plumaje plummage
la población population, 16.2
pobre poor
la poción potion
 poco(a) little, small (amount)
 poco a poco little by little
 poder (irreg.) to be able, I-7.1
 puede ser maybe, 16.2
el poder extranjero foreign power
el poema poem
polar polar
el/la policía police officer, 16.1
 policíaco(a) detective (adj.)
 las novelas policíacas mysteries, detective fiction
político(a) political
los políticos (parientes) in-laws, 6
el pollo chicken, I-15.2
el polo pole
 polvo: en polvo powdered, 2.2
el poncho poncho, cape
 poner (irreg.) to put, I-8.1
 poner al fuego to put on the fire, 9.2
 poner la mesa to set the table
 ponerse to put on, I-16.1
popular popular, I-2.1
la popularidad popularity
poquito más a little more
por about, for, by
 por consiguiente consequently
 por ejemplo for example
 por encima over, I-7.2
 por eso therefore
 por favor please, I-BV
 por lo menos at least
 ¿por qué? why?
 por supuesto of course
la porcelana porcelain
la porción portion
porque because
la portería goal, I-7.1
el/la portero(a) goalkeeper, goalie, I-7.1
 posible possible, 11
 positivo(a) positive
 postizo(a) false
el postre dessert, I-5.2
el/la practicante hospital nurse
 practicar to practice
 precario(a) precarious
el precepto precept
el precio price, I-13.1
 precioso(a) beautiful, I-6.2
la precipitación precipitation
 precisamente precisely
 precolombino(a) pre-Columbian
 predominante predominant
la preferencia preference
 preferir (ie, i) to prefer, I-7
el prefijo prefix
 el prefijo del país country code, 1.1
 el prefijo telefónico area code, 1.1
la pregunta question
 preguntar to ask
el premio prize
la prenda garment, article of clothing
 preocuparse to worry
la preparación preparation
 preparar to prepare, I-4.1
la presencia presence
 presentar to present, I-12
el presente present
el/la presidente(a) president
la presión pressure, 5.2
 la presión arterial blood pressure, 4.2
 presunto(a) presumed
 pretender (ie) to seek
el pretendiente suitor
 primario(a) primary, elementary
la primavera spring, I-7.2
 primer, primero(a) first, I-BV

 primitivo(a) primitive
el/la primo(a) cousin, I-6.1
 principal main
el principiante, la principianta beginner, I-9.1
 principio: al principio in the beginning
la prioridad priority
la prisa haste, hurry
 darse prisa to rush, hurry
 de prisa fast
el/la prisionero(a) prisoner
 privado(a) private, I-5.1
la privatización privatization
 privatizar to privatize
 probable probable, 11
 probar (ue) to try; to taste
el problema problem
la procesión procession
el proceso process
 producir (zc) to produce
 productivo(a) productive
el producto product
el/la productor(a) producer
la profesión profession; career, 16.1
 profesional professional (adj.)
el/la profesional professional (person)
el/la profesor(a) teacher, I-2.1
el/la profeta prophet
 profundo(a) profound
el programa program
el/la programador(a) programmer, 16.1
el progreso progress
 prohibido(a) forbidden, 10.2
 prohibir to prohibit
la promesa promise
el/la prometido(a) fiancé(e)
la propiedad property
el/la propietario(a) owner
la propina tip, I-12.2
 propio(a) one's own
 ¡Próspero Año Nuevo! Happy New Year!, 12.2
la protección protection
 protectora: la crema protectora sunblock, I-11.1
 proteger to protect
la proteína protein, I-10.2
 protestante Protestant
el provecho benefit, advantage
 buen provecho enjoy your meal
 proveer to provide

VOCABULARIO ESPAÑOL-INGLÉS

la **provincia** provence
la **proximidad** proximity, nearness
próximo(a) next, I-14.2
la **prueba** test
publicado(a) published
la **publicidad** advertising
el **público** public; audience, I-12.2
público(a) public (adj.)
el **pueblo** town, I-5.1; people
puede ser maybe, **16.2**
el **puente** bridge
el **puerco** pork
la **puerta** gate, I-8.1; door, **5.1**
   la **puerta de salida** departure gate, I-8.1; exit door
el **puerto** port
puertorriqueño(a) Puerto Rican, I-2
pues well
el **puesto** stall, **2.1**
la **pulgada** inch
pulmonar pulmonary
la **pulsación** beat
el **pulso** pulse, **4.2**
el **punto** stitch, **4.2**; dot
   en punto on the dot, I-3.1

Q

que that
¿qué? what?; how?, I-BV
   ¿Qué es? What is it?, I-BV
   ¿Qué hora es? What time is it?, I-2
   ¿Qué tal? How are you?, I-BV
   ¿Qué tiempo hace? What's the weather like?, I-9.1
quedar(se) to stay, remain, **Me queda bien.** It fits me., I-13.2
   quedar empatado(a) to be tied (sports), I-7.1
querer (irreg.) to want, I-7; to love, **1.2**
   querer decir to mean
el **queso** cheese, I-15.2
¿quién? who?, I-BV
   ¿De parte de quién? Who is calling?, **1.1**
   ¿Quién es? Who is it?, I-BV
la **química** chemistry, I-2.2

el/la **químico** chemist
químico(a) chemical
la **quinceañera** young woman's fifteenth birthday, **12.1**
quinientos five hundred
quinto(a) fifth, I-5.1
el **quiosco** newsstand, I-14.1
el **quirófano** operating room, **4.2**
Quisiera... I would like...
quitar del fuego to take off the fire, **9.2**
quizá(s) perhaps, **16.2**

R

el **radiador** radiator, **5.2**
radical radical
radioactivo(a) radioactive
la **radiografía** X ray, **4.2**
rallar to grate, **9.2**
la **rama** branch
el/la **ranchero(a)** rancher
la **ranura** slot (for money), **1.1**
rápidamente quickly
rápido fast, I-9.1
la **raqueta** racket, I-11.2
el **rasgo** feature
el **ratón** mouse
la **raya** part (in hair), **8.1**
   a rayas striped, I-13.2
el **rayo** ray, **4.2**
   los rayos equis X ray, **4.2**
la **razón** reason
razonable reasonable
real real, actual
realista realistic
realizar to carry out, put into effect
realmente really; actually
la **rebaja** reduction
la **rebanada** slice, **9.2**
rebanar to slice, **9.2**
la **rebelión** rebellion
el **recado** message
recambio: de recambio spare (tire), **5.1**
la **recepción** reception, **6.1**
el/la **recepcionista** receptionist, **6.1**
el/la **receptor(a)** catcher (baseball), I-7.2
la **receta** prescription, I-10.2; recipe
recetar to prescribe, I-10

recibir to receive, I-5.2
el **recibo** receipt
el/la **recién casado(a)** newlywed, **15.2**
reciente recent
recientemente recently
reclamar to claim, I-8.2
el **reclamo de equipaje** baggage claim, I-8.2
recoger to pick up, collect, I-8.2
la **recomendación** recommendation
recomendar (ie) to recommend, **13.2**
reconocer (zc) to recognize
reconstruir (y) to reconstruct
recordar (ue) to remember
el **recorrido** distance traveled, trip
   de largo recorrido long-distance
recortar to trim, **8.2**
el **recorte** trim, **8.2**
el **recurso** resource
   el servicio de recursos humanos human resources department, **16.2**
   los recursos naturales natural resources
la **red** net, I-7.2; network
la **rededicación** rededication
redondo(a) round
reducido(a) reduced
reducir (zc) to reduce
   reducir la fractura to set the bone, **4.2**
referir (ie, i) to refer
reflejar to reflect
el **refrán** proverb
el **refresco** soft drink, I-4.1
el **refrigerador** refrigerator, **9.1**
el **refugio** refuge
el **regalo** gift, I-6.2
   el regalo de Navidad Christmas present, **12.2**
regatear to bargain
el **regateo** bargaining
el **régimen** regimen
la **región** region
la **regla** rule
el **reglamento** rule
regresar to return
el **regreso** return
regulador regulating (adj.)
regular fair, passing (grade); to regulate (verb)
reinar to reign

VOCABULARIO ESPAÑOL-INGLÉS

el **reino** kingdom
la **relación** relationship
relacionar to relate
relativamente relatively
religioso(a) religious
rellenar to fill
el/la **remitente** sender, 3.1
remontar to go back (to some date in time)
remoto(a) remote
repartir to deliver, 3.2
el **reparto** delivery, 3.2
repetir (i, i) to repeat, I-15
la **representación** performance, I-12.2
    dar una representación to put on a performance, I-12.2
el/la **representante** representative
representar to represent
la **reproducción** reproduction
el **reptil** reptile
la **república** republic
repuesto: de repuesto spare (tire), 5.1
requerir (ie, i) to require, 16.2
resbalarse to slip, 4.1
la **reserva** reserve
la **reservación** reservation
reservado(a) reserved, I-14.2
reservar to reserve, 6.1
el **resfriado** (head) cold
la **residencia** residence, home
residencial residential
resolver (ue) to resolve
el **respaldo** seat back, 7.1
el **respeto** respect
la **respiración** breathing
respirar to breathe
responder to respond, answer
la **responsabilidad** responsibility
el **restaurante** restaurant, I-12.2
los **restos** remains
la **restricción** restriction
el **resultado** result
resultar to result
la **resurrección** resurrection
retirar to withdraw, 14.2
    retirar del fuego to take off the fire, 9.2
    retirarse to retire
el **retiro** withdrawal, 14.2
    el formulario de retiro withdrawal slip, 14.2
el **retraso** delay, I-14.2
    con retraso late, I-14.2
el **retrato** portrait

reunirse to get together, 12.1
revés: al revés the contrary
revisar to inspect, I-8; to check, 5.2
el/la **revisor(a)** (train) conductor, I-14.2; auditor, 16.1
la **revista** magazine, I-5.2
revolucionario(a) revolutionary
revolver (ue) to stir, 9.1
revueltos scrambled (eggs)
el **rey** king
los **Reyes Magos** Three Wise Men, 12.2
    el Día de los Reyes Day of the Three Kings
rico(a) rich; tasty, I-15.2
rigor: de rigor essential
riguroso(a) rigorous
el **río** river, I-16.2
el **rito** rite
el **rizado** curling, 8
rizado(a) curly, 8.1
el **rizador** curling iron, 8.2
rizar to curl, 8
el **rizo** curl, 8.1
robar to steal, I-7.2
rodar (ue) to shoot a movie
la **rodilla** knee, 4.1
rogar (ue) to beg; to request, 12
rojo(a) red, I-13.2
el **rollo** roll (of paper), I-16.2
el/la **romano(a)** Roman
romántico(a) romantic
romperse to break, 4.1
la **ropa** clothes, I-8.2
    poner la ropa en la maleta to pack
la **rotación** rotation
el **rótulo** sign, 10.2
rubio(a) blond(e), I-1.1
la **rueda** wheel; roller, I-9.2
el **ruido** noise
la **ruina** ruin
el **rulo** hair roller, 8.2
rumbo a toward, in the direction of
la **ruta** route
rutinario(a) routine

S

el **sábado** Saturday, I-BV
la **sábana** sheet, 6.2

saber (irreg.) to know (how), I-9.1
sacar (qu) to get, receive, I-3.2; to take out, 13.2
    sacar notas buenas (malas) to get good (bad) grades, I-3.2
el **sacerdote** priest
el **saco** jacket, I-13.1; sack
    el saco de dormir sleeping bag, I-16.2
el **sacramento** sacrament
sacrificar to sacrifice
el **sacrificio** sacrifice
sagrado(a) sacred
la **sal** salt, I-15.1
la **sala** living room, I-4.1
    la sala de clase classroom, I-3.1
    la sala de emergencia emergency room, 4.1
    la sala de espera waiting room, I-14.1
    la sala de operaciones operating room, 4.2
    la sala de recepción waiting room, 4.2
    la sala de recuperación recovery room, 4.2
    la sala de restablecimiento recovery room, 4.2
    la sala de urgencias emergency room, 4.1
el **salario** salary
la **salchicha** sausage, 9.1
el **saldo** sale; balance (bank), 14.2
la **salida** departure, I-8.1; exit, 7.1
    el tablero de llegadas y salidas arrival and departure board, I-8.1
    la puerta de salida departure gate, I-8.1
    la salida de emergencia emergency exit, 7.1
salir (irreg.) to leave, I-8.1; to go out
el **salón de clase** classroom, I-3.1
el **salón del hotel** hotel ballroom, 12.1
la **salsa** sauce
saltar (de) to jump (out of)
la **salud** health

VOCABULARIO ESPAÑOL-INGLÉS

estar de buena salud to be in good health
saludable healthy
saludar to greet, 11.1
el saludo greeting
las sandalias sandals, I-13.1
la sandía watermelon, 9.2
el sándwich sandwich, I-5.2
la sangre blood
la sanidad health
el/la santo(a) saint
el/la sartén frying pan, 9.1
satisfacer to satisfy
el saxofón saxophone
el secador hair dryer, 8.2
la secadora clothes dryer, 13.2
secar to dry
la sección section
    la sección de no fumar no smoking section, I-8.1
seco(a) dry
el/la secretario(a) secretary, 16.1
el secreto secret, 11.1
el sector section
secundario(a) secondary, I-1.1
    la escuela secundaria high school, I-1.1
secuoya: árboles secuoyas sequoia trees
la sed thirst, I-15.1
    tener sed to be thirsty, I-15.1
el sedán sedan, 5.1
el/la sefardí Sephardic Jew
el segmento segment
segregar to segregate
seguida: en seguida at once, immediately, 1.2
seguir (i, i) to follow, I-15; to continue, 10.2
según according to
segundo(a) second, I-5.1
la seguridad security, I-8.1
    el cinturón de seguridad seat belt, 5.1
    el control de seguridad security control, I-8.1
el seguro social social security
seguro(a) reliable, dependable; sure; safe, 12
seis six, I-BV
la selección selection
la selva rainforest
el sello stamp, 3.1
el semáforo traffic light, 10.1
la semana week, I-11.2

la semana pasada last week, I-11.2
la Semana Santa Holy Week
el semestre semester
el/la senador(a) senator
sencillo(a) one-way, I-14.1; single, 6.1
la senda path, 13.1
el sendero path, 13.1
la sensación sensation
sensible sensitive
sentarse (ie) to sit down, I-16.1
    Me sienta bien. It fits me well. I-13.1
el sentido sense; way, direction, 10.2
    de sentido único one way
sentirse (ie, i) to feel, 12
la señal dial tone, 1.1; signal, 7.1
    la señal de no fumar no smoking signal, 7.1
señalar to point out
el/la señor(a) Mr., sir, (Mrs., ma'am)
la señorita Miss, I-BV
separado(a) separated
separar to separate
septiembre September, I-BV
séptimo(a) seventh, I-5.1
ser (irreg.) to be, I-1
    ser una lástima to be a pity, 12
el ser being
    el ser viviente living being
la serie series
    la Serie Mundial World Series
serio(a) serious, I-1.2
el servicio service
    el servicio de primer socorro first-aid service, 4.1
    el servicio de primeros auxilios first-aid service, 4.1
    el servicio de recursos humanos human resources department, 16.2
    la estación de servicio service station, 5.2
el/la servidor(a) servant
    su seguro(a) servidor(a) your humble servant

la servilleta napkin, I-15.1
servir (i, i) to serve, I-15.1
sesenta sixty, I-BV
la sesión show (movies), I-12.1
setenta seventy, I-BV
severo(a) severe
el sexo gender
sexto(a) sixth, I-5.1
si if
sí yes; used for emphasis
el SIDA AIDS
siempre always, I-5.2
la sierra mountain range
la siesta nap, I-11.1
    echar (tomar) una siesta to take a nap, I-11.1
siete seven, I-BV
el siglo century
el significado meaning
significar to mean
siguiente following
la silla chair, I-BV
    la silla de ruedas wheelchair, 4.1
    la silla plegable folding chair, I-11.1
el sillín seat
simpático(a) pleasant, likeable
simple simple
simplemente simply
sin without
    sin embargo nevertheless
    sin escala nonstop
    sin que without, 15
la sinagoga synagogue
sincero(a) sincere, I-1.2
sino but
el sinónimo synonym
el síntoma symptom, I-10.2
la sirena siren
el sistema system
    el sistema nervioso nervous system
la situación situation
situar to situate
el slálom slalom, I-9.1
el sobre envelope, 3.1
    sobre above, over, 7.1; about
    sobre todo especially, above all
el/la sobrecargo flight attendant, 7.1
sobresaliente outstanding
sobrevolar to fly over, 7.2

el/la **sobrino(a)** nephew (niece), I-6.1
   los sobrinos niece(s) and nephew(s), I-6.1
social social
la **sociedad** society
la **sociología** sociology, I-2.2
el/la **sociólogo(a)** sociologist
el/la **socorrista** first aid worker, 4.1
el **socorro** help
el **sodio** sodium
sofisticado(a) sophisticated
el **sol** sun, I-11.1
   Hay (Hace) sol. It's sunny., I-11.1
   tomar el sol to sunbathe, I-11.1
solamente only, 10.2
el/la **soldado** soldier
solemne solemn
soler (ue) to tend to, to be accustomed to, to be in the habit of
   solemos decir we usually say
   suelen servir they usually serve
solicitar (trabajo) to apply for (work), 16
la **solicitud de empleo** job application, 16.2
sólido(a) solid
solitario(a) solitary, lone
solo(a) alone
sólo only
la **solución** solution
la **sombra** shade
el **sombrero** hat, I-13.1
la **sombrilla** umbrella, I-11.1
somos we are, I-2.2
son they/you (pl. form.) are, I-2.1
sonar (ue) to ring, 1.1
   Suena ocupado. It is busy., 1.1
el **sonido** sound
la **sopa** soup, I-5.2
soplar to blow
soportar to support
el **soroche** mountain sickness
sorprender to surprise, I-13
la **sortija** ring, 15.1
   la **sortija de compromiso** engagement ring, 15.1
el **sostén** support
sostener to sustain

soy I am, I-1.2
su his, her, your (form.), their
suave soft
la **subcultura** subculture
subir to go up, I-5.1; to take up, 6.1
   subir a to get on, to board, I-8.1
subscribir to subscribe
subsistir to continue to exist
la **substancia** substance
subterráneo(a) underground, I-12
el **subtítulo** subtitle
los **suburbios** suburbs, I-5.1
sucesivo(a) successive
sucio(a) dirty, 13.2
la **sucursal** branch (office)
sudamericano(a) South American
el/la **suegro(a)** father-in-law (mother-in-law)
el **suelo** ground, I-7
   tocar el suelo to touch the ground
el **sueño** dream
la **suerte** luck, 15.2
   tener suerte to be lucky
el **suéter** sweater, I-13.1
suficiente sufficient, enough, 5.1
sufrir to suffer
sugerir (ie, i) to suggest, 12
suizo(a) Swiss
sumamente extremely
sumo(a) highest, greatest
súper super, 5.2
la **superficie** surface
superior superior; higher; top, upper
el **supermercado** supermarket, 2.1
supervisar to supervise
supuesto: por supuesto of course
el **sur** south, 10.1
   La América del Sur South America, I-8.1
el **suroeste** southwest
suspenso(a) failing (grade)
la **sustancia** substance
sustituir (y) to substitute
la **sutura** stitch, 4.2

T

el **T shirt** T shirt, I-13.1
el **tabaco** tobacco
la **tabla hawaiiana** surfing
el **tablero** backboard (basketball), I-7.2
   el **tablero de llegadas y salidas** arrival and departure board, I-8.1
   el **tablero indicador** scoreboard, I-7.1
la **tableta** tablet
el **tacón** heel, I-13.2
la **tajada** slice, 2.2
tal such
   tal vez perhaps, 16
el **talco** talcum powder
el **talento** talent
talentoso(a) talented; gifted
la **talla** size, I-13.1
el **taller** artisan's shop, 16.1
el **talón** luggage claims ticket, I-8.1
el **talonario** checkbook, 14.2
el **tamaño** size, I-13.1
también also, too, I-1.1
tampoco neither, either
   Ni yo tampoco. Me neither., I-13
tan so
   tan pronto como as soon as, 15
el **tanque** tank, 5.2
el **tanto** score, point, I-7.1
la **tapa** cover, 9
tapar to cover, 9.2
la **taquilla** ticket office, I-12.1
tarde late, I-8.1
la **tarde** afternoon
   esta tarde this afternoon, I-11.2
la **tarifa** fare, rate
la **tarjeta** card, I-5.2; registration card, 6.1
   la **tarjeta de crédito** credit card, I-13.1
   la **tarjeta de embarque** boarding card, I-8.1
   la **tarjeta postal** postcard, I-5.2
la **tasa de cambio** exchange rate, 14.1
el **taxi** taxi, I-8.1
la **taza** cup, I-15.1
te you (fam. pron.)

VOCABULARIO ESPAÑOL-INGLÉS

el **té** tea
teatral theatrical, I-12.2
el **teatro** theater, I-12.2
la **tecla** key, **1.1**
el **teclado** keypad, **1.1**
la **técnica** technique
técnico(a) technical
el/la **técnico(a)** technician, **4.2**
la **telecomunicación** telecommunication
telefonear to telephone, **1.1**
telefónico(a) pertaining to the telephone, **1.1**
el/la **telefonista** telephone operator
el **teléfono** telephone, I-4.1
    por teléfono on the phone, I-4.1
el **telégrafo** telegraph
la **telenovela** soap opera, I-5.2
el **telesilla** chair lift, I-9.1
el **telesquí** ski lift, I-9.1
la **televisión** television, I-4.1
el **televisor** television set, **6.2**
el **telón** curtain, I-12.2
el **tema** theme, subject
temer to be afraid, **11**
temerario(a) reckless
la **temperatura** temperature, I-9.1
la **tempestad** storm
templado(a) temperate
el **templo** temple
temprano early
tender (ie) to tend
    tender la cama to make the bed, **6.2**
el **tenedor** fork, I-15.1
tener (irreg.) to have, I-6.1
    tener ... años to be ... years old, I-6.1
    tener cuidado to be careful
    tener hambre to be hungry, I-15.1
    tener lugar to take place, **12.2**
    tener miedo to be afraid, **11**
    tener que to have to, I-6
    tener que ver con to have to do with
    tener sed to be thirsty, I-15.1
el **tenis** tennis, I-11.2
    el juego de tenis tennis game, I-11.2

la **cancha de tenis** tennis court, I-11.2
los **tenis** tennis shoes, I-13.1
la **tensión arterial** blood pressure, **4.2**
la **teoría** theory
tercer, tercero(a) third, I-5.1
terminar to end, finish
el **término** term, word
    a término medio medium (meat)
la **ternera** veal chop, **2.1**
la **terraza** terrace
el **terreno** land, terrain
el **territorio** territory
terrorista terrorist
el **tesoro** treasure
el **tiempo** half (soccer game), I-7.1; weather; time
    a tiempo on time, I-8.1
    a tiempo completo full-time, **16.2**
    a tiempo parcial part-time, **16.2**
    al mismo tiempo at the same time
    hace mucho tiempo a long time ago
la **tienda** store, I-4.1; tent
    armar una tienda to put up a tent, I-16.2
    la tienda de abarrotes grocery store
    la tienda de campaña tent, I-16.2
    la tienda de departamentos department store
    la tienda de ropa para caballeros (señores) men's clothing store, I-13.1
    la tienda de ropa para damas (señoras) women's clothing store, I-13.1
    la tienda por departamentos department store, **16.1**
la **tierra** land, Earth, **16.2**
    la Tierra Santa Holy Land
el **tigre** tiger
las **tijeras** scissors, **8.2**
el **timbre** tone
tímido(a) timid, shy, I-1.2
el **tímpano** eardrum

tinto(a) red
la **tintorería** dry cleaners, **13.2**
el/la **tío(a)** uncle (aunt), I-6.1
    los tíos aunt(s) and uncle(s), I-6.1
típicamente typically
típico(a) typical
el **tipo** type
    ¿Cuál es el tipo de cambio? What is the exchange rate?, **14.1**
    el tipo de cambio exchange rate, **14.1**
tirar to throw, I-7.2
    tirar con el pie to kick, I-7.2
titulado(a) entitled
el **título** degree
    el título universitario university diploma, **16.2**
la **tiza** chalk, I-BV
la **toalla** towel, **6.2**
    la toalla playera beach towel, I-11.1
el **tobillo** ankle, **4.1**
tocar to play (an instrument), I-4.2; to touch, I-7
el **tocino** bacon
todavía yet, still
    todavía no not yet, **6**
todo everything (noun)
    en todas partes everywhere
    sobre todo especially
    todo(a) every, all (adj.), I-4.2
    todo el mundo everybody
tomar to take, I-3.2; to drink, I-4.1
    tomar el sol to sunbathe, I-11.1
    tomar una ducha to take a shower, I-16.2
el **tomate** tomato
la **tonelada** ton
el **tono** dial tone, **1.1**; pitch
    el tono de ocupado busy tone, **1**
la **tonsura** tonsure
torcer (ue) to twist, **4.1**
el/la **torero(a)** bullfighter
el **toro** bull
la **toronja** grapefruit, **9.1**
la **torre** tower
    la torre de control control tower, **7.2**
tórrido(a) torrid
la **torta** cake, **12.1**
la **tortilla** tortilla, I-15.2

VOCABULARIO ESPAÑOL-INGLÉS

torturar to torture
la tos cough, I-10.1
    tener tos to have a cough, I-10.1
    toser to cough, I-10.1
    tostadito(a) tanned
el tostón fried plantain slice
el total total, 6.1
    totalmente totally
    tóxico(a) toxic
el/la trabajador(a) worker, 16.1
    trabajar to work, I-4.1
el trabajo work, job, 16.1
    el trabajo a tiempo completo (parcial) full-time (part-time) job, 16.2
la tradición tradition
    tradicional traditional
la traducción translation
    traer (irreg.) to bring, I-8
el tráfico traffic, 5.1
la tragedia tragedy
el traje suit, I-13.1
    el traje de baño bathing suit, I-11.1
    el traje pantalón pantsuit
    tranquilamente peacefully
    tranquilo(a) calm, peaceful, I-14.2
    transbordar to transfer, I-14.2
el tránsito traffic, 5.1
    transmitir to transmit
el transporte transportation, I-12
    trasero(a) back, rear
    trasladar to transfer
el tratado treatise
el tratamiento treatment
    tratar to deal with; to treat
    tratar de to be about; to try
    través: a través de through, across
    treinta thirty, I-BV
el tren train, I-14.1
    el tren de vía estrecha narrow-gauge train
    subir al tren to get on the train, I-14.2
la trenza braid, 8.1
    tres three, I-BV
la tribu tribe
el tribunal court, 16.1
el trigo wheat
la trigonometría trigonometry, I-2.2
la tripulación crew, I-8.2
    triste sad, I-10.1

    triunfante triumphant
    triunfar to win, triumph
el trocito little piece, 9.2
la trompeta trumpet, I-4.2
el tronco trunk
    tropical tropical
el truco trick, device
    tu your (sing. fam.)
    tú you (sing. fam.)
el tubo tube, I-16.2
la tumba tomb, 12.1
la turbulencia turbulence
    turbulento(a) turbulent
el turismo tourism
el/la turista tourist, I-12.2
    tutear to be on familiar terms with, 11

U

    u or (used instead of o before words beginning with o or ho)
    Ud(s)., usted(es) you (sing. [pl.] form), I-2.2
    último(a) last
    un(a) a, an, I-BV
    único(a) only
la unidad unit
    la unidad de cuidado intensivo intensive care area, 4.2
el uniforme uniform
    llevar uniforme to wear a uniform
    unir to unite
la universidad university
    universitario(a) pertaining to the university, 16.2
    el título universitario university diploma, 16.2
    uno one, I-BV
    el uno del otro each other, 11.1
    unos cuantos a few
    uruguayo(a) Uruguayan
    usado(a) used
    usar to use, I-11.1
el uso use
    usted(es), Ud(s) you (sing. [pl.] form.), I-2.2
    útil useful
    utilizar to use
la uva grape, 2.1

V

    va he/she/it goes (is going)
la vaca cow
las vacaciones vacation
el vacío vacuum
el vagón train car, I-14.1
    valiente brave, valient
    valer to be worth
    vale la pena it's worth it
el valle valley, 7.2
el valor value
    vamos we go, (are going)
    van they/you (pl. form.) go (are going), I-4.1
la variación variation
    variar to vary
la variedad variety
    vario(a) various, varied; several (pl.)
el varón male
    vas you (sing. fam.) go (are going)
el vaso (drinking) glass, I-5.2
el váter toilet, 6.2
la vegetación vegetation
el vegetal vegetable, I-15.2
el/la vegetariano(a) vegetarian
el vehículo vehicle
    veinte twenty, I-BV
la vela candle, 12.1
la velocidad speed, 10.2
    la velocidad máxima speed limit, 10.2
    vencer to overcome, conquer
la venda band-aid, 4.2
el vendaje bandage, 4.2
el/la vendedor(a) salesperson
    vender to sell, I-5.2
    venenoso(a) poisonous
    venezolano(a) Venezuelan
    venir (irreg.) to come, 8
la venta sale
    en venta for sale
la ventaja advantage
la ventanilla ticket window, I-9.1; window, 3.2
    ver (irreg.) to see, to watch, I-5.2
el verano summer, I-11.1
el verbo verb
la verdad truth, I-1.1
    ¿No es verdad? Isn't it true?, I-1.1
    ¿verdad? right?, I-1.1
    verde green, I-13.2

VOCABULARIO ESPAÑOL-INGLÉS   **509**

    verdadero(a) real, true
la **verdulería** greengrocer shop, **2.1**
el/la **verdulero(a)** greengrocer
la **verdura** vegetable, I-15.2
    verificar to check, **5.2**; to verify, **14.2**
    versátil versatile
la **versión** version
el **vestido** dress, I-13.1
        el vestido de boda wedding dress
    vestirse (i, i) to get dressed, I-16.1
la **vez** time
        veces: a veces sometimes, I-5.2
        de vez en cuando now and then
        en vez de instead of
la **vía** track, I-14.1
        de vía estrecha narrow-guage (train)
    viajar to travel
el **viaje** trip, I-8.1
        el viaje de novios honeymoon trip, **15.2**
        hacer un viaje to take a trip, I-8.1
el/la **viajero(a)** traveler
la **víbora** snake
la **vibración** vibration
    vibrar to vibrate
la **victoria** victory
    victorioso(a) victorious
la **vida** life
    viejo(a) old, I-6.1
el **viento** wind, I-11.1
        Hace viento. It's windy., I-11.1
el **viernes** Friday, I-BV
    vigilar to guard
el **vinagre** vinegar
el **vino** wine
el **violín** violin, I-4.2
    virar to turn
el **virus** virus
la **visita** visit
la **víspera de Navidad** Christmas Eve, **12.2**
la **vista** view, I-6.2
la **vitamina** vitamin, I-10.2
la **vitrina** shop window, I-13.1
el/la **viudo(a)** widower (widow)
la **vivienda** housing
    vivir to live, I-5.1

    vivo(a) living; bright, vivid
        el ser vivo living being
el **vocabulario** vocabulary
    volar (ue) to fly
    volcán volcano
el **vólibol** volleyball, I-7.2
el **volumen** volume
    volver (ue) to go back, I-7.1
    vosotros(as) you (pl. fam.)
    voy I go (am going)
el **vuelo** flight, I-8.1
        el número del vuelo flight number, I-8.1,
        el asistente (la asistenta) de vuelo flight attendant, I-8.2
la **vuelta** turn; rotation
        dar vuelta to go around
    vuestro(a) your (pl. fam.)

Y

    y and, I-1.2
    ya already, **6.1**
        ya no no longer, **12.1**
el **yate** yacht
el **yen** yen
el **yeso** cast, **4.2**
    yo I, I-1.2

Z

la **zanahoria** carrot, **2.2**
el **zapato** shoe, I-13.1
el **zíper** zipper, I-13.2
la **zona** district, zone
        la zona postal ZIP code, **3.1**
la **zoología** zoology
el **zoológico** zoo
el **zumo de naranja** orange juice

510   VOCABULARIO ESPAÑOL-INGLÉS

VOCABULARIO INGLÉS-ESPAÑOL

The *Vocabulario inglés-español* contains all productive vocabulary from Levels 1 and 2. The numbers following each entry indicate the chapter and vocabulary section in which the word is introduced. For example, **2.2** means that the word first appeared actively in Level 2, *Capítulo 2, Palabras* 2. Boldface numbers without a *Palabras* reference indicate vocabulary introduced in the grammar sections of the given chapter of Level 2. Numbers preceded by I indicate vocabulary introduced in Level I; I-BV refers to the Level 1 introductory *Bienvenidos* chapter.

The following abbreviations are used in this glossary.

adj.	adjective
adv.	adverb
conj.	conjunction
dem. adj.	demonstrative adjective
dem. pron.	demonstrative pronoun
dir. obj.	direct object
f.	feminine
fam.	familiar
form.	formal
ind. obj.	indirect object
inf.	infinitive
inform.	informal
interr.	interrogative
interr. adj.	interrogative adjective
interr. pron.	interrogative pronoun
inv.	invariable
irreg.	irregular
m.	masculine
n.	noun
past. part.	past participle
pl.	plural
poss. adj.	possessive adjective
prep.	preposition
pron.	pronoun
sing.	singular
subj.	subject
subjunc.	subjunctive

A

a, an un(a), I-BV
about a eso de, I-3.1
above sobre, 7.1; arriba, 8.2
to accelerate acelerar, 5.1
accident el accidente, 4.1
account la cuenta, 14.2
accountant el/la contable, 16.1
to ache doler (ue), I-10.2
   My_____ hurts, aches. Me duele_____., I-10
active activo(a), 16.2
actor el actor, I-12.2
actress la actriz, I-12.2
to add agregar (gue), 9.2
address la dirección, 3.1
adhesive bandage la venda, 4.2
admission ticket la entrada, I-12.2
admitting office (hospital) la oficina de recepción, 4.2
to adore adorar, 1.2
to advise aconsejar, 12.2
aerobic aeróbico(a), I-10.2
aerogram el aerograma, 3.1
afro hairstyle el peinado afro, 8.1
after después de, I-4.1; después de que, 15
afternoon la tarde
   Good afternoon. Buenas tardes., I-BV
   this afternoon esta tarde, I-11.2
agent el/la agente, I-8.1
agriculture la agricultura, 16.2
aisle el pasillo, 2.1; 7.1
air el aire, 5.2; aéreo(a), 3.2
   air conditioning el aire acondicionado, 6.2
   air mail, by por correo aéreo, 3.2
airline la línea aérea, I-8.1
airplane el avión, I-8.1
   by (air)plane en avión, I-8.1
airport el aeropuerto, I-8.1
algebra el álgebra (f.), I-2.2
allergy la alergia, I-10.2
already ya, 6.1
also también, I-1.1
altar el altar, 15.2
although aunque, 15
altitude la altura, la altitud, 7.2
always siempre, I-5.2
am soy, I-1.2
ambulance la ambulancia, 4.1
American americano(a), I-1.2
and y, I-1.2
anesthetist el/la anestesista, 4.2
to anger enojar, enfadar, I-13
ankle el tobillo, 4.1
to announce anunciar, 15.1
announcement el anuncio, 7.1
to annoy enojar, enfadar, I-13
anorak el anorak, I-9.1
to answer contestar, 1.2
answering machine el contestador automático, 1.1
apartment el apartamento, I-5.1
to applaud aplaudir, I-12.2
apple la manzana, 2.1
application la solicitud, 16.2
   job application la solicitud de empleo, 16.2
to apply for (work) solicitar (trabajo), 16
to approach acercarse (qu), 11.2
April abril (m.), I-BV
architecture la arquitectura, 16.2
area code la clave de área, el código de área, el prefijo telefónico, 1.1
Argentinian argentino(a), I-2.1
arithmetic la aritmética, I-2.2
arm el brazo, 4.1
around alrededor de, I-6.2; a eso de (time), I-3.1
arrival la llegada, I-8.1
   arrival and departure board el tablero de llegadas y salidas, I-8.1
to arrive llegar, I-3.1
art el arte, I-2.2
arterial arterial, 4.2
artisan el/la artesano(a), 16.1
   artisan's shop el taller, 16.1
artist el/la artista, I-12.2
as soon as en cuanto, 1.2; tan pronto como, 15
to ask for pedir (i, i), I-15.1
to assist asistir, I-5.2
at a
   at once en seguida, I-16.1
   at the (m. sing.) al
to attend asistir, I-5.2
attendant el/la empleado(a), 5.2
attractive atractivo(a), I-1.2
audience el público, I-12.2
auditor el/la revisor(a), 16.1
August agosto (m.), I-BV
aunt la tía, I-6.1
   aunt(s) and uncle(s) los tíos, I-6.1
author el/la autor(a), I-12.2
automatic automático(a), 1.1
autumn el otoño, I-7.1
avenue la avenida, I-5.1
avocado el aguacate, 9.2

B

back la espalda, 11.2
backboard (basketball) el tablero, I-7.2
backpack la mochila, I-BV
bad malo(a), I-1
bad-mannered malcriado(a), 11.1
bag la bolsa, 2.2
   plastic bag la bolsa de plástico, 2.2
baggage el equipaje, I-8.1
   baggage claim el reclamo de equipaje, I-8.2
   hand baggage el equipaje de mano, I-8.1
bakery la panadería, 2.1
balance (bank) el saldo, 14.2
balcony el balcón, I-6.2
ball el balón, I-7.1; la pelota, I-7.2; la bola, I-11.2
ballpoint pen el bolígrafo, I-BV
banana el plátano, la banana, 9.2
band-aid la venda, 4.2
bandage el vendaje, 4.2
bangs el flequillo, 8.1
bank el banco, I-14.1
   bank clerk el/la empleado(a) del banco, 14.1
   bank statement el estado de cuenta, 14.2
bank (of a river) la orilla, I-16.2
banquet el banquete, 15.2
baptism el bautizo, 12.1
to baptize bautizar, 12.1
bar (of soap) la barra, I-16.2; la pastilla, 6.2
barber el/la barbero(a), 8.2

VOCABULARIO INGLÉS-ESPAÑOL

base la base, I-7.2
baseball el béisbol, I-7.2
basket el cesto, el canasto, I-7.2; la canasta, 2.2
basketball el baloncesto, el básquetbol, I-7.2
bat el bate, I-7.2
bathing suit el traje de baño, I-11.1; el bañador, I-11.1
bathroom el cuarto de baño, I-5.1; el baño, 6.2
bathtub la bañera, 6.2
batter (baseball) el/la bateador(a), I-7.2
battery la batería, 5.2
to **be** ser (irreg.), I-1; estar (irreg.), I-4.1
   to be . . . years old tener . . . años, I-6.1; cumplir, 12.1
   to be a pity ser una lástima, 12
   to be able poder (irreg.), I-7.1
   to be afraid temer, tener miedo, 11
   to be born nacer (zc), 12.1
   to be called llamarse, I-16.1
   to be glad about alegrarse de, 12
   to be hungry tener hambre, I-15.1
   to be named llamarse, I-16.1
   to be on familiar terms with tutear, 11
   to be thirsty tener sed, I-15.1
   to be tied (sports) quedar empatado(a), I-7.1
beach la playa, I-11.1
   beach resort el balneario, I-11.1
   beach towel la toalla playera, I-11.1
   beach (adj.) playero(a), I-11.1
bean la habichuela, el frijol, I-15.2
beautiful precioso(a), I-6.2
bed la cama, I-10.1
bedroom el cuarto de dormir, el dormitorio, I-5.1
beef la carne de res, 2.1
before antes de que, 15.1
to **beg** rogar (ue), 12
to **begin** empezar (ie)(c), comenzar (ie)(c), I-7.1

beginner el principiante, la principianta, I-9.1
to **behave** comportarse, 11.1
behavior el comportamiento, 11.1
behind atrás, 8.2; detrás de, 10.1
to **believe** creer (y), 12
bell pepper el pimiento, 9.2
bellhop el botones, el mozo, 6.1
below bajo, I-9.1
   below zero bajo cero, I-9.1
belt el cinturón, I-13.1
   seat belt el cinturón de seguridad, 5.1
bench el banco, I-BV
berth la litera, I-14.2
best man el padrino
better mejor, 11
bicycle la bicicleta, I-6.2
big gran, grande, I-2.1
bill la cuenta, I-12.2; la nota, 6.1 (money); el billete, 14.1
biologist el/la biólogo(a), I-2.2
biology la biología, I-2.2
birth el nacimiento, 12.1
birthday el cumpleaños, I-6.2
   Happy Birthday. Feliz Cumpleaños., 12.1
black negro(a), I-13.2
   black bean la habichuela negra, el frijol negro, 9.2
blade la cuchilla, la hoja, I-9.2
bleach el blanqueador, 13.2
to **block** bloquear, parar, I-7.1
block (city) la manzana, la cuadra, 10.1
blond(e) rubio(a), I-1.1
blood pressure la tensión arterial, la presión arterial, 4.2
blouse la blusa, I-13.1
blue azul, I-13.2
   blue jeans el blue jean, I-13.1
board el tablero, I-8.1
   arrival and departure board el tablero de llegadas y salidas, I-8.1
to **board** abordar, subir a, I-8.1
boarding house la pensión, I-16.2
boarding pass la tarjeta de embarque, el pase de abordar, I-8.1

boastful fanfarrón (fanfarrona), I-9.1
boat el barco
   small boat el barquito, I-11.1
bobby pin la horquilla, 8.2
to **boil** hervir (ie), 9.1
bone el hueso
   to set the bone reducir la fractura, 4.2
book el libro, I-BV
bookbag la mochila, I-BV
boot la bota, I-9.1
to **bore** aburrir, I-13
boring aburrido(a), I-1.1
to **bother** molestar, I-13
bottle la botella, 2.2
box la caja, 2.2
boy el muchacho, I-BV; el niño, 1.2
boyfriend el novio, 15.1
braid la trenza, 8.1
brake el freno, 5.1
to **brake** frenar, 5.1
branch (of candelabra) el brazo, 12.2
bread el pan, I-15.2
to **break** romperse, 4.1
breakfast el desayuno, I-5.2
   to eat breakfast desayunarse, I-16
bridesmaid la dama de honor, 15.2
to **bring** traer (irreg.), I-8
to **broil** asar, 9.1
broker el/la cambista, 14.1
brother el hermano, I-2.1
brown castaño(a), 8.1; marrón, I-13
brush el cepillo, I-16.2
to **brush one's hair** cepillarse, I-16.1
building el edificio, I-5.1
bumper el parachoques
bun (hair) el moño, 8.1
burner (stove) el/la hornillo(a), 9.1
to **bury** enterrar (ie), 12.1
bus el autobús, el bus, I-3.1
   to miss the bus perder el autobús, I-12.1
busy ocupado(a), 1.1
   busy signal; el tono de ocupado, 1
   It is busy. Suena ocupado., 1.1

VOCABULARIO INGLÉS-ESPAÑOL

The line is busy. La línea está ocupada., **1.1**
butcher shop la carnicería, **2.1**
butter la mantequilla, **2.1**
button el botón, I-13.2
to **buy** comprar, I-5.2
by (plane, car, etc.) en

C

cake la torta, **12.1**
calculator la calculadora, I-BV
call la llamada, **1.1**
to **call by telephone** llamar por teléfono, **1.1**
   Who is calling? ¿De parte de quién?, **1.1**
caller el/la interlocutor(a), **1.1**
calorie la caloría, I-10.2
camel el camello, **12.2**
camp el campamento, I-16.2
to **camp** acampar, I-16.2
camping el camping, I-16.2
   to go camping ir de camping, I-16.2
can la lata, el bote, **2.2**
candelabra el candelabro, **12.2**
candidate el/la candidato(a), el/la aspirante, **16.2**
candle la vela, **12.1**
canteen la cantimplora, I-16.2
cap el gorro, I-9.1
captain el/la comandante, I-8.2
car el coche, el carro, I-3.1; **(train)** el vagón, I-14.1; el coche, I-14.2
   sports car el coche deportivo, **5.1**
carbohydrate el carbohidrato, I-10.2
card la tarjeta, I-13.1
   credit card la tarjeta de crédito, I-13.1
career la profesión, **16.1**
careful: Be careful! ¡Cuidado!, **10.2**
carefully con cuidado, **5.1**
carpenter el/la carpintero(a), **16.2**
carrot la zanahoria, **2.2**
to **carry** llevar, I-3.2
   carry-on luggage el equipaje de mano, I-8.1

cart el carrito, **2.1**
cash el dinero en efectivo, **14.1**
to **cash** cobrar, **14.2**
cash register la caja, I-13.1
cashier el/la cajero(a), **6.1**
   cashier desk la caja, **6.1**
cast el yeso, **4.2**
cat el/la gato(a), I-6.1
to **catch** atrapar, I-7.2
catcher el/la cátcher, el/la receptor(a), I-7.2
cauliflower la coliflor, **9.1**
to **celebrate** celebrar, **12.1**
celebration of lights la fiesta de las luces, **12.2**
celery el apio
cellular celular, **1.1**
cemetery el cementerio, el camposanto, **12.1**
centigrade el centígrado, I-9.1
ceremony la ceremonia, **15.2**
certified mail por correo certificado, por correo recomendado, **3.2**
chair la silla, I-BV
   chair lift el telesilla, I-9.1
   folding chair la silla plegable, I-11.1
chalk la tiza, I-BV
chalkboard la pizarra, I-BV; el pizarrón, I-3.2
to **change** cambiar, **6.2**
channel el canal, **7.1**
chaperone la dueña, **15.1**
charge el gasto, **6.1**
cheap barato(a), I-13.1
check el cheque, **14.1**
to **check** revisar, verificar, **5.2**
   to check (luggage) facturar, I-8.1
checkbook el talonario, la chequera, **14.2**
checking account la cuenta corriente, **14.2**
checkstand la caja, **2.2**
cheek la mejilla, **4.1**
cheese el queso, I-15.2
chemistry la química, I-2.2
cherry la cereza, **9.2**
chest el pecho, I-10.2
chicken el pollo, I-15.2
chignon el moño, **8.1**
children los hijos, I-6.1
chills los escalofríos, I-10.1
chop la chuleta, **2.1**

Christmas la Navidad, **12.2**
   Christmas Eve la víspera de Navidad, la Nochebuena, **12.2**
   Christmas present el regalo de Navidad, el aguinaldo, **12.2**
   Christmas tree el árbol de Navidad, **12.2**
   Merry Christmas Feliz Navidad, **12.2**
church la iglesia, **10.1**
city la ciudad, I-5.1
   city hall la alcaldía, el ayuntamiento, **16.1**
   city hall employee el/la funcionario(a), **16.1**
to **claim** reclamar, I-8.2
clam la almeja, **9.2**
class la clase, I-2.1
classic clásico(a), I-4
classroom la sala de clase, el salón de clase, I-3.1
to **clean** limpiar, **5.2**
clerk el/la dependiente, **16.1**
client el/la cliente, **6.1**
clinic la clínica, I-10.2
close íntimo(a), **11.2**
closet el armario, **6.2**
clothes la ropa, I-8.2
   clothes dryer la secadora, **13.2**
   clothes hanger la percha, el colgador, el gancho, **6.2**
clothing store la tienda de ropa, I-13.1
cloud la nube, I-11.1
cloudy nublado(a), I-11.1
   It's cloudy. Está nublado., I-11.1
club (golf) el palo, el bastón, I-11.2
cockpit la cabina de vuelo (mando), **7.1**
cocktail el cóctel, **15**
coconut el coco, **9.2**
code el prefijo, **1.1**
   country code el prefijo del país, **1.1**
coffee el café, I-5.2
coin la moneda, **1.1**
cold (medical) el catarro, la gripa, I-10.1; **(weather)** el frío, I-9.1
   It's cold. Hace frío., I-9.1

VOCABULARIO INGLÉS-ESPAÑOL

to **collect** recoger, I-8.2
Colombian colombiano(a), I-1
color el color, I-13.2
    cream-, wine-, coffee-, olive-, maroon-, turquoise- colored de color crema, vino, café, oliva, brown, turquesa, I-13.2
comb el peine, I-16.2
to **comb one's hair** peinarse, I-16.1
to **come** venir (irreg.)
    to come on stage entrar en escena, I-12.2
compartment el compartimiento, I-14.2
complicated complicado(a)
computer la computadora, I-BV; el ordenador
    computer sciences la informática, 16.1
concert el concierto, I-12.2
conductor el/la director(a), I-12.2; **(train)** el/la revisor(a), I-14.2
to **confide** confiar, 11.1
congratulations la enhorabuena, felicitaciones, 15.2
container el envase, 2.2
to **continue** seguir (i, i), 10.2
control tower la torre de control, 7.2
controller el/la controlador(a), 16.1
conversation la conversación, 1.2
convertible el descapotable, 5.1
cook el/la cocinero(a), I-15.1
to **cook** cocinar, 9.1
cookie el bizcocho, 12.1
copilot el/la co-piloto, I-8.2
cordless inalámbrico(a), 1.1
corn el maíz, 9.2
corner la esquina, 5.1
to **correspond** corresponder, 3
correspondence la correspondencia, 3.1
corridor el pasillo, I-14.2
to **cost** costar (ue), I-13.1
cough la tos, I-10.1
    to have a cough tener tos, I-10.1
counselor el/la consejero(a) de orientación, el/la orientador(a), 16.1

counter el mostrador, I-8.1
country el campo, I-5.1
coupe el cupé, 5.1
couple la pareja, 15.1
course el curso, I-2.1
court la corte, el tribunal, 16.1; **(sports)** la cancha, I-7.2
    tennis court la cancha de tenis, I-11.2
courteous cortés, 11.1
courtesy la cortesía, 11
cousin el/la primo(a), I-6.1
cover la tapa, 9
to **cover** tapar, 9.2
covered cubierto(a), I-9.2
cream la crema, 2.2
credit card la tarjeta de crédito, 6.1
crew la tripulación, I-8.2
to **cross** cruzar (c), 10.1
crosswalk el paso de peatones, 10.1
crutch la muleta, 4.1
cucumber el pepino, 9.1
cup la taza, I-15.1
curl el rizo, el bucle, 8.1
to **curl** rizar, 8
curling el rizado, 8
    curling iron el rizador, 8.2
curly rizado(a), crespo(a), 8.1
curriculum vitae el historial profesional, el currículo profesional, 16.2
curtain el telón, I-12.2
custom la costumbre, II.2
customer el/la cliente, I-5.2
customs la aduana, I-8.2
to **cut** cortar, 4.1

D

dad el papá, I-5.2
to **dance** bailar, I-4.2
dark moreno(a), I-1.1
date (calendar) la fecha, I-BV; **(appointment)** la cita, 15.1
    What is today's date? ¿Cuál es la fecha de hoy?, I-BV
daughter la hija, I-6.1
day el día, I-BV
    the day before yesterday anteayer, I-11.2
dead person el/la muerto(a), el/la difunto(a), 12.1

December diciembre (m.), I-BV
to **dedicate (oneself)** dedicar(se), 16.2
degree el grado, I-9.1
delay el retraso, la demora, I-14.2
delicious delicioso(a), I-15.2
to **delight** encantar, I-13
to **deliver** repartir, entregar, 3.2
delivery la entrega, el reparto, 3.2
to **demand** exigir, 12
deodorant el desodorante, I-16.2
department store la tienda por departamentos, 16.1
departure la salida, I-8.1
    arrival and departure board el tablero de llegadas y salidas, I-8.1
    departure gate la puerta de salida, I-8.1
deposit el depósito, el ingreso,
to **deposit** depositar, ingresar, 14.2
dessert el postre, I-5.2
destination el destino, I-8.1
detergent el detergente, 2.2
diagnosis la diagnosis, I-10.2
dial (of telephone) el disco, 1.1
    dial tone la señal, el tono, 1.1
to **dial** discar, 1; marcar, 1.1
to **dice** picar, 9.2
to **die** morir (ue, u), I-15
diet la dieta, I-10.2
difficult difícil, I-2.1
dining car el coche-comedor, I-14.2
dining room el comedor, I-5.1
dinner la cena, I-5.2
direction: la dirección, 10.1; el sentido, 10.2
dirty sucio(a), 13.2
discourteous descortés, 11
to **disembark** desembarcar, I-8
to **distribute** distribuir (y), 7.1
to **do** hacer (irreg.), I-8.1
    to do again volver (ue) a
doctor el/la médico(a), I-10.2
    doctor's office la consulta del médico, el consultorio del médico, I-10.2
dog el/la perro(a), I-6.1
door la puerta, 5.1
dose la dosis, I-10.2

VOCABULARIO INGLÉS-ESPAÑOL

dot punto, I-3.1
   on the dot en punto, I-3.1
double doble, 6.1
doubt la duda
   there is no doubt no hay duda
to doubt dudar, 12
dress el vestido, I-13.1
to dribble driblar con, I-7.2
drink la bebida, 7.1
to drink tomar, I-4.1; beber, I-5.2
to drive conducir (zc), 5.1; manejar, 10.2
driver el/la conductor(a), 5.1
   driver's license la licencia, el permiso de conducir, 5.1
drug la droga, I-10.2
to dry clean limpiar en seco, 13.2
dry cleaners la tintorería, 13.2
dry cleaning la limpieza en seco, 13.2
during durante, I-4.2

E

each cada, 10.2
   each other el uno del otro, 11.1
earphones los audífonos, 7.1
early temprano
east el este, 10.1
easy fácil, I-2.1
to eat comer, I-5.2
   to eat breakfast desayunarse, I-16.1
economics la economía, 16.2
education la pedagogía, 16.2
egg el huevo, I-15.2
eight ocho, I-BV
eighth octavo(a), I-5.1
eighty ochenta, I-BV
elastic elástico(a), 4.2
elbow el codo, 4.1
electric hair clipper la maquinilla, 8.2
electrician el/la electricista, 16.2
elevator el ascensor, I-5.1
to embrace abrazar (c), 11.2
emergency exit la salida de emergencia, 7.1
emergency room la sala de urgencias, la sala de emergencia, 4.1
employee el/la empleado(a), 3.2
to endorse endosar, 14.2
energy la energía, 16.2
   nuclear energy la energía nuclear, 16.2
engagement el compromiso, 15.1
   engagement ring la sortija de compromiso, 15.1
engine el motor, 7.2
English el inglés, I-2.2; inglés, inglesa
to enjoy oneself divertirse (ie, i), I-16.2
enough suficiente, 5.1
to enter entrar, I-3.1
entrance la entrada, I-6.2
envelope el sobre, 3.1
eraser la goma, I-BV
Europe Europa, 15.2
Eve: Christmas Eve la víspera de Navidad, la Nochebuena, 12.2
evening la noche
   Good evening. Buenas noches., I-BV
everyone todos, I-4.2
examination el examen, I-3.2
to examine examinar, I-10.2
exchange el cambio, 14.1
   exchange office la oficina de cambio, 14.1
   exchange rate el tipo de cambio, la tasa de cambio, 14.1
   What is the exchange rate? ¿Cuál es el tipo de cambio?, 14.1
to exchange cambiar, 6.2; intercambiar, 15.2
exercise el ejercicio, I-10.2
   aerobic exercise el ejercicio aeróbico, I-10.2
   physical exercise el ejercicio físico, I-10.2
exhibition la exposición, I-12.2
exit la salida, 7.1
   exit door la puerta de salida, 7.1
expensive caro(a), I-13.1
expert experto(a), I-9.1

F

face la cara, I-16.1
factory la fábrica, 16.1
to fall caerse (irreg.), 4.1
   to fall asleep dormirse (ue, u), I-16.1
   to fall in love enamorarse, 15.1
family la familia, I-5.1
fantastic fantástico(a), I-1.2
to farm (the land) labrar (la tierra), 16.2
farm worker el/la labrador(a), 16.2
fast rápido, I-9.1
to fasten abrocharse, 7.1
father el padre, I-6.1
February febrero (m.), I-BV
to feel sentir (ie, i), 12
fever la fiebre, I-10.1
fiancé(e) el/la novio(a), el/la comprometido(a), 15.1
fiber la fibra, I-10.2
field el campo, I-7.1
   soccer field el campo de fútbol, I-7.1
fifteenth: young woman's fifteenth birthday la quinceañera, 12.1
fifth quinto(a), I-5.1
fifty cincuenta, I-BV
figure skating el patinaje artístico, I-9.2
to fill (out) llenar, 4.2
film la película, el film(e), I-12.1
fine bien, I-BV
finger el dedo, 4.1
fire el fuego, 9.2
first primer, primero(a), I-BV
   first-aid kit el botiquín, I-16.2
   first-aid service el servicio de primeros auxilios, el servicio de primer socorro, 4.1
   first-aid worker el/la socorrista, 4.1
fish el pescado, I-15.2
   fish market la pescadería, 2.1
to fit sentar (ie) bien a, I-13.1
   It fits me. Me sienta bien., I-13.1
five cinco, I-BV

VOCABULARIO INGLÉS-ESPAÑOL   **517**

flashlight la linterna, I-16.2
flight el vuelo, I-8.1
   flight attendant el asistente, la asistenta de vuelo, I-8.2; el/la sobrecargo, **7.1**
   flight number el número del vuelo, I-8.1
floor el piso, I-5.1
flower la flor, I-6.2
flu la gripe, I-10.1
to **fluctuate** fluctuar, **14.1**
to **fly over** sobrevolar (ue), **7.2**
folding plegable, I-11.1
   folding chair la silla plegable, I-11.1
to **follow** seguir (i, i), I-15
food el comestible, **2.1**
foot el pie, I-7.1
   on foot a pie, I-3.1
football el fútbol americano
forbidden prohibido(a), **10.2**
forehead la frente, **4.1**
forest el bosque, I-16.2
fork el tenedor, I-15.1
form el formulario, **4.2**
forty cuarenta, I-BV
four cuatro, I-BV
fourth cuarto(a), I-5.1
fracture la fractura, **4.1**
free libre, I-14.2
freezer el congelador, **9.1**
French francés (francesa), I-2.2
   French fry la papa frita
frequently con frecuencia, **1**
Friday el viernes, I-BV
friend el/la amigo(a), I-1.1
from de, I-1.1
   from the (m. sing.) del
front: in front of enfrente, **8.2**; delante de, **10.1**
frozen congelado(a), **2.2**
fruit la fruta, I-15.2
to **fry** freír (i, i), I-15.1
frying pan el/la sartén, **9.1**
full-time a tiempo completo, **16.2**
fun divertido(a), I-1.1

G

game el partido, I-7.1; el juego, I-11.2
   tennis game el juego de tenis, I-11.2
garage el garaje, I-6.2
garden el jardín, I-6.2
garlic el ajo, **9.2**
gas la gasolina, **5.2**
   gas station la gasolinera, **5.2**
gate la puerta, I-8.1
   departure gate la puerta de salida, I-8.1
geography la geografía, I-2.2
geometry la geometría, I-2.2
to **get** sacar (qu), I-3.2
   to get dressed vestirse (i, i), I-16.1
   to get engaged comprometerse, **15.1**
   to get good (bad) grades sacar notas buenas (malas), I-3.2
   to get hurt lastimarse, **4.1**
   to get married casarse, **15.1**
   to get off the train bajar(se) del tren, I-14.2
   to get on subir a, I-8.1
   to get on the train subir al tren, I-14.2
   to get together reunirse, **12.1**
   to get up levantarse, I-16.1
gift el regalo, I-6.2
girl la muchacha, I-BV; la niña, **1.2**
girlfriend la novia, **15.1**
to **give** dar (irreg.), I-4.2
glass (drinking) el vaso, I-5.2
glasses (eye) las gafas, I-9.1
glove el guante, I-7.2
to **go** ir (irreg.), I-4.1
   to go back volver (ue), I-7.1
   to go camping ir de camping
   to go down bajar, I-9.1
   to go for a swim bañarse, I-16.2
   to go home ir a casa, I-4.2
   to go out salir (irreg.)
   to go to bed acostarse (ue), I-16.1
   to go up subir, I-5.1
   to go with hacer juego con, I-13.2
goal el gol, la portería, I-7.1
goalkeeper el/la portero(a), I-7.1
godfather el padrino, **12.1**
godmother la madrina, **12.1**
golf el golf, I-11.2
golf bag la bolsa de golf, I-11.2
golf course el campo de golf, I-11.2
golf game el juego de golf, I-11.2
good bueno(a), I-1.2
   Good evening., Good night. Buenas noches., I-BV
   Good afternoon. Buenas tardes., I-BV
   Good morning. Buenos días., I-BV
good-bye adiós, chao, I-BV
grade la nota, I-3.2; la calificación
grandchild el/la nieto(a), I-6.1
grandfather el abuelo, I-6.1
grandmother la abuela, I-6.1
grandparents los abuelos, I-6.1
grape la uva, **2.1**
grapefruit la toronja, **9.1**
to **grate** rallar, **9.2**
green (color) verde, I-13.2; **(golf)** el green, I-11.2
greengrocer shop la verdulería, **2.1**
to **greet** saludar, **11.1**
grey gris, I-13.2
grill la parrilla, **9.1**
grocery store la tienda de abarrotes
ground el suelo, I-7
   ground floor la planta baja, I-5.1
guest el/la huésped, **6.1**; el/la invitado(a), **15.2**
guitar la guitarra, I-4.2

H

hair el pelo, I-16.1; el cabello, **8.1**
   hair clip la pinza para el cabello, **8.2**
   hair dryer el secador, **8.2**
   hair roller el rulo, **8.2**
   hair salon la peluquería, **8.2**
   hair spray la laca, **8.2**
   hair stylist el/la peluquero(a), **8.2**
haircut el corte de pelo, **8.2**
half (soccer) El tiempo, I-7.1
ham el jamón, I-15.2

hammock la hamaca, I-11.1
hand la mano, I-7.1
handle el mango, I-11.2
to **hang up** colgar (ue), **1**
Hanukkah Hanuka, **12.2**
happiness la felicidad, **15.2**
happy contento(a), I-10.1; alegre, **1.2**; Feliz, **12.1**.
   Happy Birthday. Feliz Cumpleaños., **12.1**
   Happy New Year! ¡Próspero año nuevo!, **12.2**
hat el sombrero, I-13.1
to **have** tener (irreg.), I-6.1
   to have just (done something) acabar de, **8.2**
   to have one's birthday cumplir años, **12.1**
   to have to tener que, I-6
he él, I-1.1
head la cabeza, I-7.1
headache el dolor de cabeza, I-10.1
headlight el faro
to **hear** oír (y)
health la salud
heat el calor, I-11.1
Hebrew hebreo(a), **12.2**
heel el tacón, I-13.2
helicopter el helicóptero, **7.2**
hello hola, Buenos días, I-BV
high alto(a), I-3
   high school el colegio, la escuela secundaria
   high tableland el altiplano, **7.2**
highway la carretera, **10.2**
hike la caminata, I-16.2
   to take a hike dar una caminata, I-16.2
hill la colina, I-16.2
history la historia, I-2.2
hit (baseball) el hit, I-7.2
to **hit** golpear, I-11.2; **(baseball)** batear, I-7.2
hole el hoyo, I-11.2
home la casa, I-4.2
   home economics la economia domestica, I-22
   home plate el platillo, I-7.2
   home run el jonrón, I-7.2
   at home en casa, I-4.2
honest honesto(a), I-1.2
honeymoon la luna de miel, **15.2**

honeymoon trip el viaje de novios, **15.2**
hood el capó, **5.1**
hoop el aro, I-7.2
hope: I hope (that) ojalá (que), **16**
horn la bocina, el claxon, **5.1**
hospital el hospital, I-10.2
hot: It's hot. Hace calor., I-11.1
hotel el hotel, **6.1**
   hotel ballroom el salón del hotel, **12.1**
house la casa, I-4.1
how? ¿qué?, I-BV; ¿cómo?, I-1.1
   How are you? ¿Qué tal?, I-BV
   how much? ¿cuánto(a)?, I-BV
   How much do I owe you? ¿Cuánto le debo?, **2.2**
   How much does it cost? ¿Cuánto cuesta?, I-13.1; ¿A cuánto está(n)?, ¿Cuánto es?, **2.2**
   How much is it? ¿Cuánto es?, I-BV
hug el abrazo, **11.2**
   to hug abrazar (c), **11.2**
human humano(a), **16.2**, I-15.1
   human resources department el departamento (servicio) de personal, el departamento de recursos humanos, **16.2**
hunger el hambre, I-15.1
   to be hungry tener hambre, I-15.1
to **hurt** doler (ue), I-10.2
   My_____hurts, aches. Me duele_____., I-10
   to hurt oneself hacerse daño, **4.1**
husband el marido, el esposo, I-6.1

I

I yo, I-1.2
ice el hielo, I-9.2
   ice cream el helado, I-5.2
   ice skating el patinaje sobre hielo, I-9.2
ill-bred malcriado(a), **11.1**
immediately en seguida, I-16
important importante, **11**
impossible imposible, **11**

improbable improbable, **11**
in en, I-1.1
individual el/la individuo(a), **7**
inning la entrada, I-7.2
to **insert** introducir (zc) (j), **1.1**
inside dentro de, **7.1**
to **insist** insistir, **11.1**
to **inspect** revisar, I-8; inspeccionar, I-8.2
inspection el control, I-8.1
   passport inspection el control de pasaportes, I-8.1
   security inspection el control de seguridad, I-8.1
instructions las instrucciones, I-5.2
to **insure** asegurar, **3.2**
intelligent inteligente, I-2.1
intensive intensivo(a), **4.2**
   intensive care area la unidad de cuidado intensivo, **4.2**
to **interest** interesar, I-13.1
interesting interesante, I-2.1
intersection el cruce, **5.1**; la bocacalle, **10.1**
intimate íntimo(a), **11.2**
invitation la invitación, I-5.2
to **invite** invitar (a), I-4.2
iron la plancha, **13.2**
   to iron planchar, **13.2**
is es, I-1.1; está, I-4.1
   It looks good on me. Me queda bien., I-13.2
Italian el italiano, (language) I-2.2

J

jack el gato
jacket la chaqueta, el saco, el blusón, I-13.1
January enero (m.), I-BV
jar el frasco, **2.2**
jazz (adj.) de jazz, I-4
jet el avión reactor, el jet, **7.2**
Jew el/la judío(a), **12.2**
job el trabajo, el empleo, **16.1**
   job application la solicitud de empleo, **16.2**
judge el/la juez, **16.1**
July julio (m.), I-BV
June junio (m.), I-BV

VOCABULARIO INGLÉS-ESPAÑOL   **519**

K

key la tecla, **1.1**; la llave, **6.1**
keypad el teclado, **1.1**
kilogram el kilo(gramo), **2.2**
kind amable, I-2.1
kiss el beso (besito), **11.2**
kitchen la cocina, I-4.1
knapsack la mochila, I-BV
knee la rodilla, **4.1**
knife el cuchillo, I-15.1
to know (a person) conocer (zc) (a), I-9.1
    to know (how) saber (irreg.), I-9.1

L

laboratory el laboratorio, **16.2**
lake el lago, **7.2**
lamb el cordero, **9.1**
land la tierra, **16.2**
to land aterrizar (c), I-8.2
landing el aterrizaje, **7.2**
lane (of highway) el carril, **10.2**
language la lengua, I-2.2
    native language la lengua materna
to last durar, **12.2**
last: last night anoche, I-11.2
last week la semana pasada, I-11.2
last year el año pasado, I-11.2
late tarde, I-8.1; con retraso, con una demora, I-14.2
Latin el latín, I-2.2
laundromat la lavandería, **13.2**
laundry el lavado, **8.2**
lavatory el aseo, el lavabo, **7.1**
lawyer el/la abogado(a), **16.1**
leaded con plomo, **5.2**
to learn aprender, I-5.2
to leave salir (irreg.), I-8.1; abandonar, **6.1**
    to leave (something behind) dejar, I-12.2
left la izquierda, I-5.1
    to the left a la izquierda, I-5.1
leg la pierna, **4.1**
lemon el limón, **9.1**
lemonade la limonada, I-BV
lesson la lección, I-3.2
letter la carta, I-5.2
lettuce la lechuga, I-15.2
level el nivel, **7.2**
    sea level el nivel del mar, **7.2**
library la biblioteca, I-4.1
life la vida
    life vest el chaleco salvavidas, **7.1**
light la luz, **10.1**
to light encender (ie), **12.2**
to like gustar, I-13.1
lime la lima, **9.1**
line la línea, **1.1**
    line (of people) la cola, I-12.1
    The line is busy. La línea está ocupada., **1.1**
lip el labio, **4.1**
liquid líquido(a), **2.2**
to listen escuchar, I-4.1
little poco(a), I-5.2
to live vivir, I-5.1
living room la sala, I-4.1
lobster la langosta, **2.1**
lock (of hair) la mecha
long largo(a), I-13.2
to look at mirar, I-3.2
    to look at oneself mirarse, I-16.1
to look for buscar (qu), **16.2**
to lose perder (ie), I-7.1
to love querer (irreg.), **1.2**
low bajo(a), **15.2**
luck la suerte, **15.2**
luggage el equipaje, I-14.1
    carry-on luggage el equipaje de mano, I-8.1
lunch el almuerzo, I-5.2

M

ma'am señora, I-BV
magazine la revista, I-5.2
maid la camarera, **6.2**
    maid of honor la madrina, **15.2**
mail el correo, **3.2**
    air mail por correo aéreo, **3.2**
    certified mail por correo certificado, por correo recomendado, **3.2**
    mail carrier el/la cartero, **3.2**
    regular mail por correo ordinario, **3.2**
mailbox el buzón, **3.1**
to make hacer (irreg.), I-8.1
    to make a basket encestar, I-7.2
    to make a call hacer una llamada, **1.1**
    to make the bed hacer (tender) la cama, **6.2**
man el caballero, I-13.1
manner la manera, I-1.1
    manners los modales, **11.1**
many muchos(as), I-5
March marzo (m.), I-BV
market el mercado, **2.1**
married couple el matrimonio, **15.1**
Mass la misa, **12.2**
    midnight Mass la misa del gallo, **12.2**
to match hacer juego con, I-13.2
material la materia, I-2.2
mathematics las matemáticas, I-2.2
maximum máximo(a), **10.2**
May mayo (m.), I-BV
    May I talk to (name of person)? ¿Está (el nombre de una persona)?, **1.1**
maybe puede ser, **16.2**
mayonnaise la mayonesa, **2.2**
Me neither. (Ni) yo tampoco, I-13
meal la comida, I-5.2
means: by no means de ninguna manera, I-1.1
meat la carne, I-5.2
mechanic el/la mecánico, **16.1**
medical kit el botiquín, I-16.2
medication el medicamento, I-10.2
medicine la medicina, I-10
medium (meat) a término medio, I-15.2
menorah la menora, **12.2**
menu el menú, I-12.2
merchant el/la comerciante, el/la mercader, **16.1**
Merry Christmas Feliz Navidad, **12.2**
Mexican mexicano(a), I-1.1
microwave oven el horno de microondas, **9.1**
midday el mediodía, I-2
midnight la medianoche, I-2
milk la leche, I-5.2

520   VOCABULARIO INGLÉS-ESPAÑOL

mineral mineral, **2.2**
mirror el espejo, I-16.1
Miss señorita, I-BV
to miss the bus perder el autobús, I-12.1
mom la mamá, I-5.2
moment momento, I-8.1
　One moment, please. Un momento, por favor., **1.1**
Monday el lunes, I-BV
money el dinero, **14.1**
mood humor, I-10
　in a bad mood de mal humor, I-10
　in a good mood de buen humor, I-10
more más, **9.1**
morning la mañana
　Good morning. Buenos días., I-BV
　this morning esta mañana, I-11.2
mother la madre, I-6.1
motorbike el ciclomotor, I-6.2
mountain la montaña, I-9.1
　mountain range la cordillera, **7.2**
mouth la boca, I-10.2
movie la película, I-5.2, el film
　movie theater el cine, I-12.1
　to show a movie dar una película,
Mr. señor, I-BV
Mrs. señora, I-BV
mural el mural, I-12.2
museum el museo, I-12.2
music la música, I-2.2
musical musical, I-12.2
musician el/la músico, I-12.2
mussel el mejillón, **9.2**
mustache el bigote, **8.1**

N

name el nombre, **3.1**
nap la siesta, I-11.1
　to take a nap echar (tomar) una siesta, I-11.1
napkin la servilleta, I-15.1
narrow estrecho(a), I-13.2
national nacional, **13.1**
nationality la nacionalidad, I-1
necessary necesario(a), **11.1**
neck el cuello, **8.2**

necktie la corbata, I-13.1
to need necesitar, **8.2**
neither: Me neither. Ni yo tampoco., I-13
nephew el sobrino, I-6.1
nervous nervioso(a), I-10.1
net la red, I-7.2
never nunca, I-13.1; jamás, **6**
new nuevo(a), I-6.2
newlywed el/la novio(a), el/la recién casado(a), **15.1**
news las noticias, I-5.2
newspaper el periódico, I-5.2
newsstand el quiosco, I-14.1
next próximo(a), I-14.2
Nice to meet you. Mucho gusto., I-BV
niece la sobrina, I-6.1
　niece(s) and nephew(s) los sobrinos, I-6.1
night la noche
　Good night. Buenas noches., I-BV
　last night anoche, I-11.2
nine nueve, I-BV
ninety noventa, I-BV
ninth noveno(a), I-5.1
no no
　by no means de ninguna manera, I-1.1
　no longer ya no, **12.1**
　no one, nobody nadie, I-13
　no smoking section la sección de no fumar, I-8.1
　no smoking signal la señal de no fumar, **7.1**
noncarbonated soft drink el refresco, I-4.1
noon el mediodía, I-2
north el norte, **10.1**
not no
　not yet todavía no, **6**
notebook el cuaderno, I-BV; la libreta, I-3.2
notes los apuntes, I-3.2
nothing nada, I-13.1
novel la novela, I-5.2
November noviembre (m.), I-BV
now ahora, I-BV
　now and then de vez en cuando, **1**
nuclear nuclear, **16.2**
　nuclear energy la energía nuclear, **16.2**

number el número, I-8.1
　flight number el número del vuelo, I-8.1
　seat number el número del asiento, I-8.1
　telephone number el número de teléfono, **1.1**
nurse el/la enfermero(a), I-10.2

O

occupied ocupado(a), I-14.2
October octubre (m.), I-BV
of de, I-1.1
　of the (m. sing.) del
to offer one's hand dar la mano, **11.2**
office la oficina, **16.1**
often a menudo, **1**
oil el aceite, I-15.2
old viejo(a), I-6.1
older mayor, **11.1**
on board a bordo, **7.1**
one uno, I-BV
　one hundred cien(to), I-BV
　One moment, please. Un momento, por favor., **1.1**
onion la cebolla, **9.1**
only solamente, **10.2**
to open abrir, I-8.2
operating room la sala de operaciones, el quirófano, **4.2**
operating table la mesa de operaciones, **4.2**
operator el/la operador(a), **16.1**
opposite contrario(a), I-7; enfrente de, **10.1**
orange la naranja (fruit), **2.1**; anaranjado(a) (color), I-13.2
orchestra la orquesta, I-12.2
　orchestra seat la butaca, I-12.1
orthopedic ortopédico(a), **4.2**
orthopedist el/la ortopedista, **4.2**
other otro(a), I-2.2
out (baseball) el out, I-7.2
outdoors al aire libre, I-9.2
outfielder (baseball) el/la jardinero(a), I-7.2
outskirts las afueras, I-5.1
oven el horno, **9.1**
over por encima, I-7.2

VOCABULARIO INGLÉS-ESPAÑOL

overcoat el abrigo, I-13.1
to overtake adelantar, 5.1
oxygen el oxígeno, 7.1
    oxygen mask la máscara de oxígeno, 7.1

P

to pack one's suitcase hacer la maleta, I-8
package el paquete, 2.2
painter el/la pintor(a), 16.1
painting el cuadro, I-12.2
pantihose las medias, I-13.1
pants los pantalones, I-13.1
papaya la papaya, 9.2
paper el papel, I-BV
    sheet of paper la hoja de papel, I-BV
    toilet paper el papel higiénico, I-16.2
parasol el parasol, I-11.1
parents los padres, I-6.1
park el parque, I-6.2
to park aparcar, estacionar, 5.1
    parking meter el parquímetro, 10.1
part la parte
    part (in hair) la raya, 8.1
    part-time a tiempo parcial, 16.2
party la fiesta, I-4.2
to pass pasar, I-7.2
passbook la libreta, 14.2
passenger el/la pasajero(a), I-8.1
passport el pasaporte, I-8.1
    passport inspection el control de pasaportes, I-8.1
pastry el pastel, 12.1
    pastry shop la pastelería, 2.1
path la senda, el sendero, 13.1
patient el/la enfermo(a), I-10.1
to pay pagar, I-13.1
pea el guisante, 9.1
peach el melocotón, 9.1
peak el pico, 7.2
pear la pera
pedestrian el peatón, 10.1
to peel pelar, 9.2
pencil el lápiz, I-5.2
people la gente, 16.2
pepper la pimienta, I-15.1

performance la representación, el espectáculo, I-12.2
perhaps tal vez, quizá(s), 16.2
person la persona, 11.1
pharmacist el/la farmacéutico(a), I-10.2
pharmacy la farmacia, I-10.2
physical físico(a), I-10.2
    physical education la educación física, I-2.2
physics la física, I-2.2
piano el piano, I-4.2
to pick up recoger, I-8.2; descolgar (ue), 1.1
picture el cuadro, I-12.2
pie el pastel, 2.1
piece, little el pedacito, el trocito, 9.2
pill la pastilla, la píldora, el comprimido, I-10.2
pillow la almohada, 6.2
pilot el/la piloto, I-8.2
to pinch apretar (ie), I-13.2
    It (They) pinch(es) me. Me aprieta(n)., I-13.2
pineapple la piña, 2.1
pitcher (sports) el/la pícher, el/la lanzador(a), I-7.2
pity la lástima, 12
    to be a pity ser una lástima, 12
place el lugar, 12.2
    to take place tener lugar, 12.2
plaid a cuadros, I-13.2
plain la llanura, 7.2
plane el avión, I-8
    by plane en avión, I-8
plant la planta, I-6.2
plastic de plástico, 2.2
    plastic bag la bolsa de plástico, 2.2
plate el plato, I-15.1
    home plate el platillo, I-7.1
to play jugar (ue) (a sport), I-7.1; tocar (an instrument), I-4.2
player el/la jugador(a), I-7.1
please por favor, I-BV
plumber el/la plomero(a), el/la fontanero(a), 16.2
point (score) el tanto, I-7.1
pole el bastón, I-9.1
police officer el policía, la mujer policia 16.1
polite educado(a), 11.1

pony tail la cola de caballo, 8.1
pool la alberca, la piscina, I-11.2
popular popular, I-2.1
population la población, 16.2
pork el cerdo, 2.1
portable stove el hornillo, I-16.2
porter el/la maletero(a), el mozo, I-14.1
possible posible, 11
post office la oficina de correos, 3.2
    post office box el apartado postal, la casilla, 3.2
postage el franqueo
postal employee el/la empleado(a) de correo, 3.2
postcard la tarjeta postal, I-5.2
pot la olla, la cazuela, 9.1
potato la papa, I-5.2; la patata, 2.1
powdered en polvo, 2.2
to practice (a profession) ejercer (una profesión), 16.2
prawn el camarón, 2.1
to prefer preferir (ie, i), I-7
to prepare preparar, I-4.1
to prescribe recetar, I-10
prescription la receta, I-10.2
present el regalo, 12.2
    Christmas present el regalo de Navidad, el aguinaldo, 12.2
pressure la presión, 5.2
pretty bonito(a), I-6.2
price el precio, I-13.1
priest el cura, 12.1
principal el/la director(a), 16.1
private particular, privado(a), I-5.1
probable probable, 11
profession la profesión, 16.1
programmer el/la programador(a), 16.1
prop las hélices, 7.2
protein la proteína, I-10.2
provided that con tal que, 15
public publico(a) (adj.), 1.1
Puerto Rican puertorriqueño(a), I-2
pulse el pulso, 4.2
to push empujar, 2.1
    push button de (a) botones, 1.1

VOCABULARIO INGLÉS-ESPAÑOL

to **put** poner (irreg.), I-8.1
   to put in meter, I-7.1
   to put in a plaster cast enyesar, 4.2
   to put on (clothes) ponerse, I-16.1
   to put on the fire poner al fuego, 9.2
   to put on a performance dar una representación, I-12.2
   to put up a tent armar una tienda, I-16.2

Q

quarter: a quarter to (past) menos (y) cuarto, I-2
quite bastante, I-1.1

R

racket la raqueta, I-11.2
radiator el radiador, 5.2
railroad el ferrocarril, I-14.2
railway platform el andén, I-14.1
railway track la vía, I-14.1
to **rain** llover (ue), I-11.1
   It's raining. Llueve., I-11.1
raincoat la gabardina, I-13.1
to **raise** levantar, 13.1
rare (meat) casi crudo, I-15.2
rather bastante, I-1.1
raw crudo(a), I-15.2
ray el rayo, 4.2
razor la navaja, I-16.1
to **read** leer (y), I-5.2
to **receive** sacar (qu), I-3.2; recibir, I-6
receiver (of telephone) el auricular, la bocina, 1.1; **(person)** el/la destinatario(a), 3.1
reception la recepción, 6.1
receptionist el/la recepcionista, 6.1
to **recommend** recomendar (ie), 13.2
to **reconcile** conciliar, 14.2
record el disco, I-4.1
recovery room la sala de recuperación, la sala de restablecimiento, 4.2

red rojo(a), I-13.2
to **reduce** reducir (zc)
referee el/la árbitro(a), I-7.1
refrigerator el refrigerador, la nevera, 9.1
registration card la tarjeta, la ficha, 6.1
regular (gas) normal, 5.2
   regular mail por correo ordinario, 3.2
to **remain** quedarse
to **rent** alquilar, I-11.1
to **repeat** repetir (i, i), I-15
to **request** rogar (ue), 12
to **require** requerir (ie, i), 16.2
reservation la reservación
to **reserve** reservar, 6.1
reserved reservado(a), I-14.2
restaurant el restaurante, I-12.2
to **return (something)** devolver (ue), I-7.2
rib la costilla, 9.1
rice el arroz, I-15.2
right la derecha, I-5.1
   right away en seguida, 1.2
   right? ¿verdad?, I-1.1
   right now en este momento
   to the right a la derecha, I-5.1
ring el anillo, la sortija, 15.1
   engagement ring la sortija de compromiso, 15.1
   wedding ring el anillo de boda, 15.1
to **ring** sonar (ue), 1.1
rink la pista de patinaje, el patinadero, I-9.2
river el río, I-16.2
roast suckling pig el lechón, 2.1
rock (music) (adj.) de rock, I-4
roll (of paper) el rollo, I-16.2
roller la rueda, I-9.2
roller skating el patinaje sobre ruedas, I-9.2
room el cuarto, la habitación, I-5.1
   classroom la sala de clase, el salon de clase, I-3.2
   double room el cuarto doble, 6.1
   single room el cuarto sencillo, 6.1
   waiting room la sala de espera, I-14.1

roundtrip (adj.) de ida y vuelta, I-14.1
row la fila, I-8
to **run** correr, I-7.2
runway la pista, 7.2

S

sad triste, I-10.1
safe seguro(a), 12
salad la ensalada, I-5.2
salesperson el/la dependiente, I-13.1
salt la sal, I-15.1
sand la arena, I-11.1
sandals las sandalias, I-13.1
sandwich el sándwich, el bocadillo, I-5.2
sanitary higiénico(a), 2.2
Saturday el sábado, I-BV
to **save** ahorrar, 14.2
saucer el platillo, I-15.1
sausage la salchicha, 9.1
savings account la cuenta de ahorros, 14.2
to **say** decir (irreg.), I-9
   to say good-bye despedirse (i, i), 11.1
scale la báscula, I-8.1
scar la cicatriz, 4.1
schedule el horario, I-14.1
school el colegio, la escuela, I-1.1; escolar (adj.), I-3.1
   high school la escuela secundaria, el colegio, I-1.1
science la ciencia, I-2.2
scissors las tijeras, 8.2
to **score (sports)** marcar, I-7.1
scoreboard el tablero indicador, I-7.1
screen la pantalla, I-8.1
sculptor el/la escultor(a), I-12.2
sea el mar, I-11.1
   sea level el nivel del mar, 7.2
search busca, 16.2
   in search of en busca de, 16.2
season la estación, I-9.1
seat el asiento, I-8.1
   seat belt el cinturón de seguridad, 5.1
   seat (in theater) la localidad, I-12.1

VOCABULARIO INGLÉS-ESPAÑOL   **523**

seat number el número del asiento, I-8.1
seat back el respaldo, **7.1**
second segundo(a), I-5.1
secondary secundario(a), I-1.1
secret el secreto, **11.1**
secretary el/la secretario(a), **16.1**
security la seguridad, I-8.1
  security control el control de seguridad, I-8.1
sedan el sedán, **5.1**
to **see** ver, I-5.2
  See you later. Hasta la vista., Hasta luego., I-BV
  See you soon. Hasta pronto., I-BV
  See you tomorrow. Hasta mañana., I-BV
to **sell** vender, I-5.2; despachar, I-10.2
to **send** enviar, **3.1**; mandar, **11**
sender el remitente, **3.1**
September septiembre (m.), I-BV
serious serio(a), I-1.2
to **serve** servir (i, i), I-15.1
  service station la estación de servicio, **5.2**
to **set the bone** reducir la fractura, **4.2**
seven siete, I-BV
seventh séptimo(a), I-5.1
seventy setenta, I-BV
shampoo el champú, I-16.2
to **shake hands** estrechar la mano, **11.2**
to **shave** afeitarse, I-16.1
  shaving cream la crema de afeitar, I-16.2
she ella, I-1.2
sheet la hoja, I-BV
  sheet (bed) la sábana, **6.2**
  sheet of paper la hoja de papel, I-BV
shellfish el marisco, I-15.2
to **shine** brillar, I-11.1
to **shift gears** cambiar de velocidad, **5.1**
shirt la camisa, I-13.1
shoes el zapato, I-13.1
shop window el escaparate, la vitrina, I-13.1
shopping de compras, I-13.1

shopping center el centro comercial, I-4.1
short (person) bajo(a), I-1.1; **(length)** corto(a), I-13.2
shoulder el hombro, **4.1**
show el espectáculo, (movies) la sesión, I-12.1, I-12.2
to **show** mostrar (ue), I-12
  to show a movie dar una película, I-12
shower la ducha, I-16.2
  to take a shower tomar una ducha, I-16.2
shrimp la gamba, **9.2**; el camarón
to **shrink** encogerse, **13.2**
shy tímido(a), I-1.2
sick enfermo(a), I-10.1
  sick person el/la enfermo(a), I-10.2
side: to the side of al lado de, **8.2**
sideburn la patilla, **8.1**
sidewalk la acera, **10.1**
sign el rótulo, **10.2**
to **sign** firmar, **14.2**
signal: busy signal el tono de ocupado, **1**
simple sencillo(a)
sincere sincero(a), I-1.2
to **sing** cantar, I-4.2
single sencillo(a), **6.1**
sir señor, I-BV
sister la hermana, I-2.1
to **sit down** sentarse (ie), I-16.1
six seis, I-BV
sixth sexto(a), I-5.1
sixty sesenta, I-BV
size el tamaño, la talla, I-13.1
skate el patín, I-9.2
to **skate** patinar, I-9
skateboard el monopatín, I-9.2
skater el/la patinador(a), I-9.2
skating el patinaje, I-9.2
  figure skating el patinaje artístico, I-9.2
  ice skating el patinaje sobre hielo, I-9.2
  roller skating el patinaje sobre ruedas, I-9.2
  skating rink el patinadero, la pista de patinaje, I-9.2
ski el esquí, I-9.1
  ski lift el telesquí, I-9.1
  ski pole el bastón, I-9.1

ski resort la estación de esquí, I-9-1
ski slope la pista de esquí, I-9
to **ski** esquiar, I-9.1
skier el/la esquiador(a), I-9.1
skiing el esquí, I-9.1
  cross-country skiing el esquí nórdico, el esquí de fondo, I-9.1
  downhill skiing el esquí alpino, el esquí de descenso, I-9.1
to **skindive** bucear, I-11.1
skindiving el buceo, I-11.1
skirt la falda, I-13.1
sky el cielo, I-11.1
slalom el slálom, I-9.1
slap la palmadita, **11.2**
to **slap gently** dar palmaditas, **11.2**
to **sleep** dormir (ue, u), I-7
sleeping bag el saco de (para) dormir, I-16.2
sleeping car el coche-cama, I-14.2
sleeve la manga, I-13.2
  long (short)-sleeved de manga larga (corta), I-13.2
slice la tajada, la lonja, **2.2**; la rebanada, **9.2**
to **slice** rebanar, **9.2**
to **slip** resbalarse, **4.1**
slope la cuesta, I-9.1; la pista (de esquí) (ski)
slot (for money) la ranura, **1.1**
small pequeño(a), I-2.1; **(amount)** poco(a), I-5.2
smoking (no smoking) section la seción de (no) fumar, I-8.1
snack la merienda, I-4.1
to **sneeze** estornudar, I-10.1
snow la nieve, I-9.1
to **snow** nevar (ie), I-9.1
  It's snowing. Nieva., I-9
snowfall la nevada, I-9.1
so that para que, de manera que, de modo que, **15.2**
soap el jabón, I-16.2
  powdered soap el jabón en polvo, **2.2**
soap opera la telenovela, I-5.2
soccer el fútbol, I-7.1

soccer field el campo de fútbol, I-7.1
social science las ciencias sociales, I-2.2
social studies la educación cívica, I-2.2
sociology la sociología, I-2.2
socks los calcetines, I-13.1
soda la gaseosa, I-5.2
soft drink la gaseosa, I-5.2
some algún, alguno(a), **2.1**
somebody alguien, I-13
something algo, I-9.1
    Something more? ¿Algo más?, **2.2**
sometimes a veces, I-5.2
son el hijo, I-6.1
soon: as soon as tan pronto como, **15**
sore throat el dolor de garganta, I-10.1
soup la sopa, I-5.2
south el sur, **10.1**
    South America la América del Sur, I-8.1
Spanish español(a); (language) el español, I-2.2
spare tire la llanta de repuesto (de recambio), **5.1**
to **speak** hablar, I-3.1
    They are speaking. Están hablando., **1.1**
specialist especialista, **16.2**
spectator el/la espectador(a), I-7
speed la velocidad, **10.2**
    speed limit la velocidad máxima, **10.2**
to **spend** (time) pasar, **15.2**
spoon la cuchara, I-15.1
sports los deportes, I-2.2
    sports broadcast la emisión deportiva, I-5.2
    sports car el coche deportivo, **5**
spring la primavera, I-7.2
squid el calamar, **9.2**
stadium el estadio, I-7.1
stage la escena, I-12.2
    to **come on stage** entrar en escena, I-12.2
stain la mancha, **13.2**
stained manchado(a), **13.2**
stairway la escalera, I-5.1
stall el puesto, **2.1**

stamp el sello, la estampilla, **3.1**
starch el almidón, **13.2**
station la estación, I-12.1
    service station la estación de servicio, **5.2**
    train station la estación de ferrocarril, I-14.1
statue la estatua, I-12.2
to **stay** quedarse
    to **stay in bed** guardar cama, I-10.1
to **steal** robar, I-7.2
steak el biftec, I-15.2
stereophonic estereofónico(a), **7.1**
to **stir** revolver (ue), **9.1**
stitch el punto, la sutura, **4.2**
stockings las medias, I-13.1
stomach el estómago, I-10.1
    stomachache el dolor de estómago, I-10.1
stop la parada, I-14.2
to **stop** parar, I-7.1
store la tienda, I-4.1
    grocery store la tienda de abarrotes, **2.1**
    department store la tienda de departamento (por departamentos), **16.1**
    men's clothing store la tienda de ropa para caballeros (señores), I-13.1
    women's clothing store la tienda de ropa para damas (señoras), I-13.1
stove la estufa, **9.1**
straight (direction) derecho, **10.1**; (hair) liso(a), lacio(a), **8.1**
straw la paja, **12.2**
strawberry la fresa, **2.1**
street la calle, I-5.1
stretcher la camilla, **4.1**
string bean la judía verde, **2.1**
striped a rayas, I-13.2
student el/la alumno(a), I-1.1; el/la estudiante
to **study** estudiar, I-3.2
subject la asignatura, la disciplina, I-2.2
suburbs los suburbios, I-5.1
subway el metro, I-12.1
sufficient suficiente, **5.1**
sugar el azúcar, **9.1**

to **suggest** sugerir (ie, i), **12**
suit el traje, I-13.1
suitcase la maleta, I-8.1
    to **pack one's suitcase** hacer la maleta, I-8
summer el verano, I-11.1
sun el sol, I-11.1
to **sunbathe** tomar el sol, I-11.1
sunblock la crema protectora, I-11.1
Sunday el domingo, I-BV
sunglasses los anteojos de (para el) sol, I-11.1
sunny: It's sunny. Hay (Hace) sol., I-11.1
suntan lotion la crema bronceadora, I-11.1
super súper, **5.2**
    super highway la autopista, la autovía, **10.2**
supermarket el supermercado, el hipermercado, **2.1**
sure seguro(a), **12**
surgeon el/la cirujano(a), **4.2**
to **surprise** sorprender, I-13
sweater el suéter, el jersey, I-13.1
sweetheart el/la enamorado(a), **15**
to **swim** nadar, I-11.1
swimsuit el traje de baño, el bañador, I-11.1
swimming pool la piscina, la alberca, I-11.2
swollen hinchado(a), **4.1**
symptom el síntoma, I-10.2

T

T-shirt el T shirt, I-13.1
table la mesa, I-12.2
tablecloth el mantel, I-15.1
tableland la meseta, **7.2**
tablet la pastilla, I-16.2
to **take** tomar, I-3.2
    to **take a bath** bañarse, I-16
    to **take a hike** dar una caminata, I-16.2
    to **take a nap** echar (tomar) una siesta, I-11.1
    to **take a shower** tomar una ducha, I-16.2
    to **take a trip** hacer un viaje, I-8.1

to take off (airplane) despegar (gu), I-8.2
to take off the fire quitar del fuego, retirar del fuego, 9.2
to take out sacar (qu), 13.2
to take place tener lugar, 12.2
to take up subir, 6.1
takeoff el despegue, 7.2
tall alto(a), I-1.1
tank el tanque, 5.2
tape la cinta, I-4.1
taxi el taxi, I-8.1
to teach enseñar, I-3.2
teacher el/la profesor(a), I-2.1
team el equipo; de equipo (adj.), I-7.1
teaspoon la cucharita, I-15.1
technician el/la técnico(a), 4.2
telephone el teléfono, I-4.1; telefónico(a) (adj.), 1.1
  telephone book la guía telefónica, 1.1
  telephone booth la cabina telefónica, 1.1
to telephone telefonear, 1.1
television la televisión, I-4.1
  television set el televisor, 6.2
to tell decir (irreg.), I-9
teller el/la cajero(a), 14.1
temperature la temperatura, I-9.1
ten diez, I-BV
tennis el tenis, I-11.2
  tennis court la cancha de tenis, I-11.2
  tennis game el juego de tenis, I-11.2
  tennis shoes los tenis, I-13.1
tent la tienda de campaña, la carpa, I-16.2
  to put up a tent armar una tienda, I-16.2
tenth décimo(a), I-5.1
test el examen, I-3.2
thank you gracias, I-BV
that eso; aquel, aquella, I-9.2
the el, la, I-1.1
theater el teatro, I-12.2
theatrical teatral, I-12.2
then luego, 10.2
there is/are hay, I-5.1
third tercer, tercero(a), I-5.1
thirst la sed, I-15.1

thirsty: to be thirsty tener sed, I-15.1
thirty treinta, I-BV
this este (esta), I-9
thousand mil, I-BV
three tres, I-BV
  Three Wise Men los Reyes Magos, 12.2
throat la garganta, I-10.2
  sore throat el dolor de garganta, I-10.1
  to have a sore throat tener dolor de garganta, I-10.1
to throw tirar, lanzar, I-7.1; echar, 3.1
Thursday el jueves, I-BV
ticket el boleto, el billete I-8.1
  one-way ticket el billete sencillo, I-14.1
  round-trip ticket el billete de ida y vuelta, I-14.1
  ticket window la ventanilla, I-9.1, la taquilla; la boletería, I-12.1
tied (score) empatado(a), I-7
tight estrecho(a), I-13.2
time tiempo
  At what time? ¿A qué hora?, I-2
  full-time a tiempo completo, 16.2
  on time a tiempo, I-8.1
  part-time a tiempo parcial, 16.2
timid tímido(a), I-1.2
tip la propina, I-12.2
tire el neumático, la goma, la llanta, 5.1
  spare tire la llanta de repuesto (de recambio), 5.1
tired cansado(a), I-10.1
to a; con destino a
  to the (m. sing.) al
toast (to one's health) el brindis, 15.2
to toast (to one's health) brindar, 15.2
today hoy, I-BV
together junto(a), 15.1
toilet el inodoro, el váter, 6.2
  toilet paper el papel higiénico, I-16.2
toll el peaje, 10.2
  toll booth la garita de peaje, 10.2

tomb la tumba, 12.1
tomorrow mañana, 3.1
tone el tono, 1
tonight esta noche, I-11.2
too también, I-1.1
too (much) demasiado, I-13.2
tooth el diente, I-16.1
toothpaste la pasta dentífrica, I-16.2
tortilla la tortilla, I-15.2
total el total, el monto, 6.1
to touch tocar, I-7
tourist el/la turista, I-12.2
towel la toalla, I-11.1
  beach towel la toalla playera, I-11.1
town el pueblo, I-5.1
trade el oficio, la compra y venta, 16.1
traffic la circulación, el tráfico, el tránsito, 5.1
  traffic light el semáforo, 10.1
trailer la caravana, la casa-remolque, 13.1
train el tren, I-14.1
  train station la estación de ferrocarril, I-14.1
to transfer transbordar, I-14.2
transportation el transporte, I-12
traveler el/la viajero(a)
  traveler's check el cheque de viajero, 14.1
tray table la mesita, 7.1
tree el árbol, I-6.2
  Christmas tree el árbol de Navidad, 12.2
trigonometry la trigonometría, I-2.2
trim el recorte, 8.2
to trim recortar, 8.2
trip el viaje, I-8.1
  to take a trip hacer un viaje, I-8.1
true verdadero(a), I-4.2
  Isn't it true? ¿No es verdad?, I-1.1
trumpet la trompeta, I-4.2
trunk (of a car) el/la maletero(a), 5.1
truth la verdad, I-1.1
tube el tubo, I-16.2
Tuesday el martes, I-BV
tuna el atún, 2.2

526 VOCABULARIO INGLÉS-ESPAÑOL

to turn doblar, 5.1
    to turn around dar la vuelta, 10.1
    to turn off apagar, 9.2
    turn signal el intermitente, la direccional, 5.1
    twenty veinte, I-BV
to twist torcer (ue), 4.1
two dos, I-BV

U

umbrella la sombrilla, I-11.1
uncle el tío, I-6.1
    uncle(s) and aunt(s) los tíos, I-6.1
under debajo de, 7.1
underground subterráneo(a), I-12
undershirt la camiseta, I-13.1
to understand comprender, I-5.2
unemployed desocupado(a), desempleado(a), 16.2
    unemployed person el/la desempleado(a), 16.2
unemployment el desempleo
university la universidad; universitario(a) (adj.), 16.2
    university diploma el título universitario, 16.2
unleaded sin plomo, 5.2
unless a menos que, 15
unpleasant antipático(a), I-1.1
until hasta, I-BV; hasta que, 15
to use usar, I-11.1
usher el paje de honor, 15.2

V

valley el valle, 7.2
veal la ternera, 2.1
vegetable la legumbre, la verdura, el vegetal, I-15.2
to verify verificar, 14.2
very muy, I-BV
view la vista, I-6.2
violin el violín, I-4.2
vitamin la vitamina, I-10.2
volleyball el vólibol, I-7.2

W

to wait for esperar
waiter el mesero, I-12.2
waiting room la sala de recepción, 4.2
waitress la mesera, I-12.2
to wake up despertarse (ie), I-16.1
to walk caminar, 4.2; andar (irreg.), 4.2
to want querer (irreg.), I-7; desear, 11
wash el lavado, 8.2
to wash (oneself) lavar(se), I-16.1
washing machine la máquina de lavar, 13.2
to watch ver, I-5.2
water el agua (f.), I-11.1
    water skiing (n.) el esquí acuático, I-11.1
    to go water skiing esquiar en el agua, I-11.1
watermelon la sandía, 9.2
wave la ola, I-11.1; la onda, 8.1
way la manera, I-1.1; el sentido, 10.2
we nosotros(as), I-2.2
    we are somos, I-2.2; estamos
to wear llevar
wedding la boda, el enlace nupcial, 15.1; el matrimonio, 15.2
    wedding ring el anillo (la sortija) de boda, 15.1
Wednesday el miércoles, I-BV
week la semana, I-11.2
    last week la semana pasada, I-11.2
    this week esta semana, I-11.2
to weigh pesar, 3.2
welcome la bienvenida, 7.1
to welcome dar la bienvenida, 7.1
well bien, I-BV
    well done (meat) bien cocido (hecho), I-15.2
well-mannered educado(a), 11.1
west el oeste, 10.1
what? ¿cuál?, ¿qué?, I-BV; ¿cómo?, I-1.1
    What is it? ¿Qué es?, I-BV
    What is today's date? ¿Cuál es la fecha de hoy?, I-BV
    What time is it? ¿Qué hora es?, I-2
    What's the weather like? ¿Qué tiempo hace?, I-9.1
wheel la rueda, I-9.2
wheelchair la silla de ruedas, 4.1
when cuando, 15
    when? ¿cuándo?, I-3.1
where? ¿dónde?, I-1.2; ¿adónde?, I-4
which? ¿cuál?, I-BV
while mientras, 2.2
white blanco(a), I-13.2
who? ¿quién?, I-BV
    Who is calling? ¿De parte de quién?, 1.1
    Who is it (he, she)? ¿Quién es?, I-BV
wide ancho(a), I-13.2
wife la esposa, la mujer, I-6.1
to win ganar, I-7.1
wind el viento, I-11.1
window la ventanilla, 3.2
windshield el parabrisas, 5.2
    windshield wiper el limpiaparabrisas
windsurfboard la plancha de vela, I-11.1
windy: It's windy. Hace viento., I-11.1
wing el ala (f.), 7.2
winter el invierno, I-9.1
to wish desear, 11
to withdraw retirar, 14.2
withdrawal el retiro, 14.2
    withdrawal slip el formulario de retiro, 14.2
without sin (que), 15
woman la mujer, I-6.1
wool la lana, 13.2
work la obra, I-12.2; el trabajo, 16.1
to work trabajar, I-4.1
worker el/la obrero(a), el/la trabajador(a), 16.1
wrinkled arrugado(a), 13.2
wrist la muñeca, 4.1
to write escribir, I-5.2
writing pad el bloc, I-3.2
wrong equivocado(a), 1.1

X

X ray los rayos equis, la radiografía, 4.2

Y

year el año, I-11.2
   Happy New Year! ¡Próspero año nuevo!, **12.2**
   last year el año pasado, I-11.2
   this year este año, I-11.2
yellow amarillo(a), I-13.2
yesterday ayer, I-11.1
   the day before yesterday anteayer, I-11.2
   yesterday afternoon ayer por la tarde, I-11.2
   yesterday morning ayer por la mañana, I-11.2
you Ud(s)., usted(es) (sing. [pl.] form.), I-2.2
   you are es (sing. form), I-1.1; son (pl. form.), I-2.1; está (sing. form), I-4.1; están (pl. form.), I-4.1
   you go van (pl. form.), I-4.1
You're welcome. De nada., No hay de qué., I-BV
young joven, I-6.1
young person el/la joven, **15.1**
younger menor, **11.1**
youth hostel el albergue juvenil, I-16.2

Z

zero cero, I-BV
zip code la zona postal, el código postal, **3.1**
zipper la cremallera, el zíper, I-13.2

ÍNDICE GRAMATICAL

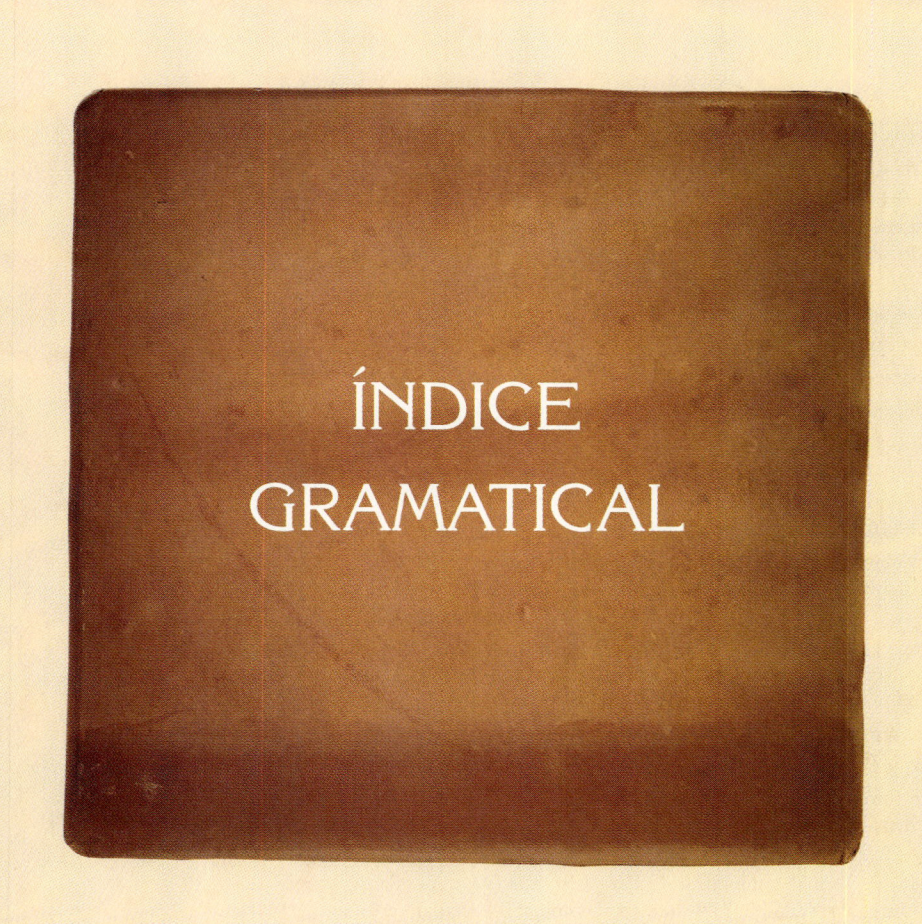

acabar de plus infinitive, 201 (8)

adjectives comparative and superlative: regular forms, 64 (3); irregular forms, 89 (4)

adverbial clauses using the subjunctive in, 398 (15)

***-ar* verbs** imperfect tense, 10 (1); future tense, 62 (3); conditional tense, 122 (5); present perfect tense, 148 (6); present progressive tense, 174 (7); formal commands, 234-6 (9); informal commands, 260 (10); present subjunctive, 285 (11); imperfect subjunctive, 373 (14)

aunque using the subjunctive with, 400 (15)

comparative see adjectives

comparing equal quantities with nouns, 177 (7)

conditional tense see regular, irregular, and stem-changing verbs

conditions expressing with *si* clauses, 377 (14)

decir imperfect tense, 11 (1); future tense, 87 (4); conditional tense, 124 (5); present perfect tense, 151 (6); present progressive tense, 174 (7); informal command, 236 (10); present subjunctive, 286 (11); imperfect subjunctive, 374 (14)

direct object pronouns with indirect object pronouns, 126 (5); placement with present participle and infinitive, 198 (8); with affirmative and negative commands, 264 (10)

***-er* verbs** imperfect tense, 11 (1); future tense, 62 (3); conditional tense, 122 (5); present perfect tense, 148 (6); present progressive tense, 174 (7); formal commands, 234 (9); informal commands, 260 (10); present subjunctive, 286 (11); imperfect subjunctive, 373 (14)

future tense see regular, irregular, and stem-changing verbs

haber present tense, 148 (6); used to form present perfect tense, 148 (6)

hacer future tense, 87 (4); conditional tense, 124 (5); formal command, 236 (9); informal command, 261 (10); present subjunctive, 286 (11); imperfect subjunctive, 374 (14)

imperative formal commands: regular verbs, 234 (9); stem-changing verbs, 234-235 (9); irregular verbs, 237 (9); informal commands, regular verbs, 260 (10); stem-changing verbs, 260 (10); irregular verbs, 261 (10); negative, 263 (10)

imperfect tense contrasted with the preterite, 36 (2); narrating a sequence of events, 39 (2); verbs most often expressed in the imperfect, 41 (2); see also regular, irregular, and stem-changing verbs

indirect object pronouns with direct object pronouns, 126 (5); placement with present participle and infinitive, 198 (8); with affirmative and negative commands, 264 (10)

infinitive versus the subjunctive, 350 (13)

ir imperfect tense, 13 (1); formal command, 237 (9); informal command, 260 (10); present subjunctive, 287 (11); imperfect subjunctive, 374 (14)

***-ir* verbs** imperfect tense, 11 (1); future tense, 62 (3); conditional tense, 122 (5); present perfect tense, 148 (6); present progressive tense, 174 (7); formal commands, 234 (9); informal commands, 260 (10); present subjunctive, 286 (11); imperfect subjunctive, 373 (14)

irregular verbs imperfect tense: *decir*, 11 (1); *ir*, 13 (1); *poder*, 11 (1); *querer*, 11 (1); *ser*, 13 (1); future tense: *poder*, 86 (4); *poner*, 86 (4); *saber*, 86 (4); *salir*, 86 (4); *tener*, 86 (4); *venir*, 86 (4); *decir*, 87 (4); *hacer*, 87 (4); *querer*, 87 (4); conditional tense: *decir*, 124 (5); *hacer*, 124 (5); *poder*, 124 (5); *poner*, 124 (5); *querer*, 124 (5);

530 ÍNDICE GRAMATICAL

saber, 124 (5); *salir,* 124 (5); *tener,* 124 (5); present perfect tense: *abrir,* 151 (6); *cubrir,* 151 (6); *decir,* 151 (6); *devolver,* 151 (6); *escribir,* 151 (6); *hacer,* 151 (6); *morir,* 151 (6); *poner,* 151 (6); *ver,* 151 (6); *volver,* 151 (6); formal commands: *conducir,* 236 (9); *dar,* 237 (9); *decir,* 236 (9); *estar,* 237 (9); *hacer,* 236 (9); *ir,* 237 (9); *poner,* 236 (9); *saber,* 237 (9); *salir,* 236 (9); *ser,* 237 (9); *venir,* 236 (9); informal commands: *decir,* 261 (10); *hacer,* 261 (10); *ir,* 261 (10); *poner,* 261 (10); *salir,* 261 (10); *ser,* 261 (10); *tener,* 261 (10); *venir,* 261 (10); present subjunctive: *conducir,* 286 (11); *decir,* 286 (11); *hacer,* 286 (11); *oír,* 286 (11); *poner,* 286 (11); *salir,* 286 (11); *tener,* 286 (11); *traer,* 286 (11); *venir,* 286 (11); *dar,* 287 (11); *estar,* 287 (11); *ir,* 287 (11); *saber,* 287 (11); *ser,* 287 (11); review of preterite tense, 352 (13); imperfect subjunctive: *andar,* 374 (14); *decir,* 374 (14); *conducir,* 374 (14); *estar,* 374 (14); *hacer,* 374 (14); *ir,* 374 (14); *leer,* 374 (14); *oír,* 374 (14); *poder,* 374 (14); *poner,* 374 (14); *querer,* 374 (14); *saber,* 374 (14); *ser,* 374 (14); *tener,* 374 (14); *venir,* 374 (14)

ojalá using the subjunctive with, 425 (16)

passive voice with *se* 238 (9)

poder imperfect tense, 11 (1); future tense, 86 (4); conditional tense, 124 (5); imperfect subjunctive, 374 (14)

poner future tense, 86 (4); conditional tense, 124 (5); present perfect tense, 151 (6); formal command, 236 (9); informal command, 261 (10); present subjunctive, 262 (11); imperfect subjunctive, 374 (14)

present perfect tense see regular, irregular, and stem-changing verbs

present progressive tense see regular, irregular, and stem-changing verbs

preterite tense review of irregular verbs, 352 (13)

pronouns direct and indirect object pronouns, 126 (5); *se* with two object pronouns, 152 (6); placement of direct and indirect object pronouns with present participle and infinitive, 198 (8); direct and indirect object pronouns with affirmative and negative commands, 264 (10)

querer imperfect tense, 11 (1); future tense, 87 (4); conditional tense, 124 (5); imperfect subjunctive, 374 (14)

quizá(s) using the subjunctive with, 425 (16)

regular verbs imperfect tense: *-ar* verbs, 10 (1); *-er* and *-ir* verbs, 11 (1); future tense: *-ar, -er,* and *-ir* verbs, 62 (3); conditional tense: *-ar, -er,* and *-ir* verbs, 122 (5); present perfect tense: *-ar, -er,* and *-ir* verbs, 148 (6); present progressive tense: *-ar, -er,* and *-ir* verbs, 174 (7); formal commands: *-ar, -er,* and *-ir* verbs, 234 (9); informal commands: *-ar, -er,* and *-ir* verbs, 260 (10); present subjunctive: *-ar, -er,* and *-ir* verbs, 286 (11); imperfect subjunctive, 373 (14)

relative clauses using the subjunctive in, 424 (16)

saber future tense, 86 (4); conditional tense, 124 (5); formal command, 237 (9); present subjunctive, 287 (11); imperfect subjunctive, 374 (14)

salir future tense, 86 (4); conditional tense, 124 (5); formal command, 236 (9); informal command, 261 (10); present subjunctive, 286 (11)

se with two object pronouns, 152 (6); with passive voice, 238 (9)

ser imperfect tense, 13 (1); formal command, 237 (9); informal command, 261 (10); present subjunctive, 287 (11); imperfect subjunctive, 374 (14)

ÍNDICE GRAMATICAL **531**

si expressing conditions with *si* clauses, 377

stem-changing verbs imperfect tense: (e>ie) *querer*, 11 (1); (o>ue) *poder*, 11 (1); present progressive tense: (e>i) *decir*, 175 (7); *pedir*, 175 (7); *repetir*, 175 (7); *sentir*, 175 (7); *servir*, 175 (7); (o>u) *dormir*, 175 (7); *morir*, 175 (7); formal commands, 234 (9); informal commands, 260 (10); present subjunctive tense: (e>i) *pedir*, 312 (12); *sentir*, 312 (12); (e>ie) *cerrar*, 312 (12); *perder*, 312 (12); (o>u) *dormir*, 312 (12); (o>ue) *encontrar*, 312 (12); *poder*, 312 (12); imperfect subjunctive, 373 (14)

subjunctive when to use, 285 (11); expressing wishes, preferences, and demands, 288 (11); giving advice and making suggestions, 313 (12); expressing doubt or uncertainty, 315 (12); expressing emotional reactions to the actions of others, 316 (12); versus the infinitive, 350 (13); speaking about the past, 373 (14); in adverbial clauses, 398 (15); using the subjunctive with *aunque*, 400 (15); using the subjunctive with time expressions, 401 (15); using the subjunctive in relative clauses, 424 (16); using the subjunctive with *ojalá, tal vez, quizá(s)*, 425 (16); see also regular, irregular, and stem-changing verbs

superlative see adjectives

tal vez using the subjunctive with, 425 (16)

tanto... como comparing equal quantities using nouns, 176 (7)

tener future tense, 86 (4); conditional tense, 124 (5); informal command, 261 (10); present subjunctive, 286 (11); imperfect subjunctive, 374 (14)

time expressions used with present perfect tense, 149 (6); using the subjunctive with, 401 (15)

venir (e>ie) future tense, 86 (4); formal command, 236 (9); informal command, 261 (10); present subjunctive, 286 (11); imperfect subjunctive, 374 (14)

Photography
Front Cover: Ron Watts/Westlight
Algaze, M./The Image Works: 182R; Arizona Daily Star: 324B; AT&T: 22; Aubrey, Daniel: 147, 161, 243B, 360-361, 377; Baird, David/Tony Stone Images: 402; Balterman, Lee/FPG: 133; Banus, Jose Luis/FPG: R48TL; Bavendam, Fred/Peter Arnold, Inc.: 340-341; Bertinetti, M./Photo Researchers: 178B; Bettmann: 108T, 223, 336, 383B; Boxer, Tim/Archive Photos: 446T; John Boykin: 275; Bronfman, Larry/Archive Photos: 204L, 204CL; Burckhalter, David: Photo 96-97; Cameramann/The Image Works: 398; Club Telemundo: 241; Cohen, Stuart/Comstock: 206, 399; Cooper, Martha/Peter Arnold, Inc.: 204BR; Crandall, Rob/The Image Works: 337T; Bob Daemmrich Photography: R18; De Wys, Leo/Leo De Wys, Inc.: 405; Diesendruck, Ary/Tony Stone Images: 135TR; Jeffrey Dunn/Stock Boston: 295T; Durrance, Richard S./National Geographic: 357; Dykinga, J.: R50-R51; Elmore, Steven D./The Stock Market: 302-303; Englebert, Victor/Photo Researchers: 95L; Everton, Macduff/The Image Works: 224-225; Focus: xiiiB, 177, 353L, 359B, 428B; Frazier, David R./Photo Researchers: 23; Frerck, Robert/Glencoe: R42-R43; Frerck, Robert/Odyssey: 22-23, 37B, 46L, 48B, 65, 110, 149R, 157, 160-161, 160T, 160B, 183B, 206C, 220, 244, 245B, 247B, 246T, 246-247, 250-251, 255B, 267T, 270C, 273TR, 273TL, 272B, 336T, 337B, 349T, 349B, 356T, 356B, 358T, 360L, 382, 384B, 400, 410-411, 429T; Frerck, Robert/The Stock Market: 352; Froomer, Brett/The Image Bank: 20; Fuller, Tim/Tim Fuller Photography: viiB, viiiC, ixB, xT, xB, xiB, xiiiT, xivTR, xvB, R55L, R55R, 4, 9T, 16, 17, 18, 19, 21, 22, 23, 30, 36, 41, 42, 43, 47, 48-49, 48T, 51, 52-53, 57, 66T, 67B, 70, 71T, 72-73, 73TR, 74B, 75, 90T, 92, 93, 94T, 95TR, 96BL, 97B, 102, 104, 112-113, 122, 123, 126, 128T, 129T, 134TL, 135TL, 136TR, 136C, 137, 142, 149L, 150, 152, 153C, 153B, 154, 156T, 164-165, 173, 176, 192, 193, 196, 197, 199, 201, 202T, 203, 205, 208TL, 208-209, 210, 215, 217, 234, 235, 255T, 258TL, 258TR, 260, 262T, 264, 266B, 267B, 283T, 283, 289, 291, 292T, 295, 296, 297, 298-299, 300, 311B, 313, 314B, 317, 318, 321, 324L, 325BL, 330, 334, 339, 348, 355, 361B, 379, 384T, 386, 392, 393BR, 399T, 401, 404T, 411TL, 414-415, 419T, 423T, 424, 426, 432B, 433BR, 434, 438, 439; General Electric Company, reproduced with permission of the copyright owner: 351; Glencoe: 62, 66B, 68, 180, 181B, 246B, 258B, 314T, 331, 350, 358, 413, 423B, 435; Glencoe/ Scribner-Macmillan: xiT, xiiCL, 61T, 208BR, 209T, 209B, 259, 261T, 262B, 263, 272T, 325T, 333, 361C, 425; Gscheidle, Gerhard: 31T, 237, 238; Goldin, Carlos: 2-3, 188-189; Gottschalk, Manfred/West Light: 274; Grames, Eberhard/The Stock Market: 443; Harrington III, Blaine/The Stock Market: 172; Heimann, Anne/The Stock Market: 345T; Hewlett Packard: 429B; Hill, Jr., W./The Image Works: 109T; Humberto, Carlos/The Stock Market: 445; Inman, Nick: viiiT, viiiB, xiiB, xivTL, R40, R54, 8, 10, 11, 14, 25, 39, 45, 46R, 60, 71B, 73TL, 73CR, 85, 90B, 94B, 97TR, 125, 127TR, 129B, 134CL, 136BR, 155, 158, 159B, 168, 174T, 178T, 185TL, 202B, 206T, 207, 208CR, 211, 239, 240T, 243C, 248, 249, 254, 266T, 270L, 270R, 284T, 290, 292B, 294, 345B, 363, 368R, 378, 393T, 393BL 442; Johnson, Jeff S./World Transport Photography, Inc.: 181T; Kanus, H./Superstock: 109B; Lehmann, Yoram/Peter Arnold, Inc.: 163; Lessin, Leonard/Peter Arnold, Inc.: 107; Levenson, Alan/Tony Stone Images: 108B; Lloyd, Harvey/The Stock Market: 361T; Mangino/The Image Works: 373; Mason, Don/The Stock Market: 245C; Mason, John F./The Stock Market: 240B; Mathers, Michael/Peter Arnold, Inc.: 233B; Mazzatenta, Louis O./National Geographic: 388-389; McCain, Edward: 284B, 311T, 323T, 324-325; McDonald, Dennis: 183T; McIntyre, Will & Deni/Photo Researchers: 67T; Meadows, Matt/Peter Arnold, Inc.: 258CL; Menzel, Peter: xC, 9B, 26-27, 35, 38B, 72, 89, 128B, 130, 131, 132, 134-135, 143, 174B, 184-185, 184C, 187, 243T, 268B, 306, 307, 322, 384-385; Meyers, Jonathan/FPG: 272-273, 323B; Mug Shots/The Stock Market: 408; NASA: 427L; O'Rourke, Randy/The Stock Market: 310; Philips, Mark/Superstock, Inc.: xvT, 433TR; Photo Researchers: 61B; Pfriender, Stephanie/The Stock Market: 204TR; Picture Box/Viesti Associates: 268T; Rumack, Gary: xivB, 329, 403, 407, 409, 410TL, 411TR, 411CR; Sanders, David/Arizona Daily Star: 228; Sauer, Jennifer: 423; Schroeder-Eastwood/Superstock, Inc.: 419C; Share, Jed/Westlight: 448; Smestad, Mark: xiiTR, R36, R48TR, R48BL, 12, 37T, 38T, 76-77, 99, 156B, 159T, 247T, 258CR, 271, 276-277, 287, 298B, 293, 316, 353R, 354, 432-433, 444; Smith, Jeff/Fotosmith: 81, 127C, 127L, 338, 374, 381; Sorensen, Chris/The Stock Market: 185TR; Stein, Art/Photo Researchers: 49; Superstock, Inc.: R34-R35, 236; Svensson, Erik/The Stock Market: 233T; Michael Taufic/The Stock Market: 404B; Ventura, Michael/Tony Stone Images: 419B; Viesti, Joe/Viesti Associates: 430B; Villota, L./The Stock Market: 74T, 383T; Wassman, Bill/The Stock Market: 138-139, 364-365; Welsch, Ulrike/Photo Researchers: 13, 96TL; Werner, Mike & Carol/Comstock: R48BR; White, Jeanne/Photo Researchers: 61C; Wide World: 427R, 427C; Wiltsie, Gordon/Peter Arnold Inc.: 359T; Wojnarowicz/Image Works: 153T; Xerox: 430T.

Fine Art
Photo courtesy The Art Institute of Chicago: 222; ©1993 Artists Rights Society (ARS), New York/SPADEM, Paris: 15, 446BL, 446BR, 447T, 447B; Glencoe: 245T; Lessing, Erich/Art Resource, NY: R49; National Gallery of Art, Washington: R44, 261B; Scala/Art Resource, NY: 31B; Schalkwijk, Bob: 111.

Illustration
Briseño, José Luis: 118-119; Castro, Antonio: 2-3, 304-305, 306, 308-309, 319, 342-343, 344, 416-417; Gregory, Lane: 81, 82-83; Hicks, Gail: 144-145, 346-347, 369-370, 394-395, 396; Loccisano, Karen: 40, 78-79, 80, 146, 194-195, 252-253, 254; Catalina Osuna: 28-29; Phillips, Gary: 281-282, 366-367, 390-391, 420-421; Pond & Giles: 106, 226, 227T, 231T, 335; Roberge, Beth: 58-59; Sanfilippo, Margaret: R52, R53, 6-7, ..32-33, 140-141, 166-167, 190-191, 278-279; Spellman, Susan: 54-55, 84, 172, 226CL, 227C, 227B, 230, 231B, 232; Torrisi, Gary: 114-115, 116, 170-171, 256-257

Realia
Realia courtesy of the following: AeroPeru: 179; Antenas Tecno: 21; AT&T: 101; Arras Nupciales: 403; Automundo: 117; Auto Pecos: 121; Ballet Folklórico: 200; Bancahsa: 375; Banco Bilbao Vizcaya: 384; Banco Cafetero: 385; Banco Gallego: 387; Banco Santander: 372; Bayer Aspirin: 105; Blanco y Negro: R39; Budget: 440; Central Cultural Universitario: 422; Cepsa: 125; CIGA Hotels: 162; Continente: 34, 47; Cristóbal Inn: 162; Della Novia: 392, 412; Dolores: 248; Ediciones Arribas: R37; Elle: R57; Elevage Hotel: 161; Eres: R38; Fiat: 123; Fibra Optica: 5; Fiesta Americana Cancún: 397; Fiesta Planners: 326; Foresta Restaurants: 405; Gallina Blanca: 239; General Motors: 131; Gofy Restaurante: R39; Guía del Ocio: R47, R56; Hallmark-Primor cards: 87, 301; Hola: 288, 351, 362; Hotel Apoquindo: 151; Hoteles Paraíso Radisson: 147; Hotel Principado: 214; Iberia: 175; Juárez, Rosalío C.: 269; Locatel: 8; L'Oreal: 193; Médica Sur: 86; Mexicana: R41, 188; Navarro, Ruíz: R37; Nexus: 203; Novias Vogue: 409; Orly: 402; Oso-Pez: 315; Panadol: 91; Pemex: 133; Plaza Hotel: 161; PolySwing: 197; Publix: 229; Restaurante Botín: R45; Servicio Postal Mexicana: 57; Subdirección General de Medios de Promoción: R36; SDFN: 382; Turespaña: 270, 271; Universidad Del Valle De Mexico: 426; Vanidades: 241; VISA: 376.

Fabric designs: Guatemalan–contemporary fabric: 44; Mexican–Los Colores Museum, Corrales, New Mexico: 92; Peruvian–private collection: 18; Spanish–Musée national des Tissus, Lyon, France: 68.

Maps
Eureka Cartography, Berkeley, CA.

T = top C = center B = bottom L = left R = right